Lecture Notes in Computer Science   **14656**

The series Lecture Notes in Computer Science (LNCS), including its subseries Lecture Notes in Artificial Intelligence (LNAI) and Lecture Notes in Bioinformatics (LNBI), has established itself as a medium for the publication of new developments in computer science and information technology research, teaching, and education.

LNCS enjoys close cooperation with the computer science R & D community, the series counts many renowned academics among its volume editors and paper authors, and collaborates with prestigious societies. Its mission is to serve this international community by providing an invaluable service, mainly focused on the publication of conference and workshop proceedings and postproceedings. LNCS commenced publication in 1973.

Marc Joye · Gregor Leander
Editors

Advances in Cryptology – EUROCRYPT 2024

43rd Annual International Conference on the Theory
and Applications of Cryptographic Techniques
Zurich, Switzerland, May 26–30, 2024
Proceedings, Part VI

 Springer

Editors
Marc Joye ⓘ
Zama
Paris, France

Gregor Leander ⓘ
Ruhr University Bochum
Bochum, Germany

ISSN 0302-9743 ISSN 1611-3349 (electronic)
Lecture Notes in Computer Science
ISBN 978-3-031-58750-4 ISBN 978-3-031-58751-1 (eBook)
https://doi.org/10.1007/978-3-031-58751-1

This Springer imprint is published by the registered company Springer Nature Switzerland AG
The registered company address is: Gewerbestrasse 11, 6330 Cham, Switzerland

Paper in this product is recyclable.

Preface

EUROCRYPT 2024 is the 43rd Annual International Conference on the Theory and Applications of Cryptographic Techniques. It was held in Zurich, Switzerland, during May 26–30, 2024. EUROCRYPT is an annual conference organized by the International Association for Cryptologic Research (IACR).

EUROCRYPT 2024 received 501 submissions, out of which 469 formally went to the review process. Every submission was assigned in a double blind way to three program committee members and, in some cases, one or two extra reviewers were added. The IACR version of the HotCRP software was used for the whole review process. In total, 1436 reviews were produced and 5200+ comments were made during the whole process. After a first round, 290 papers were pre-selected by the program committee to enter the second round. These remaining papers were offered a rebuttal to answer questions and requests for clarification from the reviewers. After several weeks of subsequent discussions, the committee ultimately selected 105 papers for acceptance.

The program committee was made up of 110 top cryptography researchers, all expert in their respective fields. For some papers, external sub-referees were appointed by the committee members. We warmly thank all the committee members and their sub-referees for the hard work in the peer review and their active participation in the discussions. We greatly benefited from the help of the area chairs: Shweta Agrawal for "Public Key Primitives with Advanced Functionalities", Serge Fehr for "Theoretical Foundations", Pierre-Alain Fouque for "Secure and Efficient Implementation, Cryptographic Engineering, and Real-World Cryptography", María Naya-Plasencia for "Symmetric Cryptology", Claudio Orlandi for "Multi-Party Computation and Zero-Knowledge", and Daniel Wichs for "Classic Public Key Cryptography". They each led the discussions and the paper selection in their respective area. The previous program chairs for IACR flagship conferences were also very helpful; in particular, we are grateful to Carmit Hazay and Martijn Stam for sharing their experience with EUROCRYPT 2023.

The IACR aims to support open and reproducible research within the field of cryptography. For the first time for a flagship conference, authors of accepted papers were invited to submit artifacts associated with their papers, such as software or datasets, for review, in a collaborative process between authors and the artifact review committee. We thank Martin Albrecht for having accepted to chair the artifact committee.

Three papers were awarded this year. The Best Paper Awards went to Pierrick Dartois, Antonin Leroux, Damien Robert and Benjamin Wesolowski for their paper "SQIsignHD: New Dimensions in Cryptography" and to Itai Dinur for his paper "Tight Indistinguishability Bounds for the XOR of Independent Random Permutations by Fourier Analysis". The Early-Career Best Paper Award was given to Maria Corte-Real Santos, Jonathan Komada Eriksen, Michael Meyer, and Krijn Reijnders for their paper "AprèsSQI: Extra Fast Verification for SQIsign Using Extension-Field Signing".

In addition to the contributed papers, EUROCRYPT 2024 featured two invited talks: "Cryptography in the Wild" by Kenny Paterson and "An Attack Became a Tool: Isogeny-based Cryptography 2.0" by Wouter Castryck. The conference also included a panel discussion on the future of publications; the panel was moderated by Anne Canteaut. The traditional rump session featuring short and entertaining presentations was held on Wednesday 29th.

Several people were key to the success of the conference. Our two general chairs, Julia Hesse and Thyla van der Merwe, did a fantastic job with the overall organization of EUROCRYPT 2024. Kevin McCurley ensured everything went smoothly with the review software and in the collection of the final papers. The conference relied on sponsors to help ensure student participation and reduce costs. We gratefully acknowledge the financial support of (in alphabetical order): Apple, AWS, CASA, City of Zürich, Concordium, Cosmian, Ethereum Foundation, Fair Math, Google, Huawei, IBM, Input/Output, NTT Research, SandboxAQ, Swiss National Science Foundation, Starkware, TII, Zama, and ZISC.

May 2024

Marc Joye
Gregor Leander

Organization

General Co-chairs

Thyla van der Merwe   Google, Switzerland
Julia Hesse   IBM Research Zurich, Switzerland

Program Co-chairs

Marc Joye   Zama, France
Gregor Leander   Ruhr-University Bochum, Germany

Area Chairs

Shweta Agrawal   IIT Madras, India
Serge Fehr   CWI Amsterdam and Leiden University,
                                 The Netherlands
Pierre-Alain Fouque   Université de Rennes, CNRS and Inria, France
María Naya-Plasencia   Inria, France
Claudio Orlandi   Aarhus University, Denmark
Daniel Wichs   Northeastern University and NTT Research, USA

Program Committee

Martin R. Albrecht   King's College London and SandboxAQ, UK
Diego F. Aranha   Aarhus University, Denmark
Nuttapong Attrapadung   AIST, Japan
Christof Beierle   RUB, Germany
Sonia Belaïd   CryptoExperts, France
Tim Beyne   KU Leuven, Belgium
Olivier Blazy   Ecole Polytechnique, France
Jeremiah Blocki   Purdue University, USA
Alexandra Boldyreva   Georgia Tech University, USA
Xavier Bonnetain   Inria, France
Jonathan Bootle   IBM Research Europe – Zurich, Switzerland
Christina Boura   University of Versailles, France

André Schrottenloher	Inria, Université de Rennes, IRISA, France
Peter Schwabe	MPI-SP, Germany, and Radboud University, The Netherlands
Yannick Seurin	Ledger, France
Mark Simkin	Ethereum Foundation, Denmark
Pratik Soni	University of Utah, USA
Akshayaram Srinivasan	University of Toronto, Canada
Damien Stehlé	CryptoLab, France
Siwei Sun	Chinese Academy of Sciences, China
Berk Sunar	Worcester Polytechnic Institute, USA
Yosuke Todo	NTT Social Informatics Laboratories, Japan
Junichi Tomida	NTT Social Informatics Laboratories, Japan
Serge Vaudenay	EPFL, Switzerland
Frederik Vercauteren	KU Leuven, Belgium
Ivan Visconti	University of Salerno, Italy
David Wu	UT Austin, USA
Mark Zhandry	NTT Research, USA

External Reviewers

Marius A. Aardal
Aysajan Abdin
Ittai Abraham
Damiano Abram
Hamza Abusalah
Anasuya Acharya
Léo Ackermann
Amit Agarwal
Ahmet Agirtas
Prabhanjan Ananth
Yoshinoro Aono
Ananya Appan
Nicolas Aragon
Arasu Arun
Gennaro Avitabile
Renas Bacho
Youngjin Bae
David Balbas
Marshall Ball
Fabio Banfi
Zhenzhen Bao
Manuel Barbosa

Augustin Bariant
Cruz Barnum
Khashayar Barooti
James Bartusek
Balthazar Bauer
Amit Behera
Shalev Ben-David
Shany Ben-David
Omri Ben-Eliezer
Loris Bergerat
Ward Beullens
Varsha Bhat
Ritam Bhaumik
Kaartik Bhushan
Alexander Bienstock
Alexander Block
Erica Blum
Jan Bobolz
Nicolas Bon
Charlotte Bonte
Carl Bootland
Joppe Bos

Katharina Boudgoust

Alexandre Bouez

Clemence Bouvier

Cyril Bouvier

Pedro Branco

Nicholas Brandt

Lennart Braun

Alessio Caminata

Matteo Campanelli

Sébastien Canard

Kevin Carrier

Ignacio Cascudo

Gaëtan Cassiers

Guilhem Castagnos

Wouter Castryck

Pierre-Louis Cayrel

André Chailloux

Debasmita Chakraborty

Hubert Chan

Anirudh Chandramouli

Rahul Chatterjee

Rohit Chatterjee

Mingjie Chen

Yanlin Chen

Yilei Chen

Yu Long Chen

Jesús-Javier Chi-Domínguez

Ilaria Chillotti

Hyeongmin Choe

Wonseok Choi

Wutichai Chongchitmate

Arka Ra Choudhuri

Hao Chung

Kai-Min Chung

Michele Ciampi

Sebastian Clermont

Benoît Cogliati

Daniel Collins

Brice Colombier

Sandro Coretti

Alain Couvreur

Daniele Cozzo

Wei Dai

Quang Dao

Debajyoti Das

Sourav Das

Pratish Datta

Emma Dauterman

Gareth T. Davies

Leo de Castro

Thomas De Cnudde

Paola de Perthuis

Giovanni Deligios

Cyprien Delpech de Saint Guilhem

Rafael del Pino

Amit Deo

Julien Devevey

Siemen Dhooghe

Zijing Di

Emanuele Di Giandomenico

Christoph Dobraunig

Rafael Dowsley

Leo Ducas

Jesko Dujmovic

Betül Durak

Avijit Dutta

Christoph Egger

Martin Ekera

Felix Engelmann

Simon Erfurth

Reo Eriguchi

Jonathan Komada Eriksen

Hülya Evkan

Thibauld Feneuil

Giacomo Fenzi

Rex Fernando

Valerie Fetzer

Rune Fiedler

Ben Fisch

Matthias Fitzi

Nils Fleischhacker

Pouyan Forghani

Boris Fouotsa

Cody Freitag

Sapir Freizeit

Daniele Friolo

Paul Frixons

Margot Funk

Phillip Gajland

Daniel Gardham

Rachit Garg
Francois Garillot
Gayathri Garimella
John Gaspoz
Robin Geelen
Paul Gerhart
Diana Ghinea
Satrajit Ghosh
Ashrujit Ghoshol
Emanuele Giunta
Kristian Gjøsteen
Aarushi Goel
Evangelos Gkoumas
Eli Goldin
Rishab Goyal
Adam Groce
Ziyi Guan
Zichen Gui
Antonio Guimaraes
Felix Günther
Kanav Gupta
Nirupam Gupta
Kamil Doruk Gur
Hosein Hadipour
Mohammad Hajiabadi
Ghaith Hammouri
Guillaume Hanrot
Keisuke Hara
Patrick Harasser
Dominik Hartmann
Keitaro Hashimoto
Rachelle Heim
Nadia Heninger
Alexandra Henzinger
Julius Hermelink
Julia Hesse
Hans Heum
Shuichi Hirahara
Taiga Hiroka
Marc Houben
James Hsin-Yu Chiang
Kai Hu
Yungcong Hu
Tao Huang
Zhenyu Huang

Loïs Huguenin-Dumittan
James Hulett
Atsunori Ichikawa
Akiko Inoue
Tetsu Iwata
Joseph Jaeger
Jonas Janneck
Dirmanto Jap
Samuel Jaques
Ruta Jawale
Corentin Jeudy
Ashwin Jha
Dan Jones
Philipp Jovanovic
Bernhard Jungk
Fatih Kaleoglu
Chethan Kamath
Jiayi Kang
Minsik Kang
Julia Kastner
Hannah Keller
Qiao Kexin
Mustafa Khairallah
Dmitry Khovratovich
Ryo Kikuchi
Jiseung Kim
Elena Kirshanova
Fuyuki Kitagawa
Michael Klooß
Christian Knabenhans
Lisa Kohl
Sebastian Kolby
Dimitris Kolonelos
Chelsea Komlo
Anders Konring
Nishat Koti
Mukul Kulkarni
Protik Kumar Paul
Simran Kumari
Norman Lahr
Russell W. F. Lai
Baptiste Lambin
Oleksandra Lapiha
Eysa Lee
Joohee Lee

Jooyoung Lee
Seunghoon Lee
Ryan Lehmkuhl
Tancrède Lepoint
Matthieu Lequesne
Andrea Lesavourey
Baiyu Li
Shun Li
Xingjian Li
Zengpeng Li
Xiao Liang
Chuanwei Lin
Fuchun Lin
Yao-Ting Lin
Fukang Liu
Peiyuan Liu
Qipeng Liu
Patrick Longa
Julian Loss
Paul Lou
George Lu
Steve Lu
Zhenghao Lu
Reinhard Lüftenegger
Vadim Lyubashevsky
Fermi Ma
Varun Madathil
Christian Majenz
Giulio Malavolta
Mary Maller
Nathan Manohar
Mario Marhuenda Beltrán
Ange Martinelli
Elisaweta Masserova
Takahiro Matsuda
Christian Matt
Noam Mazor
Pierrick Méaux
Jeremias Mechler
Jonas Meers
Willi Meier
Kelsey Melissaris
Nikolas Melissaris
Michael Meyer
Pierre Meyer

Charles Meyer-Hilfiger
Peihan Miao
Chohong Min
Brice Minaud
Kazuhiko Minematsu
Tomoyuki Morimae
Hiraku Morita
Mahnush Movahedi
Anne Mueller
Michael Naehrig
Marcel Nageler
Vineet Nair
Yusuke Naito
Varun Narayanan
Hugo Nartz
Shafik Nassar
Patrick Neumann
Lucien K. L. Ng
Ruth Ng
Dinh Duy Nguyen
Jérôme Nguyen
Khoa Nguyen
Ky Nguyen
Ngoc Khanh Nguyen
Phong Nguyen
Phuong Hoa Nguyen
Thi Thu Quyen Nguyen
Viet-Sang Nguyen
Georgio Nicolas
Guilhem Niot
Julian Nowakowski
Koji Nuida
Sabine Oechsner
Kazuma Ohara
Olya Ohrimenko
Jean-Baptiste Orfila
Astrid Ottenhues
Rasmus Pagh
Arghya Pal
Tapas Pal
Mahak Pancholi
Omkant Pandey
Lorenz Panny
Jai Hyun Park
Nikitas Paslis

Alain Passelègue

Rutvik Patel

Shravani Patil

Sikhar Patranabis

Robi Pedersen

Alice Pellet-Mary

Hilder V. L. Pereira

Guilherme Perin

Léo Perrin

Thomas Peters

Richard Petri

Krzysztof Pietrzak

Benny Pinkas

Guru-Vamsi Policharla

Eamonn Postlethwaite

Thomas Prest

Ludo Pulles

Kirthivaasan Puniamurthy

Luowen Qian

Kexin Qiao

Xianrui Qin

Willy Quach

Rahul Rachuri

Rajeev Raghunath

Ahmadreza Rahimi

Markus Raiber

Justin Raizes

Bhavish Raj Gopal

Sailaja Rajanala

Hugues Randriam

Rishabh Ranjan

Shahram Rasoolzadeh

Christian Rechberger

Michael Reichle

Krijn Reijnders

Jean-René Reinhard

Bhaskar Roberts

Andrei Romashchenko

Maxime Roméas

Franck Rondepierre

Schuyler Rosefield

Mike Rosulek

Dragos Rotaru

Yann Rotella

Lior Rotem

Lawrence Roy

Ittai Rubinstein

Luigi Russo

Keegan Ryan

Sayandeep Saha

Yusuke Sakai

Matteo Salvino

Simona Samardjiska

Olga Sanina

Antonio Sanso

Giacomo Santato

Paolo Santini

Maria Corte-Real Santos

Roozbeh Sarenche

Pratik Sarkar

Yu Sasaki

Rahul Satish

Sarah Scheffler

Dominique Schröder

Jacob Schuldt

Mark Schultz-Wu

Gregor Seiler

Sruthi Sekar

Nicolas Sendrier

Akash Shah

Laura Shea

Yixin Shen

Yu Shen

Omri Shmueli

Ferdinand Sibleyras

Janno Siim

Tjerand Silde

Jaspal Singh

Nitin Singh

Rohit Sinha

Luisa Siniscalchi

Naomi Sirkin

Daniel Slamanig

Daniel Smith-Tone

Yifan Song

Yongsoo Song

Eduardo Soria-Vazquez

Nick Spooner

Mahesh Sreekumar Rajasree

Sriram Sridhar

Srivatsan Sridhar
Lukas Stennes
Gilad Stern
Marc Stöttinger
Bing Sun
Ling Sun
Ajith Suresh
Elias Suvanto
Jakub Szefer
Akira Takahashi
Abdullah Talayhan
Abdul Rahman Taleb
Suprita Talnikar
Tianxin Tang
Samuel Tap
Stefano Tessaro
Jean-Pierre Tillich
Ivan Tjuawinata
Patrick Towa
Kazunari Tozawa
Bénédikt Tran
Daniel Tschudi
Yiannis Tselekounis
Ida Tucker
Nirvan Tyagi
LaKyah Tyner
Rei Ueno
Gilles Van Assche
Wessel Van Woerden
Nikhil Vanjani
Marloes Venema
Michiel Verbauwhede
Javier Verbel
Tanner Verber
Damien Vergnaud
Fernando Virdia
Damian Vizár
Benedikt Wagner
Roman Walch
Julian Wälde

Alexandre Wallet
Chenghong Wang
Mingyuan Wang
Qingju Wang
Xunhua Wang
Yuyu Wang
Alice Wanner
Fiona Weber
Christian Weinert
Weiqiangg Wen
Chenkai Weng
Ivy K. Y. Woo
Lichao Wu
Keita Xagawa
Aayush Yadav
Anshu Yadav
Saikumar Yadugiri
Shota Yamada
Takashi Yamakawa
Hailun Yan
Yibin Yang
Kevin Yeo
Eylon Yogev
Yang Yu
Chen Yuan
Mohammad Zaheri
Gabriel Zaid
Riccardo Zanotto
Arantxa Zapico
Maryam Zarezadeh
Greg Zaverucha
Marcin Zawada
Runzhi Zeng
Tina Zhang
Yinuo Zhang
Yupeng Zhang
Yuxi Zheng
Mingxun Zhou
Chenzhi Zhu

Contents – Part VI

Multi-party Computation and Zero-Knowledge (II/II)

Jolt: SNARKs for Virtual Machines via Lookups 3
Arasu Arun, Srinath Setty, and Justin Thaler

Constant-Size zk-SNARKs in ROM from Falsifiable Assumptions 34
Helger Lipmaa, Roberto Parisella, and Janno Siim

Lower-Bounds on Public-Key Operations in PIR 65
Jesko Dujmovic and Mohammad Hajiabadi

Fast Public-Key Silent OT and More from Constrained Naor-Reingold 88
Dung Bui, Geoffroy Couteau, Pierre Meyer, Alain Passelègue, and Mahshid Riahinia

Best-of-Both-Worlds Multiparty Quantum Computation with Publicly Verifiable Identifiable Abort 119
Kai-Min Chung, Mi-Ying Huang, Er-Cheng Tang, and Jiapeng Zhang

The Hardness of LPN over Any Integer Ring and Field for PCG Applications 149
Hanlin Liu, Xiao Wang, Kang Yang, and Yu Yu

Unlocking the Lookup Singularity with Lasso 180
Srinath Setty, Justin Thaler, and Riad Wahby

Efficient Pre-processing PIR Without Public-Key Cryptography 210
Ashrujit Ghoshal, Mingxun Zhou, and Elaine Shi

Strong Batching for Non-interactive Statistical Zero-Knowledge 241
Changrui Mu, Shafik Nassar, Ron D. Rothblum, and Prashant Nalini Vasudevan

Two-Round Maliciously-Secure Oblivious Transfer with Optimal Rate 271
Pedro Branco, Nico Döttling, and Akshayaram Srinivasan

Succinct Homomorphic Secret Sharing 301
Damiano Abram, Lawrence Roy, and Peter Scholl

How to Garble Mixed Circuits that Combine Boolean and Arithmetic
Computations 331
   Hanjun Li and Tianren Liu

Classic Public Key Cryptography (I/II)

M &M'S: Mix and Match Attacks on Schnorr-Type Blind Signatures
with Repetition 363
   Khue Do, Lucjan Hanzlik, and Eugenio Paracucchi

The Supersingular Endomorphism Ring and One Endomorphism Problems
are Equivalent 388
   Aurel Page and Benjamin Wesolowski

Evaluating the Security of CRYSTALS-Dilithium in the Quantum Random
Oracle Model 418
   Kelsey A. Jackson, Carl A. Miller, and Daochen Wang

Crypto Dark Matter on the Torus: Oblivious PRFs from Shallow PRFs
and TFHE 447
   Martin R. Albrecht, Alex Davidson, Amit Deo, and Daniel Gardham

Author Index 477

Multi-party Computation
and Zero-Knowledge (II/II)

Jolt: SNARKs for Virtual Machines via Lookups

Arasu Arun[1], Srinath Setty[2($\boxtimes$)], and Justin Thaler[3,4]

[1] New York University, New York, USA
[2] Microsoft Research, New York, USA
srinath@microsoft.com
[3] a16z crypto research, Washington, USA
[4] Georgetown University, Washington, USA

Abstract. Succinct Non-interactive Arguments of Knowledge (SNARKs) allow an untrusted prover to establish that it correctly ran some "witness-checking procedure" on a witness. A zkVM (short for zero-knowledge virtual machine) is a SNARK that allows the witness-checking procedure to be specified as a computer program written in the assembly language of a specific instruction set architecture (ISA).

A *front-end* converts computer programs into a lower-level representation such as an arithmetic circuit or generalization thereof. A SNARK for circuit-satisfiability can then be applied to the resulting circuit.

We describe a new front-end technique called Jolt that applies to a variety of ISAs. Jolt arguably realizes a vision called the *lookup singularity*, which seeks to produce circuits that only perform lookups into pre-determined lookup tables. The circuits output by Jolt primarily perform lookups into a gigantic lookup table, of size more than 2^{128}, that depends only on the ISA. The validity of the lookups are proved via a new *lookup argument* described in a companion work called Lasso [STW23]. Although size-2^{128} tables are vastly too large to materialize in full, the tables arising in Jolt are structured, avoiding costs that grow linearly with the table size.

We describe performance and auditability benefits of Jolt compared to prior zkVMs, focusing on the popular RISC-V ISA as a concrete example. The dominant cost for the Jolt prover applied to this ISA (on 64-bit data types) is equivalent to cryptographically committing to under eleven 256-bit field elements per step of the RISC-V CPU. This compares favorably to prior zkVM provers, even those focused on far simpler VMs.

1 Introduction

A SNARK (succinct non-interactive argument of knowledge) is a cryptographic protocol that lets an untrusted prover $\mathcal{P}$ convince a verifier $\mathcal{V}$ that they know

---

The full version of this work is presented in [AST23], and is accompanied by its companion work, Lasso [STW23].

© International Association for Cryptologic Research 2024
M. Joye and G. Leander (Eds.): EUROCRYPT 2024, LNCS 14656, pp. 3–33, 2024.
https://doi.org/10.1007/978-3-031-58751-1_1

a witness w satisfying some property. A trivial proof is for $\mathcal{P}$ to send w to $\mathcal{V}$, who can then directly check that w satisfies the claimed property. A SNARK achieves the same effect, but with better costs to the verifier. Specifically, the term *succinct* roughly means that the proof should be shorter than this trivial proof (i.e., the witness w itself), and verification should be much faster than direct witness checking.

As an example, the prover could be a cloud service provider running an expensive computation on behalf of its client (the verifier). A SNARK gives the client confidence that the prover ran the computation honestly. Alternatively, in a blockchain setting, the witness could be a list of valid digital signatures authorizing several transactions. A SNARK can be used to prove that one *knows* the (valid) signatures, so that the signatures themselves do not have to be stored and verified by all blockchain nodes. Instead, only the SNARK needs to be stored and verified on-chain.

1.1   SNARKs for Virtual Machine Abstractions

A popular approach to SNARK design today is to prove the correct execution of *computer programs*. This means that the prover proves that it correctly ran a specified computer program Ψ on a witness. In the example above, Ψ might take as input a list of blockchain transactions and associated digital signatures authorizing each of them, and verify that each of the signatures is valid.

Many projects today accomplish this via a CPU abstraction, also often called a *virtual machine* (VM). Here, a VM abstraction entails fixing a set of *primitive instructions*, known as an instruction set architecture (ISA), analogous to assembly instructions in processor design. A full specification of the VM also includes the number of registers and the type of memory that is supported. The program Ψ to be proved is written in this language.

Systems that generate proofs for these VM abstractions are commonly called "zkVMs". While this is a misnomer as they do not necessarily provide zero-knowledge, we stick with this terminology throughout this work due to its popularity. To list a few examples, several so-called "zkEVM" projects seek to achieve "byte-code level compatibility" with the Ethereum Virtual Machine (EVM). This means that the set of primitive instructions is the 141 opcodes available on the EVM and the types of memory supported are those required in the EVM (such as a stack containing 256-bit elements, a byte-addressable memory, and a key-value store with 256-bit keys and values).

Many other zkVM projects choose (or design) ISAs for their purported "SNARK-friendliness", or for surrounding infrastructure and tooling, or for a combination thereof. For example, Cairo-VM is a very simple virtual machine designed specifically for compatibility with SNARK proving [GPR21, AGL+22]. Another example is the RISC Zero project, which uses the RISC-V instruction set. RISC-V is popular in the computer architecture community, and comes with a rich ecosystem of compiler tooling. Other zkVM projects include Polygon Miden,[1] Valida,[2] and many others.

Front-End, Back-End Paradigm. SNARKs are built using protocols that perform certain probabilistic checks, so to apply SNARKs to program executions, one must express the execution of a program in a specific form that is amenable to probabilistic checking (e.g., as arithmetic circuits or generalizations thereof). Accordingly, most SNARKs consist of a so-called *front-end* and *back-end*: the front-end transforms a witness-checking computer program Ψ into an equivalent circuit-satisfiability instance, and the back-end allows the prover to establish that it knows a satisfying assignment to the circuit.

Typically, the circuit will "execute" each step of the compute program one at a time (with the help of untrusted "advice inputs"). Executing a step of the CPU conceptually involves two tasks: (1) identify which primitive instruction should be executed at this step, and (2) execute the instruction and update the CPU state appropriately. Existing front-ends implement these tasks by carefully devising gates or so-called constraints that implement each instruction. This is time-intensive and potentially error-prone. As we show in this work, it also leads to circuits that are substantially larger than necessary.

Pros and Cons of the zkVM Paradigm. One major benefit of zkVMs that use pre-existing ISAs is that they can exploit extant compiler infrastructure and tooling. This applies, for example, to the RISC-V and EVM instruction set, and leads to a developer-friendly toolchain without building the infrastructure from scratch. One can directly invoke existing compilers that transform witness-checking programs written in high-level languages down to assembly code for the ISA, and also benefit from prior audits or other verification efforts of these compilers.

Another benefit of zkVMs is that a single circuit can suffice for running all programs up to a certain time bound, whereas alternative approaches may require re-running a front-end for every program. Finally, frontends for VM abstractions output circuits with repeated structure. For a given circuit size, backends targeting circuits with repeated structure [Set20, BSBHR19, WTS+18] can be much faster than backends that do not leverage repeated structure [CHM+20, GWC19, Gro16].

However, zkVMs also have downsides that render them less efficient for some applications. Circuits implementing a VM abstraction must pay for their generality – they must support all possible sequences of CPU instructions as opposed to being tailored for a specific program. This leads to an overhead in circuit size and ultimately, proving costs.

---

[1] https://polygon.technology/polygon-miden.
[2] https://github.com/valida-xyz/valida-compiler/issues/2.

Another issue is that implementing certain important operations in a zkVM (e.g., cryptographic operations such as Keccak hashing or ECDSA signature verification) is extremely expensive-e.g., ECDSA signature verification takes up to 100 microseconds to verify on real CPUs, which translates to millions of RISC-V instructions.[3] This is why zkVM projects contain so-called gadgets or built-ins, which are hand-optimized circuits and lookup tables computing specific functionalities.

The Conventional Wisdom on zkVMs. The prevailing viewpoint today is that simpler VMs can be turned into circuits with fewer gates per step of the VM. This is most apparent in the design of particularly simple and ostensibly SNARK-friendly VMs such as TinyRAM [BSCG+13a] and the Cairo-VM [4]. However, this comes at a cost, because primitive operations that are standard in real-world CPUs require many primitive instructions to implement on the simple VM. In part to minimize the overheads in implementing standard operations on such limited VMs, many projects have designed domain specific languages (DSLs) that are exposed to the programmer who writes the witness-checking program.

Moreover, existing zkVMs remain expensive for the prover, even for very simple ISAs. For example, the prover for Cairo-VM programs described in [GPR21, AGL+22] cryptographically commits to 51 field elements per step of the Cairo-VM. This means that a single primitive instruction for the Cairo-VM may cause the prover to execute millions of instructions on real CPUs. This severely limits the applicability of SNARKs for VM abstractions, to applications involving only very simple witness-checking procedures.

1.2   Jolt: a0- New Paradigm for zkVM Design

In this work, we introduce a new paradigm in zkVM design. The result is zkVMs with much faster provers, as well as substantially improved auditability and extensibility (i.e., a simple workflow for adding additional primitive instructions to the VM). Our techniques are general. As a concrete example, we instantiate them for the RISC-V instruction set (with multiplication extension [WA17]), a popular open-source ISA developed by the computer architecture community without SNARKs in mind.

Our results upend the conventional wisdom that simpler instruction sets necessarily lead to smaller circuits and associated faster provers. First, our prover is

---

[3] See https://github.com/risc0/risc0/tree/v0.16.0/examples/ecdsa.

[4] The Cairo-VM has 3 registers, memory that is read-only (each cell can only be written to once) and must be "continuous", and the primitive instructions are roughly addition and multiplication over a finite field, jumps, and function calls. Even the high-level language only exposes write-once (also known as immutable) memory to the programmer and does not offer signed integer data types. See https://www.cairo-lang.org/ for information on the high-level language and [GPR21, AGL+22] and https://github.com/lambdaclass/cairo-vm for information on the virtual machine.

faster per step of the VM than existing SNARK provers for much simpler VMs. Second, the complexity of our prover primarily depends on the size (i.e., number of bits) of the inputs to each instruction. This holds so long as all of the primitive instructions satisfy a natural notion of structure, called *decomposability*. Roughly speaking, decomposability means that one can evaluate the instruction on a given pair of inputs (x, y) by breaking x and y up into smaller chunks, evaluating a small number of functions of each chunk, and combining the results. A primary contribution of our work is to show that decomposability is satisfied by all instructions in the RISC-V instruction set.

Lookup Arguments and Lasso. In a lookup argument, there is a predetermined "table" T of size N, meaning that $T \in \mathbb{F}^N$. An (*unindexed*) lookup argument allows the prover to commit to any vector $a \in \mathbb{F}^m$ and prove that every entry of a resides somewhere in the table. That is, for every $i \in \{1, \ldots, m\}$, there exists some k such that $a_i = T[k]$. In an *indexed* lookup argument, the prover commits not only to $a \in \mathbb{F}^m$, but also a vector $b \in \mathbb{F}^m$, and the prover proves that for every i, $a_i = T[b_i]$. In this setting, we call a the vector of *lookups* and b the vector of associated *indices*.

In a companion paper [STW23], we describe a new lookup argument called Lasso (which applies to both indexed and unindexed lookups). One distinguishing feature of Lasso is that it applies even to tables that are far too large for anyone to materialize in full, so long as the table satisfies the *decomposability* condition mentioned earlier.

Lookup Every Instruction! Say $\mathcal{P}$ claims to have run a certain computer program for m steps, and that the program is written in the assembly language for a VM. Today, front-ends produce a circuit that, for each step of the computation: (1) identifies what instruction to execute at that step, and then (2) executes that instruction. The second step is essentially a switch statement with a case for each instruction, as the circuit should handle any possible instruction in the ISA. This leads to a wasteful blowup in circuit size. Jolt's core idea is to replace step 2 with a single lookup. For each instruction f, the table stores the entire evaluation table of f: that is, if f operates on two 64-bit inputs, this table stores $f(x, y)$ for every pair of inputs $(x, y) \in \{0, 1\}^{64} \times \{0, 1\}^{64}$. This table has size 2^{128}. In this work, we show that all RISC-V instructions are *decomposable*.

In a research forum post in 2022, Barry Whitehat articulated a goal of designing front-ends that produce circuits that *only* perform lookups [Whi], terming it the *lookup singularity*. Circuits that only perform lookups are much simpler to understand and formally verify than circuits consisting of many gates that are often hand-optimized. Arguably, Jolt realizes the vision of the lookup singularity. The bulk of the prover work in Jolt lies in the lookup argument, Lasso. On top of this, the Jolt front-end only performs simple logic to handle memory reads and writes. These are very basic and overall captured in fewer that 50 R1CS constraints!

1.3   Costs of Jolt

Polynomial Commitments and MSMs. A central component of most SNARKs is a cryptographic protocol called a *polynomial commitment scheme* (see Definition 8). Such a scheme allows an untrusted prover to succinctly commit to a polynomial p and later reveal an evaluation $p(r)$ for a point r chosen by the verifier along with a *proof* that the claimed evaluation is correct. In Jolt, as with most SNARKs, the bottleneck for the prover is the polynomial commitment scheme.

Many popular polynomial commitments are based on multi-exponentiations (also known as multi-scalar multiplications, or MSMs). This means that the commitment to a polynomial p (with n coefficients $c_0, \ldots, c_{n-1}$ over an appropriate basis) is $\prod_{i=0}^{n-1} g_i^{c_i}$, for some public generators $g_1, \ldots, g_n$ of a multiplicative group $\mathbb{G}$. Examples include KZG [KZG10], Bulletproofs/IPA [BCC+16,BBB+18], Hyrax [WTS+18], and Dory [Lee21].[5]

The naive MSM algorithm performs n group exponentiations and n group multiplications (note that each group exponentiation is about $400\times$ slower than a group multiplication). But Pippenger's MSM algorithm saves a factor of about $\log(n)$ relative to the naive algorithm. This factor can be well over $10\times$ in practice.

Working Over Large Fields, But Committing to Small Elements. If all exponents appearing in the multi-exponentiation are "small", one can save another factor of $10\times$ relative to applying Pippenger's algorithm to an MSM involving random exponents. This is analogous to how computing $g_i^{2^{16}}$ is $10\times$ faster than computing $g_i^{2^{160}}$: the first requires 16 squaring operations, while the second requires 160 such operations. In other words, if one is promised that all field elements (i.e., exponents) to be committed via an MSM are in the set $\{0, 1, \ldots, K\} \subset \mathbb{F}$, the number of group operations required to compute the MSM depend only on K and not on the size of $\mathbb{F}$.[6]

Quantitatively, if all exponents are upper bounded by some value K, with $K \ll n$, then Pippenger's algorithm only needs (about) one group *operation* per term in the multi-exponentiation. More generally, with any MSM-based commitment scheme, Pippenger's algorithm allows the prover to commit to roughly $k \cdot \log(n)$-bit field elements (meaning field elements in $\{0, 1, \ldots, n\}$) with only k group *operations* per committed field element. So for size-n MSMs, one can commit to $\log(n)$ bits with a *single* group operation.

Polynomial Evaluation Proofs. For many polynomial commitment schemes, the evaluation proof computation is a low-order cost [WTS+18,BBHR18,Lee21].

---

[5] In Hyrax and Dory, the prover does $\sqrt{n}$ MSMs each of size $\sqrt{n}$.

[6] Of course, the cost of each group operation depends on the size of the group's base field, which is closely related to that of the scalar field $\mathbb{F}$. However, the *number* of group operations to compute the MSM depends only on K, not on $\mathbb{F}$.

Moreover, evaluation proofs exhibit excellent batching properties, whereby the prover can commit to many polynomials and only produce a single evaluation proof across all of them [BGH19, Lee21, KST22, BDFG20]. So in many contexts, computing opening proofs is not a bottleneck even when a scheme such as Bulletproofs/IPA is employed. For these reasons, our accounting in this work ignores the cost of polynomial evaluation proofs.

The Ultimate Cost of Jolt. For RISC-V instructions on 64-bit data types supporting both the base integer instructions and the multiplication extension, the Jolt prover commits to about 80 field elements per step of the RISC-V CPU, with only a dozen being as large as 2^{64}. Table 2 provides the complete distribution. With an MSM-based polynomial commitment, the Jolt prover costs are roughly that of committing to under eleven arbitrary (256-bit) field elements per CPU step.

1.4   Comparison of Prover Costs to Prior Works

This section compares Jolt's commitment cost with other proof systems and zkVM protocols.

Plonk [GWC19] is a popular backend that can prove statements about certain generalizations of arithmetic circuit satisfiability. When Plonk is applied to an arithmetic circuit (i.e., consisting of addition and multiplication gates of fan-in two), the Plonk prover commits to 11 field elements per gate of the circuit, and 7 of these 11 field elements are random. Thus, the Jolt prover costs are roughly equivalent to applying the Plonk backend to an arithmetic circuit with only about one gate per step of the RISC-V CPU.

A more apt comparison is to the RISC Zero project[7], which currently targets the RISC-V ISA on 32-bit data types. A direct comparison is complicated, in part because RISC Zero uses FRI as its (univariate) polynomial commitment scheme, which is based on FFTs and Merkle-hashing, avoiding the use of elliptic curve groups. Still, a crude comparison can be made by using how many field elements the RISC Zero prover commits to, which is at least 275 31-bit field elements per CPU step [Sol23]. At least on small instances, the prover bottleneck is Merkle-hashing the result of various FFTs [Sol23], and one can hash 8 different 31-bit field elements with the same cost as hashing one 256-bit field element. This is roughly equivalent to committing to about $275 \cdot 1/8 \approx 34$ different 256-bit field elements per CPU step. Thus, Jolt commits to significantly fewer elements per CPU step (11 versus 34 in 256-bit equivalents) while also supporting 64-bit architectures.

A final comparison point is to the SNARK for the Cairo-VM described in the Cairo whitepaper [GPR21]. The prover in that SNARK commits to about 50 field

---

[7] https://www.risczero.com/.

elements per step of the Cairo Virtual Machine, using FRI as the polynomial commitment scheme. StarkWare currently works over a 251-bit field.[8] This field size may be larger than necessary (it is chosen to match the field used by certain ECDSA signatures), but the provided arithmetization of Cairo-VM *requires* a field of size at least 2^{63}. So the commitment costs for the prover are at least equivalent to committing to $50 \cdot 64/256 \approx 13$ 256-bit field elements.[9] Jolt's prover costs per CPU compare favorably to this, despite the RISC-V instruction set being vastly more complicated than the Cairo-VM (and with the Cairo-VM instruction set specifically designed to be ostensibly "SNARK-friendly").

Verifier Costs of Jolt. For RISC-V programs running for at most T steps, the dominant costs for the Jolt verifier are performing $O(\log(T) \log\log(T))$ hash evaluations and field operations,[10] plus checking one evaluation proof from the chosen polynomial commitment scheme (when applied to a multilinear polynomial over at most $O(\log T)$ variables). Verifier costs can be further reduced, and the SNARK rendered zero-knowledge, via composition with a zero-knowledge SNARK with smaller proof size.

1.5   Technical Details: CPU Instructions as Structured Polynomials

As mentioned, Lasso is most efficient when applied to lookup tables satisfying a property called *decomposability*. Intuitively, this refers to tables t such that one lookup into t of size N can be answered with a small number (say, about c) of lookups into much smaller tables $t_1, \ldots, t_\ell$, each of size $N^{1/c}$. Furthermore, if a certain polynomial $\widetilde{t}_i$ associated with each t_i can be evaluated at any desired point r using, say, $O(\log(N)/c)$ field operations,[11] then no one needs to cryptographically commit to any of the tables (neither to t itself, nor to $t_1, \ldots, t_\ell$). Specifically, $\widetilde{t}_i$ can be any so-called *low-degree extension* polynomial of t_i. In Jolt, we will exclusively work with a specific low-degree extension of t_i, called the *multilinear extension*, and denoted $\widetilde{t}_i$.

---

[8] See, for example, https://github.com/starkware-libs/starkex-contracts/blob/master/audit/EVM_STARK_Verifier_v4.0_Audit_Report.pdf.

[9] Furthermore, in order to control proof size, StarkWare currently uses a "FRI blowup factor" of 16, compared to RISC Zero's choice of 4. This adds at least an extra factor of 4 to the prover time per field element committed, relative to RISC Zero's.

[10] As described in Appendix G.3 of the full version [AST23], Lasso can use any so-called *grand product argument*. The $O(\log(T) \log\log(T))$ verifier cost are due to the choice of grand product argument from [SL20, Section 6]. Other choices of lookup argument offer different tradeoffs between commitment costs for the prover, versus proof size and verifier time.

[11] The Lasso verifier has to evaluate $\widetilde{t}_i$ at a random point r on its own, so we need this computation to be fast enough that we are satisfied with the resulting verifier runtime. For all tables arising in Jolt, the verifier can compute all necessary $\widetilde{t}_i$ polynomial evaluations in $O(\log(N))$ total field operations.

Hence, to take full advantage of Lasso, we must show two things:

- The evaluation table t of each RISC-V instruction has is decomposable in the above sense. That is, one lookup into t, which has size N, can be answered with a small number of lookups into much smaller tables $t_1, \dots, t_\ell$, each of size $N^{1/c}$. For most RISC-V instructions, ℓ equals one or two, and about c lookups are performed into each table.

- For each of the small tables t_i, the multilinear extension $\widetilde{t_i}$ is evaluatable at any point, using just $O(\log(N)/c)$ field operations.

Establishing the above is the main technical contribution of our work. It turns out to be quite straightforward for certain instructions (e.g., bitwise AND), but more complicated for others (e.g., bitwise shifts, comparisons).

1.6   Decomposable Instructions

Suppose that table t contains all evaluations of some primitive instruction $f \colon \{0,1\}^n \to \mathbb{F}$. Decomposability of the table t is equivalent to the following property of f: for any n-bit input x to f, x can be decomposed into c "chunks", $X_0, \dots, X_{c-1}$, each of size n/c, and such that the following holds. There are ℓ functions $f_0, \dots, f_{\ell-1}$ such that $f(x)$ can be derived in a relatively simple manner from $f_i(x_j)$ as i ranges over $0, \dots, \ell-1$ and j ranges over $0, \dots, c-1$. Then the evaluation table t of f is decomposable: one lookup into t can be answered with c total lookups into $\ell \cdot c$ lookups into the evaluation tables of $f_0, \dots, f_{\ell-1}$.

Bitwise AND is a clean example by which to convey intuition for why the evaluation tables of RISC-V instructions are decomposable. Suppose we have two field elements x and y in $\mathbb{F}$, both in $\{0, \dots, 2^{64} - 1\}$. We refer to x and y as 64-bit field elements (we clarify here that "64 bits" does *not* refer to the size of the *field* $\mathbb{F}$, which may, for example, be a 256-bit field. Rather to the fact that x and y are both in the much smaller set $\{0, \dots, 2^{64} - 1\} \subset \mathbb{F}$, no matter how large $\mathbb{F}$ may be).

Our goal is to determine the 64-bit field element z whose binary representation is given by the bitwise AND of the binary representations of x and y. That is, if $x = \sum_{i=0}^{63} 2^i \cdot x_i$ and $y = \sum_{i=0}^{63} 2^i \cdot y_i$ for $(x_0, \dots, x_{63}) \in \{0,1\}^{64}$ and $(y_0, \dots, y_{63}) \in \{0,1\}^{64}$, then $z = \sum_{i=0}^{63} 2^i \cdot x_i \cdot y_i$.

One way to compute z is as follows. Break x and y into 8 chunks of 8 bits each compute the bitwise AND of each chunk, and concatenate the results to obtain z. Equivalently, we can express

$$z = \sum_{i=0}^{7} 2^{8 \cdot i} \cdot \mathsf{AND}(X_i, Y_i), \tag{1}$$

where each $X_i, Y_i \in \{0, \ldots, 2^8 - 1\}$ is such that $x = \sum_{i=0}^{7} 2^{8 \cdot i} \cdot X_i$ and $y = \sum_{i=0}^{7} 2^{8 \cdot i} \cdot Y_i$. These X_i's and Y_i's represent the decomposition of x and y into 8-bit limbs.[12]

In this way, one lookup into the evaluation table of bitwise-AND, which has size 2^{128}, can be answered by the prover providing $X_1, \ldots, X_8, Y_1, \ldots Y_8 \in \{0, \ldots, 2^8 - 1\}$ as untrusted advice, and performing 8 lookups into the size-2^{16} table t_1 containing all evaluations of bitwise-AND over pairs of 8-bit inputs. The results of these 8 lookups can easily be collated into the result of the original lookup, via Eq. (1). No party has to commit to the size-2^{16} table t_1 because for any input $(r_0', \ldots, r_7', r_0'', \ldots, r_7'') \in \mathbb{F}^{16}$, the multilinear extension $\widetilde{t_1}(r_0', \ldots, r_7', r_0'', \ldots, r_7'') = \sum_{i=0}^{7} 2^i \cdot r_i' \cdot r_i''$, can be evaluated directly by the verifier with only 14 field multiplications and 6 field additions.

Challenges for Other Instructions. One may initially expect that correct execution of RISC-V operations capturing 64-bit addition and multiplication would be easy prove, because large prime-order fields come with addition and multiplication operations that behave like integer addition and multiplication until the result of the operation overflows the field characteristic. Unfortunately, the RISC-V instructions capturing addition and multiplication have specified behavior upon overflow (beyond 64 bits, not 256 bits!) that differs from that of field addition and multiplication. Resolving this discrepancy is one key challenge that we overcome.

2   Technical Preliminaries

2.1   Multilinear Extensions

An ℓ-variate polynomial $p \colon \mathbb{F}^\ell \to \mathbb{F}$ is said to be *multilinear* if p has degree at most one in each variable. Let $f \colon \{0,1\}^\ell \to \mathbb{F}$ be any function mapping the ℓ-dimensional Boolean hypercube to a field $\mathbb{F}$. A polynomial $g \colon \mathbb{F}^\ell \to \mathbb{F}$ is said to *extend* f if $g(x) = f(x)$ for all $x \in \{0,1\}^\ell$. It is well-known that for any $f \colon \{0,1\}^\ell \to \mathbb{F}$, there is a unique *multilinear* polynomial $\widetilde{f} \colon \mathbb{F} \to \mathbb{F}$ that extends f. The polynomial $\widetilde{f}$ is referred to as the *multilinear extension* (MLE) of f.

Multilinear Extensions of Vectors. Given a vector $u \in \mathbb{F}^m$, we will often refer to the *multilinear extension of u* and denote this multilinear polynomial by $\widetilde{u}$. Assuming for simplicity that m is a power of two, $\widetilde{u}$ is obtained by viewing u as a function mapping $\{0,1\}^{\log m} \to \mathbb{F}$ in the natural way[13]: the function interprets its $(\log m)$-bit input $(i_0, \ldots, i_{\log m - 1})$ as the binary representation of an integer i

---

[12] Just as "digits" refers to a base-10 decomposition of an integer or field element, "limbs" refer to a decomposition into a different base, in this case base 2^8.

[13] All logarithms in this paper are to base 2.

between 0 and $m-1$, and outputs u_i. $\tilde{u}$ is defined to be the multilinear extension of this function.

Lagrange Interpolation. An explicit expression for the MLE of any function is given by the following standard lemma (see [Tha22, Lemma 3.6]).

Lemma 1. *Let $f: \{0,1\}^\ell \to \mathbb{F}$ be any function. Then the following multilinear polynomial $\tilde{f}$ extends f:*

$$\tilde{f}(x_0,\ldots,x_{\ell-1}) = \sum_{w\in\{0,1\}^\ell} f(w) \cdot \chi_w(x_0,\ldots,x_{\ell-1}), \tag{2}$$

where, for any $w = (w_0,\ldots,w_{\ell-1})$, $\chi_w(x_0,\ldots,x_{\ell-1}) := \prod_{i=0}^{\ell}(x_i w_i + (1-x_i)(1-w_i))$. Equivalently,

$$\chi_w(x_0,\ldots,x_{\ell-1}) = \widetilde{\mathsf{EQ}}(x_0,\ldots,x_{\ell-1},w_0,\ldots,w_{\ell-1}).$$

The polynomials $\{\chi_w : w \in \{0,1\}^\ell\}$ are called the *Lagrange basis polynomials* for ℓ-variate multilinear polynomials. The evaluations $\{\tilde{f}(w) : w \in \{0,1\}^\ell\}$ are sometimes called the coefficients of $\tilde{f}$ *in the Lagrange basis*, terminology that is justified by Eq. (2).

Lasso can make use of any commitment schemes for *multilinear* polynomials g.[14] Here an ℓ-variate multilinear polynomial $g: \mathbb{F}^\ell \to \mathbb{F}$ is a polynomial of degree at most one in each variable.

We employ standards definitions of SNARKs, Polynomial Commitments, Polynomial IOPs, and R1CS constraints and provide them in Appendix A of the full version [AST23] for completeness.

2.2   Lookup Arguments

Lookup arguments allow a prover to commit to two vectors $a \in \mathbb{F}^m$ and $b \in \mathbb{F}^m$ (with a polynomial commitment scheme) and prove that each entry a_i of vector a resides in index b_i of a pre-determined lookup table $T \in \mathbb{F}^N$. That is, for each $i = 1,\ldots,m$, $a_i = T[b_i]$. Here, to emphasize the interpretation of T as a table, we use square brackets $T[i]$ to denote the i'th entry of T. Here, if $b_i \notin \{1,\ldots,N\}$, then $t[b_i]$ is undefined, and hence $a_i \neq T[b_i]$. We refer to a as the vector of *looked-up values* and b as the vector of *indices*.

Definition 1 (Lookup arguments, indexed variant). *Let $PC = $ (Gen, Commit, Open, Eval) be an extractable polynomial commitment scheme for*

---

[14] Any univariate polynomial commitment scheme can be transformed into a multilinear one, though the transformations introduce some overhead (see, e.g., [CBBZ23, BCHO22, ZXZS20]).

multilinear polynomials over $\mathbb{F}$. *A lookup argument (for* indexed lookups*) for table* $T \in \mathbb{F}^N$ *is a SNARK for the relation*

$$\{(\mathsf{pp}, \mathcal{C}_1, \mathcal{C}_2, w = (a, b)) : a, b \in \mathbb{F}^m \wedge a_i = T[b_i] \forall i \in \{1, \ldots, n\}$$
$$\wedge \; \mathsf{Open}(\mathsf{pp}, \mathcal{C}_1; \tilde{a}) = 1 \wedge \mathsf{Open}(\mathsf{pp}, \mathcal{C}_2; \tilde{b}) = 1\}.$$

Here $w = (a, b) \in \mathbb{F}^m \times \mathbb{F}^m$ *is the witness, while* pp, $\mathcal{C}_1$, *and* $\mathcal{C}_2$ *are public inputs.*

Definition 1 captures so-called *indexed* lookup arguments (this terminology was introduced in our companion work, Lasso [STW23]. Other works consider *unindexed* lookup arguments, in which only the vector vector $a \in \mathbb{F}^m$ of looked-up values is committed, and the prover claims that *there exists* a vector b of indices such that $a_i = T[b_i]$ for all $i = 1, \ldots, m$.

Definition 2 (Lookup arguments, unindexed variant). *Let* $PC = (\mathsf{Gen}, \mathsf{Commit}, \mathsf{Open}, \mathsf{Eval})$ *be an extractable polynomial commitment scheme for multilinear polynomials over* $\mathbb{F}$. *A lookup argument (for* indexed lookups*) for table* $T \in \mathbb{F}^N$ *is a SNARK for the relation*

$$\{(\mathsf{pp}, \mathcal{C}_1, \mathcal{C}_2, a) : a \in \mathbb{F}^m \wedge \forall i \in \{1, \ldots, n\}, \exists b_i \text{ such that } a_i = T[b_i] \wedge \mathsf{Open}(\mathsf{pp}, \mathcal{C}_1, \tilde{a}) = 1\}.$$

Here $a \in \mathbb{F}^m \times \mathbb{F}^m$ *is the witness, while* pp *and* $\mathcal{C}_1$ *are public inputs.*

Jolt primarily requires indexed lookups. However, a few instructions require range checks, which are naturally handled by unordered lookups (to prove that a value is in the range $\{0, \ldots 2^L - 1\}$, perform an unordered lookup into the table T with $T[i] = i$ for $i = \{0, \ldots, 2^L - 1\}$).

There are natural reductions in both directions, i.e., unindexed lookup arguments can be transformed into index lookup arguments and vice versa.

A Companion Work: Lasso. Our companion work Lasso introduces a family of lookup arguments called Lasso. The lookup arguments in this family are the first that do not require any party to cryptographically commit to the table vector $T \in \mathbb{F}^N$, so long as T satisfies one of the two structural properties defined below.

Definition 3 (MLE-structured tables). *We say that a vector* $T \in \mathbb{F}^N$ *is MLE-structured if for any input* $r \in \mathbb{F}^{\log(N)}$, $\widetilde{T}(r)$ *can be evaluated with* $O(\log N)$ *field operations.*

Definition 4 (Decomposable tables). *Let* $T \in \mathbb{F}^N$. *For a small constant* c, *we say that* T *is c-decomposable if there exist a constant* k *and constant* $\alpha \leq kc$ *tables* $T_1, \ldots, T_\alpha$ *each of size* $N^{1/c}$ *and each MLE-structured, as well as a multilinear* α-*variate polynomial* g *such that the following holds. As in Sect. 2.1, let us view* T *as a function mapping* $\{0, 1\}^{\log N}$ *to* $\mathbb{F}$ *in the natural way, and view* each T_i as a function mapping $\{0, 1\}^{\log(N)/c} \to \mathbb{F}$. Then for any $r \in \{0, 1\}^{\log N}$, writing $r = (r_1, \ldots, r_c) \in \{0, 1\}^{\log(N)/c}$,

$$T[r] = g(T_1[r_1], \ldots, T_k[r_1], T_{k+1}[r_2], \ldots, T_{2k}[r_2], \ldots, T_{\alpha-k+1}[r_c], \ldots, T_\alpha[r_c]).$$

We refer to $T_1, \ldots, T_\alpha$ as sub-tables.

For any constant $c > 0$ and any c-decomposable table, our companion paper gives a lookup argument called Lasso, in which the prover commits to roughly $3cm + cN^{1/c}$ field elements. Moreover, all of these field elements are *small*, meaning that they are all in $\{0, \ldots, m\}$ (specifically, they are counts for the number of times each entry of each subtable is read), or are elements of the subtables $T_1, \ldots, T_\alpha$. The verifier performs $O(\log(m) \log \log(m))$ hash evaluations and field operations, processes one evaluation proof from the polynomial commitment scheme applied to a multilinear polynomial in $\log m$ variables, and evaluates $\widetilde{T}_1, \ldots, \widetilde{T}_\alpha$ each at a single randomly chosen point.

The Relationship Between MLE-Structured and Decomposable Tables. For any decomposable table $T \in \mathbb{F}^N$, there is some low-degree extension $\hat{T}$ of T (namely, an extension of degree at most k in each variable) that can be evaluated in $O(\log N)$ time. Specifically, the extension polynomial is

$$\hat{T}(r) = g(\widetilde{T}_1(r_1), \ldots, \widetilde{T}_\alpha(r_c)).$$

In general, $\hat{T}$ is not necessarily multilinear, so a table being decomposable does not necessarily imply that it is MLE-structured. In Jolt, we show *all* lookup tables used are *both* c-decomposable (for any integer $c > 0$) as well as MLE-structured.

Lasso with Small Tables ($c = 1$). A special case of Lasso used throughout this work is with a lookup table of small size (say, under 2^{22}) that does not need to be decomposed. Equivalently, this can be thought of as a decomposition with $c = 1$. Such tables are used to range-check small values like bytes, chunks and timestamps.

Remark 1. To show that a value x is in a table of size under 2^{22}, the lookup proof requires the prover to commit to only *one* additional element, the value of which is bounded by the total number of lookup queries made (specifically the *access count* of the subtable).

2.3   Memory Checking

Any SNARK for VM execution has to perform *memory-checking*. This means that the prover must be able to commit to an execution trace for the VM (that is, a step-by-step record of what the VM did over the course of its execution), and the verifier has to find a way to confirm that the prover maintained memory correctly throughout the entire execution trace. In other words, the value purportedly returned by any read operation in the execution trace must equal the value most recently written to the appropriate memory cell. We use the term *memory-checking argument* to refer to a SNARK for the above functionality. Note that a lookup table $T \in \mathbb{F}^N$ can be viewed as a read-only memory of size N, with memory cell i initialized to $T[i]$. Hence, a lookup argument for indexed lookups (Definition 1) is equivalent the a memory-checking argument for read-only memories.

A variety of memory-checking arguments have been described in the research literature [ZGK+18,BCG+18,BFR+13,BSCGT13] (with the underlying techniques rediscovered multiple times). The most efficient are based on lightweight fingerprinting techniques for the closely related problem of *offline memory checking* [Lip89,BEG+91]. In this work, we use such an argument due to Spice [SAGL18], but optimize it using Lasso. For completeness, we an provide overview of other memory-checking arguments in Appendix G, and Spice's in particular in Appendix G.3 of the full version [AST23].

3   An Overview of RISC-V and Jolt's Approach

This section first provides a brief overview of the RISC-V instruction set architecture considered in this work. Our goal is to convey enough about the architecture that readers who have not previously encountered it can follow this paper. A complete specification can be found at [WA17].[15] We also stick to regular control flow and do not support external events and other unusual run-time conditions like exceptions, traps, interrupts and CSR registers.

Informally, the RISC-V ISA consists of a CPU and a read-write memory, collectively called the *machine*.

Definition 5 (Machine state). *The machine state consists of $(PC, \mathcal{R}, \mathcal{M})$. $\mathcal{R}$ denotes the 32 integer registers, each of W bits, where W is 32 or 64. $\mathcal{M}$ is a linear read-write byte-addressable array consisting of a fixed number of total locations with each location storing one byte. The PC, also of W bits, is a separate register that stores the memory location of the instruction to be executed.*

Assembly programs consist of a sequence of instructions, each of which operate on the machine state. The instruction to be executed at a step is the one stored at the address pointed to by the PC . Unless specified by the instruction, the PC is advanced to the next memory location after executing the instruction. The RISC-V ISA specifies that all instructions are 32 bits long (i.e., 4 bytes), so advancing the PC to the next memory location entails incrementing PC by 4.

---

[15] Another helpful resource for interested readers is Lectures 5–8 at https://inst.eecs.berkeley.edu/~cs61c/resources/su18_lec/.

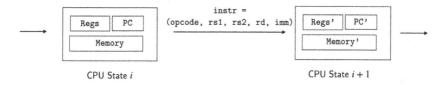

(a) The CPU state and instruction formats.

CPU step transition:

1. Read the instruction at location PC in the program code.

   Parse instruction as [opcode, rs1, rs2, rd, imm].

2. Read the W-bit values stored in registers rs1, rs2.

3. If required, write to or read from memory.

   The value written and memory location accessed are derived from the values stored in rs1, rs2, imm.

4. Perform the instruction's function on the values read from registers and imm to get the output.

   Examples of functions are arithmetic, logical and comparison operations.

5. Store output to register rd.

   Only a few instructions, like STOREs, do not involve rd.

6. Update PC.

   PC is usually incremented by 4, but instructions like jumps and branches update PC in other ways.

(b) The broad stages of a CPU step transition.

Fig. 1. A model of RISC-V's CPU state and transition function. Note that the transition function is deterministic and all information required, such as the location of memory accessed, is derived from the CPU state and instr.

While RISC-V uses multiple formats to store instructions in memory, we can abstract away the details and represent all instructions in the following 5-tuple format.

Definition 6 (5-tuple RISC-V instruction format). *Any RISC-V instruction can be written in the following format: [opcode, rs1, rs2, rd, imm]. That is, each instruction specifies an operation code uniquely identifying its function, at most two source registers rs1, rs2, a destination register rd, and a constant value imm (standing for "immediate") provided in the program code itself.*

Figure 1 provides a schematic of the CPU state change and instruction format. Operations read the source registers, perform some computation, and can do any or all of the following: read from memory, write to memory, store a value in rd, or update the PC. For example, the logical left-shift instruction "(SLL, r5, r8, r2, -)" reads the value stored in the fifth register, performs a logical left shift on the value by the length stored in the eighth register, and stores the result in second register (and does not involve any immediates). As another example, the branch instruction "(BEQ, r5, r8, -, imm)" sets PC to be PC + imm if the values stored in the fifth and eighth registers are equal, or routinely increments PC by 4, otherwise (and does not involve the destination register).

Unsigned and Signed Data Types. For the RISC-V ISA, data in registers has no type. A register simply stores W bits. However, different instructions can be conceptualized as interpreting register values in different ways. Specifically, some instructions operate upon unsigned data types, while others operate over signed data types. All RISC-V instructions involving signed data types interpret the bits in a register as an integer via two's complement representation.[16] For many instructions (such as ADD and SUB), the use of two's complement has the consequence that the instruction operates identically regardless of whether or not the inputs are interpreted as signed or unsigned. For some instructions, like multiplication (MUL and MULU) and integer comparison (SLT and SLTU), there will be two different RISC-V instructions, one for signed and one for unsigned. See Appendix D of the full version [AST23] for more information on two's complement notation and arithmetic.

Let z be a W-bit data type with constituent bits $[z_{W-1}, \ldots, z_0]$ such that $z = \sum_{i=0}^{W-1} 2^i \cdot z_i$. When discussing instructions interpreting their W-bit inputs as signed data types represented in twos-complement format, we refer to z_{W-1} as the sign bit of z, and denote this by z_s. (Concretely, the sign bit of a 64-bit register value z will be $z_s = z_{63}$.) We use $z_{<s}$ to refer to $[z_{W-2}, \ldots, z_0] \in \{0,1\}^{W-1}$.

Sign and Zero Extensions. A "sign-extension" of an L-bit value z to W bits (where $L < W$) is the W-bit value $z_{\text{sign-ext}}$ with bits $[z_s, \ldots, z_s, z_{L-1}, \ldots, z_0]$. That is, the sign bit of z is replicated to fill the higher-order bits of z until it reaches length W. A "zero-extension" is when, instead of the sign bit, the 0 bit is used. This results in W-bit $z_{\text{zero-ext}}$ with bits $[0, \ldots, 0, z_{L-1}, \ldots, z_0]$.

3.1 Performing Instruction Logic Using Lookups

As described in Sect. 2.2, the Jolt paradigm avoids the complexity of implementing each instruction's logic as constraints in a circuit by encapsulating instruction execution into a lookup table. Specifically, we identify an "evaluation table" for each operation opcode, $T_{\text{opcode}}[x \parallel y] = r$, that contains the required result for all possible inputs x, y. Jolt combines the tables for all instructions into

---

[16] See https://en.wikipedia.org/wiki/Two%27s_complement for an overview of how two's complement maps bit vectors in $\{0,1\}^L$ to integers in $\{-2^L, \ldots, 2^L - 1\}$ and vice versa.

one table and thus makes only one lookup query per step to this table as $T_{\text{risc-v}}[\text{opcode} \parallel x \parallel y] = r$. Given a processor and instruction set, this table is fixed and independent of the program or inputs. The key contribution of Jolt is to design these enormous tables with a certain *decomposability* structure (see Definition 4) that allows for efficient lookup arguments using Lasso.

Preparing Operands and the Lookup Query. The main responsiblity of the constraint system is to prepare the appropriate operands x, y at each step before the lookup. This is efficient to do as the operands only come from the set {value in rs1, value in rs2, imm, PC}. This means, for example, that the instructions ADD and ADDI are expressed by the same lookup table as they only differ in whether the second operand comes from register rs2 or is imm, respectively. With the operands prepared, the lookup query is then committed to by the prover and fed to the lookup argument for verification. The query is of the form opcode $\parallel$ z where z is generally $x \parallel y$ or $(x + y)$ or $(x \times y)$, making it either $2 \cdot W$ or $W + 1$ bits in length. The prover provides as advice the claimed entry, result, in the lookup table corresponding to the query.

The trace of all lookup queries and entries is sent to Lasso. As described in Definition 4, Lasso requires the query to be split into "chunks" which are fed into different subtables. The prover provides these chunks as advice, which are c in number for some small constant c, and hence approximately W/c or $2W/c$ bits long, depending on the structure of z. The constraint system must verify that the chunks correctly constitute z, but need not perform any range checks as the Lasso algorithm itself later implicitly enforces these on the chunks.

3.2   Using Memory-Checking

The machine state transition involves reading from and writing to three conceptually separate parts of memory: (1) the program code, (2) the registers and (3) the random access memory. As discussed in Sect. 2.3, the most efficient way to enforce correct reads and writes is by using the offline memory checking techniques. These techniques are used for reading from the program code, reading and writing to registrers, and performing load and store operations from the RAM. Unlike other operations, loads and stores do not involve lookups to a large table to perform their core function. As is standard in zkVM design, Jolt conceptualizes the memory-checking procedure as a black box that guarantees correctness of all the memory reads and writes required by the CPU execution, and hence the proof proceeds assuming these operations are correct.

At the start of the proof, the prover commits to the transcript of *all* memory accesses in the form of two sequences: the sequence of reads RS and that of writes WS. Each access is represented as a 3-tuple of field elements (a, v, t) where a is the address read from (or written to), v is the value read (or written) and t is the "timestamp". In writes, the timestamp is the current CPU step counter, and in reads, the timestamp is that of the preceding write to that address.

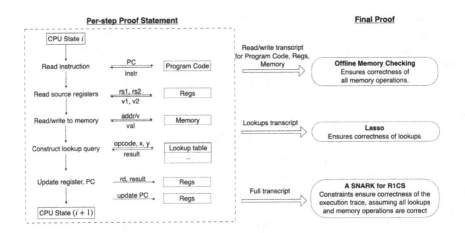

Fig. 2. Proving the correctness of CPU execution using offline memory checking (Sect. 3.2) and lookups (Sect. 3.1).

The offline memory-checking procedure takes these sequences and their commitments as inputs and convinces the verifier that they are consistent: that is, the value read from an address is always the latest value written to that address. The constraint system also takes the transcript of all reads and writes and performs various checks, such as ensuring the address read from or written to is the one deterministically computed by the corresponding step's operation and CPU state. See Appendix C.3 of the full version [AST23] for the list of constraints enforced.

Supporting Byte-Addressable Memory. RISC-V requires that memory be byte-addressable (as opposed to word-addressable). A load or store operation may read up to $W/8$ (which equals four and eight for 32-bit and 64-bit processors, respectively) bytes in a given instruction. Thus, when writing a W-bit value v, the prover must provide its byte-decomposition $[v_1 \ldots v_{W/8}]$ as each byte is stored in a separate address in memory. Jolt enforces range-checks on the provided bytes through lookups performed using Lasso. Certain load instructions also require the values read from memory to be sign-extended to W bits. This is enforced using lookups to small tables to obtain the sign bit. See Appendix C.2 of the full version [AST23] for more details.

3.3   Formatting Assembly Code

Before the proof starts, the assembly code is formatted into the 5-tuple form of Definition 6: ⟨opcode, rs1, rs2, rd, imm⟩. Instructions may need to sign-extend or zero-extend imm to W bits. This is a deterministic choice that depends only on the instruction (and is independent of the rest of the program or inputs).

Additionally, in our design, each instruction may also comes with a number of one-bit "flags" that guide the constraint system. For example, in our design, opflag[5] is 1 to indicate whether the instruction is a jump instruction, and opflags[7] is 1 if and only if the lookup's result is to be stored in rd. Note that these flags are fixed for any given instruction. See Appendix C.1 of the full version [AST23] for a list of all the fourteen flags used in Jolt.

Putting this together, before the proof starts, the prover and verifier convert the RISC-V assembly code to the 5-tuple format, along with the flags packed into one "packed_flags"value. These six elements are then stored in consecutive locations of a read-only section of memory and accessed using standard offline memory-checking techniques in the constraint system. Jolt thus performs six memory-checking reads per CPU step to read each element of the tuple. As the program code is read-only, the prover's cost involves committing to the elements of the tuple, along with the read timestamp for the address PC .

4 Analyzing MLE-Structure and Decomposability

This section illustrates the process of designing MLE-structured tables and decomposing them as per Definition 4 required by Lasso. We first establish notation and then design the tables for three important functions that are used as building blocks for the tables of many RISC-V instructions: equality, less than, and shifts. The MLE-structured tables and their decomposition for other instructions such as arithmetic ones (like ADD, SUB), logical ones (like AND, OR, XOR), and jumps and branches are described in Appendix B of the full version [AST23]. Load and store instructions do not perform any lookups.

Notation. Let z be a field element in $\{0, 1, \ldots, 2^W - 1\} \subset \mathbb{F}$. We denote the binary representation of z as $\mathsf{bin}(z) = [z_{W-1}, \ldots, z_0] \in \{0, 1\}^W$. Here, z_0 is the least significant bit (LSB), while z_{W-1} is the most significant bit (MSB). That is, $z = \sum_{i=0}^{W-1} 2^i z_i$. We refer to the "sign-bit" of z as $z_s = z_{W-1}$. We use $z_{<i}$ and $z_{>i}$ to refer to the subsequences $[z_{i-1}, \ldots, z_0]$ and $[z_{W-1}, \ldots, z_{i+1}]$, respectively.[17]

Concatenation of Bit Vectors. Given two bit vectors $x, y \in \{0, 1\}^W$, we use $x \parallel y$ to refer to the number whose binary representation is the concatenation $[x_{W-1}, \ldots, x_0 \parallel y_{W-1}, \ldots, y_0]$. Under this definition, it holds that $\mathsf{int}(x \parallel y) = \mathsf{int}(x) \cdot 2^W + \mathsf{int}(y)$.

Decomposing Bit Vectors into Chunks. For a constant c, and any $x \in \{0, 1\}^L$, we divide the bits of input x naturally into chunks

$$x = [x_{W-1} \ldots x_0] = X_{c-1} \parallel \ldots \parallel X_2 \parallel X_0, \tag{3}$$

---

[17] In the above paragraphs, we used an italicized z to denote both a field element in $\{0, \ldots, 2^W - 1\}$ and a vector in $\{0, 1\}^W$. Throughout the paper, which of the two sets any variable z resides in will be clear from context.

with each $X_i \in \{0,1\}^{W/c}$. In the following discussions, we assume c divides W for simplicity. However, this is not necessary and is in fact more efficient to set $c = 3$ for $W = 32$ and $c = 6$ for $W = 64$, resulting in differing chunk lengths.

Three Instructive Functions and Associated Lookup Tables

Let field $\mathbb{F}$ be a prime order field of size at least 2^W. Let x and y denote field elements that are guaranteed to be in the set $\{0, 1, \ldots, 2^W - 1\}$.

4.1   The Equality Function

MLE-Structured. The equality function EQ takes as inputs two vectors $x, y \in \{0, 1\}^W$ of identical length and outputs 1 if they are equal, and 0 otherwise. We will use a subscript to clarify the number of bits in each input to EQ, e.g., EQ_W denotes the equality function defined over domain $\{0, 1\}^W \times \{0, 1\}^W$. It is easily confirmed that the multilinear extension of EQ_W is as follow:

$$\widetilde{\mathsf{EQ}}_W(x, y) = \prod_{j=0}^{W-1} (x_j y_j + (1 - x_j)(1 - y_j)). \tag{4}$$

Indeed, the right hand side is clearly a multilinear polynomial in x and y, and if $x, y \in \{0, 1\}^W$, it equals 1 if and only if $x = y$. Hence, the right hand side must equal the unique multilinear extension of the equality function. Clearly, it can be evaluated at any point $(x, y) \in \mathbb{F}^W \times \mathbb{F}^W$ with $O(W)$ field operations.

Decomposability. To determine whether two W-bit inputs $x, y \in \{0, 1\}^W$ are equal, one can decompose x and y into c chunks of length W/c, compute equality of each chunk, and multiply the results together.

Let $x = [X_{c-1}, \ldots, X_0]$ and $y = [Y_{c-1}, \ldots, Y_0]$ denote the decomposition of x and y into c chunks each, as per Eq. (3). Let EQ_W denote the "big" table of size $N = 2^{2W}$ indexed by pairs (x, y) with $x, y \in \{0, 1\}^W$, such that $\mathsf{EQ}_W[x \parallel y] = \widetilde{\mathsf{EQ}}_W(x, y)$. Let $\mathsf{EQ}_{W/c}$ denote the "small" table of size $N^{2W/c}$ indexed by pairs (X, Y) of chunks $X, Y \in \{0, 1\}^{W/c}$, such that $\mathsf{EQ}_{W/c}[X \parallel Y] = 1$ if $X = Y$ and $\mathsf{EQ}_{W/c}[X \parallel Y] = 0$ otherwise. The table below asserts that evaluating the equality function on x and y is equivalent to evaluating the equality function on each chunk $X_i \parallel Y_i$ and multiplying the results.

CHUNKS	SUBTABLES	FULL TABLE
$C_i = X_i \parallel Y_i$	$\mathsf{EQ}_{W/c}[X_i \parallel Y_i] = \widetilde{\mathsf{EQ}}_{W/c}(X_i, Y_i)$	$\mathsf{EQ}_W[x, y] = \prod_{i=0}^{c-1} \mathsf{EQ}_{W/c}[X_i \parallel Y_i]$

The (lone) subtable $\mathsf{EQ}_{W/c}$ is MLE-structured by Eq. (4).

4.2   Less Than Comparision

To show that an L-bit value x is less than another L-bit value y, it suffices to enforce an L-bit range check on $y - x$. However, this doesn't work when x and y are treated as two-complement signed numbers and we thus use a lookup table. We explain below how this table is designed through unsigned less-than comparisons (LTU) and show how to adapt it to perform signed comparisons (LTS) in Appendix B.5 of the full version [AST23].

MLE-Structured. The comparison of two unsigned data types $x, y \in \{0, 1, \ldots, 2^{W-1}\}$ is involved in many instructions. For example, SLTU outputs 1 if $x < y$ and 0 otherwise, where the inequality interprets x and y as integers in the natural way. Note that the inequality computed here is strict. Consider the following $2W$-variate multilinear polynomial (LTU below stands for "less than unsigned"):

$$\widetilde{\mathsf{LTU}}_i(x, y) = (1 - x_i) \cdot y_i \cdot \widetilde{\mathsf{EQ}}_{W-i-1}(x_{>i}, y_{>i}).   (5)$$

Clearly, this polynomial satisfies the following two properties:

(1) Suppose $x \geq y$. Then $\widetilde{\mathsf{LTU}}_i(x, y) = 0$ for all i.

(2) Suppose $x < y$. Let k be the first index (starting from the MSB of x and y) such that $x_k = 0$ and $y_k = 1$. Then $\widetilde{\mathsf{LTU}}_k(x, y) = 1$ and $\widetilde{\mathsf{LTU}}_i(x, y) = 0$ for all $i \neq k$.

Based on the above properties, it is easy to check that

$$\widetilde{\mathsf{LTU}}(x, y) = \sum_{i=0}^{W-1} \widetilde{\mathsf{LTU}}_i(x, y).   (6)$$

Indeed, the right hand side is clearly multilinear, and by the two properties above, it equals $\widetilde{\mathsf{LTU}}(x, y)$ whenever $x, y \in \{0, 1\}^W$. It is not difficult to see that the right hand side of Eq. (6) can be evaluated at any point $(x, y) \in \mathbb{F}^W \times \mathbb{F}^W$ with $O(W)$ field operations as the set $\{\widetilde{\mathsf{EQ}}_{W-i}(x_{>i}, y_{>i})\}_{i=0}^{W-1}$ can be computed in $O(W)$ total steps using the recurrence relation

$$\widetilde{\mathsf{EQ}}_{W-i-1}(x_{>i}, y_{>i}) = \widetilde{\mathsf{EQ}}_{W-i-2}(x_{>(i+1)}, y_{>(i+1)}) \cdot \widetilde{\mathsf{EQ}}(x_i, y_i).   (7)$$

See [Tha22, Figure 3.3] for a depiction of this procedure.

Decomposing $\widetilde{\mathsf{LTU}}$. A similar reasoning to the derivation of Eq. (6) reveals the following. As usual, break x and y into c chunks, $X_{c-1} \parallel \cdots \parallel X_0$ and $Y_{c-1} \parallel \cdots \parallel Y_0$. Let $\mathsf{LTU}_{W/c}[X_i \parallel Y_i] = \widetilde{\mathsf{LTU}}_{W/c}(X_i, Y_i)$ denote the subtable with entry 1 if $X_i < Y_i$ when interpreted as unsigned (W/c)-bit data types, and

0 otherwise. Then

$$\mathsf{LTU}_W[x \parallel y] = \sum_{i=0}^{c-1} \mathsf{LTU}_{W/c}[X_i \parallel Y_i] \cdot \mathsf{EQ}_{W/c}[X_{>i} \parallel Y_{>i}]$$

$$= \sum_{i=0}^{c-1} \left(\mathsf{LTU}_{W/c}[X_i \parallel Y_i] \cdot \prod_{j<i} \mathsf{EQ}_{W/c}(X_j \parallel Y_j) \right)$$

Thus, evaluating $\mathsf{LTU}(x, y)$ can be done by evaluating $\mathsf{LTU}_{W/c}$ and $\mathsf{EQ}_{W/c}$ on each chunk (X_i, Y_i) ($\mathsf{EQ}_{W/c}$ need not be evaluated on the lowest-order chunk (X_c, Y_c)). This is summarized in the table below.

CHUNKS	SUBTABLES	FULL TABLE
$C_i = X_i \parallel Y_i$	$\mathsf{LTU}_{W/c}[X_i \parallel Y_i]$, $\mathsf{EQ}_{W/c}[X_i \parallel Y_i]$	$\mathsf{LTU}_W[x \parallel y] = \sum_{i=0}^{c-1} \mathsf{LTU}_{W/c}[X_i \parallel Y_i] \cdot \prod_{j<i} \mathsf{EQ}_{W/c}[X_j \parallel Y_j]$

The two subtables LTU and EQ are MLE-structured by Eqs. (4) and (6).

4.3   Shift Left Logical

MLE-Structured. SLL takes a W-bit integer x and a $\log(W)$-bit integer y, and shifts the binary representation of x to the left by length y. Bits shifted beyond the MSB of x are ignored, and the vacated lower bits are filled with zeros.[18] For a constant k, let

$$\widetilde{\mathsf{SLL}}_k(x) = \sum_{j=k}^{W-1} 2^j \cdot x_{j-k}. \tag{8}$$

It is straightforward to check that the right hand side of Eq. (8) is multilinear (in fact, linear) function in x, and that when evaluated at $x \in \{0,1\}^W$, it outputs the unsigned W-bit data type whose binary representation is the same as that of the output of the SLL instruction on inputs x and k, $\mathsf{SLL}(x, k)$.

Now consider

$$\widetilde{\mathsf{SLL}}(x, y) = \sum_{k \in \{0,1\}^{\log W}} \widetilde{eq}(y, k) \cdot \widetilde{\mathsf{SLL}}_k(x). \tag{9}$$

It is straightforward to check that the right hand side of Eq. (9) is multilinear in (x, y), and that, when evaluated at $x \in \{0,1\}^W \times \{0,1\}^{\log W}$, it outputs the unsigned W-bit data type $\mathsf{SLL}(x, y)$.

Decomposability. We split the value to be shifted, x, into c chunks, $X_1, \ldots, X_c$, each consisting of $W' = W/c$ bits. y has only one chunk, Y_0, consisting of the

---

[18] For $L = 32$-bit data types, the RISC-V manual says that the "shift amount is encoded in the lower $5 = \log(W)$ bits".

lowest order $\log W$ bits. As explained below, we decompose a lookup into the evaluation table of SLL into a lookup into c different subtables, each of size $2^{W'+\log W}$. For $W = 64$, a reasonable setting of c would be 4 (instead of the usual $c = 6$ for most other instructions), ensuring that $2^{W'+\log W} = 2^{20}$.

Conceptually, each chunk X_i of X needs to determine how many of its input bits goes "out of range" after the shift of length y. By out of range, we mean that shifting x left by y bits causes those bits to overflow the MSB of x and hence not contribute to the output of the instruction.

For chunks $i = 0, \ldots, (c-1)$ and shift length $k \in \{0, 1\}^{\log W}$, define:

$$m_{i,k} = \min\{W', \max\{0, (\text{int}(k) + W' \cdot (i+1)) - W\}\}$$

Here, $m_{i,k}$ equals the number of bits from the i'th chunk that go out of range. Let $m'_{i,k} = W' - m_{i,k} - 1$ denote the index of the highest-order bit within the i'th chunk that does *not* go out of range. Then the evaluation table of SLL decomposes into c smaller tables $\text{SLL}_0, \ldots, \text{SLL}_{c-1}$ as follows.

CHUNKS	SUBTABLES		FULL TABLE
$C_i = X_i \parallel Y_0$	$\text{SLL}_i[X_i \parallel Y_0] =$		$\text{SLL}[x \parallel y] = \sum_{i=0}^{c-1} 2^{i \cdot W'} \cdot \text{SLL}_i[X_i \parallel Y_c]$
	$\sum_{k \in \{0,1\}^{\log W}} \widetilde{\text{EQ}}(Y_0, k) \cdot \left(\sum_{j=0}^{m'_{i,k}} 2^{j+\text{int}(k)} \cdot X_{i,j} \right)$		

Note that each SLL_i can be evaluated at any input $(x, y) \in \mathbb{F}^{W'} \times \mathbb{F}^{\log W}$ in $O(W')$ field operations. Indeed, the set $\{\widetilde{\text{EQ}}(Y_0, k)\}_{k \in \{0,1\}^{\log W}}$ can be computed in $O(W)$ field operations via the recurrence in Eq. (7). Similarly, the set $\{2^{j+\text{int}(k)}\}_{i \in \{0,\ldots,c-1\}, k \in \{0,1\}^{\log W}}$ can be computed with $O(W)$ field operations. It follows that $\text{SLL}_0(x \parallel y), \ldots, \text{SLL}_{c-1}(x \parallel y)$ can be evaluated in $O(W)$ field operations in total.

4.4   The Multiplication Extension

On top of the base integer instruction set, RISC-V supports various instructions to multiply, divide and find the remainder with two operands in an optional "M" extension. Jolt can handle all of these instructions, most with no additional overhead. The only caveat is that six of these are split into via several "pseudoinstructions". For example, division is handled by having P provide the quotient and remainder as untrusted advice in one pseudoinstruction, and they are checked for correctness by performing multiplication and addition with more pseudoinstructions. Appendix E of the full version [AST23] describes these techniques along with the tables for each new instruction.

5 Putting It All Together: A SNARK for RISC-V Emulation

The overall architecture of Jolt is depicted in Fig. 2. The Jolt prover executes the program to obtain the trace, and calls the provers for each module (memory-checking, lookups and constraint satisfaction) to obtain three proofs that together form the Jolt proof. This involves the prover cryptographically committing to the execution trace z of the VM on the appropriate input (or more precisely, its multilinear extension polynomial $\tilde{z}$, using any multilinear polynomial commitment scheme). We leave a detailed discussion of the R1CS and memory-checking modules of Jolt to Appendix F of the full version [AST23], and focus on a particular aspect of the lookup argument here.

5.1 Combining Instruction Lookup Tables into One

The previous sections so far explained that the evaluation table of each individual RISC-V instruction is both MLE-structured and decomposable. But Lasso is a lookup argument for a single decomposable table. We now explain how to bridge this gap, and thus make Jolt use "just one lookup table".

Closely related issues have been addressed in earlier work on zkVMs. Specifically, the fact that the evaluation tables of different RISC-V instructions have different decompositions into subtables is analogous to the following issue dealt with in earlier approaches to front-end design for zkVMs: different instructions are computed by different circuits, and while only one instruction is executed per step of the VM, in general it is not known until runtime which instruction will be executed at any given step. Appendix F of the full version [AST23] discusses techniques used in existing works, such as the re-ordering approach of vRAM [ZGK+18], to solve this problem.

Conceptually, the approach we use expresses the concatenation of the evaluation tables of each instruction (and of which we have shown to be decomposable) as itself decomposable, analogous to how the concatenation of MLE-structured tables is itself MLE-structured. To this end, it is convenient to treat each instruction as leading to $2c - 1$ different lookups into subtables ($2c - 1$ here comes from the maximum number of subtable lookups across all instructions, namely due to SLT as described in Sect. 4). For instructions that require fewer than $2c - 1$ lookups into subtables, the extraneous lookup results can be set to 0, thereby avoiding any cryptographic work on the part of the prover if using an MSM-based commitment scheme (we will explain below how to ensure that these extraneous subtable lookup results will be ignored by all subtables).

There will be a single collation polynomial g (Definition 4) for all instructions, but g will take as input not only the results of relevant subtable lookups, but also 8 additional variables that, when assigned values in $\{0, 1\}$, are interpreted as the bit-representation of the opcode. Denoting these variables as $w = (w_1, \ldots, w_8)$, and letting $g_i(z)$ denote the collation polynomial for the i'th instruction, and letting x denote a vector of $2c - 1$ variables, interpreted as specifying the results of $2c - 1$ subtable lookups, we define

$$g(w, x) = \sum_{y \in \{0,1\}^8} \widetilde{\mathsf{EQ}}(w, y) \cdot g_{\mathsf{int}(y)}(x).$$

This definition ensures that for any instruction i, $g(\mathsf{bin}(i), x) = g_i(x)$, i.e., collation for each instruction is performed correctly by g.

The core of Lasso is to invoke a grand product argument for each subtable (as explained in Appendix G.3 of the full version [AST23], this is due to the use of memory-checking techniques to verify that the sequences of reads from the subtable are consistent). We can modify the circuit used to compute these products for each subtable to take as input the bits of the opcode associated with each lookup. This way, the circuit can simply ignore any lookups associated with opcodes that do not access the subtable associated with the circuit.

To minimize the size of this circuit, rather than having the prover commit to the 8 bits of the opcode, it may be preferable to instead have the prover commit to some additional Boolean flags (beyond the Boolean circuit flags already described in Sect. 3.3), so that each subtable's circuit only needs to inspect fewer than 8 Boolean flags to determine whether or not a given lookup operation actually is intended to access the subtable.

6   Qualitative Cost Estimation

The overall architecture of Jolt is depicted in Fig. 2. In this section, we analyze the cost of a lookup and of the prover's per-step work in Jolt.

6.1   Cost of a Lookup

We first briefly state the costs incurred by the prover when making a lookup query in terms of the bit-lengths of the elements to be committed to. A Lasso lookup into a decomposed table involves committing to the following elements for some fixed Lasso parameter c:

1. Chunks of the operands x, y or of $x + y$ or $x \times y$. (Each $< 2W/c$ bits.)

2. The outputs of the subtables involved in the lookup. (Each $< W/c$ bits.)

3. Access counts of each subtable at that step. (Each $< \log T$ bits.)

4. Elements involved in the range checks of the chunks. (Each $< \log T$ bits.)

In the worst case (the LTU table, to be precise), each step involves at most $2c - 1$ total elements. We use this scenario when reporting costs in Sect. 6.2. Note that the chunks need to be range-checked as it is possible for the prover to provide invalid chunks x_i, y_i but together form a valid lookup index $x_i \parallel y_i$. These range checks are a special case of Lasso with parameter $c = 1$ and, from Remark 1, each involve committing to a single element bounded by the step counter.

With parameters $(W = 32, c = 3)$, a lookup requires committing to 6 elements of at most 11 bits, 6 elements of at most 22 bits, and 12 elements that are equal to the step counter.

6.2 Overall Prover Costs in Jolt

From Fig. 2, the broad steps involved are committing to the transcripts and then proving satisfaction of the constraint system, lookup arguments and offline memory-checking procedures. The prover's field operation costs and the verifier's costs are presented in Table 1. = We note here that the constraint system is a uniform circuit consisting of under 50 R1CS constraints per CPU step. In Appendix C.3 and F of the full version [AST23], we describe the constraints and how Spartan is used to prove that they are satisfied. As discussed in Sect. 1.3, the dominating cost for the prover is in producing commitments.

Table 1. Field operation costs involved in Jolt for a program that runs in n steps with memory of size M. Cryptographic group operation costs are described in Tables 2 and 3. Lasso is run with parameter c and Jolt performs at most one Lasso lookup per step. We assume that memory-checking and Lasso protocols implement the optimized variant of the GKR protocol due to Thaler [Tha13]. We assume Spartan is instantiated with a polynomial commitment scheme with $O(\log n)$-verification time opening proofs.

Jolt field operation costs			
Module	Dominating Cost	$\mathcal{P}$ Cost	$\mathcal{V}$ Cost
Memory-checking	$13 \cdot n$ memory operations on an $(M + \lvert\mathsf{code}\rvert + 32)$-sized memory	$O(n + M)$	$O(\log^2 (n + M))$
Lasso lookups	n lookups on a decomposable table of size $O(2^{128})$	$O(c^2 n)$	$O(\log^2 n)$
Constraint checking	Spartan proof on a uniform R1CS with $\approx 50 \cdot n$ constraints	$O(n)$	$O(\log n)$

The rest of this section analyzes the elements that are committed to in Jolt. Table 2 provides a upper bound on the elements committed per step grouped by their bit-lengths. We measure bit-length as that is the main factor determining the commitment cost when using Pippenger's multi-scalar multiplication algorithm.[19] We provide below a brief overview of the elements involved and leave a more detailed discussion to Appendix C of the full version [AST23].

---

[19] In Pippenger's multi-scalar multiplication algorithm to commit to elements, committing to an N-bit element costs roughly $\mathsf{ceil}(N/22)$ group operations. This makes committing to a 32-bit element cost two group operations while a 256-bit element costs 12 group operations.

Table 2. An approximate spread of the spread of elements committed to in Jolt in lookup-based operations (i.e., excluding loads and stores which do not involve lookups) by their bit-length. We assume that the program code is under 2^{22} bytes long, and the program finishes in under 2^{22} CPU steps. The Lasso parameter $c = 3$ when $W = 32$ and $c = 6$ when $W = 64$. We approximate the per-step committments costs in terms of the cost of committing to a 256-bit element when using Pippenger's MSM algorithm: an n-bit number involves $\lceil n/22 \rceil$ group operations to commit to.

Per-step Commitment Costs for Non-Memory Operations			
Bit-length	Number of Elements	In RV32 $W = 32, c = 3$	In RV64 $W = 64, c = 6$
1	22	22	22
$[2, 12]$	9	9	9
$(2W/c) \approx 22$	5c	15	30
$\log(T)$	9+4c	21	33
W	12	12	12
Total Elements	$52 + 9c$	79	106
In 256-bit commit equivalents:		< 8 elements	< 11 elements

Elements Involved in CPU Execution. First, let's look at the elements involved in satisfying the CPU step circuit's constraints before looking at the elements needed for the Lasso argument. The smallest of these are the 1-bit circuit flags (Sect. 3.3) and the opcode bits (Sect. 5), and the 5-bit elements indexing the source (rs1, rs2) and destination (rd) registers read from the instruction. Slightly larger elements are the PC (which could be as large as $\log |\text{program\_code}|$ bits) and the step counter, both of which we assume to be under 2^{22} to simplify our analysis. Finally, the largest elements involved are the W-bit ones specifying the values stored in the two source registers, the sign-extended imm read from the program code, the lookup output, (which is generally stored in the destination register), and the advice element involved (only) in division and reminder operations. However, an instruction uses at most 4 of these elements (specifically, this is because the division/remainder instructions do use advice never use imm). Beyond this, there are more (eight to be specific) W-bit values that arise as auxiliary witness values involved in constraint satisfaction. These can be thought of as the internal wires of the circuit representing each step's constraint checks.

6.3   Cost of Memory Operations

Load and store operations do not involve large lookups to perform the core instruction logic. Rather, the main cost here is performing memory-checking operations, one for each byte of memory involved in the load/store. This can be up to four for 32-bit processors and eight for 64-bit processors. The elements involved on top of the non-lookup elements of the non-memory instructions are

Table 3. The spread of elements committed per memory operation with the extra overhead elements per byte of load or store. See Appendix C.2 and Table 5 of the full version [AST23] for more details on the exact procedure and elements involved. Note that the per-step costs are independent of the total size of the memory . We approximate these costs in terms of the cost of committing to a 256-bit element when using Pippenger's MSM algorithm, assuming that the program code is under 2^{22} bytes long and the program finishes executing in under 2^{22} CPU steps.

Base Costs per Memory Instruction		**Overhead per Byte**	
Bit-length	Number of Elements	for Loads	for Stores
1	23	1	1
$[2, 12]$	4	1	1
$(2W/c) \approx 22$	2	1	1
$\log(T)$	8	2	3
W	10	–	–
Total Elements	47	5	6
In 256-bit equivalents (both RV32, RV64)	$\approx 5 - 6$ elements	≈ 0.5 elements	≈ 0.5 elements

the actual bytes read/written, the timestamps involved in memory-checking (one for each byte), and the cost of range checking these bytes and timestamps. Memory operations also commit to fewer W-bit elements as they don't involve computing the lookup query or reading the lookup output. Stores, which are memory "writes", require 8-bit range checks of the bytes written. These range-checks are again very efficient in Lasso (see Remark 1) and only involve committing to a single element of value at most the number of steps up to that point.

Acknowledgements and Disclosures. Justin Thaler was supported in part by NSF CAREER award CCF-1845125 and by DARPA under Agreement No. HR00112020022. Any opinions, findings and conclusions or recommendations expressed in this material are those of the author and do not necessarily reflect the views of the United States Government or DARPA.

Disclosures. Thaler is a Research Partner at a16z crypto and is an investor in various blockchain-based platforms, as well as in the crypto ecosystem more broadly (for general a16z disclosures, see https://www.a16z.com/disclosures/.)

References

[AGL+22] Avigad, J., Goldberg, L., Levit, D., Seginer, Y., Titelman, A.: A verified algebraic representation of cairo program execution. In: Proceedings of the 11th ACM SIGPLAN International Conference on Certified Programs and Proofs, pp. 153–165 (2022)

[AST23] Arun, A., Setty, S., Thaler, J.: Jolt: snarks for virtual machines via lookups. Cryptology ePrint Archive, Report 2023/1217 (2023)

[BBB+18] Bünz, B., Bootle, J., Boneh, D., Poelstra, A., Wuille, P., Maxwell, G.: Bulletproofs: Short proofs for confidential transactions and more. In: Proceedings of the IEEE Symposium on Security and Privacy (S&P) (2018)

[BBHR18] Ben-Sasson, E., Bentov, I., Horesh, Y., Riabzev, M.: Fast Reed-Solomon interactive oracle proofs of proximity. In: Proceedings of the International Colloquium on Automata, Languages and Programming (ICALP) (2018)

[BCC+16] Bootle, J., Cerulli, A., Chaidos, P., Groth, J., Petit, C.: Efficient zero-knowledge arguments for arithmetic circuits in the discrete log setting. In: Proceedings of the International Conference on the Theory and Applications of Cryptographic Techniques (EUROCRYPT) (2016)

[BCG+18] Bootle, J., Cerulli, A., Groth, J., Jakobsen, S., Maller, M.: Arya: nearly linear-time zero-knowledge proofs for correct program execution. In: Proceedings of the International Conference on the Theory and Application of Cryptology and Information Security (ASIACRYPT) (2018)

[BCHO22] Bootle, J., Chiesa, A., Hu, Y., Orru, M.: Gemini: elastic snarks for diverse environments. In: Proceedings of the International Conference on the Theory and Applications of Cryptographic Techniques (EUROCRYPT) (2022)

[BDFG20] Boneh, D., Drake, J., Fisch, B., Gabizon, A.: Halo Infinite: Recursive zk-SNARKs from any Additive Polynomial Commitment Scheme. Cryptology ePrint Archive, Report 2020/1536 (2020)

[BEG+91] Blum, M., Evans, W., Gemmell, P., Kannan, S., Naor, M.: Checking the correctness of memories. In: Proceedings of the IEEE Symposium on Foundations of Computer Science (FOCS) (1991)

[BFR+13] Braun, B., Feldman, A.J., Ren, Z., Setty, S., Blumberg, A.J., Walfish, M.: Verifying computations with state. In: Proceedings of the ACM Symposium on Operating Systems Principles (SOSP) (2013)

[BFS20] Bünz, B., Fisch, B., Szepieniec, A.: Transparent SNARKs from DARK compilers. In: Proceedings of the International Conference on the Theory and Applications of Cryptographic Techniques (EUROCRYPT) (2020)

[BGH19] Bowe, S., Grigg, J., Hopwood, D.: Recursive proof composition without a trusted setup. Cryptology ePrint Archive, Report 2019/1021 (2019)

[BGtR23] Bruestle, J., Gafni, P., the RISC Zero Team: Scalable, transparent arguments of RISC-V integrity, RISC Zero zkVM (2023)

[BSBHR19] Ben-Sasson, E., Bentov, I., Horesh, Y., Riabzev, M.: Scalable zero knowledge with no trusted setup. In: Boldyreva, A., Micciancio, D. (eds.) CRYPTO 2019. LNCS, vol. 11694, pp. 701–732. Springer, Cham (2019). https://doi.org/10.1007/978-3-030-26954-8_23

[BSCG+13a] Ben-Sasson, E., Chiesa, A., Genkin, D., Tromer, E., Virza, M.: SNARKs for C: verifying program executions succinctly and in zero knowledge. In: Canetti, R., Garay, J.A. (eds.) CRYPTO 2013. LNCS, vol. 8043, pp. 90–108. Springer, Heidelberg (2013). https://doi.org/10.1007/978-3-642-40084-1_6

[BSCG+13b] Ben-Sasson, E., Chiesa, A., Genkin, D., Tromer, E., Virza, M.: Tinyram architecture specification, vol. 991. en. In:(Aug. 2013), pp. 16 (2013)

[BSCGT13] Ben-Sasson, E., Chiesa, A., Genkin, D., Tromer, E.: Fast reductions from rams to delegatable succinct constraint satisfaction problems. In: Proceedings of the 4th conference on Innovations in Theoretical Computer Science, pp. 401–414 (2013)

[BSCTV14] Ben-Sasson, E., Chiesa, A., Tromer, E., Virza, M.: Scalable zero knowledge via cycles of elliptic curves. In: Garay, J.A., Gennaro, R. (eds.) CRYPTO 2014. LNCS, vol. 8617, pp. 276–294. Springer, Heidelberg (2014). https://doi.org/10.1007/978-3-662-44381-1_16

[CBBZ23] Chen, B., Bünz, B., Boneh, D., Zhang, Z.: HyperPlonk: plonk with linear-time prover and high-degree custom gates. In: Hazay, C., Stam, M. (eds.) EUROCRYPT 2023. LNCS, vol. 14005, pp. 499–530. Springer, Cham (2023). https://doi.org/10.1007/978-3-031-30617-4_17

[CHM+20] Chiesa, A., Hu, Y., Maller, M., Mishra, P., Vesely, N., Ward, N.: Marlin: preprocessing zkSNARKs with universal and updatable SRS. In: Canteaut, A., Ishai, Y. (eds.) EUROCRYPT 2020. LNCS, vol. 12105, pp. 738–768. Springer, Cham (2020). https://doi.org/10.1007/978-3-030-45721-1_26

[CMT12] Cormode, G., Mitzenmacher, M., Thaler, J.: Practical verified computation with streaming interactive proofs. In: Proceedings of the Innovations in Theoretical Computer Science (ITCS) (2012)

[ET18] Eberhardt, J., Tai, S.: Zokrates - scalable privacy-preserving off-chain computations. In: 2018 IEEE International Conference on Internet of Things (iThings) and IEEE Green Computing and Communications (GreenCom) and IEEE Cyber, Physical and Social Computing (CPSCom) and IEEE Smart Data (SmartData), pp. 1084–1091 (2018)

[FS86] Fiat, A., Shamir, A.: How to prove yourself: practical solutions to identification and signature problems. In: Proceedings of the International Cryptology Conference (CRYPTO), pp. 186–194 (1986)

[GKR08] Goldwasser, S., Kalai, Y.T., Rothblum, G.N.: Delegating computation: interactive proofs for muggles. In: Proceedings of the ACM Symposium on Theory of Computing (STOC) (2008)

[GPR21] Goldberg, L., Papini, S., Riabzev, M.: Cairo–a Turing-complete stark-friendly CPU architecture. Cryptology ePrint Archive (2021)

[Gro16] Groth, J.: On the size of pairing-based non-interactive arguments. In: Fischlin, M., Coron, J.-S. (eds.) EUROCRYPT 2016. LNCS, vol. 9666, pp. 305–326. Springer, Heidelberg (2016). https://doi.org/10.1007/978-3-662-49896-5_11

[GWC19] Gabizon, A., Williamson, Z.J., Ciobotaru, O.: PLONK: Permutations over Lagrange-bases for oecumenical noninteractive arguments of knowledge. ePrint Report 2019/953 (2019)

[KST22] Kothapalli, A., Setty, S., Tzialla, I.: Nova: recursive zero-knowledge arguments from folding schemes. In: Dodis, Y., Shrimpton, T. (eds.) CRYPTO 2022. LNCS, vol. 13510, pp. 359–388. Springer, Cham (2022). https://doi.org/10.1007/978-3-031-15985-5_13

[KZG10]   Kate, A., Zaverucha, G.M., Goldberg, I.: Constant-size commitments to polynomials and their applications. In: Abe, M. (ed.) ASIACRYPT 2010. LNCS, vol. 6477, pp. 177–194. Springer, Heidelberg (2010). https://doi.org/10.1007/978-3-642-17373-8_11

[Lee21]   Lee, J.: Dory: efficient, transparent arguments for generalised inner products and polynomial commitments. In: Nissim, K., Waters, B. (eds.) TCC 2021. LNCS, vol. 13043, pp. 1–34. Springer, Cham (2021). https://doi.org/10.1007/978-3-030-90453-1_1

[LFKN90] Lund, C., Fortnow, L., Karloff, H., Nisan, N.: Algebraic methods for interactive proof systems. In: Proceedings of the IEEE Symposium on Foundations of Computer Science (FOCS) (1990)

[Lip89]   Lipton, R.J.: Fingerprinting sets. Princeton University, Department of Computer Science (1989)

[SAGL18] Setty, S., Angel, S., Gupta, T., Lee, J.: Proving the correct execution of concurrent services in zero-knowledge. In: Proceedings of the USENIX Symposium on Operating Systems Design and Implementation (OSDI) (2018)

[Set20]   Setty, S.: Spartan: efficient and general-purpose zkSNARKs without trusted setup. In: Micciancio, D., Ristenpart, T. (eds.) CRYPTO 2020. LNCS, vol. 12172, pp. 704–737. Springer, Cham (2020). https://doi.org/10.1007/978-3-030-56877-1_25

[SL20]   Setty, S., Lee, J.: Quarks: quadruple-efficient transparent zkSNARKs. Cryptology ePrint Archive, Report 2020/1275 (2020)

[Sol23]   Solberg, T..: RISC Zero prover protocol & analysis (2023). https://github.com/ingonyama-zk/papers/blob/main/risc0_protocol_analysis.pdf

[STW23]   Setty, S., Thaler, J., Wahby, R.S.: Lasso: Unlocking the lookup singularity. Cryptology ePrint Archive, Report 2023/1216 (2023)

[Tha13]   Thaler, J.: Time-optimal interactive proofs for circuit evaluation. In: Canetti, R., Garay, J.A. (eds.) CRYPTO 2013. LNCS, vol. 8043, pp. 71–89. Springer, Heidelberg (2013). https://doi.org/10.1007/978-3-642-40084-1_5

[Tha22]   Thaler, J.: Proofs, arguments, and zero-knowledge. Found. Trends Priv. Secur. 4(2–4), 117–660 (2022)

[WA17]   Waterman, A., Asanovic, K.: The RISC-V instruction set manual (2017). https://riscv.org/wp-content/uploads/2017/05/riscv-spec-v2.2.pdf

[Whi]   Whitehat, B.: Lookup singularity. https://zkresear.ch/t/lookup-singularity/65/7

[WTS+18] Wahby, R.S., Tzialla, I., Shelat, A., Thaler, J., Walfish, M.: Doubly-efficient zkSNARKs without trusted setup. In: Proceedings of the IEEE Symposium on Security and Privacy (S&P) (2018)

[ZGK+18] Zhang, Y., Genkin, D., Katz, J., Papadopoulos, D., Papamanthou, C.: vRAM: faster verifiable RAM with program-independent preprocessing. In: Proceedings of the IEEE Symposium on Security and Privacy (S&P) (2018)

[ZXZS20] Zhang, J., Xie, T., Zhang, Y., Song, D.: Transparent polynomial delegation and its applications to zero knowledge proof. In: Proceedings of the IEEE Symposium on Security and Privacy (S&P) (2020)

Constant-Size zk-SNARKs in ROM
from Falsifiable Assumptions

Helger Lipmaa[1]($\boxtimes$) , Roberto Parisella[2] , and Janno Siim[2]

[1] University of Tartu, Tartu, Estonia
helger.lipmaa@gmail.com
[2] Simula UiB, Bergen, Norway

Abstract. We prove that the seminal KZG polynomial commitment scheme (PCS) is black-box extractable under a simple falsifiable assumption ARSDH. To create an interactive argument, we construct a compiler that combines a black-box extractable non-interactive PCS and a polynomial IOP (PIOP). The compiler incurs a minor cost per every committed polynomial. Applying the Fiat-Shamir transformation, we obtain slightly less efficient variants of well-known PIOP-based zk-SNARKs, such as Plonk, that are knowledge-sound in the ROM under the ARSDH assumption. Importantly, there is no need for idealized group models or knowledge assumptions. This results in the first known zk-SNARKs in the ROM from falsifiable assumptions with both an efficient prover and constant-size argument.

Keywords: Black-box knowledge-soundness · polynomial commitment scheme · polynomial IOP · witness-extended emulation · zk-SNARKs

1 Introduction

Zero-knowledge Succinct Arguments of Knowledge (zk-SNARKs) allow to give a short proof of computational statements without leaking any information besides the truth of the statements. Especially in the blockchain world, efficient zk-SNARKs have found wide-scale use [3,27,40] and thus are of great practical importance. Many recent zk-SNARKs are based on a combination of a polynomial commitment scheme (PCS, [26]) and an information-theoretically secure non-succinct proof system like polynomial IOP [10] (interactive oracle proof).

A PCS allows the prover to make a short commitment to a polynomial and later open it at a point chosen by the verifier. The very first PCS, KZG [26], uses one group element for commitment and opening and two pairing operations for verification. KZG is also additively homomorphic and efficiently batchable [8,26,42], making it ideal for zk-SNARKs with multiple PCS openings. On the negative side, it lacks a transparent setup, meaning that the public key cannot be generated from a public source of randomness. However, the public key is updatable, making it possible to generate it in a distributed way by different parties making sequential updates to the public key. The public key is secure if at least one honest party contributes with an update. Thus, KZG is preferred for

© International Association for Cryptologic Research 2024
M. Joye and G. Leander (Eds.): EUROCRYPT 2024, LNCS 14656, pp. 34–64, 2024.
https://doi.org/10.1007/978-3-031-58751-1_2

communication and *verifier*-efficient updatable and universal zk-SNARKs such as [12,14,19,34,38]. Universal means that the public key of the zk-SNARK, also known as the structured reference string (SRS), can be reused for many different relations that one wants to prove (but up to some relation size bound).

As mentioned, many recent works in communication-efficient updatable and universal zk-SNARKs start by constructing an information-theoretically secure proof system in some idealized model. For example, DARK [10] uses polynomial IOP, Marlin [14] uses Algebraic Holographic Proof (AHP), Lunar [12] and Basilisk [38] use Polynomial Holographic IOP (PHP), and Plonk [19] uses idealized low-degree protocols. In all such information-theoretic models is that the prover sends polynomial oracles to the verifier and the verifier can make queries to the oracles. One can transform information-theoretic proofs into succinct SNARKs using an extractable PCS. The prover commits to each polynomial oracle and opens commitments at queries chosen by the verifier. Vampire [34] is a recent exception to this paradigm, giving a direct proof in AGM.

The knowledge-soundness of PCS-based zk-SNARKs relies on PCS's extractability: given that the prover succeeds in convincing the verifier after sending a polynomial commitment and an opening, there exists an extractor that can efficiently extract a committed polynomial that is consistent with the commitment. Unfortunately, it is only known [14] how to prove that KZG is extractable under knowledge assumptions or in idealized models like the generic group model (GGM) and the algebraic group model (AGM, [18]). For brevity, we use the acronym IGM (idealized group model) to denote any of the GGM, the AGM, or just knowledge assumptions. Hence, the knowledge-soundness of known KZG-based zk-SNARKs relies indirectly on the IGM.

On top of that, the same zk-SNARKs use the Fiat-Shamir transform, which means that they additionally rely on another strong idealization, the random oracle model (ROM). We end up in a highly undesirable situation, where efficient zk-SNARKs used in practice depend on two different idealized models. Both models, the IGM and the ROM, are known to be uninstantiable, with several papers attacking either separately. The AGM and GGM were intensively cryptanalyzed in 2022 [43,45]. Zhandry and Zhang [44] recently showed that the ROM is strictly milder heuristic than Shoup's formalization of GGM [39]. Knowledge assumptions, formalized as extractable one-way functions, are known to be impossible for auxiliary input of unbounded polynomial length if a particular class of indistinguishability obfuscators exist [6].

Efficient non-updatable and non-universal (not based on PCSs) zk-SNARKs are known [20,23,37] that use the IGM but not the ROM. The most efficient known updatable and universal zk-SNARKs [24] that rely on an IGM and do not use the ROM are too inefficient for practice.

While non-falsifiable assumptions are needed in the standard model [13,21], one can obtain zk-SNARKs for NP in the ROM from falsifiable assumptions. We know two types of verifier-efficient zk-SNARKs in the ROM from falsifiable assumptions. First, the zk-SNARK of Lai and Malavolta [28] that uses Probabilistically Checkable Proofs (PCPs). Unfortunately, PCPs are inefficient [4] (e.g., the PCP proof length is at least $\Theta(N \log^3 N)$ with a large constant, where N is the witness size), and thus this solution only has a theoretical value. In addition, PCP-based zk-SNARKs are based on inefficient arithmetizations (mathematical representation of a relation). Second, one can combine a verifier-efficient PCS in the ROM from falsifiable assumptions with a polynomial IOP. Unfortunately, the known PCSs do not result in constant-size zk-SNARKs. For example, Dory [29] and [11] have an efficient prover but log-length arguments.

It is unknown if zk-SNARKs with an efficient, say $O_\lambda(N \log N)^1$, prover and $O_\lambda(1)$ argument size are possible in the ROM under falsifiable assumption. Constructing one—especially with a small constant in both $O_\lambda(\cdot)$-s—is an important open problem: it allows one to base zk-SNARKs on more secure foundations without sacrificing efficiency. Ideally, one would like to prove an already well-established zk-SNARK (such as Plonk) to be secure under weaker assumptions since an efficient arithmetization (say, R1CS or Plonk's arithmetization) and much infrastructure already accompanies it.

We propose the following two questions.

- **Theoretical:** Does a zk-SNARK with $O_\lambda(1)$ proof size and an efficient prover/verifier exist that is secure in the ROM under falsifiable assumptions?
- **Practical:** Is the KZG-based Plonk secure in the ROM under falsifiable assumptions?

We answer positively to the first question and achieve notable progress on the second.

Our Contributions. In this work, we consider non-interactive (univariate) PCSs over a field $\mathbb{F}$ where both the commitment and opening phases are non-interactive (a single message). The KZG [26] is a prime example. Assume n is a degree bound on committed polynomials. Although the commitment and opening phases are non-interactive, as a whole a non-interactive PCS can be viewed as a three-round protocol:

1. the prover sends a commitment C to some polynomial $f(X) \in \mathbb{F}[X]$ of degree at most n,
2. the verifier responds with an evaluation point $\alpha \in \mathbb{F}$, and
3. the prover sends $\eta = f(\alpha)$ and an opening proof π.

Note that some other PCSs, such as the one in DARK [10], have an interactive opening phase. In the following, unless specified otherwise, we mean a non-interactive PCS when we write PCS.

We define computational k-special-soundness and black-box extractability for PCS by following the definitions of k-special-soundness and black-box extractability for proof systems.

More precisely, a PCS satisfies computational $(n+1)$-special-soundness if there exists an efficient extractor, such that: if an efficient adversary produces

---

[1] Here, $O_\lambda(\cdot)$ is the common "Big O" notation, but we ignore $\mathsf{poly}(\lambda)$ factors.

$n + 1$ accepting PCS transcripts $(C, \alpha_j, \eta_j, \pi_j)$ with the same commitment C but distinct evaluation points α_j, then the extractor extracts a polynomial f of degree at most n, that is consistent with the commitment C and satisfies $f(\alpha_j) = \eta_j$ for all $j = 1, \ldots, n + 1$. We prove that KZG is computationally $(n + 1)$-special-sound under a new but falsifiable and standard-looking assumption ARSDH (*Adaptive Rational Strong Diffie-Hellman*). ARSDH is an adaptive variant of the known assumption RSDH (*Rational Strong Diffie-Hellman*) of González and Ráfols [22]. Interestingly, our special-soundness reduction uses the techniques of [42] to combine $n + 1$ openings to a single batch opening.

We prove that ARSDH is secure in the AGM with oblivious sampling (AGMOS) [32]. AGMOS is a more realistic version of AGM that additionally allows the adversary to sample group elements without knowing their discrete logarithms. We emphasize that our special-soundness proof does not depend on the AGMOS; we use the AGMOS only as a sanity check for the *falsifiable* ARSDH assumption. We also prove that ARSDH implies the strong Diffie-Hellman assumption and thus implies the evaluation binding of KZG (it is difficult to open a polynomial commitment to two different values at the same evaluation point).

Next, we define black-box extractability for non-interactive PCS. A non-interactive PCS is black-box extractable if there exists an expected probabilistic polynomial time (PPT) black-box extractor $\mathsf{Ext_{bb}}$, such that for each efficient adversary $(\mathcal{A}, \mathsf{P}^*)$, where $\mathcal{A}$ produces commitments and P^* produces openings: given a maliciously generated transcript $\mathsf{tr_0} = (C, \alpha_0, \eta_0, \pi_0)$, for randomly sampled α_0, and an oracle access to P^*, the extractor outputs a polynomial f, such that if the PCS verifier accepts $\mathsf{tr_0}$ then f agrees with $\mathsf{tr_0}$ (C is a commitment of f and $f(\alpha_0) = \eta_0$). The evaluation point α_0 is sampled uniformly and independently from C from some super-polynomially large subset[2] $\mathcal{F}$ of $\mathbb{F}$.

We prove that every computationally $(n + 1)$-special-sound non-interactive PCS is black-box extractable. Let ck be a commitment key. The black-box extractor $\mathsf{Ext_{bb}^{P^*}}(\mathsf{ck}, \mathsf{tr_0})$ rejects if the PCS verifier V rejects $\mathsf{tr_0}$. Otherwise, $\mathsf{Ext_{bb}}$ invokes another extractor $\mathsf{Ext_{rw}^{P^*}}(\mathsf{ck}, \mathsf{tr_0})$ that outputs n transcripts $\mathbf{tr} = (\mathsf{tr_1}, \ldots, \mathsf{tr_n})$. $\mathsf{Ext_{bb}}$ rejects if V rejects $\mathsf{tr_j}$ for some $j \geq 1$. Otherwise, $\mathsf{Ext_{bb}}$ uses the special-soundness extractor (that exists since PCS is special sound) on input $\mathsf{tr_0} \| \mathbf{tr}$ to extract f. One complication is that $\mathsf{Ext_{rw}}$ (described in the next paragraph) is an expected PPT algorithm. To prove that $\mathsf{Ext_{bb}}$ works, we need to define a special-soundness reduction $\mathcal{A_{ss}}$, which internally runs $\mathsf{Ext_{rw}}$. However, special-soundness holds against strict PPT adversaries. To resolve this mismatch, we prove a general result that if a falsifiable security game [21,35] (one where an efficient challenger interacts with an adversary) holds respect to any strict PPT adversary, then it also holds against any expected PPT adversary.

The most challenging part of the reduction is the rewinding extractor $\mathsf{Ext_{rw}}$. $\mathsf{Ext_{rw}}$ has the following goal: given that the adversary can produce a single transcript $\mathsf{tr_0} = (C, \alpha_0, \ldots)$, accepted by the PCS verifier, $\mathsf{Ext_{rw}}$ produces with an

---

[2] In zk-SNARKs in the literature, one can have say $\mathcal{F} = \mathbb{F}$, $\mathcal{F} = \mathbb{F}^*$, $\mathcal{F} = \mathbb{F} \setminus \mathbb{H}$ for a multiplicative subgroup of $\mathbb{H}$, etc.

overwhelming probability n more accepting transcripts that share the same commitment but have pairwise distinct second elements α_j. For a fixed commitment C, $\mathsf{Ext}_{\mathsf{rw}}$ runs P^* with distinct random evaluation points α until it obtains n accepting transcripts. The proof that $\mathsf{Ext}_{\mathsf{rw}}$ produces a correct output with an overwhelming probability in expected PPT is technical but similar to proofs of other such extractors (especially [1]).

Given the above, we can conclude that the KZG PCS is black-box extractable under the ARSDH assumption.

Compiler. Following earlier works like [10,12,14], we present a general compiler, which combines a non-interactive PCS and a polynomial IOP [10] into an interactive argument.

Polynomial IOP [10] is an idealized information-theoretic proof system, where in each round of a protocol, the prover sends a polynomial oracle to the verifier, and the verifier replies with a challenge. The verifier can also query the oracles. Query points are revealed to the prover, who can use them to construct polynomial oracles of the subsequent rounds. For example, in Plonk [19], several polynomials are opened at $\mathfrak{z} \leftarrow_{\!s} \mathbb{F}$, and one polynomial is opened at $\omega \cdot \mathfrak{z}$, where ω is a known value (a primitive root of unity). In Vampire [34], some polynomials are opened at whole (known) subgroups. Finally, the verifier either rejects or accepts the proof based on the responses from the oracles.

Bünz et al. (DARK, [10]) prove that when combining a polynomial IOP with a knowledge sound PCS (the prover knows the committed polynomial), one obtains an interactive argument system for the same relation. In DARK, the opening phase is an interactive argument for proving knowledge of the committed polynomial. This is a crucial difference with our work, where commitment and opening phases are non-interactive.

Our compiler follows the execution of the polynomial IOP protocol but with the following differences. First, when the polynomial IOP prover sends a polynomial oracle f, the argument's prover sends a commitment of f, the argument's verifier responds with $\chi \leftarrow_{\!s} \mathcal{F}$ ($\mathcal{F}$ is some superpolynomial size set), and the prover opens the commitment at the point χ.[3] Second, when the polynomial IOP verifier wants to query one of its oracles g, it sends the query point α to the prover, which then opens the commitment of g at point α.

Our compiler's security relies on the knowledge soundness of the polynomial IOP and on the PCS's black-box extractability and evaluation binding. We prove that the compiled argument satisfies witness-extended emulation (WEE, [30]). Intuitively, given an adversary that breaks witness-extended emulation of the argument, we can construct an adversary that breaks the knowledge soundness of the polynomial IOP. When the argument's prover (potentially malicious) outputs a commitment and successfully opens it at an extraction point χ, the reduction

---

[3] Alternatively, one can define the following version of the KZG commitment secure in the ROM. The commitment phase is (C, η, π), where $\chi = H(C)$, and H is a random oracle. This guarantees extractability. Now, in the opening phase one can use arbitrary evaluation points α' that do not have to be uniformly random.

extracts the polynomial f and sends it to the polynomial IOP verifier. The evaluation binding property guarantees that the queries that the polynomial IOP verifier makes to f are consistent with the evaluations that the argument's prover outputs. Otherwise, if $f(\alpha) \neq \eta$ for some claimed evaluation η outputted by the argument's prover, we get a collision (contradicting evaluation binding).

We can use the polynomial IOP of popular zk-SNARKs like [19] and Marlin [14] and apply our compiler with KZG. Our compiler adds only a small overhead. First, our compiler is for polynomial IOP, so it works only for polynomial IOP variants of such zk-SNARKs. Second, we must open each committed polynomial at one more random point. This results in a public coin argument, secure under the falsifiable ARSDH assumption, with $O_\lambda(1)$ proof size, $O_\lambda(N \log N)$ prover's computation time, $O_\lambda(|\mathbb{x}| + \log N)$ verifier's computation time, and $O_\lambda(N)$ length structured reference string (SRS). Here, N denotes the circuit size representing the proven relation, and $|\mathbb{x}|$ is the statement size. Importantly, the compiled variant will be universal and updatable. Some care must be taken with zero-knowledge since we introduce additional queries to the polynomial IOPs. However, this can be adjusted by introducing additional randomness to the polynomials, which adds minor extra cost. We did not try to find a generic approach as is seems to be better to be handled it in a case-by-case basis.

To our knowledge, this is the first argument system with a constant proof size and an efficient prover and verifier in the ROM under falsifiable assumptions. After applying the Fiat-Shamir heuristic, we obtain a SNARK that is secure in the ROM under the ARSDH assumption. This answers the first question we proposed in the introduction.

As for the second question (is Plonk secure in the ROM under falsifiable assumptions?), we obtain partial success. Our compiler outputs a version of Plonk, which is less efficient by a small constant factor. For each polynomial committed by the prover, we will have an additional opening proof (1 group element) and an evaluation of the polynomial (1 field element). Note that the evaluation point χ does not add to the communication size since the prover and the verifier compute χ locally using a hash function when applying the Fiat-Shamir heuristic. Plonk's (or Marlin's) efficiency also relies on several small optimizations: batching of commitment openings and the so-called Maller's trick [19]. We leave it an open question if our notion of extractability is sufficient to prove the security of such optimizations. We also leave it as an open question if it is possible to tightly reduce the soundness of our SNARK to the underlying ARSDH assumption.

Extractability in AGM(OS). The extractability of the KZG PCS in the AGM was proven in [14]. They also proposed a slightly less efficient version of KZG, where a knowledge component accompanies each commitment. In that case, extractability is possible under a knowledge assumption, but the commitment length is two group elements instead of one (i.e., the extra cost is one group element). When using our extraction technique, we get purely rewinding-based extractability with the cost of one group element and one field element.

Lipmaa et al. [32] recently proposed AGMOS (AGM with oblivious sampling). AGMOS is a more realistic variant of the AGM [18] that gives the adversary additional power to obliviously sample group elements without knowing their discrete logarithms. Moreover, [32] pointed out that researchers use KZG extractability in two different senses. In many papers (e.g., [14]), KZG extractability means extracting the polynomial after both the commitment and opening phase. In other papers, it means the ability of polynomial extraction after the commitment phase only. For example, Lunar [12] and Plonk [19] assume that one can extract the polynomial directly after the commitment phase; however, this results [32] in a spurious knowledge assumption that is secure in the AGM but insecure in the standard model.

Lipmaa et al. [32] analyzed KZG in AGMOS and provided an AGMOS proof that f can be extracted from the KZG commitment C and an acceptable opening (η, π) of the commitment at any evaluation point α. In particular, α does not have to be sampled from a set of superpolynomial size (one can pick $\alpha = 0$, for example). We work without using any idealized group model like AGM(OS), but we pay by having the random evaluation requirement.

2   Preliminaries

Let λ denote the security parameter. PPT stands for probabilistic polynomial time, and DPT for deterministic polynomial time. We say *expected PPT* when referring to probabilistic Turing machines whose expected running time is bounded by a polynomial in the security parameter. All adversaries are implicitly assumed to be non-uniform. Other algorithms are uniform. $\mathbb{F}$ is a finite field of prime order p; let $\mathbb{F}^* := \mathbb{F} \setminus \{0\}$. We denote by $\mathbb{F}_{\leq n}[X]$ the ring of univariate polynomials with variable X over $\mathbb{F}$ of degree $\leq n$. When a is uniformly sampled from a set A, we write $a \leftarrow_s A$. A negligible function δ is a function such that, for every polynomial f, there exists an integer N_f such that, if $\lambda > N_f$, then $|\delta(\lambda)| \leq 1/f(\lambda)$. We write $\delta(\lambda) \approx_\lambda 0$, when $\delta(\lambda)$ is a negligible function. By $f(\lambda) \in \mathsf{poly}(\lambda)$, we mean that the function $f(\lambda)$ is asymptotically bounded by some polynomial.

Assume n is a power of two. Let ω be the n-th primitive root of unity modulo p and let $\mathbb{H} = \langle \omega \rangle$ be the multiplicative subgroup of $\mathbb{F}$ generated by ω. (ω exists, given that $n \mid (p-1)$.)

For $j \in [1, n]$, let $\ell_j(X)$ be the j-th *Lagrange polynomial*, that is, the unique degree $n - 1$ polynomial, such that $\ell_j(\omega^{j-1}) = 1$ and $\ell_i(\omega^{j-1}) = 0$ for $i \neq j$. It is well known that $\ell_j(X) = \left((X^n - 1)\omega^{j-1} \right) / \left(n(X - \omega^{j-1}) \right)$ for $X \neq \omega^{j-1}$.

Bilinear Groups. A bilinear group generator $\mathsf{Pgen}(1^\lambda)$ returns $\mathsf{p} = (p, \mathbb{G}_1, \mathbb{G}_2, \mathbb{G}_T, \hat{e}, [1]_1, [1]_2)$, where $\mathbb{G}_1$, $\mathbb{G}_2$, and $\mathbb{G}_T$ are additive cyclic (thus, abelian) groups of prime order p, $\hat{e} : \mathbb{G}_1 \times \mathbb{G}_2 \to \mathbb{G}_T$ is a non-degenerate efficiently computable bilinear pairing, and $[1]_\iota$ is a fixed generator of $\mathbb{G}_\iota$. While $[1]_\iota$ is a part of p, for the sake of clarity, we often give it as an explicit input to different algorithms. The bilinear pairing is of Type-3, that is, there is no efficient isomorphism between

$\mathbb{G}_1$ and $\mathbb{G}_2$. We use the standard bracket notation, that is, for $\iota \in \{1, 2, T\}$ and $x \in \mathbb{Z}_p$, we write $[x]_\iota$ to denote $x[1]_\iota$. We denote $\hat{e}([x]_1, [y]_2)$ by $[x]_1 \bullet [y]_2$ and assume $[1]_T = [1]_1 \bullet [1]_2$. Thus, $[x]_1 \bullet [y]_2 = [xy]_T$ for any $x, y \in \mathbb{F}$.

Let $d_1(\lambda), d_2(\lambda) \in \mathsf{poly}(\lambda)$. Pgen is (d_1, d_2)-*PDL (Power Discrete Logarithm* [31]*) secure* if for any PPT $\mathcal{A}$, $\mathsf{Adv}^{\mathrm{pdl}}_{d_1, d_2, \mathsf{Pgen}, \mathcal{A}}(\lambda) :=$

$$\Pr\left[\mathcal{A}(\mathsf{p}, [(\sigma^i)_{i=0}^{d_1}]_1, [(\sigma^i)_{i=0}^{d_2}]_2) = \sigma \,\middle|\, \mathsf{p} \leftarrow \mathsf{Pgen}(1^\lambda); \sigma \leftarrow_\$ \mathbb{F}^*\right] \approx_\lambda 0 \ .$$

Let $d(\lambda) \in \mathsf{poly}(\lambda)$. Pgen is d-*SDH (Strong Diffie-Hellman,* [7]*) secure* in $\mathbb{G}_1$, if for any PPT $\mathcal{A}$, $\mathsf{Adv}^{\mathrm{sdh}}_{\mathsf{Pgen}, 1, d, \mathcal{A}}(\lambda) :=$

$$\Pr\left[\begin{array}{c} \sigma + c \neq 0 \wedge \\ [\varphi]_1 = \frac{1}{\sigma+c} \cdot [1]_1 \end{array} \,\middle|\, (c, [\varphi]_1) \leftarrow \mathcal{A}(\mathsf{p}, ([\sigma^i]_1)_{i=0}^d, [1, \sigma]_2) \begin{array}{c} \mathsf{p} \leftarrow \mathsf{Pgen}(1^\lambda); \sigma \leftarrow_\$ \mathbb{Z}_p; \end{array}\right] \approx_\lambda 0 \ .$$

A security game is *falsifiable* if it can be expressed as an interaction between an efficient challenger and an adversary [21,35]. In the full version [33], we show that if a falsifiable game is secure respect to any strict PPT adversary, it is also secure respect to any expected PPT adversary. We use that result in several of our reductions.

2.1   Polynomial Commitment Schemes

In a *non-interactive* (univariate) polynomial commitment scheme (PCS, [26]), the prover commits to a polynomial $f \in \mathbb{F}_{\leq n}[X]$ and later opens it to $f(\alpha)$ for $\alpha \in \mathbb{F}$ chosen by the verifier. A (non-randomized) non-interactive polynomial commitment scheme [26] consists of the following algorithms:

Setup $\mathsf{Pgen}(1^\lambda) \mapsto \mathsf{p}$: Given 1^λ, return system parameters p.

Commitment key generation $\mathsf{KGen}(\mathsf{p}, n) \mapsto (\mathsf{ck}, \mathsf{tk})$: Given a system parameter p and an upperbound n on the polynomial degree, return $(\mathsf{ck}, \mathsf{tk})$, where ck is the commitment key and tk is the trapdoor. We assume ck implicitly contains p. In the context of this paper, we do not use the trapdoor.

Commitment $\mathsf{Com}(\mathsf{ck}, f) \mapsto C$: Given a commitment key ck and a polynomial $f \in \mathbb{F}_{\leq n}[X]$, return a commitment C.

Opening $\mathsf{Open}(\mathsf{ck}, C, \alpha, f) \mapsto (\eta, \pi)$: Given a commitment key ck, a commitment C, an evaluation point $\alpha \in \mathbb{F}$, and a polynomial $f \in \mathbb{F}_{\leq n}[X]$, return (η, π), where $\eta \leftarrow f(\alpha)$ and π is an evaluation proof.

Verification $\mathsf{V}(\mathsf{ck}, C, \alpha, \eta, \pi) \mapsto \{0, 1\}$: Given a commitment key ck, a commitment C, an evaluation point α, a purported evaluation $\eta =^? f(\alpha)$, and an evaluation proof π, return 1 (accept) or 0 (reject).

Thus, in a non-interactive PCS, both the commitment and the opening are non-interactive (it only consists of a single message that can be verified non-interactively). In an *interactive PCS*, either opening or verification (or both) is an interactive protocol. Most of the known PCSs, like FRI [2], Bulletproofs [9], and DARK [10], are interactive. Univariate KZG [26] and multivariate PST [36] are two well-known non-interactive PCSs.

A non-interactive PCS PC is complete, if for any λ, $p \leftarrow \mathsf{Pgen}(1^\lambda)$, $n \in \mathrm{poly}(\lambda)$, $\alpha \in \mathbb{F}$, and $f \in \mathbb{F}_{\leq n}[X]$,

$$\Pr\left[\, \mathsf{V}(\mathsf{ck}, C, \alpha, \eta, \pi) = 1 \,\middle|\, (\mathsf{ck}, \mathsf{tk}) \leftarrow \mathsf{KGen}(p, n); (\eta, \pi) \leftarrow \mathsf{Open}(\mathsf{ck}, C, \alpha, f) \,\right] = 1.$$

Definition 1. *A non-interactive polynomial commitment scheme* PC *is* (non-black-box) extractable *for* Pgen, *if for any* $n \in \mathrm{poly}(\lambda)$, *and PPT adversary* $\mathcal{A}$, *there exists a PPT extractor* $\mathsf{Ext}_\mathcal{A}$, *such that* $\mathsf{Adv}^{\mathrm{ext}}_{\mathsf{Pgen}, \mathsf{PC}, n, \mathcal{A}, \mathsf{Ext}_\mathcal{A}}(\lambda) :=$

$$\Pr\left[\begin{array}{l} \mathsf{V}(\mathsf{ck}, C, \alpha, \eta, \pi) = 1 \wedge \\ \left(\begin{array}{l} C \neq \mathsf{Com}(f(X)) \vee \\ \deg f > n \vee f(\alpha) \neq \eta \end{array}\right) \end{array} \middle| \begin{array}{l} p \leftarrow \mathsf{Pgen}(1^\lambda); (\mathsf{ck}, \mathsf{tk}) \leftarrow \mathsf{KGen}(p, n); \\ r \leftarrow \mathsf{RND}_\lambda(\mathcal{A}); (C, \alpha, \eta, \pi) \leftarrow \mathcal{A}(\mathsf{ck}; r); \\ f(X) \leftarrow \mathsf{Ext}_\mathcal{A}(\mathsf{ck}; r) \end{array}\right] \approx_\lambda 0\ ,$$

where $r \leftarrow \mathsf{RND}_\lambda(\mathcal{A})$ *denotes sampling random coins for* $\mathcal{A}$.

A weaker property is evaluation binding [26], which does not include extractability, but disallows opening the same evaluation point to different evaluations.

Definition 2. *A polynomial commitment scheme* PC *is* evaluation binding *for* Pgen, *if for any* $n \in \mathrm{poly}(\lambda)$, *and PPT adversary* $\mathcal{A}$, $\mathsf{Adv}^{\mathrm{evbind}}_{\mathsf{Pgen}, \mathsf{PC}, n, \mathcal{A}}(\lambda) :=$

$$\Pr\left[\begin{array}{l} \mathsf{V}(\mathsf{ck}, C, \alpha, \eta, \pi) = 1 \wedge \\ \mathsf{V}(\mathsf{ck}, C, \alpha, \eta', \pi') = 1 \wedge \eta \neq \eta' \end{array} \middle| \begin{array}{l} p \leftarrow \mathsf{Pgen}(1^\lambda); (\mathsf{ck}, \mathsf{tk}) \leftarrow \mathsf{KGen}(p, n); \\ (C, \alpha, \eta, \pi, \eta', \pi') \leftarrow \mathcal{A}(p, \mathsf{ck}) \end{array}\right] \approx_\lambda 0.$$

The seminal (non-randomized) KZG [26] polynomial commitment scheme is defined as follows:

KZG.Pgen(λ): return $p \leftarrow \mathsf{Pgen}(1^\lambda)$.
KZG.KGen(p, n): tk $= \sigma \leftarrow_{\$} \mathbb{Z}_p^*$; ck $\leftarrow (p, [(\sigma^i)_{i=0}^n]_1, [1, \sigma]_2)$; return (ck, tk).
KZG.Com(ck, f): return $C \leftarrow [f(\sigma)]_1 = \sum_{j=0}^n f_j [\sigma^j]_1$.
KZG.Open(ck, C, α, f): $\eta \leftarrow f(\alpha)$; $\varphi(X) \leftarrow (f(X) - \eta)/(X - \alpha)$; $\pi \leftarrow [\varphi(\sigma)]_1$; return (η, π).
KZG.V(ck, C, α, η, π): Return 1 iff $(C - \eta[1]_1) \bullet [1]_2 = \pi \bullet [\sigma - \alpha]_2$.

KZG's security is based on the fact that $(X - \alpha) \mid (f(X) - \eta) \Leftrightarrow f(\alpha) = \eta$. KZG is evaluation binding under the n-SDH assumption [26] and non-black-box extractable in the AGM [14] under the PDL assumption and in AGMOS under the PDL and TOFR (see the full version [33]) assumptions.

2.2 Succinct Zero-Knowledge Arguments

Indexed Relation. We consider relations that depend on the pairing description $p \leftarrow \mathsf{Pgen}(1^\lambda)$. An indexed relation $\mathcal{R}_p$ is a relation of triples (i, x, w), where i is an index (e.g., an arithmetic circuit), x is a statement (e.g., a public input to the circuit) and w is an NP-witness (e.g., a private input to the circuit) for the language $\mathcal{L}(\mathcal{R}_p) := \{(i, x) : (i, x, w) \in \mathcal{R}_p\}$. We denote $\mathbb{I}(\mathcal{R}_p) = \{i : (i, x, w) \in \mathcal{R}_p\}$. We also consider subrelations $\mathcal{R}_{p,n} \subset \mathcal{R}_p$, where the size of index i is bounded by n.

Argument System. Groth et al. [24] introduced the notion of (preprocessing) zk-SNARKs with specializable universal structured reference string (SRS). This notion formalizes the idea that the key generation for $\mathcal{R}_{p,n}$ can be seen as the sequential combination of two steps. First, a probabilistic algorithm KGen generates a SRS for $\mathcal{R}_{p,n}$ (e.g., for satisfiability of any circuit with $\leq n$ gates) and second, a deterministic algorithm Derive specializes the universal SRS into one for a specific $i \in \mathbb{I}(\mathcal{R}_{p,n})$ (e.g., for a fixed circuit with $\leq n$ gates).

Let (P, V) be a pair of interactive algorithms where V outputs the final message (typically either 0 or 1, unless V is malicious). We denote by $\mathsf{tr} \leftarrow \langle P(x), V(y) \rangle$ the protocol transcript when P gets an input x and V gets an input y. For simplicity we sometimes write $\langle P(x), V(y) \rangle = b$ when we compare V's last message to b.

A *succinct zero-knowledge argument system* $\Pi = (\mathsf{Pgen}, \mathsf{KGen}, \mathsf{Derive}, P, V)$ *with specializable universal SRS for a relation family* $(\mathsf{Pgen}, \{\mathcal{R}_{p,n}\}_{p \in \mathrm{range}(\mathsf{Pgen}), n \in \mathbb{N}})$ consists of the following algorithms.

Setup: Given 1^λ, return system parameters $\mathsf{p} \leftarrow \mathsf{Pgen}(1^\lambda)$.

Universal SRS Generation: a probabilistic algorithm $\mathsf{KGen}(\mathsf{p}, n) \rightarrow (\mathsf{srs}, \mathsf{td}_{srs})$ that takes as input public parameters p and an upper bound n on the index size, and outputs srs together with a trapdoor. We assume that srs contains p.

SRS Specialization: a deterministic algorithm $\mathsf{Derive}(\mathsf{srs}, i) \rightarrow (\mathsf{ek}_i, \mathsf{vk}_i)$ that takes as input a universal SRS srs and an index $i \in \mathbb{I}(\mathcal{R}_{p,n})$, and outputs a specialized SRS $\mathsf{srs}_i := (\mathsf{ek}_i, \mathsf{vk}_i)$. Here ek_i is for the prover, and vk_i is for the verifier. We assume that ek_i and vk_i contain p.

Prover/Verifier: a pair of interactive algorithms $\langle P(\mathsf{ek}_i, x, w), V(\mathsf{vk}_i, x) \rangle = b$, where P takes a proving key ek_i for an index i, a statement x, and a witness w, s.t. $(i, x, w) \in \mathcal{R}_{p,n}$, and V takes a verification key vk_i for an index i and a statement x, and either accepts ($b = 1$) or rejects ($b = 0$) the argument.

Π must satisfy the following four requirements.

Completeness. For all $\mathsf{p} \in \mathrm{range}(\mathsf{Pgen})$, $n \in \mathbb{N}$, $(i, x, w) \in \mathcal{R}_{p,n}$,

$$\Pr \left[\langle P(\mathsf{ek}_i, x, w), V(\mathsf{vk}_i, x) \rangle = 1 \,\middle|\, \begin{array}{l} (\mathsf{srs}, \mathsf{td}_{srs}) \leftarrow \mathsf{KGen}(\mathsf{p}, n); \\ (\mathsf{ek}_i, \mathsf{vk}_i) \leftarrow \mathsf{Derive}(\mathsf{srs}, i) \end{array} \right] = 1 \ .$$

Witness-Extended Emulation. Π satisfies witness-extended emulation if for every DPT P^* there exists an expected polynomial time emulator Emu, such that for any λ, PPT adversary $\mathcal{A}$, PPT distinguisher $\mathcal{D}$, and $n \in \mathsf{poly}(\lambda)$,

$\mathsf{Adv}^{\mathsf{wee}}_{\mathsf{Pgen},\Pi,n,\mathsf{P}^*,\mathcal{A},\mathcal{D}}(\lambda) := |\varepsilon_0 - \varepsilon_1| \approx_\lambda 0$, where

$$\varepsilon_0 := \Pr\left[\begin{array}{c}\mathbb{i} \in \mathbb{I}(\mathcal{R}_{\mathsf{p},n}) \wedge \\ \mathcal{D}(\mathsf{tr}) = 1\end{array} \middle| \begin{array}{l}\mathsf{p} \leftarrow \mathsf{Pgen}(1^\lambda); (\mathsf{srs}, \mathsf{td}_{srs}) \leftarrow \mathsf{KGen}(\mathsf{p}, n); \\ (\mathbb{i}, \mathbb{x}, \mathsf{st}) \leftarrow \mathcal{A}(\mathsf{p}, \mathsf{srs}); (\mathsf{ek}_\mathbb{i}, \mathsf{vk}_\mathbb{i}) \leftarrow \mathsf{Derive}(\mathsf{srs}, \mathbb{i}); \\ \mathsf{tr} \leftarrow \langle \mathsf{P}^*(\mathsf{p}, \mathsf{srs}, \mathbb{x}, \mathsf{st}), \mathsf{V}(\mathsf{vk}_\mathbb{i}, \mathbb{x})\rangle\end{array}\right],$$

$$\varepsilon_1 := \Pr\left[\begin{array}{c}\mathbb{i} \in \mathbb{I}(\mathcal{R}_{\mathsf{p},n}) \wedge \\ \mathcal{D}(\mathsf{tr}) = 1 \wedge \\ \left(\begin{array}{c}\mathsf{V}_{\mathsf{check}}(\mathsf{srs}, \mathsf{tr}) = 1 \\ \Rightarrow (\mathbb{i}, \mathbb{x}, \mathbb{w}) \in \mathcal{R}\end{array}\right)\end{array} \middle| \begin{array}{l}\mathsf{p} \leftarrow \mathsf{Pgen}(1^\lambda); (\mathsf{srs}, \mathsf{td}_{srs}) \leftarrow \mathsf{KGen}(\mathsf{p}, n); \\ (\mathbb{i}, \mathbb{x}, \mathsf{st}) \leftarrow \mathcal{A}(\mathsf{p}, \mathsf{srs}); \\ (\mathsf{ek}_\mathbb{i}, \mathsf{vk}_\mathbb{i}) \leftarrow \mathsf{Derive}(\mathsf{srs}, \mathbb{i}); \\ (\mathsf{tr}, \mathbb{w}) \leftarrow \mathsf{Emu}^{\langle \mathsf{P}^*(\mathsf{p}, \mathsf{srs}, \mathbb{x}, \mathsf{st}), \mathsf{V}(\mathsf{vk}_\mathcal{R}, \mathbb{x})\rangle}(\mathsf{p}, \mathsf{srs}, \mathbb{x})\end{array}\right],$$

where Emu has access to a transcript oracle that can be rewound to any round and run again with fresh random coins of the verifier. $\mathsf{V}_{\mathsf{check}}(\mathsf{srs}, \mathsf{tr})$ outputs 1 if the transcript is accepted by the verifier and 0 otherwise.

Honest Verifier Zero-Knowledge. Π is ε-statistical *honest verifier zero-knowledge* if there exists a PPT simulator Sim, s.t. for all unbounded algorithms $\mathcal{D} = (\mathcal{D}_1, \mathcal{D}_2)$, all $\mathsf{p} \in \mathsf{range}(\mathsf{Pgen})$, all $n \in \mathsf{poly}(\lambda)$, $|\varepsilon_0(\lambda) - \varepsilon_1(\lambda)| \leq \varepsilon(\lambda)$, where

$$\varepsilon_0(\lambda) := \Pr\left[\begin{array}{c}\mathcal{D}_2(\mathsf{st}, \mathsf{tr}) = 1 \wedge \\ \mathcal{R}_{\mathsf{p},n}(\mathbb{i}, \mathbb{x}, \mathbb{w})\end{array} \middle| \begin{array}{l}(\mathsf{srs}, \mathsf{td}_{srs}) \leftarrow \mathsf{KGen}(\mathsf{p}, n); (\mathbb{i}, \mathbb{x}, \mathbb{w}, \mathsf{st}) \leftarrow \mathcal{D}_1(\mathsf{srs}); \\ (\mathsf{ek}_\mathbb{i}, \mathsf{vk}_\mathbb{i}) \leftarrow \mathsf{Derive}(\mathsf{srs}, \mathbb{i}); \\ \mathsf{tr} \leftarrow \langle \mathsf{P}(\mathsf{ek}_\mathbb{i}, \mathbb{x}, \mathbb{w}), \mathsf{V}(\mathsf{vk}_\mathbb{i}, \mathbb{x})\rangle\end{array}\right],$$

$$\varepsilon_1(\lambda) := \Pr\left[\begin{array}{c}\mathcal{D}_2(\mathsf{st}, \mathsf{tr}) = 1 \wedge \\ \mathcal{R}_{\mathsf{p},n}(\mathbb{i}, \mathbb{x}, \mathbb{w})\end{array} \middle| \begin{array}{l}(\mathsf{srs}, \mathsf{td}_{srs}) \leftarrow \mathsf{KGen}(\mathsf{p}, n); (\mathbb{i}, \mathbb{x}, \mathbb{w}, \mathsf{st}) \leftarrow \mathcal{D}_1(\mathsf{srs}); \\ (\mathsf{ek}_\mathbb{i}, \mathsf{vk}_\mathbb{i}) \leftarrow \mathsf{Derive}(\mathsf{srs}, \mathbb{i}); \\ \mathsf{tr} \leftarrow \langle \mathsf{Sim}(\mathsf{srs}, \mathsf{td}_{srs}, \mathbb{i}, \mathbb{x}), \mathsf{V}(\mathsf{vk}_\mathbb{i}, \mathbb{x})\rangle\end{array}\right].$$

We say that Π has statistical honest verifier zero-knowledge when $\varepsilon(\lambda)$ is negligible and perfect zero-knowledge when $\varepsilon(\lambda) = 0$.

Succinctness. Π is *succinct* if the running time of V is $\mathsf{poly}(\lambda + |\mathbb{x}| + \log |\mathbb{w}|)$ and the communication size is $\mathsf{poly}(\lambda + \log |\mathbb{w}|)$.

Π is *updatable* [24], if the SRS can be sequentially updated by many updaters, such that knowledge-soundness holds if either the original SRS creator or one of the updaters is honest.

When we have a public-coin protocol with a constant number of rounds, we can apply the Fiat-Shamir heuristic [17] to obtain a zk-SNARK.

3   ARSDH: Underlying Security Assumption

For a set $\mathcal{S}$, $\mathbf{Z}_\mathcal{S}(X) := \prod_{s \in \mathcal{S}}(X - s)$ is its vanishing polynomial. We need a new assumption, ARSDH, an adaptive version of the following known assumption.

Definition 3 (RSDH [22]). *Let $n \in \mathsf{poly}(\lambda)$ and Pgen be a bilinear-group generator. Let $\mathcal{S} = \{\alpha_j\} \subset \mathbb{F}$ be any set of size $n + 1$. Then, the $\mathcal{S}$-RSDH (Rational Strong Diffie-Hellman) assumption holds for Pgen in $\mathbb{G}_1$, if for any PPT $\mathcal{A}$, the following probability is negligible:* $\mathsf{Adv}^{\mathsf{rsdh}}_{\mathsf{Pgen},1,n,\mathcal{S},\mathcal{A}}(\lambda) :=$

$$\Pr\left[\begin{array}{c}[g]_1 \neq [0]_1 \wedge \\ [g]_1 \bullet [1]_2 = [\varphi]_1 \bullet [\mathbf{Z}_\mathcal{S}(\sigma)]_2\end{array} \middle| \begin{array}{c}\mathsf{p} \leftarrow \mathsf{Pgen}(1^\lambda); \sigma \leftarrow_\$ \mathbb{Z}_p; \\ \mathsf{ck} \leftarrow ([(\sigma^i)^n_{i=0}]_1, [(\sigma^i)^{n+1}_{i=0}]_2); \\ [g, \varphi]_1 \leftarrow \mathcal{A}(\mathsf{ck}, \mathcal{S})\end{array}\right].$$

(The condition $[g]_1 \bullet [1]_2 = [\varphi]_1 \bullet [\mathbf{Z}_{\mathcal{S}}(\sigma)]_2$ is equivalent to $\frac{1}{\mathbf{Z}_{\mathcal{S}}(\sigma)} \cdot [g]_1 = [\varphi]_1$.)

Definition 4 (New Assumption ARSDH). *The* adaptive $(n + 1)$-RSDH *assumption holds for* Pgen *in* $\mathbb{G}_1$ *if* $\mathcal{S}$-RSDH *holds for* Pgen *in* $\mathbb{G}_1$ *even when the adversary can choose itself a set* $\mathcal{S}$ *of size* $n + 1$. *That is, if for any PPT* $\mathcal{A}$, *the following probability is negligible:* $\mathsf{Adv}^{\mathsf{arsdh}}_{\mathsf{Pgen},1,n,\mathcal{A}}(\lambda) :=$

$$
\Pr \left[
\begin{array}{l}
\mathcal{S} \subset \mathbb{F} \wedge |\mathcal{S}| = n + 1 \wedge [g]_1 \neq [0]_1 \wedge \\
[g]_1 \bullet [1]_2 = [\varphi]_1 \bullet [\mathbf{Z}_{\mathcal{S}}(\sigma)]_2
\end{array}
\left|
\begin{array}{l}
\mathsf{p} \leftarrow \mathsf{Pgen}(1^\lambda); \sigma \leftarrow_\$ \mathbb{Z}_p; \\
\mathsf{ck} \leftarrow ([(\sigma^i)^n_{i=0}]_1, [1, \sigma]_2); \\
(\mathcal{S}, [g, \varphi]_1) \leftarrow \mathcal{A}(\mathsf{ck})
\end{array}
\right.
\right] .
$$

The $(\mathcal{S}\text{-})$RSDH assumption from [22] is stronger than ARSDH in the sense that it gives the adversary $[(\sigma^i)^n_{i=0}]_1, [(\sigma^i)^{n+1}_{i=0}]_2$ as an input. The additional input elements were needed for the assumption to be publicly verifiable, meaning breaking the success of the adversary can be tested only by knowing ck (knowing σ itself is unnecessary). In our application, public verification is not important. On the other hand, [22] assumed $\mathcal{S}$-RSDH (for a specific set $\mathcal{S}$) while ARSDH must be secure against an adverary that adaptively chooses $\mathcal{S}$.

In our constructions, we need both ARSDH and SDH. The latter is needed for the evaluation binding of the KZG commitment. To simplify the assumption zoo, we prove the following lemma. Note that the adaptive choice of $\mathcal{S}$ in ARSDH is needed for the reduction to work (in addition to being needed in Sect. 4.1).

Lemma 1. $(n + 1)$-ARSDH *implies* $(n + 1)$-SDH.

Proof. Let $\mathcal{A}$ be an $(n + 1)$-SDH adversary. We construct the following $(n + 1)$-ARSDH adversary $\mathcal{B}(\mathsf{ck})$:

1. Obtain $(c, [\varphi]_1 = \frac{1}{\sigma+c}[1]_1) \leftarrow \mathcal{A}(\mathsf{ck})$.
2. Abort if $\mathcal{A}(\mathsf{ck})$ did not succeed, i.e., if $[\varphi]_1 \bullet [\sigma + c]_2 \neq [1]_T$ or $\sigma + c = 0$.
3. Choose *any* set $\mathcal{S}$ of size $n + 1$ that contains $-c$, but not σ.
4. Set $g(X) \leftarrow \mathbf{Z}_{\mathcal{S}}(X)/(X + c) \in \mathbb{F}[X]$, with degree n.
5. Return $(\mathcal{S}, [g(\sigma), \varphi]_1)$.

Clearly, $\mathcal{B}$ has broken RSDH since $\frac{1}{\mathbf{Z}_{\mathcal{S}}(\sigma)}[g(\sigma)]_1 = [\varphi]_1$ and $g(\sigma) \neq 0$. □

In particular, this means that ARSDH implies that KZG is evaluation binding. In the full version [33], we prove the security of ARSDH in the algebraic group model with oblivious sampling (AGMOS) [32]. This is the recent variant of AGM [18], which additionally allows oblivious sampling of group elements. It does not mean that the security of our protocols relies on AGM/AGMOS. Instead, we use AGMOS only as an additional sanity check.

4   Special Soundness of KZG

In the following sections, we define two security notions for non-interactive polynomial commitment schemes: special soundness and black-box extractability (BBE). We prove that KZG satisfies both notions under ARSDH.

We model a non-interactive polynomial commitment scheme (e.g., KZG) as a three-message protocol, where the first message is a commitment, the second is the verifier's query (evaluation point) α, and the third is an evaluation η together with an evaluation proof π.

Notation. We call $\mathsf{tr} := (C, \alpha, \eta, \pi)$ a *transcript*. For a fixed ck, tr is *accepting* if $\mathsf{V}(\mathsf{ck}, \mathsf{tr}) = 1$. Let $n \geq 1$ be an integer. We say that an $(n+1)$-tuple $\mathbf{tr} = \{\mathsf{tr}_j = (C_j, \alpha_j, \eta_j, \pi_j) : j \in [0, n]\}$ is *admissible*, if (1) $C_i = C_j =: C$ for all $i, j \in [0, n]$, and (2) $\alpha_i \neq \alpha_j$ for $i \neq j$. We say $\mathbf{tr}$ is *accepting* if each tr_j is accepting.

For a non-interactive PCS PC, $\lambda \in \mathbb{N}$, $n \in \mathsf{poly}(\lambda)$, $\mathsf{p} \in \mathsf{Pgen}(1^\lambda)$, $\mathsf{ck} \in \mathsf{PC.KGen}(\mathsf{p}, n)$ (that encodes implicitly information about PC, λ, n, and p), and an admissible $(n+1)$-tuple $\mathbf{tr}$, we define the following two relations:

$$
\begin{aligned}
\mathcal{R}_{\mathsf{ck}} &:= \{(C, f) : C = \mathsf{PC.Com}(\mathsf{ck}, f) \wedge \deg f \leq n\} \; , \\
\mathcal{R}_{\mathsf{ck},\mathbf{tr}} &:= \{(C, f) : (C, f) \in \mathcal{R}_{\mathsf{ck}} \wedge \forall j \in [0, n]. f(\alpha_j) = \eta_j\} \; .
\end{aligned}
\tag{1}
$$

That is, (C, f) belongs to $\mathcal{R}_{\mathsf{ck}}$ if $f(X)$ is a valid opening of C. Moreover, (C, f) belongs to $\mathcal{R}_{\mathsf{ck},\mathbf{tr}}$ if it belongs to $\mathcal{R}_{\mathsf{ck}}$ and in addition, $f(\alpha_j) = \eta_j$ for all $j \in [0, n]$.

4.1 Special Soundness

Next, we define a variant of the standard special soundness [15] notion for *non-interactive* polynomial commitment schemes.

Definition 5 (Special Soundness). *Let* $n \in \mathsf{poly}(\lambda)$ *with* $n \geq 1$. *A non-interactive polynomial commitment scheme* PC *is computationally* $(n+1)$-*special-sound for* Pgen, *if there exists a PPT extractor* $\mathsf{Ext}_{\mathsf{ss}}$, *such that for any PPT adversary* $\mathcal{A}_{\mathsf{ss}}$, $\mathsf{Adv}^{\mathsf{ss}}_{\mathsf{Pgen},\mathsf{PC},\mathsf{Ext}_{\mathsf{ss}},n+1,\mathcal{A}_{\mathsf{ss}}}(\lambda) :=$

$$
\Pr \left[\begin{array}{l} \mathbf{tr} = (\mathsf{tr}_j)_{j=0}^n \wedge \\ \forall j \in [0, n]. \begin{pmatrix} \mathsf{tr}_j = (C, \alpha_j, \eta_j, \pi_j) \\ \wedge \mathsf{V}(\mathsf{ck}, \mathsf{tr}_j) = 1 \end{pmatrix} \\ \wedge (\forall i \neq j. \alpha_i \neq \alpha_j) \wedge (C, f) \notin \mathcal{R}_{\mathsf{ck},\mathbf{tr}} \end{array} \middle| \begin{array}{l} \mathsf{p} \leftarrow \mathsf{Pgen}(1^\lambda); \\ (\mathsf{ck}, \mathsf{tk}) \leftarrow \mathsf{KGen}(\mathsf{p}, n); \\ \mathbf{tr} \leftarrow \mathcal{A}_{\mathsf{ss}}(\mathsf{ck}); \\ f \leftarrow \mathsf{Ext}_{\mathsf{ss}}(\mathsf{ck}, \mathbf{tr}) \end{array} \right] \approx_\lambda 0 \; .
$$

Intuitively, this definition states that if $\mathcal{A}_{\mathsf{ss}}$ produces an accepting admissible $(n+1)$-tuple $\mathbf{tr}$, then one can extract a degree-$\leq n$ polynomial $f(X)$ that agrees with all the transcripts (i.e., with all $n + 1$ polynomial openings).

Theorem 1. *If the* $(n + 1)$-*ARSDH assumption holds, then KZG for degree* $\leq n$ *polynomials is computationally* $(n + 1)$-*special-sound: There exists a DPT extractor* $\mathsf{Ext}_{\mathsf{ss}}$, *such that for any PPT* $\mathcal{A}_{\mathsf{ss}}$, *there exists a PPT* $\mathcal{B}$, *such that* $\mathsf{Adv}^{\mathsf{ss}}_{\mathsf{Pgen},\mathsf{PC},\mathsf{Ext}_{\mathsf{ss}},n+1,\mathcal{A}_{\mathsf{ss}}}(\lambda) \leq \mathsf{Adv}^{\mathsf{arsdh}}_{\mathsf{Pgen},1,n+1,\mathcal{B}}(\lambda)$.

We fix some notation and state a technical lemma before proving Theorem 1. Let $\mathcal{I} := [0, n]$ and fix any set $\mathcal{S} := \{\alpha_j\}_{j \in \mathcal{I}}$ with $\alpha_i \neq \alpha_j$. As before, let $\mathbf{Z}_{\mathcal{S}}(X) := \prod_{j \in \mathcal{I}}(X - \alpha_j)$ be the vanishing polynomial of $\mathcal{S}$. For $j \in \mathcal{I}$, let

$$
\ell_j^{\mathcal{I}}(X) := \prod_{i \neq j \in \mathcal{I}} \frac{X - \alpha_i}{\alpha_j - \alpha_i}
$$

be the jth Lagrange polynomial of $\mathcal{S}$ over $\mathcal{I}$. Let

$$\mathsf{d}_j^{\mathcal{I}} := \frac{1}{\mathbf{Z}_{\mathcal{S}\setminus\{\alpha_j\}}(\alpha_j)} = \frac{1}{\prod_{i\neq j\in\mathcal{I}}(\alpha_j-\alpha_i)} .$$

Clearly,

$$\ell_j^{\mathcal{I}}(X) = \frac{\mathbf{Z}_{\mathcal{S}}(X)\mathsf{d}_j^{\mathcal{I}}}{X-\alpha_j} . \tag{2}$$

In Lemma 2, we generalize a batching technique of Tomescu et al. [42] from the case $\alpha_j \in \langle\omega\rangle$ to any $\alpha_j \in \mathbb{F}$.[4]

Lemma 2 (Batching lemma). *Let* $\mathcal{S} = \{\alpha_j\}_{j\in\mathcal{I}}$ *with* $\alpha_i \neq \alpha_j$. *Assume that for all* $j \in \mathcal{I}$,

$$[\mathsf{c} - \eta_j]_1 \bullet [1]_2 = [\varphi_j]_1 \bullet [\sigma - \alpha_j]_2 \tag{3}$$

for some $[\mathsf{c}]_1$, $[\varphi_j]_1$, *and* η_j. *Then,*

$$[\mathsf{c} - L(\sigma)]_1 \bullet [1]_2 = [\varphi]_1 \bullet [\mathbf{Z}_{\mathcal{S}}(\sigma)]_2 , \tag{4}$$

where $[\varphi]_1 := \sum_{j\in\mathcal{I}} \mathsf{d}_j^{\mathcal{I}}[\varphi_j]_1$ *and* $L(X) := \sum_{j\in\mathcal{I}} \eta_j \ell_j^{\mathcal{I}}(X)$ *is the low-degree extension of* $\{\eta_j\}$.

Proof. Let us first handle the case $\sigma = \alpha_{j_0}$ for some j_0. In this case, Eq. (3) tells us that $\mathsf{c} = \eta_{j_0}$. Moreover, $\ell_j^{\mathcal{I}}(\sigma) = 0$ for $j \neq j_0$ while

$$\ell_{j_0}^{\mathcal{I}}(X) = \mathsf{d}_{j_0}^{\mathcal{I}} \prod_{i\neq j_0}(X - \alpha_i) = \frac{\mathbf{Z}_{\mathcal{S}\setminus\{\sigma\}}(X)}{\mathbf{Z}_{\mathcal{S}\setminus\{\sigma\}}(\sigma)} .$$

Since $\mathsf{d}_{j_0}^{\mathcal{I}} = 1/\mathbf{Z}_{\mathcal{S}\setminus\{\sigma\}}(\sigma)$, we get that $L(\sigma) = \sum_{j\in\mathcal{I}} \eta_j \ell_j^{\mathcal{I}}(\sigma) = \eta_{j_0} = \mathsf{c}$ and Eq. (4) holds.

From now on, assume $\sigma \notin \mathcal{S}$. Define implicitly $\varphi := (\mathsf{c} - L(\sigma))/\mathbf{Z}_{\mathcal{S}}(\sigma) = \mathsf{c}/\mathbf{Z}_{\mathcal{S}}(\sigma) - L(\sigma)/\mathbf{Z}_{\mathcal{S}}(\sigma)$. From Eq. (2), we get

$$\frac{L(\sigma)}{\mathbf{Z}_{\mathcal{S}}(\sigma)} = \frac{\sum_{j\in\mathcal{I}} \eta_j \ell_j^{\mathcal{I}}(\sigma)}{\mathbf{Z}_{\mathcal{S}}(\sigma)} = \frac{\sum_{j\in\mathcal{I}} \eta_j \mathbf{Z}_{\mathcal{S}}(\sigma)\mathsf{d}_j^{\mathcal{I}}/(\sigma-\alpha_j)}{\mathbf{Z}_{\mathcal{S}}(\sigma)} = \sum_{j\in\mathcal{I}} \frac{\mathsf{d}_j^{\mathcal{I}}\eta_j}{\sigma-\alpha_j} .$$

We also get from Eq. (2) that $\frac{1}{\mathbf{Z}_{\mathcal{S}}(X)} = \frac{1}{\mathbf{Z}_{\mathcal{S}}(X)} \sum_{j\in\mathcal{I}} \ell_j^{\mathcal{I}}(X) = \sum_{j\in\mathcal{I}} \frac{\mathsf{d}_j^{\mathcal{I}}}{X-\alpha_j}$. Thus, $\mathsf{c}/\mathbf{Z}_{\mathcal{S}}(\sigma) = \sum_{j\in\mathcal{I}} \mathsf{d}_j^{\mathcal{I}}\mathsf{c}/(\sigma - \alpha_j)$. Hence,

$$\varphi = \sum_{j\in\mathcal{I}} \frac{\mathsf{d}_j^{\mathcal{I}}\mathsf{c}}{\sigma-\alpha_j} - \sum_{j\in\mathcal{I}} \frac{\mathsf{d}_j^{\mathcal{I}}\eta_j}{\sigma-\alpha_j} = \sum_{j\in\mathcal{I}} \mathsf{d}_j^{\mathcal{I}} \frac{\mathsf{c}-\eta_j}{\sigma-\alpha_j} = \sum_{j\in\mathcal{I}} \mathsf{d}_j^{\mathcal{I}}\varphi_j .$$

The last equality holds since $\varphi_j = (\mathsf{c} - \eta_j)/(\sigma - \alpha_j)$. This proves the lemma. $\square$

Proof (Of Theorem 1). Let $\mathcal{A}_{\mathsf{ss}}$ be any PPT adversary in the computational special soundness game. We construct the following extractor $\mathsf{Ext}_{\mathsf{ss}}$. (See Fig. 1 for a formal description.) Let $n \in \mathsf{poly}(\lambda)$, $\mathsf{p} \leftarrow \mathsf{Pgen}(1^\lambda)$, and $(\mathsf{ck}, \mathsf{tk}) \leftarrow \mathsf{KGen}(\mathsf{p}, n)$. $\mathsf{Ext}_{\mathsf{ss}}$ obtains ck and $\mathbf{tr}$, where $\mathbf{tr}$ is an $(n + 1)$-tuple of transcripts $\mathsf{tr}_j = ([\mathsf{c}]_1, \alpha_j, \eta_j, [\varphi_j]_1)$. Define $\mathcal{S} := \{\alpha_j\}_{j\in\mathcal{I}}$.[5] When $\mathcal{A}_{\mathsf{ss}}$ produces a successful

---

[4] [42] used this technique of batching polynomial commitment openings to improve on efficiency, while we use it for the security proof. Without using Lemma 2, we have a somewhat uglier assumption, where $\mathcal{A}_{\mathsf{ss}}$ returns $[\varphi_j]_1$ for every $j \in \mathcal{I}$, and $n + 1$ equalities $[g]_1 \bullet [1]_2 = [\varphi_j]_1 \bullet [\sigma - \alpha_j]_2$ hold individually.

[5] Note that if $\mathcal{S}$ contains σ then $\mathcal{A}_{\mathsf{ss}}$ has broken the $(n, 1)$-PDL assumption, and thus also the ARSDH assumption. However, the following proof also goes through when $\mathcal{S}$ contains σ, and thus we do not have to consider the case $\sigma \in \mathcal{S}$ separately.

attack, α_j are pairwise different (**tr** is admissible), and the KZG verifier accepts each transcript. That is, for all $j \in \mathcal{I}$, Eq. (3) holds.

$\mathsf{Ext_{ss}}(\mathsf{ck} = ([(\sigma^i)_{i=0}^n]_1, [1, \sigma]_2), \mathbf{tr})$	$\mathcal{B}(\mathsf{ck} = ([(\sigma^i)_{i=0}^n]_1, [1, \sigma]_2))$
	$\mathbf{tr} \leftarrow \mathcal{A}_{ss}(\mathsf{ck}); \quad /\!/ \; \mathsf{tr}_j = ([\mathsf{c}]_1, \alpha_j, \eta_j, [\varphi_j]_1)$
if $\exists i \neq j.\alpha_i = \alpha_j$ **then return** $\bot$;	**if** $\exists i \neq j.\alpha_i = \alpha_j$ **then return** $\bot$;
if $\exists j \in \mathcal{I} : \mathsf{V}(\mathsf{ck}, \mathsf{tr}_j) = 0$ **then**	**if** $\exists j \in \mathcal{I} : \mathsf{V}(\mathsf{ck}, \mathsf{tr}_j) = 0$ **then**
return $\bot$;	**return** $\bot$;
$L(X) \leftarrow \sum_{j \in \mathcal{I}} \eta_j \ell_j^{\mathcal{I}}(X) \in \mathbb{F}_{\leq n}[X]$;	$L(X) \leftarrow \sum_{j \in \mathcal{I}} \eta_j \ell_j^{\mathcal{I}}(X) \in \mathbb{F}_{\leq n}[X]$;
$[g]_1 \leftarrow [\mathsf{c} - L(\sigma)]_1$;	$[g]_1 \leftarrow [\mathsf{c} - L(\sigma)]_1$;
if $[g]_1 = [0]_1$ **then return** $L(X)$;	**if** $[g]_1 = [0]_1$ **then return** $\bot$;
return $\bot$;	$[\varphi]_1 \leftarrow \sum_{j \in \mathcal{I}} \mathsf{d}_j^{\mathcal{I}} [\varphi_j]_1$;
	return $(\mathcal{S} \leftarrow \{\alpha_j\}, [g, \varphi]_1)$;

Fig. 1. The extractor $\mathsf{Ext_{ss}}$ and the ARSDH reduction $\mathcal{B}$ in the proof of Theorem 1

$\mathsf{Ext_{ss}}$ interpolates a polynomial $L(X)$ of degree $\leq n$ such that $L(\alpha_j) = \eta_j$ for every $j \in \mathcal{I}$. That is, $L(X) = \sum_{j \in \mathcal{I}} \eta_j \ell_j^{\mathcal{I}}(X)$. If $[\mathsf{c}]_1 = [L(\sigma)]_1$, $\mathsf{Ext_{ss}}$ outputs $L(X)$. Observe that in this case, $\deg L(X) \leq n$ and $L(\alpha_j) = \eta_j$ for all $j \in \mathcal{I}$; thus, $(C, L) \in \mathcal{R}_{\mathsf{ck,tr}}$ as required in Definition 5. Otherwise, $\mathsf{Ext_{ss}}$ outputs $\bot$.

Let bad be the event that $\mathsf{c} \neq L(\sigma)$ but the verifier accepts all transcripts in **tr**. In Fig. 1, we depict a reduction $\mathcal{B}$ that breaks ARSDH whenever bad happens. $\mathcal{B}$ runs $\mathcal{A}_{ss}$ to obtain transcripts and then computes $L(X)$ just as the extractor. If $[\mathsf{c}]_1 = [L(\sigma)]_1$, $\mathcal{B}$ outputs $\bot$ (in this case, the extractor succeeds). Otherwise, $\mathcal{B}$ proceeds and computes $[g]_1 \leftarrow [\mathsf{c} - L(\sigma)]_1$ and $[\varphi]_1 \leftarrow \sum_{j \in \mathcal{I}} \mathsf{d}_j^{\mathcal{I}} [\varphi_j]_1$. Since Eq. (3) holds for all $j \in \mathcal{I}$, we get from Lemma 2 that Eq. (4) holds, that is, $[g]_1 \bullet [1]_2 = [\varphi]_1 \bullet [\mathbf{Z}_{\mathcal{S}}(\sigma)]_2$. When bad happens, $[g]_1 \neq [0]_1$ and thus $\mathcal{B}$ breaks the ARSDH assumption by returning $[g, \varphi]_1$. Thus, $\Pr[\mathcal{B} \text{ breaks ARSDH}] = \Pr[\text{bad}]$. Summarizing, $\mathsf{Adv}_{\mathsf{Pgen}, \mathsf{PC}, \mathsf{Ext_{ss}}, n+1, \mathcal{A}_{ss}}^{ss}(\lambda) \leq \mathsf{Adv}_{\mathsf{Pgen}, 1, n+1, \mathcal{B}}^{\mathsf{arsdh}}(\lambda)$. $\quad\square$

5 Rewinding Lemma

Next, we prove a generic information-theoretical rewinding lemma. Intuitively, if the adversary can produce an accepting transcript for a random challenge α_0, there exists an efficient extractor that can recover n more accepting transcripts for $n \in \mathsf{poly}(\lambda)$. Note that ε_{ss} is a function of p since $|\mathcal{F}_\mathsf{p}|$ is a function of p.

Theorem 2. *Fix $\mathcal{F}_\mathsf{p}$ as a function of p. For all DPT P^* and $n \in \mathsf{poly}(\lambda)$, there exists an expected PT extractor $\mathsf{Ext_{rw}}$, such that for any unbounded $\mathcal{A}$, $\varepsilon_{ss}(\mathsf{p}) > 1 - n/|\mathcal{F}_\mathsf{p}|$, where for every $\mathsf{p} \in \mathsf{Pgen}(1^\lambda)$, $\varepsilon_{ss}(\mathsf{p}) :=$*

$$
\Pr \left[\begin{array}{l|l} \mathsf{V}(\mathsf{ck}, \mathsf{tr}_0) = 1 \Rightarrow & (\mathsf{ck}, \mathsf{tk}) \leftarrow \mathsf{KGen}(\mathsf{p}, n); (C, \mathsf{st}) \leftarrow \mathcal{A}(\mathsf{ck}); \\ \forall j \in [1, n].\mathsf{V}(\mathsf{ck}, \mathsf{tr}_j) = 1 & \alpha_0 \leftarrow_\$ \mathcal{F}_\mathsf{p}; (\eta_0, \pi_0) \leftarrow \mathsf{P}^*(\mathsf{st}, \alpha_0); \\ & \mathsf{tr}_0 \leftarrow (C, \alpha_0, \eta_0, \pi_0); \\ & \mathbf{tr} \leftarrow \mathsf{Ext_{rw}}^{\mathsf{P}^*(\mathsf{st}, \cdot)}(\mathsf{ck}, \mathsf{tr}_0) \end{array} \right],
$$

and $\mathbf{tr} = (\mathsf{tr}_1, \ldots, \mathsf{tr}_n)$ *consists of transcripts* $\mathsf{tr}_j = (C, \alpha_j, \eta_j, \pi_j)$ *for* $j \in [1, n]$, *where* C *is the same as in* tr_0 *and* $\alpha_j \in \mathcal{F}_\mathsf{p}$ *are pairwise distinct. In particular,* Ext_rw *makes an expected number of* n *queries to* P^*.

Proof. Our proof strategy roughly follows [1]. In Fig. 2, we depict the extractor Ext_rw. Intuitively, Ext_rw runs $\mathsf{P}^*(\mathsf{st}, \cdot)$ on distinct uniformly random challenges $\alpha \in \mathcal{F}_\mathsf{p}$ until it either finds n additional accepting transcripts or the whole challenge set $\mathcal{F}_\mathsf{p}$ is exhausted.

$\mathsf{Ext}_\mathsf{rw}^{\mathsf{P}^*(\mathsf{st}, \cdot)}(\mathsf{ck}, \mathsf{tr}_0)$

Parse $\mathsf{tr}_0 = (C, \alpha_0, \eta_0, \pi_0)$;
if $\mathsf{V}(\mathsf{ck}, C, \alpha_0, \eta_0, \pi_0) = 0$ **then return** $\perp$; **fi**
$j \leftarrow 1; \mathcal{T} \leftarrow \mathcal{F}_\mathsf{p} \setminus \{\alpha_0\}$;
while $j \le n \land \mathcal{T} \ne \emptyset$ **do**
$\quad \alpha \leftarrow_\$ \mathcal{T}; (\eta, \pi) \leftarrow \mathsf{P}^*(\mathsf{st}, \alpha)$;
$\quad$ **if** $\mathsf{V}(\mathsf{ck}, C, \alpha, \eta, \pi) = 1$ **then** $\mathsf{tr}_j \leftarrow (C, \alpha, \eta, \pi); j \leftarrow j + 1;$ **fi**
$\quad \mathcal{T} \leftarrow \mathcal{T} \setminus \{\alpha\}$;
endwhile
if $j < n$ **then return** $\perp$; **fi**
return $\mathbf{tr} \leftarrow (\mathsf{tr}_1, \ldots, \mathsf{tr}_n)$;

Fig. 2. Extractor Ext_rw from Theorem 2.

Let r_p, r_ck, and $r_\mathcal{A}$ be the randomizers used in creating $\mathsf{p} \leftarrow \mathsf{Pgen}(1^\lambda; r_\mathsf{p})$, $\mathsf{ck} \leftarrow \mathsf{KGen}(\mathsf{p}, n; r_\mathsf{ck})$, and $(C, \mathsf{st}) \leftarrow \mathcal{A}(\mathsf{ck}; r_\mathcal{A})$. Consider a Boolean matrix H where the rows are indexed by the set $\mathsf{Rows} := \{\bar{r} = (r_\mathsf{p}, r_\mathsf{ck}, r_\mathcal{A}) : r_\mathsf{p}, r_\mathsf{ck}, r_\mathcal{A} \in \{0, 1\}^{\mathsf{poly}(\lambda)}\}$ and the columns are indexed by the verifier challenges from $\mathcal{F}_\mathsf{p}$. We implicitly set $H_{\bar{r}, \alpha} = 1$ iff $\mathsf{V}(\mathsf{ck}, C, \alpha, \eta, \pi) = 1$, where the parameters $(\mathsf{p}, \mathsf{ck}, C, \mathsf{st})$ are created using the coins $\bar{r}$ and $(\eta, \pi) \leftarrow \mathsf{P}^*(\mathsf{st}, \alpha)$.

Probability Analysis. Consider the game described in the lemma's statement. W.r.t. this game, let A be the event that $\mathsf{V}(\mathsf{ck}, \mathsf{tr}_0) = 1$ and let B be the event that $\forall j \in [1, n], \mathsf{V}(\mathsf{ck}, \mathsf{tr}_j) = 1$. Then,

$$\varepsilon_\mathsf{ss}(\mathsf{p}) = \Pr[A \Rightarrow B] = \Pr[A \land (A \Rightarrow B)] + \Pr[\neg A \land (A \Rightarrow B)]$$
$$= \Pr[A \land B] + \Pr[\neg A] .$$

Let $R := |\mathsf{Rows}|$. For $j \le |\mathcal{F}_\mathsf{p}|$, let R_j be the number of rows in H with exactly j ones. Thus, $\Pr[A] = \left(\sum_{j=1}^{|\mathcal{F}_\mathsf{p}|} j R_j\right) / (R \cdot |\mathcal{F}_\mathsf{p}|)$ is the fraction of ones in H. The event $A \land B$ happens iff tr_0 is accepting and it comes from a row $\bar{r} \in \mathsf{Rows}$ with at least $n + 1$ ones. Thus,

$$\Pr[A \land B] = \frac{\sum_{j=n+1}^{|\mathcal{F}_\mathsf{p}|} j R_j}{R \cdot |\mathcal{F}_\mathsf{p}|} = \frac{\sum_{j=1}^{|\mathcal{F}_\mathsf{p}|} j R_j}{R \cdot |\mathcal{F}_\mathsf{p}|} - \frac{\sum_{j=1}^{n} j R_j}{R \cdot |\mathcal{F}_\mathsf{p}|} = \Pr[A] - \frac{\sum_{j=1}^{n} j R_j}{R \cdot |\mathcal{F}_\mathsf{p}|} .$$

Next, $\sum_{j=1}^{n} jR_j$ is largest when all R rows have exactly n ones, i.e., $R_n = R$ and $R_j = 0$ for $j < n$. Thus, $(\sum_{j=1}^{n} jR_j)/(R \cdot |\mathcal{F}_p|) \leq nR/(R \cdot |\mathcal{F}_p|) = n/|\mathcal{F}_p|$ and $\Pr[A \wedge B] \geq \Pr[A] - n/|\mathcal{F}_p|$. Finally, $\varepsilon_{ss}(p) \geq (\Pr[A] - n/|\mathcal{F}_p|) + \Pr[\neg A] = 1 - n/|\mathcal{F}_p|$.

Expected Number of Queries. Let Q denote the number of queries Ext_{rw} makes to P^*. Since the total running time of Ext_{rw} is $\mathrm{poly}(\lambda) \cdot Q$, it is sufficient to only analyze Q. Consider the case that $H_{\bar{r},\alpha_0} = 1$ (therefore, A happened); then, the extractor in Fig. 2 will not abort on the second step but enters the **while** loop. The **while** loop in the extractor can be viewed as sampling without replacement from a finite binary-classified population.

Recall the negative hypergeometric distribution (NHG) is the distribution of X in the next game: given a bin with N balls of which K are marked, X is the number of sampled balls from the bin (without replacements) until we get $k \leq K$ marked balls. The expected value of X is $\mathbb{E}[\mathrm{NHG}_{N,K,k}] = k(N+1)/(K+1)$. The number of iterations of the **while** loop corresponds to an NHG random variable with the following parameters, where $\delta_{\bar{r}}$ is the fraction of ones in $H_{\bar{r}}$ ($\bar{r}$th row).

- $N = |\mathcal{F}_p| - 1$ (the number of possible challenges except α_0),
- $K = \delta_{\bar{r}}|\mathcal{F}_p| - 1$ (the number of ones in $H_{\bar{r}}$, except the entry $H_{\bar{r},\alpha_0}$),
- $k = n$ (the additional number of accepting transcripts Ext_{rw} needs to find).

If there are at least $n + 1$ entries in the row $\bar{r}$, the expected number of iterations in the **while** loop to get n ones is $k(N+1)/(K+1) = n|\mathcal{F}_p|/(\delta_{\bar{r}}|\mathcal{F}_p|) = n/\delta_{\bar{r}}$. On the other hand, if there are less than $n + 1$ ones in the row ϱ, then the **while** loop checks all the $|\mathcal{F}_p| - 1$ entries in the row. In this case, $K = \delta_{\bar{r}}|\mathcal{F}_p| - 1 \leq n - 1$ and thus $|\mathcal{F}_p| \leq n/\delta_{\bar{r}}$. Thus, the expected number of iterations in the **while** loop satisfies $|\mathcal{F}_p| - 1 < n/\delta_{\bar{r}}$. Hence, $\mathbb{E}[Q \mid A \wedge \bar{r}] \leq n/\delta_{\bar{r}}$.

The conditional probability, given the row $\bar{r}$, that the extractor does not abort before entering the **while** loop is $\delta_{\bar{r}} = \Pr[A \mid \bar{r}]$. Thus, conditioned on the row $\bar{r}$, the expected number of calls that the extractor makes is $\mathbb{E}[Q \mid \bar{r}] \leq \delta_{\bar{r}} \cdot n/\delta_{\bar{r}} = n$. The expected number of calls of Ext_{rw} can be computed as the average expected number of calls over the choice of $\bar{r}$:

$$\mathbb{E}[Q] = \sum_{\bar{r} \in \mathsf{Rows}} \mathbb{E}[Q|\bar{r}] \Pr[\bar{r}] \leq \sum_{\varrho=1}^{|\mathsf{Rows}|} \frac{n}{|\mathsf{Rows}|} = n .$$

The claim follows.   □

6   Black-Box Extractability

Definition. For a single transcript tr, we write that $(C, f) \in \mathcal{R}_{ck,tr}$ iff $(C, f) \in \mathcal{R}_{ck} \wedge f(\alpha) = \eta$. (This is a particular case of Eq. (1) for $n = 0$.)

Definition 6 (Black-Box Extractability). *A non-interactive polynomial commitment scheme* PC *is black-box extractable (BBE) for* Pgen, *if there exists*

$\mathsf{Ext}_{\mathsf{bb}}^{\mathsf{P}^*(\mathsf{st},\cdot)}(\mathsf{ck},\mathsf{tr}_0)$	$\mathcal{A}_{\mathsf{ss}}(\mathsf{ck})$
	$(C,\mathsf{st}) \leftarrow \mathcal{A}(\mathsf{ck}); \alpha_0 \leftarrow_{\$} \mathcal{F}_{\mathsf{p}};$
	$(\eta_0,\pi_0) \leftarrow \mathsf{P}^*(\mathsf{st},\alpha_0);$
	$\mathsf{tr}_0 \leftarrow (C,\alpha_0,\eta_0,\pi_0);$
$1:$ **if** $\mathsf{V}(\mathsf{ck},\mathsf{tr}_0) = 0$	**if** $\mathsf{V}(\mathsf{ck},\mathsf{tr}_0) = 0$
$\qquad$ **then return** $\perp;$ **fi**	$\qquad$ **then return** $\perp;$ **fi**
$2:$ $\mathsf{tr} \leftarrow \mathsf{Ext}_{\mathsf{rw}}^{\mathsf{P}^*(\mathsf{st},\cdot)}(\mathsf{ck},\mathsf{tr}_0);$	$\mathsf{tr} \leftarrow \mathsf{Ext}_{\mathsf{rw}}^{\mathsf{P}^*(\mathsf{st},\cdot)}(\mathsf{ck},\mathsf{tr}_0);$
$3:$ **if** $\exists j \in [1,n].\mathsf{V}(\mathsf{ck},\mathsf{tr}_j) = 0$	**if** $\exists j \in [1,n].\mathsf{V}(\mathsf{ck},\mathsf{tr}_j) = 0$
$\qquad$ **then return** $\perp;$ **fi**	$\qquad$ **then return** $\perp;$ **fi**
$\qquad f \leftarrow \mathsf{Ext}_{\mathsf{ss}}(\mathsf{ck},\mathsf{tr}_0\|\mathsf{tr});$	
$4:$ **return** $f;$	**return** $(\mathsf{tr}_0\|\mathsf{tr});$

Fig. 3. The black-box extractor $\mathsf{Ext}_{\mathsf{bb}}$ and the special-soundness adversary $\mathcal{A}_{\mathsf{ss}}^{\mathsf{P}^*(\mathsf{st},\cdot)}$ from Theorem 3.

an expected PPT black-box extractor $\mathsf{Ext}_{\mathsf{bb}}$, *such that for all PPT* $\mathcal{A}$, *DPT* P^*, $n \in \mathsf{poly}(\lambda)$, *and* $\mathcal{F}_{\mathsf{p}} \subseteq \mathbb{F}$ *of size* $|\mathcal{F}_{\mathsf{p}}| = \lambda^{\omega(1)}$, $\mathsf{Adv}_{\mathsf{Pgen},\mathsf{PC},\mathsf{Ext},n,\mathcal{A},\mathsf{P}^*}^{\mathsf{bbe}}(\lambda) =$

$$\Pr\left[\begin{array}{l} \mathsf{V}(\mathsf{ck},\mathsf{tr}_0) = 1 \wedge \\ (C,f) \notin \mathcal{R}_{\mathsf{ck},\mathsf{tr}_0} \end{array} \middle| \begin{array}{l} \mathsf{p} \leftarrow \mathsf{Pgen}(1^\lambda); (\mathsf{ck},\mathsf{tk}) \leftarrow \mathsf{KGen}(\mathsf{p},n); (C,\mathsf{st}) \leftarrow \mathcal{A}(\mathsf{ck}); \\ \alpha_0 \leftarrow_{\$} \mathcal{F}_{\mathsf{p}}; (\eta_0,\pi_0) \leftarrow \mathsf{P}^*(\mathsf{st},\alpha_0); \mathsf{tr}_0 \leftarrow (C,\alpha_0,\eta_0,\pi_0); \\ f \leftarrow \mathsf{Ext}_{\mathsf{bb}}^{\mathsf{P}^*(\mathsf{st},\cdot)}(\mathsf{ck},\mathsf{tr}_0); \end{array} \right] \approx_\lambda 0 \ .$$

$\mathsf{Ext}_{\mathsf{bb}}$ *can invoke* $\mathsf{P}^*(\mathsf{st},\cdot)$ *with any challenge* $\tilde{\alpha} \in \mathcal{F}_{\mathsf{p}}$ *to which* $\mathsf{P}^*(\mathsf{st},\tilde{\alpha})$ *returns some tuple* $(\tilde{\eta},\tilde{\pi})$.

Note that st can contain information about ck and C. In Definition 6, P^* being deterministic means that we can rewind and restart P^* many times on the same state st, but different challenges.

We balanced Definition 6 so that it is weak enough for KZG to satisfy it and strong enough so that the SNARK compiler in Sect. 7 can use it. A crucial difference between Definition 1 and Definition 6 is that the evaluation point is sampled randomly from a large set in the latter. We need this property to prove Theorem 2. This difference with Definition 1 is why we must open each polynomial at a random evaluation point in our compiler in Sect. 7.

In the full version [33], we show that if the PCS is binding and BBE, it also has non-adaptive evaluation binding. This is a slightly weaker form of evaluation binding than usual, where the game picks the evaluation point randomly.

Security Reduction. We prove that if a non-interactive polynomial commitment scheme is computationally special-sound, it is also black-box extractable, as in Definition 6. The proof of Theorem 3 per se is not complicated if one assumes the results of Sects. 4 and 5.

Theorem 3. *If a non-interactive PCS* PC *is computational* $(n+1)$-*special-sound, it is black-box extractable.*

Proof. Assume PC is special-sound (see Definition 5) and let $\mathsf{Ext_{ss}}$ be the guaranteed PPT special soundness extractor. Let $\mathsf{Ext_{rw}}$ be the rewinding extractor from Fig. 2. Let $\mathcal{A}$ and P^* be the adversaries in the definition of black-box extraction.

Figure 3 depicts the new black-box extractor $\mathsf{Ext_{bb}}$. If the verifier does not accept tr_0, there is no need to extract, and $\mathsf{Ext_{bb}}$ outputs $\bot$. Otherwise, $\mathsf{Ext_{bb}}$ calls $\mathsf{Ext_{rw}}$ to obtain n more accepting transcripts $\mathbf{tr}$, resulting in an $(n+1)$-tuple $\mathsf{tr}_0\|\mathbf{tr}$ of admissible transcripts. $\mathsf{Ext_{bb}}$ runs $\mathsf{Ext_{ss}}$ on $\mathsf{tr}_0\|\mathbf{tr}$, obtaining a polynomial f. If both $\mathsf{Ext_{rw}}$ and $\mathsf{Ext_{ss}}$ succeed, then $\mathsf{Ext_{bb}}$ outputs f. Since $\mathsf{Ext_{rw}}$ runs in the expected PPT and $\mathsf{Ext_{ss}}$ in strict PPT, $\mathsf{Ext_{bb}}$ runs in expected PPT.

We next bound the probability that when running $\mathsf{Ext_{bb}}$, $\mathsf{V}(\mathsf{ck}, \mathsf{tr}_0) = 1$ but $(C, f) \notin \mathcal{R}_{\mathsf{ck},\mathsf{tr}_0}$. Looking at Fig. 3, we can see that there are two different ways for this to happen.

(i) $\mathsf{Ext_{bb}}$ returns $\bot$ in step 3. This corresponds to the event $\mathbf{F_{rw}}$ ("failure in rewinding") that $\mathsf{V}(\mathsf{ck}, \mathsf{tr}_0) = 1$ but $\mathsf{V}(\mathsf{ck}, \mathsf{tr}_j) = 0$ for some $j \in [1, n]$.

(ii) $\mathsf{Ext_{bb}}$ reaches step 4 and returns f, such that $(C, f) \notin \mathcal{R}_{\mathsf{ck},\mathsf{tr}_0}$. This corresponds to the event $\mathbf{F_{ss}}$ ("failure in special soundness") that $\forall j \in [0, n].\mathsf{V}(\mathsf{ck}, \mathsf{tr}_j) = 1$ but $(C, f) \notin \mathcal{R}_{\mathsf{ck},\mathsf{tr}_0}$.

We next bound the probabilities that $\mathbf{F_{rw}}$ or $\mathbf{F_{ss}}$ happen.

Event $\mathbf{F_{rw}}$. By Theorem 2, $\mathbf{F_{rw}}$ happens with probability at most $n/|\mathcal{F}_{\mathsf{p}}|$.

Event $\mathbf{F_{ss}}$. We bound the probability that $\mathbf{F_{ss}}$ happens by relying on special soundness (Definition 5). In Fig. 3, we depict a special soundness adversary $\mathcal{A}_{\mathsf{ss}}$ that runs $\mathcal{A}$ and P^* internally. $\mathcal{A}_{\mathsf{ss}}$ first runs $\mathcal{A}$ and P^* to create tr_0 as in Definition 6. Crucially, $\mathcal{A}_{\mathsf{ss}}$ creates tr_0 from the correct distribution for $\mathsf{Ext_{bb}}$. Then, $\mathcal{A}_{\mathsf{ss}}$ executes $\mathsf{Ext_{bb}}$ up to step 3 Finally, $\mathcal{A}_{\mathsf{ss}}$ outputs tr_0 together with n transcripts computed by $\mathsf{Ext_{rw}}$. (However, it does not run $\mathsf{Ext_{ss}}$.)

According to the special soundness definition, the event that the extractor outputs $f(X)$ such that $(C, f) \notin \mathcal{R}_{\mathsf{ck},\mathsf{tr}_0}$, but $\forall j \in [0, n].\mathsf{V}(\mathsf{ck}, \mathsf{tr}_j) = 1$ is bounded $\mathsf{Adv}^{\mathsf{ss}}_{\mathsf{Pgen},\mathsf{PC},\mathsf{Ext_{ss}},n+1,\mathcal{A}_{\mathsf{ss}}}(\lambda)$. This corresponds precisely to the event $\mathbf{F_{ss}}$. Thus, $\Pr[\mathbf{F_{ss}}] \leq \mathsf{Adv}^{\mathsf{ss}}_{\mathsf{Pgen},\mathsf{PC},\mathsf{Ext_{ss}},n+1,\mathcal{A}_{\mathsf{ss}}}(\lambda)$. However, $\mathcal{A}_{\mathsf{ss}}$ is an expected PPT adversary, but special soundness is defined only for strict PPT adversary. We observe that special soundness is a falsifiable assumption (it can be written as an interaction between a PPT challenger and an adversary, Appendix A [33]). According to Lemma 6 [33], since $\mathsf{Adv}^{\mathsf{ss}}_{\mathsf{Pgen},\mathsf{PC},\mathsf{Ext_{ss}},n+1,\mathcal{A}'}(\lambda)$ is negligible for any PPT $\mathcal{A}'$, then also $\mathsf{Adv}^{\mathsf{ss}}_{\mathsf{Pgen},\mathsf{PC},\mathsf{Ext_{ss}},n+1,\mathcal{A}_{\mathsf{ss}}}(\lambda)$ is a negligible function.

Summing up the above results, we get the claim of the theorem. $\square$

Corollary 1. *If $(n+1)$-ARSDH holds, then KZG for degree $\leq n$ polynomials is black-box extractable.*

Proof. Follows directly from Theorems 1 and 3. $\square$

7   Application to SNARKs

7.1   Polynomial IOP

The following definition of polynomial IOP (PIOP) roughly follows [41].

Definition 7 (Polynomial IOP with Preprocessing). *Let $\mathcal{R}$ be an indexed relation, $\mathbb{F}$ a finite field, and $d \in \mathbb{N}$ a degree bound. A polynomial IOP for $\mathcal{R}$ with degree bound d is a tuple of PPT algorithms $\Pi_{\mathsf{IOP}} = (\mathsf{IOP.I}, \mathsf{IOP.P}, \mathsf{IOP.V})$, satisfying the following. 1. $\mathsf{IOP.I}$ takes i for input and outputs a list of polynomials of degree at most d. 2. $\mathsf{IOP.V}$ gets oracle access to these polynomials. 3. $(\mathsf{IOP.P}, \mathsf{IOP.V})$ run a Rnds-round interactive protocol. 4. In each round, $\mathsf{IOP.P}$ sends polynomials $f_i(X) \in \mathbb{F}[X]$ of degree at most d to $\mathsf{IOP.V}$. 5. $\mathsf{IOP.V}$ is an oracle machine with access to a list of oracles, containing one oracle for each polynomial it has received from the prover (and indexer). 6. At the end of each round, $\mathsf{IOP.V}$ can query oracles associated with $f_i(X)$ on a point $\alpha_j \in \mathbb{F}$; the oracle responds with the value $f_i(\alpha_j)$. 7. In the subsequent round, $\mathsf{IOP.V}$ sends oracle queries and challenges $z_k \in \mathbb{F}$ to $\mathsf{IOP.P}$. 8. $\mathsf{IOP.V}$ is public coin.*

On common input x and prover's witness w, the protocol transcript is denoted by the random variable $\langle \mathsf{IOP.P}(\mathsf{x}, \mathsf{w}), \mathsf{IOP.V}(\mathsf{x}) \rangle = \mathsf{tr}$. When the verifier accepts the transcript, we conveniently write $\mathsf{tr} = 1$. $\mathsf{IOP.V}^{\mathsf{I(i)}}$ denotes that the verifier has oracle access to the polynomials outputted by the indexer.

A polynomial IOP must satisfy the following properties.

Perfect Completeness: for all $(\mathsf{i}, \mathsf{x}, \mathsf{w}) \in \mathcal{R}$,

$$\Pr\left[\langle \mathsf{IOP.P}(\mathsf{x}, \mathsf{w}), \mathsf{IOP.V}^{\mathsf{I(i)}}(\mathsf{x}) \rangle = 1\right] = 1 \ .$$

Knowledge Soundness: There exists a PPT algorithm Ext^6, such that for any interactive algorithm $\mathcal{A}$, $\mathsf{i} \in \mathbb{I}(\mathcal{R})$, and input $\mathsf{x} \in \{0,1\}^{\mathsf{poly}(\lambda)}$ (not necessarily in the language), the following holds: $\mathsf{Adv}^{\mathsf{ks}}_{\Pi, \mathsf{Ext}, \mathcal{A}}(\lambda) :=$

$$\Pr\left[\mathsf{tr} = 1 \wedge (\mathsf{i}, \mathsf{x}, \mathsf{w}) \notin \mathcal{R} \mid \mathsf{tr} \leftarrow \langle \mathcal{A}(\mathsf{i}, \mathsf{x}), \mathsf{IOP.V}^{\mathsf{I(i)}}(\mathsf{x}) \rangle; \mathsf{w} \leftarrow \mathsf{Ext}(\mathsf{i}, \mathsf{x}, \mathsf{tr})\right] \approx_\lambda 0 \ .$$

7.2 Compiling Polynomial IOPs into Arguments

We present a compiler that compiles a PIOP and a non-interactive polynomial commitment scheme (as defined in Sect. 2.1) into an interactive argument.

The SRS is the public key of the commitment scheme, and in the preprocessing phase, the commitments of the indexer's polynomials are published. The interactive part of the argument runs PIOP, except with the following two changes:

– If the PIOP prover sends some polynomial f to the PIOP verifier, then P and V execute the following three-message subprotocol: the prover sends a commitment of f to the verifier, the verifier samples a new extraction point[7] $\chi \leftarrow_{\$} \mathcal{F}$ (here $|\mathcal{F}| = \lambda^{\omega(1)}$), and the prover opens the commitment of f at

---

[6] Note that [10] allowed the extractor to rewind. We are unaware of any concrete polynomial IOP, which would need that. Thus, for the sake of simplicity we use a straight-line extractor.

[7] In practice, $\mathcal{F} = \mathbb{F}$. After using Fiat-Shamir, the extraction point is a hash.

this point. The verifier checks that the opening proof verifies. We can think of this protocol as an interactive commitment phase of a new polynomial commitment scheme KZG^+.

- If the PIOP verifier queries a previously sent polynomial f at some point α, the verifier sends α to the prover and the prover opens the commitment to f at the evaluation point α. The verifier checks that the opening proof verifies.

The rest of the PIOP is executed truthfully. In particular, the verifier checks that the PIOP verifier accepts the corresponding PIOP transcript that can be easily compiled from the verifier's responses and evaluations sent by the prover.

It is important to observe that even if the original PIOP has zero knowledge, the compiled argument might not have. We make new queries (with extraction points) to the polynomials, which leak additional information. However, in efficient zk-SNARKs like Plonk, this can be tackled by adding extra randomness to polynomials to account for one more opening point.

For simplicity, we assume that the PIOP prover sends a single polynomial in each round. This assumption is without loss of generality: We can always write an equivalent PIOP, where instead of sending many polynomials per round, the prover sends each in a separate round, and the verifier's intermediate responses are random challenges never used by the prover. In the compiled argument, these challenges can be removed, meaning there is no increase in the number of rounds.

Compiler Description. We introduce more notation to make it easier to explain rewinding. Let $(\mathsf{IOP.I}, \mathsf{IOP.P}, \mathsf{IOP.V})$ be a polynomial IOP. We denote by $\mathsf{st}_{r-1}^{\mathsf{V}}$ the verifier's state at the beginning of round r. The verifier's initial state is $\mathsf{st}_0^{\mathsf{V}} = \mathrm{x}$. On input $(\mathsf{st}_{r-1}^{\mathsf{V}}, \mathsf{coins}_r)$, V outputs query points $\boldsymbol{\alpha}_r$, other challenge values z_r, and labels[8] $\boldsymbol{g}_r$ for the oracles that need to be evaluated. More precisely, $\boldsymbol{g}_r$ is a vector of length $\ell_r = |\boldsymbol{g}_r| = |\boldsymbol{\alpha}_r|$ containing labels for V's oracles that need to be queried. An oracle can be from the prover or from the indexer (the same oracle may appear even multiple times in $\boldsymbol{g}_r$). The verifier queries $\eta_{r,i} \leftarrow g_{r,i}(\alpha_{r,i})$ for all $i \in [1, \ell_r]$, where $g_{r,i}$ is a label for one of V's oracles.

We depict the compiler, with full details, in Fig. 4. Here, $\Pi_{\mathsf{IOP}} = (\mathsf{IOP.I}, \mathsf{IOP.P}, \mathsf{IOP.V})$ is a Rnds-round PIOP for $\mathcal{R}_{\mathsf{p},n}$ and PC is a non-interactive polynomial commitment scheme.

Security. We prove that if the PIOP is knowledge sound, the commitment scheme is evaluation binding and black-box extractable, then the compiled (interactive) argument system has witness-extended emulation.

Theorem 4. *If the non-interactive polynomial commitment scheme* PC *is black-box extractable and evaluation-binding, and if the* Rnds*-round PIOP* Π_{IOP} *for* $\mathcal{R}$ *is knowledge-sound, then the argument* Π *described in Fig. 4 is a public-coin interactive argument system for* $\mathcal{R}$ *that has witness-extended emulation.*

---

[8] They have to be labels, not polynomials, since technically V does not know the polynomials themselves. For simplicity, we will ignore this difference in the notation.

Pgen(1^λ): run p $\leftarrow$ PC.Pgen(1^λ) of the PCS.

KGen(p, n): run (ck, tk) $\leftarrow$ PC.KGen(p, n).

Derive(ck, $i \in \mathbb{I}(\mathcal{R}_{p,n})$): run $(\iota_1(X), \ldots, \iota_\ell(X)) \leftarrow$ IOP.I(i) and compute
   $c_j \leftarrow$ PC.Com(ck, $\iota_j(X)$) for $j = 1, \ldots, \ell$. Return ek$_i \leftarrow$ ck and
   vk$_i \leftarrow (c_1, \ldots, c_\ell)$.

$\langle$P(ek$_i$, x, w), V(vk$_i$, x)$\rangle$:
   - For each $r \in [1, \mathsf{Rnds}]$, P and V run the following subprotocol:
     1. P sends $C_r \leftarrow$ PC.Com(ck, f_r).
        // where $f_r \in \mathbb{F}_{\leq n}[X]$ is sent by IOP.P in the r-th PIOP round
     2. V sends $\chi_r \leftarrow_\$ \mathcal{F}$.
     3. P sends $(\eta_{\chi_r}, \pi_{\chi_r}) \leftarrow$ PC.Open(ck, C_r, χ_r, f_r).
     4. V sends random coins coins$_r$ of IOP.V.
     5. P computes $(\boldsymbol{z}_r, \boldsymbol{\alpha}_r, \boldsymbol{g}_r) \leftarrow$ IOP.V(st$^V_{r-1}$, coins$_r$) and
        sends a vector of openings $(\boldsymbol{\eta}_r, \boldsymbol{\pi}_r)$, where $(\eta_{r,i}, \pi_{r,i}) \leftarrow$
        PC.Open(ck, $C_r, \alpha_{r,i}, g_{r,i}$) for each $i \in [1, \ell_r]$. // $\ell_r = |\boldsymbol{g}_r| = |\boldsymbol{\alpha}_r|$.
     6. P and V update their states.
   - V uses PC.V to check that all the openings are valid and IOP.V to
     check that the opened PIOP transcript is valid.

Fig. 4. Public-coin interactive argument system $\Pi = $ (Pgen, KGen, Derive, P, V, Sim)
for the relation $\mathcal{R}_{p,n}$.

Proof. Let P*, $\mathcal{A}$, $\mathcal{D}$ denote the adversaries from the WEE definition (Sect. 2.2).
We construct a WEE emulator Π.Emu for the argument system Π. Π.Emu is
defined in Fig. 5, having black-box rewindable access to P*.

We denote the state of the prover P* (containing the state st from $\mathcal{A}$, P*'s
internal configuration, and messages from V) at the beginning of the round r
subprotocol by st$^{(1)}_{r-1}$ and after receiving the challenge $\chi_r \leftarrow_\$ \mathcal{F}$ by st$^{(2)}_{r-1}$. Note
that Π.Emu has only an oracle access to P* and does not see P*'s state. We use
the state notation only for showing that Π.Emu rewinds the deterministic P* to
a particular state. We give an overview of Π.Emu depicted in Fig. 5.

Π.Emu black-box executes the prover's first round P*(st$^{(1)}_0$) and gets a commitment C_1 to an unknown polynomial. The initial state is st$^{(1)}_0 = $ (p, ck, x, st),
where st is the state information sent from $\mathcal{A}$. Then, Π.Emu plays the argu-
ment's verifier, sampling $\chi_1 \leftarrow_\$ \mathcal{F}$ and running P*(st$^{(1)}_0$, χ_1) to obtain an opening
$(\eta_{\chi_1}, \pi_{\chi_1})$. If Π.Emu received a valid opening for χ, it runs the black-box extractor PC.Ext$_{bb}$ of PC to obtain a polynomial f_1, such that $(C_1, f_1) \in \mathcal{R}_{ck}$. We show
later that Ext extracts a valid polynomial with overwhelming probability. This
follows from the definition of black-box extractability (Definition 6), which can
be invoked because χ_1 is an extraction point sampled from a superpolynomial
size set. Then, Π.Emu samples coins$_1$ for IOP.V and uses them to compute eval-
uation points $\boldsymbol{\alpha}_1$, challenges $\boldsymbol{z}_1$, and oracle labels $\boldsymbol{g}_1$ that have to be evaluated
on $\boldsymbol{\alpha}_1$. It runs P* on coins$_1$ to get openings $(\boldsymbol{\eta}_1, \boldsymbol{\pi}_1)$.

$\Pi.\mathsf{Emu}^{\langle P^*(p,\mathsf{ck},\mathbb{x},\mathsf{st}),V(\mathsf{vk}_i,\mathbb{x})\rangle}(p,\mathsf{ck},\mathbb{x})$

---

1 : $\mathsf{colsn} \leftarrow \mathbf{false}$;
2 : $\mathbf{for}\ r = 1\ \mathbf{to}\ \mathsf{Rnds}\ \mathbf{do}$ // P^*'s initial state is $\mathsf{st}_0^{(1)} = (p, \mathsf{ck}, \mathbb{x}, \mathsf{st})$
3 :   Run $P^*(\mathsf{st}_{r-1}^{(1)})$ and receive C_r;
4 :   Sample extraction point $\chi_r \leftarrow_\$ \mathcal{F}$;
5 : $(\eta_{\chi_r}, \pi_{\chi_r}) \leftarrow P^*(\mathsf{st}_{r-1}^{(1)}, \chi_r)$;   // P^*'s new state is denoted $\mathsf{st}_{r-1}^{(2)}$
6 : $\mathsf{tr}_{\mathsf{PC}} \leftarrow (C_r, \chi_r, \eta_{\chi_r}, \pi_{\chi_r})$;
7 : $\mathbf{if}\ \mathsf{PC.V}(\mathsf{ck}, \mathsf{tr}_{\mathsf{PC}}) = 1\ \mathbf{then}$
8 : $f_r(X) \leftarrow \mathsf{PC.Ext}_{\mathsf{bb}}^{P^*(\mathsf{st}_{r-1}^{(1)}, \cdot)}(\mathsf{ck}, \mathsf{tr}_{\mathsf{PC}})$;
9 : $\mathbf{if}\ (C_r, f_r) \in \mathcal{R}_{\mathsf{ck}}\ \mathbf{then}$
10 : $\mathsf{ext\text{-}fail}_r \leftarrow \mathbf{false}$;
11 : $\mathbf{else}\ \mathsf{ext\text{-}fail}_r \leftarrow \mathbf{true}; \mathbf{fi}$
12 : $\mathbf{fi}$
13 :   Sample coins_r for IOP.V; $(\alpha_r, z_r, g_r) \leftarrow \mathsf{IOP.V}(\mathsf{st}_{r-1}^V, \mathsf{coins}_r)$;
14 : $(\eta_r, \pi_r) \leftarrow P^*(\mathsf{st}_{r-1}^{(2)}, \mathsf{coins}_r)$;   // P^*'s new state is denoted $\mathsf{st}_r^{(1)}$
15 : $\mathsf{st}_r^V \leftarrow (\mathsf{st}_{r-1}^V, \mathsf{coins}_r, \eta_r, \pi_r)$;
16 : $\mathbf{if}\ (\mathsf{PC.V}(\mathsf{ck}, \mathsf{tr}_{\mathsf{PC}}) = 1) \wedge \neg (\mathsf{ext\text{-}fail}_r)\ \mathbf{then}$
17 :   Compute $\tilde{\eta}_r \leftarrow (g_{r,1}(\alpha_{r,1}), \ldots, g_{r,\ell_r}(\alpha_{r,\ell_r}))$;
18 : $\mathbf{if}\ \eta_r \neq \tilde{\eta}_r\ \mathbf{then}\ \mathsf{colsn} \leftarrow \mathbf{true}; \mathbf{fi}$
19 : $\mathbf{fi}$
20 : $\mathbf{endfor}$
21 : $\mathsf{tr} \leftarrow (\mathsf{tr}_1, \ldots, \mathsf{tr}_{\mathsf{Rnds}})$, where $\mathsf{tr}_i = (C_i, \chi_i, \eta_{\chi_i}, \pi_{\chi_i}, \mathsf{coins}_i, \eta_i, \pi_i)$;
22 : $\mathsf{tr}_{\mathsf{IOP}} \leftarrow (f_1, \alpha_1, z_1, g_1, \ldots, f_{\mathsf{Rnds}}, \alpha_{\mathsf{Rnds}}, z_{\mathsf{Rnds}}, g_{\mathsf{Rnds}})$;
23 : $\mathbf{if}\ \vee_{i=1}^{\mathsf{Rnds}} \mathsf{ext\text{-}fail}_i\ \mathbf{then\ return}\ (\mathsf{tr}, \bot); \mathbf{fi}$
24 : $\mathbf{if}\ \mathsf{colsn}\ \mathbf{then\ return}\ (\mathsf{tr}, \bot); \mathbf{fi}$
25 : $\mathbb{w} \leftarrow \mathsf{Ext}(\mathbb{x}, \mathsf{tr}_{\mathsf{IOP}})$, where Ext is the PIOP knowledge extractor.
26 : $\mathbf{if}\ (i, \mathbb{x}, \mathbb{w}) \notin \mathcal{R}\ \mathbf{then\ return}\ (\mathsf{tr}, \bot); \mathbf{fi}$
27 : $\mathbf{return}\ (\mathsf{tr}, \mathbb{w})$;

Fig. 5. Emulator $\Pi.\mathsf{Emu}$ for the compiled argument Π.

If f_1 was correctly extracted, $\Pi.\mathsf{Emu}$ computes $\eta_{1,i} \leftarrow g_{1,i}(\alpha_{1,i})$, evaluating all the polynomials that the verifier indicated (g_1 may include a label for f_1 or indexer's polynomials) at the respective evaluation points. $\Pi.\mathsf{Emu}$ checks if the openings returned by P^* are compatible with the one it can compute itself using f_1. If so, then $\Pi.\mathsf{Emu}$ has successfully simulated the first round of the PIOP, $(f_1, \alpha_1, z_1, g_1)$. Otherwise, if one of the openings is incompatible, we get a contradiction with the evaluation binding of PC, as we prove later. After updating the state of IOP.V, $\Pi.\mathsf{Emu}$ proceeds to simulate the subsequent rounds similarly. Finally, the emulator runs the PIOP extractor on the PIOP transcript to recover the witness $\mathbb{w}$. $\Pi.\mathsf{Emu}$ outputs the argument's transcript and $\mathbb{w}$.

Note that the transcript that $\Pi.\mathsf{Emu}$ outputs is distributed as the one resulted from an honest protocol execution between P^* and V. Therefore, real and emulated transcripts are perfectly indistinguishable. Let $\mathbf{D}_0$ be the event "$i \in \mathbb{I}(\mathcal{R}_{p,n}) \wedge \mathcal{D}(\mathsf{tr}) = 1$" with the real transcript tr and $\mathbf{D}_1$ the same event when tr is emulated. Additionally, let $\mathbf{V}$ be the event that "$V_{\mathsf{check}}(\mathsf{ck}, \mathsf{tr}) = 1$" and $\mathbf{W}$ the event $(i, \mathbb{x}, \mathbb{w}) \in \mathcal{R}$ when the emulator outputs tr and $\mathbb{w}$. Then,

$$\mathsf{Adv}^{\mathsf{wee}}_{\mathsf{Pgen},\Pi,n,\mathsf{P^*},\mathcal{A},\mathcal{D}}(\lambda) = \Pr[\mathbf{D}_0] - \Pr[\mathbf{D}_1 \wedge (\mathbf{V} \Rightarrow \mathbf{W})]$$
$$= \Pr[\mathbf{D}_1] - \Pr[\mathbf{D}_1 \wedge (\neg\mathbf{V} \vee \mathbf{W})]$$
$$= \Pr[\mathbf{D}_1 \wedge \mathbf{V} \wedge \neg\mathbf{W}] \leq \Pr[\mathbf{V} \wedge \neg\mathbf{W}] \ .$$

Thus, to conclude the proof, we need to bound the probability that Π.Emu computes a valid transcript but fails to extract a witness. This can be divided into the following disjoint events.

1. Π.Emu computes a valid transcript, but on the line 23 in Fig. 5 it returns $(\mathsf{tr}, \bot)$. Namely, there exists r, for which $\mathsf{PC.Ext}_{\mathsf{bb}}$ failed to extract a polynomial f_r such that $(C_r, f_r) \in \mathcal{R}_{\mathsf{ck}}$, and consequently the corresponding variable ext-fail$_r$ is set to **true**. We denote this event $\mathbf{F}^{(r)}_{\mathsf{bbe}}$ (failure in the black box extraction). Let $\mathbf{F}_{\mathsf{bbe}} = \mathbf{F}^{(1)}_{\mathsf{bbe}} \vee \ldots \vee \mathbf{F}^{(\mathsf{Rnds})}_{\mathsf{bbe}}$ be the event that extraction fails in any of the rounds.
2. Π.Emu computes a valid transcript, but on the line 24 in Fig. 5 it returns $(\mathsf{tr}, \bot)$. We denote the event by $\mathbf{F}_{\mathsf{eb}}$ (failure in evaluation binding). In that case ext-fail$_r$ = false for all r, but colsn = true. The variable colsn is set to true if some evaluation $\eta_{r,\alpha}$ sent by $\mathsf{P^*}$ is different from $\tilde{\eta}_{r,\alpha} = g_{r,i}(\alpha_{r,i})$, where $g_{r,i}(X)$ is either a publicly-known indexer polynomial or one of the extracted polynomials and $\alpha_{r,i} \in \boldsymbol{\alpha}_r$ is one of the query points.
3. Π.Emu computes a valid transcript, but on the line 26 in Fig. 5 it returns $(\mathsf{tr}, \bot)$. We denote this event by $\mathbf{F}_{\mathsf{iop}}$ (failure in the PIOP extraction). In that case, $\mathsf{tr}_{\mathsf{IOP}}$ compiled by the emulator is a valid PIOP transcript because polynomials have been successfully extracted, and there are no collisions, but the PIOP extractor still failed to extract the witness.

We prove that each of the three events happens with a negligible probability. We bound the first event by the probability of breaking black-box extractability. We show this first for a fixed round r.

Lemma 3. *There exists a expected PPT $\mathcal{A}_r$ such that* $\Pr\left[\mathbf{F}^{(r)}_{\mathsf{bbe}}\right] \leq$ $\mathsf{Adv}^{\mathsf{bbe}}_{\mathsf{Pgen},\mathsf{PC},\mathsf{Ext},n,\mathcal{A}_r,\mathsf{P^*}}(\lambda)$.

Proof. We construct a reduction to the black-box extractability property of PC. Let $\mathcal{A}$, $\mathsf{P^*}$ be the adversaries in the WEE definition as above.

To construct a reduction, we need to construct a black-box extractability adversary $\mathcal{A}_r$ (we use $\mathsf{P^*}$ as the deterministic black-box extractability adversary). The adversary $\mathcal{A}_r$ runs Π.Emu until the line 2 in r-th execution of **for**loop. That is, until the emulator gets C_r. At that point, $\mathcal{A}_r$ outputs $(C_r, \mathsf{st}^{(1)}_{r-1})$.

We now plug $\mathcal{A}_r$ and $\mathsf{P^*}$ into the black-box extractability game. Let us recall the game. The adversary $\mathcal{A}_r(\mathsf{ck})$ outputs $(C_r, \mathsf{st}^{(1)}_{r-1})$ on a correctly sampled ck. Then the game picks $\chi \leftarrow_{\$} \mathscr{F}_{\mathsf{p}}$, sets $(\eta_{r,\chi}, \pi_{r,\chi}) \leftarrow \mathsf{P^*}(\mathsf{st}^{(1)}_{r-1}, \chi)$ and defines $\mathsf{tr}_{\mathsf{PC}} \leftarrow (C_r, \chi, \eta_{r,\chi}, \pi_{r,\chi})$. Finally, $\mathsf{PC.Ext}^{\mathsf{P^*}(\mathsf{st}^{(1)}_{r-1}, \cdot)}_{\mathsf{bb}}(\mathsf{ck}, \mathsf{tr}_{\mathsf{PC}})$ outputs a polynomial $f_r(X)$. According to the definition, probability that $\mathsf{PC.V}(\mathsf{ck}, \mathsf{tr}_{\mathsf{PC}}) = 1$ and $(C_r, f_r) \notin \mathcal{R}_{\mathsf{ck},\mathsf{tr}}$ is bounded by $\mathsf{Adv}^{\mathsf{bbe}}_{\mathsf{Pgen},\mathsf{PC},\mathsf{Ext},n,\mathcal{A}_r,\mathsf{P^*}}(\lambda)$.

By construction of $\mathcal{A}_r$ and P^* the latter event is implied by the event $\mathbf{F}_{\mathsf{bbe}}$. Therefore, $\Pr[\mathbf{F}_{\mathsf{bbe}}] \leq \mathsf{Adv}^{\mathsf{bbe}}_{\mathsf{Pgen},\mathsf{PC},\mathsf{Ext},n,\mathcal{A}_r,\mathsf{P}^*}(\lambda)$. $\qquad\qquad\square$

From the above it follows that $\Pr[\mathbf{F}_{\mathsf{bbe}}] \leq \sum_{r=1}^{\mathsf{Rnds}} \mathsf{Adv}^{\mathsf{bbe}}_{\mathsf{Pgen},\mathsf{PC},\mathsf{Ext},n,\mathcal{A}_r,\mathsf{P}^*}(\lambda) \leq$ $\mathsf{Rnds} \cdot \mathsf{Adv}^{\mathsf{bbe}}_{\mathsf{Pgen},\mathsf{PC},\mathsf{Ext},n,\bar{\mathcal{A}},\mathsf{P}^*}(\lambda)$ for some $\bar{\mathcal{A}} \in \{\mathcal{A}_1,\ldots,\mathcal{A}_{\mathsf{Rnds}}\}$.

The second type of abortion can only happen with negligible probability due to the evaluation binding property (Sect. 2.1) of PC, which requires that it is computationally hard to open a commitment for two different evaluations at the same point. We prove it in the following lemma.

Lemma 4. *There exists a expected PPT* $\mathcal{B}$ *such that* $\Pr[\mathbf{F}_{\mathsf{eb}}] \leq \mathsf{Adv}^{\mathsf{evbind}}_{\mathsf{Pgen},\mathsf{PC},n,\mathcal{B}}(\lambda)$.

Proof. Recall that if $\Pi.\mathsf{Emu}$ aborts on the line 24, then $\mathsf{colsn} = \mathsf{true}$, but $\mathsf{ext\text{-}fail}_r = \mathsf{false}$ for all $r \in [1,\mathsf{Rnds}]$. It means that in each subprotocol the extraction of the polynomial was successful (for all r, $(C_r, f_r) \in \mathcal{R}_{\mathsf{ck}}$), but for some rth subprotocol $\eta_{r,\alpha} \neq \tilde{\eta}_{r,\alpha} = g_{r,i}(\alpha_{r,i})$ for some $i \in [1,\ell_r]$ and a polynomial $g_{r,i}$, which is either one of the extracted polynomials or a publicly known indexer polynomial.

Given $\Pi.\mathsf{Emu}$ as defined in Fig. 5, we construct an adversary $\mathcal{B}$ that breaks evaluation binding whenever the event $\mathbf{F}_{\mathsf{eb}}$ happens. $\mathcal{B}$ gets (p,ck) as input and starts by internally running the WEE adversary $\mathcal{A}(\mathsf{p},\mathsf{ck})$ to obtain $(\mathbf{x},\mathsf{st})$. After this $\mathcal{B}$ runs $\Pi.\mathsf{Emu}$ until at some round r, P^* outputs $(\boldsymbol{\pi}_r, \boldsymbol{\eta}_r)$ such that $\boldsymbol{\eta}_r \neq \tilde{\boldsymbol{\eta}}_r$. In this case, there exists $\alpha_{r,i} \in \boldsymbol{\alpha}_r$ such that $\eta_{r,i} \neq \tilde{\eta}_{r,i} = g_{r,i}(\alpha_{r,i})$ for some $(C, g_{r,i}) \in \mathcal{R}_{\mathsf{ck}}$. Here, C could be a commitment produced by an indexer (in that case $g_{r,i}(X)$ is publicly known) or one of the commitments sent by the prover (in that case $(C, g_{r,i}) \in \mathcal{R}_{\mathsf{ck}}$ since the extraction succeeded). $\mathcal{B}$ computes an opening proof $\tilde{\pi}_{r,i}$ using $\mathsf{PC.Open}(\mathsf{ck}, C, \alpha_{r,i}, g_{r,i})$ and outputs $(C, \alpha_{r,i}, \eta_{r,i}, \pi_{r,i}, \tilde{\eta}_{r,i}, \tilde{\pi}_{r,i})$.

The event $\mathbf{F}_{\mathsf{eb}}$ implies the following:

- The argument's verifier V accepts, thus $\mathsf{PC.V}(\mathsf{ck}, C, \alpha_{r,i}, \eta_{r,i}, \pi_{r,i}) = 1$.
- The extraction of polynomials was successful and thus $(C, g_{r,i}) \in \mathcal{R}_{\mathsf{ck}}$. By the completeness property of the commitment scheme, $\mathsf{PC.V}(\mathsf{ck}, C, \alpha_{r,i}, \tilde{\eta}_{r,i}, \tilde{\pi}_{r,i}) = 1$.
- Since $\mathsf{colsn} = \mathsf{true}$, $\eta_{r,i} \neq \tilde{\eta}_{r,i}$.

It follows that $\mathcal{B}$ breaks evaluation binding when the event $\mathbf{F}_{\mathsf{eb}}$ happens. We get $\Pr[\mathbf{F}_{\mathsf{eb}}] \leq \mathsf{Adv}^{\mathsf{evbind}}_{\mathsf{Pgen},\mathsf{PC},n,\mathcal{B}}(\lambda)$. $\qquad\qquad\square$

Recall, $\mathbf{F}_{\mathsf{iop}}$ is the event that $\mathsf{tr}_{\mathsf{IOP}}$ is accepting, but the PIOP extractor in Step 25 returns w such that $(\mathsf{i},\mathsf{x},\mathsf{w}) \notin \mathcal{R}$. We bound the probability of this event in the following lemma.

Lemma 5. *There exists an interactive algorithm* $\mathcal{C}$ *(potentially unbounded) such that* $\Pr[\mathbf{F}_{\mathsf{iop}}] \leq \mathsf{Adv}^{\mathsf{ks}}_{\Pi_{\mathsf{IOP}},\mathsf{Ext},\mathcal{C}}(\lambda)$.

Proof. The knowledge soundness of PIOP holds for any fixed $i \in \mathbb{I}(\mathcal{R})$ and $x \in \{0,1\}^{\mathsf{poly}(\lambda)}$. If it holds for any fixed input, then it will also hold when x and i are sampled. We sample $p \leftarrow \mathsf{Pgen}(1^\lambda)$, $(ck, tk) \leftarrow \mathsf{KGen}(p, n)$, and $(i, x, st) \leftarrow \mathcal{A}_1(ck)$.

We will construct an adversary $\mathcal{C}$ against the knowledge soundness of PIOP that takes (i, x) as an input. The adversary $\mathcal{C}$ runs identically to the **for**loop in $\Pi.\mathsf{Emu}$ except for two notable difference. First, instead of sampling coins$_r$ by itself, it sends f_r to IOP.V and receives back (α_r, z_r, g_r). It then computes coins$_r$ corresponding to (α_r, z_r, g_r). We assume that this is efficient since we deal with public coin protocols. Second, it aborts the protocol if either the verification of the commitment opening fails, extraction of a polynomial fails (ext-fail$_r = $ **true**), or there is a collision (colsn $= $ **true**). Complete details of $\mathcal{C}$ can be found in Fig. 6.

$\langle \mathcal{C}(i, x), \mathsf{V}^{\mathsf{I}(i)}(x) \rangle \quad /\!/ \ p \leftarrow \mathsf{Pgen}(1^\lambda); \ (ck, tk) \leftarrow \mathsf{KGen}(p, n); \ (i, x, st) \leftarrow \mathcal{A}_1(ck)$

1 : **for** $r = 1$ **to** Rnds **do** $\quad /\!/ \ P^*$'s initial state is $\mathsf{st}_0^{(1)} = (p, ck, x, st)$

2 :   Run $P^*(\mathsf{st}_{r-1}^{(1)})$ and receive C_r;

3 :   Sample extraction point $\chi_r \leftarrow_{\$} \mathcal{F}$;

4 : $(\eta_{\chi_r}, \pi_{\chi_r}) \leftarrow P^*(\mathsf{st}_{r-1}^{(1)}, \chi_r)$; $\quad /\!/ \ P^*$'s new state is denoted $\mathsf{st}_{r-1}^{(2)}$

5 : $\mathsf{tr_{PC}} \leftarrow (C_r, \chi_r, \eta_{\chi_r}, \pi_{\chi_r})$;

6 :   **if** $\mathsf{PC.V}(ck, \mathsf{tr_{PC}}) = 1$ **then**

7 : $f_r(X) \leftarrow \mathsf{PC.Ext}_{\mathsf{bb}}^{P^*(\mathsf{st}_{r-1}^{(1)}, \cdot)}(ck, \mathsf{tr_{PC}})$;

8 :   **if** $(C_r, f_r) \in \mathcal{R}_{ck}$ **then**

9 :   Send $f_r(X)$ to IOP.V; Receive (α_r, z_r, g_r) from IOP.V;

10 :   Compute coins$_r$ such that $(\alpha_r, z_r, g_r) = \mathsf{IOP.V}(\mathsf{st}_{r-1}^{\mathsf{V}}, \mathsf{coins}_r)$;

11 : $(\eta_r, \pi_r) \leftarrow P^*(\mathsf{st}_{r-1}^{(2)}, \mathsf{coins}_r)$; $\quad /\!/ \ P^*$'s new state is denoted $\mathsf{st}_r^{(1)}$

12 :   Compute $\tilde{\eta}_r \leftarrow (g_{r,1}(\alpha_{r,1}), \ldots, g_{r,\ell_r}(\alpha_{r,\ell_r}))$;

13 :   **if** $\eta_r \neq \tilde{\eta}_r$ **then** abort; **fi**

14 :   **else** abort; **fi**

15 :   **else** abort; **fi**

16 : $\mathsf{st}_r^{\mathsf{V}} \leftarrow (\mathsf{st}_{r-1}^{\mathsf{V}}, \mathsf{coins}_r, \eta_r, \pi_r)$;

17 : **endfor**

Fig. 6. The adversary $\mathcal{C}$ against knowledge soundness of PIOP. We have *highlighted* the main differences compared to $\Pi.\mathsf{Emu}$.

In case the extraction of f_r is successful in each round and there are no collisions, the resulting PIOP transcript $\mathsf{tr_{IOP}}$ is accepting. The probability of the PIOP extractor failing in this case corresponds precisely to the event $\mathbf{F_{iop}}$. Thus, $\Pr[\mathbf{F_{iop}}] \leq \mathsf{Adv}_{\Pi_{\mathsf{IOP}}, \mathsf{Ext}, \mathcal{C}}^{\mathsf{ks}}(\lambda)$. $\qquad \square$

By combining the results of all the lemmas above, we get that $\Pr[\mathbf{V} \wedge \neg \mathbf{W}] \leq$ Rnds $\cdot \mathsf{Adv}_{\mathsf{Pgen}, \mathsf{PC}, \mathsf{Ext}, n, \bar{\mathcal{A}}, P^*}^{\mathsf{bbe}}(\lambda) + \mathsf{Adv}_{\mathsf{Pgen}, \mathsf{PC}, n, \mathcal{B}}^{\mathsf{evbind}}(\lambda) + \mathsf{Adv}_{\Pi_{\mathsf{IOP}}, \mathsf{Ext}, \mathcal{C}}^{\mathsf{ks}}(\lambda)$. Finally, we must consider that $\bar{\mathcal{A}}$ and $\mathcal{B}$ are expected PPT algorithms, but BBE and evaluation binding holds against strict PPT adversaries.

Both BBE and evaluation binding can be viewed as falsifiable assumptions. They can be written as an interaction between an efficient challenger and an adversary (see the full version [33] for a formal definition). According to assumptions of our theorem, for any (strict) PPT $\mathcal{A}'$ and $\mathcal{B}'$, $\mathsf{Adv}^{\mathsf{bbe}}_{\mathsf{Pgen},\mathsf{PC},\mathsf{Ext},n,\mathcal{A}',\mathsf{P}*}(\lambda)$ and $\mathsf{Adv}^{\mathsf{evbind}}_{\mathsf{Pgen},\mathsf{PC},n,\mathcal{B}'}(\lambda)$ are negligible functions in λ. Thus, applying Lemma 6 [33], $\mathsf{Adv}^{\mathsf{bbe}}_{\mathsf{Pgen},\mathsf{PC},\mathsf{Ext},n,\bar{\mathcal{A}},\mathsf{P}*}(\lambda)$ and $\mathsf{Adv}^{\mathsf{evbind}}_{\mathsf{Pgen},\mathsf{PC},n,\mathcal{B}}(\lambda)$ are also negligible. The claim of the theorem follows since $\mathsf{Adv}^{\mathsf{ks}}_{\Pi_{\mathsf{IOP}},\mathsf{Ext},\mathcal{C}}(\lambda)$ is negligible according to the knowledge soundness of PIOP. □

As previously argued, KZG PCS has black-box extractability and evaluation binding under the ARSDH assumption. Thus, we get the following result.

Corollary 2. *If the* ARSDH *assumption holds and if a* Rnds-*round Polynomial IOP for* $\mathcal{R}$ *has negligible knowledge error, then the argument* Π *described in Fig. 4, instantiated with KZG PCS, is a public-coin interactive argument for* $\mathcal{R}$ *that has witness-extended emulation.*

Finally, if we use, for example, Plonk's PIOP, then we obtain a public coin interactive argument with a constant proof size under a falsifiable assumption. The resulting argument retains Plonk's original asymptotic efficiency features. Below, $O_\lambda(\cdot)$ is the common "Big-O" notation, but we ignore $\mathsf{poly}(\lambda)$ factors.

Corollary 3. *Let* N *be the number of gates in an arithmetic circuit that describes a relation* $\mathcal{R}$, *and let* $|x|$ *denote the statement size. If the* ARSDH *assumption holds, then there exists a public coin argument system for* $\mathcal{R}$ *with* $O_\lambda(1)$ *proof size,* $O_\lambda(N)$ *SRS size,* $O_\lambda(|x| + \log N)$ *verifier's running time,* $O_\lambda(N \log N)$ *prover's running time, and a universal and updatable SRS.*

By applying the Fiat-Shamir transform, one can obtain a constant size SNARK, which is secure in the random oracle model assuming ARSDH. We recall the good, and often necessary practice, to instantiate the so-called strong Fiat-Shamir transform: hashing the common input with the current portion of the transcript to obtain the following challenge. As noted in [5,16,25] the usage of weak Fiat-Shamir transform, where only the transcript is hashed, can be exploited to break adaptive soundness of the resulting SNARK.

References

1. Attema, T., Cramer, R., Kohl, L.: A compressed Σ-protocol theory for lattices. In: Malkin, T., Peikert, C. (eds.) CRYPTO 2021, Part II. LNCS, vol. 12826, pp. 549–579. Springer, Cham (2021). https://doi.org/10.1007/978-3-030-84245-1_19
2. Ben-Sasson, E., Bentov, I., Horesh, Y., Riabzev, M.: Fast Reed-Solomon interactive oracle proofs of proximity. In: Chatzigiannakis, I., Kaklamanis, C., Marx, D., Sannella, D. (eds.) ICALP 2018. LIPIcs, vol. 107, pp. 14:1–14:17. Schloss Dagstuhl, July 2018. https://doi.org/10.4230/LIPIcs.ICALP.2018.14

3. Ben-Sasson, E., et al.: Zerocash: decentralized anonymous payments from bitcoin. In: 2014 IEEE Symposium on Security and Privacy, pp. 459–474. IEEE Computer Society Press, May 2014. https://doi.org/10.1109/SP.2014.36

4. Ben-Sasson, E., Chiesa, A., Genkin, D., Tromer, E.: On the concrete efficiency of probabilistically-checkable proofs. In: Boneh, D., Roughgarden, T., Feigenbaum, J. (eds.) STOC 2013, Palo Alto, CA, USA, 1–4 June 2013, pp. 585–594. ACM Press. https://doi.org/10.1145/2488608.2488681

5. Bernhard, D., Pereira, O., Warinschi, B.: How not to prove yourself: pitfalls of the Fiat-Shamir heuristic and applications to Helios. In: Wang, X., Sako, K. (eds.) ASIACRYPT 2012. LNCS, vol. 7658, pp. 626–643. Springer, Heidelberg (2012). https://doi.org/10.1007/978-3-642-34961-4_38

6. Bitansky, N., Canetti, R., Paneth, O., Rosen, A.: On the existence of extractable one-way functions. In: Shmoys, D.B. (ed.) 46th ACM STOC, pp. 505–514. ACM Press, May/June 2014. https://doi.org/10.1145/2591796.2591859

7. Boneh, D., Boyen, X.: Short signatures without random oracles and the SDH assumption in bilinear groups. J. Cryptol. **21**(2), 149–177 (2008). https://doi.org/10.1007/s00145-007-9005-7

8. Boneh, D., Drake, J., Fisch, B., Gabizon, A.: Efficient polynomial commitment schemes for multiple points and polynomials. Cryptology ePrint Archive, Report 2020/081 (2020). https://eprint.iacr.org/2020/081

9. Bünz, B., Bootle, J., Boneh, D., Poelstra, A., Wuille, P., Maxwell, G.: Bulletproofs: short proofs for confidential transactions and more. In: 2018 IEEE Symposium on Security and Privacy, pp. 315–334. IEEE Computer Society Press, May 2018. https://doi.org/10.1109/SP.2018.00020

10. Bünz, B., Fisch, B., Szepieniec, A.: Transparent SNARKs from DARK compilers. In: Canteaut, A., Ishai, Y. (eds.) EUROCRYPT 2020. LNCS, vol. 12105, pp. 677–706. Springer, Cham (2020). https://doi.org/10.1007/978-3-030-45721-1_24

11. Bünz, B., Maller, M., Mishra, P., Tyagi, N., Vesely, P.: Proofs for inner pairing products and applications. In: Tibouchi, M., Wang, H. (eds.) ASIACRYPT 2021. LNCS, vol. 13092, pp. 65–97. Springer, Cham (2021). https://doi.org/10.1007/978-3-030-92078-4_3

12. Campanelli, M., Faonio, A., Fiore, D., Querol, A., Rodríguez, H.: Lunar: a toolbox for more efficient universal and updatable zkSNARKs and commit-and-prove extensions. In: Tibouchi, M., Wang, H. (eds.) ASIACRYPT 2021. LNCS, vol. 13092, pp. 3–33. Springer, Cham (2021). https://doi.org/10.1007/978-3-030-92078-4_1

13. Campanelli, M., Ganesh, C., Khoshakhlagh, H., Siim, J.: Impossibilities in succinct arguments: black-box extraction and more. In: El Mrabet, N., De Feo, L., Duquesne, S. (eds.) AFRICACRYPT 2023. LNCS, vol. 14064, pp. 465–489. Springer, Cham (2023). https://doi.org/10.1007/978-3-031-37679-5_20

14. Chiesa, A., Hu, Y., Maller, M., Mishra, P., Vesely, N., Ward, N.: Marlin: preprocessing zkSNARKs with universal and updatable SRS. In: Canteaut, A., Ishai, Y. (eds.) EUROCRYPT 2020. LNCS, vol. 12105, pp. 738–768. Springer, Cham (2020). https://doi.org/10.1007/978-3-030-45721-1_26

15. Cramer, R., Damgård, I., Schoenmakers, B.: Proofs of partial knowledge and simplified design of witness hiding protocols. In: Desmedt, Y.G. (ed.) CRYPTO 1994. LNCS, vol. 839, pp. 174–187. Springer, Heidelberg (1994). https://doi.org/10.1007/3-540-48658-5_19

16. Dao, Q., Miller, J., Wright, O., Grubbs, P.: Weak Fiat-Shamir attacks on modern proof systems. In: 44th IEEE Symposium on Security and Privacy, SP 2023, San Francisco, CA, USA, 21–25 May 2023, pp. 199–216. IEEE (2023). https://doi.org/10.1109/SP46215.2023.10179408

17. Fiat, A., Shamir, A.: How to prove yourself: practical solutions to identification and signature problems. In: Odlyzko, A.M. (ed.) CRYPTO 1986. LNCS, vol. 263, pp. 186–194. Springer, Heidelberg (1987). https://doi.org/10.1007/3-540-47721-7_12

18. Fuchsbauer, G., Kiltz, E., Loss, J.: The algebraic group model and its applications. In: Shacham, H., Boldyreva, A. (eds.) CRYPTO 2018. LNCS, vol. 10992, pp. 33–62. Springer, Cham (2018). https://doi.org/10.1007/978-3-319-96881-0_2

19. Gabizon, A., Williamson, Z.J., Ciobotaru, O.: PLONK: permutations over Lagrange-bases for Oecumenical noninteractive arguments of knowledge. Cryptology ePrint Archive, Report 2019/953 (2019). https://eprint.iacr.org/2019/953

20. Gennaro, R., Gentry, C., Parno, B., Raykova, M.: Quadratic span programs and succinct NIZKs without PCPs. In: Johansson, T., Nguyen, P.Q. (eds.) EUROCRYPT 2013. LNCS, vol. 7881, pp. 626–645. Springer, Heidelberg (2013). https://doi.org/10.1007/978-3-642-38348-9_37

21. Gentry, C., Wichs, D.: Separating succinct non-interactive arguments from all falsifiable assumptions. In: Fortnow, L., Vadhan, S.P. (eds.) 43rd ACM STOC, pp. 99–108. ACM Press, June 2011. https://doi.org/10.1145/1993636.1993651

22. González, A., Ràfols, C.: Shorter pairing-based arguments under standard assumptions. In: Galbraith, S.D., Moriai, S. (eds.) ASIACRYPT 2019. LNCS, vol. 11923, pp. 728–757. Springer, Cham (2019). https://doi.org/10.1007/978-3-030-34618-8_25

23. Groth, J.: On the size of pairing-based non-interactive arguments. In: Fischlin, M., Coron, J.-S. (eds.) EUROCRYPT 2016. LNCS, vol. 9666, pp. 305–326. Springer, Heidelberg (2016). https://doi.org/10.1007/978-3-662-49896-5_11

24. Groth, J., Kohlweiss, M., Maller, M., Meiklejohn, S., Miers, I.: Updatable and universal common reference strings with applications to zk-SNARKs. In: Shacham, H., Boldyreva, A. (eds.) CRYPTO 2018. LNCS, vol. 10993, pp. 698–728. Springer, Cham (2018). https://doi.org/10.1007/978-3-319-96878-0_24

25. Haines, T., Lewis, S.J., Pereira, O., Teague, V.: How not to prove your election outcome. In: 2020 IEEE Symposium on Security and Privacy, pp. 644–660. IEEE Computer Society Press, May 2020. https://doi.org/10.1109/SP40000.2020.00048

26. Kate, A., Zaverucha, G.M., Goldberg, I.: Constant-size commitments to polynomials and their applications. In: Abe, M. (ed.) ASIACRYPT 2010. LNCS, vol. 6477, pp. 177–194. Springer, Heidelberg (2010). https://doi.org/10.1007/978-3-642-17373-8_11

27. Kosba, A.E., Miller, A., Shi, E., Wen, Z., Papamanthou, C.: Hawk: the blockchain model of cryptography and privacy-preserving smart contracts. In: 2016 IEEE Symposium on Security and Privacy, pp. 839–858. IEEE Computer Society Press, May 2016. https://doi.org/10.1109/SP.2016.55

28. Lai, R.W.F., Malavolta, G.: Subvector commitments with application to succinct arguments. In: Boldyreva, A., Micciancio, D. (eds.) CRYPTO 2019. LNCS, vol. 11692, pp. 530–560. Springer, Cham (2019). https://doi.org/10.1007/978-3-030-26948-7_19

29. Lee, J.: Dory: efficient, transparent arguments for generalised inner products and polynomial commitments. In: Nissim, K., Waters, B. (eds.) TCC 2021. LNCS, vol. 13043, pp. 1–34. Springer, Cham (2021). https://doi.org/10.1007/978-3-030-90453-1_1

30. Lindell, Y.: Parallel coin-tossing and constant-round secure two-party computation. In: Kilian, J. (ed.) CRYPTO 2001. LNCS, vol. 2139, pp. 171–189. Springer, Heidelberg (2001). https://doi.org/10.1007/3-540-44647-8_10

31. Lipmaa, H.: Progression-free sets and sublinear pairing-based non-interactive zero-knowledge arguments. In: Cramer, R. (ed.) TCC 2012. LNCS, vol. 7194, pp. 169–189. Springer, Heidelberg (2012). https://doi.org/10.1007/978-3-642-28914-9_10

32. Lipmaa, H., Parisella, R., Siim, J.: Algebraic group model with oblivious sampling. In: Rothblum, G., Wee, H. (eds.) TCC 2023. LNCS, vol. 14372, pp. 363–392. Springer, Cham (2023). https://doi.org/10.1007/978-3-031-48624-1_14

33. Lipmaa, H., Parisella, R., Siim, J.: Constant-size zk-SNARKs in ROM from falsifiable assumptions. Technical report, 2024/173, IACR, 5 February 2024. https://eprint.iacr.org/2024/173

34. Lipmaa, H., Siim, J., Zajac, M.: Counting vampires: from univariate sumcheck to updatable ZK-SNARK. In: Agrawal, S., Lin, D. (eds.) ASIACRYPT 2022. LNCS, vol. 13792, pp. 249–278. Springer, Cham (2022). https://doi.org/10.1007/978-3-031-22966-4_9

35. Naor, M.: On cryptographic assumptions and challenges. In: Boneh, D. (ed.) CRYPTO 2003. LNCS, vol. 2729, pp. 96–109. Springer, Heidelberg (2003). https://doi.org/10.1007/978-3-540-45146-4_6

36. Papamanthou, C., Shi, E., Tamassia, R.: Signatures of correct computation. In: Sahai, A. (ed.) TCC 2013. LNCS, vol. 7785, pp. 222–242. Springer, Heidelberg (2013). https://doi.org/10.1007/978-3-642-36594-2_13

37. Parno, B., Howell, J., Gentry, C., Raykova, M.: Pinocchio: nearly practical verifiable computation. In: 2013 IEEE Symposium on Security and Privacy, pp. 238–252. IEEE Computer Society Press, May 2013. https://doi.org/10.1109/SP.2013.47

38. Ràfols, C., Zapico, A.: An algebraic framework for universal and updatable SNARKs. In: Malkin, T., Peikert, C. (eds.) CRYPTO 2021. LNCS, vol. 12825, pp. 774–804. Springer, Cham (2021). https://doi.org/10.1007/978-3-030-84242-0_27

39. Shoup, V.: Lower bounds for discrete logarithms and related problems. In: Fumy, W. (ed.) EUROCRYPT 1997. LNCS, vol. 1233, pp. 256–266. Springer, Heidelberg (1997). https://doi.org/10.1007/3-540-69053-0_18

40. StarkWare: ethSTARK documentation. Cryptology ePrint Archive, Report 2021/582 (2021). https://eprint.iacr.org/2021/582

41. Szepieniec, A., Zhang, Y.: Polynomial IOPs for linear algebra relations. Technical report, 2020/1022, IACR, 24 August 2020. https://ia.cr/2020/1022. Last checked modification from June 9, 2021

42. Tomescu, A., Abraham, I., Buterin, V., Drake, J., Feist, D., Khovratovich, D.: Aggregatable subvector commitments for stateless cryptocurrencies. In: Galdi, C., Kolesnikov, V. (eds.) SCN 2020. LNCS, vol. 12238, pp. 45–64. Springer, Cham (2020). https://doi.org/10.1007/978-3-030-57990-6_3

43. Zhandry, M.: To label, or not to label (in generic groups). In: Dodis, Y., Shrimpton, T. (eds.) CRYPTO 2022. LNCS, vol. 13509, pp. 66–96. Springer, Cham (2022). https://doi.org/10.1007/978-3-031-15982-4_3

44. Zhang, C., Zhandry, M.: The relationship between idealized models under computationally bounded adversaries abstract. In: Guo, J., Steinfeld, R. (eds.) ASIACRYPT 2023. LNCS, vol. 14443, pp. 390–419. Springer, Cham (2023). https://doi.org/10.1007/978-981-99-8736-8_13
45. Zhang, C., Zhou, H.S., Katz, J.: An analysis of the algebraic group model. In: Agrawal, S., Lin, D. (eds.) ASIACRYPT 2022. LNCS, vol. 13794, pp. 310–322. Springer, Cham (2022). https://doi.org/10.1007/978-3-031-22972-5_11

Lower-Bounds on Public-Key Operations in PIR

Jesko Dujmovic[1,2]([✉]) and Mohammad Hajiabadi[3]

[1] Helmholtz Center for Information Security (CISPA), Saarbrücken, Germany
`jesko.dujmovic@cispa.de`
[2] Saarbrücken Graduate School of Computer Science, Saarbrücken, Germany
[3] University of Waterloo, Waterloo, Canada
`mdhajiabadi@uwaterloo.ca`

Abstract. Private information retrieval (PIR) is a fundamental cryptographic primitive that allows a user to fetch a database entry without revealing to the server which database entry it learns. PIR becomes nontrivial if the server communication is less than the database size. We show that building (even) very weak forms of PIR protocols requires that the amount of public-key operations scale linearly in the database size.

We then use this bound to examine the related problem of communication efficient oblivious transfer (OT) extension.

Oblivious transfer is a crucial building block in secure multi-party computation (MPC). In most MPC protocols, OT invocations are the main bottleneck in terms of computation and communication. OT extension techniques allow one to minimize the number of public-key operations in MPC protocols. One drawback of all existing OT extension protocols is their communication overhead. In particular, the sender's communication is roughly double what is information-theoretically optimal.

We show that OT extension with close to optimal sender communication is impossible, illustrating that the communication overhead is inherent. Our techniques go much further; we can show many lower bounds on communication-efficient MPC. E.g. we prove that to build high-rate string OT with generic groups, the sender needs to do linearly many group operations.

Keywords: Private Information Retrieval · PIR · Lower Bounds · OT Extension · Generic group model · GGM · Communication Complexity

1 Introduction

Secure Multi-Party Computation (MPC), allows two parties to jointly evaluate a function f while leaking nothing about their input to the other party beyond the output of f. A central goal of modern cryptography is to construct efficient MPC protocols. This goal is important not only from a theoretical but also from a practical viewpoint. The computational efficiency of all MPC protocols

© International Association for Cryptologic Research 2024
M. Joye and G. Leander (Eds.): EUROCRYPT 2024, LNCS 14656, pp. 65–87, 2024.
https://doi.org/10.1007/978-3-031-58751-1_3

is typically bottlenecked by public-key operations (e.g., group operations, oblivious transfers (OT)). OT extension is a technique toward reducing public-key operations [3,29], allowing one to get the results of many OTs at the cost of performing only a few OTs and some symmetric-key operations. This technique has revolutionized the practical development of MPC, leading to protocols which employ a small number of public-key operations for sophisticated tasks.

A significant limitation of existing OT extension techniques are their high communication cost: for performing ℓ 1-out-of-2 bit OTs, the sender communicates at least 2ℓ bits. This severely limits the use of OT extension in MPC settings where a low amount of communication is required 'by design' (e.g., Private-Information Retrieval (PIR)). The overarching goal of our paper is to understand communication-computation tradeoffs in such MPC settings. We show that in many such situations, performing many public-key operations is provably unavoidable. To put our results in context, let us illustrate how communication efficient OT would impact private information retrieval.

Private-Information Retrieval (PIR). Private information retrieval [15,33] is a fundamental cryptographic primitive that allows a user to fetch a database entry without revealing to the server which database entry it learns. PIR becomes nontrivial if the server-to-user communication is strictly less than the database size (and ideally growing sub-linearly or even polylogarithmically in the database size). In some applications, one may need extra properties, such as an overall (as opposed to server-to-user) sub-linear communication or server privacy. Throughout the paper, we require neither of these unless otherwise stated. Since we prove lower bounds, this makes our results stronger. A truly efficient PIR protocol has significant real-world applications such as private certificate retrieval or private DNS lookups. By now, we know how to build PIR with communication complexity polylogarithmic in n from a wide range of assumptions [10,12,19,27,30]. While the amount of communication is attractively low, the computation overhead leaves much to be desired. [19] demonstrates that a communication efficient OT would imply PIR.

Computational Complexity of PIR. In (single-server) PIR protocols, the running time of the server cannot be sub-linear in n, the database size, without preprocessing [4]. If it was sub-linear the server could not read all the entries, leaking information about the user's index i. Faced with this lower-bound, and the fact that PIR requires public-key assumptions [18], one may wish to settle for the next best thing: making the number of public-key operations independent of n. Somehow curiously, in all existing PIR protocols based on Diffie-Hellman or OT related assumptions [12,19], not only the server's running time, but the number of public-key operations performed by the server grows at least linearly with n. There is no evidence, however, if this is inherent, and in fact, it has remained an open problem whether one can build a PIR protocol where the number of public-key operations is sub-linear in n.

Is it possible construct PIR with a sub-linear amount of public-key operations and an arbitrarily large number of symmetric-key operations?

OT Extension. A major tool used for minimizing computation is OT extension. Existing OT extension techniques induce at least a linear amount of communication for the sender, making them unsuitable for PIR applications. Specifically, under existing constructions, an extended OT sender needs to communicate at least as many bits as its total input length. Beaver's seminal construction [3] works by encoding all the sender messages into a garbled circuit, which the receiver can evaluate only on the labels that correspond to her choice bits; the IKNP protocol [29] establishes correlated randomness between the sender and the receiver, allowing the sender to XOR his messages with the corresponding masks such that the receiver can only de-mask the correct messages. In both these protocols, the sender's outgoing protocol messages information-theoretically determine the entire sender's input, causing the communication overhead. This state of affairs raises the following natural question.

Is it possible construct OT extension where the sender communication is close to optimal?

In the above question, by 'optimal sender communication' we mean the best information-theoretically achievable communication: which is ℓ bits for the sender for performing ℓ 1-out-2 single-bit OTs. Since OT extension is crucially used in many MPC protocols, understanding its communication complexity is of both practical and theoretical value.

Having optimal sender communication for OT extension is reminiscent of rate-1 string OT: building 1-out-of-2 string OTs for a pair of ℓ-bit strings, where (roughly speaking) the sender communication grows as $\ell + \lambda$ (as opposed to $2\ell + \lambda$), where λ is the security parameter. Two-round rate-1 OT has found a number of applications, notably in the construction of PIR protocols with poly-logarithmic communication [1,8,12,19,21,30]. We know how to build rate-1 OT from a wide variety of assumptions [1,12,19,21,30], but all these constructions make at least a linear number of public-key operations. In particular, computational efficiency (e.g., sub-linear number of public-key operations) and communication efficiency (e.g., sub-linear communication) seem to have largely been in conflict with each other — for reasons we have not been to justify so far. The goal of our paper is to elucidate this conflicting situation.

1.1   Our Results

We answer both of the above questions, and several other related ones, negatively. In particular, we give a lower-bound on the number of public-key operations that need to be performed by servers in PIR protocols, and use this lower-bound to derive similar results for related primitives. Our core idea is based on a compilation technique that allows one to remove public-key operation queries from a PIR protocol at the cost of proportionally increasing the communication complexity in the public-key operation free protocol. As applications of our main theorem, we obtain results that settle several open problems in MPC.

In the statement below, by an SO oracle we mean a *simulatable oracle*: roughly speaking, one that can be simulated via lazy sampling. Examples of such oracles include generic-group oracles, public-key encryption oracles, etc. See Sect. 2 for more details. Also, we use the term a "party's SO bit complexity" to indicate the total bit size of all SO queries made by the party.

Theorem 1 (Informal Main Theorem). *If there exists a PIR for n-bit databases with oracle access to simulatable oracle SO, arbitrary oracle O, server communication of $\eta < cn$ for $c < 1$, $r \in o(n)$ rounds of interaction with the user, and $q \in o(n)$ bits of communication with the SO oracle, then there exists a PIR with oracle access to O, server communication $\overline{\eta} \leq \overline{c}n$ for $\overline{c} < 1$, and no calls to SO.*

We derive the following corollary.

Corollary 1. *There exists no n-bit PIR protocol built solely[1] from a simulatable oracle SO and a random oracle O with o(n) round complexity, with o(n) server's SO bit complexity and with $\eta \leq cn$ server's communication for $c < 1$.*

For example, letting SO be a generic group oracle (GGM), we rule out all n-bit PIR protocols that have $o(n)$ rounds and where the server's communication and the server's total number of GGM queries are, respectively, cn and $o(n)$ for $c < 1$. This holds irrespective of the number of RO queries the protocol is allowed to make. This closely matches the known upper-bounds, as [19,35] give n-bit PIR protocols based on the DDH assumption with server communication of $O(\lambda)$ and with the sever making $O(n)$ group operations.

The strength of the main theorem lies in its flexibility in instantiating the oracle SO: for example, one may let SO be an FHE oracle, and obtain similar results as long as the amount of server's communication with the FHE oracle respects the bounds. The work of [35] shows how to obtain PIR generically from (additively) homomorphic encryption, where the sever performs $O(n)$ homomorphic additions. Our work shows that this is close to optimal.

We will show that our computational lower-bounds for PIRs give rise to communication lower-bounds for OT extension.

Corollary 2 (OT Extension: Communication Lower-Bounds). *There exists no ℓ-batch k-bit OT extension protocol with round complexity $r \in o(k\ell)$ and with server communication $\eta < c2k\ell$ for $c < 1$.*

In the above corollary, by ℓ-batch k-bit OT we mean performing ℓ OTs for pairs of k-bit strings. The IKNP protocol [29] in the ℓ single-bit OT case achieves sender communication of $> 2\ell$. Our result shows that the IKNP's sender communication complexity is close to optimal.

Finally, we relate PIR to other MPC protocols such as rate-1 OT to arrive at the following corollary. For brevity, we describe the statements when O is the GGM oracle, and only for rate-1 OT. In fact, we can show that achieving any rate strictly greater than $1/2$ (measured as the information-theoretically optimal sender communication size divided by the sender's communication size in the actual protocol) requires making an almost linear number of group operations.

---

[1] By "solely" we mean that the parties also have access to a PSPACE oracle. This stops the party from using any hardness assumptions other than the ones provided by the oracles.

Corollary 3 (String OT Corollary). *There exists no ℓ-bit string OT protocol in the GGM+RO model with sender communication of $\eta \leq c2\ell$ and $o(\ell)$ calls to the generic group for $c < 1$.*

Similar results can be proven about unbalanced PSI, see Sect. 5.2 for details.

2 Technical Overview

First, we will give a quick example of how to simulate a generic group efficiently to illustrate a simulatable oracle. Then, we sketch the proof of the main theorem. We proceed by showing why the main theorem is useful by demonstrating a few MPC protocols which imply non-trivial PIR, allowing us to apply our lower-bounds to them.

2.1 Generic Group Model

A generic group of order p is the group $\mathbb{Z}_p$ together with the random injective encoding function $\sigma \colon \mathbb{Z}_p \to S$, where $S = \{0, \ldots, p-1\}$. The algorithms can access this group via the oracle Add which decodes two encoded elements, computes a linear combination of them and gives back the encoded result. More formally, $\mathsf{Add} \colon \mathbb{Z}_p^2 \times S^2 \to S$, $(a_1, a_2, \ell_1, \ell_2) \mapsto \sigma(a_1 v_1 + a_2 v_2)$, where $v_i = \sigma^{-1}(\ell_i)$ for $i \in \{1, 2\}$.[2] This way the algorithms interacting with the oracle can only access encodings instead of the real group.

To simulate a GGM oracle efficiently, the simulator dynamically generates the encoding function σ. More specifically, it maintains a partial set L of $\mathbb{Z}_p$-label pairs sampled by the simulator so far. (It is initially empty.) Whenever a query $(a_1, a_2, \ell_1, \ell_2)$ is made, the simulator checks if $(*, \ell_1) \in L$ (meaning that if for some v_1, $(v_1, \ell_1) \in L$); if not, the simulator samples a random v_1 from $\mathbb{Z}_p$ subject to $(v_1, *) \notin L$, and adds (v_1, ℓ_1) to L. The simulator does the same thing for ℓ_2. Now assuming $(v_1, \ell_1) \in L$ and $(v_2, \ell_2) \in L$, letting $a_3 = a_1 v_1 + a_2 v_2$ if $(a_3, \ell_3) \in L$ for some ℓ_3, the simulator responds to the query with ℓ_3; else, the simulator samples a random ℓ_3 subject to $(*, \ell_3) \notin L$, adds (a_3, ℓ_3) to L, and responds to the query with ℓ_3.

Other simulatable oracles that are useful in our main theorem are black-box oblivious transfer [26], black-box public-key encryption [26], and ideal obfuscation [31].

2.2 Proof Sketch of Main Theorem

The observation that leads to the main theorem is that in PIR protocols the server does not need to be secure. This means the protocol would still be secure if the user learned all of the servers oracle queries. Also, the user knows all of

---

[2] One may set S to be a random subset of size p of a larger set $\{0, 1\}^u$ for $u > \log p$. Our analysis will remain unchanged, so we simply assume $S = \{0, \ldots, p-1\}$. See [41] for differences between various models.

its own oracle queries. Therefore, the user can just simulate the oracle for both of the parties. For this the server just has to send all of its queries to the user. This modification increases the server communication roughly by the amount that the server would have communicated to the oracle. We will prove that this transformation preserves user security. Since we require the oracle communication to be in $o(n)$ and the server communication to be $< cn$ for some $c < 1$, the modified protocol will have no oracle queries and the server communication will be $< \bar{c}n$ for $\bar{c} < 1$. Moreover, in the actual compiled protocol, to enable the compiled user to distinguish query messages from normal protocol messages, we append a flag bit to the end of each server's protocol messages — causing a dependency on r, the number of rounds, in Theorem 1.

2.3 PIR Related Protocols

Now we exhibit a few protocols which imply non-trivial PIR, allowing us to apply our impossibility results for PIR to these protocols.

Low Sender-Communication OT. We show that an ℓ-batch k-bit OT protocol with sender communication $< c2k\ell$ for $c < 1$ implies a PIR. The transformation works as follows: suppose w.l.o.g the database size is $2k\ell$. The server runs the OT protocol and encodes the first half of the database into the messages $(m_i^{(0)})_{i \in [\ell]}$ and the second half into $(m_i^{(1)})_{i \in [\ell]}$. Now, if a user wants to look up the j-th element of the database, it acquires $(m_i^{(0)})_{i \in [\ell]}$ if $j \leq k\ell$ and $(m_i^{(1)})_{i \in [\ell]}$ otherwise. The database entry that the client wants to learn is contained in the OT output. The server communication is $< c2k\ell$ and the user's input j is hidden from the server by the OT's receiver security.

Low Total Communication OT. We next attempt to prove lower-bounds for the case where the OT protocol has low total communication (as opposed to low sender communication). For convenience we focus on ℓ-batch single-bit OT. By low total communication we mean an amount that is close the information-theoretically optimal communication, which is 2ℓ bits. The techniques for low sender-communication as above do not apply outright because the sender might cause the bulk of communication itself, an amount close to 2ℓ bits. We get around this issue via the following intuitive idea: When an OT protocol has low total communication it must have either low sender communication, from which we already showed how to obtain a non-trivial PIR, or it must have low receiver communication. In the latter case, we swap the roles of the two different parties with a role-flipping trick implicitly in [29] and explicitly in [39]. This role flipping trick turns the low receiver communication into low sender communication, which we can then turn into a non-trivial PIR. Figure 1 depicts the construction for $\ell = 1$. In essence, we show how to turn a communication-efficient OT into a sender-communication-efficient OT by introducing an additioal round.

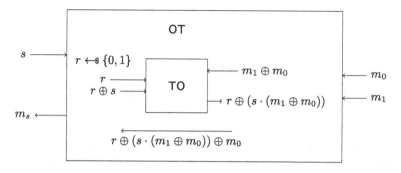

Fig. 1. Similar to [39] a visual representation of how to build an oblivious transfer OT from an oblivious transfer TO that goes in the opposite direction.

OT Extension. The above results immediately imply communication lower bounds for OT extension: showing that performing OT extension for ℓ-batch k-bit OTs with $c2k\ell$ bits of sender communication for $c < 1$, and with an $O(\lambda)$ (and even $o(k\ell)$) number of public-key operations is impossible.

Unbalanced PSI. Private set intersection (PSI) is an MPC protocol between two parties each holding a set and the party called the receiver learns the intersection of the two sets. No other information should be revealed to is to any of the parties. In Unbalanced PSI, a special case of PSI, the receiver set is much smaller than the sender set and the communication should only scale with the receiver set. To build a non-trivial PIR from such a protocol, for a client index i, the client sets $x := i$ (padding it out if necessary), and for a database DB, the server forms the set $\{i \mid \mathsf{DB}[i] = 1\}$. An answer to $x \in^? S$ reveals $\mathsf{DB}[i]$. This observation allows us to prove that in unbalanced PSI with sub-linear communication, the receiver should perform close to linear public-key operations. This shows that the large number of public-key operations used in unbalanced PSI protocols of [12,19,21] is inherent.

Non-Trivial PIR implies Oblivious Transfer. We know that non-trivial PIR implies oblivious transfer [18], and this is used to get our final impossibility results. The transformation utilizes the user security of the PIR protocol and deploys a compression argument to argue information loss. The entropy garnered from the information loss is then fed into a randomness extractor, the output of which can be used to guarantee sender security in the resulting oblivious transfer protocol.

2.4 Oracles

Notice that all these transformations only make black-box use of the protocols they transform. This means that if the starting protocol uses some oracle other than the one we want to remove, say the random oracle [6], then the resulting protocol will also use the random oracle even if we remove other oracle queries.

3   Related Work

Technique. Our 'compilation-out' techniques bear some similarities to ideas used by Gennaro and Trevisan [25] for giving lower-bounds on the query complexity of PRGs from OWPs. Essentially, they showed that if the number of queries is 'small', they can be encoded as part of the input, hence getting rid of OWP calls in the construction of a PRG. Gennaro et al. [24] built on that idea to give lower-bounds on the efficiency of various cryptographic primitives. These works mostly deal with non-interactive primitives. Our techniques are used in a different way in that we leverage the lack of security requirements for a party to get rid of oracle calls of an interactive protocol.

Private-Information Retrieval. In all but this section of the paper we talk about non-trivial single-server private information retrieval, which is why we will sometimes leave out the descriptor "single-server". Traditionally, PIR [15,33] is a protocol between one user and possibly multiple servers. Just like in the non-trivial single-server case the user with an index $i \in [n]$ learns the i-th element of a database $DB \in \{0,1\}^n$ held by all the servers without disclosing i to the servers. In other words, if the caveat of non-triviality is not made, then not only the server communication needs to be sub-linear in n, but also the total communication. Thus, a non-trivial PIR is a weaker primitive than PIR. Multi-server PIR protocols assume some kind of non-collusion between the servers, which allows them to achieve statistical security as opposed to computational security in the single-server case.

By now PIR is a well studied primitive; here we focus on the single server setting. We know how to build PIR with communication complexity polylogarithmic in n from a wide range of assumptions [10,12,19,30]. In the last few years, we have also made progress towards practically efficient PIR [16,17,28,32,37,42,43] and asymptotically efficient PIR [7,11,34] when the server and the client (or sometimes only the server) are allowed to preprocess the database. We even know some lower bounds for different preprocessing settings [5,16,17,36,40]. Preprocessing, however, only makes sense if one expects to use the PIR multiple times. We focus on a single query PIR and uniquely distinguish between public-key and symmetric key operations.

OT Extension. The intuition behind OT extension is that it only uses very few calls to an OT functionality to implement many more OTs. An equivalent description is that an OT extension protocol is an OT protocol that can make calls to an OT functionality. The protocol becomes valuable if the number of OT calls in the protocol is much less than the 'size' of the OT being implemented. OT calls are typically modelled as oracle calls to an OT functionality or the OT hybrid model.

Beaver [3] constructed the first OT extension protocol, which makes non-black-box use of pseudorandom generators and which has two rounds. Ishai et al. [29] give the first OT extension protocol only making black-box use of symmetric-key cryptography while increasing the rounds to three. Garg et al. [22]

show that three rounds are necessary in the OT hybrid model when only making black-box use of symmetric-key cryptography.

Rate-1 String OT. The notion of rate-1 OT has applications beyond the construction of PIR with polylog communication. In particular, a generalization of this notion, called trapdoor hash, has been used as a building block to build non-interactive zero knowledge for NP [9]. This has made the notion of rate-1 OT appealing from both a theoretical and practical points of view.

Unbalanced Private-Set Intersection (PSI). Private keyword search allows a receiver, with a single element x, to learn whether x is a member of a large set S held by a sender, or sometimes called PIR for keywords [14]. This is an instance of the so-called unbalanced PSI problem, defined earlier. A desirable feature of such unbalanced PSI protocols is sub-linear communication: the total amount of communication must be sub-linear the larger set size. We have protocols, from a wide variety of cryptographic assumptions, for unbalanced PSI whose communication complexity grows only polylogarithmically with the larger set size [12, 19, 21, 30].

Again, the Diffie-Hellman-based protocols come with a high sender computation cost: the number of group operations grows at least linearly in the bigger set size. As in PIR, one can prove that the strict running time of the sender in unbalanced PSI cannot be sub-linear in $|S_1|$, but that does not mean the number of public-key operations must also grow with n — especially, if the sender is allowed to make an arbitrarily-large number of symmetric-key operations. In fact, while the protocols in [12, 19, 21] induce little communication, the large number of public-key operations involved is a major bottleneck.

In the absence of the sub-linear communication requirement, one may use oblivious-transfer (OT) extension techniques [3, 29] to design unbalanced PSI protocols with a number of public-key operations independent of $|S_1|$. These protocols can be made concretely efficient as well (e.g., [13]). However, all these OT-extension-based protocols fail to achieve sub-linear communication.

4 Preliminaries

We denote the security parameter by λ. We say a function negl is negligible if for any polynomial poly we have $\mathsf{negl}(\lambda) \in o(\frac{1}{\mathsf{poly}(\lambda)})$. For two integers i and i', we define $[i, i'] := \{i, i+1, \dots, i'\}$. We let $[n] := \{1, \dots, n\}$.

For $i \in \{r, s\}$, denoting receiver (r) and sender (s), we let $\mathsf{view}_i^{\varPi}(1^\lambda, x, y)$ denote the view of Party i in an honest execution of the protocol $\varPi$ on 1^λ and on the parties' respective inputs, where the view contains the private input and the random coins of the respective party, the protocol's transcript, and the transcript of oracle queries and their responses. We may omit the security parameter 1^λ whenever it is clear from the context.

4.1   Oblivious Transfer

Definition 1 (Oblivious Transfer (OT)). *An ℓ-batch k-bit string OT protocol* OT *is a protocol between two interactive PPT programs* (OTR, OTS), *where* OTR *and* OTS *denote, respectively, the receiver and the sender.*

OTR$(1^\lambda, 1^\ell, 1^k, s)$: *An interactive algorithm that takes in a security parameter 1^λ, batching parameter 1^ℓ, message parameter 1^k, and choice vector $s \in \{0,1\}^\ell$, and outputs $m \in \{0,1\}^\ell$.*
OTS$(1^\lambda, 1^\ell, 1^k, m^{(0)}, m^{(1)})$: *An interactive algorithm that takes in a security parameter 1^λ, batching parameter 1^ℓ, message parameter 1^k and two message vectors $m^{(0)}, m^{(1)} \in \mathsf{M}^\ell$, for $\mathsf{M} = \{0,1\}^k$, and outputs $\perp$*

We require the following.

Correctness. OT *is $\alpha(\cdot)$-correct if for any λ, $s \in \{0,1\}^\ell$, $(m_i^{(0)}, m_i^{(1)})_{i \in [\ell]} \in (\mathsf{M} \times \mathsf{M})^\ell$, the probability over an honest interaction between* OTR$(1^\lambda, 1^k, 1^\ell, s)$ *and* OTS$(1^\lambda, 1^k, 1^\ell, m^{(0)}, m^{(1)})$ *that* OTR *outputs $(m_1^{(s_1)} \ldots m_\ell^{(s_\ell)})$ is $\geq \alpha(\lambda)$. The protocol is perfectly correct if $\alpha = 1$. By default we require prefect correctness.*

Semi-Honest Receiver Security. *For any strings $s_0, s_1 \in \{0,1\}^\ell$, $m^{(0)}, m^{(1)} \in \mathsf{M}^\ell$ we have that* $\mathsf{view}_s^{\mathsf{OT}}(s_0, (m^{(0)}, m^{(1)}))$ *and* $\mathsf{view}_s^{\mathsf{OT}}(s_1, (m^{(0)}, m^{(1)}))$ *are computationally indistinguishable.*

Semi-Honest Sender Security. *For any $s \in \{0,1\}^\ell$ and $m^{(0)}, m^{(1)}, z^{(0)}, z^{(1)} \in \mathsf{M}^\ell$ such that $\{(m_i^{s_i})\} = \{(z_i^{s_i})\}$, we have that the two views* $\mathsf{view}_r^{\mathsf{OT}}(s, (m^{(0)}, m^{(1)}))$ *and* $\mathsf{view}_r^{\mathsf{OT}}(s, (z^{(0)}, z^{(1)}))$ *are computationally indistinguishable.*

OT Terminologies. We may sometimes refer to an ℓ-batch single-bit OT as an ℓ-batch OT. Also, whenever we say a k-bit string OT we mean $\ell = 1$.

We define notions of *rate* as asymptotic ratios between the actual communication under a given protocol and the best achievable communication under a (possibly) insecure protocol; i.e., for ℓ-batch single-bit OT the sender must communicate at least ℓ bits to the receiver, if perfect correctness is required. Therefore, the optimal download communication is ℓ. Similarly, the optimal total communication is 2ℓ.

Expected Download Rate. An ℓ-batch single-bit OT protocol has expected download rate c if for all λ, s, $m^{(0)}$, $m^{(1)}$, and all but finitely many ℓ

$$\frac{\ell}{d(\lambda, \ell)} \geq c,$$

where $d(\lambda, \ell)$ is expected communication from OTS$(1^\lambda, 1^\ell, m^{(0)}, m^{(1)})$ to OTR$(1^\lambda, 1^\ell, s)$.

Expected (Overall) Rate. An ℓ-batch single-bit OT protocol has expected (overall) rate c if for all λ, s, $m^{(0)}$, $m^{(1)}$, and all but finitely many ℓ

$$\frac{2\ell}{t(\lambda, \ell)} \geq c,$$

where $t(\lambda, \ell)$ is the expected total communication.

We now define the notion of OT extension in the black-box OT model, which is stronger than the OT-hybrid model.

Definition 2 (Black-Box OT Extension). *A black-box OT extension* $\mathsf{OTExt}^{\mathsf{OT}} = (\mathsf{OTRExt}^{\mathsf{OT}}, \mathsf{OTSExt}^{\mathsf{OT}})$ *is an ℓ-batch k-bit OT protocol that for a fixed polynomial* poly, *independent of ℓ, makes at most* $\mathsf{poly}(\lambda)$ *calls to the base single-bit OT oracle* $\mathsf{OT} = (\mathsf{OTR}, \mathsf{OTS})$.

4.2 Private-Information Retrieval (PIR)

Definition 3 (Non-Trivial PIR). *A non-trivial (single-server) private information retrieval* ntPIR *is an interactive protocol between two interactive PPT programs* $(\mathsf{PIRU}, \mathsf{PIRS})$, *where* PIRU *and* PIRS *denote, respectively, the client (user) and the server.*

$\mathsf{PIRU}(1^\lambda, 1^n, i)$: *An interactive algorithm that takes in a security parameter 1^λ, the database size n, and a choice index $i \in [n]$, and at the end of the interaction outputs $y \in \{0, 1\}$.*

$\mathsf{PIRS}(1^\lambda, 1^n, \mathsf{DB})$: *An interactive algorithm that takes in a security parameter 1^λ, database size n and a database $\mathsf{DB} \in \{0, 1\}^n$, and outputs $\perp$.*

We require the following properties.

Correctness. The PIR protocol is $\alpha(\cdot)$-correct if for any λ, n, $i \in [n]$ and $\mathsf{DB} \in \{0, 1\}^n$, the probability over an honest interaction between $\mathsf{PIRU}(1^\lambda, 1^n, i)$ and $\mathsf{PIRS}(1^\lambda, 1^n, \mathsf{DB})$ that PIRU outputs DB_i is $\geq \alpha(\lambda)$. The protocol is perfectly correct if $\alpha = 1$. By default we require perfect correctness.

Semi-Honest Client Security. For any n, $i, i' \in [n]$, $\mathsf{DB} \in \{0, 1\}^n$, $\mathsf{view}_s^{\mathsf{ntPIR}}(i, \mathsf{DB})$ and $\mathsf{view}_s^{\mathsf{ntPIR}}(i', \mathsf{DB})$ are computationally indistinguishable.

Non-Trivial Expected Download Communication. There exists a polynomial poly such that for all sufficiently large λ, for all $n \geq \mathsf{poly}(\lambda)$, for all $i \in [n]$, and $\mathsf{DB} \in \{0, 1\}^n$, the expected communication from $\mathsf{PIRS}(1^\lambda, 1^n, i)$ to $\mathsf{PIRU}(1^\lambda, 1^n, \mathsf{DB})$ is $d(\lambda, n) < n$.

The following result shows that non-trivial PIR implies public-key cryptography in a black-box way. We use this theorem for our lower-bound results.

Theorem 2 ([18]). *There exists a black-box construction of OT from a non-trivial PIR protocol.*

5   Protocols that Imply Non-Trivial PIR

We substantiate the relevence of non-trivial PIR by showing that communication-efficient versions of some popular MPC protocols can be transformed into non-trivial PIR in a black-box manner. These transformations later let us transfer the lower-bounds regarding PIR to these protocols.

In the following, we focus on different variants of oblivious transfer and unbalanced private set intersection to demonstrate the concept. The same ideas apply to many other protocols such as vector oblivious linear evaluation and oblivious polynomial evaluation.

5.1   Oblivious Transfer

We show how to transform a protocol for k-bit string oblivious transfer $\mathsf{OT} = (\mathsf{OTR}, \mathsf{OTS})$ that makes calls to an oracle $\mathcal{O}$ into a PIR protocol $(\mathsf{PIRU}, \mathsf{PIRS})$ with database size $n = 2k$ that makes calls to the same oracle $\mathcal{O}$ in a black-box manner. The construction is folklore and works by splitting the database in half, using each half as one of the two strings, and choosing the OT choice bit based on the PIR client's index accordingly.

- $\mathsf{PIRU}^{\mathcal{O}}(1^\lambda, 1^n, i)$: For $n = 2k$, set the choice bit $b \leftarrow \lfloor (i-1)/k \rfloor$. Run the OT receiver $m_b \leftarrow \mathsf{OTR}^{\mathcal{O}}(1^\lambda, b)$ to get the chosen string m_b. Return $m_b[i - kb]$
- $\mathsf{PIRS}^{\mathcal{O}}(1^\lambda, 1^n, \mathsf{DB})$: Let strings $m_0 \leftarrow \mathsf{DB}[1, \ldots, k]$ and $m_1 \leftarrow \mathsf{DB}[k + 1, \ldots, 2k]$. Run the OT sender $\mathsf{OTS}^{\mathcal{O}}(1^\lambda, m_0, m_1)$.

Lemma 1 (Folklore). *The PIR protocol* $(\mathsf{PIRU}, \mathsf{PIRS})$ *has the same correctness error, the same sender/receiver query complexity, and the same sender/receiver communication as those of the OT protocol* OT.

That means if the expected sender communication in OT *is less than* $n = 2k$, *then* $(\mathsf{PIRU}, \mathsf{PIRS})$ *is a non-trivial PIR protocol.*

Proof of Correctness. Correctness follows from the correctness of the OT protocol and for $b = \lfloor (i-1)/k \rfloor$ we have $m_b[i - kb] = \mathsf{DB}[kb + 1, \ldots, kb + k][i - kb] = \mathsf{DB}[i]$. $\qquad\square$

Proof of Client Security. Suppose there exists $i, i' \in [N]$, $\mathsf{DB} \in \{0,1\}^N$ such that an adversary $\mathcal{A}$ can distinguish $\mathsf{view}_s^{\mathsf{PIR}}(i, \mathsf{DB})$ from $\mathsf{view}_s^{\mathsf{PIR}}(i', \mathsf{DB})$ with non-negligible probability. Then $\lfloor (i-1)/k \rfloor \neq \lfloor (i'-1)/k \rfloor$ else $\mathsf{view}_s^{\mathsf{PIR}}(i, \mathsf{DB})$ and $\mathsf{view}_s^{\mathsf{PIR}}(i', \mathsf{DB})$ follow the exact same distribution. The same adversary $\mathcal{A}$ distinguishes between $\mathsf{view}_s^{\mathsf{OT}}(\lfloor (i-1)/k \rfloor, (\mathsf{DB}[1, \ldots, k], \mathsf{DB}[k+1, \ldots, 2k]))$ and $\mathsf{view}_s^{\mathsf{OT}}(\lfloor (i'-1)/k \rfloor, (\mathsf{DB}[1, \ldots, k], \mathsf{DB}[k+1, \ldots, 2k]))$ with the same non-negligible probability since the views are exactly the same as $\mathsf{view}_s^{\mathsf{PIR}}(i, \mathsf{DB})$ and $\mathsf{view}_s^{\mathsf{PIR}}(i', \mathsf{DB})$ respectively. $\qquad\square$

Remark 1. One can transform any ℓ-batch k-bit OT protocol into a $k\ell$-bit string OT protocol by reusing the same choice bit across all the ℓ batches. This works without any issues because we only talk about semi-honest security.

OT With Low Total Communications. Using the symmetric nature of OT we transform an OT protocol with low communication (not just low sender communication) into a low sender communication OT protocol in a black-box manner. This allows us to apply our PIR lower-bounds to OT with low expected communication. Our transformation works by noting that every communication efficient OT protocol has either low sender or low receiver communication; if the receiver communication is low, our transformation will swap the roles of the sender and receiver, to obtain an OT protocol with low sender communication, as desired.

The following transformation was implicitly used in [29] and explicitly in [39]. The transformation works as follows: Let $\mathsf{OT} = (\mathsf{OTR}, \mathsf{OTS})$ be an ℓ-batch single-bit OT with expected total communication $t(\lambda, \ell)$, expected download communication $d(\lambda, \ell)$, expected upload communication $u(\lambda, \ell)$, and oracle accesses to $\mathcal{O}$. We define a $\mathsf{OT}' = (\mathsf{OTR}', \mathsf{OTS}')$ as follows

$\mathsf{OTR}'^{\mathcal{O}}(1^\lambda, 1^\ell, s)$:

1. If the expected download communication of OT is $d(\lambda, \ell) < u(\lambda, \ell) + \ell$:
   (a) Run $(m_1', \ldots, m_\ell') \leftarrow \mathsf{OTR}^{\mathcal{O}}(1^\lambda, 1^\ell, s)$, the ℓ-batch OT receiver on the choice string s.
   (b) Return $(m_1', \ldots, m_\ell')$
2. Else:
   (a) Sample $r \xleftarrow{\$} \{0,1\}^\ell$ uniformly at random.
   (b) Run $\mathsf{OTS}^{\mathcal{O}}(1^\lambda, 1^\ell, r, s\oplus r)$, the ℓ-batch OT sender on messages $m_0 = r$ and $m_1 = r \oplus s$.
   (c) Receive v in the round after OTS is done.
   (d) Return $v \oplus r$

$\mathsf{OTS}'^{\mathcal{O}}(1^\lambda, 1^\ell, m^{(0)}, m^{(1)})$:

1. If the expected download communication of OT is $d(\lambda, \ell) < u(\lambda, \ell) + \ell$:
   (a) Run $\mathsf{OTS}^{\mathcal{O}}(1^\lambda, 1^\ell, m^{(0)}, m^{(1)})$, the ℓ-batch OT sender on messages $m_0 = m^{(0)}$ and $m_1 = m^{(1)}$.
   (b) Return
2. Else:
   (a) Run $z \leftarrow \mathsf{OTR}^{\mathcal{O}}(1^\lambda, 1^\ell, m^{(1)} \oplus m^{(0)})$, the ℓ-batch OT receiver on the choice string $m^{(1)} \oplus m^{(0)}$ to receive the string z.
   (b) Send $z \oplus m^{(0)}$ in the round after OTR is done
   (c) Return

Lemma 2. *The constructed OT protocol* $\mathsf{OT}' = (\mathsf{OTR}', \mathsf{OTS}')$ *has the same correctness as the base OT* $\mathsf{OT} = (\mathsf{OTR}, \mathsf{OTS})$. *Moreover,* $\mathsf{OT}' = (\mathsf{OTR}', \mathsf{OTS}')$ *is secure if* $\mathsf{OT} = (\mathsf{OTR}, \mathsf{OTS})$ *is secure.*

Assuming $\mathsf{OT} = (\mathsf{OTR}, \mathsf{OTS})$ *has expected overall rate* $r > 2/3$, *the constructed OT has expected download rate* $w > 1/2$.

Correctness. If $d(\lambda, \ell) < u(\lambda, \ell) + \ell$ then both parties behave exactly like OT and therefore correctness is inherited.

If $d(\lambda, \ell) \geq u(\lambda, \ell) + \ell$ the sender OTS' learns

$$\left(r_1 \oplus s_1 \cdot (m_1^{(1)} \oplus m_1^{(0)}), \ldots, r_\ell \oplus s_\ell \cdot (m_\ell^{(1)} \oplus m_\ell^{(0)})\right)$$

it then sends back

$$\left(r_1 \oplus s_1 \cdot (m_1^{(1)} \oplus m_1^{(0)}) \oplus m_1^{(0)}, \ldots, r_\ell \oplus s_\ell \cdot (m_\ell^{(1)} \oplus m_\ell^{(0)}) \oplus m_\ell^{(0)}\right)$$

then the receiver OTR' computes

$$\left(s_1 \cdot (m_1^{(1)} \oplus m_1^{(0)}) \oplus m_1^{(0)}, \ldots, s_\ell \cdot (m_\ell^{(1)} \oplus m_\ell^{(0)}) \oplus m_\ell^{(0)}\right)$$
$$= \left(m_1^{(s_1)}, \ldots, m_\ell^{(s_\ell)}\right)$$

$\square$

Security. The security in the case that $d(\lambda, \ell) < u(\lambda, \ell) + \ell$ directly follows from the security of OT.

In the other case it follows from the security of OT and the work of [39] which proves that this exact construction is secure. For receiver security we have that the sender (according to sender security of OT) only learns z. Each bit z_i is either r_i or $s_i \oplus r_i$, in both cases it is uniformly random because r is uniformly random. Sender security of OT' follows because the execution of OT leaks nothing to the receiver (according to the receiver security of OT). That means all the receiver learns is $z \oplus m^{(0)}$. By correctness of OT' this is exactly $(m_1^{(s_1)} \oplus r_1, \ldots, m_\ell^{(s_\ell)} \oplus r_\ell)$ and therefore contains no information about $(m_1^{(1-s_1)}, \ldots, m_\ell^{(1-s_\ell)})$. $\square$

Expected Download Communication. Let r be the rate, $t(\lambda, n)$ be the expected total communication which is the sum of the expected receiver-to-sender communication $u(\lambda, \ell)$ and the expected sender-to-receiver communication $d(\lambda, \ell)$. Then for all but finitely many ℓ we have $t(\lambda, \ell) < \frac{2\ell}{r}$. In the following, the expected sender-to-receiver communication of OT' will be called $d'(\lambda, \ell)$.

If $d(\lambda, \ell) < u(\lambda, \ell) + \ell$ then

$$d'(\lambda, \ell) = d(\lambda, \ell) = t(\lambda, \ell) - u(\lambda, \ell) \leq t(\lambda, \ell) - d(\lambda, \ell) + \ell \qquad \Leftrightarrow$$
$$d'(\lambda, \ell) \leq \frac{t(\lambda, \ell) + \ell}{2}$$

Else the new expected sender-to-receiver communication is

$$d'(\lambda, \ell) = u(\lambda, \ell) + \ell = t(\lambda, \ell) - d(\lambda, \ell) + \ell \leq t(\lambda, \ell) - u(\lambda, \ell) - \ell + \ell \qquad \Leftrightarrow$$
$$d'(\lambda, \ell) \leq \frac{t(\lambda, \ell) + \ell}{2}$$

Either way, $d'(\lambda, \ell) \leq \frac{t(\lambda, \ell) + \ell}{2}$ which means that for all but finitely many ℓ we have $d'(\lambda, \ell) < (\frac{1}{r} + \frac{1}{2})\ell$. Therefore, the expected download rate is $\frac{2}{(\frac{1}{r} + \frac{1}{2})}$ which is $> 1/2$ for $r > 2/3$. $\square$

5.2 Unbalanced Private-Set Intersection

In unbalanced private set intersection we have a set A of n λ-bit messages, held by a sender $\mathsf{PSIS}(1^\lambda, 1^n, A)$, and a singleton set B, held by a receiver $\mathsf{PSIR}(1^\lambda, 1^n, B)$. The goal is for the receiver to learn $A \cap B$ while the sender should learn nothing. Semi-honest receiver security can be defined along the lines of receiver (client) security of PIR (Definition 3).

We show how to transform a protocol for unbalanced private-set intersection $\mathsf{PSI} = (\mathsf{PSIS}, \mathsf{PSIR})$ that makes calls to oracle $\mathcal{O}$ into a PIR protocol $(\mathsf{PIRU}, \mathsf{PIRS})$ that makes calls to the same oracle $\mathcal{O}$ in a black-box manner. We do this by simply encoding the PIR-database and the PIR-query as sets.

– $\mathsf{PIRU}^{\mathcal{O}}(1^\lambda, 1^n, i)$: Set $A := \{i\}$. Run the PSI receiver $I \leftarrow \mathsf{PSIR}^{\mathcal{O}}O(1^\lambda, A)$ to get the intersection I. Return 1 if $\{i\} = I$ and 0 otherwise.
– $\mathsf{PIRS}^{\mathcal{O}}(1^\lambda, 1^n, \mathsf{DB})$: Form the set $B := \{x \mid \mathsf{DB}[x] = 1\}$. Run the PSI sender $\mathsf{PSIS}^{\mathcal{O}}(1^\lambda, B)$.

Lemma 3 (Folklore). *The PIR protocol* $(\mathsf{PIRU}, \mathsf{PIRS})$ *has the same correctness error, sender and receiver communication and sender and receiver query complexity as those of* PSI. *Moreover, the resulting PIR protocol has client security if* PSI *provides receiver security.*

That means if the sender communication in PSI *is less than* n, *then* $(\mathsf{PIRU}, \mathsf{PIRS})$ *is a non-trivial PIR protocol.*

Proof of Correctness. Correctness follows from the correctness of the PSI protocol and the intersection of $\{i\}$ and B being $\{i\}$ if $i \in B \Leftrightarrow \mathsf{DB}[i] = 1$ and $\emptyset$ otherwise.

Proof of Client Security. Suppose there exists $i, i' \in [n]$, $\mathsf{DB} \in \{0,1\}^n$ such that an adversary $\mathcal{A}$ can distinguish $\mathsf{view}_s^{\mathsf{PIR}}(i, \mathsf{DB})$ from $\mathsf{view}_s^{\mathsf{PIR}}(i', \mathsf{DB})$ with non-negligible probability. The same adversary $\mathcal{A}$ distinguishes between $\mathsf{view}_s^{\mathsf{PSI}}(\{i\}, B)$ and $\mathsf{view}_s^{\mathsf{PSI}}(\{i'\}, B)$ with the same non-negligible probability since the views are exactly the same. □

6 Lower-Bounds on the Number Oracle Queries in PIR

In this section, we show how to transform a private information retrieval (PIR) protocol with access to some *simulatable* oracle SO into one that does not query that oracle. To have something concrete in mind one may imagine SO being the generic group model, though the technique is much more general. We will later go into common instantiations of the oracle. This transformation allows us to transfer lower-bounds from PIR without oracle access to PIR with oracle access.

Simulatable Oracles. A simulatable oracle is an oracle SO which can efficiently be simulated by a stateful simulator Sim. More formally, a computationally unbounded adversary $\mathcal{A}$ cannot win the following game with a non-negligible advantage in polynomially many rounds r, where Sim is a PPT algorithm:

1. Sample random bit $b \xleftarrow{\$} \{0,1\}$.
2. Initialize the state of the oracle as st $\leftarrow \perp$.
3. Initialize the state of the adversary ast $\leftarrow \perp$.
4. The adversary produces a first query qu.
5. For $i \in [r]$:
   (a) If $b = 0$:
       – Let the response be resp $\leftarrow$ SO(qu)
   (b) Else:
       – Let response and new oracle state be (resp, st) $\leftarrow$ Sim(qu, st)
   (c) Let new query and adversary state be (qu, ast) $\leftarrow \mathcal{A}$(ast, resp)
6. Let the adversary output its guess $b' \leftarrow \mathcal{A}$(ast).
7. The adversary wins if $b = b'$.

Typical examples of simulatable oracles include the random oracle and the generic group oracle.

Construction 1. *Let* PIR $:=$ (PIRU$^{\text{SO,O}}$, PIRS$^{\text{SO,O}}$) *be a bit PIR protocol that uses a simulatable oracle* SO *and another oracle* O. *We show how to compile out the* SO-*calls of* (PIRU$^{\text{SO,O}}$, PIRS$^{\text{SO,O}}$), *obtaining an* SO-*free PIR protocol* $\overline{\text{PIR}} :=$ ($\overline{\text{PIRU}}^{\text{O}}$, $\overline{\text{PIRS}}^{\text{O}}$).

For notational convenience, in the following whenever calling PIRU *or* PIRS, *we omit the private-state part of the input.*

The protocol messages sent from $\overline{\text{PIRU}}$ *to* $\overline{\text{PIRS}}$ *are tagged with either 'protocol' (or bit zero) signifying a normal protocol message, or with 'query' (or bit 1) signifying a query message.*

$\overline{\text{PIRU}}^{\text{O}}(1^\lambda, 1^n, i)$:
   – *Initialize the state of the simulatable oracle* st $\leftarrow \perp$.
   – *Run the interactive PPT* PIRU$^{\text{SO,O}}$ *with the following interactions:*
      1. *When* PIRU$^{\text{SO,O}}$ *calls* O *on a query* qu *forward the query to* O *and respond with the received response.*
      2. *When* PIRU$^{\text{SO,O}}$ *calls* SO *on a query* qu, *simulate the response and update the oracle simulators state* (resp, st) $\leftarrow$ Sim(qu, st).
      3. *Upon* $\overline{\text{PIRU}}$ *receiving a message of the form* ('query', msgs), *interpret* msgs *as a query* qu, *simulate the oracle response and update the oracle simulators state as* (resp, st) $\leftarrow$ Sim(qu, st) *and return* resp *to the sender* $\overline{\text{PIRS}}$. *If the message has the form* ('protocol', msgs), *run* PIRU$^{\text{SO,O}}$ *on the protocol message* msgs *until it produces the next message* msgr *and send that to* $\overline{\text{PIRS}}$. *The oracle queries are handled as described above.*

$\overline{\text{PIRS}}^{\text{O}}(1^\lambda, 1^n, \text{DB})$:
   – *Run the interactive PPT* PIRS$^{\text{SO,O}}$ *with the following interactions:*

1. When $\mathsf{PIRS^{SO,O}}$ *calls* O *on a query* qu, *forward the query to* O *and respond with the received response.*
2. *When* $\mathsf{PIRS^{SO,O}}$ *calls* SO *on a query* qu, *send a tagged query pair* (*'query'*, qu) *to* $\overline{\mathsf{PIRU}}$ *and use the response* msgr *as a query response for* qu *to* PIRS.
3. *Else, run* $\mathsf{PIRS^{SO,O}}$ *until it produces a message* msgs *and send the tagged message* (*'protocol'*, msgs) *to* $\overline{\mathsf{PIRU}}$, *then wait for the response* msgr *and continue.*

Theorem 3. *If* PIR *is a non-trivial private information retrieval with server communication of* $\eta < cn$ *for* $c < 1$, $r \in o(n)$ *rounds of interaction with the user, and* $q \in o(n)$ *bits of communication with the* SO *oracle then* $\overline{\mathsf{PIR}}$ *is a non-trivial private information retrieval with server communication* $\overline{\eta} \leq \overline{c}n$ *for* $\overline{c} < 1$ *and no calls to* SO.

Server Communication. The server's additional communication overhead includes 1 bit per round as well as a total of $O(q)$ bits. Since the number rounds is $o(n)$, the total server communication complexity becomes $cn + o(n)$, which is less than $\overline{c}n$ for some $\overline{c} < 1$. □

Correctness. Notice that the above protocol will have different output from an execution of PIR either

1. if a with Sim simulated oracle behave differently from the real oracle behaviour
   or
2. if a message in the execution of PIR happens to start with t.

Both of these events happen with negligible probability. Therefore, if PIR has statistical correctness then so does $\overline{\mathsf{PIR}}$. □

Client Security. Suppose there exists $i, i' \in [n]$, $\mathsf{DB} \in \{0,1\}^n$ such that an adversary $\overline{\mathcal{A}}$ can distinguish $\mathsf{view}_s^{\overline{\mathsf{PIR}}}(i, \mathsf{DB})$ from $\mathsf{view}_s^{\overline{\mathsf{PIR}}}(i', \mathsf{DB})$ with non-negligible probability. We construct a new adversary $\mathcal{A}$ to distinguish between $\mathsf{view}_s^{\mathsf{PIR}}(i, \mathsf{DB})$ and $\mathsf{view}_s^{\mathsf{PIR}}(i', \mathsf{DB})$. The new adversary $\mathcal{A}$ gets as input a view v either from $\mathsf{view}_s^{\mathsf{PIR}}(i, \mathsf{DB})$ or $\mathsf{view}_s^{\mathsf{PIR}}(i', \mathsf{DB})$ and does the following:

1. Generate an empty view $\overline{v}$.
2. Copy all O-oracle calls from v to $\overline{v}$.
3. Run PIRS on the randomness and DB as defined in the view v and simulate its interaction as follows:
   (a) For PIRS's calls to the SO oracle with query qu and gets response resp enter (*'query'*, qu) as a server message into $\overline{v}$ and resp as a user message.
   (b) For PIRS's messages msgs enter (*'protocol*, msgs) in the transcript $\overline{v}$ as a server message and enter the users response msgr as a users message.
4. Run $b \leftarrow \overline{\mathcal{A}}(\overline{v})$, on the view $\overline{v}$ produced by $\overline{\mathsf{PIR}}$
5. Return b

$\mathcal{A}$ will distinguish $\mathsf{view}_s^{\mathsf{PIR}}(i, \mathsf{DB})$ and $\mathsf{view}_s^{\mathsf{PIR}}(i', \mathsf{DB})$ with negligibly close to the probability as $\overline{\mathcal{A}}$ can distinguish $\overline{\mathsf{view}}_s^{\mathsf{PIR}}(i, \mathsf{DB})$ from $\overline{\mathsf{view}}_s^{\mathsf{PIR}}(i', \mathsf{DB})$. This is because $\overline{v}$ follows the same distribution as $\mathsf{view}_s^{\mathsf{PIR}}(i, \mathsf{DB})$ (except that the SO queries are produced by the real oracle, not the simulator) if v was from $\mathsf{view}_s^{\mathsf{PIR}}(i, \mathsf{DB})$ and $\overline{v}$ follows the same distribution as $\mathsf{view}_s^{\mathsf{PIR}}(i', \mathsf{DB})$ (same caveat here) if v was from $\mathsf{view}_s^{\mathsf{PIR}}(i', \mathsf{DB})$. If the adversary could notice the simulation of SO then it would break its simulatability.   □

Remark 2. Theorem 3 is applicable to any two-PC protocol with one-sided receiver security. Of course, in the absence of further restrictions, such protocols are trivial to realize (e.g., by the sender sending its input in the clear to the receiver). One restriction that makes the problem non-trivial is to require the sender-to-receiver communication to be sub-linear in the sender's input size, as in PIR.

The utility of Theorem 3, beyond PIR itself, becomes apparent when one considers other protocols that imply non-trivial PIR while instantiating their underlying oracles via ideal forms of powerful primitives. We first discuss the implications of the theorem in terms of particular instantiations of the oracle, and in the next section we consider protocols that imply PIR.

Theorem 3 allows us to also rule out powerful non-black-box techniques for building PIR. We demonstrate this by letting SO include an OT oracle and an ideal obfuscation oracle that can obfuscate circuits with generic OT gates and random oracle gates. (See [2,20] for capturing similar non-black-box techniques via oracle-aided circuits.)

Corollary 4. *For any constants $c < 1$, there exists no n-bit PIR protocol with server communication $\eta \leq cn$, round complexity $r \in o(n)$, and with oracle access to a PSPACE-complete oracle, a random oracle, a generic OT oracle, and an obfuscation oracle for circuits with OT and random oracle gates, and where the server only communicates $q \in o(n)$ bits to the ideal obfuscation and OT oracles.*

Proof. In Lemma 1 we show an OT protocol with the above mentioned characteristics implies a non-trivial PIR. Let SO consist of an OT oracle [26] and an ideal obfuscation oracle [2,31] for obfuscating circuits with OT/RO gates. (Such an SO oracle is simulatable.) By invoking Theorem 3 one gets a non-trivial PIR with oracle access to the random oracle and an PSPACE-complete oracle. This in turn can be transformed into an OT protocol (while retaining the O oracles) via [18]. The existence of such an object however was ruled out by [26].   □

Back to the black-box setting, other illustrative examples include the use of GGMs for building non-trivial PIR.

Corollary 5. *For any constants $c < 1$, a non-trivial n-bit PIR protocol with server communication of cn, round complexity $r \in o(n)$ and where the server makes sublinear in n many generic group queries requires MPC-hard assumptions, beyond the generic group.*

Proof. In Theorem 3, if one instantiates SO by a generic group [38] and let the O oracle be empty, then one gets a non-trivial PIR without any oracle calls. This in turn can be transformed into an OT protocol without any oracles via [18]. OT is an MPC-complete protocol.   □

The above corollary is almost tight as there exists GGM-based PIR protocols with a linear number of GGM queries.

Lemma 4 ([19]). *Based on the DDH assumption, there exists a non-trivial n-bit PIR protocol with server communication of $O(\lambda)$ and with the sever making $O(n)$ group operations.*

Finally, we may derive a statement for FHE oracles.

Corollary 6. *For any constants $c < 1$, a non-trivial n-bit PIR protocol with server communication of cn, round complexity $r \in o(n)$ where the server makes $q \in o(n)$ black-box use of fully homomorphic encryption[3] requires MPC-hard assumptions, even beyond the fully homomorphic encryption.*

Proof. Let SO be an FHE oracle [23] (defined similarly to a generic PKE oracle of [26]). Let the O oracle be empty. Invoking Theorem 3 one gets a non-trivial PIR without any oracle calls. This in turn can be transformed into an OT protocol without oracles via [18]. OT is an MPC-complete protocol.   □

7   Communication Lower-Bounds for OT Extension

Theorem 3 provides lower-bounds on the computational complexity of PIR protocols. In this section, we show that these computational lower-bounds give rise to communication lower-bounds for OT extension (i.e., the number of bits that an extended OT sender needs to communicate). The result of this section implies that the communication complexity of the sender in the IKNP OT extension protocol [29] is close to optimal.

Corollary 7 (OT Extension: Sender Communication Lower-Bound). *For any constants $c < 1$, there exist no ℓ-batch k-bit OT extension protocol with sender communication $\eta < c2k\ell$, round complexity $r \in o(k\ell)$, and with the sender making $q \in o(k\ell)$ OT calls.*

Proof. OT extension is just an OT protocol that makes use of only a black-box OT and a random oracle. An ℓ-batch k-bit OT naturally gives rise to a $k\ell$-bit string OT. In Lemma 1 we show that such an OT protocol implies a non-trivial PIR for databases of $2\ell k$ bits. Under the resulting PIR protocol, the server communication is $\eta < c2k\ell$, round complexity $r \in o(k\ell)$, and the server communicates a total of $o(k\ell)$ bits with the OT oracle. Invoking Theorem 3, by instantiating SO with a generic OT oracle [26] and O with the random oracle [6] and by also including a PSPACE-complete oracle, we get a non-trivial PIR with

---

[3] This means the server communicates at most q bits to the FHE oracle.

oracle access to the random oracle and a PSPACE-complete oracle. This in turn can be transformed into an OT protocol (while retaining the O oracles) via [18]. The existence of such an object however was ruled out by [26].   □

Corollary 8 (OT Extension: Total Communication Lower-Bound). *For any constants $c < 1$, there exist no ℓ-batch k-bit OT extension protocol with total communication $\eta < \frac{3}{2}c(\ell + k\ell)$, round complexity $r \in o(k\ell)$, and with the sender making $q \in o(k\ell)$ $O\tilde{T}$ calls.*

Proof. Follows from Lemma 2 and Corollary 7.   □

Acknowledgements. We thank the anonymous reviewers for their valuable comments and suggestions.

J.D.: Funded by the European Union (ERC, LACONIC, 101041207). Views and opinions expressed are however those of the author(s) only and do not necessarily reflect those of the European Union or the European Research Council. Neither the European Union nor the granting authority can be held responsible for them.

M. Hajiabadi supported in part by an NSERC Discovery Grant 03270, and a Meta Research Award.

References

1. Aggarwal, D., Dottling, N., Dujmovic, J., Hajiabadi, M., Malavolta, G., Obremski, M.: Algebraic restriction codes and their applications. In: Braverman, M. (ed.), 13th Innovations in Theoretical Computer Science Conference, ITCS 2022, January 31–3 February 2022, Berkeley, CA, USA, volume 215 of LIPIcs, pp. 2:1–2:15. Schloss Dagstuhl - Leibniz-Zentrum für Informatik (2022)

2. Asharov, G., Segev, G.: Limits on the power of indistinguishability obfuscation and functional encryption. In: Guruswami, V. (ed.) 56th Annual Symposium on Foundations of Computer Science, pp. 191–209. IEEE Computer Society Press, October 2015

3. Beaver, D.: Correlated pseudorandomness and the complexity of private computations. In: 28th Annual ACM Symposium on Theory of Computing, pp. 479–488. ACM Press, May 1996

4. Beimel, A., Ishai, Y., Malkin, T.: Reducing the servers computation in private information retrieval: PIR with preprocessing. In: Bellare, M. (ed.) CRYPTO 2000. LNCS, vol. 1880, pp. 55–73. Springer, Heidelberg (2000). https://doi.org/10.1007/3-540-44598-6_4

5. Beimel, A., Ishai, Y., Malkin, T.: Reducing the servers' computation in private information retrieval: PIR with preprocessing. J. Cryptol. **17**(2), 125–151 (2004)

6. Bellare, M., Rogaway, P.: Random oracles are practical: a paradigm for designing efficient protocols. In: Denning, D.E., Pyle, R., Ganesan, R., Sandhu, R.S., Ashby, V. (eds.), ACM CCS 93: 1st Conference on Computer and Communications Security, pp. 62–73. ACM Press, November 1993

7. Boyle, E., Ishai, Y., Pass, R., Wootters, M.: Can we access a database both locally and privately? In: Kalai, Y., Reyzin, L. (eds.) TCC 2017. LNCS, vol. 10678, pp. 662–693. Springer, Cham (2017). https://doi.org/10.1007/978-3-319-70503-3_22

8. Brakerski, Z., Branco, P., Dottling, N., Pu, S.: Batch-OT with optimal rate. In: Dunkelman, O., Dziembowski, S. (eds.) Advances in Cryptology – EUROCRYPT 2022. EUROCRYPT 2022. LNCS, vol. 13276, pp. 157–186. Springer, Cham (2022). https://doi.org/10.1007/978-3-031-07085-3_6

9. Brakerski, Z., Koppula, V., Mour, T.: NIZK from LPN and trapdoor hash via correlation intractability for approximable relations. In: Micciancio, D., Ristenpart, T. (eds.) CRYPTO 2020. LNCS, vol. 12172, pp. 738–767. Springer, Cham (2020). https://doi.org/10.1007/978-3-030-56877-1_26

10. Cachin, C., Micali, S., Stadler, M.: Computationally private information retrieval with polylogarithmic communication. In: Stern, J. (ed.) EUROCRYPT 1999. LNCS, vol. 1592, pp. 402–414. Springer, Heidelberg (1999). https://doi.org/10.1007/3-540-48910-X_28

11. Canetti, R., Holmgren, J., Richelson, S.: Towards doubly efficient private information retrieval. In: Kalai, Y., Reyzin, L. (eds.) TCC 2017. LNCS, vol. 10678, pp. 694–726. Springer, Cham (2017). https://doi.org/10.1007/978-3-319-70503-3_23

12. Chase, M., Garg, S., Hajiabadi, M., Li, J., Miao, P.: Amortizing rate-1 OT and applications to PIR and PSI. In: Nissim, K., Waters, B. (eds.) TCC 2021. LNCS, vol. 13044, pp. 126–156. Springer, Cham (2021). https://doi.org/10.1007/978-3-030-90456-2_5

13. Chase, M., Miao, P.: Private set intersection in the internet setting from lightweight oblivious PRF. In: Micciancio, D., Ristenpart, T. (eds.) CRYPTO 2020. LNCS, vol. 12172, pp. 34–63. Springer, Cham (2020). https://doi.org/10.1007/978-3-030-56877-1_2

14. Chor, B., Gilboa, N., Naor, M.: Private information retrieval by keywords. Cryptology ePrint Archive, Report 1998/003 (1998). https://eprint.iacr.org/1998/003

15. Chor, B., Kushilevitz, E., Goldreich, O., Sudan, M.: Private information retrieval. In: 36th Annual Symposium on Foundations of Computer Science, pp. 41–50. IEEE Computer Society Press, October 1995

16. Corrigan-Gibbs, H., Henzinger, A., Kogan, D.: Single-server private information retrieval with sublinear amortized time. In: Dunkelman, O., Dziembowski, S. (eds.) Advances in Cryptology – EUROCRYPT 2022. EUROCRYPT 2022. LNCS, vol. 13276, pp. 3–33. Springer, Cham (2022). https://doi.org/10.1007/978-3-031-07085-3_1

17. Corrigan-Gibbs, H., Kogan, D.: Private information retrieval with sublinear online time. In: Canteaut, A., Ishai, Y. (eds.) EUROCRYPT 2020. LNCS, vol. 12105, pp. 44–75. Springer, Cham (2020). https://doi.org/10.1007/978-3-030-45721-1_3

18. Di Crescenzo, G., Malkin, T., Ostrovsky, R.: Single database private information retrieval implies oblivious transfer. In: Preneel, B. (ed.) EUROCRYPT 2000. LNCS, vol. 1807, pp. 122–138. Springer, Heidelberg (2000). https://doi.org/10.1007/3-540-45539-6_10

19. Döttling, N., Garg, S., Ishai, Y., Malavolta, G., Mour, T., Ostrovsky, R.: Trapdoor hash functions and their applications. In: Boldyreva, A., Micciancio, D. (eds.) CRYPTO 2019. LNCS, vol. 11694, pp. 3–32. Springer, Cham (2019). https://doi.org/10.1007/978-3-030-26954-8_1

20. Garg, S., Hajiabadi, M., Mahmoody, M., Mohammed, A.: Limits on the power of garbling techniques for public-key encryption. In: Shacham, H., Boldyreva, A. (eds.) CRYPTO 2018. LNCS, vol. 10993, pp. 335–364. Springer, Cham (2018). https://doi.org/10.1007/978-3-319-96878-0_12

21. Garg, S., Hajiabadi, M., Ostrovsky, R.: Efficient range-trapdoor functions and applications: rate-1 OT and more. In: Pass, R., Pietrzak, K. (eds.) TCC 2020. LNCS, vol. 12550, pp. 88–116. Springer, Cham (2020). https://doi.org/10.1007/978-3-030-64375-1_4

22. Garg, S., Mahmoody, M., Masny, D., Meckler, I.: On the round complexity of OT extension. In: Shacham, H., Boldyreva, A. (eds.) CRYPTO 2018. LNCS, vol. 10993, pp. 545–574. Springer, Cham (2018). https://doi.org/10.1007/978-3-319-96878-0_19

23. Garg, S., Mahmoody, M., Mohammed, A.: Lower bounds on obfuscation from all-or-nothing encryption primitives. In: Katz, J., Shacham, H. (eds.) CRYPTO 2017. LNCS, vol. 10401, pp. 661–695. Springer, Cham (2017). https://doi.org/10.1007/978-3-319-63688-7_22

24. Gennaro, R., Gertner, Y., Katz, J.: Lower bounds on the efficiency of encryption and digital signature schemes. In: 35th Annual ACM Symposium on Theory of Computing, pp. 417–425. ACM Press, June 2003

25. Gennaro, R., Trevisan, L.: Lower bounds on the efficiency of generic cryptographic constructions. In: 41st Annual Symposium on Foundations of Computer Science, pp. 305–313. IEEE Computer Society Press, November 2000

26. Gertner, Y., Kannan, S., Malkin, T., Reingold, O., Viswanathan, M.: The relationship between public key encryption and oblivious transfer. In: 41st Annual Symposium on Foundations of Computer Science, pp. 325–335. IEEE Computer Society Press, November 2000

27. Henzinger, A., Hong, M.M., Corrigan-Gibbs, H., Meiklejohn, S., Vaikuntanathan, V.: One server for the price of two: simple and fast single-server private information retrieval. Cryptology ePrint Archive, Report 2022/949 (2022). https://eprint.iacr.org/2022/949

28. Henzinger, A., Hong, M.M., Corrigan-Gibbs, H., Meiklejohn, S., Vaikuntanathan, V.: One server for the price of two: simple and fast single-server private information retrieval. In: Calandrino, J.A., Troncoso, C. (eds.), 32nd USENIX Security Symposium, USENIX Security 2023, Anaheim, CA, USA, 9–11 August 2023. USENIX Association (2023)

29. Ishai, Y., Kilian, J., Nissim, K., Petrank, E.: Extending oblivious transfers efficiently. In: Boneh, D. (ed.) CRYPTO 2003. LNCS, vol. 2729, pp. 145–161. Springer, Heidelberg (2003). https://doi.org/10.1007/978-3-540-45146-4_9

30. Ishai, Y., Paskin, A.: Evaluating branching programs on encrypted data. In: Vadhan, S.P. (ed.) TCC 2007. LNCS, vol. 4392, pp. 575–594. Springer, Heidelberg (2007). https://doi.org/10.1007/978-3-540-70936-7_31

31. Jain, A., Lin, H., Luo, J., Wichs, D.: The pseudorandom oracle model and ideal obfuscation. In: Handschuh, H., Lysyanskaya, A. (eds.) Advances in Cryptology – CRYPTO 2023. CRYPTO 2023. LNCS, vol. 14084, pp. 233–262. Springer, Cham (2023). https://doi.org/10.1007/978-3-031-38551-3_8

32. Kogan, D., Corrigan-Gibbs, H.: Private blocklist lookups with checklist. In: Bailey, M., Greenstadt, R. (eds.) USENIX Security 2021: 30th USENIX Security Symposium, pp. 875–892. USENIX Association, August 2021

33. Kushilevitz, E., Ostrovsky, R.: One-way trapdoor permutations are sufficient for non-trivial single-server private information retrieval. In: Preneel, B. (ed.) EUROCRYPT 2000. LNCS, vol. 1807, pp. 104–121. Springer, Heidelberg (2000). https://doi.org/10.1007/3-540-45539-6_9

34. Lin, W.-K., Mook, E., Wichs, D.: Doubly efficient private information retrieval and fully homomorphic RAM computation from ring LWE. In: Saha, B., Servedio, R.A. (eds.) Proceedings of the 55th Annual ACM Symposium on Theory of Computing, STOC 2023, Orlando, FL, USA, 20–23 June 2023, pp. 595–608. ACM (2023)

35. Ostrovsky, R., Skeith, W.E.: A survey of single-database private information retrieval: techniques and applications. In: Okamoto, T., Wang, X. (eds.) PKC 2007. LNCS, vol. 4450, pp. 393–411. Springer, Heidelberg (2007). https://doi.org/10.1007/978-3-540-71677-8_26

36. Persiano, G., Yeo, K.: Limits of preprocessing for single-server PIR. In: Naor, J.S., Buchbinder, N. (eds.) Proceedings of the 2022 ACM-SIAM Symposium on Discrete Algorithms, SODA 2022, Virtual Conference/Alexandria, VA, USA, 9–12 January 2022, pp. 2522–2548. SIAM (2022)

37. Shi, E., Aqeel, W., Chandrasekaran, B., Maggs, B.: Puncturable pseudorandom sets and private information retrieval with near-optimal online bandwidth and time. In: Malkin, T., Peikert, C. (eds.) CRYPTO 2021. LNCS, vol. 12828, pp. 641–669. Springer, Cham (2021). https://doi.org/10.1007/978-3-030-84259-8_22

38. Shoup, V.: Lower bounds for discrete logarithms and related problems. In: Fumy, W. (ed.) EUROCRYPT 1997. LNCS, vol. 1233, pp. 256–266. Springer, Heidelberg (1997). https://doi.org/10.1007/3-540-69053-0_18

39. Wolf, S., Wullschleger, J.: Oblivious transfer is symmetric. In: Vaudenay, S. (ed.) EUROCRYPT 2006. LNCS, vol. 4004, pp. 222–232. Springer, Heidelberg (2006). https://doi.org/10.1007/11761679_14

40. Yeo, K.: Lower bounds for (Batch) PIR with private preprocessing. In: Hazay, C., Stam, M. (eds.) Advances in Cryptology – EUROCRYPT 2023. EUROCRYPT 2023. LNCS, vol. 14004, pp. 518–550. Springer, Cham (2023). https://doi.org/10.1007/978-3-031-30545-0_18

41. Zhandry, M.: To label, or not to label (in generic groups). In: Dodis, Y., Shrimpton, T. (eds.) Advances in Cryptology – CRYPTO 2022. CRYPTO 2022. LNCS, vol. 13509, pp. 66–96. Springer, Cham (2022). https://doi.org/10.1007/978-3-031-15982-4_3

42. Zhou, M., Lin, WK., Tselekounis, Y., Shi, E.: Optimal single-server private information retrieval. In: Hazay, C., Stam, M. (eds.) Advances in Cryptology – EUROCRYPT 2023. EUROCRYPT 2023. LNCS, vol. 14004, pp. 395–425. Springer, Cham (2023). https://doi.org/10.1007/978-3-031-30545-0_14

43. Zhou, M., Park, A., Shi, E., Zheng, W.: PIANO: extremely simple, single-server PIR with sublinear server computation. IACR Cryptol. ePrint Arch., p. 452 (2023)

Fast Public-Key Silent OT and More from Constrained Naor-Reingold

Dung Bui[1]([envelope]), Geoffroy Couteau[1], Pierre Meyer[2], Alain Passelègue[3,4], and Mahshid Riahinia[4]

[1] Université Paris Cité, CNRS, IRIF, Paris, France
{bui,couteau}@irif.fr
[2] Aarhus Universitet, Aarhus, Denmark
pierre.meyer@cs.au.dk
[3] CryptoLab Inc., Lyon, France
alain.passelegue@cryptolab.co.kr
[4] ENS de Lyon, Laboratoire LIP (U. Lyon, CNRS, ENSL, Inria, UCBL), Lyon, France
mahshid.riahinia@ens-lyon.fr

Abstract. Pseudorandom Correlation Functions (PCFs) allow two parties, given correlated evaluation keys, to locally generate arbitrarily many pseudorandom correlated strings, e.g. Oblivious Transfer (OT) correlations, which can then be used by the two parties to jointly run secure computation protocols. In this work, we provide a novel and simple approach for constructing PCFs for OT correlation, by relying on constrained pseudorandom functions for a class of constraints containing a weak pseudorandom function (wPRF). We then show that tweaking the Naor-Reingold pseudorandom function and relying on low-complexity pseudorandom functions allow us to instantiate our paradigm. We further extend our ideas to obtain efficient *public-key* PCFs, which allow the distribution of correlated keys between parties to be non-interactive: each party can generate a pair of public/secret keys, and any pair of parties can locally derive their correlated evaluation key by combining their secret key with the other party's public key.

In addition to these theoretical contributions, we detail various optimizations and provide concrete instantiations of our paradigm relying on the Boneh-Ishai-Passelègue-Sahai-Wu wPRF and the Goldreich-Applebaum-Raykov wPRF. Putting everything together, we obtain public-key PCFs with a throughput of 15k–40k OT/s, which is of a similar order of magnitude to the state-of-the-art *interactive* PCFs and about 4 orders of magnitude faster than state-of-the art *public-key* PCFs.

As a side result, we also show that public-key PCFs can serve as a building block to construct reusable designated-verifier non-interactive zero-knowledge proofs (DV-NIZK) for NP. Combined with our instantiations, this yields simple and efficient reusable DV-NIZKs for NP in pairing-free groups.

1 Introduction

Efficient procedures to generate correlated randomness are at the heart of modern secure computation. Starting with the seminal work of Beaver [14], many

© International Association for Cryptologic Research 2024
M. Joye and G. Leander (Eds.): EUROCRYPT 2024, LNCS 14656, pp. 88–118, 2024.
https://doi.org/10.1007/978-3-031-58751-1_4

protocols achieving impressive performances have been designed in a model where the parties are given access to a trusted source of correlated randomness [43,44,46,49,54,61,67,76]. As an example, $O(n)$ instances of a random oblivious transfer suffice to evaluate any size-n circuit using the seminal GMW protocol [52], using as little as four bits of communication per AND gate.

Due to the efficiency of protocols in the correlated randomness model, a popular paradigm in secure computation is to divide the protocol into two phases: in the *preprocessing* phase, which is independent of the inputs (and can be executed ahead of time), long correlated random strings are securely generated using a dedicated protocol. Then, in the *online* phase, this correlated randomness is consumed by a fast and lightweight protocol. Traditional approaches for generating the correlated randomness were based on oblivious transfer extension [55] or somewhat homomorphic encryption [44]. They incur a large $\Omega(\lambda \cdot n)$ communication overhead for n-gate circuits and typically form the main efficiency bottleneck of the protocol.

Generating Pseudorandom Correlations. Recently, a new paradigm has emerged which enables the *silent* generation of long correlated *pseudo*random strings [22,24,25], removing essentially all of the communication in the preprocessing phase. Concretely, this is made possible by the mean of cryptographic primitives, such as *pseudorandom correlation generators* (PCG) [25] and *pseudorandom correlated functions* (PCFs) [26].

A PCG is a pair of algorithms (PCG.Gen, PCG.Expand) where PCG.Gen produces two short keys (k_0, k_1), and PCG.Expand(σ, k_σ) produces a long string y_σ such that (y_0, y_1) form pseudorandom samples from the target correlation. PCGs enable silent secure computation as follows: using a small distributed protocol to securely generate the keys (k_0, k_1), two parties can afterwards locally expand them into long correlated pseudorandom strings without any further communication. The online phase proceeds as before.

PCGs suffer from a considerable limitation: after distributing the keys, the parties are bound to generate *all at once* a priori *fixed amount* of correlated randomness. PCFs overcome this issue: a PCF is a pair of algorithms (PCF.Gen, PCF.Eval) where PCF.Gen produces two short keys (k_0, k_1), and PCF.Eval(σ, k_σ, x) outputs y_σ^x where for each new input x, (y_0^x, y_1^x) appears like a fresh sample from the target correlation. Hence, after distributively generating the keys (k_0, k_1) once and for all, two parties can generate on-the-fly any amount of target correlations in all their future secure computations.

The line of work on PCGs and PCFs has been fairly successful: modern PCG protocols for the oblivious transfer (OT) correlation (often called *silent OT extension*) can stretch up to 10M OT/s on one core of a standard laptop [23, 39,73] from keys in the 10~20kB range, and the fastest PCFs for OT [23] can generate up to 100k OT/s on one core of a standard laptop.

Public-Key Silent OT. The silent generation of correlated randomness from PCGs or PCFs requires two parties to engage in an interactive protocol to securely generate the PCG/PCF keys. *Public-key* PCFs reduce this interactive phase to a bare minimum, by replacing it with a public-key setup. More precisely, after publishing their public keys online, any pair of parties on a network can start generating correlated randomness, without *any interaction* beyond the initial PKI. Public-key silent correlated randomness generation is somewhat of a holy grail in this line of work: it would represent a major step towards bridging the usability gap between secure communication (since PKI suffices to enable efficient pairwise secure communication) and secure computation, but public-key PCFs for OTs have so far proven considerably harder to achieve than standard PCG and PCFs. Until recently, we simply had no public key silent OT construction, beyond heavy-hammer constructions from obfuscation or threshold multikey FHE.

This changed recently with the result of [70], which achieved the first practical public-key silent OT, assuming the quadratic residuosity assumption and the existence of correlation-robust hash functions. However, the efficiency of the new construction of [70] still lags way behind that of state-of-the-art PCFs for OTs. Concretely, their construction relies on a new distributed discrete logarithm protocol that allows two parties, given multiplicative shares of a value G^x (where G generates a suitable DLog-easy group), to non-interactively compute additive shares of x. The public-key silent OT construction of [70] has public keys of size around 1kB for one of the parties, and about 50kB for the other. In terms of computational efficiency, the cost of generating a single OT correlation is dominated by λ exponentiations with an exponent in $\mathbb{Z}_{N \cdot 2^\lambda}$, where N is an RSA modulus. Using $\lambda = 128$ and $\log N = 3072$, this translates to 128 exponentiations with 3200-bit exponents and takes about one second on one core of a standard laptop, which is between four and five orders of magnitude slower than the state-of-the-art PCF of [23]. In summary, as of today, the fundamental goal of obtaining concretely efficient and usable public-key silent OTs remains open.

Our Results. As our main contribution, we construct the first concretely efficient public-key PCF for oblivious transfers. Our approach departs significantly from all previous works, and we obtain several additional contributions. Our new public-key PCF features public key sizes in the 30kB range, and the cost of generating each OT is dominated by *a single exponentiation* over a standard 256-bit elliptic curve. Using fast curves such as Curve25519 [16] or FourQ [32], we estimate a throughput of 15k to 40k OT/s on one core of a standard laptop, about four orders of magnitude faster than the best previous public-key PCF, and approaching the efficiency of the best PCF overall. Our results enable for the first time all users of a network, after a simple PKI setup, to efficiently generate arbitrary amounts of pairwise OT correlations without any interaction. The security of our construction reduces to four assumptions: the Decisional Composite Residuosity assumption, the sparse power-DDH assumption (a new —static, falsifiable, secure in the GGM—variant of DDH that we introduce), correlation-robust hash function, and a suitable weak pseudorandom function (which we instantiate using either the Goldreich-Applebaum-Raykov weak PRF [10, 50] or the Boneh-Ishai-Passelègue-Sahai-Wu weak PRF [21]).[1] Table 1 provides a comparison between our results and others.

At the heart of our result is a new construction of efficient *constrained pseudorandom functions* from the Naor-Reingold PRF [66], for a class of constraints we term *inner-product membership* (IPM) constraints. Informally, CPRFs are pseudorandom functions where given a *constrained key* K_C for some predicate C, one can locally evaluate the PRF at all points x where $C(x) = 0$, while the output of the function still looks random on inputs x where $C(x) = 1$. A constrained key for the class IPM is associated to a vector z and a set S, and allows evaluating the PRF on an input x if and only if $\langle x, z \rangle \in S$. Along the way to our efficient public-key PCF, we achieve several results of independent interest:

- We show how a simple tweak to the Naor-Reingold PRF yields a constrained PRF (CPRF) for IPM constraints, in the random oracle model. IPM constraints capture several predicates of interest, and in particular, we obtain the first puncturable pseudorandom function (CPRF for the class of point functions) in the complexity class NC^1.
- Observing that several low-complexity PRFs can be expressed as IPM constraints, we obtain a *pseudorandomly* constrained PRF: a constrained key is associated to a (low-complexity) PRF, and allows evaluating the CPRF on inputs x for which the low-complexity PRF evaluates to 0.
- We then show that pseudorandomly constrained PRFs yield *precomputable* PCFs. The notion of precomputability for PCFs was recently introduced in [38] together with a proof-of-concept (inefficient) construction from DCR. In a precomputable PCF, one of the parties can locally generate a PCF key and precompute its entire share of the correlated randomness *even before knowing the identity of the other party*. This pushes to an extreme the possibility of preparing secure computation protocols ahead of time, by allowing one party to execute the entire preprocessing before knowing its input, the function, and the identity of its opponent. Combining these results, we obtain the first *concretely efficient* precomputable PCF, from the sparse DDH assumption, in the random oracle model. While the resulting construction is not a public-key PCF, distributing the key generation of our precomputable PCF is also very simple, requiring only n parallel calls to an oblivious transfer protocol (with $n = 256$ in our most efficient instantiation).

Eventually, we explore an application of public-key PCF to *designated-verifier zero-knowledge proofs* (DV-NIZKs). A DV-NIZK allows any prover to demonstrate the truth of a statement using a single message, such that the proof can be verified using a secret verification key. DV-NIZKs are believed to be easier to obtain than standard NIZKs, in the following sense: they are known to exist under the plain CDH assumption in pairing-free groups [35,59,72], while NIZKs are only known in pairing groups, or using subexponential hardness assumptions [36,57]. Yet, efficiency-wise, we do not know of any concretely efficient

---

[1] The DCR assumption in our construction can be replaced by the DDH assumption over subgroups of finite fields, but at the cost of a less efficient construction.

construction of DV-NIZKs in pairing-free groups (efficient NIZKs are known in pairing groups [34,53,60], and known DV-NIZKs in pairing-free groups rely on the hidden bit model, for which no concretely efficient instantiation is known). We show how, using a public-key PCF, one can compile any Σ-protocol with binary challenge into a DV-NIZK. Plugging our construction of public-key PCF, we obtain a new DV-NIZK from polynomial assumptions over pairing-free groups for all languages that admit a bit Σ-protocol, with communication comparable to that of the Σ-protocol. Conceptually, our result can be seen as observing that a public-key PCF suffices to upgrade *non-reusable* DV-NIZKs (which exist from public key encryption [41]) into *reusable* DV-NIZKs.

Organization of the Paper. Due to space limitation, we provide a detailed technical overview explaining the core techniques of all our contributions. Detailed constructions and proofs are provided in the full version of our paper and follow from the ideas described in this technical overview.

Table 1. Comparison of state-of-the-art PCFs and PK-PCFs for OT correlations

	Public-Key Setup?	Key Size (reusable part if pk)	Total number of OTs (for 128-bit security)	Assumptions	Throughput
[23]	✗	<1 MB	2^{30}	EA-LPN	100 kOT/s
[70]	✓	50 kB	$\_^{\dagger\dagger}$	DCR	1 OT/s
This Paper	✓	30,2 kB (12,1 kB)	$2^{44,5}$	BIPSW wPRF, spDDH[†], DCR, RO*	10–15 kOT/s[‡]
	✓	18 kB (12,2 kB)	2^{40}	GAR wPRF, spDDH[†], DCR, RO*	15–40 kOT/s[‡]
	✓	18,9 kB (12,2 kB)	2^{45}	GAR wPRF, spDDH[†], DCR, RO*	15–40 kOT/s[‡]

†† The number of OTs derived from a single PCF key has no bearing on the security level if the underlying Paillier ciphertexts are chosen to achieve 128-bit security.

* RO: Random Oracle.

† spDDH: sparse power DDH.

‡ Lower range estimates per core based on using curve25519 on an AWS platform; higher range estimates based on using FourQ on a Haswell architecture.

2   Technical Overview

In this section, we provide a detailed overview of our results. We start by describing our main paradigm about constructing PCF for OT correlations from Pseudorandomly Constrained PRFs in Sect. 2.1. Then, in Sect. 2.2, we explain how to modify the Naor-Reingold PRF in order to obtain a CPRF for the class of inner-product membership predicates, and show that various weak PRF constructions can be expressed as such predicates in Sect. 2.3, leading to instantiations of pseudorandomly constrained PRFs and therefore of PCFs.

Next, we focus on optimizing the resulting PCFs. In Sects. 2.4–2.5,we provide several optimizations which benefit the most efficient instantiations of our paradigm and detail our optimized PCF construction. Concrete parameters are provided in Sect. 2.6.

We then describe in Sect. 2.7 how our PCF can be turned into an efficient public-key PCF by relying on ideas borrowed from [70], and how to optimize the resulting construction. Finally, in Sect. 2.8, we explain how our public-key PCF can be used to construct reusable designated-verifier NIZKs.

2.1 A PCF for OT from Pseudorandomly Constrained PRFs

Let $F = (F.\mathsf{KeyGen}, F.\mathsf{Eval})$ be a (weak, strong) PRF with key space $\mathcal{K}$ and binary outputs. For a key $K \in \mathcal{K}$, let $F_K : x \mapsto F.\mathsf{Eval}(K, x)$. Also, let $\mathsf{CPRF} = (\mathsf{CPRF.KeyGen}, \mathsf{CPRF.Eval}, \mathsf{CPRF.Constrain}, \mathsf{CPRF.CEval})$ denote a constrained PRF for the class $\mathcal{F} = \{F_K\}_{K \in \mathcal{K}} \cup \{1 - F_K\}_{K \in \mathcal{K}}$, i.e., $\mathcal{F}$ contains all predicates "$F.\mathsf{Eval}(K, x)$ evaluates to b" for $b \in \{0, 1\}$ and $K \in \mathcal{K}$. Then, we construct a (weak, strong) pseudorandom correlation function for oblivious transfer correlation as follows:

- The sender gets two independent master secret keys $(\mathsf{msk}_0, \mathsf{msk}_1)$ of the CPRF. On an input x, this party evaluates the CPRF on x using both keys to obtain two pseudorandom outputs (y_0, y_1).
- The receiver gets a random (weak) PRF key $K \xleftarrow{\$} \mathcal{K}$, and two constrained keys: ck_0 that is msk_0 constrained at "$F_K(x) = 0$", and ck_1 that is msk_1 constrained at "$F_K(x) = 1$". On an input x, this party computes $b \leftarrow F_K(x)$, and sets $y_b \leftarrow \mathsf{CPRF.CEval}(\mathsf{ck}_b, x)$. It then outputs (b, y_b).

Correctness is straightforward: for any x, the predicate $F_K(x) = b$ is satisfied for some $b \in \{0, 1\}$, hence the constrained key ck_b yields the correct output y_b by the correctness of the CPRF. *Sender security* follows from the fact that the two constrained keys are constrained at F_K and $1 - F_K$, respectively, hence both constrains can never be satisfied at the same time. Thus, by the security of the CPRF, when $F_K(x) = b$, the value y_{1-b} is indistinguishable from random for the receiver. *Receiver security* follows from the (weak) pseudorandomness of F, which entails that $b = F_K(x)$ is pseudorandom from the sender's perspective.

We sketch the full construction below (we omit the public parameters pp output by the CPRF for simplicity):

- $\mathsf{PCF.Gen}(1^\lambda)$: For $b \in \{0, 1\}$, run $\mathsf{msk}_b \leftarrow \mathsf{CPRF.KeyGen}(1^\lambda)$. Then sample a secret key $K \xleftarrow{\$} F.\mathsf{KeyGen}(1^\lambda)$ for the PRF F. Compute $\mathsf{ck}_0 \leftarrow \mathsf{CPRF.Constrain}(\mathsf{msk}_0, f_K)$ and $\mathsf{ck}_1 \leftarrow \mathsf{CPRF.Constrain}(\mathsf{msk}_1, 1 - f_K)$. Output $k_0 \leftarrow (\mathsf{msk}_0, \mathsf{msk}_1)$ and $k_1 \leftarrow (K, \mathsf{ck}_0, \mathsf{ck}_1)$.
- $\mathsf{PCF.Eval}(\sigma, k_\sigma, x)$:
  - If $\sigma = 0$, parse $k_0 = (\mathsf{msk}_0, \mathsf{msk}_1)$, and compute $y_b \leftarrow \mathsf{CPRF.Eval}(\mathsf{msk}_0, x)$ for $b \in \{0, 1\}$, and output (y_0, y_1).
  - If $\sigma = 1$, parse $k_1 = (K, \mathsf{ck}_0, \mathsf{ck}_1)$, and compute $b \leftarrow F_K(x)$. Set $y_b \leftarrow \mathsf{CPRF.CEval}(\mathsf{ck}_b, x)$, and output (b, y_b).

We further observe that the resulting PCF is *precomputable* as recently defined in [38]. Informally, it allows one of the parties to locally generate its own PCF key and compute its correlated randomness entirely, before even knowing the identity of the other party. In the above construction, the sender can precompute all pairs (y_0, y_1) ahead of time, and it is therefore precomputable.

We note that the fact that CPRFs for a class containing a PRF yield a PCF is not entirely new; for example, a similar observation was briefly mentioned in [13]. However, the few known constructions of sufficiently expressive CPRFs [11,28,38] are too expensive, and using them within the above transformation yields PCFs that are much less flexible than generic constructions based on homomorphic secret sharing or threshold FHE (that are not restricted to the OT correlation), and much less efficient than state-of-the-art PCFs [23,26]. Our key contribution is identifying that a simple tweak to the Naor-Reingold PRF [66] yields an extremely efficient pseudorandomly constrained PRF.

2.2 A CPRF for Inner-Product Membership from the Naor-Reingold PRF

Let us first recall the Naor-Reingold PRF [66], whose input domain is $\mathcal{X} = \{0,1\}^n$. Let $\mathbb{G} = \mathbb{G}(\lambda)$ be a family of cyclic groups of prime order $p = p(\lambda)$.

- $F.\mathsf{KeyGen}(1^\lambda)$: Sample $g \xleftarrow{\$} \mathbb{G}$ and $a_1, a_2, \cdots, a_n \xleftarrow{\$} \mathbb{Z}_p^*$. Output $\mathsf{msk} \leftarrow (g, a_1, \cdots, a_n)$.
- $F.\mathsf{Eval}(\mathsf{msk}, x)$: On input $x = (x_1, \cdots, x_n) \in \{0,1\}^n$, output $g^{\prod_{i=1}^n a_i^{x_i}}$.

Evaluating the Naor-Reingold PRF requires a few multiplications, followed by a single exponentiation. Its security reduces to the Decisional Diffie-Hellman assumption over $\mathbb{G}$.

A No-Evaluation-Secure CPRF for Inner-Product. As a warm-up, we define the class of predicates

$$C_z : x \to \begin{cases} 0 & \text{if } \langle x, z \rangle = 0 \\ 1 & \text{otherwise.} \end{cases}$$

That is, a constrained key for z allows evaluating the PRF on all inputs x where $\langle x, z \rangle = 0$. Now, consider the following extension of the Naor-Reingold PRF:

- $F.\mathsf{Constrain}(\mathsf{msk}, z)$: Sample $r \xleftarrow{\$} \mathbb{Z}_p^*$ and define $(\alpha_1, \cdots, \alpha_n) \leftarrow (r^{z_1} \cdot a_1, \cdots, r^{z_n} \cdot a_n)$. Output $\mathsf{ck} = (g, \alpha_1, \cdots, \alpha_n)$.
- $F.\mathsf{CEval}(\mathsf{ck}, x)$: On input $x = (x_1, \cdots, x_n) \in \{0,1\}^n$, output $g^{\prod_{i=1}^n \alpha_i^{x_i}}$.

Here, each key a_i is *blinded* by a term r^{z_i}, and the outputs of the Eval and CEval algorithms coincide when the blinding terms cancel out which happens precisely when the inner product $\langle x, z \rangle$ is equal to 0 modulo the order of r. For a safe prime p with $p - 1 = 2q$, the order of r is q or $2q$ with overwhelming probability, so with $q \gg n$, $\langle x, z \rangle = 0 \bmod q$ iff $\langle x, z \rangle = 0$ over the integers.

$$F.\mathsf{CEval}(\mathsf{ck}, x) = g^{\prod_{i=1}^n \alpha_i^{x_i}} = g^{\prod_{i=1}^n (r^{z_i} \cdot a_i)^{x_i}} = g^{r^{\sum_{i=1}^n x_i z_i} \prod_{i=1}^n a_i^{x_i}}$$

$$= (g^{\prod_{i=1}^n a_i^{x_i}})^{r^{\langle x, z \rangle}} = (F.\mathsf{Eval}(\mathsf{msk}, x))^{r^{\langle x, z \rangle}}$$

$$= F.\mathsf{Eval}(\mathsf{msk}, x) \text{ iff } \langle x, z \rangle = 0 \ .$$

Furthermore, when the adversary makes no query to the evaluation oracle, it can be shown that the pseudorandomness of the above construction on a challenge input x where $\langle x, z \rangle \neq 0$ holds as long as $g^{r^{\langle x, z \rangle}}$ looks random for a uniformly random $r \in \mathbb{Z}_p^*$. Indeed, the constrained key owner can compute $r^{\langle x, z \rangle} \prod_{i=1}^{n} a_i^{x_i}$ and knows g, x, z. The actual evaluation is $g^{\prod_{i=1}^{n} a_i^{x_i}}$ and the constrained key reveals no information about r since a_i are uniformly random in $\mathbb{Z}_p^*$.

Before we move on, we make three observations:

- The algorithm $F.\mathsf{CEval}$ does not need to know z. Hence, our CPRF for inner products is also constraint-hiding.
- We described the construction for an input and a constrain $x, z \in \{0, 1\}^n$ for simplicity, and to match with the original construction of Naor and Reingold. However, the construction extends immediately to the setting where $x, z \in [\pm B]^n$, where B is some polynomial-size bound (the security of the original Naor-Reingold construction for inputs of this form was shown in [1] to reduce to a variant of the Diffie-Hellman assumption). We then have $|\langle x, z \rangle| \leq n \cdot B^2$ and assuming $n \cdot B^2 \ll q$, the inner product is computed over the integers.
- Eventually, we also consider a straightforward modification of the construction where both parties apply an arbitrary public preprocessing function $\mathsf{p}(\cdot)$ on the input x before feeding it into Eval or CEval. This allows to force the input x to have a specific format.

From No-Evaluation Security to Full Security. While the above construction can be attacked if the adversary makes an evaluation query, we recall that any no-evaluation secure CPRF can be turned into an adaptively secure CPRF (with any number of evaluation queries) in the random oracle model by hashing the output, as in [11]. Hence, proving no-evaluation security suffices for our goal.

From Inner Product to Inner Product Membership. We just turned the Naor-Reingold PRF into a CPRF, but it is restricted so far to a small class of functions (inner product predicates) which is of course too limited to instantiate our template PCF construction from Sect. 2.1. Our next observation is that this class can be significantly expanded by adding elements of the form $g^{r^{-t}}$ to the constrained key to help the evaluator cancel out some r^t terms. Indeed, if the evaluator uses $g^{r^{-t}}$ instead of g as the basis for exponentiation, the computation of $F.\mathsf{CEval}(\mathsf{ck}, x)$ becomes

$$F.\mathsf{CEval}(\mathsf{ck}, x) = (g^{r^{-t}})^{r^{\langle x, z \rangle} \cdot \prod_{i=1}^{n}(r^{z_i} \cdot a_i)^{x_i}}$$
$$= (g^{r^{\langle x, z \rangle - t}})^{\prod_{i=1}^{n}(r^{z_i} \cdot a_i)^{x_i}}$$
$$= (F.\mathsf{Eval}(\mathsf{msk}, x))^{r^{\langle x, z \rangle - t}} ,$$

which is the same as $F.\mathsf{Eval}(\mathsf{msk}, x)$ iff $t = \langle x, z \rangle$. What makes this observation particularly powerful is that the evaluator can be given terms of the form $g^{r^{-t}}$ *for multiple values of* t, and choose upon evaluation the term $g^{r^{-t}}$ for $t = \langle x, z \rangle$.

This yields a CPRF for the class of predicates

$$C_{z,S} : x \to \begin{cases} 0 & \text{if } \langle x, z \rangle \in S \\ 1 & \text{otherwise} \end{cases}$$

where $S \subseteq \mathbb{Z}_{p-1}$ is a polynomial size subset. The full construction is given below:

- $F.\text{Constrain}(\text{msk}, z, S)$: sample $r \xleftarrow{\$} \mathbb{Z}_p^*$. For every $t \in S$, define $g_t \leftarrow g^{r^{-t}}$ and define $(\alpha_1, \cdots, \alpha_n) \leftarrow (r^{z_1} \cdot a_1, \cdots, r^{z_n} \cdot a_n)$. Output $\text{ck} = ((g_t)_{t \in S}, \alpha_1, \cdots, \alpha_n)$.
- $F.\text{CEval}(\text{ck}, x)$: on input $x = (x_1, \cdots, x_n) \in [\pm B]^n$, set $t \leftarrow \langle x, z \rangle$ and output $g_t^{\prod_{i=1}^n \alpha_i^{x_i}}$.

Note that our prior claim that the constrained key contains no information about r does not longer hold as it now contains $g^{r^{-t}}$ for all $t \in S$, hence no-evaluation security is no longer unconditional. We show that this construction is (no-evaluation) secure under a variant of the Diffie-Hellman assumption which we call *sparse power-DDH* assumption and which states that given $g^{r^{-t}}$ for various $t \in S$, it is infeasible to distinguish $g^{r^{-t}}$ for $t \notin S$ from uniformly random group elements.[2] The sparse power-DDH assumption is a static falsifiable assumption. It generalizes in a natural way the power-DDH assumption (which states that given g^{r^i} for $i = 1$ to n, it is infeasible to distinguish $g^{r^{n+1}}$ from random), and is easily proven to hold in the generic group model since all exponents are distinct univariate monomials (e.g., using [20, Corollary A.3], and observing that it is a special case of the uber-assumption family).

On IPM Predicates. The inner product membership predicate captures several predicates of interest. We already mentioned inner-product equality (in which case our CPRF is constraint-hiding), and it also captures inner-product *in*equality. Moreover, this class captures puncturing, which, to our knowledge, yields the first candidate puncturable pseudorandom function in the complexity class NC^1 (assuming that the hash function is instantiated with an NC^1 function).[3] Since puncturable PRFs have independent applications, for instance in the context of indistinguishability obfuscation (which is typically first built for NC^1 before being bootstrapped to P), we expect that this result could have other applications. Furthermore, the IPM predicates capture several variants of puncturing, such as puncturing a Hamming ball, and many more. Most importantly, and as we explain in the following section, this class of predicates captures several candidate weak pseudorandom functions from the literature, which makes it powerful enough to instantiate the PCF for OT correlation outlined in Sect. 2.1.

---

[2] By $t \notin S$, we mean $t \notin S$ but still $t \in \mathcal{R}$, for some small support $\mathcal{R}$ denoting the (polynomial-sized) range of possible values for the inner-product $\langle z, x \rangle$, e.g., $\mathcal{R} = \{-n \cdot B^2, \ldots, n \cdot B^2\}$ for $x, z \in [\pm B]^n$.

[3] It is not too hard to build a PPRF in NC^1 by following the blueprint of the GGM PRF [51] but using a λ-ary tree instead of a binary tree and instantiating the PRG with an NC^0 PRG with polynomial stretch. However, such constructions are inherently limited to superpolynomial-size domains, while our construction can handle subexponential-size domains.

2.3   Inner-Product Membership Weak Pseudorandom Functions

We observe that several known candidate weak PRFs can be expressed as IPM predicates. In this section, we provide a non-exhaustive list of such constructions. Notably, we show that the BIPSW [21] and the XOR-MAJ [9,50] candidate weak PRFs fall into this category and lead to efficient instantiations of our paradigm. We write IPM-wPRF to denote a weak PRF expressed as an IPM predicate.

The Learning-with-Rounding wPRF. Given a modulus q and a smaller modulus $q' \ll q$, the well-known candidate wPRF of [12] is given by $F_z(x) = \lfloor \langle x, z \rangle \rceil_{q'}$, where $x, z \in \mathbb{Z}_q^n$, and $\lfloor \cdot \rceil_{q'}$ denotes an appropriate procedure for rounding to an element of $\mathbb{Z}_{q'}$. This candidate was shown in [12] to be a secure wPRF under the standard LWE assumption, provided that q, q' are superpolynomial. This proof was further refined in [3] to show that a polynomial-size modulus suffices for the reduction. While the proof does not extend to the case $q' = 2$, no known efficient attack is known, and the learning-with-rounding (LWR) assumption is now widely conjectured to hold even outside of the regime where it reduces to LWE. When q is polynomial and $q' = 2$, we can define S as $S = \{s \in \mathbb{Z}_{n \cdot q^2} : \lfloor (s \bmod q) \rceil_2 = 0\}$ to rewrite this wPRF as an IPM-wPRF (with $|S| \approx n \cdot q^2/2$). Due to the q^2 overhead in the size of S, for standard choices of the modulus q, our construction with this candidate does not yield a very efficient instantiation. But, it forms a basis for our next candidate.

The BIPSW wPRF. In [21], the authors introduced several new low-complexity wPRF candidates, together with some preliminary analysis to back up the security claims. Five years later, these candidates have received some attention, both by cryptanalysts [30,58] and in the context of a range of applications, from secure computation to side-channel security [2,45,48]. As the authors observed, one of their candidates (that we denote as BIPSW) can be rephrased as an LWR-style wPRF: $F_z(x) = \lfloor \langle x, z \rangle \bmod 6 \rceil$, with $x, z \in \{0, 1\}^n$, and with the rounding function defined as $\lfloor s \rceil = 0$ if $(s \bmod 6) \in \{0, 1, 2\}$, and $\lfloor s \rceil = 1$ if $(s \bmod 6) \in \{3, 4, 5\}$. The authors initially suggested a key length $n = 384$ as a conservative choice for security. Several attacks were later shown, in [30] and very recently in [58], suggesting that the key length should be increased to $n = 770$. We note that the BIPSW candidate fits particularly well in our framework: it can be written as an IPM-wPRF by defining $S = \{s \leq n : \exists k \leq n/6, i \in \{0, 1, 2\}, s = 6k + i\}$. The size of S is $n/2$, which is as low as $|S| = 385$ for $n = 770$.

The Goldreich-Applebaum-Raykov wPRF. In [50], Goldreich suggested an approach for building one-way functions by evaluating a fixed low-arity predicate on fixed random small subsets of the input bits (*i.e.*, $f(x) = (P(x[S_1]), \cdots, P(x[S_m]))$, where P is a predicate and $S_1, \cdots, S_n$ are fixed random subsets, also $x[S_i]$ denotes the substring of the bits of x indexed by S_i). Later works suggested that for a suitable choice of P, these *random local functions* can also be conjectured to be a pseudorandom generator when $m > |x|$. The construction of Goldreich has ever since been featured extensively in cryptography, both by cryptanalysts [7–9,19,31,33,42,47,62–65,68,69,74,75,77] and in numerous cryptographic applications such as low-complexity cryptography, secure computation, obfuscation, and many more [4,6,10,27,56] (see [5] for a survey from 2015). In [10], Applebaum and Raykov showed how Goldreich's random local functions can also yield plausible candidate wPRFs for suitable choices of P, when $|S_i| = \Omega(\log n)$. We denote this candidate wPRF as Goldreich-Applebaum-Raykov(GAR) wPRF.

We outline how the GAR wPRF can be expressed as an IPM-wPRF. The core idea is to view the random input x as an *encoding* of a subset $S_x \subset [n]$ of size $|S_x| = \Omega(\log n)$, and to preprocess x using some fixed preprocessing function g such that $\langle g(x), z \rangle = z[S_x]$. To do so, we let $|x| = \log^2(n)$ and parse x as a $k = \Omega(\log(n))$-tuple of distinct indices $j_1, \cdots, j_k \in [n]$ by keeping only the distinct j's from the $\log(n)$ strings $j \in \{0,1\}^{\log(n)}$ (viewed as elements of $[n]$). Then, we let $g(x)$ be the length-n vector defined as follows: the vector $g(x)$ is 0 everywhere, except that it has the entry $2^{\ell-1}$ at position j_ℓ for $\ell = 1, \ldots, k$. Observe that with this encoding, computing $\langle g(x), z \rangle$ returns $\sum_{\ell=1}^{k} z_{j_\ell} \cdot 2^{\ell-1}$, which is exactly the integer whose binary representation encodes the subset S_x of the bits of z. Now, for any choice of $\log(n)$-ary predicate P, we define $S = \{s \in [2^k] : P(s) = 0\}$. Observe that checking whether $\langle g(x), z \rangle \in S$ is equivalent to computing $P(z[S_x])$, where S_x is the $\Omega(\log n)$-sized subset defined by x. Hence, up to the preprocessing of the input x (which is for free in our construction), the GAR wPRF can be expressed as an IPM-wPRF. As long as the arity of P is $k = O(\log(n))$, we have $|S| = O(2^k) = \mathsf{poly}(n)$.

This yields a generic construction that works for any choice of predicate with sufficiently low arity. Directly instantiating this construction does not yield a very competitive PCF. However, our next observation is that for the most standard and well-studied choices of predicate P, the generic construction can be considerably improved.

The XOR-MAJ wPRF. The previous construction works for arbitrary predicates P, provided that P takes at most $O(\log n)$ bits as input. In this section, we observe that when P is of the form $P(x_0, x_1) = \mathsf{SYM}_0(x_0) \oplus \mathsf{SYM}_1(x_1)$, where $\mathsf{SYM}_0, \mathsf{SYM}_1$ are arbitrary symmetric functions, then there exists an improved construction that handles predicates of *arbitrary* locality. This capture in particular the XOR-MAJ predicate, which computes the XOR between the parity of the x_0 input and the majority of the x_1 input. XOR-MAJ is probably the most common choice of predicate for the GAR wPRF, and its properties have been studied extensively [9,33,47,63,64,75,77].

We briefly outline how to express the GAR wPRF with the XOR-MAJ predicate as an IPM-wPRF (the generalization to other symmetric functions is immediate). Assume that the predicate is $P = \mathsf{XOR_k}\text{-}\mathsf{MAJ_\ell}$, which takes as input a $(k + \ell)$-bit subset z of the bits of the secret key, and outputs $\mathsf{XOR}(z_1, \cdots, z_k) \oplus \mathsf{MAJ}(z_{k+1}, \cdots, z_{k+\ell})$. Similarly to before, we parse a random input x as an encoding of two random disjoint subsets $(S_{0,x}, S_{1,x})$ of $[n]$, of size k and ℓ respectively. Then, we let $\mathsf{p}(x)$ denote the length-n vector with 1's at all entries indexed by $S_{1,x}$, value $\ell + 1$ at all entries indexed by $S_{0,x}$, and 0's everywhere else. Observe that this encodings yields

$$\langle \mathsf{p}(x), z \rangle = \mathsf{HW}((z_i)_{i \in S_{1,x}}) + (\ell + 1) \cdot \mathsf{HW}((z_i)_{i \in S_{0,x}}),$$

where $\mathsf{HW}(\cdot)$ denotes the Hamming weight. Furthermore, since $|S_{1,x}| = \ell$, every integer $\langle \mathsf{p}(x), z \rangle$ computed as above uniquely determines the pair $(\mathsf{HW}((z_i)_{i \in S_{1,x}}), \mathsf{HW}((z_i)_{i \in S_{0,x}})))$. In turn, symmetric functions such as XOR and MAJ are uniquely determined by the Hamming weight of their inputs (in particular, $\mathsf{XOR}(z)$ returns $\mathsf{HW}(z) \bmod 2$ and $\mathsf{MAJ}(z)$ returns 1 iff $\mathsf{HW}(z) > \ell/2$). Then, using the fact that $A \oplus B = 0$ iff $A = B$, we define S as follows:

$$S = \{s = s_1 + (\ell+1)s_0 \in [\ell + (\ell+1) \cdot k] \; : \; [\mathsf{HW}(s_1) \bmod 2] = [\mathsf{HW}(s_0) > \ell/2]\}.$$

Compared to the previous construction, this new construction is tailored to XOR-MAJ (or more generally to predicates of the form $P(x_0, x_1) = \mathsf{SYM}_0(x_0) \oplus \mathsf{SYM}_1(x_1)$[4].). However, for a predicate of locality $\ell + k$, the size of S scales as $O(\ell \cdot k)$, which is an exponential improvement over the $2^{\ell+k}$ cost of the generic construction. While the GAR wPRF is typically considered in the low-locality setting, our construction allows simultaneously relying on a particularly conservative parameter setting, using XOR-MAJ with locality $O(\sqrt{n})$ (in this parameter regime, the GAR wPRF is generally conjectured to provide subexponential security $2^{O(\sqrt{n})}$), and keeping S to a small size $|S| = O(n)$. Together with the BIPSW wPRF candidate, this instantiation yields the most efficient concrete instantiations of our framework. To give a single data point, using the state-of-the-art cryptanalysis on Goldreich-style local wPRFs, we can set the key length n to 256 and use the $\mathsf{XOR}_{10}\text{-}\mathsf{MAJ}_{64}$ predicate to achieve 128 bits of security for up to 2^{40} queries to the wPRF, and have $|S| = 357$.

Other Candidates. Before moving on, we note that several other candidate wPRFs can be shown to fit in the IPM-wPRF framework: candidates based on sparse LPN or variable-density LPN [26], and the BFLK candidate $f_{A,B} : x \mapsto (\bigoplus_{i \in A} x_i) \oplus \mathsf{MAJ}((x_i)_{i \in B})$ from [17]. These candidates yield less competitive instantiations of our framework, and we do not discuss them further here. However, this suggests two interesting open questions for future work:

- Finding the best-possible IPM-wPRF (*i.e.* the one achieving the best possible tradeoffs between security and key size + size of S), and
- All candidates considered in this work are *weak* PRFs. Whether there exists *strong* IPM-PRFs remains an interesting open question (though we note that any IPM-wPRF can be generically upgraded to a strong PRF when instantiating the preprocessing function p with a random oracle).

2.4 Optimizations

The above framework can be largely improved by various optimizations. In this section, we sketch several of them that allow improving the performance of our PCF. We provide a detailed description of the optimizations in the full version.

---

[4] Even more generally, the construction can be adapted to handle the XOR of any number N of symmetric predicates with respective locality $\ell_1, \cdots, \ell_N$, with $|S| = O(\prod_{i=1}^{N} \ell_i)$.

Halving the Key Size. When we instantiate the framework of Sect. 2.1 using our Naor-Reingold CPRF, the sender key consists of two master secret keys $(g, a_1, \cdots, a_n)$ and $(h, a'_1, \cdots, a'_n)$, and the receiver key for the predicate $F_{z,S} : x \mapsto \langle x, z \rangle \in_? S$ consists of $(r^{z_i} \cdot a_i)_{i \in [n]}, ((r')^{z_i} \cdot a'_i)_{i \in [n]}, (g^{r^{-t}})_{t \in S}$, and $(h^{(r')^{-t}})_{t \in [\pm n \cdot B^2] \setminus S}$ (where r, r' are random elements of $\mathbb{Z}_p^*$ and B is a bound on the entries of x, z). Thanks to the random self-reducibility of DDH, the two master secret keys can use the same elements $(a_1, \cdots, a_n)$ provided that they use different bases g, h. For the same reason, we can also set $r = r'$ without any security loss. This reduces the sender key size by a factor two, and significantly compresses the receiver key size as well. Concretely, we have:

- Sender key: $(g, h, a_1, \cdots, a_n)$,
- Receiver key: $(r^{z_i} \cdot a_i)_{i \le n}, (g_t)_{t \in [\pm n \cdot B^2]}$,

where $g_t \leftarrow g^{r^{-t}}$ if $t \in S$, and $g_t \leftarrow h^{r^{-t}}$ if $t \in [\pm n \cdot B^2] \setminus S$. The resulting construction is secure under the same assumptions as the basic construction.

Reusing the g_t's. We observe that the value z (which relates to underlying PRF key used by the receiver) is known only to the receiver, while the set S is public (and relates to the definition of the PRF). In a multiparty setting where the sender wants to compute PCF keys with multiple receivers, we can exploit this observation to define the g_t's once for all, and pass them as common parameters to be used by all receivers. This requires adding two additional terms $(a_{0,j}, a'_{0,j})$ in the sender key for each receiver R_j, to re-randomize the bases g, h. That is, the sender now computes its pseudorandom OT messages as

$$s_{0,j}^x \leftarrow g^{a_{0,j}} \cdot \prod_{i=1}^n a_i^{x_i} \qquad\qquad s_{1,j}^x \leftarrow h^{a'_{0,j}} \cdot \prod_{i=1}^n (a'_i)^{x_i},$$

where $g^{a_{0,j}}$ and $h^{a'_{0,j}}$ play the role of fresh new bases for each receiver R_j (the receiver CEval has to be adapted accordingly). With this change, the g_t's can be viewed as public parameters (or as a "public key" associated to the sender).

Compressing the a_i's. When instantiating the group with a suitable elliptic curve, the size of the a_i's is typically 2λ bits (to achieve λ bits of security against generic discrete log attacks). To further reduce the key size, the a_i's can be generated from a pseudorandom generator in a two-step fashion: first, the sender receives a λ-bit seed seed and computes $(g, h, \mathsf{seed}_1, \cdots, \mathsf{seed}_n) \leftarrow \mathsf{PRG}(\mathsf{seed})$, where $\mathsf{PRG} : \{0,1\}^\lambda \mapsto \{0,1\}^{(4+n)\cdot\lambda}$ (each seed_i is in $\{0,1\}^\lambda$). Second, define $a_i \leftarrow \mathsf{PRG}'(\mathsf{seed}_i)$, where $\mathsf{PRG}' : \{0,1\}^\lambda \mapsto \{0,1\}^{2\lambda}$. This approach enables compressing both the sender key and the receiver key:

- The sender key is now simply the λ-bit seed seed.
- The receiver key is still $(r^{z_i} \cdot a_i)_{i \le n}$ (together with the public g_t terms), except that whenever $z_i = 0$, we have $r^{z_i} \cdot a_i = a_i$, which we can send in compressed form by replacing it with seed_i, which is twice smaller. When z_i is a bitstring (which is the case for the BIPSW and XOR-MAJ wPRFs), this reduces the size of about half of the $r^{z_i} \cdot a_i$ to that of seed_i, resulting in a 25% reduction of the key length.

Exploiting the Structure in S. Assume that S contains all integers s (from some bounded range $\{0, \cdots, m \cdot R\}$) such that $(s \bmod m) < m/2$, where m is some fixed value; we say that S is m-antiperiodic. Then we *almost* have:

$$s \notin S \iff (s - m) \in S \ ,$$

where the *almost* stems from the fact that the equivalence breaks down at the extremities: for example, $s = m/2 + 1 \notin S$, yet $s - m \notin S$ because $s - m$ is outside of the bounded range $\{0, \cdots, m \cdot R\}$. Nevertheless, we can recover the equivalence by slightly extending S into $S' = S \cup \{-m/2, \cdots, -1\}$ (the equivalence becomes: for every $s \in \{0, \cdots, R \cdot m\}$, $s \notin S' \iff (s - m) \in S'$).

In this case, we observe that it is not necessary to include in the receiver key both $(g_t)_{t \in S}$ and $(g_t)_{t \notin S}$. Indeed, as we are constraining before a key msk_0 with respect to the predicate "$\langle x, z \rangle \in S$", and a second key msk_1 with respect to the predicate "$\langle x, z \rangle \notin S$", we can then rewrite the second constraint as "$\langle x, z \rangle - m \in S$". Concretely, we now deal a single key msk to the sender, but we add an $(n+1)$-th element a_{n+1} to act as a *shift*. The keys become:

- Sender key: $\mathsf{msk} = (g, a_1, \cdots, a_n, a_{n+1})$
- Receiver key: $\mathsf{ck} = (g, r^{z_1} \cdot a_1, \cdots, r^{z_n} \cdot a_n, r^{-m} \cdot a_{n+1}), (g_t)_{t \in S'}$.

Given msk, on input x the sender computes their two OT inputs as $s_b \leftarrow F.\mathsf{Eval}(\mathsf{msk}, x|b)$ for $b = 0, 1$. That is, we have:

$$s_b \leftarrow g^{\prod_{i=1}^{n} a_i^{x_i} \cdot a_{n+1}^b} \text{ for } b = 0, 1.$$

Now, because of the term $r^{-m} \cdot a_{n+1}$ in the key of the receiver, for every string x, there is only a single $b \in \{0, 1\}$ such that $\langle x|b, z| - m \rangle \in S$, i.e. such that $\langle x, z \rangle - b \cdot m \in S'$. Compared to the previous construction, this (almost) halves the number of group elements g_t in the receiver key, going from $m \cdot R$ to $(m/2) \cdot (R+1)$.

The BIPSW wPRF and the XOR-MAJ wPRF satisfy this property: the set S is m-antiperiodic with $m = 6$ for BIPSW, and $m = 49$ for our parameter choice with XOR-MAJ. Hence, they can benefit from this optimization.

2.5   Final PCF Construction

We are now fully equipped to describe our final PCF construction. Concrete parameters for both instantiations based on the BIPSW and the XOR-MAJ are provided in the next section. Let the input domain be $\{0, 1\}^\ell$. Let F be an IPM-wPRF with preprocessing function $\mathsf{p} : \{0, 1\}^\ell \mapsto [0, B]^n$ (for some polynomial bound B), key space $\{0, 1\}^n$ and associated set S; that is, given a key $z \xleftarrow{\$} \{0, 1\}^n$ and an input $x \in \{0, 1\}^\ell$, $F_z(x)$ outputs 1 iff $\langle \mathsf{p}(x), z \rangle \in S$. We assume that S is m-antiperiodic for some integer m (*i.e.* $S = \{s \in \{0, \cdots, R\} : s \bmod m < m/2\}$ for some polynomial bound R). Define $S' \leftarrow S \cup \{-m/2, \cdots, -1\}$. Fix a family of cyclic groups $\mathbb{G} = \mathbb{G}(\lambda)$ of order $p = p(\lambda)$. Let $G_0 : \{0, 1\}^\lambda \mapsto \mathbb{Z}_p^* \times \{0, 1\}^{n \cdot \lambda}$, $G_1 : \{0, 1\}^\lambda \mapsto \mathbb{Z}_p^*$, and $G_2 : \{0, 1\}^\lambda \mapsto \{0, 1\}^n$ be three pseudorandom generators. Let $H : \mathbb{G} \mapsto \{0, 1\}^\lambda$ be a hash function.

- PCF.Gen(1^λ) : sample seed $\overset{\$}{\leftarrow} \{0,1\}^\lambda$. let $(g, \mathsf{seed}_1, \cdots, \mathsf{seed}_{n+1}) \leftarrow G_0(\mathsf{seed})$ and $a_i \leftarrow \mathbb{G}_1(\mathsf{seed}_i)$ for $i = 1$ to $n + 1$. Sample $\mathsf{seed}_z \in \{0,1\}^\lambda$, $r \overset{\$}{\leftarrow} \mathbb{Z}_p^*$, and let $z \leftarrow G_2(\mathsf{seed}_z)$. For $i = 1$ to n, set $v_i \leftarrow \mathsf{seed}_i$ if $z_i = 0$, and $v_i \leftarrow r \cdot a_i$ otherwise. Set $v_{n+1} \overset{\$}{\leftarrow} r^{-m} \cdot a_{n+1}$. Define $g_t \leftarrow g^{r^{-t}}$ for every $t \in S'$. Output $k_0 \leftarrow \mathsf{seed}$ and $k_1 \leftarrow (\mathsf{seed}_z, v_1, \cdots, v_{n+1}, (g_t)_{t \in S'})$.
- PCF.Eval($0, k_0, x$) : recompute $(g, \mathsf{seed}_1, \cdots, \mathsf{seed}_{n+1}) \leftarrow G_0(k_0)$ and $a_i \leftarrow \mathbb{G}_1(\mathsf{seed}_i)$ for $i = 1$ to $n + 1$. Let $(y_1, \cdots, y_n) \leftarrow \mathsf{p}(x)$. Define

$$s_b \leftarrow H\left(g^{\prod_{i=1}^{n} a_i^{y_i} \cdot a_{n+1}^b}\right) \text{ for } b = 0, 1.$$

Output (s_0, s_1).
- PCF.Eval($1, k_1, x$) : parse k_1 as $(\mathsf{seed}_z, v_1, \cdots, v_{n+1}, (g_t)_{t \in S'})$. Let $(y_1, \cdots, y_n) \leftarrow \mathsf{p}(x)$. Recompute $z \leftarrow G_2(\mathsf{seed}_z)$. For $i = 1$ to $n+1$, set $\alpha_i \leftarrow \mathbb{G}_1(v_i)$ if $z_i = 0$ or $i = n+1$, and $\alpha_i \leftarrow v_i$ else. Let $b \leftarrow F_z(x)$ and $t \leftarrow \langle \mathsf{p}(x), z \rangle - b \cdot m$. Note that by definition, this means that $t \in S'$. Define

$$s_b \leftarrow H\left(g_t^{\prod_{i=1}^{n} \alpha_i^{y_i} \cdot \alpha_{n+1}^b}\right).$$

Output (b, s_b).

To state our main theorem, we define the sparse power-DDH assumption with respect to S'. For a group $\mathbb{G}_\lambda = \langle g \rangle$ of prime order p, the sparse power-DDH assumption with respect to S' over a support $[0, R]$ states that

$$\left(g, (g^{r \cdot a^i})_{i \in S'}, (g^{r \cdot a^i})_{i \in [0,R] \setminus S'}\right) \overset{c}{\approx} \left(g, (g^{r \cdot a^i})_{i \in S'}, (g^{t_i})_{i \in [0,R] \setminus S'}\right),$$

where $\overset{c}{\approx}$ denotes computational indistinguishability, $a, r \overset{\$}{\leftarrow} \mathbb{Z}_p^*$, and $t_i \overset{\$}{\leftarrow} \mathbb{Z}_p^*$ for all $i \in [0, R] \setminus S'$. Note that the bound R and the set S' are fixed parameters of the construction; hence, this assumption is a static, falsifiable variant of the power-DDH assumption used in several previous works (e.g. [11]). It can be shown to hold in the generic group model. We obtain the following theorem:

Theorem 1 (informal). *Assuming that the sparse power-DDH assumption with respect to S' holds, that (G_0, G_1, G_2) are pseudorandom generators, that F is a secure IPM-wPRF, and modeling H as a random oracle, then the above construction is a weak pseudorandom correlation function for the oblivious transfer correlation.*

Note that, in the random oracle model, the construction can be upgraded to a strong PCF by first hashing the inputs [26] and can also be proven secure under a weaker *search* version of the sparse power-DH assumption.

Distributed Key Generation. A useful feature of our PCF is that it admits a very efficient two-round distributed key generation algorithm. Concretely, and borrowing the notations from the construction above, the OT sender can simply generate seed and r themself, and send $(g_t)_{t \in S'}$ to the OT receiver directly, together with $v_{n+1} = r^{-m} \cdot a_i$. Then, the OT receiver samples seed_z. Eventually, to obtain the missing v_i's, observe that $v_i = \mathsf{seed}_i$ if $z_i = 0$, and $v_i = r \cdot a_i$ otherwise. Therefore, the sender and the receiver simply run n parallel instances of an oblivious transfer protocol, where the sender input pairs $(\mathsf{seed}_i, r \cdot a_i)$, and the receiver uses selection bits z_i. Security follows immediately from the security of the oblivious transfer protocol. Using a two-round OT protocol, the entire distributed key generation can be done in two rounds, and the communication boils down to n parallel OTs plus sending $|S'|$ group elements.

2.6   Concrete Parameters

With all the above optimizations in mind, we provide two concrete instantiations of PCF for the OT correlation, using either the BIPSW wPRF candidate, or the XOR-MAJ wPRF candidate.

Curve and Exponentiations. To estimate the runtime of our constructions, we rely mainly on the website zka.lc, which provides an extensive list of benchmarks for standard operations on various curves and over various platforms. According to the benchmarks of zka.lc, computing one exponentiation represents about $50\mu s$ of computation on one core of an AWS platform using curve25519 [16]. Note that in our construction, the sender must compute two exponentiations (to compute (s_0, s_1)) while the receiver computes a single exponentiation. However, the two sender exponentiations use a fixed basis g. Hence, the exponentiations can be significantly sped up with precomputation (in contrast, the receiver does an exponentiation with a basis g_t which is chosen based on the input). In our instantiations, exponentiations will generally dominate the runtime. Using more efficient curves, such as Microsoft's FourQ curve [32], the exponentiation time can be reduced to about $15\mu s$ on a Haswell architecture (note that the curve offers slightly less security compared to curve25519, about 122 bits instead of 128).

Parameters with BIPSW. For BIPSW, we used the state-of-the-art cryptanalysis from the works of [30,58], and set the key length to $n = 770$, which achieves 128 bits of security according to these attacks. We note that this parameter choice ignores some significant polynomial factors in the cost estimation (that come from a nearest neighbor search), hence our parameter choice takes a bit of margin. Furthermore, the recent attack of [58] has a much higher memory requirement compared to previous attack. On the other hand, we warn the reader that the BIPSW candidate is a relatively young wPRF and while a total break would be surprising at this point, the state of cryptanalysis is likely to improve over the years. With $n = 770$, S is 6-antiperiodic and we have $|S'| = 388$ With this parameter choice, the precomputable PCF has the following efficiency features:

- Key size: the receiver key size is 30.2 kB (and the sender key size is 16 Bytes). Out of that, 12.1 kB are public parameters $(g_t)_{t \in S'}$, which the sender can reuse with other receivers.

- Computation: computing s_b involves 385 multiplications over $\mathbb{Z}_p^*$, one exponentiation, and one hash. This translates to about 10k OT/s per core using curve25519 on an AWS platform, or about 15k OT/s per core using a curve such as FourQ on a Haswell architecture.

Parameters with XOR-MAJ. For the GAR wPRF instantiated with the XOR-MAJ predicate, we rely on the state-of-the-art cryptanalysis results from [9,33,74,77]. Specifically, according to Table 1 of [74], for a candidate to achieve λ bits of security with a key of length $n = \lambda^\delta$ and a bound n^{1+e} on the number of queries, the underlying predicate P must have

- rational degree at least $\frac{\delta}{\delta-1} \cdot e + 1$, and
- resiliency at least $2e + 1$.

A k-variable Boolean function P has rational degree d if it is the smallest integer for which there exist degree d polynomials g and h, not both zero, such that $P \cdot g = h$.[5] A k-variate boolean function is t-resilient if it has no nontrivial correlation with any linear combination of at most t of its inputs. We note that Table 1 of [74] ignores the guess-and-decode attack of [77], because their attack does not have a closed-form formula. However, Both the guess-and-determine attack of [33] and the guess-and-decode attack of [77] are specifically targeted at predicates with a very small locality (the papers consider localities from 5 to 8), and their complexity scales very poorly for predicates with a larger locality. As we will see shortly, our candidates have considerably higher locality (e.g. 74 in our main instantiation) and after selecting them, we verified individually that they yield concrete instances which are (way) out of reach of the guess-and-determine and the guess-and-decode attacks. In the following, we therefore use the two criteria above to select our candidates.

The algebraic immunity and resiliency of the XOR-MAJ predicate have been studied in several papers. To match the above two constraints, it suffices to use the $\mathsf{XOR}_{\ell_1}\text{-}\mathsf{MAJ}_{\ell_2}$ predicate with $\ell_1 = 2 \cdot (e+1)$ and $\ell_2 = 2\delta e/(\delta-1)$. We outline below a concrete choice of parameters for illustration: set $\delta = 1.143$. This yields $\delta/(\delta-1) = 8$ and $n = \lambda^\delta = 256$ using $\lambda = 128$. We get $\ell_2 = 16e$, and $|S'| = 16e^2 + 33e + 2$. Setting $e = 4$, the parties can generate up to $n^{1+e} = 2^{40}$ pseudorandom OTs and $|S'| = 390$. With this parameter choice, the precomputable PCF has the following efficiency features:

- Key size: the receiver key size is 18 kB (and the sender key size is 16 Bytes). Out of that, 12.2 kB are public parameters $(g_t)_{t \in S'}$, which the sender can reuse with other receivers.
- Computation: computing s_b involves 74 multiplications over $\mathbb{Z}_p^*$, one exponentiation, and one hash. This translates to about 15k OT/s per core using curve25519 on an AWS platform, or about 40k OT/s per core using a curve such as FourQ on a Haswell architecture.

---

[5] Table 1 of [74] mentions only the degree of the predicate, but strengthening the requirement to the rational degree is known to be necessary [9,47].

Note that other choices of parameters can yield different trade-offs, such as achieving slightly smaller key size, slightly more OTs, or slightly less computation. For example, using $\delta = 1.2858$ yields $n = 512$, $|S'| = 222$, a slightly larger key size 18.9 kB, 46 multiplications instead of 74, and a bound of 2^{45} on the target number of OTs.

2.7 Public Key PCF

We finally describe a *public key PCF*. Informally, a public key PCF allows users to generate a pair of public/secret keys, and then to broadcast their public key using a single message, while storing their secret key locally. Then, any pair of users can *non-interactively* obtain a PCF key pair (k_0, k_1) by combining their secret key and the other party's public key.

While the distributed key generation protocol described in Sect. 2.5 is particularly efficient, it requires two rounds of interaction. The protocol we now describe uses a *single* round of interaction. A major advantage of such protocol is that they enable n parties over a network to execute $\Omega(n^2)$ pairwise PCF key generations (to set up an OT channel between each pair of parties) using only $O(n)$ communication in total (this is similar to how non-interactive key exchange enable n^2 pairs of parties to agree on shared keys using $O(n)$ communication).

A Simple Construction. In our interactive protocol, sending $(g_t)_{t \in S'}$ does not require interaction: the interaction stems entirely from the OTs. We start with a protocol that replaces the two-round OT with the non-interactive OT protocol of Bellare and Micali [15]. The objective is, for the sender with input r, and the receiver with input z_i, to distributively generate keys $a_i \in \mathbb{Z}_p^*$ and $\alpha_i = r^{z_i} \cdot a_i \in \mathbb{Z}_p^*$ respectively. These values can be viewed as multiplicative shares over $\mathbb{Z}_p^*$ of r^{z_i} (up to inverting a_i locally). We observe that if DDH holds over (a suitable subgroup of) $\mathbb{Z}_p^*$, such multiplicative shares can be directly obtained via the Bellare-Micali protocol. Concretely, let $\mathbb{G}'$ be a suitable cyclic subgroup of $\mathbb{Z}_p^*$ where DDH is conjectured to hold, and let (G, H) be two random generators of $\mathbb{G}'$, and let $r \in \mathbb{G}'$. The protocol simply consists in having the sender send an ElGamal encryption of r, while the receiver sends a Pedersen commitment to z_i:

- **Sender to receiver:** pick a random coin ρ, and sends the ElGamal ciphertext $(C_0, C_1) \leftarrow (G^\rho, H^\rho \cdot r)$.
- **Receiver to sender:** pick n random coins $(\theta_1, \cdots, \theta_n)$ and send the Pedersen commitments $(H_1, \cdots, H_n) \leftarrow (H^{z_i} \cdot G^{\theta_i})_{i \leq n}$.
- **Output:** for $i = 1$ to n, the sender outputs $a_i \leftarrow H_i^\rho$, and the receiver outputs $\alpha_i \leftarrow C_1^{z_i} \cdot C_0^{\theta_i}$.

Observe that $\alpha_i = C_1^{z_i} \cdot C_0^{\theta_i} = G^{\rho \theta_i} \cdot H^{\rho z_i} r^{z_i} = a_i \cdot r^{z_i}$. Furthermore, r is computationally indistinguishable from a random element of $\mathbb{G}'$ under the DDH assumption over $\mathbb{G}'$, and the protocol statistically hides z_i.

A first downside of this protocol is that we cannot set $\mathbb{Z}_p^* = \mathbb{G}'$, since DDH is easy over $\mathbb{Z}_p^*$ (it can be broken by computing the Legendre symbol). However, assuming that $p = 2q + 1$ is a safe prime (q is prime), we can set $\mathbb{G}'$ to be the subgroup QR_p of quadratic residues modulo p, where DDH is widely conjectured to hold (for a sufficiently large p). This implies that the protocol generates a (pseudo)random *square* r, instead of a random element of $\mathbb{Z}_p^*$. This does not harm the security of the CPRF but changes slightly the underlying sparse power-DDH variant: using r of the form w^2 for a (pseudo)random element w when computing $g_t \leftarrow g^{r^{-t}} = g^{w^{-2t}}$ for $t \in S'$ amounts exactly to relying on the sparse power-DDH assumption with respect to the set $2 \cdot S' = \{2 \cdot t : t \in S'\}$.

A more concerning downside is the size of p: due to subexponential-time algorithms for discrete logarithm over finite fields, p should be taken much larger than 256 bits, at the very least 1024 bits. This forces the group $\mathbb{G}$, over which we instantiate our PCF, to have order $p \geq 2^{1024}$, which considerably harms efficiency (both for key size and computation), and prevents us in particular to rely on efficient 256-bit elliptic curves. We circumvent this issue by setting p to a smaller value (e.g. a 256-bit prime), and relying on Paillier encryption.

A More Efficient Variant. Assume for simplicity that $p = 2q+1$ for a prime q (the construction also works fine with any large prime factor of $p-1$). At a high level, we perform the Bellare-Micali-style non-interactive protocol over a Paillier group (similarly as in [70]) followed by a post-processing operation which:

- converts the multiplicative shares over the Paillier group to subtractive shares modulo N (where N is an RSA modulus) using a distributed discrete log algorithm,
- converts the shares modulo N to shares modulo q using the fact that subtractive shares modulo N are with very high probability shares over $\mathbb{Z}$ when the shared value is sufficiently smaller than the modulus,
- converts the additive shares modulo q into multiplicative shares over $\mathbb{Z}_p^*$ via exponentiation.

Let QR_p denote the set of quadratic residues modulo p, which has order q. Let G be a basis of QR_p. Instead of sampling $r \xleftarrow{\$} \mathsf{QR}_p$ directly, Alice samples $\Delta \xleftarrow{\$} \mathbb{Z}_q$ and sets $r \leftarrow G^\Delta \bmod p$ (this yields the same distribution). Let N be a public RSA modulus, whose factorization is unknown to both parties. The protocol proceeds almost as the previous protocol, except that Alice sends a Paillier-ElGamal encryption of Δ (viewed as an integer in $\{0, \cdots, q-1\}$) instead of an ElGamal encryption of r. Let $(\mathbf{G}, \mathbf{H})$ be two random elements of $\mathbb{Z}_{N^2}$. Our protocol borrows ideas from [70]. It builds upon a *distributed discrete logarithm* algorithm DDLOG over $\mathbb{Z}_{N^2}$, which has the following features: given respective multiplicative shares $(S^{\mathsf{send}}, S^{\mathsf{rec}})$ of a value $(1 + N)^m$ modulo N^2, the sender and the receiver can locally compute $v^{\mathsf{send}} \leftarrow \mathsf{DDLOG}(\mathsf{send}, S^{\mathsf{send}})$ and $v^{\mathsf{rec}} \leftarrow \mathsf{DDLOG}(\mathsf{rec}, S^{\mathsf{rec}})$ which form subtractive shares of m over $\mathbb{Z}_N$ (*i.e.* $v^{\mathsf{send}} - v^{\mathsf{rec}} = m \bmod N$). Furthermore, if $m < N/2^\lambda$ (when viewed as an integer in $\{0, \cdots, N-1\}$), it holds with probability at least $1 - 2^{-\lambda}$ that $v^{\mathsf{send}} - v^{\mathsf{rec}} = m$ *over the integers*. The work of [70] described an efficient implementation of DDLOG, whose cost boils down to one inversion and one multiplication over $\mathbb{Z}_N$. Given this procedure, our protocol proceeds as follows:

- **Sender to receiver:** pick a random coin ρ, and sends the Paillier-ElGamal ciphertext $(C_0, C_1) \leftarrow (\mathbf{G}^\rho \bmod N, \mathbf{H}^\rho \cdot (1+N)^\Delta \bmod N^2)$.
- **Receiver to sender:** pick n random coins $(\theta_1, \cdots, \theta_n)$ and send the Pedersen commitments $(H_1, \cdots, H_n) \leftarrow (\mathbf{H}^{z_i} \cdot \mathbf{G}^{\theta_i} \bmod N^2)_{i \leq n}$.
- **Output:** for $i = 1$ to n, the sender computes $\mathbf{G}_i^{\mathsf{send}} \leftarrow H_i^\rho$, and the receiver computes $\mathbf{G}_i^{\mathsf{rec}} \leftarrow C_1^{z_i} \cdot C_0^{\theta_i}$. Observe that

$$\mathbf{G}_i^{\mathsf{rec}} = C_1^{z_i} \cdot C_0^{\theta_i} = G^{\rho\theta_i} \cdot H^{\rho z_i}(1+N)^{\Delta \cdot z_i} = \mathbf{G}_i^{\mathsf{send}} \cdot (1+N)^{\Delta \cdot z_i} \bmod N^2.$$

Using DDLOG, both parties locally compute values $(v_i^{\mathsf{send}}, v_i^{\mathsf{rec}})$ such that $v_i^{\mathsf{send}} - v_i^{\mathsf{rec}} = b \cdot \Delta \bmod N$. Assuming that $q < N/2^\lambda$,[6] it holds that $v_i^{\mathsf{send}} - v_i^{\mathsf{rec}} = b \cdot \Delta$ over $\mathbb{Z}$ with probability at least $1 - 1/2^\lambda$. Eventually, the sender outputs $a_i \leftarrow G^{v_i^{\mathsf{send}}}$ and the receiver outputs $\alpha_i \leftarrow G^{v_i^{\mathsf{rec}}}$. Observe that

$$a_i = G^{v_i^{\mathsf{send}}} = G^{v_i^{\mathsf{rec}} + b \cdot \Delta} = \alpha_i \cdot r^b \bmod p.$$

A Balancing Optimization. In the above protocol, the size of the public keys is quite unbalanced: the sender public key contains a single Paillier-ElGamal ciphertext (in addition to $(g_t)_{t \in S'}$), while the receiver public key contains n Pedersen commitments over $\mathbb{Z}_{N^2}$ (where n is the wPRF key length, e.g. $n = 256$ for our XOR-MAJ candidate, or $n = 770$ for our BIPSW candidate). We now describe an optimization which reduces the receiver key size by a factor k, at the cost of increasing the Paillier-ElGamal ciphertext by a factor k^2. Taking $k = O(n^{1/3})$, this yields a variant in which both public keys contain $O(n^{2/3})$ elements of $\mathbb{Z}_{N^2}$. We note that our balancing optimization also applies to the public key PCF of [70], thus enables reducing their public key size to $O(n^{2/3})$.

The main idea of the optimization is to compress the receiver public key by replacing the Pedersen commitments with a multi-Pedersen commitment. Fix a compression parameter k (which we assume to divide n for simplicity) and public random elements $(\mathbf{G}, \mathbf{H}_1, \cdots, \mathbf{H}_k) \in \mathbb{Z}_{N^2}^{k+1}$. We let the sender commits to z by batches of k values z_i at once, as follows:

- **Receiver to sender:** pick n/k random coins $(\theta_1, \cdots, \theta_{n/k})$ and send the Pedersen commitments $(H_1, \cdots, H_{n/k}) \leftarrow (\mathbf{G}^{\theta_{i+1}} \cdot \prod_{j=1}^k \mathbf{H}_j^{z_{j+k \cdot i}} \bmod N^2)_{0 \leq i < n/k}$.

Suppose the parties want to retrieve multiplicative shares of $(1+N)^{\Delta \cdot z_i} \bmod N^2$. The main observation is that this can be done using the randomness-reuse variant of Paillier-ElGamal, putting $(1 + N)^\Delta$ in the first "slot": the sender picks a random coin ρ_1 and computes

$$(C_0, (C_1^j)_{j \leq k}) \leftarrow (\mathbf{G}^{\rho_1} \bmod N, \mathbf{H}_1^{\rho_1} \cdot (1+N)^\Delta, \mathbf{H}_2^{\rho_1}, \cdots, \mathbf{H}_k^{\rho_1} \bmod N^2).$$

---

[6] In practice, we take $\log q = 256$ and $\log N = 3072$.

Then, given this extended ciphertext and $H_1 = \mathbf{G}^{\theta_1} \cdot \prod_{j=1}^{k} \mathbf{H}_j^{z_j} \bmod N^2$, the parties retrieve multiplicative shares of $(1 + N)^{\Delta \cdot z_1}$ by computing

$$\mathbf{G}_1^{\text{send}} \leftarrow H_1^{\rho_1}, \qquad\qquad \mathbf{G}_1^{\text{rec}} \leftarrow C_0^{\theta_1} \cdot \prod_{j \leq k} (C_1^j)^{z_j}.$$

The above only yields shares of $(1 + N)^{\Delta \cdot z_1}$. To extract shares of $(1 + N)^{\Delta \cdot z_j}$ for $j = 2, \cdots, k$, the sender must proceed similarly as above, using extended Paillier-ElGamal ciphertexts, but this time placing $(1 + N)^{\Delta}$ in the j-th slot. In total, the sender computes k length-$(k + 1)$ extended ciphertexts, for a total of k elements of $\mathbb{Z}_N$ and k^2 elements of $\mathbb{Z}_{N^2}$ (these $k + k^2$ elements can be reused across all n/k batches). The full sender public key is given below:

- **Sender to receiver:** pick random coins ρ_j for $j = 1$ to k, and constructs the extended Paillier-ElGamal ciphertexts as follows for $j = 1$ to k:

$$C_0^j \leftarrow \mathbf{G}^{\rho_j} \bmod N$$
$$(C_1^{j,1} \cdots, C_1^{j,k}) \leftarrow (\mathbf{H}_1^{\rho_j}, \cdots, \mathbf{H}_j^{\rho_j} \cdot (1 + N)^{\Delta}, \cdots, \mathbf{H}_k^{\rho_j}) \bmod N^2$$

Efficiency. Without the balancing optimization, sender's public key consists of $|S'|$ elements of $\mathbb{G}$, one element of $\mathbb{Z}_N$, and one element of $\mathbb{Z}_{N^2}$, and receiver's public key consists of n elements of $\mathbb{Z}_{N^2}$. To provide concrete estimates, we use our XOR-MAJ parameter set with $n = 256$ and $|S'| = 390$. We set $\lambda = 128$, $\log |\mathbb{G}| = 2\lambda$, and $\log N = 3072$. With these parameters, the sender public key size is 13.3 kB, and the receiver public key size is 192 kB. Using the balancing optimization, the public key of the sender consists in $|S'|$ elements of $\mathbb{G}$, k element of $\mathbb{Z}_N$, and k^2 element of $\mathbb{Z}_{N^2}$, and the public key of the receiver consists in n/k elements of $\mathbb{Z}_{N^2}$. With the XOR-MAJ parameter set and using $k = 5$, the sender key increases to 32.8 kB while the receiver key is reduced to 38.4 kB.

Regarding computation, the cost of deriving the PCF keys from the public and secret keys is dominated by $n + 1$ exponentiations modulo N^2 and n exponentiations modulo p for the sender, and $2n$ exponentiations modulo N^2 and n exponentiations modulo p for the receiver. Using the balancing optimization, the number of exponentiations modulo N^2 increases to $n + k^2$ for the sender, and decreases to $n \cdot (1 + 1/k)$ for the receiver. Using $n = 256$ and $k = 5$, this translates to respectively 281 and 307 exponentiations over $\mathbb{Z}_{N^2}$.

Using $\log N = 3072$, an exponentiation modulo N^2 takes of the order of 5ms on one core a standard laptop, which translates to $1 \sim 2$ seconds of computation (note that this is a rough back-of-the-envelope estimation, true estimates may vary). Observe that this can be easily sped up using multiple cores, and that this is a one-time preprocessing phase to generate the shared PCF keys. After generating the PCF keys once, the parties can directly start generating OT correlations. Also, the computational efficiency can be significantly improved by sampling ρ and the θ_i's as 256-bit integers. This improves computation by one to two orders of magnitude, at the (reasonable) cost of having to assume the security of the small-exponent indistinguishability assumption (see e.g. [29,37] for discussions on this assumption and relations to other assumptions).

2.8   Application: A Simple Reusable DV-NIZK Reusable

As a final contribution, we provide a way to use our PK-PCF in order to construct *reusable* DV-NIZKs from three ingredients: (1) A Σ-protocol [40] with 1-bit challenges for an NP-complete language $\mathcal{L}$, for example Blum's protocol for graph Hamiltonicity [18], (2) a public key PCF for OT correlation where the key evaluation of each party can be *silently* obtained from their own secret key and public key of the other, and (3) a *non-reusable* DV-NIZK with computational adaptive soundness knowledge and adaptive zero-knowledge properties. Note that this last ingredient can be constructed from public-key encryption and λ invocations of Σ-protocol [71].

The main idea behind our construction is the following. The designated verifier samples a PCF key pair $(\mathsf{sk}_V, \mathsf{pk}_V)$ and outputs a CRS containing their public key. A prover with statement x and witness w can then sample their own PCF key pair $(\mathsf{sk}_P, \mathsf{pk}_P)$ to produce a shared evaluation key with the designated prover. It then runs the Σ-protocol by computing a first message a. The challenge being binary, there are 2 possible third message for a transcript starting with a. We let z_b the third message for challenge $b \in \{0,1\}$. Doing this λ-times lead to 2λ triplets $(a_i, b, z_{i,b})_{i \in [\lambda], b \in \{0,1\}}$. The prover then uses their PCF evaluation key to compute 2λ pseudorandom masks $r_{i,b}$ by evaluating the PCF on input $x|i|b$ (or $H(x|i|b)$ if the PCF is only weakly-secure). The prover finally outputs $\mathsf{pk}_P, (a_i, z_{i,0} \oplus r_{i,0}, z_{i,1} \oplus r_{i,1})$ as their proof.

The correctness of the PCF and Σ-protocol guarantee that the designated verifier can recover 1 mask out of each pair $(r_{i,0}, r_{i,1})$ and then can verify λ-transcripts, while security guarantees that the prover cannot predict which of the two is recovered by the verifier and that the non-revealed $r_{i,b}$ is pseudorandom, therefore providing soundness and zero-knowledge. A minor issue remains: one needs to prevent the prover to sample maliciously their PCF key pair such that it can predict the challenge bit. We show that it is sufficient to require the prover to additionally provide a proof (using a non-reusable DV-NIZK) that their PCF public key was generated from a honest execution of the PCF key generation algorithm (with possibly bad randomness).

3   Preliminaries

We use λ to denote the security parameter. For a natural integer $n \in \mathbb{N}$, the set $\{1, \ldots, n\}$ is denoted by $[n]$. We mostly use bold lowercase letters (e.g., $\mathbf{r}$) to denote vectors. For a finite set S, we write $x \xleftarrow{\$} S$ to denote that x is sampled uniformly at random from S. For an algorithm $\mathcal{A}$, we denote by $y \leftarrow \mathcal{A}(x)$ the output y after running $\mathcal{A}$ on input x. We consider GenPar as a probabilistic polynomial-time (PPT) algorithm that on input 1^λ for $\lambda \in \mathbb{N}$, outputs $(\mathbb{G}, g, p)$, where $\mathbb{G}$ is a cyclic group of prime order p generated by g.

We assume familiarity with the following notions, and refer to the full version of our paper for definitions: Pseudorandom Functions (PRF), Constrained Pseudorandom Functions (CPRF), and Pseudorandom Correlation Functions (PCF).

4   Constraining the Naor-Reingold PRF

In this section, we provide an overview of how we obtain a constrained PRF in the ROM from the Naor-Reingold PRF for the class of inner-product membership constraints, defined below. We refer the reader to the full version of our paper for more details and further optimizations of our construction.

We define the class of inner-product membership (IPM) constraints as $\mathsf{IPM} = \{C_{\mathbf{z}}^S \mid \mathbf{z} \in \mathcal{R}^n, S \subseteq \mathcal{I}\}$, for some sets $\mathcal{R}$ and $\mathcal{I}$, and $n > 0$, where $C_{\mathbf{z}}^S : \mathcal{R}^n \to \{0,1\}$ is defined as $C_{\mathbf{z}}^S(\mathbf{x}) = 0$ iff $\langle \mathbf{z}, \mathbf{x} \rangle \in S$ for an input $\mathbf{x} \in \mathcal{R}^n$. In the following construction, we only consider binary inputs, i.e., $\mathcal{R} = \{0,1\}$.

In Fig. 1, we describe our construction for constraining the Naor-Reingold PRF for the class of inner-product membership constraints.

Naor-Reingold CPRF for IPM (Binary Inputs)

Requires:

- p is a safe prime, i.e., $p = 2q + 1$ for some prime q.
- The input and constraint space is $\{0,1\}^n$.
- The inner-product space is $\mathcal{I} = \{0,1,\ldots,n\}$.

CPRF.KeyGen(1^λ):

- Run $(\mathbb{G}, g, p) \xleftarrow{\$} \mathsf{GenPar}(1^\lambda)$.
- Sample $\mathbf{a} = (a_0, \ldots, a_n) \xleftarrow{\$} \mathbb{Z}_p^{n+1}$.
- Set and output $\mathsf{msk} = \mathbf{a}$ and $\mathsf{pp} = (\mathbb{G}, g, p)$.

CPRF.Eval($\mathsf{pp}, \mathsf{msk}, \mathbf{x} \in \{0,1\}^n$):

- Parse $\mathsf{pp} = (\mathbb{G}, g, p)$ and $\mathsf{msk} = \mathbf{a}$.
- Output $y = g^{a_0 \cdot \prod_{i=1}^n a_i^{x_i}}$.

CPRF.Constrain($\mathsf{pp}, \mathsf{msk}, (\mathbf{z}, S)$):

- Parse $\mathsf{pp} = (\mathbb{G}, g, p)$, and $\mathsf{msk} = \mathbf{a}$.
- Sample $r \xleftarrow{\$} \mathbb{Z}_p^*$.
- For $i \in [n]$, set $\alpha_i := a_i \cdot r^{-z_i}$.
- Let $\boldsymbol{\alpha} = (\alpha_1, \ldots, \alpha_n)$.
- For $s \in S$, compute $g_s := g^{a_0 \cdot r^s}$.
- Output $\mathsf{ck} = (\boldsymbol{\alpha}, (g_s)_{s \in S}, \mathbf{z})$.

CPRF.CEval($\mathsf{pp}, \mathsf{ck}, \mathbf{x} \in \{0,1\}^n$):

- Parse $\mathsf{pp} = (\mathbb{G}, g, p)$, and $\mathsf{ck} = (\boldsymbol{\alpha}, (g_s)_{s \in S}, \mathbf{z})$.
- Let $s_{\mathbf{x}} := \langle \mathbf{z}, \mathbf{x} \rangle$.
- If $\langle \mathbf{z}, \mathbf{x} \rangle \in S$,

  output $y = (g_{s_{\mathbf{x}}})^{\prod_{i=1}^n \alpha_i^{x_i}}$.
- Otherwise, return $\perp$.

Fig. 1. Naor-Reingold CPRF for IPM constraints over binary inputs.

The above construction is no-evaluation secure under the sparse power-DDH assumption. Please see the full version of the paper for the definition of this assumption and the proof of the following theorem.

Theorem 2 (No-Evaluation Security). *Assuming the hardness of sparse power-DDH, the construction in Fig. 1 is a single-key, no-evaluation secure CPRF for the class of* IPM *constraints.*

Achieving Selective and Adaptive Security. As shown in [11], our no-evaluation secure CPRF for IPM constraints (Fig. 1) can be modified to achieve adaptive security using a hash function modeled as a random oracle. In order to do so, we can simply hash the output of our no-evaluation secure CPRF. Modeling the hash function as a random oracle, the output of the evaluation function is perfectly random as long as an adversary cannot efficiently find two values $\mathbf{x} \neq \mathbf{x}' \in \mathbb{Z}_p^n$ for which it holds that $s_\mathbf{x} = s_{\mathbf{x}'} \notin S$ and $u_\mathbf{x} = u_{\mathbf{x}'}$. Since each a_i (therefore each α_i) is a random element of $\mathbb{Z}_p$, the probability that $u_\mathbf{x} = u_{\mathbf{x}'}$ for any $\mathbf{x} \neq \mathbf{x}' \in \mathbb{Z}_p^n$ is $1/p$. Therefore, the probability of finding a collision is negligible. The proof of adaptive security proceeds in the same way as in [11] (Sect. 4.3).

5   Fast PCFs for OTs from Pseudorandomly Constrained PRFs

In this section, we briefly introduce a general framework for building programmable PCFs for OT correlations from CPRFs and this framework is presented Fig. 2. We refer to the full version of our paper for more results and details. In particular, a detailed discussion of the following topics is provided in the full version: We provide a general framework for building programmable PCFs from CPRFs supporting classes of "pseudorandom constraints". We then introduce a more specific template, which uses an "inner product membership (weak) PRF" to ensure these pseudorandom constraints can be expressed as "inner-product membership" constraints (which is the class tolerated by the Naor-Reingold CPRF Sect. 4). Next, we show that many weak PRFs based on LWR or random CSPs are inner product membership weak PRFs. Finally, we show that, when instantiated with the Naor-Reingold CPRF, our PCF admits a 2-round low-communication protocol for securely distributing the PCF key generation.

Definition 1 (1-in-2 Pseudorandomly Constrained PRF). *A weakly/ strongly pseudorandomly constrained PRF (PR-CPRF) is a constrained PRF with domain* $\{0,1\}^{n(\lambda)}$ *that supports the class of constraints of the form:*

$$\mathcal{C}_\lambda = \left\{ \begin{array}{l} C_k \colon \{0,1\}^{n(\lambda)} \to \{0,1\} \\ x_0 \ldots x_{n-1} \mapsto F_{in}(k, x_0 \ldots x_{n-2}) \oplus x_{n-1} \end{array} : k \in \mathcal{K}_\lambda \right\}$$

where $F_{in} \colon \mathcal{K}_\lambda \times \{0,1\}^{n(\lambda)-1} \to \{0,1\}$ *is a weak/strong pseudorandom function.*

PCF Precomputable PCF for OT from PR-CPRFs

Requires: PR-CPRF = (KeyGen, Eval, Constrain, CEval) is a weakly/strongly pseudorandomly constrained PRF with input space $\{0,1\}^{n(\lambda)+1}$ and characterized by inner weak/strong PRF $F_{\mathsf{in}} \colon \mathcal{K}_\lambda \times \{0,1\}^{n(\lambda)} \to \{0,1\}$.

PCF.Gen$_0(1^\lambda)$:

1. Run $(\mathsf{pp}, \mathsf{msk}) \xleftarrow{\$} \mathsf{KeyGen}(1^\lambda)$.
2. Set and output $k_0 = (\mathsf{pp}, \mathsf{msk})$.

PCF.Gen$_1(1^\lambda, k_0)$:

1. Sample $k \xleftarrow{\$} \mathcal{K}_\lambda$.
2. Parse $k_0 = (\mathsf{pp}, \mathsf{msk})$.
3. Run $\mathsf{ck} \leftarrow \mathsf{Constrain}(\mathsf{msk}, C_k)$.
4. Set and output $k_1 = (\mathsf{ck}, k, \mathsf{pp})$.

PCF.Eval$(1^\lambda, \sigma, k_\sigma, x = (x_0 \ldots x_{n-1}))$:

1. If $\sigma = 0$:
   (a) Parse $k_0 = (\mathsf{pp}, \mathsf{msk})$.
   (b) $r_0 \leftarrow \mathsf{Eval}(\mathsf{pp}, \mathsf{msk}, x_0 \ldots x_{n-1}0)$.
   (c) $r_1 \leftarrow \mathsf{Eval}(\mathsf{pp}, \mathsf{msk}, x_0 \ldots x_{n-1}1)$.
   (d) Set and output $y_0 \leftarrow (r_0, r_1)$.

2. If $\sigma = 1$:
   (a) Parse $k_1 = (\mathsf{ck}, k, \mathsf{pp})$.
   (b) $b \leftarrow F_{\mathsf{in}}(k, x_0 \ldots x_{n-1})$.
   (c) $r \leftarrow \mathsf{CEval}(\mathsf{pp}, \mathsf{ck}, x_0 \ldots x_{n-1}b)$.
   (d) Run and output $y_1 \leftarrow (b, r)$.

Fig. 2. Pre-computable wPCF/PCF for OT from weakly/strongly PR-CPRF.

6 Public-Key PCF for OT Correlations

This section provides efficient public-key PCFs for OT correlations. The content is available in the full version.

7 DV-NIZKs from PK-PCFs

This section introduces to a new construction of *reusable* DV-NIZK argument of knowledge from a compiler that combines a sigma protocol for general NP language and a public-key PCF. The content is available in the full version.

Acknowledgments. Geoffroy Couteau and Dung Bui were supported by the French Agence Nationale de la Recherche (ANR), under grant ANR-20-CE39-0001 (project SCENE), and by the France 2030 ANR Project ANR22-PECY-003 SecureCompute. Dung Bui was supported by DIM Math Innovation 2021 (N°IRIS: 21003816) from the Paris Mathematical Sciences Foundation (FSMP) funded by the Paris Ile-deFrance Region. Pierre Meyer was supported by the European Research Council (ERC) under the European Union's Horizon 2020 research and innovation programme under grants agreement number 852952 (HSS) and 803096 (SPEC). Alain Passelègue and Mahshid Riahinia were supported by the French ANR RAGE project (ANR-20-CE48-0011) and the France 2030 ANR Project (ANR22-PECY-003) SecureCompute.

References

1. Abdalla, M., Benhamouda, F., Passelègue, A.: An algebraic framework for pseudorandom functions and applications to related-key security. In: Gennaro, R., Robshaw, M. (eds.) CRYPTO 2015. LNCS, vol. 9215, pp. 388–409. Springer, Heidelberg (2015). https://doi.org/10.1007/978-3-662-47989-6_19

2. Albrecht, M.R., Davidson, A., Deo, A., Gardham, D.: Crypto dark matter on the torus: oblivious PRFs from shallow PRFs and FHE. Cryptology ePrint Archive, Report 2023/232 (2023). https://eprint.iacr.org/2023/232

3. Alwen, J., Krenn, S., Pietrzak, K., Wichs, D.: Learning with rounding, revisited. In: Canetti, R., Garay, J.A. (eds.) CRYPTO 2013. LNCS, vol. 8042, pp. 57–74. Springer, Heidelberg (2013). https://doi.org/10.1007/978-3-642-40041-4_4

4. Applebaum, B.: Pseudorandom generators with long stretch and low locality from random local one-way functions. In: Karloff, H.J., Pitassi, T. (eds.) 44th ACM STOC (2012). https://doi.org/10.1145/2213977.2214050

5. Applebaum, B.: The cryptographic hardness of random local functions – survey. Cryptology ePrint Archive (2015). https://eprint.iacr.org/2015/165

6. Applebaum, B.: Exponentially-hard gap-CSP and local PRG via local hardcore functions. In: FOCS (2017). https://doi.org/10.1109/FOCS.2017.82

7. Applebaum, B., Bogdanov, A., Rosen, A.: A dichotomy for local small-bias generators. J. Cryptol. (2016). https://doi.org/10.1007/s00145-015-9202-8

8. Applebaum, B., Kachlon, E.: Sampling graphs without forbidden subgraphs and unbalanced expanders with negligible error. In: Zuckerman, D. (ed.) 60th FOCS 2019 (2019). https://doi.org/10.1109/FOCS.2019.00020

9. Applebaum, B., Lovett, S.: Algebraic attacks against random local functions and their countermeasures. In: Wichs, D., Mansour, Y. (eds.) 48th ACM STOC, pp. 1087–1100. ACM Press (2016). https://doi.org/10.1145/2897518.2897554

10. Applebaum, B., Raykov, P.: Fast pseudorandom functions based on expander graphs. In: Hirt, M., Smith, A. (eds.) TCC 2016. LNCS, vol. 9985, pp. 27–56. Springer, Heidelberg (2016). https://doi.org/10.1007/978-3-662-53641-4_2

11. Attrapadung, N., Matsuda, T., Nishimaki, R., Yamada, S., Yamakawa, T.: Constrained PRFs for NC^1 in traditional groups. In: Shacham, H., Boldyreva, A. (eds.) CRYPTO 2018. LNCS, vol. 10992, pp. 543–574. Springer, Cham (2018). https://doi.org/10.1007/978-3-319-96881-0_19

12. Banerjee, A., Peikert, C., Rosen, A.: Pseudorandom functions and lattices. In: Pointcheval, D., Johansson, T. (eds.) EUROCRYPT 2012. LNCS, vol. 7237, pp. 719–737. Springer, Heidelberg (2012). https://doi.org/10.1007/978-3-642-29011-4_42

13. Bartusek, J., Garg, S., Masny, D., Mukherjee, P.: Reusable Two-round MPC from DDH. In: Pass, R., Pietrzak, K. (eds.) TCC 2020. LNCS, vol. 12551, pp. 320–348. Springer, Cham (2020). https://doi.org/10.1007/978-3-030-64378-2_12

14. Beaver, D.: Precomputing oblivious transfer. In: Coppersmith, D. (ed.) CRYPTO 1995. LNCS, vol. 963, pp. 97–109. Springer, Heidelberg (1995). https://doi.org/10.1007/3-540-44750-4_8

15. Bellare, M., Micali, S.: Non-interactive oblivious transfer and applications. In: Brassard, G. (ed.) CRYPTO 1989. LNCS, vol. 435, pp. 547–557. Springer, New York (1990). https://doi.org/10.1007/0-387-34805-0_48

16. Bernstein, D.J.: Curve25519: new Diffie-Hellman speed records. In: Yung, M., Dodis, Y., Kiayias, A., Malkin, T. (eds.) PKC 2006. LNCS, vol. 3958, pp. 207–228. Springer, Heidelberg (2006). https://doi.org/10.1007/11745853_14

17. Blum, A., Furst, M., Kearns, M., Lipton, R.J.: Cryptographic primitives based on hard learning problems. In: Stinson, D.R. (ed.) CRYPTO 1993. LNCS, vol. 773, pp. 278–291. Springer, Heidelberg (1994). https://doi.org/10.1007/3-540-48329-2_24

18. Blum, M.: How to prove a theorem so no one else can claim it. In: International Congress of Mathematicians (1986)

19. Bogdanov, A., Qiao, Y.: On the security of Goldreich's one-way function. In: Dinur, I., Jansen, K., Naor, J., Rolim, J. (eds.) APPROX/RANDOM -2009. LNCS, vol. 5687, pp. 392–405. Springer, Heidelberg (2009). https://doi.org/10.1007/978-3-642-03685-9_30

20. Boneh, D., Boyen, X., Goh, E.-J.: Hierarchical identity based encryption with constant size ciphertext. In: Cramer, R. (ed.) EUROCRYPT 2005. LNCS, vol. 3494, pp. 440–456. Springer, Heidelberg (2005). https://doi.org/10.1007/11426639_26

21. Boneh, D., Ishai, Y., Passelègue, A., Sahai, A., Wu, D.J.: Exploring crypto dark matter: new simple PRF candidates and their applications. In: Beimel, A., Dziembowski, S. (eds.) TCC 2018. LNCS, vol. 11240, pp. 699–729. Springer, Cham (2018). https://doi.org/10.1007/978-3-030-03810-6_25

22. Boyle, E., Couteau, G., Gilboa, N., Ishai, Y.: Compressing vector OLE. In: Lie, D., Mannan, M., Backes, M., Wang, X. (eds.) ACM CCS 2018, pp. 896–912. ACM Press (2018). https://doi.org/10.1145/3243734.3243868

23. Boyle, E., et al.: Correlated pseudorandomness from expand-accumulate codes. In: Dodis, Y., Shrimpton, T. (eds.) CRYPTO 2022, Part II. LNCS, vol. 13508, pp. 603–633. Springer, Cham (2022). https://doi.org/10.1007/978-3-031-15979-4_21

24. Boyle, E., et al.: Efficient two-round OT extension and silent non-interactive secure computation. In: Cavallaro, L., Kinder, J., Wang, X., Katz, J. (eds.) ACM CCS 2019, pp. 291–308. ACM Press (2019). https://doi.org/10.1145/3319535.3354255

25. Boyle, E., Couteau, G., Gilboa, N., Ishai, Y., Kohl, L., Scholl, P.: Efficient pseudorandom correlation generators: silent OT extension and more. In: Boldyreva, A., Micciancio, D. (eds.) CRYPTO 2019, Part III. LNCS, vol. 11694, pp. 489–518. Springer, Cham (2019). https://doi.org/10.1007/978-3-030-26954-8_16

26. Boyle, E., Couteau, G., Gilboa, N., Ishai, Y., Kohl, L., Scholl, P.: Correlated pseudorandom functions from variable-density LPN. In: 61st FOCS, pp. 1069–1080. IEEE Computer Society Press (2020). https://doi.org/10.1109/FOCS46700.2020.00103

27. Boyle, E., Couteau, G., Gilboa, N., Ishai, Y., Orrù, M.: Homomorphic secret sharing: optimizations and applications. In ACM CCS 2017. ACM Press (2017). https://doi.org/10.1145/3133956.3134107

28. Brakerski, Z., Vaikuntanathan, V.: Constrained key-homomorphic PRFs from standard lattice assumptions. In: Dodis, Y., Nielsen, J.B. (eds.) TCC 2015, Part II. LNCS, vol. 9015, pp. 1–30. Springer, Heidelberg (2015). https://doi.org/10.1007/978-3-662-46497-7_1

29. Chaidos, P., Couteau, G.: Efficient designated-verifier non-interactive zero-knowledge proofs of knowledge. In: Nielsen, J.B., Rijmen, V. (eds.) EUROCRYPT 2018. LNCS, vol. 10822, pp. 193–221. Springer, Cham (2018). https://doi.org/10.1007/978-3-319-78372-7_7

30. Cheon, J.H., Cho, W., Kim, J.H., Kim, J.: Adventures in crypto dark matter: attacks and fixes for weak pseudorandom functions. In: Garay, J.A. (ed.) PKC 2021. LNCS, vol. 12711, pp. 739–760. Springer, Cham (2021). https://doi.org/10.1007/978-3-030-75248-4_26

31. Cook, J., Etesami, O., Miller, R., Trevisan, L.: On the one-way function candidate proposed by goldreich. ACM Trans. Comput. Theory (2014)

32. Costello, C., Longa, P.: FourQ: four-dimensional decompositions on a Q-curve over the mersenne prime. In: Iwata, T., Cheon, J.H. (eds.) ASIACRYPT 2015. LNCS, vol. 9452, pp. 214–235. Springer, Heidelberg (2015). https://doi.org/10.1007/978-3-662-48797-6_10

33. Couteau, G., Dupin, A., Méaux, P., Rossi, M., Rotella, Y.: On the concrete security of Goldreich's pseudorandom generator. In: Peyrin, T., Galbraith, S. (eds.) ASIACRYPT 2018. LNCS, vol. 11273, pp. 96–124. Springer, Cham (2018). https://doi.org/10.1007/978-3-030-03329-3_4

34. Couteau, G., Hartmann, D.: Shorter non-interactive zero-knowledge arguments and ZAPs for algebraic languages. In: Micciancio, D., Ristenpart, T. (eds.) CRYPTO 2020. LNCS, vol. 12172, pp. 768–798. Springer, Cham (2020). https://doi.org/10.1007/978-3-030-56877-1_27

35. Couteau, G., Hofheinz, D.: Designated-verifier pseudorandom generators, and their applications. In: Ishai, Y., Rijmen, V. (eds.) EUROCRYPT 2019. LNCS, vol. 11477, pp. 562–592. Springer, Cham (2019). https://doi.org/10.1007/978-3-030-17656-3_20

36. Couteau, G., Jain, A., Jin, Z., Quach, W.: A note on non-interactive zero-knowledge from CDH. In: Handschuh, H., Lysyanskaya, A. (eds.) CRYPTO 2023. LNCS, vol. 14084, pp. 731–764. Springer, Cham (2023). https://doi.org/10.1007/978-3-031-38551-3_23

37. Couteau, G., Klooß, M., Lin, H., Reichle, M.: Efficient range proofs with transparent setup from bounded integer commitments. In: Canteaut, A., Standaert, F.-X. (eds.) EUROCRYPT 2021. LNCS, vol. 12698, pp. 247–277. Springer, Cham (2021). https://doi.org/10.1007/978-3-030-77883-5_9

38. Couteau, G., Meyer, P., Passelègue, A., Riahinia, M.: Constrained pseudorandom functions from homomorphic secret sharing. In: Hazay, C., Stam, M. (eds.) EUROCRYPT 2023. LNCS, vol. 14006, pp. 194–224. Springer, Cham (2023). https://doi.org/10.1007/978-3-031-30620-4_7

39. Couteau, G., Rindal, P., Raghuraman, S.: Silver: silent VOLE and oblivious transfer from hardness of decoding structured LDPC codes. In: Malkin, T., Peikert, C. (eds.) CRYPTO 2021. LNCS, vol. 12827, pp. 502–534. Springer, Cham (2021). https://doi.org/10.1007/978-3-030-84252-9_17

40. Cramer, R., Damgård, I., Schoenmakers, B.: Proofs of partial knowledge and simplified design of witness hiding protocols. In: Desmedt, Y.G. (ed.) CRYPTO 1994. LNCS, vol. 839, pp. 174–187. Springer, Heidelberg (1994). https://doi.org/10.1007/3-540-48658-5_19

41. Cramer, R., et al.: Bounded CCA2-secure encryption. In: Kurosawa, K. (ed.) ASIACRYPT 2007. LNCS, vol. 4833, pp. 502–518. Springer, Heidelberg (2007). https://doi.org/10.1007/978-3-540-76900-2_31

42. Cryan, M., Miltersen, P.B.: On pseudorandom generators in NC^0. In: Sgall, J., Pultr, A., Kolman, P. (eds.) MFCS 2001. LNCS, vol. 2136, pp. 272–284. Springer, Heidelberg (2001). https://doi.org/10.1007/3-540-44683-4_24

43. Damgård, I., Nielsen, J.B., Nielsen, M., Ranellucci, S.: The TinyTable protocol for 2-party secure computation, or: gate-scrambling revisited. In: Katz, J., Shacham, H. (eds.) CRYPTO 2017. LNCS, vol. 10401, pp. 167–187. Springer, Cham (2017). https://doi.org/10.1007/978-3-319-63688-7_6

44. Damgård, I., Pastro, V., Smart, N., Zakarias, S.: Multiparty computation from somewhat homomorphic encryption. In: Safavi-Naini, R., Canetti, R. (eds.) CRYPTO 2012. LNCS, vol. 7417, pp. 643–662. Springer, Heidelberg (2012). https://doi.org/10.1007/978-3-642-32009-5_38

45. Dinur, I., et al.: MPC-friendly symmetric cryptography from alternating moduli: candidates, protocols, and applications. In: Malkin, T., Peikert, C. (eds.) CRYPTO 2021. LNCS, vol. 12828, pp. 517–547. Springer, Cham (2021). https://doi.org/10. 1007/978-3-030-84259-8_18

46. Dittmer, S., Ishai, Y., Lu, S., Ostrovsky, R.: Authenticated garbling from simple correlations. In: Dodis, Y., Shrimpton, T. (eds.) CRYPTO 2022. LNCS, vol. 13510, pp. 57–87. Springer, Cham (2022). https://doi.org/10.1007/978-3-031-15985-5_3

47. Dupin, A., Méaux, P., Rossi, M.: On the algebraic immunity-resiliency trade-off, implications for goldreich's pseudorandom generator. Des. Codes Cryptogr. 1–45 (2023)

48. Duval, S., Méaux, P., Momin, C., Standaert, F.X.: Exploring crypto-physical dark matter and learning with physical rounding. IACR TCHES **2021**(1), 373–401 (2021). https://doi.org/10.46586/tches.v2021.i1.373-401

49. Frederiksen, T.K., Keller, M., Orsini, E., Scholl, P.: A unified approach to MPC with preprocessing using OT. In: Iwata, T., Cheon, J.H. (eds.) ASIACRYPT 2015. LNCS, vol. 9452, pp. 711–735. Springer, Heidelberg (2015). https://doi.org/10. 1007/978-3-662-48797-6_29

50. Goldreich, O.: Candidate one-way functions based on expander graphs. Cryptology ePrint Archive (2011). https://eprint.iacr.org/2000/063

51. Goldreich, O., Goldwasser, S., Micali, S.: On the cryptographic applications of random functions (extended abstract). In: Blakley, G.R., Chaum, D. (eds.) CRYPTO 1984. LNCS, vol. 196, pp. 276–288. Springer, Heidelberg (1985). https://doi.org/ 10.1007/3-540-39568-7_22

52. Goldreich, O., Micali, S., Wigderson, A.: How to play any mental game or A completeness theorem for protocols with honest majority. In: 19th ACM STOC. ACM Press (1987). https://doi.org/10.1145/28395.28420

53. Groth, J., Sahai, A.: Efficient non-interactive proof systems for bilinear groups. In: Smart, N. (ed.) EUROCRYPT 2008. LNCS, vol. 4965, pp. 415–432. Springer, Heidelberg (2008). https://doi.org/10.1007/978-3-540-78967-3_24

54. Hazay, C., Scholl, P., Soria-Vazquez, E.: Low cost constant round MPC combining BMR and oblivious transfer. J. Cryptol. (2020). https://doi.org/10.1007/s00145-020-09355-y

55. Ishai, Y., Kilian, J., Nissim, K., Petrank, E.: Extending oblivious transfers efficiently. In: Boneh, D. (ed.) CRYPTO 2003. LNCS, vol. 2729, pp. 145–161. Springer, Heidelberg (2003). https://doi.org/10.1007/978-3-540-45146-4_9

56. Jain, A., Lin, H., Sahai, A.: Indistinguishability obfuscation from well-founded assumptions. In: 53rd ACM STOC. ACM Press (2021). https://doi.org/10.1145/3406325.3451093

57. Jain, A., Jin, Z.: Non-interactive zero knowledge from sub-exponential DDH. In: Canteaut, A., Standaert, F.-X. (eds.) EUROCRYPT 2021. LNCS, vol. 12696, pp. 3–32. Springer, Cham (2021). https://doi.org/10.1007/978-3-030-77870-5_1

58. Johansson, T., Meier, W., Nguyen, V.: Differential cryptanalysis of mod-2/mod-3 constructions of binary weak PRFs. In: 2023 IEEE International Symposium on Information Theory (ISIT). IEEE (2023)

59. Katsumata, S., Nishimaki, R., Yamada, S., Yamakawa, T.: Designated verifier/prover and preprocessing NIZKs from Diffie-Hellman assumptions. In: Ishai, Y., Rijmen, V. (eds.) EUROCRYPT 2019. LNCS, vol. 11477, pp. 622–651. Springer, Cham (2019). https://doi.org/10.1007/978-3-030-17656-3_22

60. Kiltz, E., Wee, H.: Quasi-adaptive NIZK for linear subspaces revisited. In: Oswald, E., Fischlin, M. (eds.) EUROCRYPT 2015, Part II. LNCS, vol. 9057, pp. 101–128. Springer, Heidelberg (2015). https://doi.org/10.1007/978-3-662-46803-6_4

61. Lindell, Y., Pinkas, B., Smart, N.P., Yanai, A.: Efficient constant round multiparty computation combining BMR and SPDZ. In: Gennaro, R., Robshaw, M. (eds.) CRYPTO 2015, Part II. LNCS, vol. 9216, pp. 319–338. Springer, Heidelberg (2015). https://doi.org/10.1007/978-3-662-48000-7_16

62. Lombardi, A., Vaikuntanathan, V.: Limits on the locality of pseudorandom generators and applications to indistinguishability obfuscation. In: Kalai, Y., Reyzin, L. (eds.) TCC 2017, Part I. LNCS, vol. 10677, pp. 119–137. Springer, Cham (2017). https://doi.org/10.1007/978-3-319-70500-2_5

63. Méaux, P.: On the fast algebraic immunity of threshold functions. Crypt. Commun. **13** (5), 741–762 (2021)

64. Méaux, P.: On the algebraic immunity of direct sum constructions. Discret. Appl. Math. **320**, 223–234 (2022)

65. Mossel, E., Shpilka, A., Trevisan, L.: On e-biased generators in NC0. In: 44th FOCS, pp. 136–145. IEEE Computer Society Press (2003). https://doi.org/10.1109/SFCS.2003.1238188

66. Naor, M., Reingold, O.: Number-theoretic constructions of efficient pseudo-random functions. In: 38th FOCS, pp. 458–467. IEEE Computer Society Press (1997). https://doi.org/10.1109/SFCS.1997.646134

67. Nielsen, J.B., Nordholt, P.S., Orlandi, C., Burra, S.S.: A new approach to practical active-secure two-party computation. In: Safavi-Naini, R., Canetti, R. (eds.) CRYPTO 2012. LNCS, vol. 7417, pp. 681–700. Springer, Heidelberg (2012). https://doi.org/10.1007/978-3-642-32009-5_40

68. ODonnell, R., Witmer, D.: Goldreich's prg: evidence for near-optimal polynomial stretch. In: 2014 IEEE 29th Conference on Computational Complexity (CCC), pp. 1–12. IEEE (2014)

69. Oliveira, I.C., Santhanam, R., Tell, R.: Expander-based cryptography meets natural proofs. In: ITCS 2019, vol. 124, pp. 18:1–18:14. LIPIcs (2019). https://doi.org/10.4230/LIPIcs.ITCS.2019.18

70. Orlandi, C., Scholl, P., Yakoubov, S.: The rise of Paillier: homomorphic secret sharing and public-key silent OT. In: Canteaut, A., Standaert, F.-X. (eds.) EUROCRYPT 2021, Part I. LNCS, vol. 12696, pp. 678–708. Springer, Cham (2021). https://doi.org/10.1007/978-3-030-77870-5_24

71. Pass, R., Shelat, A., Vaikuntanathan, V.: Construction of a non-malleable encryption scheme from any semantically secure one. In: Dwork, C. (ed.) CRYPTO 2006. LNCS, vol. 4117, pp. 271–289. Springer, Heidelberg (2006). https://doi.org/10.1007/11818175_16

72. Quach, W., Rothblum, R.D., Wichs, D.: Reusable designated-verifier NIZKs for all NP from CDH. In: Ishai, Y., Rijmen, V. (eds.) EUROCRYPT 2019, Part II. LNCS, vol. 11477, pp. 593–621. Springer, Cham (2019). https://doi.org/10.1007/978-3-030-17656-3_21

73. Raghuraman, S., Rindal, P., Tanguy, T.: Expand-convolute codes for pseudorandom correlation generators from LPN. In: Handschuh, H., Lysyanskaya, A. (eds.) CRYPTO 2023. LNCS, vol. 14084, pp. 602–632. Springer, Cham (2023). https://doi.org/10.1007/978-3-031-38551-3_19

74. Ünal, A.: New baselines for local pseudorandom number generators by field extensions. Cryptology ePrint Archive (2023)

75. Ünal, A.: Worst-case subexponential attacks on PRGs of constant degree or constant locality. In: Hazay, C., Stam, M. (eds.) EUROCRYPT 2023, Part I. LNCS, vol. 14004, pp. 25–54. Springer, Cham (2023). https://doi.org/10.1007/978-3-031-30545-0_2

76. Wang, X., Ranellucci, S., Katz, J.: Global-scale secure multiparty computation. In: ACM CCS 2017, pp. 39–56. ACM Press (2017). https://doi.org/10.1145/3133956. 3133979
77. Yang, J., Guo, Q., Johansson, T., Lentmaier, M.: Revisiting the concrete security of Goldreich's pseudorandom generator. IEEE Trans. Inf. Theory **68**(2), 1329–1354 (2021)

Best-of-Both-Worlds Multiparty Quantum Computation with Publicly Verifiable Identifiable Abort

Kai-Min Chung[1]([✉]), Mi-Ying Huang[2][ORCID], Er-Cheng Tang[3][ORCID], and Jiapeng Zhang[2]

[1] Academia Sinica, Taipei, Taiwan
kmchung@iis.sinica.edu.tw
[2] University of Southern California, Los Angeles, USA
[3] University of Washington, Seattle, USA

Abstract. Alon et al. (CRYPTO 2021) introduced a multiparty quantum computation protocol that is secure with identifiable abort (MPQC-SWIA). However, their protocol allows only inside MPQC parties to know the identity of malicious players. This becomes problematic when two groups of people disagree and need a third party, like a jury, to verify who the malicious party is. This issue takes on heightened significance in the quantum setting, given that quantum states may exist in only a single copy. Thus, we emphasize the necessity of a protocol with *publicly verifiable identifiable abort* (PVIA), enabling outside observers with only classical computational power to agree on the identity of the malicious party in case of an abort. However, achieving MPQC with PVIA poses significant challenges due to the no-cloning theorem, and previous works proposed by Mahadev (STOC 2018) and Chung et al. (Eurocrypt 2022) for classical verification of quantum computation fall short.

In this paper, we obtain the first MPQC-PVIA protocol assuming post-quantum oblivious transfer and a classical broadcast channel. The core component of our construction is a new authentication primitive called *auditable quantum authentication* (AQA) that identifies the malicious sender with overwhelming probability. Additionally, we provide the first MPQC protocol with best-of-both-worlds (BoBW) security, which guarantees output delivery with an honest majority and remains secure with abort even if the majority is dishonest. Our best-of-both-worlds MPQC protocol also satisfies PVIA upon abort.

1 Introduction

Secure multiparty computation (MPC) allows two or more parties to compute a function on their joint private inputs securely [28]. Most of the MPC literature studies classical functionality over classical inputs with different notions of security, such as *full security*, *security with abort*, and *security with identifiable abort* [22,25,26].

Recently, secure multiparty quantum computation (MPQC) has raised research interest. Most of the works consider the fully quantum setting i.e.,

© International Association for Cryptologic Research 2024
M. Joye and G. Leander (Eds.): EUROCRYPT 2024, LNCS 14656, pp. 119–148, 2024.
https://doi.org/10.1007/978-3-031-58751-1_5

the functionality, including inputs and outputs, is quantum. Like in the classical setting, it is known that an honest majority is both sufficient [9,16], and necessary [4] to achieve full security, which guarantees output delivery for everyone. In light of this, the study of MPQC protocols in the dishonest majority setting has focused on the weaker notion of *security with abort* [6,17,18], which allows all honest parties to abort when they detect an attack. However, such a notion is vulnerable to a denial-of-service attack because an attacker can repeatedly induce aborts. For this reason, a more recent work [3] has proposed an MPQC protocol with identifiable abort (MPQC-SWIA) that allows all honest parties to agree on the identity of a corrupted party in case of an abort. Regrettably, the identification mechanism of [3] only allows the participants of the protocol to identify a malicious party. This is unsatisfactory in many practical scenarios because during a dispute, external observers are aware that two groups of people are in disagreement, but it is unclear which side is acting maliciously. Consider an instance where a client accuses a tech company of failing to provide a service and, therefore, refuses payment. Conversely, the company asserts that they have indeed provided the service. In such cases, it becomes vital to employ a publicly verifiable protocol to assess their integrity. This is especially important in the quantum setting, where each party may possess only one copy of their quantum input. Once the quantum inputs are ruined, it results in the irreversible loss of inputs for honest parties. Therefore, we consider a notion of security called *publicly verifiable identifiable abort* (PVIA) that allows everyone, including outside observers, to identify the malicious party. We ask:

Is it possible to construct MPQC with publicly verifiable identifiable abort (PVIA)?

In the classical setting, one can turn MPC-SWIA into MPC-PVIA almost for free. A publicly verifiable protocol can be obtained by requiring each party to broadcast their messages and proofs to outside observers. Unfortunately, this simple solution does not work in the quantum setting due to the no-cloning theorem. One may be tempted to turn to classical verification of quantum computation (CVQC) [14,24] in order to achieve public verifiability. However, this approach is restricted to computation that is performed by a single quantum party with classical outputs, and it is unclear how it can be adapted to fit into the setting of MPQC. Furthermore, all existing MPQC protocols face an inherent difficulty in achieving PVIA because their sender-receiver mechanism cannot differentiate a malicious sender from a malicious receiver. To address this issue, we propose a new primitive called Auditable Quantum Authentication (AQA), which subverts the traditional sender-receiver mechanism and holds the sender accountable for his behavior.

While PVIA security can act as insurance for honest parties when a dishonest majority is present, it is desirable to have a stronger security notion, such as full security, if it turns out that the honest parties outnumber the malicious ones. An intriguing scenario involves reducing the maximal number of malicious parties allowed for security with abort while conditionally offering full security.

Such a notion is called best-of-both-worlds (BoBW) security[1]. In the classical setting, [21] constructs, for every threshold $t < \frac{n}{2}$, an MPC protocol that achieves security with abort against $n-1-t$ malicious parties and achieves full security tolerating t malicious parties. [23] proved that these corruption thresholds are optimal. In the quantum setting, none of the existing MPQC protocols satisfy BoBW security. Therefore, we ask:

Is it possible to construct a single MPQC that achieves full security under an honest majority and is secure with abort under a dishonest majority?

1.1   Our Results

We answer both questions affirmatively. First, we design protocols in the preprocessing model, which features an offline setup that prepares input-independent auxiliary quantum states. After the setup, we require that the parties exchange only classical bits. With this approach, the parties can create classical proofs that are accessible to everyone, which in turn facilitates PVIA. Moreover, combined with quantum error correction code (QECC), the setup can create quantum states that enable distributed computation and ultimately achieve best-of-both-worlds security. Finally, we show that our offline setup can be instantiated without requiring any trusted third party.

Our first result is an MPQC protocol secure with publicly verifiable identifiable abort (PVIA) under a trusted setup. Similar to existing MPQC works [3,6,17,18], we assume that parties have access to an ideal functionality cMPC for classical MPC (this model is known as the MPC-hybrid model; see Sect. 4.2). Here, the classical MPC is assumed to be PVIA-secure. Such an MPC can be based on post-quantum oblivious transfer (OT) and classical broadcast channel.

Theorem 1 (MPQC-PVIA with trusted setup, informal). *There exists a multiparty quantum computation protocol secure with publicly verifiable identifiable abort supporting poly-size quantum circuits in the preprocessing MPC-hybrid model.*

To achieve Theorem 1, we propose and construct a new primitive called auditable quantum authentication (AQA) that allows a classical auditor to decide the integrity of a quantum message sender. Then, in our MPQC-PVIA protocol, the actions of the trusted auditor will be taken by classical MPC.

Our second result is a best-of-both-worlds (BoBW) MPQC protocol that achieves full security against t corruptions and satisfies security with abort against $n-1-t$ corruptions under a trusted setup. We call t as the BoBW threshold. Here, we assume our underlying classical MPC to be BoBW-secure with threshold t as well, which can be based on post-quantum OT for $t < \frac{n}{3}$ and additionally requires a classical broadcast channel for $\frac{n}{3} \le t < \frac{n}{2}$.

---

[1] There are different flavors of best-of-both-worlds security. For example, [8,23] consider MPC protocols with full security against $\lfloor \frac{n-1}{2} \rfloor$ malicious parties and $(1/p)$-security with abort against $n-1$ malicious parties. The notion of $(1/p)$-security only requires an inverse polynomial error in distinguishing the real/ideal world.

Theorem 2 (BoBW-MPQC with trusted setup, informal). *There exists a best-of-both-worlds multiparty quantum computation protocol of threshold t supporting poly-size quantum circuits for any $t < \frac{n}{2}$ in the preprocessing MPC-hybrid model.*

The key to arriving at best-of-both-worlds security is our protocol's compatibility with decentralized quantum computation using QECC. In particular, no single party in our protocol holds all the quantum information of a piece of data during the computation step, as opposed to prior security-with-abort protocols [3,6,17].

Combining these two results, we obtain a BoBW-MPQC-PVIA protocol that achieves full security against t corruptions and satisfies PVIA security against $n - 1 - t$ corruptions under a trusted setup. The underlying classical MPC should be BoBW-PVIA-secure, which can be based on a post-quantum OT and a classical broadcast channel.

Theorem 3 (BoBW-MPQC-PVIA with trusted setup, informal). *There exists a best-of-both-worlds multiparty quantum computation protocol secure with publicly verifiable identifiable abort of threshold t supporting poly-size quantum circuits for every $t < \frac{n}{2}$ in the preprocessing MPC-hybrid model.*

Furthermore, we can instantiate the setups, thus obtaining the above three results without needing a trusted setup.

Theorem 4 (BoBW-MPQC-PVIA without trusted setup, informal). *Theorems 1,2,3 hold in the (standard) MPC-hybrid model.*

Our main technique for instantiating the setup is to leverage MPQC secure with identifiable abort (SWIA) protocols. Interestingly, the properties of both BoBW and PVIA can be preserved under our instantiation. Note that our instantiation is based on an MPQC-SWIA protocol which, contrasting with the previous result [3], only assumes classical MPC.

Table 1. Comparison of MPQC protocols.

	Dishonest-Majority Regime	Honest-Majority Regime	Assumptions
[9]	No Security	Full Security	cMPC
[6,17]	Security with Abort $\begin{pmatrix} \leq n-1 \\ \text{corruptions} \end{pmatrix}$	Security with Abort	cMPC
[3]	Identifiable Abort $\begin{pmatrix} \leq n-1 \\ \text{corruptions} \end{pmatrix}$	Identifiable Abort	cMPC+FHE
This Work $(0 \leq t < \frac{n}{2})$	Publicly Verifiable Identifiable Abort $\begin{pmatrix} \leq n-1-t \\ \text{corruptions} \end{pmatrix}$	Full Security $\begin{pmatrix} \leq t \\ \text{corruptions} \end{pmatrix}$	cMPC

2   Technical Overview

In this section, we first explain why PVIA does not follow directly from existing works. Then, we put forth a novel primitive called Auditable Quantum Authentication (AQA), which ensures the secure transmission of quantum outputs and the public identification of malicious identities within a protocol. Following a high-level understanding of AQA, we then incorporate the input encoding and computation steps together to realize MPQC-PVIA. Finally, we discuss the difficulty of achieving best-of-both-worlds security and elucidate our approach to attaining a BoBW-MPQC protocol.

2.1   Why is MPQC-PVIA Hard to Achieve?

A first observation is that classical techniques for public verifiability cannot apply to their quantum counterparts. Existing methods for classical MPC-PVIA protocols are to commit to classical messages, provide zero-knowledge arguments over the commitments, and let outside observers check whether any party deviates from the protocol. There are several issues when adapting to MPQC in the fully quantum setting. If one considers classical commitments to quantum messages [24], one cannot fulfill MPQC with purely quantum outputs because such classical commitment schemes always end with measurements. Instead, one may have to consider quantum commitments [20]. However, quantum commitments are unlikely to be duplicated and broadcast to each party for verification because of the no-cloning theorem. In addition, zero-knowledge arguments for quantum computation (e.g., [11]) only apply to problems with a classical description. Those arguments cannot prove relations involving quantum commitments.

Another difficulty arises because we require the outside observers of MPQC to have only classical computational power. Although there is research on classical verification of quantum computation (CVQC), a seemingly similar task, CVQC needs to be more relaxed because it can only resolve computations with classical outputs conducted by a single quantum prover. The techniques of CVQC fail in the fully quantum setting. Moreover, CVQC already produces an inverse polynomial soundness error when extended from decisional problems [24] to sampling problems [14]. Thus, there is little hope that CVQC can aid the construction of MPQC-PVIA.

One may try to upgrade MPQC-SWIA to MPQC-PVIA directly, but there is still a gap between them. The MPQC-SWIA protocol by [3] is based on a Sequential Authentication primitive that outputs two suspects whenever message tampering is detected. However, it gives no information about the *exact* party that deviates from the protocol. The resulting MPQC-SWIA allows honest parties to agree on the same malicious party when protocol aborts, but an outside observer only sees two groups of people accusing each other. This outcome arises from the conventional utilization of quantum authentication codes[2],

---

[2] The prevalent approach in most existing works involves employing authentication codes in this manner [3,6,17].

where the sender sends an authenticated state to the receiver, and the receiver is in charge of measuring the authentication checksum to validate the state. However, this kind of validation mechanism relies on the synergy of both sender and receiver over a single-copy state, which makes it challenging to achieve public verifiability. To address this, we subvert the old idea and creatively combine quantum authentication codes with quantum teleportation in a white-box manner.

2.2   Our Solution: Auditable Quantum Authentication (AQA)

The primary goal of AQA is to establish a mechanism where the sender of an authenticated state is held responsible for his own sending action through a test performed by someone trustworthy. In a normal quantum authentication scheme, the receiver of an authenticated state runs the decoding algorithm to obtain either the original message or an authentication failure symbol. To learn the true authentication outcome, an outside observer has to trust the party who executes the decoding algorithm. This would require trust in the receiver, who might be malicious. To resolve this issue, we propose an *auditable* quantum authentication scheme that separates the authenticity check from the message decoding process. Importantly, the AQA scheme is equipped with a *classical* auditing algorithm that decides message authenticity and outputs a decoding key for the receiver to recover the message. With AQA, an outside observer can learn the authentication outcome by trusting a classical auditor who executes the auditing algorithm. Later on, we can replace the classical auditor with a publicly verifiable classical MPC (cMPC) to completely remove the need of trust.

AQA is designed to be cooperated by three parties: a sender, a receiver, and a classical auditor. We define AQA as consisting of five algorithms: Setup, Enc, Send, Audit, Recv. In the beginning, Setup prepares initial states for all the parties, and Enc produces an authenticated state σ for the sender. The sender runs Send(σ) to generate a classical proof pf showing that the quantum message has been delivered. Next, the auditor runs Audit(pf) to verify the proof and produce a decoding key dk. Afterward, the receiver can run Recv(dk) to obtain the quantum message. The security of AQA entails that Recv(dk) produces the correct quantum message (up to a negligible error) whenever Audit(pf) outputs a positive verification outcome.

Constructing a (Simplified) AQA. We will start with a normal quantum authentication scheme (Gen,Enc,Dec), the Clifford code [2] in particular. We aim to keep the encoding procedure Enc and split its decoding procedure into several parts. The decoding procedure of Clifford code applies a secret Clifford gate $F^{\dagger M,T}$ to an authenticated state $\sigma^{M,T}$ and measures T register in the computational basis. An authentication failure occurs if the measurement result is not all zeros. Otherwise, the content of the M register will be the message state. To make this authentication scheme classically auditable, we consider the following alternative decoding procedure that involves 4 algorithms. We take $|M| = 1$ and $|T| = \lambda$ as an example Fig. 1.

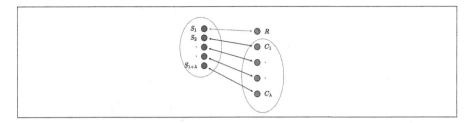

Fig. 1. AQA Setup: Each edge represents an EPR pair. The nodes on the left contain halves of EPR pairs $\{e_0^i\}_{i\in[\lambda+1]}$, and the nodes on the right contain the other halves of EPR pairs $\{e_1^i\}_{i\in[\lambda+1]}$. The encircled vertices (the sending register S and checking register C) are given to the sender. The lonely vertex (receiving register R) is given to the receiver.

Setup:

- Generate EPR pairs $\{(e_0^i, e_1^i)\}_{i\in[\lambda+1]}$ of length $\lambda + 1$. Put $\{e_0^i\}_{i\in[\lambda+1]}$, $\{e_1^i\}_{i\in\{2,\cdots,\lambda+1\}}$, e_1^1 into the sending, checking, receiving registers S, C, R respectively.
- Apply the secret Clifford gate $F^\dagger \leftarrow \mathscr{C}_{\lambda+1}$ to R, C.

Send:

- Sending: Teleport the authenticated state σ through the sending register S.
- Proving: Measure the checking register C in the computational basis.
- Set classical proof as the teleportation Pauli P and measurement result c.

Audit:

- Compute the Pauli $F^\dagger P F$ and express it as a tensor product of two Pauli gates $\hat{P}_R, \hat{P}_C$ that act on $1, \lambda$ qupits respectively.
- Report an authentication failure if $c \neq x(\hat{P}_C)$. Set the decoding key as $\hat{P}_R$.

Recv:

- Apply $\hat{P}_R^{\dagger}{}^R$ and output the state on the receiving register R.

Running these 4 algorithms in a row is equivalent to running the decoding procedure of Clifford code. This follows almost directly from quantum teleportation: If we denote $F^\dagger \sigma = (\rho^M, \tau^T)$ and if teleporting σ through S during Send yields teleportation result P, then the state in R, C would collapse from $F^\dagger(\{e_1^i\}_{i\in[\lambda+1]})$ to

$$F^\dagger P(\sigma) = (F^\dagger P F)(F^\dagger(\sigma)) = (\hat{P}_R \otimes \hat{P}_C)(\rho, \tau) = (\hat{P}_R(\rho), \hat{P}_C(\tau))$$

This shows that the measurement result of the checking register C equals $x(\hat{P}_C)$ if and only if the measurement result of τ equals all zeros. The current decoding procedure includes a classical algorithm Audit that determines the authentication outcome, so we can set our simplified AQA as these 4 algorithms plus the encoding algorithm of Clifford code.

Proving Security of AQA. For the security of AQA, it's crucial for Recv to recover the original message whenever Audit doesn't indicate an authentication failure upon receiving proof from an adversarial sender. Take, for instance, a malicious sender who alters the authenticated message σ prior to the execution of Send. In such a specific scenario, the security of the simplified AQA is derived from the established equivalence between the processes (Send, Audit, Recv) and Dec mentioned in the preceding paragraph and grounded on the efficacy of (Enc, Dec) as a quantum authentication scheme. However, the simplified AQA is presented mainly as an explanation of how we achieve the audit functionality, and is not yet secure against arbitrary malicious senders. To further protect against adversaries employing arbitrary attacks, our formal AQA in Sect. 5 additionally integrates quantum one-time pads. To offer a high-level intuition, the use of quantum one-time pads can split the attack of the malicious sender into a combination of Pauli attacks. Since the malicious sender knows nothing about the random Clifford key F, the Clifford twirl will transform Pauli attacks into random Pauli operators distributed across the states, breaking the consistency of P and c.

2.3   From AQA to MPQC-PVIA

From the previous section, we see that transmission of quantum information can be audited by a classical party. We now build an MPQC-PVIA protocol with AQA where the auditing is performed by a publicly verifiable classical MPC.

MPQC-PVIA with Setup. The MPQC-PVIA consists of two phases: an offline setup and an online phase. The offline setup generates EPR pairs that would allow each party to send their input to the server (who is a designated party, say P_1), and runs the setup of AQA. During the online phase, every party teleports their input to P_1 and P_1 only obtains a ciphertext of the joint inputs. Next, P_1 performs quantum computation on the ciphertext as instructed by classical MPC. Finally, P_1 sends the output ciphertexts to other parties using AQA, which is audited by classical MPC. These three steps in the online phase are called input encoding, computation, and output delivery, respectively.

We now move on to examine security. In our protocol, the parties' inputs are gathered towards P_1, and the quantum computation is solely performed by P_1. Thus, only P_1 can launch an effective attack. The attack would ruin P_1's ciphertext, and P_1 would ultimately face an authentication error when transmitting the ciphertext with AQA. In this case, the classical MPC that runs the audit algorithm can publicly output P_1 as malicious. As a result, our protocol achieves MPQC while maintaining PVIA security.

Instantiable Setup. Next, we show how to instantiate our setup with an MPQC protocol secure with identifiable abort (SWIA). Note that we refine a slightly different version of MPQC-SWIA, thereby circumventing the need for the post-quantum Fully Homomorphic Encryption (FHE) assumption needed in [3].

MPQC-SWIA guarantees that whenever an abort happens, cMPC will output a partition of parties with all honest parties staying in the same group.

Our approach for instantiating the setup is to run MPQC-SWIA hierarchically to prepare the states that the setup would generate. The hierarchical MPQC-SWIA maintains a grouping between parties, where all parties are initially in the same group. Each group will try to run MPQC-SWIA by themselves, and a group breaks into two whenever MPQC-SWIA fails. At some point, all parties must have succeeded in running MPQC-SWIA within their group (or they will continue running MPQC-SWIA within descent subgroups), so they can proceed to execute the online MPQC-PVIA protocol. By employing the security of MPQC-PVIA with preprocessing, it is guaranteed that either the honest parties obtain their outputs, or some malicious party in the group that contains all honest parties will be publicly identified Fig. 2.

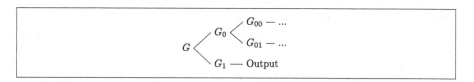

Fig. 2. Hierarchical MPQC-SWIA parties try to run the offline setup using MPQC-SWIA. Initially, G contains all the parties. When the first MPQC-SWIA run by G terminates with a failure, parties in G separate into two groups G_0 and G_1, who run another MPQC-SWIA within their own group. In this figure, G_1 executes MPQC-SWIA successfully and obtains the setup output. They can proceed to execute the online MPQC-PVIA protocol.

2.4 Best-of-Both-Worlds Security

One advantage of our protocol design is its flexibility to provide best-of-both-worlds security. That is, we construct an MPQC protocol that simultaneously achieves full security when there are at most $t < \frac{n}{2}$ corruptions and satisfies security with publicly verifiable identifiable abort against at most $n - 1 - t$ corrupted parties.

Prior to this work, the honest-majority and the dishonest-majority worlds were once separated because of a tension between sharing and extracting quantum information. We elaborate on it as follows. MPQC protocols that obtain full security in an honest majority setting [9] are based on verifiable quantum secret sharing (VQSS). In these protocols, each party individually creates VQSS of their input and distributes the shares across parties. The problem is that the secret shares sent between malicious parties are private information. Once the number of corrupted parties reaches one-half, the simulator cannot extract the adversary's input from the available secret shares. This is also why current MPQC protocols designed for a dishonest majority need every quantum message to be transmitted through all parties: the simulator can extract inputs when the quantum message passes through an honest party. As a result, protocols against a dishonest majority cannot divide a piece of quantum information across multiple parties, and a single malicious party is sufficient to destroy the information subjected to the computation.

Our solution to this tension is to utilize the offline-online structure of our protocol and incorporate quantum error correction codes (QECC). First, our offline setup[3] prepares QECC codewords on EPR pairs and distributes the codewords evenly across parties. Afterward, the parties can perform distributed computation over QECC codewords in the online protocol. In this protocol, the honestly-generated QECC codewords facilitate the sharing of quantum information. Moreover, to extract quantum information even in the presence of a malicious majority, the setup can entangle a trapdoor with the states prepared for the parties and use the trapdoor to extract online inputs. We see that the offline setup acts as a vital piece of machinery that allows information extraction while preparing for the online distributed computation.

Our BoBW-MPQC protocol is reminiscent of the classical BoBW-cMPC protocols [8,21,23]. A key difference is that the classical protocols need to broadcast secret sharings and invoke the ideal functionality on the inputs multiple times, both of which are infeasible in MPQC due to no-cloning. Our protocol does not follow the same pattern, and we achieve the same goal in the merit of quantum teleportation.

3   Preliminary

Let $[n] = \{1, \cdots, n\}$. We denote by $A_{[n]}$ the tuple $(A_1, \cdots, A_n)$. Uniform sampling from a set S is denoted by $s \leftarrow S$. A function $f \colon \mathbb{N} \to [0,1]$ is called negligible if for every polynomial $\text{poly}(\cdot)$ and all sufficiently large n, we have $f(n) < |1/\text{poly}(n)|$. We use $\text{negl}(\cdot)$ to denote an unspecified negligible function.

Quantum states are written in lowercase Greek alphabets, e.g., ρ, σ. Quantum operations are written in uppercase Latin alphabets, e.g., U, V. We write ρ^M and U^M to specify that ρ is stored in register M and U operates on register M. The notation (ρ, σ) denotes a state on two registers that may be entangled. The letters QPT stands for quantum polynomial time.

Fix a prime p. A qupit in pure state $|\phi\rangle$ is a unit vector in the p-dimensional Hilbert space $\mathbb{C}^p$ and can be identified with the density operator $\text{Mixed}\,[|\phi\rangle] := |\phi\rangle\langle\phi|$. The set of n-qupit mixed states, denoted $\mathcal{D}^n$, consists of positive semi-definite operators on $\mathbb{C}^{p^n}$ with trace 1. We sometimes identify a mixed state ρ with its purification, which is a pure state $|\phi\rangle$ such that $\text{Mixed}\,[|\phi\rangle]$ has partial trace ρ. We also consider sub-normalized mixed states, which are positive semi-definite operators with trace at most 1. We identify a distribution $\{\rho_j\}$ of sub-normalized states with the state $\mathbb{E}_j \rho_j$. Two sequences of sub-normalized states $\rho(n), \sigma(n) \in \mathcal{D}^{\text{poly}(n)}$ are said to be statistically indistinguishable, denoted $\rho \approx \sigma$, if they have trace distance $\text{tr}|\rho(n) - \sigma(n)| = \text{negl}(n)\text{tr}(\rho(n))$.

---

[3] Similar to previous subsection, this setup can be instantiated using MPQC-SWIA.

3.1   Quantum Computation

A quantum operation is a completely positive, trace preserving (CPTP) map acting on mixed states. Any such map can be represented as $\{A_j\}$ which maps a mixed state ρ to the mixed state $\sum_j A_j \rho A_j^\dagger$. Each A_j defines a completely positive (CP) map $\rho \mapsto A_j \rho A_j^\dagger$. For example, measurement in the computation basis $\{|j\rangle\}_{j \in \mathbb{Z}_p}$ is a CPTP map, whereas each projector $|j\rangle\langle j|$ is only a CP map.

Consider the phase $\omega = e^{2\pi i/p}$, the shift operator $\mathsf{X} : |j\rangle \mapsto |j+1\rangle$ and the clock operator $\mathsf{Z} : |j\rangle \mapsto \omega^j |j\rangle$. Write $\mathsf{X}^{(x_1,\cdots,x_n)}\mathsf{Z}^{(z_1,\cdots,z_n)} = \bigotimes_{j \in [n]} \mathsf{X}^{x_j}\mathsf{Z}^{z_j}$ where each $x_j, z_j \in \mathbb{Z}_p$. We define the Pauli basis $\mathscr{P}_n^* = \{\mathsf{X}^x\mathsf{Z}^z \mid x, z \in \mathbb{Z}_p^n\}$, which is a basis for the space of linear operators on $\mathbb{C}^{p^n}$. Decomposing a linear operator according to this basis is called the Pauli decomposition. We identify the Pauli $P_a = \mathsf{X}^{x_a}\mathsf{Z}^{z_a} \in \mathscr{P}_n^*$ with the string $(z_a, x_a) = (z(P_a), x(P_a)) \in \mathbb{Z}_p^{2n}$. Define the Pauli group $\mathscr{P}_n$ as $\{\omega^k \mathsf{X}^x\mathsf{Z}^z \mid k \in \mathbb{Z}_p,\ x, z \in \mathbb{Z}_p^n\}$ and the Clifford group $\mathscr{C}_n$ as the normalizer of $\mathscr{P}_n$ in the unitary group quotient by global phases. That is, a unitary $C \in \mathscr{C}_n$ if and only if for all $A \in \mathscr{P}_n$, $CAC^\dagger \in \mathscr{P}_n$.

The Clifford group is generated by the Fourier transform gate $\mathsf{H} : |j\rangle \mapsto \frac{1}{\sqrt{p}}\sum_k \omega^{jk}|k\rangle$, the phase gate $\mathsf{S} : |j\rangle \mapsto \omega^{j(j-1)/2}|j\rangle$ and the sum gate $\mathsf{CX} : |j,k\rangle \mapsto |j, k+j\rangle$ [15]. When $p = 2$, the phase gate is defined as $\mathsf{S} : |j\rangle \mapsto i^j|j\rangle$ instead. One can sample uniformly random Clifford gates in polynomial time [19,27]. We denote $\mathsf{CX}_{(b_1,\cdots,b_n)}^{R_0,\cdots,R_n}$ as the abbreviation of $\mathsf{CX}^{b_1}{}^{R_0,R_1} \cdots \mathsf{CX}^{b_n}{}^{R_0,R_n}$.

Universal quantum computation can be carried out with Clifford gates and T gates, where $\mathsf{T} : |j\rangle \mapsto e^{\frac{2\pi i \eta_j}{p^2}}|j\rangle$ with $\eta_j = p\binom{j}{3} - j\binom{p}{3} + \binom{p+1}{4}$ [12]. When $p = 2$, the T gate is defined as $\mathsf{T} : |j\rangle \mapsto e^{\frac{\pi i j}{4}}|j\rangle$ instead. Although T gate is not in the Clifford group, it can be applied using classically controlled (i.e., adaptive) Clifford operations with the help of the T state $|\mathsf{T}\rangle = \mathsf{T}|+\rangle$, where $|+\rangle = \frac{1}{\sqrt{p}}\sum_{j=0}^{p-1}|j\rangle$. T states can be purified from noisy ones using classically controlled Clifford gates [10,12].

3.2   Quantum One-Time Pad

Definition 1. *A quantum one-time pad (QOTP) with key $P \in \mathscr{P}_n$ is a symmetric-key encryption scheme that consists of the following two algorithms.*

- *Encryption: $\mathsf{QOPT.Enc}_P(\rho) := P\rho P^\dagger$.*
- *Decryption: $\mathsf{QOPT.Dec}_P(\rho) := P^\dagger \rho P$.*

It is well known that the ciphertext under QOTP is maximally mixed:

Lemma 1. (Pauli Twirl). *For every $|\phi\rangle^{M,N} = \sum_u |u\rangle^M \otimes |\phi_u\rangle^N$, it holds that*

$$\underset{P \leftarrow \mathscr{P}_n}{\mathbb{E}} \; \mathsf{Mixed}\left[P^M|\phi\rangle^{M,N}\right] = \left(\underset{r \leftarrow \mathbb{Z}_p^n}{\mathbb{E}} \; \mathsf{Mixed}\left[|r\rangle\right]\right)^M \otimes \left(\sum_u \mathsf{Mixed}\left[|\phi_u\rangle\right]\right)^N$$

The same result holds when P is randomly sampled from the Clifford group $\mathscr{C}_n$. Moreover, it is well known that QOTP can split a quantum attack into a probabilistic combination of Pauli attacks. This work considers a specific scenario where an untrusted party measures a state which is protected under QOTP. We formulate the following lemma, which shows that any attack would be equivalent to a probabilistic combination of Pauli attacks that cause different shifts. We prove the lemma in the full version of this paper.

Lemma 2. (Pauli Twirl with Measurement). *Let* $|\phi\rangle^{M,N} = \sum_{u \in \mathbb{Z}_p^n} |u\rangle^M \otimes |\phi_u\rangle^N$ *be a state and* $v \in \mathbb{Z}_p^n$ *be the target measurement result. For any attack* $A^{M,N} = \sum_{Q \in \mathscr{P}_n^*} \left(Q^M \otimes A_Q^N\right)$ *applied on the QOTP-protected state, we have*

$$\mathop{\mathbb{E}}_{P \leftarrow \mathscr{P}_n} \mathsf{Mixed}\left[|v + x(P)\rangle\langle v + x(P)|^M A^{M,N} P^M |\phi\rangle^{M,N}\right]$$

$$= \mathop{\mathbb{E}}_{r \leftarrow \mathbb{Z}_p^n} \sum_u \mathsf{Mixed}\left[\left(\sum_{x(Q)=v-u} Q \otimes A_Q\right)(|r\rangle \otimes |\phi_u\rangle)\right]$$

3.3 Quantum Authentication Code

Quantum authentication code detects whether unauthorized alterations have been made to the data. When alternation is detected, the algorithm will output a rejection symbol $\perp$.

Definition 2 (Quantum Authentication Code, [5]). *A quantum authentication code consists of three algorithms. The key generation algorithm* Gen *takes in the security parameter* 1^λ *and the message size* 1^ℓ *and outputs a random secret key* sk. *The encoding algorithm* Enc *maps a secret key* sk *and a quantum message on* M *to a quantum ciphertext on* MT. *The decoding algorithm* Dec *maps a secret key* sk *and a quantum ciphertext on* MT *to a quantum message* M. *These algorithms should satisfy the following properties.*

- *Completeness: For every secret key* sk, *it holds that* $\mathsf{Dec}_{sk} \circ \mathsf{Enc}_{sk} = \mathbb{1}$.
- *Security: For any quantum map* $\mathcal{A}$, *there exists two CP maps* $\mathcal{A}_{\mathsf{Acc}}$ *and* $\mathcal{A}_{\mathsf{Rej}}$ *such that* $\mathcal{A}_{\mathsf{Acc}} + \mathcal{A}_{\mathsf{Rej}}$ *is trace preserving and that for any (possibly entangled) states* $\rho, \rho_{\mathsf{aux}}$,

$$\left\{(\rho', \rho'_{\mathsf{aux}}) \;\middle|\; \begin{matrix} \mathsf{sk} \leftarrow \mathsf{Gen}(1^\lambda, 1^\ell) \\ \sigma \leftarrow \mathsf{Enc}(\mathsf{sk}, \rho) \\ (\sigma', \rho'_{\mathsf{aux}}) \leftarrow \mathcal{A}(\sigma, \rho_{\mathsf{aux}}) \\ \rho' \leftarrow \mathsf{Dec}(\mathsf{sk}, \sigma') \end{matrix}\right\} \underset{\mathsf{negl}(\lambda)}{\approx} \left(\left(\rho, \mathcal{A}_{\mathsf{Acc}}(\rho_{\mathsf{aux}})\right) + \left(|\perp\rangle\langle\perp|, \mathcal{A}_{\mathsf{Rej}}(\rho_{\mathsf{aux}})\right)\right)$$

Here, we recall the Clifford authentication code from [2]. The key generation algorithm outputs a uniformly random Clifford gate $E^{M,T}$. The encoding procedure augments the message state ρ^M with traps $|0\rangle^{\otimes \lambda^T}$ and applies $E^{M,T}$.

The decoding procedure applies $E^\dagger$ followed by measuring the register T in the computational basis. If the measurement results are not all zero, the content of M is replaced with $|\perp\rangle$. The Clifford authentication code satisfies Definition 2. The following lemma is crucial to its proof, and we will use the lemma directly later on.

Lemma 3 (Pauli Partitioning by Clifford, [2,13]). *For every Pauli operators $Q, Q' \in \mathscr{P}_n$ that do not lie in $\{\omega^k I \mid k \in \mathbb{Z}_p\}$, it holds that*

$$\Pr_{C \leftarrow \mathscr{C}_n} \left[C^\dagger Q C = Q' \right] = \text{negl}(n).$$

The Clifford code also supports homomorphic computation for any Clifford operator. Consider a Clifford-code ciphertext $\text{Enc}_E(\rho^M)$ with secret key $\text{sk} = E$. To perform a Clifford gate G on ρ, it suffices to update the secret key as $\text{sk}' = EG^\dagger$. This works because we have $\text{Enc}_{\text{sk}}(\rho) = E(\rho, |0\rangle^{\otimes\lambda}) = EG^\dagger(G\rho, |0\rangle^{\otimes\lambda}) = \text{Enc}_{\text{sk}'}(G(\rho))$.

3.4 Quantum Error-Correction Code

Quantum error correction code protects quantum states from errors as long as the number of errors is limited. In this work, it suffices to consider erasure errors.

Definition 3 (Quantum Error Correction Code). *A $[[n, k]]_p$ quantum error correction code consists of two algorithms. The encoding algorithm* $\text{QECC.Enc} : \mathcal{D}^k \rightarrow \mathcal{D}^n$ *encodes a k-qupit message into a n-qupit codeword. The decoding algorithm* $\text{QECC.Dec} : \mathcal{D}^n \times \{0,1\}^n \rightarrow \mathcal{D}^k$ *takes a modified codeword and its location of errors and outputs a k-qupit message. A quantum error correction code is said to correct t erasure errors, if for any $\rho \in \mathcal{D}^k$ and any quantum channel Δ^R acting on $|R| < t$ qupits, it holds that*

$$\text{QECC.Dec} \left(\Delta^R \text{QECC.Enc}(\rho), \mathbb{1}_R \right) = \rho$$

where $\mathbb{1}_R$ specifies the locations of R among the n qupits.

To arrive at best-of-both-worlds security for any threshold $t < \frac{n}{2}$, we can use the quantum polynomial code of [1], which satisfies other desirable properties.

Lemma 4 (Polynomial Code, [1]). *For every $t < \frac{n}{2}$ and prime $p > n$, there exists a $[[n, 1]]_p$ quantum error correction code that corrects t erasure errors with the following additional properties:*

- *Syntax:* QECC.Enc *applies a Clifford gate to input ρ and ancilla $|0\rangle^{\otimes(n-1)}$.*
- *Fault-Tolerant Computation:* X, Z, CX, H *gates and measurement in the computational basis can be applied to the message ρ by locally applying some of these operators to the individual components of the codeword using ancillas.*

A state injection technique shows that the S gate can be performed through X, Z, CX^{-1} gates and measurements in the computational basis using ancillas. Hence, the entire Clifford group $\mathscr{C}_n = \langle S, H, CX \rangle$ can be applied fault-tolerantly using ancillas under the polynomial code.

3.5   Quantum Teleportation

Quantum teleportation allows parties to transmit quantum messages using only classical communication and pre-shared quantum states. Below, an EPR pair $(e_S{}^{S_1, \cdots, S_n}, e_R{}^{R_1, \cdots, R_n})$ of length n stands for the state $\bigotimes_{j \in [n]} |\Phi^+\rangle^{S_j, R_j}$ where $|\Phi^+\rangle = \frac{1}{\sqrt{p}} \Sigma_{j=0}^{p-1} |j, j\rangle$.

Definition 4 (Quantum Teleportation Without Measurement). *Let (e_S, e_R) be an EPR pair of length n independent to a state $\psi \in \mathcal{D}^n$. Quantum teleportation consists of two algorithms. We will also abbreviate TP.Send as* TP.

- *TP.Send$(\psi^M, e_S{}^S)$ applies* $\mathsf{H}^M \mathsf{CX}^{\dagger M,S}$ *to $(\psi^M, e_S{}^S)$ and outputs M, S.*
- *TP.Recv$(z, x, e_R{}^R)$ applies $(\mathsf{X}^x \mathsf{Z}^z)^\dagger$ to $e_R{}^R$ and outputs R.*

When we speak of teleporting a state ψ^M via register S, we mean to apply TP.Send^{M,S}, measure (M, S) in the computational basis and interpret the measurement result (z, x) as the Pauli $\mathsf{X}^x \mathsf{Z}^z$. The following lemma states that the teleportation result $\mathsf{X}^x \mathsf{Z}^z$ can help recover the original quantum message ψ.

Lemma 5 *Let (ψ, τ) be a purified state independent of (e_S, e_R). Then*

$$\left(\mathsf{TP.Send}(\psi^M, e_S{}^S), e_R{}^R, \tau^N\right) = \frac{1}{p^n} \sum_{x, z \in \mathbb{Z}_p^n} |z\rangle^M \otimes |x\rangle^S \otimes \left((\mathsf{X}^x \mathsf{Z}^z)\, \psi^R, \tau^N\right)$$

4   Model and Definition

We focus on interactive protocols between n parties $\mathsf{P}_1, \cdots, \mathsf{P}_n$ with quantum computational power. They can communicate using pairwise authenticated quantum channels and a broadcast channel for classical messages. We work in the synchronous communication model where the protocol proceeds in rounds, and each message will certainly arrive at the end of each round. In addition, we consider the presence of a protocol observer O who passively receives and records classical information from the broadcast channel all the time.[4] The adversary $\mathcal{A}$ can statically corrupt a set $I \subset \{\mathsf{P}_1, \cdots, \mathsf{P}_n\}$ of up to $n - 1$ parties.

The quantum computation to be performed is modeled as a quantum circuit C, which takes n parts of quantum inputs and produces n parts of quantum outputs. Without loss of generality, we assume that the corresponding inputs and outputs have equal size. We always apply [10,12] to convert C into the following format, incurring only a polynomial growth in description size. The ancilla ϕ_{anc} consists of $|0\rangle$ and $|T\rangle$ states, and the circuit operates on a total of $\ell_{\mathsf{total}} = \sum_i \ell_i + d$ qupits.

---

[4] Alternatively, one can assume a public bulletin board from which the observer can retrieve the broadcast information.

Specification of Quantum Circuit C

1. Take input registers $R_1, \cdots, R_n$ where $|R_i| = \ell_i$.
2. Initialize register $N = (N_1, \cdots, N_d)$ as some ancilla (magic) state ϕ_{anc} where $|N_i| = 1$.
3. For $k = d, \cdots, 1$, perform the following computation, denoted as $C[k]$:
   (a) Measure N_k in the computational basis and obtain a pit b_k.
   (b) Compute a classical circuit $f_k(b_k, \cdots, b_d)$ that outputs a Clifford gate G_{k-1}.
   (c) Apply G_{k-1} $\in$ $\mathscr{C}_{\ell_1 + \cdots + \ell_n + k - 1}$ on   registers $(R_1, \cdots, R_n, N_1, \cdots, N_{k-1})$.
4. Output registers $R_1, \cdots, R_n$.

4.1   The Ideal World of BoBW-MPQC-PVIA

A multi-party quantum computation protocol is defined using the real vs. ideal paradigm. In the ideal world, the parties delegate the computation C to a trusted party T. The only way for the corrupted parties to interrupt the delegation is to ask T to abort, in which case T publicly announces their identities. The ideal world of best-of-both-worlds multi-party quantum computation secure with publicly verifiable identifiable abort is formally defined as follows. We denote its joint output distribution as $\mathsf{Ideal}^{\mathsf{MPQC}}_{\mathcal{A}_I(\rho_{\mathsf{aux}})}(1^\lambda, t, C, \rho_1, \cdots, \rho_n)$.

$\mathsf{Ideal}^{\mathsf{MPQC}}$: Best-of-Both-Worlds Multi-party Quantum Computation with Publicly Verifiable Identifiable Abort

Common input:
    The security parameter 1^λ, BoBW threshold t and quantum circuit C.
Input:
    P_i holds input ρ_i. $\mathcal{A}_I$ holds input ρ_{aux} and controls parties in I.
T receives inputs and performs computation:
    Each party P_i sends some $\tilde{\rho}_i$ as input to T. Honest parties choose $\tilde{\rho}_i = \rho_i$.
    T computes $(\rho'_1, \cdots, \rho'_n) \leftarrow C(\tilde{\rho}_1, \cdots, \tilde{\rho}_n)$.
T sends back outputs:
    T sends ρ'_i to all $P_i \in I$.
    $P_i \in I$ can send **abort** message to T.
    Let J be the set of parties who indeed do so.
    If $|J| > t$, T publicly aborts to J.
    If $|J| \leq t$, T sends ρ'_i to all $P_i \notin I$.
Output:
    Honest parties output whatever output received from T.
    The observer O outputs whatever public information received from T.
    The adversary $\mathcal{A}_I$ outputs a function of his view.

For a protocol Π, we denote by $\mathsf{Real}^{\Pi}_{\mathcal{A}_I(\rho_{\mathsf{aux}})}(1^\lambda, \rho_1, \cdots, \rho_n)$ the joint output distribution of the honest parties, the observer, and the adversary at the end of protocol Π when executed by $\mathsf{P}_i(\rho_i)$ in the presence of an adversary $\mathcal{A}_I(\rho_{\mathsf{aux}})$ corrupting parties in I. For a protocol Π with a trusted setup Σ, we define $\mathsf{Real}^{\Pi \circ \Sigma}_{\mathcal{A}_I(\rho_{\mathsf{aux}})}(1^\lambda, \rho_1, \cdots, \rho_n)$ similarly with Σ being executed by a trusted party prior to Π.

Definition 5. *We say that a protocol Π is a best-of-both-worlds multi-party quantum computation secure with publicly verifiable identifiable abort (BoBW-MPQC-PVIA) of threshold t over a circuit C, if for every $|I| \leq n-1-t$ and every non-uniform (QPT) adversary $\mathcal{A}_I$ corrupting parties in I, there is a non-uniform (QPT) simulator Sim_I corrupting parties in I, such that for any quantum inputs $\rho_i \in \mathcal{D}^{\ell_i}$, $i \in [n]$,*

$$\mathsf{Real}^{\Pi}_{\mathcal{A}_I(\rho_{\mathsf{aux}})}(1^\lambda, \rho_1, \cdots, \rho_n) \approx \mathsf{Ideal}^{\mathsf{MPQC}}_{\mathsf{Sim}_I(\rho_{\mathsf{aux}})}(1^\lambda, t, C, \rho_1, \cdots, \rho_n)$$

If the protocol Π has a trusted setup Σ, the indistinguishability requirement is replaced with

$$\mathsf{Real}^{\Pi \circ \Sigma}_{\mathcal{A}_I(\rho_{\mathsf{aux}})}(1^\lambda, \rho_1, \cdots, \rho_n) \approx \mathsf{Ideal}^{\mathsf{MPQC}}_{\mathsf{Sim}_I(\rho_{\mathsf{aux}})}(1^\lambda, t, C, \rho_1, \cdots, \rho_n)$$

Definition 6. *We say that Π is a multi-party quantum computation secure with publicly verifiable identifiable abort (MPQC-PVIA) over a circuit C if Definition 5 holds for $t = 0$.*

4.2 (Preprocessing) MPC-Hybrid Model

Following [3,6,17,18], we assume an ideal functionality cMPC for *reactive*[5] classical multiparty computation within our MPQC protocol. The ideal world of classical MPC is similar to that of MPQC defined in section Sect. 4.1, but allows only classical messages and classical computation. In additional to producing n private outputs, the classical computation is allowed to generate an additional output which the ideal functionality publicly outputs if there is no abort. In our presentation, we will simply view cMPC as a trusted classical party. We refer this setting as the MPC-hybrid model. The preprocessing MPC-hybrid model extends the MPC-hybrid model by allowing an input-independent trusted setup to be executed prior to the actual protocol.

One can instantiate the MPC ideal functionality using a post-quantum best-of-both-worlds MPC protocol with publicly verifiable identifiable abort and publicly verifiable output. In the literature [3,6,17], post-quantum MPCs are typically derived from classical MPC protocols featuring black-box, straight-line simulations and reductions in the CRS model to circumvent the challenging issue of quantum rewinding in proving post-quantum security. In our case, we begin with the MPC-PVIA protocol of [7] Theorem 1.3 that has black-box, straight-line simulations and reductions and then apply the [21] compiler to obtain BoBW security. To facilitate straight-line simulation, we replace the commitment scheme in

---

[5] The functionality can be equipped with an internal state that may be taken into account when it is called next time.

[21] with a UC-secure commitment scheme akin to the one in [7]. The resulting BoBW-MPC-PVIA protocol achieves post-quantum security in the CRS model, assuming post-quantum OT and a classical broadcast channel.[6]

5   Auditable Quantum Authentication (AQA)

This section presents a new primitive called *Auditable Quantum Authentication* (AQA) that lets a sender send quantum messages to a receiver and be accountable for his sending action. AQA is designed to identify the malicious sender only, while the receiving behavior is automatically guaranteed by successfully passing the test. In contrast to traditional quantum authentication codes like the Clifford or Trap codes, which necessitate the receiver to verify the checking bits, AQA adopts a different approach. It obliges the sender to generate the proof that should be verified by the auditor.

Definition 7 (Auditable Quantum Authentication). *An auditable quantum authentication scheme consists of the following five algorithms:*

- Setup$(1^\lambda, 1^\ell) \to (\mathsf{sk}, \phi_S, \phi_R)$ *takes as input the security parameter λ and the message length ℓ and outputs a classical secret key* sk, *a quantum sending state* ϕ_S *and a quantum receiving state* ϕ_R.
- Enc$(\mathsf{sk}, \rho) \to \sigma$ *takes as input a classical secret key* sk, *a quantum message state* $\rho \in \mathcal{D}^\ell$ *and outputs a quantum authenticated state* σ.
- Send$(\sigma, \phi_S) \to \mathsf{pf}$ *takes as input a quantum authenticated state* σ, *a quantum sending state* ϕ_S *and outputs a classical proof* pf.
- Audit$(\mathsf{sk}, \mathsf{pf}) \to \mathsf{dk}$ *is a classical algorithm that takes as input a secret key* sk, *a proof* pf *and outputs a decryption key* dk. *When the proof is invalid,* dk *will be set as* $\perp$.
- Recv$(\mathsf{dk}, \phi_R) \to \rho'$ *takes as input a classical decryption key* dk, *a quantum receiving state* ϕ_R *and outputs a quantum message state* ρ'. *When* $\mathsf{dk} = \perp$, ρ' *will be set as* $\perp$.

These algorithms should satisfy the following properties:

- *Sender completeness: For every quantum message state* $\rho \in \mathcal{D}^\ell$, *it holds that*

$$\Pr\left[\mathsf{dk} \neq \perp \;\middle|\; \begin{array}{c} (\mathsf{sk}, \phi_S, \phi_R) \leftarrow \mathsf{Setup}(1^\lambda, 1^\ell) \\ \sigma \leftarrow \mathsf{Enc}(\mathsf{sk}, \rho) \\ \mathsf{pf} \leftarrow \mathsf{Send}(\sigma, \phi_S) \\ \mathsf{dk} \leftarrow \mathsf{Audit}(\mathsf{sk}, \mathsf{pf}) \end{array}\right] = 1$$

- *Receiver security: There exists algorithms* $\widetilde{\mathsf{Setup}}, \widetilde{\mathsf{Enc}}, \widetilde{\mathsf{Audit}}$ *such that* $\mathsf{Recv} \circ \widetilde{\mathsf{Enc}} = \mathbb{1}$ *and that for every completely positive map* $\mathcal{A}$ *and every possibly*

---

[6] Note that [7] additionally assumes a 2-correlation robust hash function for the practical efficiency of garbled circuits, which can be avoided if we only aim for feasibility.

entangled quantum states ρ, ρ_{aux}, it holds that

$$\left\{ (dk,\phi_A) \;\middle|\; \begin{array}{c} (\text{sk},\phi_S,\phi_R)\leftarrow\text{Setup}(1^\lambda,1^\ell) \\ \sigma\leftarrow\text{Enc}(\text{sk},\rho) \\ (\text{pf},\phi_A)\leftarrow\mathcal{A}(\sigma,\phi_S,\phi_R,\rho_{\text{aux}}) \\ dk\leftarrow\text{Audit}(\text{sk},\text{pf}) \end{array} \right\} \underset{\text{negl}(\lambda)}{\approx} \left\{ (dk,\phi_A) \;\middle|\; \begin{array}{c} (\text{sk},\phi_S,\sigma)\leftarrow\widetilde{\text{Setup}}(1^\lambda,1^\ell) \\ (dk,\phi_R)\leftarrow\widetilde{\text{Enc}}(\rho) \\ (\text{pf},\phi_A)\leftarrow\mathcal{A}(\sigma,\phi_S,\phi_R,\rho_{\text{aux}}) \\ dk\leftarrow\bot \; if \; \bot\leftarrow\widetilde{\text{Audit}}(\text{sk},\text{pf}) \end{array} \right\}$$

Sender completeness guarantees that the honest sender always passes the audit. Receiver security is defined through the indistinguishability of two kinds of executions, implying that whatever property is satisfied by the right-hand side will also hold up to a negligible error for the left-hand side.

In particular, receiver security captures the following properties. First, it guarantees that the sender's inputs (σ, ϕ_S) are as if they can be generated independently of ρ, and hence contain no information about the message ρ. Similarly, the receiver's input ϕ_R is as if it already encodes ρ. Second, dk is the only information required for the receiver to recover ρ from ϕ_R, and the honest receiver always obtains the true message given that the audit accepts. Third, all the adversarial sender can do, even if the sender and the receiver collude, is to completely destroy dk at the cost of making the audit output $\bot$ at the same time Fig. 3.

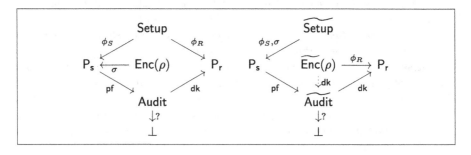

Fig. 3. AQA real execution (left) and fake execution (right)

5.1 Construction

Construction 1. Clifford-Form AQA

- Setup$(1^\lambda, 1^\ell)$:
  1. Sample random Clifford $F \leftarrow \mathscr{C}_{\ell+\lambda}$ and random Pauli $P_M, P_S \leftarrow \mathscr{P}_{\ell+\lambda}$, $P_R \leftarrow \mathscr{P}_\ell, P_C \leftarrow \mathscr{P}_\lambda$.
  2. Prepare EPR pairs $(\hat{\mathcal{S}}^{\hat{S}}, (\hat{\mathcal{R}}^{\hat{R}}, \hat{\mathcal{C}}^{\hat{C}}))$ with $|\hat{S}| = \ell + \lambda$, $|\hat{R}| = \ell$, $|\hat{C}| = \lambda$.

3. Apply $P_S{}^{\hat{S}} P_R{}^{\hat{R}} P_C{}^{\hat{C}} F^\dagger{}^{\hat{R},\hat{C}}$. Name the resulting state as $\phi_S{}^{\hat{S},\hat{C}}$ and $\phi_R{}^{\hat{R}}$.
4. Output $(\mathsf{sk}, \phi_S, \phi_R)$ where $\mathsf{sk} = (F, P_M, P_S, P_C, P_R)$.

- $\mathsf{Enc}(\mathsf{sk}, \rho)$: Parse $\mathsf{sk} = (F, P_M, P_S, P_C, P_R)$ and output $\sigma = P_M F(\rho \otimes 0^\lambda) F^\dagger P_M^\dagger$.

- $\mathsf{Send}(\sigma^{\hat{M}}, \phi_S{}^{\hat{S},\hat{C}})$:
  1. Teleport $\sigma^{\hat{M}}$ via $\hat{S}$ and obtain the teleportation result $\hat{P}$.
  2. Measure $\hat{C}$ in the computational basis and obtain measurement result $\hat{c}$.
  3. Output $\mathsf{pf} = (\hat{P}, \hat{c})$.

- $\mathsf{Audit}(\mathsf{sk}, \mathsf{pf})$:
  1. Parse $\mathsf{sk} = (F, P_M, P_S, P_C, P_R)$ and $\mathsf{pf} = (\hat{P}, \hat{c})$.
  2. Compute the quantum one-time pad $P_{M,S} := \mathsf{TP}(P_M \otimes P_S)\mathsf{TP}^\dagger$. Set the decoded teleportation result $\hat{P}'$ as the Pauli with string representation $\big(z(\hat{P}), x(\hat{P})\big) \oplus x(P_{M,S})$.
  3. Split the twirled Pauli $F^\dagger \hat{P}' F \in \mathscr{P}_{\ell+\lambda}$ as $\hat{P}'_R, \hat{P}'_C$ that act on ℓ, λ qupits respectively.
  4. If $\hat{c} \neq x(\hat{P}'_C) \oplus x(P_C)$, output $\mathsf{dk} = \perp$. Otherwise, output $\mathsf{dk} = P_R \hat{P}'_R$.

- $\mathsf{Recv}(\mathsf{dk}, \phi_R)$: If $\mathsf{dk} \neq \perp$, parse dk as a Pauli gate and output $\rho' = \mathsf{dk}^\dagger(\phi_R)\mathsf{dk}$.

In light of the homomorphic property of the Clifford code (Section 3.3), we additionally define EncG which extracts the encoding Clifford gate from the secret key. It will be useful in applications that make use of homomorphic computation.

- $\mathsf{EncG}(\mathsf{sk})$: Parse $\mathsf{sk} = (F, P_M, P_S, P_C, P_R)$ and output $P_M F$.

5.2   Security

Theorem 5. *Construction 1 is an Auditable Quantum Authentication scheme.*

Proof. We take the following steps. First, we analyze the state (dk, ϕ_A) that results from executing $(\mathsf{Setup}, \mathsf{Enc}, \mathcal{A}, \mathsf{Audit})$ in a row. Second, we prove sender completeness by plugging in $\mathcal{A} = \mathsf{Send}$. Third, we show that the distribution of (dk, ϕ_A) generated above is indistinguishable from a simpler state. Last, we construct $\widetilde{\mathsf{Setup}}, \widetilde{\mathsf{Enc}}, \widetilde{\mathsf{Audit}}$ that satisfy the requirements of receiver security.

Step 1. Without loss of generality, we assume that $\mathcal{A}$ has the same output length in ϕ_A as the input length. We can also assume that $\mathcal{A}(\sigma^{\hat{M}}, \phi_S{}^{\hat{S},\hat{C}}, \phi_R{}^{\hat{R}}, \rho_{\mathrm{aux}}{}^{\hat{W}})$ produces the classical proof pf by measuring the registers $(\hat{M}, \hat{S}, \hat{C})$ in the computational basis. Moreover, we can assume that the CP map $\mathcal{A}$ takes the form $\tau \mapsto A\tau A^\dagger$ because every CP map can be decomposed into a sum of such operators and indistinguishability of subnormalized states extends under addition. We denote the Pauli decomposition of $A' = A\,\mathsf{TP}^{\dagger\,\hat{M},\hat{S}}$ as $\sum_{Q \in \mathscr{P}_*} Q^{\hat{M},\hat{S},\hat{C}} \otimes A'_Q{}^{\hat{R},\hat{W}}$.

By definition, the execution of Setup and Enc yields a random classical key $\mathsf{sk} = (F, P_M, P_S, P_C, P_R)$ and quantum state

$$\left(\sigma^{\hat{M}}, \phi_S^{\hat{S},\hat{C}}, \phi_R^{\hat{R}}\right) = \mathsf{Mixed}\left[\left(P_M F\left(\rho, |0\rangle^{\otimes\lambda}\right)^{\hat{M}}, P_S \hat{S}^{\hat{S}}, (P_R \otimes P_C) F^\dagger\left(\hat{R}, \hat{C}\right)^{\hat{R},\hat{C}}\right)\right]$$

After the execution of $\mathcal{A}$, the joint state is

$$\mathbb{E}_{\mathsf{sk}}\, \mathsf{Mixed}\left[A\left(P_M F\left(\rho, |0\rangle^{\otimes\lambda}\right)^{\hat{M}}, P_S \hat{S}^{\hat{S}}, (P_R \otimes P_C) F^\dagger\left(\hat{R}, \hat{C}\right)^{\hat{R},\hat{C}}, \rho_{\mathsf{aux}}^{\hat{W}}\right) \otimes |\mathsf{sk}\rangle\right]$$

$$=\mathbb{E}_{\mathsf{sk}}\, \mathsf{Mixed}\left[A'\left(\mathsf{TP}\left(P_M F\left(\rho, |0\rangle^{\otimes\lambda}\right)^{\hat{M}}, P_S \hat{S}^{\hat{S}}\right), (P_R \otimes P_C) F^\dagger\left(\hat{R}, \hat{C}\right)^{\hat{R},\hat{C}}, \rho_{\mathsf{aux}}^{\hat{W}}\right) \otimes |\mathsf{sk}\rangle\right]$$

$$=\mathbb{E}_{\mathsf{sk}}\, \mathsf{Mixed}\left[A'\left(P_{M,S}\mathsf{TP}\left(F\left(\rho, |0\rangle^{\otimes\lambda}\right)^{\hat{M}}, \hat{S}^{\hat{S}}\right), (P_R \otimes P_C) F^\dagger\left(\hat{R}, \hat{C}\right)^{\hat{R},\hat{C}}, \rho_{\mathsf{aux}}^{\hat{W}}\right) \otimes |\mathsf{sk}\rangle\right]$$

$$=\mathbb{E}_{\mathsf{sk}}\, \mathsf{Mixed}\left[A'\left(\sum_P \frac{1}{p^{\ell+\lambda}}\left(P_{M,S}|z(P), x(P)\rangle^{\hat{M},\hat{S}}, (P_R \otimes P_C) F^\dagger P F\left(\rho, |0\rangle^{\otimes\lambda}\right)^{\hat{R},\hat{C}}, \rho_{\mathsf{aux}}^{\hat{W}}\right)\right) \otimes |\mathsf{sk}\rangle\right]$$

The first and second equalities follows from the definitions of A' and $P_{M,S}$, and the last equality is by quantum teleportation. Let us define the linear functions

$$L_F(P) := \left(z(P), x(P), x(F^\dagger P F)_{[\ell+1:\ell+\lambda]}\right) \in \mathbb{Z}_p^{2\ell+3\lambda}$$

$$K_F(P) := \left(F^\dagger P F\right)_{[1:\ell]} \in \mathscr{P}_\ell$$

for every Clifford operator F. The joint state can be simplified as

$$\mathbb{E}_{\mathsf{sk}}\, \mathsf{Mixed}\left[A'\left(\sum_P \frac{1}{p^{\ell+\lambda}}\left((P_{M,S} \otimes P_C)|L_F(P)\rangle^{\hat{M},\hat{S},\hat{C}}, P_R K_F(P)(\rho)^{\hat{R}}, \rho_{\mathsf{aux}}^{\hat{W}}\right)\right) \otimes |\mathsf{sk}\rangle\right]$$

The next step is to apply Audit, which checks whether the value stored in $(\hat{M}, \hat{S}, \hat{C})$ is equal to $L_F(\hat{P}) \oplus x(P_{M,S} \otimes P_C)$ for some $\hat{P} \in \mathscr{P}_{\ell+\lambda}$. If there is such a $\hat{P}$, then Audit outputs $\mathsf{dk} = P_R K_F(\hat{P})$; otherwise, it outputs $\mathsf{dk} = \bot$. To analyze the resulting state post-selected on finding $\hat{P}$, we can apply Pauli twirl with target measurement result $L_F(\hat{P})$ (lemma 2) using the Pauli decomposition of A'. We obtain

$$\mathop{\mathbb{E}}_{r,F,P_R} \sum_P \mathsf{Mixed}\left[\sum_{x(Q)=L_F(\hat{P}/P)} \frac{1}{p^{\ell+\lambda}} Q|r\rangle \otimes A'_Q\left(P_R K_F(P)(\rho), \rho_{\mathsf{aux}}\right) \otimes |P_R K_F(\hat{P})\rangle\right]$$

$$= \mathop{\mathbb{E}}_{r,F,P_R} \sum_P \mathsf{Mixed}\left[\sum_{x(Q)=L_F(\hat{P}/P)} \frac{1}{p^{\ell+\lambda}} Q|r\rangle \otimes A'_Q\left(P_R(\rho), \rho_{\mathsf{aux}}\right) \otimes |P_R K_F(\hat{P}/P)\rangle\right]$$

$$= \frac{1}{p^{2(\ell+\lambda)}} \mathop{\mathbb{E}}_{r,F,P_R} \sum_P \mathsf{Mixed}\left[\sum_{x(Q)=L_F(P)} Q|r\rangle \otimes A'_Q\left(P_R(\rho), \rho_{\mathsf{aux}}\right) \otimes |P_R K_F(P)\rangle\right]$$

where we change variables $P_R \leftarrow P_R K_F(P)$ in the second line and $P \leftarrow \hat{P}/P$ in the third line. Summing the post-selected states corresponding to every Pauli $\hat{P} \in \mathscr{P}_{\ell+\lambda}$, we obtain the state conditioned that Audit accepts as

$$\mathop{\mathbb{E}}_{r,F,P_R} \sum_P \mathsf{Mixed}\left[\sum_{x(Q)=L_F(P)} Q|r\rangle^{\hat{M},\hat{S},\hat{C}} \otimes A'_Q\left(P_R(\rho)^{\hat{R}}, \rho_{\mathsf{aux}}^{\hat{W}}\right) \otimes |P_R K_F(P)\rangle\right] \quad (1)$$

Similarly, the state conditioned that Audit rejects is

$$
\mathop{\mathbb{E}}_{r,F,P_R} \sum_{x \notin \text{RANGE}(L_F)} \text{Mixed} \left[\sum_{x(Q)=x} Q|r\rangle^{\hat{M},\hat{S},\hat{C}} \otimes A'_Q \left(P_R(\rho)^{\hat{R}}, \rho_{\text{aux}}^{\hat{W}} \right) \otimes |\bot\rangle \right] \quad (2)
$$

Step 2. To see sender completeness, we take $\mathcal{A} = \text{Send}$, which applies $\text{TP}^{\hat{M},\hat{S}}$ followed by measuring $(\hat{M}, \hat{S}, \hat{C})$ in the computational basis. The induced $A' = A \, \text{TP}^\dagger$ is a measurement in the computational basis, and the Pauli decomposition of A' involves only terms with $x(Q) = 0 \in \text{RANGE}(L_F)$. For such A', expression (2) shows that Audit never outputs $\bot$.

Step 3. We claim that (1)+(2) is statistically indistinguishable to (3)+(4).

$$
\mathop{\mathbb{E}}_{r,P_R} \text{Mixed} \left[\sum_{x(Q)=0} Q|r\rangle^{\hat{M},\hat{S},\hat{C}} \otimes A'_Q \left(P_R(\rho)^{\hat{R}}, \rho_{\text{aux}}^{\hat{W}} \right) \otimes |P_R\rangle \right] \quad (3)
$$

$$
\mathop{\mathbb{E}}_{r,P_R} \sum_{x \neq 0} \text{Mixed} \left[\sum_{x(Q)=x} Q|r\rangle^{\hat{M},\hat{S},\hat{C}} \otimes A'_Q \left(P_R(\rho)^{\hat{R}}, \rho_{\text{aux}}^{\hat{W}} \right) \otimes |\bot\rangle \right] \quad (4)
$$

The trace distance between (1) and (3) is

$$
\text{tr} \left| \mathop{\mathbb{E}}_{F,r,P_R} \sum_{P \neq I} \text{Mixed} \left[\sum_{x(Q)=L_F(P)} Q|r\rangle \otimes A'_Q \left(P_R(\rho), \rho_{\text{aux}} \right) \otimes |P_R K_F(P)\rangle \right] \right|
$$

$$
\leq \sum_{x \neq 0} \sum_{P \neq I} \mathop{\mathbb{E}}_{F,r,P_R} 1_{L_F(P)=x} \, \text{tr} \left| \text{Mixed} \left[\sum_{x(Q)=x} Q|r\rangle \otimes A'_Q \left(P_R(\rho), \rho_{\text{aux}} \right) \otimes |P_R K_F(P)\rangle \right] \right|
$$

$$
= \sum_{x \neq 0} \mathop{\mathbb{E}}_{r,P_R} \left(\sum_{P \neq I} \mathop{\text{Pr}}_F [L_F(P) = x] \right) \text{tr} \left(\text{Mixed} \left[\sum_{x(Q)=x} Q|r\rangle \otimes A'_Q \left(P_R(\rho), \rho_{\text{aux}} \right) \right] \right)
$$

$$
= \sum_{x \neq 0} \mathop{\mathbb{E}}_{r,P_R} \text{Pr} \left[x \in \text{RANGE}(L_F) \right] \text{tr} \left(\text{Mixed} \left[\sum_{x(Q)=x} Q|r\rangle \otimes A'_Q \left(P_R(\rho), \rho_{\text{aux}} \right) \right] \right)
$$

$$
\quad (5)
$$

which follows from the triangle inequality, the positivity of Mixed $[\cdot]$, and the observation that each x has at most one P such that $L_F(P) = x$. Similarly, the trace distance between (2) and (4) is

$$
\mathop{\mathbb{E}}_{r,P_R} \sum_{x \neq 0} (1 - \text{Pr}[x \notin \text{RANGE}(L_F)]) \, \text{tr} \left(\text{Mixed} \left[\sum_{x(Q)=x} Q|r\rangle \otimes A'_Q \left(P_R(\rho), \rho_{\text{aux}} \right) \right] \right)
$$

which is equal to (5). By the triangle inequality, the trace distance between (1)+(2) and (3)+(4) is upper bounded by

$$\sum_{x \neq 0} \mathop{\mathbb{E}}_{r, P_R} 2 \Pr\left[x \in \text{RANGE}(L_F)\right] \operatorname{tr}\left(\text{Mixed}\left[\sum_{x(Q)=x} Q|r\rangle \otimes A'_Q\left(P_R(\rho), \rho_{\text{aux}}\right)\right]\right)$$

$$\leq \text{negl}(\lambda) \sum_{x \neq 0} \mathop{\mathbb{E}}_{s, P_R} \operatorname{tr}\left(\text{Mixed}\left[\sum_{x(Q)=x} Q|r\rangle \otimes A'_Q\left(P_R(\rho), \rho_{\text{aux}}\right)\right]\right) \leq \text{negl}(\lambda) \operatorname{tr}\left((3)+(4)\right).$$

The first inequality follows from the Pauli partitioning by Clifford (lemma 3). This establishes the statistical indistinguishability between (1)+(2) and (3)+(4).

Step 4. Finally, we construct $\widetilde{\text{Setup}}, \widetilde{\text{Enc}}, \widetilde{\text{Audit}}$ and prove receiver security.

$\widetilde{\text{Setup}}(1^\lambda, 1^\ell)$:
1. Sample a random string sk $\leftarrow \mathbb{Z}_p^{2\ell+3\lambda}$.
2. Output $(\text{sk}, \phi_S, \sigma)$, where $(\sigma^{\hat{M}}, \phi_S^{\hat{S}, \hat{C}})$ is the result of applying $\text{TP}^{\dagger \hat{M}, \hat{S}}$ to $|\text{sk}\rangle^{\hat{M}, \hat{S}, \hat{C}}$.

$\widetilde{\text{Enc}}(\rho)$:
1. Sample a random Pauli dk $\leftarrow \mathscr{P}_\ell$.
2. Output (dk, σ) where $\sigma = \text{dk}(\rho)\text{dk}^\dagger$.

$\widetilde{\text{Audit}}(\text{sk}, \text{pf})$:
1. Parse $\text{pf} = (\hat{P}, \hat{c})$.
2. Output $\perp$ if $(z(\hat{P}), x(\hat{P}), \hat{c}) \neq \text{sk}$.

It is direct to see that $\text{Recv} \circ \widetilde{\text{Enc}} = \mathbb{1}$. We now analyze the state (dk, ϕ_A) that results from executing $(\widetilde{\text{Setup}}, \widetilde{\text{Enc}}, \mathcal{A})$ in a row and replacing $\text{dk} \leftarrow \perp$ if $\perp \leftarrow \widetilde{\text{Audit}}$. The execution of $\widetilde{\text{Setup}}$ and $\widetilde{\text{Enc}}$ yields random classical keys $\text{sk} = r$, $\text{dk} = P$ and quantum state

$$\left(\sigma^{\hat{M}}, \phi_S^{\hat{S}, \hat{C}}, \phi_R^{\hat{R}}\right) = \text{Mixed}\left[\left(\text{TP}^{\dagger \hat{M}, \hat{S}}|r\rangle^{\hat{M}, \hat{S}, \hat{C}}, P\rho^{\hat{R}}\right)\right]$$

After the execution of $\mathcal{A}$, the joint state is

$$\mathop{\mathbb{E}}_{r, P} \text{Mixed}\left[A\left(\text{TP}^{\dagger \hat{M}, \hat{S}}|r\rangle^{\hat{M}, \hat{S}, \hat{C}}, P\rho^{\hat{R}}, \rho_{\text{aux}}^{\hat{W}}\right) \otimes |r\rangle \otimes |P\rangle\right]$$

$$= \mathop{\mathbb{E}}_{r, P} \text{Mixed}\left[A'\left(|r\rangle^{\hat{M}, \hat{S}, \hat{C}}, P\rho^{\hat{R}}, \rho_{\text{aux}}^{\hat{W}}\right) \otimes |r\rangle \otimes |P\rangle\right]$$

The next step is to apply $\widetilde{\text{Audit}}$, which corresponds to the projection $|r\rangle\langle r|^{\hat{M}, \hat{S}, \hat{C}}$. The state conditioned that $\widetilde{\text{Audit}}$ accepts can be analyzed through Pauli twirl with target measurement result 0 (lemma 2), which yields exactly (3). Similarly, the state conditioned that $\widetilde{\text{Audit}}$ rejects is exactly (4). Hence, (dk, ϕ_A) generated from $(\text{Setup}, \text{Enc}, \mathcal{A}, \text{Audit})$ and from $(\widetilde{\text{Setup}}, \widetilde{\text{Enc}}, \mathcal{A}, \widetilde{\text{Audit}})$ are indistinguishable, which establishes receiver security.

6   MPQC-PVIA with Trusted Setup

Here, we present our MPQC protocol with a trusted setup. We make use of the Clifford-form AQA developed in the previous section together with cMPC to achieve PVIA security. For simplicity, we work with qubits i.e., $p = 2$ here. The protocol is divided into two parts:

1. An offline phase using a trusted setup: a trusted setup Σ^{PVIA} prepares EPR pairs $(\mathcal{S}_i, \mathcal{R}_i)$ of length ℓ_i and distributes the sending side $\mathcal{S}_i$ to party P_i. Next, the trusted setup encodes all of the receiving sides $\mathcal{R}_1, \cdots, \mathcal{R}_n$ and the ancilla ϕ_{anc} into a single ciphertext σ, which is sent to the server. This server can be any participant in the MPQC game; for simplicity, we can assume it's the first party. The above quantum states will later be utilized in the input encoding stage. The trusted setup then executes AQA.Setup to obtain portals for the output delivery stage. Finally, the trusted setup transmits information related to the secret keys to cMPC.
2. An online phase: every party acts as a client who teleports their input to the server. Directed by cMPC, the server evaluates the circuit on the ciphertext σ. Finally, the server returns the outputs to all clients using AQA.

Protocol 1. $(\Sigma^{\mathsf{PVIA}}, \Pi^{\mathsf{PVIA}})$ for MPQC-PVIA with Trusted Setup

---

Common Input: A quantum circuit C in the format of Section 4. **Trusted**

Setup Σ^{PVIA}:

1. Prepare EPR pairs $(\mathcal{S}_i^{S_i}, \mathcal{R}_i^{R_i})$ with $|S_i| = |R_i| = \ell_i$.
2. Initialize the ancilla register $N = (N_1, \cdots, N_d)$ as ϕ_{anc}.
3. Initialize the trap register $T = (T_1, \cdots, T_{n+d})$ as $|0\rangle^{\otimes(n+d)\lambda}$.
4. Sample $(\mathsf{sk}_i, \phi_{S,i}, \phi_{R,i}) \leftarrow \mathsf{AQA.Setup}(1^\lambda, 1^{\ell_i})$.
5. Sample Clifford $E \leftarrow \mathscr{C}_{\ell_{\mathsf{total}}+(n+d)\lambda}$ and apply $E^{R_1, \cdots, R_n, N, T}$ with result σ.
6. Send $(\sigma^{R_1, \cdots, R_n, N, T}, \phi_{S,1}, \cdots, \phi_{S,n})$ to server. Send $(\mathcal{S}_i^{S_i}, \phi_{R,i})$ to client i.
7. Send the secrets $(E, \mathsf{sk}_1, \cdots, \mathsf{sk}_n)$ to cMPC.

Online Input: Client i receives $\rho_i \in \mathcal{D}^{\ell_i}$.

Protocol Π^{PVIA}:

Input Encoding:

1. Client i teleports ρ_i via $\mathcal{S}_i^{S_i}$ and sends the teleportation result P_i to cMPC.
2. cMPC sets the key $E_d = E^{R_1, \cdots, R_n, N, T} P_1^{R_1} \cdots P_n^{R_n}$.

Computation:

3. For $k = d, \cdots, 1$:
   (a) cMPC sends the gate $V_k = (E_{k-1}'^{R_{[n]}, N_{[k-1]}, T_{[n+k-1]}} \otimes P_k' \mathsf{CX}_{c_k}^{N_k, T_{n+k}})$ $E_k^{\dagger R_{[n]}, N_{[k]}, T_{[n+k]}}$ to the server using a random Clifford $E_{k-1}' \leftarrow \mathscr{C}_{\Sigma_i \ell_i + (k-1)+(n+k-1)\lambda}$, a random Pauli $P_k' \leftarrow \mathscr{P}_{1+\lambda}^*$, and a random string $c_k \leftarrow \{0, 1\}^\lambda$.

(b) Server applies V_k to registers $(R_{[n]}, N_{[k]}, T_{[n+k]})$, measures (N_k, T_{n+k}) in the computational basis and sends the measurement outcome $r_k \in \{0,1\}^{1+\lambda}$ to cMPC.

(c) cMPC sets $b_k \in \{0,1\}$ as the solution to $r_k \oplus x(P'_k) = b_k(1, c_k)$ if there is a solution. Otherwise, cMPC publicly outputs the server as malicious and aborts.

(d) cMPC computes $G_{k-1} = f_k(b_k, \cdots, b_d)$ and sets the key $E_{k-1} = E'_{k-1}G^\dagger_{k-1}$.

Output Delivery:

4. cMPC sends server $V' = \mathsf{AQA.EncG(sk_1)}^{R_1, T_1} \cdots \mathsf{AQA.EncG(sk_n)}^{R_n, T_n}$ $E_0^{\dagger R_1, \cdots, R_n, T_1, \cdots, T_n}$.

5. Server applies $V'^{R_1, \cdots, R_n, T_1, \cdots, T_n}$ with result $(\hat{\sigma}_1^{\hat{M}_1}, \cdots, \hat{\sigma}_n^{\hat{M}_n})$ where $\hat{M}_i := (R_i, T_i)$.

6. Server computes $\mathsf{pf}_i \leftarrow \mathsf{AQA.Send}(\hat{\sigma}_i, \phi_{S,i})$ and sends the result to cMPC.

7. cMPC computes $\mathsf{dk}_i \leftarrow \mathsf{AQA.Audit(sk_i, pf}_i)$. If $\mathsf{dk}_i = \bot$, cMPC publicly outputs the server as malicious and aborts. Otherwise, cMPC sends dk_i to client i.

8. Client i outputs $\rho'_i \leftarrow \mathsf{AQA.Recv(dk}_i, \phi_{R,i})$.

6.1 Security

Theorem 6. ($\Sigma^{\mathsf{PVIA}}, \Pi^{\mathsf{PVIA}}$) *is a multi-party quantum computation secure with publicly verifiable identifiable abort in the preprocessing MPC-hybrid model as defined in Definition 6. i.e., For every non-uniform* (QPT) *adversary $\mathcal{A}$ corrupting party set I with $|I| \leq n-1$, there is a non-uniform* (QPT) *adversary $\mathsf{Sim}_\mathcal{A}$ corrupting I, such that for any (possibly entangled) states $\rho_1, \cdots \rho_n, \rho_{\mathsf{aux}}$,*

$$\{\mathsf{Real}^{\Pi^{\mathsf{PVIA}} \circ \Sigma^{\mathsf{PVIA}}}_{\mathcal{A}(\rho_{\mathsf{aux}})}(1^\lambda, C, \rho_1, \cdots, \rho_n)\} \approx \{\mathsf{Ideal}^{\mathsf{MPQC}}_{\mathsf{Sim}_\mathcal{A}(\rho_{\mathsf{aux}})}(1^\lambda, 0, C, \rho_1, \cdots, \rho_n)\}$$

Below is the simulator we use for Theorem 6. We refer the readers to our full version for the proof.

Simulator 1. $\mathsf{Sim}^{\mathsf{PVIA}}_{\mathcal{A}(\rho_{\mathsf{aux}})}$ for MPQC-PVIA with Trusted Setup

---

1. Fake setup (if client i is corrupted):
   (a) Prepare EPR pairs on registers $(S_i, \tilde{R}_i)$ with $|S_i| = |\tilde{R}_i| = \ell_i$.
   (b) Prepare EPR pairs on registers $(\tilde{S}_i, \hat{R}_i)$ with $|\tilde{S}_i| = |\hat{R}_i| = \ell_i$.
   (c) Send $(S_i, \hat{R}_i)$ to $\mathcal{A}$.
2. Fake setup (if server is corrupted):
   (a) Sample $(\mathsf{sk}_i, \phi_{S,i}, \sigma_i^{R_i, T_i}) \leftarrow \widetilde{\mathsf{AQA.Setup}}(1^\lambda, 1^{\ell_i})$ for $i \in [n]$.
   (b) Initialize registers (N_k, T_{n+k}) with random $\tilde{r}_k \leftarrow \{0,1\}^{\lambda+1}$ for $k \in [d]$.

(c) Sample random Clifford gates $V_k \leftarrow \mathscr{C}_{\ell_{\text{total}}+(n+k)\lambda}$ for $k = 0, 1, \cdots, d$.

(d) Apply $V_d^{\dagger R_{[n]}, N_{[d]}, T_{[n+d]}} \cdots V_1^{\dagger R_{[n]}, N_{[1]}, T_{[n+1]}} V_0^{\dagger R_{[n]}, T_{[n]}}$ with resulting state σ.

(e) Send $(\sigma^{R_1, \cdots, R_n, N, T}, \phi_{S,1}, \cdots, \phi_{S,n})$ to $\mathcal{A}$.

3. Input extraction: Receive P_i from $\mathcal{A}$ and extract the input $\tilde{\rho}_i^{\tilde{R}_i} = P_i^{\dagger} \tilde{\mathcal{R}}_i^{\tilde{R}_i}$.

4. Invoke the ideal functionality: Send $\tilde{\rho}_i$ to T and receive output $\tilde{\rho}_i'$ from T.

5. Check the abort decision (if server is corrupted):
   (a) For $k = d, \cdots, 1$, send V_k to $\mathcal{A}$ and receive r_k in return.
       If $r_k \neq \tilde{r}_k$, send **abort** to T in the name of the server.
   (b) Send V_0 to $\mathcal{A}$.
   (c) For $i \in [n]$, receive pf_i from $\mathcal{A}$.
       If $\bot \leftarrow \mathsf{AQA}.\widehat{\mathsf{Audit}}(\mathsf{sk}_i, \mathsf{pf}_i)$, send **abort** to T in the name of the server.

6. Output delivery: Teleport $\tilde{\rho}_i'$ via $\tilde{S}_i$, obtain its result $\tilde{P}_i$ and send $\mathsf{dk}_i = \tilde{P}_i$ to $\mathcal{A}$ if the server did not send **abort** in the previous step.

7. Output $\mathcal{A}$'s output.

---

7 BoBW-MPQC-PVIA with Trusted Setup

In this section, we describe our construction of best-of-both-worlds multi-party quantum computation protocol secure with publicly verifiable identifiable abort (BoBW-MPQC-PVIA). The protocol is similar to the MPQC-PVIA protocol but with n servers instead. P_j will be assigned as server j. The protocol is divided into two parts:

1. An offline setup: a setup Σ^{BoBW} prepares EPR pairs $(\mathcal{S}_i, \mathcal{R}_i)$ of length ℓ_i and distributes the sending side $\mathcal{S}_i$ to party P_i. Next, the setup uses a QECC scheme to encode every $\mathcal{R}_i$ into $\{\mathcal{R}_i^{(j)}\}_{j \in [n]}$ and the ancilla ϕ_{anc} into $\{\phi_{\mathsf{anc}}^{(j)}\}_{j \in [n]}$. Afterwards, the setup encrypts the j-th part of the QECC codewords into a Clifford ciphertext and send it to server j. The setup then executes $\mathsf{AQA}.\mathsf{Setup}$ to prepare for the output delivery stage. Finally, the setup sends the secret keys to cMPC.

2. An online phase: every party acts as a client who teleports their input to the servers. Directed by cMPC, the servers evaluate the circuit in a fault-tolerant manner. Each server j operates only on the ciphertext that encrypts the j-th part of the QECC codewords. Finally, the servers returns the outputs to the clients using AQA.

Theorem 7. *For every $t < \frac{n}{2}$, there is a best-of-both-worlds multi-party quantum computation secure with publicly verifiable identifiable abort of threshold t in the preprocessing MPC-hybrid model as in Definition 5.*

We refer the readers to our full version for the formal protocol and proof. They bear resemblance to those of Theorem 6 with the additional use of a $[[n, 1]]_p$ polynomial code that corrects t erasure errors, which exists by Lemma 4.

8   BoBW-MPQC-PVIA Without Trusted Setup

So far, we have demonstrated an BoBW-MPQC-PVIA protocol Π^{BoBW} in the preprocessing model with a trusted setup Σ^{BoBW}. Now, we will illustrate how to instantiate the preprocessing phase *without* a trusted setup. Our approach involves using MPQC-SWIA e.g., [3] to implement the preprocessing phase. Note that [3] requires a post-quantum fully homomorphic encryption assumption to achieve the security; however, we do not need this assumption when we want to compute circuits that have no inputs and apply only Clifford gates to $|0\rangle$'s and $|T\rangle$'s. We defer the explicit MPQC-SWIA construction to the full version of this paper. We reformulate MPQC-SWIA as the following lemma.

Lemma 6. (MPQC-SWIA). *There is a multi-party quantum computation Π^{SWIA} secure with identifiable abort in the MPC-hybrid model that computes quantum circuit C, given that C takes no inputs and only applies Clifford to ancillary $|0\rangle$ and $|T\rangle$ states. That is, for every non-uniform (QPT) adversary $\mathcal{A}$ corrupting party set I, there is a non-uniform (QPT) adversary $\mathsf{Sim}_{\mathcal{A}}^{\mathsf{SWIA}}$ corrupting I, such that*

$$\{\mathsf{Real}_{\mathcal{A}(\rho_{\mathsf{aux}})}^{\Pi^{\mathsf{SWIA}}}(1^\lambda, C)\} \approx \{\mathsf{Ideal}_{\mathsf{Sim}_{\mathcal{A}(\rho_{\mathsf{aux}})}^{\mathsf{SWIA}}}^{\mathsf{SWIA}}(1^\lambda, C)\}$$

$\mathsf{Ideal}^{\mathsf{SWIA}}$: Multi-party Quantum Computation Secure with Identifiable Abort

Common input:
   The security parameter 1^λ and a quantum circuit C with no inputs.
Input:
   $\mathcal{A}_I$ holds input ρ_{aux} and controls parties in I.
Execution of $\mathsf{T}^{\mathsf{SWIA}}$:
   $\mathsf{T}^{\mathsf{SWIA}}$ computes $(\rho_1', \rho_2', \cdots, \rho_n', r_{\mathsf{cMPC}}') \leftarrow C$, where r_{cMPC}' is classical.
   $\mathsf{T}^{\mathsf{SWIA}}$ sends ρ_i' to all $\mathsf{P}_i \in I$. Every $\mathsf{P}_i \in I$ can send **abort** to $\mathsf{T}^{\mathsf{SWIA}}$.
   Let I_{abort} be the set of parties who indeed send the **abort** message.
   If I_{abort} is non-empty, $\mathsf{T}^{\mathsf{SWIA}}$ sends the partition $\{I_{\mathsf{abort}}, \mathsf{P}_{[n]} \backslash I_{\mathsf{abort}}\}$ to all parties.
   Otherwise, $\mathsf{T}^{\mathsf{SWIA}}$ sends ρ_i' to all $\mathsf{P}_i \notin I$ and sends r_{cMPC}' to cMPC.
Output:
   Honest parties output whatever output received from $\mathsf{T}^{\mathsf{SWIA}}$.
   The adversary $\mathcal{A}_I$ outputs a function of his view.

We say an execution succeeds if every party receives their part of the circuit output. Whenever the execution fails, all parties get to know how they have been partitioned into two groups. An honest party can infer that the group he does not belong to (i.e., I_{abort}) is the set of malicious parties who interfered the computation.

In contrast to [3] where the partition information serves the purpose of SWIA, we utilize the partition information to design a preprocessing procedure that *always* succeeds. Such a preprocessing procedure will be suitable for replacing the setup of MPQC-PVIA.

8.1   Protocol

First, we let the parties run MPQC-SWIA over the setup circuit Σ^{BoBW} that the trusted setup is supposed to run. If the MPQC-SWIA fails, the parties will be divided into two groups. Each group will then ignore other groups and run MPQC-SWIA independently. By iterating this process, each party will eventually find a group in which the MPQC-SWIA succeeds and receive an output of the setup circuit. This constitutes our preprocessing procedure. Note that we do not publicly identify anyone during this stage.

After obtaining the output of the setup circuit, every party can run the protocol Π^{BoBW} within their group to obtain their MPQC output. It is reasonable for each group to operate independently, as they view other groups as untrustworthy. Parties within a group can set the inputs of the parties outside the group as some default inputs such as $|0\rangle$. Moreover, MPQC-SWIA guarantees that the honest parties are always in the same group, so they will jointly compute their outputs. Our approach circumvents the false accusation problem encountered in [3] because the parties in our protocol no longer accuse between groups. Instead, each group runs its own Π^{BoBW}, which only aborts dishonest members.

Protocol 2. Π^{MPQC} for BoBW-MPQC-PVIA

Input:

1. Everyone holds the threshold t and the circuit description C.
2. Party P_i holds private input $\rho_i \in \mathcal{D}^{\ell_i}$.

Protocol:

1. Set $G = \{\{\mathsf{P}_1, \cdots, \mathsf{P}_n\}\}$ as the initial partition of parties (i.e., no partition) and mark the set $\{\mathsf{P}_1, \cdots, \mathsf{P}_n\} \in G$ as unfinished.
2. Repeat the following as long as G contains a set S that is unfinished:
   (a) The parties in S run Π^{SWIA} over the setup circuit $\Sigma^{\mathsf{BoBW}}(t, C_S)$, where C_S is the circuit that prepares default inputs (e.g., $|0\rangle$) for parties not in S and runs C afterwards.
   (b) If Π^{SWIA} succeeds or if $|S| = 1$, parties in S has obtained the output of the setup circuit. In this case, mark S as finished.
   (c) Otherwise, Π^{SWIA} instructs to partition S into $\{S_0, S_1\}$ of S. In this case, replace S with S_0 and S_1 in G, and mark both S_0, S_1 as unfinished.
3. Run $\Pi^{\mathsf{BoBW}}(t, C_S)$ within every set $S \in G$.
4. Let J be the union of all corruption lists output by all executions of Π^{BoBW}. We note that every corruption list is public and only contains the parties that participate.

Output:

1. If $|J| > t$, every party outputs J as malicious and aborts.
2. Otherwise, P_i outputs the result obtained from his execution of Π^{BoBW}.

Theorem 8. Π^{MPQC} *is a best-of-both-worlds multi-party quantum computation with publicly verifiable identifiable abort of threshold t in the MPC-hybrid model.*

Proof sketch. We want to show that the real world and the ideal world are indistinguishable using the following simulator. Let $\mathsf{Sim}^{\mathsf{BoBW}}$ be the simulator for $(\Sigma^{\mathsf{BoBW}}, \Pi^{\mathsf{BoBW}})$. We regard $\mathcal{A}$ as a stateful adversary throughout.

Simulator 2. $\mathsf{Sim}^{\mathsf{MPQC}}_{\mathcal{A}(\rho_{\mathsf{aux}})}$ for BoBW-MPQC-PVIA

---

1. Set $S = \{\mathsf{P}_1, \cdots, \mathsf{P}_n\}$ as the initial group that contains all the honest parties.
2. Repeat the following as long as the inner $\mathsf{Ideal}^{\mathsf{SWIA}}$ fails:
   (a) Run a simulated $\mathsf{Ideal}^{\mathsf{SWIA}}$ that computes the first part of $\mathsf{Sim}^{\mathsf{BoBW}}_{\mathcal{A}}(C_S)$, which is a circuit that resembles the setup circuit $\Sigma^{\mathsf{BoBW}}(C_S)$ but prepares different states.
   (b) Run $\mathsf{Sim}^{\mathsf{SWIA}}_{\mathcal{A}}$ who interacts with the simulated $\mathsf{Ideal}^{\mathsf{SWIA}}$.
   (c) Upon failure, let I_{abort} be the set of parties instructed by $\mathsf{Sim}^{\mathsf{SWIA}}_{\mathcal{A}}$ to send abort. Run $\mathcal{A}$ to complete the steps in the protocol that involve only the malicious group I_{abort}.
   (d) Set S as the updated group $S \backslash I_{\mathsf{abort}}$ that contains all the honest parties.
3. For every corrupted party not in S, send their default input to the ideal functionality.
4. Run the remaining part of $\mathsf{Sim}^{\mathsf{BoBW}}_{\mathcal{A}}(C_S)$, which interacts with the ideal functionality.
5. Let J be the union of all corrupted lists output by all executions of Π^{BoBW}. Make all parties in J send abort to the ideal functionality.
6. Output the output of $\mathcal{A}$.

We show indistinguishability by gradually modifying the real world. Since the sub-protocols Π^{SWIA} are executed sequentially, we can apply Lemma 6 to replace them with ideal executions of $\mathsf{Ideal}^{\mathsf{SWIA}}$ one by one, incurring only a negligible difference. Similarly, we can apply Theorem 7 to replace the real executions of Π^{BoBW} with ideal executions of $\mathsf{Ideal}^{\mathsf{MPQC}}$ one by one. Next, we replace the ideal execution of $\mathsf{Ideal}^{\mathsf{MPQC}}$ that involves only the group S that contains all honest parties with an ideal execution of $\mathsf{Ideal}^{\mathsf{MPQC}}$ that involves all parties, where parties not in S always send default inputs. Also, for every corruption list output by a group other than S, we let the malicious parties in the list send abort to the above $\mathsf{Ideal}^{\mathsf{MPQC}}$. It is direct to see that such a replacement always produces the same outputs and abort decisions. Merging all the simulators and ideal functionalities except for $\mathsf{Ideal}^{\mathsf{MPQC}}$ in the last hybrid world gives us simulator 2. Thus, the real and ideal worlds are indistinguishable. □

Acknowledgement. The authors would like to thank Andrea Coladangelo for useful discussions. This research is supported by NSF CAREER award 2141536, the Air Force Office of Scientific Research under award number FA2386-20-1-4066, and NSTC TACC project under Grant no. NSTC 112-2634-F-001-001-MBK.

References

1. Aharonov, D., Ben-Or, M.: Fault-tolerant quantum computation with constant error. In: Proceedings of the Twenty-ninth Annual ACM Symposium on Theory of Computing, pp. 176–188 (1997). https://doi.org/10.1145/258533.258579
2. Aharonov, D., Ben-Or, M., Eban, E., Mahadev, U.: Interactive proofs for quantum computations. arXiv preprint arXiv:1704.04487 (2017). https://doi.org/10.48550/arXiv.1704.04487
3. Alon, B., Chung, H., Chung, K.-M., Huang, M.-Y., Lee, Y., Shen, Y.-C.: Round efficient secure multiparty quantum computation with identifiable abort. In: Malkin, T., Peikert, C. (eds.) Advances in Cryptology – CRYPTO 2021: 41st Annual International Cryptology Conference, CRYPTO 2021, Virtual Event, August 16–20, 2021, Proceedings, Part I, pp. 436–466. Springer International Publishing, Cham (2021). https://doi.org/10.1007/978-3-030-84242-0_16
4. Ambainis, A., Buhrman, H., Dodis, Y., Rohrig, H.: Multiparty quantum coin flipping. In: Proceedings of 19th IEEE Annual Conference on Computational Complexity, 2004, pp. 250–259. IEEE (2004). https://doi.org/10.1109/CCC.2004.1313848
5. Barnum, H., Crépeau, C., Gottesman, D., Smith, A., Tapp, A.: Authentication of quantum messages. In: The 43rd Annual IEEE Symposium on Foundations of Computer Science, 2002. Proceedings, pp. 449–458. IEEE (2002). https://doi.org/10.1109/SFCS.2002.1181969
6. Bartusek, J., Coladangelo, A., Khurana, D., Ma, F.: On the round complexity of secure quantum computation. In: Malkin, T., Peikert, C. (eds.) CRYPTO 2021. LNCS, vol. 12825, pp. 406–435. Springer, Cham (2021). https://doi.org/10.1007/978-3-030-84242-0_15
7. Baum, C., Orsini, E., Scholl, P., Soria-Vazquez, E.: Efficient constant-round MPC with identifiable abort and public verifiability. In: Micciancio, D., Ristenpart, T. (eds.) CRYPTO 2020. LNCS, vol. 12171, pp. 562–592. Springer, Cham (2020). https://doi.org/10.1007/978-3-030-56880-1_20
8. Beimel, A., Lindell, Y., Omri, E., Orlov, I.: 1/p-Secure multiparty computation without an honest majority and the best of both worlds. J. Cryptol. 33(4), 1659–1731 (2020). https://doi.org/10.1007/s00145-020-09354-z
9. Ben-Or, M., Crepeau, C., Gottesman, D., Hassidim, A., Smith, A.: Secure multiparty quantum computation with (only) a strict honest majority. In: 2006 47th Annual IEEE Symposium on Foundations of Computer Science (FOCS'06). IEEE (2006). https://doi.org/10.1109/FOCS.2006.68
10. Bravyi, S., Kitaev, A.: Universal quantum computation with ideal clifford gates and noisy ancillas. Phys. Rev. A 71, 022316 (2005). https://doi.org/10.1103/PhysRevA.71.022316
11. Broadbent, A., Ji, Z., Song, F., Watrous, J.: Zero-knowledge proof systems for qma. In: 2016 IEEE 57th Annual Symposium on Foundations of Computer Science (FOCS), pp. 31–40. IEEE (2016). https://doi.org/10.1109/FOCS.2016.13
12. Campbell, E.T., Anwar, H., Browne, D.E.: Magic-state distillation in all prime dimensions using quantum reed-muller codes. Phys. Rev. X 2(4), 041021 (2012). https://doi.org/10.1103/PhysRevX.2.041021
13. Chau, H.F.: Unconditionally secure key distribution in higher dimensions by depolarization. IEEE Trans. Inf. Theory 51(4), 1451–1468 (2005). https://doi.org/10.1109/TIT.2005.844076

14. Chung, K.M., Lee, Y., Lin, H.H., Wu, X.: Constant-round blind classical verification of quantum sampling. In: Annual International Conference on the Theory and Applications of Cryptographic Techniques, pp. 707–736. Springer (2022). https://doi.org/10.1007/978-3-031-07082-2_25

15. Clark, S.: Valence bond solid formalism for d-level one-way quantum computation. J. Phys. A: Math. Gen. **39**(11), 2701 (2006). https://doi.org/10.1088/0305-4470/39/11/010

16. Crépeau, C., Gottesman, D., Smith, A.: Secure multi-party quantum computation. In: Proceedings of the Thiry-fourth Annual ACM symposium on Theory of computing - STOC '02. ACM Press (2002). https://doi.org/10.1145/509907.510000

17. Dulek, Y., Grilo, A.B., Jeffery, S., Majenz, C., Schaffner, C.: Secure multi-party quantum computation with a dishonest majority. In: Advances in Cryptology - EUROCRYPT 2020 (2020). https://doi.org/10.1007/978-3-030-45727-3_25

18. Dupuis, F., Nielsen, J.B., Salvail, L.: Actively secure two-party evaluation of any quantum operation. In: Safavi-Naini, R., Canetti, R. (eds.) CRYPTO 2012. LNCS, vol. 7417, pp. 794–811. Springer, Heidelberg (2012). https://doi.org/10.1007/978-3-642-32009-5_46

19. Gu, T., Yuan, X., Wu, B.: Efficient measurement schemes for bosonic systems. Quant. Sci. Technol. **8**(4), 045008 (2023). https://doi.org/10.1088/2058-9565/ace6cd

20. Gunn, S., Ju, N., Ma, F., Zhandry, M.: Commitments to quantum states. In: Proceedings of the 55th Annual ACM Symposium on Theory of Computing, pp. 1579–1588 (2023). https://doi.org/10.1145/3564246.3585198

21. Ishai, Y., Katz, J., Kushilevitz, E., Lindell, Y., Petrank, E.: On achieving the "best of both worlds" in secure multiparty computation. SIAM J. Comput. **40**(1), 122–141 (2011). https://doi.org/10.1137/100783224

22. Ishai, Y., Ostrovsky, R., Zikas, V.: Secure multi-party computation with identifiable abort. In: Garay, J.A., Gennaro, R. (eds.) CRYPTO 2014. LNCS, vol. 8617, pp. 369–386. Springer, Heidelberg (2014). https://doi.org/10.1007/978-3-662-44381-1_21

23. Katz, J.: On achieving the "best of both worlds" in secure multiparty computation. In: Proceedings of the Thirty-ninth Annual ACM Symposium on Theory of Computing, pp. 11–20 (2007). https://doi.org/10.1145/1250790.1250793

24. Mahadev, U.: Classical verification of quantum computations. In: 2018 IEEE 59th Annual Symposium on Foundations of Computer Science (FOCS), pp. 259–267. IEEE (2018). https://doi.org/10.1109/FOCS.2018.00033

25. Micali, S., Goldreich, O., Wigderson, A.: How to play any mental game. In: Proceedings of the Nineteenth ACM Symposium on Theory of Computing, STOC, pp. 218–229. ACM (1987). https://doi.org/10.1145/28395.28420

26. Rabin, T., Ben-Or, M.: Verifiable secret sharing and multiparty protocols with honest majority. In: Proceedings of the Twenty-first Annual ACM symposium on Theory of Computing, pp. 73–85 (1989). https://doi.org/10.1145/73007.73014

27. Van Den Berg, E.: A simple method for sampling random clifford operators. In: 2021 IEEE International Conference on Quantum Computing and Engineering (QCE), pp. 54–59. IEEE (2021). https://doi.org/10.1109/QCE52317.2021.00021

28. Yao, A.C.C.: How to generate and exchange secrets. In: 27th Annual Symposium on Foundations of Computer Science (sfcs 1986), pp. 162–167 (1986). https://doi.org/10.1109/SFCS.1986.25

The Hardness of LPN over Any Integer Ring and Field for PCG Applications

Hanlin Liu[1,4] [ID], Xiao Wang[2(✉)] [ID], Kang Yang[3(✉)] [ID], and Yu Yu[1,4(✉)] [ID]

[1] Shanghai Jiao Tong University, Shanghai, China
{hans1024,yyuu}@sjtu.edu.cn
[2] Northwestern University, Evanston, USA
wangxiao@northwestern.edu
[3] State Key Laboratory of Cryptology, Beijing, China
yangk@sklc.org
[4] Shanghai Qi Zhi Institute, Shanghai, China

Abstract. Learning parity with noise (LPN) has been widely studied and used in cryptography. It was recently brought to new prosperity since Boyle et al. (CCS'18), putting LPN to a central role in designing secure multi-party computation, zero-knowledge proofs, private set intersection, and many other protocols. In this paper, we thoroughly studied the security of LPN problems in this particular context. We found that some important aspects have long been ignored and many conclusions from classical LPN cryptanalysis do not apply to this new setting, due to the low noise rates, extremely high dimensions, various types (in addition to $\mathbb{F}_2$) and noise distributions.

– For LPN over a field, we give a parameterized reduction from exact-noise LPN to regular-noise LPN. Compared to the recent result by Feneuil, Joux and Rivain (Crypto'22), we significantly reduce the security loss by paying only a small additive price in dimension and number of samples.
– We analyze the security of LPN over a ring $\mathbb{Z}_{2^\lambda}$. Existing protocols based on LPN over integer rings use parameters as if they are over fields, but we found an attack that effectively reduces the weight of a noise by half compared to LPN over fields. Consequently, prior works that use LPN over $\mathbb{Z}_{2^\lambda}$ overestimate up to 40 bits of security.
– We provide a complete picture of the hardness of LPN over integer rings by showing: 1) the equivalence between its search and decisional versions; 2) an efficient reduction from LPN over $\mathbb{F}_2$ to LPN over $\mathbb{Z}_{2^\lambda}$; and 3) generalization of our results to any integer ring.

Finally, we provide an all-in-one estimator tool for the bit security of LPN parameters in the context of PCG, incorporating the recent advanced attacks.

1 Introduction

The learning parity with noise (LPN) assumption states that it is hard to distinguish LPN samples $(\mathbf{A}, \mathbf{A} \cdot \mathbf{s} + \mathbf{e})$ from random samples, where $\mathbf{A}$ is a public

© International Association for Cryptologic Research 2024
M. Joye and G. Leander (Eds.): EUROCRYPT 2024, LNCS 14656, pp. 149–179, 2024.
https://doi.org/10.1007/978-3-031-58751-1_6

	Protocol	LPN type
[17, 82]	(C)OT	$\mathbb{F}_2$
[69]	VOLE	$\mathbb{F}_{2^{61}-1}$ and $\mathbb{Z}_{2^{64}}$
[76]	ZK	$\mathbb{F}_2$ and $\mathbb{F}_{2^{61}-1}$
[45]	ZK	$\mathbb{F}_{2^{128}}$
[10]	ZK	$\mathbb{F}_{2^{40}}$ and $\mathbb{F}_{2^{61}-1}$
[8]	ZK	$\mathbb{Z}_{2^{72}}$
[9]	ZK	$\mathbb{Z}_{2^{104}}$
[34, 29]	MPC	$\mathbb{F}_2$, $\mathbb{F}_{2^{40}}$ and $\mathbb{F}_{2^{128}}$
[68, 23, 66]	PSI	$\mathbb{F}_{2^{128}}$

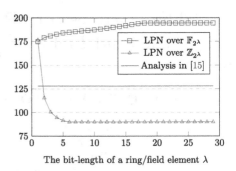

(a) Prior works in the PCG framework and their required LPN variants over different fields and rings.

(b) **The bit-security from our analysis for LPN over $\mathbb{F}_{2^\lambda}$ and $\mathbb{Z}_{2^\lambda}$.** Parameters $N = 2^{10}, k = 652, t = 106$ are used.

Fig. 1. LPN assumptions in prior works, and our analysis on one set of parameters. For a set of parameters (N, k, t), N is the number of samples, k is the dimension and t is the Hamming weight of a noise vector.

matrix, s is a random secret and e is a noise vector sampled from a sparse distribution. The LPN assumption has been applied to build various primitives, e.g., symmetric encryption and authentication (e.g., [49] and follow-up works), public key encryption [4], commitment scheme [53], garbled circuits [5], oblivious transfer [32] and collision-resistant hash functions [21,84]. All these primitives adopt LPN over binary field $\mathbb{F}_2$ with moderate dimensions.

The recent work by Boyle et al. [15] introduced the pseudorandom correlation generator (PCG) paradigm that can produce a large batch of correlated randomness, e.g., (correlated) oblivious transfer ((C)OT) and (vector) oblivious linear evaluation ((V)OLE), at a small communication. The core of the PCG idea is to build a pseudorandom generator (PRG) with a simple internal structure from LPN assumptions and then privately evaluate such a PRG using function secret sharing [20]. The sparsity of a noise e translates to communication efficiency, while the efficiency of LPN encoding translates to computational efficiency. Later, the PCG paradigm was used to build a series of concretely efficient protocols [1,14,16–19,27,67,69,76,82] with sublinear communication for generating random (C)OT or (V)OLE correlations. These PCG-like protocols have gained a lot of interests in designing various concretely efficient protocols, including secure multi-party computation (MPC) (e.g., [28–31,34,48,56,64,74,75,81]), zero-knowledge (ZK) proofs (e.g., [8–10,35,36,76,78,80]), privacy-preserving machine learning [51,69,77], private set intersection (PSI) [23,66,68], etc.

Although widely used in many constructions and some real-world applications, these protocols often use LPN variations that are not much studied in cryptanalysis, especially compared to the classical LPN assumption over $\mathbb{F}_2$ [4,43,46,73]. Furthermore, prior analyses on the classical LPN problems do not directly cover the LPN variants used in the PCG setting because of their unique features:

- **Value type.** Protocols often require an LPN assumption over a ring other than $\mathbb{F}_2$, including a finite field or even an integer ring[1] like $\mathbb{Z}_{2^\lambda}$.
- **Noise distribution.** Most existing analyses focus on a Bernoulli or exact noise distribution. However, most PCG-like protocols, for better performance, adopt a regular noise distribution, where the noise vector is divided into consecutive equal-sized sub-vectors, and each sub-vector has a single noisy coordinate in a random position.

  There are some recent exceptions. [42] showed a generalized reduction in LPN, which can imply a reduction from exact-noise LPN to regular-noise LPN but with a very large security loss; [24] showed an attack specific to regular noises but not for parameters usable in PCG applications; [22] also introduced an algebraic attack which, as we will show in this paper, can be cheaply mitigated without significantly increasing the communication.
- **Dimension and noise rate.** Most applications require an LPN assumption with very high dimension (e.g., millions) and low noise rate (e.g., $1/10^5$), which is out of the typically reported range of parameters considered for coding-theoretic primitives.

At this point, all implementations of PCG-like protocols use the LPN parameters from the original work by Boyle et al. [15], who analyzed the concrete security of LPN over $\mathbb{F}_{2^{128}}$. However, as we summarize in Table 1a, follow-up works used the same analysis to choose parameters for many different variants of LPN over $\mathbb{F}_2$, $\mathbb{F}_p$, and $\mathbb{Z}_{2^\lambda}$, many of which were not covered by the original analysis. It was not clear how large a gap in security when using LPN parameters over a field for LPN over another field or ring.

1.1 Our Contributions

In this paper, we put forth a set of LPN analyses specific to the setting of PCG applications. From the theoretical perspective, we show a tighter reduction from exact-noise LPN to regular-noise LPN and a complete categorization between LPN over integer rings and prime fields. From the concrete side, we summarize and incorporate all existing LPN attacks applicable to the PCG setting into one estimator tool that can be used for researchers to select LPN parameters. In particular, we find that existing PCG applications use parameters more expensive than necessary for fields and less security than needed for integer rings. Below we provide more details of our contributions.

The Hardness of LPN Under Regular Noise Distributions. Recently, Feneuil et al. [42] observed that, as a special case in their main theorem, an exact noise vector (of Hamming weight t) is also regular with some probability (estimated to e^{-t} in Sect. 3), and thus (T, ϵ)-hard[2] LPN under an exact noise

---

[1] By integer ring we refer to $\mathbb{Z}_N$ for any composite number N, which is used to distinguish from polynomial rings.

[2] We classify a problem as (T, ϵ)-hard when, for any probabilistic algorithm $\mathcal{B}$ with a running time of T, the algorithm's capacity to solve this problem is limited to a success probability of at most ϵ.

Table 1. Comparison between our analysis and [15] for the bit-security of an LPN problem with dimension k, number of samples N and Hamming weight of noises t over different rings. The bit-security considers an exact noise distribution; the values in brackets denote the decrease of bit-security due to the usage of a regular noise distribution. The sets of LPN parameters are adopted from [15].

LPN			This work					[15]
N	k	t	$\mathbb{F}_{2^{128}}$	$\mathbb{F}_{2^8}$	$\mathbb{Z}_{2^{128}}$	$\mathbb{Z}_4$	$\mathbb{F}_2$	Any field
2^{10}	652	57	111 (-0)	104 (-0)	54 (-2)	68 (-2)	94 (-4)	80
2^{12}	1589	98	100 (-0)	92 (-0)	53 (-0)	63 (-1)	83 (-3)	80
2^{14}	3482	198	101 (-0)	97 (-0)	58 (-1)	67 (-1)	86 (-3)	80
2^{16}	7391	389	103 (-0)	101 (-0)	63 (-1)	72 (-2)	91 (-4)	80
2^{18}	15336	760	105 (-0)	105 (-0)	68 (-1)	76 (-1)	95 (-3)	80
2^{20}	32771	1419	107 (-6)	107 (-6)	73 (-1)	81 (-1)	99 (-2)	80
2^{22}	67440	2735	108 (-4)	108 (-4)	75 (-1)	84 (-1)	104 (-5)	80

distribution implies $(T, e^t \cdot \epsilon)$-hard LPN under a regular noise distribution. However, the security loss is sometimes unaffordable as LPN may not have security beyond e^t in many practical settings. To reduce the security loss, we introduce a tunable parameter $\alpha \geq 2$ and divide a noise vector into αt blocks (each denoted by e_i). Furthermore, instead of hoping that every e_i has the exact weight 1, we relax the condition to that the weight of e_i is *at most* 1. For each block, we add an extra sample with noise $\tilde{e}_i$ such that vector $(e_i, \tilde{e}_i)$ has the exact weight 1, which allows us to obtain a regular noise vector. As a result, we prove that if the exact-noise LPN problem over an arbitrary field $\mathbb{F}$ with sample number N, dimension k and weight t is (T, ϵ)-hard, then the regular-noise LPN problem over $\mathbb{F}$ with sample number $(N + \alpha t)$, dimension $(k + \alpha t)$ and weight (αt) is $(T - \mathsf{poly}(k, N), 2^{\frac{t}{\alpha}} \cdot \epsilon)$-hard, where the security loss is reduced by at least 2^α, while the dimension and number of samples are increased by only αt.

We note that our reduction is not contradictory, but rather complementary, to a very recent work by Briaud and Øygarden [22]. In particular, they proposed a new algebraic attack that can take advantage of regular noise distributions, and demonstrated that the algebraic attack on regular-noise LPN is more efficient than other existing attacks, in the scenarios characterized by small code rates (particularly, some primal-LPN parameter sets). Whereas our reduction establishes an asymptotic connection, suggesting that LPN with regular noise could be as hard as that with exact noise, albeit with some security loss.

The Hardness of LPN over Integer Rings. Although having been used in protocol design [8,9,69], LPN problems over integer rings (e.g., $\mathbb{Z}_{2^\lambda}$) have received relatively limited attention in research. One notable exception is the work of Akavia [2], which explored a generalized LPN assumption over an integer ring within the context of the random samples access model. However, the work does not consider the hardness of LPN problems over integer rings in the PCG setting. As a result, all existing works for PCG-like protocols and applications select the parameters assuming that LPN over an integer ring is as secure as LPN over a finite field.

In this paper, we provide a complete relationship between LPN over fields and that over integer rings, with both asymptotic reduction and concrete analysis. From the theoretic side, we show the equivalence of related problems as shown in Fig. 2. On the concrete side, our analysis (in Fig. 1b and in Tables 1 and the full version of the paper [58, Table 2]) shows that LPN over an integer ring is significantly more vulnerable to attacks than LPN over a finite field of similar size. *What's more, we show that although LPN over a finite field becomes harder to attack as the field size increases, LPN over an integer ring becomes easier to attack as the ring size increases!*

1. Focusing on the most commonly used ring $\mathbb{Z}_{2^\lambda}$, we show a concrete attack that can solve a t-noise LPN over $\mathbb{Z}_{2^\lambda}$ by solving a $\left(\frac{2^{(\lambda-1)}}{2^\lambda-1} \cdot t\right)$-noise (which approximates to $t/2$) LPN over $\mathbb{F}_2$. This means that LPN over an integer ring is concretely weaker than LPN over a finite field and we need to double the weight of noise vectors to cover this attack. The impact to existing cryptographic protocols is significant. It will lead to roughly $2\times$ more communication and computation.

2. On the positive side, we provide an evidence that the LPN problem over an integer ring is generally hard. In particular, we show a reduction between t-noise LPN over $\mathbb{F}_2$ and $(\lambda \cdot t)$-noise LPN over a ring $\mathbb{Z}_{2^\lambda}$, which means that LPN over an integer ring is asymptotically as hard as classical LPN. This "efficient" reduction requires a different noise distribution: instead of sampling t locations and putting a uniform non-zero entry from $\mathbb{Z}_{2^\lambda}$ in each location, we need to independently sample λ weight-t noises $e_0, \ldots, e_{\lambda-1}$ over $\mathbb{F}_2$, and define the final noise vector as $e = \sum_{i \in [\lambda]} 2^i \cdot e_i$ with weight $\leq \lambda \cdot t$. This noise distribution may be interesting, as it can be used in the design of PCG-like protocols by adopting the upper bound $\lambda \cdot t$ to run these protocols. This change of distributions is crucial: without such change, the most favorable reduction we can identify shifts from t-noise LPN over $\mathbb{F}_2$ to $(2^\lambda \cdot t)$-noise LPN over $\mathbb{Z}_{2^\lambda}$, which is exponentially worse than the above. Another interesting fact is that the above reductions only require the code matrix $\mathbf{A}$ to be Boolean, which eliminates the need for integer multiplication during LPN encoding. Prior work [27] observed that using a Boolean code matrix is not vulnerable to existing linear-test attacks for LPN over finite fields; here we show that for LPN over integer rings, using a Boolean matrix is provably secure assuming that classical LPN over $\mathbb{F}_2$ is hard.

3. While the above reductions focus on the decisional version of LPN, we also give a reduction from computational LPN over $\mathbb{Z}_{2^\lambda}$ to that over $\mathbb{F}_2$. Thus, we show the equivalence between computational and decisional versions of LPN over $\mathbb{Z}_{2^\lambda}$ as shown in Fig. 2. We also generalize all the results to any integer ring. In particular, we show a concrete attack that can solve a t-noise LPN over a ring $\mathbb{Z}_{p^{\lambda_1} q^{\lambda_2}}$ by solving either a $\left(\frac{p-1}{p} \cdot t\right)$-noise LPN over $\mathbb{F}_p$ or a $\left(\frac{q-1}{q} \cdot t\right)$-noise LPN over $\mathbb{F}_q$, where p, q are two primes. This attack works for both computational and decisional versions of LPN. We also give a reduction from t-noise LPN over $\mathbb{F}_p$ and t-noise LPN over $\mathbb{F}_q$ to $((\lambda_1 + \lambda_2) \cdot t)$-noise LPN

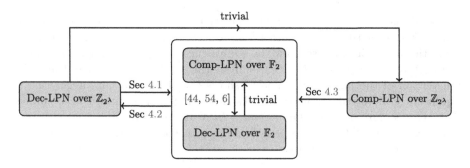

Fig. 2. The reduction relations between computational and decisional versions of LPN over $\mathbb{F}_2$ and $\mathbb{Z}_{2^\lambda}$ in the presence of Bernoulli and exact noise distributions.

over $\mathbb{Z}_{p^{\lambda_1}q^{\lambda_2}}$. Given these reductions over $\mathbb{Z}_{p^{\lambda_1}q^{\lambda_2}}$, one can easily generalize them to any integer ring.

Concrete Security of LPN for PCG. Finally, we maintain an easy-to-use tool to estimate the costs of the advanced attacks (Pooled Gauss, SD, ISD and algebraic attacks) on the concrete security of LPN problems related to the PCG setting, and will integrate new attacks found in the future into the estimator tool[3]. Prior to this work, most PCG-like protocols use the analysis from [15] for all LPN variants. We refined their analysis and incorporated attacks on integer rings and regular noises. See Table 1 and the full version of the paper [58, Table 2] for some representative parameters originally proposed in [15].

In the process of summarizing existing attacks, we also made an interesting observation in the context of PCG. Statistical decoding (SD) and information set decoding (ISD) are both important attack techniques for the exact-noise LPN problems. We observe that in the context of PCG, ISD attacks are almost always better than the SD attacks, including the recent work of SD 2.0 by Carrier et al. [25]. We formalize this observation by showing that both the optimal SD and SD 2.0 attacks (adapted to the low-noise setting) require more cost, compared to the Prange's original ISD algorithm [65] for a large set of commonly used parameters. Note that our findings do not diminish the relevance of SD 2.0; rather, they arise from differences in parameter settings between our work and [25]. This also shows the disparity of cryptanalysis between classical LPN problems with high noise rates and low-noise LPN problems used in PCG-like protocols.

Subsequent Works. The estimator tool has been used in subsequent works (e.g., [50]) to choose LPN parameters for PCG-like protocols. Our attack on integer rings has subsequently been noted by multiple works. Baum et al. [9] addressed this attack by a countermeasure: sampling the non-zero values in the noise vector only from invertible elements in $\mathbb{Z}_{2^\lambda}$ (i.e., odd values). This plausibly prevents the attack, and we did not find an efficient attack against LPN over

---

[3] Available at www.lpnestimator.com.

$\mathbb{Z}_{2^\lambda}$ with the countermeasure. Besides, the updated version by Boyle et al. [19] and the work by Lin et al. [57] adopted the same countermeasure to address our attack. It seems to be hard to prove that LPN over $\mathbb{F}_2$ implies LPN over $\mathbb{Z}_{2^\lambda}$ with random-odd noises, even if a significant security loss is allowed. This is because two noise vectors in two adjacent hybrids have the strong correlation, when a random odd value is sampled for each noisy coordinate. If one is desirable to obtain a tight reduction from LPN over $\mathbb{F}_2$ to that over $\mathbb{Z}_{2^\lambda}$, it may choose the noise distribution in the form of $e = \sum_{i\in[\lambda]} 2^i \cdot e_i$ with independent and random weight-t noises e_i for $i \in [\lambda]$.

2 Preliminary

2.1 Notation

We denote by log the logarithm in base 2. For $a, b \in \mathbb{N}$ with $a \le b$, we write $[a, b] = \{a, \ldots, b\}$ and use $[n]$ to denote $[0, n-1]$ for simplicity. We use $x \leftarrow S$ to denote sampling x uniformly at random from a set S and $x \leftarrow \mathcal{D}$ to denote sampling x according to a distribution $\mathcal{D}$. For a ring $\mathcal{R}$, we denote by $|\mathcal{R}|$ the size of $\mathcal{R}$. We will use bold lower-case letters like a for column vectors, and bold upper-case letters like $\mathbf{A}$ for matrices. By slightly abusing the notation, for a vector a, we use $|a|$ to denote the Hamming weight of a, and denote by $a[i]$ the i-th component of a. For two vectors x, y, we denote by $\langle x, y \rangle$ the inner product of x and y. For a vector $a \in (\mathbb{Z}_{2^\lambda})^k$, we use $\mathsf{BitDecomp}(a)$ to denote the bit-decomposition of a, and its output is denoted by $(a^0, a^1, \cdots, a^{\lambda-1})$ such that $a^i \in \mathbb{F}_2^k$ for $i \in [\lambda]$ and $(a^0[j], a^1[j], \ldots, a^{\lambda-1}[j])$ is the bit-decomposition of ring element $a[j] \in \mathbb{Z}_{2^\lambda}$ for $j \in [k]$. Let $\mathsf{BitDecomp}^{-1}(a^0, a^1, \cdots, a^{\lambda-1}) = \sum_{i=0}^{\lambda-1} 2^i \cdot a^i \in (\mathbb{Z}_{2^\lambda})^k$ be the inverse of $\mathsf{BitDecomp}(a)$. We use $\mathsf{poly}(\cdot)$ to denote a polynomial function. For two distributions X and Y, we denote by $X \approx_c Y$ that X is computationally indistinguishable from Y. We will use the following lemma:

Lemma 1 (see, e.g., [83]). *For any $\mu \in (0, 1)$, if each coordinate of a vector $v \in \mathbb{F}_2^t$ is independently set to 1 with probability μ, then the probability that $|v| = \lceil \mu t \rceil$ is at least $\Omega(1/\sqrt{t})$.*

2.2 Learning Parity with Noise

Recently, variants of the learning parity with noise (LPN) assumption [13] are used to build PCG-like protocols with sublinear communication for generating (C)OT and (V)OLE correlations. The LPN variants are defined over a general finite ring $\mathcal{R}$. The known LPN-based PCG-like protocols mainly consider three cases for the choices of ring $\mathcal{R}$:

- Case 1 that $\mathcal{R} = \mathbb{F}_2$ is used to design the COT protocols [16–18,27,67,82], which is in turn able to be transformed into standard OT protocols.

- Case 2 that $\mathcal{R}$ is a finite field $\mathbb{F}$ with $|\mathbb{F}| > 2$ is used to construct the VOLE protocols [15–18,27,67,69,76] and the OLE protocols [1,14,18,19].
- Case 3 that $\mathcal{R} = \mathbb{Z}_{2^\lambda}$ (e.g., $\lambda \in \{32, 64, 128\}$) is used to obtain the VOLE protocols [8,9,57,69].

When considering more general rings such as $\mathcal{R} = \mathbb{Z}_{p^\lambda}$ for a prime $p > 2$ and $\mathcal{R} = \mathbb{Z}_{p^{\lambda_1} q^{\lambda_2}}$ for two primes p, q, the LPN problems over such rings may be interesting for future protocols. Following prior works (e.g., [17,18]), we define the (primal-)LPN and dual-LPN assumptions over a general ring $\mathcal{R}$ as follows:

Definition 1 (LPN). *Let $\mathcal{D}(\mathcal{R}) = \{\mathcal{D}_{t,N}(\mathcal{R})\}_{t,N \in \mathbb{N}}$ denote a family of distributions over a ring $\mathcal{R}$ such that for any $t, N \in \mathbb{N}$, $\mathsf{Im}(\mathcal{D}_{t,N}(\mathcal{R})) \subseteq \mathcal{R}^N$. Let $\mathbf{C}$ be a probabilistic code generation algorithm such that $\mathbf{C}(k, N, \mathcal{R})$ outputs a matrix $\mathbf{A} \in \mathcal{R}^{N \times k}$. For dimension $k = k(\kappa)$, number of samples $N = N(\kappa)$, Hamming weight of a noise vector $t = t(\kappa)$, and a ring $\mathcal{R}$, we say that the decisional $(\mathcal{D}, \mathbf{C}, \mathcal{R})$-LPN$(N, k, t)$ problem is (T, ϵ)-hard if for every probabilistic distinguisher $\mathcal{B}$ running in time T, we have*

$$\left| \Pr_{\mathbf{A},s,e} [\mathcal{B}(\mathbf{A}, b = \mathbf{A} \cdot s + e) = 1] - \Pr_{\mathbf{A},u} [\mathcal{B}(\mathbf{A}, u) = 1] \right| \leq \epsilon,$$

where $\mathbf{A} \leftarrow \mathbf{C}(k, N, \mathcal{R})$, $s \leftarrow \mathcal{R}^k$, $e \leftarrow \mathcal{D}_{t,N}(\mathcal{R})$ and $u \leftarrow \mathcal{R}^N$. We say that the computational $(\mathcal{D}, \mathbf{C}, \mathcal{R})$-LPN$(k, N, t)$ problem is (T, ϵ)-hard if for every probabilistic algorithm $\mathcal{B}$ running in time T, we have

$$\Pr_{\mathbf{A},s,e} [\mathcal{B}(\mathbf{A}, b = \mathbf{A} \cdot s + e) = (s, e)] \leq \epsilon,$$

where $\mathbf{A}, s, e$ are defined as above.

In the above definition, both T and ϵ are functions of computational security parameter κ. Following the previous work, we consider the following families of noise distributions:

- **Bernoulli.** Let $\mathsf{Ber}(\mathcal{R}) = \{\mathsf{Ber}_{\mu,N}(\mathcal{R})\}_{\mu,N}$ be the family of Bernoulli distributions. In particular, $\mathsf{Ber}_{\mu,N}(\mathcal{R})$ is a Bernoulli distribution with parameters μ, N over a ring $\mathcal{R}$, such that each component in a noise vector sampled from $\mathsf{Ber}_{\mu,N}(\mathcal{R})$ is a uniform element in $\mathcal{R}$ with probability μ and 0 otherwise. Following prior works (e.g., [15,27,37,52]), we adopt such Bernoulli definition which samples a uniform element in $\mathcal{R}$ with probability μ. Note that the definition is equivalent to sampling a uniform *non-zero* element in $\mathcal{R}$ with probability $\mu(|\mathcal{R}| - 1)/|\mathcal{R}|$ for each component. One notational benefit we enjoy with this definition is that if e follows $\mathsf{Ber}_{\mu,N}(\mathcal{R})$ then any bit vector, formed by taking one bit from each corresponding component in e, follows $\mathsf{Ber}_{\mu,N}(\mathbb{F}_2)$ for the same parameter μ.
- **Exact.** Let $\mathsf{HW}(\mathcal{R}) = \{\mathsf{HW}_{t,N}(\mathcal{R})\}_{t,N}$ be the family of exact noise distributions. In particular, for $\mathsf{HW}_{t,N}(\mathcal{R})$, each component of a noise vector is a uniform non-zero element in t random positions and zero elsewhere. Informally, we refer to LPN with exact noise distributions as exact-LPN.

- **Regular.** To achieve better efficiency, a series of works, e.g., [7, 14–18, 24, 47, 76, 82], adopt the family of *regular* noise distributions, denoted by RHW($\mathcal{R}$) = $\{\text{RHW}_{t,N}(\mathcal{R})\}_{t,N}$. In addition to fixed Hamming weight, the noise vector is further divided into t consecutive sub-vectors of size $\lfloor N/t \rfloor$, where each sub-vector has a single noisy coordinate. Sometimes, we refer to LPN with regular noise distributions as regular-LPN.

The existing LPN-based PCG-like protocols adopt the latter two noise distributions, and the standard LPN assumption adopts the Bernoulli distribution. While the standard LPN assumption uses random linear codes to instantiate $\mathbf{C}$ (i.e., sampling $\mathbf{A}$ uniformly at random), multiple LPN-based protocols adopt other kinds of linear codes to obtain faster computation, including local linear codes [4], quasi-cyclic codes [60], MDPC codes [63], expand-accumulate codes [16] etc. We do not analyze the hardness of LPN problems based on quasi-cyclic codes, which needs to take into account the effect of the DOOM attack [70] that allows providing $\sqrt{N}$ computational speedup. We are not aware that other kinds of linear codes listed as above lead to significantly better attacks, compared to random linear codes. The reductions given in this work focus on the case of random linear codes, and we leave that extending them to other linear codes as a future work. To simplify the notation, we often omit $\mathbf{C}$ from the $(\mathcal{D}, \mathbf{C}, \mathcal{R})$-LPN$(N, k, t)$ problem, and only write $(\mathcal{D}, \mathcal{R})$-LPN$(N, k, t)$.

Below, we define the dual-LPN assumption over a general finite ring $\mathcal{R}$ with a family $\mathcal{D}$ of noise distributions, where both the decisional version and search version are described. Dual-LPN is also known as syndrome decoding.

Definition 2 (Dual LPN). *Let $\mathcal{D}(\mathcal{R})$ and $\mathbf{C}$ be as in Definition 1. For two integers N, n with $N > n$, we define*

$$\mathbf{C}^{\perp}(N, n, \mathcal{R}) = \left\{ \mathbf{H} \in \mathcal{R}^{n \times N} : \mathbf{H} \cdot \mathbf{A} = \mathbf{0}, \; \mathbf{A} \in \mathbf{C}(N - n, N, \mathcal{R}), \text{rank}(\mathbf{H}) = n \right\}.$$

For output length $n = n(\kappa)$, number of samples $N = N(\kappa)$, noise-vector Hamming weight $t = t(\kappa)$, we say that the decisional $(\mathcal{D}, \mathbf{C}^{\perp}, \mathcal{R})$-dual-LPN$(N, n, t)$ problem is (T, ϵ)-hard if for every probabilistic distinguisher $\mathcal{B}$ running in time T:

$$\left| \Pr_{\mathbf{H},\mathbf{e}} [\mathcal{B}(\mathbf{H}, \mathbf{H} \cdot \mathbf{e}) = 1] - \Pr_{\mathbf{H},\mathbf{u}} [\mathcal{B}(\mathbf{H}, \mathbf{u}) = 1] \right| \leq \epsilon,$$

where $\mathbf{H} \leftarrow \mathbf{C}^{\perp}(N, n, \mathcal{R})$, $\mathbf{e} \leftarrow \mathcal{D}_{t,N}(\mathcal{R})$ and $\mathbf{u} \leftarrow \mathcal{R}^N$.
We say that the computational $(\mathcal{D}, \mathbf{C}^{\perp}, \mathcal{R})$-dual-LPN$(N, n, t)$ problem is (T, ϵ)-hard if for every probabilistic algorithm $\mathcal{B}$ running in time T, we have

$$\Pr_{\mathbf{H},\mathbf{e}} [\mathcal{B}(\mathbf{H}, \mathbf{H} \cdot \mathbf{e}) = \mathbf{e}] \leq \epsilon,$$

where $\mathbf{H}, \mathbf{e}$ are defined as above.

For any fixed code generation algorithm $\mathbf{C}$ and noise distribution $\mathcal{D}$, the dual-LPN problem defined as above is equivalent to the primal-LPN problem from Definition 1 with dimension $k = N - n$ and the number of samples N. The direction transforming an LPN instance into a dual-LPN instance directly follows the simple fact that $\mathbf{H} \cdot (\mathbf{A} \cdot \boldsymbol{s} + \boldsymbol{e}) = (\mathbf{H} \cdot \mathbf{A}) \cdot \boldsymbol{s} + \mathbf{H} \cdot \boldsymbol{e} = \mathbf{H} \cdot \boldsymbol{e}$, as $\mathbf{H}$ is the parity-check matrix of the code generated by $\mathbf{A}$. The reverse direction can be obtained in a way similar to [62, Lemma 4.9].

3   The Hardness of LPN with Regular Noise Distributions

A series of MPC and ZK protocols (e.g., [7–10, 14–18, 24, 35, 36, 47, 76, 78, 80, 82]) rely on the hardness of LPN problems with regular noise distributions. Multiple prior works, e.g., [15–18, 24, 82], believe that regular-LPN problems are not significantly easier than exact-LPN problems, or even harder than exact-LPN for a part of parameter sets. However, no reduction from exact-LPN to regular-LPN was provided, until the recent work by Feneuil, Joux and Rivain [42]. They introduced a reduction from a (dual)-LPN problem with a regular noise distribution to that with an exact noise distribution, which is summarized in the following theorem.[4]

Theorem 1 (Theorem 1 of [42], adapted). *If an exact-LPN problem* (HW, $\mathbb{F}$)- LPN(N, k, t) *is* (T, ϵ)*-hard, the regular-LPN problem* (RHW, $\mathbb{F}$)- LPN(N, k, t) *is*

$$\left(T, \epsilon \cdot \binom{N}{t} \bigg/ \left(\frac{N}{t} \right)^t \right) \text{-hard.}$$

The statement also holds for dual-LPN.

The above reduction suffers from a significant security loss, i.e., the penalty factor

$$p_t = \binom{N}{t} \bigg/ \left(\frac{N}{t} \right)^t = \left(\frac{t^t}{t!} \right) \cdot \prod_{i=1}^{t-1} \left(1 - \frac{i}{N} \right) = e^{t - \Theta(\ln t) - \Theta(t^2/N)} = e^{t \cdot (1 - o(1))},$$

where the Stirling's approximation $\ln(t!) = t \cdot \ln t - t + \Theta(\ln t)$ is used, and $4^{-x} \leq 1 - x \leq e^{-x}$ for $0 \leq x \leq 1/2$. Here we focus on the case of $t = o(N)$, which is satisfied by low-noise LPN problems used in the PCG setting. Meanwhile, it is not hard to see that for many non-trivial parameter selections, we have $\epsilon > e^{-t}$. Let us analyze the following dual-LPN problem

$$[\mathbf{H}_1 \ \mathbf{H}_2] \cdot \begin{pmatrix} \boldsymbol{e}_1 \\ \boldsymbol{e}_2 \end{pmatrix} = \mathbf{H}_1 \cdot \boldsymbol{e}_1 + \mathbf{H}_2 \cdot \boldsymbol{e}_2 = \boldsymbol{y},$$

where $\mathbf{H}_1 \in \mathbb{F}_q^{n \times n}$, $\mathbf{H}_2 \in \mathbb{F}^{n \times (N-n)}$, $\boldsymbol{e}_1 \in \mathbb{F}^n$ and $\boldsymbol{e}_2 \in \mathbb{F}^{N-n}$. A polynomial-time attack simply bets $\boldsymbol{e}_2 = \mathbf{0}$ and computes $\boldsymbol{e}_1 = \mathbf{H}_1^{-1} \cdot \boldsymbol{y}$ (without loss of generality,

---

[4]   In particular, [42] considers a d-split noise, which consists of d blocks of length N/d and each block has weight t/d. For $d = t$, it corresponds to the (most often used) case of regular noise.

assuming that $\mathbf{H}_1$ is invertible), which succeeds with probability

$$\binom{n}{t} \bigg/ \binom{N}{t} = \prod_{i=1}^{N-n} \left(\frac{n-t+i}{n+i}\right) > \left(1 - \frac{t}{n+1}\right)^{N-n} \approx e^{-\frac{t(N-n)}{n+1}} .$$

If $N \leq 2n$, a larger penalty factor p_t only implies that the regular-LPN problem (RHW, $\mathbb{F}$)-LPN(N,k,t) becomes $(\text{poly}(\kappa), p_t \cdot \epsilon)$-hard, where $p_t \cdot \epsilon > 1$. Thus, this motivates us to decrease the penalty factor to yield more conservative (yet still meaningful) results.

Prior work [42] incurs a significant security loss, because it simply uses $1/p_t$ to account for the probability that an exact noise vector is regular at the same time. We provide a new reduction with a new parameter α such that [42, Theorem 1] can be seen as a special case of $\alpha = 1$. More importantly, with large α, we are able to reduce the security loss dramatically by dividing the exponent by α, while paying only an additive price αt in dimension and number of samples.

At a high level, we give an overview of the proof idea. Given exact-LPN samples $(\mathbf{A}, \boldsymbol{b} = \mathbf{A} \cdot \boldsymbol{s} + \boldsymbol{e})$ with dimension k and noise weight t, we divide them into αt blocks, i.e., $(\mathbf{A}_i, \boldsymbol{b}_i = \mathbf{A}_i \cdot \boldsymbol{s} + \boldsymbol{e}_i)$ for $i \in [1, \alpha t]$, where α is an additional parameter. Instead of hoping that every $\boldsymbol{e}_i$ has exact weight 1 (as done by Feneuil et al. in [42]), we relax the condition to $|\boldsymbol{e}_i| \leq 1$, which occurs with higher probability (and hence less security loss), especially for large α. For each block, we add an extra random sample $(\boldsymbol{a}_i, v_i = \langle \boldsymbol{a}_i, \boldsymbol{s}\rangle + \tilde{e}_i)$ such that the vector $(\boldsymbol{e}_i^\mathsf{T}, \tilde{e}_i)$ has the exact weight 1 (i.e., the resulting noise vector is regular). This is possible if the dimension of the target regular-LPN problem is $k + \alpha t$. That is, the additional αt values would help to simulate αt values $\{v_i\}$ almost perfectly.

Theorem 2. *Let $t, N \in \mathbb{N}$, and $\alpha \geq 2$ such that $\alpha t \in \mathbb{N}$ and $(\alpha t)|N$. If the exact-LPN problem (HW, $\mathbb{F}$)-LPN(N,k,t) is (T,ϵ)-hard, then the regular-LPN problem (RHW, $\mathbb{F}$)-LPN$(N+\alpha t, k+\alpha t, \alpha t)$ is $(T - \text{poly}(N,k), 2^{\frac{1}{\alpha}} \cdot \epsilon)$-hard, where $\mathbb{F}$ is any finite field.*

Proof. Let $N = \alpha t m$ for some $m \in \mathbb{N}$. We parse the exact-LPN samples of (HW, $\mathbb{F}$)-LPN(N,k,t) as αt blocks:

$$\mathbf{A} \stackrel{\text{def}}{=} \begin{bmatrix} \mathbf{A}_1 \in \mathbb{F}^{m \times k} \\ \vdots \\ \mathbf{A}_{\alpha t} \in \mathbb{F}^{m \times k} \end{bmatrix}, \quad \boldsymbol{b} \stackrel{\text{def}}{=} \begin{bmatrix} \boldsymbol{b}_1 = (\mathbf{A}_1 \cdot \boldsymbol{s} + \boldsymbol{e}_1) \in \mathbb{F}^m \\ \vdots \\ \boldsymbol{b}_{\alpha t} = (\mathbf{A}_{\alpha t} \cdot \boldsymbol{s} + \boldsymbol{e}_{\alpha t}) \in \mathbb{F}^m \end{bmatrix}, \quad \text{where } \boldsymbol{s} \leftarrow \mathbb{F}^k.$$

Let $\mathcal{E}$ be the event (not explicitly stated hereafter) that for every $i \in [1, \alpha t]$, the $\boldsymbol{e}_i$'s weight $|\boldsymbol{e}_i| \leq 1$. Then, we have that $\mathcal{E}$ occurs with probability

$$\Pr_{(\boldsymbol{e}_1^\mathsf{T},\ldots,\boldsymbol{e}_{\alpha t}^\mathsf{T}) \leftarrow \mathsf{HW}_{t,N}(\mathbb{F})} [\mathcal{E}] = \frac{\binom{\alpha t}{t} \cdot \left(\frac{N}{\alpha t}\right)^t}{\binom{N}{t}} = \prod_{i=1}^{t-1} \frac{(1 - \frac{i}{\alpha t})}{(1 - \frac{i}{N})} > \frac{4^{\sum\limits_{i=1}^{t-1} -\frac{i}{\alpha t}}}{1} = 2^{\frac{1}{\alpha} - \frac{t}{\alpha}},$$

where the inequality is due to $1 - x \geq 4^{-x}$ for $0 \leq x \leq 1/2$, and $x = \frac{i}{\alpha t} < \frac{1}{\alpha} \leq 1/2$. Our analysis is conditioned on $\mathcal{E}$, and thus incurs a security loss of factor $2^{\frac{1}{\alpha} - \frac{t}{\alpha}}$. Sample row vectors $r_1^{\mathsf{T}}, \ldots, r_{\alpha t}^{\mathsf{T}} \leftarrow \mathbb{F}^{k+\alpha t}$. Condition on that they are linearly independent, which has probability more than $1 - |\mathbb{F}|^{-k}$ (see, e.g., [55,83]), pick any full-rank matrix $\mathbf{B} \in \mathbb{F}^{k \times (k+\alpha t)}$ such that $\mathbf{M}$ defined below has full rank

$$\mathbf{M} \stackrel{\text{def}}{=} \begin{bmatrix} \mathbf{B}^{\mathsf{T}} & r_1 & \ldots & r_{\alpha t} \end{bmatrix}^{\mathsf{T}} \in \mathbb{F}^{(k+\alpha t) \times (k+\alpha t)}.$$

We denote the secret of a regular LPN instance by $x \leftarrow \mathbb{F}^{k+\alpha t}$, subject to $\mathbf{B} \cdot x = s$. For each $i \in [1, \alpha t]$, we also define a random element $u_i \in \mathbb{F} \backslash \{0\}$ as follows:

$$u_i \stackrel{\text{def}}{=} \begin{cases} \text{the non-zero entry of } e_i, \text{ if } |e_i| = 1 \\ \text{sample a fresh } u_i \leftarrow \mathbb{F} \backslash \{0\}, \text{ if } |e_i| = 0 \end{cases} \text{(recall } |e_i| \leq 1 \text{ conditioned on } \mathcal{E}).$$

Let $\mathbf{C}_i \stackrel{\text{def}}{=} \begin{bmatrix} \mathbf{A}_i \cdot \mathbf{B} \\ r_i^{\mathsf{T}} - 1^{\mathsf{T}} \cdot (\mathbf{A}_i \cdot \mathbf{B}) \end{bmatrix}$, $b_i' \stackrel{\text{def}}{=} \begin{bmatrix} b_i = \mathbf{A}_i \cdot \mathbf{B} \cdot x + e_i \\ v_i = r_i^{\mathsf{T}} \cdot x + u_i - 1^{\mathsf{T}} \cdot b_i \end{bmatrix}$ for $i \in [1, \alpha t]$,

where 1^{T} is the all-ones row vector (i.e., every component is 1). It is easy to verify that $b_i' = \mathbf{C}_i \cdot x + \begin{bmatrix} e_i \\ u_i - 1^{\mathsf{T}} \cdot e_i \end{bmatrix}$ and the noise vector $(e_i^{\mathsf{T}}, u_i - 1^{\mathsf{T}} \cdot e_i)$ has an exact weight 1.[5] Now we argue $(\mathbf{C}_i, b_i')$ can be efficiently simulated. Since x is uniform over $\mathbb{F}^{k+\alpha t}$, we have that $\mathbf{M} \cdot x$ is uniformly random over $\mathbb{F}^{k+\alpha t}$ for any full-rank matrix $\mathbf{M}$. Therefore, $(r_1^{\mathsf{T}} \cdot x, \ldots, r_{\alpha t}^{\mathsf{T}} \cdot x)$ is uniformly random over $\mathbb{F}^{\alpha t}$, even conditioned on $\mathbf{M}$, $\mathbf{B} \cdot x$ and other variables (e.g., all the $\mathbf{A}_i$'s, e_i's, u_i's). Thus, even without knowledge of u_i and e_i, the reduction can perfectly simulate the additional sample $v_i = r_i^{\mathsf{T}} \cdot x + u_i - 1^{\mathsf{T}} \cdot b_i$ by sampling $v_i \in \mathbb{F}$ uniformly at random.

However, $(\mathbf{C}_i, b_i')$ doesn't constitute the i-th block of the regular-LPN instance, since $\mathbf{A}_i \cdot \mathbf{B}$ (as part of $\mathbf{C}_i$) is *not* uniform over $\mathbb{F}^{m \times (k+\alpha t)}$ (but sampled from a k-dimensional subspace). We first complete the rest proof for the special case $\mathbb{F} = \mathbb{F}_2$ and then proceed to the general case of any finite field $\mathbb{F}$ with $|\mathbb{F}| > 2$.

CASE 1: $\mathbb{F} = \mathbb{F}_2$. In this case, we have that u_i is always 1 (i.e., the only non-zero element in $\mathbb{F}_2$). We sample a random matrix $\mathbf{P}_i \leftarrow \mathbb{F}^{m \times \alpha t}$ for each $i \in [1, \alpha t]$. We define the following LPN samples, which have the same weight-1 noise $(e_i^{\mathsf{T}}, u_i - 1^{\mathsf{T}} \cdot e_i)$ as $(\mathbf{C}_i, b_i')$.

$$\left(\begin{bmatrix} [\mathbf{A}_i \| \mathbf{P}_i] \cdot \mathbf{M} \\ r_i^{\mathsf{T}} - 1^{\mathsf{T}} \cdot (\mathbf{A}_i \cdot \mathbf{B}) \end{bmatrix}, \begin{bmatrix} b_i \\ v_i \end{bmatrix} + \begin{bmatrix} \mathbf{P}_i \cdot \begin{bmatrix} 1^{\mathsf{T}} \cdot b_1 + v_1 - 1 \\ \vdots \\ 1^{\mathsf{T}} \cdot b_{\alpha t} + v_{\alpha t} - 1 \end{bmatrix} \\ 0 \end{bmatrix} \right), \tag{1}$$

---

[5] Strictly speaking, the noise vector is ensured to have Hamming weight 1, but its coordinates may not take non-zero values with equal probability. The issue can be easily addressed by shuffling the matrices and samples accordingly.

which can be verified by comparing their difference, i.e.,

$$[\mathbf{A}_i \| \mathbf{P}_i] \cdot \mathbf{M} \cdot \boldsymbol{x} + \boldsymbol{e}_i$$

$$= (\mathbf{A}_i \cdot \mathbf{B} \cdot \boldsymbol{x} + \boldsymbol{e}_i) + \mathbf{P}_i \cdot \begin{bmatrix} \boldsymbol{r}_1^\mathsf{T} \cdot \boldsymbol{x} \\ \vdots \\ \boldsymbol{r}_{\alpha t}^\mathsf{T} \cdot \boldsymbol{x} \end{bmatrix} = \boldsymbol{b}_i + \mathbf{P}_i \cdot \begin{bmatrix} \mathbf{1}^\mathsf{T} \cdot \boldsymbol{b}_1 + v_1 - 1 \\ \vdots \\ \mathbf{1}^\mathsf{T} \cdot \boldsymbol{b}_{\alpha t} + v_{\alpha t} - 1 \end{bmatrix}.$$

Furthermore, the matrices in (1) are $2/|\mathbb{F}|^k$-close to uniform ones, which is proved in the following Lemma 2. Therefore, for each $i \in [1, \alpha t]$, the LPN samples in (1) constitute the i-th block of a regular-LPN instance $(\mathrm{RHW}, \mathbb{F})$-$\mathrm{LPN}(N + \alpha t, k + \alpha t, \alpha t)$. Therefore, we just feed all αt blocks as per (1) to the solver against $(\mathrm{RHW}, \mathbb{F})$-$\mathrm{LPN}(N + \alpha t, k + \alpha t, \alpha t)$. If it returns $\boldsymbol{x}$, then we recover the secret vector $\boldsymbol{s} := \mathbf{B} \cdot \boldsymbol{x}$ of the exact-LPN instance $(\mathrm{HW}, \mathbb{F})$-$\mathrm{LPN}(N, k, t)$. Quantitatively, if one breaks $(\mathrm{RHW}, \mathbb{F})$-$\mathrm{LPN}(N + \alpha t, k + \alpha t, \alpha t)$ with probability p, then it can also break $(\mathrm{HW}, \mathbb{F})$-$\mathrm{LPN}(N, k, t)$ with probability at least $2^{\frac{1}{\alpha} - \frac{t}{\alpha}} \cdot (p - 2 \cdot |\mathbb{F}|^{-k}) \geq p \cdot 2^{-\frac{t}{\alpha}}$.

CASE 2: $|\mathbb{F}| > 2$. In this case, we have that u_i is uniform over $\mathbb{F} \backslash \{0\}$. The reduction can be oblivious of u_i by letting the secret absorb u_i. We define $\boldsymbol{x}'$ such that $\mathbf{B} \cdot \boldsymbol{x}' \equiv \mathbf{B} \cdot \boldsymbol{x}$ and for all $i \in [1, \alpha t]$, $\boldsymbol{r}_i^\mathsf{T} \cdot \boldsymbol{x}' \equiv \boldsymbol{r}_i^\mathsf{T} \cdot \boldsymbol{x} + u_i - 1$, i.e.,

$$\mathbf{M} \cdot \boldsymbol{x}' \equiv \mathbf{M} \cdot \boldsymbol{x} + \left(\boldsymbol{h} \overset{\text{def}}{=} \underbrace{[0, \ldots, 0}_{k}, (u_1 - 1), \ldots, (u_{\alpha t} - 1)]^\mathsf{T} \right),$$

which is always possible by letting $\boldsymbol{x}' \overset{\text{def}}{=} \boldsymbol{x} + \mathbf{M}^{-1} \cdot \boldsymbol{h}$ for any invertible $\mathbf{M}$. Therefore, the reduction in Case 1 still works in Case 2 by considering $\boldsymbol{x}'$ instead of $\boldsymbol{x}$, where $\mathbf{B} \cdot \boldsymbol{x}' = \boldsymbol{s}$ and $\boldsymbol{r}_i^\mathsf{T} \cdot \boldsymbol{x}' = \mathbf{1}^\mathsf{T} \cdot \boldsymbol{b}_i + v_i - 1$ just like in Case 1. □

Lemma 2. *Let $\mathbf{A}_i$, $\mathbf{P}_i$, $\boldsymbol{r}_i^\mathsf{T}$ for $i \in [1, \alpha t]$, $\mathbf{B}$ and $\mathbf{M}$ be as defined in the proof of Theorem 2. Then,*

$$\mathsf{SD}\left(\left(\begin{bmatrix} [\mathbf{A}_1 \| \mathbf{P}_1] \cdot \mathbf{M} \\ \boldsymbol{r}_1^\mathsf{T} - \mathbf{1}^\mathsf{T}(\mathbf{A}_1 \mathbf{B}) \end{bmatrix}, \ldots, \begin{bmatrix} [\mathbf{A}_{\alpha t} \| \mathbf{P}_{\alpha t}] \cdot \mathbf{M} \\ \boldsymbol{r}_{\alpha t}^\mathsf{T} - \mathbf{1}^\mathsf{T}(\mathbf{A}_{\alpha t} \mathbf{B}) \end{bmatrix} \right), (U_\mathbb{F}^{(m+1) \times (k + \alpha t)})^{\alpha t} \right) \leq 2 \cdot |\mathbb{F}|^{-k},$$

where $\mathsf{SD}(\cdot, \cdot)$ denotes the statistical distance between two distributions, and $U_\mathbb{F}^{m \times n}$ denotes the uniform distribution over $\mathbb{F}^{m \times n}$.

The proof of Lemma 2 is given in the full version of the paper [58]. We also obtain a similar result for dual-LPN in the following Corollary 1 via the reductions between LPN and dual-LPN (see Sect. 2.2).

Corollary 1. *Let $t, N \in \mathbb{N}$ and $\alpha \geq 2$ such that $\alpha t \in \mathbb{N}$ and $(\alpha t) | N$. If the exact-dual-LPN problem $(\mathrm{HW}, \mathbb{F})$-$\mathrm{dual\text{-}LPN}(N, n, t)$ is (T, ϵ)-hard, then the regular-dual-LPN problem $(\mathrm{RHW}, \mathbb{F})$-$\mathrm{dual\text{-}LPN}(N + \alpha t, n, \alpha t)$ is $(T - \mathrm{poly}(N, n), 2^{\frac{t}{\alpha}} \cdot \epsilon)$-hard.*

The reduction underlying Theorem 2 can be generalized to that from standard LPN (with Bernoulli or exact noise distributions) to LPN with d-split noise distributions (refer to Footnote 4). To avoid redundancy, we sketch how to adapt the proof. Similar to the proof of Theorem 2, for each i-th block $(1 \leq i \leq \alpha d)$, introduce t/d additional random samples in the form of

$$\{(\boldsymbol{a}_{i,j}, v_{i,j} = \langle \boldsymbol{a}_{i,j}, \boldsymbol{s} \rangle + \tilde{e}_{i,j})\}_{j \in [1, t/d]}$$

such that the vector $(\boldsymbol{e}_i^\mathsf{T}, \tilde{e}_{i,1}, \cdots \tilde{e}_{i,t/d})$ possesses an exact weight of t/d. This incurs less security loss than Theorem 2 as it only requires $|\boldsymbol{e}_i^\mathsf{T}| \leq t/d$ (instead of $|\boldsymbol{e}_i^\mathsf{T}| \leq 1$) when the dimension of the target αd-split LPN problem is $k + \alpha t$. Consequently, the additional αt dimensions help to realize the almost-perfect simulation of αt values $\{v_{i,j}\}$.

4   The Hardness of LPN over Integer Rings

LPN over an integer ring (e.g., $\mathbb{Z}_{2^\lambda}$) has been used in VOLE and ZK protocols [8, 9,57,69], where these VOLE protocols could also benefit other works that need VOLE over integer rings like the MPC protocol SPDZ$_{2^k}$ [28,30]. The current security estimate of LPN over $\mathbb{Z}_{2^\lambda}$ in prior works is directly adapted from that for LPN over a field $\mathbb{F}$ of size $|\mathbb{F}| \approx 2^\lambda$ [15]. As we will show in this section the hardness of LPN over $\mathbb{Z}_{2^\lambda}$ is more related to that over $\mathbb{F}_2$ (rather than that over the λ-bit field). As depicted in Fig. 2, we provide the following reductions between the hardness of LPN over $\mathbb{Z}_{2^\lambda}$ and that over $\mathbb{F}_2$.

- **Decisional LPN over $\mathbb{Z}_{2^\lambda}$ → Decisional LPN over $\mathbb{F}_2$.** We show that distinguishing LPN over $\mathbb{Z}_{2^\lambda}$ with noise weight t is no harder than distinguishing LPN over $\mathbb{F}_2$ with noise weight $\frac{2^{(\lambda-1)}}{2^\lambda - 1} \cdot t \approx t/2$. This reduction directly gives an attack that reduces the noise weight by half for an LPN instance over $\mathbb{Z}_{2^\lambda}$.
- **Decisional LPN over $\mathbb{F}_2$ → Decisional LPN over $\mathbb{Z}_{2^\lambda}$.** We show that distinguishing LPN over $\mathbb{F}_2$ with noise weight t is no harder than the distinguishing attack on LPN over $\mathbb{Z}_{2^\lambda}$ with 1) non-standard Bernoulli-like integer noise of weight at most $\lambda \cdot t$; and 2) standard Bernoulli noise of weight $\approx 2^\lambda \cdot t$.
- **Computational LPN over $\mathbb{Z}_{2^\lambda}$ → Computational LPN over $\mathbb{F}_2$.** We show that a secret recovery attack on LPN over $\mathbb{Z}_{2^\lambda}$ with noise weight t is no harder than that on LPN over $\mathbb{F}_2$ with noise weight roughly $t/2$. While a generic reduction requires $k^{\omega(\lambda)}$-hardness for LPN over $\mathbb{Z}_{2^\lambda}$, we also give more efficient reductions for their weakly one-wayness that is more relevant to practical attacks and security estimates. We also discuss how to optimize the secret recovery attack on LPN over $\mathbb{Z}_{2^\lambda}$ based on that over $\mathbb{F}_2$ in practice.

We give similar reductions for LPN over a ring $\mathbb{Z}_{p^{\lambda_1} q^{\lambda_2}}$ (for any distinct primes p, q) in the full version of the paper [58, Appendix A], which can be further generalized to any ring $\mathbb{Z}_N$ for an integer N. All these reductions focus on the case of (primal)-LPN, and are easy to be generalized to the case of dual-LPN. When we give the reductions between different computational LPN variants, we assume that LPN over a field in consideration has a unique solution in the average case (except for a negligible fraction), which will simplify the analysis. Note that this is true for most interesting parameter regimes of LPN, which give rise to crypto-graphic applications (e.g., PCG and public-key encryption), as demonstrated in the full version of the paper [58, Lemma 3]. For the concrete security of an LPN instance $\mathsf{LPN}(N,k,t)$ over $\mathbb{Z}_{2^\lambda}$, we can first reduce it to $\mathsf{LPN}(N,k,\frac{2^{(\lambda-1)}}{2^\lambda-1}t)$ over $\mathbb{F}_2$, and then estimate the bit security of the LPN instance over $\mathbb{F}_2$ as demon-strated in Sect. 5. Thus, we omit the detailed analysis of concrete LPN over $\mathbb{Z}_{2^\lambda}$. In the *subsequent work*, Baum et al. [9] gave a countermeasure by sampling an invertible element in $\mathbb{Z}_{2^\lambda}$ at random for each noisy coordinate to resist our attack. Given the countermeasure, we can reduce an LPN problem over a ring $\mathbb{Z}_{2^\lambda}$ to that over $\mathbb{F}_2$ with the same noise weight, using the same approach shown in Sect. 4.1. In other words, LPN over $\mathbb{Z}_{2^\lambda}$ is no harder than LPN over $\mathbb{F}_2$ under the same parameters. Therefore, when estimating the bit security of LPN over $\mathbb{Z}_{2^\lambda}$, one needs to use the cost attacking LPN over $\mathbb{F}_2$ as an upper bound.

4.1   Reduction from Decisional LPN over $\mathbb{Z}_{2^\lambda}$ to LPN over $\mathbb{F}_2$

We start with a simple observation that the distinguishing attack on LPN over $\mathbb{Z}_{2^\lambda}$ can be based on that over $\mathbb{F}_2$ with roughly halved noise weight. Specifically, we have the following theorem.

Theorem 3. *If the decisional exact-LPN problem* $(\mathsf{HW}, \mathbb{Z}_{2^\lambda})\text{-}\mathsf{LPN}(N,k,t)$ *is* (T,ϵ)*-hard, then the decisional exact-LPN problem* $(\mathsf{HW}, \mathbb{F}_2)\text{-}\mathsf{LPN}(N,k,\frac{2^{(\lambda-1)}}{2^\lambda-1}t)$ *is* $(T - \text{poly}(N,k), O(\sqrt{t} \cdot \epsilon))$*-hard.*

The above statement can be generalized to the case of Bernoulli distributions. If the decisional LPN problem $(\mathsf{Ber}, \mathbb{Z}_{2^\lambda})\text{-}\mathsf{LPN}(N,k,\mu)$ *is* (T,ϵ)*-hard, then the decisional LPN problem* $(\mathsf{Ber}, \mathbb{F}_2)\text{-}\mathsf{LPN}(N,k,\mu)$ *is* $(T - \text{poly}(N,k), O(\epsilon))$*-hard.*

Proof. Given LPN samples over a ring $\mathbb{Z}_{2^\lambda}$ $(\mathbf{A}, \boldsymbol{b} = \mathbf{A} \cdot \boldsymbol{s} + \boldsymbol{e})$, we observe that least significant bits (LSBs) of these samples $(\mathbf{A}^0 := \mathbf{A} \mod 2, \boldsymbol{b}^0 := \boldsymbol{b} \mod 2)$ constitute exactly the LPN samples over $\mathbb{F}_2$ for noise $\boldsymbol{e}^0 = \boldsymbol{e} \mod 2$. In case that $\boldsymbol{e} \leftarrow \mathsf{HW}_{t,N}(\mathbb{Z}_{2^\lambda})$, the noise vector $\boldsymbol{e}^0$ follows a Bernoulli-like distribution over $\mathbb{F}_2^N$, which is sampled by first picking t out of N coordinates at random and then filling in these t coordinates with random non-zero elements over $\mathbb{Z}_{2^\lambda}$ (and the rest with zeros). Thus, overall $\boldsymbol{e}^0$ has expected weight $t' = \frac{2^{(\lambda-1)}}{2^\lambda-1} \cdot t$, where $\frac{2^{(\lambda-1)}}{2^\lambda-1}$ is the probability that a random non-zero element of $\mathbb{Z}_{2^\lambda}$ is odd. By Lemma 1, this implies that with probability $\Omega(1/\sqrt{t})$, the noise vector $\boldsymbol{e}^0$ follows the exact noise distribution $\mathsf{HW}_{t',N}(\mathbb{F}_2)$. On the other hand, the LSBs of $(\mathbf{A}, \boldsymbol{u})$ with a uniform $\boldsymbol{u} \in \mathbb{Z}_{2^\lambda}$ are uniform as well. Therefore, one can use the solver of $(\mathsf{HW}, \mathbb{F}_2)\text{-}\mathsf{LPN}(N,k,t')$ to distinguish $(\mathbf{A}^0, \boldsymbol{b}^0)$ from uniform samples. The proof for the second statement is likewise, except when taking the LSBs of $\boldsymbol{e} \leftarrow \mathsf{Ber}_{\mu,N}(\mathbb{Z}_{2^\lambda})$ we immediately get $\boldsymbol{e}^0 \sim \mathsf{Ber}_{\mu,N}(\mathbb{F}_2)$ as desired. □

Despite the preserved noise probability μ in the case of Bernoulli distribution, we note that $\mathsf{Ber}_{\mu,N}(\mathbb{Z}_{2^\lambda})$ has expected weight $(1 - 2^{-\lambda})\mu N$, while $\mathsf{Ber}_{\mu,N}(\mathbb{F}_2)$ has expected weight $\mu N/2$ that is roughly $2\times$ smaller than $\mathsf{Ber}_{\mu,N}(\mathbb{Z}_{2^\lambda})$. We can transform regular-LPN samples into exact-LPN samples by randomly shuffling these samples, and thus obtain a reduction from the decisional regular-LPN problem $(\mathsf{RHW}, \mathbb{Z}_{2^\lambda})\text{-LPN}(N, k, t)$ to the decisional exact-LPN problem $(\mathsf{HW}, \mathbb{F}_2)\text{-LPN}(N, k, \frac{2^{(\lambda-1)}}{2^\lambda-1}t)$. The reductions directly give an efficient attack to reduce the noise weight of an exact-LPN or regular-LPN instance over a ring $\mathbb{Z}_{2^\lambda}$ by half.

4.2   Reduction from LPN over $\mathbb{F}_2$ to Decisional LPN over $\mathbb{Z}_{2^\lambda}$

We first show that the LPN assumption over $\mathbb{F}_2$ implies that over $\mathbb{Z}_{2^\lambda}$ under the standard Bernoulli noise distribution. However, we achieve the goal by paying a price in the security loss due to the dependence among different noise vectors. As a result, we get the very conservative statement that decisional LPN over $\mathbb{F}_2$ with noise weight t is no harder than decisional LPN over $\mathbb{Z}_{2^\lambda}$ with noise weight roughly $2^\lambda t$. We then introduce more useful Bernoulli-like noise distributions to enable more efficient reductions. In particular, we can reduce to an LPN over $\mathbb{Z}_{2^\lambda}$ with noise weight λt.

Theorem 4. *If decisional* $(\mathsf{Ber}, \mathbb{F}_2)\text{-LPN}(N, k, \mu/2^\lambda)$ *is* (T, ϵ)*-hard, then decisional* $(\mathsf{Ber}, \mathbb{Z}_{2^\lambda})\text{-LPN}(N, k, \mu)$ *is* $(T - \mathrm{poly}(N, k), \lambda \cdot \epsilon)$*-hard.*

Proof. Let $(\mathbf{A}, \mathbf{b} = \mathbf{A} \cdot \mathbf{s} + \mathbf{e})$ be LPN samples over $\mathbb{Z}_{2^\lambda}$. Decompose the matrix and vectors into λ ones over $\mathbb{F}_2$ as follows: $(\mathbf{A}^0, \mathbf{A}^1, \cdots, \mathbf{A}^{\lambda-1}) :=$ $\mathsf{BitDecomp}(\mathbf{A})$, $(\mathbf{s}^0, \mathbf{s}^1, \cdots, \mathbf{s}^{\lambda-1}) := \mathsf{BitDecomp}(\mathbf{s})$, $(\mathbf{e}^0, \mathbf{e}^1, \cdots, \mathbf{e}^{\lambda-1}) :=$ $\mathsf{BitDecomp}(\mathbf{e})$ and $(\mathbf{b}^0, \mathbf{b}^1, \cdots, \mathbf{b}^{\lambda-1}) := \mathsf{BitDecomp}(\mathbf{b})$. Therefore, for $i \in [\lambda]$, $\mathbf{b}^i$ depends only on $\mathbf{A}$, $(\mathbf{s}^i, \ldots, \mathbf{s}^0)$, $(\mathbf{e}^i, \ldots, \mathbf{e}^0)$, and we write it as $\mathbf{b}^i = \mathbf{A}^0 \cdot \mathbf{s}^i + \mathbf{e}^i + f_i(\mathbf{A}, \mathbf{S}(0, i-1), \mathbf{E}(0, i-1)) \mod 2$, where $\mathbf{S}(0, i-1) \overset{\mathrm{def}}{=} (\mathbf{s}^{i-1}, \ldots, \mathbf{s}^0)$, and $\mathbf{E}(0, i-1) \overset{\mathrm{def}}{=} (\mathbf{e}^{i-1}, \ldots, \mathbf{e}^0)$, and f_i sums up the other terms not depending on $\mathbf{s}^i$ and $\mathbf{e}^i$. Define the hybrid distributions $H_0, H_1, \cdots, H_\lambda$, where each $H_i = (\mathbf{A}, \mathbf{b}^0, \cdots, \mathbf{b}^{i-1}, \mathbf{u}_i \cdots, \mathbf{u}_{\lambda-1})$ and $\mathbf{u}_j \leftarrow \mathbb{F}_2^N$ for $j \in [\lambda]$ is sampled independently at random. Note that all the $\mathbf{s}^i$'s are independent and uniformly random. Therefore, for $i \in [\lambda]$, by the decisional $(\mathsf{Ber}, \mathbb{F}_2)$-LPN assumption,

$$\big(\mathbf{A}^0, \mathbf{u}_i, \mathbf{S}(0, i-1), \mathbf{E}(0, i-1)\big) \approx_c \big(\mathbf{A}^0, \mathbf{A}^0 \cdot \mathbf{s}^i + \mathbf{e}^i \mod 2, \mathbf{S}(0, i-1), \mathbf{E}(0, i-1)\big)$$

where $\mathbf{S}(0, i-1)$ is independent of any other variables, and the actual noise rate of LPN is that of $\mathbf{e}^i$ conditioned on $\mathbf{E}(0, i-1)$ (see analysis blow). This implies

$$\big(\mathbf{A}, \mathbf{b}^0, \cdots, \mathbf{b}^{i-1}, \mathbf{u}_i + f_i(\mathbf{A}, \mathbf{S}(0, i-1), \mathbf{E}(0, i-1)) \mod 2\big) \approx_c \big(\mathbf{A}, \mathbf{b}^0, \cdots, \mathbf{b}^{i-1}, \mathbf{b}^i\big)$$

which in turn implies $H_i \approx_c H_{i+1}$, where $\mathbf{b}^0, \ldots, \mathbf{b}^{i-1}, f_i(\mathbf{A}, \mathbf{S}(0, i-1), \mathbf{E}(0, i-1))$ can be efficiently computed from $\mathbf{A}, \mathbf{S}(0, i-1), \mathbf{E}(0, i-1)$.

Therefore, if all the adjacent H_i and H_{i+1} are computationally indistinguishable except with probability ϵ, then H_0 and H_λ are computationally indistinguishable by a hybrid argument except with probability $\lambda \cdot \epsilon$. It thus remains to estimate the noise rate needed by the LPN assumption. Consider a single noise sample $(e^0[j], e^1[j], \ldots, e^{\lambda-1}[j]) \leftarrow \mathsf{Ber}_{\mu,N}(\mathbb{Z}_{2^\lambda})$, where $e^i[j]$ is the j-th entry of e^i. Conditioned on any non-zero $(e^0[j], \ldots, e^{i-1}[j])$, $e^i[j]$ is uniformly random and thus unconditionally masks the corresponding $b^i[j]$. Otherwise, we have that

$$\Pr\left[e^i[j] = 1 \mid (e^0[j], \ldots, e^{i-1}[j]) = 0^i\right] = \frac{\mu \cdot 2^{-(i+1)}}{1 - \mu + \mu \cdot 2^{-i}} \geq \mu \cdot 2^{-(i+1)}$$

is the noise rate needed to keep the computational indistinguishability between H_i and H_{i+1}, which reaches its minimum $\mu \cdot 2^{-\lambda}$ when $i = \lambda - 1$.   □

Based on the above theorem, we easily obtain the following corollary, with its proof given in the full version of the paper [58].

Corollary 2. *If decisional* $(\mathsf{Ber}, \mathbb{F}_2)$-$\mathsf{LPN}(N, k, \mu/2^\lambda)$ *is hard, then computational* $(\mathsf{HW}, \mathbb{Z}_{2^\lambda})$-$\mathsf{LPN}(N, k, t = (1 - 2^{-\lambda})\mu N)$ *is hard.*

The dependency among the noise vectors $\{e^i\}$ incurs a significant loss during the reduction. This motivates us to introduce two specific noise distributions, i.e., $\mathsf{IndBer}_{\mu,N}(\mathbb{Z}_{2^\lambda})$ and $\mathsf{IndHW}_{t,N}(\mathbb{Z}_{2^\lambda})$, where Ind refers that the noise's bit-decomposition $e^0, \ldots, e^{\lambda-1}$ are independent and identically distributed, and parameter μ (resp., t) is noise rate (resp., weight) of each e^i.

- $\mathsf{IndBer}_{\mu,N}(\mathbb{Z}_{2^\lambda})$ is bit-wise independent. By $e \leftarrow \mathsf{IndBer}_{\mu,N}(\mathbb{Z}_{2^\lambda})$, we mean that $e := \sum_{i=0}^{\lambda-1} 2^i \cdot e^i \in \mathbb{Z}_{2^\lambda}$ with $e^i \leftarrow \mathsf{Ber}_{\mu,N}(\mathbb{F}_2)$ for $i \in [\lambda]$. The noise rate of $\mathsf{IndBer}_{\mu,N}(\mathbb{Z}_{2^\lambda})$ is the probability that a coordinate of e is non-zero, i.e., $1 - (1 - \mu/2)^\lambda \leq \lambda\mu/2$ by Bernoulli's inequality. Therefore, the expected Hamming weight of $e \leftarrow \mathsf{IndBer}_{\mu,N}(\mathbb{Z}_{2^\lambda})$ is λt where $t = \mu N/2$.
- $\mathsf{IndHW}_{t,N}(\mathbb{Z}_{2^\lambda})$ decomposes into λ independent vectors from $\mathsf{HW}_{t,N}(\mathbb{F}_2)$. By $e \leftarrow \mathsf{IndHW}_{t,N}(\mathbb{Z}_{2^\lambda})$, we mean that $e := \sum_{i=0}^{\lambda-1} 2^i \cdot e^i$ with $e^i \leftarrow \mathsf{HW}_{t,N}(\mathbb{F}_2)$ for $i \in [\lambda]$. It is easy to see that the Hamming weight of e is at most λt.

Although $\mathsf{IndBer}_{\mu,N}(\mathbb{Z}_{2^\lambda})$ and $\mathsf{IndHW}_{t,N}(\mathbb{Z}_{2^\lambda})$ have not been used in existing protocols, LPN with such noise distributions can be used to design PCG-like VOLE protocols by running these protocols with maximum weight λt. The PCG-like VOLE protocols employing the non-standard noise distributions are approximately $\lambda/2$ times less efficient than the state-of-the-art protocol [9] using LPN with regular noise distributions over $\mathbb{Z}_{2^\lambda}$. Despite their lower efficiency, these PCG-like VOLE protocols enjoy (1) that the underlying LPN problem over $\mathbb{Z}_{2^\lambda}$ is tightly equivalent to LPN over $\mathbb{F}_2$; (2) a simpler approach to detect malicious behaviors. Below, we show that decisional LPN over $\mathbb{F}_2$ with noise weight t is *tightly* equivalent to decisional LPN over $\mathbb{Z}_{2^\lambda}$ with noise weight roughly λt under the new noise distributions. The proof of Theorem 5 is detailed in the full version of the paper [58].

Theorem 5. *Let* $(\mathcal{D}_1, \mathcal{D}_2, w) \in \{(\mathsf{Ber}, \mathsf{IndBer}, \mu), (\mathsf{HW}, \mathsf{IndHW}, t)\}$ *and we have:*

- *If decisional* $(\mathcal{D}_1, \mathbb{F}_2)$-$\mathsf{LPN}(N, k, w)$ *is* (T, ϵ)-*hard, then decisional* $(\mathcal{D}_2, \mathbb{Z}_{2^\lambda})$-$\mathsf{LPN}(N, k, w)$ *is* $(T - \mathsf{poly}(N, k), \lambda \cdot \epsilon)$-*hard.*

Algorithm 1: $\mathcal{A}_{\mathrm{LPN}_{2^\lambda}}$, the secret recovery algorithm on LPN over $\mathbb{Z}_{2^\lambda}$ ($\lambda \geq 2$) with oracle access to $\mathcal{A}_{\mathrm{LPN}_2}$ (the solver for LPN over $\mathbb{F}_2$).

Input: $(\mathcal{D}, \mathbb{Z}_{2^\lambda})$-LPN$(N, k, t)$ samples $(\mathbf{A}, \boldsymbol{b} = \mathbf{A} \cdot \boldsymbol{s} + \boldsymbol{e} \mod 2^\lambda)$

Output: $\boldsymbol{s} \in \mathbb{Z}_{2^\lambda}$

1 $(\mathbf{A}^0, \mathbf{A}^1, \cdots, \mathbf{A}^{\lambda-1}) := \mathsf{BitDecomp}(\mathbf{A})$;

2 $(\boldsymbol{b}^0, \boldsymbol{b}^1, \cdots, \boldsymbol{b}^{\lambda-1}) := \mathsf{BitDecomp}(\boldsymbol{b})$;

3 $(\boldsymbol{s}^0, \boldsymbol{e}^0) \leftarrow \mathcal{A}_{\mathrm{LPN}_2}(\mathbf{A}^0, \boldsymbol{b}^0)$;

4 $\boldsymbol{b}' := (\boldsymbol{b} - \mathbf{A} \cdot \boldsymbol{s}^0 - \boldsymbol{e}^0)/2 \mod 2^{(\lambda-1)}$;

5 **Return** $\boldsymbol{s} = \boldsymbol{s}^0 + 2 \cdot \mathcal{A}_{\mathrm{LPN}_{2^{(\lambda-1)}}}\left(\mathbf{A}' := \sum_{i=0}^{\lambda-2} 2^i \cdot \mathbf{A}^i \in \mathbb{Z}_{2^{\lambda-1}}, \boldsymbol{b}'\right)$.

- *If decisional* $(\mathcal{D}_2, \mathbb{Z}_{2^\lambda})$-LPN$(N, k, w)$ *is* (T, ϵ)-*hard, then decisional* $(\mathcal{D}_1, \mathbb{F}_2)$-LPN$(N, k, w)$ *is* $(T - \mathsf{poly}(N, k), \epsilon)$-*hard.*

On the Choice of Matrix A. As we can see from the proofs of Theorem 4, Theorem 5 and Theorem 6 (shown in Sect. 4.3), all the reductions only rely on that $\mathbf{A}^0$ is uniformly distributed over $\mathbb{F}_2^{N \times k}$ while $\mathbf{A}^1, \cdots, \mathbf{A}^{\lambda-1}$ can be arbitrary (or even zero matrix), where $(\mathbf{A}^0, \mathbf{A}^1, \ldots, \mathbf{A}^{\lambda-1}) := \mathsf{BitDecomp}(\mathbf{A})$. In other words, it suffices to use a Boolean matrix $\mathbf{A} = \mathbf{A}^0$, and the choices of $\mathbf{A}^1, \ldots, \mathbf{A}^{\lambda-1}$ do not introduce any further hardness to the LPN problem over $\mathbb{Z}_{2^\lambda}$. Overall, we give a positive result that LPN over a ring $\mathbb{Z}_{2^\lambda}$ with Boolean matrices is secure if the corresponding LPN over binary field $\mathbb{F}_2$ is secure.

4.3   Reduction from Computational LPN over $\mathbb{Z}_{2^\lambda}$ to LPN over $\mathbb{F}_2$

In the computational setting, we show that an LPN instance over $\mathbb{Z}_{2^\lambda}$ can be efficiently translated to λ instances of LPN over $\mathbb{F}_2$, which are independent except that they share the same random matrix $\mathbf{A}^0$ over $\mathbb{F}_2$ and that the noise vectors of the λ instances are somehow correlated. We refer to the proof of Theorem 6 on how to address the correlation issue. Here we give a reduction from computational LPN over a ring $\mathbb{Z}_{2^\lambda}$ to that over $\mathbb{F}_2$ by extending the corresponding reduction between their decisional versions shown in Sect. 4.1. Algorithm 1 shows how computational LPN over $\mathbb{Z}_{2^\lambda}$ is reduced to that over $\mathbb{Z}_{2^{\lambda-1}}$. The correctness of this reduction is analyzed in Lemma 3, and its proof is available in the complete version of the paper [58]. Note that by recursion, $\mathcal{A}_{\mathrm{LPN}_{2^\lambda}}$ degenerates to secret recovery algorithm for LPN over $\mathbb{F}_2$ when $\lambda = 1$. Without loss of generality, we assume that $\mathcal{A}_{\mathrm{LPN}_2}$ returns the noise vector in addition to the recovered secret.

Lemma 3. *Let* $(\mathbf{A}, \boldsymbol{b} = \mathbf{A} \cdot \boldsymbol{s} + \boldsymbol{e} \mod 2^\lambda)$ *be the LPN samples over* $\mathbb{Z}_{2^\lambda}$, *then* $(\mathbf{A}', \boldsymbol{b}')$ *as defined in Algorithm 1 constitute the LPN samples over* $\mathbb{Z}_{2^{(\lambda-1)}}$, *where* $\mathbf{A}' = \sum_{i=0}^{\lambda-2} 2^i \cdot \mathbf{A}^i \mod 2^{(\lambda-1)}$, $\boldsymbol{b}' = \mathbf{A}' \cdot \boldsymbol{s}' + \boldsymbol{e}' \mod 2^{(\lambda-1)}$, $\boldsymbol{s}' = \sum_{i=1}^{\lambda-1} 2^{i-1} \cdot \boldsymbol{s}^i \mod 2^{(\lambda-1)}$ *and* $\boldsymbol{e}' = \sum_{i=1}^{\lambda-1} 2^{i-1} \cdot \boldsymbol{e}^i \mod 2^{(\lambda-1)}$.

Below, we show that $(\epsilon^{\lambda+1})$-hard computational LPN over $\mathbb{Z}_{2^\lambda}$ implies (2ϵ)-hard LPN over $\mathbb{F}_2$. Here $\lambda = O(1)$ needs to be small in general for polynomial hardness, and it can be up to $\lambda = k^{\Theta(1)}$ for sub-exponential hardness, e.g., $\lambda = k^{0.25}$ and $\epsilon = 2^{-k^{0.25}}$. The proofs of Theorem 6 and Theorem 7 are detailed in the full version of the paper [58].

Theorem 6. *If computational $(D_1, \mathbb{Z}_{2^\lambda})$-LPN$(N, k, w)$ is $(\lambda \cdot T + \mathrm{poly}(N, k), \epsilon^{\lambda+1})$-hard, then computational $(D_2, \mathbb{F}_2)$-LPN(N, k, w) is $(T, 2\epsilon)$-hard, where $(D_1, D_2, w) \in \{(\mathsf{Ber}, \mathsf{Ber}, \mu), (\mathsf{IndBer}, \mathsf{Ber}, \mu), (\mathsf{IndHW}, \mathsf{HW}, t)\}$.*

Theorem 7. *If computational $(\mathsf{HW}, \mathbb{Z}_{2^\lambda})$-LPN$(N, k, t)$ is $(\lambda \cdot T + \mathrm{poly}(N, k), \epsilon^{\lambda+1})$-hard, then computational $(\mathsf{HW}, \mathbb{F}_2)$-LPN$(N, k, t')$ is $(T, \frac{2\epsilon}{1-\exp(-\delta^2 t/6)})$-hard, where $t' = \frac{2^{(\lambda-1)}}{2^\lambda - 1}(1 + \delta)t$ for any constant $\delta > 0$.*

Recall that we can transform regular-LPN samples into exact-LPN samples by randomly shuffling these samples. Therefore, we are able to obtain a reduction from the computational regular-LPN problem $(\mathsf{RHW}, \mathbb{Z}_{2^\lambda})$-LPN$(N, k, t)$ to the computational exact-LPN problem $(\mathsf{HW}, \mathbb{F}_2)$-LPN$(N, k, \frac{2^{(\lambda-1)}}{2^\lambda - 1}(1 + \delta)t)$. The above reduction suffers a significant security loss by exponent factor $1/(\lambda + 1)$ since computationally intractable problems typically require a small success probability for efficient adversaries. In the setting of practical key recovery attacks, however, we often expect the success probability to be $(1 - 1/\mathrm{poly}(k))$ or even overwhelming. In this case, we get more efficient reductions as below. The proofs of Theorem 8 and Theorem 9 are provided in the full version of the paper [58].

Theorem 8. *If the computational $(D_1, \mathbb{F}_2)$-LPN(N, k, w) problem can be broken by $\mathcal{A}_{LPN_2}$ in time T with success probability at least $(1 - \epsilon)$, then the computational $(D_2, \mathbb{Z}_{2^\lambda})$-LPN$(N, k, w)$ problem can be broken by $\mathcal{A}_{LPN_{2^\lambda}}$ (see Algorithm 1) in time $\lambda \cdot T + \mathrm{poly}(N, k)$ with success probability at least $1 - (\lambda+1)\sqrt{\epsilon}$, where $(D_1, D_2, w) \in \{(\mathsf{Ber}, \mathsf{Ber}, \mu), (\mathsf{Ber}, \mathsf{IndBer}, \mu), (\mathsf{HW}, \mathsf{IndHW}, t)\}$.*

Theorem 9. *If the computational $(\mathsf{HW}, \mathbb{F}_2)$-LPN$(N, k, t')$ problem can be broken by $\mathcal{A}_{LPN_2}$ in time T with success probability at least $(1 - \epsilon/2)$, then the computational $(\mathsf{HW}, \mathbb{Z}_{2^\lambda})$-LPN$(N, k, t)$ problem can be broken by $\mathcal{A}_{LPN_{2^\lambda}}$ (see Algorithm 1) in time $\lambda \cdot T + \mathrm{poly}(N, k)$ with success probability at least $1 - (\lambda+1)\sqrt{\epsilon}$, where $t' = \frac{2^{\lambda-1}}{2^\lambda-1}(1 + \delta)t$ for any δ and ϵ satisfying $\delta^2 t \geq 6\ln(2/\epsilon)$.*

Optimized Attacks on $(\mathsf{Ber/HW}, \mathbb{Z}_{2^\lambda})$**-LPN.** In practice, we optimize the attacks on $(\mathsf{Ber/HW}, \mathbb{Z}_{2^\lambda})$-LPN by exploiting the correlations among the noise vectors of the λ instances (i.e., $e^0, \ldots, e^{\lambda-1}$). In particular, Algorithm 1 recovers the corresponding secrets $s^0, s^1, \cdots, s^{\lambda-1}$ sequentially. That means when the attacker works on the $(i + 1)$-th LPN instance, it has already seen $e^0, \ldots, e^{i-1}$ from the previous i broken instances. As analyzed in the proof of Theorem 4, for any single noise sample $(e^0[j], e^1[j], \ldots, e^{\lambda-1}[j]) \leftarrow \mathsf{Ber}_{\mu, N}(\mathbb{Z}_{2^\lambda})$, $e^i[j]$ is uniformly random conditioned on any non-zero $(e^0[j], \ldots, e^{i-1}[j])$, and thus sample $b^i[j]$ is useless (encrypted by one-time padding) and should be discarded. In other words, the effective noise rate of the i-th LPN instance is roughly $\mu \cdot 2^{-(i+1)}$ given the attacker's knowledge about $e^0, \ldots, e^{i-1}$. Therefore, the success rate of solving the $(\mathsf{Ber}, \mathbb{Z}_{2^\lambda})$-LPN$(N, k, \mu)$ instance is roughly the product of the λ instances of $(\mathsf{Ber}, \mathbb{F}_2)$-LPN with continuously halving noise rates μ, $\mu/2$, ..., $\mu/2^{\lambda-1}$. For instance, if solving these instances can succeed with probability ϵ, $\epsilon^{2^{-1}}$, ..., $\epsilon^{2^{-(\lambda-1)}}$ respectively, then it leads to a success probability of approximately ϵ^2 (instead of $\epsilon^{\lambda+1}$). The optimization for reducing $(\mathsf{HW}, \mathbb{Z}_{2^\lambda})$-LPN to $(\mathsf{HW}, \mathbb{F}_2)$-LPN is likewise.

5 Concrete Analysis of Low-Noise LPN over Finite Fields

Recently, a series of works [14–18, 27, 67, 69, 76, 82] use the (dual-)LPN problem with very low noise rate over finite fields to construct concretely efficient PCG-like protocols, which extend a small number of correlations (e.g., COT, VOLE and OLE) to a large number of correlations with sublinear communication. These protocols can be used as building blocks to design a variety of MPC and ZK protocols. Therefore, the hardness of (dual-)LPN problems is crucial to guarantee the security of all the protocols.

Before our work, almost all of the known PCG-like protocols based on (dual-)LPN adopt the formulas by Boyle et al. [15] to select the concrete parameters for some specified security level. Boyle et al. [15] obtained the formulas by analyzing three attacks: Pooled Gauss [40], ISD [65] and SD [3]. However, we found some imprecisions for their analysis, which are outlined as follows:

- When analyzing the hardness of LPN with exact noise distribution $\mathsf{HW}_{t,N}(\mathbb{F})$, the formula against Pooled Gauss attack is obtained by viewing $\mathsf{HW}_{t,N}(\mathbb{F})$ as a Bernoulli distribution $\mathsf{Ber}_{t/N,N}(\mathbb{F})$, which makes the formula not accurate.
- When analyzing the hardness of LPN against ISD attacks, the formula is obtained by an upper bound of the complexity of the Prange's ISD algorithm [65] to solve LPN problems over a large field. This does not cover the advanced ISD variants [11, 38, 59, 71]. Additionally, their analysis does not capture the impact of field sizes when calculating the ISD cost.
- When analyzing the hardness of LPN against SD attacks, each parity-check vector is assumed to be independently in compliance with a Bernoulli distribution, which is inaccurate [33].

We also give more accurate formulas on the hardness of low-noise (dual-)LPN problems, where the recent SD improvement called SD 2.0 [25] is also included. Very recently, Meyer-Hilfiger and Tillich [61] shown that the SD 2.0 algorithm can be modified to obtain the same complexity under a weaker assumption. For LPN with exact noise distributions, we compare our more accurate costs of Pooled Gauss, SD and ISD attacks with that by Boyle et al. [15] in the full version of the paper [58, Tables 6 and 7], where all the LPN parameters are adopted from [15]. Under the same LPN parameters, while Boyle et al. [15] showed that either Pooled Gauss attack or SD attack has the lowest cost, our analysis shows that ISD attack has the lowest cost. [58, Tables 6 and 7] also show that the ISD attack has lower cost for smaller field size, which is also observed in prior works such as [42]. This justifies that it is not accurate to use the same formulas for all field sizes as in [15].

Under the Gilbert-Varshamov (GV) bound[6], Carrier et al. [25] shown that SD 2.0 outperforms all ISD algorithms for the case that the code rate $k/N < 0.3$. However, we observe that the SD 2.0 algorithm [25] does not behave better when solving the low-noise LPN problems used in the PCG-like protocols. This is because the collision technique[7] (a subroutine of SD 2.0) takes exponential time $2^{\theta(k)}$ that is much larger than the subexponential time $2^{O(k\mu)}$ to solve the low-noise LPN problem with ISD, where $\mu = 1/k^c$ is the noise rate (i.e., t/N) for constant $0 < c < 1$. Thus, in SD 2.0, we incorporate other collision techniques that are known to perform better for low-noise LPN (e.g., the one used in low-weight parity-check attack shown in [15, Sect. 2.3], originated from [85]). In the full version of the paper [58, Appendix B.2], we prove that the SD 2.0 attack [25] (that improves the SD attack) adapted to the low-noise setting require more cost than the ISD attack against $(\mathsf{HW}, \mathbb{F})$-$\mathsf{LPN}(N, k, t)$ with field size $|\mathbb{F}| \geq 4t$.

The previous analysis [15] focuses on exact noise distributions, but the recent PCG-like protocols mainly adopt regular noise distributions to achieve better efficiency. To close the gap, our analysis includes two aspects to capture the regular structure of noises. On the one hand, we transform a regular-LPN problem $(\mathsf{RHW}, \mathbb{F}_2)$-$\mathsf{LPN}(N, k, t)$ into an exact-LPN problem $(\mathsf{HW}, \mathbb{F}_2)$-$\mathsf{LPN}(N - t, k - t, t)$ based on the approach in prior works [22,41]. Then, we solve the $(\mathsf{HW}, \mathbb{F}_2)$-$\mathsf{LPN}(N - t, k - t, t)$ problem by applying established attacks, independent of the regular structure. This transformation from regular-LPN to exact-LPN works for LPN over $\mathbb{F}_2$, but fails to work for LPN over larger fields (see more details in Sect. 5.1). On the other hand, our analysis includes the recent algebraic attack by Briaud and Øygarden [22], which exploits the regular structure of noises. This attack is able to obtain lower cost for regular-LPN problems with small code rate k/N for some parameter sets. Recently, Carozza, Couteau and Joux [24] also proposed new attacks tailored to LPN with regular noises, but focus on the parameter selection satisfies the condition $(N/t)^t \leq 2^{N-k} \leq \binom{N}{t}$, which notably differs from the parameter selection used in the PCG setting. Thus, we do not cover their attacks.

For regular noise distributions, we give the costs of different attacks against LPN problems with the parameters given in [15], which is shown in Tables 2 and the full version of the paper [58, Table 4]. For the case of $\log|\mathbb{F}| = 128$ and $(N, k, t) = (2^{20}, 32771, 1419)$ or $(N, k, t) = (2^{22}, 67440, 2735)$, the algebraic attack achieves the lowest cost among these attacks. When the LPN parameters listed in Table 2 achieve the bit security at most 111, we have two choices to achieve 128-bit security: (a) increasing the dimension k; (b) increasing the noise weight t. When only increasing weight t, the algebraic attack would have a

---

[6] The GV bound decoding over $\mathbb{F}_2$ is to solve LPN instances that achieve the GV relative distance $t/N = \mathbf{H}^{-1}(1 - k/N)$, where $\mathbf{H}(\mu) = \mu \cdot \log(1/\mu) + (1 - \mu) \cdot \log(1/(1 - \mu))$ is the binary entropy function and $\mathbf{H}^{-1}$ is the inverse of $\mathbf{H}$.

[7] The collision technique refers to the process of finding parity check vectors.

Table 2. The bit-security of LPN problems over finite fields with number of samples N, dimension k and Hamming weight of noises t for a regular noise distribution. The abbreviation "AGB" denotes the recent algebraic attack [22].

Regular LPN over a field $\mathbb{F}$			This work ($\log |\mathbb{F}| = 128$)					This work ($\log |\mathbb{F}| = 1$)				
N	k	t	Gauss	SD	SD 2.0	ISD	AGB	Gauss	SD	SD 2.0	ISD	AGB
2^{10}	652	57	111	184	184	111	111	106	183	108	90	101
2^{12}	1589	98	100	151	151	100	107	96	146	130	80	103
2^{14}	3482	198	101	149	149	101	110	97	143	136	83	106
2^{16}	7391	389	103	147	147	103	111	99	141	138	87	108
2^{18}	15336	760	105	146	146	105	107	101	140	138	92	104
2^{20}	32771	1419	107	145	145	107	102	104	139	139	97	98
2^{22}	67440	2735	108	138	138	108	104	103	133	133	99	103

Table 3. Comparison of dimensions between exact-LPN problems and regular-LPN problems over finite fields for 128-bit security level.

#Samples	Weight	Dimension for $\log |\mathbb{F}| = 128$		Dimension for $\log |\mathbb{F}| = 1$	
N	t	Exact-LPN	Regular-LPN	Exact-LPN	Regular-LPN
2^{12}	172	1321	1377 (+4.2%)	1549	1657 (+7.0%)
2^{14}	338	2895	2909 (+0.5%)	3373	3655 (+8.3%)
2^{16}	667	6005	6091 (+1.4%)	6956	7560 (+8.7%)
2^{18}	1312	12160	14796 (+21.7%)	13898	15996 (+15.1%)
2^{20}	2467	25346	30978 (+22.2%)	28289	33354 (+17.9%)
2^{22}	4788	50854	75396 (+48.3%)	55408	80074 (+44.5%)

significantly lower cost than other attacks for some parameter sets (see the full version of the paper [58, Table 8]), which has been observed in [22]. To resist the algebraic attack and the attack strategy based on the above regular-to-exact transformation, a better choice is to increase dimension k. For example, as shown in Table 3, we need to increase the dimension of LPN problems with a regular noise distribution by 0.5%–48.3% to achieve the same 128-bit security as LPN problems with an exact noise distribution. The increase of dimension k has a negligible impact on the efficiency of PCG-like protocols, due to the usage of the Bootstrapping-iteration technique [82]. For dual-LPN problems, we note that the algebraic attack [22] has significantly more cost than Pooled Gauss and ISD attacks for all the listed parameters, as the code rate is constant (typically 1/2 or 3/4).

In this section, we aim to give more accurate formulas by adjusting the known attacks to analyze the cost of low-noise LPN problems in the PCG setting. In particular, we provide an estimator tool (see Footnote 3), which incorporates the advanced attacks being applicable to LPN problems in the PCG setting, to automatically evaluate the bit security of low-noise LPN problems. This will help future works to select LPN parameters when designing or applying PCG-like protocols. While the recent estimator tool by Esser and Bellini [39] focuses on ISD attacks to analyze the hardness of classical LPN problems over $\mathbb{F}_2$ with an exact noise distribution in the traditional public-key setting, our estimator tool covers Pooled Gauss, SD, SD 2.0, ISD and algebraic attacks to evaluate the hardness of low-noise LPN problems over an arbitrary finite field (or integer ring) with a regular or exact noise distribution in the PCG setting.

In Sect. 5.1, we first show that $(\mathsf{RHW}, \mathbb{F}_2)\text{-LPN}(N, k, t)$ is not harder than $(\mathsf{HW}, \mathbb{F}_2)\text{-LPN}(N - t, k - t, t)$, and also give an overview of the algebraic attack. For LPN over larger fields, we do not find such an efficient transformation from regular-LPN to exact-LPN. Therefore, we are able to analyze the costs of Pooled Gauss, SD and ISD attacks against LPN problems in a similar way for both exact and regular noise distributions. Then, in the full version of the paper [58, Appendix B], we show the imprecisions of the previous analysis [15] and give more accurate formulas against Pooled Gauss, SD and ISD attacks for the hardness of low-noise LPN problems.

5.1 The Hardness of LPN with Regular Noise Distributions

Transformation from Regular-LPN to Exact-LPN over $\mathbb{F}_2$. Building upon prior works [22,41], we transform a regular-LPN problem $(\mathsf{RHW}, \mathbb{F}_2)\text{-LPN}(N, k, t)$ into an exact-LPN problem $(\mathsf{HW}, \mathbb{F}_2)\text{-LPN}(N - t, k - t, t)$. The reduction is useful for the case of $2^{N-k} > \binom{N}{t}$ which is satisfied by the LPN parameters in the PCG setting. In this case, both regular-LPN and exact-LPN problems have unique solutions for these parameters, and thus the solution of $(\mathsf{HW}, \mathbb{F}_2)\text{-LPN}(N - t, k - t, t)$ is always that of $(\mathsf{RHW}, \mathbb{F}_2)\text{-LPN}(N, k, t)$.

Let $m = \lfloor N/t \rfloor$. Given a $(\mathsf{RHW}, \mathbb{F}_2)\text{-LPN}(N, k, t)$ instance $(\mathbf{A}, \boldsymbol{b})$ with $\boldsymbol{b} = \mathbf{A} \cdot \boldsymbol{s} + \boldsymbol{e} \in \mathbb{F}_2^N$ and $\boldsymbol{s} \in \mathbb{F}_2^k$, we define

$$
\mathbf{A} \stackrel{\text{def}}{=} \begin{bmatrix} \mathbf{A}_1 \\ \vdots \\ \mathbf{A}_t \end{bmatrix}, \; \boldsymbol{e} \stackrel{\text{def}}{=} \begin{bmatrix} \boldsymbol{e}_1 \\ \vdots \\ \boldsymbol{e}_t \end{bmatrix} \text{ and } \boldsymbol{b} \stackrel{\text{def}}{=} \begin{bmatrix} \boldsymbol{b}_1 = \mathbf{A}_1 \cdot \boldsymbol{s} + \boldsymbol{e}_1 \\ \vdots \\ \boldsymbol{b}_t = \mathbf{A}_t \cdot \boldsymbol{s} + \boldsymbol{e}_t \end{bmatrix},
$$

where $\mathbf{A}_i \in \mathbb{F}_2^{m \times k}$, $\boldsymbol{e}_i \in \mathbb{F}_2^m$ and $\boldsymbol{b}_i \in \mathbb{F}_2^m$ for $i \in [1, t]$. Note that the Hamming weight of each sub-vector $\boldsymbol{e}_i$ is exactly 1. We use $\mathbf{A}_i[j]$ to denote the j-th row vector of $\mathbf{A}_i$, and recall that $\boldsymbol{b}_i[j]$ and $\boldsymbol{e}_i[j]$ is the j-th component of vectors $\boldsymbol{b}_i$ and $\boldsymbol{e}_i$ respectively. Then, for each $i \in [1, t]$, we can obtain the following equation:

$$
\sum_{j=1}^{m} \boldsymbol{b}_i[j] = \sum_{j=1}^{m} \mathbf{A}_i[j] \cdot \boldsymbol{s} + \sum_{j=1}^{m} \boldsymbol{e}_i[j] = \left(\sum_{j=1}^{m} \mathbf{A}_i[j] \right) \cdot \boldsymbol{s} + 1 .
$$

Therefore, we extract t linear relations about the secret and reduce the dimension of $\boldsymbol{s}$ by t. Specifically, we replace $\boldsymbol{s}[0], \ldots, \boldsymbol{s}[t-1]$ with a linear function of other components in $\boldsymbol{s}$, allowing us to eliminate $\boldsymbol{s}[0], \ldots, \boldsymbol{s}[t-1]$ from $\boldsymbol{s}$.

We eliminate the correlation by removing one sample within each block, where correlation indicates that the noise bit of the removed sample is fully determined by the remaining $m-1$ samples in the same block. After removing the t samples, we show that the remaining samples, permuted randomly, still constitute an LPN instance. For the remaining samples in each block $i \in [1, t]$, we denote by w_i the Hamming weight of the noise sub-vector. Then we have that w_i follows a Bernoulli distribution, i.e., $\Pr[w_i = 1] = 1 - 1/m$ and $\Pr[w_i = 0] = 1/m$. By a union bound, we have that the resulting noise vector follows the exact noise distribution $\mathsf{HW}_{t,N-t}(\mathbb{F}_2)$, with probability at least $(1 - 1/m)^t \geq 1 - t/m$, which is close to 1 as $m = \lfloor N/t \rfloor$ is sufficiently large for the LPN parameters used in the PCG setting. Thus, the resulting LPN instance is an exact-LPN instance $(\mathsf{HW}, \mathbb{F}_2)\text{-}\mathsf{LPN}(N-t, k-t, t)$. Therefore, we can use the bit security of an exact-LPN instance $(\mathsf{HW}, \mathbb{F}_2)\text{-}\mathsf{LPN}(N-t, k-t, t)$, based on all known attacks against exact-LPN, to estimate that of a regular-LPN instance $(\mathsf{RHW}, \mathbb{F}_2)\text{-}\mathsf{LPN}(N, k, t)$. We can convert a dual-LPN problem into an LPN problem using the approach in [62]. Thus, we are also able to perform the above transformation for dual-LPN problems over $\mathbb{F}_2$.

For LPN problems over a field $\mathbb{F}$ with $|\mathbb{F}| > 2$, the above transformation fails to work. For each noisy coordinate, a regular-LPN instance now samples a random element in $\mathbb{F}\backslash\{0\}$ rather than only 1. In this case, for each block $i \in [1, t]$, we have that $\sum_{j=1}^{m} \boldsymbol{b}_i[j] = (\sum_{j=1}^{m} \mathbf{A}_i[j]) \cdot \boldsymbol{s} + r$ where $r \in \mathbb{F}\backslash\{0\}$ is random and unknown. Now, we have to guess the random element r, which succeeds with probability at most $\frac{1}{|\mathbb{F}|-1}$. For all t blocks, we can succeed in guessing all random elements in t noisy coordinates with probability at most $\frac{1}{(|\mathbb{F}|-1)^t} \leq \frac{1}{2^t}$. Besides, we are able to perform the above transformation for a part of blocks. However, it does not allow us to decrease the cost of solving a regular-LPN problem by guessing the random elements located in noisy coordinates and performing the above transformation. In conclusion, we choose to use the known attacks of Pooled Gauss, SD and ISD against exact-LPN to estimate the cost of regular-LPN against these attacks for the case of larger fields.

The Recent Algebraic Attack Against Regular-LPN. Recently, Briaud and Øygarden [22] introduced a new algebraic attack that is tailored to LPN problems with regular noise distributions. Specifically, their attack solves a polynomial system involving the coordinates of a regular noise vector $\boldsymbol{e}$, leveraging the quadratic system that captures the regular structure. This algebraic attack, as described in [22], converts solving a dual-LPN problem over a field $\mathbb{F}$ into solving a polynomial system of degree 2 involving the coordinates of an error vector. In particular, the polynomial system consists of n parity-check equations (represented as $\mathbf{H} \cdot \boldsymbol{e} = \boldsymbol{y}$) along with another quadratic system that encodes the regular structure of a noise vector $\boldsymbol{e} = (\boldsymbol{e}_1, \ldots, \boldsymbol{e}_t)$ where $\boldsymbol{e}_i$ is defined as above. In more detail, for each sub-vector $\boldsymbol{e}_i \in \mathbb{F}^m$ with $m = \lfloor N/t \rfloor$, all quadratic equations of the form $\boldsymbol{e}_i[j_1] \cdot \boldsymbol{e}_i[j_2] = 0$ for $j_1 < j_2$ are involved. For the case of $\mathbb{F}_2$, a variation of the quadratic system is employed by introducing *additional* structural equations of the form $(\boldsymbol{e}_i[j])^2 = \boldsymbol{e}_i[j]$ and $\sum_{j=1}^{m} \boldsymbol{e}_i[j] = 1$, which guarantees that every $\boldsymbol{e}_i$ is a unit vector. Standard algorithms such as XL/Gröbner bases [12, 26, 72, 79] are then applied to solve the degree-2 polynomial system. Furthermore, a hybrid approach is proposed to reduce the computation complexity. This approach involves guessing some error-free positions of the noise error e, inspired from the regular version of Prange's algorithm [47]. It is not easy to give a succinct formula to compute the cost of their algebraic attack. Instead, we choose to provide an estimator tool (see Footnote 3), which allows us to automatically estimate the cost of the algebraic attack.

Compared to linear attacks such as Pooled Gauss, SD and ISD attacks, their algebraic attack achieves lower cost when solving regular-LPN problems with small code rate for some parameter sets (see Table 2 and the full version of the paper [58, Table 8]). The algebraic attack does not outperform ISD attacks for dual-LPN problems used in PCG-like protocols that have constant code rate (i.e., 1/2 or 3/4). Given the number of samples (corresponding to the number of PCG correlations), we are able to increase the dimension k and keep the noise weight t unchanged to resist the algebraic attack [22] against LPN problems, while keeping the efficiency essentially unchanged due to the usage of bootstrapping iterations [82].

Acknowledgements. Work of Yu Yu is supported by the National Key Research and Development Program of China (Grant No. 2020YFA0309705) and the National Natural Science Foundation of China (Grant Nos. 62125204 and 61872236). Yu Yu's work has also been supported by the New Cornerstone Science Foundation through the XPLORER PRIZE. Work of Kang Yang is supported by the National Natural Science Foundation of China (Grant Nos. 62102037 and 61932019). Work of Xiao Wang is supported in part by DARPA under Contract No. HR001120C0087, NSF awards #2016240 and #2236819. The views, opinions, and/or findings expressed are those of the author(s) and should not be interpreted as representing the official views or policies of the Department of Defense or the U.S. Government.

References

1. Abram, D., Scholl, P.: Low-communication multiparty triple generation for SPDZ from ring-LPN. In: Hanaoka, G., Shikata, J., Watanabe, Y. (eds.) PKC 2022, Part I. LNCS, vol. 13177, pp. 221–251. Springer, Heidelberg (2022). https://doi.org/10.1007/978-3-030-97121-2_9

2. Akavia, A.: Learning noisy characters, multiplication codes, and cryptographic hardcore predicates. Ph.D. thesis, Massachusetts Institute of Technology (2008). https://people.csail.mit.edu/akavia/AkaviaPhDThesis.pdf

3. Al Jabri, A.: A statistical decoding algorithm for general linear block codes. In: Honary, B. (ed.) 8th IMA International Conference on Cryptography and Coding. LNCS, vol. 2260, pp. 1–8. Springer, Heidelberg (2001). https://doi.org/10.1007/3-540-45325-3_1

4. Alekhnovich, M.: More on average case vs approximation complexity. In: 44th FOCS, pp. 298–307. IEEE Computer Society Press (2003). https://doi.org/10.1109/SFCS.2003.1238204

5. Applebaum, B.: Garbling XOR gates "for free" in the standard model. J. Cryptol. **29**(3), 552–576 (2016). https://doi.org/10.1007/s00145-015-9201-9

6. Applebaum, B., Ishai, Y., Kushilevitz, E.: Cryptography with constant input locality. In: Menezes, A. (ed.) CRYPTO 2007. LNCS, vol. 4622, pp. 92–110. Springer, Heidelberg (2007). https://doi.org/10.1007/978-3-540-74143-5_6

7. Augot, D., Finiasz, M., Sendrier, N.: A family of fast syndrome based cryptographic hash functions. In: Dawson, E., Vaudenay, S. (eds.) Mycrypt 2005. LNCS, vol. 3715, pp. 64–83. Springer, Heidelberg (2005). https://doi.org/10.1007/11554868_6

8. Baum, C., Braun, L., Munch-Hansen, A., Razet, B., Scholl, P.: Appenzeller to Brie: efficient zero-knowledge proofs for mixed-mode arithmetic and Z2k. In: Vigna, G., Shi, E. (eds.) ACM CCS 2021, pp. 192–211. ACM Press, November 2021. https://doi.org/10.1145/3460120.3484812

9. Baum, C., Braun, L., Munch-Hansen, A., Scholl, P.: Mozℤ_2^{k}arella: efficient vector-OLE and zero-knowledge proofs over ℤ_2^k. In: Dodis, Y., Shrimpton, T. (eds.) CRYPTO 2022, Part IV. LNCS, vol. 13510, pp. 329–358. Springer, Heidelberg (2022). https://doi.org/10.1007/978-3-031-15985-5_12

10. Baum, C., Malozemoff, A.J., Rosen, M.B., Scholl, P.: Mac'n'Cheese: zero-knowledge proofs for boolean and arithmetic circuits with nested disjunctions. In: Malkin, T., Peikert, C. (eds.) CRYPTO 2021, Part IV. LNCS, vol. 12828, pp. 92–122. Springer, Heidelberg, Virtual Event (2021). https://doi.org/10.1007/978-3-030-84259-8_4

11. Becker, A., Joux, A., May, A., Meurer, A.: Decoding random binary linear codes in $2^{n/20}$: how $1 + 1 = 0$ improves information set decoding. In: Pointcheval, D., Johansson, T. (eds.) EUROCRYPT 2012. LNCS, vol. 7237, pp. 520–536. Springer, Heidelberg (2012). https://doi.org/10.1007/978-3-642-29011-4_31

12. Beullens, W.: Improved cryptanalysis of UOV and Rainbow. In: Canteaut, A., Standaert, F.X. (eds.) EUROCRYPT 2021, Part I. LNCS, vol. 12696, pp. 348–373. Springer, Heidelberg (2021). https://doi.org/10.1007/978-3-030-77870-5_13

13. Blum, A., Furst, M.L., Kearns, M.J., Lipton, R.J.: Cryptographic primitives based on hard learning problems. In: Stinson, D.R. (ed.) CRYPTO 1993. LNCS, vol. 773, pp. 278–291. Springer, Heidelberg (1994). https://doi.org/10.1007/3-540-48329-2_24

14. Bombar, M., Couteau, G., Couvreur, A., Ducros, C.: Correlated pseudorandomness from the hardness of quasi-abelian decoding. In: Handschuh, H., Lysyanskaya, A. (eds.) CRYPTO 2023, Part IV, pp. 567–601. LNCS, Springer, Heidelberg (2023). https://doi.org/10.1007/978-3-031-38551-3_18

15. Boyle, E., Couteau, G., Gilboa, N., Ishai, Y.: Compressing vector OLE. In: Lie, D., Mannan, M., Backes, M., Wang, X. (eds.) ACM CCS 2018, pp. 896–912. ACM Press, October 2018. https://doi.org/10.1145/3243734.3243868

16. Boyle, E., et al.: Correlated pseudorandomness from expand-accumulate codes. In: Dodis, Y., Shrimpton, T. (eds.) CRYPTO 2022, Part II. LNCS, vol. 13508, pp. 603–633. Springer, Heidelberg (2022). https://doi.org/10.1007/978-3-031-15979-4_21

17. Boyle, E., et al.: Efficient two-round OT extension and silent non-interactive secure computation. In: Cavallaro, L., Kinder, J., Wang, X., Katz, J. (eds.) ACM CCS 2019, pp. 291–308. ACM Press, November 2019. https://doi.org/10.1145/3319535.3354255

18. Boyle, E., Couteau, G., Gilboa, N., Ishai, Y., Kohl, L., Scholl, P.: Efficient pseudorandom correlation generators: silent OT extension and more. In: Boldyreva, A., Micciancio, D. (eds.) CRYPTO 2019, Part III. LNCS, vol. 11694, pp. 489–518. Springer, Heidelberg (2019). https://doi.org/10.1007/978-3-030-26954-8_16

19. Boyle, E., Couteau, G., Gilboa, N., Ishai, Y., Kohl, L., Scholl, P.: Efficient pseudo-random correlation generators from ring-LPN. In: Micciancio, D., Ristenpart, T. (eds.) CRYPTO 2020, Part II. LNCS, vol. 12171, pp. 387–416. Springer, Heidelberg (2020). https://doi.org/10.1007/978-3-030-56880-1_14

20. Boyle, E., Gilboa, N., Ishai, Y.: Function secret sharing. In: Oswald, E., Fischlin, M. (eds.) EUROCRYPT 2015, Part II. LNCS, vol. 9057, pp. 337–367. Springer, Heidelberg (2015). https://doi.org/10.1007/978-3-662-46803-6_12

21. Brakerski, Z., Lyubashevsky, V., Vaikuntanathan, V., Wichs, D.: Worst-case hardness for LPN and cryptographic hashing via code smoothing. In: Ishai, Y., Rijmen, V. (eds.) EUROCRYPT 2019, Part III. LNCS, vol. 11478, pp. 619–635. Springer, Heidelberg (2019). https://doi.org/10.1007/978-3-030-17659-4_21

22. Briaud, P., Øygarden, M.: A new algebraic approach to the regular syndrome decoding problem and implications for PCG constructions. In: Hazay, C., Stam, M. (eds.) EUROCRYPT 2023, Part V. LNCS, vol. 14008, pp. 391–422. Springer, Heidelberg (2023). https://doi.org/10.1007/978-3-031-30589-4_14

23. Bui, D., Couteau, G.: Improved private set intersection for sets with small entries. In: Boldyreva, A., Kolesnikov, V. (eds.) PKC 2023, Part II. LNCS, vol. 13941, pp. 190–220. Springer, Heidelberg (2023). https://doi.org/10.1007/978-3-031-31371-4_7

24. Carozza, E., Couteau, G., Joux, A.: Short signatures from regular syndrome decoding in the head. In: Hazay, C., Stam, M. (eds.) EUROCRYPT 2023, Part V. LNCS, vol. 14008, pp. 532–563. Springer, Heidelberg (2023). https://doi.org/10.1007/978-3-031-30589-4_19

25. Carrier, K., Debris-Alazard, T., Meyer-Hilfiger, C., Tillich, J.P.: Statistical decoding 2.0: reducing decoding to LPN. In: Agrawal, S., Lin, D. (eds.) ASIACRYPT 2022, Part IV. LNCS, vol. 13794, pp. 477–507. Springer, Heidelberg (2022). https://doi.org/10.1007/978-3-031-22972-5_17

26. Coppersmith, D.: Solving homogeneous linear equations over $GF(2)$ via block Wiedemann algorithm. Math. Comput. 62(205), 333–350 (1994)

27. Couteau, G., Rindal, P., Raghuraman, S.: Silver: silent VOLE and oblivious transfer from hardness of decoding structured LDPC codes. In: Malkin, T., Peikert, C. (eds.) CRYPTO 2021, Part III. LNCS, vol. 12827, pp. 502–534. Springer, Heidelberg, Virtual Event (2021). https://doi.org/10.1007/978-3-030-84252-9_17

28. Cramer, R., Damgård, I., Escudero, D., Scholl, P., Xing, C.: SPD $\mathbb{Z}_{2^k}$: efficient MPC mod 2^k for dishonest majority. In: Shacham, H., Boldyreva, A. (eds.) CRYPTO 2018, Part II. LNCS, vol. 10992, pp. 769–798. Springer, Heidelberg (2018). https://doi.org/10.1007/978-3-319-96881-0_26

29. Cui, H., Wang, X., Yang, K., Yu, Y.: Actively secure half-gates with minimum overhead under duplex networks. In: Hazay, C., Stam, M. (eds.) EUROCRYPT 2023, Part II. LNCS, vol. 14005, pp. 35–67. Springer, Heidelberg (2023). https://doi.org/10.1007/978-3-031-30617-4_2

30. Damgård, I., Escudero, D., Frederiksen, T.K., Keller, M., Scholl, P., Volgushev, N.: New primitives for actively-secure MPC over rings with applications to private machine learning. In: 2019 IEEE Symposium on Security and Privacy, pp. 1102–1120. IEEE Computer Society Press, May 2019. https://doi.org/10.1109/SP.2019.00078

31. Damgård, I., Pastro, V., Smart, N.P., Zakarias, S.: Multiparty computation from somewhat homomorphic encryption. In: Safavi-Naini, R., Canetti, R. (eds.) CRYPTO 2012. LNCS, vol. 7417, pp. 643–662. Springer, Heidelberg (2012). https://doi.org/10.1007/978-3-642-32009-5_38

32. David, B., Dowsley, R., Nascimento, A.C.A.: Universally composable oblivious transfer based on a variant of LPN. In: Gritzalis, D., Kiayias, A., Askoxylakis, I.G. (eds.) CANS 2014. LNCS, vol. 8813, pp. 143–158. Springer, Heidelberg (2014). https://doi.org/10.1007/978-3-319-12280-9_10

33. Debris-Alazard, T., Tillich, J.: Statistical decoding. In: ISIT 2017 (2017). https://doi.org/10.1109/ISIT.2017.8006839

34. Dittmer, S., Ishai, Y., Lu, S., Ostrovsky, R.: Authenticated garbling from simple correlations. In: Dodis, Y., Shrimpton, T. (eds.) CRYPTO 2022, Part IV. LNCS, vol. 13510, pp. 57–87. Springer, Heidelberg (2022). https://doi.org/10.1007/978-3-031-15985-5_3

35. Dittmer, S., Ishai, Y., Lu, S., Ostrovsky, R.: Improving line-point zero knowledge: two multiplications for the price of one. In: Yin, H., Stavrou, A., Cremers, C., Shi, E. (eds.) ACM CCS 2022, pp. 829–841. ACM Press, November 2022. https://doi.org/10.1145/3548606.3559385

36. Dittmer, S., Ishai, Y., Ostrovsky, R.: Line-point zero knowledge and its applications. In: 2nd Conference on Information-Theoretic Cryptography (2021). https://doi.org/10.4230/LIPICS.ITC.2021.5

37. Dodis, Y., Kalai, Y.T., Lovett, S.: On cryptography with auxiliary input. In: Mitzenmacher, M. (ed.) 41st ACM STOC, pp. 621–630. ACM Press, May/June 2009. https://doi.org/10.1145/1536414.1536498

38. Dumer, I.: On minimum distance decoding of linear codes. In: Proceedings of 5th Joint Soviet-Swedish International Workshop Information Theory (1991)

39. Esser, A., Bellini, E.: Syndrome decoding estimator. In: Hanaoka, G., Shikata, J., Watanabe, Y. (eds.) PKC 2022, Part I. LNCS, vol. 13177, pp. 112–141. Springer, Heidelberg (2022). https://doi.org/10.1007/978-3-030-97121-2_5

40. Esser, A., Kübler, R., May, A.: LPN decoded. In: Katz, J., Shacham, H. (eds.) CRYPTO 2017, Part II. LNCS, vol. 10402, pp. 486–514. Springer, Heidelberg (2017). https://doi.org/10.1007/978-3-319-63715-0_17

41. Esser, A., May, A., Zweydinger, F.: McEliece needs a break - solving McEliece-1284 and quasi-cyclic-2918 with modern ISD. In: Dunkelman, O., Dziembowski, S. (eds.) EUROCRYPT 2022, Part III. LNCS, vol. 13277, pp. 433–457. Springer, Heidelberg, May/June 2022. https://doi.org/10.1007/978-3-031-07082-2_16

42. Feneuil, T., Joux, A., Rivain, M.: Syndrome decoding in the head: shorter signatures from zero-knowledge proofs. In: Dodis, Y., Shrimpton, T. (eds.) CRYPTO 2022, Part II. LNCS, vol. 13508, pp. 541–572. Springer, Heidelberg (2022). https://doi.org/10.1007/978-3-031-15979-4_19

43. Finiasz, M., Sendrier, N.: Security bounds for the design of code-based cryptosystems. In: Matsui, M. (ed.) ASIACRYPT 2009. LNCS, vol. 5912, pp. 88–105. Springer, Heidelberg (2009). https://doi.org/10.1007/978-3-642-10366-7_6

44. Fischer, J.B., Stern, J.: An efficient pseudo-random generator provably as secure as syndrome decoding. In: Maurer, U.M. (ed.) EUROCRYPT 1996. LNCS, vol. 1070, pp. 245–255. Springer, Heidelberg (1996). https://doi.org/10.1007/3-540-68339-9_22

45. Franzese, N., Katz, J., Lu, S., Ostrovsky, R., Wang, X., Weng, C.: Constant-overhead zero-knowledge for RAM programs. In: Vigna, G., Shi, E. (eds.) ACM CCS 2021, pp. 178–191. ACM Press, November 2021. https://doi.org/10.1145/3460120.3484800

46. Hamdaoui, Y., Sendrier, N.: A non asymptotic analysis of information set decoding. Cryptology ePrint Archive, Report 2013/162 (2013). https://eprint.iacr.org/2013/162

47. Hazay, C., Orsini, E., Scholl, P., Soria-Vazquez, E.: TinyKeys: a new approach to efficient multi-party computation. In: Shacham, H., Boldyreva, A. (eds.) CRYPTO 2018, Part III. LNCS, vol. 10993, pp. 3–33. Springer, Heidelberg (2018). https://doi.org/10.1007/978-3-319-96878-0_1

48. Hazay, C., Scholl, P., Soria-Vazquez, E.: Low cost constant round MPC combining BMR and oblivious transfer. J. Cryptol. **33**(4), 1732–1786 (2020). https://doi.org/10.1007/s00145-020-09355-y

49. Hopper, N.J., Blum, M.: Secure human identification protocols. In: Boyd, C. (ed.) ASIACRYPT 2001. LNCS, vol. 2248, pp. 52–66. Springer, Heidelberg (2001). https://doi.org/10.1007/3-540-45682-1_4

50. Hou, X., et al.: CipherGPT: secure two-party GPT inference. Cryptology ePrint Archive, Paper 2023/1147 (2023). https://eprint.iacr.org/2023/1147

51. Huang, Z., Lu, W.J., Hong, C., Ding, J.: Cheetah: lean and fast secure two-party deep neural network inference. In: Butler, K.R.B., Thomas, K. (eds.) USENIX Security 2022, pp. 809–826. USENIX Association, August 2022

52. Jain, A., Lin, H., Sahai, A.: Indistinguishability obfuscation from well-founded assumptions. In: Khuller, S., Williams, V.V. (eds.) 53rd ACM STOC, pp. 60–73. ACM Press, June 2021. https://doi.org/10.1145/3406325.3451093

53. Jain, A., Krenn, S., Pietrzak, K., Tentes, A.: Commitments and efficient zero-knowledge proofs from learning parity with noise. In: Wang, X., Sako, K. (eds.) ASIACRYPT 2012. LNCS, vol. 7658, pp. 663–680. Springer, Heidelberg (2012). https://doi.org/10.1007/978-3-642-34961-4_40

54. Katz, J., Shin, J.S., Smith, A.: Parallel and concurrent security of the HB and HB+ protocols. J. Cryptol. **23**(3), 402–421 (2010). https://doi.org/10.1007/s00145-010-9061-2

55. Keller, M., Orsini, E., Scholl, P.: Actively secure OT extension with optimal overhead. In: Gennaro, R., Robshaw, M.J.B. (eds.) CRYPTO 2015, Part I. LNCS, vol. 9215, pp. 724–741. Springer, Heidelberg (2015). https://doi.org/10.1007/978-3-662-47989-6_35

56. Keller, M., Orsini, E., Scholl, P.: MASCOT: faster malicious arithmetic secure computation with oblivious transfer. In: Weippl, E.R., Katzenbeisser, S., Kruegel, C., Myers, A.C., Halevi, S. (eds.) ACM CCS 2016, pp. 830–842. ACM Press, October 2016. https://doi.org/10.1145/2976749.2978357

57. Lin, F., Xing, C., Yao, Y.: More efficient zero-knowledge protocols over $\mathbb{Z}_{2^k}$ via galois rings. Cryptology ePrint Archive, Report 2023/150 (2023). https://eprint.iacr.org/2023/150

58. Liu, H., Wang, X., Yang, K., Yu, Y.: The hardness of LPN over any integer ring and field for PCG applications. Cryptology ePrint Archive, Report 2022/712 (2022). https://eprint.iacr.org/2022/712

59. May, A., Meurer, A., Thomae, E.: Decoding random linear codes in $\tilde{\mathcal{O}}(2^{0.054n})$. In: Lee, D.H., Wang, X. (eds.) ASIACRYPT 2011. LNCS, vol. 7073, pp. 107–124. Springer, Heidelberg (2011). https://doi.org/10.1007/978-3-642-25385-0_6

60. Melchor, C.A., Blazy, O., Deneuville, J., Gaborit, P., Zémor, G.: Efficient encryption from random quasi-cyclic codes. IEEE Trans. Inf. Theory **64**(5), 3927–3943 (2018). https://doi.org/10.1109/TIT.2018.2804444

61. Meyer-Hilfiger, C., Tillich, J.: Rigorous foundations for dual attacks in coding theory. In: Rothblum, G.N., Wee, H. (eds.) TCC 2023. LNCS, vol. 14372, pp. 3–32. Springer, Heidelberg (2023). https://doi.org/10.1007/978-3-031-48624-1_1

62. Micciancio, D., Mol, P.: Pseudorandom knapsacks and the sample complexity of LWE search-to-decision reductions. In: Rogaway, P. (ed.) CRYPTO 2011. LNCS, vol. 6841, pp. 465–484. Springer, Heidelberg (2011). https://doi.org/10.1007/978-3-642-22792-9_26

63. Misoczki, R., Tillich, J., Sendrier, N., Barreto, P.S.L.M.: MDPC-McEliece: new McEliece variants from moderate density parity-check codes. In: Proceedings of the 2013 IEEE International Symposium on Information Theory, 2013. pp. 2069–2073. IEEE (2013). https://doi.org/10.1109/ISIT.2013.6620590

64. Nielsen, J.B., Nordholt, P.S., Orlandi, C., Burra, S.S.: A new approach to practical active-secure two-party computation. In: Safavi-Naini, R., Canetti, R. (eds.) CRYPTO 2012. LNCS, vol. 7417, pp. 681–700. Springer, Heidelberg (2012). https://doi.org/10.1007/978-3-642-32009-5_40

65. Prange, E.: The use of information sets in decoding cyclic codes. IRE Trans. Inf. Theory 8, 5–9 (1962). https://doi.org/10.1109/TIT.1962.1057777

66. Raghuraman, S., Rindal, P.: Blazing fast PSI from improved OKVS and subfield VOLE. In: Yin, H., Stavrou, A., Cremers, C., Shi, E. (eds.) ACM CCS 2022, pp. 2505–2517. ACM Press, November 2022. https://doi.org/10.1145/3548606.3560658

67. Raghuraman, S., Rindal, P., Tanguy, T.: Expand-convolute codes for pseudorandom correlation generators from LPN. In: CRYPTO 2023, Part IV, pp. 602–632. LNCS, Springer, Heidelberg (2023). https://doi.org/10.1007/978-3-031-38551-3_19

68. Rindal, P., Schoppmann, P.: VOLE-PSI: fast OPRF and circuit-PSI from vector-OLE. In: Canteaut, A., Standaert, F.X. (eds.) EUROCRYPT 2021, Part II. LNCS, vol. 12697, pp. 901–930. Springer, Heidelberg (2021). https://doi.org/10.1007/978-3-030-77886-6_31

69. Schoppmann, P., Gascón, A., Reichert, L., Raykova, M.: Distributed vector-OLE: improved constructions and implementation. In: Cavallaro, L., Kinder, J., Wang, X., Katz, J. (eds.) ACM CCS 2019, pp. 1055–1072. ACM Press, November 2019. https://doi.org/10.1145/3319535.3363228

70. Sendrier, N.: Decoding one out of many. In: Yang, B.Y. (ed.) Post-Quantum Cryptography - 4th International Workshop, PQCrypto 2011, pp. 51–67. Springer, Heidelberg, November/December 2011. https://doi.org/10.1007/978-3-642-25405-5_4

71. Stern, J.: A method for finding codewords of small weight. In: Coding Theory and Applications, vol. 388 (1988). https://doi.org/10.1007/BFB0019850

72. Thomé, E.: Subquadratic computation of vector generating polynomials and improvement of the block Wiedemann algorithm. J. Symb. Comput. 33(5), 757–775 (2002). https://doi.org/10.1006/JSCO.2002.0533

73. Torres, R.C., Sendrier, N.: Analysis of information set decoding for a sub-linear error weight. In: Takagi, T. (ed.) Post-Quantum Cryptography - 7th International Workshop, PQCrypto 2016, pp. 144–161. Springer, Heidelberg (2016). https://doi.org/10.1007/978-3-319-29360-8_10

74. Wang, X., Ranellucci, S., Katz, J.: Authenticated garbling and efficient maliciously secure two-party computation. In: Thuraisingham, B.M., Evans, D., Malkin, T., Xu, D. (eds.) ACM CCS 2017, pp. 21–37. ACM Press, October/November 2017. https://doi.org/10.1145/3133956.3134053

75. Wang, X., Ranellucci, S., Katz, J.: Global-scale secure multiparty computation. In: Thuraisingham, B.M., Evans, D., Malkin, T., Xu, D. (eds.) ACM CCS 2017, pp. 39–56. ACM Press, October/November 2017. https://doi.org/10.1145/3133956.3133979

76. Weng, C., Yang, K., Katz, J., Wang, X.: Wolverine: fast, scalable, and communication-efficient zero-knowledge proofs for boolean and arithmetic circuits. In: 2021 IEEE Symposium on Security and Privacy, pp. 1074–1091. IEEE Computer Society Press, May 2021. https://doi.org/10.1109/SP40001.2021.00056

77. Weng, C., Yang, K., Xie, X., Katz, J., Wang, X.: Mystique: efficient conversions for zero-knowledge proofs with applications to machine learning. In: Bailey, M., Greenstadt, R. (eds.) USENIX Security 2021, pp. 501–518. USENIX Association, August 2021

78. Weng, C., Yang, K., Yang, Z., Xie, X., Wang, X.: AntMan: interactive zero-knowledge proofs with sublinear communication. In: Yin, H., Stavrou, A., Cremers, C., Shi, E. (eds.) ACM CCS 2022, pp. 2901–2914. ACM Press, November 2022. https://doi.org/10.1145/3548606.3560667

79. Wiedemann, D.H.: Solving sparse linear equations over finite fields. IEEE Trans. Inf. Theory **32**(1), 54–62 (1986)

80. Yang, K., Sarkar, P., Weng, C., Wang, X.: QuickSilver: efficient and affordable zero-knowledge proofs for circuits and polynomials over any field. In: Vigna, G., Shi, E. (eds.) ACM CCS 2021, pp. 2986–3001. ACM Press, November 2021. https://doi.org/10.1145/3460120.3484556

81. Yang, K., Wang, X., Zhang, J.: More efficient MPC from improved triple generation and authenticated garbling. In: Ligatti, J., Ou, X., Katz, J., Vigna, G. (eds.) ACM CCS 2020, pp. 1627–1646. ACM Press, November 2020. https://doi.org/10.1145/3372297.3417285

82. Yang, K., Weng, C., Lan, X., Zhang, J., Wang, X.: Ferret: fast extension for correlated OT with small communication. In: Ligatti, J., Ou, X., Katz, J., Vigna, G. (eds.) ACM CCS 2020, pp. 1607–1626. ACM Press, November 2020. https://doi.org/10.1145/3372297.3417276

83. Yu, Y., Steinberger, J.P.: Pseudorandom functions in almost constant depth from low-noise LPN. In: Fischlin, M., Coron, J.S. (eds.) EUROCRYPT 2016, Part II. LNCS, vol. 9666, pp. 154–183. Springer, Heidelberg (2016). https://doi.org/10.1007/978-3-662-49896-5_6

84. Yu, Y., Zhang, J., Weng, J., Guo, C., Li, X.: Collision resistant hashing from sub-exponential learning parity with noise. In: Galbraith, S.D., Moriai, S. (eds.) ASIACRYPT 2019, Part II. LNCS, vol. 11922, pp. 3–24. Springer, Heidelberg (2019). https://doi.org/10.1007/978-3-030-34621-8_1

85. Zichron, L.: Locally computable arithmetic pseudorandom generators. Master's thesis, School of Electrical Engineering, Tel Aviv University (2017)

Unlocking the Lookup Singularity with Lasso

Srinath Setty[1]([envelope]), Justin Thaler[2], and Riad Wahby[3]

[1] Microsoft Research, Redmond, USA
srinath@microsoft.com
[2] a16z crypto research and Georgetown University, Washington DC, USA
[3] Carnegie Mellon University, Pittsburgh, USA

Abstract. This paper introduces Lasso, a new family of lookup arguments, which allow an untrusted prover to commit to a vector $a \in \mathbb{F}^m$ and prove that all entries of a reside in some predetermined table $t \in \mathbb{F}^n$. Lasso's performance characteristics unlock the so-called "lookup singularity". Lasso works with any multilinear polynomial commitment scheme, and provides the following efficiency properties.

- For m lookups into a table of size n, Lasso's prover commits to just $m + n$ field elements. Moreover, the committed field elements are *small*, meaning that, no matter how big the field $\mathbb{F}$ is, they are all in the set $\{0, \ldots, m\}$. When using a multiexponentiation-based commitment scheme, this results in the prover's costs dominated by only $O(m+n)$ group *operations* (e.g., elliptic curve point additions), plus the cost to prove an evaluation of a multilinear polynomial whose evaluations over the Boolean hypercube are the table entries. This represents a significant improvement in prover costs over prior lookup arguments (e.g., plookup, Halo2's lookups, logUp).

- Unlike all prior lookup arguments, if the table t is structured (in a precise sense that we define), then no party needs to commit to t, enabling the use of much larger tables than prior works (e.g., of size 2^{128} or larger). Moreover, Lasso's prover only "pays" in runtime for table entries that are accessed by the lookup operations. This applies to tables commonly used to implement range checks, bitwise operations, big-number arithmetic, and even transitions of a full-fledged CPU such as RISC-V. Specifically, for any integer parameter $c > 1$, Lasso's prover's dominant cost is committing to $3 \cdot c \cdot m + c \cdot n^{1/c}$ field elements. Furthermore, all these field elements are "small", meaning they are in the set $\{0, \ldots, \max\{m, n^{1/c}, q\} - 1\}$, where q is the maximum value in any of the sub-tables that collectively capture t (in a precise manner that we define).

1 Introduction

Suppose that an untrusted prover $\mathcal{P}$ claims to know a witness w satisfying some property. For example, w might be a pre-image of a designated value y of a cryptographic hash function h, i.e., a w such that $h(w) = y$. A trivial proof is for $\mathcal{P}$ to send w to the verifier $\mathcal{V}$, who checks that w satisfies the claimed property.

M. Joye and G. Leander (Eds.): EUROCRYPT 2024, LNCS 14656, pp. 180–209, 2024.
https://doi.org/10.1007/978-3-031-58751-1_7

A zero-knowledge succinct non-interactive argument of knowledge (zkSNARK) achieves the same, but with better verification costs (and proof sizes) and privacy properties. Succinct means that verifying a proof is much faster than checking the witness directly (this also implies that proofs are much smaller than the size of the statement proven). Zero-knowledge means that the verifier does not learn anything about the witness beyond the validity of the statement proven.

Fast Algorithms via Lookup Tables. A common technique in the design of fast algorithms is to use *lookup tables*. These are pre-computed tables of values that, once computed, enable certain operations to be computed quickly. For example, in *tabulation-based universal hashing* [25,27], the hashing algorithm is specified via some small number c of tables $T_1, \ldots, T_c$, each of size $n^{1/c}$. Each cell of each table is filled with a random q-bit number in a preprocessing step. To hash a key x of length n, the key is split into c "chunks" $x_1, \ldots, x_c \in \{0,1\}^{n/c}$, and the hash value is defined to be the bitwise XOR of c *table lookups* i.e., $\oplus_{i=1}^{c} T_i[x_i]$.

Lookup tables are also useful in the context of SNARKs. Recall that to apply SNARKs to prove the correct execution of computer programs, one must express the execution of the program in a specific form that is amenable to probabilistic checking (e.g., as arithmetic circuits or generalizations thereof). Lookup tables can facilitate the use of substantially smaller circuits.

For example, imagine that a prover wishes to establish that at no point in a program's execution did any integer ever exceed 2^{128}, say, because were that to happen then an uncorrected "overflow error" would occur. A naive approach to accomplish this inside a circuit-satisfiability instance is to have the circuit take as part of its "non-deterministic advice inputs" 128 field elements for each number x arising during the execution. If the prover is honest, these 128 advice elements will be set to the binary representation of x. The circuit must check that all of the 128 advice elements are in $\{0,1\}$ and that they indeed equal the binary representation of x, i.e., $x = \sum_{i=0}^{127} 2^i \cdot b_i$, where $b_0, \ldots, b_{127}$ denotes the advice elements. This is very expensive: a simple overflow check turns into at least 129 constraints and an additional 128 field elements in the prover's witness that must be cryptographically committed by the prover.[1]

Lookup tables offer a better approach. Imagine for a moment that the prover and the verifier initialize a lookup table containing all integers between 0 and $2^{128} - 1$. Then the overflow check above amounts to simply confirming that x is in the table, i.e., the overflow check *is* a single table lookup. Of course, a table of size 2^{128} is far too large to be explicitly represented—even by the prover. This paper describes techniques to enable such a table lookup without requiring

---

[1] As we explain later (Remark 1.2), for certain commitment schemes, the prover's cost to commit to vectors consisting of many $\{0,1\}$ values can be much cheaper than if the to vectors contain arbitrary field elements. However, other SNARK prover costs (e.g., number of field operations) will grow linearly with the number of advice elements and constraints in the circuit to which the SNARK is applied, irrespective of whether the advice elements are $\{0,1\}$-valued.

a table such as this to be explicitly materialized, by either the prover or the verifier.

Table lookups are now used pervasively in deployed applications that employ SNARKs. They are very useful for representing "non-arithmetic" operations efficiently inside circuits [6,17,18]. The above example is often called a *range check* for the range $\{0, 1, \ldots, 2^{128} - 1\}$. Other example operations for which lookups are useful include bitwise operations such as XOR and AND [6], and any operations that require big-number arithmetic.

Lookup Arguments. To formalize the above discussion regarding the utility of lookup tables in SNARKs, a (non-interactive) *lookup argument* is a SNARK for the following claim made by the prover.

Definition 1 (Statement proven in a lookup argument). *Given a commitment cm_a and a public set T of N field elements, represented as vector $t = (t_0, \ldots, t_{N-1}) \in \mathbb{F}^N$ to which the verifier has (possibly) been provided a commitment cm_t, the prover knows an opening $a = (a_0, \ldots, a_{m-1}) \in \mathbb{F}^m$ of cm_a such that all elements of a are in T. That is, for each $i = 0, \ldots, m - 1$, there is a $j \in \{0, \ldots, N - 1\}$ such that $a_i = t_j$.*

The set T in Definition 1 is the contents of a lookup table and the vector a is the sequence of "lookups" into the table. The prover in the lookup argument proves to the verifier that every element of a is in T.

A flurry of works (Caulk [37], Caulk+ [26], flookup [16], Baloo [38], and cq [14]) have sought to give lookup arguments in which the prover's runtime is sublinear in the table size N. This is important in applications where the lookup table itself is much larger than the number of lookups into that table. As a simple example, if the verifier wishes to confirm that $a_0, \ldots, a_{m-1}$ are all in a large range (say, in $\{0, 1, \ldots, 2^{32} - 1\}$), then performing a number of cryptographic operations linear in N will be slow or possibly untenable. For performance reasons, these papers also express a desire for the commitment scheme used to commit to a and t to be additively homomorphic. However, these prior works all require generating a structured reference string of size N as well as an additional pre-processing work of $O(N \log N)$ group exponentiations. This limits the size of the tables to which they can be applied. For example, the largest structured reference strings generated today are many gigabytes in size and still only support $N < 2^{30}$.[2]

Indexed Lookup Arguments. Definition 1 is a standard formulation of lookup arguments in SNARKs (e.g., see [38]). It treats the table as an unordered list of values—T is a *set* and, accordingly, reordering the vector t does not alter the validity of the prover's claim. However, for reasons that will become apparent shortly (§1.3), we consider a variant notion to be equally natural. We refer to this variant as an *indexed lookup argument* (and refer to the standard variant in Definition 1 as an unindexed lookup argument.) In an indexed lookup argument, in addition to a commitment to $a \in \mathbb{F}^m$, the verifier is handed a commitment to

---

[2] See, for example, https://setup.aleo.org/stats.

a second vector $b \in \mathbb{F}^m$. The prover claims that for all $i = 1, \ldots, m$, $a_i = t_{b_i}$. We refer to a as the vector of *looked-up values*, and b as the vector of *indices*.

Definition 2 (Statement proven in an indexed lookup argument). *Given commitment cm_a and cm_b, and a public array T of N field elements, represented as vector $t = (t_0, \ldots, t_{N-1}) \in \mathbb{F}^N$ to which the verifier has (possibly) been provided a commitment cm_t, the prover knows an opening $a = (a_0, \ldots, a_{m-1}) \in \mathbb{F}^m$ of cm_a and $b = (b_0, \ldots, b_{m-1}) \in \mathbb{F}^m$ of cm_b such that for each $i = 0, \ldots, m-1$, $a_i = T[b_j]$, where $T[b_j]$ is short hand for the b_j'th entry of t.*

Any indexed lookup argument can easily be turned into an unindexed lookup argument: the unindexed lookup argument prover simply commits to a vector b such that $a_i = T[b_j]$ for all i, and then applies the indexed lookup argument to prove that indeed this holds. There is also a generic transformation that turns any unindexed lookup argument into an indexed one, at least in fields of large enough characteristic (see [32]). However, the protocols we describe in this work directly yield indexed lookup arguments, without invoking this transformation. Accordingly, our primary focus in this work is on indexed lookup arguments.

1.1 Lasso: A New Lookup Argument

Lasso's starting point is a polynomial commitment scheme for sparse multilinear polynomials. In particular, Lasso builds on Spark, an optimal polynomial commitment scheme for sparse multilinear polynomials from Spartan [28].

Lasso can be instantiated with any multilinear polynomial commitment scheme. Furthermore, Lasso can be used with any SNARK, including those that prove R1CS or Plonkish satisfiability. This is particularly seamless for SNARKs that have the prover commit to the witness using a multilinear polynomial commitment scheme. This includes many known prover-efficient SNARKs [10,20,28,31,36]. If a SNARK does not natively use multilinear polynomial commitments (e.g., Marlin [11], Plonk [19]), then one would need an auxiliary argument that the commitment cm_a used in Lasso is a commitment to the multilinear extension of the vector of all lookups performed in the SNARK.

Below, we provide an overview of Lasso's technical components.

(1) A stronger analysis of Spark, an optimal commitment scheme for sparse polynomials. A sparse polynomial commitment allows an untrusted prover to cryptographically commit to a *sparse* multilinear polynomial g and later provide a requested evaluation $g(r)$ along with a proof that the provided value is indeed equal to the committed polynomial's evaluation at r. Crucially, we require that the the prover's runtime depends only on the sparsity of the polynomial.[3] Spartan [28] provides such a commitment scheme, which it calls Spark.

---

[3] For multilinear polynomials, m-sparse refers to polynomials $g : \mathbb{F}^\ell \to \mathbb{F}$ in ℓ variables such that $g(x) \neq 0$ for at most m values of $x \in \{0,1\}^\ell$. That is, g has at most m non-zero coefficients in the so-called multilinear Lagrange basis. There are $n := 2^\ell$ Lagrange basis polynomials, so if $m \ll 2^\ell$, then only a tiny fraction of the possible coefficients are non-zero. In contrast, if $m = \Theta(2^\ell)$, then g is a *dense* polynomial.

Spartan assumed that certain metadata associated with the sparse polynomial is committed honestly, which was sufficient for its purposes. But, as we see later, Lasso requires an *untrusted* prover to commit to sparse polynomials (and the associated metadata).

A naive extension Spark to handle a maliciously committed metadata incurs concrete and asymptotic overheads, which is undesirable. Nevertheless, we prove that Spark in fact satisfies a stronger security property without any modifications (i.e., it is secure even if the metadata is committed by a potentially malicious party). This provides the first "standard" sparse polynomial commitment scheme with optimal prover costs, a result of independent interest. Furthermore, we specialize Spark for Lasso's use to obtain concrete efficiency benefits.

(2) Surge: A generalization of Spark. We reinterpret Spark sparse polynomial commitment scheme as a technique for computing the inner product of an m-sparse committed vector of length N with a dense—but highly structured—lookup table of size N (the table is represented as a vector of size N). Specifically, in the sparse polynomial commitment scheme, the table consists of all $(\log N)$-variate Lagrange basis polynomials evaluated at a specific point $r \in \mathbb{F}^{\log N}$. Furthermore, this table is a *tensor product* of $c \geq 2$ smaller tables, each of size $N^{1/c}$ (here, c can be set to any desired integer in $\{1, \ldots, \log N\}$). We further observe that many other lookup tables can similarly be decomposed has product-like expressions of $O(c)$ tables of size $N^{1/c}$, and that Spark extends to support all such tables.

Exploiting this perspective, we describe Surge, a generalization of Spark that allows an untrusted prover to commit to any sparse vector and establish the sparse vector's inner product with any dense, structured vector. We refer to the structure required for this to work as *Spark-only structure* (SOS). We also refer to this property as *decomposability*. In more detail, an SOS table T is one that can be decomposed into $\alpha = O(c)$ "sub-tables" $\{T_1, \ldots, T_\alpha\}$ of size $N^{1/c}$ satisfying the following properties. First, any entry $T[j]$ of T can be expressed as a simple expression of a corresponding entry into each of $T_1, \ldots, T_\alpha$. Second, the so-called *multilinear extension polynomial* of each T_i can be evaluated quickly (for any such table, we call T_i *MLE-structured*, where MLE stands for multilinear extension). For example, as noted above, the table T arising in Spark itself is simply the tensor product of MLE-structured sub-tables $\{T_1, \ldots, T_\alpha\}$, where $\alpha = c$.

(3) Lasso: A lookup argument for SOS tables and small/unstructured tables. We observe that Surge directly provides a lookup argument for tables with SOS structure. We call the resulting lookup argument Lasso. Lasso has the important property that *all* field elements committed by the prover are "small", meaning they are in the set $\{0, 1, \ldots, \max\{m, N^{1/c}, q\} - 1\}$, where q is such that $\{T_1, \ldots, T_\alpha\}$ all have entries in the set $\{0, 1, \ldots, q - 1\}$. As elaborated upon shortly (Sect. 1.2), this property of Lasso has substantial implications for prover efficiency.

Lasso has new and attractive costs when applied to small and unstructured tables in addition to large SOS ones. Specifically, by setting $c = 1$, the Lasso prover commits to only about $m + N$ field elements, and all of the committed elements are $\{0, 1, \ldots, \max\{m, N, q\}\}$ where q is the size of the largest value in the table.[4,5] Lasso is the first lookup argument with this property, which substantially speeds up commitment computation when m, N, and q are all much smaller than the size of the field over which the commitment scheme is defined. For $c > 1$, the number of field elements that the Lasso prover commits to is $3cm + \alpha \cdot N^{1/c}$.

(4) GeneralizedLasso: Beyond SOS and small/unstructured tables. Finally, we describe a lookup argument that we call GeneralizedLasso, which applies to any MLE-structured table, not only decomposable ones.[6] The main disadvantage of GeneralizedLasso relative to Lasso is that cm out of the $3cm + cN^{1/c}$ field elements committed by the GeneralizedLasso prover are random rather than small. The proofs are also somewhat larger, as GeneralizedLasso involves one extra invocation of the sum-check protocol compared to Lasso.

GeneralizedLasso is reminiscent of a sum-check based SNARK (e.g., Spartan [28]) and is similarly built from a combination of the sum-check protocol and the Spark sparse polynomial commitment scheme. There are two key differences: (1) In GeneralizedLasso, the (potentially adversarial) prover commits to a sparse polynomial, rather than an honest "setup algorithm" committing to a sparse polynomial in a preprocessing step in the context of Spartan (where the sparse polynomial encodes the circuit or constraint system of interest); and (2) invoking the standard linear-time sum-check protocol [13,24,33] makes the prover incur costs linear in the *table size* rather than the number of lookups. To address (1), we invoke our stronger security analysis of Spark. To address (2), we introduce a new variant of the sum-check protocol tailored for our setting, which we refer to as the *sparse-dense* sum-check protocol. Conceptually, GeneralizedLasso can be viewed as using the sparse-dense sum-check protocol to reduce lookups into any MLE-structured table into lookups into a decomposable table (namely, a certain lookup table arising within the Spark polynomial commitment scheme).

Additional discussion of the benefits and costs of GeneralizedLasso relative to Lasso can be found in the full version of this paper [32].

1.2   Additional Discussion of Lasso's Costs

Polynomial Commitments and MSMs. As indicated above, a central component of most SNARKs is a cryptographic protocol called a *polynomial commitment*

---

[4] Lasso makes blackbox use of any so-called grand product argument. If using the grand product argument from [30, Section 6], a low-order number, say at most $O(m/\log^3 m)$, of large field elements need to be committed (see the full version of this paper [32] for discussion).

[5] If Lasso is used as an indexed lookup argument, the prover commits to $m + N$ field elements. If used as an unindexed lookup argument, the number can increase to $2m + N$ because in the unindexed setting one must "charge" for the prover to commit to the index vector $b \in \mathbb{F}^m$.

[6] In fact, GeneralizedLasso applies to any table with *some* low-degree extension, not necessarily its multilinear one, that is evaluable in logarithmic time.

scheme. Such a scheme allows an untrusted prover to succinctly commit to a polynomial p and later reveal an evaluation $p(r)$ for a point r chosen by the verifier (the prover will also return a *proof* that the claimed evaluation is indeed equal to the committed polynomial's evaluation at r). In Lasso, the bottleneck for the prover is the polynomial commitment scheme.

Many popular polynomial commitments are based on multiexponentiations (also known as multi-scalar multiplications, or MSMs). This means that the commitment to a polynomial p (with n coefficients $c_0, \ldots, c_{n-1}$ over an appropriate basis) is $\prod_{i=0}^{n-1} g_i^{c_i}$, for some public generators $g_1, \ldots, g_n$ of a multiplicative group $\mathbb{G}$. Examples include KZG [21], IPA [5,8], Hyrax [35], and Dory [23].[7]

The naive MSM algorithm performs n group exponentiations and n group multiplications (note that each group exponentiation is about 400× slower than a group multiplication). But Pippenger's MSM algorithm saves a factor of about $\log(n)$ relative to the naive algorithm. This factor can be well over 10× in practice.

Working Over Large Fields, But Committing to Small Elements. If all exponents appearing in the multiexponentiation are "small", one can save another factor of 10 relative to applying Pippenger's algorithm to an MSM involving random exponents. This is analogous to how computing $g_i^{2^{16}}$ is 10× faster than computing $g_i^{2^{160}}$: the first requires 16 squaring operations, while the second requires 160 such operations. In other words, if one is promised that all field elements (i.e., exponents) to be committed via an MSM are in $\{0, 1, \ldots, K\} \subset \mathbb{F}$, the number of group operations required to compute the MSM depends only on K and not on the size of $\mathbb{F}$.[8]

Quantitatively, if all exponents are upper bounded by some value K, with $K \ll n$, then Pippenger's algorithm only needs (about) one group *operation* per term in the multiexponentiation.[9] More generally, with any MSM-based commitment scheme, Pippenger's algorithm allows the prover to commit to roughly $k \cdot \log(n)$-bit field elements (meaning field elements in $\{0, 1, \ldots, n\}$) with only k group operations per committed field element.

Polynomial Evaluation Proofs. In any SNARK or lookup argument, the prover not only has to commit to one or more polynomials, but also reveal to the verifier an evaluation of the committed polynomials at a point of the verifier's choosing. This requires the prover to compute a so-called evaluation proof, which establishes that the returned evaluation is indeed consistent with the committed polynomial. For some polynomial commitment schemes, such as Bulletproofs/IPA [5,8], producing evaluation proofs is quite slow and this cost can

---

[7] In Hyrax and Dory, the prover does $\sqrt{n}$ MSMs each of size $\sqrt{n}$.

[8] Of course, the cost of each group operation depends on the size of the group's base field, which is closely related to that of the scalar field $\mathbb{F}$. However, the *number* of group operations to compute the MSM depends only on K, not on $\mathbb{F}$.

[9] To be very precise, if $K \leq n$, then Pippenger's algorithm performs only $(1 + o(1))n$ group operations.

bottleneck the prover. However, for others, evaluation proof computation is a low-order cost [2,35].

Moreover, evaluation proofs exhibit excellent batching properties (whereby the prover can commit to many polynomials and only produce a single evaluation proof across all of them) [4,7,22]. So in many contexts, computing opening proofs is not a bottleneck even when using a scheme such as Bulletproofs/IPA.

For all of the above reasons, our accounting of prover cost in this work generally ignores the cost of polynomial evaluation proofs.

Summarizing Lasso's Prover Costs. Based on the above accounting, Lasso's prover costs when applied to a lookup table T can be summarized as follows.

- Setting the parameter $c = 1$, the Lasso prover commits to just $m + N$ field elements (using any multilinear polynomial commitment scheme), all of which are in $\{0, \ldots, m\}$.[10] Using an MSM-based commitment scheme, this translates to very close to $m + N$ group operations.
- For $c > 1$, the Lasso prover applied to any decomposable table commits to $3cm + \alpha N^{1/c}$ field elements, all of which are in the set $\{0, \ldots, \max\{m, N^{1/c}, q\} - 1\}$, where q is the largest value in any of the α sub-tables $T_1, \ldots, T_\alpha$. This cost accounting does not "charge" the prover for committing a of lookup results. We do so because the natural formulation of lookup arguments as a self-contained problem (Definition 2) considers the commitment to a to be part of the problem statement
- The GeneralizedLasso prover applies to any MLE-structured table, and commits to the same number of field elements as the Lasso prover, but cm of them are random field elements, instead of small ones.

In all cases above, no party needs to cryptographically commit to the table T or subtables $T_1, \ldots, T_\alpha$, so long as they are MLE-structured. The full version of this paper [32] compares these costs with those of existing lookup arguments.

1.3   A Companion Work: Jolt, and the Lookup Singularity

In the context of SNARKs, a *front-end* is a transformation or compiler that turns any computer program into an *intermediate representation*—typically a variant of circuit-satisfiability—so that a back-end (i.e., a SNARK for circuit-satisfiability) can be applied to establish that the prover correctly ran the computer program on a witness. A companion paper called Jolt [1] (for "Just One Lookup Table") shows that Lasso's ability to handle gigantic tables without either prover or verifier ever materializing the whole table (so long as the table is modestly "structured") enables substantial improvements in the front-end design. Jolt shows that for each of the RISC-V instructions, the resulting table has the structure that we require to apply Lasso. This leads to a front-end for VMs such as RISC-V that outputs much smaller circuits than prior front-ends, and has additional benefits such as easier auditability.

---

[10] In fact, for any $k \geq 1$, at most m/k of these field elements are larger than k.

2   Technical Overview

Suppose that the verifier has a commitment to a table $t \in \mathbb{F}^n$ as well as a commitment to another vector $a \in \mathbb{F}^m$. Suppose that a prover wishes to prove that all entries in a are in the table t. A simple observation in prior works [37,38] is that the prover can prove that it knows a sparse matrix $M \in \mathbb{F}^{m \times n}$ such that for each row of M, only one cell has a value of 1 and the rest are zeros and that $M \cdot t = a$, where $\cdot$ is the matrix-vector multiplication.[11] This turns out to be equivalent, up to negligible soundness error, to confirming that

$$\sum_{y \in \{0,1\}^{\log N}} \widetilde{M}(r,y) \cdot \tilde{t}(y) = \tilde{a}(r), \tag{1}$$

for an $r \in \mathbb{F}^{\log m}$ chosen at random by the verifier. Here, $\widetilde{M}$, $\tilde{a}$ and $\tilde{t}$ are the so-called *multilinear extension polynomials* (MLEs) of M, t, and a (see Thaler [34]).

Lasso proves Eq. (1) by having the prover commit to the sparse polynomial $\widetilde{M}$ using Spark and then prove the equation directly with a generalization of Spark called Surge. This provides the most efficient lookup argument when either the table t is "decomposable" (we discuss details of this below), or when t is unstructured but small. It turns out most tables that occur in practice (e.g., the ones that arise in Jolt are decomposable). When t is not decomposable, but still structured, a generalization of Lasso, which we refer to as GeneralizedLasso, proves Eq. (1) using a combination of a new form of the sum-check protocol (which we refer to as the sparse-dense sum-check protocol) and the Spark polynomial commitment scheme. We defer further details of GeneralizedLasso to the full version of this paper [32].

2.1   Starting Point: Spark Sparse Polynomial Commitment Scheme

Lasso's starting point is Spark, an optimal sparse polynomial commitment scheme from Spartan [28]. It allows an untrusted prover to prove evaluations of a sparse multilinear polynomial with costs proportional to the size of the dense representation of the sparse multilinear polynomial. Spartan established security of Spark under the assumption that certain metadata associated with a sparse polynomial is committed honestly, which sufficed for its application in the context of Spartan. In this paper, perhaps surprisingly, we prove that Spark remains secure even if that metadata is committed by an untrusted party (e.g., the prover), providing a standard commitment scheme for sparse polynomials.

The Spark sparse polynomial commitment scheme works as follows. The prover commits to a unique dense representation of the sparse polynomial g,

---

[11] Lasso's approach to prove $M \cdot t = a$ deviates significantly from the approaches in Baloo [38] and Caulk [37] despite Lasso starting with the same observation. In particular, Lasso's approach originates in Spartan [28], a work that predates Baloo and Caulk. Moreover, if one only demands a quasilinear prover time rather than linear, one can prove that $M \cdot t = a$ via "Spark-naive" [28, §7.1], even when M is committed by an untrusted prover.

using any polynomial commitment scheme for "dense" (multilinear) polynomials. The dense representation of g is effectively a list of all of the monomials of g with a non-zero coefficient (and the corresponding coefficient). More precisely, the list specifies all *multilinear Lagrange basis polynomials* with non-zero coefficient. Details as to what are the multilinear Lagrange basis polynomials are not relevant to this overview (but can be found elsewhere [32,34]).

When the verifier requests an evaluation $g(r)$ of the committed polynomial g, the prover returns the claimed evaluation v and needs to prove that v is indeed equal to the committed polynomial evaluated at r. Let c be such that $N = m^c$. As explained below, there is a simple and natural algorithm that takes as input the dense representation of g, and outputs $g(r)$ in $O(c \cdot m)$ time. Spark amounts to the bespoke SNARK establishing that the prover correctly ran this sparse-polynomial-evaluation algorithm on the committed description of g. Note that this perspective on Spark is somewhat novel, though it is partially implicit in the scheme itself and in an exposition of [34, Section 16.2].

A Time-Optimal Algorithm for Evaluating a Multilinear Polynomial of Sparsity m. We first describe a naive solution and then describe an optimal solution in Spark. Note that Spark provides a time-optimal algorithm when c is a constant.

A Naive Solution. Consider an algorithm that iterates over each Lagrange basis polynomials specified in the dense representation, evaluates that basis polynomial at r, multiplies by the corresponding coefficient, and adds the result to the evaluation. Unfortunately, a naive evaluation of a $(\log N)$-variate Lagrange basis polynomial at r takes $O(\log N)$ time, resulting in a total runtime of $O(m \cdot \log N)$.

Eliminating the Logarithmic Factor. The key to achieving time $O(c \cdot m)$ is to ensure that each Lagrange basis polynomial can be evaluated in $O(c)$ time. This is done as follows. This procedure is reminiscent of Pippenger's algorithm for multiexponentiation, with m being the size of the multiexponentiation, and Lagrange basis polynomials with non-zero coefficients corresponding to exponents.

Decompose the $\log N = c \cdot \log m$ variables of r into c blocks, each of size $\log m$, writing $r = (r_1, \ldots, r_c) \in \left(\mathbb{F}^{\log m}\right)^c$. Then any $(\log N)$-variate Lagrange basis polynomial evaluated at r can be expressed as a product of c "smaller" Lagrange basis polynomials, each defined over only $\log m$ variables, with the i'th such polynomial evaluated at r_i. There are only $2^{\log m} = m$ multilinear Lagrange basis polynomials over $\log m$ variables. Moreover, there are now-standard algorithms that, for any input $r_i \in \mathbb{F}^{\log m}$, run in time m and evaluate all m of the $(\log m)$-variate Lagrange basis polynomials at r_i. Hence, in $O(c \cdot m)$ total time, one can evaluate *all* m of these basis polynomials at each r_i, storing the results in a (write-once) memory M.

Given M, the time-optimal algorithm can evaluate *any* given $\log(N)$-variate Lagrange basis polynomial at r by performing c lookups into memory, one for each block r_i, and multiplying together the results.[12] Note that we chose to decompose the $\log N$ variables into c blocks of length $\log m$ (rather than more,

---

[12] This is also closely analogous to the behavior of tabulation hashing discussed earlier in §1, which is why we chose to highlight this example from algorithm design.

smaller blocks, or fewer, bigger blocks) to balance the runtime of the two phases of the algorithm, namely:

- The time required to "write to memory" the evaluations of all $(\log m)$-variate Lagrange basis polynomials at $r_1, \ldots, r_c$.
- The time required to evaluate $g(r)$ given the contents of memory.

In general, if we break the variables into c blocks of size $\ell = \log(N)/c = \log(m)$, the first phase requires time $c \cdot 2^\ell = cm$, and the second requires time $O(m \cdot c)$.

How the Spark Prover Proves it Correctly Ran the Above Time-Optimal Algorithm. To enable an untrusted prover to efficiently prove that it correctly ran the above algorithm to compute an evaluation of a sparse polynomial g at r, Spark uses *offline memory checking* [3] to prove read-write consistency. Furthermore, the contents of the memory is determined succinctly by r, so the verifier does not need any commitments to the contents of the memory. Spark effectively forces the prover to commit to the "execution trace" of the algorithm (which has size $O(c \cdot m)$, because the algorithm runs in time $O(c)$ for each of the m Lagrange basis polynomials with non-zero coefficient) plus $c \cdot N^{1/c} = O(c \cdot m)$. The latter term arises because at the end of m operations, the offline memory-checking technique requires the prover to supply certain access counts indicating the number of times a particular memory location was read during the course of the protocol. Moreover, note that this memory has size $c \cdot N^{1/c}$ if the algorithm breaks the $\log N$ variables into c blocks of size $\log(N)/c$. As we will see later, this is why Lasso's prover cryptographically commits to $3 \cdot c \cdot m + c \cdot N^{1/c}$ field elements.

Remark 1 The cost incurred by Spark's prover to "replay" to provide access counts at the very end of the algorithm's execution can be amortized over multiple sparse polynomial evaluations. In particular, if the prover proves an evaluation of k sparse polynomials in the same number of variables, the aforementioned cost in the offline memory checking is reused across all k sparse polynomials.

2.2   Surge: A Generalization of Spark

Re-imagining Spark. A sparse polynomial commitment scheme can be viewed as having the prover commit to an m-sparse vector u of length N, where m is the number of non-zero coefficients of the polynomial, and N is the number of elements in a suitable basis. For univariate polynomials in the standard monomial basis, N is the degree, m is the number of non-zero coefficients, and u is the vector of coefficients. For an ℓ-variate multilinear polynomial g over the Lagrange basis, $N = 2^\ell$, m is the number of evaluation points over the Boolean hypercube $x \in \{0,1\}^\ell$ such that $g(x) \neq 0$, and u is the vector of evaluations of g at all evaluation points over the hypercube $\{0,1\}^\ell$.

An evaluation query to g at input r returns the inner product of the sparse vector u with the dense vector t consisting of the evaluations of all basis polynomials at r. In the multilinear case, for each $S \in \{0,1\}^\ell$, the S'th entry of t

is $\chi_S(r)$. In this sense, *any* sparse polynomial commitment scheme achieves the following: it allows the prover to establish the value of the inner product $\langle u, t \rangle$ of a sparse (committed) vector u with a dense, structured vector t.

Spark → Surge. To obtain Surge from Spark, we critically examine the type of structure in t that is exploited by Spark, and introduce Surge as a natural generalization of Spark that supports any table t with this structure. More importantly, we observe that many lookup tables critically important in practice (e.g., those that arise in Jolt) exhibit this structure.

In more detail, the Surge prover establishes that it correctly ran a natural $O(c \cdot m)$-time algorithm for computing $\langle u, t \rangle$. This algorithm is a natural analog of the sparse polynomial evaluation algorithm described in Sect. 2.1: it iterates over every non-zero entry u_i of u, quickly computes $t_i = T[i]$ by performing one lookup into each of $O(c)$ "sub-tables" of size $N^{1/c}$, and quickly "combines" the result of each lookup to obtain t_i and hence $u_i \cdot t_i$. In this way, this algorithm takes just $O(c \cdot m)$ time to compute the desired inner product $\sum_{i:\ u_i \neq 0} u_i \cdot t_i$.

Details of the Structure Needed to Apply Surge. In the case of Spark itself, the dense vector t is simply the *tensor product* of smaller vectors, $t_1, \ldots, t_c$, each of size $N^{1/c}$. Specifically, Spark breaks r into c "chunks" $r = (r_1, \ldots, r_c) \in \left(\mathbb{F}^{(\log N)/c} \right)^c$, where r is the point at which the Spark verifier wants to evaluate the committed polynomial. Then t_i contains the evaluations of all $((\log N)/c)$-variate Lagrange basis polynomials evaluated at r_i. And for each $S = (S_1, \ldots, S_c) \in \left(\{0, 1\}^{(\log N)/c} \right)^c$, the S'th entry of t is: $\prod_{i=1}^{c} t_i(r_i)$.

In general, Spark applies to any table vector t that is "decomposable" in a manner similar to the above. Specifically, suppose that $k \geq 1$ is an integer and there are $\alpha = k \cdot c$ tables $T_1, \ldots, T_\alpha$ of size $N^{1/c}$ and an α-variate multilinear polynomial g such that the following holds. For any $r \in \{0, 1\}^{\log N}$, write $r = (r_1, \ldots, r_c) \in \left(\{0, 1\}^{\log(N)/c} \right)^c$, i.e., break r into c pieces of equal size. Suppose that $\forall r \in \{0, 1\}^{\log N}$,

$$T[r] = g\left(T_1[r_1], \ldots, T_k[r_1], T_{k+1}[r_2], \ldots, T_{2k}[r_2], \ldots, T_{\alpha-k+1}[r_c], \ldots, T_\alpha[r_c] \right). \tag{2}$$

Simplifying slightly, Surge allows the prover to commit to a m-sparse vector $u \in \mathbb{F}^N$ and prove that the inner product of u and the table T (or more precisely the associated vector t) equals some claimed value. And the cost for the prover is dominated by the following operations.

- Committing to $3 \cdot \alpha \cdot m + \alpha \cdot N^{1/c}$ field elements, where $2 \cdot \alpha \cdot m + \alpha \cdot N^{1/c}$ of the committed elements are in the set $\{0, 1, \ldots, \max\{m, N^{1/c}\} - 1\}$, and the remaining $\alpha \cdot m$ of them are elements of the sub-tables $T_1, \ldots, T_\alpha$. For many lookup tables T, these elements are themselves in the set $\{0, 1, \ldots, N^{1/c} - 1\}$.
- Let b be the number of monomials in g. Then the Surge prover performs $O(k \cdot \alpha N^{1/c}) = O(b \cdot c \cdot N^{1/c})$ field operations. In many cases, the factor of b in the number of prover field operations can be removed.

We refer to tables that can be decomposed into sub-tables of size $N^{1/c}$ as per Eq. (2) as having *Spark-only structure* (SOS), or being *decomposable*.

3   A Stronger Analysis of **Spark**

We prove a substantial strengthening of a result from Spartan [28, Lemma 7.6]. In particular, we prove that in Spartan's sparse polynomial commitment scheme, which is called **Spark**, one does not need to assume that certain metadata associated with a sparse polynomial is committed honestly (in the case of Spartan, the metadata is committed by the setup algorithm, so it was sufficient for its purposes). We thereby obtain the first "standard" polynomial commitment scheme with prover costs *linear* in the number of non-zero coefficients. We prove this result without any substantive changes to **Spark**.

For simplicity, we make a minor change that does not affect costs nor analysis: we have the prover commit to metadata associated with the sparse polynomial at the time of proving an evaluation rather than when the prover commits to the sparse polynomial (the metadata depends only on the sparse polynomial, and in particular, it is independent of the point at which the sparse polynomial is evaluation, so the metadata can be committed either in the commit phase or when proving an evaluation). Our text below is adapted from an exposition of Spartan's result by Golovnev et al. [20]. It is natural for the reader to conceptualize the **Spark** sparse polynomial commitment scheme as a bespoke SNARK for a prover to prove it correctly ran the sparse $(\log N)$-variate multilinear polynomial evaluation algorithm described in Sect. 2.1 using c memories of size $N^{1/c}$.

3.1   A (slightly) Simpler Result: $c = 2$

We first prove a special case of the final result, the proof of which exhibits all of the ideas and techniques. This special case (Theorem 1) describes a transformation from any commitment scheme for dense polynomials defined over $\log m$ variables to one for sparse multilinear polynomials defined over $\log N = 2 \log m$ variables. It is the bespoke SNARK mentioned above for $c = 2$ memories of size $N^{1/2}$.

The dominant costs for the prover in **Spark** is committing to 7 dense multilinear polynomials over $\log(m)$-many variables, and 2 dense multilinear polynomials over $\log(N^{1/c})$-many variables. In dense ℓ-variate multilinear polynomial commitment schemes, the prover time is roughly linear in 2^ℓ. Hence, so long as $m \geq N^{1/c}$, the prover time is dominated by the commitments to the 7 dense polynomials over $\log(m)$-many variables. This ensures that the prover time is linear in the sparsity of the committed polynomial as desired (rather than linear in $2^{2 \log m} = m^2$, which would be the runtime of applying a dense polynomial commitment scheme directly to the sparse polynomial over $2 \log m$ variables).

The Full Result. If we wish to commit to a sparse multilinear polynomial over ℓ variables, let $N := 2^\ell$ denote the dimensionality of the space of ℓ-variate multilinear polynomials. For any desired integer $c \geq 2$, our final, general, result replaces these two memories (each of size equal to $N^{1/2}$) with c memories of size equal to $N^{1/c}$. Ultimately, the prover commits to $(3c + 1)$ many dense $(\log m)$-variate multilinear polynomials, and c many dense $(\log(N^{1/c}))$-variate polynomials. We begin with $c = 2$ before stating and proving the full result.

Theorem 1 (Special case of Theorem 2 with $c = 2$). *Let* $\mathsf{M} = N^{1/2}$. *Given a polynomial commitment scheme for* $(\log \mathsf{M})$-*variate multilinear polynomials with the following parameters (where* $\mathsf{M} > 0$ *and WLOG a power of 2): (1) the size of the commitment is* $\mathsf{c}(\mathsf{M})$; *(2) the running time of the commit algorithm is* $\mathsf{tc}(\mathsf{M})$; *(3) the running time of the prover to prove a polynomial evaluation is* $\mathsf{tp}(\mathsf{M})$; *(4) the running time of the verifier to verify a polynomial evaluation is* $\mathsf{tv}(\mathsf{M})$; *and (5) the proof size is* $\mathsf{p}(\mathsf{M})$, *there exists a polynomial commitment scheme for multilinear polynomials over* $2 \log \mathsf{M} = \log N$ *variables that evaluate to a non-zero value at at most m locations over the Boolean hypercube* $\{0,1\}^{2 \log \mathsf{M}}$, *with the following parameters: (1) the size of the commitment is* $7\mathsf{c}(m) + 2\mathsf{c}(\mathsf{M})$; *(2) the running time of the commit algorithm is* $O(\mathsf{tc}(m) + \mathsf{tc}(\mathsf{M}))$; *(3) the running time of the prover to prove a polynomial evaluation is* $O(\mathsf{tp}(m) + \mathsf{tc}(\mathsf{M}))$; *(4) the running time of the verifier to verify a polynomial evaluation is* $O(\mathsf{tv}(m) + \mathsf{tv}(\mathsf{M}))$; *and (5) the proof size is* $O(\mathsf{p}(m) + \mathsf{p}(\mathsf{M}))$.

Representing Sparse Polynomials with Dense Polynomials. Let D denote a $(2 \log \mathsf{M})$-variate multilinear polynomial that evaluates to a non-zero value at at most m locations over $\{0,1\}^{2 \log \mathsf{M}}$. For any $r \in \mathbb{F}^{2 \log \mathsf{M}}$, we can express the evaluation of $D(r)$ as follows. Interpret $r \in \mathbb{F}^{2 \log \mathsf{M}}$ as a tuple (r_x, r_y) in a natural manner, where $r_x, r_y \in \mathbb{F}^{\log \mathsf{M}}$. Then by multilinear Lagrange interpolation, we can write

$$D(r_x, r_y) = \sum_{(i,j) \in \{0,1\}^{\log \mathsf{M}} \times \{0,1\}^{\log \mathsf{M}} : D(i,j) \neq 0} D(i,j) \cdot \widetilde{eq}(i, r_x) \cdot \widetilde{eq}(j, r_y). \quad (3)$$

Lemma 1. *Let* $\mathsf{to-field}$ *be the canonical injection from* $\{0,1\}^{\log \mathsf{M}}$ *to* $\mathbb{F}$ *and* $\mathsf{to-bits}$ *be its inverse. Given a* $2 \log \mathsf{M}$-*variate multilinear polynomial D that evaluates to a non-zero value at at most m locations over* $\{0,1\}^{2 \log \mathsf{M}}$, *there exist three* $(\log m)$-*variate multilinear polynomials* $\mathsf{row}, \mathsf{col}, \mathsf{val}$ *such that the following holds for all* $r_x, r_y \in \mathbb{F}^{\log \mathsf{M}}$.

$$D(r_x, r_y) = \sum_{k \in \{0,1\}^{\log m}} \mathsf{val}(k) \cdot \widetilde{eq}(\mathsf{to-bits}(\mathsf{row}(k)), r_x) \cdot \widetilde{eq}(\mathsf{to-bits}(\mathsf{col}(k)), r_y).$$

$$(4)$$

Moreover, the polynomials' coefficients in the Lagrange basis can be computed in $O(m)$ time.

Proof. Since D evaluates to a non-zero value at at most m locations over $\{0,1\}^{2 \log \mathsf{M}}$, D can be represented uniquely with m tuples of the form $(i, j, D(i,j)) \in (\{0,1\}^{\log \mathsf{M}}, \{0,1\}^{\log \mathsf{M}}, \mathbb{F})$. By using the natural injection $\mathsf{to-field}$ from $\{0,1\}^{\log \mathsf{M}}$ to $\mathbb{F}$, we can view the first two entries in each of these tuples as elements of $\mathbb{F}$ (let $\mathsf{to-bits}$ denote its inverse). Furthermore, these tuples can be represented with three m-sized vectors $R, C, V \in \mathbb{F}^m$, where tuple k (for all $k \in [m]$) is stored across the three vectors at the kth location in the vector, i.e., the first entry in the tuple is stored in R, the second entry in C, and the third entry in V. Take row as the unique MLE of R viewed as a function $\{0, 1\}^{\log m} \to \mathbb{F}$. Similarly, col is the unique MLE of C, and val is the unique MLE of V. The lemma holds by inspection since Eqs. (3) and (4) are both multilinear polynomials in r_x and r_y and agree with each other at every pair $r_x, r_y \in \{0, 1\}^{\log M}$.

Conceptually, the sum in Eq. (4) is *exactly* what the sparse polynomial evaluation algorithm described in Sect. 2.1 computes term-by-term. Specifically, that algorithm (using $c = 2$ memories) filled up one memory with the quantities $\widetilde{eq}(i, r_x)$ as i ranges over $\{0, 1\}^{\log M}$ (see Eq. (3)), and the other memory with the quantities $\widetilde{eq}(j, r_x)$, and then computed each term of Eq. (4) via one lookup into each memory, to the respective memory cells with (binary) indices to−bits(row(k)) and to−bits(col(k)), followed by two field multiplications.

Commit Phase. To commit to D, the committer can send commitments to the three $(\log m)$-variate multilinear polynomials row, col, val from Lemma 1. Using the provided polynomial commitment scheme, this costs $O(m)$ finite field operations, and the size of the commitment to D is $O_\lambda(c(m))$.

Intuitively, the commit phase commits to a "dense" representation of the sparse polynomial, which simply lists all the Lagrange basis polynomial with non-zero coefficients (each specified as an element in $\{0, \ldots, M - 1\}^2$), along with the associated coefficient. This is exactly the input to the sparse polynomial evaluation algorithm described in Sect. 2.1.

In the evaluation phase described below, the prover proves that it correctly ran the sparse polynomial evaluation algorithm (§2.1) on the committed polynomial in order to evaluate it at the requested evaluation point $(r_x, r_y) \in \mathbb{F}^{2 \log M}$.

A First Attempt at the Evaluation Phase. Given $r_x, r_y \in \mathbb{F}^{\log M}$, to prove an evaluation of a committed polynomial, i.e., to prove that $D(r_x, r_y) = v$ for a purported evaluation $v \in \mathbb{F}$, consider the polynomial IOP in Fig. 1, where the verifier has oracle access to the three $(\log m)$-variate multilinear polynomial oracles that encode D (namely row, col, val). Here, the oracles E_{rx} and E_{ry} should be thought of as the (purported) multilinear extensions of the values returned by each memory reads that the algorithm of Sect. 2.1 performed into each of its two memories, step-by-step over the course of its execution.

If the prover is honest, it is easy to see that it can convince the verifier about the correct of evaluations of D. Unfortunately, the two oracles that the prover sends in the first step of the depicted polynomial IOP can be completely arbitrary. To fix this, $\mathcal{V}$ must *additionally* check that the following two conditions hold. (1) $\forall k \in \{0, 1\}^{\log m}$, $E_{rx}(k) = \widetilde{eq}(\text{to−bits}(\text{row}(k)), r_x)$; and (2) $\forall k \in \{0, 1\}^{\log m}$, $E_{ry}(k) = \widetilde{eq}(\text{to−bits}(\text{col}(k)), r_y)$.

A core insight of Spartan [28] is to check these two conditions using memory-checking techniques [3]. These techniques amount to an efficient randomized

1. $\mathcal{P} \to \mathcal{V}$: two $(\log m)$-variate multilinear polynomials E_{rx} and E_{ry} as oracles. These polynomials are purported to respectively equal the multilinear extensions of the functions mapping $k \in \{0,1\}^{\log m}$ to $\widetilde{eq}(\text{to-bits}(\text{row}(k)), r_x)$ and $\widetilde{eq}(\text{to-bits}(\text{col}(k)), r_y)$.
2. $\mathcal{V} \leftrightarrow \mathcal{P}$: run the sum-check reduction to reduce the check that

$$v = \sum_{k \in \{0,1\}^{\log m}} \text{val}(k) \cdot E_{rx}(k) \cdot E_{ry}(k)$$

to checking if the following hold, where $r_z \in \mathbb{F}^{\log m}$ is chosen at random by the verifier over the course of the sum-check protocol:

- $\text{val}(r_z) \overset{?}{=} v_{\text{val}}$;
- $E_{rx}(r_z) \overset{?}{=} v_{E_{rx}}$ and $E_{ry}(r_z) \overset{?}{=} v_{E_{ry}}$. Here, v_{val}, $v_{E_{rx}}$, and $v_{E_{ry}}$ are values provided by the prover at the end of the sum-check protocol.
3. $\mathcal{V}$: check if the three equalities hold with an oracle query to each of $\text{val}, E_{rx}, E_{ry}$.

Fig. 1. A first attempt at a polynomial IOP for revealing a requested evaluation of a $(2\log(M))$-variate multilinear polynomial p over $\mathbb{F}$ such that $p(x) \neq 0$ for at most m values of $x \in \{0,1\}^{2\log(M)}$.

procedure to confirm that every memory read over the course of an algorithm's execution returns the value last written to that location. We take a detour to introduce new results that we rely on here.

Detour: Offline Memory Checking. Recall that in the offline memory checking algorithm of [3], a *trusted checker* issues operations to an untrusted memory. For our purposes, it suffices to consider only operation sequences in which each memory address is initialized to a certain value, and all subsequent operations are read operations. To enable efficient checking using multiset-fingerprinting techniques, the memory is modified so that in addition to storing a value at each address, the memory also stores a timestamp with each address. Moreover, each read operation is followed by a write operation that updates the timestamp associated with that address (but not the value stored there).

In prior descriptions of offline memory checking [3,12,29], the trusted checker maintains a single timestamp counter and uses it to compute write timestamps, whereas in Spark and our description below, the trusted checker does not use any local timestamp counter; rather, each memory cell maintains its own counter, which is incremented by the checker every time the cell is read.[13] For this reason,

---

[13] The same timestamp update procedure was used in Spartan's use of Spark [28, §7.2.3]. The purpose was to achieve a concrete efficiency benefit. In particular, Spartan used a separate timestamp counter for each cell and considered the case where all read timestamps were guaranteed to be computed honestly. In this case, the write timestamp is the result of incrementing an honestly returned read timestamp, which allows Spartan to not explicitly materialize write timestamps. Here, we are interested in the case where read timestamps themselves are not computed honestly.

we depart from the standard terminology in the memory-checking literature and henceforth refer to these quantities as *counters* rather than timestamps.

The memory-checking procedure is captured in the codebox below.

Local State of the Checker: Two sets: RS and WS, which are initialized as follows.[14] RS = {}, and for an M-sized memory, WS is initialized to the following set of tuples: for all $i \in [N^{1/c}]$, the tuple $(i, v_i, 0)$ is included in WS, where v_i is the value stored at address i, and the third entry in the tuple, 0, is an "initial count" associated with the value (intuitively capturing the notion that when v_i was written to address i, it was the first time that address was accessed). Here, [M] denotes the set $\{0, 1, \ldots, M - 1\}$.

Read Operations and An Invariant. For a read operation at address a, suppose that the untrusted memory responds with a value-count pair (v, t). Then the checker updates its local state as follows:

---

1. RS $\leftarrow$ RS $\cup \{(a, v, t)\}$;
2. store $(v, t + 1)$ at address a in the untrusted memory; and
3. WS $\leftarrow$ WS $\cup \{(a, v, t + 1)\}$.

The following lemma captures the invariant maintained on the sets of the checker:

Lemma 2. *Let* $\mathbb{F}$ *be a prime order field. Assuming that the domain of counts is* $\mathbb{F}$ *and that* m *(the number of reads issued) is smaller than the field characteristic* $|\mathbb{F}|$. *Let* WS *and* RS *denote the multisets maintained by the checker in the above algorithm at the conclusion of* m *read operations. If for every read operation, the untrusted memory returns the tuple last written to that location, then there exists a set* S *with cardinality* M *consisting of tuples of the form* (k, v_k, t_k) *for all* $k \in [M]$ *such that* WS = RS $\cup$ S. *Moreover,* S *is computable in time linear in* M.

Conversely, if the untrusted memory ever returns a value v *for a memory call* $k \in [M]$ *such* v *does not equal the value initially written to cell* k, *then there does not exist any set* S *such that* WS = RS $\cup$ S.

Proof. If for every read operation, the untrusted memory returns the tuple last written to that location, then it is easy to see the existence of the desired set S. It is simply the current state of the untrusted memory viewed as the set of address-value-count tuples.

We now prove the other direction in the lemma. For notational convenience, let WS$_i$ and RS$_i$ $(0 \leq i \leq m)$ denote the multisets maintained by the trusted

---

[14] The checker in [3] maintains a fingerprint of these sets, but for our exposition, we let the checker maintain full sets.

checker at the conclusion of the ith read operation (i.e., WS_0 and RS_0 denote the multisets before any read operation is issued). Suppose that there is some read operation i that reads from address k, and the untrusted memory responds with a tuple (v, t) such that v differs from the value initially written to address k. This ensures that $(k, v, t) \in \mathsf{RS}_j$ for all $j \geq i$, and in particular that $(k, v, t) \in \mathsf{RS}$, where recall that RS is the read set at the conclusion of the m read operations. Hence, to ensure that there exists a set S such that $\mathsf{RS} \cup S = \mathsf{WS}$ at the conclusion of the procedure (i.e., to ensure that $\mathsf{RS} \subseteq \mathsf{WS}$), there must be some other read operation during which address k is read, and the untrusted memory returns tuple $(k, v, t - 1)$.[15] This is because we have assumed that the value v was not written in the initialization phase, and outside of the initialization phase, the only way that the checker writes (k, v, t) to memory is if a read to address k returns tuple $(v, t - 1)$.

Accordingly, the same reasoning as above applies to tuple $(k, v, t - 1)$. That is, to ensure that $\mathsf{RS} = \mathsf{WS}$ at the conclusion of the procedure, there must be some other read operation at which address k is read, and the untrusted memory returns tuple $(k, v, t - 2)$. And so on. We conclude that for *every* field element in $\mathbb{F}$ of the form $t - i$ for $i = 1, 2, \ldots, \mathrm{char}(\mathbb{F})$, there is some read operation that returns (k, v, t'). Since there are m many read operations and the characteristic of field is greater than m, we obtain a contradiction.

Remark 2. The proof of Lemma 2 implies that, if the checker ever performs a read to an "invalid" memory cell k, meaning a cell indexed by $k \notin [\mathsf{M}]$, then regardless of the value and timestamp returned by the untrusted prover in response to that read, there does not exist any set S such that $\mathsf{WS} = \mathsf{RS} \cup S$.

Counter Polynomials. To aid the polynomial evaluation proof of the sparse polynomial the prover commits to additional multilinear polynomials beyond E_{rx} and E_{ry}. We now describe how these additional polynomials are constructed.

Observe that given the size M of memory and a list of m addresses involved in read operations, one can compute two vectors $C_r \in \mathbb{F}^m, C_f \in \mathbb{F}^\mathsf{M}$ defined as follows. For $k \in [m]$, $C_r[k]$ stores the count that would have been returned by the untrusted memory if it were honest during the kth read operation. Similarly, for $j \in [\mathsf{M}]$, let $C_f[j]$ store the final count stored at memory location j of the untrusted memory (if the untrusted memory were honest) at the termination of the m read operations. Computing these two vectors requires computation comparable to $O(m)$ operations over $\mathbb{F}$.

Let $\mathsf{read\_cts} = \widetilde{C_r}, \mathsf{write\_cts} = \widetilde{C_r} + 1, \mathsf{final\_cts} = \widetilde{C_f}$. We refer to these polynomials as *counter polynomials*, which are unique for a given memory size M and a list of m addresses involved in read operations.

The Actual Evaluation Proof. To prove the evaluation of a given $(2 \log \mathsf{M})$-variate multilinear polynomial D that evaluates to a non-zero value at at

---

[15] Recall here that counter arithmetic is done over $\mathbb{F}$, i.e., t and $t - 1$ are in $\mathbb{F}$.

most m locations over $\{0,1\}^{2\log M}$, the prover sends the following polynomials in addition to E_{rx} and E_{ry}: two $(\log m)$-variate multilinear polynomials as oracles $(\mathsf{read\_cts_{row}}, \mathsf{read\_cts_{col}})$, and two $(\log M)$-variate multilinear polynomials $(\mathsf{final\_cts_{row}}, \mathsf{final\_cts_{col}})$, where $(\mathsf{read\_cts_{row}}, \mathsf{final\_cts_{row}})$ and $(\mathsf{read\_cts_{col}}, \mathsf{final\_cts_{col}})$ are respectively the counter polynomials for the m addresses specified by row and col over a memory of size M. After that, in addition to performing the polynomial IOP depicted earlier in the proof (Fig. 1), the core idea is to check if the two oracles sent by the prover satisfy the conditions identified earlier using Lemma 2.

Lemma 3. *Given a $(2\log M)$-variate multilinear polynomial, suppose that $(\mathsf{row}, \mathsf{col}, \mathsf{val})$ denote multilinear polynomials committed by the commit algorithm. Furthermore, $(E_{\mathsf{rx}}, E_{\mathsf{ry}}, \mathsf{read\_cts_{row}}, \mathsf{final\_cts_{row}}, \mathsf{read\_cts_{col}}, \mathsf{final\_cts_{col}})$ denotes the additional polynomials sent by the prover at the beginning of the evaluation proof. For any $r_x \in \mathbb{F}^{\log M}$, suppose that*

$$\forall k \in \{0,1\}^{\log m}, \ E_{\mathsf{rx}}(k) = \widetilde{eq}(\mathsf{to-bits}(\mathsf{row}(k)), r_x). \tag{5}$$

Then the following holds: $\mathsf{WS} = \mathsf{RS} \cup S$, *where*

- $\mathsf{WS} = \{(\mathsf{to-field}(i), \widetilde{eq}(i, r_x), 0) : i \in \{0,1\}^{\log(M)}\} \cup \{(\mathsf{row}(k), E_{\mathsf{rx}}(k), \mathsf{write\_cts_{row}} (k) = \mathsf{read\_cts_{row}}(k) + 1) : k \in \{0,1\}^{\log m}\}$;
- $\mathsf{RS} = \{(\mathsf{row}(k), E_{\mathsf{rx}}(k), \mathsf{read\_cts_{row}}(k)) : k \in \{0,1\}^{\log m}\}$; *and*
- $S = \{(\mathsf{to-field}(i), \widetilde{eq}(i, r_x), \mathsf{final\_cts_{row}}(i)) : i \in \{0,1\}^{\log(M)}\}$.

Meanwhile, if Eq. (5) does not hold, then there is no set S such that $\mathsf{WS} = \mathsf{RS} \cup S$, where WS and RS are defined as above.

Similarly, for any $r_y \in \mathbb{F}^{\log M}$, checking that $\forall k \in \{0,1\}^{\log m}, \ E_{\mathsf{ry}}(k) = \widetilde{eq}(\mathsf{to-bits}(\mathsf{col}(k)), r_y)$ is equivalent (in the sense above) to checking that $\mathsf{WS}' = \mathsf{RS}' \cup S'$, where

- $\mathsf{WS}' = \{(\mathsf{to-field}(j), \widetilde{eq}(j, r_y), 0) : j \in \{0,1\}^{\log(M)}\} \cup \{(\mathsf{col}(k), E_{\mathsf{ry}}(k), \mathsf{write\_cts_{col}} (k) = \mathsf{read\_cts_{col}}(k) + 1) : k \in \{0,1\}^{\log m}\}$;
- $\mathsf{RS}' = \{(\mathsf{col}(k), E_{\mathsf{ry}}(k), \mathsf{read\_cts_{col}}(k)) : k \in \{0,1\}^{\log m}\}$; *and*
- $S' = \{(\mathsf{to-field}(j), \widetilde{eq}(j, r_y), \mathsf{final\_cts_{col}}(j)) : j \in \{0,1\}^{\log(M)}\}$.

Proof. The result follows from an application of the invariant in Lemma 2.

Here, we clarify the following subtlety. The expression $\mathsf{to-bits}(\mathsf{row}(k))$ appearing in Eq. (5) is not defined if $\mathsf{row}(k)$ is outside of $[\mathsf{M}]$ for any $k \in \{0,1\}^{\log m}$. But in this event, Remark 2 nonetheless implies the conclusion of the theorem, namely that there is no set S such that $\mathsf{WS} = \mathsf{RS} \cup S$. The analogous conclusion holds by the same reasoning if $\mathsf{col}(k)$ is outside of $[\mathsf{M}]$ for any $k \in \{0,1\}^{\log m}$.

There is no direct way to prove that the checks on sets in Lemma 3 hold. Instead, we rely on public-coin, multiset hash functions to compress RS, WS, and S into a single element of $\mathbb{F}$ each. Specifically:

// During the commit phase, $\mathcal{P}$ has committed to three $(\log m)$-variate multilinear polynomials row, col, val.

1. $\mathcal{P} \rightarrow \mathcal{V}$: four $(\log m)$-variate multilinear polynomials E_{rx}, E_{ry}, read_cts$_{\text{row}}$, read_cts$_{\text{col}}$ and two $(\log M)$-variate multilinear polynomials final_cts$_{\text{row}}$, final_cts$_{\text{col}}$.

2. Recall that Claim 1 (see Equation (4)) shows that $D(r_x, r_y) = \sum_{k \in \{0,1\}^{\log m}} \text{val}(k) \cdot E_{rx}(k) \cdot E_{ry}(k)$ assuming that
   - $\forall k \in \{0,1\}^{\log m}$, $E_{rx}(k) = \widetilde{eq}(\text{to-bits}(\text{row}(k)), r_x)$; and
   - $\forall k \in \{0,1\}^{\log m}$, $E_{ry}(k) = \widetilde{eq}(\text{to-bits}(\text{col}(k)), r_y)$.

   Hence, $\mathcal{V}$ and $\mathcal{P}$ apply the sum-check protocol to the polynomial $\text{val}(k) \cdot E_{rx}(k) \cdot E_{ry}(k)$, which reduces the check that $v = \sum_{k \in \{0,1\}^{\log m}} \text{val}(k) \cdot E_{rx}(k) \cdot E_{ry}(k)$ to checking that the following equations hold, where $r_z \in \mathbb{F}^{\log m}$ chosen at random by the verifier over the course of the sum-check protocol:
   - $\text{val}(r_z) \overset{?}{=} v_{\text{val}}$; and
   - $E_{rx}(r_z) \overset{?}{=} v_{E_{rx}}$ and $E_{ry}(r_z) \overset{?}{=} v_{E_{ry}}$. Here, v_{val}, $v_{E_{rx}}$ and $v_{E_{ry}}$ are values provided by the prover at the end of the sum-check protocol.

3. $\mathcal{V}$: check if the three equalities above hold with one oracle query each to each of val, E_{rx}, E_{ry}.

4. // The following checks if E_{rx} is well-formed as per the first bullet in Step 2 above.

5. $\mathcal{V} \rightarrow \mathcal{P}$: $\tau, \gamma \in_R \mathbb{F}$.

6. $\mathcal{V} \leftrightarrow \mathcal{P}$: run a sum-check-based protocol for "grand products" ([33, Proposition 2] or [30, Section 5 or 6]) to reduce the check that $\mathcal{H}_{\tau,\gamma}(\text{WS}) = \mathcal{H}_{\tau,\gamma}(\text{RS}) \cdot \mathcal{H}_{\tau,\gamma}(S)$, where RS, WS, S are as defined in Claim 3 and $\mathcal{H}$ is defined in Claim 4 to checking if the following hold, where $r_M \in \mathbb{F}^{\log M}$, $r_m \in \mathbb{F}^{\log m}$ are chosen at random by the verifier over the course of the sum-check protocol:
   - $\widetilde{eq}(r_M, r_x) \overset{?}{=} v_{eq}$
   - $E_{rx}(r_m) \overset{?}{=} v_{E_{rx}}$
   - $\text{row}(r_m) \overset{?}{=} v_{\text{row}}$; read_cts$_{\text{row}}(r_m) \overset{?}{=} v_{\text{read\_cts}_{\text{row}}}$; and final_cts$_{\text{row}}(r_M) \overset{?}{=} v_{\text{final\_cts}_{\text{row}}}$

7. $\mathcal{V}$: directly check if the first equality holds, which can be done with $O(\log M)$ field operations; check the remaining equations hold with an oracle query to each of E_{rx}, row, read_cts$_{\text{row}}$, final_cts$_{\text{row}}$.

8. // The following steps check if E_{ry} is well-formed as per the second bullet in Step 2 above.

9. $\mathcal{V} \rightarrow \mathcal{P}$: $\tau', \gamma' \in_R \mathbb{F}$.

10. $\mathcal{V} \leftrightarrow \mathcal{P}$: run a sum-check-based reduction for "grand products" ([33, Proposition2] or [30, Sections 5 and 6]) to reduce the check that $\mathcal{H}_{\tau',\gamma'}(\text{WS}') = \mathcal{H}_{\tau',\gamma'}(\text{RS}') \cdot \mathcal{H}_{\tau',\gamma'}(S')$, where RS', WS', S' are as defined in Claim 3 and $\mathcal{H}$ is defined in Claim 4 to checking if the following hold, where $r'_M \in \mathbb{F}^{\log M}$, $r'_m \in \mathbb{F}^{\log m}$ are chosen at random by the verifier in the sum-check protocol:
    - $\widetilde{eq}(r'_M, r_y) \overset{?}{=} v'_{eq}$
    - $E_{ry}(r'_m) \overset{?}{=} v_{E_{ry}}$
    - $\text{col}(r'_m) \overset{?}{=} v_{\text{col}}$; read_cts$_{\text{col}}(r'_m) \overset{?}{=} v_{\text{read\_cts}_{\text{col}}}$; and final_cts$_{\text{col}}(r'_M) \overset{?}{=} v_{\text{final\_cts}_{\text{col}}}$

11. $\mathcal{V}$: directly check if the first equality holds, which can be done with $O(\log M)$ field operations; check the remaining equations hold with an oracle query to each of E_{ry}, col, read_cts$_{\text{col}}$, final_cts$_{\text{col}}$.

Fig. 2. Evaluation procedure of the Spark sparse polynomial commitment scheme.

Lemma 4 (*[28]). Given two multisets A, B where each element is from $\mathbb{F}^3$, checking that $A = B$ is equivalent to checking the following, except for a soundness error of $O((|A| + |B|)/|\mathbb{F}|)$ over the choice of γ, τ: $\mathcal{H}_{\tau,\gamma}(A) = \mathcal{H}_{\tau,\gamma}(B)$, where $\mathcal{H}_{\tau,\gamma}(A) = \prod_{(a,v,t) \in A} (h_\gamma(a, v, t) - \tau)$, and $h_\gamma(a, v, t) = a \cdot \gamma^2 + v \cdot \gamma + t$. That is, if $A = B$, $\mathcal{H}_{\tau,\gamma}(A) = \mathcal{H}_{\tau,\gamma}(B)$ with probability 1 over randomly chosen values τ and γ in $\mathbb{F}$, while if $A \neq B$, then $\mathcal{H}_{\tau,\gamma}(A) = \mathcal{H}_{\tau,\gamma}(B)$ with probability at most $O(|A| + |B|)/|\mathbb{F}|)$.*

Intuitively, Lemma 4 gives an efficient randomized procedure for checking whether two sequences of tuples are permutations of each other. First, the procedure Reed-Solomon fingerprints each tuple (see [34, §2.1] for an exposition). This is captured by the function h_γ and intuitively replaces each tuple with a single field element, such that distinct tuples are unlikely to collide. Second, the procedure applies a permutation-independent fingerprinting procedure $H_{r,\gamma}$ to confirm the resulting two sequences of fingerprints are permutations of each other.

We are now ready to depict a polynomial IOP for proving evaluations of a committed sparse multilinear polynomial. Given $r_x, r_y \in \mathbb{F}^{\log M}$, to prove that $D(r_x, r_y) = v$ for a purported evaluation $v \in \mathbb{F}$, consider the polynomial IOP given in Fig. 2, which assumes that the verifier has an oracle access to multilinear polynomial oracles that encode D (namely, row, col, val)

Completeness. Perfect completeness follows from perfect completeness of the sum-check protocol and the fact that the multiset equality checks using their fingerprints hold with probability 1 over the choice of τ, γ if the prover is honest.

Soundness. Applying a standard union bound to the soundness error introduced by probabilistic multiset equality checks with the soundness error of the sum-check protocol [24], we conclude that the soundness error for the depicted polynomial IOP as at most $O(m)/|\mathbb{F}|$.

Round and Communication Complexity. There are three invocations of the sum-check protocol. First, the sum-check protocol is applied on a polynomial with $\log m$ variables where the degree is at most 3 in each variable, so the round complexity is $O(\log m)$ and the communication cost is $O(\log m)$ field elements. Second, four sum-check-based "grand product" protocols are computed in parallel. Two of the grand products are over vectors of size M and the remaining two are over vectors of size m. Third, the depicted IOP runs four additional "grand products", which incurs the same costs as above. In total, with the protocol of [30, Section 6] for grand products, the round complexity of the depicted IOP is $\tilde{O}(\log m + \log(N))$ and the communication cost is $\tilde{O}(\log m + \log N)$ field elements, where the $\tilde{O}$ notation hides doubly-logarithmic factors. The prover commits to an extra $O(m/\log^3 m)$ field elements.

Verifier Time. The verifier's runtime is dominated by its runtime in the grand product sum-check reductions, which is $\tilde{O}(\log m)$ field operations.

Prover Time. Using linear-time sum-checks [33] in all three sum-check reductions (and using the linear-time prover in the grand product protocol [30,33]), the prover's time is $O(N)$ finite field operations for unstructured tables.

Finally, to prove Theorem 1, applying the compiler of [9] to the depicted polynomial IOP with the given dense polynomial commitment primitive, followed by the Fiat-Shamir transformation [15], provides the desired non-interactive argument of knowledge for proving evaluations of committed sparse multilinear polynomials, with efficiency claimed in the theorem statement.

The full version of this paper [32] provides details of the grand product argument.

Additional Discussion and Intuition. As previously discussed, the protocol in Fig. 2 allows the prover to prove that it correctly ran the sparse polynomial evaluation algorithm described in Sect. 2.1 on the committed representation of the sparse polynomial. The core of the protocol lies in the memory-checking procedure, which enables the untrusted prover to establish that it produced the correct value upon every one of the algorithm's reads into the $c = 2$ memories of size $\mathsf{M} = N^{1/2}$. Intuitively, the values that the prover cryptographically commits to in the protocol are simply the values and counters returned by the aforementioned read operations (including a final "read pass" over both memories, which is required by the offline memory-checking procedure).

A key and subtle aspect of the above is that the prover does *not* have to cryptographically commit to the values written to memory in the algorithm's first phase, when it initializes the two memories (aka lookup tables, albeit dynamically determined by the evaluation point (r_x, r_y)), of size $\mathsf{M} = N^{1/2}$. This is because these lookup tables are MLE-structured, meaning that the verifier can evaluate the multilinear extension of these tables on its own. The whole point of cryptographically committing to these values is to let the verifier evaluate the multilinear extension thereof at a randomly chosen point in the grand product argument. Since the verifier can perform this evaluation quickly on its own, there is no need for the prover in the protocol of Fig. 2 to commit to these values.

3.2 The General Result

Theorem 1 gives a commitment scheme for m-sparse multilinear polynomials over $\log N = 2\log(\mathsf{M})$ many variables, in which the prover commits to 7 dense multilinear polynomials over $\log m$ many variables, and 2 dense polynomials over $\log(\mathsf{M})$ many variables.

Suppose we want to support sparse polynomials over $c\log(\mathsf{M})$ variables for constant $c > 2$, while ensuring that the prover still only commits to $3c + 1$ many dense multilinear polynomials over $\log m$ many variables, and c many over $\log(N^{1/c})$ many variables. We can proceed as follows.

The Function eq *and its Tensor Structure.* Recall that $\mathsf{eq}_s \colon \{0,1\}^s \times \{0,1\}^s \to \{0,1\}$ takes as input two vectors of length s and outputs 1 if and only if the vectors are equal. (In this section, we find it convenient to make explicit the number of variables over which eq is defined by including a subscript s.) Recall from the definition of $\widetilde{\text{eq}}$ polynomial [32, 34] that $\widetilde{\text{eq}}_s(x, e) = \prod_{i=1}^{s} (x_i e_i + (1 - x_i)(1 - e_i))$.

Equation (3) expressed the evaluation $\widetilde{D}(r_x, r_y)$ of a sparse $2\log(\mathsf{M})$-variate multilinear polynomial $\widetilde{D}$ as

$$\widetilde{D}(r_x, r_y) = \sum_{(i,j) \in \{0,1\}^{\log(\mathsf{M})} \times \{0,1\}^{\log(\mathsf{M})}} D(i,j) \cdot \widetilde{\text{eq}}_{\log(\mathsf{M})}(i, r_x) \cdot \widetilde{\text{eq}}_{\log(\mathsf{M})}(j, r_y). \quad (6)$$

The last two factors on the right hand side above have effectively factored $\widetilde{\text{eq}}_{2\log(\mathsf{M})}((i,j),(r_x,r_y))$ as the product of two terms that each test equality over $\log(\mathsf{M})$ many variables, namely: $\widetilde{\text{eq}}_{2\log(\mathsf{M})}((i,j),(r_x,r_y)) = \widetilde{\text{eq}}_{\log(\mathsf{M})}(i,r_x) \cdot \widetilde{\text{eq}}_{\log(\mathsf{M})}(j,r_y)$.

Within the sparse polynomial commitment scheme, this ultimately led to checking two different memories, each of size M, one of which we referred to as the "row" memory, and one as the "column" memory. For each memory checked, the prover had to commit to three $(\log m)$-variate polynomials, e.g., E_{rx}, row, read_cts$_{\text{row}}$, and one $\log(\mathsf{M})$-variate polynomial, e.g., final_cts$_{\text{row}}$.

Supporting $\log N = c\log \mathsf{M}$ *variables rather than* $2\log \mathsf{M}$. If we want to support polynomials over $c\log(\mathsf{M})$ variables for $c > 2$, we simply factor $\widetilde{\text{eq}}_{c\log(\mathsf{M})}$ into a product of c terms that test equality over $\log(\mathsf{M})$ variables each. For example, if $c = 3$, then we can write: $\widetilde{\text{eq}}_{3\log(\mathsf{M})}((i,j,k),(r_x,r_y,r_z)) = \widetilde{\text{eq}}_{\log(\mathsf{M})}(i,r_x) \cdot \widetilde{\text{eq}}_{\log(\mathsf{M})}(j,r_y) \cdot \widetilde{\text{eq}}_{\log(\mathsf{M})}(k,r_z)$.

Hence, if D is a $(3\log \mathsf{M})$-variate polynomial, we obtain the following analog of Eq. (6):

$$\widetilde{D}(r_x, r_y, r_z) = \sum_{(i,j,k) \in \{0,1\}^{\log(\mathsf{M})} \times \{0,1\}^{\log(\mathsf{M})} \times \{0,1\}^{\log(\mathsf{M})}} D(i,j,k) \cdot \widetilde{\text{eq}}_{\log(\mathsf{M})}(i,r_x) \cdot \widetilde{\text{eq}}_{\log(\mathsf{M})}(j,r_y) \cdot \widetilde{\text{eq}}_{\log(\mathsf{M})}(k,r_z). \quad (7)$$

Based on the above equation, straightforward modifications to the sparse polynomial commitment scheme lead to checking c different untrusted memories, each of size M, rather than two. For example, when $c = 3$, the first memory stores all evaluations of $\widetilde{\text{eq}}_{\log(\mathsf{M})}(i, r_x)$ as i ranges over $\{0,1\}^{\log m}$, the second stores $\widetilde{\text{eq}}_{\log(\mathsf{M})}(j, r_y)$ as j ranges over $\{0,1\}^{\log m}$, and the third stores $\widetilde{\text{eq}}_{\log(\mathsf{M})}(k, r_z)$ as k ranges over $\{0,1\}^{\log m}$. These are exactly the contents of the three lookup tables of size $N^{1/c}$ used by the sparse polynomial evaluation algorithm of Sect. 2.1 when $c = 3$.

For each memory checked, the prover has to commit to three multilinear polynomials defined over $\log(m)$-many variables, and one defined over $\log(\mathsf{M}) = \log(N)/c$ variables. We obtain the following theorem.

Theorem 2. *Given a polynomial commitment scheme for* $(\log \mathsf{M})$-*variate multilinear polynomials with the following parameters (where* M *is a positive integer and WLOG a power of 2): (1) the size of the commitment is* $\mathsf{c}(\mathsf{M})$; *(2) the running time of the commit algorithm is* $\mathsf{tc}(\mathsf{M})$; *(3) the running time of the prover to prove a polynomial evaluation is* $\mathsf{tp}(\mathsf{M})$; *(4) the running time of the verifier* *to verify a polynomial evaluation is* $\mathsf{tv}(M)$*; and (5) the proof size is* $\mathsf{p}(M)$*, there exists a polynomial commitment scheme for* $(c \log M)$*-variate multilinear polynomials that evaluate to a non-zero value at at most* m *locations over the Boolean hypercube* $\{0,1\}^{c \log M}$*, with the following parameters: (1) the size of the commitment is* $(3c+1)\mathsf{c}(m) + c \cdot \mathsf{c}(M)$*; (2) the running time of the commit algorithm is* $O\left(c \cdot (\mathsf{tc}(m) + \mathsf{tc}(M))\right)$*; (3) the running time of the prover to prove a polynomial evaluation is* $O\left(c\,(\mathsf{tp}(m) + \mathsf{tc}(M))\right)$*; (4) the running time of the verifier to verify a polynomial evaluation is* $O\left(c\,(\mathsf{tv}(m) + \mathsf{tv}(M))\right)$*; and (5) the proof size is* $O\left(c\,(\mathsf{p}(m) + \mathsf{p}(M))\right)$*.*

3.3   Specializing the **Spark** Sparse Commitment Scheme to **Lasso**

In Lasso, if the prover is honest then the sparse polynomial commitment scheme is applied to the multilinear extension of a matrix M with m rows and N columns, where m is the number of lookups and N is the size of the table. If the prover is honest then each row of M is a unit vector.

In fact, we require the commitment scheme to enforce these properties even when the prover is potentially malicious. Achieving this simplifies the commitment scheme and provides concrete efficiency benefits. It also keeps Lasso's polynomial IOP simple as it does not need additional invocations of the sum-check protocol to prove that M satisfies these properties.

First, the multilinear polynomial $\mathsf{val}(k)$ is fixed to 1, and it is not committed by the prover. Recall from Lemma 1 that $\mathsf{val}(k)$ extends the function that maps a bit-vector $k \in \{0,1\}^{\log m}$ to the value of the k'th non-zero evaluation of the sparse function. Since M is a $\{0,1\}$-valued matrix, $\mathsf{val}(k)$ is just the constant polynomial that evaluates to 1 at all inputs.

Second, for any $k = (k_1, \ldots, k_{\log m}) \in \{0,1\}^{\log m}$, the k'th non-zero entry of M is in row $\mathsf{to-field}(k) = \sum_{j=1}^{\log m} 2^{j-1} \cdot k_j$. Hence, in Eq. (4) of Lemma 1, $\mathsf{to-bits}(\mathsf{row}(k))$ is simply k.[16] This means that $E_{rx}(k) = \widetilde{\mathsf{eq}}(k, r_x)$, which the verifier can evaluate on its own in logarithmic time. With this fact in hand, the prover does not commit to E_{rx} nor prove that it is well-formed.

In terms of costs, these effectively remove the contribution of the first $\log m$ variables of $\widetilde{M}$ to the costs. Hence, the costs are that of applying the commitment scheme to an m-sparse $\log(N)$-variate polynomial (with val fixed to 1). This means that, setting $c = 2$ for illustration, the prover commits to 6 multilinear polynomials with $\log(m)$ variables each and to two multilinear polynomials with $(1/2) \log N$ variables each.

[32, Figure 3] describes Spark specialized for Lasso to commit to $\widetilde{M}$. The prover commits to $3c$ dense $(\log(m))$-variate multilinear polynomials, called $\mathsf{dim}_1, \ldots, \mathsf{dim}_c$ (the analogs of the row and col polynomials of Sect. 3.1), $E_1, \ldots, E_c$, and $\mathsf{read\_cts}_1, \ldots, \mathsf{read\_cts}_c$, as well as c dense multilinear polynomials in $\log(N^{1/c}) = \log(N)/c$ variables, called $\mathsf{final\_cts}_1, \ldots, \mathsf{final\_cts}_c$. Each dim_i is purported to be the memory cell from the i'th memory that the sparse

---

[16] More precisely, this holds if we define r_x to be in $\mathbb{F}^{\log m}$ and r_y to be in $\mathbb{F}^{\log N}$, rather than defining them both to be in $\mathbb{F}^{\log M} = \mathbb{F}^{(1/2)(\log m + \log n)}$.

polynomial evaluation algorithm (Sect. 2.1) reads at each of its m time steps, $E_1, \ldots, E_c$ the values returned by those reads, and $\mathsf{read\_cts}_1, \ldots, \mathsf{read\_cts}_c$ the associated counts. $\mathsf{final\_cts}_1, \ldots, \mathsf{final\_cts}_c$ are purported to be to counts returned by the memory checking procedure's final pass over each of the c memories.

If the prover is honest, then $\dim_1, \ldots, \dim_c$ each map $\{0,1\}^{\log m}$ to $\{0, \ldots, N^{1/c} - 1\}$, and $\mathsf{read\_cts}_1, \ldots, \mathsf{read\_cts}_c$ each map $\{0,1\}^{\log m}$ to $\{0, \ldots, m-1\}$; $\mathsf{final\_cts}_1, \ldots, \mathsf{final\_cts}_c$ each map $\{0,1\}^{\log m}$ to $\{0, \ldots, m-1\}$. In fact, for any integer $j > 0$, at most m/j out of the m evaluations of each counter polynomial $\mathsf{read\_cts}_i$ and $\mathsf{final\_cts}_i$ can be larger than j.

4   Surge: A Generalization of Spark, Providing Lasso

The technical core of the Lasso lookup argument is Surge, a generalization of Spark. In particular, Lasso is simply a straightforward use of Surge.

Recall from Sect. 3 that Spark allows the untrusted Lasso prover to commit to $\widetilde{M}$, purported to be the multilinear extension of an $m \times N$ matrix M, with each row equal to a unit vector, such that $M \cdot t = a$. The commitment phase of Surge is same as that of Spark. Surge generalizes Spark in that the Surge prover proves a larger class of statements about the committed polynomial $\widetilde{M}$ (Spark focused only on proving *evaluations* of the sparse polynomial $\widetilde{M}$).

Overview of Lasso. In Lasso, after committing to $\widetilde{M}$, the Lasso verifier picks a random $r \in \mathbb{F}^{\log m}$ and seeks to confirm that

$$\sum_{j \in \{0,1\}^{\log N}} \widetilde{M}(r, j) \cdot t(j) = \widetilde{a}(r). \tag{8}$$

Indeed, if $M \cdot t$ and a are the same vector, then Eq. (8) holds for every choice of r, while if $Mt \neq a$, then by the Schwartz-Zippel lemma, Eq. (8) holds with probability at most $\frac{\log m}{|\mathbb{F}|}$. So up to soundness error $\frac{\log m}{|\mathbb{F}|}$, checking that $Mt = a$ is equivalent to checking that Eq. (8) holds.

In Lasso, the verifier obtains $\widetilde{a}(r)$ via the polynomial commitment to $\widetilde{a}$. Then, the prover establishes Eq. (8) using Surge. Specifically, Surge generalizes Spark's procedure for generating evaluation proofs, to directly produce a proof as to the value of the left hand side of Eq. (8). Essentially, the proof *proves* that the prover correctly ran a (very efficient) algorithm for evaluating the left hand side of Eq. (8).

A Roughly $O(\alpha m)$-time Algorithm for Computing the LHS of Eq. (8). From Eq. (3), $\widetilde{M}(r, y) = \sum_{(i,j) \in \{0,1\}^{\log m + \log N}} M_{i,j} \cdot \widetilde{eq}(i, r) \cdot \widetilde{eq}(j, y)$.

Hence, letting $\mathsf{nz}(i)$ denote the unique column in row i of M that contains a non-zero value (namely, the value 1), the left hand side of Eq. (8) equals

$$\sum_{i \in \{0,1\}^{\log m}} \widetilde{eq}(i, r) \cdot T[\mathsf{nz}(i)]. \tag{9}$$

Suppose that T is a SOS table. This means that there is an integer $k \geq 1$ and $\alpha = k \cdot c$ tables $T_1, \ldots, T_\alpha$ of size $N^{1/c}$, as well as an α-variate multilinear polynomial g such that the following holds. Suppose that for every $r = (r_1, \ldots, r_c) \in \left(\{0,1\}^{\log(N)/c}\right)^c$,

$$T[r] = g\left(T_1[r_1], \ldots, T_k[r_1], T_{k+1}[r_2], \ldots, T_{2k}[r_2], \ldots, T_{\alpha-k+1}[r_c], \ldots, T_\alpha[r_c]\right).$$
(10)

For each $i \in \{0,1\}^{\log m}$, decompose $\mathsf{nz}(i)$ and $(\mathsf{nz}_1(i), \ldots, \mathsf{nz}_c(i)) \in [N^{1/c}]^c$. Then Expression (9) equals

$$\sum_{i \in \{0,1\}^{\log m}} \widetilde{\mathsf{eq}}(i, r) \cdot g\left(T_1[\mathsf{nz}_1(i)], \ldots, T_k[\mathsf{nz}_1(i)], T_{k+1}[\mathsf{nz}_2(i)], \ldots, \right.$$

$$\left. T_{2k}[\mathsf{nz}_2(i)], \ldots, T_{\alpha-k+1}[\mathsf{nz}_c(i)], \ldots, T_\alpha[\mathsf{nz}_c(i)]\right).$$
(11)

The algorithm to compute Expression (11) simply initializes all tables $T_1, \ldots, T_\alpha$, then iterates over every $i \in \{0,1\}^m$ and computes the i'th term of the sum with a single lookup into each table (of course, the algorithm evaluates g at the results of the lookups into $T_1, \ldots, T_\alpha$, and multiplies the result by $\widetilde{\mathsf{eq}}(i, r)$).

Description of Surge. The commitment to $\widetilde{M}$ in Surge consists of commitments to c multilinear polynomials $\dim_1, \ldots, \dim_c$, each over $\log m$ variables. $\dim_i$ is purported to be the multilinear extension of nz_i.

The verifier chooses $r \in \{0,1\}^{\log m}$ at random and requests that the Surge prover prove that the committed polynomial $\widetilde{M}$ satisfy Eq. (9). The prover does so by proving it ran the aforementioned algorithm for evaluating Expression (11). Following the memory-checking procedure in Sect. 3, with each table $T_i \colon i = 1, \ldots, \alpha$ viewed as a memory of size $N^{1/c}$, this entails committing for each i to $\log(m)$-variate multilinear polynomials E_i and $\mathsf{read\_cts}_i$ (purported to capture the value and count returned by each of the m lookups into T_i) and a $\log(N^{1/c})$-variate multilinear polynomial $\mathsf{final\_cts}_i$ (purported to capture the final count for each memory cell of T_i.)

Let $\widetilde{t}_i$ be the mutlilinear extension of the vector t_i whose j'th entry is $T_i[j]$. The sum-check protocol is applied to compute

$$\sum_{j \in \{0,1\}^{\log m}} \widetilde{\mathsf{eq}}(r, j) \cdot g\left(E_1(j), \ldots, E_\alpha(j)\right).$$
(12)

At the end of the sum-check protocol, the verifier needs to evaluate $\widetilde{\mathsf{eq}}(r, r') \cdot g(E_1(r'), \ldots, E_\alpha(r'))$ at a random point $r' \in \mathbb{F}^{\log m}$, which it can do with one evaluation query to each E_i (the verifier can compute $\widetilde{\mathsf{eq}}(r, r')$ on its own in $O(\log m)$ time).

The verifier must still check that each E_i is well-formed i.e., that $E_i(j)$ equals $T_i[\dim_i(j)]$ for all $j \in \{0,1\}^{\log m}$. This is done exactly as in Spark to confirm that for each of the α memories, $\mathsf{WS} = \mathsf{RS} \cup S$ (see Lemmas 3 and 4, and [32, Figure 3]). At the end of this procedure, for each $i = 1, \ldots, \alpha$, the verifier needs to evaluate each of $\dim_i$, $\mathsf{read\_cts}_i$, $\mathsf{final\_cts}_i$ at a random point, which it can do with one query to each. The verifier also needs to evaluate the multilinear extension $\widetilde{t}_i$ of each sub-table T_i for each $i = 1, \ldots, \alpha$ at a single point. T being SOS guarantees that the verifier can compute each of these evaluations in $O(\log(N)/c)$ time.

Prover Time. Besides committing to the polynomials $\dim_i, E_i, \text{read\_cts}_i$, final_cts_i for each of the α memories and producing one evaluation proof for each (in practice, these would be batched), the prover must compute its messages in the sum-check protocol used to compute Expression (12) and the grand product arguments (which can be batched). Using the linear-time sum-check protocol [13, 28, 33], the prover can compute its messages in the sum-check protocol used to compute Expression (12) with $O(b \cdot k \cdot \alpha \cdot m)$ field operations, where recall that $\alpha = k \cdot c$ and b is the number of monomials in g. If $k = O(1)$, then this is $O(b \cdot c \cdot m)$ time. For many tables of practical interest, the factor b can be eliminated (e.g., if the *total degree* of g is a constant independent of b, such as 1 or 2). The costs for the prover in the memory checking argument is similar to Spark: $O(\alpha \cdot m + \alpha \cdot N^{1/c})$ field operations, plus committing to a low-order number of field elements.

Verification Costs. The sum-check protocol used to compute Expression (12) consists of $\log m$ rounds in which the prover sends a univariate polynomial of degree at most $1 + \alpha$ in each round. Hence, the prover sends $O(c \cdot k \cdot \log m)$ field elements, and the verifier performs $O(k \cdot \log m)$ field operations. The costs of the memory checking argument for the verifier are identical to Spark.

Completeness and Knowledge Soundness of the Polynomial IOP. Completeness holds by design and by the completeness of the sum-check protocol, and of the memory checking argument.

By the soundness of the sum-check protocol and the memory checking argument, if the prover passes the verifier's checks in the polynomial IOP with probability more than an appropriately chosen threshold $\gamma = O(m + N^{1/c}/|\mathbb{F}|)$, then $\sum_{y \in \{0,1\}^{\log N}} \widetilde{M}(r, y)T[y] = v$, where $\widetilde{M}$ is the multilinear extension of the following matrix M. For $i \in \{0,1\}^{\log m}$, row i of M consists of all zeros except for entry $M_{i,j} = 1$, where $j = (j_1, \ldots, j_c) \in \{0, 1, \ldots, N^{1/c}\}^c$ is the unique column index such that $j_1 = \dim_1(i), \ldots, j_c = \dim_c(i)$.

Theorem 3. *Figure 3 is a complete and knowledge-sound polynomial IOP for establishing that the prover knows an $m \times N$ matrix $M \in \{0,1\}^{m \times N}$ with exactly one entry equal to 1 in each row, such that*

$$\sum_{y \in \{0,1\}^{\log N}} \widetilde{M}(r, y)T[y] = v. \tag{13}$$

The discussion surrounding Eq. (8) explained that checking that $Mt = a$ is equivalent, up to soundness error $\log(m)/|\mathbb{F}|$, to Eq. (13) holding for a random $r \in \mathbb{F}^{\log m}$. Combining this with Theorem 3 implies that the protocol in [32, Figure 5] i.e., Lasso, is a lookup argument.

T is an SOS lookup table of size N i.e., there are $\alpha = kc$ tables $T_1, \ldots, T_\alpha$, each of size $N^{1/c}$, such that for any $r \in \{0,1\}^{\log N}$, $T[r] = g(T_1[r_1], \ldots, T_k[r_1], T_{k+1}[r_2], \ldots, T_{2k}[r_2], \ldots, T_{\alpha-k+1}[r_c], \ldots, T_\alpha[r_c])$. During the commit phase, $\mathcal{P}$ commits to c multilinear polynomials $\dim_1, \ldots, \dim_c$, each over $\log m$ variables. $\dim_i$ is purported to provide the indices of $T_{(i-1)k+1}, \ldots, T_{ik}$ read by the natural algorithm computing $\sum_{i \in \{0,1\}^{\log m}} \widetilde{\mathsf{eq}}(i, r) \cdot T[\mathsf{nz}[i]]$ (Equation (11)).

// $\mathcal{V}$ requests $\langle u, t \rangle$, where the ith entry of t is $T[i]$ and the yth entry of u is $\widetilde{M}(r, y)$.

1. $\mathcal{P} \rightarrow \mathcal{V}$: 2α different $(\log m)$-variate multilinear polynomials $E_1, \ldots, E_\alpha$, $\mathsf{read\_cts}_1, \ldots \mathsf{read\_cts}_\alpha$ and α different $(\log(N)/c)$-variate multilinear polynomials $\mathsf{final\_cts}_1, \ldots, \mathsf{final\_cts}_\alpha$.
   // E_i is purported to specify the values of each of the m reads into T_i.
   // $\mathsf{read\_cts}_1, \ldots \mathsf{read\_cts}_\alpha$ and $\mathsf{final\_cts}_1, \ldots, \mathsf{final\_cts}_\alpha$, are "counter polynomials" for each of the α sub-tables T_i.

2. $\mathcal{V}$ and $\mathcal{P}$ apply the sum-check protocol to the polynomial $h(k) := \widetilde{\mathsf{eq}}(r, k) \cdot g(E_1(k), \ldots, E_\alpha(k))$, which reduces the check that $v = \sum_{k \in \{0,1\}^{\log m}} g(E_1(k), \ldots, E_\alpha(k))$ to checking that the following equations hold, where $r_z \in \mathbb{F}^{\log m}$ chosen at random by the verifier over the course of the sum-check protocol:
   - $E_i(r_z) \stackrel{?}{=} v_{E_i}$ for $i = 1, \ldots, \alpha$. Here, $v_{E_1}, \ldots, v_{E_\alpha}$ are values provided by the prover at the end of the sum-check protocol.

3. $\mathcal{V}$: check if the above equalities hold with one oracle query to each E_i.

4. // The following checks if E_i is well-formed, i.e., that $E_i(j)$ equals $T_i[\dim_i(j)]$ for all $j \in \{0,1\}^{\log m}$.

5. $\mathcal{V} \rightarrow \mathcal{P}$: $\tau, \gamma \in_R \mathbb{F}$.
   //In practice, one would apply a single sum-check protocol to a random linear combination of the below polynomials. For brevity, we describe the protocol as invoking c independent instances of sum-check.

6. $\mathcal{V} \leftrightarrow \mathcal{P}$: For $i = 1, \ldots, \alpha$, run a sum-check-based protocol for "grand products" ([33, Proposition2] or [30, Section 5 or 6]) to reduce the check that $\mathcal{H}_{\tau,\gamma}(\mathsf{WS}) = \mathcal{H}_{\tau,\gamma}(\mathsf{RS}) \cdot \mathcal{H}_{\tau,\gamma}(S)$, where $\mathsf{RS}, \mathsf{WS}, S$ are as defined in Claim 3 and $\mathcal{H}$ is defined in Claim 4 to checking if the following hold, where $r_i'' \in \mathbb{F}^\ell, r_i''' \in \mathbb{F}^{\log m}$ are chosen at random by the verifier over the course of the sum-check protocol:
   - $E_i(r_i''') \stackrel{?}{=} v_{E_i}$
   - $\dim_i(r_i''') \stackrel{?}{=} v_i$; $\mathsf{read\_cts}_i(r_i''') \stackrel{?}{=} v_{\mathsf{read\_cts}_i}$; and $\mathsf{final\_cts}_i(r_i'') \stackrel{?}{=} v_{\mathsf{final\_cts}_i}$

7. $\mathcal{V}$: Check the equations hold with an oracle query to each of $E_i, \dim_i, \mathsf{read\_cts}_i, \mathsf{final\_cts}_i$.

Fig. 3. Surge's polynomial IOP for proving that $\sum_{y \in \{0,1\}^{\log N}} \widetilde{M}(r, y) T[y] = v$.

References

1. Arun, A., Setty,S., Thaler, J.: Jolt: SNARKs for virtual machines via lookups. In: EUROCRYPT, pp. xx–yy. Springer, Cham (2024)
2. Ben-Sasson, E., Bentov, I., Horesh, Y., Riabzev., M., In: Fast reed-solomon interactive oracle proofs of proximity. In: ICALP (2018)

3. Blum, M., Evans, W., Gemmell, P., Kannan, S., Naor, M.: Checking the correctness of memories. In: FOCS (1991)

4. Boneh, D., Drake, J., Fisch, B., Gabizon, A.: Halo infinite: recursive zk-SNARKs from any additive polynomial commitment scheme. In: Cryptology ePrint Archive, Report 2020/1536 (2020)

5. Bootle, J., Cerulli, A., Chaidos, P., Groth, J., Petit, C.: Efficient zero-knowledge arguments for arithmetic circuits in the discrete log setting. In: Fischlin, M., Coron, J.-S. (eds.) EUROCRYPT 2016. LNCS, vol. 9666, pp. 327–357. Springer, Heidelberg (2016). https://doi.org/10.1007/978-3-662-49896-5_12

6. Bootle, J., Cerulli, A., Groth, J., Jakobsen, S., Maller., M.: Arya: nearly linear-time zero-knowledge proofs for correct program execution. In: ASIACRYPT (2018)

7. Bowe, S., Grigg, J., Hopwood, D.: Recursive proof composition without a trusted setup. Cryptology ePrint Archive, Report 2019/1021 (2019)

8. Bünz, B., Bootle, J., Boneh, D., Poelstra, A., Wuille, P., Maxwell, G.: Bulletproofs: short proofs for confidential transactions and more. In: S&P (2018)

9. Bünz, B., Fisch, B., Szepieniec, A.: Transparent SNARKs from DARK compilers. In: Canteaut, A., Ishai, Y. (eds.) EUROCRYPT 2020. LNCS, vol. 12105, pp. 677–706. Springer, Cham (2020). https://doi.org/10.1007/978-3-030-45721-1_24

10. B. Chen, B. Bünz, D. Boneh, and Z. Zhang. HyperPlonk: Plonk with linear-time prover and high-degree custom gates. In: Hazay, C., Stam, M. (eds.) EUROCRYPT. Springer, Cham (2023). https://doi.org/10.1007/978-3-031-30617-4_17

11. Chiesa, A., Hu, Y., Maller, M., Mishra, P., Vesely, N., Ward, N.: Marlin: preprocessing zkSNARKs with universal and updatable SRS. In: Canteaut, A., Ishai, Y. (eds.) EUROCRYPT 2020. LNCS, vol. 12105, pp. 738–768. Springer, Cham (2020). https://doi.org/10.1007/978-3-030-45721-1_26

12. Clarke, D., Devadas, S., Dijk, M.V., Gassend, B., Edward, G., Mit, S.: Incremental multiset hash functions and their application to memory integrity checking. In: ASIACRYPT (2003)

13. Cormode, G., Thaler, J., Yi, K.: Verifying computations with streaming interactive proofs. Proc. VLDB Endow. 5(1), 25–36 (2011)

14. Eagen, L., Fiore, D., Gabizon, A.: CQ: cached quotients for fast lookups. Cryptology ePrint Archive (2022)

15. Fiat, A., Shamir, A.: How to prove yourself: practical solutions to identification and signature problems. In: Odlyzko, A.M. (ed.) CRYPTO 1986. LNCS, vol. 263, pp. 186–194. Springer, Heidelberg (1987). https://doi.org/10.1007/3-540-47721-7_12

16. Gabizon, A., Khovratovich, D.: Flookup: fractional decomposition-based lookups in quasi-linear time independent of table size. Cryptology ePrint Archive (2022)

17. Gabizon, A., Williamson, Z.: Proposal: the TurboPlonk program syntax for specifying SNARK programs (2020)

18. Gabizon, A., Williamson, Z.J.: plookup: a simplified polynomial protocol for lookup tables (2020)

19. Gabizon, A., Williamson, Z.J., Ciobotaru, O.: PLONK: permutations over Lagrange-bases for oecumenical noninteractive arguments of knowledge. ePrint Report 2019/953 (2019)

20. Golovnev, A., Lee, J., Setty, S., Thaler, J., Wahby, R.S.: Brakedown: linear-time and post-quantum snarks for R1CS. Cryptology ePrint Archive (2021)

21. Kate, A., Zaverucha, G.M., Goldberg, I.: Constant-size commitments to polynomials and their applications. In: ASIACRYPT, pp. 177–194 (2010)

22. Kothapalli, A., Setty, S., Tzialla, I.: Nova: recursive zero-knowledge arguments from folding schemes. In: CRYPTO. Springer, Cham (2022). https://doi.org/10.1007/978-3-031-15985-5_13

23. Lee, J.: Dory: efficient, transparent arguments for generalised inner products and polynomial commitments. In: Nissim, K., Waters, B. (eds.) TCC 2021. LNCS, vol. 13043, pp. 1–34. Springer, Cham (2021). https://doi.org/10.1007/978-3-030-90453-1_1

24. Lund, C., Fortnow, L., Karloff, H., Nisan, N.: Algebraic methods for interactive proof systems. In: FOCS, October 1990

25. Pătraşcu, M., Thorup, M.: Twisted tabulation hashing. pp. 209–228 (2013)

26. Posen, J., Kattis, A.A.: Caulk+: table-independent lookup arguments. Cryptology ePrint Archive (2022)

27. Pătraşcu, M., Thorup, M.: The power of simple tabulation hashing. J. ACM (JACM) **59**(3), 1–50 (2012)

28. Setty, S.: Spartan: efficient and general-purpose zkSNARKs without trusted setup. In: Micciancio, D., Ristenpart, T. (eds.) CRYPTO 2020. LNCS, vol. 12172, pp. 704–737. Springer, Cham (2020). https://doi.org/10.1007/978-3-030-56877-1_25

29. Setty, S., Angel, S., Gupta, T., Lee, J.: Proving the correct execution of concurrent services in zero-knowledge. In: OSDI, October 2018

30. Setty, S., Lee, J.: Quarks: quadruple-efficient transparent zkSNARKs. Cryptology ePrint Archive, Report 2020/1275 (2020)

31. Setty, S., Thaler, J., Wahby, R.: Customizable constraint systems for succinct arguments. Cryptology ePrint Archive (2023)

32. Setty, S., Thaler, J., Wahby, R.: Unlocking the lookup singularity with Lasso. Cryptology ePrint Archive (2023)

33. Thaler, J.: Time-optimal interactive proofs for circuit evaluation. In: Canetti, R., Garay, J.A. (eds.) CRYPTO 2013. LNCS, vol. 8043, pp. 71–89. Springer, Heidelberg (2013). https://doi.org/10.1007/978-3-642-40084-1_5

34. Thaler, J.: Proofs, arguments, and zero-knowledge. Found. Trends Privacy Secur. **4**(2–4), 117–660 (2022)

35. Wahby, R.S., Tzialla, I., Shelat, A., Thaler, J., Walfish, M.: Doubly-efficient zkSNARKs without trusted setup. In: S&P (2018)

36. T. Xie, Y. Zhang, and D. Song. Orion: Zero knowledge proof with linear prover time. In: Dodis, Y., Shrimpton, T. (eds.) CRYPTO. Springer, Cham (2022). https://doi.org/10.1007/978-3-031-15985-5_11

37. Zapico, A., Buterin, V., Khovratovich, D., Maller, M., Nitulescu, A., Simkin, M.: Caulk: lookup arguments in sublinear time. Cryptology ePrint Archive (2022)

38. Zapico, A., Gabizon, A., Khovratovich, D., Maller, M., Ràfols, C.: Baloo: nearly optimal lookup arguments. Cryptology ePrint Archive (2022)

Efficient Pre-processing PIR Without Public-Key Cryptography

Ashrujit Ghoshal$^{(\boxtimes)}$, Mingxun Zhou, and Elaine Shi

Carnegie Mellon University, Pittsburgh, USA
{aghoshal,mingxunz,rshi}@andrew.cmu.edu

Abstract. Classically, Private Information Retrieval (PIR) was studied in a setting without any pre-processing. In this setting, it is well-known that 1) public-key cryptography is necessary to achieve non-trivial (i.e., sublinear) communication efficiency in the single-server setting, and 2) the total server computation per query must be linear in the size of the database, no matter in the single-server or multi-server setting. Recent works have shown that both of these barriers can be overcome if we are willing to introduce a pre-processing phase. In particular, a recent work called PIANO showed that using only one-way functions, one can construct a single-server preprocessing PIR with $\widetilde{O}(\sqrt{n})$ bandwidth and computation per query, assuming $\widetilde{O}(\sqrt{n})$ client storage. For the two-server setting, the state-of-the-art is defined by two incomparable results. First, PIANO immediately implies a scheme in the two-server setting with the same performance bounds as stated above. Moreover, Beimel et al. showed a two-server scheme with $O(n^{1/3})$ bandwidth and $O(n/\log^2 n)$ computation per query, and one with $O(n^{1/2+\epsilon})$ cost both in bandwidth and computation—both schemes provide information theoretic security.

In this paper, we show that assuming the existence of one-way functions, we can construct a two-server preprocessing PIR scheme with $\widetilde{O}(n^{1/4})$ bandwidth and $\widetilde{O}(n^{1/2})$ computation per query, while requiring only $\widetilde{O}(n^{1/2})$ client storage. We also construct a new single-server preprocessing PIR scheme with $\widetilde{O}(n^{1/4})$ *online* bandwidth and $\widetilde{O}(n^{1/2})$ *offline* bandwidth and *computation* per query, also requiring $\widetilde{O}(n^{1/2})$ client storage. Specifically, the online bandwidth is the bandwidth required for the client to obtain an answer, and the offline bandwidth can be viewed as background maintenance work amortized to each query. Our new constructions not only advance the theoretical understanding of preprocessing PIR, but are also concretely efficient because the only cryptography needed is pseudorandom functions.

Author ordering is randomized. Full version: https://eprint.iacr.org/2023/1574.

Supplementary Information The online version contains supplementary material available at https://doi.org/10.1007/978-3-031-58751-1_8.

M. Joye and G. Leander (Eds.): EUROCRYPT 2024, LNCS 14656, pp. 210–240, 2024.
https://doi.org/10.1007/978-3-031-58751-1_8

1   Introduction

Private Information Retrieval (PIR), originally formulated by Chor, Goldreich, Kushilevitz, and Sudan [10], studies the following important problem. Imagine that a server holds a public database denoted $DB \in \{0,1\}^n$. A client with small local storage wants to query the database, while hiding its queries from the server. PIR has wide applications in practice. For example, it enables private contact discovery [11,14], privacy-preserving light-weight clients for cryptocurrencies, private DNS queries [18,39,43], private web search [21], and so on.

Classical PIR Without Pre-processing. A naïve solution for PIR is to have the client linearly scan through the entire database for each query. Unfortunately, this would incur linear bandwidth. A series of works spanning over two decades [1,6,8–10,19,20,26,30–32,35,36,40] starting with Chor et al. [10] showed how to construct PIR with non-trivial bandwidth. Specifically, in the single-server setting, it is well-known that with various cryptographic assumptions (e.g., Φ-hiding, LWE, Damgård-Jurik, DDH, QR), we can achieve $\widetilde{O}_\lambda(1)$ bandwidth per query [6,16,22,33] where $\widetilde{O}_\lambda(\cdot)$ hides polylogarithmic factors and the dependence on the security parameter λ. In the two-server setting, Dvir and Gopi [17] showed that information-theoretic PIR is possible with $n^{O(\sqrt{\log \log n / \log n})}$ bandwidth per query. All the aforementioned works studied PIR in the *classical setting without preprocessing*. More specifically, the classical setting assumes that the server stores only the original database, and need not store per-client state. Unfortunately, the classical setting suffers from the following inherent limitations.

1. First, Beimel, Ishai, and Malkin [2] proved that any classical PIR scheme without preprocessing must suffer from linear (in n) server computation per query. Intuitively, if there is any location that the server does not look at during a query, then the client cannot be asking for that location.
2. Second, in a single-server setting, it is known that any PIR scheme with non-trivial (i.e., sublinear) bandwidth would imply oblivious transfer [15], i.e., some form of public-key cryptography is needed.

Pre-processing Sublinear PIR Without Public-Key Cryptography. To get around the aforementioned barriers, earlier works have suggested a pre-processing model. Specifically, we consider a model with a one-time pre-processing phase upfront, followed by an *unbounded* number of queries. The pre-processing model was first proposed by Beimel, Ishai, and Malkin [2] and Corrigan-Gibbs and Kogan [13].

In a pre-processing model, we focus on exploring the efficiency of PIR with *sublinear computation*, and *without the use of public-key cryptography*—to get around the aforementioned barriers, In particular, the requirement of sublinear computation is especially important in practical scenarios where the database is large—for example, in a private DNS application, the database can be several hundred Gigabytes. Further, we restrict ourselves to Minicrypt (i.e., allowing

PRFs but not using any public-key cryptography)—this is not only motivated by theoretical interest, but also the promise of concretely faster constructions since modern processors have hardware acceleration for AES operations.

Earlier works showed that under a global, server-side preprocessing, one can overcome the linear computation barrier [2,12,13,27–29,39,42,43]; and further, assuming a client-specific preprocessing, we can overcome both of the aforementioned barriers [34,43]. So far, we know the following pre-processing PIR schemes which enjoy sublinear pre-processing without the use of public-key cryptography. Beimel et al. [2] showed by leveraging a global server-side pre-processing, it is possible to construct an information theoretic 2-server PIR with $O(n^{1/3})$ bandwidth, $O(n/\log^2 n)$ computation, while consuming $O(n^2)$ server storage. The same work also showed an incomparable information-theoretic scheme with $O(n^{1/2+\epsilon})$ cost in both computation and bandwidth, while incurring $n^{1+\epsilon'}$ server storage where ϵ' is a constant dependent on ϵ.

Under a client-specific pre-processing model, the recent work PIANO [43] and the subsequent work of Mughees et al. [34] constructed single-server PIR schemes with $\widetilde{O}(\sqrt{n})$ bandwidth and server computation, $\widetilde{O}_\lambda(\sqrt{n})$ client computation per query, while consuming $\widetilde{O}_\lambda(\sqrt{n})$ client storage. Their one-time preprocessing is done by letting the client streamingly download the whole database and dynamically update the client's local state. Interestingly, their schemes relied only on one-way functions (OWFs) and do not make use of public-key cryptography. By contrast, classical (single-server) PIR with non-trivial bandwidth implies oblivious transfer [15], i.e., we cannot get classical single-server PIR in a blackbox way from OWF [24]. The reason why Piano [43] and Mughees et al. [34] got away using only OWF is because their schemes require that the client make a streaming pass over the entire database during preprocessing; however, the cost of this preprocessing can be amortized over an unbounded number of subsequent queries.

1.1   Our Results

We show new results that improve the state of our understanding regarding pre-processing PIR. In all of our constructions, the server only needs to store the original database and need not store any per-client state.

Main Result 1. First, we construct a two-server pre-processing PIR scheme with asymptotically better bandwidth than prior work, relying only on the existence of PRFs (which is equivalent to the existence of one-way functions). Our result is stated in the following theorem.

Theorem 1 (Two-server pre-processing PIR with improved bandwidth). *Assume the existence of one-way functions. There exists a two-server pre-processing PIR scheme with $O_\lambda(n^{1/4})$ bandwidth and $O_\lambda(n^{1/2})$ computation per query, while incurring $\widetilde{O}_\lambda(n^{1/2})$ client storage.*

In comparison with the prior work of Beimel et al. [2], our Theorem 1 achieves significant asymptotic improvements in both bandwidth, computation, and server-side storage. On the other hand, we need to assume one-way functions whereas

Table 1. Comparison of single-server and two-server pre-processing PIR schemes (for unbounded queries). Any single-server scheme immediately implies a two-server result with the same performance bounds. n is the size of the database and m is the number of clients. The computation overhead counts both the client and the server's computation, and here we report the expected computation. The server space counts only the extra storage needed on top of storing the original database.

Scheme	Assumpt.	Compute	Comm.	Space		#	Concrete
				client	server	servers	eff
With public-key cryptography							
[12]	LWE	$\tilde{O}_\lambda(\sqrt{n})$	$\tilde{O}_\lambda(\sqrt{n})$	$\tilde{O}_\lambda(\sqrt{n})$	$\tilde{O}_\lambda(m \cdot n)^*$	1	✗
[27,42]	LWE	$\tilde{O}_\lambda(\sqrt{n})$	$\tilde{O}_\lambda(1)$	$\tilde{O}_\lambda(\sqrt{n})$	$\tilde{O}_\lambda(m \cdot n)^*$	1	✗
[29]	Ring-LWE	$\text{poly}((\log n)^{1/\epsilon})$	$\text{poly}((\log n)^{1/\epsilon})$	0	$n^{1+\epsilon}$	1	✗
[39]	LWE	$\tilde{O}_\lambda(\sqrt{n})$	$\tilde{O}_\lambda(1)$	$\tilde{O}_\lambda(\sqrt{n})$	0	2	✗
[28]	Various	$\tilde{O}_\lambda(\sqrt{n})$	$\tilde{O}_\lambda(1)$	$\tilde{O}_\lambda(\sqrt{n})$	0	2	✓
Our work	Various	$\tilde{O}_\lambda(\sqrt{n})$	$\tilde{O}(\sqrt{n})$ offline $\tilde{O}_\lambda(1)$ online	$\tilde{O}_\lambda(\sqrt{n})$	0	1	✓
Without public-key cryptography							
[2]	None	$O(n/\log^2 n)$	$O(n^{1/3})$	0	$O(n^2)$	2	✗
[2]	None	$O(n^{1/2+\epsilon})$	$O(n^{1/2+\epsilon})$	0	$O(n^{1+\epsilon'})^{**}$	2	✗
[13]	OWF	$\tilde{O}_\lambda(\sqrt{n})$	$\tilde{O}(\sqrt{n})$	$\tilde{O}_\lambda(\sqrt{n})$	0	2	✓
[25]	OWF	$O(n)$	$\tilde{O}_\lambda(1)$	$\tilde{O}_\lambda(\sqrt{n})$	0	2	✓
[34,43]	OWF	$\tilde{O}_\lambda(\sqrt{n})$	$O(\sqrt{n})$	$\tilde{O}_\lambda(\sqrt{n})$	0	1	✓
Our work	OWF	$O_\lambda(\sqrt{n})$	$O_\lambda(n^{1/4})$	$\tilde{O}_\lambda(\sqrt{n})$	0	2	✓
Our work	OWF	$O_\lambda(\sqrt{n})$	$O(\sqrt{n})$ offline $O_\lambda(n^{1/4})$ online	$\tilde{O}_\lambda(\sqrt{n})$	0	1	✓

$*$: In the unbounded query setting, some earlier works [12,27,42] require that the next pre-processing is persistently piggybacked on the current window of $O(\sqrt{n})$ operations, and the pre-processing consumes $O_\lambda(n)$ server space per client to evaluate under FHE an $\tilde{O}(n)$-sized circuit containing a sorting network. $**$: $\epsilon' > 0$ depends on ϵ.

Beimel et al. [2]'s schemes are information theoretic; further, we additionally require $\tilde{O}(\sqrt{n})$ space on each client. However, our construction that gives Theorem 1 is simple and concretely efficient, which is another advantage over Beimel et al..

Main Result 2. Second, we construct a new pre-processing PIR scheme in the single-server setting that improves the *online* bandwidth in comparison with the state-of-the-art. In this theorem, we differentiate between online bandwidth and offline bandwidth. The online bandwidth is the bandwidth necessary for the client to obtain an answer to its query, so it matters to the response time of the client. The offline bandwidth is the cost of background maintenance work amortized to each query, and is not on the critical path of the client's response time.

Theorem 2 (Single-server preprocessing PIR with improved online bandwidth). *Assume the existence of one-way functions. There exists a single-server pre-processing PIR scheme with* $O_\lambda(n^{1/4})$ *online bandwidth,* $O(n^{1/2})$

offline bandwidth, $O_\lambda(n^{1/2})$ server computation and $\widetilde{O}_\lambda(n^{1/2})$ client computation per query, while incurring $\widetilde{O}(n^{1/2})$ client storage.

In comparison with the state-of-the-art scheme PIANO, Theorem 2 improves the online bandwidth cost from $\widetilde{O}(\sqrt{n})$ to $\widetilde{O}_\lambda(n^{1/4})$, while keeping all other costs the same. Moreover, recall that earlier works [12,13], proved the time-space product lower bound, showing that the product of the client space and the online server time has to be at least linear in n. In this sense, Theorem 2 is tight (upto polylogarithmic factors) in terms of this time-space product.

Similar to Piano [43] and Mughees et al. [34], our 1-server result adopts the same model where the client is allowed to make a streaming pass over the database during preprocessing (while consuming small client space). Otherwise, we would encounter the well-known OT barrier [15].

We evaluate the concrete performance of our 1-server scheme in Sect. 6.

Additional Results. While our main results focus on constructions in Minicrypt, if we are willing to assume classical PIR with $\widetilde{O}_\lambda(1)$ bandwidth (which is known from various assumptions such as LWE, Φ-hiding, Damgård-Jurik, DDH, QR) [6,16,22,33], our techniques would then give rise to a concretely efficient single-server PIR scheme with $\widetilde{O}_\lambda(1)$ *online* bandwidth, $\widetilde{O}(\sqrt{n})$ offline bandwidth and computation per query, consuming $\widetilde{O}_\lambda(\sqrt{n})$ client storage. In comparison, although the earlier works by Zhou et al. [42] and Lazzaretti and Papamanthou [27] claim to achieve polylogarithmic (online and offline) bandwidth, their schemes suffer from a significant drawback, that is, the server would have to persistently store at least n amount of state per client! Specifically, Zhou et al. [42] and Lazzaretti and Papamanthou [27] require the pre-processing phase of the next epoch be piggybacked on the queries of the current epoch; however, their pre-processing phase requires that the server allocate at least n amount of space per client, to perform homomorphic evaluation of a circuit which is super-linear in size. So far, in the unbounded query setting, it is not known how to get polylogarithmic overall bandwidth (including offline and online) per query *under any assumption*, assuming that the server stores only the original database. We state this additional result in the following theorem.

Theorem 3. *Assume the existence of a classical single-server PIR scheme (i.e., without pre-processing) that enjoys $\widetilde{O}_\lambda(1)$ bandwidth per query. Then, there exists a single-server pre-processing PIR scheme with $\widetilde{O}_\lambda(1)$ online bandwidth, $\widetilde{O}_\lambda(\sqrt{n})$ computation, $\widetilde{O}(\sqrt{n})$ offline bandwidth, and requiring $\widetilde{O}_\lambda(\sqrt{n})$ client storage.*

1.2   Technical Highlights

The earlier work of Shi et al. [39] showed that assuming the existence of a privately puncturable PRF [3–5,7], one can construct an efficient 2-server pre-processing PIR scheme with $\widetilde{O}_\lambda(\sqrt{n})$ computation per query and requiring $\widetilde{O}_\lambda(\sqrt{n})$ client storage. Further, the communication per query is only polylogarithmically larger than the size of a punctured key, which can be as small as $\widetilde{O}_\lambda(1)$

using known constructions [3–5,7]. Unfortunately, the only known techniques for constructing a privately puncturable PRF [3–5,7] requires two layers of fully homomorphic encryption, and it is not known whether privately puncturable PRFs can be built from only one-way functions. The elegant TreePIR work of Lazzaretti and Papamanthou [28] showed how to replace the privately puncturable PRF with a weaker primitive called a "weak privately puncturable PRF". Unfortunately, their approach relies on recursing on a classical PIR scheme for a $\sqrt{n}$-sized database, and because this database is *dynamically constructed* during the scheme, it is not possible to pre-process it. Therefore, Lazzaretti and Papamanthou [28]'s techniques fundamentally also require public-key cryptography.

Privately Programmable Pseudorandom Set with List Decoding. Our main contribution is to come up with a new abstraction called a *Privately Programmable Pseudorandom Set with List Decoding* (PPPS). Given a PPPS key sk, we can expand the key sk to a pseudorandom set denoted Set(sk) of size $\sqrt{n}$. Further, deciding whether any element in $\{0, 1, \ldots, n-1\}$ is in the set takes only constant time. Importantly, we can call a Program algorithm to program sk such that the new set is almost the same as the original Set(sk), except that the one element in the set is now changed to another specified element. The programmed key does not leak information about which element is programmed.

Our notion of PPPS is otherwise very similar to the earlier work of Zhou et al. [42], except that we make a relaxation on the correctness when decoding a programmed key—this relaxation is the crucial reason why we can construct it from only one-way functions, whereas Zhou et al. [42]'s construction relies on LWE. More specifically, we do not require that one can correctly recover the programmed set given a programmed key sk'. Instead, we allow *list-decoding*, that is, given a programmed key sk', decoding outputs a list of candidate sets, among which one must be the true programmed set. Moreover, the list-decoding of our PPPS construction is structured, allowing succinct representation and efficient computation.

Using only one-way functions, we construct a PPPS scheme with list decoding for a pseudorandom set of size $\sqrt{n}$, where the programmed key has size $O_\lambda(n^{1/4})$.

Using such a PPPS scheme, we show how to get a two-server scheme with $O_\lambda(n^{1/4})$ communication and $\widetilde{O}_\lambda(n^{1/2})$ computation per query, using only $\widetilde{O}_\lambda(n^{1/2})$ client space (Theorem 1). Unlike TreePIR [28], our scheme need not recurse on a classical PIR scheme, and thus we do not need public-key operations.

A New Broken Hint Technique. To get our single-server scheme (Theorem 2), we encounter some further challenges. In particular, it would have been easy to make the scheme work if our PPPS scheme supported programming a key twice at two points. Specifically, in our construction, when the client consumes a pseudorandom set (represented by sk) in the hint table containing the current query x, it needs to replace the replaced entry with another randomly sampled PPPS key sk subject to containing the query x. One way to achieve this is to fetch an unconsumed key from a backup table, and program the key to contain x. However, later, when the client consumes this already-programmed key in another query y, it needs to program the point y to some other random point in order not to leak the query y.

Unfortunately, our PPPS construction does not support programming twice. Interestingly, earlier works [27,42] also encountered a similar challenge of needing to program a key twice, but there it was resolved using different techniques that relied on the LWE assumption, which would not work in our setting.

The way we resolve the problem is to introduce a new technique of allowing *broken* entries in the hint table. Basically, if the client consumes some PPPS key sk in the hint table, it simply replaces the consumed sk with a new entry sampled according to the desired distribution (required for privacy). However, since the client did not perform any preparation work during the pre-processing phase for this new entry, consuming this entry later in a new query would result in an incorrect answer, i.e., the replaced entry is *broken*. Fortunately, we can amplify correctness through repetition. We defer the details to the subsequent technical sections.

Other Applications of the Broken Hint Technique. The broken hint technique can also lead to other interesting applications. For example, recall that TreePIR is a 2-server pre-processing scheme [28]. With our new broken hint technique, we can convert TreePIR to a single-server scheme which enjoys the efficiency stated in Theorem 3.

Further Improvements. The approach of using broken entries introduces a super-logarithmic blowup in the bandwidth and computation costs, due the repetition needed for correctness amplification. In Appendix B of the online full version, we suggest an improved scheme that avoids this super-logarithmic blowup and gets us the tighter bounds stated in Theorem 2, but the resulting scheme is somewhat more complex to describe.

2   Formal Definitions

Single-Server Pre-processing PIR. We first define a single-server pre-processing PIR scheme. A single-server pre-processing PIR scheme consists of two stateful algorithms: the client and the server. The scheme consists of the two following phases.

1. **Pre-processing:** The pre-processing is run only once at the beginning. The client receives no input, while the server receives a database $DB \in \{0,1\}^n$ as input. The client and server interact and the client may store some information in its local storage. We refer to this information as "hints".
2. **Queries:** This phase is repeated for every index x of the DB that the client wants to read. For every query, the client sends a single message to the server, and the server responds with a single message. The client then performs some computation and outputs an answer β.

Correctness. Given a database DB with entries indexed by $0, 1, \ldots, n-1$, correctness entails that the query for an index $x \in \{0, 1, \ldots, n-1\}$ by the client in the query phase, results in an answer $\mathsf{DB}[x]$ (the x-th bit of DB) output by the client. Formally, correctness requires that for any security parameter $\lambda \in \mathbb{N}$, for any n, q which are polynomially bounded in λ, there exists a negligible function negl such that for any database $\mathsf{DB} \in \{0,1\}^n$, for any sequence of queries $x_1, x_2, \ldots, x_q \in \{0, 1, \ldots, n-1\}$, an honest execution of the PIR scheme with DB and queries $x_1, x_2, \ldots, x_q$ returns all correct answers with probability at least $1 - \mathsf{negl}(\lambda)$.

Privacy. Privacy of a PIR scheme entails that for any index x queried by the client to the server, the view of the server must not leak information about the query x. Formally, we define the privacy of a single-server PIR scheme as follows.

A single-server PIR scheme satisfies privacy if and only if there exists a probabilistic polynomial-time simulator $\mathsf{Sim}(1^\lambda, n)$ such that for any probabilistic polynomial-time adversary $\mathcal{A}$ acting as the server, any polynomially bounded n and q, any database $\mathsf{DB} \in \{0,1\}^n$, $\mathcal{A}$'s views in the following two experiments are computationally indistinguishable:

- Real: an honest client interacts with $\mathcal{A}(1^\lambda, n, \mathsf{DB})$ who acts as the server and may arbitrarily deviate from the prescribed protocol. In every query step $t \in [q]$, $\mathcal{A}$ may adaptively choose the next query $x_t \in \{0, 1, \ldots, n-1\}$ for the client, and the client is invoked with x_t as input.
- Ideal: the simulated client $\mathsf{Sim}(1^\lambda, n)$ interacts with $\mathcal{A}(1^\lambda, n, \mathsf{DB})$ who acts as the server and may arbitrarily deviate from the prescribed protocol. In every query step $t \in [q]$, $\mathcal{A}$ may adaptively choose the next query $x_t \in \{0, 1, \ldots, n-1\}$ for the client, and the client is invoked without x_t as input.

Two-Server Pre-processing PIR. In the two-server setting, there are two non-colluding servers, and the client may interact with both servers in both the preprocessing and query phases. The two servers do not interact with each other.

Correctness is defined in the same way as the single-server setting. For privacy, we want the definition of the single-server setting to hold for each individual server.

Additional Notation. In the formal sections later, for clarity we distinguish between a statistical security parameter denoted κ and a computational security parameter denoted λ.

3 Privately Programmable Pseudorandom Set with List Decoding

3.1 Definition

Distribution of Set $\mathcal{D}_n$. We want to construct a pseudorandom set whose distribution emulates a set $S \subset \{0, 1, \ldots, n-1\}$ of size $\sqrt{n}$ sampled from the following distribution denoted $\mathcal{D}_n$—we assume that n is a perfect forth ($n^{1/4}$ is an integer):

- Divide the n elements into $\sqrt{n}$ chunks indexed with $0, 1, \ldots, \sqrt{n} - 1$, where chunk i contains the elements $[\ell \cdot \sqrt{n}, (\ell + 1) \cdot \sqrt{n} - 1]$
- For each chunk $\ell \in \{0, 1, \ldots, \sqrt{n} - 1\}$, sample a random offset $\delta_\ell \xleftarrow{\$} \{0, 1, \ldots, \sqrt{n} - 1\}$.
- Output the following set $S := \{\ell \cdot \sqrt{n} + \delta_\ell\}_{\ell \in \{0,1,\ldots,\sqrt{n}-1\}}$.

Offset Representation of a Set. For convenience, in the rest of the section, we will always use an offset representation of a set, i.e., we will represent a set as

$$S := \{\delta_0, \ldots, \delta_{\sqrt{n}-1}\}$$

where each $\delta_i \in \{0, \ldots, \sqrt{n} - 1\}$ represents the relative offset of the i-th element inside the i-th chunk.

Privately Programmable Pseudorandom Set with List Decoding. We introduce a new abstraction called a privately programmable pseudorandom set with list decoding that we utilize in our PIR constructions that follow. Intuitively, this primitive provides an algorithm to generate a secret key that represents pseudorandom subset of $\{0, \ldots, n - 1\}$ with a specific distribution. Further, the primitive allows, given a key for a pseudorandom set, to produce a key for pseudorandom set that is the same as the starting set except for being programmed at a particular location with a specified value – with the guarantee that the new key does not reveal the programmed location. Moreover, this primitive has a list decoding algorithm, that given a programmed key outputs a list of sets such that one of them is the one is the correct set that the key represents.

Formally, define a privately programmable pseudorandom set (PPPS) with list decoding which emulates the distribution $\mathcal{D}_n$:

- $\mathsf{sk} \leftarrow \mathsf{Gen}(1^\lambda, n)$: takes in the security parameter 1^λ, the size of the set n, and outputs a secret key sk.
- $S \leftarrow \mathsf{Set}(\mathsf{sk})$: takes in a secret key sk, and expands it to a random set S of size $\sqrt{n}$. We sometimes write $\mathsf{Set}(\mathsf{sk})[i]$ to denote the element in the i-th chunk for this set.
- $\mathsf{sk}', i \leftarrow \mathsf{Program}(\mathsf{sk}, \ell, \delta_\ell)$: takes in a secret key sk, a chunk identifier $\ell \in \{0, 1, \ldots, \sqrt{n}-1\}$, a desired offset δ_ℓ within the specified chunk ℓ, and outputs a programmed key sk', and some auxiliary information i that indicates which of the decoded set will be correct.
- $\{S_0, \ldots, S_{L-1}\} \leftarrow \mathsf{ListDecode}(\mathsf{sk}')$: takes in a programmed key sk' and outputs a list of sets $S_0, S_2, \ldots, S_{L-1}$, such that one of them is the correctly programmed set corresponding to the key sk'.

Correctness. Correctness requires that for any $\lambda, n \in \mathbb{N}$, for any $\ell, \delta_\ell \in \{0, 1, \ldots, \sqrt{n} - 1\}$, the following holds with probability 1: let $\mathsf{sk} \leftarrow \mathsf{Gen}(1^\lambda, n)$, $\mathsf{sk}', i \leftarrow \mathsf{Program}(\mathsf{sk}, \ell, \delta_\ell)$, $S_0, \ldots, S_{L-1} \leftarrow \mathsf{ListDecode}(\mathsf{sk}')$, it must be that S_i is equal to the $\mathsf{Set}(\mathsf{sk})$ but replacing the ℓ-th element with δ_ℓ instead.

Pseudorandomness. We say that a PPPS scheme emulates $\mathcal{D}_n$ iff the following two distributions are computationally indistinguishable:

- Sample $S \xleftarrow{\$} \mathcal{D}_n$ and output S;
- Sample sk $\leftarrow$ Gen$(1^\lambda, n)$, output Set(sk).

Private Programmability. We require that there exists a probabilistic polynomial time simulator Sim such that for any $n \in \mathbb{N}$ that is a perfect square and polynomially bounded in λ, any $\ell \in \{0, 1, \ldots, \sqrt{n}-1\}$, any index x that belongs to the ℓ-th chunk, the outputs of the following experiments be computationally indistinguishable:

- Real. Sample sk $\leftarrow$ Gen$(1^\lambda, n)$ subject to $x \in$ Set(sk), let $\delta_\ell \xleftarrow{\$} \{0, 1, \ldots, \sqrt{n}-1\}$, and let sk$'$, _ $\leftarrow$ Program(sk, ℓ, δ_ℓ), output sk$'$.
- Ideal. Output Sim$(1^\lambda, n)$.

Efficiency. In our PIR scheme later, we need a programmed key sk$'$ to have size at most $O_\lambda(n^{1/4})$. Further, the size of the decoded list $L = n^{1/4}$. Naïvely, since each set has size $\sqrt{n}$, it would take $n^{3/4}$ space to represent the L decoded sets. However, we want our scheme to satisfy a non-trivial notion of efficiency, that is, it takes only $O(\sqrt{n})$ space to represent all L decoded sets. Specifically, the compression is possible because the L decoded sets are correlated.

3.2 Construction

Intuition. In our construction, we will divide the $\sqrt{n}$ *chunks* into $n^{1/4}$ *superblocks* where the i-th superblock contains the i-th group of $n^{1/4}$ consecutive chunks.

To program a PPPS key in some chunk ℓ with the specified offset $\tilde{\delta}$, we first expand the PPPS key to $n^{1/4}$ superblock keys denoted $k_0, \ldots, k_{n^{1/4}-1}$. Let i be the superblock corresponding to chunk ℓ. We then replace k_i with a randomly sampled superblock key $\tilde{k}_i$. We than expand k_i into $n^{1/4}$ offsets denoted $\delta_0, \ldots, \delta_{n^{1/4}-1}$, one corresponding to each chunk contained in the i-th superblock. Suppose chunk ℓ corresponds to the j-th chunk within the i-th superblock. We then replace δ_j with the desired $\tilde{\delta}$. The programmed key is the combination of $k_0, \ldots, k_{i-1}, \tilde{k}_i, k_{i+1}, \ldots, k_{n^{1/4}-1}$, and $\delta_0, \ldots, \delta_{j-1}, \tilde{\delta}, \delta_{j+1}, \ldots, \delta_{n^{1/4}-1}$. Given this programmed key, we do not know which superblock should contain the expanded offsets $\delta_0, \ldots, \delta_{j-1}, \tilde{\delta}, \delta_{j+1}, \ldots, \delta_{n^{1/4}-1}$. However, we can generate a list of $n^{1/4}$ candidate sets by plugging in the offsets $\delta_0, \ldots, \delta_{j-1}, \tilde{\delta}, \delta_{j+1}, \ldots, \delta_{n^{1/4}-1}$ into each of the $n^{1/4}$ superblocks. One of them must be the true programmed set.

Detailed PPPS Construction. Henceforth, let $\mathsf{PRF}_1 : \{0,1\}^\lambda \times \{0,1\}^{\frac{\log n}{4}} \to \{0,1\}^\lambda$, and $\mathsf{PRF}_2 : \{0,1\}^\lambda \times \{0,1\}^{\frac{\log n}{4}} \to \{0,1\}^{\frac{\log n}{2}}$ be two pseudorandom functions.

- Gen$(1^\lambda, n)$: Sample a PRF_1 key sk and output sk.
- Set(sk):

1. First, expand sk to $n^{1/4}$ superblock keys:

$$\forall i \in \{0, \ldots, n^{1/4} - 1\} : \ k_i = \mathsf{PRF}_1(\mathsf{sk}, i) \tag{1}$$

2. Next, for each superblock $i \in \{0, \ldots, n^{1/4} - 1\}$, compute the pseudorandom offset for each of its $n^{1/4}$ chunks, that is:

$$\forall i, j \in \{0, \ldots, n^{1/4} - 1\} : \ \delta_{i,j} = \mathsf{PRF}_2(k_i, j) \tag{2}$$

3. Define the alias $\delta_{i \cdot n^{1/4} + j} := \delta_{i,j}$, and output $S := \{\delta_\ell\}_{\ell \in \{0, \ldots, \sqrt{n} - 1\}}$.

– Program$(\mathsf{sk}, \ell, \widetilde{\delta})$:
  1. Expand sk to $n^{1/4}$ superblock keys denoted $k_0, \ldots, k_{n^{1/4} - 1}$ as in Eq. (1).
  2. Let $i := \lfloor \ell / n^{1/4} \rfloor$ be the superblock containing the ℓ-th chunk, let $j := \ell$ mod $n^{1/4}$ be the index of chunk ℓ within superblock i.
  3. Sample a fresh PRF key $\widetilde{k}_i$ to replace k_i with.
  4. For $j' \in \{0, 1, \ldots, n^{1/4} - 1\}$, compute $\delta_{j'} = \mathsf{PRF}_2(k_i, j')$.
  5. Output the following:

$$\mathsf{sk}' := \left(\begin{array}{c} (k_0, \ldots, k_{i-1}, \widetilde{k}_i, k_{i+1}, \ldots, k_{n^{1/4} - 1}), \\ (\delta_0, \ldots, \delta_{j-1}, \widetilde{\delta}, \delta_{j+1}, \ldots, \delta_{n^{1/4} - 1}), \end{array} \right), \quad i$$

– ListDecode(sk'):
  1. Parse $\mathsf{sk}' = (\{k_i\}_{i \in \{0, \ldots, n^{1/4} - 1\}}, \{\delta_j^*\}_{j \in \{0, \ldots, n^{1/4} - 1\}})$.
  2. $\forall i, j \in \{0, \ldots, n^{1/4} - 1\}$, compute $\delta_{i,j}$ like in Eq. (2), let S be the matrix $S := \{\delta_{i,j}\}_{i,j \in \{0, 1, \ldots, n^{1/4} - 1\}}$.
  3. For $i \in \{0, \ldots, n^{1/4} - 1\}$, let S_i be the same as S except for substituting the i-th row with $\{\delta_j^*\}_{j \in \{0, \ldots, n^{1/4} - 1\}}$. In other words,

$$S_i := \begin{pmatrix} \delta_{0,0}, & \cdots, & \delta_{0,n^{1/4} - 1}, \\ \cdots, & \cdots, & \cdots, \\ \delta_{i-1,0}, & \cdots, & \delta_{i-1,n^{1/4} - 1}, \\ \delta_0^*, & \cdots, & \delta_{n^{1/4} - 1}^*, \\ \delta_{i+1,0}, & \cdots, & \delta_{i+1,n^{1/4} - 1}, \\ \cdots, & \cdots, & \cdots, \\ \delta_{n^{1/4} - 1,0}, & \cdots, & \delta_{n^{1/4} - 1,n^{1/4} - 1}, \end{pmatrix}$$

  4. Output $(\mathsf{Flatten}(S_0), \ldots, \mathsf{Flatten}(S_{n^{1/4} - 1}))$ where Flatten outputs the vector obtained from concatenating all rows of the matrix,

Size of Programmed Key and Efficiency of ListDecode. Clearly, the programmed key sk' output by Program has size $O_\lambda(n^{1/4})$. It is also easy to have a succinct representation of size $O(\sqrt{n})$ of all $n^{1/4}$ candidate sets output by ListDecode. Specifically, one can first compute the common set S of size $\sqrt{n}$ (we abuse the notation that this set is derived from flattening the matrix S in ListDecode). Then, the symmetric difference between the i-th candidate set and the common set S is just $2n^{1/4}$ elements (those elements in the i-th superblocks).

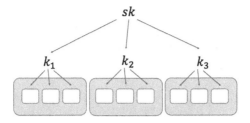

Fig. 1. Two-layer set representation. The first layer key expands to $n^{1/4}$ superblock keys. Each superblock key further expands to $n^{1/4}$ offsets, one for each chunk in the superblock.

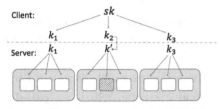

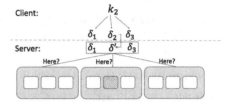

Step 1: The client expands the PPPS key to $n^{1/4}$ superblock keys and replaces the key corresponding to x's superblock with a random key.

Step 2: The client expands the replaced superblock key to $n^{1/4}$ offsets and replaces x's offset to a random one. The server constructs the candidate sets by plugging these offsets into every superblock.

Fig. 2. Illustration about how PPPS is used in our PIR schemes. The client programs the key and the server will decode the list of candidate sets.

So the succinct representation (and hence the efficient algorithm) of ListDecode takes $O_\lambda(\sqrt{n})$ space and time.

Efficient Set Membership. The above construction also supports $O_\lambda(1)$-time set membership query. Given a secret key sk that has not been programmed, to check if some element $x \in \mathsf{Set(sk)}$ or not, one simply has to check

$$\mathsf{PRF}_2(\mathsf{PRF}_1(\mathsf{sk}, \lfloor \ell/n^{1/4} \rfloor), \quad \ell \bmod n^{1/4}) \overset{?}{=} x \bmod n^{1/2} \text{ where } \ell = \lfloor x/n^{1/2} \rfloor$$

3.3 Proof of Correctness

To see correctness, let $\mathsf{sk} \leftarrow \mathsf{Gen}(1^\lambda, n)$, let $\mathsf{sk}', i^* \leftarrow \mathsf{Program(sk}, \ell, \delta_\ell)$. Recall that sk' can be parsed as $\mathsf{sk}' = (\{k_i\}_{i \in \{0,\dots,n^{1/4}-1\}}, \{\delta_i^*\}_{i \in \{0,\dots,n^{1/4}-1\}})$, and by construction, we know that $i^* = \lfloor \ell/n^{1/4} \rfloor$ is the index of the superblock that contains the chunk ℓ. Let $j^* := \ell \bmod n^{1/4}$. Let $S_\emptyset := \mathsf{Set(sk)}$, and we can view $S_\emptyset$ as a $n^{1/4} \times n^{1/4}$ matrix. The correct programmed set S^* is $S_\emptyset$ but replacing the element at index (i^*, j^*) with δ_ℓ.

Below, we show that the set S_i output by ListDecode is the same as S^*. By construction, in the ListDecode(sk') algorithm, the intermediate set S is the same as $S_\emptyset$ except for the i^*-th row. Further, the i^*-th row of $S_\emptyset$ is the same as $\{\delta_j^*\}_{j \in \{0,\ldots,n^{1/4}-1\}}$ but replacing the j^*-th element with δ_ℓ. Additionally, the S_i output by ListDecode is obtained by replacing the i^*-th row of S with $\{\delta_i^*\}_{i \in \{0,\ldots,n^{1/4}-1\}}$.

3.4   Proof of Security

We now prove pseudorandomness and private programmability assuming the security of the underlying PRF_1 and PRF_2.

Pseudorandomness. Pseudorandomness follows directly from the pseudorandomness of the underlying PRFs.

Private Programmability. We can consider the following sequence of hybrid experiments. Fix an arbitrary chunk identifier ℓ and an index x that belongs to the ℓ-th chunk. Throughout, let $i^* = \lfloor \ell/n^{1/4} \rfloor$, let $j^* = \ell \mod n^{1/4}$.

Experiment Real. Recall the definition of the real experiment. Sample a PRF key sk such that $\mathsf{PRF}_2(\mathsf{PRF}_1(\mathsf{sk}, i^*), j^*) = x \mod \sqrt{n}$. Let $\delta_\ell \xleftarrow{\$} \{0, 1, \ldots, \sqrt{n}-1\}$, and let $\mathsf{sk}', \_ \leftarrow \mathsf{Program}(\mathsf{sk}, \ell, \delta_\ell)$, output sk'.

Experiment Hyb. Same as Real except with the following modification: when executing the $\mathsf{Program}(\mathsf{sk}, \ell, \delta_\ell)$ algorithm instead of using the $k_0, \ldots, k_{n^{1/4}-1}$ keys that are expanded using $\mathsf{PRF}_1(\mathsf{sk}, \cdot)$, sample $k_0, \ldots, k_{n^{1/4}-1}$ at random subject to $\mathsf{PRF}_2(k_{i^*}, j^*) = x \mod \sqrt{n}$.

Lemma 1. *Suppose that PRF_1 is secure. Then, Hyb is computationally indistinguishable from Real.*

Proof. Suppose there is an efficient adversary $\mathcal{A}$ that can distinguish Real and Hyb with non-negligible probability. We can construct the following efficient reduction $\mathcal{B}$ which can distinguish a PRF from a random function with non-negligible probability. Basically, $\mathcal{B}$ is interacting with its own challenger who either answers queries using a PRF or using a truly random function. $\mathcal{B}$ will query its own challenger on the inputs $0, 1, \ldots, n^{1/4} - 1$, and it will obtain $k_0, \ldots, k_{n^{1/4}-1}$ from its challenger. It will check if k_{i^*} satisfies the relation $\mathsf{PRF}(k_{i^*}, j^*) = x \mod \sqrt{n}$. If not, $\mathcal{B}$ aborts and outputs 0. Otherwise, it runs the Program algorithm where it plugs in the terms $k_0, \ldots, k_{n^{1/4}-1}$ as the superblock keys. It gives the resulting sk' to $\mathcal{A}$. Henceforth, we use $b = 0$ to denote the world in which $\mathcal{B}$'s challenger uses a truly random function, and we use $b = 1$ to denote the world in which $\mathcal{B}$'s challenger uses a randomly sampled PRF function. We use the notation $\Pr_b[\cdot]$ to denote the probability of events in world $b \in \{0, 1\}$. Let G be the good event that the relation $\mathsf{PRF}(k_{i^*}, j^*) = x \mod \sqrt{n}$ is satisfied.

$$\Pr_b[\mathcal{B} \text{ outputs } 1] = 0 \cdot \Pr_b[\overline{G}] + \Pr_b[\mathcal{A} \text{ outputs } 1|G] \cdot \Pr_b[G]$$

We know that $\Pr_0[G] = 1/\sqrt{n}$ which is non-negligible. If the PRF is secure, then it must be that $|\Pr_1[G] - \Pr_0[G]| \leq \mathsf{negl}(\lambda)$ due to a straightforward reduction to PRF security. Therefore, we have that

$$\left| \Pr_1[\mathcal{B} \text{ outputs } 1] - \Pr_0[\mathcal{B} \text{ outputs } 1] \right|$$

$$= \left| \Pr_1[\mathcal{A} \text{ outputs } 1|G] \cdot \Pr_1[G] - \Pr_0[\mathcal{A} \text{ outputs } 1|G] \cdot \Pr_0[G] \right|$$

$$\geq \left| \Pr_1[\mathcal{A} \text{ outputs } 1|G] - \Pr_0[\mathcal{A} \text{ outputs } 1|G] \right| \cdot \frac{1}{\sqrt{n}} - \mathsf{negl}(\lambda)$$

Observe also that in world 0, conditioned on G, $\mathcal{A}$'s view in the experiment is identically distributed as Hyb. In world 1, conditioned on G, $\mathcal{A}$'s view in the experiment is identically distributed as Real. Therefore, the term

$$\left| \Pr_1[\mathcal{A} \text{ outputs } 1|G] - \Pr_0[\mathcal{A} \text{ outputs } 1|G] \right|$$

represents $\mathcal{A}$'s advantage in distinguishing Real and Hyb. We can now conclude that if $\mathcal{A}$ can distinguish Real and Hyb with non-negligible probability, then $\mathcal{B}$ can break PRF security with non-negligible probability.   ∎

Experiment Ideal. The Ideal experiment is almost the same as Hyb except with the following modification: when outputting the sk', instead of using the $\delta_0, \ldots, \delta_{j^*-1}, \delta_{j^*+1}, \delta_{n^{1/4}-1}$ terms derived from evaluating $\mathsf{PRF}_2(k_{i^*}, \cdot)$ at the points $0, 1, \ldots, j^* - 1, j^* + 1, \ldots, n^{1/4} - 1$, we now sample $\delta_0, \ldots, \delta_{j^*-1}, \delta_{j^*+1}, \delta_{n^{1/4}-1}$ at random from $\{0, \ldots, n^{1/2} - 1\}$ instead.

Observe that in the Ideal experiment, we no longer make use of knowledge of the query x. Therefore, the description of the Ideal experiment also uniquely specifies the simulator Sim we want to construct.

Lemma 2. *Suppose that* PRF_2 *is secure. Then,* Ideal *is computationally indistinguishable from* Hyb.

Proof. It suffices to show that the following to probability ensembles are computationally indistinguishable for any fixed $\delta^* \in \{0, 1, \ldots, \sqrt{n} - 1\}$, and $j^* \in \{0, 1, \ldots, n^{1/4} - 1\}$.

1. Distr$_0$: Output a randomly sampled vector $\delta_0, \ldots, \delta_{n^{1/4}-1} \in \{0, 1, \ldots, \sqrt{n} - 1\}^{n^{1/4}}$.
2. Distr$_1$: Sample a PRF key k subject to $\mathsf{PRF}_2(k, j^*) = \delta^*$. Sample $\delta' \in \{0, 1, \ldots, \sqrt{n} - 1\}$ at random. For $j \in \{0, 1, \ldots, n^{1/4} - 1\}$, compute $\delta_j = \mathsf{PRF}_2(k, j)$. Output $\delta_0, \ldots, \delta_{j^*-1}, \delta', \delta_{j^*+1}, \ldots, \delta_{n^{1/4}-1}$.

If there is an efficient adversary $\mathcal{A}$ that can distinguish between the above Distr$_0$ and Distr$_1$ with non-negligible probability, we can construct an efficient reduction $\mathcal{B}$ that can distinguish whether it is interacting with a random oracle or a randomly chosen PRF function. Basically, $\mathcal{B}$ sends the inputs $0, \ldots, n^{1/4} - 1$

to the oracle it is interacting with, and gets back $\delta_0, \ldots, \delta_{n^{1/4}-1}$. If $\delta_{j^*} \neq \delta^*$, then $\mathcal{B}$ aborts and outputs 0. Otherwise, it replaces δ_{j^*} with a random value from $\{0, \ldots, n^{1/2} - 1\}$ and gives the resulting vector to $\mathcal{A}$. Suppose $\mathcal{B}$ is interacting with a random oracle, then conditioned on the good event $\delta_{j^*} = \delta^*$, $\mathcal{A}$'s view is identically distributed as Distr_0. On the other hand, suppose $\mathcal{B}$ is interacting with a PRF, then conditioned on the good event $\delta_{j^*} = \delta^*$, $\mathcal{A}$'s view is identically distributed as Distr_1. The rest of the proof can be completed due to a similar probability calculation as Lemma 1. ∎

4 Our Two-Server PIR Scheme

4.1 Construction

Intuition. The scheme has three major components.

- *Preprocessing.* The client randomly samples $\tilde{O}(\sqrt{n})$ privately programmable pseudorandom sets, each of size $\sqrt{n}$. It queries the right server for the sets' parities, storing them along with the keys. Moreover, the client queries the right server for the values of logarithmic numbers of randomly sampled indices for each $\sqrt{n}$-size chunk. Those entries are stored as the "replacement" entries.
- *Online Query.* Given a query x, the client finds a set S such that $x \in S$. The client then finds a replacement entry r that resides in the same chunk as x. The client privately programs the set, intending to change it from S to $(S/\{x\}) \cup \{r\}$. Once the client knows the parity for this new set, it can computes $\mathsf{DB}[x]$ because it already knows $\mathsf{DB}[r]$ and the parity for S. The client uses the PPPS programming function to program the set, and sends the programmed key sk' to the left server. The *left server* runs the list decoding algorithm, then computes and returns all $n^{1/4}$ candidate sets' parities. The client knows that there is one candidate parity corresponding to the correct set $(S/\{x\}) \cup \{r\}$, which is enough to compute the answer.
- *Refresh.* Each query consumes a set. After each query, the client just samples a new set conditioned on it containing the query x, and queries the *right server* for its parity with the same query technique mentioned above. The new set will replace the consumed set.

Detailed Algorithm for Bounded, Random Queries. We describe the detailed construction for $Q = \sqrt{n} \log \kappa \cdot \alpha$ random, distinct queries in Fig. 3. We can easily extend such a scheme to support unbounded, arbitrary queries using known techniques [42]. For completeness, we explain how the extension works shortly after.

Efficiency. Observe that the list decoding produces $n^{1/4}$ candidate sets each of size $\sqrt{n}$. Naively, expanding all sets and computing their corresponding parities takes $O_\lambda(n^{3/4})$ time. We are still going to rely on the fact that ListDecode has an $O(\sqrt{n})$-size succinct representation to optimize the computation. Recall that we can first compute the common set of size $\sqrt{n}$, and then the symmetric difference

---

Two-server scheme for $Q = \sqrt{n} \log \kappa \cdot \alpha$ queries

Offline preprocessing.

- *Hint table.* Let $M_1 = \sqrt{n} \log \kappa \cdot \alpha(\kappa)$. For each $i \in [M_1]$, sample a fresh PPPS key sk_i, send sk_i to the <u>right server</u> and receive a parity $p_i := \oplus_{j \in \mathsf{Set}(\mathsf{sk}_i)} \mathsf{DB}[j]$ back. Let $T := \{(\mathsf{sk}_i, p_i)\}_{i \in [M_1]}$ denote the client's *hint table*.

- *Replacement entries.* For each chunk $\ell \in \{0, \ldots, \sqrt{n} - 1\}$, repeat the following $M_2 = 3 \log \kappa \cdot \alpha(\kappa)$ times: sample a random index $r_1 \in \{0, \ldots, n - 1\}$ in chunk ℓ, send r_1 to the <u>left server</u>, and receive $\mathsf{DB}[r_1]$. Store the tuple $(r_1, \mathsf{DB}[r_1])$. Similarly, for each chunk $\ell \in \{0, \ldots, \sqrt{n} - 1\}$, repeat the following M_2 times: sample a random index r_2 in chunk ℓ, send r_2 to the <u>right server</u>, and receive $\mathsf{DB}[r_2]$. Store the tuple $(r_2, \mathsf{DB}[r_2])$.

Query for index $x \in \{0, 1, \ldots, n - 1\}$.

1. **Step 1: (Client Querying)**
   - Find the first entry (sk, p) in the hint table such that $x \in \mathsf{Set}(\mathsf{sk})$. [a]
   - Find the first unconsumed replacement entries $(r_1, \mathsf{DB}[r_1])$ retrieved from right server, such that r_1 is in $\mathsf{chunk}(x)$. [b]
   - $(\mathsf{sk}_1', j_1) \leftarrow \mathsf{Program}(\mathsf{sk}, \mathsf{chunk}(x), r_1 \bmod \sqrt{n})$.
   - Send sk_1' to the left server.

2. **Step 2: (Client Reconstructing)**
   - Receive $(\beta_{0,1}, \ldots, \beta_{n^{1/4}-1,1})$ from the left server.
   - Save the answer as $y = p \oplus \mathsf{DB}[r_1] \oplus \beta_{j_1,1}$.

3. **Step 3: (Client Refreshing)**
   - Sample sk_2 such that $x \in \mathsf{Set}(\mathsf{sk}_2)$.
   - Find the first unconsumed replacement entries $(r_2, \mathsf{DB}[r_2])$ retrieved from left server, such that r_2 is in $\mathsf{chunk}(x)$.
   - $(\mathsf{sk}_2', j_2) \leftarrow \mathsf{Program}(\mathsf{sk}_2, \mathsf{chunk}(x), r_2 \bmod \sqrt{n})$.
   - Send sk_2' to right server.
   - Receive $(\beta_{0,2}, \ldots, \beta_{n^{1/4}-1,2})$ from the right server.
   - Replace the hint (sk, p) with $(\mathsf{sk}_2, \mathsf{DB}[r_2] \oplus \beta_{j_2,2} \oplus y)$ in the table.

4. **Server Responding: (Same for Left and Right Server)**
   - Upon receiving sk', compute $(S_0, S_1, \ldots, S_{n^{1/4}-1}) \leftarrow \mathsf{ListDecode}(\mathsf{sk}')$.
   - Return $(\beta_0, \ldots, \beta_{n^{1/4}-1})$ to the client where $\beta_i = \oplus_{i \in S_b} \mathsf{DB}[i]$.

---

[a] In a rare case, if not found, let sk be a freshly sampled PPPS key subject to $x \in \mathsf{Set}(\mathsf{sk})$, and let $p = 0$.

[b] In a rare case, if such an r_1 is not found, let it be a random index in $\mathsf{chunk}(x)$, and use 0 whenever $\mathsf{DB}[r_1]$ is needed later.

Fig. 3. Two-server preprocessing PIR with $O_\lambda(n^{1/4})$ communication, $O_\lambda(n^{1/2})$ computation based on PRFs.

between each possible decoding set and the common set will only contain $2n^{1/4}$ elements. Therefore, to compute the parities for all $n^{1/4}$ possible sets, we first compute the parity for the common set S, which takes $O_\lambda(\sqrt{n})$ time. Then, it takes $O_\lambda(n^{1/4})$ time to enumerate the symmetric difference between the i-th set and the common set, which suffices to compute the parity for the i-th set. So the total computation time will be $O_\lambda(\sqrt{n})$.

Supporting Unbounded, Arbitrary Queries. For completeness, we review the techniques described in previous works for upgrading the scheme for Q random, distinct queries to a scheme supporting unbounded, arbitrary queries. We can easily get rid of the distinct query assumption in the following way: we require the client to store a local cache of size Q for caching the most recent Q queries. If the client wants a repeated query, it can lookup in the cache and make a distinct fake query.

Further, we can assume that the queries are random without loss of generality as follows: we can let the client and the servers agree on a small-domain pseudorandom permutation (PRP) [23,38] (which is implied by one-way functions [23]) upfront and the server can permute the database according to the PRP. Another option is let one of the servers build the database as a key-value storage and use a cuckoo hash table [37,41] directly based on a PRF to locate the queries, and share it with the other server. Notice that, in both implementations, the client can still make queries adaptively depending on the real query sequence and the responses, which is sufficient for practical usage. Then, as long as the client makes the queries independent of the randomness of the PRP/PRF, those queries can be considered as uniformly random. This assumption is only needed for the correctness.

Lastly, we can remove the bounded Q query assumption as follows: we use a pipelining trick suggested in earlier works [42,43]. Essentially, we can spread the pre-processing for the next window of Q queries over the current window of Q queries.

Theorem 4. *Let $\alpha(\kappa)$ be any superconstant function. Suppose that $\mathsf{PRF}_1, \mathsf{PRF}_2$ are secure pseudorandom functions, and that n is bounded by $\mathsf{poly}(\lambda)$ and $\mathsf{poly}(\kappa)$. The two-server scheme in Fig. 3 that supports $Q = \sqrt{n} \log \kappa \cdot \alpha$ random, distinct queries is private, and correct with probability $1 - \mathsf{negl}(\lambda) - \mathsf{negl}(\kappa)$ for some negligible function $\mathsf{negl}(.)$. Further, it achieves the following performance bounds:*

- *$O_\lambda(\sqrt{n} \log \kappa \alpha(\kappa))$ client storage and no additional server storage;*
- ***Pre-processing Phase:***
  - *$O_\lambda(n \log \kappa \cdot \alpha)$ server time and $O_\lambda(\sqrt{n} \log \kappa \cdot \alpha)$ client time;*
  - *$O_\lambda(\sqrt{n} \log \kappa \cdot \alpha)$ communication;*
- ***Query Phase:***
  - *$O_\lambda(\sqrt{n})$ expected client time and $O_\lambda(\sqrt{n})$ server time per query;*
  - *$O_\lambda(n^{1/4})$ communication per query.*

Therefore, the amortized communication per query is $O_\lambda(n^{1/4})$, and the amortized server computation and expected client computation per query is $O_\lambda(\sqrt{n})$.

Proof. We defer the privacy and correctness proofs to Sect. 4.2 and Sect. 4.3 respectively. Here, we focus on proving the efficiency claims.

The client stores $M_1 = \sqrt{n} \log \kappa \cdot \alpha$ number of PPPS keys, and $M_2 = 3 \log \kappa \cdot \alpha$ number of replacement entries per chunk. Therefore, the space required is $O_\lambda(\sqrt{n} \log \kappa \cdot \alpha)$.

During the offline phase, the client sends M_1 PPPS keys to the right server, and sends M_2 indices per chunk to either server for constructing replacement entries. Therefore, the offline communication is bounded by $O_\lambda(\sqrt{n} \log \kappa \cdot \alpha)$. The right server needs to expand the sets for each PPPS key received and evaluate the xor-sums. Both servers need to return the bits for the replacement entries. Therefore, the total server computation is bounded by $O_\lambda(n \log \kappa \cdot \alpha)$.

During the query phase, the client sends one programmed PPPS key to each server, and the size of a programmed key is at most $O_\lambda(n^{1/4})$. Each server sends back the xor-sums of $n^{1/4}$ candidate sets. Each candidate set has size $n^{1/2}$, however, all $n^{1/4}$ candidate sets has a succinct representation of size only $n^{1/2}$, and server can compute this succinct representation in time $O_\lambda(n^{1/2})$. Further, it is not hard to see that due to the structure of the candidate sets, the server can compute all $n^{1/4}$ xor-sums in time only $O(n^{1/2})$. Therefore, the servers' running time is bounded by $O_\lambda(n^{1/2})$ during each query. The client needs to find a matched hint, and compute $O(1)$ xor operations during each query. Its running time is dominated by the cost of finding a matched hint, which can be done by invoking the set membership operation for each of the M_1 hints. Using Lemma 3 and the pseudorandomness property of the PPPS, the expected number of hints checked until a key sk such that Set(sk) contains the current query is found is $O(\sqrt{n})$. The expected number of tries till success is $\sqrt{n}$. Therefore, the client's expected running time per query is upper bounded by $O_\lambda(\sqrt{n})$. ∎

4.2 Privacy Proof

Suppose that the underlying PPPS scheme satisfies private programmability. Below, we prove the privacy of our two-server PIR scheme.

In the pre-processing phase, the server sends the sets Set(sk_i) only to the right server, thereby no information about these sets is leaked to the left server. Similarly, no information about the indices r_1 is leaked to the right server and no information about the indices r_2 is leaked to the left server. We will first the lemma about the distribution of client's hint table, when the adversary controls either of the left or right server.

Lemma 3. *Recall that in each time step t, the adversary $\mathcal{A}$ adaptively chooses a query $x_t \in \{0, 1, \ldots, n-1\}$ for the client. At the end of each time step t, the client's hint table is distributed as a table of size M_1 where each entry is a freshly sampled PPPS key, even when conditioned on $\mathcal{A}$'s view so far.*

Proof. Suppose the above statement holds at the end of time step $t-1$. We prove that it still holds at the end of time step t. Since the hint table is distributed as a fresh randomly sampled table even when conditioned on $\mathcal{A}$'s view at the end of $t-1$, we may henceforth assume an arbitrary fixed query x_t. The distribution of the hint table before the t-th query can be equivalently rewritten as:

– First, sample the decision whether any of the M_1 entries contains the current query x_t, and if so, which is the first entry (denoted i^*) that contains x_t. If not found, we assume $i^* = M_1 + 1$.

– For each $i < i^*$, sample a random PPPS key subject to not containing x_t.
– For each $i = i^*$, sample a random PPPS key subject to containing x_t.
– For each $i > i^*$, sample a random PPPS key.

Using the above interpretation, it is easy to see that the distribution of the hint table after the t-th query is unaltered no matter which of the two servers $\mathcal{A}$ controls.   ∎

Left Server Privacy. We first construct the following simulator for proving left server privacy.

Simulator Construction

– During the pre-processing phase, for each chunk ℓ, sample M_2 random indices belonging to ℓ, send them to $\mathcal{A}$.
– During each query, call the simulator of the PPPS scheme which outputs sk', send sk' to $\mathcal{A}$.

Indistinguishability of Real and Ideal. We now prove the indistinguishability of the Real and Ideal for both the servers assuming the private programmability of the underlying PPPS scheme.

First, due to Lemma 3, we can equivalently rewrite the Real experiment for the right server as follows: at the end of each time step, resample the entire hint table freshly at random before continuing to answer more queries. As a result, the view of $\mathcal{A}$ who controls the right server is distributed as:

– *Pre-processing phase.* For each chunk ℓ, send M_2 random indices in chunk ℓ to $\mathcal{A}$.
– *Each time step t.*
  • sample a PPPS key sk at random subject to containing the query x_t; sample δ at random from $\{0, \ldots, \sqrt{n} - 1\}$.
  • call $\mathsf{sk}', \_ \leftarrow \mathsf{Program}(\mathsf{sk}, \mathsf{chunk}(x_t), \delta)$;
  • send sk' to $\mathcal{A}$.

One way to see this is to think of the distribution of the table as the equivalent distribution in the proof of Lemma 4. Further, observe that each $r_2 \bmod \sqrt{n}$ in the scheme is distributed randomly from the perspective of the left server, since they were only sent to the right server during the pre-processing phase.

Therefore, the rest of the proof follows due to a straightforward hybrid argument where we replace the programmed keys (denoted sk' earlier) sent to the right server in all time steps one by one with a simulated key, relying on the private programmability of the underlying PPPS.

Right Server Privacy. We first construct the following simulator for proving right server privacy.

Simulator Construction

- During the pre-processing phase, send M_1 randomly sampled PPPS keys to $\mathcal{A}$. Further, for each chunk ℓ, sample M_2 random indices in ℓ, send them to $\mathcal{A}$.
- During each query, call the simulator of the PPPS scheme which outputs sk', send sk' to $\mathcal{A}$.

Indistinguishability of Real and Ideal. We now prove the indistinguishability of the Real and Ideal for both the servers assuming the private programmability of the underlying PPPS scheme. The view of $\mathcal{A}$ who controls the right server is distributed as:

- *Pre-processing phase.* Sample M_1 random PPPS keys, and send them to $\mathcal{A}$. Further, for each chunk ℓ, send M_2 random indices in chunk ℓ to $\mathcal{A}$.
- *Each time step t.*
  - sample a PPPS key sk at random subject to containing the query x_t; sample δ at random from $\{0, \ldots, \sqrt{n} - 1\}$.
  - call sk', _ ← Program(sk, chunk(x_t), δ);
  - send sk' to $\mathcal{A}$.

To see the above, observe that each $r_1 \bmod \sqrt{n}$ in the scheme is distributed randomly from the perspective of the right server, since they were only sent to the left server during the pre-processing phase.

Therefore, the rest of the proof follows due to a straightforward hybrid argument where we replace the programmed keys (denoted sk' earlier) sent to the right server in all time steps one by one with a simulated key, relying on the private programmability of the underlying PPPS.

4.3 Correctness Proof

We show that with $Q = \sqrt{n} \log \kappa \cdot \alpha$ random, distinct queries, the probability of ever having correctness error is negligibly small. An error can happen if one of the following bad events take place:

- *No matched hint.* During some query for x, no hint is found that contains the query x.
- *Depleting replacement entries.* During some query for x, there is no more replacement entry of the form $(r_1, \mathsf{DB}[r_1])$ or $(r_2, \mathsf{DB}[r_2])$ corresponding to chunk(x).

Below, we show that the probability of each bad event during a window of Q random, distinct queries is negligibly small.

Probability of No Matched Hint. Due to Lemma 3, for any fixed time step t, we can assume the client's hint table contains freshly sampled PPPS keys and is independent of the current query x_t. Due to the pseudorandomness property of the PPPS, the sets generated by the keys in the hint table are computationally indisintinguishable from M_1 sets independently sampled from the distribution $\mathcal{D}_n$. Below we calculate the probability that a fixed element x_t is not in any of the M_1 sets sampled independently from $\mathcal{D}_n$—the probability that x_t is not contained in any entry in the client's hint table can only be negligibly different.

The probability that one set sampled from $\mathcal{D}_n$ contains x_t is $1/\sqrt{n}$. Therefore, the probability that none of the M_1 sets contains x_t is $(1 - 1/\sqrt{n})^{M_1}$, and given the choice of $M_1 = \sqrt{n}\log \kappa\alpha(\kappa)$ where $\alpha(\kappa)$ is a super-constant function, this probability is negligibly small in κ.

Finally, taking a union bound over all polynomially many time steps, the probability of ever not having a matched hint is negligibly small in κ.

Probability of Depleting Replacement Entries. One can only deplete the replacement entries of some chunk ℓ if the chunk ℓ is encountered more than M_2 times. With Q random distinct queries, each query will hit a random chunk. The expected number of hits per chunk is therefore $Q/\sqrt{n} = \log \kappa \cdot \alpha$. By the Chernoff bound, the probability that the number of visits to some fixed chunk ℓ exceeds $M_2 = 3\log \kappa\cdot\alpha$ is negligibly small in κ as long as $\alpha(\kappa)$ is a super-constant function.

Finally, taking a union bound over all chunks and all polynomially many time steps, the probability of ever depleting replacement entries of any chunk is negligibly small in κ.

5   Our Single-Server PIR Scheme

5.1   Construction

Notation. For $x \in \{0, 1, \ldots, n - 1\}$, we define $\mathsf{chunk}(x) := \lfloor x/n^{1/2}\rfloor$ and $\mathsf{superblock}(x) := \lfloor \mathsf{chunk}(x)/n^{1/4}\rfloor$. We assume $(\mathsf{Gen}, \mathsf{Set}, \mathsf{Program}, \mathsf{Decode})$ is a PPPS scheme over the distribution $\mathcal{D}_n$ as described in Sect. 3.

Intuition. The major differences between our single-server scheme and the two-server scheme are summarized below.

- *Preprocessing.* The two server scheme allows the client to do preprocessing with one server and do online queries with another server. Our single-server scheme uses the technique from Piano [43] such that the client makes a streaming pass over the whole database (retrieving from the only server) and runs the preprocessing locally.
- *Query and Refresh.* The two-server scheme allows the client to replace a consumed set with a new set on-the-fly, because the client can query another server for the new parity. Instead, in the single-serve scheme, we use a new <u>broken hint</u> idea. The client still generates a new set after the query, but it only marks the new set as "broken hint" since the parity is unknown. To ensure correctness, the client now *uses all the matched sets* given one query, and as long as there is one non-broken hint, the answer can be computed correctly.

Single-Server Scheme for $Q = \sqrt{n}/2$ Queries [a]

Notation. κ denotes a *statistical* security parameter, λ denotes a computational security parameter. We use $\alpha(\kappa)$ to denote an arbitrarily small super-constant function.

Preprocessing.

- Client samples $M_1 = 2\sqrt{n} \log \kappa \cdot \alpha(\kappa)$ master PPPS keys denoted $\mathsf{sk}_1, \ldots, \mathsf{sk}_{M_1} \in \{0,1\}^\lambda$. Initialize the parities $p_1, \ldots, p_{M_1}$ to zeros.
- Client downloads the whole DB from the server in a streaming way: when the client has the j-th chunk $\mathsf{DB}[j\sqrt{n} : (j+1)\sqrt{n}]$:
  - *Update primary table:* for $i \in [M_1]$, let $p_i \leftarrow p_i \oplus \mathsf{DB}[\mathsf{Set}(\mathsf{sk}_i)[j]]$.
  - *Store replacement entries:* sample and store $M_2 = 3 \log \kappa \cdot \alpha(\kappa)$ tuples of the form $(r, \mathsf{DB}[r])$ where r is a random index from the j-th chunk.
  - Delete $\mathsf{DB}[j\sqrt{n} : (j+1)\sqrt{n}]$ from the local storage.
- At this moment, let $T := \{(\mathsf{sk}_i, p_i)\}_{i \in [M_1]}$ denote the client's *hint table*. Mark all the hints as "good".

Query for index $x \in \{0, 1, \ldots, n-1\}$.

1. Client: For each matched entry (sk_i, p_i) such that $x \in \mathsf{Set}(\mathsf{sk}_i)$ in the hint table, do the following unless there are already $M_3 = 3 \log \kappa \cdot \alpha$ matched entries:
   - For the first good (i.e., non-broken) matched entry, find the first unconsumed replacement entry $(r, \mathsf{DB}[r])$ for $\mathsf{chunk}(x)$. [b]
   - Otherwise, sample a random index r in $\mathsf{chunk}(x)$.
   - $(\mathsf{sk}', i^*) \leftarrow \mathsf{Program}(\mathsf{sk}_i, \mathsf{chunk}(x), r \bmod \sqrt{n})$.
   - Send sk' to the server, and receive $\{\beta_i\}_{i \in \{0, \ldots, n^{1/4}-1\}}$ from the server.
   - For the first good matched entry, save the answer $p_i \oplus \beta_{i^*} \oplus \mathsf{DB}[r]$.
   - Sample a fresh PPPS key $\mathsf{sk}_{\mathrm{new}}$ subject to $x \in \mathsf{Set}(\mathsf{sk})$, and replace the consumed entry (sk_i, p_i) with $(\mathsf{sk}_{\mathrm{new}}, 0)$ and mark the entry as *broken*.
2. Client: If less than M_3 keys are sent in the previous step, send more dummy programmed keys to the server until there are M_3 keys sent [c].
3. Client: Output the saved answer. If no answer was saved, output 0.
4. Server: for each sk' received, let $S_0, \ldots, S_{n^{1/4}-1} \leftarrow \mathsf{ListDecode}(\mathsf{sk}')$. For each $i \in \{0, \ldots, n^{1/4} - 1\}$, send the xor-sum $\oplus_{j \in S_i} \mathsf{DB}[j]$ to the client [d].

---

[a] We first present the scheme supporting distinct and random queries. As mentioned, these restrictions can be removed by applying PRP and local caching.
[b] If not found, treat it as the otherwise case.
[c] The dummy key is constructed as sampling a random PPPS key sk subject to $x \in \mathsf{Set}(\mathsf{sk})$ and call $\mathsf{sk}', \_ \leftarrow \mathsf{Program}(\mathsf{sk}, \mathsf{chunk}(x), \delta')$.
[d] We use the normal representation of the set S_i and not the offset representation.

Fig. 4. Our single-server pre-processing PIR scheme.

Detailed Algorithm for Bounded, Random Queries. In Fig. 4, we describe our algorithm which supports $Q = \sqrt{n}/2$ random and distinct queries. It is well-known how to upgrade such an algorithm to support an *unbounded* number of *arbitrary* queries [42]. For completeness, we briefly describe the upgrade shortly after.

Efficiency. Observe that although the list decoding produces $n^{1/4}$ candidate sets each of size $\sqrt{n}$, all $n^{1/4}$ sets can actually be represented using only $O(\sqrt{n})$ space. Further, computing the parities of all sets takes only $O(\sqrt{n})$ time. This is because all $n^{1/4}$ sets are derived from some common set S, but replacing offsets within each of the $n^{1/4}$ superblocks with another random vector $\delta_0, \ldots, \delta_{n^{1/4}-1}$. We give a full efficiency analysis in the proof of Theorem 5.

Supporting Unbounded, Arbitrary Queries. We can easily get rid of the distinct query assumption in the following way: we can require the client to store a local cache of size Q for caching the most recent Q queries. If the client wants a repeated query, it can lookup in the cache and make a dummy query.

Further, we can assume that the queries are random without loss of generality as follows: we can let the client and the server agree on a pseudorandom permutation (PRP) [23,38] upfront and the server can permute the database according to the PRP. Another option is let the server build the database as a key-value storage and use a cuckoo hash table [37,41] directly based on a PRF to locate the queries. Notice that, in both implementations, the client can still make queries adaptively depending on the real query sequence and the responses, which is sufficient for practical usage. Then, as long as the client makes the queries independent of the randomness of the PRP/PRF, those queries can be considered as uniformly random. This assumption is only needed for the correctness.

Lastly, we can remove the bounded Q query assumption as follows: the straightforward way is that once the client finishes a window of Q queries, the client and the server reruns the preprocessing phase again, using fresh randomness. The drawback is that the client has to wait a long time before starting the next window. As previous work pointed out [42,43], we can easily avoid this drawback through a simple pipelining trick, by spreading the preprocessing work of the next Q window over the current Q window of queries.

Theorem 5. *Let $\alpha(\kappa)$ be any super-constant function. Suppose that $\mathsf{PRF}_1, \mathsf{PRF}_2$ are secure pseudorandom functions, and n is bounded by $\mathsf{poly}(\lambda)$ and $\mathsf{poly}(\kappa)$. The single-server scheme in Fig. 4 that supports $\sqrt{n}/2$ random, distinct queries is private, and correct with probability $1 - \mathsf{negl}(\lambda) - \mathsf{negl}(\kappa)$ for some negligible function $\mathsf{negl}(\cdot)$. Further, it achieves the following performance bounds:*

- $O_\lambda(\sqrt{n}\log\kappa \cdot \alpha)$ *client storage and no additional server storage;*
- ***Pre-processing Phase:***
  - $O(n)$ *server time and* $O_\lambda(n\log\kappa \cdot \alpha)$ *client time;*
  - $O(n)$ *communication;*
- ***Query Phase:***
  - $O_\lambda(\sqrt{n}\log\kappa \cdot \alpha)$ *expected client time and* $O_\lambda(\sqrt{n}\log\kappa \cdot \alpha)$ *server time per query;*
  - $O_\lambda(n^{1/4}\log\kappa \cdot \alpha)$ *communication per query.*

Therefore, the amortized online communication per query is $O_\lambda(n^{1/4} \log \kappa \cdot \alpha)$, the amortized offline communication per query is $O(\sqrt{n})$, the amortized client and server computation per query is $O_\lambda(\sqrt{n} \log \kappa \cdot \alpha)$.

Proof. We defer the privacy and the correctness proof to Sect. 5.2 and Sect. 5.3 respectively. The client only stores $M_1 = 2\sqrt{n} \log \kappa\alpha$ λ-bit keys and store in total $\sqrt{n} \cdot M_2 = 3\sqrt{n} \log \kappa \cdot \alpha$ index-value pairs. So the storage is $O_\lambda(\sqrt{n} \log \kappa \cdot \alpha)$. The pre-processing phase's performance bounds follow straightforward by the algorithm descriptions.

For the query phase, the client first enumerates all M_1 hints to find x, which takes $O_\lambda(\sqrt{n} \log \kappa \cdot \alpha)$ time. For all the $M_3 = \Theta(\log \kappa \cdot \alpha)$ found hints, the Program algorithm takes $O_\lambda(n^{1/4})$ client computation. For the server, during the query phase, the client sends M_3 programmed PPPS key to the server, the size of which is $O_\lambda(n^{1/4})$. The server sends back the xor-sum of $n^{1/4}$ candidate sets for each key after running ListDecode. Even though each candidate set has size $n^{1/2}$, all the candidate sets have a succinct representation of size $n^{1/2}$ and server can compute this representation in time $O_\lambda(n^{1/2})$. Further, as observed in Theorem 4, due to the structure of the candidate sets, the sever can compute all the $n^{1/4}$ xor-sums in time only $O(n^{1/2})$. Hence, the server's running time $O_\lambda(\sqrt{n})$.

The client needs to find M_3 matched hints, compute $O(\log \kappa \cdot \alpha)$ xor operations during each query and for the matched hints, it needs to sample fresh PPPS key $\mathsf{sk}_{\mathsf{new}}$ subject to $x \in \mathsf{Set}(\mathsf{sk}_{\mathsf{new}})$. The client's computation time is dominated by this sampling step. We consider the expected computation time: each key in the hint table will have $1/\sqrt{n}$ probability to be replaced in this and each sampling takes $O_\lambda(\sqrt{n})$ expected time to finish using Lemma 4 and pseudorandomness of PPPS, the expected number of keys checked until a key sk such that $\mathsf{Set}(\mathsf{sk})$ contains the current query is found is $O(\sqrt{n})$. So the total expected time for the query phase is $O_\lambda(\sqrt{n} \log \kappa\alpha)$ per query. The server time is $O_\lambda(\sqrt{n}(\log \kappa \cdot \alpha))$ per query. The online communication per query is $O_\lambda(n^{1/4}(\log \kappa \cdot \alpha))$. ∎

5.2 Privacy Proof

Suppose that the underlying PPPS scheme satisfies private programmability. Below, we prove the privacy of our single-server PIR scheme.

In the pre-processing phase, the server observes a single scan over the database, and thus no information is leaked. The rest of the proof will therefore focus on the query phase.

Lemma 4. *Recall that in each time step t, the adversary $\mathcal{A}$ adaptively chooses a query $x_t \in \{0, 1, \ldots, n-1\}$ for the client. At the end of each time step t, the client's hint table is distributed as a table of size M_1 where each entry is a freshly sampled PPPS key, even when conditioned on $\mathcal{A}$'s view so far.*

Proof. Suppose the above statement holds at the end of time step $t-1$. We prove that it still holds at the end of time step t. Since the hint table is distributed as a fresh randomly sampled table even when conditioned on $\mathcal{A}$'s view at the end of $t-1$, we may henceforth assume an arbitrary fixed query x_t. The distribution of the hint table before the t-th query can be equivalently rewritten as:

- First, sample the indices of the entries (henceforth denoted I) that contain the query x_t. Specifically, each $i \in [M_1]$ is chosen into the set I independently with probability $1/\sqrt{n}$.
- For each $i \notin I$, sample a random PPPS key subject to not containing x_t.
- For each $i \in I$, sample a random PPPS key subject to containing x_t.

Using the above interpretation, it is easy to see that the distribution of the hint table after the t-th query is unaltered.   ∎

Simulator Construction and the Ideal Experiment. Consider the following simulator construction which does not make use of the queries: in every time step t, call the simulator Sim of the PPPS scheme, and let the output be sk'. Send sk' to the server.

Indistinguishability of Real and Ideal. We now prove the indistinguishability of the Real and Ideal assuming the private programmability of the underlying PPPS scheme.

First, due to Lemma 4, we can equivalently rewrite the Real experiment as follows: at the end of each time step, resample the entire hint table freshly at random before continuing to answer more queries. As a result, the messages sent to $\mathcal{A}$ in each time step t is distributed as

Repeat M_3 times:
- sample a PPPS key sk at random subject to containing the query x_t; sample δ at random from $\{0, \ldots, \sqrt{n} - 1\}$.
- call $sk', \_ \leftarrow \mathsf{Program}(sk, \mathsf{chunk}(x_t), \delta)$;
- send sk' to $\mathcal{A}$.

One way to see this is to think of the distribution of the table as the equivalent distribution in the proof of Lemma 4.

Therefore, the rest of the proof follows due to a straightforward hybrid argument where we replace the programmed keys (denoted sk' earlier) sent to the server in all time steps one by one with a simulated key, relying on the private programmability of the underlying PPPS.

5.3   Correctness Proof

For the correctness analysis, we may assume that every set is sampled independently from $\mathcal{D}_n$. Due to the pseudorandomness property of the PPPS, this will only affect the correctness probability by a negligible amount.

Recall that we have a window of $Q = \sqrt{n}/2$ random, distinct queries. There are only two bad events that can cause correct failure: 1) the client cannot find a good hint that contains the query index; 2) the client runs out of replacements in a chunk.

We first analyze the second bad event, i.e., depleting replacement entries For every query, at most one replacement entry is consumed. Therefore, the second bad event only happens when the client makes more than M_2 queries in one chunk. The analysis is the same as analysis of depleting replacement entries in the proof of correctness for our 2-server scheme (see Sect. 4.3).

The first bad event, i.e., no matched good hint, can only arise from the following events: 1) there are no good hints left that match the query; 2) there are more than M_3 matched hints but the first M_3 matched hints are all broken.

Fix a sequence of query $x_1, \ldots, x_m$ and consider the error probability for x_m. Consider the initial hint table in which each entry represents a random set sampled from $\mathcal{D}_n$. If a hint in the initial hint table contains x_m and does not contain $x_1, \ldots, x_{m-1}$, this hint will remain good until the query for x_m. We have that, for any hint

$$\Pr[\text{ the hint contains } x_m] = 1/\sqrt{n} \ .$$

Further, conditioned on a hint containing x_m, if x_i and x_m are not in the same chunk, then the hint contains x_i with probability $1/\sqrt{n}$ because each chunk has its own randomness. Moreover, if x_i and x_m are in the same chunk, this hint definitely will not contain x_i. Hence, we have that

$$\Pr\left[\text{ hint is broken} \mid \text{the hint contains } x_m\right]$$
$$\leq \Pr\left[\exists i \in \{1, \ldots, m-1\} \text{ hint contains } x_i \mid \text{ the hint contains } x_m\right]$$
$$\leq (m-1)/\sqrt{n} \leq Q/\sqrt{n} \leq 1/2 \ .$$

Therefore,

$$\Pr[\text{ hint is good and contains } x_m]$$
$$\geq \Pr\left[\text{ hint is good} \mid \text{ the hint contains } x_m\right] \cdot \Pr\left[\text{ the hint contains } x_m\right] \geq 1/(2\sqrt{n}) \ .$$

Then, the probability that there is no good hint matching x_m in the table is at most

$$\left(1 - \frac{1}{2\sqrt{n}}\right)^{M_1} = \left(1 - \frac{1}{2\sqrt{n}}\right)^{2\sqrt{n}\ln\kappa\cdot\alpha(\kappa)}$$
$$\leq (1/e)^{\ln\kappa\alpha(\kappa)} = \kappa^{-\alpha(\kappa)}.$$

Now let us argue that for query x_m, the probability of more than M_3 hints being matched is small. Due to the Lemma 4, we may assume that at the beginning of each query, the hint table contains freshly and independently chosen sets. Each set sampled from $\mathcal{D}_n$ contains the query with probability $1/\sqrt{n}$. The expected number of hints that match the query is therefore $M_1/\sqrt{n} = 2\log\kappa \cdot \alpha$. Using the Chernoff bound, we have that the probability of more than more than $M_3 = 3\log\kappa \cdot \alpha$ hints being matched is bounded by a negligibly small function in κ.

Finally, we can apply a union bound over all $\sqrt{n}/2$ queries and conclude that the probability of the first bad event (i.e., no matched good hint) ever happening is negligibly small in κ.

6   Evaluation

We implement our optimized single-server PIR scheme (Appendix B of the online full version) and compare it against a state-of-the-art preprocessing single server PIR scheme (Piano [43]). We show that the performance of our scheme is reasonably efficient and practical, while having a huge advantage in the online communication.

Implementation and Parameters. We implement our scheme with Go, based on the open-sourced code base of Piano [43]. Our code base is open-sourced[1]. We set $Q = \sqrt{n}\ln n$, set the correctness failure parameter κ to 40 and set the computational security parameter λ to 128. We adjust the chunk size and also superblock size by constant factors to optimize the overall performance. The parameter combination ensures the failure probability is bounded by $2^{-\kappa} = 2^{-40}$ for all queries. We use 128-bit keys and use AES to instantiate the PRF.

Evaluation Setup. We evaluate our scheme and the baseline scheme on a single AWS m5.8xlarge instance with 128 GB of RAM and run the experiment on local network. In this case, the network will not be the bottleneck. However, we do expect that our scheme can perform relatively better compared to Piano in a network-constrained environment.

6.1   Experiments Results

We evaluate the schemes under two scenarios: 1) a 64 GB database with 4.2 billions of 16-byte entries; 2) a 100 GB database with 1.6 billions of 64-byte entries. As the same as Piano, we use 8-thread parallelization during the preprocessing phase, and only use a single thread during the online phase.

In Table 2, we show the cost for the one-time preprocessing, the online query cost, and also the amortized offline cost. Notice that the amortized offline cost can also be considered as the background maintenance cost that is not on the critical path of the query.

Computation Costs. As seen in Table 2, our scheme is worse compared to Piano in terms of computation cost. The offline time is worse by around $1.4\times$ (the same for the maintenance time), and the per query online time is worse by around $3.0\times$. Although the two schemes have the same asymptotic computation costs, our scheme is more complicated, resulting in a larger constant factor. The most significant factor is that our scheme needs to make at least two PRF evaluations per hint, while Piano only makes one PRF evaluation. Also, Piano further optimizes the PRF evaluations. This explains the $3.0\times$ gap.

Communication Costs. Our scheme has the same offline communication cost (same streaming preprocessing) and a much better online communication compared to Piano. The asymptotic online communication is $O_\lambda(n^{1/4})$ for our scheme

---

[1] https://github.com/wuwuz/QuarterPIR.

Table 2. Performance of our scheme and Piano on 64 GB and 100 GB sized databases. The 64 GB database has 16-byte entries and the 100 GB database has 64-byte entries. "Am." is an abbreviation of "Amortized". We report the online costs as well as the offline costs amortized over $Q = \sqrt{n} \ln n$ queries.

	64GB		100GB	
	Piano	Ours	Piano	Ours
Preprocessing				
Client time	81min	114min	32min	46min
Communication	64GB	64GB	100GB	100GB
Per query				
Online Time	14.0ms	42.7ms	11.9ms	46.3ms
Online Communication	256KB	5KB	100KB	8KB
Am. Offline Time	3.3ms	4.7ms	2.2ms	3.2ms
Am. Offline Communication	46KB	46KB	120.5KB	120.5KB
Client Storage	419MB	684MB	839MB	1.8GB

and is $O(\sqrt{n})$ for Piano. Thus, given a bigger n, the gap will be bigger. The concrete performance also depends on many other factors, including the size of the entries, the size of the chunk and the size of the superblock. We see a 12× gap when n is 1.6 billions in the 100 GB database case (with a larger entry size) and a 51× gap when n is 4.2 billions in the 64 GB database case (with a smaller entry size).

Storage Costs. Our scheme has worse storage cost compared to Piano. In our experiment, the gap is 1.6×–2.1×. Our optimized scheme needs to additionally store the superblock parity for each hint, and also stores the constraints generated during the query phase, compared to Piano.

Acknowledgments. This work is in part supported by a grant from ONR, a grant from the DARPA SIEVE program under a subcontract from SRI, a gift from Cisco, Samsung MSL, NSF awards under grant numbers 1705007, 2128519 and 2044679.

References

1. Beigel, R., Fortnow, L., Gasarch, W.I.: A nearly tight bound for private information retrieval protocols. In: Electronic Colloquium on Computational Complexity (ECCC) (2003)
2. Beimel, A., Ishai, Y., Malkin, T.: Reducing the servers computation in private information retrieval: PIR with preprocessing. In: Bellare, M. (ed.) CRYPTO 2000. LNCS, vol. 1880, pp. 55–73. Springer, Heidelberg (2000). https://doi.org/10.1007/3-540-44598-6_4

3. Boneh, D., Kim, S., Montgomery, H.: Private puncturable PRFs from standard lattice assumptions. In: Coron, J.-S., Nielsen, J.B. (eds.) EUROCRYPT 2017. LNCS, vol. 10210, pp. 415–445. Springer, Cham (2017). https://doi.org/10.1007/978-3-319-56620-7_15

4. Boneh, D., Lewi, K., Wu, D.J.: Constraining pseudorandom functions privately. In: Fehr, S. (ed.) PKC 2017. LNCS, vol. 10175, pp. 494–524. Springer, Heidelberg (2017). https://doi.org/10.1007/978-3-662-54388-7_17

5. Brakerski, Z., Tsabary, R., Vaikuntanathan, V., Wee, H.: Private constrained PRFs (and more) from LWE. In: Kalai, Y., Reyzin, L. (eds.) TCC 2017. LNCS, vol. 10677, pp. 264–302. Springer, Cham (2017). https://doi.org/10.1007/978-3-319-70500-2_10

6. Cachin, C., Micali, S., Stadler, M.: Computationally private information retrieval with polylogarithmic communication. In: Stern, J. (ed.) EUROCRYPT 1999. LNCS, vol. 1592, pp. 402–414. Springer, Heidelberg (1999). https://doi.org/10.1007/3-540-48910-X_28

7. Canetti, R., Chen, Y.: Constraint-hiding constrained PRFs for NC^1 from LWE. In: Coron, J.-S., Nielsen, J.B. (eds.) EUROCRYPT 2017. LNCS, vol. 10210, pp. 446–476. Springer, Cham (2017). https://doi.org/10.1007/978-3-319-56620-7_16

8. Chang, Y.-C.: Single database private information retrieval with logarithmic communication. In: Wang, H., Pieprzyk, J., Varadharajan, V. (eds.) ACISP 2004. LNCS, vol. 3108, pp. 50–61. Springer, Heidelberg (2004). https://doi.org/10.1007/978-3-540-27800-9_5

9. Chor, B., Gilboa, N.: Computationally private information retrieval. In: STOC (1997)

10. Chor, B., Goldreich, O., Kushilevitz, E., Sudan, M.: Private information retrieval. In: FOCS (1995)

11. Connell, G.: Technology deep dive: Building a faster ORAM layer for enclaves. https://signal.org/blog/building-faster-oram/

12. Corrigan-Gibbs, H., Henzinger, A., Kogan, D.: Single-server private information retrieval with sublinear amortized time. In: Dunkelman, O., Dziembowski, S. (eds.) EUROCRYPT 2022. Lecture Notes in Computer Science, vol. 13276, pp. 3–33. Springer, Cham (2022). https://doi.org/10.1007/978-3-031-07085-3_1

13. Corrigan-Gibbs, H., Kogan, D.: Private information retrieval with sublinear online time. In: Canteaut, A., Ishai, Y. (eds.) EUROCRYPT 2020. LNCS, vol. 12105, pp. 44–75. Springer, Cham (2020). https://doi.org/10.1007/978-3-030-45721-1_3

14. Demmler, D., Rindal, P., Rosulek, M., Trieu, N.: PIR-PSI: scaling private contact discovery. Proc. Priv. Enhancing Technol. **2018**(4), 159–178 (2018)

15. Di Crescenzo, G., Malkin, T., Ostrovsky, R.: Single database private information retrieval implies oblivious transfer. In: Preneel, B. (ed.) EUROCRYPT 2000. LNCS, vol. 1807, pp. 122–138. Springer, Heidelberg (2000). https://doi.org/10.1007/3-540-45539-6_10

16. Döttling, N., Garg, S., Ishai, Y., Malavolta, G., Mour, T., Ostrovsky, R.: Trapdoor hash functions and their applications. In: Boldyreva, A., Micciancio, D. (eds.) CRYPTO 2019. LNCS, vol. 11694, pp. 3–32. Springer, Cham (2019). https://doi.org/10.1007/978-3-030-26954-8_1

17. Dvir, Z., Gopi, S.: 2-server PIR with subpolynomial communication. J. ACM **63**(4) (2016)

18. Feamster, N.: Oblivious DNS deployed by Cloudflare and Apple. https://medium.com/noise-lab/oblivious-dns-deployed-by-cloudflare-and-apple-1522ccf53cab

19. Gasarch, W.I.: A survey on private information retrieval. Bull. EATCS **82**, 72–107 (2004)

20. Gentry, C., Ramzan, Z.: Single-database private information retrieval with constant communication rate. In: Caires, L., Italiano, G.F., Monteiro, L., Palamidessi, C., Yung, M. (eds.) ICALP 2005. LNCS, vol. 3580, pp. 803–815. Springer, Heidelberg (2005). https://doi.org/10.1007/11523468_65

21. Henzinger, A., Dauterman, E., Corrigan-Gibbs, H., Zeldovich, N.: Private web search with Tiptoe. In: 29th ACM Symposium on Operating Systems Principles (SOSP), Koblenz, Germany (2023)

22. Henzinger, A., Hong, M.M., Corrigan-Gibbs, H., Meiklejohn, S., Vaikuntanathan, V.: One server for the price of two: simple and fast single-server private information retrieval. Cryptology ePrint Archive, Paper 2022/949 (2022). https://eprint.iacr.org/2022/949

23. Hoang, V.T., Morris, B., Rogaway, P.: An enciphering scheme based on a card shuffle. In: Safavi-Naini, R., Canetti, R. (eds.) CRYPTO 2012. LNCS, vol. 7417, pp. 1–13. Springer, Heidelberg (2012). https://doi.org/10.1007/978-3-642-32009-5_1

24. Impagliazzo, R., Rudich, S.: Limits on the provable consequences of one-way permutations. In: Proceedings of the 21st Annual ACM Symposium on Theory of Computing, Seattle, Washington, USA, 14–17 May 1989, pp. 44–61. ACM (1989)

25. Kogan, D., Corrigan-Gibbs, H.: Private blocklist lookups with checklist. In: 30th USENIX Security Symposium (USENIX Security 2021), pp. 875–892. USENIX Association (2021). https://www.usenix.org/conference/usenixsecurity21/presentation/kogan

26. Kushilevitz, E., Ostrovsky, R.: Replication is not needed: single database, computationally-private information retrieval. In: FOCS (1997)

27. Lazzaretti, A., Papamanthou, C.: Single server PIR with sublinear amortized time and polylogarithmic bandwidth. Cryptology ePrint Archive, Paper 2022/830 (2022). https://eprint.iacr.org/2022/830

28. Lazzaretti, A., Papamanthou, C.: TreePIR: sublinear-time and polylog-bandwidth private information retrieval from DDH. In: Handschuh, H., Lysyanskaya, A. (eds.) CRYPTO 2023. LNCS, vol. 14082, pp. 284–314. Springer, Cham (2023). https://doi.org/10.1007/978-3-031-38545-2_10

29. Lin, W.K., Mook, E., Wichs, D.: Doubly efficient private information retrieval and fully homomorphic ram computation from ring LWE. In: STOC (2023)

30. Lipmaa, H.: First CPIR protocol with data-dependent computation. In: Lee, D., Hong, S. (eds.) ICISC 2009. LNCS, vol. 5984, pp. 193–210. Springer, Heidelberg (2010). https://doi.org/10.1007/978-3-642-14423-3_14

31. Melchor, C.A., Crespin, B., Gaborit, P., Jolivet, V., Rousseau, P.: High-speed private information retrieval computation on GPU. In: Proceedings of the 2008 Second International Conference on Emerging Security Information, Systems and Technologies, SECURWARE 2008, Washington, DC, USA, pp. 263–272. IEEE Computer Society (2008)

32. Melchor, C.A., Gaborit, P.: A lattice-based computationally-efficient private information retrieval protocol. IACR Cryptology ePrint Archive 2007, 446 (2007)

33. Menon, S.J., Wu, D.J.: SPIRAL: fast, high-rate single-server PIR via FHE composition. In: IEEE S&P (2022)

34. Mughees, M.H., Sun, I., Ren, L.: Simple and practical amortized sublinear private information retrieval. Cryptology ePrint Archive, Paper 2023/1072 (2023)

35. Olumofin, F., Goldberg, I.: Revisiting the computational practicality of private information retrieval. In: Danezis, G. (ed.) FC 2011. LNCS, vol. 7035, pp. 158–172. Springer, Heidelberg (2012). https://doi.org/10.1007/978-3-642-27576-0_13

36. Ostrovsky, R., Skeith, W.E.: A survey of single-database private information retrieval: techniques and applications. In: Okamoto, T., Wang, X. (eds.) PKC 2007. LNCS, vol. 4450, pp. 393–411. Springer, Heidelberg (2007). https://doi.org/10.1007/978-3-540-71677-8_26

37. Pagh, R., Rodler, F.F.: Cuckoo hashing. J. Algorithms **51**(2), 122–144 (2004)

38. Ristenpart, T., Yilek, S.: The mix-and-cut shuffle: small-domain encryption secure against N queries. In: Canetti, R., Garay, J.A. (eds.) CRYPTO 2013. LNCS, vol. 8042, pp. 392–409. Springer, Heidelberg (2013). https://doi.org/10.1007/978-3-642-40041-4_22

39. Shi, E., Aqeel, W., Chandrasekaran, B., Maggs, B.: Puncturable pseudorandom sets and private information retrieval with near-optimal online bandwidth and time. In: Malkin, T., Peikert, C. (eds.) CRYPTO 2021. LNCS, vol. 12828, pp. 641–669. Springer, Cham (2021). https://doi.org/10.1007/978-3-030-84259-8_22

40. Sion, R., Carbunar, B.: On the computational practicality of private information retrieval. In: Network and Distributed Systems Security Symposium (NDSS) (2007)

41. Yeo, K.: Cuckoo hashing in cryptography: optimal parameters, robustness and applications. arXiv preprint arXiv:2306.11220 (2023)

42. Zhou, M., Lin, W.K., Tselekounis, Y., Shi, E.: Optimal single-server private information retrieval. In: Hazay, C., Stam, M. (eds.) EUROCRYPT 2023. LNCS, vol. 14004, pp. 395–425. Springer, Cham (2023). https://doi.org/10.1007/978-3-031-30545-0_14

43. Zhou, M., Park, A., Shi, E., Zheng, W.: Piano: extremely simple, single-server PIR with sublinear server computation. In: IEEE S& P (2024)

Strong Batching for Non-interactive Statistical Zero-Knowledge

Changrui Mu[1]([envelope]), Shafik Nassar[2], Ron D. Rothblum[3],
and Prashant Nalini Vasudevan[1]

[1] National University of Singapore, Singapore, Singapore
changrui.mu@u.nus.edu, prashant@comp.nus.edu.sg
[2] UT Austin, Austin, USA
shafik@cs.utexas.edu
[3] Technion, Haifa, Israel
rothblum@cs.technion.ac.il

Abstract. A zero-knowledge proof enables a prover to convince a verifier that $x \in S$, without revealing anything beyond this fact. By running a zero-knowledge proof k times, it is possible to prove (still in zero-knowledge) that k separate instances $x_1, \ldots, x_k$ are all in S. However, this increases the communication by a factor of k. Can one do better? In other words, is (non-trivial) zero-knowledge *batch verification* for S possible?

Recent works by Kaslasi et al. (TCC 2020, Eurocrypt 2021) show that any problem possessing a *non-interactive statistical* zero-knowledge proof (**NISZK**) has a non-trivial statistical zero-knowledge batch verification protocol. Their results had two major limitations: (1) to batch verify k inputs of size n each, the communication in their batch protocol is roughly $\mathrm{poly}(n, \log k) + O(k)$, which is better than the naive cost of $k \cdot \mathrm{poly}(n)$ but still scales linearly with k, and, (2) the batch protocol requires $\Omega(k)$ rounds of interaction.

In this work we remove both of these limitations by showing that any problem in **NISZK** has a *non-interactive* statistical zero-knowledge batch verification protocol with communication $\mathrm{poly}(n, \log k)$.

Keywords: Batch Verification · SZK · Zero-knowledge Proofs

1 Introduction

Zero-knowledge proofs, introduced in the groundbreaking work of Goldwasser, Micali, and Rackoff [18], allow a prover to convince a verifier that a given statement "$x \in S$" is true, without revealing anything beyond its validity. Since their inception, zero-knowledge proofs have had a profound impact on cryptography, complexity theory, and more generally throughout theoretical computer science.

The full version is available at [25].

M. Joye and G. Leander (Eds.): EUROCRYPT 2024, LNCS 14656, pp. 241–270, 2024.
https://doi.org/10.1007/978-3-031-58751-1_9

Remarkably, these proof-systems are now being used in practical systems as well.[1]

In this work, we study *batch verification* of zero-knowledge proofs: assuming that S has a zero-knowledge proof, can one prove, still in zero-knowledge, that $x_1, \ldots, x_k$ all belong to S? The immediate answer to this question is yes – one can simply prove separately that each $x_i \in S$, and the resulting protocol only has a linear in k loss in zero-knowledge error. What we ask however, is whether there is a protocol that can do so with much shorter communication.

We focus on the setting of *statistical zero-knowledge (SZK) proofs* – these are proof-systems in which both the soundness and zero-knowledge properties hold in a strong information-theoretic sense. Statistical zero-knowledge proofs are known for most of the commonly studied problems in cryptography and are closely related to constructions of encryption and signature schemes. In particular, the study of batch verification of zero-knowledge proofs is motivated by their enabling of batch proofs that public-keys, ciphertexts or signatures are well-formed, and more generally, for better understanding the rich structure[2] of **SZK**.

The question of batch verification for statistical zero-knowledge proofs was raised in a recent pair of works by Kaslasi *et al.* [22,23]. These works showed that every problem possessing a *non-interactive* **SZK** proof, has an interactive **SZK** proof-system for batch verification, with non-trivial communication complexity. Recall that non-interactive statistical zero-knowledge proofs (**NISZK**) [15,35], similarly to their computational counterparts [2], are defined in the *common random string* model, in which all parties have access to a common random string (aka a CRS).[3]

Thus, [22,23] construct **SZK** batch verification protocols for every problem in **NISZK**. However, their results suffer from some important drawbacks. First, the communication complexity of their protocol is (up to poly-logarithmic factors) $\text{poly}(n) + O(k)$. This is better than the naive protocol which has communication $\text{poly}(n) \cdot k$, but the improvement is still limited. We call a batching protocol achieving such communication a *weak batching protocol*, since, ideally, we would like the dependence on k to be much smaller. Second, while the starting point is a problem that has a *non-interactive* **SZK** proof, the resulting batch protocol is highly interactive, requiring $\Omega(k)$ rounds of interaction, which can be exorbitant for large values of k.

Our Results. In this work, we improve on the results of [22,23] and construct a *strong* batch verification protocol in which the communication only grows *poly-logarithmically with k*. Furthermore, the resulting protocol is non-interactive (in the CRS model).

---

[1] See https://zkproof.org and references therein.

[2] See Vadhan's thesis [38] for further background.

[3] As is typically done in the statistical setting (see [15]), we focus on the case that the CRS is a *uniform* random string (rather than the related common "reference" string model, which is sometimes considered in the computational setting).

Theorem 1 (Batch Proofs for NISZK). *Suppose* $\Pi \in$ **NISZK** *and* $k = k(n) \in \mathbb{N}$ *such that* $k(n) \leq 2^{n^{0.01}}$, *where* n *denotes the length of a single instance of* Π. *Then,* $\Pi^{\otimes k}$ *has an* **NISZK** *protocol in which the communication complexity and the length of the common random string is* $\mathrm{poly}(n, \log k)$. *The completeness, soundness, and zero-knowledge errors are all negligible in* n *and* k, *and the verifier runs in time* $\mathrm{poly}(n, k)$.

Here and throughout, $\Pi^{\otimes k}$ denotes the set of k-tuples of inputs $(x_1, \ldots, x_k)$ (of equal length), all of which belong to Π.[4] We remark that a $\mathrm{poly}(n)$ dependence in the communication complexity is inevitable, even when $k = 1$, assuming the existence of a sub-exponentially hard problem in **NISZK** (this follows from known limitations on laconic provers [13,17]).

In addition, our protocol is significantly simpler than those in [22,23]. The main technical observations underlying it are that:

1. Hash functions with bounded independence (specifically 4-wise independence suffices) preserve very specific types of entropies, and,
2. A cascade of such hash functions can be derandomized while still preserving this behaviour.

We elaborate on these points next.

1.1 Technical Overview

In this section, we provide an overview of our construction of batch **NISZK** protocols for any problem in **NISZK**.

Batching Protocol for Permutations. The starting point of our protocol is the same as those of [22,23]. In particular, [22] first demonstrate a very simple batching protocol for a specific promise problem in **NISZK**, denoted PERM, of checking whether a given *length-preserving* circuit $C : \{0,1\}^n \rightarrow \{0,1\}^n$ is a permutation (these are the YES instances of the problem) or a 2-to-1 function (these are the NO instances). Hereon, we will use the notation $N = 2^n$. Overloading notation, we will use C to also represent the distribution induced by evaluating the circuit on a uniformly random input.

A straightforward **NISZK** protocol for (a single instance of) PERM is to have the CRS contain a random string $r \in \{0,1\}^n$ and the proof is an $x \in \{0,1\}^n$ such that $C(x) = r$. This simple protocol clearly has perfect completeness and soundness error $1/2$ (which can be amplified by repetition). The protocol is perfectly zero-knowledge since the simulator can just sample x at random and output $(x, r = C(x))$. The communication complexity and CRS length are both n, corresponding to the input and output length of C – significantly, these are otherwise independent of the size of C.

This protocol can be easily extended to prove that circuits $C_1, \ldots, C_k$ all belong to PERM as follows. The CRS is again a uniformly random $r \in \{0,1\}^n$,

---

[4] In the technical sections we refer to promise problems, in which the formal definition of $\Pi^{\otimes k}$ requires that all k inputs satisfy the promise of Π, see Sect. 2.

but now the proof is a string $x \in \{0,1\}^n$ such that $(C_k \circ C_{k-1} \circ \cdots \circ C_1)(x) = r$ (here $\circ$ denotes composition of functions). Completeness and zero-knowledge are as before. As for soundness, observe that even if one of the C_i's is 2-to-1, then the composed circuit has an image of size at most $2^n/2$ and so with probability at least $1/2$, the CRS string r is sampled outside the image and so a suitable preimage x does not exist.

Approximate Injectivity. If the problem PERM were **NISZK**-complete, we would be done – given k instances of any **NISZK** problem Π, we could reduce each of them to an instance of PERM, and run the above batch **NISZK** protocol. Unfortunately, PERM is not known to be **NISZK**-complete, and in fact seems unlikely to be, as it has a *perfect* zero-knowledge proof.

Still, [22,23] identify a closely related problem that they show to be **NISZK**-complete. This problem is called *Approximate Injectivity*, denoted by $\mathsf{AI}_{L,\delta}$, and is specified by two parameters L and δ.[5] In the $\mathsf{AI}_{L,\delta}$ problem, the instance is a circuit $C : \{0,1\}^n \to \{0,1\}^m$, where $m \geq n$, and:

- YES instances are circuits that are injective on all except a δ-fraction of inputs; that is, for all except $\delta \cdot N$ elements $x \in \{0,1\}^n$, there is no $x' \neq x$ such that $C(x) = C(x')$.
- NO instances are circuits where for all except a δ-fraction of inputs x, there are at least L elements x' such that $C(x) = C(x')$.

They then show that, even for sub-exponential values of L and δ, the problem $\mathsf{AI}_{L,\delta}$ is **NISZK**-complete.

For this overview, it will be convenient to focus first on an exact variant of $\mathsf{AI}_{L,\delta}$ that we will call *Exact Injectivity*, denoted EI_L. Here YES instances are required to be *fully* injective, whereas NO instances are exactly L-to-1. We will describe how to construct a batch **NISZK** protocol for this problem, and later describe how to make this work with just approximate injectivity.

Batch Protocol for Exact Injectivity. We would now like to design an **NISZK** protocol that distinguishes between the YES case where input circuits $C_1, \ldots, C_k : \{0,1\}^n \to \{0,1\}^m$ are all injective, and the NO case where at least one of them is highly non-injective (i.e., it is L-to-1). Simply composing the circuits as we did in the protocol for PERM does not work, even syntactically, since the co-domain of each circuit C_i is larger than the domain of C_{i+1}. Since it is in general unclear how to injectively map the co-domain of the former to the domain of the latter, a natural approach is to perform this mapping at random.

Thus, consider selecting hash functions $h_1, \ldots, h_k : \{0,1\}^m \to \{0,1\}^n$ from a suitable hash function family (e.g., of bounded independence), and applying these in between consecutive applications of the C_i's. This defines the following "chain" circuit:

$$C(x) = (h_k \circ C_k \circ \cdots \circ h_2 \circ C_2 \circ h_1 \circ C_1)(x).$$

---

[5] The **NISZK** hardness of AI also follows from the instance dependent universal one-way hashing constructed in the earlier work of Ong and Vadhan [29].

Before continuing, looking ahead, a major problem with this approach is that even if each hash function requires merely a constant number of bits to represent it, and if the hash functions are chosen independently, then they must be communicated between the parties, which implies that communication (or CRS length) still scales linearly with k. Getting around this requires an entirely separate set of techniques that we describe towards the end of this section. For now, we ignore this issue and focus on simply constructing a **NISZK** protocol with short prover to verifier communication.

Does Naive Hashing Work? Clearly, if even one of the C_i's is L-to-1, then similarly to the case of PERM, the size of the range of the chain circuit C is at most N/L. So in the NO case we have what we want, but what about the YES case? Can we argue that if $C_1, \ldots, C_k$ are all injective then C is also injective (with high probability)? Unfortunately, the answer is negative. Even if the functions h_i were chosen completely at random, by the birthday bound, a very large number of collisions is likely to occur. Let alone further compositions, the expected size of the range of even $(h_1 \circ C_1)$ is only $(1 - (1 - 1/N)^N) \cdot N \approx (1 - 1/e) \cdot N$, which is a constant factor smaller than N. These collisions from the h_i's skew the output distribution of C, and after a large ($k \gg n$) number of compositions it is unclear whether we will be able to distinguish between the YES and NO cases. Indeed, even if each composition decreases the entropy of the resulting circuit by merely $1/p(n)$ for some polynomial p, after $k \gg p$ steps, the two cases become indistinguishable.

Prior work [22, 23] handled this using a delicate interactive protocol in which information is only gradually revealed both to the prover and the verifier. This gradual process handled each circuit in the chain, in order, via a constant-round interactive protocol. In each round, the collisions coming out of the corresponding hash h_i were "nipped at the bud" (i.e., immediately when they appeared). This approach led to a total of $\Omega(k)$ rounds, which, in particular, also meant that the communication complexity was $\Omega(k)$.

At this point we depart from the [22, 23] approach. We show that as a matter of fact, in the YES case, even though there are many collisions in C, its output distribution still has higher entropy (for a particular notion of entropy) than in the NO case. Given such a gap between YES and NO instances, we then construct an **NISZK** protocol that takes advantage of this. We find the fact that we can control the output distribution of the circuit even after a huge number of compositions (i.e., even if k is sub-exponential in n) quite surprising, and we elaborate on this below.

The Range of C. To see why C stands any chance of having high entropy when all the C_i's are injective, it is useful to think about the size of its range. As observed earlier, even if C_1 is injective and h_1 is a completely random function, the expected size of the range of $(h_1 \circ C_1)$ is, with good probability, close to $(1 - 1/e) \cdot N$. This is computed as follows:

- There are N elements $y \in \{0,1\}^m$ that are in the range of C_1, since it is injective.

- For any $z \in \{0,1\}^n$, the probability there exists a y in the image of C_1 with $h_1(y) = z$ is:

$$\left(1 - (1 - 1/N)^N\right) \approx 1 - 1/e.$$

- The expected number of z's in the range of $(h_1 \circ C_1)$ is thus $\approx (1 - 1/e) \cdot N$.

It can also be shown that the size of this range concentrates around this expectation. The expected size of the range of $(h_2 \circ C_2 \circ h_1 \circ C_1)$ will also be a constant factor smaller than $(1 - 1/e) \cdot N$. If this trend continues, then after k compositions there is no hope that C will have a large range.

Fortunately, it does not. Suppose that the function $(C_i \circ h_{i-1} \circ \cdots \circ C_1)$ has range of size $S \ll N$, for some i and hash functions $h_1, \ldots, h_{i-1}$. Then, the expected size of the range of $(h_i \circ C_i \circ \cdots)$ when h_i is completely random is computed as:

- For any $z \in \{0,1\}^n$, the probability there exists a y in the image of $(C_i \circ \cdots)$ with $h_i(y) = z$ can be approximated using the Taylor series as:

$$\left(1 - (1 - 1/N)^S\right) \approx \frac{S}{N} - O\left(\frac{S^2}{N^2}\right).$$

- The expected number of z's in the range of $(h_i \circ C_i \circ \cdots)$ is thus $\approx S - O(S^2/N)$.

So if (S^2/N) is smaller than $o(S)$, the size of the range does *not* shrink by a constant factor. In other words, as we keep composing with $(h_2 \circ C_2)$, $(h_3 \circ C_3)$, etc., the size of the range of the composed circuit might quickly drop to $o(N)$, but after that the rate of its decrease goes down, and the size of the range nearly stabilises. By careful arguments along these lines, it can in fact be shown that, with high probability, the size of the range of C is at least $\Omega(N/k)$.

Entropies of C. The arguments so far indicate that if all the C_i's are injective, the range of C is of size at least $\Omega(N/k)$, whereas if even one of them is L-to-1, it is at most N/L. If L is much larger than k (as can be arranged[6]), there is a significant gap between these numbers. While this is encouraging, it is insufficient for an **NISZK** protocol. The problem of distinguishing between circuits whose range is large and ones whose range is small is, in fact, **NP**-hard[7], and thus unlikely to have an **SZK** protocol (let alone an **NISZK** one).

We do, however, know how to construct **NISZK** protocols that distinguish between circuits whose output distribution has large entropy, and circuits with a small range. To help with precision, we define the following notions of entropy of a distribution D. Below, D_x denotes the probability mass placed on the element x by D.

---

[6] Recall that $k \leq 2^{n^\varepsilon}$, for some small $\varepsilon > 0$, and as noted earlier, the problem $\mathsf{AI}_{L,\delta}$ is **NISZK**-hard [23] even for some sub-exponential values of L.

[7] This **NP**-hardness can be shown by reducing from **SAT**. Given a SAT formula ϕ, construct a circuit that takes input (x, y) where $x, y \in \{0,1\}^n$, and outputs 0^n if $\phi(x) = 0$, and y otherwise. If ϕ is not satisfiable, the size of the range of this circuit is 1, whereas if it has even one satisfying assignment, it is 2^n. So an algorithm that can distinguish between these two cases can be used to solve **SAT**.

- *Max Entropy:* $H_0(D) = \log |\text{Supp}(D)|$.
- *Shannon Entropy:* $H_1(D) = \sum_x -D_x \log D_x$.

Circuit C having a small range corresponds to $H_0(C)$ being small. Following the work of Goldreich *et al.* [15], we know **NISZK** protocols that can distinguish between circuits with large and small *Shannon* entropies. As the max entropy is always larger than the Shannon entropy, this immediately gives us an **NISZK** protocol that can distinguish between circuits with large Shannon entropy and those with small range.

So if we can show that in the YES case the composed circuit C has high Shannon entropy, we would be done. We show this by proving a stronger statement. We consider the following notion of entropy that is a lower bound on the Shannon entropy[8]:

- *Rényi Entropy:* $H_2(D) = -\log \sum_x D_x^2$.

We show that in the YES case (i.e., when $C_1, \ldots, C_k$ are injective), C actually has large Rényi entropy. We consider this notion of entropy for two reasons. First, the quantity inside the log above (i.e., $\sum_x D_x^2$, aka the collision probability of D) is simpler and easier to work with. The more important reason, however, is the following. Eventually, we are going to derandomise the construction of C so that we don't need $\Omega(k)$ bits to describe all the functions h_i. We show that the derandomization procedure we use more-or-less preserves the Rényi entropy of C. It is not at all clear, however, whether the process preserves the Shannon entropy. So it would not have been sufficient to show that C has high Shannon entropy, and we do need it to have high Rényi entropy.

Preservation of Rényi Entropy. Next we describe how we bound the Rényi entropy of C, arguing in terms of its collision probability, denoted by $\mathbf{cp}(C)$. Note that $H_2(D) = -\log(\mathbf{cp}(D))$. For each $i \in [0, k]$, define the following distribution:

$$D_i \equiv (h_i \circ C_i \circ \cdots \circ h_1 \circ C_1)(x),$$

where x is uniformly random. To show that the Rényi entropy of C is high if all the C_i's are injective, we proceed inductively, and show that C's collision probability is small. First, D_0 is simply the uniform distribution over $\{0, 1\}^n$, and its collision probability is $1/N$. We then show that for each $i \in [k]$:

$$\mathop{\mathbf{E}}_{h_i} [\mathbf{cp}(D_i)] \leq \mathbf{cp}\big(C_i(D_{i-1})\big) + \frac{1}{N} = \mathbf{cp}(D_{i-1}) + \frac{1}{N},$$

where the inequality follows from the law of total expectation and the pairwise independence of h_i, and the equality follows from the fact that C_i is injective. This shows that the expected collision probability of $D_k \equiv C$ is at most $(k+1)/N$. We then similarly bound the variances of the $\mathbf{cp}(D_i)$'s, and inductively use concentration bounds to show that, with high probability, the collision probability

---

[8] Technically, this is only one of a family of measures called Rényi entropies, of which the Shannon entropy is also one. We simply refer to this as Rényi entropy for convenience.

of D_k is not much larger than $O(k/N)$. The above bound on the expectation can be shown as long as the h_i's are drawn from a family that is pairwise-independent. And for the bound on the variance, it is sufficient that they are 4-wise independent.

So the Rényi entropy of C, with high probability over the choice of $h_1, \ldots, h_k$, is not much less than $(n - \log k)$. If at least one of the C_i's was L-to-1, then C has a range of size at most N/L, and thus max entropy of at most $(n - \log L)$. So as long as $k \ll L$, there is a gap between these bounds and we have an **NISZK** protocol that distinguishes between these cases. For any $k < 2^{n^{o(1)}}$, there is a setting of $L \gg k$ and δ for which $\mathsf{AI}_{L,\delta}$ is **NISZK**-hard, and so we can support batching of k instances of any **NISZK** problem with this approach.

Dealing with Approximate Injectivity. So far, however, we have ignored the fact that in the actual **NISZK**-complete problem $\mathsf{AI}_{L,\delta}$, the circuits are only *approximately* injective or L-to-1. In the NO case, the approximation is not an issue as it only slightly increases the size of the range of the circuit. In the YES case, however, we need to be careful.

To be more precise, recall that YES instances of $\mathsf{AI}_{L,\delta}$ are circuits where up to a δ fraction of inputs may not be mapped injectively. When this happens, the relation $\mathbf{cp}(C_i(D_{i-1})) = \mathbf{cp}(D_{i-1})$ that we used to inductively bound the collision probabilities of D_i breaks down – composition with C_i does not necessarily preserve collision probabilities any more. For instance, suppose C_1 is such that it maps $(1 - \delta)N$ inputs injectively, and maps all of the remaining δN inputs to 0^m. The collision probability of $C_1(x)$ is now at least δ^2, which could already be much larger than $O(k/N)$ and $O(L/N)$.

However, while the collision probability of $C_1(x)$ is not small, it is, in fact, close to another distribution whose collision probability is small. Consider a function $\hat{C}_1$ that satisfies the following two properties:

- $\hat{C}_1 : \{0,1\}^n \to \{0,1\}^m$ is injective.
- For any x that C_1 maps injectively, $\hat{C}_1(x) = C_1(x)$.

Fix any such function. Note that the statistical distance between $C_1(x)$ and $\hat{C}_1(x)$ is at most δ – the probability mass from all the inputs on which C_1 and $\hat{C}_1$ might disagree. And also, the collision probability of $\hat{C}_1(x)$ is $1/N$, as $\hat{C}_1$ is injective.

Recall that our earlier approach was to show that the collision probability of D_k is small. While we cannot hope for this any more following the above observations, we may still endeavour to show that D_k is *close to* a distribution whose collision probability is small. This would also be sufficient for constructing an **NISZK** protocol, using a simple reduction to the Statistical Difference from Uniform (SDU) problem (also complete for **NISZK** [15]) by hashing and using the Leftover Hash Lemma.

So far using the closeness of C_1 and $\hat{C}_1$, for any h_1, we can show the following bound on statistical distance from the data processing inequality:

$$\Delta(h_1 \circ C_1, h_1 \circ \hat{C}_1) \leq \delta.$$

So $D_1 \equiv (h_1 \circ C_1)$ is indeed close to a distribution whose collision probability is small. To take this argument further, similarly define $\hat{C}_i$ for the other circuits C_i, and define the following corresponding distributions:

$$\hat{D}_i \equiv (h_i \circ \hat{C}_i \circ \cdots \circ h_1 \circ \hat{C}_1)(x).$$

We have shown above that for any choice of h_1, the distributions D_1 and $\hat{D}_1$ are close. We would like to argue that for any choices of $h_1, \ldots, h_k$, the distributions D_k and $\hat{D}_k$ are close. It is not straightforward to argue this for further compositions, however. Ideally, we would like to also say, for instance, that for any h_1 and h_2, the distributions of $(h_2 \circ C_2 \circ h_1 \circ \hat{C}_1)$ and $(h_2 \circ \hat{C}_2 \circ h_1 \circ \hat{C}_1)$ are close, to enable a hybrid argument where we slowly replace the C_i's with the $\hat{C}_i$'s. This is, however, not true. Consider an h_1 that maps all inputs to an x on which C_2 is not injective. Then, the distance between $(C_2 \circ h_1 \circ \hat{C}_1)$ and $(\hat{C}_2 \circ h_1 \circ \hat{C}_1)$ can be very large.

Pathological cases like this can be avoided if the distribution of $(h_1 \circ \hat{C}_1)$ has high entropy. Roughly, if this distribution has high entropy, then it cannot place too much probability mass on the elements on which C_2 and $\hat{C}_2$ differ. Observe that the distance between $(C_2 \circ h_1 \circ \hat{C}_1)$ and $(\hat{C}_2 \circ h_1 \circ \hat{C}_1)$ is upper bounded by this probability mass. Using such arguments, we can show that if $\hat{D}_1 \equiv (h \circ \hat{C}_1)$ has high Rényi entropy, then the distance between D_2 and $\hat{D}_2$ is small.

Note that for any choice of $h_1, \ldots, h_k$, the entropy of any $\hat{D}_i$ is at least that of $\hat{D}_k$, as entropy cannot be increased by composition with deterministic functions. We can then proceed inductively to show that for any hash functions $h_1, \ldots, h_k$ for which $\hat{D}_k$ has high Rényi entropy, the distance between D_k and $\hat{D}_k$ is small.

That is, for any such choice of hash functions (which happens with high probability), C is close to a distribution that has high Rényi entropy. This implies, in particular, that with high probability C will be close to a distribution that has high Shannon entropy. This latter statement seems sufficient for our purposes, but is not. We will actually need the former stronger statement to perform the derandomization of C as discussed next.

Derandomizing the Reduction. What we have so far is a randomized reduction from $\mathsf{AI}_{L,\delta}^{\otimes k}$ to a problem in which the YES instances are circuits that are close to having high Rényi entropy, and NO instances are circuits that have low max entropy. As noted earlier, although throughout the previous discussion we have assumed that the hash functions $h_1, \ldots, h_k$ are truly random, it suffices to use 4-wise independent hash functions to bound the collision probability. This still yields a reduction that uses a lot of randomness. Namely, since we need to sample k independent 4-wise independent hash functions, the randomness grows linearly with k. Recall that our goal is to construct an **NISZK** protocol with a CRS of size $\mathrm{poly}(n, \log k)$. In our protocol, both the verifier and prover run the reduction using randomness from the CRS, therefore we cannot afford to sample k independent hash functions for this reduction.

It is natural to try to reduce the randomness by using correlated hash functions, but one has to be extremely careful as in each step we apply the hash function to a potentially correlated input.

We explain how to overcome this problem in the exact injectivity case, since that captures the main idea of the derandomization. We recall that our reduction outputs a chain

$$C(x) = (h_k \circ C_k \circ \cdots \circ h_2 \circ C_2 \circ h_1 \circ C_1)(x).$$

alternating between the input circuits and the random hash functions. We can view the description of the hash functions $h_1, \ldots, h_k$ as additional input to the circuit C and denote

$$C_{h_1,\ldots,h_k}(x) = (h_k \circ C_k \circ \cdots \circ h_2 \circ C_2 \circ h_1 \circ C_1)(x).$$

Completeness of our protocol relies on the guarantee that if all of the circuits $C_1, \ldots, C_k$ are injective then with high probability over $h_1, \ldots, h_k$, the circuit $C_{h_1,\ldots,h_k}$ would have a small collision probability.

Once an input x is fixed, the circuit C can be modeled as a small-width *Read Once Branching Program* (ROBP), with $h_1, \ldots, h_k$ as the inputs. The key observation is that the collision probability of C can therefore also be computed using a small-width ROBP. Hence, we can use Nisan's [28] pseudorandom generator (PRG) for ROBP to sample the $h_1, \ldots, h_k$, while nearly preserving the collision probability, and thus keeping the same guarantee even when sampling pseudorandom $h_1, \ldots, h_k$. We remark that here we crucially use the fact that the collision probability can be computed via a local process (namely sampling two inputs and checking for a collision). This does not seem to be the case for other notions of entropy (e.g., Shannon entropy), for which we do not know a similar derandomization.

In more detail, for any two fixed inputs x_1, x_2, we can define a ROBP $M_{x_1,x_2}(h_1, \ldots, h_k)$ of length k and width 2^{2n} that outputs 1 if and only if $C_{h_1,\ldots,h_k}(x_1) = C_{h_1,\ldots,h_k}(x_2)$. The collision probability can thus be written as

$$\mathbf{cp}(C_{h_1,\ldots,h_k}) = \Pr_{x_1,x_2 \leftarrow \{0,1\}^n} [M_{x_1,x_2}(h_1, \ldots, h_k) = 1].$$

Using the linearity of expectation, the expected collision probability over the choice of $h_1, \ldots, h_k$ is

$$\mathop{\mathbf{E}}_{h_1,\ldots,h_k} [\mathbf{cp}(C_{h_1,\ldots,h_k})] = \mathop{\mathbf{E}}_{x_1,x_2 \leftarrow \{0,1\}^n} \left[\Pr_{h_1,\ldots,h_k} [M_{x_1,x_2}(h_1, \ldots, h_k) = 1] \right].$$

If we employ a PRG for ROBP, with error ε, the collision probability increases by at most ε more than if $h_1, \ldots, h_k$ were sampled uniformly at random. Since the seed length in Nisan's PRG only depends logarithmically on ε, we can afford to use $\varepsilon = 2^{-\Omega(n)}$ and so the collision probability is indeed preserved up to very small factors. Thus, using Nisan's PRG reduces the seed length to $\mathrm{poly}(n, \log k)$, as desired.

The Protocol. To summarize, given k instances of any **NISZK** problem Π, both the verifier and the prover first reduce the instances to $\mathsf{AI}_{L,\delta}$ instances $C_1, \ldots, C_k : \{0,1\}^n \to \{0,1\}^m$. Then they utilize $\mathrm{poly}(n, \log k)$ bits from CRS as the seed for Nisan's PRG. The output of the PRG is then used to sample 4-wise independent hash functions, denoted as $h_1, \ldots, h_k : \{0,1\}^m \to \{0,1\}^n$. These functions are used to construct the chain circuit $C(x) = (h_k \circ C_k \circ \cdots \circ h_2 \circ C_2 \circ h_1 \circ C_1)(x)$.

In the YES case (i.e. when all instances are YES instances of Π), with probability all but negligible in n, k, there exists a $\hat{C}$ such that:

- $\hat{C}$ has high Rényi entropy.
- The distribution of C is very close to that of $\hat{C}$.

As a consequence, C can be reduced to a YES instance of SDU by hashing its output with an appropriate pairwise-independent hash function. In the NO case (i.e. some instances are NO instances of Π), the max entropy $H_0(C)$ will be small. As a result, applying the same reduction on C will yield a NO instance of SDU.

The prover and verifier then run the **NISZK** protocol for SDU on this instance. This uses an additional poly(n) bits from the CRS and poly(n) bits of communication. Here we crucially use the fact that the communication of the **NISZK** protocol for SDU only depends on the input/output size of the circuit, rather than the size of its description $\big($as in our case the former is poly(n) whereas the latter is $k \cdot$ poly$(n)\big)$. The negligible error associated with the reduction is incorporated into the completeness error of the protocol.

1.2 Related Works

The two closest relevant works, already mentioned above are [22,23], where the former constructed an *honest-verifier* **SZK** protocol for batch verification of **NISZK**, whereas the latter constructed a *malicious-verifier* (and public-coin) protocol. We remark that our **NISZK** protocol can be transformed into an interactive public-coin (malicious verifier) **SZK** protocol using standard transformations [16].

If one drops the zero-knowledge requirement and merely strives for short communication, batch verification is possible for every problem in **NP** (or more generally **PSPACE**), using the **IP** = **PSPACE** Theorem [24,36]. That protocol however has an exponential-time prover. Reingold, Rothblum and Rothblum [31,32,34] constructed batch verification protocol for every problem in **UP** (i.e., **NP** problems in which YES instances have a unique witness) in which the honest prover runs in polynomial-time given the witnesses. Curiously, this line of work also started with a protocol achieving weak batching [32] (i.e., with an additive linear dependence on k) and gradually improved to a poly-logarithmic dependence on k [31,34].

A separate and exciting line of work has constructed non-interactive *computationally sound* batch verification protocols for all of **NP** (aka batch arguments or BARGs for short) [5–9,20,21,30,39]. In contrast to the **NISZK** setting, these results focus on protocols for all of **NP** but only offer computational soundness and rely on unproven cryptographic assumptions such as LWE. A recent work by Bitansky *et al.* [1] has shown that different notions of batch proofs automatically yield hiding properties such as witness indistinguishibilty and, under suitable cryptographic assumptions, even full fledged zero-knowledge.

Lastly, we mention the work of Goel *et al.* [12] who construct efficient zero-knowledge proofs for *disjunctions*, whereas batch verification can be viewed as zero-knowledge proofs for *conjuctions*; and the works of Brakerski *et al.* [4] and Nassar *et al.* [26] who construct computationally sound protocols for *monotone policies* within **NP**.

1.3   Discussion and Open Problems

Theorem 1 introduces a *non-interactive* batching verification protocol for the **NISZK** class, achieving substantial communication efficiency compared to independent executions. This is an encouraging indication for the possibility of batch verification in zero-knowledge proofs. Below are some natural open problems for future investigation:

1. Theorem 1 gives a *non-interactive* batching verification protocol for problems in **NISZK**. The most pressing open question is whether a similar result holds for **SZK** – namely, for every $\Pi \in$ **SZK** does there exist an **SZK** proof for $\Pi^{\otimes k}$ with communication $\text{poly}(n, \log k)$? Or, alternatively, one that features less strigent, yet non-trivial, communication such as sub-linear dependence on k?

2. As highlighted in [22], one avenue of research focuses on prover efficiency. It is known that problems in **SZK** $\cap$ **NP** have **SZK** protocol where the prover is efficient given an **NP**-witness [27]. All the current batch protocols for **NISZK** proceed by reducing to **NISZK**-complete problems and thus do not preserve this efficiency. Is it possible to construct batch protocols even for **NISZK** $\cap$ **NP** that preserve prover efficiency?

3. Is it possible to improve the multiplicative overhead in our construction to be a fixed constant? That is, can we achieve communication $O(c) + \text{polylog}(n, k)$, where c is the communication for a single instance? This might necessitate avoiding the complete problems, since the reduction introduces a polynomial overhead (or, alternatively, achieving the result only for a limited class of problems).

   Pushing things even further, can we push the constant to be close to 1 (aka a "rate-1" batch-proof)? Results of this flavor have been recently achieved in the computational setting [9, 30].

4. Our protocol shows an efficient closure property of **NISZK** for conjunctions. What about more general efficient forms of closure: given a formula $\phi : \{0,1\}^k \to \{0,1\}$, does there exist an **SZK** protocol for $\phi(b_1, \ldots, b_k)$, where $b_i = 1 \leftrightarrow x_i \in S$, with sublinear in k communication?

2   Preliminaries

For any $N \in \mathbb{N}$, we denote the set of numbers $\{1, \ldots, N\}$ by $[N]$. For convenience, we may write a boolean circuit C with n input bits and m output bits as C :

$[N] \rightarrow [M]$ where $N = 2^n, M = 2^m$. For any circuit $C : [N] \rightarrow [M]$ and any set $S \subseteq [N]$, we denote by $C(S)$ the set of images of inputs in S, that is $C(S) = \{C(x) : x \in S\}$. For an element $y \in [M]$, we denote by $C^{-1}(y)$ the set of preimages of y. For any set S, we denote by U_S the uniform distribution over S. For any positive integer n, we denote by U_n the uniform distribution of $\{0, 1\}^n$.

A *promise problem* is a pair $\Pi = (Y, N)$ of disjoint sets (i.e., $Y \cap N = \emptyset$). We use $x \in \Pi$ to denote that $x \in Y \cup N$ and say that x satisfies the promise. We denote by $\text{YES}(\Pi) = Y$ and refer to this set as the "YES" instances and by $\text{NO}(\Pi) = N$ the "NO" instances.

Definition 1. *Let Π be a promise problem, and let $k = k(n) \in \mathbb{N}$. We define the promise problem $\Pi^{\otimes k}$ where*

$$\text{YES}\left(\Pi^{\otimes k}\right) = \left\{(x_1, \ldots, x_k) \in \left(\text{YES}(\Pi)\right)^k : |x_1| = \cdots = |x_k|\right\}$$

and

$$\text{NO}\left(\Pi^{\otimes k}\right) = \left\{(x_1, \ldots, x_k) \in \Pi^k : |x_1| = \cdots = |x_k|\right\} \setminus \text{YES}\left(\Pi^{\otimes k}\right).$$

2.1 Probability Theory Background

Lemma 1 (Chebyshev's inequality). *Let X be a random variable. Then, for every $\alpha > 0$:*

$$\Pr\left[|X - \mathbf{E}[X]| \geq \alpha\right] \leq \frac{\mathbf{Var}[X]}{\alpha^2}.$$

Definition 2 (Statistical Distance). *The* statistical distance *between two distributions X and Y over a finite domain D is defined as*

$$\Delta(X, Y) = \max_{S \subseteq U}(X(S) - Y(S)) = \frac{1}{2}\sum_{u \in U}|X(u) - Y(u)|.$$

Fact 1. *Let D be a domain and X be a distribution over D. If $|\text{Supp}(X)| < \delta \cdot |D|$ then $\Delta(X, U_D) > 1 - \delta$.*

Definition 3. *The* collision probability *of a distribution X is defined as*

$$\mathbf{cp}(X) = \Pr_{x, x' \leftarrow X}[x = x'].$$

Definition 4. *Consider a random variable X over domain D. For any $x \in D$, denote by $p_x = \Pr[X = x]$. We recall the following notions of entropy of X:*

- *Max Entropy: $H_0(X) = \log\left(|\{x \mid p_x \neq 0\}|\right)$.*
- *Shannon Entropy: $H_1(X) = -\sum_{x \in D} p_x \log(p_x)$.*
- *Renyi Entropy: $H_2(X) = -\log\left(\sum_{x \in D} p_x^2\right) = -\log\left(\mathbf{cp}(X)\right)$.*

Technically, all of the above (as well as the notion of "min-entropy" which we do not use in this work) are usually referred to as Renyi entropies of various orders. For convenience, we use this term only for H_2 and the terms above for the others.

Fact 2. *For any random variable X, we have: $H_2(X) \leq H_1(X) \leq H_0(X)$.*

2.2 Hash Functions with Bounded Independence

Definition 5. *(ℓ-wise Independent Hash Functions). For $\ell = \ell(n) \in \mathbb{N}$ and $m = m(n) \in \mathbb{N}$, a family of functions $F = (F_n)_{n \in \mathbb{N}}$, where $F_n = \{f : \{0,1\}^m \to \{0,1\}^n\}$ is called ℓ-wise independent if for every $n \in \mathbb{N}$ and every ℓ distinct domain elements $x_1, x_2, \ldots, x_\ell \in \{0,1\}^m$, and every $y_1, y_2, \ldots, y_\ell \in \{0,1\}^n$, it holds that:*

$$\Pr_{f \xleftarrow{\$} F_n} \left[\bigwedge_{i=1}^{\ell} f(x_i) = y_i \right] = 2^{-\ell \cdot n}.$$

Lemma 2 (See, e.g., [37, Sect. 3.5.5]). *For every $\ell = \ell(n) \in \mathbb{N}$ and $m = m(n) \in \mathbb{N}$, there exists a family of ℓ-wise independent hash functions $F(\ell) = \{f : \{0,1\}^m \to \{0,1\}^n\}$ where a random function from $F_{n,m}$ can be selected using $O(\ell \cdot \max(n, m))$ random bits, and given a description of $f \in F(\ell)$ and $x \in \{0,1\}^m$, the value $f(x)$ can be computed in time $\text{poly}(n, m, \ell)$.*

Lemma 3 (Leftover Hash Lemma [19], see also [37, Sect. 6.2]). *For any polynomial $k = k(n)$ and $\varepsilon = \varepsilon(n) \in (0,1)$, if $\mathcal{H} = \{h : \{0,1\}^n \to \{0,1\}^m\}$ is a family of pairwise independent hash functions such that $m = k - 2\log(1/\varepsilon)$, then for any distribution X over $\{0,1\}^n$ such that $\mathbf{cp}(X) < 2^{-k}$ it holds that*

$$\Delta\Big((H, H(X)), (H, U_m)\Big) \leq \varepsilon,$$

where H distributed uniformly over $\mathcal{H}$.

Remark 1. The Leftover Hash Lemma is typically described with respect to sources that have large *min-entropy*. However, examining the proof given in [37, Sect. 6.2] shows that an upper bound on the collision probability suffices.

3   Non-Interactive Statistical Zero-Knowledge

In this section, we present the formal definitions of **NISZK** and some of its complete problems that are useful in our work. In Sect. 3.1, we define a new problem that is more directly useful, and prove that it is complete for **NISZK**.

Definition 6 (NISZK). *Let $c = c(n) \in [0,1]$, $s = s(n) \in [0,1]$ and $z = z(n) \in [0,1]$. A non-interactive statistical zero-knowledge proof (**NISZK**) with completeness error c, soundness error s and zero-knowledge error z for a promise problem Π, consists of a probabilistic polynomial-time verifier V, a computationally unbounded prover P and a polynomial $\ell = \ell(n)$ such that the following properties hold:*

- *Completeness: For any $x \in \text{YES}_n(\Pi)$:*

$$\Pr_{r \leftarrow \{0,1\}^{\ell(|x|)}} [\mathsf{V}(x, r, \pi) \text{ accepts}] \geq 1 - c(n),$$

where $\pi = \mathsf{P}(x, r)$.

– **Soundness:** *For any $x \in \mathrm{NO}_n(\Pi)$:*

$$\Pr_{r \leftarrow \{0,1\}^{\ell(|x|)}}[\exists \pi^* \ s.t. \ \mathsf{V}(x, r, \pi^*) \ accepts] \leq s(n),$$

– **Zero Knowledge:** *There exists a probabilistic polynomial-time algorithm* Sim *(called the simulator) such that for any $x \in \mathrm{YES}_n(\Pi)$:*

$$\Delta\Big((U_\ell, \mathsf{P}(x, U_\ell)), \mathsf{Sim}(x)\Big) \leq z(n),$$

where U_ℓ denotes a random variable distributed uniformly over $\{0,1\}^{\ell(n)}$.

Unless otherwise specified, we assume by default that $c(\cdot), s(\cdot)$ and $z(\cdot)$ are negligible in the input size, and say that Π has an **NISZK** protocol if the latter holds. We further use **NISZK** to denote the class of all such promise problems.

We note that parallel repetition of **NISZK** reduces the completeness and soundness errors at an exponential rate, while increasing the zero-knowledge error at only a linear rate.[9] We recall some known complete problems for **NISZK** that are useful in our work.

Definition 7 (Statistical Difference from Uniform [15]). *The* Statistical Difference from Uniform *problem, denoted* SDU, *is a promise problem defined by the following sets:*

$$\mathrm{YES}_n(\mathsf{SDU}) = \{ circuit \ C \ : \ \Delta(C, U_n) < 1/n \};$$
$$\mathrm{NO}_n(\mathsf{SDU}) = \{ circuit \ C \ : \ \Delta(C, U_n) > 1 - 1/n \},$$

where C is a circuit that outputs n bits. The size *of an instance C is its output length n.*

Lemma 4 (SDU is NISZK-complete [15]). *The promise problem* SDU *is complete for* **NISZK**. *Moreover, the* **NISZK** *protocol for* SDU *only needs black-box access to the instance circuit; and for a parameter s that is any polynomial in the input and output sizes of the circuit in the instance, there are such protocols with the following properties:*

– *the communication complexity and the length of the common random string are* $\mathrm{poly}(s)$,
– *the completeness, soundness, and zero-knowledge errors are* 2^{-s}.

We note that the "moreover" part is not stated explicitly in [15], but follows by examining their proof.

---

[9] We remark that this property does not hold for interactive zero-knowledge proofs [11,14]. The reason that it works for **NISZK** is that in **NISZK** the verifier cannot cheat as there is no interaction [3].

Definition 8 (Approximate Injectivity [22,23]). *For any $L = L(n) \in \mathbb{N}$ and any $\delta = \delta(n) \in [0,1]$, the* Approximate Injectivity *problem* $\mathsf{AI}_{L,\delta}$ *is a promise problem defined as follows over circuits taking n bits of input and outputting $3n$ bits:*

$$\mathrm{YES}_n(\mathsf{AI}_{L,\delta}) = \left\{ circuit\ C\ :\ \Pr_{x \leftarrow \{0,1\}^n} \left[|C^{-1}(C(x))| > 1 \right] \leq \delta \right\};$$

$$\mathrm{NO}_n(\mathsf{AI}_{L,\delta}) = \left\{ circuit\ C\ :\ \Pr_{x \leftarrow \{0,1\}^n} \left[|C^{-1}(C(x))| < L \right] \leq \delta \right\}.$$

Lemma 5 (AI is NISZK-hard [22,23], see also [29, Theorem 2]). *For any $L(n) < 2^{n^{0.1}}$ and non-increasing $\delta(n) > 2^{-n^{0.1}}$, the problem $\mathsf{AI}_{L,\delta}$ is* **NISZK**-*hard.*

Remark 2. In [22,23], the definition of the AI problem does not restrict the output length of the circuits to $3n$ as Definition 8 does. This restricted version, however, is equivalent in complexity to the unrestricted version. An instance $C : \{0,1\}^n \to \{0,1\}^m$ of the unrestricted AI problem can be reduced to an instance $\hat{C}$ of the restricted version as follows:

- If $m > 3n$, $\hat{C}$ takes as input $(x,y) \in \{0,1\}^{n+(m-3n)/2}$ and outputs $(C(x), y)$.
- If $m < 3n$, $\hat{C}(x)$ outputs $C(x)$ padded with $(3n - m)$ zeroes.

Neither of these transformations change its membership in YES(AI) or NO(AI), and the resulting circuits are of size $O(m + n)$ larger than that of C.

3.1   Smooth Entropy Approximation

We start by defining smoothened versions of the various entropy measures defined in Sect. 2, again slightly modified from usual convention to fit our application.

Definition 9 (Smooth Entropy [33]). *For any $\varepsilon \geq 0$, the ε-smooth Rényi entropy of a random variable X is defined as:*

$$H_2^\varepsilon(X) = \max_{Y \in \mathcal{B}_\varepsilon(X)} H_2(Y),$$

where $\mathcal{B}_\varepsilon(X)$ is the set of all distributions within statistical distance ε of X.

We define the following variant of the Entropy Approximation problem [15] using the smooth Rényi and max entropies. Similar problems can be defined with other entropy measures as well [10]. We show in Lemma 6 below that this problem has an **NISZK** protocol, and that it is, in fact, **NISZK**-complete, as stated in Theorem 2.

Definition 10 (Smooth Entropy Approximation). *For any $\varepsilon = \varepsilon(n) \in [0,1]$, the ε-Smooth Entropy Approximation problem, denoted by SEA_ε, is a promise problem defined by the following sets:*

$$\mathsf{YES}_n(\mathsf{SEA}_\varepsilon) = \{(C,k) \mid H_2^\varepsilon(C) \geq k+1\};$$
$$\mathsf{NO}_n(\mathsf{SEA}_\varepsilon) = \{(C,k) \mid H_0(C) \leq k-1\},$$

where C is a circuit that takes n bits as input and outputs $m \leq 3n$ bits, and k is a positive real number that is at most the output length of C. The input and output sizes of an instance (C,k) refer to the input and output lengths of C, respectively.

Lemma 6 (NISZK Protocol for SEA). *Consider any $m = m(n)$ and $\varepsilon = \varepsilon(n)$ such that $\varepsilon(n) < o\left(1/\max(n,m) \cdot \log^2 m\right)$. Then, SEA_ε has an NISZK protocol where, for any instance (C,k) with input and output lengths n and m, respectively, the communication complexity and the length of the common random string are $\mathrm{poly}(n,m)$. The completeness, soundness, and zero-knowledge errors of this protocol are all $2^{-\Omega(\max(n,m))}$.*

Proof. We show a reduction from SEA to SDU that preserves the input and output lengths of the circuit up to a $\mathrm{poly}(n,m)$ blowup. The rest follows from Lemma 4. For any m and $k \leq m$, let $H_{m,k} = \left\{h : \{0,1\}^m \to \{0,1\}^k\right\}$ be the pairwise-independent family of hash functions promised by Lemma 2, where each hash function is described by $O(\max(m,k)) = O(m)$ bits.

Consider an instance (C,k) of $\mathsf{SEA}_{\varepsilon,g}$ where the input length of C is n and its output length is m. Construct the circuit C' that corresponds to $20 \log m$ copies of C evaluated independently. Its input length is $n' = n \cdot (20 \log m)$, and its output length is $m' = m \cdot (20 \log m)$. Similarly, let $k' = k \cdot (20 \log m)$. The reduction, on input (C,k), outputs a circuit $\widehat{C}$ that works as follows:

- It takes as input a description h of a hash function in $H_{m',k'}$ and an $x \in \{0,1\}^{n'}$.
- It outputs $\left(h, h\big(C'(x)\big)\right)$.

The output length of $\widehat{C}$ is $\hat{m} = O(m') + k' < O(\max(n',m'))$. Its input length is also $O(\max(n',m'))$.

Suppose $(C,k) \in \mathsf{YES}(\mathsf{SEA}_\varepsilon)$. That is, $H_2^\varepsilon(C) \geq k+1$, and thus $H_2^{\varepsilon'}(C') \geq k' + 20 \log m$, where $\varepsilon' = \varepsilon \cdot (20 \log m)$. This implies that there is a distribution Y that is at most ε'-far from C' that has $\mathbf{cp}(Y) \leq 2^{-(k'+20\log m)}$. Let H denote the random variable corresponding to a uniformly random $h \in H_{m',k'}$. By the leftover hash lemma (Lemma 3), the statistical distance between $(H, H(Y))$ and (H, U_k) is at most $2^{-(20\log m)/2}$. Thus, the distance between $(H, H(C))$ and (H, U_k) is at most $\varepsilon' + 2^{-10\log m} < 1/\hat{m}$. So $\widehat{C} \in \mathsf{YES}(\mathsf{SDU})$.

Suppose $(C,k) \in \mathsf{NO}(\mathsf{SEA}_\varepsilon)$. That is, $H_0(C) \leq k-1$. This means that C has support of size at most 2^{k-1}, and C' has support of size at most $2^{k'-20\log m}$. This implies that the support size of $(H, H(C'))$ is at most $|H_{m,k}| \cdot 2^{k'-20\log m} =$

$2^{-20 \log m} \cdot 2^{\hat{m}}$. This implies that the distance of $(H, H(C'))$ from (H, U_k) is at least $(1 - 2^{-20 \log m}) \geq (1 - 1/\hat{m})$. Thus, $\widehat{C} \in \mathtt{NO(SDU)}$. $\square$

Theorem 2 (SEA is NISZK-complete). *For any $\varepsilon(n) \in \left(2^{-n^{0.1}}, o(1/n)\right)$, the problem SEA_ε is **NISZK**-complete under randomized reductions.*

Proof (Proof of Theorem 2). By Lemma 6, for any $\varepsilon(n) < o(1/n)$, we know that SEA_ε is contained in **NISZK**. We now show a reduction from $\mathsf{AI}_{L,\delta}$. Specifically, for any $L = L(n)$ and $\delta = \delta(n)$, with $\varepsilon(n) = \delta(n)$, we claim that if C is a YES instance of $\mathsf{AI}_{L,\delta}$, then $(C, n-1)$ is a YES instance of SEA_ε, and the same for NO instances.

Suppose $C : \{0,1\}^n \rightarrow \{0,1\}^{3n}$ is a YES instance of $\mathsf{AI}_{L,\delta}$. Consider any injective function $\hat{C}$ on the same domain and co-domain that agrees with C on all inputs on which C is injective. Then, the statistical distance between the output distributions of C and $\hat{C}$ is at most δ. Further, the Rényi entropy of $\hat{C}$ is n. So $H_2^\varepsilon(C) = n$. Thus, $(C, n-1)$ is a YES instance of SEA_ε.

Suppose C is a NO instance of $\mathsf{AI}_{L,\delta}$. Then, the size of its range is at most $(1 - \delta) \cdot (N/L) + \delta N \leq N \cdot (\delta + 1/L)$. So $H_0(C) \leq n - \log L + \log(1 + \delta L)$. As long as $L \geq 8$ and $\delta L \leq 1$, this is at most $(n-2)$, and $(C, n-1)$ is a NO instance of SEA_ε for any ε.

Therefore, for any $\varepsilon(n) \in (2^{-n^{0.1}}, 1/8)$, choosing $\delta(n) = \varepsilon(n)$ and $L(n) = 1/\varepsilon(n)$, we get a reduction to SEA_ε from $\mathsf{AI}_{L,\delta}$, which is hard for **NISZK**. So for such ε, the problem SEA_ε is also hard for **NISZK** (Lemma 5). This completes the proof of the theorem. $\square$

4   Derandomizing Batch Reductions

In this section, we set up a framework for derandomizing the specific kinds of randomized reductions that we perform in Sect. 5. These reductions result in a sequential composition of circuits alternated with randomly chosen hash functions from some hash family. We refer to the composition as a *chaining circuit*. Due to page constraints, we only formally define chaining circuits and state our derandomization lemma. The formal proofs are deferred to the full version [25].

Definition 11 (Randomized Chaining Circuit). *Let $R : \{0,1\}^d \times \{0,1\}^m \rightarrow \{0,1\}^n$ be a Boolean circuit family and denote $R_\rho(y) := R(\rho, y)$ for each $(\rho, y) \in \{0,1\}^d \times \{0,1\}^m$, and let $C_1, \ldots, C_k : \{0,1\}^n \rightarrow \{0,1\}^m$ be a sequence of Boolean circuits. A circuit $\bar{C} : \{0,1\}^n \times \{0,1\}^{dk} \rightarrow \{0,1\}^n$ of the following form is called a randomized chaining circuit:*

$$\bar{C}(x, \rho_1, \ldots, \rho_k) = (R_{\rho_k} \circ C_k \circ \ldots \circ R_{\rho_1} \circ C_1)(x).$$

The parameter k is called the chain length.

Lemma 7. *For any $n, d, k \in \mathbb{N}$, $t \in \mathbb{R}$ and $\varepsilon, \delta \in (0,1)$, suppose $C : \{0,1\}^n \times \{0,1\}^{dk} \to \{0,1\}^n$ is a randomized chaining circuit such that:*

$$\Pr_{\rho \leftarrow \{0,1\}^{dk}} [H_2(C_\rho) > t] > 1 - \delta.$$

Then there exists a PRG $G : \{0,1\}^{seed} \to \{0,1\}^{dk}$ with $seed = \log(k) \cdot \log(k \cdot 2^n \cdot 2^d / \varepsilon) \cdot \mathrm{polylog}(d)$ such that for any $s > 0$,

$$\Pr_{\rho \leftarrow G(U_{seed})} [H_2(C_\rho) > t - s] > 1 - \delta',$$

where $\delta' = \frac{1}{2^s} + (\delta + \varepsilon) \cdot 2^{t-s}$.

5 Batching AI by Direct Composition

In this section, we show how to reduce k size-n instances of AI to a single instance of the Smooth Entropy Approximation (SEA) problem. Crucially, the length of inputs and outputs of the circuit in the resulting SEA instance is still only n. The **NISZK** protocol for this SEA instance (Lemma 6) then gives a batch protocol for AI, and thus any problem in **NISZK**.

Theorem 3. *Consider functions $k(n)$, $L(n)$, and $\delta(n) \leq 1/L(n)$, and let $\varepsilon(n) = (\delta(n)^{1/2} \cdot k(n) \cdot L(n)^{1/2})$. There is a $\mathrm{poly}(n, k)$ algorithm that, given $k = k(n)$ circuits $(C_1, \ldots, C_k)$, each taking n input bits, outputs a tuple (C, t) such that:*

- *If all of the C_i's are YES instances of $\mathsf{AI}_{L,\delta}$, then except with probability $O(k(n)^3 / L(n))$, the instance (C, t) is a YES instance of SEA_ε.*
- *If some C_i is a NO instance of $\mathsf{AI}_{L,\delta}$, then (C, t) is a NO instance of SEA_ε.*

Further, the input and output lengths of C are both n, and the algorithm uses $n \cdot \mathrm{poly}(\log k, \log n)$ bits of randomness.

Before proceeding to the proof, we restate and prove our main theorem about batching **NISZK** proofs.

Theorem 1 (Batch Proofs for NISZK). *Suppose $\Pi \in$ **NISZK** and $k = k(n) \in \mathbb{N}$ such that $k(n) \leq 2^{n^{0.01}}$, where n denotes the length of a single instance of Π. Then, $\Pi^{\otimes k}$ has an **NISZK** protocol in which the communication complexity and the length of the common random string is $\mathrm{poly}(n, \log k)$. The completeness, soundness, and zero-knowledge errors are all negligible in n and k, and the verifier runs in time $\mathrm{poly}(n, k)$.*

Proof (Proof of Theorem 1). Given k instances of Π of size n, set the parameters $L = \max(2^{\log^3(n)}, k^{\log \log k})$, $\delta = 1/L^4$, and $\varepsilon = (\delta^{1/2} \cdot k \cdot L^{1/2})$. Note that we still have $L < 2^{n^{0.1}}$ and $\delta > 2^{-n^{0.1}}$ as needed for the **NISZK**-hardness of $\mathsf{AI}_{L,\delta}$ (Lemma 5), while also satisfying the conditions required by Theorem 3. Further, ε and (k^3/L) are both negligible in both k and n. The prover and verifier in our **NISZK** protocol run as follows:

1. Using Lemma 5, reduce the k instances of Π respectively to k instances of $\mathsf{AI}_{L,\delta}$ of size $\mathrm{poly}(n, \log k)$ each.[10]
2. Reduce these k instances of $\mathsf{AI}_{L,\delta}$ to a single instance of SEA_ε with input and output length $\mathrm{poly}(n, \log k)$, using the reduction promised by Theorem 3. Here, both the prover and verifier will use $\mathrm{poly}(n, \log k)$ bits from the common random string as the randomness for the reduction. The probability that the reduction fails is at most $O(k^3/L)$ for YES instances, and 0 for NO instances.
3. Run the **NISZK** protocol for SEA_ε (with input and output lengths $\mathrm{poly}(n)$) promised by Lemma 6. This protocol has all errors bounded by $2^{-n^{\Omega(1)}}$, negligible in k and n.

Completeness, soundness, and zero-knowledge errors are negligible in k and n following those of the protocol for SEA, and using the fact that the reduction to SEA only fails with negligible probability. Overall, the length of the CRS is $\mathrm{poly}(n, \log k)$ and the communication complexity of the protocol is $\mathrm{poly}(n, \log k)$.   □

Reduction from $\mathsf{AI}_{L,\delta}^{\otimes k}$ to SEA

Input: $C_1, \ldots, C_k$, where each C_i is a circuit $C_i : \{0,1\}^n \to \{0,1\}^{3n}$ (k instances of $\mathsf{AI}_{L,\delta}$)

Output: (C, t), where C is a circuit $C : \{0,1\}^n \to \{0,1\}^n$ (one instance of SEA)

Ingredients:

- $\mathcal{H} = \left\{ h : \{0,1\}^{3n} \to \{0,1\}^n \right\}$ is a family of efficient 4-wise independent hash functions as guaranteed to exist by Lemma 2. A random function from this family is selected using $d = O(n)$ random bits. For any string $r \in \{0,1\}^d$, we will denote by h_r the function in $\mathcal{H}$ selected by this string.
- $G : \{0,1\}^s \to \{0,1\}^{dk}$ is the PRG promised by Lemma 7, with the parameters there instantiated as: n, d, k, and $\varepsilon = 2^{-5n}$. This implies a seed length of $s = (n + \log(k)) \cdot \log(k) \cdot \mathrm{polylog}(n)$.

Procedure:

1. Sample random $\rho \leftarrow \{0,1\}^s$.
2. Compute $(r_1, \ldots, r_k) \leftarrow G(\rho)$, where each $r_i \in \{0,1\}^d$.
3. Define circuit C as $C(x) = (h_{r_k} \circ C_k \circ h_{r_{k-1}} \circ C_{k-1} \circ \cdots \circ h_{r_1} \circ C_1)(x)$.
4. Output (C, t), where $t = (n - \log L + 2)$.

Fig. 1. Reducing k instances of AI to one instance of SEA

---

[10] The $\log(k)$ factor comes from our setting of the parameter L of $\mathsf{AI}_{L,\delta}$, see [23, Lemma 4.3]. It is important to note, however, that given that $k(n) \leq 2^{n^{0.01}}$, it holds $\mathrm{poly}(n, \log k) = \mathrm{poly}(n)$.

We now present, in Fig. 1, the reduction that establishes Theorem 3. Then we state Lemmas 8 and 9 about its properties. These lemmas together imply Theorem 3, as we show below. We present the proof of Lemma 9 immediately after, and prove Lemma 8 in Sect. 5.1. For the rest of the section we adopt the notation $N = 2^n$ and $L = 2^\ell$.

Lemma 8. *Let (C, t) be the output of the reduction in Fig. 1 on input circuits $(C_1, \ldots, C_k)$. For any L and δ, if all of the C_i's are YES-instance of $\mathsf{Al}_{L,\delta}$, then for any $c > 1$:*

$$\Pr\left[H_2^\varepsilon(C) < n - c \cdot \log k\right] < O\left(\frac{1}{k^{c-3}}\right),$$

where $\varepsilon = \delta^{1/2} \cdot k^{1+c/2}$.

Lemma 9. *Let (C, t) be the output of the reduction in Fig. 1 on input circuits $(C_1, \ldots, C_k)$. For any L and δ such that $\delta \cdot L \leq 1$, if at least one of the C_i's is a NO-instance of $\mathsf{Al}_{L,\delta}$, then:*

$$H_0(C) \leq n - \ell + 1.$$

Proof (Proof of Lemma 9). Suppose C_{i*} is a NO-instance of $\mathsf{Al}_{L,\delta}$. This implies that:

$$|\mathrm{Supp}(C_{i*})| \leq (1 - \delta) \cdot N \cdot \frac{1}{L} + \delta \cdot N \cdot 1 \leq N \cdot \left(\frac{1}{L} + \delta\right).$$

So even if all the other C_i's and the hash functions chosen in the reduction are injective, the number of possible images of C is at most this (since merely composing functions cannot increase the support size). So the max entropy of C can be bounded as:

$$H_0(C) = \log(|\mathrm{Supp}(C)|) \leq \log N + \log\left(\frac{1}{L} + \delta\right)$$
$$= \log N - \log L + \log(1 + \delta L)$$
$$\leq n - \ell + 1.$$

$\square$

Proof (Proof of Theorem 3). Let (C, t) be the output of the reduction in Fig. 1 on input $(C_1, \ldots, C_k)$. Note that $t = n - \ell + 2$. By Lemma 9, if even one of the C_i's is a NO-instance of $\mathsf{Al}_{L,\delta}$, then $H_0(C) \leq t - 1$, and thus (C, t) is a NO-instance of SEA_ε for any ε.

Suppose all the C_i's are YES instances of $\mathsf{Al}_{L,\delta}$. Applying Lemma 8 with $c = (\ell - 3)/\log k$, we get that:

$$\Pr\left[H_2^\varepsilon(C) \geq n - \ell + 3\right] > 1 - O\left(\frac{k^3}{L}\right),$$

where $\varepsilon < \delta^{1/2} \cdot k \cdot L^{1/2}$. Thus, (C, t) is a YES-instance of SEA_ε for such a value of ε. The input and output lengths of C and the randomness complexity of the reduction may be verified in a straightforward manner to be n and $\mathrm{poly}(n, \log k)$, respectively. This proves the theorem. $\square$

5.1   Proof of Lemma 8

For convenience, we set up the following notation in the context of the reduction in Fig. 1. For any circuit C, denote by $inj(C)$ the set of inputs on which C is injective. The input to the reduction are the circuits $C_1, \ldots, C_k : \{0,1\}^n \to \{0,1\}^{3n}$, which are all YES instances of $\mathsf{AI}_{L,\delta}$. The output is (C, t), where $C : \{0,1\}^n \to \{0,1\}^n$. We will denote the process of sampling the hash functions in the reduction by $(h_1, \ldots, h_k) \leftarrow G$ – this indicates first computing $(r_1, \ldots, r_k) \leftarrow G(\rho)$ for a uniformly random ρ, and setting h_i to be h_{r_i}. We will denote sampling k uniformly random hash functions from $\mathcal{H}$ by $(h_1, \ldots, h_k) \leftarrow \mathcal{H}^k$. For any tuple of hash functions $\overline{h} = (h_1, \ldots, h_k)$, we will denote the circuit constructed by using these for the composition by $C_{\overline{h}}$ or $C_{h_1, \ldots, h_k}$. That is,

$$C_{h_1, \ldots, h_k}(x) = (h_k \circ C_k \circ h_{k-1} \circ C_{k-1} \circ \cdots \circ h_1 \circ C_1)(x).$$

The reduction samples $\overline{h} = (h_1, \ldots, h_k) \leftarrow G$ and outputs $C_{\overline{h}}$. Our approach is to show that, with high probability over $\overline{h}$, the output distribution of the circuit $C_{\overline{h}}$ is close to that of a different function $\hat{C}_{\overline{h}} : \{0,1\}^n \to \{0,1\}^n$, which has high Rényi entropy. We start by defining this function. For each C_i, we define its *injective completion*, denoted $\hat{C}_i : \{0,1\}^n \to \{0,1\}^{3n}$, to be the lexicographically smallest function[11] that has the following two properties:

- $\hat{C}_i$ is injective.
- For all $x \in inj(C_i)$, we have $\hat{C}_i(x) = C_i(x)$.

Note that $\hat{C}_i$ always exists because the co-domain of C_i is larger than its domain. For any tuple of hash functions $\overline{h}$, the function $\hat{C}_{\overline{h}}$ is defined as:

$$\hat{C}_{h_1, \ldots, h_k}(x) = (h_k \circ \hat{C}_k \circ h_{k-1} \circ \hat{C}_{k-1} \circ \cdots \circ h_1 \circ \hat{C}_1)(x).$$

The proof now proceeds by showing the following:

1. For $(h_1, \ldots, h_k) \leftarrow G$, with high probability, $\hat{C}_{\overline{h}}$ has high Rényi entropy.
2. For any $\overline{h}$ for which $\hat{C}_{\overline{h}}$ has high Rényi entropy, the distribution of $C_{\overline{h}}$ is close to that of $\hat{C}_{\overline{h}}$.

Together, these imply that with $\overline{h} \leftarrow G$, with high probability, $C_{\overline{h}}$ has high smooth Rényi entropy, which proves the lemma. We now state these claims formally, show how to use them to prove the lemma, and then prove the claims.

Proposition 1. *For any $s \in (3, n)$, we have:*

$$\Pr_{(h_1, \ldots, h_k) \leftarrow G} \left[H_2(\hat{C}_{h_1, \ldots, h_k}) < n - \log k - s \right] < O\left(\frac{k^2}{2^s} \right).$$

---

[11] Any function that satisfies the two stated properties will do for our purpose, and the injective completion may be defined to be any such function.

Proposition 2. *For any* $(h_1, \ldots, h_k)$ *for which* $H_2(\hat{C}_{h_1,\ldots,h_k}) \geq t$, *we have:*

$$\Delta(\hat{C}_{h_1,\ldots,h_k}, C_{h_1,\ldots,h_k}) \leq k \cdot \delta^{1/2} \cdot 2^{(n-t)/2}.$$

Proof (Proof of Lemma 8). Setting $s = (c-1) \cdot \log k$, we get the following from Proposition 1:

$$\Pr_{(h_1,\ldots,h_k) \leftarrow G} \left[H_2(\hat{C}_{h_1,\ldots,h_k}) \geq n - c \cdot \log k \right] > 1 - O\left(\frac{1}{k^{c-3}}\right).$$

For any $(h_1, \ldots, h_k)$ for which the above event happens, Proposition 2 implies that:

$$\Delta(\hat{C}_{h_1,\ldots,h_k}, C_{h_1,\ldots,h_k}) \leq \delta^{1/2} \cdot k^{1+c/2},$$

which proves the lemma.   □

5.2 Proof of Proposition 1

We prove the claim by first showing a similar bound when the hash functions are sampled completely at random, and then derandomizing this using G.

Claim 1. $\Pr_{(h_1,\ldots,h_k) \leftarrow \mathcal{H}^k} H_2(\hat{C}_{h_1,\ldots,h_k}) < n - \log k - 3 < O\left(\frac{k^3}{2^n}\right).$

Proof (Proof of Proposition 1). Note that $\hat{C}_{h_1,\ldots,h_k}$ is a chaining circuit (as in Definition 11), and so we can use the derandomization techniques from Sect. 4 to derandomize Claim 1. Specifically, applying Lemma 7 with $\hat{C}_{h_1,\ldots,h_k}$ as the chaining circuit, with $t = n - \log k - 3$, $\delta = O(k^3/2^n)$, and $\varepsilon = 2^{-5n}$ (as in our reduction), we get the following conclusion:

$$\Pr_{(h_1,\ldots,h_k) \leftarrow G} [H_2(\hat{C}_{h_1,\ldots,h_k}) < n - \log k - 3 - (s-3)]$$

$$< \frac{1}{2^{s-3}} + \left(O\left(\frac{k^3}{2^n}\right) + \frac{1}{2^{5n}}\right) \cdot 2^{n-\log k - s}$$

$$= O\left(\frac{k^2}{2^s}\right).$$

□

Recall that $\mathcal{H}$ is a 4-wise independent family of hash functions mapping $\{0,1\}^{3n}$ to $\{0,1\}^n$. We prove Claim 1 by showing that most functions from $\mathcal{H}$ nearly preserve the collision probability of their input distribution. Given any distribution D over $\{0,1\}^{3n}$, denote by $h(D)$ the distribution obtained by applying the function h to a sample from D. We first show the following claim, use it to prove Claim 1, and then complete its proof.

Claim 2. *If $H_2(D) \geq t$ and $\mathcal{H}$ is a 4-wise independent family of hash functions, then:*

$$\Pr_{h \leftarrow \mathcal{H}} \left[H_2(h(D)) < t - \frac{2^{t+2}}{2^n} \right] \leq \frac{4}{2^{2t-n}}.$$

This claim is only interesting when $t > n/2$. In our applications of it, we will be using values of t that are very close to n, and it gives rather strong bounds.

Proof (Proof of Claim 1). For $i \in [0, k]$, define distribution D_i as the output distribution of $(h_i \circ \hat{C}_i \circ \cdots \circ h_1 \circ \hat{C}_1)(x)$ when x is uniformly random. We will prove the claim by induction on the D_i's. To start with, note that D_0 is the uniform distribution over $\{0,1\}^n$, and so $H_2(D_0) = n$.

For any i, since $\hat{C}_i$ is injective, we have $H_2(\hat{C}_i(D_{i-1})) = H_2(D_{i-1})$. Applying Claim 2 with any $t \in [n - \log k - 3, n - \log k - 2]$, we get that if $H_2(\hat{C}_i(D_{i-1})) = H_2(D_{i-1}) > t$, then $H_2(D_i) < (t - 1/k)$ with probability at most $2^8 \cdot k^2/2^n$. Starting from D_0 and $t = (n - \log k - 2)$ and applying this iteratively, and using a union bound, we get that the probability that $H_2(D_k) < n - \log k - 3$ is at most $O(k^3/2^n)$, as needed. $\qquad\square$

Proof (Proof of Claim 2). Our approach will be to show that the expected collision probability of $h(D)$ is not much larger than $\mathbf{cp}(D)$, and that its variance is small. We can then bound the probability that $\mathbf{cp}(h(D))$ is much larger than $\mathbf{cp}(D)$ using Chebyshev's inequality (Lemma 1). Recall that $\mathcal{H}$ is a set of 4-wise independent hash functions whose co-domain is of size $N = 2^n$.

We set up the following notation:

- Denote by $c = \mathbf{cp}(D)$ denote the collision probability of D.
- For any $h \in \mathcal{H}$, denote by Q_h the collision probability of $h(D)$.

The hypothesis of the claim implies that:

$$c \leq 2^{-t}. \tag{1}$$

By the definition of collision probability, we have for any h:

$$Q_h = \Pr_{x_1, x_2 \leftarrow D} [h(x_1) = h(x_2)].$$

Its expectation can be calculated as follows:

$$\begin{aligned}
\mathbf{E}_{h \leftarrow \mathcal{H}}[Q_h] &= \Pr_{h, x_1, x_2} [h(x_1) = h(x_2)] \\
&= \Pr[x_1 = x_2] \cdot 1 + \Pr[x_1 \neq x_2] \cdot \Pr[h(x_1) = h(x_2) \mid x_1 \neq x_2] \\
&= c + \frac{1-c}{N}, \tag{2}
\end{aligned}$$

where in the last equality we used the fact that $\mathcal{H}$ is a pairwise independent family. Next we calculate its second moment. If Q_h is the collision probability of

$h(D)$, then Q_h^2 is the probabilty that when two pairs of samples from $h(D)$ are picked, both pairs are colliding. Thus, we have:

$$\mathbf{E}\left[Q_h^2\right] = \Pr_{h,x_1,x_2,x_3,x_4} [h(x_1) = h(x_2) \wedge h(x_3) = h(x_4)]$$

$$= \sum_i \Pr[E_i] \cdot \Pr[h(x_1) = h(x_2) \wedge h(x_3) = h(x_4) \mid E_i], \qquad (3)$$

where E_i's are any set of disjoint events whose union is the entire sample space. We will employ a set of such events E_i as follows, and in each case we will bound the following quantities:

$$p_i = \Pr[E_i] \quad \text{and} \quad q_i = \Pr[h(x_1) = h(x_2) \wedge h(x_3) = h(x_4) \mid E_i].$$

Throughout the following analysis, we use the fact that h is from a family of 4-wise independent hash functions, and $\mathbf{cp}(D) = c$.

- $E_1 \equiv ((x_1 = x_2) \wedge (x_3 = x_4))$: In this case, hashes are always equal. The probability this event happens is simply the square of the collision probability. So we have:

$$p_1 = c^2;$$
$$q_1 = 1.$$

- $E_2 \equiv ((x_1 = x_2) \wedge (x_3 \neq x_4))$: In this case, $h(x_1)$ is always equal to $h(x_2)$, and the event $h(x_3) = h(x_4)$ is independent of this. So we have:

$$p_2 = c \cdot (1 - c);$$
$$q_2 = \frac{1}{N}.$$

- $E_3 \equiv ((x_1 \neq x_2) \wedge (x_3 = x_4))$: The probabilities here are the same as for E_2.
- $E_4 \equiv (x_1 \neq x_2) \wedge (x_3 \neq x_4) \wedge (\{x_1, x_2\} = \{x_3, x_4\})$: In this case, either $x_1 = x_3$ and $x_2 = x_4$, or the other way round. Further, the events $h(x_1) = h(x_2)$ and $h(x_3) = h(x_4)$ are the same. We have:

$$p_4 \leq \Pr[x_1 = x_3 \wedge x_2 = x_4] + \Pr[x_1 = x_4 \wedge x_2 = x_3] = 2c^2;$$
$$q_4 = \frac{1}{N}.$$

- $E_5 \equiv (x_1 \neq x_2) \wedge (x_3 \neq x_4) \wedge (\{x_1, x_2\} \neq \{x_3, x_4\})$: In this case, it could be that all the x_i's are distinct, but it could also be that $x_1 = x_3$ and $x_2 \neq x_4$ (or the other way round, etc.). In any case, the events $h(x_1) = h(x_2)$ and $h(x_3) = h(x_4)$ are always independent due to the 4-wise independence of $\mathcal{H}$. We have:

$$p_5 \leq 1;$$
$$q_5 = \frac{1}{N^2}.$$

With the above analysis and Eq. (3), we can bound the second moment of Q_h as:

$$\mathbf{E}\left[Q_n^2\right] \le c^2 + \frac{2c(1-c)}{N} + \frac{2c^2}{N} + \frac{1}{N^2}.$$

The variance of Q_h can now be bounded as:

$$\begin{aligned}
\mathbf{Var}\left[Q_h^2\right] &= \mathbf{E}\left[Q_h^2\right] - \mathbf{E}\left[Q_h\right]^2 \\
&\le \left(c^2 + \frac{2c(1-c)}{N} + \frac{2c^2}{N} + \frac{1}{N^2}\right) - \left(c + \frac{1-c}{N}\right)^2 \\
&= c^2 + \frac{2c(1-c)}{N} + \frac{2c^2}{N} + \frac{1}{N^2} - c^2 - \left(\frac{1-c}{N}\right)^2 - \frac{2c(1-c)}{N} \\
&= \frac{2c^2}{N} + \frac{1}{N^2} - \left(\frac{1}{N^2} + \frac{c^2}{N^2} - \frac{2c}{N^2}\right) \\
&\le \frac{2c^2}{N} + \frac{2c}{N^2} \\
&\le \frac{4c^2}{N},
\end{aligned}$$
(4)

where in the last inequality we used the fact that $c \ge 1/N$. From Eqs. (1), (2) and (4), we get:

$$\mathbf{E}\left[Q_h\right] \le 2^{-t} + \frac{1}{N};$$
$$\mathbf{Var}\left[Q_h\right] \le \frac{2^{-(2t-2)}}{N}.$$

Applying Chebychev's inequality (Lemma 1),

$$\Pr_h\left[Q_h > 2^{-t} + \frac{2}{N}\right] \le \frac{2^{-(2t-2)}}{N} \cdot N^2 = \frac{4}{2^{2t-n}}.$$

Using the fact that $\log_2(1+x) \le 2x$, we have:

$$\begin{aligned}
\Pr\left[H_2(h(D)) < t - \frac{2^{t+2}}{2^n}\right] &\le \Pr\left[H_2(h(D)) < t - \log\left(1 + \frac{2^{t+1}}{N}\right)\right] \\
&= \Pr\left[Q_h > 2^{-t} + \frac{2}{N}\right] \\
&\le \frac{4}{2^{2t-n}},
\end{aligned}$$

which proves the claim. $\square$

5.3   Proof of Proposition 2

Fix some $h_1, \ldots, h_k$ for which $H_2(\hat{C}_{h_1,\ldots,h_k}) \ge t$. To help with the proof, we define the following sets of distributions for $i \in [0, k]$, with x chosen uniformly at random:

$$D_i = (h_i \circ C_i \circ \cdots \circ h_1 \circ C_1)(x).$$
$$\hat{D}_i = (h_i \circ \hat{C}_i \circ \cdots \circ h_1 \circ \hat{C}_1)(x).$$

Here, D_0 and $\hat{D}_0$ are both the uniform distribution over $\{0,1\}^n$, and D_k and $\hat{D}_k$ are the distributions whose distance we need to bound to show the claim. The hypothesis of the claim is that $H_2(\hat{D}_k) \geq t$. We will prove the claim inductively, with the identity of D_0 and $\hat{D}_0$ as the base case, and using the following claims for the inductive steps.

Claim 3. *For any $i \in [k]$, we have:*

$$\Delta\left(D_i, \hat{D}_i\right) \leq \Delta\left(C_i(D_{i-1}), \hat{C}_i(\hat{D}_{i-1})\right).$$

Proof. D_i and $\hat{D}_i$ are sampled, respectively, by applying the same function h_i to a sample from $C_i(D_{i-1})$ and $\hat{C}_i(\hat{D}_{i-1})$. Thus, the claim follows from the data processing inequality. $\square$

Claim 4. *For any $i \in [k]$, we have:*

$$\Delta\left(C_i(D_{i-1}), \hat{C}_i(\hat{D}_{i-1})\right) \leq \Delta\left(D_{i-1}, \hat{D}_{i-1}\right) + \delta^{\frac{1}{2}} \cdot 2^{\frac{n-t}{2}}.$$

Proof. We start by observing that the hypothesis of the claim – $H_2(\hat{C}_{h_1,\ldots,h_k}) \geq t$ – also implies that for all $i \in [0,k]$, we have $H_2(\hat{D}_i) \geq t$. This is because all the h_i's and $\hat{C}_i$'s are fixed deterministic functions, and applying them can only decrease the entropy of a distribution.

For any $x \in inj(C_i)$, by definition, $C_i(x) = \hat{C}_i(x)$. Thus, we have:

$$\Delta\left(C_i(\hat{D}_{i-1}), \hat{C}_i(\hat{D}_{i-1})\right) \leq \Pr_{x \leftarrow \hat{D}_{i-1}}\left[x \notin inj(C_i)\right]. \tag{5}$$

Denote the quantity in the right-hand side above by p, which we will now bound. As C_i is a YES instance of $\mathsf{AI}_{L,\delta}$, the number of x's not in $inj(C_i)$ is at most δN. The least possible collision probability achievable for $\hat{D}_{i-1}$ with a probability mass of p on this set is achieved when the mass is distributed uniformly across it. Thus, due to the contribution to collision probability from this set alone, we get:

$$\mathbf{cp}(\hat{D}_{i-1}) \geq \left|\overline{inj(C_i)}\right| \cdot \left(\frac{p}{\left|\overline{inj(C_i)}\right|}\right)^2 \geq \frac{p^2}{\delta N}.$$

On the other hand, we know that $\mathbf{cp}(\hat{D}_{i-1}) \leq 2^{-t}$. This gives us:

$$p \leq (2^{-t} \cdot \delta N)^{1/2} = \delta^{1/2} \cdot 2^{(n-t)/2}. \tag{6}$$

Next, by the data processing inequality, we have:

$$\Delta\left(C_i(D_{i-1}), C_i(\hat{D}_{i-1})\right) \leq \Delta\left(D_{i-1}, \hat{D}_{i-1}\right). \tag{7}$$

Putting together Eqs. (5) to (7) and using the triangle inequality gives us the claim. $\square$

Proof (Proof of Proposition 2). Starting with the fact that $\Delta(D_0, \hat{D}_0) = 0$ and applying Claims 3 and 4 inductively k times proves the claim.   □

Acknowledgements. We thank Or Keret for helpful comments.

Shafik Nassar and Ron Rothblum were funded by the European Union (ERC, FASTPROOF, 101041208). Views and opinions expressed are however those of the author(s) only and do not necessarily reflect those of the European Union or the European Research Council. Neither the European Union nor the granting authority can be held responsible for them. Shafik Nassar is also supported in part by NSF CNS-1908611, CNS-2318701, and CNS-2140975.

Prashant Nalini Vasudevan is supported by the National Research Foundation, Singapore, under its NRF Fellowship programme, award no. NRF-NRFF14-2022-0010.

References

1. Bitansky, N., Kamath, C., Paneth, O., Rothblum, R., Vasudevan, P.N.: Batch proofs are statistically hiding. Electron. Colloquium Comput. Complex. **TR23-077** (2023)
2. Blum, M., Feldman, P., Micali, S.: Non-interactive zero-knowledge and its applications (extended abstract). In: Proceedings of the 20th Annual ACM Symposium on Theory of Computing, pp. 103–112. ACM (1988). https://doi.org/10.1145/62212.62222
3. Blum, M., Santis, A., Micali, S., Persiano, G.: Noninteractive zero-knowledge. SIAM J. Comput. **20**(6), 1084–1118 (1991). https://doi.org/10.1137/0220068
4. Brakerski, Z., Brodsky, M.F., Kalai, Y.T., Lombardi, A., Paneth, O.: SNARGs for monotone policy batch NP. In: Handschuh, H., Lysyanskaya, A. (eds.) Advances in Cryptology - CRYPTO 2023 - 43rd Annual International Cryptology Conference. LNCS, vol. 14082, pp. 252–283. Springer, Cham (2023). https://doi.org/10.1007/978-3-031-38545-2_9
5. Brakerski, Z., Holmgren, J., Kalai, Y.T.: Non-interactive delegation and batch NP verification from standard computational assumptions. In: Proceedings of the 49th Annual ACM SIGACT Symposium on Theory of Computing, STOC 2017, pp. 474–482. ACM (2017). https://doi.org/10.1145/3055399.3055497
6. Choudhuri, A.R., Garg, S., Jain, A., Jin, Z., Zhang, J.: Correlation intractability and SNARGs from sub-exponential DDH. In: Handschuh, H., Lysyanskaya, A. (eds.) Advances in Cryptology - CRYPTO 2023 - 43rd Annual International Cryptology Conference. LNCS, vol. 14084, pp. 635–668. Springer, Cham (2023). https://doi.org/10.1007/978-3-031-38551-3_20
7. Choudhuri, A.R., Jain, A., Jin, Z.: Non-interactive batch arguments for NP from standard assumptions. In: Malkin, T., Peikert, C. (eds.) CRYPTO 2021. LNCS, vol. 12828, pp. 394–423. Springer, Cham (2021). https://doi.org/10.1007/978-3-030-84259-8_14
8. Choudhuri, A.R., Jain, A., Jin, Z.: SNARGs for P from LWE. In: 62nd IEEE Annual Symposium on Foundations of Computer Science, FOCS 2021, pp. 68–79. IEEE (2021). https://doi.org/10.1109/FOCS52979.2021.00016
9. Devadas, L., Goyal, R., Kalai, Y., Vaikuntanathan, V.: Rate-1 non-interactive arguments for batch-NP and applications. In: 63rd IEEE Annual Symposium on Foundations of Computer Science, FOCS 2022, pp. 1057–1068. IEEE (2022). https://doi.org/10.1109/FOCS54457.2022.00103

10. Dvir, Z., Gutfreund, D., Rothblum, G.N., Vadhan, S.P.: On approximating the entropy of polynomial mappings. In: Innovations in Computer Science - ICS 2011, pp. 460–475. Tsinghua University Press (2011)
11. Feige, U., Shamir, A.: Witness indistinguishable and witness hiding protocols. In: Proceedings of the Twenty-Second Annual ACM Symposium on Theory of Computing, STOC 1990, pp. 416–426. Association for Computing Machinery, New York, NY, USA (1990). https://doi.org/10.1145/100216.100272
12. Goel, A., Hall-Andersen, M., Kaptchuk, G., Spooner, N.: Speed-stacking: fast sublinear zero-knowledge proofs for disjunctions. In: Hazay, C., Stam, M. (eds.) Advances in Cryptology - EUROCRYPT 2023 - 42nd Annual International Conference on the Theory and Applications of Cryptographic Techniques. LNCS, vol. 14005, pp. 347–378. Springer, Cham (2023). https://doi.org/10.1007/978-3-031-30617-4_12
13. Goldreich, O., Håstad, J.: On the complexity of interactive proofs with bounded communication. Inf. Process. Lett. **67**(4), 205–214 (1998). https://doi.org/10.1016/S0020-0190(98)00116-1
14. Goldreich, O., Krawczyk, H.: On the composition of zero-knowledge proof systems. SIAM J. Comput. **25**(1), 169–192 (1996). https://doi.org/10.1137/S0097539791220688
15. Goldreich, O., Sahai, A., Vadhan, S.: Can statistical zero knowledge be made non-interactive? or On the relationship of SZK and *NISZK*. In: Wiener, M. (ed.) CRYPTO 1999. LNCS, vol. 1666, pp. 467–484. Springer, Heidelberg (1999). https://doi.org/10.1007/3-540-48405-1_30
16. Goldreich, O., Sahai, A., Vadhan, S.P.: Honest-verifier statistical zero-knowledge equals general statistical zero-knowledge. In: Proceedings of the Thirtieth Annual ACM Symposium on the Theory of Computing, Dallas, pp. 399–408. ACM (1998). https://doi.org/10.1145/276698.276852
17. Goldreich, O., Vadhan, S., Wigderson, A.: On interactive proofs with a Laconic prover. Comput. Complex. **11**(1/2), 1–53 (2002). https://doi.org/10.1007/s00037-002-0169-0
18. Goldwasser, S., Micali, S., Rackoff, C.: The knowledge complexity of interactive proof systems. SIAM J. Comput. **18**(1), 186–208 (1989). https://doi.org/10.1137/0218012
19. Håstad, J., Impagliazzo, R., Levin, L.A., Luby, M.: A pseudorandom generator from any one-way function. SIAM J. Comput. **28**(4), 1364–1396 (1999). https://doi.org/10.1137/S0097539793244708
20. Kalai, Y., Lombardi, A., Vaikuntanathan, V., Wichs, D.: Boosting batch arguments and RAM delegation. In: Proceedings of the 55th Annual ACM Symposium on Theory of Computing, STOC 2023, pp. 1545–1552. ACM (2023). https://doi.org/10.1145/3564246.3585200
21. Kalai, Y.T., Vaikuntanathan, V., Zhang, R.Y.: Somewhere statistical soundness, post-quantum security, and SNARGs. In: Nissim, K., Waters, B. (eds.) TCC 2021. LNCS, vol. 13042, pp. 330–368. Springer, Cham (2021). https://doi.org/10.1007/978-3-030-90459-3_12
22. Kaslasi, I., Rothblum, G.N., Rothblum, R.D., Sealfon, A., Vasudevan, P.N.: Batch verification for statistical zero knowledge proofs. In: Pass, R., Pietrzak, K. (eds.) TCC 2020. LNCS, vol. 12551, pp. 139–167. Springer, Cham (2020). https://doi.org/10.1007/978-3-030-64378-2_6
23. Kaslasi, I., Rothblum, R.D., Vasudevanr, P.N.: Public-coin statistical zero-knowledge batch verification against malicious verifiers. In: Canteaut, A., Standaert, F.-X. (eds.) EUROCRYPT 2021. LNCS, vol. 12698, pp. 219–246. Springer, Cham (2021). https://doi.org/10.1007/978-3-030-77883-5_8

24. Lund, C., Fortnow, L., Karloff, H.J., Nisan, N.: Algebraic methods for interactive proof systems. J. ACM **39**(4), 859–868 (1992). https://doi.org/10.1145/146585.146605

25. Mu, C., Nassar, S., Rothblum, R.D., Vasudevan, P.N.: Strong batching for non-interactive statistical zero-knowledge. IACR Cryptol. ePrint Arch. (2024). https://eprint.iacr.org/2024/229

26. Nassar, S., Waters, B., Wu, D.J.: Monotone policy BARGs from BARGs and additively homomorphic encryption. IACR Cryptol. ePrint Arch. (2023). https://eprint.iacr.org/2023/1967

27. Nguyen, M., Vadhan, S.P.: Zero knowledge with efficient provers. In: Proceedings of the 38th Annual ACM Symposium on Theory of Computing, pp. 287–295. ACM (2006). https://doi.org/10.1145/1132516.1132559

28. Nisan, N.: Pseudorandom generators for space-bounded computation. Combinatorica **12**(4), 449–461 (1992). https://doi.org/10.1007/BF01305237

29. Ong, S.J., Vadhan, S.: An equivalence between zero knowledge and commitments. In: Canetti, R. (ed.) TCC 2008. LNCS, vol. 4948, pp. 482–500. Springer, Heidelberg (2008). https://doi.org/10.1007/978-3-540-78524-8_27

30. Paneth, O., Pass, R.: Incrementally verifiable computation via rate-1 batch arguments. In: 63rd IEEE Annual Symposium on Foundations of Computer Science, FOCS 2022, pp. 1045–1056. IEEE (2022). https://doi.org/10.1109/FOCS54457.2022.00102

31. Reingold, O., Rothblum, G.N., Rothblum, R.D.: Efficient batch verification for UP. In: 33rd Computational Complexity Conference, CCC 2018. LIPIcs, vol. 102, pp. 22:1–22:23. Schloss Dagstuhl - Leibniz-Zentrum für Informatik (2018). https://doi.org/10.4230/LIPIcs.CCC.2018.22

32. Reingold, O., Rothblum, G.N., Rothblum, R.D.: Constant-round interactive proofs for delegating computation. SIAM J. Comput. **50**(3) (2021). https://doi.org/10.1137/16M1096773

33. Renner, R., Wolf, S.: Smooth Renyi entropy and applications. In: International Symposium on Information Theory, ISIT 2004, Proceedings, pp. 233– (2004). https://doi.org/10.1109/ISIT.2004.1365269

34. Rothblum, G.N., Rothblum, R.D.: Batch verification and proofs of proximity with polylog overhead. In: Pass, R., Pietrzak, K. (eds.) TCC 2020. LNCS, vol. 12551, pp. 108–138. Springer, Cham (2020). https://doi.org/10.1007/978-3-030-64378-2_5

35. De Santis, A., Di Crescenzo, G., Persiano, G., Yung, M.: Image density is complete for non-interactive-SZK. In: Larsen, K.G., Skyum, S., Winskel, G. (eds.) ICALP 1998. LNCS, vol. 1443, pp. 784–795. Springer, Heidelberg (1998). https://doi.org/10.1007/BFb0055102

36. Shamir, A.: IP = PSPACE. J. ACM **39**(4), 869–877 (1992). https://doi.org/10.1145/146585.146609

37. Vadhan, S.P.: Pseudorandomness. Found. Trends® Theor. Comput. Sci. **7**(1–3), 1–336 (2012). https://doi.org/10.1561/0400000010

38. Vadhan, S.P.: A study of statistical zero-knowledge proofs. Ph.D. thesis, Massachusetts Institute of Technology (1999)

39. Waters, B., Wu, D.J.: Batch arguments for NP and more from standard bilinear group assumptions. In: Dodis, Y., Shrimpton, T. (eds.) Advances in Cryptology - CRYPTO 2022 - 42nd Annual International Cryptology Conference. LNCS, vol. 13508, pp. 433–463. Springer, Cham (2022). https://doi.org/10.1007/978-3-031-15979-4_15

Two-Round Maliciously-Secure Oblivious Transfer with Optimal Rate

Pedro Branco[1(✉)], Nico Döttling[2], and Akshayaram Srinivasan[3]

[1] Max Planck Institute for Security and Privacy, Bochum, Germany
pedrodemelobranco@gmail.com
[2] Helmholtz Center for Information Security (CISPA), Saarbrücken, Germany
[3] University of Toronto, Toronto, Canada

Abstract. We give a construction of a two-round batch oblivious transfer (OT) protocol in the CRS model that is UC-secure against malicious adversaries and has (near) optimal communication cost. Specifically, to perform a batch of k oblivious transfers where the sender's inputs are bits, the sender and the receiver need to communicate a total of $3k + o(k) \cdot \mathsf{poly}(\lambda)$ bits. We argue that $3k$ bits are required by any protocol with a black-box and straight-line simulator. The security of our construction is proven assuming the hardness of Quadratic Residuosity (QR) and the Learning Parity with Noise (LPN).

1 Introduction

Oblivious transfer (OT) is a two-party protocol between a sender and a receiver. The receiver's private input in this protocol is a bit $b \in \{0, 1\}$ and the sender's private input are two bits (m_0, m_1). At the end of the protocol, the receiver learns m_b and the sender does not get any output. For security, we require that the sender learns no information about the receiver's choice bit b and the receiver should not learn any information about the sender's other bit, namely, m_{1-b}. We also consider a natural extension where the sender's private inputs are two strings rather than bits and the receiver learns one of the two strings. This extension is known as the string OT protocol.

Oblivious transfer is a foundational cryptographic primitive that is used as the core building block in the construction of secure computation protocols [4,24,28,30,36]. In many applications, including secure computation and OT extension [3,26], we require the sender and the receiver to execute k oblivious transfers in parallel. This is known as the batch setting and such protocols are called batch OT protocols.

A large body of work focused on minimizing the round-complexity of oblivious transfer (e.g., [2,21,31,34]). We now know constructions of round-optimal (i.e., two-round) oblivious transfer protocols in the CRS model that are UC-secure against malicious adversaries based on standard cryptographic assumptions such as CDH, LPN, QR, and LWE [21,34].

M. Joye and G. Leander (Eds.): EUROCRYPT 2024, LNCS 14656, pp. 271–300, 2024.
https://doi.org/10.1007/978-3-031-58751-1_10

Communication Complexity. Recently, the communication complexity of OT has received a lot of attention [1,6–10,18,22,23,26]. This line of research has culminated with the works of Gentry et al. [25], Brakerski et al. [13,14], and Branco et al. [16] which focused on minimizing the communication complexity of batch OT protocols. They gave constructions of two-round semi-honest and statistical sender private batch OT protocols with (near) optimal communication cost. Specifically, the communication complexity of these protocols was $2k+o(k)\cdot$ poly(λ) where k is the batch size and λ is the security parameter. These works further argued that any batch OT protocol requires at least $2k$ bits to ensure correctness.

We observe that at least $3k$ bits of communication is needed to prove security against malicious adversaries via a black-box and straight-line simulator.[1] Indeed, the first-round message from the receiver should contain enough information for the simulator to extract all its choice bits and the sender's message should contain enough information for the simulator to extract both the sender's inputs. By standard incompressibility argument, it follows that the communication complexity should be at least $3k$ bits. Given this lower bound, a natural question is to give a construction with matching communication cost.

Prior Work. Though not explicitly stated, we observe that the techniques introduced in prior works can be used to construct a malicious-secure, two-round batch OT protocol with optimal communication.

1. **Spooky Encryption.** Spooky encryption [19] is a generalization of fully homomoprhic encryption with the following property. Let $(\mathsf{pk}_1, \mathsf{sk}_1)$ and $(\mathsf{pk}_2, \mathsf{sk}_2)$ be independently sampled public-key, secret-key pairs for a spooky encryption scheme. Given $\mathsf{Enc}(\mathsf{pk}_1, x_1)$, $\mathsf{Enc}(\mathsf{pk}_2, x_2)$ and a two-party function f, there is a special homomorphic operation that generates $\mathsf{Enc}(\mathsf{pk}_1, y_1)$ and $\mathsf{Enc}(\mathsf{pk}_2, y_2)$ such that $y_1 \oplus y_2 = f(x_1, x_2)$. Let us now see how to use spooky encryption to construct a batch OT protocol with optimal communication. In the first round, the receiver samples $(\mathsf{pk}_1, \mathsf{sk}_1)$ of a spooky encryption scheme and a PRG seed s_1. It generates $\mathsf{Enc}(\mathsf{pk}_1, s_1)$ and sends this ciphertext along with $\mathbf{b}' = \mathsf{PRG}(s_1) \oplus \mathbf{b}$ where $\mathbf{b}$ denotes the vector of choice bits of the receiver. In the second round, the sender samples $(\mathsf{pk}_2, \mathsf{sk}_2)$ of the spooky encryption scheme and PRG seed s_2. It generates $\mathsf{Enc}(\mathsf{pk}_2, s_2)$. Let f be a two-party function that takes in s_1 and s_2 and computes $\mathsf{PRG}(s_1) \circ \mathsf{PRG}(s_2)$ where $\circ$ denotes the point-wise product of the two strings. The sender homomorphically evaluates f on $\mathsf{Enc}(\mathsf{pk}_1, s_1)$ and $\mathsf{Enc}(\mathsf{pk}_2, \mathsf{sk}_2)$ to obtain $\mathsf{Enc}(\mathsf{pk}_1, \mathbf{y}_1)$ and $\mathsf{Enc}(\mathsf{pk}_2, \mathbf{y}_2)$ such that $\mathbf{y}_1 \oplus \mathbf{y}_2 = f(s_1, s_2)$. It decrypts the second ciphertext using sk_2 to learn $\mathbf{y}_2$. Note that if the sender sends $\mathsf{Enc}(\mathsf{pk}_2, s_2)$ to the receiver, the receiver can obtain $\mathbf{y}_1$. Observe that $\mathbf{y}_1 = \mathbf{y}_2 \oplus \mathsf{PRG}(s_1) \circ \mathsf{PRG}(s_2)$. Hence, we can use this to generate random OT correlations where the receiver's choice bits are given by $\mathsf{PRG}(s_1)$ and the sender's random input bits are

---

[1] Straight-line simulation is required to show UC-security.

$(\mathbf{y}_2, \mathbf{y}_2 \oplus \mathsf{PRG}(s_2))$. Further, the sender can derandomize this random OT correlation to actual OT using the receiver's first round message $\mathbf{b}'$. The receiver can then use $\mathbf{y}_1$ to recover the inputs of the sender corresponding to its choice bits $\mathbf{b}$. To protect against malicious adversaries, we add additional NIZK proofs (that are known from LWE [33]) showing that the receiver's and the sender's encryptions are generated correctly. This protocol has a total communication cost of $3k + \mathsf{poly}(\lambda)$ bits. Dodis et al. [19] gave a construction of spooky FHE under LWE with super-polynomial modulus-to-noise ratio.

2. **Pseudorandom Correlation Generators.** Orlandi et al. [32] constructed a non-interactive protocol for generating the seeds of a pseudorandom correlation generator (PCG) for computing correlated oblivious transfer. These short seeds can be locally expanded to give many instances of correlated OT.[2] These can be further transformed to standard OT correlations using a correlation-robust hash function [26]. Generically, the entire protocol requires at least three rounds in the CRS model (one round to generate the seeds and two more rounds to derandomize from random OT correlations to actual OTs). However, if we open up the protocol of [32], we note that the OT protocol can in fact be implemented in two rounds as the receiver can already compute its random choice bits after the CRS is known. One caveat, though, is that [32] requires a way to publicly generate random Goldwasser-Micali ciphertexts encrypting random bits. This would either need a random oracle, or a uniform CRS with length proportional to the number of OTs which is non-reusable. Boyle et al. [7] gave a two-round protocol for generating many instances of correlated OTs with small communication using LPN in the random oracle model.

To conclude, we know how to build optimal-rate maliciously-secure OT in two rounds in the standard model i) from LWE with super-polynomial modulus to noise ratio, ii) group based assumptions (namely DCR and QR) with a large CRS (that is, a CRS which grows with the batch size) that is non-reusable, or a random oracle, or (iii) LPN assumption in the random oracle model.

Given the above state-of-the-art, the main question we would like to address in this work is the following:

Can we construct a malicious-secure, two-round batch oblivious transfer protocol with (near) optimal communication cost with a short resuable CRS under assumptions that are weaker than LWE?

Our Results. We answer the above question affirmatively and give a construction of a two-round batch OT protocol in the CRS model with (near) optimal communication and satisfying UC-security against malicious adversaries. The security of our construction is based on the Quadratic Residuosity (QR) and Learning Parity with Noise (LPN) assumptions. Formally,

---

[2] Correlated OTs are generated by sampling a fixed offset $\Delta \leftarrow \{0,1\}^\lambda$ and generating several instances of the form $(b, v + b \cdot \Delta)$ where $b \leftarrow \{0,1\}$ and $v \leftarrow \{0,1\}^\lambda$. The receiver gets $(b, v + b \cdot \Delta)$ and the sender gets (v, Δ).

Theorem 1. *Assume the hardness of Quadratic Residuosity and the Learning Parity with Noise. There exists a two-round protocol for computing batch of k oblivious transfers in the CRS model with total communication cost of $3k + o(k) \cdot \mathrm{poly}(\lambda)$ bits when the sender's private inputs are bits and $k + 2km + o(k) \cdot \mathrm{poly}(\lambda)$ bits when the sender's private inputs are strings of length m. The protocol achieves UC-security against malicious adversaries.*

2   Technical Overview

A recent line of work [13,14,16,25] studies the hardness assumptions needed to construct communication-optimal 2-message batch OT, that is batch OT protocols in which the amortized communication cost per OT approaches 2 bits. Such protocols cannot be maliciously secure under straight-line simulation, as the total amount of communication is insufficient to encode both the sender's and receiver's inputs in an information-theoretic sense.

2.1   Warmup: The PVW Protocol

The starting point of our construction is the well-known protocol of Peikert, Vaikuntanathan and Waters [34], in the following referred to as the PVW protocol. We will consider a simple variant of the PVW protocol in the QR setting which can be described as follows on a high-level[3]. Let $N = pq$ be a product of two safe primes and let $g \in \mathbb{QR}_N$ be a random generator of the group of quadratic residues in $\mathbb{Z}_N^*$, and let $u \in \mathbb{J}_N$ be a uniformly random element with Jacobi symbol 1. The common reference string consists of the N, g and u.

The receiver, given a choice bit $b \in \{0,1\}$ picks a random $x \leftarrow_{\$} \mathbb{Z}_N$, sets $h = g^x \cdot u^b$ and sends h to the sender. The sender, on input two messages $m_0, m_1 \in \{0,1\}$ picks a random $r \leftarrow_{\$} \mathbb{Z}_N$ and computes $c = g^r$, $c_0 = h^r \cdot (-1)^{m_0}$ and $c_1 = (h \cdot u^{-1})^r \cdot (-1)^{m_1}$. He then sends c, c_0 and c_1 to the receiver, who can recover $(-1)^{m_b}$ (and thus m_b) by computing c_b/c^x.

Security against a malicious receiver can (roughly) be argued by choosing the value u in the CRS as $u = g^y \cdot (-1)$ (for a random $y \leftarrow_{\$} \mathbb{Z}_N^*$), which is indistinguishable from a random $u \in \mathbb{Z}_N^*$ under the QR assumption. Given the factorization $N = pq$ as a trapdoor, a simulator can now extract the choice bit b from h by testing whether h is a quadratic residue. Finally, we can argue that the values $c = g^r$, c_0 and c_1 statistically hide m_{1-b} as

$$c_0 = h^r(-1)^{m_0} = (g^r)^{x+by} \cdot (-1)^{br+m_1}$$
$$c_1 = (h \cdot u^{-1})^r \cdot (-1)^{m_1} = (g^r)^{x+(1-b)y} \cdot (-1)^{(1-b)r+m_1}.$$

We can rewrite this as

$$c_b = (g^r)^x \cdot (-1)^{m_b}$$
$$c_{1-b} = (g^r)^{x+y} \cdot (-1)^{r+m_{1-b}}.$$

---

[3] The QR-based construction in [34] is based on Cocks' cryptosystem, but we will describe a version here based on the Brakerski Goldwasser encryption scheme [15].

Since p and q are safe primes, it holds that the group order of $\mathbb{QR}_N$ is odd, from which is follows that $(-1)^r$ is uniformly random in $\{-1, 1\}$ given g^r as $g \in \mathbb{QR}_N$. Hence, the distribution of c_{1-b} is independent of m_{1-b} and the claim follows.

Security against a malicious sender can be argued by modifying the CRS such that $u = g^y$ is a random quadratic residue, which is indistinguishable from a random u under the QR assumption. Hence, the term h now statistically hides b. The senders input can be extracted by decrypting c_0 and c_1 using c, x and y.

The communication complexity of this protocol is far from constant; for a single bit OT, the receiver needs to send 1 group element, whereas the sender transmits 3 group elements. Using ciphertext compression techniques introduced in [22] (which we discuss in the next paragraph), the sender's communication complexity may further be improved to 1 single group element and two additional bits.

To improve the communication complexity further, we will need to consider the batch setting, i.e. a setting in which the protocol parties run many independent OT instances in parallel.

2.2   Batch OT with Trapdoor Hash Functions

To make progress towards optimal communication complexity for the sender, in other words optimal download complexity, we will consider a batch variant of the PVW protocol based on a primitive called *trapdoor hash functions (TDH)* [22].

Trapdoor Hash Functions. In broad terms, a trapdoor hash function is a hash function that supports the generation of additional *hinting keys* that encode a secret function f. Using this hinting key and the hash key, a hash evaluator can release fine-grained *hints* along with a hash value of some input x. Using the hash value, the hints, and secret state needed to generate the hinting key, one can recover the output of f applied on x. The important efficiency requirement is that the size of the hints only grow with the length of the output of f and are otherwise, independent of the input length.

In a bit more detail, TDH consists of a setup algorithm Setup, which produces a public hashing key hk, and a hashing algorithm H which takes hk and an input x and produces a succinct hash value h. In addition to these, there are three more algorithms KeyGen, Enc and Dec with the following syntax.

- KeyGen takes as input a hashing key hk and some function $f : \{0, 1\}^n \rightarrow \{0, 1\}$ *which outputs a single bit*, and produces an hinting key ek and a corresponding trapdoor td.
- The encryption or hinting algorithm Enc takes a hinting key ek and an input **x** and produces a *binary* hint $z \in \{0, 1\}$.
- The decryption algorithm Dec takes a trapdoor td and a hash value h and produces an offset $v \in \{0, 1\}$.

In terms of security, we only require that the hinting key ek computationally hides the function f. In terms of correctness, we require that it holds for all supported functions f and all inputs $\mathbf{x}$ that

$$\mathsf{Enc}(\mathsf{ek}, \mathbf{x}) = \mathsf{Dec}(\mathsf{td}, \mathsf{H}(\mathsf{hk}, \mathbf{x})) \oplus f(\mathbf{x}),$$

where $\mathsf{hk} \leftarrow \mathsf{Setup}(1^\lambda, n)$ and $(\mathsf{ek}, \mathsf{td}) \leftarrow \mathsf{KeyGen}(\mathsf{hk}, f)$. In other words, $\mathsf{Enc}(\mathsf{ek}, \mathbf{x})$ produces a simple XOR-encryption of $f(\mathbf{x})$ under a key which can be recovered from $\mathsf{H}(\mathsf{hk}, \mathbf{x})$ using the trapdoor td. This property can also be interpreted as the ability to *perfectly simulate* the hint $\mathsf{Enc}(\mathsf{ek}, \mathbf{x})$ given only the succinct hash value $\mathsf{H}(\mathsf{hk}, \mathbf{x})$, the trapdoor td and the bit $f(\mathbf{x})$. Conversely, it allows us to perfectly simulate $\mathsf{Dec}(\mathsf{td}, \mathbf{x})$ without td, given only $h = \mathsf{H}(\mathsf{hk}, \mathbf{x})$, ek, $f(x)$ and $\mathbf{x}$.

Döttling et al. [22] provide a number of instantiations of TDH from DDH, LWE and QR. Looking ahead, in this work our goal is to construct *maliciously secure* OT. For this reason we will require the above correctness property of TDH to hold perfectly, which is the case for the QR-based construction in [22], but not for their DDH-based construction.

We will thus briefly discuss the QR-based TDH of [22]. The setup algorithm Setup generates an RSA-modulus $N = p \cdot q$ with two random safe primes p and q. It further generates n random quadratic residues $g_1, \ldots, g_n \in \mathbb{QR}_N$. The hashing key hk consists of N and $g_1, \ldots, g_n$. To hash a message $\mathbf{x} \in \{0,1\}^n$, the hash algorithm H computes

$$h = \prod_{i=1}^{n} g_i^{x_i}.$$

This construction only supports $\mathbb{F}_2$-linear functions $f : \{0,1\}^n \to \{0,1\}$, i.e. inner product functions $f(x) = \langle \mathbf{t}, \mathbf{x} \rangle$ for some vector $\mathbf{t} \in \mathbb{F}_2^n$. The key generation algorithm KeyGen, given a hashing $\mathsf{hk} = (N, g_1, \ldots, g_n)$ and such a vector $\mathbf{t} = (t_1, \ldots, t_n)$ (describing the function $f(\mathbf{x}) = \langle \mathbf{t}, \mathbf{x} \rangle$) chooses a uniformly random $r \in \mathbb{Z}_n$ and computes $h_1 = g_1^r \cdot (-1)^{t_1}, \ldots, h_n = g_n^r \cdot (-1)^{t_n}$. The hinting key ek is then given by $h_1, \ldots, h_n$, whereas the trapdoor td is the value r. We can routinely argue that ek hides $\mathbf{t}$ via the QR assumption.

To construct the hinting algorithm Enc, we will make use of an efficient "rounding" or "shrinking" algorithm $\mathsf{Shrink} : \mathbb{Z}_N^* \to \{0,1\}$ with the property that for all $h \in \mathbb{Z}_N^*$ it holds that $\mathsf{Shrink}(h \cdot (-1)) = \mathsf{Shrink}(h) \oplus 1$. Now, given $\mathsf{ek} = (h_1, \ldots, h_n)$ and $\mathbf{x}$ the hinting algorithm computes and outputs

$$c = \mathsf{Shrink}\left(\prod_{i=1}^{n} h_i^{x_i}\right).$$

The decryption algorithm, given a hash value h and a trapdoor $\mathsf{td} = r$ computes and outputs $v = \mathsf{Shrink}(h^r)$. To see that this construction satisfies the correctness property, note that

$$\mathsf{Enc}(\mathsf{ek}, \mathbf{x}) = \mathsf{Shrink}\left(\prod_{i=1}^{n} h_i^{x_i}\right)$$

$$= \mathsf{Shrink}\left(\prod_{i=1}^{n} (g_i^r \cdot (-1)^{t_i})^{x_i}\right)$$

$$= \mathsf{Shrink}\left(\left(\prod_{i=1}^{n} g_i^{x_i}\right)^r \cdot (-1)^{\sum_{i=1}^{n} t_i x_i}\right)$$

$$= \mathsf{Shrink}\left(h^r \cdot (-1)^{\langle \mathbf{t}, \mathbf{x}\rangle}\right)$$

$$= \mathsf{Shrink}(h^r) \oplus \langle \mathbf{t}, \mathbf{x}\rangle$$

$$= \mathsf{Dec}(\mathsf{td}, h) \oplus \langle \mathbf{t}, \mathbf{x}\rangle.$$

PVW with Trapdoor Hash Functions. We will now discuss a new batched variant of the PVW protocol using TDH which achieves optimal communication complexity for the sender. The new protocol proceeds as follows.

The CRS consist of a hashing key hk for a TDH that supports inner product functions (such as the one discussed in the last paragraph) and m uniformly random vectors $\mathbf{t}_1, \ldots, \mathbf{t}_m \in \mathbb{F}_2^n$.

The receiver, on input choice bits $b_1, \ldots, b_m$ generates hinting keys and trapdoors $(\mathsf{ek}_i, \mathsf{td}_i) \leftarrow \mathsf{KeyGen}(\mathsf{hk}, b_i \cdot \mathbf{t}_i)$ for $i = 1, \ldots, m$ and sends $\mathsf{ek}_1, \ldots, \mathsf{ek}_m$ to the sender.

The sender, on input pairs of bits $(m_{1,0}, m_{1,1}), \ldots, (m_{m,0}, m_{m,1})$ and given the hashing key hk and the hinting keys $\mathsf{ek}_1, \ldots, \mathsf{ek}_m$ proceeds as follows. He picks a uniformly random $\mathbf{r} \in \mathbb{F}_2^n$ and computes $h \leftarrow \mathsf{H}(\mathsf{hk}, \mathbf{r})$. He then proceeds to compute

$$w_{i,0} \leftarrow \mathsf{Enc}(\mathsf{ek}_i, \mathbf{r}) \oplus m_{i,0}$$
$$w_{i,1} \leftarrow \mathsf{Enc}(\mathsf{ek}_i, \mathbf{r}) \oplus \langle \mathbf{t}_i, \mathbf{r}\rangle \oplus m_{i,1},$$

for $i = 1, \ldots, m$. He then sends the hash value h and the pairs $(w_{1,0}, w_{1,1}), \ldots, (w_{m,0}, w_{m,1})$ to the receiver.

The receiver then computes and outputs $m_i' \leftarrow \mathsf{Dec}(\mathsf{td}_i, h) \oplus w_{i,b_i}$ for $i = 1, \ldots, m$. We will first argue correctness of this protocol. Note that it holds that

$$m_i' = \mathsf{Dec}(\mathsf{td}_i, h) \oplus w_{i,b_i}$$
$$= \mathsf{Dec}(\mathsf{td}_i, h) \oplus \mathsf{Enc}(\mathsf{ek}_i, \mathbf{r}) \oplus b_i \cdot \langle \mathbf{t}_i, \mathbf{r}\rangle \oplus m_{i,b_i}$$
$$= m_{i,b_i},$$

as $\mathsf{Enc}(\mathsf{ek}_i, \mathbf{r}) = \mathsf{Dec}(\mathsf{td}_i, h) \oplus \langle b_i \cdot \mathbf{t}_i, \mathbf{r}\rangle$ by the correctness of the TDH.

This protocol is not readily maliciously secure. However, assume for a moment there was an additional mechanism in place against a malicious sender which ensures that $h = \mathsf{H}(\mathsf{hk}, \mathbf{r})$ for some $\mathbf{r}$ without revealing $\mathbf{r}$, and further enables a simulator to extract $\mathbf{r}$. This could in principle be achieved via (designated verifier) zero-knowledge proofs of knowledge. Given $\mathbf{r}$, we can simulate the receiver's behavior (without knowledge of the b_i or td_i) by extracting the messages

$$m'_{i,0} \leftarrow \mathsf{Enc}(\mathsf{ek}_i, \mathbf{r}) \oplus w_{i,0}$$
$$m'_{i,1} \leftarrow \mathsf{Enc}(\mathsf{ek}_i, \mathbf{r}) \oplus \langle \mathbf{t}_i, \mathbf{r} \rangle \oplus w_{i,1}$$

for all $i = 1, \ldots, m$. By the correctness property of the TDH it holds that

$$\mathsf{Dec}(\mathsf{td}_i, h) \oplus w_{i,b_i} = \mathsf{Enc}(\mathsf{ek}_i, \mathbf{r}) \oplus b_i \langle \mathbf{t}_i, \mathbf{r} \rangle \oplus w_{i,b_i} = m'_{i,b_i},$$

i.e. we can replace the receiver's output by m'_{i,b_i}, and this modification is perfectly indistinguishable from the receivers view. At this point, the simulation does not rely on the b_i or td_i anymore. Hence, we can use the function hiding property of the TDH to generate the hinting keys ek_i independently of the b_i, and hence simulate the protocol.

In turn, to establish security against a malicious receiver we need an additional mechanism which ensures well-formedness of hk and the ek_i and lets us extract the b_i and td_i from the receiver. Once such a mechanism is in place, we can argue security against a malicious receiver as follows. Note that by the correctness of the TDH a simulator in possession of the trapdoors td_i can equivalently compute the ciphertexts $w_{i,b}$ (for $i = 1, \ldots, m$ and $b \in \{0, 1\}$) via $w_{i,b} = \mathsf{Dec}(\mathsf{td}_i, h) \oplus (b \oplus b_i) \cdot \langle \mathbf{t}_i, \mathbf{r} \rangle \oplus m_{i,b}$. Consequently, for the message $m_{i,1-b_i}$, which should remain hidden from the receiver, it holds that

$$w_{i,1-b_i} = \mathsf{Dec}(\mathsf{td}_i, h) \oplus \langle \mathbf{t}_i, \mathbf{r} \rangle \oplus m_{i,1-b_i}.$$

That is, from the receiver's view the message $m_{i,1-b_i}$ is masked by the term $\langle \mathbf{t}_i, \mathbf{r} \rangle$. Note that the succinct hash value h is the only additional information the receiver learns about $\mathbf{r}$ besides the inner products $\langle \mathbf{t}_i, \mathbf{r} \rangle$. Furthermore, note that the hash value $h = \mathsf{H}(\mathsf{hk}, \mathbf{r})$ does not depend on the random vectors $\mathbf{t}_1, \ldots, \mathbf{t}_m$. Hence, given that m is sufficiently smaller than $n - \mathsf{bitlength}(h)$, we can appeal to the leftover hash lemma [20,35] to argue that the inner products $\langle \mathbf{t}_i, \mathbf{r} \rangle$ are statistically close to uniform given h, and consequently we can simulate the $w_{i,1-b_i}$ by choosing them uniformly at random.

While this protocol makes progress towards our goal of optimal *maliciously secure* OT, it has several glaring problems.

Most obviously, we have not specified how the additional extraction mechanism require for simulation affect the communication complexity of the protocol. We will postpone the discussion of this issue as there is another, far more severe issue with the above protocol: With the parameter choice discussed above we can achieve optimal amortized download complexity for the sender, however we have done so at the expense of the upload complexity! Specifically, in order to be able to extract a sufficient number of masks, we need to make n sufficiently larger than m. But looking at the TDH construction from QR above, this means that each hinting key ek_i consists of n group elements, while at the same time the receiver sends m hinting keys, which means in order to get m bit OTs, the receiver needs to send $\Omega(m^2)$ group elements. This means the total communication complexity of this protocol is *asymptotically worse* than repeating the simple QR-based PVW protocol above m times!

The underlying issue here is that our information theoretic argument for sender security runs into an entropy barrier; we cannot extract more than n random bits from $\mathbf{r}$. Consequently, to bypass this barrier and make this approach work we need to settle on a computational argument, that is we need to derive computationally secure masks from $\mathbf{r}$.

2.3   Computational Sender Security via LPN

This is where the *Learning Parity with Noise* (LPN) assumption comes into play. The basic observation is that, using nearly the same construction as above, the LPN assumption lets us extract more entropy than there is if we are able to deal with additional errors. The *decisional LPN assumption* postulates that for any polynomial bound m the samples $(\mathbf{t}_1, \langle \mathbf{t}_1, \mathbf{r} \rangle + f_1), \ldots, (\mathbf{t}_m, \langle \mathbf{t}_m, \mathbf{r} \rangle + f_m)$ are pseudorandom, where the $\mathbf{r} \leftarrow_{\$} \mathbb{F}_2^n$ and the $\mathbf{t}_i \leftarrow_{\$} \mathbb{F}_2^n$ are chosen uniformly random and the f_i are independent and follow a Bernoulli distribution, that is each f_i is 0 with probability $1 - \delta$ and 1 with probability δ. We will choose a slightly sub-constant δ, hence there will not be too many faulty positions.

A moment of reflection exposes that we cannot simply add noise terms f_i into the construction in the last paragraph, as LPN requires the secret $\mathbf{r}$ to be uniform, whereas $\mathbf{r}$ in the construction above "loses" entropy as the hash value $h = \mathsf{H}(\mathsf{hk}, \mathbf{r})$ is leaked. However, we have also seen in the last paragraph that we can use the leftover hash lemma to extract a uniformly random vector from $\mathbf{r}$ in the presence of the leakage $h = \mathsf{H}(\mathsf{hk}, \mathbf{r})$. Hence, we will modify the construction such that it first extracts an LPN secret $\hat{\mathbf{r}}$ from $\mathbf{r}$, and then expands $\hat{\mathbf{r}}$ via LPN. We can achieve this via a single linear function!

We will now discuss the necessary modifications to the protocol in the last paragraph in more detail. Let n' be sufficiently smaller than $n - \mathsf{bitlength}(h)$. We will first discuss how CRS generation has to be modified. Instead of choosing the $\mathbf{t}_i \in \mathbb{F}_2^n$ uniformly random, we will choose a uniformly random matrix $\mathbf{V} \in \mathbb{F}_2^{n' \times n}$ and uniformly random vectors $\hat{\mathbf{t}}_1, \ldots, \hat{\mathbf{t}}_m$ and set $\mathbf{t}_i \leftarrow \mathbf{V}^\top \cdot \hat{\mathbf{t}}_i$ for $i = 1, \ldots, m$. Note that this is equivalent to putting the random matrix $\mathbf{V}$ and the random vectors $\hat{\mathbf{t}}_1, \ldots, \hat{\mathbf{t}}_m$ into the CRS and letting the parties compute the $\mathbf{t}_i$.

Both the receiver's first and second phase are as before, we will only modify the sender's algorithm. As before, the sender picks a uniformly random $\mathbf{r} \in \mathbb{F}_2^n$ and computes $h \leftarrow \mathsf{H}(\mathsf{hk}, \mathbf{r})$ and $z_i \leftarrow \mathsf{Enc}(\mathsf{ek}_i, \mathbf{r})$ for $i = 1, \ldots, m$. However, the computation of the $w_{i,b}$ is now modified by introducing noise terms. Specifically, for $i = 1, \ldots, m$ the sender computes

$$w_{i,0} \leftarrow z_i \oplus f_{i,0} \oplus m_{i,0}$$
$$w_{i,1} \leftarrow z_i \oplus \langle \mathbf{t}_i, \mathbf{r} \rangle \oplus f_{i,1} \oplus m_{i,1},$$

where the $f_{i,b}$ are chosen from a Bernoulli distribution with parameter δ. As before, he then sends the hash value h and the pairs $(w_{1,0}, w_{1,1}), \ldots, (w_{m,0}, w_{m,1})$ to the receiver.

We will first analyze correctness of this protocol. Letting $m'_i \leftarrow \mathsf{Dec}(\mathsf{td}_i, h) \oplus w_{i,b_i}$ for $i = 1, \ldots, m$ be the receiver's outputs, we can establish using the correctness of the TDH that

$$m'_i = m_{i,b_i} \oplus f_{i,b_i},$$

which means that each output of the receiver will be faulty with (small) probability δ. We will later describe a mechanism that deals with the errors and merely observe now that if the total number of errors is sufficiently small, we will be able to afford a relatively costly mechanism (in terms of communication complexity) to correct the errors.

At this point we will only examine security against malicious receivers. We do this in a few hybrid steps. As before, via the correctness property of the TDH we can simulate the $w_{i,b}$ via

$$w_{i,b_i} \leftarrow \mathsf{Dec}(\mathsf{td}_i, h) \oplus f_{i,b_i} \oplus m_{i,b_i}$$
$$w_{i,1-b_i} \leftarrow \mathsf{Dec}(\mathsf{td}_i, h) \oplus \langle \mathbf{t}_i, \mathbf{r} \rangle \oplus f_{i,1-b_i} \oplus m_{i,1-b_i}.$$

First note that it holds by our choice of the $\mathbf{t}_i = \mathbf{V}^\top \hat{\mathbf{t}}_i$ that

$$\langle \mathbf{t}_i, \mathbf{r} \rangle = \langle \mathbf{V}^\top \hat{\mathbf{t}}_i, \mathbf{r} \rangle = \langle \hat{\mathbf{t}}_i, \mathbf{Vr} \rangle.$$

That is, we can equivalently compute $w_{i,1-b_i}$ via

$$w_{i,1-b_i} \leftarrow \mathsf{Dec}(\mathsf{td}_i, h) \oplus \langle \hat{\mathbf{t}}_i, \mathbf{Vr} \rangle \oplus f_{i,1-b_i} \oplus m_{i,1-b_i}.$$

As before, noting that $\mathbf{r}$ has high conditional min-entropy given the succinct hash $h = \mathsf{H}(\mathsf{hk}, \mathbf{r})$ and that h is independent of $\mathbf{V}$, we can invoke the leftover hash lemma and replace $\mathbf{Vr}$ with a uniformly random $\hat{\mathbf{r}} \leftarrow_\$ \mathbb{F}_2^{n'}$ while introducing only a negligible statistical distance in the view of a malicious receiver. That is, we compute $w_{i,1-b_i}$ via

$$w_{i,1-b_i} \leftarrow \mathsf{Dec}(\mathsf{td}_i, h) \oplus \langle \hat{\mathbf{t}}_i, \hat{\mathbf{r}} \rangle \oplus f_{i,1-b_i} \oplus m_{i,1-b_i}.$$

Now, as $\hat{\mathbf{r}}$ is independent of h, we can rely on the pseudorandomness of LPN to replace the $\langle \hat{\mathbf{t}}_i, \hat{\mathbf{r}} \rangle \oplus f_{i,1-b_i}$ with uniformly random and independent $u_i \leftarrow_\$ \{0,1\}$. That is, we compute $w_{i,1-b_i}$ via

$$w_{i,1-b_i} \leftarrow \mathsf{Dec}(\mathsf{td}_i, h) \oplus u_i \oplus m_{i,1-b_i}.$$

But this means that $w_{i,1-b_i}$ itself is independently uniformly random in $\{0,1\}$, i.e. we can equivalently just choose $w_{i,1-b_i} \leftarrow_\$ \{0,1\}$. We can conclude that in this final hybrid the sender's message is independent of the $m_{i,1-b_i}$, and we have thus established security against malicious receivers (given that we have a mechanism to extract the td_i and b_i).

We will now briefly consider the communication complexity of our current protocol. The modification discussed in this paragraph (omitting the issue of errors) does not affect the download communication complexity, the sender still sends (amortized) 2 bits per OT. However, the upload communication complexity is now just $O(n \cdot m)$ group elements, where $n = \mathsf{poly}(\lambda)$ is a fixed polynomial, independent of m.

2.4 Key-Homomorphic Trapdoor Hash Functions

We will now discuss an additional mechanism which lets us further compress the upload communication complexity. The starting observation here is that each hinting key ek_i only "encrypts" a single bit b_i, but consists of n group elements. To address this issue, we will pursue a *hybrid encryption approach* similar to [13], i.e. we will encrypt the bits b_i under a symmetric key encryption scheme with optimal rate along with TDH hinting keys which encrypt the corresponding secret key, and then let the sender *homomorphically expand* these ciphertexts into the actual hinting keys ek_i.

Consequently, to implement this approach we need to add homomorphic capabilities to our underlying trapdoor hash functions for linear functions. We call this primitive *key-homomorphic trapdoor hash functions*. Recall that our trapdoor hash functions allow for hints which let the receiver learn linear functions $f(\mathbf{r}) = \langle \mathbf{t}, \mathbf{r} \rangle$ of then sender's input $\mathbf{r}$, i.e. it holds that

$$\mathsf{Enc}(\mathsf{ek}, \mathbf{r}) = \mathbf{Dec}(\mathsf{td}, \mathsf{H}(\mathsf{hk}, \mathbf{r})) \oplus \langle \mathbf{t}, \mathbf{r} \rangle,$$

where $(\mathsf{ek}, \mathsf{td}) \leftarrow \mathsf{KeyGen}(\mathsf{hk}, \mathbf{t})$.

In a key-homomorphic trapdoor hash function, we require keys to support homomorphic operations, that is, given ek_1 and ek_2 with $(\mathsf{ek}_1, \mathsf{td}_1) \leftarrow \mathsf{KeyGen}(\mathsf{hk}, \mathbf{t}_1)$ and $(\mathsf{ek}_2, \mathsf{td}_2) \leftarrow \mathsf{KeyGen}(\mathsf{hk}, \mathbf{t}_2)$, one can efficiently derive a key ek^* corresponding to $\mathbf{t}_1 \oplus \mathbf{t}_2$, given only hk, ek_1 and ek_2, and likewise a trapdoor td^* from hk, td_1 and td_2 such that

$$\mathsf{Enc}(\mathsf{ek}^*, \mathbf{r}) = \mathbf{Dec}(\mathsf{td}^*, \mathsf{H}(\mathsf{hk}, \mathbf{r})) \oplus \langle \mathbf{t}_1 \oplus \mathbf{t}_2, \mathbf{r} \rangle.$$

More formally, we require a key-homomorphic evaluation algorithm Eval along with a corresponding decryption algorithm Dec' such that the following holds. Eval takes as input a vector $\mathbf{d} = (d_1, \ldots, d_k) \in \mathbb{F}_2^k$ and hinting keys $\mathsf{ek}_1, \ldots, \mathsf{ek}_k$ and outputs a hinting key ek^*, while Dec' also takes the vector $\mathbf{d}$ and trapdoors $\mathsf{td}_1, \ldots, \mathsf{td}_k$ as well as a hash value h and outputs a trapdoor td^*, such that it holds that

$$\mathsf{Enc}(\mathsf{Eval}(\mathbf{d}, \mathsf{ek}_1, \ldots, \mathsf{ek}_k), \mathbf{r}) = \mathsf{Dec}'(\mathbf{d}, \mathsf{td}_1, \ldots, \mathsf{td}_k, h) \oplus \left\langle \sum_{i=1}^{k} d_i \mathbf{t}_i, \mathbf{r} \right\rangle.$$

Turning to the construction of key-homomorphic TDH, we observe that the construction of TDH from QR [22] we discussed above readily supports key homomorphism. Specifically, given two hinting keys $\mathsf{ek}_1 = (h_{1,i} = g_i^{r_1} \cdot (-1)^{t_{1,i}})_{i \in [n]}$ and $\mathsf{ek}_2 = (h_{2,i} = g_i^{r_2} \cdot (-1)^{t_{2,i}})_{i \in [n]}$, it holds that

$$h_{1,i} \cdot h_{2,i} = g_i^{r_1}(-1)^{t_{1,i}} \cdot g_i^{r_2}(-1)^{t_{2,i}} = g_i^{r_1+r_2} \cdot (-1)^{t_{1,i}+t_{2,i}},$$

i.e. $\mathsf{ek}^* = (h_{1,i} \cdot h_{2,i})_{i \in [n]}$ is a hinting key for $\mathbf{t}_1 \oplus \mathbf{t}_2$, and the corresponding trapdoor is $\mathsf{td}^* = r_1 + r_2$.

2.5 Compressing the Receiver's Message via LPN and Key-Homomorphic TDH

We will use the LPN assumption once more, this time in conjunction with the key-homomorphism property of the trapdoor hash function to implement a hybrid encryption approach which enables the receiver to transmit the encoding keys corresponding to his choice bits in a *compressed* form, which can then be locally expanded by the sender. In essence, this approach is an adaptation of the LPN-based compression mechanisms of [13]. Specifically, we can think of the hinting keys of a key-homomorphic TDH as ciphertexts of a homomorphic encryption scheme encrypting a vector $\mathbf{t}$. Following the blueprint of [13], we let the receiver provide TDH hinting keys which encode an LPN secret, and additionally provide LPN ciphertexts of the actual choice bits along with. Given this information, the sender will then be able to homomorphically derive hinting keys that encode the actual choice bits.

For simplicity, we start be considering a single $\mathbf{t}$. Assume the common reference string contains uniformly random vectors $\mathbf{d}_1, \ldots, \mathbf{d}_\ell \in \mathbb{F}_2^n$. The receiver will choose an LPN secret $\mathbf{s} \leftarrow_{\$} \mathbb{F}_2^n$ and compute hinting keys $\mathsf{ek}_0, \mathsf{ek}_1, \ldots, \mathsf{ek}_n$, where ek_0 encodes $\mathbf{t}$ and ek_i encodes $s_i \cdot \mathbf{t}$ for $0 < i \leq n$. The receiver further encrypts his choice bits $b_1, \ldots, b_\ell$ to

$$c_i \leftarrow \langle \mathbf{s}, \mathbf{d_i} \rangle + e_i + b_i$$

for $i = 1, \ldots, k$. Here the $e_i \in \{0, 1\}$ are chosen from a Bernoulli distribution with slightly sub-constant parameter ϵ, that is each e_i is independently 1 with probability ϵ and otherwise 0.

The receiver now sends sends the hinting keys $\mathsf{ek}_0, \mathsf{ek}_1, \ldots, \mathsf{ek}_n$ and the ciphertexts $c_1, \ldots, c_\ell$ to the sender. Sender can compute expanded encoding keys via

$$\mathsf{ek}'_j = \mathsf{Eval}((c_j, \mathbf{d}_j), \mathsf{ek}_0, \mathsf{ek}_1, \ldots, \mathsf{ek}_n)$$

for $j = 1, \ldots, \ell$. By the homomorphic correctness of the TDH, ek'_j is a hinting key for the vector

$$c_j \cdot \mathbf{t} + \sum_{i=1}^{n} d_{j,i} s_i \mathbf{t} = (c_j + \langle \mathbf{s}, \mathbf{d} \rangle) \cdot \mathbf{t}$$
$$= (\langle \mathbf{s}, \mathbf{d}_j \rangle + e_j + b_j + \mathbf{s}, \mathbf{d} \rangle) \cdot \mathbf{t}$$
$$= (b_j + e_j) \cdot \mathbf{t}.$$

Consequently, if $e_j = 0$, which holds except with sub-constant probability ϵ, the sender obtains the correct hinting key for $b_j \cdot \mathbf{t}$. The sender now proceeds analogous to the previous protocol. He chooses uniform vectors $\mathbf{r}_1, \ldots, \mathbf{r}_\ell$ and computes hash values $h_j \leftarrow \mathsf{H}(\mathsf{hk}, \mathbf{r}_j)$ for $j = 1, \ldots, \ell$. Furthermore, he computes

$$w_{j,0} \leftarrow \mathsf{Enc}(\mathsf{ek}'_j, \mathbf{r}_j) \oplus f_{j,0} \oplus m_{j,0}$$
$$w_{j,1} \leftarrow \mathsf{Enc}(\mathsf{ek}'_j, \mathbf{r}_j) \oplus \langle \mathbf{t}, \mathbf{r}_j \rangle \oplus f_{j,1} \oplus m_{j,1},$$

for $j = 1, \ldots, \ell$. He then sends the $h_1, \ldots, h_\ell$ and $(w_{j,0}, w_{j,1})_{j \in [\ell]}$ to the receiver.

Using the trapdoors $\mathsf{td}_0, \mathsf{td}_1, \ldots, \mathsf{td}_n$ corresponding to $\mathsf{ek}_0, \mathsf{ek}_1, \ldots, \mathsf{ek}_n$ the receiver then computes

$$m'_{j,b_j} \leftarrow \mathsf{Dec}'((c_j, \mathbf{d}_j), \mathsf{td}_0, \ldots, \mathsf{td}_n, h_j) \oplus w_{j,b_j}$$

for $j = 1, \ldots, \ell$. This concludes the outline of the protocol.

We will first look at correctness of this protocol. By the homomorphic correctness of TDH it holds that

$$
\begin{aligned}
m'_{j,b_j} =& \mathsf{Dec}'((c_j, \mathbf{d}_j), \mathsf{td}_0, \ldots, \mathsf{td}_n, h_j) \oplus w_{j,b_j} \\
=& \mathsf{Dec}'((c_j, \mathbf{d}_j), \mathsf{td}_0, \ldots, \mathsf{td}_n, \mathsf{H}(\mathsf{hk}, \mathbf{r}_j)) \\
& \oplus \mathsf{Enc}(\mathsf{Eval}((c_j, \mathbf{d}_j), \mathsf{ek}_0, \mathsf{ek}_1, \ldots, \mathsf{ek}_n), \mathbf{r}_j) \oplus b_j \cdot \langle \mathbf{t}, \mathbf{r}_j \rangle \oplus f_{j,b_j} \oplus m_{j,b_j} \\
=& (b_j \oplus e_j) \cdot \langle \mathbf{t}, \mathbf{r}_j \rangle \oplus b_j \cdot \langle \mathbf{t}, \mathbf{r}_j \rangle \oplus f_{j,b_j} \oplus m_{j,b_j} \\
=& e_j \cdot \langle \mathbf{t}, \mathbf{r}_j \rangle \oplus f_{j,b_j} \oplus m_{j,b_j}.
\end{aligned}
$$

Consequently, if both e_j and f_{j,b_j} are 0, which happens except with (small) probability $\leq \delta + \epsilon$, the receiver obtains the correct output m_{j,b_j}.

For simplicity, we only considered a single vector $\mathbf{t}$ in this sketch; this is insufficient to get optimal download communication as the sizes of the hash values h_j are not amortized. Hence, in the full protocol we need to use all the vectors $\mathbf{t}_1, \ldots, \mathbf{t}_m$.

The Full Protocol. For the full protocol, it will be convenient to arrange both the receiver's choice bits and the sender's messages in a matrix form. That is, the receiver's choice bits are $b_{i,j}$ and the sender's messages are $(m_{i,j,0}, m_{i,j,1})$ for $i \in [m]$ and $j \in [\ell]$. I.e., we will get $m \cdot \ell$ batch OTs.

The full protocol is summarized as follows.

- The common reference string contains the hashing key hk, random vectors $\mathbf{t}_1, \ldots, \mathbf{t}_m \in \mathbb{F}_2^n$ as in Sect. 2.3, and uniformly random $\mathbf{d}_{i,j} \in \mathbb{F}_2^n$ for $i \in [m]$ and $j \in [\ell]$.
- The receiver generates hinting keys $\mathsf{ek}_{i,k}$ encoding $s_k \cdot \mathbf{t}_i$ for $i \in [m]$ and $k \in [n]$ together with a corresponding trapdoor $\mathsf{td}_{i,k}$. The receiver further encrypts each $b_{i,j}$ to
$$c_{i,j} \leftarrow \langle \mathbf{s}, \mathbf{d}_{i,j} \rangle + e_{i,j} + b_{i,j}.$$
The receiver sends the $\mathsf{ek}_{i,k}$ and the $c_{i,j}$ to the sender.
- The sender homomorphically derives hinting keys $\mathsf{ek}'_{i,j}$ corresponding to $(b_{i,j} \oplus e_{i,j}) \cdot \mathbf{t}_i$ from the $\mathsf{ek}_{i,k}$, $\mathbf{d}_{i,j}$ and the $c_{i,j}$ as described above. The

sender now chooses $\mathbf{r}_1, \ldots, \mathbf{r}_\ell \leftarrow_{\$} \{0,1\}^n$ uniformly at random and computes $h_j \leftarrow \mathsf{Hash}(\mathsf{hk}, \mathbf{r}_j)$. He further computes

$$w_{i,j,0} \leftarrow \mathsf{Enc}(\mathsf{ek}'_{i,j}, \mathbf{r}_j) \oplus f_{i,j,0} \oplus m_{i,j,0}$$
$$w_{i,j,1} \leftarrow \mathsf{Enc}(\mathsf{ek}'_{i,j}, \mathbf{r}_j) \oplus \langle \mathbf{t}_i, \mathbf{r}_j \rangle \oplus f_{i,j,1} \oplus m_{i,j,1},$$

for $i \in [m]$ and $j \in [\ell]$.
- The receiver recovers the $m'_{i,j,b_{i,j}}$ via

$$m'_{i,j,b_{i,j}} \leftarrow \mathsf{Dec}'(\mathsf{Eval}((c_{i,j}, \mathbf{d}_{i,j}), \mathsf{td}_{i,0}, \ldots, \mathsf{td}_{i,n}), h_j) \oplus w_{i,j,b_{i,j}}.$$

The correctness analysis is identical to the one provided in the last paragraph, i.e. it holds that $m'_{i,j,b_{i,j}} = m_{i,j,b_{i,j}}$, except with probability $\delta + \epsilon$ over the choice of the e_j and $f_{i,j}$.

In terms of security, note the following. Once we extract the $\mathbf{r}_j$ and the locations of the errors $f_{i,j}$, we can simulate the output of the receiver without knowledge of the LPN secret $\mathbf{s}$ or the choice-bits $b_{i,j}$. Consequently, we can use the LPN assumption to replace the $c_{i,j}$ with uniformly random values.

In terms of security against a malicious receiver, we now have to extract the trapdoors $\mathsf{td}_{i,k}$ and the LPN secret $\mathbf{s}$, as well as the locations of the errors $e_{i,j}$. Once these are known, we can simulate the sender's messages without knowledge of the secrets $\mathbf{r}_1, \ldots, \mathbf{r}_\ell$, but only the corresponding LPN samples $\langle \mathbf{t}_i, \mathbf{r}_j \rangle \oplus f_{i,j,1-b_{i,j}}$ as well as the hash-values $h_1, \ldots, h_\ell$. The rest of the argument proceeds analogous to the argument given in Sect. 2.3.

Communication Complexity. We will now take at look at the communication complexity of this protocol.

- The receiver's message consists of $m \cdot n$ hinting keys $\mathsf{ek}_{i,j}$ (each consisting of $O(n)$ group elements) and $m \cdot \ell$ bits $c_{i,j}$. Hence the upload rate of this protocol is

$$\rho_{up} = \frac{m \cdot n^2 \mathsf{poly}(\lambda) + m \cdot \ell}{m \cdot \ell} = 1 + \frac{n^2 \mathsf{poly}(\lambda)}{\ell} = 1 + \frac{\mathsf{poly}(\lambda)}{\ell},$$

as we can choose the LPN dimension n as a fixed polynomial in the security parameter.
- The sender's message consists of ℓ hash values h_j (each consisting of $O(1)$ group elements) and $2 \cdot m \cdot \ell$ bits $w_{i,j,0}$ and $w_{i,j,1}$. Hence the download rate becomes

$$\rho_{down} = \frac{\ell \cdot \mathsf{poly}(\lambda) + 2 m \cdot \ell}{m \cdot \ell} = 2 + \frac{\mathsf{poly}(\lambda)}{m}.$$

Consequently, by choosing $\ell, m = \mathsf{poly}(\lambda)$ as sufficiently large polynomials, we will obtain asymptotically optimal rate.

2.6   Correcting Errors and Achieving Malicious Security

We will now briefly discuss which additional mechanisms need to be deployed in order to make this protocol both *correct* and *maliciously secure*. Taking the analysis of the communication complexity in the last Section as a guideline, we can afford to "spend" additional $m \cdot \mathsf{poly}(\lambda)$ bits of communication in the receiver's message, and $\ell \cdot \mathsf{poly}(\lambda)$ bits on top of the sender's message.

The additional mechanism will ensure the following properties:

1. For every error location (i, j) for which $e_{i,j} = 1$ we need to "flip" the receiver's output.
2. For every error location $(i, j, b_{i,j})$ (where $b_{i,j}$ is the receiver's choice bit at i, j) where $f_{i,j,b_{i,j}} = 1$, we need to signal to the receiver that an error occurred at this location so that the corresponding output can be corrected.
3. For every "column" $j \in [\ell]$ we need to make the $\mathbf{r}_j$ corresponding to the $h_j = \mathsf{H}(\mathsf{hk}, \mathbf{r}_j)$ extractable. Furthermore, we need to make the LPN secret $\mathbf{s}$ and the *support* of the error vector $\mathbf{e}_j = (e_{1,j}, \ldots, e_{m,j})$ extractable. Since $\mathbf{e}_i$ has Hamming weight at most $2\epsilon m$, we can describe it via a succinct list of indices of length $2\epsilon m$. Furthermore, we need to make the support of the error vectors $\mathbf{f}_{j,0} = (f_{1,j,0}, \ldots, f_{m,j,0})$ and $\mathbf{f}_{j,1} = (f_{1,j,1}, \ldots, f_{m,j,1})$ extractable. Since each of this vectors has Hamming weight at most $2\delta m$, we can describe each of them via a list of length $2\delta m$.
4. For every "row" $i \in [m]$ and for $k \in \{0, \ldots, n\}$ we need to make the trapdoors $\mathsf{td}_{i,k}$ corresponding to the hinting keys $\mathsf{ek}_{i,k}$ extractable and ensure that the $\mathsf{ek}_{i,k}$ were generated correctly with respect to the LPNs secret $\mathbf{s}$, and the vectors $\mathbf{t}_i$ which are taken from the common reference string.

Property 4 can be achieved succinctly via a computationally secure rate-1 conditional disclosure of secrets (CDS) scheme, which can routinely implemented from general purpose non-interactive secure computation (NISC) protocol (with malicious UC-security) and pseudorandom functions. This protocol can be run "piggy-back" style with the main protocol, so it does not increase the round complexity.

We will thus focus on properties 1,2 and 3. We will address these issues *simultaneously* using also a general purpose NISC protocol with malicious UC-security. The key insight is that both our corrections and checks do not need to be performed "globally", but merely "column"-wise. Hence the NISC for each column can be succinct. Similarly important, these 2-message NISC protocols can also be piggy-backed with the main protocol, so they will neither increase the round complexity.

We will need an additional mechanism which lets us correct the LPN errors $e_{i,j}$ on the receiver's choice-bits. A mechanism achieving this was recently proposed in [13]. For every column j the sender chooses a fresh key K_j for a puncturable pseudorandom function [5,11,29] which is puncturable in $2\epsilon m$ positions. We need to modify the protocol such that the $w_{i,j,0}$ and $w_{i,j,1}$ are computed via

$$w_{i,j,0} \leftarrow \mathsf{Enc}(\mathsf{ek}'_{i,j}, \mathbf{r}_j) \oplus f_{i,j,0} \oplus m_{i,j,0} \oplus \mathsf{PRF}_{K_j}(i)$$
$$w_{i,j,1} \leftarrow \mathsf{Enc}(\mathsf{ek}'_{i,j}, \mathbf{r}_j) \oplus \langle \mathbf{t}_i, \mathbf{r}_j \rangle \oplus f_{i,j,1} \oplus m_{i,j,1} \oplus \mathsf{PRF}_{K_j}(i).$$

Furthermore, we will need to make the vectors $\mathbf{t}_1, \ldots, \mathbf{t}_m$, which are part of the CRS, available to the NISC computation. However, since we need to NISC protocol to have sublinear communication complexity in m, we cannot make the $\mathbf{t}_i$ explicit inputs to the NISC. However, each NISC_j will only need to access a few of the $\mathbf{t}_i$. Hence, we will bind to the $\mathbf{t}_i$ via a vector commitment with succinct opening [17], and instead of providing all the $\mathbf{t}_i$ to NISC_j, we will let the receiver only input a small number of the $\mathbf{t}_i$ (needed to correct the receiver's errors) together with a succinct opening of the vector commitment. In the same manner, we will use vector commitments with succinct opening to bind to the vectors $\mathbf{d}_{i,j}$ given in the CRS and to the ciphertexts $c_{i,j}$.

We will now describe the NISC functionality NISC_j for column j.

The functionality for column j takes as input from the receiver the LPN secret s, the error vector $\mathbf{e}_j$ (represented by a succinct list of length at most $2\epsilon m$). Furthermore, for every index i in the support of $\mathbf{e}_j$ the receiver inputs $\mathbf{t}_i$ together with a succinct opening of the corresponding vector commitment.

The sender provides as input $\mathbf{r}_j$, and the error vectors $\mathbf{f}_{j,0}$ and $\mathbf{f}_{j,1}$ (each represented by a succinct list of length $2\delta m$), as well as the key K_j. For every index i in the support of either $\mathbf{f}_{j,0}$ or $\mathbf{f}_{j,1}$, the sender also inputs $c_{i,j}$ (together with a succinct opening of the corresponding vector commitment) and $\mathbf{d}_{i,j}$ (also with an opening of the corresponding vector commitment).

The functionality performs the following computations. It punctures K_j at the support of $\mathbf{e}_j$ yielding a key $K_j^\odot$, computes offsets $\gamma_{i,j} = \mathsf{PRF}_{K_j}(i) \oplus \langle \mathbf{t}_i, \mathbf{r}_j \rangle$ for i in the support of $\mathbf{e}_j$, as well as $h_j = \mathsf{H}(\mathsf{hk}, \mathbf{r}_j)$. For every index i in the support of either $\mathbf{f}_{j,0}$ or $\mathbf{f}_{j,1}$, the functionality decrypts $c_{i,j}$ via $b_{i,j} \leftarrow \langle s, \mathbf{d}_{i,j} \rangle \oplus e_{i,j} \oplus c_{i,j}$. If i is in the support of $\mathbf{f}_{j,b_{i,j}}$, it sets $\beta_{i,j} = 1$ and otherwise $\beta_{i,j} = 0$. Note that the $(\beta_{i,j})_{i \in [m]}$ can be described by a succinct list of length at most $4\delta m$.

The functionality then outputs $K_j^\odot$, $(\gamma_{i,j})_{i \in [m]}$, h_j as well as $(\beta_{i,j})_{i \in [m]}$ to the receiver.

Now the receiver proceeds as follows. For every i not in the support of $\mathbf{e}_j$, he uses the punctured key $K_j^\odot$ to remove the mask $\mathsf{PRF}_{K_j}(i)$ from $w_{i,j,b_{i,j}}$ and use $\beta_{i,j}$ to correct a potential error. Specifically, he computes

$$m'_{i,j,b_{i,j}} \leftarrow \mathsf{Dec}'(\mathsf{Eval}((c_{i,j}, \mathbf{d}_{i,j}), \mathsf{td}_{i,0}, \ldots, \mathsf{td}_{i,n}), h_j) \oplus w_{i,j,b_{i,j}} \oplus \mathsf{PRF}_{K_j^\odot}(i) \oplus \beta_{i,j}.$$

For every i in the support of $\mathbf{e}_j$, the receiver can correct $w_{i,j,b_{i,j}}$ via $\gamma_{i,j}$, i.e. he computes

$$m'_{i,j,b_{i,j}} \leftarrow \mathsf{Dec}'(\mathsf{Eval}((c_{i,j}, \mathbf{d}_{i,j}), \mathsf{td}_{i,0}, \ldots, \mathsf{td}_{i,n}), h_j) \oplus w_{i,j,b_{i,j}} \oplus \gamma_{i,j} \oplus \beta_{i,j}.$$

We will first discuss correctness of the modified scheme. First note that by construction it holds that $\beta_{i,j} = f_{i,j,b_{i,j}}$. Hence, for i not in the support of $\mathbf{e}_j$ it holds that

$$m'_{i,j,b_{i,j}} = \mathsf{Dec}'(\mathsf{Eval}((c_{i,j}, \mathbf{d}_{i,j}), \mathsf{td}_{i,0}, \ldots, \mathsf{td}_{i,n}), h_j) \oplus w_{i,j,b_{i,j}} \oplus \mathsf{PRF}_{K_j^\odot}(i) \oplus \beta_{i,j}$$

$$= m_{i,j,b_{i,j}} \oplus f_{i,j,b_{i,j}} \oplus \beta_{i,j}$$

$$= m_{i,j,b_{i,j}}$$

as desired. Here, the first equality follows from

$$w_{i,j,b_{i,j}} = \mathsf{Enc}(\mathsf{ek}'_{i,j}, \mathbf{r}_j) \oplus b_{i,j} \langle \mathbf{t}_i, \mathbf{r}_j \rangle \oplus f_{i,j,b_{i,j}} \oplus m_{i,j,b_{i,j}} \oplus \mathsf{PRF}_{K_j}(i).$$

For i in the support of $\mathbf{e}_j$, it holds that

$$\begin{aligned}
m'_{i,j,b_{i,j}} &= \mathsf{Dec}'(\mathsf{Eval}((c_{i,j}, \mathbf{d}_{i,j}), \mathsf{td}_{i,0}, \ldots, \mathsf{td}_{i,n}), h_j) \oplus w_{i,j,b_{i,j}} \oplus \gamma_{i,j} \oplus \beta_{i,j} \\
&= e_{i,j} \langle \mathbf{t}_i, \mathbf{r}_j \rangle \oplus f_{i,j,b_{i,j}} \oplus m_{i,j,b_{i,j}} \oplus \mathsf{PRF}_{K_j}(i) \oplus \gamma_{i,j} \oplus \beta_{i,j} \\
&= \langle \mathbf{t}_i, \mathbf{r}_j \rangle \oplus \oplus m_{i,j,b_{i,j}} \oplus \mathsf{PRF}_{K_j}(i) \oplus \gamma_{i,j} \\
&= \langle \mathbf{t}_i, \mathbf{r}_j \rangle \oplus \oplus m_{i,j,b_{i,j}} \langle \mathbf{t}_i, \mathbf{r}_j \rangle \\
&= m_{i,j,b_{i,j}},
\end{aligned}$$

where the second equality follows from $\beta_{i,j} = f_{i,j,b_{i,j}}$, the third equality from $e_{i,j} = 1$ for i in the support of $\mathbf{e}_j$, and the fourth equality from the definition of $\gamma_{i,j}$. Hence the modified scheme is correct.

The security proof proceeds along similar lines as in [13], in that we can replace the PRF outputs $\mathsf{PRF}_{K_j}(i)$ at punctured points i by uniformly random values to make the programming via the $\gamma_{i,j}$ undetectable.

Concerning the additional communication overhead induced by these modifications, note the following. For every $j \in [\ell]$, **NISC**$_j$ takes inputs of size sub-linear in m and only performs a few local computations. Hence, using a NISC protocol such as [27] (which can be instantiated using any 2-message OT protocol), we obtain for each NISC$_j$ a communication overhead sub-linear in m, hence by choosing m and ℓ as sufficiently large polynomials, we achieve amortized upload complexity approaching 1 bit, and amortized download complexity approaching 2 bits.

This concludes the outline.

2.7   Discussion

A natural question arising considering the results of our work is whether trapdoor hash function TDH in our protocol can be instantiated from assumptions other than QR, e.g. via the DDH-based trapdoor hash function given in [22]. A point of notice is that our construction makes critical use of perfect correctness properties of the underlying TDH, as it allows us to simulate the views of malicious parties. The DDH-based construction in [22] has a correctness error, and mitigating this correctness error requires the "assistance" of the evaluator. This is highly problematic for the case of malicious evaluators, since we cannot rely on tools such as NIZK proofs to enforce honest behaviour by the evaluator as this would ruin the rate of the TDH. Consequently, trying to instantiate this blueprint with TDH that have an additional correctness error is beyond the scope of this work.

3   Key-Homomorphic Trapdoor Hash Function

We start by defining key-homomorphic trapdoor hash (KH-TDH). This primitive is similar to the one presented in [22] except that it allows for homomorphic operations over evaluation keys. Here, we define homomorphism just for linear functions which is enough for our application.

Definition 2 (Key-Homomorphic Trapdoor Hash Function). *Let $n \in \mathbb{N}$. A key-homomorphic trapdoor hash function (KH-TDH) is a tuple of algorithms* (Setup, KeyGen, Eval, H, Enc, Dec)

- Setup$(1^\lambda, L)$ *takes as input a security parameter and an integer $L \in \mathbb{N}$. It outputs a hash key* hk.
- KeyGen(hk, $\mathbf{z}$, $\mathbf{t}$) *takes as input a hash key* hk *and two vectors* $\mathbf{z} \in \{0,1\}^n$ *and* $\mathbf{t} \in \{0,1\}^L$. *It outputs a evaluation key* ek *and a trapdoor* td.
- Eval(ek, $(\mathbf{d}, c)$, $\mathbf{t}$) *takes as input an evaluation key* ek, *a linear function* $(\mathbf{d}, c) \in \{0,1\}^n \times \{0,1\}$ *and a vector* $\mathbf{t} \in \{0,1\}^L$. *It outputs a new evaluation key* ek'.
- H(hk, $\mathbf{r}$) *takes as input a hash key* hk *and a vector* $\mathbf{r} \in \{0,1\}^L$. *It outputs a hash value* h.
- Enc(ek', $\mathbf{r}$) *takes as input an evaluation key* ek' *and a vector* $\mathbf{r} \in \{0,1\}^L$. *It outputs an encoding* $a \in \{0,1\}$.
- Dec(td, $(\mathbf{d}, c)$, h) *takes as input a trapdoor* td, *a linear function* $(\mathbf{d}, c) \in \{0,1\}^n \times \{0,1\}$ *and a hash value* h. *It outputs an encoding* $a' \in \{0,1\}$.

Correctness. For all integers $n, L \in \mathbb{N}$, all vectors $\mathbf{z} \in \{0,1\}^n$, $\mathbf{t} \in \{0,1\}^L$, $\mathbf{r} \in \{0,1\}^L$ and all linear functions $(\mathbf{d}, c) \in \{0,1\}^n \times \{0,1\}$ we have that

$$
\Pr \left[a + a' = (\mathbf{z} \cdot \mathbf{d}^T + c) \cdot (\mathbf{t} \cdot \mathbf{r}^T) : \begin{array}{c} \mathsf{hk} \leftarrow \mathsf{Setup}(1^\lambda, L) \\ (\mathsf{ek}, \mathsf{td}) \leftarrow \mathsf{KeyGen}(\mathsf{hk}, \mathbf{z}, \mathbf{t}) \\ \mathsf{ek'} \leftarrow \mathsf{Eval}(\mathsf{ek}, (\mathbf{d}, c), \mathbf{t}) \\ h \leftarrow \mathsf{H}(\mathsf{hk}, \mathbf{r}) \\ a \leftarrow \mathsf{Enc}(\mathsf{ek'}, \mathbf{r}) \\ a' \leftarrow \mathsf{Dec}(\mathsf{td}, (\mathbf{d}, c), h) \end{array} \right] = 1
$$

Receiver Privacy. For all $\lambda \in \mathbb{N}$, all $n, L \in \mathbb{N}$, all vectors $\mathbf{z}_0, \mathbf{z}_1 \in \{0,1\}^n$ and $\mathbf{t} \in \{0,1\}^L$ and all PPT adversaries $\mathcal{A}$, we have that

$$
\Pr \left[b \leftarrow \mathcal{A}(\mathsf{hk}, \mathsf{ek}) : \begin{array}{c} \mathsf{hk} \leftarrow \mathsf{Setup}(1^\lambda, L) \\ b \leftarrow_\$ \{0,1\} \\ (\mathsf{ek}, \mathsf{td}) \leftarrow \mathsf{KeyGen}(\mathsf{hk}, \mathbf{z}_b, \mathbf{t}) \end{array} \right] \leq \frac{1}{2} + \mathsf{poly}(\lambda).
$$

Sender Security. For all $\lambda \in \mathbb{N}$, all $n, L \in \mathbb{N}$ such that $L = \omega(\lambda)$, all vectors $\mathbf{r} \leftarrow_\$ \{0,1\}^L$ and all PPT adversaries $\mathcal{A}$, we have that

$$
\Pr \left[b \leftarrow \mathcal{A}(\mathsf{hk}, h) : \begin{array}{c} \mathsf{hk} \leftarrow \mathsf{Setup}(1^\lambda, n, L) \\ b \leftarrow_\$ \{0,1\} \\ h \leftarrow \mathsf{H}(\mathsf{hk}, \mathbf{r}) \text{ if } b = 0 \\ h \leftarrow \{0,1\}^\lambda \text{ if } b = 1 \end{array} \right] \leq \frac{1}{2} + \mathsf{poly}(\lambda).
$$

3.1   Construction from QR

We recall the shrinking mechanism of [22] (formalized in [12]). Let a (packed) ciphertext $\mathsf{ct} = (g^r, (-1)^{b_1} h_1^r, \ldots, (-1)^{b_k} h_k^r) = (c_1, c_{2,1}, \ldots, c_{2,k})$ and let $<$ be an order over $\mathbb{J}_N$ (e.g., the lexicographic order). The shrinking mechanism of [22] simply outputs 0 if $c_{2,i} < -c_{2,i}$ and outputs 1 otherwise. We will denote this procedure by $\mathsf{Shrink_{QR}} : \mathbb{J}_N \to \{0,1\}$. Note that this procedure is completely deterministic.

Lemma 3 (Linear Homomorphism). *For any* $x \in \mathbb{J}_N$ *we have that* $\mathsf{Shrink_{QR}}(x \cdot (-1)) \mod 2 = \mathsf{Shrink_{QR}}(x) + 1 \mod 2$

Proof. If $x < -x$ then $\mathsf{Shrink_{QR}}(x) = 0$ and $\mathsf{Shrink_{QR}}(x \cdot (-1)) = 1$. Then $\mathsf{Shrink_{QR}}(x \cdot (-1)) = \mathsf{Shrink_{QR}}(x) + 1$. The other case follows using a similar reasoning.

In this section we present our key-homomorphic TDH from QR. The construction shares similarities with the one from [22]. The main difference is that we show keys are linearly homomorphic.

Construction 1 *Let* $L, n \in \mathsf{poly}(\lambda)$. *Let* $\mathsf{Shrink_{QR}}$ *be the algorithm described above.* $\mathsf{Setup}(1^\lambda, L)$:

- *Generate two safe prime numbers* P, Q *and compute* $N = P \cdot Q$. *Sample* $\mathbf{g} = (g_1, \ldots, g_L) \leftarrow_{\$} \mathbb{QR}_N^L$.
- *Output* $\mathsf{hk} = (N, \mathbf{g})$.

$\mathsf{KeyGen}(\mathsf{hk}, \mathbf{z} \in \{0,1\}^n, \mathbf{t} \in \{0,1\}^L)$:

- *Parse* hk *as* $(N, \mathbf{g})$, $\mathbf{z} = (z_1, \ldots, z_n)$ *and* $\mathbf{t} = (t_1, \ldots, t_L)$.
- *Sample* $\mathbf{s} = (s_1, \ldots, s_n) \leftarrow_{\$} [(N-1)/2]$.
- *For all* $i \in [n]$ *and all* $j \in [L]$ *compute* $y_{j,i} = g_j^{s_i} (-1)^{z_i \cdot t_j} \mod N$.
- *Output* $\mathsf{ek} = \{y_{j,i}\}_{i \in [n], j \in [L]}$ *and* $\mathsf{td} = (\mathbf{s}, \mathbf{t})$.

$\mathsf{Eval}(\mathsf{ek}, (\mathbf{d} \in \{0,1\}^n, c \in \{0,1\}), \mathbf{t})$:

- *Parse* ek *as* $\{y_{j,i}\}_{i \in [n], j \in [L]}$, $\mathbf{d} = (d_1, \ldots, d_n)$.
- *For all* $j \in [L]$ *compute* $w_j = \prod_{i=1}^n y_{j,i}^{d_i} \cdot (-1)^{c \cdot \mathbf{t}} \mod N$.
- *Output* $\mathsf{ek}' = \{w_j\}_{j \in [L]}$.

$\mathsf{H}(\mathsf{hk}, \mathbf{r} \in \{0,1\}^L)$:

- *Parse* hk *as* $(N, \mathbf{g})$ *where* $\mathbf{g} = (g_1, \ldots, g_L)$.
- *Output* $h = \prod_{j=1}^L g_j^{r_j} \mod N$.

$\mathsf{Enc}(\mathsf{ek}', \mathbf{r} \in \{0,1\}^L)$:

- *Parse* ek' *as* $\{w_j\}_{j \in [L]}$.
- *Output* $a = \mathsf{Shrink_{QR}}(\prod_{j=1}^L w_j^{r_j} \mod N)$.

$\mathsf{Dec}(\mathsf{td}, (\mathbf{d} \in \{0,1\}^n, c \in \{0,1\}), h):$

- *Parse* td *as* $(\mathbf{s}, \mathbf{t})$.
- *Compute* $s' = \mathbf{s} \cdot \mathbf{d}^T \in \mathbb{Z}_N$.
- *Output* $a' = \mathsf{Shrink}_{\mathsf{QR}}(h^{s'} \bmod N)$.

We now analyze correctness of the scheme.

Lemma 4. *The scheme presented in Construction 1 is correct.*

Proof. First note that

$$\prod_{j=1}^{L} w_j^{r_j} \bmod N = \prod_{j=1}^{L} \left(\prod_{i=1}^{n} y_{j,i}^{d_i} \cdot (-1)^{c \cdot \mathbf{t}} \right)^{r_j} = \prod_{j=1}^{L} \left(\prod_{i=1}^{n} \left(g_j^{s_i} (-1)^{z_i \cdot t_j} \right)^{d_i} \cdot (-1)^{c \cdot \mathbf{t}} \right)^{r_j}$$

$$= (-1)^{(\mathbf{z} \cdot \mathbf{d}^T + c) \cdot (\mathbf{t} \cdot \mathbf{r}^T)} \prod_{j=1}^{L} g_j^{(\mathbf{s} \cdot \mathbf{d}^T) \cdot r_j}.$$

On the other hand

$$h^{s'} \bmod N = \left(\prod_{j=1}^{L} g_j^{r_j} \right)^{\mathbf{s} \cdot \mathbf{d}^T} \bmod N.$$

Hence by the linear homomorphic correctness of $\mathsf{Shrink}_{\mathsf{QR}}$ (Lemma 3) we have that

$$a + a' \bmod 2 = \mathsf{Shrink}_{\mathsf{QR}} \left(\prod_{j=1}^{L} w_j^{r_j} \bmod N \right) + \mathsf{Shrink}_{\mathsf{QR}}(h^{s'} \bmod N)$$

$$= (\mathbf{z} \cdot \mathbf{d}^T) \cdot (\mathbf{t} \cdot \mathbf{r}^T) \bmod 2.$$

Lemma 5 (Receiver Security). *The scheme presented in Construction 1 is receiver secure assuming that the QR assumption holds.*

This is a direct consequence of the QR assumption.

Lemma 6 (Sender Security). *The scheme presented in Construction 1 is sender secure assuming that $L = \Omega(\mathsf{poly}(\lambda))$.*

Let $q, L \in \mathbb{N}$ such that $L = \Omega(\lambda)$. To prove this lemma, recall that the leftover hash lemma states that for $\mathbf{s} \leftarrow_\$ \{0,1\}^L$ and for $\mathbf{b} \leftarrow_\$ \mathbb{Z}_q^L$ then

$$(\mathbf{b}, \mathbf{s} \cdot \mathbf{b}^T) \approx_s (\mathbf{b}, u)$$

where $U \leftarrow_\$ \mathbb{Z}_q$.

Proof. Let $g_1, \ldots, g_L \leftarrow_\$ \mathbb{QR}_N$, then there exists a $\mathbf{b} \in \mathbb{Z}_{\phi(N)/4}$ such that $g^{b_i} = g_i$. Then the leftover hash lemma states that $g^u \approx_s g^{\mathbf{r} \cdot \mathbf{b}^T}$ for $u \leftarrow_\$ \mathbb{Z}_{\phi(N)/4}$.

Batch KH-TDH. We also define a batch version of the algorithms described above. Let $\mu \in \mathbb{N}$. For a set of vectors $\mathbf{t}_1, \ldots, \mathbf{t}_\mu \in \{0, 1\}^L$ we define $\mathsf{ek} = (\mathsf{ek}_1, \ldots, \mathsf{ek}_\mu) \leftarrow \mathsf{KeyGen}(\mathsf{hk}, \mathbf{z} \in \{0, 1\}^n, \mathbf{t}_1, \ldots, \mathbf{t}_\mu)$ where $\mathsf{ek}_i \leftarrow \mathsf{KeyGen}(\mathsf{hk}, \mathbf{z} \in \{0, 1\}^n, \mathbf{t}_i)$ for all $i \in [\mu]$. Additionally, we define $\mathsf{ek}' = (\mathsf{ek}'_1, \ldots, \mathsf{ek}'_\mu) \leftarrow \mathsf{Eval}(\mathsf{ek}, (\mathbf{D} \in \{0, 1\}^{n \times \mu}, \mathbf{c} \in \{0, 1\}^\mu))$ as $\mathsf{ek}'_i \leftarrow \mathsf{Eval}(\mathsf{ek}, (\mathbf{d}_i \in \{0, 1\}^n, c_i \in \{0, 1\}))$ where $\mathbf{d}_i$ is the i-th column of $\mathbf{D}$. All other algorithms are defined analogously.

Communication Complexity. We now analyze the communication complexity of our construction. Let $n, L, \mu \in \mathbb{N}$ defined as above.

- $\mathsf{hk} = L \cdot \mathsf{poly}(\lambda)$.
- $|\mathsf{td}| = n \cdot L \cdot \mathsf{poly}(\lambda)$ (in the batch version it has size $\mu \cdot L \cdot n \cdot \mathsf{poly}(\lambda)$).
- $|\mathsf{ek}| = L \cdot n \cdot \mathsf{poly}(\lambda)$ (in the batch version it has size $\mu \cdot L \cdot n \cdot \mathsf{poly}(\lambda)$).
- $|h| = \mathsf{poly}(\lambda)$.
- $|a| = |a'| = 1$ (in the batch version they have size μ).

Local Decryption. We define an additional property for our KH-TDH called local decryption. A KH-TDH is local decryptable if there exists an algorithm LocDec such that for all $\lambda \in \mathbb{N}$ we have that

$$\Pr \left[\mathbf{z} \cdot \mathbf{d}^T + c \leftarrow \mathsf{LocDec}(\mathsf{td}, \mathbf{d}, \mathsf{ek}') : \begin{array}{l} \mathsf{hk} \leftarrow \mathsf{Setup}(1^\lambda, L) \\ (\mathsf{ek}, \mathsf{td}) \leftarrow \mathsf{KeyGen}(\mathsf{hk}, \mathbf{z}, \mathbf{t}) \\ \mathsf{ek}' \leftarrow \mathsf{Eval}(\mathsf{ek}, (\mathbf{d}, c)) \end{array} \right] = 1.$$

In this batch version, given a batch of encoding keys $\mathsf{ek}' = (\mathsf{ek}'_1, \ldots, \mathsf{ek}'_\mu)$ (obtained by evaluating $\mathbf{D} \in \{0, 1\}^{n \times \mu}$ instead of a single vector $\mathbf{d}$), the LocDec algorithm can decrypt only one of ek'_i given the i-th column of $\mathbf{D}$.

It is easy to see that Construction 1 fulfills this definition. We explicitly present the LocDec algorithm.

$\mathsf{LocDec}(\mathsf{td}, \mathbf{d}, \mathsf{ek}')$:

- Parse ek' as $\{w_j\}_{j \in [L]}$ and td as $(\mathbf{s}, \mathbf{t})$.
- Compute $s' = \mathbf{s} \cdot \mathbf{d}^T$.
- For all $j \in [L]$ compute $a_j = w_j / g_j^{s'} \mod N$.
- For all $i \in \mathsf{Supp}(\mathbf{t})$, if $a_i = 1$, output 0. Else if $a_i = -1$, output 1.

Upon evaluation $\mathsf{Eval}(\mathsf{ek}, (\mathbf{d}, c))$ we obtain the encoding key $\mathsf{ek}' = (g_1^{r'} \cdot (-1)^{(\mathbf{z} \cdot \mathbf{d}^T + c) \cdot t_1}, \ldots, g_L^{r'} \cdot (-1)^{(\mathbf{z} \cdot \mathbf{d}^T + c) \cdot t_L})$ where $r' = \mathbf{s} \cdot \mathbf{d}^T$. Correctness of LocDec follows easily.

Moreover, note that, since $|\mathsf{td}| = n \cdot L \cdot \mathsf{poly}(\lambda)$, the algorithm described above can be computed by a circuit of size $n \cdot L \cdot \mathsf{poly}(\lambda)$.

4   Composable Oblivious Transfer with Optimal Rate

In this section we present our optimal-rate OT scheme that achieves UC-security against malicious adversaries under the QR and LPN assumptions. Before we present our OT construction, we enumerate the necessary ingredients as well as an auxiliary ideal functionality. Additionally, we show that this ideal functionality can be implemented with sublinear communication (with respect to the total communication of the OT protocol).

4.1   Ingredients

For our construction we need the following ingredients

- Let $L, n, \mu, t_1, t_2 \in \mathbb{N}$ such that $\nu = \sqrt{\mu}$.
- A key-homomorphic TDH scheme TDH = (Setup, KeyGen, Eval, H, Enc, LocDec, Dec).
- A puncturable PRF PRF = (KeyGen, Eval, Puncture, EvalPunct) such that PRF.Eval : $([\nu] \times [\nu] \times \{0,1\}) \to \{0,1\}$.
- A PRG PRG : $\{0,1\}^\lambda \to \{0,1\}^{2\cdot\mu}$.
- A functional LOT = (Setup, H, Enc, Dec) for the function $F_{\mathbf{r}_i,\mathsf{K},b}(\mathbf{t}_j) = F(\mathbf{t}_j, (\mathbf{r}_i, i, \mathsf{K}, b)) = \mathsf{PRF.Eval}(\mathsf{K}, (i, j, b)) + (\mathbf{r}_i \cdot \mathbf{t}_j^T) \mod 2$.
- A vector commitment VC = (Com, Open, Verify) with local openings.

Auxiliary Ideal Functionality. We present an auxiliary ideal functionality that we will use in our OT protocol. This functionality implements four procedures: i) It checks if the receiver's TDH message is well-formed. ii) It checks if the sender's TDH hash is well-formed. iii) It corrects the receiver's LPN errors. And iv) it corrects the sender's LPN errors.

For technical reasons, we define an ideal functionality that simultaneously implements these four procedures as it becomes easier to guarantee consistency of inputs for different procedures. Additionally, it gives the simulator enough power to extract the receiver's and sender's inputs that will allow for the simulation to go through in the security proof.

$\mathcal{G}_{\mathsf{aux}}$ *ideal functionality.* Consider the ideal functionality $\mathcal{G}_{\mathsf{aux}}$ such that: Receiver's Input. An LPN secret $\mathbf{s} \in \{0,1\}^n$, random coins $r \in \{0,1\}^\lambda$, a set of indices $S = \mathsf{Supp}(\mathbf{e})$, vectors $\mathbf{t}_1, \ldots, \mathbf{t}_\nu \in \{0,1\}^L$, a hash key hk, a LOT hash h_{LOT} and a VC commitments , and ,'. Sender's Input. An encoding key ek, a PRG seed seed, hash values $h_1, \ldots, h_\nu$, vectors $\mathbf{r}_1, \ldots, \mathbf{r}_\nu \in \{0,1\}^L$ and $\mathbf{t}_1', \ldots, \mathbf{t}_\nu' \in \{0,1\}^L$, a hash key hk', two support sets $T_0 = \mathsf{Supp}(\mathbf{f}_0), T_1 = \mathsf{Supp}(\mathbf{f}_1)$, vectors $\{\mathbf{d}_{i,j}\}_{(i,j)\in T_0\cup T_1}$, uncompressed ciphertexts $\{\gamma_{i,j}\}_{(i,j)\in T_0\cup T_1}$, openings $\{\delta_{i,j}\}_{i,j\in T_0\cup T_1}$ and $\{\phi_{i,j}\}_{i,j\in T_0\cup T_1}$ and a LOT hash h_{LOT}.

The functionality $\mathcal{G}_{\mathsf{aux}}$ implements the following functions:

F_{Cons} : This function checks consistency of inputs from the receiver and the sender.

- If hk $\neq$ hk' or $\mathbf{t}_1, \ldots, \mathbf{t}_\nu \neq \mathbf{t}_1', \ldots, \mathbf{t}_\nu'$ or $h_{\mathsf{LOT}} \neq h'_{\mathsf{LOT}}$ abort.

F_{CDS}: This function checks if the receiver's TDH messsage is well-formed.

- Take as input $\mathbf{s} \in \{0,1\}^n$, $r \in \{0,1\}^\lambda$, $\mathbf{t}_1, \ldots, \mathbf{t}_\nu \in \{0,1\}^L$ from the receiver. Take as input ek and seed from the sender.
- Parse ek $= (\text{ek}_1, \ldots, \text{ek}_\nu)$.
- If for all $i \in [\nu]$ $\text{ek}_i \leftarrow$ TDH.KeyGen$(\text{hk}, \mathbf{s}, \mathbf{t}_i : r)$ return seed to the receiver.
- Else abort.

F_{DVNIZK} : This function checks if the sender's message is well-formed.

- Take as input $h_1, \ldots, h_\nu$ and $\mathbf{r}, \ldots, \mathbf{r}_\nu$ from the sender.
- If for all $i \in [\nu]$ $h_i \leftarrow$ TDH.H$(\text{hk}, \mathbf{r}_i)$ return $h_1, \ldots, h_\nu$ to the receiver. Else abort.

F_{RecErr} : This function corrects the errors introduced by the receiver.

- Take as input a set of indices $S = \text{Supp}(\mathbf{e})$ from the receiver. Take as input a PRF key K, a LOT hash h'_{LOT} and vectors $\mathbf{r}_1, \ldots, \mathbf{r}_\nu$ from the sender.
- Compute $\text{K}^* \leftarrow$ PRF.Puncture$(\text{K}, \{(i,j,b) : (i,j) \in S, b \in \{0,1\}\})$.
- For all $(i,j) \in S$ compute $\text{lotct}_{0,i,j} \leftarrow$ LOT.Enc$(\text{crs}, h_{\text{LOT}}, j, (\text{K}, i, 0))$ and $\text{lotct}_{1,i,j} \leftarrow$ LOT.Enc$(\text{crs}, h_{\text{LOT}}, j, (\text{K}, i, 1))$.
- Output $(h_{\text{LOT}}, \text{K}^*, \{\text{lotct}_{b,i,j}\}_{\beta \in \{0,1\}, (i,j) \in S}$ to the receiver.

F_{SendErr} : This function corrects the errors introduced by the sender.

- Take as input $S = \text{Supp}(\mathbf{e})$, td, $\mathbf{s} \in \{0,1\}^n$, , and ,$'$ from the receiver. Take as input a support set $T = T_0 \cup T_1$, vectors $\{\mathbf{d}_{i,j}\}_{(i,j) \in T}$, uncompressed ciphertexts $\{\gamma_{i,j}\}_{(i,j) \in T}$, and openings $\{\delta_{i,j}\}_{(i,j) \in T}$ and $\{\phi_{i,j}\}_{(i,j) \in T}$ from the sender.
- For all $(i,j) \in T$ do the following:
  - If $1 \neq$ VC.Verify$(\text{crs}_{\text{VC}}, , , \gamma_{i,j}, (i,j), \delta_{i,j})$ or $1 \neq$ VC.Verify$(\text{crs}_{\text{VC}}, ,', \mathbf{d}_{i,j},$ $(i,j), \phi_{i,j})$ abort the protocol.
  - Decrypt $b'_{i,j} \leftarrow$ TDH.LocDec$(\text{td}, \mathbf{d}_{i,j}, \gamma_{i,j})$.
  - If $(i,j) \in T_{b'_{i,j}}$ and $(i,j) \notin S$, add $(i,j) \in \bar{T}$.
  - Else if $(i,j) \in T_{1-b'_{i,j}}$ and $(i,j) \in S$, add $(i,j) \in \bar{T}$.
- Output $\bar{T}$ to the receiver.

Receiver's Output. A seed seed $\in \{0,1\}^\lambda$, hash values $\{h_i\}_{i \in [\nu]}$, a punctured key K*, LOT ciphertexts $\{\text{lotct}_{b,i,j}\}_{\beta \in \{0,1\}, (i,j) \in S}$ and a set $\bar{T}$.

The following lemma states that the functionality described above can be implemented using a two-round protocol with communication sublinear in $\nu^2 = \mu$.

Lemma 7. *The functionality $\mathcal{G}$ can be implemented using a two-round NISC protocol with communication complexity of $\nu \cdot \text{poly}(n, L, t_1, t_2, \lambda)$.*

Proof. It is enough to show that there is a circuit $\mathcal{C}$ with size $\nu \cdot \text{poly}(n, L, t_1, t_2, \lambda)$ that implements the functionality described above.

To analyze the size of the circuit, we analyze each component individually. The total size of $\mathcal{C}$ will be the sum of all these components.

F_{Cons} can be implemented using a circuit of size $\nu \cdot L \cdot \mathsf{poly}(\lambda)$ (this is just the equality circuit).

For F_{CDS}, note that each $\mathsf{ek}_i \leftarrow \mathsf{TDH.KeyGen}(\mathsf{hk}, \mathbf{s}, \mathbf{t}_i)$ can be implemented using a circuit of size $n \cdot L \cdot \mathsf{poly}(\lambda)$ by the definition of $\mathsf{TDH.KeyGen}$, that is, independent of ν. Thus, repeating this process ν times, we conclude that F_{CDS} can be implemented using a circuit of size $\nu \cdot n \cdot L \cdot \mathsf{poly}(\lambda)$.

Analogously, for F_{CDS}, we have that each $h_i \leftarrow \mathsf{TDH.H}(\mathsf{hk}, \mathbf{r}_i)$ can be implemented using a circuit of size $L \cdot \mathsf{poly}(\lambda)$. Thus F_{CDS} can be implemented using a circuit of size $\nu \cdot L \cdot \mathsf{poly}(\lambda)$.

Let $t_1 = |S| = |\mathsf{Supp}(\mathbf{e})|$. To puncture the K on the set $\{(i,j,b) : (i,j) \in S, b \in \{0,1\}\}$ a circuit of size $\mathsf{poly}(t_1, \lambda)$ is needed. Moreover, for a fixed (i,j,b), $\mathsf{lotct}_{b,i,j} \leftarrow \mathsf{LOT.Enc}(\mathsf{crs}, h_{\mathsf{LOT}}, j, (\mathsf{K}, i, b))$ can be implemented using a circuit of size $\mathsf{poly}(L, \lambda)$ by the definition of LOT. Repeating this process t_1 times, we obtain a circuit of size $\mathsf{poly}(L, t_1, \lambda)$. Moreover, fetching each $\mathbf{r}_i$ requires $\nu \cdot \mathsf{poly}(\lambda)$. Hence the total size of this circuit is $\nu \cdot \mathsf{poly}(L, t_1, \lambda)$.

For F_{SendErr} :, note that each $b'_{i,j} \leftarrow \mathsf{TDH.LocDec}(\mathbf{s}, \mathbf{d}_{i,j}, \gamma_{i,j})$ requires a circuit of size $\mathsf{poly}(n, \lambda)$. Repeating this $|T|$ (where $|T| = |T_0 \cup T_1| \leq 2 \cdot t_2$) we obtain a circuit of size $\mathsf{poly}(n, t_2)$.

Finally, the total size of the circuit can be upperbounded by $\nu \cdot \mathsf{poly}(n, L, t_1, t_2, \lambda)$ and the result follows.

4.2   Universally Composable Oblivious Transfer with Optimal Rate

We are now ready to present our OT scheme. We first present the scheme, then we analyze it.

Construction 2 *Let* $L, n, \mu, t_1, t_2 \in \mathsf{poly}(\lambda)$. *Let* $\nu = \sqrt{\mu}$. *Let* $\chi_{\mu,t}$ *be the uniform distribution over the binary vectors of size* μ *and hamming weight* t. *In the scheme, parties execute* μ *independent OTs. We now describe the scheme in full detail.*
$\mathsf{Setup}(1^\lambda)$:

- *Run* $\mathsf{hk} \leftarrow \mathsf{TDH.Setup}(1^\lambda, L)$.
- *Sample vectors* $\hat{\mathbf{t}}_1, \ldots, \hat{\mathbf{t}}_\nu \leftarrow_\$ \{0,1\}^\ell$ *and a matrix* $\mathbf{V} \leftarrow_\$ \mathbb{F}_2^{\ell \times L}$, *for* $i = 1, \ldots, \nu$ *set* $\mathbf{t}_i \leftarrow \hat{\mathbf{t}}_i \cdot \mathbf{V}$. *Additionally sample an LPN matrix* $\mathbf{D} = (\mathbf{D}_1, \ldots, \mathbf{D}_\nu) \leftarrow_\$ \{0,1\}^{n \times \mu}$, *where each* $\mathbf{D}_i \in \{0,1\}^{n \times \nu}$.
- *Compute* $\mathsf{crs}_{\mathsf{LOT}} \leftarrow \mathsf{LOT.Setup}(1^\lambda)$.
- *Output* $\mathsf{crs} = (\mathsf{hk}, \{\mathbf{t}_i\}_{i \in [\nu]}, \mathbf{D}, \mathsf{crs}_{\mathsf{LOT}})$

$\mathsf{R}_1(\mathsf{crs}, \mathbf{b} \in \{0,1\}^\mu)$:

- *Parse* crs *as* $(\mathsf{hk}, \{\mathbf{t}_i\}_{i \in [\sqrt{\mu}]}, \mathbf{D}, \mathsf{crs}_{\mathsf{LOT}})$ *and* $\mathbf{b}$ *as* $(b_{1,1}, b_{1,2}, \ldots, b_{\nu,\nu})$.
- *Sample* $\mathbf{s} \leftarrow_\$ \{0,1\}^n$ *and* $\mathbf{e} \leftarrow_\$ \chi_{\mu,t}$.
- *Compute* $\mathbf{c} = \mathbf{s} \cdot \mathbf{D} + \mathbf{e} + \mathbf{b}$ *and* $(\mathsf{ek}, \mathsf{td}) \leftarrow \mathsf{TDH.KeyGen}(\mathsf{hk}, \mathbf{s}, (\mathbf{t}_1, \ldots, \mathbf{t}_\nu); r)$ *using random coins* $r \leftarrow_\$ \{0,1\}^\lambda$.
- *Compute* $h_{\mathsf{LOT}} \leftarrow \mathsf{LOT.H}(\mathsf{crs}_{\mathsf{LOT}}, (\mathbf{t}_1, \ldots, \mathbf{t}_\nu \cdot))$.

- *For all $i \in [\nu]$ compute $\mathsf{ek}'_i \leftarrow \mathsf{TDH.Eval}(\mathsf{ek}, \mathbf{D}_i, \mathbf{c}_i)$ and set $\mathsf{ek}'_i = (\gamma_{i,1}, \ldots, \gamma_{i,\nu})$. Compute $, \leftarrow \mathsf{VC.Com}(\mathsf{crs}_{\mathsf{VC}}, \mathsf{EK})$ where $\mathsf{EK} = (\mathsf{ek}_1, \ldots, \mathsf{ek}_\nu)$ and $,' \leftarrow \mathsf{VC.Com}(\mathsf{crs}_{\mathsf{VC}}, \mathbf{D})$.*
- *Set $S = \mathsf{Supp}(\mathbf{e})$. Send $(S, \mathbf{s}, r, (\mathbf{t}_1, \ldots, \mathbf{t}_\nu), \mathsf{hk}, h_{\mathsf{LOT}}, , , ')$ to $\mathcal{G}_{\mathsf{aux}}$.*
- *Output $\mathsf{ot}_1 = (\mathsf{ek}, \mathbf{c})$ and $\mathsf{st} = \mathsf{td}$.*

$\mathsf{S}(\mathsf{ot}_1, (\mathbf{m}_0, \mathbf{m}_1) \in \{0,1\}^\mu \times \{0,1\}^\mu)$:

- *Parse $\mathbf{m}_0 = (m_{0,1,1}, \ldots, m_{0,\nu,\nu})$ and $\mathbf{m}_1 = (m_{1,1,1}, \ldots, m_{1,\nu,\nu})$. Parse ot_1 as $(\mathsf{ek}, \mathbf{c})$ where $\mathbf{c} = (\mathbf{c}_1, \ldots, \mathbf{c}_\nu)$ and $\mathbf{c}_i \in \{0,1\}^\nu$.*
- *For all $i \in [\nu]$ sample $\mathbf{r}_i \leftarrow_\$ \{0,1\}^L$. Compute $h_i \leftarrow_\$ \mathsf{TDH.H}(\mathsf{hk}, \mathbf{r}_i)$. Compute $\mathsf{ek}'_i \leftarrow \mathsf{TDH.Eval}(\mathsf{ek}, \mathbf{D}_i, \mathbf{c}_i)$. Finally compute $\mathbf{z}_i \leftarrow \mathsf{TDH.Enc}(\mathsf{ek}'_i, \mathbf{r}_i)$.*
- *Sample a puncturable PRF key $\mathsf{K} \leftarrow_\$ \{0,1\}^\lambda$.*
- *For all $i \in [\nu]$ parse $\mathbf{z}_i = (z_{i,1}, \ldots, z_{i,\nu})$. For all $\beta \in \{0,1\}$ sample $\mathbf{f}_\beta \leftarrow_\$ \chi_{\mu,t_2}$ such that $\mathbf{f} = (f_{i,j})_{i,j\in[\nu]}$. For all $j \in [\nu]$ compute*

$$w_{0,i,j} = z_{i,j} + m_{0,i,j} + f_{0,i,j} + \mathsf{PRF.Eval}(\mathsf{K}, (i,j,0)) \bmod 2$$

and

$$w_{1,i,j} = z_{i,j} + (\mathbf{r}_i \cdot \mathbf{t}_j^T) + m_{1,i,j} + f_{1,i,j} + \mathsf{PRF.Eval}(\mathsf{K}, (i,j,1)) \bmod 2.$$

- *Sample a PRG seed $\mathsf{seed} \leftarrow_\$ \{0,1\}^\lambda$ and compute $\bar{\mathbf{w}} = (w_{0,1,1}, w_{1,1,1}, w_{0,1,2}, \ldots, w_{1,\nu,\nu}) + \mathsf{PRG}(\mathsf{seed})$.*
- *Compute $h_{\mathsf{LOT}} \leftarrow \mathsf{LOT.H}(\mathsf{crs}_{\mathsf{LOT}}, (\mathbf{t}_1, \ldots, \mathbf{t}_\nu))$.*
- *Set $T_0 = \mathsf{Supp}(\mathbf{f}_0)$, $T_1 = \mathsf{Supp}(\mathbf{f}_1)$ and $T = T_0 \cup T_1$.*
- *For all $i \in [\nu]$, set $\mathsf{ek}'_i = (\gamma_{i,1}, \ldots, \gamma_{i,\nu})$. Compute $(, \mathsf{st}_{\mathsf{VC}}) \leftarrow \mathsf{VC.Com}(\mathsf{crs}_{\mathsf{VC}}, \mathsf{EK})$ where $\mathsf{EK} = (\mathsf{ek}_1, \ldots, \mathsf{ek}_\nu)$. Additionally, for all $(i,j) \in T$ compute $\delta_{i,j} \leftarrow \mathsf{VC.Open}(\mathsf{crs}, , , \mathsf{st}, (i,j))$. Additionally, compute $(,', \mathsf{st}'_{\mathsf{VC}}) \leftarrow \mathsf{VC.Com}(\mathsf{crs}_{\mathsf{VC}}, \mathbf{D})$ and for all $(i,j) \in T$ compute $\phi_{i,j} \leftarrow \mathsf{VC.Open}(\mathsf{crs}, ,', \mathsf{st}', (i,j))$.*
- *Send $(\mathsf{ek}, \mathsf{seed}, \{h_i \mathbf{r}_i, \mathbf{t}_i\}_{i,\in[\nu]}, \mathsf{hk}, T_0, T_1, \{\mathbf{d}_{i,j}, \gamma_{i,j}, \delta_{i,j}, \phi_{i,j}\}_{(i,j)\in T}, h_{\mathsf{LOT}})$ to $\mathcal{G}_{\mathsf{aux}}$.*
- *Output $\mathsf{ot}_2 = (\{h_i\}_{i\in[\nu]}, \bar{\mathbf{w}})$.*

$\mathsf{R}_2(\mathsf{ot}_2, \mathsf{st})$:

- *Parse ot_2 as $(\{h_i\}_{i\in[\nu]}, \bar{\mathbf{w}})$ and st as $(\{\mathsf{st}_i\}_{i\in[\mu]}$.*
- *Obtain $(\mathsf{seed}, \{h'_i\}_{i\in[\nu]}, \mathsf{K}^*, \{\mathsf{lotct}_{b,i,j}\}_{\beta\in\{0,1\},(i,j)\in S}, \bar{T})$ from $\mathcal{G}_{\mathsf{aux}}$.*
- *Compute $(w_{0,1,1}, w_{1,1,1}, w_{0,1,2}, \ldots, w_{1,\nu,\nu}) = \bar{\mathbf{w}} + \mathsf{PRG}(\mathsf{seed})$.*
- *If there is $i \in [\nu]$ such that $h_i \neq h'_i$, abort the protocol.*
- *For all $i \in [\mu]$ compute $\mathbf{a}_i \leftarrow \mathsf{TDH.Dec}(\mathsf{td}, (\mathbf{D}_i, \mathbf{c}_i,), h_i)$. Parse $\mathbf{a}_i = (a_{i,1}, \ldots, a_{i,\nu})$.*
- *For all $(i,j) \in S = \mathsf{Supp}(\mathbf{e})$ and all $\beta \in \{0,1\}$ compute*

$$y_{i,j,b} \leftarrow \mathsf{LOT.Dec}(\mathsf{crs}_{\mathsf{LOT}}, \{\mathbf{t}_1, \ldots, \mathbf{t}_\nu\}, \mathsf{lotct}_{\beta,i,j}, i).$$

– *For all $i, j \in [\mu]$ compute*

$$m'_{i,j} = \begin{cases} w_{b_{i,j},i,j} + a_{i,j} + y_{i,j,b_{i,j}} \bmod 2, \text{ if } j \in \mathsf{Supp}(\mathbf{e}_i) \\ w_{b_{i,j},i,j} + a_{i,j} + \mathsf{PRF.Eval}(\mathsf{K}^*, (i,j,b_{i,j})) \bmod 2, \text{ otherwise} \end{cases}.$$

– *Finally, output $m_{i,j}$ where*

$$m_{i,j} = \begin{cases} m'_{i,j} + 1 \bmod 2, \text{ if } (i,j) \in \bar{T} \\ m'_{i,j}, \text{ otherwise} \end{cases}.$$

Communication Complexity. We now analyze the communication complexity for our protocol. For this analysis, we instantiate the ideal functionality $\mathcal{G}_{\mathsf{aux}}$ using a two-round protocol as in Lemma 7. Recall that, using Lemma 7, the ideal functionality $\mathcal{G}_{\mathsf{aux}}$ can be instantiated using a two-round protocol with total communication complexity $\nu \cdot \mathsf{poly}(n, L, t_1, t_2, \lambda)$. Let $\mathsf{nisc}_1, \mathsf{nisc}_2$ be the receiver's and sender's message in this protocol, respectively.

– **Receiver's Message.** The receiver's message is composed by $(\mathsf{ek}, \mathbf{c})$ and nisc_1 where
  - $|\mathsf{ek}| = \nu \cdot L \cdot n \cdot P_1(\lambda)$ for some polynomial P_1
  - $|\mathbf{c}| = \nu^2 = \mu$
  - $|\mathsf{nisc}_1| = \nu \cdot P_2(n, L, t_1, t_2, \lambda)$ for some polynomial P_2.

  Hence, the upload rate ρ_{up} of the protocol is

  $$\rho_{\mathsf{up}} = \frac{\nu \cdot L \cdot n \cdot P_1(\lambda) + \nu^2 + \nu \cdot P_2(n, L, t_1, t_2, \lambda)}{\nu^2} = 1 + \frac{L \cdot n \cdot P_1(\lambda) + P_2(n, L, t_1, t_2, \lambda)}{\nu}.$$

  Setting ν, n, L, t_1, t_2 such that $o(\nu) = L \cdot n \cdot P_1(\lambda)$ and $o(\nu) = P_2(n, L, t_1, t_2)^4$ then $\rho_{\mathsf{up}} \to 1$ for large enough ν.

– **Sender's Message.** The sender's message is composed by $(\{h_i\}_{i \in [\nu]}, \bar{\mathbf{w}})$ and nisc_2 where
  - $|\{h_i\}_{i \in [\nu]}| = \nu \cdot \mathsf{poly}(\lambda) = \nu \cdot n \cdot Q_1(\lambda)$ for some polynomial Q_1.
  - $|\bar{\mathbf{w}}| = 2 \cdot \nu^2 = 2 \cdot \mu$.
  - $|\mathsf{nisc}_2| = \nu \cdot \mathsf{poly}(n, L, t_1, t_2, \lambda) = \nu \cdot Q_2(n, L, t_1, t_2, \lambda)$ for some polynomial Q_2.

  Hence the download rate ρ_{down} of the protocol is

  $$\rho_{\mathsf{down}} = \frac{\nu \cdot Q_1(\lambda) + 2\nu^2 + \nu \cdot Q_2(n, L, t_1, t_2, \lambda)}{\nu^2} = 2 + \frac{Q_1(\lambda) + Q_2(n, L, t_1, t_2, \lambda)}{\nu}.$$

  A similar choice of parameters as in the previous case, yields that $\rho_{\mathsf{up}} \to 2$ for large enough ν.

Analysis. We now analyze the correctness and security of our scheme. Proofs are presented in the full version of the paper.

---

[4] For this to happen, we just have to set $o(\nu) = n, L, t_1, t_2$ accordingly.

Theorem 8 (Correctness). *The scheme presented in Construction 2 is correct.*

Theorem 9 (Security). *The scheme presented in Construction 2 implements the functionality $\mathcal{F}_{OT}$ in the $\mathcal{G}_{aux}$ hybrid model.*

The proof of this theorem follows from Lemmas 10 and 11 presented below.

Lemma 10 (Receiver Security). *Assume that TDH is receiver secure, VC is position binding and that the LPN assumption holds. Then the scheme presented in Construction 2 is secure against malicious senders in the $\mathcal{G}_{aux}$ hybrid model.*

Lemma 11 (Sender Security). *Assume that TDH is sender secure, PRF is pseudorandom at punctured points, LOT is sender secure and that the (entropic) LPN assumption holds. Then the scheme presented in Construction 2 is secure against malicious receivers in the $\mathcal{G}_{aux}$ hybrid model.*

Acknowledgement. Pedro Branco is funded by the Deutsche Forschungsgemeinschaft (DFG, German Research Foundation) - Project number 537717419 and partially funded by the German Federal Ministry of Education and Research (BMBF) in the course of the 6GEM research hub under grant number 16KISK038. Nico Döttling: Funded by the European Union (ERC, LACONIC, 101041207). Views and opinions expressed are however those of the author(s) only and do not necessarily reflect those of the European Union or the European Research Council. Neither the European Union nor the granting authority can be held responsible for them.

References

1. Aggarwal, D., Döttling, N., Dujmovic, J., Hajiabadi, M., Malavolta, G., Obremski, M.: Algebraic restriction codes and their applications. In: Braverman, M. (ed.) 13th Innovations in Theoretical Computer Science Conference (ITCS 2022). Leibniz International Proceedings in Informatics (LIPIcs), vol. 215, pp. 2:1–2:15. Schloss Dagstuhl – Leibniz-Zentrum für Informatik, Dagstuhl (2022). https://drops.dagstuhl.de/opus/volltexte/2022/15598
2. Aiello, W., Ishai, Y., Reingold, O.: Priced oblivious transfer: how to sell digital goods. In: Pfitzmann, B. (ed.) Advances in Cryptology. EUROCRYPT 2001. LNCS, vol. 2045, pp. 119–135. Springer, Heidelberg (2001). https://doi.org/10.1007/3-540-44987-6_8
3. Beaver, D.: Correlated pseudorandomness and the complexity of private computations. In: Miller, G.L. (ed.) Proceedings of the Twenty-Eighth Annual ACM Symposium on the Theory of Computing, Philadelphia, 22–24 May 1996, pp. 479–488. ACM (1996). https://doi.org/10.1145/237814.237996
4. Benhamouda, F., Lin, H.: k-round multiparty computation from k-round oblivious transfer via garbled interactive circuits. In: Nielsen, J.B., Rijmen, V. (eds.) Advances in Cryptology. EUROCRYPT 2018, Part II. LNCS, vol. 10821, pp. 500–532. Springer, Heidelberg (2018). https://doi.org/10.1007/978-3-319-78375-8_17
5. Boneh, D., Waters, B.: Constrained pseudorandom functions and their applications. In: Sako, K., Sarkar, P. (eds.) Advances in Cryptology. ASIACRYPT 2013, Part II. LNCS, vol. 8270, pp. 280–300. Springer, Heidelberg (2013). https://doi.org/10.1007/978-3-642-42045-0_15

6. Boyle, E., Couteau, G., Gilboa, N., Ishai, Y.: Compressing vector OLE. In: Lie, D., Mannan, M., Backes, M., Wang, X. (eds.) ACM CCS 2018: 25th Conference on Computer and Communications Security, pp. 896–912. ACM Press, Toronto (2018)

7. Boyle, E., et al.: Efficient two-round OT extension and silent non-interactive secure computation. In: Cavallaro, L., Kinder, J., Wang, X., Katz, J. (eds.) ACM CCS 2019: 26th Conference on Computer and Communications Security, pp. 291–308. ACM Press (2019)

8. Boyle, E., Couteau, G., Gilboa, N., Ishai, Y., Kohl, L., Scholl, P.: Efficient pseudorandom correlation generators: silent OT extension and more. In: Boldyreva, A., Micciancio, D. (eds.) Advances in Cryptology. CRYPTO 2019, Part III. LNCS, vol. 11694, pp. 489–518. Springer, Heidelberg (2019). https://doi.org/10.1007/978-3-030-26954-8_16

9. Boyle, E., Couteau, G., Gilboa, N., Ishai, Y., Kohl, L., Scholl, P.: Correlated pseudorandom functions from variable-density LPN. In: 61st Annual Symposium on Foundations of Computer Science, pp. 1069–1080. IEEE Computer Society Press (2020)

10. Boyle, E., Couteau, G., Gilboa, N., Ishai, Y., Kohl, L., Scholl, P.: Efficient pseudorandom correlation generators from ring-LPN. In: Shacham, H., Boldyreva, A. (eds.) Advances in Cryptology. CRYPTO 2020, Part II. LNCS, pp. 387–416. Springer, Heidelberg (2020). https://doi.org/10.1007/978-3-030-56880-1_14

11. Boyle, E., Goldwasser, S., Ivan, I.: Functional signatures and pseudorandom functions. In: Krawczyk, H. (ed.) PKC 2014: 17th International Conference on Theory and Practice of Public Key Cryptography. LNCS, vol. 8383, pp. 501–519. Springer, Heidelberg (2014). https://doi.org/10.1007/978-3-642-54631-0_29

12. Brakerski, Z., Branco, P., Döttling, N., Garg, S., Malavolta, G.: Constant ciphertext-rate non-committing encryption from standard assumptions. In: TCC 2020: 18th Theory of Cryptography Conference, Part I. LNCS, vol. 12550, pp. 58–87. Springer, Heidelberg (2020). https://doi.org/10.1007/978-3-030-64375-1_3

13. Brakerski, Z., Branco, P., Döttling, N., Pu, S.: Batch-OT with optimal rate. In: Dunkelman, O., Dziembowski, S. (eds.) Advances in Cryptology. EUROCRYPT 2022. LNCS, vol. 13276, pp. 157–186. Springer, Cham (2022). https://doi.org/10.1007/978-3-031-07085-3_6

14. Brakerski, Z., Döttling, N., Garg, S., Malavolta, G.: Leveraging linear decryption: rate-1 fully-homomorphic encryption and time-lock puzzles. In: Hofheinz, D., Rosen, A. (eds.) TCC 2019: 17th Theory of Cryptography Conference, Part II. LNCS, vol. 11892, pp. 407–437. Springer, Heidelberg (2019)

15. Brakerski, Z., Goldwasser, S.: Circular and leakage resilient public-key encryption under subgroup indistinguishability - (or: Quadratic residuosity strikes back). In: Rabin, T. (ed.) Advances in Cryptology. CRYPTO 2010. LNCS, vol. 6223, pp. 1–20. Springer, Heidelberg (2010). https://doi.org/10.1007/978-3-642-14623-7_1

16. Branco, P., Döttling, N., Srinivasan, A.: A framework for statistically sender private OT with optimal rate. In: Handschuh, H., Lysyanskaya, A. (eds.) Advances in Cryptology. CRYPTO 2023. LNCS, vol. 14081, pp. 548–576. Springer, Cham (2023). https://doi.org/10.1007/978-3-031-38557-5_18

17. Catalano, D., Fiore, D.: Vector commitments and their applications. In: Kurosawa, K., Hanaoka, G. (eds.) PKC 2013: 16th International Conference on Theory and Practice of Public Key Cryptography. LNCS, vol. 7778, pp. 55–72. Springer, Heidelberg (2013). https://doi.org/10.1007/978-3-642-36362-7_5

18. Chase, M., Garg, S., Hajiabadi, M., Li, J., Miao, P.: Amortizing rate-1 OT and applications to PIR and PSI. In: Nissim, K., Waters, B. (eds.) Theory of Cryptography. LNCS, vol. 13044, pp. 126–156. Springer, Cham (2021). https://doi.org/10.1007/978-3-030-90456-2_5

19. Dodis, Y., Halevi, S., Rothblum, R.D., Wichs, D.: Spooky encryption and its applications. In: Robshaw, M., Katz, J. (eds.) Advances in Cryptology. CRYPTO 2016, Part III. LNCS, vol. 9816, pp. 93–122. Springer, Heidelberg (2016). https://doi.org/10.1007/978-3-662-53015-3_4

20. Dodis, Y., Reyzin, L., Smith, A.: Fuzzy extractors: how to generate strong keys from biometrics and other noisy data. In: Cachin, C., Camenisch, J. (eds.) Advances in Cryptology. EUROCRYPT 2004. LNCS, vol. 3027, pp. 523–540. Springer, Heidelberg (2004). https://doi.org/10.1007/978-3-540-24676-3_31

21. Döttling, N., Garg, S., Hajiabadi, M., Masny, D., Wichs, D.: Two-round oblivious transfer from CDH or LPN. In: Rijmen, V., Ishai, Y. (eds.) Advances in Cryptology. EUROCRYPT 2020, Part II. LNCS, vol. 12106, pp. 768–797, Springer, Heidelberg (2020). https://doi.org/10.1007/978-3-030-45724-2_26

22. Döttling, N., Garg, S., Ishai, Y., Malavolta, G., Mour, T., Ostrovsky, R.: Trapdoor hash functions and their applications. In: Boldyreva, A., Micciancio, D. (eds.) Advances in Cryptology. CRYPTO 2019, Part III. LNCS, vol. 11694, pp. 3–32. Springer, Heidelberg (2019). https://doi.org/10.1007/978-3-030-26954-8_1

23. Garg, S., Hajiabadi, M., Ostrovsky, R.: Efficient range-trapdoor functions and applications: rate-1 OT and more. In: TCC 2020: 18th Theory of Cryptography Conference, Part I. LNCS, vol. 12550, pp. 88–116. Springer, Heidelberg (2020). https://doi.org/10.1007/978-3-030-64375-1_4

24. Garg, S., Srinivasan, A.: Two-round multiparty secure computation from minimal assumptions. In: Nielsen, J.B., Rijmen, V. (eds.) Advances in Cryptology. EUROCRYPT 2018, Part II. LNCS, vol. 10821, pp. 468–499. Springer, Heidelberg (2018). https://doi.org/10.1007/978-3-319-78375-8_16

25. Gentry, C., Halevi, S.: Compressible FHE with applications to PIR. In: Hofheinz, D., Rosen, A. (eds.) TCC 2019: 17th Theory of Cryptography Conference, Part II. LNCS, vol. 11892, pp. 438–464. Springer, Heidelberg (2019). https://doi.org/10.1007/978-3-030-36033-7_17

26. Ishai, Y., Kilian, J., Nissim, K., Petrank, E.: Extending oblivious transfers efficiently. In: Boneh, D. (ed.) Advances in Cryptology. CRYPTO 2003. LNCS, vol. 2729, pp. 145–161. Springer, Heidelberg (2003). https://doi.org/10.1007/978-3-540-45146-4_9

27. Ishai, Y., Kushilevitz, E., Ostrovsky, R., Prabhakaran, M., Sahai, A.: Efficient non-interactive secure computation. In: Paterson, K.G. (ed.) Advances in Cryptology. EUROCRYPT 2011. LNCS, vol. 6632, pp. 406–425. Springer, Heidelberg (2011). https://doi.org/10.1007/978-3-642-20465-4_23

28. Ishai, Y., Prabhakaran, M., Sahai, A.: Founding cryptography on oblivious transfer - efficiently. In: Wagner, D. (ed.) Advances in Cryptology. CRYPTO 2008. LNCS, vol. 5157, pp. 572–591. Springer, Heidelberg (2008). https://doi.org/10.1007/978-3-540-85174-5_32

29. Kiayias, A., Papadopoulos, S., Triandopoulos, N., Zacharias, T.: Delegatable pseudorandom functions and applications. In: Sadeghi, A.R., Gligor, V.D., Yung, M. (eds.) ACM CCS 2013: 20th Conference on Computer and Communications Security, pp. 669–684. ACM Press, Berlin (2013)

30. Kilian, J.: Founding cryptography on oblivious transfer. In: 20th Annual ACM Symposium on Theory of Computing, pp. 20–31. ACM Press, Chicago (1988)

31. Naor, M., Pinkas, B.: Efficient oblivious transfer protocols. In: Kosaraju, S.R. (ed.) 12th Annual ACM-SIAM Symposium on Discrete Algorithms, pp. 448–457. ACM-SIAM, Washington (2001)

32. Orlandi, C., Scholl, P., Yakoubov, S.: The rise of Paillier: homomorphic secret sharing and public-key silent OT. In: Canteaut, A., Standaert, F.X. (eds.) Advances in Cryptology. EUROCRYPT 2021, pp. 678–708. Springer, Cham (2021). https://doi.org/10.1007/978-3-030-77870-5_24

33. Peikert, C., Shiehian, S.: Noninteractive zero knowledge for NP from (plain) learning with errors. In: Boldyreva, A., Micciancio, D. (eds.) Advances in Cryptology. CRYPTO 2019, Part I. LNCS, vol. 11692, pp. 89–114. Springer, Heidelberg (2019). https://doi.org/10.1007/978-3-662-53015-3_4

34. Peikert, C., Vaikuntanathan, V., Waters, B.: A framework for efficient and composable oblivious transfer. In: Wagner, D. (ed.) Advances in Cryptology. CRYPTO 2008. LNCS, vol. 5157, pp. 554–571. Springer, Heidelberg (2008). https://doi.org/10.1007/978-3-540-85174-5_31

35. Regev, O.: On lattices, learning with errors, random linear codes, and cryptography. In: Gabow, H.N., Fagin, R. (eds.) 37th Annual ACM Symposium on Theory of Computing, pp. 84–93. ACM Press, Baltimore (2005)

36. Yao, A.C.C.: How to generate and exchange secrets (extended abstract). In: 27th Annual Symposium on Foundations of Computer Science, pp. 162–167. IEEE Computer Society Press, Toronto (1986)

Succinct Homomorphic Secret Sharing

Damiano Abram$^{(\boxtimes)}$ ⓘ, Lawrence Roy, and Peter Scholl ⓘ

Aarhus University, Aarhus, Denmark
{damiano.abram,peter.scholl}@cs.au.dk

Abstract. This work introduces homomorphic secret sharing (HSS) with succinct share size. In HSS, private inputs are shared between parties, who can then homomorphically evaluate a function on their shares, obtaining a share of the function output. In succinct HSS, a portion of the inputs can be distributed using shares whose size is sublinear in the number of such inputs. The parties can then locally evaluate a function f on the shares, with the restriction that f must be linear in the succinctly shared inputs.

We construct succinct, two-party HSS for branching programs, based on either the decisional composite residuosity assumption, a DDH-like assumption in class groups, or learning with errors with a superpolynomial modulus-to-noise ratio. We then give several applications of succinct HSS, which were only previously known using fully homomorphic encryption, or stronger tools:

- **Succinct vector oblivious linear evaluation (VOLE):** Two parties can obtain secret shares of a long, arbitrary vector x, multiplied by a scalar Δ, with communication sublinear in the size of the vector.
- **Batch, multi-party distributed point functions**: A protocol for distributing a batch of secret, random point functions among N parties, for any polynomial N, with communication sublinear in the number of DPFs.
- **Sublinear MPC for any number of parties:** Two new constructions of MPC with sublinear communication complexity, with N parties for any polynomial N: (1) For general layered Boolean circuits of size s, with communication $O(Ns/\log\log s)$, and (2) For layered, sufficiently wide Boolean circuits, with communication $O(Ns/\log s)$.

1 Introduction

Homomorphic secret sharing (HSS) allows two or more parties to perform a distributed computation on private inputs. HSS can be seen as a distributed

Supported by the Aarhus University Research Foundation (AUFF), the Independent Research Fund Denmark (DFF) (grant DFF-0165-00107B "C3PO"), and the DARPA SIEVE program (contract HR001120C0085 "FROMAGER"). Any opinions, findings and conclusions or recommendations expressed in this material are those of the author(s) and do not necessarily reflect the views of DARPA. Distribution Statement "A" (Approved for Public Release, Distribution Unlimited).

M. Joye and G. Leander (Eds.): EUROCRYPT 2024, LNCS 14656, pp. 301–330, 2024.
https://doi.org/10.1007/978-3-031-58751-1_11

analogue of homomorphic encryption, where instead of having a single server carry out a computation on encrypted inputs, several parties are each given a share of the inputs, and can then locally carry out homomorphic computations on the shares, to obtain a share of the desired result.

HSS was first introduced by Boyle, Gilboa and Ishai [BGI16], who showed how to build two-party HSS for branching programs based on the decisional Diffie-Hellman (DDH) assumption. A major application of the [BGI16] result was to obtain secure two-party computation for arbitrary, layered Boolean circuits of size s with a communication complexity of $O(s/\log s)$ bits. This was the first work to bypass the circuit-size barrier in secure computation, without relying on fully homomorphic encryption (FHE). Since then, many subsequent works on HSS have focused on improving efficiency and obtaining HSS under new assumptions, offering alternative approaches to sublinear secure computation without FHE.

1.1   Our Results

In this work, we introduce a new family of *succinct HSS* schemes. In succinct HSS, a subset of the inputs from one party can be shared succinctly, with a share size of $o(n)$ for n-bit inputs. This is in contrast to classical HSS, where all known constructions have share size $\Omega(n)$. We build two-party, succinct HSS for the class of *special, restricted multiplication straightline* (special RMS) programs. A function f is a special RMS program if it is an RMS program, and furthermore if $f(x,y)$ is linear in x, where x is the subset of inputs with succinct shares.

Below is an overview of our main results, including applications to distributed point functions and MPC with sublinear communication.

Bilinear HSS and Succinct VOLE. We start by building a form of HSS for bilinear functions, that is, two-party HSS where one party, Alice, holds as input a vector $x \in \mathbb{Z}_q^n$, while Bob holds a matrix $M \in \mathbb{Z}_q^{m \times n}$. The goal is to obtain additive secret shares of the bilinear function $M \cdot x$, using only a single round of interaction. We construct a succinct form of bilinear HSS, where Alice's message has size *independent of n and m*, using techniques from previous trapdoor hash functions for linear predicates [DGI+19,RS21]. We obtain instantiations based on each of the following assumptions: (1) decisional composite residuosity (DCR), (2) quadratic residuosity (QR), (3) a DDH-like assumption in class groups, or (4) learning with errors (LWE) with a superpolynomial modulus-to-noise ratio.

We show that bilinear HSS can be used to build a succinct form of *vector oblivious linear evaluation* (VOLE), that is, the functionality $f((x_0, x_1), \Delta) = x_0 \Delta + x_1$, with input vectors (x_0, x_1) from Alice and a scalar Δ from Bob: we obtain a one-round protocol, where Alice's input x_1 is sampled at random and the total communication is sublinear in the dimension of x_0. We call this primitive *succinct, half-chosen VOLE*. Half-chosen VOLE suffices for many applications of VOLE, such as designated-verifier zero-knowledge proofs [BMRS21,DIO21,YSWW21] and private set intersection [RR22].

Theorem 1 (informal). *There exists a protocol for half-chosen VOLE of length n, with one parallel message from each party, and total communication complexity $O(n^{2/3})$,[1] if one of the following assumptions holds: (1) DCR, (2) QR, (3) a DDH-like assumption in class groups, or (4) LWE with a superpolynomial modulus-to-noise ratio.*

The communication can further be reduced to $O(n^{1/2})$, by relying on a variant of bilinear HSS for structured matrices with reduced communication cost. This requires either the power-DDH assumption over Paillier groups or class groups, or a new variant of ring-LWE called the *power ring-LWE* assumption.

We note that previous constructions of laconic function evaluation (LFE) also imply succinct, bilinear HSS and half-chosen VOLE. However, LFE constructions are only known from LWE with a sub-exponential modulus-to-noise ratio [QWW18], or from ring-LWE with a polynomial modulus [Ros22]. Furthermore, the resulting bilinear HSS and half-chosen VOLE schemes would require two rounds of interaction.

Bilinear HSS + HSS for RMS $\Rightarrow$ Succinct HSS for Special RMS. We observe that existing constructions of two-party HSS for RMS programs can be upgraded to achieve succinct HSS for special RMS programs, by applying our succinct, half-chosen VOLE protocol. This leads to constructions based on DCR, class groups or LWE (here, we cannot use QR, since there is no suitable HSS for RMS programs based on QR).

Next, we present several applications of succinct HSS.

Batch, Multi-party Distributed Point Functions. A point function $f_{\alpha,\beta} : \{0,1\}^k \to \{0,1\}$ is a function, parametrized by α, β, where $f_{\alpha,\beta}(\alpha) = \beta$, and $f_{\alpha,\beta}(x) = 0$ for all $x \neq \alpha$. A distributed point function (DPF) is a way of distributing succinct shares of a secret point function to N parties, such that they can locally compute a share of $f_{\alpha,\beta}(x)$, for any public x.

Using two-party, succinct HSS, we construct a batch, N-party DPF protocol, which distributes shares for m DPFs on a domain of size 2^k, using $O(m + k) + o(m \cdot 2^k)$ communication (ignoring $\mathsf{poly}(\lambda, N)$ factors). Therefore, for sufficiently high m (but still $\mathsf{poly}(\lambda)$), the per-DPF communication becomes $\mathsf{poly}(\lambda)$. If the α, β values defining the point functions are uniformly random, the per-DPF communication even becomes $o(1)$. This effectively gives a pseudorandom correlation generator [BCG+19] for distributing a batch of random DPF instances. This was not known previously, without relying on FHE.

Sublinear MPC Without FHE. Finally, we present two new results on MPC with sublinear communication, for any (polynomial) number of parties. The following results are obtained, respectively, via our batch DPF construction and one-time truth tables [Cou19], and directly via succinct HSS.

---

[1] Ignoring factors of $\mathsf{poly}(\lambda)$, for security parameter λ.

Theorem 2 (Informal). *Let $N = \mathsf{poly}(\lambda)$, and assume either DCR or a DDH-like assumption in class groups. Then, for a sufficiently large Boolean circuit C with s gates, there exists an N-party protocol that securely computes C with semi-honest security and total communication complexity:*

1. $O(Ns/\log\log s)$, *for arbitrary layered circuits C.*
2. $O(Ns/\log s)$, *for layered circuits C that are sufficiently wide.*

For comparison with previous works, the standard, semi-honest GMW protocol with multiplication triples has $O(Ns)$ communication complexity. The result from [BGI16] for 2 parties, using HSS based on DDH, achieved $O(s/\log s)$ complexity for arbitrary layered circuits. Couteau [Cou19] used one-time truth tables to obtain $O(Ns/\log\log s)$ in the correlated randomness model, for any N. The recent work of [DIJL23] achieves $O(Ns/\log\log s)$ complexity for any N, for sufficiently wide, layered circuits using sparse LPN, while [BCM23] achieves $O(s/\log\log s)$ for arbitrary circuits and up to 5 parties.

On Malicious Security. We present all of our results in the semi-honest security model. Analogous results in the malicious model can be obtained by applying communication-preserving compilers [NN01] based on succinct zero-knowledge arguments, which can be built from collision-resistant hashing [Kil92].

1.2   Technical Overview—Construction of Succinct HSS

Homomorphic Secret Sharing. Here we briefly review the two-party HSS technique introduced by [BGI16], and subsequently extended in [BKS19, OSY21, RS21, ADOS22]. Suppose that there are secret values x and y, which are unknown to Alice and Bob. However, they both get ciphertexts c and c' encrypting x and y under some public key pk. Let k be the private counterpart of pk. The parties also have subtractive secret shares $[\![k]\!]$ of the secret key k, i.e., Alice has $[\![k]\!]_0$ and Bob has $[\![k]\!]_1$ such that $[\![k]\!]_0 - [\![k]\!]_1 = k$. Alice and Bob want to get secret shares of $x \cdot y$, without communicating.

Some properties are required of the encryption scheme. First, it must be additively homomorphic, i.e., $c \cdot c'$ consists of an encryption of $x + y$. Second, decryption is required to work in a particular way: $k \cdot x = \mathsf{DLog}(c^k)$.[2] Note that this requires some instances of discrete logarithm to be easy. For schemes based on DCR or class groups, there is a subgroup where discrete logarithm is easy, and DLog works within this group. For LWE-based schemes, the equivalent of DLog becomes scaling and rounding, which works whenever the plaintext is only hidden by small noise.

Now, Alice and Bob start by converting the ciphertext c into secret shares, by doing a distributed decryption. They first compute $\langle\!\langle k \cdot x \rangle\!\rangle = c^{[\![k]\!]}$; this is a *multiplicative sharing* of $k \cdot x$, which means that $\mathsf{DLog}(\langle\!\langle k \cdot x \rangle\!\rangle_0 / \langle\!\langle k \cdot x \rangle\!\rangle_1) =$

---

[2] Technically, this is a simplification for Damgård–Jurik-based HSS [RS21]. For other schemes, k becomes a vector, and c becomes a matrix of group elements which has k as a kind of eigenvector (in the exponent).

$k \cdot x$. Next they use a *distributed discrete-log* operation DDLog on their multiplicative shares, which has the property that $\mathsf{DDLog}(\langle\!\langle z \rangle\!\rangle_0) - \mathsf{DDLog}(\langle\!\langle z \rangle\!\rangle_1) = \mathsf{DLog}(\langle\!\langle z \rangle\!\rangle_0/\langle\!\langle z \rangle\!\rangle_1) = z$,[3] allowing the DLog shares to be computed through purely local computation. They use it to convert $\langle\!\langle k \cdot x \rangle\!\rangle$ into a subtractive sharing $[\![k \cdot x]\!] = \mathsf{DDLog}(\langle\!\langle k \cdot x \rangle\!\rangle)$. This process can then be repeated starting from $[\![k \cdot x]\!]$ (instead of $[\![k]\!]$) and c' (instead of c), to get $\langle\!\langle k \cdot x \cdot y \rangle\!\rangle = c'^{[\![k \cdot x]\!]}$ and $[\![k \cdot x \cdot y]\!] = \mathsf{DDLog}(\langle\!\langle k \cdot x \cdot y \rangle\!\rangle)$. From $[\![k \cdot x \cdot y]\!]$, there are various techniques that allow retrieving $[\![x \cdot y]\!]$. Alice and Bob have now successfully multiplied x by y.

Generalizing this technique gives two-party HSS for Restricted Multiplication Straight-line (RMS) programs. These are arithmetic circuits that support two kinds of values: (a) input ciphertexts (encryptions c of an input x under pk), and (b) memory shares (subtractive secret-sharings $[\![k \cdot x]\!]$ where x is the value and k is the private counterpart of pk); with the restriction that multiplication is only allowed between an input ciphertext and a memory share, but never between two memory shares. In the HSS scheme, multiplications between input ciphertexts and memory wires can be performed without any communication as we outlined above. Additions between memory wires come at essentially no cost thanks to the linearity of subtractive secret sharing.

We recall that RMS programs are powerful enough to implement branching programs and log-depth circuits [BGI16, Appendix A].

Succinct HSS from Half-Chosen VOLE. While the communication cost of HSS is independent of the circuit size, it still requires sending (encryptions of) both parties' inputs to each other. Even in the worst case, information theory only requires that one party send data proportional to its input size, so we sought to build *succinct HSS*, where some inputs are sent with only sublinear communication. We found a construction of succinct HSS for special RMS programs.

Special RMS programs have two different classes of inputs: Standard inputs are the usual input ciphertexts, and can be multiplied by memory values as normal. Special inputs can only be used as memory values, and can never be multiplied by memory values. A succinct HSS scheme is an HSS scheme for special RMS programs with communication sublinear in the size of the special inputs. We highlight that since HSS supports complex non-linear operations on the input ciphertexts, succinctness for these is impossible in general.

In the HSS framework outlined earlier, notice that implementing succinct HSS for a vector of special inputs $\boldsymbol{x} = (x_1, \ldots, x_n)$ boils down to succinctly obtaining shares $[\![k \cdot \boldsymbol{x}]\!] = ([\![k \cdot x_1]\!], \ldots, [\![k \cdot x_n]\!])$ of $\boldsymbol{x}$'s product with the secret key. Without loss of generality, suppose that Alice is the party who knows the input $\boldsymbol{x}$. In our construction, she will only send a compact hash of her input, so we will call her the *hasher* and Bob the *encryptor*. Since the parties already have secret shares of $[\![k]\!]$, we have that $[\![k \cdot \boldsymbol{x}]\!] = [\![k]\!]_0 \boldsymbol{x} - [\![k]\!]_1 \boldsymbol{x}$, and the hasher can locally compute the first term $[\![k]\!]_0 \boldsymbol{x}$. The second term, $-[\![k]\!]_1 \cdot \boldsymbol{x}$, is a product of a scalar $-[\![k]\!]_1$ known by the encryptor with a vector $\boldsymbol{x}$ known by the hasher. That is, they need a vector oblivious linear evaluation (VOLE), where the hasher chooses

---

[3] For HSS based on DDH, this is only possible with probability $1 - 1/\mathsf{poly}(\lambda)$.

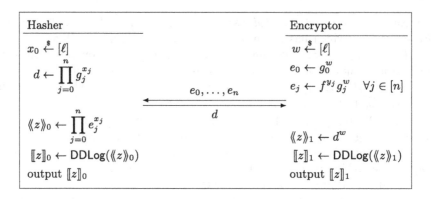

Fig. 1. Bilinear HSS for inner product.

vector $\boldsymbol{x}$ and gets $[\![\Delta \cdot \boldsymbol{x}]\!]_0$, while the encryptor chooses the scalar $\Delta = -[\![k]\!]_1$ and gets $[\![\Delta \cdot \boldsymbol{x}]\!]_1$, such that $[\![\Delta \cdot \boldsymbol{x}]\!]_0 - [\![\Delta \cdot \boldsymbol{x}]\!]_1 = k \cdot \boldsymbol{x}$. Since the hasher only chooses one vector and gets a second vector sampled pseudorandomly, we call this a *half-chosen VOLE*. See Sect. 6 for more discussion of succinct HSS.

Realizing Half-Chosen VOLE and Bilinear HSS. We consider half-chosen VOLE as a special case of a more general problem, *bilinear HSS*. The hasher and the encryptor have input vectors $\boldsymbol{x}$ and $\boldsymbol{y}$, respectively, and they want secret shares of some bilinear function of $\boldsymbol{x}$ and $\boldsymbol{y}$. We additionally require that bilinear HSS has only one simultaneous round, i.e., they must each send some hash or encryption of $\boldsymbol{x}$ and $\boldsymbol{y}$, but further communication (which might depend on both $\boldsymbol{x}$ and $\boldsymbol{y}$) is disallowed. For efficiency, we require that the communication sent by the hasher must be sublinear in their input size.

We start with a bilinear HSS protocol for the dot product $z = \langle \boldsymbol{x}, \boldsymbol{y} \rangle$. Our protocol, illustrated in Fig. 1, is inspired by existing constructions of trapdoor hash functions for linear predicates [DGI+19, RS21]. We work over a group, and assume that the elements $g_0, \ldots, g_n$ each generate the same cyclic subgroup. Moreover, we assume the existence of a subgroup generated by an element f where discrete log is easy. This is consistent with the non-interactive discrete logarithm sharing (NIDLS) framework of [ADOS22], which can be instantiated either from DCR or class groups.

In our protocol, the hasher only sends a Pedersen commitment[4]

$$d = g_0^{x_0} g_1^{x_1} \cdots g_n^{x_n}$$

---

[4] Note that in any such protocol both parties must at least commit to their inputs. If one didn't, then it could learn two different output shares $[\![z]\!]_i, [\![z']\!]_i$, and take the difference to get $z - z'$ (since the other party's share must be the same both times), which would leak.

(the *hash*) to their input $(x_1, \ldots, x_n)$ (x_0 is a random mask), which has size independent of n. Meanwhile, the encryptor picks a random private key w, and sends ElGamal-like ciphertexts $e_j = f^{y_j} g_j^w$ for $j = 0, \ldots, n$ (where $y_0 := 0$). Using the homomorphism on these ciphertexts, they can then get multiplicative shares $\langle\!\langle z \rangle\!\rangle_0 := \prod_{j=0}^n e_j^{x_j}$ and $\langle\!\langle z \rangle\!\rangle_1 := d^w$ of $z = \langle x, y \rangle$.

$$\frac{\langle\!\langle z \rangle\!\rangle_0}{\langle\!\langle z \rangle\!\rangle_1} = \frac{\prod_{j=0}^n e_j^{x_j}}{d^w} = \frac{g_0^{w \cdot x_0} \prod_{j=1}^n f^{x_j \cdot y_j} g_j^{w \cdot x_j}}{\prod_{j=0}^n g_j^{w \cdot x_j}} = \prod_{j=1}^n f^{x_j \cdot y_j} = f^{\langle x, y \rangle}$$

Finally, DDLog converts these to additive shares $[\![z]\!]$.

Note that Fig. 1 has one simultaneous round, as is required for bilinear HSS. One simultaneous round protocols often have a very useful property: the messages sent by each party can be reused. If the hasher generates l messages and the encryptor generates m messages, they can compute secret shares of all $l \cdot m$ inner products. That is, if the hasher's input vectors are the columns of a matrix X and the encryptor's input vectors are the rows of a matrix Y, then they get secret shares of the matrix product $Y \cdot X$. They get all $m \cdot l$ outputs, even though the hasher sends only l group elements and the encryptor sends only $m \cdot (n+1)$ group elements. The output can have significant length, even though we are building on an inner product protocol, which only produces a single output.

Next, we construct bilinear HSS for scalar-vector product with sublinear communication in both directions – i.e., succinct half-chosen VOLE. Let N be the length of the original vector x, and let $n = m = N^{1/3}$ and $l = N^{2/3}$. Let $Y = \Delta \cdot \mathrm{id}_n$, where Δ is the scalar input to the VOLE from Bob, and let X be an $n \times l$ matrix such that x is the columns of X stacked together. Then the result is $Y \cdot X = \Delta \cdot X$, and stacking its columns gives $\Delta \cdot x$, so we have a half-chosen VOLE. We have achieved half-chosen VOLE, while sending a total of only $l + m \cdot (n+1) \approx 2 \cdot N^{2/3}$ group elements.

We formally define bilinear HSS in Sect. 3, detail our initial construction in Sect. 4.1, and explain how to build succinct half-chosen VOLE in Sect. 5.

More Efficient Bilinear HSS. In the previous bilinear HSS construction, the hasher had to send an encryption E of the whole matrix Y, even though it was structured as a multiple of the identity matrix. If we could somehow preserve some of this structure in E, then we could compress it.

In Fig. 2, we present such a bilinear HSS construction, based on the Power-DDH assumption used by the efficient range-trapdoor functions of [GHO20]. Here, we describe its relation with Fig. 1. Run Fig. 1 with n repetitions of the encryptor, one for each of the n rows of Y. However, make two changes to reduce the entropy of E, by sampling values in a correlated manner. First, instead of sampling $g_0, \ldots, g_n$ independently, have the encryptor sample a random exponent α, and set $g_j = g^{\alpha^j}$.[5] We require that the g_j's are given to the hasher in an

---

[5] This requires some Setup to be run before the protocol starts, since the hasher must not learn α.

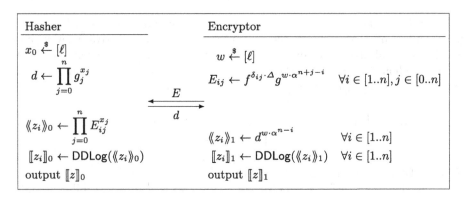

Fig. 2. Bilinear HSS for scalar-vector product from Power DDH. Before this protocol is run, the hasher must receive $g_j = g^{\alpha^j}$ for $j \in [0..n]$ from the encryptor.

initial setup phase. The Power-DDH assumption states that these are indistinguishable from random group elements. Second, sample the secret keys w_i in a correlated way, as $w_i = w \cdot \alpha^{n-i}$ for random w.

With these two changes, we have

$$E_{ij} = f^{\Delta \cdot \delta_{ij}} g_j^{w_i} = f^{\Delta \cdot \delta_{ij}} g^{w \cdot \alpha^{n+j-i}},$$

where δ_{ij} is the Kronecker delta function (1 if $i = j$, and 0 otherwise). Note that E_{ij} now only depends on $j - i$, so E is constant along diagonals, making it a Toeplitz matrix. Therefore, it can be compressed: the first row and column are enough to reconstruct the rest. This takes $2n$ group elements, as E is an $n \times (n+1)$ matrix.

Correctness still works in the same way:

$$\frac{\langle\!\langle z_i \rangle\!\rangle_0}{\langle\!\langle z_i \rangle\!\rangle_1} = \frac{\prod_{j=0}^n E_{ij}^{x_j}}{d^{w \cdot \alpha^{n-i}}} = \frac{\prod_{j=0}^n f^{\delta_{ij} \cdot \Delta \cdot x_j} g^{w \cdot \alpha^{n+j-i} \cdot x_j}}{\prod_{j=0}^n g_j^{w \cdot \alpha^{n-i} \cdot x_j}} = f^{\Delta \cdot x_i} \cdot \frac{\prod_{j=0}^n g^{w \cdot \alpha^{n+j-i} \cdot x_j}}{\prod_{j=0}^n g^{w \cdot \alpha^{n+j-i} \cdot x_j}}$$

After DDLog, the protocol outputs additive shares of the vector $\Delta \cdot \boldsymbol{x}$.

Now, we can further improve efficiency by reusing E for many different hashes. Divide $\boldsymbol{x}$ into $N^{1/2}$ blocks $\boldsymbol{x}_k$ of $n = N^{1/2}$ elements each, then compute shares of $\Delta \cdot \boldsymbol{x}_k$ for all k to get $\Delta \cdot \boldsymbol{x}$. The communication cost is $O(N^{1/2})$: $N^{1/2}$ hashes, plus a single matrix E containing $2 \cdot N^{1/2}$ group elements. We detail this construction in the full version of our paper [ARS24, Section 6.1].

LWE-Based Bilinear HSS. We also designed protocols for bilinear HSS from the learning with errors (LWE) assumption. In Fig. 3 we present a direct translation of Fig. 1 from groups to lattices. Assume that $\boldsymbol{x} \in \mathbb{Z}_p^n$ and $\boldsymbol{y} \in \mathbb{Z}_p^n$ are encoded into the larger ring $\mathbb{Z}_q$ by taking the smallest representative modulo p. Then the digest becomes the usual SIS hash function: $\boldsymbol{d} = A \cdot \boldsymbol{x} + B \cdot \boldsymbol{u}$ [Ajt96], for public random matrices $A \in \mathbb{Z}_q^{k \times n}, B \in \mathbb{Z}_q^{k \times t}$, and a small random mask $\boldsymbol{u}$. The encryption $\boldsymbol{e}, \boldsymbol{e}'$ of y becomes a dual-Regev-like ciphertext

$$\boldsymbol{e} = A^{\mathsf{T}} \cdot \boldsymbol{w} + \chi + \lceil q/p \rceil \cdot \boldsymbol{y}, \qquad \boldsymbol{e}' = B^{\mathsf{T}} \cdot \boldsymbol{w} + \chi,$$

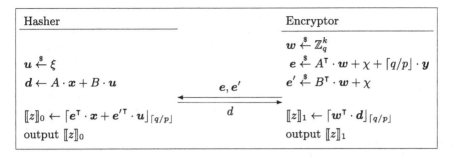

Fig. 3. Bilinear HSS for inner product (mod p) from LWE. Here $A \in \mathbb{Z}_q^{k \times n}, B \in \mathbb{Z}_q^{k \times t}$ are public random matrices, and ξ and χ are noise distributions.

Hasher	Encryptor	
$x_{-1} \xleftarrow{\$} \chi$	$w \xleftarrow{\$} R_q$	
$x_0 \xleftarrow{\$} \chi$	$e_k \xleftarrow{\$} \chi$	$\forall k \in [-n..n]$
	$\forall i \in [1..n], j \in [-1..n]:$	
$d \leftarrow \sum_{j=-1}^{n} a^{j+1} \cdot x_j$	$E_{ij} \leftarrow a^{n+j-i+1} \cdot w + e_{j-i+1} + \lceil q/p \rfloor \cdot \delta_{ij} \cdot \Delta$	
$[\![z]\!]_0 \leftarrow \lceil E \cdot x \rfloor_{\lceil q/p \rfloor}$	$[\![z_i]\!]_1 \leftarrow \lceil d \cdot a^{n-i} \cdot w \rfloor_{\lceil q/p \rfloor}$	$\forall i \in [1..n]$
output $[\![z]\!]_0$	output $[\![z]\!]_1$	

(Between Hasher and Encryptor columns: E arrow, d arrow)

Fig. 4. Bilinear HSS for scalar-vector product from Power Ring-LWE. Here $a \in R_q$ is a public ring element, and χ is a noise distribution on R_q.

where χ is a noise distribution [GPV08].

For correctness, first notice that before rounding the output shares are nearly correct, assuming that the noise distribution is sufficiently small.

$$
\begin{aligned}
e^{\mathsf{T}} \cdot x + e'^{\mathsf{T}} \cdot u - w^{\mathsf{T}} \cdot d &= (w^{\mathsf{T}} \cdot A + \chi^{\mathsf{T}} + \lceil q/p \rfloor \cdot y^{\mathsf{T}}) \cdot x + (w^{\mathsf{T}} \cdot B + \chi^{\mathsf{T}}) \cdot u \\
&\quad - w^{\mathsf{T}} \cdot (A \cdot x + B \cdot u) \\
&= \lceil q/p \rfloor \cdot y^{\mathsf{T}} \cdot x + \chi^{\mathsf{T}} \cdot x + \chi^{\mathsf{T}} \cdot u \\
&\approx \lceil q/p \rfloor \cdot (\langle x, y \rangle \bmod p)
\end{aligned}
$$

Next, if this pre-rounding correctness error is negligible compared to q/p, after rounding, the result will be correct with all but negligible probability:

$$
[\![z]\!]_0 - [\![z]\!]_1 = \lceil e^{\mathsf{T}} \cdot x + e'^{\mathsf{T}} \cdot u \rfloor_{\lceil q/p \rfloor} - \lceil w^{\mathsf{T}} \cdot d \rfloor_{\lceil q/p \rfloor} \equiv \langle x, y \rangle \mod p
$$

The communication cost is asymptotically the same as for Fig. 1, with each hash being k elements of $\mathbb{Z}_q$, and each vector y being $n + t$ elements of $\mathbb{Z}_q$. We detail this construction in the full version of our paper [ARS24, Section 4.2].

Power Ring-LWE. We also adapted the ideas from Fig. 2 to work with LWE. Our protocol is Fig. 4. Again, the main idea of the protocol is structure the ciphertexts so that E becomes a Toeplitz matrix, and so can be compressed. To support this additional structure, we need to define a new security assumption: Power Ring-LWE. In standard Ring-LWE, the adversary is given as many samples of the form $(a_i, a_i \cdot s + e_i)$ as they want, where s and all a_i are uniform and e_i is from a noise distribution χ, and they must distinguish from random. Power Ring-LWE is similar, but the public ring elements a_i are structured: they satisfy $a_i = a^i$. In this way, the digest value d becomes a polynomial evaluation[6] at a: $d = \sum_{j=-1}^{n} a^{j+1} x_j$. Note that some random values have been prepended to x to hide the hasher's input.

Also like with Fig. 2, the encryptor's secret keys w_i values are correlated by $w_i = a^{n-i} \cdot w$. Ignoring noise, this makes the ciphertexts become

$$E_{ij} \approx a^{n+j-i+1} \cdot w + \lceil q/p \rfloor \cdot \delta_{ij} \cdot \Delta,$$

which again only depends on $j - i$, so it is a Toeplitz matrix. For negligible noise-to-modulus ratio, correctness holds because

$$\left(\sum_{j=-1}^{n} E_{ij} \cdot x_j \right) - d \cdot a^{n-i} \cdot w = \sum_{j=-1}^{n} \left(a^{n+j-i+1} \cdot w + e_{j-i+1} + \lceil q/p \rfloor \cdot \delta_{ij} \cdot \Delta \right) \cdot x_j$$

$$- \sum_{j=-1}^{n} a^{n+j-i+1} \cdot x_j \cdot w$$

$$= \lceil q/p \rfloor \cdot \Delta \cdot x_i + \sum_{j=-1}^{n} e_{j-i+1} \cdot x_j$$

$$\approx \lceil q/p \rfloor \cdot (\Delta \cdot x_i \bmod p).$$

The communication cost is similar to Fig. 2, with the hasher sending a single ring element, and the encryptor sending $2n + 1$ ring elements: the first row and first column of E. We detail this construction in the full version of our paper [ARS24, Section 6.2].

1.3 Technical Overview—Applications of Succinct HSS

One main application of HSS is to MPC with sublinear communication [BGI16]. Alice and Bob divide their circuit into layers of logarithmic depth, and use HSS to evaluate each layer. Communication is only required between layers, so they only send $O(s/\log s)$ bits for a circuit with s gates.

The biggest limitation of this technique is that it only applies to two parties, since the underlying HSS only works for two parties. Recent work has addressed this gap by building truth tables for $(\log \log s)$-depth circuit blocks, which have at most $\log(s)$ inputs and so have polynomial-sized truth tables. [Cou19] showed that if the parties are given correlated randomness in the form of (batched)

---

[6] The SIS problem corresponding to d being a collision-resistant hash was defined in [CLM23]. They named it vanishing SIS, and gave some evidence for its hardness.

One-Time Truth-Tables (OTTTs)[7] for these blocks, then they can evaluate the layered circuit with $O(s/\log\log s)$ communication. However, they were unable to efficiently generate these OTTTs without using assumptions that imply FHE. [BCM23] got past this issue by generating truth tables for two parties with HSS, then evaluating them on the third party's input using a variant of PIR. Their technique can be stretched to work with 5 parties, but no further. Recently, another work [DIJL23] managed to achieve $O(s/\log\log s)$ communication— when the circuit is sufficiently wide—for any number of parties, based on a sparse variant of the learning parity with noise assumption.

Sublinear MPC from Succinct HSS. We show how to generate these OTTTs with only sublinear communication, using succinct HSS. We consider the following procedure to generate a OTTT of a function $f\colon \{0,1\}^k \to \{0,1\}$.

1. Party $\mathcal{P}_1$ generates a random mask $r_1 \in \{0,1\}^k$, and computes their permuted truth table $s_1[x] \leftarrow f(x \oplus r_1)$ for all $x \in \{0,1\}^k$.
2. For $j = 2, \ldots, N$, party $\mathcal{P}_j$ generates a random mask $r_j \in \{0,1\}^k$, and uses succinct HSS to permute the truth table as follows:
   (a) Currently, we have that $\sum_{i=1}^{j-1} s_i[x] = f(x \oplus r_1 \oplus \cdots \oplus r_{j-1})$.
   (b) For every $i < j$, parties $\mathcal{P}_i$ and $\mathcal{P}_j$ run 2-party succinct HSS on input the truth table s_i and the mask r_j. They compute secret shares $s'_{ij}[x]$ and $s'_{ji}[x]$ of $s_i[x \oplus r_j]$ for all x, so $s'_{ij}[x] - s'_{ji}[x] = s_i[x \oplus r_j]$. Party $\mathcal{P}_i$ updates their share $s_i \leftarrow s'_{ij}$.
   (c) Party $\mathcal{P}_j$ sets their share to $s_j \leftarrow -\sum_{i=1}^{j-1} s'_{ji}$.
   (d) Now $\displaystyle\sum_{i=1}^{j} s_i[x] = \sum_{i=1}^{j-1} s'_{ij}[x] - \sum_{i=1}^{j-1} s'_{ji}[x] = f\Big(x \oplus r_1 \oplus \ldots \oplus r_{j-1} \oplus r_j\Big).$
3. Each party $\mathcal{P}_i$ outputs s_i as their share of the OTTT. The loop invariant guarantees that $\sum_{i=1}^{N} s_i[x] = f(x \oplus r)$, where $r = \bigoplus_{i=1}^{N} r_i$, so these shares form a OTTT for f.

This protocol can also be batched to generate many OTTTs at once. If the underlying HSS has sublinear communication complexity in its inputs then this protocol can generate the OTTTs needed by [Cou19] with communication sublinear in the circuit size, completing their sublinear MPC protocol.

   We notice that in all HSS evaluation, the input s_i is only used linearly, as the circuit is only permuting the entries of s_i according to $x \mapsto x \oplus r_j$. In other words, given succinct HSS, s_i can be compressed. Unfortunately, the random mask r_j is used non-linearly as it defines the permutation on s_i, so it cannot be compressed in the same way. However, it is sampled randomly, so for each j, all the r_j's across all OTTTs can be compressed together using a PRF in NC_1. Since all inputs can be compressed, we achieve sublinear communication MPC. We detail this construction in the full version of our paper [ARS24, Section 8.1].

---

[7] A OTTT [IKM+13] is a truth table, permuted according to a random input mask, secret shared among all N parties.

Multiparty DPFs. In the special case of a OTTT for the function f, given by $f(0) = \beta$ and otherwise $f(x) = 0$, we get a protocol for generating a batch of multiparty DPFs using sublinear communication (the OTTT mask r corresponds to the non-zero point of the point function). Most directly, this would require giving β to $\mathcal{P}_1$, but with a minor tweak to the protocol, β can be secret shared among the N parties instead. Note that the communication complexity is polynomial in the number of parties, and that for a sufficiently large batch size the per-DPF communication can be made arbitrarily small. We detail this construction in the full version of our paper [ARS24, Section 8].

Sublinear MPC for RMS Programs. Another application of succinct HSS is to (interactively) evaluate layered RMS programs in MPC for a polynomial number of parties, with communication sublinear in the program size. A layered RMS program allows arbitrary fan-in addition gates and 2-input multiplication gates, with the restriction that every gate must output into a later layer than any of its inputs.

Our protocol for evaluating layered RMS programs works as follows. Maintain additive secret shares $y_1 + \cdots + y_N$ of every memory value in the RMS program. We can initially share the inputs as well, since $(0, \ldots, x, \ldots, 0)$ is an additive sharing of x, and every input is known by some party. We can easily evaluate addition gates directly on the shares, just by adding the shares. The difficulty comes when we need to multiply an input x by some memory value y. We implement multiplications with succinct HSS, by having the shares of y be compressed as special inputs.

In more detail, to handle the multiplications for each layer, we run a succinct HSS evaluations between every pair of parties. If party $\mathcal{P}_i$ has an input x_i, it provides x_i as a standard input to all of its succinct HSS evaluations[8] Now, every multiplication in this layer can be handled as follows. If we need to evaluate $x \cdot y$, for an input x held by party $\mathcal{P}_i$ and a memory value $y = y_1 + \cdots + y_N$:

1. For all $j \neq i$, include y_j as a special input (if it is not already included) to the succinct HSS between $\mathcal{P}_i$ and $\mathcal{P}_j$, and compute shares of $x \cdot y_j$.
2. $\mathcal{P}_i$ locally evaluates $x \cdot y_i$.
3. Sum the above shares to get shares of $x \cdot y_1 + \cdots + x \cdot y_N = x \cdot y$.

Note that all multiplications in a single layer use the same succinct HSS, so that all of these share inputs get compressed together in the succinct HSS. Therefore, for efficiency we need a sufficiently wide RMS program. Note also that the round complexity is proportional to the number of layers.

We can also use this protocol to get sublinear complexity MPC for layered circuits, as long as the layers are wide enough and even in size. Similarly to [BGI16], divide the circuit into blocks of depth $c \cdot \log s$ for some $0 < c < 1$, and convert each block into an $o(s)$-layer RMS program. Evaluate each block using the above protocol for RMS programs, and input the shares output from each layer into the next. For efficiency, however, we require hybrid encryption for the

---

[8] These input ciphertexts can sent to all parties at the start, and reused for all layers.

inputs, so the parties will instead generate symmetric-key ciphertexts from their shares, and input $\log(\lambda)$-depth PRF keys to the RMS program so that they can be decrypted. This increases the circuit depth to $c \cdot \log s + O(\log(\lambda))$, and so the RMS program will have $s^c \operatorname{poly}(\lambda)$ layers.

For sufficiently wide circuits, the symmetric-key ciphertexts become the biggest term asymptotically, and so the whole circuit can be evaluated with $O(s/\log s)$ communication. However, this construction blows up the round complexity to $d \cdot \frac{s^c \operatorname{poly}(\lambda)}{c \log s}$, if d is the depth of the original circuit. We detail this construction in the full version of our paper [ARS24, Section 9].

2 Notation and Preliminaries

We denote the security parameter by λ. For any $n \in \mathbb{N}$, we define $[n] := \{1, \ldots, n\}$ and $[0..n] := \{0, 1, \ldots, n\}$. For any $x, N \in \mathbb{N}$ where N is odd, we use $\left(\frac{x}{N}\right)$ to denote the Jacobi symbol of x and N. Given a real number x and an integer p, we use $\lceil x \rfloor_p$ to denote the integer y such that $y \cdot p$ is the multiple of p that is closest to x. We use $\lceil x \rfloor$ to denote rounding to the closest integer.

Objects in vectorial form are represented using bold font. For any vector v, we denote the i-th entry either by $v[i]$ or by v_i. Matrices are represented using capital letters. The element in the i-th row and j-th column of a matrix A is denoted by $A_{i,j}$. The transposition of a matrix A is denoted by $A^\intercal$. Unit-vectors are vectors where all the entries are zero except for, perhaps, one. We call the latter the *special position* or the *special entry*. The corresponding value is called the *non-zero element*. We denote a unit vector with special position α and non-zero element β by $u_{\alpha,\beta}$. We use $\otimes$ to denote the outer product.

For any randomised algorithm Alg, we use $y \xleftarrow{\$} \operatorname{Alg}(x)$ to mean that y is assigned the output of Alg on input x and uniformly random coins. We use instead $y \leftarrow \operatorname{Alg}(x; r)$ to mean that y is assigned the output of Alg on input x and randomness r. If Alg is deterministic, we simply write $y \leftarrow \operatorname{Alg}(x)$. Finally, for any finite set S, we write $y \xleftarrow{\$} S$ if y is assigned the value of a uniformly random element in S.

Throughout the paper, we deal with multiparty computation protocols. We denote the number of parties by N. The i-th party is denoted by $\mathcal{P}_i$. In all protocols, we assume static, semi-honest corruption.

2.1 Computational Assumptions

Throughout the paper, we will use the following standard assumptions. We denote by $N = pq$ an RSA modulus, where p and q are both random, safe primes. Recall that a safe prime is a prime number $p = 2p' + 1$ where p' is also prime. For complete definitions, see the full version of our work [ARS24, Section 2.1].

- Quadratic Residuosity (QR): a random $g \xleftarrow{\$} \mathbb{Z}_N^*$, with Jacobi symbol equal to 1, is indistinguishable from g^2, where $g \xleftarrow{\$} \mathbb{Z}_N^*$.

- Decisional Composite Residuosity (DCR): a random $g \xleftarrow{\$} \mathbb{Z}_{N^2}^*$ is indistinguishable from g^N, where $g \xleftarrow{\$} \mathbb{Z}_{N^2}^*$.
- Learning With Errors (LWE): The distribution $(A, As + e)$, for $A \xleftarrow{\$} \mathbb{Z}_q^{M \times N}, s \xleftarrow{\$} \mathbb{Z}_q^N$ and small noise vector e, is indistinguishable from uniform.

2.2   The NIDLS Framework

Some of our bilinear HSS constructions are based on the non-interactive discrete logarithm sharing (NIDLS) framework of [ADOS22]. We recall here its definition and some known instantiations.

The NIDLS framework consists of a finite commutative group G that can be decomposed as the direct product $F \times H$. The subgroup F is cyclic of known order. Furthermore, it is easy to solve discrete logarithms with respect to a generator f. The subgroup H is instead of unknown order and computing discrete logarithms over it is hard. The framework is also equipped with an upper-bound on the order of G, which we denote by ℓ, and a distribution $\mathcal{D}$ that provides (non-necessarily uniformly) random elements in G.

The most interesting property of the framework is that it allows compute discrete logarithms in a distributed way: if two parties $\mathcal{P}_0$ and $\mathcal{P}_1$ hold elements g_0 and g_1 such that $g_0 = f^m \cdot g_1$ for some $m \in \mathbb{N}$, the parties can derive a subtractive secret-sharing of m without having to interact. The operation is called *distributed discrete logarithm* or DDLog.

Definition 1 (The NIDLS Framework [ADOS22]). *The NIDLS framework consists of a triple of PPT algorithms* (Gen, $\mathcal{D}$, DDLog) *with the following syntax:*

- Gen($\mathbb{1}^\lambda$) *outputs a tuple* par $:= (G, F, H, f, q, \ell, \text{aux})$ *where*
  - G *is a finite abelian group*
  - F *and* H *are subgroups of* G *such that* $G = F \times H$
  - $F = \langle f \rangle$ *and* $|F| = q$
  - ℓ *is a positive integer*
  - aux *consists of auxiliary information*
- $\mathcal{D}(\mathbb{1}^\lambda, \text{par})$ *outputs an element* $g \in G$ *along with auxiliary information* ρ
- DDLog(par, g) *is deterministic and outputs an element* $s \in \mathbb{Z}_q$.

We additionally require the following properties:

- *For every PPT adversary* $\mathcal{A}$,

$$\Pr\left[s_0 - s_1 \not\equiv m \bmod q \;\middle|\; \begin{array}{l} \text{par} := (G, F, H, f, q, \ell, \text{aux}) \xleftarrow{\$} \text{Gen}(\mathbb{1}^\lambda) \\ (g_0, m) \xleftarrow{\$} \mathcal{A}(\mathbb{1}^\lambda, \text{par}) \\ g_1 \leftarrow f^m \cdot g_0 \\ s_0 \leftarrow \text{DDLog}(\text{par}, g_0) \\ s_1 \leftarrow \text{DDLog}(\text{par}, g_1) \end{array} \right] \leq \text{negl}(\lambda)$$

- *The following distributions are statistically indistinguishable*

$$\left\{ \mathsf{par}, g, \rho, g^r \; \middle| \; \begin{array}{l} \mathsf{par} := (G, F, H, f, q, \ell, \mathsf{aux}) \xleftarrow{\$} \mathsf{Gen}(\mathbb{1}^\lambda) \\ (g, \rho) \xleftarrow{\$} \mathcal{D}(\mathbb{1}^\lambda, \mathsf{par}) \\ r \xleftarrow{\$} [\ell] \end{array} \right\}$$

$$\left\{ \mathsf{par}, g, \rho, h \; \middle| \; \begin{array}{l} \mathsf{par} := (G, F, H, f, q, \ell, \mathsf{aux}) \xleftarrow{\$} \mathsf{Gen}(\mathbb{1}^\lambda) \\ (g, \rho) \xleftarrow{\$} \mathcal{D}(\mathbb{1}^\lambda, \mathsf{par}) \\ h \xleftarrow{\$} \langle g \rangle \end{array} \right\}$$

Known Instantiations of the Framework. We now recall the known instantiations of the framework: the Paillier group (and its generalisation Damgård-Jurik) [OSY21, RS21], Goldwasser-Micali (and some variants of its generalisation Joye-Libert) [ADOS22] and class groups [ADOS22].

The Paillier Instantiation. We consider the subgroup G of squares of $\mathbb{Z}^*_{N^2}$. Such subgroup is cyclic of order $N \cdot \phi(N)/4$ where $\phi(N)$ denotes Euler's totient function. It is possible to decompose G as the direct product of $F := \langle 1 + N \rangle$ and H, the subgroup of $2N$-th powers of $\mathbb{Z}^*_{N^2}$. It is easy to observe that $(1 + N)^a \equiv 1 + a \cdot N \bmod N^2$ for any $a \in \mathbb{N}$. From this we can easily conclude that the order of F is N and discrete logarithms are easy compute. We refer to [ADOS22] for a detailed discussion on how the distributed DLOG can be computed over Paillier. In the full version of our work (see [ARS24, Section 2.3]), we present a formal description of the Paillier instantiation of the framework (see $\mathsf{Gen}_\mathsf{Paillier}$ and $\mathcal{D}_\mathsf{Paillier}$).

The Goldwasser-Micali Instantiation. Let N be the product of two large random safe-primes. We consider the subgroup G of all elements in $\mathbb{Z}^*_N$ having Jacobi symbol equal to 1. Such group is cyclic of order $\phi(N)/4$. It is possible to decompose G as the product of $F = \{1, -1\}$ and H, the subgroup of squares of $\mathbb{Z}^*_N$. Due to the size, discrete logarithms over F are trivially to solve. The same holds for distributed DLOGs (see [ADOS22]). In the full version of our work (see [ARS24, Section 2.3]), we present a formal description of the Goldwasser-Micali instantiation of the framework (see Gen_GM and $\mathcal{D}_\mathsf{GM}$).

The Class Group Instantiation. The last known instantiation of the framework is given by class groups. Class groups are commutative groups for which it is computationally expensive to compute the order. One of the reasons why class groups are popular in cryptography is the fact that it is possible to generate the parameters of the group with a transparent setup: while the security of Paillier and Goldwasser-Micali requires that the factorisation of N is kept secret, the computational assumptions on class groups remain solid even if we leak the random coins used to sample the group (Gen_CL will provide them as part of aux).

Any class groups G can be decomposed as the product of F and H. The subgroup F is generated by a group element f of prime order q (such q does not need to be sampled at random, it can be given as input to $\mathsf{Gen_{CL}}$). Computing DLOGs over F is easy. The subgroup H has instead unknown order and, in most cases, it is not even cyclic. The sampling procedure $\mathcal{D}_{CL}$ can be instantiated in different ways: it could either be a distribution that is statistically close to uniform over G or it could be a distribution producing random (but not uniformly random) elements of high unknown order. In both cases $\mathcal{D}_{CL}$ outputs the random coins it uses as part of the auxiliary information ρ. We refer to [ADOS22] for a detailed discussion on how the distributed DLOG can be computed over class groups.

In the full version of our work [ARS24, Section 2.2], we provide a survey on computational assumptions over the NIDLS framework.

3   Defining Bilinear HSS

In this section, we provide formal definitions of bilinear HSS, describing its syntax and properties.

A bilinear HSS scheme consists of a 2-party primitive: one party is called the hasher and provides as input an n-dimensional vector $\boldsymbol{x}$, the other party is called the encryptor and provides as input a matrix M. The primitive relies on a setup that takes as input n and distributes keys to the parties. Such keys allow the hasher and the encryptor to obtain a secret-sharing of $M \cdot \boldsymbol{x}$ using a single round of interaction. Furthermore, the digest sent by the hasher will have sublinear size in n.

Definition 2 (Bilinear HSS). *Let R be a commutative ring. An R-bilinear HSS scheme for the matrix class $\mathcal{M}$ is a tuple of PPT algorithms* (Setup, Hash, Matrix, HasherEval, MatrixEval) *with the following syntax:*

- Setup *is randomised and takes as input the security parameter $\mathbb{1}^\lambda$ and the input length $\mathbb{1}^n$. The output is a hasher key* hk *and a matrix key* mk.
- Hash *is randomised and takes as input a hasher key* hk *and an input $\boldsymbol{x} \in R^n$. The output is a digest d and the hasher secret information ψ.*
- Matrix *is randomised and takes as input a matrix key* mk *and an n-column matrix $M \in \mathcal{M}$ of elements in R. The output is an encoding E and the matrix secret information ϕ.*
- HasherEval *is deterministic and takes as input a hasher key* hk, *a matrix encoding E and hasher secret information ψ. The output is a vector $\boldsymbol{s_0}$.*
- MatrixEval *is deterministic and takes as input a matrix key* mk, *a digest d and matrix secret information ϕ. The output is a vector $\boldsymbol{s_1}$.*

We require also the following properties

1. **(Correctness).** *For every $n \in \mathbb{N}$, $x \in R^n$ and n-column matrix $M \in \mathcal{M}$, we have*

$$
\Pr \left[s_0 - s_1 \neq M \cdot x \middle| \begin{array}{l} (\mathsf{hk}, \mathsf{mk}) \xleftarrow{\$} \mathsf{Setup}(\mathbb{1}^\lambda, \mathbb{1}^n) \\ (d, \psi) \xleftarrow{\$} \mathsf{Hash}(\mathsf{hk}, x) \\ (E, \phi) \xleftarrow{\$} \mathsf{Matrix}(\mathsf{mk}, M) \\ s_0 \leftarrow \mathsf{HasherEval}(\mathsf{hk}, E, \psi) \\ s_1 \leftarrow \mathsf{MatrixEval}(\mathsf{mk}, d, \phi) \end{array} \right] \leq \mathsf{negl}(\lambda).
$$

2. **(Hasher Privacy).** *No PPT adversary $\mathcal{A}$ can win the game in Fig. 5 with non-negligible advantage.*

THE GAME $\mathcal{G}_n^{\mathsf{HP}}(\lambda)$

Initialisation: This procedure is run only once at the beginning of the game.

(a) $b \xleftarrow{\$} \{0, 1\}$

(b) Activate $\mathcal{A}$ with $\mathbb{1}^\lambda$ and receive n in unary notation.

(c) $(\mathsf{hk}, \mathsf{mk}) \xleftarrow{\$} \mathsf{Setup}(\mathbb{1}^\lambda, \mathbb{1}^n)$

(d) Provide mk to the adversary.

Query: This procedure can be run multiple times and at any moment.

(a) Receive $x \in R^n$ from $\mathcal{A}$.

(b) $(d, \psi) \xleftarrow{\$} \mathsf{Hash}(\mathsf{hk}, x)$

(c) Provide the adversary with d.

Challenge: This procedure can be run only once and at any moment.

(a) Receive $x_0, x_1 \in R^n$ from $\mathcal{A}$.

(b) $(d, \psi) \xleftarrow{\$} \mathsf{Hash}(\mathsf{hk}, x_b)$

(c) Provide the adversary with d.

Win: The adversary wins if it ends its execution outputting b.

Fig. 5. The Game for Hasher Privacy

3. **(Matrix Privacy).** *No PPT adversary $\mathcal{A}$ can win the game in Fig. 6 with non-negligible advantage.*

4. **(Efficiency).** *The size of the hash d is $\mathsf{poly}(\lambda, \log|R|) \cdot o(n)$.*

Notice that hasher privacy is essentially saying that the digests sent by the hasher reveal no information about the underlying messages, even if they are all generated using the same hasher key. In a similar way, matrix privacy states that the messages sent by the encryptor leak no information about the input matrices. Again, this holds even if the matrix key is reused multiple times.

In general, both properties are guaranteed as long as the hasher key and the matrix key remain secret (similarly to what happens in every symmetric encryption scheme). We now formalise, however, stronger security notions that, if satisfied, ensure the privacy of both parties even if the keys are made public (similarly to all public key encryption schemes).

THE GAME $\mathcal{G}_n^{\mathsf{MP}}(\lambda)$

Initialisation: This procedure is run only once at the beginning of the game.

(a) $b \xleftarrow{\$} \{0,1\}$

(b) Activate $\mathcal{A}$ with $\mathbb{1}^\lambda$ and receive n in unary notation.

(c) $(\mathsf{hk}, \mathsf{mk}) \xleftarrow{\$} \mathsf{Setup}(\mathbb{1}^\lambda, \mathbb{1}^n)$

(d) Provide hk to the adversary.

Query: This procedure can be run multiple times and at any moment.

(a) Receive an n-column matrix $M \in \mathcal{M}$ from $\mathcal{A}$.

(b) $(E, \phi) \xleftarrow{\$} \mathsf{Matrix}(\mathsf{mk}, M)$

(c) Provide the adversary with E.

Challenge: This procedure can be run only once and at any moment.

(a) Receive two n-column matrices with the same number of rows $M_0, M_1 \in \mathcal{M}$ from $\mathcal{A}$.

(b) $(E, \phi) \xleftarrow{\$} \mathsf{Matrix}(\mathsf{mk}, M_b)$

(c) Provide the adversary with E.

Win: The adversary wins if it ends its execution outputting b.

Fig. 6. The Game for Matrix Privacy

Definition 3 (Strong Hasher Privacy). *Let* $(\mathsf{Setup}, \mathsf{Hash}, \mathsf{Matrix}, \mathsf{HasherEval},$ $\mathsf{MatrixEval})$ *be a bilinear HSS scheme over the ring R. We say that the scheme satisfies strong hasher privacy if, for every $n \in \mathbb{N}$ and values $\boldsymbol{x}_0, \boldsymbol{x}_1 \in R^n$, the following distributions are computationally indistinguishable*

$$\left\{ (d, \mathsf{hk}, \mathsf{mk}) \;\middle|\; \begin{array}{l} (\mathsf{hk}, \mathsf{mk}) \xleftarrow{\$} \mathsf{Setup}(\mathbb{1}^\lambda, \mathbb{1}^n) \\ (d, \psi) \xleftarrow{\$} \mathsf{Hash}(\mathsf{hk}, \boldsymbol{x}_0) \end{array} \right\} \left\{ (d, \mathsf{hk}, \mathsf{mk}) \;\middle|\; \begin{array}{l} (\mathsf{hk}, \mathsf{mk}) \xleftarrow{\$} \mathsf{Setup}(\mathbb{1}^\lambda, \mathbb{1}^n) \\ (d, \psi) \xleftarrow{\$} \mathsf{Hash}(\mathsf{hk}, \boldsymbol{x}_1) \end{array} \right\}$$

Definition 4 (Strong Matrix Privacy). *Let* $(\mathsf{Setup}, \mathsf{Hash}, \mathsf{Matrix}, \mathsf{HasherEval},$ $\mathsf{MatrixEval})$ *be a bilinear HSS scheme over the ring R. We say that the scheme satisfies strong matrix privacy if, or every $n, m \in \mathbb{N}$ and $m \times n$ matrices $M_0, M_1 \in \mathcal{M}$ over R, the following distributions are computationally indistinguishable*

$$\left\{ (E, \mathsf{hk}, \mathsf{mk}) \;\middle|\; \begin{array}{l} (\mathsf{hk}, \mathsf{mk}) \xleftarrow{\$} \mathsf{Setup}(\mathbb{1}^\lambda, \mathbb{1}^n) \\ (E, \phi) \xleftarrow{\$} \mathsf{Matrix}(\mathsf{mk}, M_0) \end{array} \right\} \left\{ (E, \mathsf{hk}, \mathsf{mk}) \;\middle|\; \begin{array}{l} (\mathsf{hk}, \mathsf{mk}) \xleftarrow{\$} \mathsf{Setup}(\mathbb{1}^\lambda, \mathbb{1}^n) \\ (E, \phi) \xleftarrow{\$} \mathsf{Matrix}(\mathsf{mk}, M_1) \end{array} \right\}$$

If strong hasher privacy and strong matrix privacy hold simultaneously, we say that we are dealing with a public-key bilinear HSS scheme. In these situations, we use pk to denote the concatenation of hk and mk. We modify the syntax of Hash and Matrix by providing them directly with pk instead of just hk and mk.

Definition 5 (Public-Key Bilinear HSS). *A bilinear HSS scheme is public-key if it simultaneously satisfies both strong hasher privacy and strong matrix privacy.*

We finally present a even stronger version of hasher privacy, which we call *transparent hasher privacy*. The latter states that the privacy of the hashed messages holds even if we provide the adversary with the random coins used to run the setup. We will use this property to build our sublinear communication MPC protocols.

Definition 6 (Transparent Hasher Privacy). *Let* (Setup, Hash, Matrix, HasherEval, MatrixEval) *be a bilinear HSS scheme over the ring R. Let $L(\lambda, n)$ denote the length of the randomness needed by* Setup($\mathbb{1}^\lambda, \mathbb{1}^n$). *We say that the scheme satisfies transparent hasher privacy if, for every $n \in \mathbb{N}$ and values $x_0, x_1 \in R^n$, the following distributions are computationally indistinguishable*

$$\left\{ (d, \rho) \;\middle|\; \begin{array}{l} \rho \xleftarrow{\$} \{0,1\}^{L(\lambda,n)} \\ (\mathsf{hk}, \mathsf{mk}) \leftarrow \mathsf{Setup}(\mathbb{1}^\lambda, \mathbb{1}^n; \rho) \\ (d, \psi) \xleftarrow{\$} \mathsf{Hash}(\mathsf{hk}, x_0) \end{array} \right\} \left\{ (d, \rho) \;\middle|\; \begin{array}{l} \rho \xleftarrow{\$} \{0,1\}^{L(\lambda,n)} \\ (\mathsf{hk}, \mathsf{mk}) \leftarrow \mathsf{Setup}(\mathbb{1}^\lambda, \mathbb{1}^n; \rho) \\ (d, \psi) \xleftarrow{\$} \mathsf{Hash}(\mathsf{hk}, x_1) \end{array} \right\}$$

A bilinear HSS scheme guarantees that the size of the digests is sublinear in the size of the hasher input n. This does not prevent however that the size of the keys and matrix encoding scales polynomially in n (we recall that the length of the hasher input is fed into Setup). If the size of the keys grows sublinearly in n, we say that the scheme satisfies key-compactness. If instead the matrix encoding of any $n \times n$ matrix in the class $\mathcal{M}$ is sublinear in n, we say that the scheme is matrix-compact. Observe that, in order for matrix compactness to be satisfied, the class of $n \times n$ matrices in $\mathcal{M}$ must contain $o(2^n)$ elements. In other words, any bilinear scheme for the class of all matrices $M \in R^{n \times n}$ cannot satisfy matrix compactness.

Definition 7 (Key-Compact Bilinear HSS). *A bilinear HSS scheme over the ring R is key-compact if, for every $\lambda, n \in \mathbb{N}$, the size of the keys (hk, mk) output by* Setup($\mathbb{1}^\lambda, \mathbb{1}^n$) *is* poly($\lambda, \log|R|$) $\cdot o(n)$.

Definition 8 (Matrix-Compact Bilinear HSS). *A bilinear HSS scheme over the ring R is matrix-compact if, for every $\lambda, n \in \mathbb{N}$, and matrix $M \in R^{n \times n}$, the size of the encoding E output by* Matrix(mk, M), *where* (hk, mk) $\xleftarrow{\$}$ Setup($\mathbb{1}^\lambda, \mathbb{1}^n$), *is* poly($\lambda, \log|R|$) $\cdot o(n)$.

4 Public-Key Bilinear HSS Constructions

In this section, we show how to build public-key bilinear HSS schemes for all matrices based on DLOG over unknown order groups (such as Paillier or class groups, see Sect. 4.1). In the full version of our work [ARS24, Section 4.2], we present another construction based on lattices.

4.1 Public-Key Bilinear HSS for All Matrices Based in the NIDLS Framework

We formalise our construction in the NIDLS framework of [ADOS22], which can be instantiated e.g. using Paillier, Goldwasser-Micali where the RSA modulus is product of safe-primes or class groups. We recall that class groups have the advantage of requiring only a transparent setup. We start by formalising the complexity assumptions we need.

New Assumptions in the NIDLS Framework

The Uniformity Assumption. We introduce a new computational assumption over the framework, we call it the *uniformity assumption.* The latter essentially says that given the parameters of the NIDLS group, a sample g_0 from $\mathcal{D}$ and the corresponding auxiliary information ρ_0[9], it is hard to distinguish between a random power of g_0 and another sample g_1 from $\mathcal{D}$ where the corresponding auxiliary information ρ_1 is kept secret.

Definition 9 (The Uniformity Assumption). *We say that the uniformity assumption holds in the NIDLS framework if the following distributions are computationally indistinguishable*

$$\left\{ \begin{array}{c} \text{par} \\ g_0, \rho_0, g_0^w \end{array} \middle| \begin{array}{l} \text{par} := (G, F, H, f, q, \ell, \text{aux}) \xleftarrow{\$} \text{Gen}(\mathbb{1}^\lambda) \\ (g_0, \rho_0) \xleftarrow{\$} \mathcal{D}(\mathbb{1}^\lambda, \text{par}) \\ w \xleftarrow{\$} [\ell] \end{array} \right\}$$

$$\left\{ \begin{array}{c} \text{par} \\ g_0, \rho_0, g_1 \end{array} \middle| \begin{array}{l} \text{par} := (G, F, H, f, q, \ell, \text{aux}) \xleftarrow{\$} \text{Gen}(\mathbb{1}^\lambda) \\ (g_0, \rho_0) \xleftarrow{\$} \mathcal{D}(\mathbb{1}^\lambda, \text{par}) \\ (g_1, \rho_1) \xleftarrow{\$} \mathcal{D}(\mathbb{1}^\lambda, \text{par}) \end{array} \right\}$$

The above assumption is useful only when the NIDLS group is not cyclic of prime order. Indeed, if that was not the case, the assumption holds information-theoretically. We observe that the subgroup of squares of the Paillier group $\mathbb{Z}_{N^2}^*$ is cyclic. If N is product of distinct safe-primes, also the subgroup of elements with Jacobi symbol 1 in $\mathbb{Z}_N^*$ is cyclic. So, in these settings the uniformity assumption holds unconditionally.

Class groups, unfortunately, are not cyclic and we could not relate uniformity to any other known assumption. We believe however that uniformity is likely to hold even in this setting. Our claim is supported by the hardness of computing discrete logarithms over class groups. We also highlight that the assumption resembles, to some extent, the DXDH assumption of [ADOS22], which says that given the description of the NIDLS group and two samples g_0, g_1 from $\mathcal{D}$, it is hard to distinguish (g_0^r, g_1^r) from (g_0^r, g_0^s) for random $r, s \xleftarrow{\$} [\ell]$. This implies that it is hard to tell whether a group element belongs to $\langle g_0 \rangle$.

Theorem 3. *If* Gen *outputs a cyclic group G of order N such that $\phi(N)/N = 1 - \text{negl}(\lambda)$, $\mathcal{D}$ is the uniform distribution over G and $|\ell - N|/N \leq \text{negl}(\lambda)$, the uniformity assumption holds information theoretically.*

---

[9] For instance, ρ_0 can represent the randomness used to produce g_0, if we aim to generate them using common random string or a random oracle.

Proof. We notice that $\mathcal{D}$ outputs a generator of G with overwhelming probability as the number of generators is $\phi(N)$ and $\phi(N)/N$ is negligible. Furthermore, the distribution of $w \bmod N$ where $w \xleftarrow{\$} [\ell]$ is statistically close to the uniform distribution over $\mathbb{Z}_N$. We conclude that the distribution of g_0^w is statistically close to the uniform distribution over G. □

The n-ary Enhanced DDH Assumption. We introduce the second assumption needed to build bilinear HSS in the NIDLS framework, we call it *enhanched DDH (EDDH) assumption*. The latter states that given the parameters of the NIDLS group and $n + 1$ group elements $g_0, \dots, g_n$ sampled from $\mathcal{D}$ (along with the corresponding auxiliary information $\rho_0, \dots, \rho_n$), it is hard to distinguish between $(g_0^w, \dots, g_n^w)$ for a random w and $(f^{r_0} \cdot g_0^w, \dots, f^{r_n} \cdot g_n^w)$ for random $r_0, \dots, r_n \in \mathbb{Z}_q$.

Definition 10 (The n-ary Enhanced DDH Assumption). *We say that the n-ary Enhanced DDH (n-EDDH) assumption holds in the NIDLS framework if the following distributions are computationally indistinguishable*

$$\left\{ \begin{array}{c} \mathsf{par} \\ g_0, \dots, g_n \\ \rho_0, \dots, \rho_n \\ g_0^w, \dots, g_n^w \end{array} \middle| \begin{array}{l} \mathsf{par} := (G, F, H, f, q, \ell, \mathsf{aux}) \xleftarrow{\$} \mathsf{Gen}(\mathbb{1}^\lambda) \\ \forall j \in [0..n] : (g_j, \rho_j) \xleftarrow{\$} \mathcal{D}(\mathbb{1}^\lambda, \mathsf{par}) \\ w \xleftarrow{\$} [\ell] \end{array} \right\}$$

$$\left\{ \begin{array}{c} \mathsf{par} \\ g_0, \dots, g_n \\ \rho_0, \dots, \rho_n \\ f^{r_0} \cdot g_0^w, \dots, f^{r_n} \cdot g_n^w \end{array} \middle| \begin{array}{l} \mathsf{par} := (G, F, H, f, q, \ell, \mathsf{aux}) \xleftarrow{\$} \mathsf{Gen}(\mathbb{1}^\lambda) \\ \forall j \in [0..n] : (g_j, \rho_j) \xleftarrow{\$} \mathcal{D}(\mathbb{1}^\lambda, \mathsf{par}) \\ w \xleftarrow{\$} [\ell] \\ \forall j \in [0..n] : r_j \xleftarrow{\$} \mathbb{Z}_q \end{array} \right\}$$

The above assumption is related to DDH. For instance, it is easy to see that if the NIDLS group has prime order, and $\mathcal{D}$ outputs a random group element without any auxiliary information, n-EDDH is implied by DDH and the hidden subgroup assumption for any polynomial $n(\lambda)$. Unfortunately, however, all known instantiations of the NIDLS framework do not have prime order (in particular, class groups, the RSA group and the Paillier group are not even cyclic). Moreover, we have often an additional issue because the distribution $\mathcal{D}$ might be different from the uniform distribution and, furthermore, it can be non-explainable (this if for instance the case, as far as we know, over class groups), meaning that, given a group element produced by $\mathcal{D}$, we are not able to simulate the corresponding auxiliary information. This fact prevents the reduction from EDDH to DDH from working as we can no longer substitute e.g. g_j with a random power of g_0 (we would not be able to simulate ρ_j).

Definition 11 (Explainable Sampler). *The distribution $\mathcal{D}$ is explainable if there exists a PPT algorithm* Explain *such that the following distributions are computationally indistinguishable*

$$\left\{ \mathsf{par}, g, \rho \;\middle|\; \begin{array}{l} \mathsf{par} := (G, F, H, f, q, \ell, \mathsf{aux}) \xleftarrow{\$} \mathsf{Gen}(\mathbb{1}^\lambda) \\ (g, \rho) \xleftarrow{\$} \mathcal{D}(\mathbb{1}^\lambda, \mathsf{par}) \end{array} \right\}$$

$$\left\{ \mathsf{par}, g, \rho' \;\middle|\; \begin{array}{l} \mathsf{par} := (G, F, H, f, q, \ell, \mathsf{aux}) \xleftarrow{\$} \mathsf{Gen}(\mathbb{1}^\lambda) \\ (g, \rho) \xleftarrow{\$} \mathcal{D}(\mathbb{1}^\lambda, \mathsf{par}) \\ \rho' \xleftarrow{\$} \mathsf{Explain}(\mathbb{1}^\lambda, \mathsf{par}, g) \end{array} \right\}$$

Enhanced DDH over Class Groups. As we have already mentioned, over class groups, the distribution $\mathcal{D}$ is not known to be explainable (unless we decide to give up on the transparent setup by not revealing the randomness ρ used by the sampling procedure). That prevents the reduction from EDDH to DDH from succeeding. We believe however that n-ary EDDH is likely to hold in this setting for any polynomial $n(\lambda)$. To support our claim, we observe that the points highlighted in [ADOS22] to argue the hardness of DXDH can also be applied to n-ary EDDH.

Enhanced DDH over the Paillier Group and the RSA Group. Compared to the class group case, analysing the hardness of EDDH over Paillier and Goldwasser-Micali is significantly easier. We show that, for any polynomial $n(\lambda)$, the n-ary EDDH assumption over the Paillier group is implied by DCR and, over Goldwasser-Micali, by the QR assumption.

Theorem 4. *The following are true.*

- *Suppose that* $\mathsf{Gen} = \mathsf{Gen}_{\mathsf{Paillier}}$ *and* $\mathcal{D} = \mathcal{D}_{\mathsf{Paillier}}$. *Then, DCR implies the n-ary EDDH assumption for any polynomial $n(\lambda)$.*
- *Suppose that* $\mathsf{Gen} = \mathsf{Gen}_{\mathsf{GM}}$ *and* $\mathcal{D} = \mathcal{D}_{\mathsf{GM}}$. *Then, QR implies the n-ary EDDH assumption for any polynomial $n(\lambda)$.*

The proof is given in the full version of our work [ARS24, Section 4.1].

The Bilinear HSS Scheme in the NIDLS Framework. We are ready to present our first bilinear HSS scheme. The construction is public-key, supports all $m \times n$ matrices over $\mathbb{Z}_q$, and is secure in the NIDLS framework under the uniformity assumption (see Definition 9), the n-ary EDDH assumption (see Definition 11) and the hidden subgroup assumption. We describe it in Fig. 7. The rationale behind the scheme is explained in Sect. 1.2. We highlight that the construction does not satisfy key-compactness.

Theorem 5. *If the n-ary EDDH assumption, the uniformity assumption and the hidden subgroup assumption hold in the NIDLS framework [ADOS22], the construction in Fig. 7 is a secure public-key bilinear HSS scheme for the class $\mathcal{M}$ of $m \times n$ matrices over $\mathbb{Z}_q$.*

Moreover, if the NIDLS framework is instantiated using Paillier or Goldwasser-Micali or class groups, the scheme satisfies transparent hasher privacy.

BILINEAR HSS FOR ALL MATRICES BASED ON DDLOG

Setup($\mathbb{1}^\lambda, \mathbb{1}^n$):

1. par $:= (G, F, H, f, q, \ell, \text{aux}) \xleftarrow{\$} \text{Gen}(\mathbb{1}^\lambda)$
2. $\forall j \in [0..n] : (g_j, \rho_j) \xleftarrow{\$} \mathcal{D}(\mathbb{1}^\lambda, \text{par})$
3. Output pk $:= (\text{par}, g_0, \ldots, g_n, \rho_0, \ldots, \rho_n)$.

Hash(pk $= (\text{par}, g_0, \ldots, g_n, \rho_0, \ldots, \rho_n), \boldsymbol{x}$):

1. $u \xleftarrow{\$} [\ell]$
2. $d \leftarrow g_0^u \cdot \prod_{j=1}^n g_j^{x_j}$
3. $\psi \leftarrow (\text{par}, u, \boldsymbol{x})$
4. Output d and ψ.

Matrix(pk $= (\text{par}, g_0, \ldots, g_n, \rho_0, \ldots, \rho_n), M$):

1. $\forall i \in [m] : w_i \xleftarrow{\$} [\ell]$
2. $\forall i \in [m] : E_{i,0} \leftarrow g_0^{w_i}$
3. $\forall i \in [m], j \in [n] : E_{i,j} \leftarrow f^{M_{i,j}} \cdot g_j^{w_i}$
4. Output $E := (E_{i,j})_{i,j}$ and $\phi = (\text{par}, w_1, \ldots, w_m, M)$.

HasherEval$(E, \psi = (\text{par}, u, \boldsymbol{x}))$:

1. $\forall i \in [m] : s_{0,i} \leftarrow \text{DDLog}(\text{par}, E_{i,0}^u \cdot \prod_{j=1}^n E_{i,j}^{x_j})$
2. Output $\boldsymbol{s_0}$

MatrixEval$(d, \phi = (\text{par}, w_1, \ldots, w_m, M))$:

1. $\forall i \in [m] : s_{1,i} \leftarrow \text{DDLog}(\text{par}, d^{w_i})$
2. Output $\boldsymbol{s_1}$

Fig. 7. Bilinear HSS for all Matrices based on DDLOG

Proof. It is trivial to see that the size of the digest d is independent of n. We start by proving correctness. We observe that, for every $i \in [m]$,

$$\left(E_{i,0}^u \cdot \prod_{j=1}^n E_{i,j}^{x_j} \right) \cdot d^{-w_i} = \left(g_0^{w_i \cdot u} \cdot \prod_{j=1}^n f^{M_{i,j} \cdot x_j} \cdot g_j^{w_i \cdot x_j} \right) \cdot \left(g_0^{-u \cdot w_i} \cdot \prod_{j=1}^n g_j^{-x_j \cdot w_i} \right)$$

$$= f^{\sum_{j=1}^n M_{i,j} \cdot x_j}$$

By the properties of the distributed DLOG procedure, we conclude that, with overwhelming probability, $\boldsymbol{s_0} - \boldsymbol{s_1} = M \cdot \boldsymbol{x}$.

We now proceed by proving the hasher privacy. We do this by relying on a sequence of $n + 1$ indistinguishably hybrids, the t-th one of these consisting of the following

Hybrid t.0.

1. pk $:= (\text{par}, g_0, \ldots, g_n, \rho_0, \ldots, \rho_n) \xleftarrow{\$} \text{Setup}(\mathbb{1}^\lambda, \mathbb{1}^n)$

2. $u \xleftarrow{\$} [\ell]$

3. $d \leftarrow g_t^u \cdot g_{t+1}^{x_{t+1}} \cdot \ldots \cdot g_n^{x_n}$

4. Output (pk, d)

Hybrid $t.1$.

1. $\mathsf{pk} := (\mathsf{par}, g_0, \ldots, g_n, \rho_0, \ldots, \rho_n) \xleftarrow{\$} \mathsf{Setup}(\mathbb{1}^\lambda, \mathbb{1}^n)$

2. $(h, \rho') \xleftarrow{\$} \mathcal{D}(\mathbb{1}^\lambda, \mathsf{par})$

3. $d \leftarrow h \cdot g_{t+1}^{x_{t+1}} \cdot \ldots \cdot g_n^{x_n}$

4. Output (pk, d)

Observe that under the uniformity assumption, the Hybrid $t.0$ is indistinguishable from Hybrid $t.1$. Furthermore, under the same assumption, Hybrid $t.1$ is indistinguishable from Hybrid $(t + 1).0$. We observe that in Hybrid 0.0, the distribution of (pk, d) is as if d was produced by $\mathsf{Hash}(\mathsf{pk}, \boldsymbol{x})$. In Hybrid $(n-1).1$, d is independent of $\boldsymbol{x}$. Hasher privacy immediately follows.

Next, we prove matrix privacy. We do this by relying on the following sequence of indistinguishably hybrids.

Hybrid 0.

1. $\mathsf{pk} := (\mathsf{par}, g_0, \ldots, g_n, \rho_0, \ldots, \rho_n) \xleftarrow{\$} \mathsf{Setup}(\mathbb{1}^\lambda, \mathbb{1}^n)$

2. $\forall i \in [m] : w_i \xleftarrow{\$} [\ell]$

3. $\forall i \in [m] : E_{i,0} \leftarrow g_0^{w_i}$

4. $\forall i \in [m], j \in [n] : E_{i,j} \leftarrow f^{M_{i,j}} \cdot g_j^{w_i}$

5. Output (pk, E)

Hybrid 1.

1. $\mathsf{pk} := (\mathsf{par}, g_0, \ldots, g_n, \rho_0, \ldots, \rho_n) \xleftarrow{\$} \mathsf{Setup}(\mathbb{1}^\lambda, \mathbb{1}^n)$

2. $\forall i \in [m] : w_i \xleftarrow{\$} [\ell]$

3. $\forall i \in [m], j \in [n] : r_{i,j} \xleftarrow{\$} \mathbb{Z}_q$

4. $\forall i \in [m] : E_{i,0} \leftarrow f^{r_{i,0}} \cdot g_0^{w_i}$

5. $\forall i \in [m], j \in [n] : E_{i,j} \leftarrow f^{M_{i,j}+r_{i,j}} \cdot g_j^{w_i}$

6. Output (pk, E)

Observe that Hybrid 0 and Hybrid 1 are indistinguishable under the n-ary EDDH assumption. We conclude the proof by observing that the distribution of (pk, E) in Hybrid 0 is exactly as if E was generated by $\mathsf{Matrix}(\mathsf{pk}, M)$. Furthermore, the distribution of (pk, E) in Hybrid 1 is independent of M as all information is masked by $(r_{i,j})_{i \in [m], j \in [n]}$. $\qquad\square$

5   Succinct Half-Chosen Vector OLE

In this section and in the full version of our paper [ARS24, Section 6], we study bilinear HSS schemes for the class $\mathcal{K}$ of matrices that are multiples of the identity. Formally, denoting the ring by R,

$$\mathcal{K} := \{k \cdot \mathsf{id}_m | m \in \mathbb{N}, k \in R\}$$

This class is particularly interesting because any bilinear HSS scheme for $\mathcal{K}$ immediately gives a "half-chosen" non-interactive Vector-OLE (VOLE) protocol: in a VOLE, one party, called the *Sender*, inputs two vectors $\boldsymbol{x}, \boldsymbol{y}$, whereas the other party, called the *Receiver*, inputs a scalar k. At the end of the protocol, the Receiver obtains $\boldsymbol{z} := k \cdot \boldsymbol{x} + \boldsymbol{y}$ without learning anything else (the Sender learns no information at all). Observe that the pair $(\boldsymbol{z}, \boldsymbol{y})$ consists of a secret-sharing of $k \cdot \boldsymbol{x}$. In a fully random VOLE protocol, on the other hand, the parties have no inputs. At the end of the protocol, the Sender will receive random vectors $\boldsymbol{x}, \boldsymbol{y}$, whereas the Receiver will obtain a random constant k along with $\boldsymbol{z} = k \cdot \boldsymbol{x} + \boldsymbol{y}$ (the parties will learn no other information). Choosing $\boldsymbol{x}$ later requires sending a full correction vector $\boldsymbol{x}' - \boldsymbol{x}$. Our VOLE protocol will be a middle ground between these two notions: the Sender will only input $\boldsymbol{x}$, and the Receiver will only input the constant k. The output will be a random secret-sharing of $k \cdot \boldsymbol{x}$.

We probably do not need to explain how important VOLE protocols are in cryptography. What we want to argue is, however, that, in many applications, we do not need a true VOLE protocol – a half-chosen VOLE is sufficient. The surprising fact is that, while it can be proven that VOLE protocols require $\Omega(n)$ communication[10] (n denotes the length of the vectors $\boldsymbol{x}, \boldsymbol{y}$ and $\boldsymbol{z}$), half-chosen VOLE protocols can achieve sublinear communication in n. This fact was not known before this work, in this section, we show how bilinear HSS allows us to achieve this.

Then, in the full version of our paper [ARS24, Section 6], we focus our energy in constructing bilinear HSS schemes for $\mathcal{K}$ where the communication complexity of the encryptor is $o(n^2)$. Due to an entropy matter, this is of course impossible to achieve in bilinear HSS scheme for all matrices.

5.1 Succinct Half-Chosen VOLE and Key-Compact, Matrix-Compact Bilinear HSS

We consider the half-chosen non-interactive Vector OLE problem (VOLE): Alice holds a vector $\boldsymbol{x} \in \mathbb{Z}_p^n$ whereas Bob holds a constant $k \in \mathbb{Z}_p$. We would like to non-interactively obtain an additive secret sharing of $k \cdot \boldsymbol{x}$. We observe that multiplying by the constant k is equivalent to multiplying by the matrix $k \cdot \mathrm{id}_n$. Now, if we would naively use the bilinear HSS schemes presented in Sect. 4 to perform such operation, the communication of Alice would be independent of n, however, the communication of Bob would be $\Omega(n^2)$. Furthermore, the size of the public key would be $O(n)$. Is it still possible to use our results to build a half-chosen non-interactive VOLE protocol with $o(n)$ total communication?

To answer this question, we rely on the fact that the messages of bilinear HSS schemes can be reused: if the ciphertext sent by Bob (encoding a matrix M) were to be reused with a new message from Alice, let's say a digest of $\boldsymbol{x}'$, the parties would still obtain a secret-sharing of $M \cdot \boldsymbol{x}'$. To achieve sublinear communication in the VOLE protocol, we can therefore apply the following trick:

---

[10] If that wasn't the case, we could send a length-n message m with $o(n)$ communication by just inputting $\boldsymbol{x} = \boldsymbol{0}$ and $\boldsymbol{y} = m$ in the VOLE protocol.

Bob will send an encoding of the matrix $k \cdot \mathsf{id}_{n^{1/3}}$, Alice will instead split its input into $n^{2/3}$ chunks of $n^{1/3}$ elements and will send a digest of each segment. By running the bilinear HSS scheme $n^{2/3}$ times, once for each digest sent by Alice, the parties will therefore obtain a secret-sharing of $k \cdot \boldsymbol{x}$. Surprisingly, the total communication is now $O(n^{2/3})$, equally distributed between Alice and Bob. The size of the public key has also decreased to $O(n^{1/3})$. In other words, our scheme would satisfy both key-compactness and matrix-compactness.

We summarise our idea in the following theorem.

Theorem 6. *Let* (Setup, Hash, Matrix, HasherEval, MatrixEval) *be a bilinear HSS scheme over R for the matrix class $\mathcal{M} \supseteq \mathcal{K}$. Suppose that the size of the HSS digest is upper bounded by $f(n) \cdot \mathsf{poly}(\lambda, \log|R|)$ and the encoding of an $n \times n$ matrix is upper bounded by $g(n) \cdot \mathsf{poly}(\lambda, \log|R|)$. Assume also that the size of the keys is upper bounded by $\kappa(n) \cdot \mathsf{poly}(\lambda, \log|R|)$. Then, there exists a bilinear HSS scheme for $\mathcal{K}$ with $g(t) \cdot \mathsf{poly}(\lambda, \log|R|)$ communication per party and $\kappa(t) \cdot \mathsf{poly}(\lambda, \log|R|)$ key size, where t is such that $n = t \cdot g(t)/f(t)$. Moreover, this transformation preserves the properties of strong hasher privacy, strong matrix privacy, and transparent hasher privacy.*

The following corollary summarises what we know so far about succinct non-interactive half-chosen VOLE with semi-honest security.

Corollary 1. *The following hold:*

- *Under DCR over the Paillier group $\mathbb{Z}_{N^2}^*$, there exists a half-chosen, semi-honest, non-interactive VOLE protocol over $\mathbb{Z}_N$ with $O(n^{2/3})$ communication per party.*
- *Under QR over the RSA group $\mathbb{Z}_N^*$ where N is the product of large safe-primes, there exists a half-chosen, semi-honest, non-interactive VOLE protocol over $\mathbb{Z}_2$ with $O(n^{2/3})$ communication per party.*
- *For any prime $q = \Omega(2^\lambda)$, under the $n^{1/3}$-ary EDDH assumption and the uniformity assumption over class groups, there exists a half-chosen, semi-honest, non-interactive VOLE protocol over $\mathbb{Z}_q$ with $O(n^{2/3})$ communication.*
- *For any integer p, under LWE with superpolynomial modulus-to-noise ratio, there exists a half-chosen, semi-honest, non-interactive VOLE protocol over $\mathbb{Z}_p$ with $O(n^{2/3})$ communication per party.*

6   Succinct HSS

In this section, we show how bilinear HSS schemes for multiples of the identity can be used to obtain particularly efficient 2-party HSS schemes for NC_1 circuits where the encoding of some of the inputs can be compressed into small digests. We call such primitive a *succinct HSS scheme*. Specifically, for any NC_1 circuit C mapping a vector in $\mathbb{Z}_q^m$ into a vector in $\mathbb{Z}_q^n$, a succinct HSS schemes allows two parties Alice and Bob, having inputs $\boldsymbol{x} \in \mathbb{Z}_q^m$ and $\boldsymbol{y} \in \mathbb{Z}_q^n$ respectively, to obtain a secret-sharing of the inner product $\langle C(\boldsymbol{x}), \boldsymbol{y} \rangle$ using a single round of interaction where the communication of Bob is independent of n. In other words, we obtain 2-party non-interactive protocols for particular classes of functions that achieve sublinear communication in the size of the inputs.

Special RMS Programs. In order to explain our idea, we need to first introduce the notion of *special restricted multiplication straightline (RMS) program*. We recall that the class of RMS programs over a ring R consists of all arithmetical circuits over R with fan-in 2, where linear operation are free, but multiplications require at least one of the factors to be an input wire. We also recall that all circuits in NC_1 can be represented as an RMS program of polynomial size [BGI16, Appendix A].

Special RMS programs generalise what we just explained. We will split the input wires into two classes: *standard inputs* and *special inputs*. Linear operations are again free, however, multiplications not only require at least one of the factors to be an input wire, but they also require the latter to be of standard type. The only operations allowed on special inputs are therefore linear gates or multiplications by a standard input. In other words, despite being input wires, special inputs are treated as any other internal wire of the RMS program. The latter are usually referred to as *memory wires*.

Definition 12 (Special RMS Program). *A special restricted multiplication straightline program (RMS) consists of a bound $B \in \mathbb{N}$, a modulus $q \in \mathbb{N}$ such that $B \leq q$ and an arithmetic circuit C with unbounded fan-out where the inputs wires are divided into two classes: standard inputs and special inputs. Furthermore, the only allowed gate types are the following:*

- ConvertInput(I_x) $\rightarrow M_x$. *Load the value of the standard input wire I_x to the memory wire M_x.*
- ConvertSpecialInput(S_x) $\rightarrow M_x$. *Load the value of the special input wire S_x to the memory wire M_x.*
- Add(M_x, M_y) $\rightarrow M_z$. *Add the values of the memory wires M_x and M_y and store the result in the memory wire M_z.*
- Mult(I_x, M_y) $\rightarrow M_z$. *Multiply the values of the standard input wire I_x by the value of the memory wire M_y. Store the result in the memory wire M_z.*
- Output(M_z) $\rightarrow z$. *Output the value of the memory wire M_z reducing it modulo q.*

All inputs must belong to $\mathbb{Z}$. If the absolute value of any wire exceeds the bound B, the output of the evaluation is $\bot$.

In the following lemma, we prove that if C is in NC_1, then the function $\langle C(\boldsymbol{x}), \boldsymbol{y} \rangle$ can be represented as a special RMS program where $\boldsymbol{y}$ are special inputs. The idea is simple: suppose for simplicity that the dimension of $\boldsymbol{y}$ is 1 and C is represented by an RMS program. We notice that $y \cdot C(x)$ can be computed by an new RMS program where every input-to-memory-wire conversion in C is substituted by a multiplication by the special input y. We provide a complete proof in the full version of our work [ARS24, Section 7].

Lemma 1. *Let R be a ring and let C be an RMS program over R taking inputs in R^m and outputting in R^n. Then, the function $f : R^m \times R^n \rightarrow R$ that maps $(\boldsymbol{x}, \boldsymbol{y})$ into $\langle C(\boldsymbol{x}), \boldsymbol{y} \rangle$ is computable by a special RMS program C' where $\boldsymbol{x}$ is the standard input and $\boldsymbol{y}$ is the special input.*

Defining Succinct HSS. Below, we formalise the definition of succinct HSS: a 2-party HSS scheme for the evaluation of special RMS programs, where the parties can compress the encodings of their special inputs into small digests. The primitive relies on a setup that takes as input an upper-bound n on the number of special inputs that can be hashed into the same digest. In order to evaluate a special RMS program where the number of special inputs exceeds n, the parties simply need to send multiple digests.

Definition 13 (Succinct HSS). *A succinct HSS scheme over $\mathbb{Z}_q$ is a tuple of PPT algorithms* (Setup, Hash, Input, Eval) *with the following syntax:*

- Setup *is randomised and takes as input the security parameter $\mathbb{1}^\lambda$ and the input length $\mathbb{1}^n$. The output is a public key* pk *and evaluation keys* ek_0 *and* ek_1.
- Hash *is randomised and takes as input a public key* pk, $b \in \{0,1\}$ *and an input $x \in \mathbb{Z}^n$. The output is a digest d and the hasher secret information ψ.*
- Input *is randomised and takes as input a public key* pk *and a value $y \in \mathbb{Z}$. The output is an encoding I of the input.*
- Eval *is deterministic and takes as input the evaluation key* ek, *the description of a special RMS program f, standard input encodings $I_1, \ldots, I_m$, digests $d_1, \ldots, d_{\ell_0}$ and hasher secret information $\psi_1, \ldots, \psi_{\ell_1}$ for some $m, \ell_0, \ell_1 \in \mathbb{N}$. The output is an element $s \in \mathbb{Z}_q$.*

We require also the following properties

1. *(**Correctness**). For every $n, m, \ell_0, \ell_1 \in \mathbb{N}$, special inputs $x_1^0, \ldots, x_{\ell_0}^0, x_1^1, \ldots,$ $x_{\ell_1}^1 \in \mathbb{Z}^n$, standard input $y \in \mathbb{Z}^m$ and special RMS program $f : \mathbb{Z}^{n \cdot (\ell_0 + \ell_1)} \times \mathbb{Z}^m \to \mathbb{Z}_q$, the following probability must be negligible.*

$$
\Pr\left[s_0 + s_1 \neq z \;\middle|\; \begin{array}{l} (\mathsf{pk}, \mathsf{ek}_0, \mathsf{ek}_1) \xleftarrow{\$} \mathsf{Setup}(\mathbb{1}^\lambda, \mathbb{1}^n) \\[4pt] \forall b \in \{0,1\}, i \in [\ell_b] : (d_i^b, \psi_i^b) \xleftarrow{\$} \mathsf{Hash}(\mathsf{pk}, b, x_i^b) \\[4pt] \forall j \in [m] : I_j \xleftarrow{\$} \mathsf{Input}(\mathsf{pk}, y_j) \\[4pt] s_0 \leftarrow \mathsf{Eval}(\mathsf{ek}_0, f, I_1, \ldots, I_m, d_1^1, \ldots, d_{\ell_1}^1, \psi_1^0, \ldots, \psi_{\ell_0}^0) \\[4pt] s_1 \leftarrow \mathsf{Eval}(\mathsf{ek}_1, f, I_1, \ldots, I_m, d_1^0, \ldots, d_{\ell_0}^0, \psi_1^1, \ldots, \psi_{\ell_1}^1) \\[4pt] z \leftarrow f(x_1^0, \ldots, x_{\ell_0}^0, x_1^1, \ldots, x_{\ell_1}^1, y) \end{array} \right]
$$

2. *(**Hasher Privacy**). For every $n \in \mathbb{N}$, $b \in \{0,1\}$ and special inputs $x_0, x_1 \in \mathbb{Z}^n$, the two values $i \in \{0,1\}$ are computationally indistinguishable in the following distribution*

$$
\left\{ (\mathsf{pk}, \mathsf{ek}_b, d) \;\middle|\; \begin{array}{l} (\mathsf{pk}, \mathsf{ek}_0, \mathsf{ek}_1) \xleftarrow{\$} \mathsf{Setup}(\mathbb{1}^\lambda, \mathbb{1}^n) \\[4pt] (d, \psi) \xleftarrow{\$} \mathsf{Hash}(\mathsf{pk}, 1 - b, x_i) \end{array} \right\}
$$

3. **(Input Privacy).** *For every* $n \in \mathbb{N}$, $b \in \{0,1\}$ *and standard inputs* $y_0, y_1 \in \mathbb{Z}$, *the two values* $i \in \{0,1\}$ *are computationally indistinguishable in the following distribution*

$$\left\{ (\mathsf{pk}, \mathsf{ek}_b, I) \,\middle|\, \begin{array}{l} (\mathsf{pk}, \mathsf{ek}_0, \mathsf{ek}_1) \xleftarrow{\$} \mathsf{Setup}(\mathbb{1}^\lambda, \mathbb{1}^n) \\ I \xleftarrow{\$} \mathsf{Input}(\mathsf{pk}, y_i) \end{array} \right\}$$

4. **(Efficiency).** *The size of the hash d is* $\mathsf{poly}(\lambda, \log|R|) \cdot o(n)$.

References

ADOS22. Abram, D., Damgård, I., Orlandi, C., Scholl, P.: An algebraic framework for silent preprocessing with trustless setup and active security. In: Dodis, Y., Shrimpton, T. (eds.) CRYPTO 2022, Part IV. LNCS, vol. 13510, pp. 421–452. Springer, Heidelberg (2022). https://doi.org/10.1007/978-3-031-15985-5_15

Ajt96. Ajtai, M.: Generating hard instances of lattice problems (extended abstract). In: 28th ACM STOC, pp. 99–108. ACM Press, May 1996

ARS24. Abram, D., Roy, L., Scholl, P.: Succinct homomorphic secret sharing. Cryptology ePrint Archive (2024). (Full version)

BCG+19. Boyle, E., Couteau, G., Gilboa, N., Ishai, Y., Kohl, L., Scholl, P.: Efficient pseudorandom correlation generators: silent OT extension and more. In: Boldyreva, A., Micciancio, D. (eds.) CRYPTO 2019, Part III. LNCS, vol. 11694, pp. 489–518. Springer, Cham (2019). https://doi.org/10.1007/978-3-030-26954-8_16

BCM23. Boyle, E., Couteau, G., Meyer, P.: Sublinear-communication secure multiparty computation does not require FHE. In: Hazay, C., Stam, M. (eds.) EUROCRYPT 2023, Part II. LNCS, vol. 14005, pp. 159–189. Springer, Heidelberg (2023). https://doi.org/10.1007/978-3-031-30617-4_6

BGI16. Boyle, E., Gilboa, N., Ishai, Y.: Breaking the circuit size barrier for secure computation under DDH. In: Robshaw, M., Katz, J. (eds.) CRYPTO 2016, Part I. LNCS, vol. 9814, pp. 509–539. Springer, Heidelberg (2016). https://doi.org/10.1007/978-3-662-53018-4_19

BKS19. Boyle, E., Kohl, L., Scholl, P.: Homomorphic secret sharing from lattices without FHE. In: Ishai, Y., Rijmen, V. (eds.) EUROCRYPT 2019, Part II. LNCS, vol. 11477, pp. 3–33. Springer, Cham (2019). https://doi.org/10.1007/978-3-030-17656-3_1

BMRS21. Baum, C., Malozemoff, A.J., Rosen, M.B., Scholl, P.: Mac′n′Cheese: zero-knowledge proofs for boolean and arithmetic circuits with nested disjunctions. In: Malkin, T., Peikert, C. (eds.) CRYPTO 2021, Part IV. LNCS, vol. 12828, pp. 92–122. Springer, Cham (2021). https://doi.org/10.1007/978-3-030-84259-8_4

CLM23. Cini, V., Lai, R.W.F., Malavolta, G.: Lattice-based succinct arguments from vanishing polynomials. In: Handschuh, H., Lysyanskaya, A. (eds.) CRYPTO 2023. LNCS, vol. 14082, pp. 72–105. Springer, Cham (2023). https://doi.org/10.1007/978-3-031-38545-2_3

Cou19. Couteau, G.: A note on the communication complexity of multiparty computation in the correlated randomness model. In: Ishai, Y., Rijmen, V. (eds.) EUROCRYPT 2019, Part II. LNCS, vol. 11477, pp. 473–503. Springer, Cham (2019). https://doi.org/10.1007/978-3-030-17656-3_17

DGI+19. Döttling, N., Garg, S., Ishai, Y., Malavolta, G., Mour, T., Ostrovsky, R.: Trapdoor hash functions and their applications. In: Boldyreva, A., Micciancio, D. (eds.) CRYPTO 2019, Part III. LNCS, vol. 11694, pp. 3–32. Springer, Cham (2019). https://doi.org/10.1007/978-3-030-26954-8_1

DIJL23. Dao, Q., Ishai, Y., Jain, A., Lin, H.: Multi-party homomorphic secret sharing and sublinear MPC from sparse LPN. In: Handschuh, H., Lysyanskaya, A. (eds.) CRYPTO 2023. Lecture Notes in Computer Science, vol. 14082, pp. 315–348. Springer, Cham (2023). https://doi.org/10.1007/978-3-031-38545-2_11

DIO21. Dittmer, S., Ishai, Y., Ostrovsky, R.: Line-point zero knowledge and its applications. In: 2nd Conference on Information-Theoretic Cryptography (ITC 2021). Schloss Dagstuhl-Leibniz-Zentrum für Informatik (2021)

GHO20. Garg, S., Hajiabadi, M., Ostrovsky, R.: Efficient range-trapdoor functions and applications: rate-1 OT and more. In: Pass, R., Pietrzak, K. (eds.) TCC 2020, Part I. LNCS, vol. 12550, pp. 88–116. Springer, Cham (2020). https://doi.org/10.1007/978-3-030-64375-1_4

GPV08. Gentry, C., Peikert, C., Vaikuntanathan, V.: Trapdoors for hard lattices and new cryptographic constructions. In: Ladner, R.E., Dwork, C. (eds.) 40th ACM STOC, pp. 197–206. ACM Press, May 2008

IKM+13. Ishai, Y., Kushilevitz, E., Meldgaard, S., Orlandi, C., Paskin-Cherniavsky, A.: On the power of correlated randomness in secure computation. In: Sahai, A. (ed.) TCC 2013. LNCS, vol. 7785, pp. 600–620. Springer, Heidelberg (2013). https://doi.org/10.1007/978-3-642-36594-2_34

Kil92. Kilian, J.: A note on efficient zero-knowledge proofs and arguments (extended abstract). In: 24th ACM STOC, pp. 723–732. ACM Press, May 1992

NN01. Naor, M., Nissim, K.: Communication preserving protocols for secure function evaluation. In: 33rd ACM STOC, pp. 590–599. ACM Press, July 2001

OSY21. Orlandi, C., Scholl, P., Yakoubov, S.: The rise of Paillier: homomorphic secret sharing and public-key silent OT. In: Canteaut, A., Standaert, F.-X. (eds.) EUROCRYPT 2021, Part I. LNCS, vol. 12696, pp. 678–708. Springer, Cham (2021). https://doi.org/10.1007/978-3-030-77870-5_24

QWW18. Quach, W., Wee, H., Wichs, D.: Laconic function evaluation and applications. In: Thorup, M. (ed.) 59th FOCS, pp. 859–870. IEEE Computer Society Press, October 2018

Ros22. Roşie, R.: Adaptively secure laconic function evaluation for NC^1. In: Galbraith, S.D. (ed.) CT-RSA 2022. LNCS, vol. 13161, pp. 427–450. Springer, Cham (2022). https://doi.org/10.1007/978-3-030-95312-6_18

RR22. Raghuraman, S., Rindal, P.: Blazing fast PSI from improved OKVS and subfield VOLE. In: Yin, H., Stavrou, A., Cremers, C., Shi, E. (eds.) ACM CCS 2022, pp. 2505–2517. ACM Press, November 2022

RS21. Roy, L., Singh, J.: Large message homomorphic secret sharing from DCR and applications. In: Malkin, T., Peikert, C. (eds.) CRYPTO 2021, Part III. LNCS, vol. 12827, pp. 687–717. Springer, Cham (2021). https://doi.org/10.1007/978-3-030-84252-9_23

YSWW21. Yang, K., Sarkar, P., Weng, C., Wang, X.: QuickSilver: efficient and affordable zero-knowledge proofs for circuits and polynomials over any field. In: Vigna, G., Shi, E. (eds.) ACM CCS 2021, pp. 2986–3001. ACM Press, November 2021

How to Garble Mixed Circuits that Combine Boolean and Arithmetic Computations

Hanjun Li[1(✉)] and Tianren Liu[2]

[1] University of Washington, Seattle, USA
hanjul@cs.washington.edu
[2] Peking University, Beijing, China
trl@pku.edu.cn

Abstract. The study of garbling arithmetic circuits is initiated by Applebaum, Ishai, and Kushilevitz [FOCS'11], which can be naturally extended to mixed circuits. The basis of mixed circuits includes Boolean operations, arithmetic operations over a large ring and bit-decomposition that converts an arithmetic value to its bit representation. We construct efficient garbling schemes for mixed circuits.

In the random oracle model, we construct two garbling schemes:
- The first scheme targets mixed circuits modulo some $N \approx 2^b$. Addition gates are free. Each multiplication gate costs $O(\lambda \cdot b^{1.5})$ communication. Each bit-decomposition costs $O(\lambda \cdot b^2 / \log b)$.
- The second scheme targets mixed circuit modulo some $N \approx 2^b$. Each addition gate and multiplication gate costs $O(\lambda \cdot b \cdot \log b / \log \log b)$. Every bit-decomposition costs $O(\lambda \cdot b^2 / \log b)$.

Our schemes improve on the work of Ball, Malkin, and Rosulek [CCS'16] in the same model.

Additionally relying on the DCR assumption, we construct in the programmable random oracle model a more efficient garbling scheme targeting mixed circuits over $\mathbb{Z}_{2^b}$, where addition gates are free, and each multiplication or bit-decomposition gate costs $O(\lambda_{\mathrm{DCR}} \cdot b)$ communication. We improve on the recent work of Ball, Li, Lin, and Liu [Eurocrypt'23] which also relies on the DCR assumption.

1 Introduction

Garbled circuit (GC) is introduced in the seminal work of Yao [1], allowing a *garbler* to efficiently transform any boolean circuit $C : \{0,1\}^{n_{\mathrm{in}}} \to \{0,1\}^{n_{\mathrm{out}}}$ into a *garbled circuit* $\tilde{C}$, along with n_{in} keys $\mathsf{K}_1, \ldots, \mathsf{K}_{n_{\mathrm{in}}}$. Each key is a function $\mathsf{K}_i : \{0,1\} \to \{0,1\}^\lambda$, mapping the i-th input bit to a short string. The output of K_i is referred to as the *label* of the i-th input wire. For any (unknown) input x, the garbled circuit $\tilde{C}$ together with input labels $\mathsf{K}_1(x_1), \ldots, \mathsf{K}_{n_{\mathrm{in}}}(x_{n_{\mathrm{in}}})$ reveal $C(x)$ but nothing else about x.

GC was originally motivated by the 2-party secure computation problem. Since then, GC has found applications to a large variety of problems, and is recognized as one of the most successful and fundamental tools in cryptography.

Hanjun Li was supported by a NSF grant CNS-2026774 and a Cisco Research Award.

M. Joye and G. Leander (Eds.): EUROCRYPT 2024, LNCS 14656, pp. 331–360, 2024.
https://doi.org/10.1007/978-3-031-58751-1_12

For practical applications, people care about the efficiency of GC, especially the communication complexity (i.e., bit length of $\tilde{C}$). A considerable amount of works [2–9] have been dedicated to optimize the *concrete* efficiency of Yao's GC construction. In the most recent construction of Rosulek and Roy [9], XOR and NOT gates involves no communication, every fan-in-2 AND gate requires $1.5\lambda + 5$ bits of communication. Despite making concrete analytic improvement, they still largely follow Yao's construction, binding tightly with boolean circuits. The class of arithmetic operations is a featuring example of computations that are expensive to express as boolean circuits.

The Arithmetic Setting. The beautiful work of Applebaum, Ishai, and Kushilevitz [10] initiated the study of garbling arithmetic circuits.

Arithmetic GC over a ring $\mathcal{R}$ is an efficient algorithm that transforms an arithmetic circuit $C : \mathcal{R}^{n_{\text{in}}} \to \mathcal{R}^{n_{\text{out}}}$ into a garbled circuit $\tilde{C}$, along with n_{in} keys $\mathsf{AK}_1, \ldots, \mathsf{AK}_{n_{\text{in}}}$. Each key is an affine function $\mathsf{AK}_i : \mathcal{R} \to \mathcal{R}^\ell$. For any (unknown) input x, the garbled circuit $\tilde{C}$ together with input labels $\mathsf{AK}_1(x_1), \ldots, \mathsf{AK}_{n_{\text{in}}}(x_{n_{\text{in}}})$ reveal $C(x)$ but nothing else about x.

The construction of AIK is a natural generalization of Yao's boolean GC. For each wire, a key $\mathsf{AK} : \mathcal{R} \to \mathcal{R}^\ell$ is sampled. The output of AK is called the label of that wire, whose length is roughly the security parameter. For any arithmetic gate g, say $\mathsf{AK}_1, \mathsf{AK}_2$ are the keys of the two input wires and AK is the key of the output wire, the garbler generates a table Tab of this gate, such that for any (unknown) $x, y \in \mathcal{R}$, the evaluator can compute $\mathsf{AK}(g(x,y))$ from $\mathsf{AK}_1(x), \mathsf{AK}_2(y), \mathsf{Tab}$, while learning no other information.

As observed by [10], to keep the table size for each gate constant, it suffices to construct the so-called *key-extension*[1] gadget. Such a gadget consists of a garbling algorithm and an evaluation algorithm. The garbling algorithm KE.Garb takes a key AK and a long key AK^{L} as input, samples a key-extension table Tab such that, $\mathsf{AK}(x), \mathsf{Tab}$ reveal $\mathsf{AK}^{\mathsf{L}}(x)$ but nothing else about $x, \mathsf{AK}^{\mathsf{L}}$.

[10] presents two constructions of key-extension gadgets. One relies on Chinese remainder theorem, enables garbling of mod-$p_1 p_2 \ldots p_k$ (the product of distinct small primes) computation. The other is based on LWE, supports bounded integer computation (computation over the integer ring $\mathbb{Z}$ when all intermediate values are guaranteed to be bounded).

Follow-up research has made improvements within this framework. Similar to FreeXOR, [12] allows free garbling of addition gates. In a different frontier, [11] presents a highly efficient arithmetic GC for bounded integer computation based on Paillier encryption. [11] also presents arithmetic GC for $\mathbb{Z}_p$ based on LWE or Paillier. However, free addition is not supported in [11]. The communication complexity of existing arithmetic GC constructions will be discussed in more detail in Sect. 1.1.

---

[1] This module is called "key shrinking" in [10]. The name "key extension" comes from [11].

Our research proceeds with this line of study within AIK's framework of arithmetic GC. Our starting point is to understand *how to garble mod-2^b arithmetic circuits,* which is not efficiently supported by previous works. In the search for mod-2^b GC, we realize that it is has a few advantage over GC for mod-p or bounded integer computation.

Match Popular Architectures. In most modern architectures, the only natively supported arithmetic operation is over $\mathbb{Z}_{2^b}$. Most existing tools (programing languages, compilers, processors, etc.) are optimized using/targeting the mod-2^b arithmetic operations. This is our initial motivation to construct the mod-2^b GC.

Mixing Boolean and Arithmetic Computation. Mixed circuits combine boolean and arithmetic computations. The basis include boolean gates, arithmetic operations, together with special gates to convert between boolean and arithmetic values: arithmetic-to-boolean conversion (bit-decomposition) and boolean-to-arithmetic conversion (bit-composition). Previous work [11,12] has considered the garbling of mixed circuits. But in their constructions, the cost of garbling bit-decomposition is expensive.

It turns out that our mod-2^b GC naturally supports *efficient* garbling of bit-decomposition and bit-composition. In fact, in our construction, the key-extension gadget is the combination of bit-decomposition and bit-composition. For example, to double the arithmetic key/label length, first bit-decompose it into boolean labels, then use bit-composition twice to obtain a longer label.

Emulate Arithmetic Computation Modulo Any Modulus N. For any constant N, mod-N computations can be efficiently emulated by mod-2^{4b} mixed circuits if $b = \lceil \log N \rceil$. To prove such a statement, it suffices to show, given $0 \le x < N^2$, how to compute $x \bmod N$ using a mod-2^{4b} mixed circuit. One step further, it is also sufficient to compute integer division $\lfloor x/N \rfloor$ using a mod-2^{4b} mixed circuit. By the rather standard multiply-and-shift trick

$$\lfloor x \cdot \lceil 2^{3b}/N \rceil / 2^{3b} \rfloor = \lfloor x/N \rfloor,$$

the quotient can be computed by first multiplying by constant $\lceil 2^{3b}/N \rceil$ then integer division by 2^{3b}. Both operations are efficient in a mod-2^{4b} mixed circuit.

1.1 Our Results

Mixed GC in the Random Oracle Model. Using only random oracle, the state-of-the-art garbling scheme for arithmetic circuit is that of [12]. They rely on Chinese remainder theorem (CRT) to garble an arithmetic circuit modulo $N = p_1, \ldots p_s \approx 2^b$, by equivalently garbling s copies of the circuit, each modulo a small prime p_i. They allow free addition and each multiplication gate costs $O(\lambda b^2 / \log b)$ bits of communication. However, bit-decomposition operation of this scheme is expensive and not explicitly considered in [12].

Our work improves the state-of-the-art in several directions.

Table 1. Comparison between our GC and previous works

	ADD gate table size	MULT gate table size	bit decomposition	ring modulus	assumption besides RO
boolean naive	λb	λb^2	free	2^b	
Karatsuba	λb	$\lambda b^{1.58}$ *	free	2^b	
FFT-based	λb	$\lambda b \log b$ *	free	2^b	
[12]	free	$\lambda b^2/\log b$	expensive †	$N = p_1 p_2 \ldots p_s \approx 2^b$	
Ours (Thm. 1)	free	$\lambda b^2/\log b$	$\lambda b^2/\log b$ ‡	$N = p^k \approx 2^b$	
Ours (Lem. 6)	$\lambda b^2/\log b$	$\lambda b^2/\log b$	$\lambda b^2/\log b$ ‡	any $N \approx 2^b$	
Ours (Thm. 2)	free	$\lambda b^{1.5}$	$\lambda b^2/\log b$ ‡	$N = p_1^{k_1} p_2^{k_2} \ldots p_s^{k_s} \approx 2^b$	
Ours (Thm. 3)	$\frac{\lambda b \log b}{\log \log b}$	$\frac{\lambda b \log b}{\log \log b}$	$\lambda b^2/\log b$ ‡	$N = p_1^{k_1} p_2^{k_2} \ldots p_s^{k_s} \approx 2^b$	
[11]	$\lambda_{\mathsf{LWE}} b$	$\lambda_{\mathsf{LWE}} b$	unknown	any $N \approx 2^b$	LWE
[11]	$\lambda(\lambda_{\mathsf{DCR}} + b)$	$\lambda(\lambda_{\mathsf{DCR}} + b)$	unknown	any $N \approx 2^b$	strong DCR §
[11]	$\lambda_{\mathsf{LWE}} b$	$\lambda_{\mathsf{LWE}} b$	$\lambda_{\mathsf{LWE}} b^2$	bounded integer	LWE
[11]	$\lambda_{\mathsf{DCR}} + b$	$\lambda_{\mathsf{DCR}} + b$	$\lambda(\lambda_{\mathsf{DCR}} + b)^2$	bounded integer	strong DCR §
Ours (Thm. 4)	free	$\lambda_{\mathsf{DCR}} b$	$\lambda_{\mathsf{DCR}} b$	2^b	DCR
Ours (Cor. 1)	$\lambda_{\mathsf{DCR}} b$	$\lambda_{\mathsf{DCR}} b$	$\lambda_{\mathsf{DCR}} b$	any $N \approx 2^b$	DCR

Constant and $\log(\lambda)$ multiplicative factors are ignored. λ_{LWE} and λ_{DCR} denote the LWE dimension and DCR key length respectively. *Due to large hidden constants, the Karatsuba's method outperforms the naive method only when b is at least a few hundreds, the FFT-base method outperforms Karatsuba's only when b is at least tens of thousands. †The cost is not explicitly stated in [12], but is no less the cost of comparison gate, which is stated to be $O(\lambda b^3/\log b)$. ‡The cost is measured when decomposing to base-p bit representation for some prime p (See Eq. 1). The cost increases to $O(\lambda b^2)$ when decomposing to base-2 bit representation. §Under the standard DCR assumption, "λ" should be replaced by "λ_{DCR}" in its cost expression.

- Our first scheme (Theorem 1) garbles arithmetic gates modulo $N = p^k \approx 2^b$, for some prime p, with the same asymptotic efficiency as [12]: addition is free, each multiplication costs $O(\lambda b^2/\log b)$ bits of communication. Additionally, our scheme supports efficient bit-decomposition gates at a cost of $O(\lambda b^2/\log b)$ communication, enabling the garbling of mixed circuits.
- Our second scheme (Theorem 2) applies CRT in a similar way to [12]. When garbling computations modulo $N = p_1^{k_1} p_2^{k_2} \ldots p_s^{k_s} \approx 2^b$, our mixed GC supports free addition and relatively efficient bit-decomposition, and garbles every multiplication gate using $O(\lambda b^{1.5})$ communication.
- Our third scheme (Theorem 3) further improves the multiplication gate cost to $O(\lambda b \log b/\log \log b)$. However, as a trade-off, addition gates are no longer free and have the same cost as multiplication gates.

Mixed GC Based on Computational Assumptions. If allowed to use public key assumptions, the state-of-the-art garbling schemes for arithmetic circuits and mixed circuits are those of [11]. Under the decisional composite residuosity (DCR) assumption, they construct a garbling scheme for bounded integers where each multiplication gate only costs $O(\lambda_{\mathsf{DCR}} + b)$. In their scheme, the addition gates cost the same as multiplication, the bit-decomposition gates have a more expensive cost of $O(\lambda_{\mathsf{DCR}}^2 \cdot b)$.

Our work improves the state-of-the-art by supporting free addition gates and more efficient bit-decomposition gates. However, as a trade-off, multiplication gates are more expensive, of size $O(\lambda_{\mathsf{DCR}} \cdot b)$.

- Our fourth scheme (Theorem 4) garbles mixed circuits modulo 2^b and allows free addition. Each multiplication gate and bit-decomposition gate costs $O(\lambda_{\mathsf{DCR}} \cdot b)$ communication.

2   Preliminaries

For any positive integer N, let $[N] := \{0, 1, \ldots, N - 1\}$, let $\mathbb{Z}_N$ denote the ring of integer modulo N. We assume modulo operation has lower priority than addition. That is, $a + b \bmod p$ should be interpreted as $(a + b) \bmod p$.

Base-p Digit Representation and Bit Representation. For any $x \in [2^b]$, the *bit representation* of x is the unique boolean vector $(x_0, \ldots, x_{b-1}) \in \{0, 1\}^n$ such that $x = \sum_i 2^i x_i$. For any $x \in [p^k]$, the *base-p digit representation* of x, is the unique vector $(x_0, \ldots, x_{k-1}) \in [p]^k$ such that $x = \sum_i p^i x_i$.

For any $x \in [p^k]$, let $(x_0, \ldots, x_{k-1})$ be its base-p digit decomposition, the *base-p bit representation* of x is the unique vector $(x_{i,j})_{i \in [k], j \in [\log p]} \in \{0, 1\}^{k \cdot \lceil \log p \rceil}$ such that $x_i = \sum_j p^i 2^j x_{i,j}$ for all $i \in [k]$. As a consequence, $x = \sum_{i,j} p^i 2^j x_{i,j}$. That is, base-$p$ bit representation is the bit representation of the base-p digit decomposition.

2.1   Computation Models

We consider *arithmetic circuits* and its generalization *mixed circuits*, where the computation can switch between arithmetic and boolean. Each wire carries a value x in either the boolean field $\mathbb{F}_2 = \{0, 1\}$ or an arithmetic ring $\mathcal{R}$. We mainly consider $\mathcal{R} = \mathbb{Z}_{p^k}$ the ring of integer modulo a prime power, and the special case $\mathcal{R} = \mathbb{Z}_{2^b}$. More specifically, we mostly focus on the following class of circuits.

Mixed Circuit. Let $\mathcal{C}_{\mathsf{mix}}(\mathcal{R})$ denote the class of circuits that mixes boolean gates and arithmetic operations over $\mathcal{R}$. A circuit in this class computes a function $f : \{0, 1\}^{n_{\mathsf{in,bool}}} \times \mathcal{R}^{n_{\mathsf{in,arith}}} \to \{0, 1\}^{n_{\mathsf{out,bool}}} \times \mathcal{R}^{n_{\mathsf{out,arith}}}$ using the gates as basis:

- $\mathsf{Add}, \mathsf{Mult} : \mathcal{R} \times \mathcal{R} \to \mathcal{R}$ compute addition and multiplication over $\mathcal{R}$.
- Bit-decomposition $\mathsf{BD} : \mathcal{R} \to \{0, 1\}^b$ computes the bit representation of an arithmetic value.
  When $\mathcal{R} = \mathbb{Z}_{2^b}$, we consider the most natural bit decomposition. That is, $\mathsf{BD}(x) = (x_0, x_1, \ldots, x_{b-1})$ such that $x = \sum_i 2^i x_i$.

When $\mathcal{R} = \mathbb{Z}_{p^k}$, the gate first decomposes the number into digits in base p, then decomposes each digit into bits. That is, $b = k \cdot \lceil \log p \rceil$, and

$$\mathsf{BD}(x) = (x_{i,j})_{i \in [k], j \in \lceil \log p \rceil} \quad \text{s.t. } x = \sum_i p^i \sum_j 2^j x_{i,j}. \tag{1}$$

– Bit-composition $\mathsf{BC} : \{0,1\}^b \to \mathcal{R}$ computes the arithmetic value from its bit representation.
– $g : \{0,1\} \times \{0,1\} \to \{0,1\}$ computes the boolean function g.

Arithmetic Circuit. Let $\mathcal{C}_{\mathsf{arith}}(\mathcal{R})$ denote the class of arithmetic circuits over $\mathcal{R}$. A circuit in this class computes a function $f : \mathcal{R}^{n_{\mathsf{in}}} \to \mathcal{R}^{n_{\mathsf{out}}}$ using the following the gates as basis:

– $\mathsf{Add}, \mathsf{Mult} : \mathcal{R} \times \mathcal{R} \to \mathcal{R}$ compute addition and multiplication over $\mathcal{R}$.

2.2 Garbled Circuits (GC)

The following definition of garbling mixed circuits has been implicitly considered in the previous works. We will not separately define arithmetic GC since it can be viewed as the special case of mixed GC.

Definition 1 (Garbling of Mixed Circuits). *A garbling scheme for $\mathcal{C}_{\mathsf{mix}}(\mathcal{R})$ consists of three efficient algorithms.*

– $\mathsf{KeyGen}(1^\lambda, 1^{n_{\mathsf{in,bool}}}, 1^{n_{\mathsf{in,arith}}})$ *samples* $n_{\mathsf{in,bool}}$ *boolean wire keys* $\mathsf{K}_1, \ldots, \mathsf{K}_{n_{\mathsf{in,bool}}}$, $n_{\mathsf{in,arith}}$ *arithmetic wire keys* $\mathsf{AK}_1, \ldots, \mathsf{AK}_{n_{\mathsf{in,arith}}}$ *and status* st*. Each boolean key* K_i *is a function from a bit to a bit string. Each arithmetic key* AK_i *is an affine function from a ring element to a vector.*
– $\mathsf{Garb}(C, \mathsf{st})$ *takes a mixed circuit* $C \in \mathcal{C}_{\mathsf{mix}}(\mathcal{R})$*, outputs a garbled circuit* $\widetilde{C}$*.*
– $\mathsf{Eval}(\widetilde{C}, \{\mathsf{l}_i\}_{i \in [n_{\mathsf{in,bool}}]}, \{\mathbf{L}_i\}_{i \in [n_{\mathsf{in,arith}}]})$ *takes a garbled circuit* $\widetilde{C}$*, boolean labels* l_i*, and arithmetic labels* $\mathbf{L}_i$*. It outputs the evaluation results* $\{y_{\mathsf{bool},i}\}$*,* $\{y_{\mathsf{arith},i}\}$*.*

Correctness. The garbling scheme is correct, if for any circuit $C \in \mathcal{C}_{\mathsf{mix}}(\mathcal{R})$ and any input x, as long as $\widetilde{C}$ and keys $\mathsf{K}_1, \ldots, \mathsf{K}_{n_{\mathsf{in,bool}}}, \mathsf{AK}_1, \ldots, \mathsf{AK}_{n_{\mathsf{in,arith}}}$ are properly generated,

$$\mathsf{Eval}(\widetilde{C}, \mathsf{l}_1, \ldots, \mathsf{l}_{n_{\mathsf{in,bool}}}, \mathbf{L}_1, \ldots, \mathbf{L}_{n_{\mathsf{in,arith}}})$$

always outputs $C(x)$, where $\mathsf{l}_i := \mathsf{K}_i(x_{\mathsf{bool},i})$, $\mathbf{L}_i := \mathsf{AK}_i(x_{\mathsf{arith},i})$ are input labels.

Security. The garbling scheme is *secure* if there exists an efficient simulator Sim such that for any circuit $C \in \mathcal{C}_{\mathsf{mix}}(\mathcal{R})$ and input x, the output of $\mathsf{Sim}(C, C(x))$ is indistinguishable from

$$(\widetilde{C}, \mathsf{l}_1, \ldots, \mathsf{l}_{n_{\mathsf{in,bool}}}, \mathbf{L}_1, \ldots, \mathbf{L}_{n_{\mathsf{in,arith}}})$$

when $\widetilde{C}, \mathsf{K}_1, \ldots, \mathsf{K}_{n_{\mathsf{in,bool}}}, \mathsf{AK}_1, \ldots, \mathsf{AK}_{n_{\mathsf{in,arith}}}$ are properly generated from C, and $\mathsf{l}_i := \mathsf{K}_i(x_{\mathsf{bool},i})$, $\mathbf{L}_i := \mathsf{AK}_i(x_{\mathsf{arith},i})$.

Gate Gadgets. The construction is mostly modular. For each gate in the basis, there is a garbling gadget for all the tasks related to this gate. Consider a general gate $g : \mathcal{R}_1^n \to \mathcal{R}_2^m$ where $\mathcal{R}_1, \mathcal{R}_2 \in \{\mathbb{Z}_2, \mathcal{R}\}$. The garbling gadget for g consists of three efficient algorithms $g.\mathsf{Garb}, g.\mathsf{Eval}, g.\mathsf{Sim}$. The garbling algorithm $g.\mathsf{Garb}$ takes input wire keys $\mathsf{K}_1, \ldots, \mathsf{K}_n$ (which are boolean keys if $\mathcal{R}_1 = \mathbb{F}_2$, arithmetic keys if $\mathcal{R}_1 = \mathcal{R}$) and output wire keys $\mathsf{K}_1', \ldots, \mathsf{K}_m'$, generates a table Tab, such that:

- *Correctness.* For any $x_1, \ldots, x_n \in \mathcal{R}_1$ and $(y_1, \ldots, y_m) = g(x_1, \ldots, x_n)$, the evaluation algorithm $g.\mathsf{Eval}(\mathsf{K}_1(x_1), \ldots, \mathsf{K}_n(x_n), \mathsf{Tab})$ will always output $(\mathsf{K}_1'(y_1), \ldots, \mathsf{K}_m'(y_m))$.
- *Handwavy Security.* For any $x_1, \ldots, x_n \in \mathcal{R}_1$, the distribution of Tab is indistinguishable from $g.\mathsf{Sim}(\mathsf{K}_1(x_1), \ldots, \mathsf{K}_n(x_n), \mathsf{K}_1'(y_1), \ldots, \mathsf{K}_m'(y_m))$ when $\mathsf{K}_1(x_1), \ldots, \mathsf{K}_n(x_n)$ are also given to the distinguisher.

As the name suggested, this security definition is imprecise. The issue is mainly caused by the global key. It can be formalized by a global simulator. The global simulator first samples a label for each wire, then samples the garbling table of each gate using the simulation algorithm of the corresponding gadget. In short, the simulation is modular, but the actual security definition is global. For simplicity, we will work in the random oracle model.[2]

There is also a modular approach [10,11] that allows the precise security definition of each gate garbling gadget, but it is incompatible with the existence of the global key. The modular approach requires the simulation algorithm of the gate gadget to sample labels on the input wires. This causes another issue that a label can not be reused by multiple gates. Thus extra work is required when a gate has fan-out greater than 1.

3 Technical Overview

This section briefly discusses AIK's framework of arithmetic GC (Sect. 3.1) and a technically less interesting extension (Sect. 3.2) discussing the sufficiency of bit-decomposition and bit-composition. The takeaway is: Mixed circuits can be efficiently garbled, as long as there are efficient garbling gadgets for bit-decomposition and bit-composition.

In Sect. 3.3, we presents a naive construction of the two garbling gadgets. The resulting GC does not have superior efficiency, but it is simple enough and will be optimized in later sections.

3.1 Background: Key-Extension Implies Arithmetic GC

We recap the framework of AIK [10] for arithmetic GC over some ring $\mathcal{R}$, with the modification that there is a global key Δ for all arithmetic wires. As observed

---

[2] In the boolean GC setting, [13] shows how random oracle can be replaced with symmetric encryption resisting a combined related-key and key-dependent message attack. Their technique are likely to work in the arithmetic GC setting as well.

by FreeXOR [4] and "FreeADD" [12], the garbling of addition gates will cost no communication if a global key is sampled.

In more detail, an arithmetic key is sampled for each wire as follows (where λ denotes the security parameter):

- A global key $\boldsymbol{\Delta} \in \mathcal{R}^{\ell}$ is sampled for all arithmetic wires, where ℓ is the label length. If $\mathcal{R} = \mathbb{Z}_{2^b}$, we will set $\ell = \lambda$. If $\mathcal{R} = \mathbb{Z}_{p^k}$, we will set $\ell = \lceil \lambda/\log p \rceil$. For each arithmetic wire, the key is an affine function $\mathsf{AK} : \mathcal{R} \to \mathcal{R}^{\ell+1}$. The output $\mathsf{AK}(x)$ consists of ℓ-dimension label and a *color number*. That is, AK can be represented by $\mathsf{AK} = (\mathbf{A} \in \mathcal{R}^{\ell}, \alpha \in \mathcal{R})$ such that

$$\mathsf{AK}(x) = (\boldsymbol{\Delta}x + \mathbf{A}, x + \alpha) \quad (\text{in } \mathcal{R}).$$

α is called the mask number of this wire. Set $\alpha = 0$ for every output wire.

The circuit is garbled gate-by-gate. The garbling gadget for arithmetic gate g consists of a garbling algorithm $g.\mathsf{Garb}$, an evaluation algorithm $g.\mathsf{Eval}$ and a simulation algorithm $g.\mathsf{Sim}$. The garbling algorithm $g.\mathsf{Garb}$ takes the keys of input wires $\mathsf{AK}_1, \mathsf{AK}_2$ and a key of output wire AK, outputs a table Tab such that:

- *Correctness.* For any $x, y \in \mathcal{R}$, $g.\mathsf{Eval}(\mathsf{AK}_1(x), \mathsf{AK}_2(y), \mathsf{Tab}) = \mathsf{AK}(g(x,y))$.
- *Handwavy Security.* For any $x, y \in \mathcal{R}$, the distribution of Tab is indistinguishable from $g.\mathsf{Sim}(\mathsf{AK}_1(x), \mathsf{AK}_2(y), \mathsf{AK}(g(x,y)))$ when $\mathsf{AK}_1(x), \mathsf{AK}_2(y)$ are also given to the distinguisher but the global arithmetic key $\boldsymbol{\Delta}$ is hidden.

If g is addition, note that

$$\mathsf{AK}_1(x) + \mathsf{AK}_2(y) - \mathsf{AK}(x+y)$$
$$= (\boldsymbol{\Delta}x + \mathbf{A}_1, x + \alpha_1) + (\boldsymbol{\Delta}y + \mathbf{A}_2, y + \alpha_2) - (\boldsymbol{\Delta}(x+y) + \mathbf{A}, x + y + \alpha)$$
$$= (\mathbf{A}_1 + \mathbf{A}_2 - \mathbf{A}, \alpha_1 + \alpha_2 - \alpha) \quad (\text{in } \mathbb{Z}_{2^d})$$

can be determined by the input/output labels. Setting it as the table will not violate security and is sufficient for correctness. A smarter solution, as suggested by [12], is to set the table Tab to be *empty*, and to change how the output wire key AK is generated. Instead of sampling AK at random, set $\mathbf{A} = \mathbf{A}_1 + \mathbf{A}_2$ and $\alpha = \alpha_1 + \alpha_2$, thus $\mathsf{AK}_1(x) + \mathsf{AK}_2(y) \bmod 2^d = \mathsf{AK}(x+y)$.

If g is multiplication, first use *randomized encoding* [14,15] to sample two affine functions (long keys) $\mathsf{AK}_1^{\mathsf{L}}, \mathsf{AK}_2^{\mathsf{L}}$ such that $\mathsf{AK}_1^{\mathsf{L}}(x), \mathsf{AK}_2^{\mathsf{L}}(y)$ reveals $\mathsf{AK}(xy)$ but nothing else about x, y, AK. This is formalized as a so-called *affinization gadget* in [10] (called "arithmetic operation gadgets" in [11]).

The affinization gadget for multiplication can be formalized by a garbling algorithm $\mathsf{Aff}_{\times}.\mathsf{Garb}$, an evaluation algorithm $\mathsf{Aff}_{\times}.\mathsf{Eval}$ and a simulation algorithm $\mathsf{Aff}_{\times}.\mathsf{Sim}$.

- Given an affine function, the garbling algorithm $\mathsf{Aff}_{\times}.\mathsf{Garb}(\mathsf{AK})$ samples two affine functions $\mathsf{AK}_1^{\mathsf{L}}, \mathsf{AK}_2^{\mathsf{L}}$ such that the output dimension of $\mathsf{AK}_i^{\mathsf{L}}$ is at most twice the output dimension of AK. (The multiplicative factors of $\mathsf{AK}_1^{\mathsf{L}}, \mathsf{AK}_2^{\mathsf{L}}$ are not necessarily the global $\boldsymbol{\Delta}$. We represent a "long key" as $\mathsf{AK}^{\mathsf{L}} = (\mathbf{A}, \mathbf{B})$ such that $\mathsf{AK}^{\mathsf{L}}(x) = \mathbf{A}x + \mathbf{B}$.)

- *Correctness.* For any x, y in the ring, given "long labels", the evaluation algorithm $\mathsf{Aff}_\times.\mathsf{Eval}(\mathsf{AK}_1^\mathsf{L}(x), \mathsf{AK}_2^\mathsf{L}(y))$ always outputs $\mathsf{AK}(xy)$.
- *Security.* For any AK, x, y, the distribution of $(\mathsf{AK}_1^\mathsf{L}(x), \mathsf{AK}_2^\mathsf{L}(y))$ is perfectly indistinguishable from $\mathsf{Aff}_\times.\mathsf{Sim}(\mathsf{AK}(xy))$. The randomness of the former comes from the randomness tape of $\mathsf{Aff}_\times.\mathsf{Garb}$.

The construction of GC is complete by the *key-extension* gadget, which allows the evaluator to compute $\mathsf{AK}_1^\mathsf{L}(x), \mathsf{AK}_2^\mathsf{L}(y)$ from $\mathsf{AK}_1(x), \mathsf{AK}_2(y)$.

The key-extension gadget can be formalized by three efficient algorithms $\mathsf{KE.Garb}, \mathsf{KE.Eval}, \mathsf{KE.Sim}$.
- Given a key AK and an affine function AK^L, the garbling algorithm $\mathsf{KE.Garb}(\mathsf{AK}, \mathsf{AK}^\mathsf{L})$ samples a table Tab.
- *Correctness.* For any x in the ring, $\mathsf{KE.Eval}(\mathsf{AK}(x), \mathsf{Tab}) = \mathsf{AK}^\mathsf{L}(x)$.
- *Handwavy Security.* For any x, the distribution of Tab is indistinguishable from $\mathsf{KE.Sim}(\mathsf{AK}(x), \mathsf{AK}^\mathsf{L}(x))$ when $\mathsf{AK}(x)$ are also given to the distinguisher but $\boldsymbol{\Delta}$ is hidden.

The garbling gadget for multiplication gates can be constructed as follows.

- Garbling algorithm $\mathsf{Mult.Garb}(\mathsf{AK}_1, \mathsf{AK}_2, \mathsf{AK})$:
  $\mathsf{Aff}_\times.\mathsf{Garb}(\mathsf{AK}) \to (\mathsf{AK}_1^\mathsf{L}, \mathsf{AK}_2^\mathsf{L})$.
  $\mathsf{KE.Garb}(\mathsf{AK}_i, \mathsf{AK}_i^\mathsf{L}) \to \mathsf{Tab}_i$ for $i \in \{1, 2\}$.
  Output $\mathsf{Tab} = (\mathsf{Tab}_1, \mathsf{Tab}_2)$.
- Evaluation algorithm $\mathsf{Mult.Eval}(\mathbf{L}_1, \mathbf{L}_2, \mathsf{Tab})$:
  $\mathsf{KE.Eval}(\mathbf{L}_i, \mathsf{Tab}_i) \to \mathbf{L}_i^\mathsf{L}$ for $i \in \{1, 2\}$.
  $\mathsf{Aff}_\times.\mathsf{Eval}(\mathbf{L}_1^\mathsf{L}, \mathbf{L}_2^\mathsf{L}) \to \mathbf{L}$.
  Output $\mathbf{L}$.
- Simulation algorithm $\mathsf{Mult.Sim}(\mathbf{L}_1, \mathbf{L}_2, \mathbf{L})$:
  $\mathsf{Aff}_\times.\mathsf{Sim}(\mathbf{L}) \to \mathbf{L}_1^\mathsf{L}, \mathbf{L}_2^\mathsf{L}$.
  $\mathsf{KE.Sim}(\mathbf{L}_i, \mathbf{L}_i^\mathsf{L}) \to \mathsf{Tab}_i$ for $i \in \{1, 2\}$.
  Output $\mathsf{Tab} = (\mathsf{Tab}_1, \mathsf{Tab}_2)$.

This arithmetic GC framework [10, 12] reduces the problem to constructing a key-extension gadget. As long as there is a secure key-extension gadget that doubles the key length (i.e., the output of AK^L can be twice as long as AK), the framework will yield an arithmetic GC of the same complexity.

Lemma 1 (informal). *If there is a secure key-extension gadget that doubles the key length whose table size is c_{KE}, there is an arithmetic GC for the same ring such that each addition gate costs no communication, and each multiplication gate costs $2 \cdot c_{\mathrm{KE}}$ communication.*

3.2   Bit-Decomposition and Bit-Composition Imply Mixed GC

We extend the AIK framework to support mixed circuit, which consists of arithmetic operation gates as described before, boolean gates such as AND, XOR, and NOT, and two conversion gates, bit-decomposition and bit-compositions.

A wire in the circuit is either an arithmetic wires as described before, or a boolean wire. The keys for arithmetic wires stay unchanged. The keys for boolean wires are sampled as follows:

– A global key $\Delta \in \{0,1\}^\lambda$ is sampled for all boolean wires.
  For each boolean wire, the key is an affine function $\mathsf{K} : \{0,1\} \rightarrow \{0,1\}^{\lambda+1}$. The output $\mathsf{K}(x)$ consists of a λ-bit label and a color bit. That is, K can be represented by $\mathsf{K} = (\mathbf{b} \in \{0,1\}^\lambda, \alpha \in \{0,1\})$ such that

$$\mathsf{K}(x) = (\Delta x \oplus \mathbf{b}, x \oplus \alpha).$$

α is called the mask bit of this wire. Set $\alpha = 0$ for every output wire.

The arithmetic operation gates are garbled as before, and we skip the rather standard boolean gate garbling gadgets. We describe gadgets for garbling bit-decomposition and bit-composition gates in more detail below.

The bit-decomposition gadget consists of $\mathsf{BD.Garb}, \mathsf{BD.Eval}, \mathsf{BD.Sim}$. The garbling algorithm $\mathsf{BD.Garb}$ takes an arithmetic key AK and b boolean keys $\mathsf{K}_0, \ldots, \mathsf{K}_{b-1}$ as inputs, outputs a table Tab, such that

– *Correctness.* For any $x \in \mathcal{R}$, $\mathsf{BD.Eval}(\mathsf{AK}(x), \mathsf{Tab}) = (\mathsf{K}_0(x_0), \ldots, \mathsf{K}_{b-1}(x_{b-1}))$.
– *Handwavy Security.* For any $x \in \mathcal{R}$, the distribution of $\mathsf{AK}(x), \mathsf{Tab}$ is indistinguishable from $\mathsf{AK}(x), \mathsf{BD.Sim}(\mathsf{AK}(x), \mathsf{K}_0(x_0), \ldots, \mathsf{K}_{b-1}(x_{b-1}))$ when the global arithmetic key Δ is hidden.

The bit-composition gadget consists of $\mathsf{BC.Garb}, \mathsf{BC.Eval}, \mathsf{BC.Sim}$. The garbling algorithm $\mathsf{BC.Garb}$ takes b boolean keys $\mathsf{K}_0, \ldots, \mathsf{K}_{b-1}$ and an arithmetic affine function AK^L as inputs, outputs a table Tab, such that

– *Correctness.* For any $x \in \mathcal{R}$, $\mathsf{BC.Eval}(\mathsf{K}_0(x_0), \ldots, \mathsf{K}_{b-1}(x_{b-1}), \mathsf{Tab}) = \mathsf{AK}^\mathsf{L}(x)$.
– *Handwavy Security.* For any $x \in \mathcal{R}$, the distribution of Tab is indistinguishable from $\mathsf{BC.Sim}(\mathsf{K}_0(x_0), \ldots, \mathsf{K}_{b-1}(x_{b-1}), \mathsf{AK}^\mathsf{L}(x))$ when $\mathsf{K}_0(x_0), \ldots, \mathsf{K}_{b-1}(x_{b-1})$ is also given to the adversary but the global key Δ is hidden.

We stress that AK^L can be an arbitrary affine function: its multiplicative factor does not have to be the global key; and its output dimension can be larger. Although for simplicity, we assume the output dimension of AK^L equals the dimension of a label. In case we need longer AK^L, we can always divide it into a few pieces and use the bit-composition gadget multiple times.

It is obvious that bit-decomposition gadget and bit-composition gadget imply key-extension gadget, and thus imply mixed GC. Previous work did not construct the key-extension gadget through this approach because bit-decomposition is expensive in their constructions.

Lemma 2 (informal). *If there are a secure bit-decomposition gadget whose table size is c_{BD} and a secure bit-composition gadget whose table size is c_{BC}, then there is a mixed GC for the same ring such that each addition gate costs no communication, and each multiplication/bit-decomposition/bit-composition gate costs $O(c_{\mathrm{BD}} + c_{\mathrm{BC}})$ communication.*

3.3   The Naive Construction

This section presents garbling gadgets for bit-decomposition and bit-composition when the ring is $\mathbb{Z}_{2^b}$. For each $x \in \mathbb{Z}_{2^b}$, let x_i denote the i-th lowest bit of x, so that $x = \sum_i 2^i x_i$. Let $x_{a:b}$ denote $\sum_{a \le i < b} 2^{i-a} x_i$, so that the bit representation of $x_{a:b}$ is a substring of the bit representation of x.

BC. The bit-composition gadget is straight-forward. Given boolean input labels $\mathsf{K}_0(x_0), \ldots, \mathsf{K}_{b-1}(x_{b-1})$, the evaluator need to compute the output label $\mathsf{AK}^\mathsf{L}(x) = \mathbf{A}x + \mathbf{B}$ (recall that in bit-composition gadget, the output key can be any affine function). The garbling algorithm BC.Garb samples additive sharing $\mathbf{B}_0, \ldots, \mathbf{B}_{b-1}$ such that $\sum_i \mathbf{B}_i = \mathbf{B}$, then generates table that allows the evaluator to compute $\mathbf{A}2^i x_i + \mathbf{B}_i$ from $\mathsf{K}_i(x_i)$. The most direct solution is to let the table contain ciphertexts

$$\mathsf{Enc}(\mathsf{K}_i(\beta), \mathbf{A}2^i\beta + \mathbf{B}_i) \text{ for all } \beta \in \{0,1\}.$$

The order of the two ciphertexts are permuted according to the mask bit in K_i, so that the evaluator can pick the right ciphertext using the color bit.

BD. The bit decomposition gadget is inspired by the following two observations.

– Let $\mathbf{L} = \mathsf{AK}(x) = \mathbf{\Delta}x + \mathbf{A}$ denote the given arithmetic label. Then

$$\mathbf{L} \bmod 2 = \mathbf{\Delta}x + \mathbf{A} \bmod 2 = \mathbf{\Delta}x_0 + \mathbf{A} \bmod 2.$$

If the table contains $\mathsf{Enc}(\mathbf{\Delta}\beta + \mathbf{A} \bmod 2, \mathsf{K}_0(\beta))$ for $\beta \in \{0,1\}$, the evaluator can properly decrypt the boolean label $\mathsf{K}_0(x_0)$ of x_0 with $\mathbf{L} \bmod 2$.
– To continue, the evaluator should be able to compute a mod-2^{b-1} arithmetic label for all but the least significant bit of x

$$\mathbf{L}^{(1)} = \mathbf{\Delta}x_{1:b} + \mathbf{A}^{(1)} \bmod 2^{b-1}.$$

Then the evaluator can iteratively compute all the boolean labels. Note that,

$$\mathbf{L} - 2\mathbf{L}^{(1)} \bmod 2^b = \mathbf{\Delta}x_0 + \mathbf{A} - 2\mathbf{A}^{(1)} \bmod 2^b. \tag{2}$$

If the table also contains ciphertexts

$$\mathsf{Enc}(\mathbf{\Delta}\beta + \mathbf{A} \bmod 2, \mathbf{\Delta}\beta + \mathbf{A} - 2\mathbf{A}^{(1)} \bmod 2^b) \text{ for } \beta \in \{0,1\},$$

the evaluator can decrypt the ciphertext to get (2) and compute $\mathbf{L}^{(1)}$.

These observations lead us to the bit-decomposition gadget in Fig. 1. For simplicity, the encryption is implemented by a secure function H which is modeled as a random oracle

$$\mathsf{Enc}(key, m) = \mathsf{H}(key, \mathsf{aux}) \oplus m, \quad \mathsf{Dec}(key, c) = \mathsf{H}(key, \mathsf{aux}) \oplus c,$$

where aux contains auxiliary information such as the id of current gate. The H queries under some auxiliary information is bounded: For each aux, the construction only queries $\mathsf{H}(key, \mathsf{aux})$ for up to two distinct key.

Garbling algorithm BD.Garb takes an arithmetic key $\mathsf{AK} = (\mathbf{A}, \alpha)$ and b boolean keys $\mathsf{K}_0, \ldots, \mathsf{K}_{b-1}$ as inputs.

- Let $\mathbf{A}^{(0)} = \mathbf{A}$. For each $1 \leq i < b$, samples $\mathbf{A}^{(i)} \leftarrow (\mathbb{Z}_{2^{b-i}})^\lambda$.
- Let $\alpha^{(0)} = \alpha$. For each $1 \leq i < b$, samples $\alpha^{(i)} \leftarrow \mathbb{Z}_{2^{b-i}}$.
- For each $0 \leq i < b$, for each $\beta \in \{0,1\}$, compute

$$\mathsf{C}_{i, \beta + \alpha^{(i)} \bmod 2} \leftarrow \mathsf{H}(\mathbf{\Delta}\beta + \mathbf{A}^{(i)} \bmod 2, (\mathsf{id}, i)) \oplus$$
$$\begin{cases} (\mathsf{K}_i(\beta), \mathbf{\Delta}\beta + \mathbf{A}^{(i)} - 2\mathbf{A}^{(i+1)} \bmod 2^{b-i}, \\ \quad\quad \beta + \alpha^{(i)} - 2\alpha^{(i+1)} \bmod 2^{b-i}) & \text{if } i < b-1 \\ \mathsf{K}_i(\beta), & \text{if } i = b-1 \end{cases}$$

- Output table $\mathsf{Tab} = (\mathsf{C}_{i,\beta})_{i \in [b], \beta \in \{0,1\}}$

Evaluation algorithm BD.Eval takes input label $(\mathbf{L}, \bar{x})$ and a table Tab as inputs.

- Let $\mathbf{L}^{(0)} := \mathbf{L}$, $\bar{x}^{(0)} = \bar{x}$.
- For $i = 0, 1, 2, \ldots, b-1$: Compute $(l_i, \mathbf{D}^{(i)}, d^{(i)}) \leftarrow \mathsf{H}(\mathbf{L}^{(i)} \bmod 2, (\mathsf{id}, i)) \oplus \mathsf{C}_{i, \bar{x}^{(i)} \bmod 2}$. If $i < b-1$, compute

$$\mathbf{L}^{(i+1)} = (\mathbf{L}^{(i)} - \mathbf{D}^{(i)} \bmod 2^{b-i})/2, \quad \bar{x}^{(i+1)} = (\bar{x}^{(i)} - d^{(i)} \bmod 2^{b-i})/2.$$

- Output boolean labels $l_0, l_1, \ldots, l_{b-1}$.

Simulation algorithm BD.Sim takes arithmetic label $(\mathbf{L}, \bar{x})$ and boolean labels $l_0, l_1, \ldots, l_{b-1}$ as inputs.

- Let $(\mathbf{L}^{(0)}, \bar{x}^{(0)}) = (\mathbf{L}, \bar{x})$.
- Sample random $\mathbf{L}^{(i)} \leftarrow (\mathbb{Z}_{2^{b-i}})^\lambda$, $\bar{x}^{(i)} \leftarrow \mathbb{Z}_{2^{b-i}}$ for each $1 \leq i < b$.
- The active ciphertexts in the table Tab are set as

$$\mathsf{C}_{i, \bar{x}^{(i)} \bmod 2} = \mathsf{H}(\mathbf{L}^{(i)} \bmod 2, (\mathsf{id}, i)) \oplus$$
$$\begin{cases} (l_i, \mathbf{L}^{(i)} - 2\mathbf{L}^{(i+1)} \bmod 2^{b-i}, \bar{x}^{(i)} - 2\bar{x}^{(i+1)} \bmod 2^{b-i}) & \text{if } i < b-1 \\ l_i & \text{if } i = b-1 \end{cases}$$

The rest are inactive ciphertexts, and are simulated as random strings.

Fig. 1. The Naive Bit-Decomposition Gadget

Lemma 3. *There are statistically secure bit-decomposition gadget (Fig. 1) and bit-composition gadget (a specialization of Fig. 2) for ring $\mathbb{Z}_{2^b}$, whose table size is $O(b^2 \lambda)$. They yield statistically secure mixed GC for $\mathbb{Z}_{2^b}$ in the random oracle model, where each addition gate costs no communication, and each multiplication/bit-decomposition/bit-composition gate costs $O(b^2 \lambda)$ communication.*

The proof of Lemma 3 is deferred to the full version[3].

---

[3] https://eprint.iacr.org/2023/1584.

4   Mixed GC for $\mathbb{Z}_{p^k}$

This section presents a mix GC for $\mathbb{Z}_{p^k}$. Recall how the arithmetic key, label, color number are defined for each arithmetic wire (where λ is the security parameter):

- A global key $\boldsymbol{\Delta} \in \mathbb{Z}_{p^k}^{\ell}$ is sampled for all arithmetic wires, where $\ell = \lceil \lambda / \log p \rceil$ is the label length.
  For each arithmetic wire, the key is an affine function $\mathsf{AK} : \mathbb{Z}_{p^k} \to \mathbb{Z}_{p^k}^{\ell+1}$. The output $\mathsf{AK}(x)$ consists of ℓ-dimension label and a *color number*. That is, AK can be represented by $\mathsf{AK} = (\mathbf{A} \in \mathbb{Z}_{p^k}^{\ell}, \alpha \in \mathbb{Z}_{p^k})$ such that

$$\mathsf{AK}(x) = (\boldsymbol{\Delta}x + \mathbf{A}, x + \alpha) \mod p^k.$$

  α is called the mask number of this wire. Set $\alpha = 0$ for every output wire.

As discussed in Sect. 3.2, it suffices to construct efficient garbling gadgets for bit-decomposition and bit-composition over ring $\mathbb{Z}_{p^k}$. The construction of the two gadgets for $\mathbb{Z}_{p^k}$ generalizes the constructions for $\mathbb{Z}_{2^b}$ in Sect. 3.3.

For each $x \in \mathbb{Z}_{p^k}$, let x_i denote the i-th lowest digit of x, so that $x = \sum_i p^i x_i$. Let $x_{a:b}$ denote $\sum_{a \le i < b} p^{i-a} x_i$, so that the base-$p$ digit representation of $x_{a:b}$ is a substring of the base-p digit representation of x. Let $x_{i,j}$ denote the j-th lowest bit of x_i, so that $x_i = \sum_j 2^j x_{i,j}$.

For each $\beta \in \mathbb{Z}_p$, let β_i denote the i-th lowest bit of β, so that $\beta = \sum_i 2^i \beta_i$. Let $\beta_{a:b}$ denote $\sum_{a \le i < b} 2^{i-a} \beta_i$, so that the bit representation of $\beta_{a:b}$ is a substring of the bit representation of β.

BC. The bit-composition gadget is straight-forward. Given boolean input labels $\mathsf{K}_{i,j}(x_{i,j})$ for $i \in [k], j \in [\log p]$, the evaluator needs to compute the output label $\mathsf{AK}^{\mathsf{L}}(x) = \mathbf{A}x + \mathbf{B}$ (recall that in the bit-composition gadget, the output key can be any affine function). The garbling algorithm $\mathsf{BC.Garb}$ samples additive sharing $\mathbf{B}_{i,j}$ such that $\sum_{i,j} \mathbf{B}_{i,j} = \mathbf{B}$, then generates a table that allows the evaluator to compute $\mathbf{A}p^i 2^j x_{i,j} + \mathbf{B}_{i,j}$ from $\mathsf{K}_{i,j}(x_{i,j})$. The most direct solution is to let the table contain ciphertexts

$$\mathsf{Enc}(\mathsf{K}_{i,j}(\beta), \mathbf{A}p^i 2^j \beta + \mathbf{B}_{i,j}) \text{ for all } \beta \in \{0,1\}.$$

The order of the two ciphertexts are permuted according to the mask bit in $\mathsf{K}_{i,j}$, so that the evaluator can pick the right ciphertext according to the color bit.

The construction is formalized in Fig. 2. The table consists of $O(k \log p)$ ciphertexts, each ciphertext is $k\lambda$-bit long, thus the table size is $O(\lambda k^2 \log p)$ bit.

BD. The bit-decomposition gadget starts with the same observations as the one in Sect. 3.3. Let $\mathbf{L} = \mathsf{AK}(x) = \boldsymbol{\Delta}x + \mathbf{A} \mod p^k$ denote the given arithmetic label. Define

$$\mathbf{L}^{(i)} = \boldsymbol{\Delta}x_{i:k} + \mathbf{A}^{(i)} \mod p^{k-i}.$$

Garbling algorithm BC.Garb takes boolean keys $\mathsf{K}_{i,j}$ for $i \in [k], j \in [\log p]$, and an arithmetic key $\mathsf{AK}^\mathsf{L} = (\mathbf{A}, \mathbf{B})$ as inputs. Let $\alpha_{i,j}$ denote the mask bit of $\mathsf{K}_{i,j}$.

- Sample random $\mathbf{B}_{i,j}$ for $i \in [k], j \in [\log p]$, satisfying $\sum_{i,j} \mathbf{B}_{i,j} \bmod p^k = \mathbf{B}$.
- For each $i \in [k], j \in [\log p]$, for each $\beta \in \{0,1\}$, compute

$$\mathsf{C}_{i,j,\beta+\alpha_{i,j} \bmod 2} \leftarrow \mathsf{H}(\mathsf{K}_{i,j}(\beta), \ (\mathsf{id}, i, j)) \oplus (\mathbf{A}p^i 2^j \beta + \mathbf{B}_{i,j} \bmod p^k)$$

- Output table $\mathsf{Tab} = (\mathsf{C}_{i,j,\beta})_{i \in [k], j \in [\log p], \beta \in \{0,1\}}$

Evaluation algorithm BC.Eval takes input labels $(\mathsf{l}_{i,j}, \bar{x}_{i,j})$ for $i \in [k], j \in [\log p]$ and a table Tab as inputs.

- For $i \in [k], j \in [\log p]$, compute $\mathbf{L}_{i,j} \leftarrow \mathsf{H}(\mathsf{l}_{i,j}, (\mathsf{id}, i, j)) \oplus \mathsf{C}_{i,j,\bar{x}_{i,j}}$.
- Output arithmetic label $\mathbf{L} = \sum_{i,j} \mathbf{L}_{i,j} \bmod p^k$.

Simulation algorithm BC.Sim takes input labels $(\mathsf{l}_{i,j}, \bar{x}_{i,j})$ for $i \in [k], j \in [\log p]$ and arithmetic label $\mathbf{L}$ as inputs.

- Sample random $\mathbf{L}_{i,j}$ for $i \in [k], j \in [\log p]$, satisfying $\sum_{i,j} \mathbf{L}_{i,j} \bmod p^k = \mathbf{L}$.
- The active ciphertexts in the table Tab are set as

$$\mathsf{C}_{i,j,\bar{x}_{i,j}} = \mathsf{H}(\mathsf{l}_{i,j}, (\mathsf{id}, i, j)) \oplus \mathbf{L}_{i,j}$$

The rest are inactive ciphertexts, and are simulated by random strings.

Fig. 2. The Naive Bit-Composition Gadget

where $\mathbf{A}^{(0)} := \mathbf{A}$ and $\mathbf{A}^{(i)}$ are randomly sampled. Thus, $\mathbf{L}^{(0)} = \mathbf{L}$. Note that,

$$\mathbf{L}^{(i)} \bmod p = \mathbf{\Delta}x_{i:k} + \mathbf{A}^{(i)} \bmod p = \mathbf{\Delta}x_i + \mathbf{A}^{(i)} \bmod p.$$

If the table contains ciphertext

$$\mathsf{Enc}(\mathbf{\Delta}x_i + \mathbf{A}^{(i)} \bmod p, \ (\text{boolean labels of } x_i, \mathbf{\Delta}x_i + \mathbf{A}^{(i)} - p\mathbf{A}^{(i+1)} \bmod p^{k-i}))$$

the evaluator can, given $\mathbf{L}^{(i)}$, computes all the boolean labels of x_i and the next label $\mathbf{L}^{(i+1)}$. This observation can be formalized as a secure bit-decomposition gadget, who has poor efficiency. The table consists of pk ciphertexts, each ciphertext is $(\lambda \log p + \lambda k)$-bit long, the total length is no less than λpk^2. Under constraint $p^k \approx 2^b$, the table size is minimized when $p = O(1)$, which is asymptotically equivalent to the naive construction in Sect. 3.3.

The bottleneck is the encryption of $\mathbf{\Delta}x_i + \mathbf{A}^{(i)} - p\mathbf{A}^{(i+1)} \bmod p^{k-i}$. To optimize the efficiency, we replace the long ciphertexts by shorter ciphertexts

$$\mathsf{Enc}(\mathbf{\Delta}x_i + \mathbf{A}^{(i)} \bmod p, \ \text{boolean labels of } x_i)$$

that only encrypts the boolean labels. Since the evaluator can computes the boolean labels of x_i, it uses a mini bit-composition gadget (Fig. 3) to compute $\mathbf{\Delta}x_i + \mathbf{A}^{(i)} - p\mathbf{A}^{(i+1)} \bmod p^{k-i}$.

The optimized construction is formalized in Fig. 4. After optimization, the table consists of $O(kp)$ ciphertexts, each of which is $O(\lambda \log p)$ bit long, and k mini-tables for the mini bit-composition, each of which is $O(\lambda k \log p)$ bit long. The total table size is $O(\lambda k(k+p) \log p)$.

Garbling algorithm $\mathsf{miniBC}_k.\mathsf{Garb}$ takes boolean keys K_j for $j \in [\log p]$, and an arithmetic key $\mathsf{AK}^{\mathsf{L}} = (\mathbf{A}, \mathbf{B})$ as inputs. Let α_j denote the mask bit of K_j.

- Sample random $\mathbf{B}_j$ for $j \in [\log p]$, satisfying $\sum_j \mathbf{B}_j \bmod p^k = \mathbf{B}$.
- For each $j \in [\log p]$, for each $\beta \in \{0, 1\}$, compute

$$\mathsf{C}_{j, \beta + \alpha_j \bmod 2} \leftarrow \mathsf{H}(\mathsf{K}_j(\beta), (\mathsf{id}, j)) \oplus (\mathbf{A}2^j \beta + \mathbf{B}_j \bmod p^k)$$

- Output table $\mathsf{Tab} = (\mathsf{C}_{j, \beta})_{j \in [\log p], \beta \in \{0, 1\}}$

Evaluation algorithm $\mathsf{miniBC}_k.\mathsf{Eval}$ takes input labels $(\mathsf{l}_j, \bar{x}_j)$ for $j \in [\log p]$ and a table Tab as inputs.

- For $j \in [\log p]$, compute $\mathbf{L}_j \leftarrow \mathsf{H}(\mathsf{l}_j, (\mathsf{id}, j)) \oplus \mathsf{C}_{j, \bar{x}_j}$.
- Output arithmetic label $\mathbf{L} = \sum_j \mathbf{L}_j \bmod p^k$.

Simulation algorithm $\mathsf{miniBC}_k.\mathsf{Sim}$ takes input labels $(\mathsf{l}_j, \bar{x}_j)$ for $j \in [\log p]$ and arithmetic label $\mathbf{L}$ as inputs.

- Sample random $\mathbf{L}_j$ for $j \in [\log p]$, satisfying $\sum_j \mathbf{L}_j \bmod p^k = \mathbf{L}$.
- The active ciphertexts in the table Tab are set as

$$\mathsf{C}_{j, \bar{x}_j} = \mathsf{H}(\mathsf{l}_j, (\mathsf{id}, j)) \oplus \mathbf{L}_j$$

The rest are simulated by random strings.

Fig. 3. The Mini Bit-Composition Gadget

Theorem 1. *There are statistically secure bit-composition gadget (Fig. 2) for ring $\mathbb{Z}_{p^k}$ whose table size is $O(\lambda k^2 \log p)$ and bit-decomposition gadget (Fig. 4) for ring $\mathbb{Z}_{p^k}$, whose table size is $O(\lambda k(k+p) \log p)$. They yield a statistically secure mixed GC for $\mathbb{Z}_{p^k}$ in the random oracle model, such that each addition gate costs no communication, and each multiplication/bit-decomposition/bit-composition gate costs $O(\lambda k(k+p) \log p)$ communication.*

The bit-composition gadget (Fig. 2) and the mini bit-composition gadget (Fig. 3) are special cases of the linear bit-composition gadget (Fig. 5), whose correctness and security will be analyzed in Sect. 4.1. The proof of the bit-decomposition gadget is similar to that of Lemma 3 in Sect. 3.3.

Under the constraint that $p^k \approx 2^b$, the asymptotic cost per gate is minimized when $p \approx b/\log^c b$ for any constant $c \geq 1$. The minimal cost is $O(\lambda b^2/\log b)$.

Garbling algorithm BD.Garb takes an arithmetic key $\mathsf{AK} = (\mathbf{A}, \alpha)$ and $k \cdot \lceil \log p \rceil$ boolean keys $\mathsf{K}_{i,j}$ for $i \in [p], j \in [\log p]$ as inputs.

- Let $\mathbf{A}^{(0)} = \mathbf{A}$. For each $1 \leq i < k$, samples $\mathbf{A}^{(i)} \leftarrow (\mathbb{Z}_{p^{k-i}})^\lambda$.
- Let $\alpha^{(0)} = \alpha$. For each $1 \leq i < k$, samples $\alpha^{(i)} \leftarrow \mathbb{Z}_{p^{k-i}}$.
- For each $i \in [k], j \in [\log p]$, for each $\beta \in [p]$, compute

$$\mathsf{C}_{i, \beta + \alpha^{(i)} \bmod p} \leftarrow \mathsf{H}(\mathbf{\Delta}\beta + \mathbf{A}^{(i)} \bmod p, \; (\mathsf{id}, i)) \oplus (\mathsf{K}_{i,j}(\beta_j) \text{ for } j \in [\log p])$$

- For each $0 \leq i < k - 1$, define affine function $\mathsf{DK}^{(i)}$

$$\mathsf{DK}^{(i)}(\beta) = (\mathbf{\Delta}\beta + \mathbf{A}^{(i)} - p\mathbf{A}^{(i+1)}, \; \beta + \alpha^{(i)} - p\alpha^{(i+1)}) \bmod p^{k-i},$$

  compute table $\mathsf{tb}_i \leftarrow \mathsf{miniBC}_{k-i}.\mathsf{Garb}(\mathsf{K}_{i,j} \text{ for } j \in [\log p], \mathsf{DK}^{(i)})$.
- Output table Tab consisting of $(\mathsf{C}_{i,\beta})_{i \in [k], \beta \in [p]}$ and $(\mathsf{tb}_i)_{i \in [k-1]}$

Evaluation algorithm BD.Eval takes input label $(\mathbf{L}, \bar{x})$ and a table Tab as inputs.

- Let $\mathbf{L}^{(0)} := \mathbf{L}, \bar{x}^{(0)} = \bar{x}$.
- For $i = 0, 1, 2, \ldots, k - 1$:
  Compute $(\mathsf{l}_{i,j} \text{ for } j \in [\log p]) \leftarrow \mathsf{H}(\mathbf{L}^{(i)} \bmod p, (\mathsf{id}, i)) \oplus \mathsf{C}_{i, \bar{x}^{(i)} \bmod p}$.
  If $i < k - 1$, compute $(\mathbf{D}^{(i)}, d^{(i)}) \leftarrow \mathsf{miniBC}_{k-i}.\mathsf{Eval}(\mathsf{l}_{i,j} \text{ for } j \in [\log p], \mathsf{tb}_i)$

$$\mathbf{L}^{(i+1)} = (\mathbf{L}^{(i)} - \mathbf{D}^{(i)} \bmod p^{k-i})/p, \qquad \bar{x}^{(i+1)} = (\bar{x}^{(i)} - d^{(i)} \bmod p^{k-i})/p.$$

- Output boolean labels $\mathsf{l}_{i,j}$ for $i \in [p], j \in [\log p]$.

Simulation algorithm BD.Sim takes arithmetic label $(\mathbf{L}, \bar{x})$ and boolean labels $\mathsf{l}_{i,j}$ for $i \in [p], j \in [\log p]$ as inputs.

- Let $(\mathbf{L}^{(0)}, \bar{x}^{(0)}) = (\mathbf{L}, \bar{x})$.
- Sample random $\mathbf{L}^{(i)} \leftarrow (\mathbb{Z}_{p^{k-i}})^\lambda, \bar{x}^{(i)} \leftarrow \mathbb{Z}_{p^{k-i}}$ for each $1 \leq i < k$.
- The active ciphertexts in the table Tab are set as

$$\mathsf{C}_{i, \bar{x}^{(i)} \bmod p} = \mathsf{H}(\mathbf{L}^{(i)} \bmod p, (\mathsf{id}, i)) \oplus (\mathsf{l}_{i,j} \text{ for } j \in [\log p])$$

  The rest are inactive ciphertexts, and are simulated by random strings.
- For each $0 \leq i < k - 1$, compute

$$(\mathbf{D}^{(i)}, d^{(i)}) \leftarrow (\mathbf{L}^{(i)} - p\mathbf{L}^{(i+1)}, \; \bar{x}^{(i)} - p\bar{x}^{(i+1)}) \bmod p^{k-i}$$

  and simulate tb_i by $\mathsf{tb}_i \leftarrow \mathsf{miniBC}_{k-i}.\mathsf{Sim}(\mathsf{l}_{i,j} \text{ for } j \in [\log p], (\mathbf{D}^{(i)}, d^{(i)}))$.

Fig. 4. The Bit-Decomposition Gadget in Ring $\mathbb{Z}_{p^k}$

Further Optimization. The bit-decomposition gadget in Fig. 4 can be further optimized. Currently, for each $i \in [k]$ the table contains ciphertexts

$$\mathsf{C}_{i, \beta + \alpha^{(i)} \bmod p} \leftarrow \mathsf{H}(\mathbf{\Delta}\beta + \mathbf{A}^{(i)} \bmod p, \; (\mathsf{id}, i)) \oplus (\mathsf{K}_{i,j}(\beta_j) \text{ for } j \in [\log p])$$

for each $j \in [\log p], \beta \in [p]$. Notice that, every potential boolean label, such as $K_{i,j}(0)$, is encrypted in $O(p)$ ciphertexts. This is rather wasteful.

For better efficiency, $C_{i,\beta+\alpha^{(i)} \bmod p}$ only encrypts a key $K_{0,\beta}$

$$C_{i,\beta+\alpha^{(i)} \bmod p} \leftarrow H(\boldsymbol{\Delta}\beta + \mathbf{A}^{(i)} \bmod p, (\mathrm{id}, i)) \oplus K_{0,\beta}.$$

The key $K_{0,\beta}$ is sampled by the garbler, and can decrypt the ciphertext

$$\mathsf{Enc}(K_{0,\beta}, (K_{i,0}(\beta_0), K_{1,\beta_{1:\log p}})),$$

which reveals the next boolean label and the next key $K_{1,\beta_{1:\log p}}$. That is, the garbler samples keys $K_{j,\beta_{j:\log p}}$ for every $j \in [\log p], \beta \in [p]$, and the table additionally includes ciphertexts

$$\mathsf{Enc}(K_{j,\beta_{j:\log p}}, (K_{i,j}(\beta_j), K_{j+1,\beta_{j+1:\log p}}))$$

for every $j \in [\log p], \beta \in [p]$. The ciphertexts should be properly shuffled, and some color bits/digits should be introduced to help the evaluation.

After optimization, the table consists of $O(kp)$ ciphertexts, each of which is $O(\lambda)$ bit long, and k mini-tables for the mini bit-composition, each of which is $O(\lambda k \log p)$ bit long. The total table size is $O(\lambda k(k \log p + p))$. It produces a statistically secure mixed GC in the random oracle model that has a marginal efficiency improvement compared to Theorem 1. But we will not explicitly state the further optimized gadget construction. The improvement is not significant enough to change the results in Table 1.

4.1 Extension: Linear BC and General BD

Our mixed GC for $\mathbb{Z}_{p^k}$ (Theorem 1) allows conversion between an arithmetic label and boolean labels of its base-p bit representation using bit-decomposition and bit-composition gadgets.

The base-p bit representation is quite useful, for example, it allows comparison between arithmetic numbers. But in many cases, we may need or may want to use the base-p' bit representation for a different base p'. The most naive solution is to use an expensive boolean circuit for base conversion. In this section, we presents an alternative solution.

BC. Let x be an arithmetic value. Given boolean labels of the base-p' bit representation of x, how to compute the $\mathbb{Z}_{p^k}$-arithmetic label of x? We ask a more general question:

> Given boolean labels of $(z_0, \ldots, z_{m-1})$, how to compute the $\mathbb{Z}_{p^k}$-arithmetic label of $\sum_i c_i z_m$, where $c_0, \ldots, c_{m-1}$ are fixed constants?

Essentially, we are asking how to garble gate $f : \{0,1\}^m \to \mathbb{Z}_{p^k}$, which is defined as $f(z_0, \ldots, z_{m-1}) = \sum_i c_i z_m \bmod p^k$.

The construction is rather straightforward. Let $K_0, \ldots, K_{m-1}$ be the input wire keys, let $\mathsf{AK}^{\mathsf{L}}(x) = \mathbf{A}x + \mathbf{B} \bmod p^k$ be the output wire key. Let

The gadget is parameterized by coefficients $c_0, \ldots, c_{m-1} \in \mathbb{Z}_{p^k}$.

Garbling algorithm linBC.Garb takes boolean keys $\mathsf{K}_0, \ldots, \mathsf{K}_{m-1}$, and an arithmetic key $\mathsf{AK}^{\mathsf{L}} = (\mathbf{A}, \mathbf{B})$ as inputs. Let α_i denote the mask bit of K_i.

- Sample random $\mathbf{B}_i$ for $i \in [m]$, satisfying $\sum_i \mathbf{B}_i \bmod p^k = \mathbf{B}$.
- For each $i \in [m]$, for each $\beta \in \{0,1\}$, compute

$$\mathsf{C}_{i,\beta+\alpha_i \bmod 2} \leftarrow \mathsf{H}(\mathsf{K}_i(\beta), \; (\mathsf{id}, i)) \oplus (\mathbf{A}c_i\beta + \mathbf{B}_i \bmod p^k)$$

- Output table $\mathsf{Tab} = (\mathsf{C}_{i,\beta})_{i \in [m], \beta \in \{0,1\}}$.

Evaluation algorithm linBC.Eval takes input labels $(\mathsf{l}_i, \bar{x}_i)$ for $i \in [m]$ and a table Tab as inputs.

- For $i \in [m]$, compute $\mathbf{L}_i \leftarrow \mathsf{H}(\mathsf{l}_i, (\mathsf{id}, i)) \oplus \mathsf{C}_{i,\bar{x}_i}$.
- Output arithmetic label $\mathbf{L} = \sum_i \mathbf{L}_i \bmod p^k$.

Simulation algorithm linBC.Sim takes input labels $(\mathsf{l}_i, \bar{x}_i)$ for $i \in [m]$ and arithmetic label $\mathbf{L}$ as inputs.

- Sample random $\mathbf{L}_i$ for $i \in [m]$, satisfying $\sum_i \mathbf{L}_i \bmod p^k = \mathbf{L}$.
- The active ciphertexts in the table Tab are set as

$$\mathsf{C}_{i,\bar{x}_i} = \mathsf{H}(\mathsf{l}_i, (\mathsf{id}, i)) \oplus \mathbf{L}_i$$

The rest are inactive ciphertexts, and are simulated by random strings.

Fig. 5. The Linear Bit-Composition Gadget over Ring $\mathbb{Z}_{p^k}$

$\mathbf{B}_0, \ldots, \mathbf{B}_{m-1}$ be an additive sharing of $\mathbf{B}$ that are sampled by the garbler. Given $\mathsf{K}_i(z_i)$, the evaluator can compute $\mathbf{L}_i = \mathbf{A}c_i z_i + \mathbf{B}_i \bmod p^k$ because the table contains

$$\mathsf{Enc}(\mathsf{K}_i(\beta), \mathbf{A}c_i\beta + \mathbf{B}_i)$$

for all $i \in [m], \beta \in \{0,1\}$. The evaluator outputs

$$\mathbf{L} := \sum_i \mathbf{L}_i \bmod p^k = \sum_i (\mathbf{A}c_i z_i + \mathbf{B}_i) \bmod p^k \tag{3}$$
$$= \mathbf{A}f(z_0, \ldots, z_{m-1}) + \mathbf{B} \bmod p^k.$$

This is formalized in Fig. 5.

Lemma 4. *For any* $f(z_0, \ldots, z_{m-1}) = \sum_i c_i z_m \bmod p^k$, *there is a secure garbling gadget for general linear bit-composition function* f *(Fig. 5), called* linear bit-composition gadget, *in the random oracle model. The table size is* $O(\lambda m k)$, *assume the output label dimension is* $\lambda/\log p$.

Proof. For any input $z_0, \ldots, z_{m-1}$, the evaluator computes $\mathbf{L}_i \leftarrow \mathsf{H}(\mathsf{l}_i, (\mathsf{id}, i)) \oplus \mathsf{C}_{i,z_i \oplus \alpha_i}$, then $\mathbf{L}_i = \mathbf{A}c_i\beta + \mathbf{B}_i \bmod p^k$. The correctness of the output is guaranteed by (3).

To prove security, is suffices to notice that $\mathbf{B}_0, \ldots, \mathbf{B}_{m-1}$ is an additive sharing implies $\mathbf{L}_0, \ldots, \mathbf{L}_{m-1}$ is an additive sharing. In other words, we know $\mathbf{L}_0, \ldots, \mathbf{L}_{m-2}$ is i.i.d. uniform in the real world because they are one-time padded by i.i.d. uniform $\mathbf{B}_0, \ldots, \mathbf{B}_{m-2}$. And $\mathbf{L}_{m-1}$ is determined by $\mathbf{L}_0, \ldots, \mathbf{L}_{m-2}$ and $\mathbf{L}$ from $\mathbf{L} := \sum_i \mathbf{L}_i \bmod p^k$. □

BD. Given the $\mathbb{Z}_{p^k}$-arithmetic label of x, if we want to compute the boolean labels of the base-p' bit representation of x:

- First compute the boolean labels of the base-p bit representation of x, using bit-decomposition gadget.
- Compute the $\mathbb{Z}_{p'^{k'}}$-arithmetic label of x, using linear bit-composition gadget.
- Compute the boolean labels of the base-p' bit representation of x, using bit-decomposition gadget.

In particular, the cost of conversion from base-p bit representation to base-2 representation is $O(\lambda b^2)$ where $2^b \approx p^k$. This is much cheaper than using the boolean circuit for base conversion.

4.2   Extension: Emulating Computations for $\mathbb{Z}_N$

Our mixed GC for $\mathbb{Z}_{p^k}$ can emulate arithmetic mod-N operations if $p^k > N^2$ and there is an efficient garbling gadget for the modulo gate $\mathsf{mod}_N : \mathbb{Z}_{p^k} \to \mathbb{Z}_{p^k}$, which is defined as $\mathsf{mod}_N(x) = x \bmod N$. The emulation is rather straightforward:

- Every number in $\mathbb{Z}_N$ is emulated by the same number in $\mathbb{Z}_{p^k}$
- Every mod-N arithmetic operation (ADD or MULT) is emulated the by the same operation over $\mathbb{Z}_{p^k}$, followed by mod_N.

Remark: The cost of emulating addition gates can be dramatically optimized. Instead of appending mod_N after every addition gate, append mod_N only if the accumulated magnitude is close to $p^k/2$ or when the fan-out includes a multiplication gate.

Garbling the modulo gate mod_N is mostly equivalent to garbling the integer division gate $\mathsf{div}_N : \mathbb{Z}_{p^k} \to \mathbb{Z}_{p^k}$, which is defined as $\mathsf{div}_N(x) = \lfloor x/N \rfloor$, since $\mathsf{mod}_N(x) = x - N \cdot \mathsf{div}_N(x)$.

Unfortunately, the garbling gadget for div_N is hard to construct.[4] We will define a similar gate div_N^* whose garbling gadget is efficient and also suffices for emulating mod-N computations. The definition of $\mathsf{div}_N^*(x)$ is inspired by a well-known optimization that reduce division by constant to multiplication and shifting.

---

[4] An efficient garbling gadget of div_N can be constructed based on the garbling gadget of div_N^*.

Lemma 5 (Generalization of [16]). *For any positive integers* $N, p, k_\mathsf{I}, k_\mathsf{E}, m$ *satisfying* $p^{k_\mathsf{I}+k_\mathsf{E}} \leq mN < p^{k_\mathsf{I}+k_\mathsf{E}} + p^{k_\mathsf{E}}$,

$$\left\lfloor \frac{x}{N} \right\rfloor = \left\lfloor \frac{mx}{p^{k_\mathsf{I}+k_\mathsf{E}}} \right\rfloor \qquad \text{for all } 0 \leq x < p^{k_\mathsf{I}}.$$

Proof. $p^{k_\mathsf{I}+k_\mathsf{E}} \leq mN < p^{k_\mathsf{I}+k_\mathsf{E}} + p^{k_\mathsf{E}}$ implies, by multiplying $\frac{x}{p^{k_\mathsf{I}+k_\mathsf{E}}N}$,

$$\frac{x}{N} \leq \frac{mx}{p^{k_\mathsf{I}+k_\mathsf{E}}} < \frac{x}{N} + \frac{x}{Np^{k_\mathsf{I}}} < \frac{x+1}{N}.$$

$\square$

Now we are ready to define the gate $\mathsf{div}_N^* : \mathbb{Z}_{p^{2k+1}} \to \mathbb{Z}_{p^{2k+1}}$. Let $k_\mathsf{E} := \lceil \log_p(N) \rceil$ be the minimum integer satisfying $p^{k_\mathsf{E}} \geq N$. Let $m = \lceil \frac{p^{k_\mathsf{I}+k_\mathsf{E}}}{N} \rceil$, thus $p^{k_\mathsf{I}+k_\mathsf{E}} \leq mN < p^{k_\mathsf{I}+k_\mathsf{E}} + N \leq p^{k_\mathsf{I}+k_\mathsf{E}} + p^{k_\mathsf{E}}$. By Lemma 5,

$$\left\lfloor \frac{x}{N} \right\rfloor = \left\lfloor \frac{mx}{p^{k+k_\mathsf{E}}} \right\rfloor$$

for any $0 \leq x < p^k$. Therefore we define $\mathsf{div}_N^* : \mathbb{Z}_{p^{2k+1}} \to \mathbb{Z}_{p^{2k+1}}$ as

$$\mathsf{div}_N^*(x) = \left\lfloor \frac{mx \bmod p^{2k+1}}{p^{k+k_\mathsf{E}}} \right\rfloor.$$

It satisfies $\mathsf{div}_N^*(x) = \lfloor x/N \rfloor$ for all $x < p^k$. Since div_N^* is the composition of multiplication in $\mathbb{Z}_{p^{2k+1}}$ and digit shifting, it can be efficiently garbled by our mixed GC for $\mathbb{Z}_{p^{2k+1}}$.

Define gate $\mathsf{mod}_N^* : \mathbb{Z}_{p^{2k+1}} \to \mathbb{Z}_{p^{2k+1}}$ as $\mathsf{mod}_N^*(x) = x - N \cdot \mathsf{div}_N^*(x)$. Then mod_N^* can be efficiently garbled by our mixed GC for $\mathbb{Z}_{p^{2k+1}}$, and $\mathsf{mod}_N^*(x) = x \bmod N$ for all $x < p^k$.

Lemma 6. *For any* $N \leq 2^b$, *there is a statistically secure mixed GC for* $\mathbb{Z}_N$ *in the random oracle model, such that each addition/multiplication/bit-decomposition/bit-composition gate costs* $O(\lambda b^2 / \log b)$ *communication. The bit-decomposition is over a prime base* $p = \Theta(b/\log b)$.

Proof. Mod-N computations can be emulated in a $\mathbb{Z}_{p^{2k+1}}$-mixed circuits. Combing with Theorem 1, the cost per gate is $O(\lambda k(k+p) \log p)$. The cost is minimized by letting $p = \Theta(b/\log b)$. $\square$

Remarks. Although Lemma 6 does not claim free addition, we observe from its construction that addition is free up to a certain extent.

In this mixed GC for $\mathbb{Z}_N$, the bit decomposition gate outputs base-p bit representations. In case a (base-2) bit representation is needed, it can be computed from the base-p bit representation by a cost of $O(\lambda b^2)$, using the trick stated in Sect. 4.1.

5   Mixed GC Based on Chinese Remainder Theorem

Chinese remainder theorem (CRT) is used in [12] to solve the following natural task: Given b, find an efficient arithmetic GC over ring $\mathbb{Z}_N$ for some $N \approx 2^b$.

Since there is no more specific constraints on N, [12] sets $N = p_1 p_2 \ldots p_s$ being the product of the first s primes. Then $s = \Theta(b/\log b)$ and $p_s = \Theta(b)$. Consider an arithmetic circuit over $\mathbb{Z}_{p_i}$, denoted by "$C \bmod p_i$", that is identical to C except the ring is replaced by $\mathbb{Z}_{p_i}$. Then

$$C(x) \bmod p_i = (C \bmod p_i)(x \bmod p_i).$$

Therefore, by CRT, the task of evaluating $C(x)$ is reduced to evaluating mod-p_i arithmetic circuit $(C \bmod p_i)(x \bmod p_i)$ for all $1 \le i \le s$. In [12], the reduction is combined with mixed GC for every ring $\mathbb{Z}_{p_i}$, resulting in an arithmetic GC for $\mathbb{Z}_N$ where each multiplication gate costs about $O(\lambda b^2/\log b)$ bits.

In this section, we will strengthen the result in two dimensions.

Based on Mod-p^k Mixed GC. [12] sets $N = p_1 p_2 \ldots p_s$ because their basic GC only supports computation modulo a prime number. In Sect. 4, we have already construct relatively efficient mixed GC for prime power rings. Therefore, we will set

$$N = p_1^{k_1} p_2^{k_2} \ldots p_s^{k_s} \approx 2^b$$

and reduce the problem of garbling mod-N computation to garbling mod-$p_i^{k_i}$ computations for each $1 \le i \le s$.

Efficient BD. In the CRT framework, if the actual value of a $\mathbb{Z}_N$-wise is x, it is not hard to get the boolean labels of the bit representation of $x \bmod p_i^{k_i}$ (via Theorem 1), for each $1 \le i \le s$. To compute the bit representation of x, the naive idea is garble the CRT algorithm.

For more efficient bit-decomposition, we make the following observation. There are constants $c_1, \ldots, c_s \in \mathbb{Z}_N$ such that, for any $x \in \mathbb{Z}_N$

$$x = \sum_i c_i x^{(i)} \bmod N,$$

where $x^{(i)} := x \bmod p_i^{k_i}$ denotes the mod-$p_i^{k_i}$ component of x. $(x^{(1)}, \ldots, x^{(s)})$ is usually called the *CRT representation* of x. The fact that x is a linear function (modulo N) on its CRT representation suggests a more efficient bit-decomposition construction in the "CRT framework".

Our new bit-decomposition construction is essentially a mixed circuit over the ring $\mathbb{Z}_{p^{2k+1}}$, where p, k satisfy $p^k > N^2 > \sum_i c_i x^{(i)}$. The input of the mixed circuits consists of the bit representation of $x^{(i)}$ for all $1 \le i \le s$. All the input wires can be merged into $\sum_i c_i x^{(i)}$ through the generalized linear BC gate (Fig. 5). Then next step is mod_N^*, whose output $\sum_i c_i x^{(i)} \bmod N$ always equals x. The last gate is the standard bit-decomposition of $\mathcal{C}_{\mathsf{mix}}(\mathbb{Z}_{p^k})$, producing the base-$p$ bit representation of x.

The linear BC costs λmk bits, where $m = \sum_i k_i \log p_i = O(b)$. The modulo gate mod_N^* and bit-decomposition gate cost $O(\lambda b(k + p))$. The overall cost is $O(\lambda b(k+p))$, which can be minimized as $O(\lambda b^2 / \log b)$ by setting $p = \Theta(b/\log b)$.

If (base-2) bit representation of x is required, the overall cost of BD is $O(\lambda b^2)$.

By combining the "CRT framework" with Theorem 1 and Lemma 6 respectively, we have two more efficient mixed GC for $\mathbb{Z}_N$.

Theorem 2. *For any b, there exist $N > 2^b$ and a statistically secure mixed GC for $\mathbb{Z}_N$ in the random oracle model, such that each addition gate costs no communication, and each multiplication gate costs $O(\lambda b^{1.5})$ communication, and each bit-decomposition/bit-composition gate costs $O(\lambda b^2 / \log b)$ communication.*

Proof. Set $N = p_1^{k_1} p_2^{k_2} \ldots p_s^{k_s} \approx 2^b$. The task of garbling mod-N mixed circuits is reduced to garbling mod-$p_i^{k_i}$ mixed circuits for all $1 \le i \le s$. Each mod-$p_i^{k_i}$ mixed circuit will be garbled the mixed GC in Theorem 1.

Thus each mod-N addition gate will cost nothing.

Each mod-N multiplication gate costs

$$\sum_i O(\lambda k_i (k_i + p_i) \log p_i).$$

We want to minimize the cost, under the constraint that $p_1^{k_1} p_2^{k_2} \ldots p_s^{k_s} \approx 2^b$.

For any i, if k_i increases by 1, then $\log N$ will increase by $\log p_i$, the total cost will increase by $O(\lambda (k_i + p_i) \log p_i)$. The "marginal cost increase per bit of N by changing k_i" is

$$\frac{\partial \mathrm{cost}(k_1, \ldots, k_s)}{\partial k_i} \bigg/ \frac{\partial \log N(k_1, \ldots, k_s)}{\partial k_i} = O(\lambda (k_i + p_i)).$$

To minimize the cost, this ratio should be roughly the same for all i.

Following this intuitive argument, we choose a constant c and let $p_i + k_i = c$ for all i. The value of c is determined by the constraint $N = p_1^{k_1} p_2^{k_2} \ldots p_s^{k_s} \approx 2^b$.

$$b \le \log \prod_{i \le s} p_i^{k_i} = \sum_{i \le s} k_i \log p_i = \sum_{i \le s} (c - p_i) \log p_i \approx \sum_{p=2}^{c} (c - p) = \Theta(c^2).$$

Thus we set $c = \Theta(\sqrt{b})$.

The cost per multiplication gate is

$$\sum_i \lambda k_i (k_i + p_i) \log p_i = \sum_i \lambda (c - p_i) c \log p_i \approx \sum_{p=2}^{c} \lambda (c - p) c = O(\lambda c^3) = O(\lambda b^{1.5}).$$

The total cost of having one BD gate in the mod-$p_i^{k_i}$ part for all $1 \le i \le s$ is also $O(\lambda b^{1.5})$. But these parallel BD gates only compute (the bit representation of) the CRT representation. To compute the bit representation, an additional cost of $O(\lambda b^2)$ (or $O(\lambda b^2 / \log b)$, if the representation can use any base) is needed.

For BC, say the boolean representation of the number has at most $O(b)$ bits. Applying linear BC (Fig. 5) for all $1 \leq i \leq s$ will cost $O(\sum_i \lambda b k_i)$ bits.

$$\sum_i \lambda b k_i = \lambda b \sum_i (c - p_i) \leq \lambda b c s = O(\lambda b^2 / \log b)$$

$\square$

Theorem 3. *For any b, there exist $N > 2^b$ and a statistically secure mixed GC for $\mathbb{Z}_N$ in the random oracle model, such that each addition/multiplication gate costs $O(\lambda b \log b / \log \log b)$ communication, each bit-decomposition costs $O(\lambda b^2 / \log b)$ communication, each bit-composition gate costs $O(\lambda b^2 / \log \log b)$ communication.*

Proof. Set $N = p_1^{k_1} p_2^{k_2} \ldots p_s^{k_s} \approx 2^b$. The task of garbling mod-N mixed circuits is reduced to garbling mod-$p_i^{k_i}$ mixed circuits for all $1 \leq i \leq s$. Each mod-$p_i^{k_i}$ mixed circuit will be garbled with the mixed GC in Lemma 6.

Each mod-N addition/multiplication gate costs

$$\sum_i O(\lambda d_i^2 / \log d_i), \text{ where } 2^{d_i} > p_i^{k_i}.$$

We want to minimize the cost, under the constraint that $p_1^{k_1} p_2^{k_2} \ldots p_s^{k_s} \approx 2^b$.

We choose a constant d such that $d = d_1 = d_2 = \cdots = d_s$, and let $k_i = \lfloor d_i / \log p_i \rfloor$. So all primes are smaller than 2^d and $s = \Theta(2^d / d)$. The value of d is determined by the constraint $N = p_1^{k_1} p_2^{k_2} \ldots p_s^{k_s} \approx 2^b$.

$$b \leq \log \prod_{i \leq s} p_i^{k_i} = \sum_{i \leq s} k_i \log p_i \leq \frac{1}{2} \sum_{i \leq s} d = \Theta(sd) = \Theta(2^d).$$

Thus we set $d = \log b + O(1)$. Then $s = O(b / \log b)$.

The cost of each mod-N addition/multiplication gate is

$$\sum_i O\left(\frac{\lambda d_i^2}{\log d_i}\right) = O\left(\frac{s \lambda d^2}{\log d}\right) = O\left(\frac{b \lambda \log b}{\log \log b}\right).$$

The cost of BD, by the same analysis as in the proof of Theorem 2, is $O(\lambda b^2)$ if the outcome is base-2 bit representation, $O(\lambda b^2 / \log b)$ if the representation can use any base.

The cost of BC is trickier to trace. For each i, the mod-$p_i^{k_i}$ computations are emulated, according to the construction of Lemma 6, by a mod-p^k mixed circuit. Such that $k = O(d / \log d) = O(\log b / \log \log b)$. For each i, using linear BC to compute the arithmetic value costs $\lambda b k$. The total cost is $s \lambda b k = \lambda b^2 / \log \log b$. But linear BC computes a linear function modulo p^k, rather than the desired modulus $p_i^{k_i}$. This issue is resolve by slightly enlarge p^k to some poly$(p_i^{k_i}, b) = b^{\Theta(1)}$ so that linear BC computes the linear function over $\mathbb{Z}$. This modification over enlarge k by a constant factor, thus will not asymptotically increase the cost of any operations.

$\square$

6 Mixed GC Based on DCR

In this section, we show how to improve the efficiency of our mixed GC construction by relying on computational assumption. The new construction is most similar to the naive mixed construction (Lemma 3 in Sect. 3.3) over ring $\mathbb{Z}_{2^b}$.

The construction is built upon the (public-key) encryption schemes described in [17,18] based on the decisional composite residuosity (DCR) assumption [17, 19]. We consider two private-key variants described below. (We provide a brief overview of the DCR assumption and more details of the private-key variants in the full version.)

The first variant Paillier consists of four algorithms. (1) Paillier.Setup($1^\lambda, 1^\varsigma$) samples public parameters pp, which defines a key space $\mathbb{Z}$, a ciphertext space $\mathbb{Z}^*_{M^{\varsigma+1}}$, and a message space $\mathbb{Z}_{M^\varsigma}$. (2) Paillier.Gen(pp) outputs a secret key sk $\in [\lfloor M/4 \rfloor]$. (3) Paillier.Enc(sk, m) outputs a ciphertext $c \in \mathbb{Z}^*_{M^{\varsigma+1}}$. (4) Paillier.Dec(sk, c) recovers the message $m \in \mathbb{Z}_{M^\varsigma}$.

The second variant DamJur is similar to the first, except in two aspects. First, the key space is $\mathbb{Z}^*_M$ instead of $\mathbb{Z}$. Second, the setup algorithm DamJur.Setup outputs a trapdoor tp in addition to the public parameters pp. The trapdoor is only used by a special inversion algorithm DamJur.Inv(tp, c), which takes any ciphertext $c \in \mathbb{Z}^*_{M^{\varsigma+1}}$ and outputs a unique secret key sk $= g \in \mathbb{Z}^*_M$, and a message $m \in \mathbb{Z}_{M^\varsigma}$ such that DamJur.Dec(sk $= g, c$) $= m$.

Both constructions have some kind of homomorphism. For any message m_1, m_2 and keys sk$_1$, sk$_2, g_1, g_2$.

$$\text{Paillier.Enc(sk}_1, m_1) \cdot \text{Paillier.Enc(sk}_2, m_2) \bmod M^{\varsigma+1}$$
$$= \text{Paillier.Enc(sk}_1 + \text{sk}_2 \text{ over } \mathbb{Z}, \ m_1 + m_2 \bmod M^\varsigma)$$
$$\text{DamJur.Enc}(g_1, m_1) \cdot \text{DamJur.Enc}(g_2, m_2) \bmod M^{\varsigma+1}$$
$$= \text{DamJur.Enc}(g_1 \cdot g_2 \bmod M, \ m_1 + m_2 \bmod M^\varsigma)$$

6.1 Bit-Composition Based on Paillier Encryption

As observed in Sect. 4.1, the more general bit-composition function $(x_0, \ldots, x_{m-1}) \rightarrow \sum_i c_i x_i \bmod 2^b$ is not harder to garble. Thus we will directly construct this more general bit-composition.

Let $\mathsf{K}_0, \ldots, \mathsf{K}_{m-1}$ be the boolean keys. Let $\mathsf{AK}^\mathsf{L} = (\mathbf{A} \in \mathbb{Z}^\ell_{2^b}, \mathbf{B} \in \mathbb{Z}^\ell_{2^b})$ be the arithmetic key. In the analysis of the complexity, we will assume $m = O(b)$ and $\ell = O(\lambda)$. For any $x_0, \ldots, x_{m-1} \in \{0, 1\}$, given $\mathsf{K}_0(x_0), \ldots, \mathsf{K}_{m-1}(x_{m-1})$ and the table, the evaluator of the bit-composition gadget should output the arithmetic label $\mathbf{L} = \mathsf{AK}^\mathsf{L}(x) = x\mathbf{A} + \mathbf{B} \bmod 2^b$ where $x = \sum_i c_i x_i \bmod 2^b$.

The construction is based on the following intuition (informally): Allow the evaluator to decrypts $x + r$ and $(x + r)\mathsf{sk}^A + \mathsf{sk}^B$. Let the table contain

$$\mathsf{ct}^A = \mathsf{Enc}(\mathsf{sk}^A, \mathbf{A}), \quad \mathsf{ct}^B = \mathsf{Enc}(-r\mathsf{sk}^B, -r\mathbf{A} + \mathbf{B})$$

using some homomorphic encryption. Then the evaluator can compute

$$(\mathsf{ct}^A)^{x+r}\mathsf{ct}^B = \mathsf{Enc}((x + r)\mathsf{sk}^A + \mathsf{sk}^B, x\mathbf{A} + \mathbf{B})$$

The gadget is parameterized by coefficients $c_0, \ldots, c_{m-1} \in \mathbb{Z}_{2^b}$.

Garbling algorithm BC.Garb takes boolean keys $\mathsf{K}_0, \ldots, \mathsf{K}_{m-1}$, and an arithmetic key $\mathsf{AK}^L = (\mathbf{A}, \mathbf{B})$ as inputs. Let α_i denote the mask bit of K_i.

- (global step) Generate $M, \zeta, g, p'q'$ using vPai.Setup, while setting ζ such that $M^\zeta \geq 2^{\ell(2b+\lambda+1)}$. Add (M, ζ, g) to the beginning of the garbled circuit.
- Sample keys $\mathsf{sk}^A, \mathsf{sk}_0^B, \ldots, \mathsf{sk}_{m-1}^B \leftarrow [p'q']$. Let $\mathsf{sk}^B := \sum_i \mathsf{sk}_i^B$.
  Sample masks $r_0, \ldots, r_{m-1} \leftarrow [2^\lambda]$, $\mathbf{R} \leftarrow [2^{b+2\lambda}]^\ell$. Let $r = \sum_i c_i r_i$. Compute

$$\mathsf{ct}^A = \mathsf{vPai.Enc}(\mathsf{sk}^A, \mathbf{A}), \qquad \mathsf{ct}^B = \mathsf{vPai.Enc}(\mathsf{sk}^B, (2^{2b+\lambda} - r\mathbf{A}) + \mathbf{B} + 2^b \mathbf{R}).$$

- For each $i \in [m]$, for each $\beta \in \{0, 1\}$, compute

$$\mathsf{C}_{i, \beta + \alpha_i \bmod 2} \leftarrow \mathsf{H}(\mathsf{K}_i(\beta), (\mathsf{id}, i)) \oplus (x_i + r_i, c_i(x_i + r_i)\mathsf{sk}^A + \mathsf{sk}_i^B \bmod p'q')$$

- Output table $\mathsf{Tab} = ((\mathsf{C}_{i,\beta})_{i \in [m], \beta \in \{0,1\}}, \mathsf{ct}^A, \mathsf{ct}^B)$.

Evaluation algorithm BC.Eval takes input labels $(l_i, \bar{x}_i)$ for $i \in [m]$ and a table Tab as inputs.

- For $i \in [m]$, compute $(\hat{x}_i, \mathsf{sk}_i) \leftarrow \mathsf{H}(l_i, (\mathsf{id}, i)) \oplus \mathsf{C}_{i, \bar{x}_i}$.
- Compute $\mathsf{sk} = \sum_i \mathsf{sk}_i$, $\hat{x} = \sum_i c_i \hat{x}_i$.
- Output label $\mathbf{L} = \hat{\mathbf{L}} \bmod 2^b$, where $\hat{\mathbf{L}} = \mathsf{vPai.Dec}(\mathsf{sk}, (\mathsf{ct}^A)^{\hat{x}} \mathsf{ct}^B)$.

Simulation algorithm BC.Sim takes input labels $(l_i, \bar{x}_i)$ for $i \in [m]$ and arithmetic label $\mathbf{L}$ as inputs.

- (global step) Sample (M, ζ, g) using the vPai.Setup.
- Sample random $\hat{x}_0, \ldots, \hat{x}_{m-1} \leftarrow [2^\lambda]$. Let $\hat{x} = \sum_i c_i \hat{x}_i$.
  Sample random $\mathsf{sk}_0, \ldots, \mathsf{sk}_{m-1} \leftarrow [M/4]$. Let $\mathsf{sk} = \sum_i \mathsf{sk}_i$.
- Sample masks $\mathbf{R} \leftarrow [2^{b+\lambda}]^\ell$, let $\hat{\mathbf{L}} = \mathbf{L} + 2^b \mathbf{R}$.
  Simulate ct^A by randomly sample $\mathsf{ct}^A \leftarrow \mathsf{QR}_{M^\zeta + 1}$. Simulate ct^B as

$$\mathsf{ct}^B = \mathsf{vPai.Enc}(\mathsf{sk}, \hat{\mathbf{L}}) / (\mathsf{ct}^A)^{\hat{x}} \quad (\text{over } \mathbb{Z}_{M^\zeta + 1}^*).$$

- The active ciphertexts in the table Tab are set as

$$\mathsf{C}_{i, \bar{x}_i} = \mathsf{H}(l_i, (\mathsf{id}, i)) \oplus (\hat{x}_i, \mathsf{sk}_i)$$

The rest are inactive ciphertexts, and are simulated by random strings.

The modifications with respect to Fig. 5 are highlighted.

Fig. 6. The Bit-Composition Gadget based on Paillier

which can be decrypted into $x\mathbf{A} + \mathbf{B}$.

To formalize the intuition: i) We will add large random noise $\mathbf{R}$, and let the evaluator get $x\mathbf{A} + \mathbf{B} + 2^b \mathbf{R}$ instead. ii) We need to construct an encryption scheme that has the required homomorphism.

As the section name suggested, the encryption scheme is (almost) Paillier. Except that we want the scheme to encrypt a vector rather than a number. We consider the following natural encoding $\mathsf{encode} : \mathbb{Z}^\ell \to \mathbb{Z}$, parameterized by ℓ and B,

$$\mathsf{encode}(v_0, \ldots, v_{\ell-1}) = \sum_{i \in [\ell]} B^i v_i,$$

together with an efficient decoder $\mathsf{decode} : [B^\ell] \to [B]^\ell$, satisfying

- For any $\mathbf{A}, \mathbf{B} \in \mathbb{Z}^\ell$, $\mathsf{encode}(\mathbf{A} + \mathbf{B}) = \mathsf{encode}(\mathbf{A}) + \mathsf{encode}(\mathbf{B})$.
- For any $\mathbf{A} \in [B]^\ell$, $\mathsf{encode}(\mathbf{A}) \in [B^\ell]$ and $\mathsf{decode}(\mathsf{encode}(\mathbf{A})) = \mathbf{A}$.

Set the parameter of the encoder by $B = 2^{2b+2\lambda+1}$. Define the following encryption scheme vPai,

- vPai.Setup(1^λ) is Paillier.Setup($1^\lambda, 1^\varsigma$), by choosing smallest ς s.t. $M^\varsigma \geq B^\ell$.
- vPai.Gen is Paillier.Gen.
- vPai.Enc(sk, $\mathbf{V}$) = Paillier.Enc(sk, $\mathsf{encode}(\mathbf{V})$).
- vPai.Dec(sk, c) = decode(Paillier.Dec(sk, c)).

Using vPai, our intuition can be formalized as a bit-composition gadget.

Lemma 7. *For any linear bit-composition function $f(z_0, \ldots, z_{m-1}) = \sum_i c_i z_m \bmod 2^b$ satisfying $\sum_i c_i \leq 2^b$ (otherwise the construction should be slightly modified), there is a secure garbling gadget for f (Fig. 6), under DCR assumption in the random oracle model. The table size is $O(m\lambda_{\mathsf{DCR}} + \ell(b + \lambda))$, which is $O(\lambda_{\mathsf{DCR}} b + \lambda^2)$ when $\ell = O(\lambda)$ and $m = O(b)$.*

The proof of Lemma 7 is deferred to the full version.

6.2 Bit-Decomposition Based on Damgård-Jurik Encryption

In the bit-decomposition gadget, the evaluator is given an arithmetic label $\mathbf{L} = \mathsf{AK}(x) = x\mathbf{\Delta} + \mathbf{A} \bmod 2^b$, and its color number $\bar{x} = x + \alpha \bmod 2^b$ together with a table generated by the garbler from $\mathsf{AK}, \mathsf{K}_0, \ldots, \mathsf{K}_{b-1}$, and should output $\mathsf{K}_0(x_0), \ldots, \mathsf{K}_{b-1}(x_b)$.

Recall our intuition behind the naive BD (Fig. 1): In each inductive step, the evaluator gets $\mathbf{L}^{(i)} = x_{i:b}\mathbf{\Delta} + \mathbf{A}^{(i)}$ and computes

$$\mathbf{L}^{(i)} \bmod 2 = x_i \mathbf{\Delta} + \mathbf{A}^{(i)} \bmod 2.$$

Using $\mathbf{L}^{(i)} \bmod 2$ as the key, the evaluator decrypts a ciphertext

$$\mathsf{H}(x_i \mathbf{\Delta} + \mathbf{A}^{(i)} \bmod 2) \oplus (\mathsf{K}(x_i), x_i \mathbf{\Delta} + \mathbf{S})$$

in the table, gets $\mathsf{K}(x_i)$ and $x_i\mathbf{\Delta} + \mathbf{S}$. The latter allows the evaluator to compute $\mathbf{L}^{(i+1)}$ and proceed to the next step.

The bottleneck is the ciphertext size. Let us replace the ciphertext by

$$\mathsf{H}(x_i \mathbf{\Delta} + \mathbf{A}^{(i)} \bmod 2) \oplus (\mathsf{K}(x_i), x_i + r, (x_i + r)\mathsf{sk}^\Delta + \mathsf{sk}^S).$$

And let the table additionally contains two ciphertexts

$$\mathsf{ct}^\Delta = \mathsf{Enc}(\mathsf{sk}^\Delta, \boldsymbol{\Delta}), \quad \mathsf{ct}^S = \mathsf{Enc}(\mathsf{sk}^S, -r\boldsymbol{\Delta} + \mathbf{S} + 2^b\mathbf{R}),$$

using a homomorphic encryption scheme. Then the evaluator can instead compute $x_i\boldsymbol{\Delta} + \mathbf{S} + 2^b\mathbf{R}$ from

$$\mathsf{Dec}((x_i + r)\mathsf{sk}^\Delta + \mathsf{sk}^S, (\mathsf{ct}^\Delta)^{x_i+r}/\mathsf{ct}^S).$$

Such modification does not improves the complexity yet, because $\mathsf{ct}^\Delta, \mathsf{ct}^S$ become the new dominating part. Notice that, all tables may share a global ct^Δ as it only depends on the global key.

For the last bottleneck ct^S, we require its distribution to be *"dense"*, in the sense that, the distribution of ct^S is statistically close to the uniform distribution over a samplable domain. This requires i) a "dense" encryption scheme, and ii) the distribution of the message $-r\boldsymbol{\Delta} + \mathbf{S} + 2^b\mathbf{R}$ is statistically close to uniform over the message space.

If our requirement is satisfied, the garbler can instead sample a random seed, and let $\mathsf{ct}^S = \mathsf{H}(\mathsf{seed})$. The ciphertext ct^S in the table can be replaced by seed. For correctness, the garbler need to reversely compute the key and message behind the ciphertext ct^S.

As discussed in [18], all of our requirements are satisfied by Damgård-Jurik encryption [17].

- *Density:* For random $g \leftarrow \mathbb{Z}_M^*$ and random $m \leftarrow [M^\varsigma]$, the distribution of ciphertext $\mathsf{DamJur.Enc}(g, m)$ is uniform in $\mathbb{Z}_{M^{\varsigma+1}}^*$.
- *Invertibility:* There is an efficient algorithm Inv, which takes a ciphertext $\mathsf{ct} \in \mathbb{Z}_{M^{\varsigma+1}}^*$ and the trapdoor tp, computes g, m such that $\mathsf{DamJur.Enc}(g, m) = \mathsf{ct}$.

Damgård-Jurik encrypts a number rather a vector. Similar to Sect. 6.1, we need a encoder-decoder pair between vectors and numbers. The encoder has to be dense in the sense that almost all encodings in the codomain are valid. Again, consider the natural encoding $\mathsf{encode} : \mathbb{Z}^{\lambda+1} \to \mathbb{Z}$, parameterized by B,

$$\mathsf{encode}(v_0, \ldots, v_\lambda) = \sum_{i \in [\lambda+1]} B^i v_i,$$

together with an efficient decoder $\mathsf{decode} : [B^\lambda] \to [B]^\lambda$.

- For security, set $B \geq 2^{b+2\lambda}$.
- For density, ensure $M^\varsigma \geq B^{\lambda+1} \geq M^\varsigma(1 - 2^{-\lambda})$.

Define the following encryption scheme vDJ,

- $\mathsf{vDJ.Setup}(1^\lambda)$ is $\mathsf{DamJur.Setup}(1^\lambda, 1^\varsigma)$, by choosing smallest ς s.t. $M^\varsigma \geq (2^{2b+\lambda+1})^{\lambda+1}$. Also let B be the largest multiple of 2^b satisfying $M^\varsigma \geq B^{\lambda+1}$. Then all the three requirements on B can be satisfied.
- $\mathsf{vDJ.Gen}$ is $\mathsf{DamJur.Gen}$.
- $\mathsf{vDJ.Enc}(\mathsf{sk}, \mathbf{V}) = \mathsf{DamJur.Enc}(\mathsf{sk}, \mathsf{encode}(\mathbf{V}))$.

Garbling algorithm BD.Garb takes an arithmetic key $\mathsf{AK} = (\mathbf{A}, \alpha)$ and b boolean keys $\mathsf{K}_0, \ldots, \mathsf{K}_{b-1}$ as inputs.

- (global step) Generate $M, \zeta, p'q'$ using vDJ.Setup, while setting ζ, B properly. Sample key $g^\Delta \leftarrow \mathbb{Z}_M^*$ and compute $\mathsf{ct}^\Delta = \mathsf{vDJ.Enc}(g^\Delta, (\mathbf{\Delta}, 1))$. Add $M, \zeta, \mathsf{ct}^\Delta$ to the beginning of the garbled circuit.
- Let $\mathbf{A}^{(0)} = \mathbf{A}$, $\alpha^{(0)} = \alpha$.
- For each $0 \le i < b$, sample $r_i \leftarrow [2^\lambda]$, $\mathsf{seed}^{(i)} \leftarrow \{0,1\}^\lambda$. Compute $\mathsf{ct}^{(i)} = \mathsf{H}(\mathsf{seed}^{(i)}, (\mathsf{id}, i)) \in \mathbb{Z}_{M^{\zeta+1}}$. Find $g^{(i)}, \mathbf{S}^{(i)}, s^{(i)}$ satisfying

$$\left(g^{(i)}, (2^{b+\lambda} - r_i(\mathbf{\Delta}, 1))\right) + (\mathbf{S}^{(i)}, s^{(i)}) = \mathsf{vDJ.Inv}(\mathsf{tp}, \mathsf{ct}^{(i)}).$$

Resample $\mathsf{seed}^{(i)}$ if $(\mathbf{S}^{(i)}, s^{(i)}) \notin [B - 2^{b+\lambda}]^{\lambda+1}$ to prevent overflow. Set

$$\mathbf{A}^{(i+1)} = \lfloor \frac{\mathbf{A}^{(i)} - \mathbf{S}^{(i)}}{2} \rfloor \bmod 2^{b-i-1} \qquad \alpha^{(i+1)} = \lfloor \frac{\alpha^{(i)} - s^{(i)}}{2} \rfloor \bmod 2^{b-i-1}.$$

- For each $0 \le i < b$, for each $\beta \in \{0,1\}$, compute

$$\mathsf{C}_{i,\beta+\alpha^{(i)} \bmod 2} \leftarrow \mathsf{H}(\mathbf{\Delta}\beta + \mathbf{A}^{(i)} \bmod 2, (\mathsf{id}, i)) \oplus (\mathsf{K}_i(\beta), \beta + r_i, (g^\Delta)^{\beta+r_i} g^{(i)})$$

- Output table $\mathsf{Tab} = ((\mathsf{C}_{i,\beta})_{i \in [b], \beta \in \{0,1\}}, (\mathsf{seed}^{(i)})_{i \in [b-1]})$

Evaluation algorithm BD.Eval takes input label $(\mathbf{L}, \bar{x})$ and a table Tab as inputs.

- Let $\mathbf{L}^{(0)} := \mathbf{L}$, $\bar{x}^{(0)} = \bar{x}$.
- For $i = 0, 1, 2, \ldots, b-1$:
  Compute $(\mathsf{l}_i, \hat{x}_i, h^{(i)}) \leftarrow \mathsf{H}(\mathbf{L}^{(i)} \bmod 2, (\mathsf{id}, i)) \oplus \mathsf{C}_{i, \bar{x}^{(i)} \bmod 2}$. If $i < b-1$, compute $\mathsf{ct}^{(i)} = \mathsf{H}(\mathsf{seed}^{(i)}, \mathsf{id}, i)$, $(\mathbf{D}^{(i)}, d^{(i)}) \leftarrow \mathsf{vDJ.Dec}(h^{(i)}, (\mathsf{ct}^\Delta)^{\hat{x}_i} \mathsf{ct}^{(i)})$

$$(\mathbf{L}^{(i+1)}, \bar{x}^{(i+1)}) = \lfloor ((\mathbf{L}^{(i)}, \bar{x}^{(i)}) - (\mathbf{D}^{(i)}, d^{(i)}) \bmod 2^{b-i})/2 \rfloor,$$

- Output boolean labels $\mathsf{l}_0, \mathsf{l}_1, \ldots, \mathsf{l}_{b-1}$.

Simulation algorithm BD.Sim takes arithmetic label $(\mathbf{L}, \bar{x})$ and boolean labels $\mathsf{l}_0, \mathsf{l}_1, \ldots, \mathsf{l}_{b-1}$ as inputs.

- (global step) Generate $M, \zeta, p'q'$ using vDJ.Setup, while setting ζ, B properly. Simulate ct^Δ as a random ciphertext.
- Let $(\mathbf{L}^{(0)}, \bar{x}^{(0)}) = (\mathbf{L}, \bar{x})$.
- Sample random $\hat{x}_i \leftarrow [2^\lambda]$, $\mathsf{seed}^{(i)} \leftarrow \{0,1\}^\lambda$, $\mathbf{D}^{(i)} \leftarrow [B]^\lambda$, $d^{(i)} \leftarrow [B]$ for each $i \in [b-1]$. Program H so that

$$\mathsf{vDJ.Enc}(h^{(i)}, (\mathbf{D}^{(i)}, d^{(i)})) = (\mathsf{ct}^\Delta)^{\hat{x}_i} \mathsf{H}(\mathsf{seed}^{(i)}, \mathsf{id}, i) \quad (\text{in } \mathbb{Z}_{M^{\zeta+1}})$$

- The active ciphertexts in the table Tab are set as

$$\mathsf{C}_{i, \bar{x}^{(i)} \bmod 2} = \mathsf{H}(\mathbf{L}^{(i)} \bmod 2, (\mathsf{id}, i)) \oplus (\mathsf{l}_i, \hat{x}_i, h^{(i)})$$

The rest are inactive ciphertexts, and are simulated by random strings.

The modifications with respect to Fig. 1 are highlighted.

Fig. 7. The Bit-Decomposition Gadget based on Damgård-Jurik

- vDJ.Dec(sk, c) = decode(vDJ.Dec(sk, c)).
- vDJ.Inv(tp, c) = (g, decode(v)) for (g, v) = DamJur.Inv(tp, c).

Now we are ready to present the bit-decomposition gadget in Fig. 7.

Lemma 8. *There is a secure bit-decomposition gadget (Fig. 7) over ring $\mathbb{Z}_{2^b}$, under DCR assumption in the programmable random oracle model. The table size is $O(b\lambda_{\mathsf{DCR}})$.*

The proof of Lemma 8 is deferred to the full version.

Combining the bit-composition gadget in Lemma 7 and the bit-decomposition gadget in Lemma 8 produces a mix GC scheme, as stated by the following theorem.

Theorem 4. *There is a secure mixed GC for $\mathbb{Z}_{2^b}$ under DCR assumption in the programmable random oracle model, such that each addition gate costs no communication, each multiplication/bit-decomposition gate costs $O(\lambda_{\mathsf{DCR}}b)$ communication, and each bit-composition gate costs $O(\lambda_{\mathsf{DCR}}b + \lambda^2)$ communication.*

Our mixed GC for $\mathbb{Z}_{2^b}$ implies a mixed GC for any $\mathbb{Z}_N$ for any $N \approx 2^b$, using the emulation technique discussed in Sect. 4.2.

Corollary 1. *For any $N \le 2^b$, there is a secure mixed GC for $\mathbb{Z}_N$ under DCR assumption in the programmable random oracle model, such that each addition/multiplication/bit-decomposition gate costs $O(\lambda_{\mathsf{DCR}}b)$ communication, and each bit-composition gate costs $O(\lambda_{\mathsf{DCR}}b + \lambda^2)$ communication.*

References

1. Yao, A.C.-C.: Protocols for secure computations (extended abstract). In: 23rd FOCS, pp. 160–164. IEEE Computer Society Press, November 1982
2. Beaver, D., Micali, S., Rogaway, P.: The round complexity of secure protocols (extended abstract). In: 22nd ACM STOC, pp. 503–513. ACM Press, May 1990
3. Naor, M., Pinkas, B., Sumner, R.: Privacy preserving auctions and mechanism design. In: Feldman, S.I., Wellman, M.P. (eds.) Proceedings of the First ACM Conference on Electronic Commerce (EC-1999), Denver, CO, USA, 3–5 November 1999, pp. 129–139. ACM (1999)
4. Kolesnikov, V., Schneider, T.: Improved garbled circuit: free XOR gates and applications. In: Aceto, L., Damgård, I., Goldberg, L.A., Halldórsson, M.M., Ingólfsdóttir, A., Walukiewicz, I. (eds.) ICALP 2008. LNCS, vol. 5126, pp. 486–498. Springer, Heidelberg (2008). https://doi.org/10.1007/978-3-540-70583-3_40
5. Pinkas, B., Schneider, T., Smart, N.P., Williams, S.C.: Secure two-party computation is practical. In: Matsui, M. (ed.) ASIACRYPT 2009. LNCS, vol. 5912, pp. 250–267. Springer, Heidelberg (2009). https://doi.org/10.1007/978-3-642-10366-7_15
6. Kolesnikov, V., Mohassel, P., Rosulek, M.: FleXOR: flexible garbling for XOR gates that beats free-XOR. In: Garay, J.A., Gennaro, R. (eds.) CRYPTO 2014. LNCS, vol. 8617, pp. 440–457. Springer, Heidelberg (2014). https://doi.org/10.1007/978-3-662-44381-1_25

7. Gueron, S., Lindell, Y., Nof, A., Pinkas, B.: Fast garbling of circuits under standard assumptions. J. Cryptol. **31**(3), 798–844 (2018)
8. Zahur, S., Rosulek, M., Evans, D.: Two halves make a whole - reducing data transfer in garbled circuits using half gates. In: Oswald, E., Fischlin, M. (eds.) EUROCRYPT 2015. LNCS, vol. 9057, pp. 220–250. Springer, Heidelberg (2015). https://doi.org/10.1007/978-3-662-46803-6_8
9. Rosulek, M., Roy, L.: Three halves make a whole? Beating the half-gates lower bound for garbled circuits. In: Malkin, T., Peikert, C. (eds.) CRYPTO 2021. LNCS, vol. 12825, pp. 94–124. Springer, Cham (2021). https://doi.org/10.1007/978-3-030-84242-0_5
10. Applebaum, B., Ishai, Y., Kushilevitz, E.: How to garble arithmetic circuits. In: Ostrovsky, R. (ed.) 52nd FOCS, pp. 120–129. IEEE Computer Society Press, October 2011
11. Ball, M., Li, H., Lin, H., Liu, T.: New ways to garble arithmetic circuits. In: Hazay, C., Stam, M. (eds.) EUROCRYPT 2023. LNCS, vol. 14005, pp. 3–34. Springer, Cham (2023). https://doi.org/10.1007/978-3-031-30617-4_1
12. Ball, M., Malkin, T., Rosulek, M.: Garbling gadgets for Boolean and arithmetic circuits. In: Weippl, E.R., Katzenbeisser, S., Kruegel, C., Myers, A.C., Halevi, S. (eds.) ACM CCS 2016, pp. 565–577. ACM Press, October 2016
13. Applebaum, B.: Garbling XOR gates "for free" in the standard model. J. Cryptol. **29**(3), 552–576 (2016)
14. Ishai, Y., Kushilevitz, E.: Randomizing polynomials: a new representation with applications to round-efficient secure computation. In: 41st FOCS, pp. 294–304. IEEE Computer Society Press, November 2000
15. Applebaum, B., Ishai, Y., Kushilevitz, E.: Cryptography in NC^0. In: 45th FOCS, pp. 166–175. IEEE Computer Society Press, October 2004
16. Granlund, T., Montgomery, P.L.: Division by invariant integers using multiplication. In: Sarkar, V., Ryder, B.G., Soffa, M.L. (eds.) Proceedings of the ACM SIGPLAN 1994 Conference on Programming Language Design and Implementation (PLDI), Orlando, Florida, USA, 20–24 June 1994, pp. 61–72. ACM (1994)
17. Damgård, I., Jurik, M.: A generalisation, a simplification and some applications of Paillier's probabilistic public-key system. In: Kim, K. (ed.) PKC 2001. LNCS, vol. 1992, pp. 119–136. Springer, Heidelberg (2001). https://doi.org/10.1007/3-540-44586-2_9
18. Brakerski, Z., Döttling, N., Garg, S., Malavolta, G.: Candidate iO from homomorphic encryption schemes. In: Canteaut, A., Ishai, Y. (eds.) EUROCRYPT 2020. LNCS, vol. 12105, pp. 79–109. Springer, Cham (2020). https://doi.org/10.1007/978-3-030-45721-1_4
19. Paillier, P.: Public-key cryptosystems based on composite degree residuosity classes. In: Stern, J. (ed.) EUROCRYPT 1999. LNCS, vol. 1592, pp. 223–238. Springer, Heidelberg (1999). https://doi.org/10.1007/3-540-48910-X_16

Classic Public Key Cryptography (I/II)

M&M'S: Mix and Match Attacks on Schnorr-Type Blind Signatures with Repetition

Khue Do$^{1,2(\boxtimes)}$, Lucjan Hanzlik[1] , and Eugenio Paracucchi^{1,2}

[1] CISPA Helmholtz Center for Information Security, Saarbrücken, Germany
{khue.do,lucjan.hanzlik,eugenio.paracucchi}@cispa.de
[2] Saarland University, Saarbrücken, Germany

Abstract. Blind signatures allow the issuing of signatures on messages chosen by the user so that they ensure *blindness* of the message against the signer. Moreover, a malicious user cannot output $\ell + 1$ signatures while only finishing ℓ signing sessions. This notion, called *one-more* unforgeability, comes in two flavors supporting either *sequential* or *concurrent* sessions. In this paper, we investigate the security of a class of blind signatures constructed from Sigma-protocols with small challenge space $\mathcal{C}_\Sigma$ (i.e., polynomial in the security parameter), using k repetitions of the protocol to decrease the chances of a cheating prover. This class of schemes includes, among others, the Schnorr blind signature scheme with bit challenges and the recently proposed isogeny-based scheme CSI-Otter (Crypto'23).

For this class of blind signatures, we show a *polynomial-time* attack that breaks one-more unforgeability for any $\ell \geq k$ concurrent sessions in time $O(k \cdot |\mathcal{C}_\Sigma|)$. Contrary to the ROS attack, ours is generic and does not require any particular algebraic structure. We also propose a computational trade-off, where, for any $t \leq k$, our attack works for $\ell = \frac{k}{t}$ in time $O(\frac{k}{t} \cdot |\mathcal{C}_\Sigma|^t)$. The consequences of our attack are as follows. Schemes in the investigated class of blind signatures should not be used concurrently without applying specific transformations to boost the security to support more signing sessions. Moreover, for the parameters proposed for CSI-Otter ($k = 128$ and $|\mathcal{C}_\Sigma| = 2$), the scheme becomes forgeable after 128 concurrent signing sessions for the basic attack and with only eight sessions in our optimized attack. We also show that for those parameters, it is even possible to compute two signatures in around 10 min with just one signing session using the computation power of the Bitcoin network. Thus, we show that, for sequential security, the parameter k must be at least doubled in the security parameter for any of the investigated schemes.

Keywords: Blind Signatures · Sigma Protocols · Group Actions · Cryptanalysis

© International Association for Cryptologic Research 2024
M. Joye and G. Leander (Eds.): EUROCRYPT 2024, LNCS 14656, pp. 363–387, 2024.
https://doi.org/10.1007/978-3-031-58751-1_13

1 Introduction

Blind signatures allow a signer to sign messages picked by third parties without actually seeing them. This property, called *blindness*, enables many privacy-preserving applications of blind signatures. The authenticity of the signer's signatures is based on a *one-more unforgeability* property, which informally states that one cannot create $\ell + 1$ valid signatures under different messages while only finishing the signing process ℓ times with the signer. If one-more unforgeability holds even if those ℓ signing queries are executed in parallel, we are talking about a *concurrently* secure blind signature scheme. Alternatively, we are talking about *sequential* unforgeable blind signatures, if the signer processes queries sequentially. Secure blind signatures can be constructed from different assumptions such as RSA [3,10], discrete logarithm [1,17,21,29], pairings [7], lattices [20,26], and isogenies [22]. The resulting schemes provide various properties, including optimal round-complexity (i.e., two-move) and security under stronger security notions.

One of the most prominent ways to construct blind signatures is to leverage the existing construction of standard digital signatures from the Sigma protocol (Σ-protocol) and the Fiat-Shamir transformation. Σ-protocols are three-move interactive protocols, where the prover creates a commitment and later answers a challenge from the verifier. If the challenge space is small (e.g., bit challenges), the prover and verifier repeat the protocol k-times in parallel to decrease the chances of a cheating prover. For Σ-protocols, one can use the Fiat-Shamir transformation to turn this protocol into a signature scheme, i.e., compute the verifier's challenge using a random oracle query on the prover's commitment and a message picked by the prover/signer. The transformation can also be applied to Σ-protocols with a small challenge space where all k commitments are queried at once to the random oracle, and the prover's responses are provided *separately* for each of the k protocol instances.

While this transformation works for standard signatures, it fails for blind signatures since the signer can break blindness by inspecting the commitment and the challenge value of the final signature. The signer can do it even if the user is the one querying the random oracle. A folklore approach to get around this problem is introducing a way to randomize the signer's commitment and output of the random oracle that the user can reverse to receive the final signature. Prominent examples using this approach are the Schnorr blind signature scheme, the Abe-Okamoto scheme in the discrete logarithm setting, and the recently proposed CSI-Otter scheme [22] based on isogenies.

Unfortunately, the Schnorr blind signature scheme and many others following the above recipe are vulnerable to the so-called ROS attack [4]. These schemes cannot be concurrently unforgeable for ℓ bigger than polylogarithmic in the security parameter. In practice, the scheme becomes unusable after approximately 8–10 concurrent signing queries, and the only way out is to either use transformations boosting the security to more signatures [9,24] or use the scheme sequentially, which limits the number of real-world applications significantly. The attack requires that there exists an algebraic structure in the space of commitments that the attacker can leverage. Such a structure does not exist, e.g., for the CSI-Otter scheme, making it potentially secure against the ROS attack and allowing for polynomially many signing queries, an open problem left by the authors [22].

1.1   Our Contribution

This paper investigates the security of three-move blind signatures built generically from (parallel repetitions of) Σ-protocols with a small challenge space $\mathcal{C}_\Sigma$ (non-negligible soundness error $1/|\mathcal{C}_\Sigma|$). For such blind signature schemes, we show a new polynomial-time attack breaking the unforgeability for $\ell = k$, where k is the number of repetitions of the base protocol. Contrary to the ROS attack, we do not require any particular algebraic structure and rely solely on the honest verifier zero-knowledge property of the Σ-protocol and queries to the random oracle (i.e., computing hash digests).

The Attack. Katsumata et al. introduced in [22] a novel blind signature scheme based on isogenies called CSI-Otter. Their construction can be interpreted as a *blinded variant* of CSI-FiSh [6], itself based on a Σ-protocol with small challenge space (bit challenge). However, the demonstrated scheme offers only provable security for a poly-logarithmic number of concurrent executions. The authors then conjectured its security for polynomially many executions based on its apparent immunity to the ROS attack, stemming from the non-algebraic structure of the protocol. We contend that this argument lacks rigor, as the ROS attack does not encompass all potential threats to the concurrent security of blind signatures in general. Thus, motivated by this observation, we elaborate a concrete attack targeting the concurrent security of this specific class of blind signatures, while being divergent from the ROS attack methodology. We use the fact that, from the user's point of view, the signer is running k instances of the Σ-protocol with challenges from $\mathcal{C}_\Sigma$. In the case of a honest user, there is no problem since we assume that the user will "glue" all k instances in the same random oracle query. However, a malicious user does not need to do it. Assume that $\mathbf{R} = (R_1, \ldots, R_k)$ is the commitment sent in the first step by the signer and $\mathbf{R}' = (R'_1, \ldots, R'_k)$ is the blinded commitment. A honest user can compute the challenge by computing $\mathbf{c}' = (c'_1, \ldots, c'_k) = \mathcal{H}(\mathbf{R}' \| m)$ and then challenges the signer with a blinded version of it. Given the signer's response, the honest user owns a signature under m.

A malicious user can generate a valid signature differently. Thanks to the honest verifier zero-knowledge property of the Σ-protocol, the adversary can simulate one of the k instances of the protocol. As a result of the simulation, it will receive a valid transcript (e^*, d^*, z^*), where $d^* \in \mathcal{C}_\Sigma$. The adversary can now compute the challenge $\mathbf{c}' = (c'_1, \ldots, c'_k) = \mathcal{H}((R'_1, \ldots, R'_{k-1}, e^*) \| m^*)$ for a random message m^* and repeat the process for a different message until $c'_k = d^*$. On average, a malicious user will only have to repeat this computation $|\mathcal{C}_\Sigma|$ times, e.g. two times for bit challenges.

The key observation, now, is that the adversary only needs the $k - 1$ first elements of the signer's response to receive a valid signature. It works since the adversary simulated the last instance and knows a proper answer z^* for the challenge $\mathbf{c}'$ it picked. This means that for the protocol instance with commitment R_k, the adversary can arbitrarily choose a challenge and still be able to receive a valid signature. In itself, this is not interesting. However, suppose the adversary executes the same attack over k concurrent sessions. In that case, the malicious user ends up with k instances of the Σ-protocol for which it can arbitrarily pick the challenge while simultaneously still being able to compute k valid signatures. Thus, the adversary can use those instances to create a one-more signature.

To be more explicit, we provide an unblind version of the attack. Suppose $\mathbf{R}_1, \ldots, \mathbf{R}_k$ are the commitment the signer creates for the k concurrent sessions the adversary executes, where $\mathbf{R}_i = (R_{i,1}, \ldots, R_{i,k})$. The adversary uses the above technique to simulate k instances of the Σ-protocol receiving (e_i, d_i, z_i). It then finds messages $m_1, \ldots, m_k$ such that for every $i \in \{1, \ldots, k\}$ we have

$$\mathcal{H}((R_{i,1}, \ldots, R_{i,k-1}, e_i) \| m_i) = (c_{i,1}, \ldots, c_{i,k-1}, d_i).$$

The adversary now picks a random message m^* and computes the challenge $\mathbf{c}^* = \mathcal{H}((R_{1,k}, \ldots, R_{k,k}) \| m^*) \in \mathcal{C}_\Sigma^k$, where $\mathbf{c}^* = (c_1^*, \ldots, c_k^*)$. Now, for the ith session, it challenges the signer with $(c_{i,1}, \ldots, c_{i,k-1}, c_i^*)$ and receives k separate responses for each of the elements of the challenge. It is easy to see now that by replacing the last entries of the response with the z_i values, the adversary will receive valid signatures for messages $m_1, \ldots, m_k$. By combining those last entries, the adversary can construct a valid signature for challenge $\mathbf{c}^*$, which means a valid forgery for message m^*.

In expectation, the adversary will have to compute the hash function $k \cdot |\mathcal{C}_\Sigma|$ times and execute k concurrent sessions for the attack to be successful. It can also be performed with fewer sessions at the expense of computation, i.e. $\frac{k}{t}$ concurrent sessions with adversary's running time $O(\frac{k}{t} \cdot |\mathcal{C}_\Sigma|^t)$. In case we want to run the attack in the sequential settings, the running time will be $O(2 \cdot |\mathcal{C}_\Sigma|^{k/2})$, i.e., exponential in k but breaking unforgeability by creating two signatures while only querying one signature. In the above attack, the adversary requires the signer to create k (respectively $\frac{k}{t}$) signatures, where all must be made using concurrent sessions. We fix this shortcoming by extending the attack so that the adversary only needs two open sessions at a given time. However, the attack still requires the signer to create k (respectively $\frac{k}{t}$) signatures.

Implications. Our results show that for practical and concurrent applications, one should not use blind signatures constructed from Σ-protocols with a small challenge space. We summarize those protocols in Table 1. Since the attack is generic and requires no unique algebraic structure, it works in various settings: Schnorr blind signature with bit challenges in the discrete logarithm setting, the Fiat-Shamir blind signatures (as in [19]) in the RSA setting, CSI-Otter [22] in the isogenies setting. For example, CSI-Otter [22] only guarantees security for polylogarithmic signatures. We demonstrate a specific attack that compromises security after only 128 signatures. This implies that the signer would need to replace its secret keys after fewer than 128 signed signatures, rendering the scheme impractical. Interestingly, the attack also works in the weaker synchronized parallel attack model from [28], where we assume that the steps of the protocol for each session are executed in order of opened sessions, i.e., in our case, this means that the challenge for the first session must be sent before the challenge for the second session, etc.

While increasing the challenge space and consequently the number of instances k makes our attack more time-consuming, an efficient way to forge a signature will always exist if the signer uses the signing keys more than k times. In practice, to use such blind signatures concurrently, one must use boosting transformations similar to the case of Schnorr blind signatures and the ROS attack. Unfortunately, this leads to a significant increase in the communication complexity and signature size.

One of the main downsides of our results is that the attack targets all known Σ-protocols for the graph isomorphism problem. This significantly influences the area of post-quantum blind signatures, where we are still trying to find more efficient alternatives for schemes based on standard lattice-based problems. Potential blind signatures from the lattice isomorphism problem [14] and the CSI-Otter scheme are vulnerable to our attack, leaving us only with relatively inefficient blind signatures from standard lattice assumptions that suffer from big signature sizes.

Table 1. Σ-protocols with small challenge space.

Σ-protocol	Hardness Assumption	Challenge space
[19]	Factoring assumption	$\{0,1\}$
[6,12]	Isogeny-based assumption	$\{0,1\}$
[14]	Lattice Isomorphism assumption	$\{0,1\}$
[25]	Lattice assumption	$\{0,1,2\}$

Case Study. We introduce our attack, targetting any blind signature scheme built from a Σ-protocol with small challenge space. To make the attack more explicit, we show how to apply it against the CSI-Otter isogeny-based blind signature scheme recently introduced at Crypto'23. With this, we solve an open problem left by the authors [22]. In particular, we show that CSI-Otter is not concurrently secure in the polynomial regime, i.e., it does not support polynomially many concurrent sessions as conjectured by the authors.

We show that for the parameters proposed by the authors (i.e., $n = 128$), CSI-Otter becomes forgeable after issuing only 128 signatures. Sacrificing a bit of computation, we can make the scheme insecure even with only eight concurrent sessions. In such a case, the adversary must perform around half a megahash, which can be done in less than a second on commodity hardware (e.g., the rate of the M1 Pro processor is 5Mh/s). Moreover, we argue that CSI-Otter is not even sequentially secure for the proposed parameters. In such a case, our attack requires around $2 \cdot 2^{64}$ hash computations, which is in the realms of the bitcoin difficulty, i.e., can be computed by the bitcoin network in around 10 min. Thus, the challenge space needs to be increased for CSI-Otter to be practically secure in the sequential setting. In particular, for n-bit security, we need at least $k = 2 \cdot n$. Interestingly, one can use the argument in [19] as long as the number of repetitions is at least doubled with the security parameter. Hence, we show that their choice of parameters is tight with our concrete attack.

Summary of Contribution. This paper analyzes the security of a specific class of blind signature schemes, i.e., schemes constructed by applying a particular transformation to a Σ-protocol with a challenge space that is polynomial in the size of the security parameter. This class captures many existing schemes, including blind Schnorr signatures with bit challenges, the Fiat-Shamir factoring-based scheme (as in [19]), and the recently proposed CSI-Otter isogeny-based scheme [22].

- We show that this class of blind signatures is vulnerable to a *polynomial-time* attack that breaks the one-more unforgeability for any $\ell > k$ of concurrent sessions, where the challenge space is $\mathcal{C}_\Sigma^k$, e.g., $|\mathcal{C}_\Sigma| = 2$ and $k = 128$ for CSI-Otter [22]. The attack is generic and does not require any particular algebraic structure. It can be improved so that, at a given time, the adversary only needs to keep two sessions open concurrently while still requiring k signatures to create a forged one.
- We then show that there exists a tradeoff between the number of sessions/signatures needed and the adversary's running time. The implications are that CSI-Otter is forgeable for the above parameters with only eight concurrent sessions in under a second on commodity hardware.
- We show that even if such schemes are only used in the impractical sequential setting, their parameters must be considered carefully. In particular, the challenge space must be at least doubled in the security parameter $k \geq 2 \cdot n$. Otherwise, for the parameters proposed in [22], the required computation needed by an adversary is comparable to the work required by Bitcoin miners (2^{66} hash operations in expectation), where the network of miners can solve such a problem in around ten minutes.

2 Background

2.1 Notation

For a set X, $|X|$ denotes the cardinality of X. For convenience, vectors will be denoted by a bold letter $\mathbf{v} = (v_1, \ldots, v_k)$. We will denote the security parameter with n, and for positive integers k we define $[k] := \{1, \ldots, k\}$. We will use $\|$ to denote the concatenation of strings. We use uppercase letters $\mathcal{A}$ or A to denote algorithms. We let $y \leftarrow \mathcal{A}(x)$ denote the output of $\mathcal{A}$ on input x and $y \leftarrow_{\$} \mathcal{A}(x)$ for the randomized algorithm. For a set X the notation $x \leftarrow_{\$} X$ means that x is uniformly sampled from X. We use st explicitly to denote the inner state of an algorithm while omitting it when the context is clear. We say that a function is negligible and denote it as $\mathsf{negl}(n)$ if it vanishes faster than the inverse of any polynomial. For a prime number p, we denote the finite field with p elements as $\mathbb{F}_p$. Given an hash function $\mathcal{H} : \{0,1\}^* \to \{0,1\}^k$ and a vector $\mathbf{R} = (R_1, \ldots, R_n)$ we define $\mathcal{H}(\mathbf{R}) := \mathcal{H}(R_1\| \ldots \|R_n)$, where the components of the vector are encoded as bit strings.

2.2 Sigma Protocols

Definition 1 (Σ-Protocol). *A sigma protocol (Σ-protocol) is a three-move interactive protocol $\Sigma = (\mathcal{G}, \mathcal{P}, \mathcal{V}, \mathcal{C})$ that consists of the following p.p.t. algorithm:*

Key Generation. *On input the security parameter 1^n, the probabilistic algorithm $\mathcal{G}$ outputs a public key pk and a secret key sk.*

Prover. *The **prover** $\mathcal{P} = (\mathsf{P}_1, \mathsf{P}_2)$ consists of two algorithms:*

 1. *$(R, \mathsf{st}) \leftarrow_{\$} \mathsf{P}_1(\mathsf{sk})$: on input a secret key sk the probabilistic algorithm P_1 outputs a **commitment** R and an internal state st.*
 2. *$s \leftarrow \mathsf{P}_2(\mathsf{sk}, c, \mathsf{st})$: on input a **challenge** $c \in \mathcal{C}$, a secret key sk and a state st, the algorithm P_2 outputs a **response** s.*

Verifier. *On input a public key pk, a commitment R, a challenge c, and a response s, the verification algorithm $\mathcal{V}$ outputs 1 to indicate the prover is valid, and 0 otherwise.*

Prover(pk, sk)		**Verifier**(pk)
$(R, \mathsf{st}) \leftarrow_{\$} \mathsf{P}_1(\mathsf{sk})$	$\xrightarrow{\quad R \quad}$	
	$\xleftarrow{\quad c \quad}$	$c \leftarrow_{\$} \mathcal{C}$
$s \leftarrow \mathsf{P}_2(\mathsf{sk}, c, \mathsf{st})$	$\xrightarrow{\quad s \quad}$	$b \leftarrow \mathcal{V}(\mathsf{pk}, R, c, s)$

Fig. 1. Interaction in a sigma protocol.

We say that a Σ-protocol is correct if for every 1^n, for every key pair $(pk, sk) \leftarrow \mathcal{G}(1^n)$, and for every transcript (R, c, s) output from the interaction in Fig. 1 between a prover and a verifier, we have $\mathcal{V}(pk, R, c, s) = 1$.

Security Notions. We briefly capture the security of a Σ-protocol in the following notions: *honest verifier zero-knowledge* and *special soundness*.

- We say that a Σ-protocol is **honest verifier zero-knowledge (HVZK)** if there exists a p.p.t. simulator Sim such that for every key pair $(\mathsf{pk}, \mathsf{sk}) \leftarrow \mathcal{G}(1^n)$, and for every challenge $c \in \mathcal{C}$, it outputs a valid transcript $(R, c, s) \leftarrow \mathsf{Sim}(\mathsf{pk}, c)$ that is indistinguishable from a real transcript.
- We say that a Σ-protocol is **(2-)special sound** if there exists a deterministic polynomial time extractor Ext such that, for every key pair $(\mathsf{pk}, \mathsf{sk}) \leftarrow \mathcal{G}(1^n)$, recovers the secret sk given two valid transcripts (R, c_1, s_1) and (R, c_2, s_2) sharing the same commitment and different challenges.

We will assume hereafter that any Σ-protocol we encounter satisfies the properties enunciated in the above security notions. Recall also that we can turn any Σ-protocols into a signature scheme using the Fiat-Shamir Transform [16,29].

2.3 Blind Signature Schemes

Definition 2 (Three-Moves Blind Signature Scheme). *A three-moves blind signature scheme* $\mathsf{BS} = (\mathcal{G}, \mathcal{S}, \mathcal{U}, \mathcal{V})$ *consists of the following p.p.t. algorithms:*

Key Generation. *On input the security parameter 1^n, the probabilistic algorithm $\mathcal{G}$ outputs a public key pk and a secret key sk.*

Signer. *The signer $\mathcal{S} = (\mathsf{S}_1, \mathsf{S}_2)$ consists of two algorithms:*
1. *$(R, \mathsf{st}_\mathsf{S}) \leftarrow_\$ \mathsf{S}_1(\mathsf{sk})$: on input a secret key sk, the probabilistic algorithm S_1 outputs an internal state st_S and a commitment R.*
2. *$s \leftarrow \mathsf{S}_2(\mathsf{sk}, c, \mathsf{st}_\mathsf{S})$: on input a challenge $c \in \mathcal{C}$, a secret key sk and an internal state st, the algorithm S_2 outputs a response s.*

User. *The user $\mathcal{U} = (\mathsf{U}_1, \mathsf{U}_2)$ consists of two algorithms:*
1. *$(c, \mathsf{st}_\mathsf{U}) \leftarrow_\$ \mathsf{U}_1(\mathsf{pk}, m, R)$: on input a public key pk, a message m and a signer commitment R, the probabilistic algorithm U_1 outputs a challenge $c \in \mathcal{C}$ and an internal state st.*
2. *$\sigma \leftarrow \mathsf{U}_2(\mathsf{pk}, s, \mathsf{st}_\mathsf{U})$: on input a public key pk, a signer response s and an internal state st_U, the probabilistic algorithm U_2 outputs a signature σ on a message m.*

Verification. *On input a public key pk, a message m, and a signature σ, the verification algorithm $\mathcal{V}$ outputs 1 to indicate the prover is valid, and 0 otherwise.*

We say that a three-moves blind signature scheme BS is correct if for every 1^n, for every key pair $(\mathsf{pk}, \mathsf{sk}) \leftarrow \mathcal{G}(1^n)$, for every message and signature pair (m, σ) generated from the interaction in Fig. 2 between an user and a signer, we have $\mathcal{V}(\mathsf{pk}, m, \sigma) = 1$. We will omit "three-moves" and will say blind signature for brevity.

Signer(pk, sk)		**User**(pk)
$(R, \mathsf{st_S}) \leftarrow\!\!\$\ \mathsf{S}_1(\mathsf{sk})$	$\xrightarrow{\quad R \quad}$	
	$\xleftarrow{\quad c \quad}$	$(c, \mathsf{st_U}) \leftarrow\!\!\$\ \mathsf{U}_1(\mathsf{pk}, R, m)$
$s \leftarrow \mathsf{S}_2(\mathsf{sk}, c, \mathsf{st_S})$	$\xrightarrow{\quad s \quad}$	$\sigma \leftarrow \mathsf{U}_2(\mathsf{pk}, s, m, \mathsf{st_U})$

Fig. 2. Interaction in a Three-move Blind Signature Scheme.

Security Notions. We capture the security of a Blind Signature Scheme BS by two security notions: *blindness* and *one-more unforgeability*. For blindness we will omit its formal definition and refer to [19] since we do not discuss blindness of the schemes and it is out of this paper's scope.

Definition 3 (One-More-Unforgeability). *Let* $\mathsf{BS} = (\mathcal{G}, \mathcal{U}, \mathcal{S}, \mathcal{V})$ *be a blind signature and n be the security parameter. We define the ℓ-one more unforgeability game ℓ-$\mathbf{OMUF_{BS}}$ with an adversary $\mathcal{A}$ (in the role of the user) as follows:*

Setup. *Sample a pair of keys* $(\mathsf{pk}, \mathsf{sk}) \leftarrow\!\!\$\ \mathcal{G}(1^n)$. *Initialize* $\ell_{\mathsf{closed}} := 0$ *and run* $\mathcal{A}$ *on input* pk.

Online Phase. $\mathcal{A}$ *is given access to oracles* sign_1 *and* sign_2, *which behave as follows.*

   Oracle sign_1: *the oracle samples a fresh session identifier* sid. *It sets* $\mathsf{open_{sid}} := \mathtt{true}$ *and generates* $(R_{\mathsf{sid}}, \mathsf{st_{sid}}) \leftarrow\!\!\$\ \mathsf{S}_1(\mathsf{sk})$. *Then it returns the response* R_{sid} *to* $\mathcal{A}$.

   Oracle sign_2: *If* $\ell_{\mathsf{closed}} < \ell$, *the oracle takes as input a challenge c and a session identifier* sid. *If* $\mathsf{open_{sid}} = \mathtt{false}$, *it returns* $\perp$. *Otherwise, it sets* $\ell_{\mathsf{closed}} := \ell_{\mathsf{closed}} + 1$ *and* $\mathsf{open_{sid}} := \mathtt{false}$. *Then it computes the response* $s \leftarrow\!\!\$\ \mathsf{S}_2(\mathsf{sk}, \mathsf{st_{sid}}, c)$ *and returns s to* $\mathcal{A}$.

Output Determination. *When* $\mathcal{A}$ *outputs distinct tuples* $(m_1, \sigma_1), \ldots,$ (m_k, σ_k), *return 1 if* $k \geq \ell_{\mathsf{closed}} + 1$ *and* $\mathcal{V}(\mathsf{pk}, \sigma_i, m_i) = 1$ *for all* $1 \leq i \leq k$. *Otherwise, return 0.*

We define the advantage of $\mathcal{A}$ *as*

$$\mathsf{Adv}_{\mathcal{A}}^{\ell\text{-}\mathbf{OMUF_{BS}}}(n) = \Pr\left[\ell\text{-}\mathbf{OMUF_{BS}}^{\mathcal{A}} = 1\right],$$

where the probability goes over the randomness of the game as well as the randomness of the adversary $\mathcal{A}$. *We say the scheme* BS *is ℓ-one-more unforgeable if for any adversary* $\mathcal{A}$ *that makes at most ℓ queries to* sign_1, *the following holds:*

$$\mathsf{Adv}_{\mathcal{A}}^{\ell\text{-}\mathbf{OMUF_{BS}}}(n) \leq \mathsf{negl}(n).$$

3   Mix-and-Match Attacks

This section presents three attacks against the one-more-unforgeability of blind signature schemes based on Σ-protocols. The first two attacks center on concurrent security, and the third focuses on sequential security. We also briefly demonstrate the first two attacks in Figs. 3 and 4.

3.1   Schnorr-Type Blind Signatures

Many blind signature schemes, such as the Schnorr Blind Signature [11], the Abe-Okamoto scheme [1] or the more recent CSI-Otter [22], are based on an underlying sigma protocol. We will call the schemes following this paradigm **Schnorr-type blind signatures**.

Definition 4. *Let* BS $= (\mathcal{G}, \mathcal{S}, \mathcal{U}, \mathcal{V})$ *be a blind signature. We say that* BS *is of Schnorr-type if there exists a sigma protocol* $\Sigma = (\mathcal{G}_\Sigma, \mathcal{P}_\Sigma, \mathcal{V}_\Sigma, \mathcal{C}_\Sigma)$ *and an hash function* $\mathcal{H} : \{0,1\}^\star \to \mathcal{C}_\Sigma$ *such that:*

1. $\mathcal{G} = \mathcal{G}_\Sigma$, *and* $\mathcal{V}_\Sigma$ *is as in the Fiat-Shamir's construction.*
2. $\mathcal{S} = \mathcal{P}_\Sigma$. *So, in particular, we have that* $\mathsf{S}_1 = \mathsf{P}_1$ *and* $\mathsf{S}_2 = \mathsf{P}_2$.
   We also require the following property on the user $\mathcal{U} = (\mathsf{U}_1, \mathsf{U}_2)$:
3. *there exists algorithms* $\mathsf{U}_1.\mathsf{BlindCom}$, $\mathsf{U}_1.\mathsf{BlindChal}$ *and* $\mathsf{U}_2.\mathsf{BlindResp}$ *such that:*

$\mathsf{U}_1(\mathsf{pk}, m, R)$	$\mathsf{U}_2(\mathsf{pk}, s, \mathsf{st_U})$
1: $(R', \mathsf{st_U}) \leftarrow_\$ \mathsf{U}_1.\mathsf{BlindCom}(R)$	*1:* $s' \leftarrow \mathsf{U}_2.\mathsf{BlindResp}(s, \mathsf{st_U})$
2: $c' \leftarrow \mathcal{H}(R' \| m)$	*2:* $\sigma \leftarrow (R', s')$
3: $c \leftarrow \mathsf{U}_1.\mathsf{BlindChal}(c', \mathsf{st_U})$	*3:* **return** σ
4: **return** $(c, \mathsf{st_U})$	

We will denote such a blind signature as BS_Σ.

Like sigma protocols, given a Schnorr-type blind signature BS_Σ with challenge space $\mathcal{C}$, we can construct (by taking parallel repetitions) another blind signature scheme with challenge space $\mathcal{C}^k$ for any $k \in \mathbb{N}$. We will denote it as BS_Σ^k.

3.2   Main Attack

In this attack, the adversary initiates k concurrent sessions and obtains $k + 1$ valid signatures.

Let $\mathsf{BS} = \mathsf{BS}_\Sigma^k = (\mathcal{G}, \mathcal{S}, \mathcal{U}, \mathcal{V})$ be a k-parallel repetition of a Schnorr-type blind signature where $k = k(n)$ is a positive integer depending on n. Let $\Sigma = (\mathcal{G}_\Sigma, \mathcal{P}_\Sigma, \mathcal{V}_\Sigma, \mathcal{C}_\Sigma)$ be the underlying sigma protocol. We have, by construction, that the challenge space of BS is equal to $\mathcal{C}_\Sigma^k$ and the signer $\mathcal{S}$ is equal to $\mathcal{P}_\Sigma^k$. The attacker $\mathcal{A}$ will proceed as follows.

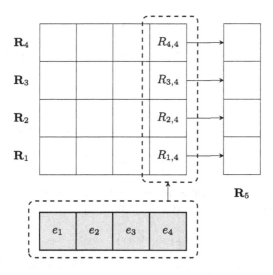

Fig. 3. The main attack depicted for the special case $k = 4$. The rows of the matrix are the signer's commitments $\mathbf{R}_1, \ldots, \mathbf{R}_4$ of the four sessions. The row at the bottom represents the simulated instances of the Σ-protocol used to replace the last instances in the signer's commitment, which are used to generate a forgery with commitment $\mathbf{R}_5$.

1. It opens k concurrent sessions $\mathsf{BS}^{(1)}, \ldots, \mathsf{BS}^{(k)}$ with $\mathcal{S}$. Let $\mathbf{R}_i$ be the commitment sent by $\mathcal{S}$ in the ith session. Since $\mathcal{S} = \mathcal{P}_\Sigma^k$, we can write

$$\mathbf{R}_i = (R_{i,1}, \ldots, R_{i,k})$$

   where $R_{i,j} \leftarrow_\$ \mathsf{P}_1(\mathsf{sk})$ for any $i, j \in [k]$.
2. From that, the attacker constructs a new fake signer commitment as

$$\mathbf{R}_{k+1} = (R_{1,k}, \ldots, R_{k,k}).$$

   Let $\mathbf{R}'_{k+1} \leftarrow \mathsf{U}_1.\mathsf{BlindCom}(\mathbf{R}_{k+1})$, $\mathbf{c}_{k+1} \leftarrow \mathsf{U}_1.\mathsf{BlindChal}(\mathbf{c}'_{k+1})$ be the blinded commitment and challenge respectively, where $\mathbf{c}'_{k+1} = \mathcal{H}(\mathbf{R}'_{k+1} \| m_{k+1})$ for a message $m_{k+1} \in \{0,1\}^\star$ picked at random.
   In addition, it computes k valid transcripts[1] (e_i, d_i, z_i), $i \in [k]$, of the underlying sigma protocol for random challenges d_i.
3. To construct a valid response for the challenge $\mathbf{c}'_{k+1}$, $\mathcal{A}$ interacts with $\mathcal{S}$ as follows. For each opened session $\mathsf{BS}^{(i)}$, the attacker replaces $\mathbf{R}_i$ with $\widetilde{\mathbf{R}}_i = (R_{i,1}, \ldots, R_{i,k-1}, e_i)$ and blinds it as

$$\mathbf{R}'_i = (R'_{i,1}, \ldots, R'_{i,k-1}, e_i), \tag{1}$$

   where, for $j \in [k-1]$, $R'_{i,j} \leftarrow \mathsf{U}_1.\mathsf{BlindCom}(R_{i,j})$. The attacker then finds a message m_i such that the last entry of $\mathbf{c}'_i = \mathcal{H}(\mathbf{R}'_i \| m_i)$ is equal to d_i. For

---

[1] This can be done because of the honest verifier zero-knowledge property of the sigma protocol.

random messages m_i this happens after $O(|\mathcal{C}_\Sigma|)$ queries of the hash function[2]. In this way, it will be able to ask the signer the response for the challenge of the forgery. $\mathcal{A}$ then sends to the signer the blinded challenge

$$\mathbf{c}_i = (c_{i,1}, \ldots, c_{i,k-1}, c_{k+1,i}),$$

where $c_{i,j} \leftarrow_\$ \mathsf{U}_1.\mathsf{BlindChal}(c'_{i,j})$ for $j \in [k-1]$, and receives the response $\mathbf{s}_i$ from $\mathcal{S}$, where $\mathbf{s}_i \leftarrow \mathsf{S}_2(\mathsf{sk}, \mathbf{c}_i)$. The attacker now blinds the response as

$$\mathbf{s}'_i = (s'_{i,1}, \ldots, s'_{i,k-1}, z_i), \tag{2}$$

where $s'_{i,j} \leftarrow_\$ \mathsf{U}_2.\mathsf{BlindResp}(s_{i,j})$ for $j \in [k-1]$, and closes session $\mathsf{BS}^{(i)}$.
4. Finally, the attacker sets the response for $\mathbf{c}'_{k+1}$ to

$$\mathbf{s}'_{k+1} = (s'_{1,k}, \ldots, s'_{k,k}), \tag{3}$$

where $s'_{i,k} \leftarrow_\$ \mathsf{U}_2.\mathsf{BlindResp}(s_{i,k})$ for $i \in [k]$. To conclude, $\mathcal{A}$ outputs $k+1$ signatures:

$$(m_i, (\mathbf{R}'_i, \mathbf{s}'_i)), \text{ for } i \in [k+1].$$

Lemma 1. *For all $i = 1, \ldots, k+1$ the pair $(\mathbf{R}'_i, \mathbf{s}'_i)$ is a valid signature for the message m_i.*

Proof. We distinguish two cases: $i \le k$ and $i = k+1$.

$i \le k$. From Eq. 1 we have $\mathbf{R}'_i = (R'_{i,1}, \ldots, R'_{i,k-1}, e_i)$ and from 2 that $\mathbf{s}'_i = (s'_{i,1}, \ldots, s'_{i,k-1}, z_i)$. Let $\mathbf{c}'_i = \mathcal{H}(\mathbf{R}'_i \| m_i)$. For $j \in [k-1]$, $R'_{i,j}$ and $s'_{i,j}$ are honestly generated following BS_Σ, therefore

$$\mathcal{V}_\Sigma(\mathsf{pk}, R'_{i,j}, c'_{i,j}, s'_{i,j}) = 1 \quad \forall j \in [k-1]$$

In addition, by construction, $c'_{i,k} = d_i$ and (e_i, d_i, z_i) is a valid transcript for Σ, hence $\mathcal{V}_\Sigma(\mathsf{pk}, e_i, d_i, z_i) = 1$. Therefore

$$\mathcal{V}_{\mathsf{BS}^k_\Sigma}(\mathsf{pk}, m_i, (\mathbf{R}'_i, \mathbf{s}'_i)) = 1.$$

$i = k+1$. Let $\mathbf{R}'_{k+1} \leftarrow \mathsf{U}_1.\mathsf{BlindCom}(\mathbf{R}_{k+1})$, $\mathbf{c}'_{k+1} = \mathcal{H}(\mathbf{R}'_{k+1} \| m_{k+1})$ and also let $\mathbf{c}_{k+1} \leftarrow \mathsf{U}_1.\mathsf{BlindChal}(\mathbf{c}'_{k+1})$ as in step 2 above. By Eq. 3 we have $\mathbf{s}'_{k+1} = (s'_{1,k}, \ldots, s'_{k,k})$ where $s_{j,k}$ is the blinded response of the signer for the challenge $c_{k+1,j}$ and commitment $R_{j,k}$. Therefore

$$\mathcal{V}_\Sigma(\mathsf{pk}, R'_{k+1,1}, c'_{k+1,j}, s'_{j,k}) = 1 \quad \forall j \in [k-1].$$

and hence $\mathcal{V}_{\mathsf{BS}^k_\Sigma}(\mathsf{pk}, m_{k+1}, (\mathbf{R}'_{k+1}, \mathbf{s}'_{k+1})) = 1$

We have just proved the following:

---

[2] Define $x = |\mathcal{C}_\Sigma|$, the probability of fail after Q queries is equal to $((x-1)/x)^Q$. This probability is negligible for $Q = O(x)$, with constant $128 \log 2$.

Theorem 1. *Let* $\mathsf{BS} = \mathsf{BS}_\Sigma^k$ *be a parallel repetition of a Schnorr-type blind signature scheme supporting at most k concurrent sessions. There exists an adversary $\mathcal{A}$ against the ℓ-one-more unforgeability game, for $\ell = k$, such that*

$$\mathsf{Adv}_{\mathcal{A}}^{\ell\text{-OMUF}_\mathsf{BS}}(n) = 1$$

and asking $O(k \cdot |\mathcal{C}_\Sigma|)$ queries to the hash function, where $\mathcal{C}_\Sigma$ is the challenge space of the base sigma protocol.

As previously mentioned in the introduction, the above attack can be generalized as follows. Instead of brute force one challenge, $\mathcal{A}$ will go for t consecutive challenges for some $1 \leq t \leq k$. In this way, by opening $s = \lceil k/t \rceil$ concurrent sessions and making $O(|\mathcal{C}_\Sigma|^t)$ queries to the hash function for each of them, it will get $s + 1$ signatures.

Theorem 2. *Let* $\mathsf{BS} = \mathsf{BS}_\Sigma^k$ *be a parallel repetition of a Schnorr-type blind signature scheme supporting at most $s = \lceil k/t \rceil$ concurrent sessions for some $1 \leq t \leq k$. There exists an adversary $\mathcal{A}$ against the ℓ-one-more unforgeability game, for $\ell = s$, such that,*

$$\mathsf{Adv}_{\mathcal{A}}^{\ell\text{-OMUF}_\mathsf{BS}}(n) = 1$$

and asking $O(s \cdot |\mathcal{C}_\Sigma|^t)$ queries to the hash function, where $\mathcal{C}_\Sigma$ is the challenge space of the base sigma protocol.

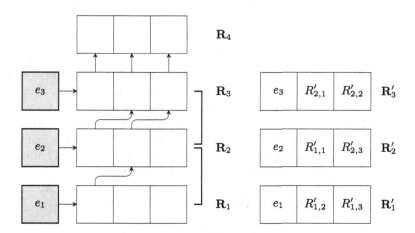

Fig. 4. The 2 out of k attack when $k = 3$. The vectors $\mathbf{R}_1, \mathbf{R}_2, \mathbf{R}_3$ are the signer commitments. The attacker will replace them with $\mathbf{R}_1', \mathbf{R}_2', \mathbf{R}_3'$ in order to get the forgery. On the right side, we depict the commitments used for the 3 standard signatures, while the left side represents the order of the challenges asked to the signer. At the top, we have the forgery with commitment $\mathbf{R}_4$ that in this scenario corresponds to $\mathbf{R}_3$.

3.3 Two Out of k Attack

In this attack, the adversary employs $k-1$ pairs of concurrent sessions, totaling k sessions, to get $k+1$ signatures. More precisely, we will construct an adversary $\mathcal{A}$ against the k-one-more unforgeability for a Schnorr-type blind signature that supports at most two concurrent sessions at a given time. Let $\mathsf{BS} = \mathsf{BS}_\Sigma^k$ be as in the previous section. For simplicity, we will present the adversary $\mathcal{A}$ in the particular case $k = 3$. However, the attack generalized easily, and we will prove its correctness for an arbitrary k. The attacker proceeds as follows.

1. It first opens two concurrent sessions $\mathsf{BS}^{(1)}, \mathsf{BS}^{(2)}$. Let $\mathbf{R}_1 = (R_{1,1}, R_{1,2}, R_{1,3})$ and $\mathbf{R}_2 = (R_{2,1}, R_{2,2}, R_{2,3})$ be the commitments sent by the signer in the first and second session respectively. Also, let $\widetilde{\mathbf{R}}_1 \leftarrow \mathsf{U}_1.\mathsf{BlindCom}(\mathbf{R}_1)$ and $\widetilde{\mathbf{R}}_2 \leftarrow \mathsf{U}_1.\mathsf{BlindCom}(\mathbf{R}_2)$ be the blinded commitments.
2. $\mathcal{A}$ now computes two valid transcripts (e_1, d_1, z_1) and (e_2, d_2, z_2) of the underlying sigma protocol for random challenges d_1 and d_2. Set $\mathbf{R}'_1 = (e_1, \widetilde{R}_{1,2}, \widetilde{R}_{1,3})$ and $\mathbf{R}'_2 = (e_2, \widetilde{R}_{1,1}, \widetilde{R}_{2,3})$. Then, the attacker searches for two messages m_1, m_2 such that $\mathbf{c}'_1 = \mathcal{H}(\mathbf{R}'_1 \| m_1)$ and $\mathbf{c}'_2 = \mathcal{H}(\mathbf{R}'_2 \| m_2)$ have the first component equal to d_1 and d_2 respectively. As before, this can be achieved with $O(|\mathcal{C}_\Sigma|)$ queries to the hash function.
3. The attacker computes $\widetilde{\mathbf{c}}_1 \leftarrow \mathsf{U}_1.\mathsf{BlindChal}(\mathbf{c}'_1)$ and $\widetilde{\mathbf{c}}_2 \leftarrow \mathsf{U}_1.\mathsf{BlindChal}(\mathbf{c}'_2)$, and sends to the signer, in the first session, the challenge $\mathbf{c}_1 = (\widetilde{c}_{2,2}, \widetilde{c}_{1,2}, \widetilde{c}_{1,3})$. Upon receiving the response $\mathbf{s}_1$ from the signer, $\mathcal{A}$ blinds it by computing $\widetilde{\mathbf{s}}_1 \leftarrow \mathsf{U}_2.\mathsf{BlindResp}(\mathbf{s}_1)$ and sets

$$\mathbf{s}'_1 = (z_1, \widetilde{s}_{1,2}, \widetilde{s}_{1,3}).$$

It outputs $(m_1, (\mathbf{R}'_1, \mathbf{s}'_1))$ and closes $\mathsf{BS}^{(1)}$.
4. Now $\mathcal{A}$ opens the third session $\mathsf{BS}^{(3)}$. Note that two concurrent sessions are open at the moment. Let $\mathbf{R}_3 = (R_{3,1}, R_{3,2}, R_{3,3})$ be the commitment sent by the signer and let $\widetilde{\mathbf{R}}_3 \leftarrow \mathsf{U}_1.\mathsf{BlindCom}(\mathbf{R}_3)$ be the blinded commitment. It creates a valid transcript of the underlying sigma protocol (e_3, d_3, z_3) for a random challenge d_3 and sets $\mathbf{R}'_3 = (e_3, \widetilde{R}_{2,1}, \widetilde{R}_{2,2})$. As before, searches for a message m_3 such that $\mathbf{c}'_3 = \mathcal{H}(\mathbf{R}'_3 \| m_3)$ has the first component equal to d_3.
5. Similarly to Step 3 above, the attacker computes $\widetilde{\mathbf{c}}_3 \leftarrow \mathsf{U}_1.\mathsf{BlindChal}(\mathbf{c}'_3)$ and sends to the signer, in the second session, the challenge $\mathbf{c}_2 = (\widetilde{c}_{3,2}, \widetilde{c}_{3,3}, \widetilde{c}_{2,3})$. Upon receiving the response $\mathbf{s}_2$ from the signer in session two, $\mathcal{A}$ computes the blinded response as $\widetilde{\mathbf{s}}_2 \leftarrow \mathsf{U}_2.\mathsf{BlindResp}(\mathbf{s}_2)$ and sets

$$\mathbf{s}'_2 = (z_2, \widetilde{s}_{1,1}, \widetilde{s}_{2,3}).$$

It outputs $(m_2, (\mathbf{R}'_2, \mathbf{s}'_2))$ and closes $\mathsf{BS}^{(2)}$.
6. Now only one session, $\mathsf{BS}^{(3)}$, is open. It sets $\mathbf{R}'_4 = \widetilde{\mathbf{R}}_3$ and $\mathbf{c}'_4 = \mathcal{H}(\mathbf{R}'_4 \| m_4)$. $\mathcal{A}$ will ask the server in $\mathsf{BS}^{(3)}$ to respond for this challenge. It hence computes $\widetilde{\mathbf{c}}_4 \leftarrow \mathsf{U}_1.\mathsf{BlindChal}(\mathbf{c}'_4)$ and sends to $\mathcal{S}$, in the third session, the challenge

$\mathbf{c}_3 = (\widetilde{c}_{4,1}, \widetilde{c}_{4,2}, \widetilde{c}_{4,3})$. Upon receiving the response $\mathbf{s}_3$ from the signer, $\mathcal{A}$ blinds it as $\widetilde{\mathbf{s}}_3$ and sets

$$\mathbf{s}'_3 = (z_3, \widetilde{s}_{2,1}, \widetilde{s}_{2,2}),$$

and

$$\mathbf{s}'_4 = (\widetilde{s}_{3,1}, \widetilde{s}_{3,2}, \widetilde{s}_{3,3})$$

It outputs $(m_3, (\mathbf{R}'_3, \mathbf{s}'_3))$, the forgery $(m_4, (\mathbf{R}'_4, \mathbf{s}'_4))$, and closes $\mathsf{BS}^{(3)}$.

Lemma 2. *For all $i = 1, \ldots, k+1$ the pair $(\mathbf{R}'_i, \mathbf{s}'_i)$ is a valid signature for the message m_i.*

Proof. We will distinguish two cases like in lemma 1.

$i \leq k$. We have by construction

$$\mathbf{R}'_i = (e_i, \underbrace{\widetilde{R}_{i-1,1}, \ldots, \widetilde{R}_{i-1,i-1}}_{i-1 \text{ terms}}, \underbrace{\widetilde{R}_{i,i+1}, \ldots, \widetilde{R}_{i,k}}_{k-i \text{ terms}}),$$

$$\mathbf{c}'_i = \mathcal{H}(\mathbf{R}'_i \| m_i) = (c'_{i,1}, \ldots, c'_{i,k}),$$

and

$$\mathbf{s}'_i = (z_i, \underbrace{\widetilde{s}_{i-1,1}, \ldots, \widetilde{s}_{i-1,i-1}}_{i-1 \text{ terms}}, \underbrace{\widetilde{s}_{i,i+1}, \ldots, \widetilde{s}_{i,k}}_{k-i \text{ terms}}).$$

Since $c'_{i,1} = d_i$ by construction, we have $\mathcal{V}_\Sigma(\mathsf{pk}, e_i, d_i, z_i) = 1$. Moreover, for all $1 \leq j \leq i-1$, we have $\mathcal{V}_\Sigma(\mathsf{pk}, \widetilde{R}_{i-1,j}, c_{i,j}, \widetilde{s}_{i-1,j}) = 1$. Similarly, $\mathcal{V}_\Sigma(\mathsf{pk}, \widetilde{R}_{i,j}, c_{i,j}, \widetilde{s}_{i,j}) = 1$ for all $i+1 \leq j \leq k$. We therefore have

$$\mathcal{V}_{\mathsf{BS}^k_\Sigma}(\mathsf{pk}, m_i, (\mathbf{R}'_i, \mathbf{s}'_i)) = 1.$$

$i = k+1$. In this case we have

$$\mathbf{R}'_{k+1} = (\widetilde{R}_{k,1}, \ldots, \widetilde{R}_{k,k}),$$

$$\mathbf{c}'_{k+1} = \mathcal{H}(\mathbf{R}'_i \| m_i) = (c'_{k,1}, \ldots, c'_{k,k})$$

and

$$\mathbf{s}'_{k+1} = (\widetilde{s}_{k,1}, \ldots, \widetilde{s}_{k,k}).$$

From the description of the attack we have $\mathcal{V}_\Sigma(\mathsf{pk}, \widetilde{R}_{k,j}, c_{k,j}, \widetilde{s}_{k,j}) = 1$ for any $j \in [k]$ and hence

$$\mathcal{V}_{\mathsf{BS}^k_\Sigma}(\mathsf{pk}, m_{k+1}, (\mathbf{R}'_{k+1}, \mathbf{s}'_{k+1})) = 1.$$

We have just proved the following theorem:

Theorem 3. *Let $\mathsf{BS} = \mathsf{BS}^k_\Sigma$ be (a parallel repetition of) a Schnorr-type blind signature scheme supporting at most two concurrent sessions. There exists an adversary $\mathcal{A}$ against the ℓ-one-more unforgeability game, for $\ell = k$, such that*

$$\mathsf{Adv}^{\ell\text{-}\mathbf{OMUF}_{\mathsf{BS}}}_{\mathcal{A}}(n) = 1$$

and asking $O(k \cdot |\mathcal{C}_\Sigma|)$ queries to the hash function, where $\mathcal{C}_\Sigma$ is the challenge space of the base sigma protocol.

3.4   One Out of One Attack

In this attack, the adversary, by opening only one session with the signer, obtains two signatures. This, however, comes with a trade-off of exponential computational cost. More precisely, suppose the attacker cannot open concurrent sessions, i.e., sequential setting. We will show how the attacker can produce two valid signatures after one session with the signer. Let $\mathsf{BS} = \mathsf{BS}_{\Sigma}^{k}$ be the blind signature scheme. Suppose, for simplicity, the number of repetition k is an even number and set $t = k/2$. We construct $\mathcal{A}$ as follows.

1. The attacker opens one session BS with the signer. Let $\mathbf{R} = (R_1, \ldots, R_k)$ be the signer commitment and let:

$$\mathbf{R}' = (R'_1, \ldots, R'_k),$$

   be the blinded commitment.

2. For any $1 \leq i \leq k$, $\mathcal{A}$ will generate k valid transcripts (r_i, d_i, z_i) for the underlining Σ-protocol, and define

$$\mathbf{R}'_1 = (r_1, \ldots, r_t, R'_1, \ldots, R'_t),$$

   and

$$\mathbf{R}'_2 = (r_{t+1}, \ldots, r_k, R'_{t+1}, \ldots, R'_k).$$

   It will then search for two messages m_1 and m_2 such that:

$$\mathbf{c}'_1 = \mathcal{H}(\mathbf{R}'_1 \| m_1) = (d_1, \ldots, d_t, c'_{1,t+1}, \ldots, c'_{1,k})$$

   and

$$\mathbf{c}'_2 = \mathcal{H}(\mathbf{R}'_2 \| m_2) = (d_{t+1}, \ldots, d_k, c'_{2,t+1}, \ldots, c'_{2,k}).$$

   This will require $O(|\mathcal{C}_{\Sigma}|^t)$ queries to the hash funcion $\mathcal{H}$.

3. The attacker now sets $\widetilde{\mathbf{c}} = (c'_{1,t+1}, \ldots, c'_{1,k}, c'_{2,t+1}, \ldots, c'_{2,k})$, then blinds it as $\mathbf{c} \leftarrow \mathsf{U}_1.\mathsf{BlindChal}(\widetilde{\mathbf{c}})$ and sends this to the signer. Upon receiving the response $\mathbf{s}$, it blinds it as $\widetilde{\mathbf{s}} \leftarrow \mathsf{U}_2.\mathsf{BlindResp}(\mathbf{s})$ and sets

$$\mathbf{s}'_1 = (z_1, \ldots, z_t, \widetilde{s}_1, \ldots, \widetilde{s}_t),$$

   and

$$\mathbf{s}'_2 = (z_{t+1}, \ldots, z_k, \widetilde{s}_{t+1}, \ldots, \widetilde{s}_k).$$

4. The attacker will close the session and output $(m_1, (\mathbf{R}'_1, \mathbf{s}'_1))$, and $(m_2, (\mathbf{R}'_2, \mathbf{s}'_2))$.

Lemma 3. *The pairs $(\mathbf{R}'_1, \mathbf{s}'_1)$ and $(\mathbf{R}'_2, \mathbf{s}'_2)$ are valid signatures for the messages m_1 and m_2 respectively.*

Proof. The proof of this theorem is analogous to that of lemma 1, and hence it will be omitted.

Theorem 4. *Let* $\mathsf{BS} = \mathsf{BS}_\Sigma^k$ *be a parallel repetition of a Schnorr-type blind signature scheme not supporting any concurrent sessions. There exists an adversary $\mathcal{A}$ against the ℓ-one-more unforgeability game, for $\ell = 1$, such that*

$$\mathsf{Adv}_{\mathcal{A}}^{\ell\text{-}\mathbf{OMUF}_{\mathsf{BS}}}(n) = 1$$

and asking $O(2 \cdot |\mathcal{C}_\Sigma|^t)$ queries to the hash function, where $\mathcal{C}_\Sigma$ is the challenge space of the base sigma protocol and $t = \lceil k/2 \rceil$.

4 Cryptanalysis of CSI-Otter

As a concrete example, we will apply our attack to the isogeny-based blind signature scheme CSI-Otter [22] as one of the state-of-the-art blind signatures based on Σ-protocols.

4.1 Cryptographic Group Actions

The scheme we will describe is based on *cryptographic group actions with twist* [8,15,27]. We will, therefore, provide some background.

Definition 5 (Group Action). *We say that a group $(G, +)$ acts on a set X if there exists a function $\star : G \times X \to X$ satisfying the following properties.*

1. *Identity: for any $x \in X$, we have $0 \star x = x$ where 0 is the identity element of G.*
2. *Compatibility: for any $g, h \in G$ and any $x \in X$, we have $(g+h)\star x = g\star(h\star x)$.*
3. *Transitivity: for every $x_1, x_2 \in X$, there exists a group element $g \in G$ such that $x_2 = g \star x_1$.*
4. *Free: for each group element $g \in G$, g is the identity element if and only if there exists some set element $x \in X$ such that $x = g \star x$.*

We will say, for brevity, that $(G, X, \star)$ is a group action.

Let $(G, X, \star)$ be a group action and $x_0 \in X$ a set element. It follows from the definition that, every $x \in X$ can be written as $x = g \star x_0$ for a (unique) $g \in G$. We define the *twist* of a set element $x = g \star x_0$ as $x^{-1} = (-g) \star x_0$.

The specific group action used in CSI-Otter is the CSIDH-512 action defined in [8]. In particular, X is the set of supersingular elliptic curves[3] over $\mathbb{F}_p$ with $\mathbb{F}_p$-rational endomorphism ring isomorphic[4] to an order $\mathcal{O} \subseteq \mathbb{Q}(\sqrt{-p})$; the group G is the ideal class group $\mathcal{C}\ell(\mathcal{O})$ acting on X via isogeny; and $x_0 = E_0$ is the curve[5] defined by:

$$E_0 : y^2 = x^3 + x.$$

We also remark that, for this specific action, the twist can be efficiently computed for every $x \in X$ [31]. For the cryptographic definitions of security, we refer to [2].

---

[3] Modulo isomorphism over $\mathbb{F}_p$.

[4] We also require that an element $\pi \in \mathcal{O}$ maps to the Frobenius endomorphism trough that isomorphism.

[5] This is in fact supersingular for primes $p \equiv 3 \pmod 4$.

4.2 The Scheme

Let $(G, X, \star)$ be a cryptographic group action with twist, and let $x_0 \in X$ be a set element. Recall that x^{-1} represents the twist of $x \in X$. We now describe the blind signature scheme presented in [22]. In the underlying sigma protocol, the prover $\mathcal{P}$ holds a secret key $\mathsf{sk} = (\delta, a_\delta) \in \{0,1\} \times G$ and a public key $\mathsf{pk} = (y_0, y_1) = (a_0 \star x_0, a_1 \star x_0)$. The interaction is described in Fig. 5. This Σ-protocol is correct, special sound and honest verifier zero-knowledge [5]. For the latter property, we can construct a simulator Sim that, given a challenge $c \in \{-1, 1\}$ and a public key (y_0, y_1), samples random $(c_0, c_1) \leftarrow_{\$} (\{-1, 1\})^2$ and $(r_0, r_1) \leftarrow_{\$} G^2$ conditioned on $c_0 \cdot c_1 = c$. It then sets $R_b = r_b \star y_b^c$ for $b \in \{0, 1\}$, and outputs the simulated transcript $((R_0, R_1),\ c,\ (r_0, r_1, c_0, c_1))$.

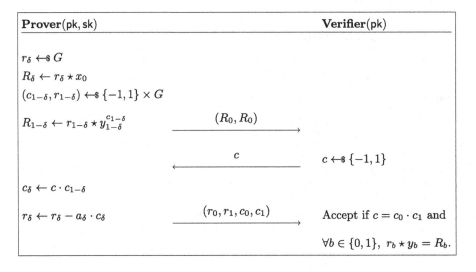

Fig. 5. The interaction between $\mathcal{P}$ and $\mathcal{V}$.

The blind signature scheme $\mathsf{BS}_\Sigma = (\mathcal{G}, \mathcal{U}, \mathcal{S}, \mathcal{V})$ is defined as follows:

$\mathcal{G}(1^n)$: On input the security parameter 1^n, it samples a bit $\delta \leftarrow_{\$} \{0, 1\}$, a pair $(a_0, a_1) \leftarrow_{\$} G^2$ and outputs a public key $\mathsf{pk} = (y_0, y_1) = (a_0 \star x_0, a_1 \star x_0)$ and secret key $\mathsf{sk} = (\delta, a_\delta)$.

$\mathsf{S}_1(\mathsf{sk})$: The signer first samples $r_\delta \leftarrow_{\$} G$ and sets $R_\delta = r_\delta \star x_0$. It then samples $(c_{1-\delta}, r_{1-\delta}) \leftarrow_{\$} \{-1, 1\} \times G$ and sets $R_{1-\delta} = r_{1-\delta} \star y_{1-\delta}^{c_{1-\delta}}$. It then outputs the signer state $\mathsf{st_S} = (r_\delta, c_{1-\delta}, r_{1-\delta})$ and the signer commitment $R = (R_0, R_1)$.

$\mathsf{U}_1(\mathsf{pk}, m, R)$: The user parses $(R_0, R_1) \leftarrow R$, samples $(e_b, t_b) \leftarrow_{\$} \{-1, 1\} \times G$, and computes $R_b' = t_b \star (R_b)^{e_b}$ for $b \in \{0, 1\}$. It then computes $c' = \mathcal{H}(R_0' \| R_1' \| m)$ and outputs the user state $\mathsf{st_U} = (e_b, t_b)_{b \in \{0,1\}}$ and user message $c = c' \cdot e_0 \cdot e_1$.

$\mathsf{S}_2(\mathsf{sk}, c, \mathsf{st_S})$: The signer parses $(r_\delta, c_{1-\delta}, r_{1-\delta}) \leftarrow \mathsf{st_S}$, sets $c_\delta = c \cdot c_{1-\delta} \in \{-1, 1\}$, and updates $r_\delta \leftarrow r_\delta - a_\delta \cdot c_\delta \in G$. It then outputs the signer response $s = (c_b, r_b)_{b \in \{0,1\}}$.

$U_2(\mathsf{pk}, s, \mathsf{st_U})$: The user parses $(e_b, t_b)_{b \in \{0,1\}} \leftarrow \mathsf{st_U}$, $(c_b, r_b)_{b \in \{0,1\}} \leftarrow s$ and sets $(c'_b, r'_b) = (c_b \cdot e_b, t_b + r_b \cdot e_b)$ for $b \in \{0, 1\}$. It then checks if

$$c'_0 \cdot c'_1 = \mathcal{H}(r'_0 \star y_0^{c'_0} \| r'_1 \star y_1^{c'_1} \| m). \tag{4}$$

If it holds, it outputs a signature $\sigma = (c'_b, r'_b)_{b \in \{0,1\}} \in (\{-1, 1\} \times G)^2$, and otherwise a $\perp$.

$\mathcal{V}(\mathsf{pk}, m, \sigma)$: The verifier outputs 1 if Eq. 4 holds, and otherwise 0.

This is, in fact, a Schnorr-type blind signature. It is clear from the construction that $\mathsf{S}_1 = \mathsf{P}_1$ and $\mathsf{S}_2 = \mathsf{P}_2$, and we have the following table for the user.

$U_1(\mathsf{pk}, m, R = (R_0, R_1))$	$U_2(\mathsf{pk}, s = (c_b, r_b)_{b \in \{0,1\}}, \mathsf{st_U})$
1 : for $b \in \{0, 1\}$	1 : for $b \in \{0, 1\}$
2 : $(e_b, t_b) \leftarrow_{\$} \{-1, 1\} \times G$	2 : $(c'_b, r'_b) \leftarrow c_b \cdot e_b, t_b + r_b \cdot e_b$
3 : $R'_b \leftarrow t_b \star (R_b)^{e_b}$	3 : $s' \leftarrow (c'_b, r'_b)_{b \in \{0,1\}}$
4 : $R' \leftarrow (R'_0, R'_1)$	4 : $c^* \leftarrow \mathcal{H}(r'_0 \star y_0^{c'_0} \| r'_1 \star y_1^{c'_1} \| m)$
5 : $c' \leftarrow \mathcal{H}(R' \| m)$	5 : if $c'_0 \cdot c'_1 = c^*$
6 : $c \leftarrow c' \cdot e_0 \cdot e_1$	6 : return $\perp$
7 : $\mathsf{st_U} \leftarrow (e_b, t_b)_{b \in \{0,1\}}$	7 : $\sigma \leftarrow s'$
8 : return $(c, \mathsf{st_U})$	8 : return σ

Blue lines represent the function $U_1.\mathsf{BlindCom}$; the line yellow represents $U_1.\mathsf{BlindChal}$ and the violet $U_2.\mathsf{BlindResp}$. It follows, now, that the blind signature BS_Σ^k is vulnerable to our attacks since the base challenge space $\mathcal{C}_\Sigma$ has cardinality 2 and k is linear in the security parameter n.

5   Discussion

This section discusses potential ways of circumventing our attack in the concurrent setting, their downsides, and implications on the efficiency and practicality of the blind signature vulnerable to our attack. We also discuss implications on sequential security, particularly a concrete treatment of those schemes in the post-quantum setting.

5.1   Concurrent Security

For our mix-and-match attack to work, the adversary must be able to initiate and finalize k signing sessions where the signer supports at least two concurrent sessions at a time. The parameter k depends on the challenge space $\mathcal{C}_\Sigma$ of the underlying Σ-protocol, e.g., in the case of CSI-Otter, the authors use the challenge space $\mathcal{C}_\Sigma = \{-1, 1\}$ and set the number of repetitions to $k = 128$. This parameter is usually polynomial in the security parameter to ensure that the soundness error for the augmented Σ-protocol is negligible while keeping it small to ensure efficiency. For almost all practical applications, the parameter $k = 128$ ensures that the soundness error of the Σ-protocol is negligible for 128-bit security. Thus, in most cases, any blind signature scheme from Σ-protocol with small challenge space will be forgeable after just around a hundred signed messages.

A potential way to circumvent our attack is to increase k since it is allowed to be polynomial in the security parameter. This way, the number of supported signatures will also be polynomial in the security parameter, where the polynomial can be freely chosen. Unfortunately, this approach will significantly decrease the efficiency of the used scheme. Let us discuss this on the CSI-Otter example. Doubling the parameter k to 256 will also double the number of signatures, allowing for one forgery, i.e., from 128 to 256 (note that we are considering the main attack here). At the same time, the communication complexity of the exchange and the signature size will also be doubled. We usually set parameters for a standard digital signature scheme so that one key pair can be used to sign around 2^{30}. To achieve a similar property while protecting against our main attack, we must set $k = 2^{30}$, leading to signatures in the gigabytes and inefficient computations.

Increasing the parameter k provides a simple fix that increases the number of concurrent sessions the blind signature can provide. Asymptotically, the scheme offers the required security, but it is impractical if we want a genuinely usable scheme supporting many signatures. Note that a signer can continuously refresh the key pair, which is not a problem for standard digital signatures but decreases the anonymity set in the blind signature setting.

An alternative approach would be to employ boosting transformations [9, 24] known and used for the Schnorr blind signature scheme vulnerable to the ROS attack. Those solutions employ cut-and-choose techniques that allow the reduction to limit the number of signing queries while providing more questions to the adversary, i.e., in the case of Schnorr signatures, the adversary is allowed to do polynomially many queries in the security parameter while at the same time, the reduction only queries the signing oracle at most a logarithmic number of times. Similar techniques could be employed for the class of blind signatures considered in this paper. Contrary to increasing the parameter k, this approach increases the communication and signature size by a smaller factor than in the previous solution, making it more efficient. However, it is still impractical and not comparable to other blind signature schemes, e.g., applying this technique to CSI-Otter would still make it less efficient than state-of-the-art schemes based on lattices.

Interestingly, [23] proposes a definition for a new version of the ROS problem called "parallel ROS" and shows that it applies to the concurrent security of CSI-Otter [22]. This attack is similar to ours, particularly in terms of efficiency. However, the only solution to the problem diverges from the fundamental concept of the ROS problem, which involves computing a signature through linear combinations of queried signatures. For this reason, we prioritized substance over form, as our generic approach enables broader application.

5.2   Sequential Security

Using the threshold variant of our attack, an adversary can compute two valid signatures using only one signing session in $O(2^{k/2})$ number of hash evaluations. Thus, launching a practical attack in the sequential setting against CSI-Otter with the proposed parameters $k = 128$ requires around $2 \cdot 2 \cdot 2^{64}$ hash evaluation in expectation. This amount of computation is less than the work required by miners to add a new block to the Bitcoin blockchain. In particular, this means that the Bitcoin mining pool can, with non-negligible probability, forge CSI-Otter signatures even in the sequential setting in around 10 min for the parameter proposed by the authors.

Our results show that assuming the underlying Σ-protocol has a negligible soundness error for a parameter k_Σ, e.g., $k_\Sigma = n$, then, we need to set the parameter k for the blind signature to $k = 2 \cdot k_\Sigma$, i.e., in the case of $k_\Sigma = n$ this will lead to $k = 2 \cdot n$. In the case of CSI-Otter, this means that to get around the above sequential attack, the parameter k must be set to $2 \cdot 128 = 256$.

The above considerations are only for the classical setting and do not treat the hash function in the post-quantum scenario. In this setting, we can accelerate the adversary's computation using Grover's algorithm on quantum computers [18]. In particular, the problem the adversary must solve is to find a message m for which $\mathcal{H}(\mathbf{R}||m) = ab$ for fixed commitments $\mathbf{R}$ and prefix a. As shown in [30] the adversary's work will be reduced to $O(2^{\frac{k}{4}})$. Therefore, the parameter k must be increased four times for the scheme to be secure against a quantum attacker.

5.3   Revisiting CSI-Otter Parameters

We will now discuss concrete parameters for CSI-Otter [22]. The authors in the original paper propose two variants: one with challenge space $\{-1, 1\}$ with $k = 128$ repetitions and an optimized variant with a challenge space of size 4 with $k = 64$ repetitions. In both cases, our main attack can forge a new signature with 128 and 64 concurrent sessions, only evaluating the hash function several hundred times. By sacrificing a bit of computation (i.e., around one hour on a commodity M1 Pro processor with a five megahash/s rate), the same concurrent attack can be executed with just 4 concurrent sessions in total for the basic version and 2 concurrent sessions for the optimized version. For the above considerations, we still assume a pre-quantum attacker.

It is evident that CSI-Otter is not concurrently secure for the proposed parameters and design. Increasing the parameter k does not solve the problem since increasing it x times also increases the communication and signature size x times, which might blow up the signature's size to Gigabytes to allow only 2^{20} signatures, making the scheme impractical. In Table 2, we provide an optimistic estimation for the scheme's efficiency after applying the proposed treatments. As argued in the introduction, CSI-Otter and, more generally, blind signatures from Σ-protocols with small challenge space should not be used concurrently without applying transformations to boost their security. Therefore, CSI-Otter can only be used as a blind signature scheme in the sequential setting.

The authors introduced the optimized variant with a challenge space of size 4 and $k = 64$ repetitions to reduce the signature size by two at the expense of the size of the secret key and communication from the signer. Further improvements with an even bigger space and smaller repetitions should be possible. Unfortunately, our attacks show that this decreases the scheme's security, allowing the adversary to forge signatures with fewer concurrent sessions and making a sequential attack more feasible. In particular, for the above case, an adversary only needs to compute $2 \cdot 4 \cdot 2^{32} = 2^{35}$ (in expectation) to forge a fresh signature with just one signing query. For the basic version of CSI-Otter, this is $2 \cdot 2 \cdot 2^{64} = 2^{66}$. The provided parameters should ensure 128-bit security, and they do if the scheme were a standard digital signature scheme. However, our attack shows that to achieve n-bit security for the blind signature scheme, we must set $k = 2 \cdot n$. Thus, the repetitions must be more than 256 for 128-bit security in both cases, making the optimized variant no longer beneficial. The number of 256 repetitions must be further increased if we want to consider the post-quantum setting where we can apply Grover's algorithm mentioned in the above section discussing sequential security.

Table 2. An optimistic estimation for the performance of the two versions of CSI-Otter [22] after applying a potential boosting transformation (e.g., [24] with some modification) resulting in approximately 128 times larger signature size and communication bandwidth. The results include our proposed countermeasures against the post-quantum sequential attack.

	Bandwidth.S	Bandwidth.U	|sk|	|pk|	|σ|
Basic version $(k = 128, \|\mathcal{C}_\Sigma\| = 2)$	8.19 Mb	8.19 Kb	16 B	128 B	4.1 Mb
Optimized version $(k = 64, \|\mathcal{C}_\Sigma\| = 4)$	32.8 Mb	8.19 Kb	16 B	512 B	2.05 Mb

6   Conclusion

We described three attacks against a class of three-move blind signature schemes based on Σ-protocol with small challenge space and parallel repetition. Unlike the ROS attack, the proposed attacks do not require any particular algebraic structure. This property is essential, as the lack of algebraic structure provides ambiguous arguments when assessing the concurrent security of the blind signature scheme. Moreover, because our attacks are generic and only rely on hash evaluation, there is a need for more rigorous treatment for the security parameter, especially when considered in the quantum setting.

We described an example case study of the CSI-Otter isogeny-based scheme and show that our mix-and-match attacks apply to this scheme. However, we highlighted that the class of aforementioned blind signature schemes is not restricted to this scheme and applies to other existing lattice-based or RSA-based constructions. CSI-Otter requires a more rigorous treatment of parameters to achieve practical sequential security. In contrast, one must apply boosting transformations for concurrent security, significantly worsening the scheme's performance, communication, and signature size, making it less attractive than other post-quantum secure candidates (e.g., scheme from lattice assumptions).

We conclude by observing that, in the isogeny-based setting, Σ-protocols with exponentially large challenge space exist, e.g., SQISign [13]. It is unclear, however, whether it is possible to turn those Σ-protocols into a blind signature or not. We leave this question to potential future work.

References

1. Abe, M., Okamoto, T.: Provably secure partially blind signatures. In: Bellare, M. (ed.) CRYPTO 2000. LNCS, vol. 1880, pp. 271–286. Springer, Heidelberg (2000). https://doi.org/10.1007/3-540-44598-6_17

2. Alamati, N., De Feo, L., Montgomery, H., Patranabis, S.: Cryptographic group actions and applications. In: Moriai, S., Wang, H. (eds.) ASIACRYPT 2020, Part II. LNCS, vol. 12492, pp. 411–439. Springer, Heidelberg (2020). https://doi.org/10.1007/978-3-030-64834-3_14

3. Bellare, M., Namprempre, C., Pointcheval, D., Semanko, M.: The one-more-RSA-inversion problems and the security of Chaum's blind signature scheme. J. Cryptol. **16**(3), 185–215 (2003). https://doi.org/10.1007/s00145-002-0120-1

4. Benhamouda, F., Lepoint, T., Loss, J., Orrù, M., Raykova, M.: On the (in)security of ROS. In: Canteaut, A., Standaert, F.X. (eds.) EUROCRYPT 2021, Part I. LNCS, vol. 12696, pp. 33–53. Springer, Heidelberg (2021). https://doi.org/10.1007/978-3-030-77870-5_2

5. Beullens, W., Katsumata, S., Pintore, F.: Calamari and Falafl: logarithmic (linkable) ring signatures from isogenies and lattices. In: Moriai, S., Wang, H. (eds.) ASIACRYPT 2020, Part II. LNCS, vol. 12492, pp. 464–492. Springer, Heidelberg (2020). https://doi.org/10.1007/978-3-030-64834-3_16

6. Beullens, W., Kleinjung, T., Vercauteren, F.: CSI-FiSh: efficient isogeny based signatures through class group computations. In: Galbraith, S.D., Moriai, S. (eds.) ASIACRYPT 2019, Part I. LNCS, vol. 11921, pp. 227–247. Springer, Heidelberg (2019). https://doi.org/10.1007/978-3-030-34578-5_9

7. Boldyreva, A.: Threshold signatures, multisignatures and blind signatures based on the gap-Diffie-Hellman-group signature scheme. In: Desmedt, Y. (ed.) PKC 2003. LNCS, vol. 2567, pp. 31–46. Springer, Heidelberg (2003). https://doi.org/10.1007/3-540-36288-6_3

8. Castryck, W., Lange, T., Martindale, C., Panny, L., Renes, J.: CSIDH: an efficient post-quantum commutative group action. In: Peyrin, T., Galbraith, S. (eds.) ASIACRYPT 2018, Part III. LNCS, vol. 11274, pp. 395–427. Springer, Heidelberg (2018). https://doi.org/10.1007/978-3-030-03332-3_15

9. Chairattana-Apirom, R., Hanzlik, L., Loss, J., Lysyanskaya, A., Wagner, B.: PI-cut-choo and friends: Compact blind signatures via parallel instance cut-and-choose and more. In: Dodis, Y., Shrimpton, T. (eds.) CRYPTO 2022, Part III. LNCS, vol. 13509, pp. 3–31. Springer, Heidelberg (2022). https://doi.org/10.1007/978-3-031-15982-4_1

10. Chaum, D.: Blind signatures for untraceable payments. In: Chaum, D., Rivest, R.L., Sherman, A.T. (eds.) CRYPTO 1982, pp. 199–203. Plenum Press, New York (1982)

11. Chaum, D., Pedersen, T.P.: Wallet databases with observers. In: Brickell, E.F. (ed.) CRYPTO 1992. LNCS, vol. 740, pp. 89–105. Springer, Heidelberg (1993). https://doi.org/10.1007/3-540-48071-4_7

12. De Feo, L., Galbraith, S.D.: SeaSign: compact isogeny signatures from class group actions. In: Ishai, Y., Rijmen, V. (eds.) EUROCRYPT 2019, Part III. LNCS, vol. 11478, pp. 759–789. Springer, Heidelberg (2019). https://doi.org/10.1007/978-3-030-17659-4_26

13. De Feo, L., Kohel, D., Leroux, A., Petit, C., Wesolowski, B.: SQISign: compact post-quantum signatures from quaternions and isogenies. In: Moriai, S., Wang, H. (eds.) ASIACRYPT 2020, Part I. LNCS, vol. 12491, pp. 64–93. Springer, Heidelberg (2020). https://doi.org/10.1007/978-3-030-64837-4_3

14. Ducas, L., van Woerden, W.P.J.: On the lattice isomorphism problem, quadratic forms, remarkable lattices, and cryptography. In: Dunkelman, O., Dziembowski, S. (eds.) EUROCRYPT 2022, Part III. LNCS, vol. 13277, pp. 643–673. Springer, Heidelberg (2022). https://doi.org/10.1007/978-3-031-07082-2_23

15. Duman, J., Hartmann, D., Kiltz, E., Kunzweiler, S., Lehmann, J., Riepel, D.: Generic models for group actions. In: Boldyreva, A., Kolesnikov, V. (eds.) PKC 2023, Part I. LNCS, vol. 13940, pp. 406–435. Springer, Heidelberg (2023). https://doi.org/10.1007/978-3-031-31368-4_15

16. Fiat, A., Shamir, A.: How to prove yourself: practical solutions to identification and signature problems. In: Odlyzko, A.M. (ed.) CRYPTO 1986. LNCS, vol. 263, pp. 186–194. Springer, Heidelberg (1987).https://doi.org/10.1007/3-540-47721-7_12

17. Fuchsbauer, G., Plouviez, A., Seurin, Y.: Blind Schnorr signatures and signed ElGamal encryption in the algebraic group model. In: Canteaut, A., Ishai, Y. (eds.) EUROCRYPT 2020, Part II. LNCS, vol. 12106, pp. 63–95. Springer, Heidelberg (2020). https://doi.org/10.1007/978-3-030-45724-2_3

18. Grover, L.K.: A fast quantum mechanical algorithm for database search. In: 28th ACM STOC, pp. 212–219. ACM Press (1996). https://doi.org/10.1145/237814.237866

19. Hauck, E., Kiltz, E., Loss, J.: A modular treatment of blind signatures from identification schemes. In: Ishai, Y., Rijmen, V. (eds.) EUROCRYPT 2019, Part III. LNCS, vol. 11478, pp. 345–375. Springer, Heidelberg (2019).https://doi.org/10.1007/978-3-030-17659-4_12

20. Hauck, E., Kiltz, E., Loss, J., Nguyen, N.K.: Lattice-based blind signatures, revisited. In: Micciancio, D., Ristenpart, T. (eds.) CRYPTO 2020, Part II. LNCS, vol. 12171, pp. 500–529. Springer, Heidelberg (2020). https://doi.org/10.1007/978-3-030-56880-1_18

21. Kastner, J., Loss, J., Xu, J.: The Abe-Okamoto partially blind signature scheme revisited. In: Agrawal, S., Lin, D. (eds.) ASIACRYPT 2022, Part IV. LNCS, vol. 13794, pp. 279–309. Springer, Heidelberg (2022). https://doi.org/10.1007/978-3-031-22972-5_10

22. Katsumata, S., Lai, Y.F., LeGrow, J.T., Qin, L.: Csi-otter: isogeny-based (partially) blind signatures from the class group action with a twist. In: Advances in Cryptology. CRYPTO 2023. Part III, pp. 729–761. Springer, Heidelberg (2023). https://doi.org/10.1007/978-3-031-38548-3_24

23. Katsumata, S., Lai, Y.F., Reichle, M.: Breaking parallel ROS: implication for isogeny and lattice-based blind signatures. Cryptology ePrint Archive, Paper 2023/1603 (2023). https://eprint.iacr.org/2023/1603

24. Katz, J., Loss, J., Rosenberg, M.: Boosting the security of blind signature schemes. In: Tibouchi, M., Wang, H. (eds.) ASIACRYPT 2021, Part IV. LNCS, vol. 13093, pp. 468–492. Springer, Heidelberg (2021). https://doi.org/10.1007/978-3-030-92068-5_16

25. Ling, S., Nguyen, K., Stehlé, D., Wang, H.: Improved zero-knowledge proofs of knowledge for the ISIS problem, and applications. In: Kurosawa, K., Hanaoka, G. (eds.) PKC 2013. LNCS, vol. 7778, pp. 107–124. Springer, Heidelberg (2013). https://doi.org/10.1007/978-3-642-36362-7_8

26. Lyubashevsky, V., Nguyen, N.K., Plançon, M.: Efficient lattice-based blind signatures via gaussian one-time signatures. In: Hanaoka, G., Shikata, J., Watanabe, Y. (eds.) PKC 2022, Part II. LNCS, vol. 13178, pp. 498–527. Springer, Heidelberg (2022). https://doi.org/10.1007/978-3-030-97131-1_17

27. Orsini, E., Zanotto, R.: Simple two-round OT in the explicit isogeny model. Cryptology ePrint Archive, Paper 2023/269 (2023). https://eprint.iacr.org/2023/269

28. Pointcheval, D.: Strengthened security for blind signatures. In: Nyberg, K. (ed.) EUROCRYPT 1998. LNCS, vol. 1403, pp. 391–405. Springer, Heidelberg (1998). https://doi.org/10.1007/BFb0054141

29. Pointcheval, D., Stern, J.: Security arguments for digital signatures and blind signatures. J. Cryptol. **13**(3), 361–396 (2000). https://doi.org/10.1007/s001450010003

30. Ramos-Calderer, S., Bellini, E., Latorre, J.I., Manzano, M., Mateu, V.: Quantum search for scaled hash function preimages. Quantum Inf. Process. **20**(5), 180 (2021). https://doi.org/10.1007/s11128-021-03118-9

31. Silverman, J.H.: The Arithmetic of Elliptic Curves, Graduate Texts in Mathematics, vol. 106. Springer, New York (1986)

The Supersingular Endomorphism Ring and One Endomorphism Problems are Equivalent

Aurel Page[1]($\boxtimes$) and Benjamin Wesolowski[2]

[1] Univ. Bordeaux, CNRS, INRIA, Bordeaux INP, IMB, UMR 5251,
33400 Talence, France
aurel.page@inria.fr85
[2] ENS de Lyon, CNRS, UMPA, UMR 5669, Lyon, France

Abstract. The supersingular Endomorphism Ring problem is the following: given a supersingular elliptic curve, compute all of its endomorphisms. The presumed hardness of this problem is foundational for isogeny-based cryptography. The One Endomorphism problem only asks to find a single non-scalar endomorphism. We prove that these two problems are equivalent, under probabilistic polynomial time reductions.

We prove a number of consequences. First, assuming the hardness of the endomorphism ring problem, the Charles–Goren–Lauter hash function is collision resistant, and the SQIsign identification protocol is sound for uniformly random keys. Second, the endomorphism ring problem is equivalent to the problem of computing arbitrary isogenies between supersingular elliptic curves, a result previously known only for isogenies of smooth degree. Third, there exists an unconditional probabilistic algorithm to solve the endomorphism ring problem in time $\tilde{O}(p^{1/2})$, a result that previously required to assume the generalized Riemann hypothesis.

To prove our main result, we introduce a flexible framework for the study of isogeny graphs with additional information. We prove a general and easy-to-use rapid mixing theorem.

1 Introduction

The endomorphism ring problem lies at the foundation of isogeny-based cryptography. On one hand, its presumed hardness is necessary for the security of all cryptosystems of this family (see for instance the reductions in [Wes22a]). On the other hand, many cryptosystems of this family can be proven secure if this problem (or some variant) is hard (the earliest example being [CLG09]). Isogeny-based cryptography takes its name from the *isogeny problem*. An isogeny is a certain kind of map between two elliptic curves, and the isogeny problem consists in finding such a map, given the two curves. Formalising the meaning of "finding an isogeny" can lead to several versions of the isogeny problem, the most prominent being the *ℓ-isogeny path problem*. In isogeny-based cryptography, one typically restricts to supersingular elliptic curves, for which this problem is believed to be hard.

© International Association for Cryptologic Research 2024
M. Joye and G. Leander (Eds.): EUROCRYPT 2024, LNCS 14656, pp. 388–417, 2024.
https://doi.org/10.1007/978-3-031-58751-1_14

Fix a supersingular elliptic curve E. An endomorphism of E is an isogeny from E to itself (or the zero morphism). The collection of all endomorphisms of E forms the endomorphism ring $\mathrm{End}(E)$. The *supersingular endomorphism ring problem*, or ENDRING, consists in computing $\mathrm{End}(E)$, when given E. Assuming the generalised Riemann hypothesis, this problem is equivalent to the ℓ-isogeny path problem (see [Wes22b], and the earlier heuristic equivalence [EHL+18]), cementing its importance in the field.

The endomorphism ring contains scalars $\mathbf{Z} \subseteq \mathrm{End}(E)$, simple elements which are always easy to compute. While ENDRING asks to find all endomorphisms, it has long been believed that finding even a single non-scalar endomorphism is hard. We call this the *one endomorphism problem*, or ONEEND. Unfortunately, former heuristic arguments suggesting that ONEEND should be as hard as ENDRING do not withstand close scrutiny, and actually fail in simple cases. Yet, the connection between these two problems bears important consequences on the hardness of ENDRING, on its connection with variants of the isogeny problem, and on the security of cryptosystems such as the CGL hash function [CLG09] or the SQIsign digital signature scheme [DKL+20].

1.1   Contributions

In this article, we prove the following theorem.

Theorem 1.1. *The* ENDRING *and* ONEEND *problems are equivalent, under probabilistic polynomial time reductions.*

Formal definitions are provided in Sect. 2, and the proof is the object of Sect. 7. The reduction from ONEEND to ENDRING is obvious, and the other direction is stated more precisely in Theorem 7.2. This reduction transforms one instance of ENDRING into polynomially many instances of ONEEND.

As a consequence of the main theorem, we prove the following:

- If ENDRING is hard, then the CGL hash function is collision resistant (Theorem 8.1), and the SQIsign identification scheme is sound when the keys are indistinguishable from uniform (Theorem 8.2, expressed for RigorousSQIsignHD [DLRW23], a variant for which keys are proved to be statistically indistinguishable from uniform). Previous security proofs relied on the hardness of ONEEND (see [DKL+20, Theorem 1]), or on flawed heuristic reductions (see [EHL+18, Algorithm 8], and the flaws discussed Sect. 1.2). This is the object of Sect. 8.1 and Sect. 8.2.
- ENDRING reduces to the isogeny problem (Theorem 8.6). Here, the isogeny problem refers to the problem of finding *any* isogeny between two elliptic curves. Previous results [EHL+18, Wes22b] only applied to isogenies of smooth degree (like the ℓ-isogeny path problem), and were conditional on the generalised Riemann hypothesis. This is the object of Sect. 8.3.
- There is an algorithm solving ENDRING in expected time $\tilde{O}(p^{1/2})$ (Theorem 8.8), where $p > 0$ is the characteristic. Previous algorithms were conditional on the generalised Riemann hypothesis (via the conditional equivalence

with the ℓ-isogeny path problem [Wes22b]; see also [FIK+23, Theorem 5.7] for a more direct approach). Previous unconditional algorithms ran in time $\tilde{O}(p)$ and only returned a full-rank subring [Koh96, Theorem 75]. This is the object of Sect. 8.4.

Our main technical tool is an equidistribution result for isogeny walks in the graph of supersingular elliptic curves equipped with an endomorphism modulo N. In fact, we prove a more general equidistribution result generalising the classical one (see [Mes86, Piz90] and Proposition 2.7), which we think is of independent interest. We state this result informally here, referring the reader to the body of the paper for a formal statement.

Definition 1.2. *Equipping the set of supersingular elliptic curves with extra data consists in defining for each such curve E a finite set $\mathcal{F}(E)$, and for every isogeny $\varphi \colon E \to E'$ a map $\mathcal{F}(\varphi) \colon \mathcal{F}(E) \to \mathcal{F}(E')$, compatible under composition of isogenies (see Definitions 2.8 and 3.1). We obtain the isogeny graph $\mathcal{G}_{\mathcal{F}}$ of pairs (E, x) where $x \in \mathcal{F}(E)$ (see Definition 3.4).*

Let $N \geq 1$ be an integer. The extra data satisfies the (mod N)-congruence property if for every curve E, pairs of endomorphisms of E that are congruent modulo N act identically on $\mathcal{F}(E)$ (see Definition 3.7).

Our equidistribution result, stated informally, reads as follows.

Theorem 1.3. *Let $N \geq 1$ be an integer. Random walks in the isogeny graph of supersingular elliptic curves equipped with extra data satisfying the (mod N)-congruence property equidistribute optimally.*

We refer to Theorem 3.10 for a formal statement. The optimality refers to the fact that the graphs can be disconnected or multipartite, resulting in the adjacency matrix having several forced eigenvalues (see Proposition 3.11 and Remark 3.12), but all the remaining eigenvalues are as small as possible. A similar general result was recently proved by Codogni and Lido [CL23], so we point out some similarities and differences. In [CL23], the extra data needs to be expressed in terms of N-torsion points (a *level structure*), whereas we allow for extra data of arbitrary nature, only requiring it to satisfy a simple property (the (mod N)-congruence property). We hope that this makes our theorem flexible, and easy to use in a variety of situations. In particular, the extra data used in our main application trivially fits within our framework; in contrast, this data is not a level structure, so does not directly fit the framework of [CL23]. Moreover, we allow p to divide N, contrary to the results in [CL23]. Both proofs use Deligne's bounds, but the proof in [CL23] is purely algebro-geometric, whereas ours proceeds via the Deuring correspondence and the Jacquet–Langlands correspondence; as a result, the two proofs could have different interesting generalisations.

1.2   Technical Overview

The ideas behind our reduction are as follows. Assume we have an oracle $\mathcal{O}$ for ONEEND and we want to compute End(E) for a given E.

The ring $\text{End}(E)$ is a lattice of dimension 4 and volume $p/4$. Computing $\text{End}(E)$ consists in finding a basis: four endomorphisms that generate all the others. Given a collection of endomorphisms, one can compute the volume of the lattice they generate, and easily check whether they generate $\text{End}(E)$.

A First Flawed Attempt. We thus need a way to generate several endomorphisms of E. Naively, one could repeatedly call $\mathcal{O}(E)$, hoping to eventually obtain a generating set. This can fail, for instance if the oracle is deterministic and $\mathcal{O}(E)$ always returns the same endomorphism.

To circumvent this issue, it was proposed in [EHL+18] to randomise the curve. More precisely, one constructs a richer, randomised oracle $\text{RICH}^{\mathcal{O}}$ from $\mathcal{O}$ as follows. On input E, walk randomly on the 2-isogeny graph, resulting in an isogeny $\varphi \colon E \to E'$. This graph has rapid mixing properties, so E' is close to uniformly distributed among supersingular curves. Now, call the oracle $\mathcal{O}$ on E', to get an endomorphism $\beta \in \text{End}(E')$. The composition $\alpha = \hat{\varphi} \circ \beta \circ \varphi$ is an endomorphism of E, the output of $\text{RICH}^{\mathcal{O}}$.

With this randomisation, there is hope that calling $\text{RICH}^{\mathcal{O}}$ repeatedly on E could yield several independent endomorphisms that would eventually generate $\text{End}(E)$. This method is essentially [EHL+18, Algorithm 8]. In that article, it is heuristically assumed that endomorphisms produced by $\text{RICH}^{\mathcal{O}}$ are very nicely distributed, and they deduce that a generating set for $\text{End}(E)$ is rapidly obtained. This heuristic has a critical flaw: one can construct oracles that contradict it. Consider an integer $M > 1$, and suppose that for any input E, the oracle $\mathcal{O}$ returns an endomorphism from the strict subring $\mathbf{Z} + M\,\text{End}(E)$. Then, the above algorithm would fail, because the randomisation $\text{RICH}^{\mathcal{O}}$ would still be stuck within the subring $\mathbf{Z} + M\,\text{End}(E)$. Worse, juggling with several related integers M, we will see that there are oracles for which this algorithm only stabilises after an exponential time.

Identifying and Resolving Obstructions. The core of our method rests on the idea that this issue is, in essence, the only possible obstruction. The key is *invariance by conjugation*. If $\varphi, \varphi' \colon E \to E'$ are two random walks of the same length, and β is an endomorphism of $\text{End}(E')$, the elements $\alpha = \hat{\varphi} \circ \beta \circ \varphi$ and $\alpha' = \hat{\varphi}' \circ \beta \circ \varphi'$ are equally likely outputs of $\text{RICH}^{\mathcal{O}}$. These two elements are conjugates of each other in $\text{End}(E)/N\,\text{End}(E)$ for any odd integer N, as

$$\alpha = \frac{\hat{\varphi} \circ \varphi'}{[\deg(\varphi')]} \circ \alpha' \circ \frac{\hat{\varphi}' \circ \varphi}{[\deg(\varphi')]} \mod N.$$

From there, one can prove that the output of $\text{RICH}^{\mathcal{O}}$ follows a distribution that is invariant by conjugation: each output is as likely as any of its conjugates, modulo odd integers N (up to some bound). Intuitively, for the outputs of $\text{RICH}^{\mathcal{O}}$ to be "stuck" in a subring (such as $\mathbf{Z} + M\,\text{End}(E)$ above), that subring must itself be stable by conjugation (modulo odd integers N). There comes the next key: every subring of $\text{End}(E)$ (of finite index not divisible by p) stable by conjugation modulo all integers is of the form $\mathbf{Z} + M \operatorname{End}(E)$. From a basis of $\mathbf{Z} + M \operatorname{End}(E)$, it is easy to recover a basis of $\operatorname{End}(E)$ essentially by dividing by M (using a method due to Robert [Rob22] that stems from the attacks on SIDH).

This intuition does not immediately translate into an algorithm, as an oracle could be "bad" without really being stuck in a subring. Imagine an oracle that outputs an element of $\mathbf{Z} + 2^e \operatorname{End}(E)$ (and not in $\mathbf{Z} + 2^{e+1} \operatorname{End}(E)$) with probability 2^{e-n} for each $e \in [0, \ldots, n-1]$, for some integer n. A sequence of samples $(\alpha_i)_i$ could eventually generate $\operatorname{End}(E)$, but only after an amount of time exponential in n. This particular case could be resolved as follows: for each sample α, identify the largest e such that $\beta = (2\alpha - \operatorname{Tr}(\alpha))/2^e$ is an endomorphism. A sequence of samples $(\beta_i)_i$ could rapidly generate $\mathbf{Z} + 2 \operatorname{End}(E)$, from which one easily recovers $\operatorname{End}(E)$. This resolution first identifies the prime 2 as the source of the obstruction, then "reduces" each sample "at 2". In general, such obstructive primes would appear as factors of $\operatorname{disc}(\alpha)$. Identifying these primes, and ensuring that each sample is "reduced" at each of them, one gets, in principle, a complete algorithm. However, factoring $\operatorname{disc}(\alpha)$ could be hard. Instead, we implement an optimistic approach: we identify obstructive pseudo-primes using a polynomial time partial-factoring algorithm. The factors may still be composite, but it is fine: the algorithm will either behave as if they were prime, or reveal a new factor.

Equidistribution in Isogeny Graphs. The technical core of our result is the proof that the distribution of $\operatorname{RICH}^\theta$ is indeed invariant by conjugation. It is a consequence of Theorem 1.3, our general equidistribution result, whose proof proceeds as follows. We use a categorical version of the Deuring correspondence to bring everything to the quaternion world. We then use a technical result to show that extra data satisfying the congruence property yield graphs isomorphic to special ones constructed from quaternionic groups. Finally, these special graphs are directly related to automorphic forms, so we can apply the Jacquet–Langlands correspondence and Deligne's bounds on coefficients of modular forms. The resulting bounds on the adjacency operators is the desired result.

2 Preliminaries

2.1 Notation

We write $\mathbf{Z}$, $\mathbf{Q}$, $\mathbf{R}$ and $\mathbf{C}$ for the ring of integers, the fields of rational, real, and complex numbers. For any prime ℓ, we write $\mathbf{Z}_\ell$ and $\mathbf{Q}_\ell$ for the ring of ℓ-adic integers and the field of ℓ-adic numbers. For any prime power q, we write $\mathbf{F}_q$ for the finite field with q elements. For any field K, we write $\overline{K}$ for its algebraic closure. For any set S, we write $\#S$ for its cardinality. We write $f = O(g)$ for the classic big O notation, and equivalently $g = \Omega(f)$ for the classic Ω notation. We also write $f = \Theta(g)$ if we have both $f = O(g)$ and $f = \Omega(g)$. We use the soft O notation $\tilde{O}(g) = \log(g)^{O(1)} \cdot O(g)$. We also write $\operatorname{poly}(f_1, \ldots, f_n) =$

$(f_1 + \cdots + f_n)^{O(1)}$. The logarithm function log is in base 2. For any ring R, we write $R^\times$ the multiplicative group of invertible elements, and $M_2(R)$ the ring of 2×2 matrices with coefficients in R.

2.2 Quaternion Algebras

A general reference for this section is [Voi21]. A *quaternion algebra over* $\mathbf{Q}$ is a ring B having a $\mathbf{Q}$-basis $1, i, j, k$ satisfying the multiplication rules $i^2 = a$, $j^2 = b$ and $k = ij = -ji$, for some $a, b \in \mathbf{Q}^\times$. Let $w = x + yi + zj + tk \in B$. The *reduced trace* of w is $\mathrm{trd}(w) = 2x$. The *reduced norm* of w is $\mathrm{nrd}(w) = x^2 - ay^2 - bz^2 - abt^2$. The reduced norm map is multiplicative. A *lattice* in a $\mathbf{Q}$-vector space V of finite dimension d is a subgroup $L \subset V$ of rank d over $\mathbf{Z}$ and such that $V = L\mathbf{Q}$. The *discriminant* of a lattice L in B is $\mathrm{disc}(L) = \det(\mathrm{trd}(b_i b_j)) \neq 0$ where (b_i) is a $\mathbf{Z}$-basis of L. When $L' \subset L$ is a sublattice, we have $\mathrm{disc}(L') = [L : L']^2 \mathrm{disc}(L)$. An *order* in B is a subring $\mathcal{O} \subset B$ that is also a lattice. A *maximal order* is an order that is not properly contained in another order. The algebra B is *ramified at* ∞ if $B \otimes \mathbf{R} \not\cong M_2(\mathbf{R})$. Let ℓ be a prime number. The algebra B is *ramified at* ℓ if $B_\ell := B \otimes \mathbf{Q}_\ell \not\cong M_2(\mathbf{Q}_\ell)$. If ℓ is unramified and $\mathcal{O}$ a maximal order, then $\mathcal{O}_\ell := \mathcal{O} \otimes \mathbf{Z}_\ell \cong M_2(\mathbf{Z}_\ell)$. The discriminant of a maximal order in B is the square of the product of the ramified primes of B. When B is ramified at ∞, the quadratic form nrd is positive definite, and for every lattice L in B, the volume $\mathrm{Vol}(L)$ satisfies $\mathrm{disc}(L) = 16 \mathrm{Vol}(B)^2$.

2.3 Elliptic Curves

A general reference for this section is [Sil86]. An *elliptic curve* over a field K is a genus 1 projective curve with a specified base point O. An elliptic curve has a unique algebraic group law with neutral element O. An algebraic morphism between elliptic curves (preserving the base point) is automatically a group morphism, and is either constant or surjective. In the latter case, we say that it is an *isogeny*. The *degree* $\deg(\varphi)$ of an isogeny φ is its degree as a rational map. An isogeny of degree d is called a *d-isogeny*. For every integer $n \neq 0$, the multiplication-by-n map $[n] \colon E \to E$ is an isogeny of degree n^2. Every isogeny $\varphi \colon E \to E'$ has a *dual isogeny* $\hat{\varphi} \colon E' \to E$ such that $\varphi\hat{\varphi} = [\deg \varphi]$ and $\hat{\varphi}\varphi = [\deg \varphi]$. An *endomorphism* is a morphism $E \to E$. We denote $\mathrm{End}(E)$ the ring of endomorphisms of E defined over $\overline{K}$. The degree map is a positive definite quadratic form on $\mathrm{End}(E)$. For $\alpha \in \mathrm{End}(E)$, the endomorphism $\alpha + \hat{\alpha}$ equals the multiplication map by an integer, the *trace* $\mathrm{Tr}(\alpha)$ of α, and we have $\mathrm{Tr}(\alpha)^2 \leq 4 \deg(\alpha)$; we also define the *discriminant* $\mathrm{disc}(\alpha) = \mathrm{Tr}(\alpha)^2 - 4 \deg(\alpha)$, which satisfies $|\mathrm{disc}(\alpha)| \leq 4 \deg(\alpha)$ and $\mathrm{disc}(\alpha + [n]) = \mathrm{disc}(\alpha)$ for all $n \in \mathbf{Z}$. If the characteristic of K is not 2 or 3, we have $\mathrm{Aut}(E) = \{\pm 1\}$ for all E, except two isomorphism classes over $\overline{K}$ having respectively $\# \mathrm{Aut}(E) = 6$ and $\# \mathrm{Aut}(E) = 4$. Assume that K has positive characteristic p and let E be an elliptic curve over K. We say that E is *supersingular* if $\mathrm{End}(E)$ is an order in a quaternion algebra. In this case, $B = \mathrm{End}(E) \otimes \mathbf{Q}$ is a quaternion algebra over $\mathbf{Q}$ with ramification set $\{p, \infty\}$, the ring $\text{End}(E)$ is a maximal order in B, and E is defined over $\mathbf{F}_{p^2}$. When we see a nonzero endomorphism $\alpha \in \text{End}(E)$ as a quaternion $a \in B$, we have $\deg(\alpha) = \text{nrd}(a)$ and $\text{Tr}(\alpha) = \text{trd}(a)$.

2.4   Computing with Isogenies

Let us formalise how one can computationally encode isogenies. All we need is a notion of *efficient representation*: some data efficiently represents an isogeny if it allows to evaluate it efficiently on arbitrary inputs.

Definition 2.1 (Efficient representation). *Let $\mathscr{A}$ be an algorithm, and let $\varphi : E \to E'$ be an isogeny over a finite field $\mathbf{F}_q$. An efficient representation of φ (with respect to $\mathscr{A}$) is some data $D_\varphi \in \{0,1\}^*$ such that*

- *$D_\varphi \in \{0,1\}^*$ has size polynomial in $\log(\deg(\varphi))$ and $\log q$, and*
- *on input D_φ and $P \in E(\mathbf{F}_{q^k})$, the algorithm $\mathscr{A}$ returns $\varphi(P)$, and runs in polynomial time in $\log(\deg(\varphi))$, $\log q$, and k.*

Remark 2.2. When we say that an isogeny is in efficient representation, the algorithm $\mathscr{A}$ is often left implicit. There are only a handful of known algorithms to evaluate isogenies, so one can think of $\mathscr{A}$ as an algorithm that implements each of these, and D_φ would start with an indicator of which algorithm to use.

Proposition 2.3. *There is an algorithm* DIVIDE *which takes as input*

- *a supersingular elliptic curve $E/\mathbf{F}_{p^2}$,*
- *an endomorphism α of E in efficient representation, and*
- *an integer N,*

and returns an efficient representation of α/N if $\alpha \in N \text{End}(E)$, and $\perp$ otherwise, and runs in time polynomial in the length of the input.

Proof. This is the division algorithm introduced by Robert [Rob22] that was derived from the attacks on SIDH [CD23, MMP+23, Rob23]. Note that in [Rob22], the algorithm is only presented for particular endomorphisms (translates of the Frobenius), but it works, mostly unchanged, in all generality. The general statement and detailed proof can be found in [HLMW23]. □

2.5   Computational Problems

The endomorphism ring problem is the following.

Problem 2.4 (ENDRING). *Given a prime p and a supersingular elliptic curve E over $\mathbf{F}_{p^2}$, find four endomorphisms in efficient representation that form a basis of $\text{End}(E)$ as a lattice.*

As the endomorphism ring problem asks to find, in a sense, all the endomorphisms, it is natural to study the problem of finding even a single one. Scalar multiplications $[m]$ for $m \in \mathbf{Z}$ are trivial to find, so we exclude them.

Problem 2.5 (ONEEND). *Given a prime p and a supersingular elliptic curve E over $\mathbf{F}_{p^2}$, find an endomorphism in $\operatorname{End}(E) \setminus \mathbf{Z}$ in efficient representation.*

There exists arbitrarily large endomorphisms, so it is convenient to introduce a bounded version of this problem. Given a function $\lambda\colon \mathbf{Z}_{>0} \to \mathbf{Z}_{>0}$, the ONEEND$_\lambda$ problem denotes the ONEEND problem where the solution α is required to satisfy $\log(\deg \alpha) \le \lambda(\log p)$ (in other words, the length of the output is bounded by a function of the length of the input).

The ℓ-isogeny path problem is a standard problem in isogeny-based cryptography. Fix a prime ℓ. An ℓ-isogeny path is a sequence of isogenies of degree ℓ such that the target of each isogeny is the source of the next.

Problem 2.6 (ℓ-ISOGENYPATH). *Given a prime p and two supersingular elliptic curves E and E' over $\mathbf{F}_{p^2}$, find an ℓ-isogeny path from E to E'.*

2.6 Probabilities

Given a random variable X with values in a discrete set $\mathscr{X}$, we say it has distribution f if $f(x) = \Pr[X = x]$ for every $x \in \mathscr{X}$. We also write $f(A) = \sum_{x \in A} f(x)$ for any $A \subseteq \mathscr{X}$. For two distributions f_1 and f_2 over the same set $\mathscr{X}$, their *statistical distance* (or *total variation distance*) is

$$\frac{1}{2}\|f_1 - f_2\|_1 = \frac{1}{2}\sum_{x \in \mathscr{X}} |f_1(x) - f_2(x)| = \sup_{A \subseteq \mathscr{X}} |f_1(A) - f_2(A)|.$$

Random walks play a key role in isogeny-based cryptography. Fix a field $\mathbf{F}_{p^2}$ and a prime number $\ell \ne p$. The supersingular ℓ-isogeny graph has vertices the (finitely many) isomorphism classes of supersingular elliptic curves over $\mathbf{F}_{p^2}$, and edges are the ℓ-isogenies between them (up to isomorphism of the target). At the heart of the Charles–Goren–Lauter hash function [CLG09], one of the first isogeny-based constructions, lies the fact that random walks in supersingular ℓ-isogeny graphs have rapid-mixing properties: they are Ramanujan graphs. This is the following well-known proposition. It is a particular case of our more general Theorem 3.10.

Proposition 2.7. *Let E be a supersingular elliptic curve over $\mathbf{F}_{p^2}$, and $\ell \ne p$ a prime number. Let $\varepsilon > 0$. There is a bound $n = O(\log_\ell(p) - \log_\ell(\varepsilon))$ such that the endpoint of a uniform random walk of length at least n from E in the ℓ-isogeny graph is at statistical distance at most ε from the stationary distribution f, which satisfies $f(E) = \frac{24}{(p-1)\#\operatorname{Aut}(E)}$.*

Proof. This is a standard consequence of Pizer's proof that the supersingular ℓ-isogeny graph is Ramanujan [Piz90]. Details can be found, for instance, in [BCC+23, Theorem 11] for the length of the walk, and in [BCC+23, Theorem 7, Item 2] for the description of the stationary distribution. ☐

The stationary distribution is at statistical distance $O(1/p)$ of the uniform distribution. Note that rejection sampling allows to efficiently transform a sampler for the stationary distribution into a sampler for the uniform distribution.

2.7 Categories

A general reference for this section is [ML98]. A *category* $\mathcal{C}$ consists of objects, for every objects $x, y \in \mathcal{C}$, a set of morphisms $\mathrm{Hom}_{\mathcal{C}}(x, y)$, sometimes denoted $f: x \to y$, an associative composition law for morphisms with compatible source and target, and an identity morphism $\mathrm{id}_x \in \mathrm{Hom}_{\mathcal{C}}(x, x)$ for every object $x \in \mathcal{C}$. Let $\mathcal{C}, \mathcal{D}$ be categories. A *functor* $\mathcal{F}: \mathcal{C} \to \mathcal{D}$ is an association of an object $\mathcal{F}(x) \in \mathcal{D}$ for every object $x \in \mathcal{C}$, and of a morphism $\mathcal{F}(f): \mathcal{F}(x) \to \mathcal{F}(y)$ for every morphism $f: x \to y$ in $\mathcal{C}$, that respects composition[1] and identities.

Let Sets be the category of sets. The following is a standard construction.

Definition 2.8. *Let* $\mathcal{C}$ *be a category and* $\mathcal{F}: \mathcal{C} \to$ Sets *be a functor. The* category of elements $\mathrm{El}(\mathcal{F})$ *is the category with*

- *objects: pairs* (c, x) *where* $c \in \mathcal{C}$ *and* $x \in \mathcal{F}(c)$;
- *morphisms* $(c, x) \to (c', x')$: *morphisms* $f \in \mathrm{Hom}_{\mathcal{C}}(c, c')$ *s.t.* $\mathcal{F}(f)(x) = x'$.

Remark 2.9. One could also use the contravariant version of this definition. All our results would hold in this setting, as one can compose $\mathcal{F}$ with the isogeny duality to reverse the direction of all morphisms.

3 Equidistribution of Elliptic Curves with Extra Data

The goal of this section is to state Theorem 3.10, whose proof is available in the full version [PW23, Section 3].

3.1 Statement of the Equidistribution Theorem

In order to avoid bad primes, we will need to restrict the possible degrees of isogenies under consideration. Let Σ be a set of primes, and let $N \geq 1$ be an integer not divisible by any prime in Σ.

Definition 3.1. *Let* $\mathrm{SS}_{\Sigma}(p)$ *denote the category with*

- *objects: supersingular elliptic curves over* $\overline{\mathbf{F}}_p$;
- *morphisms* $\mathrm{Hom}_{\Sigma}(E, E')$: *isogenies with degree a product of the primes in* Σ.

When Σ is the set of all primes, we simply write $\mathrm{SS}(p)$.

Our results are expressed in terms of categories of elements of various functors, as in Definition 2.8. For us, this is going to play the role of "equipping with extra structure": when $\mathcal{F}: \mathcal{C} \to$ Sets is a functor, $\mathrm{El}(\mathcal{F})$ is the category of "objects $c \in \mathcal{C}$ with extra structure taken from $\mathcal{F}(c)$".

Example 3.2. Assume $p \nmid N$. Let Σ be the set of primes not dividing N. Define the functor $\mathrm{Cyc}_N: \mathrm{SS}_{\Sigma}(p) \to$ Sets by:

---

[1] All our functors are covariant.

- $\text{Cyc}_N(E)$ is the set of cyclic subgroups of order N of E;
- for every isogeny $\varphi \in \text{Hom}_\Sigma(E, E')$, the map $\text{Cyc}_N(\varphi)$ is $C \mapsto \varphi(C)$.

Then $\text{El}(\text{Cyc}_N)$ is the category of supersingular elliptic curves equipped with a cyclic subgroup of order N.

Example 3.3. Let Σ be the set of primes not dividing N. Let End/N denote the functor $\text{SS}_\Sigma(p) \to \text{Sets}$ defined by

- $(\text{End}/N)(E) = \text{End}(E)/N\,\text{End}(E)$;
- for $\varphi\colon E \to E'$, the map $(\text{End}/N)(\varphi)$ is $\alpha \mapsto \varphi\alpha\hat{\varphi}$.

Then $\text{El}(\text{End}/N)$ is the category of supersingular elliptic curves equipped with an endomorphism modulo N, which will play an important role in Sect. 4.

We now introduce the graphs of interest (more generally see Definition ??).

Definition 3.4. *Let* $\mathcal{F}\colon \text{SS}_\Sigma(p) \to \text{Sets}$ *be a functor with* $\mathcal{F}(E)$ *finite for all* E. *We define the graph* $\mathcal{G}_\mathcal{F}$ *with:*

- *vertices: isomorphism classes of objects in* $\text{El}(\mathcal{F})$;
- *edges: let* $(E, x) \in \text{El}(\mathcal{F})$; *edges from* (E, x) *are isogenies* $\varphi \in \text{Hom}_\Sigma(E, E')$ *modulo automorphisms of* $(E', \mathcal{F}(\varphi)(x))$.

Let $L^2(\mathcal{G}_\mathcal{F})$ *be the space of complex functions on vertices of* $\mathcal{G}_\mathcal{F}$, *and define*

$$\langle F, G \rangle = \sum_{(E,x) \in \mathcal{G}_\mathcal{F}} \frac{F(E,x)\overline{G(E,x)}}{\#\,\text{Aut}(E,x)} \text{ for } F, G \in L^2(\mathcal{G}_\mathcal{F}).$$

For every prime ℓ, *we define the adjacency operator* A_ℓ *on* $L^2(\mathcal{G}_\mathcal{F})$ *by*

$$A_\ell F(E,x) = \sum_{(E,x) \to (E',x')} F(E', x'),$$

where the sum runs over edges of degree ℓ *leaving* (E, x).

Remark 3.5. The graphs $\mathcal{G}_\mathcal{F}$ have finitely many vertices, but infinitely many edges.

Example 3.6. Assume $p \nmid N$, and let ℓ a prime not dividing Np. The graph obtained from $\mathcal{G}_{\text{Cyc}_N}$ by keeping only the edges of degree ℓ is the ℓ-isogeny graph of supersingular elliptic curves with Borel structure studied in [Arp23] and [BCC+23]. When $N = 1$ this is the classical supersingular ℓ-isogeny graph.

We are now in position to state our equidistribution theorem.

Definition 3.7. *Let* $\mathcal{F}\colon \text{SS}_\Sigma(p) \to \text{Sets}$ *be a functor and* $N \geq 1$ *an integer. We say that* $\mathcal{F}$ *satisfies the* (mod N)-*congruence property if for every* $E \in \text{SS}(p)$ *and every* $\varphi, \psi \in \text{End}_\Sigma(E)$ *such that* $\varphi - \psi \in N\,\text{End}(E)$, *we have* $\mathcal{F}(\varphi) = \mathcal{F}(\psi)$.

Example 3.8. Assume that p does not divide N. The functor Cyc_N from Example 3.2 satisfies the (mod N)-congruence property: indeed, endomorphisms divisible by N act as 0 on N-torsion points.

Example 3.9. The functor End/N from Example 3.3 has the (mod N)-congruence property: if $\varphi, \psi \in \text{End}_\Sigma(E)$ and $\alpha, \beta \in \text{End}(E)$ satisfy $\psi = \varphi + N\beta$, then $\psi\alpha\hat{\psi} = (\varphi + N\beta)\alpha(\hat{\varphi} + N\hat{\beta}) \in \varphi\alpha\hat{\varphi} + N\text{End}(E)$, so that $(\text{End}/N)(\varphi) = (\text{End}/N)(\psi)$.

Theorem 3.10. *Let p be a prime and $N \geq 1$ an integer. Let Σ be a set of primes that do not divide N, such that Σ generates $(\mathbf{Z}/N\mathbf{Z})^\times$. Let $\mathcal{F}\colon \text{SS}_\Sigma(p) \to \text{Sets}$ be a functor satisfying the (mod N)-congruence property and such that all sets $\mathcal{F}(E)$ are finite.*

Then, for every $\ell \in \Sigma$ different from p, the adjacency operator A_ℓ on $L^2(\mathcal{G}_\mathcal{F})$ commutes with its adjoint and stabilises the following subspaces:

- *$L^2_{\deg}(\mathcal{G}_\mathcal{F})$, the subspace of functions that are constant on every connected component of the graph $\mathcal{G}^1_\mathcal{F}$ obtained from $\mathcal{G}_\mathcal{F}$ by keeping only the edges of degree 1 mod N. For all $f \in L^2_{\deg}(\mathcal{G}_\mathcal{F})$ we have $\|A_\ell f\| \leq (\ell + 1) \cdot \|f\|$.*
- *$L^2_0(\mathcal{G}_\mathcal{F})$, the orthogonal complement of $L^2_{\deg}(\mathcal{G}_\mathcal{F})$. For all $f \in L^2_0(\mathcal{G}_\mathcal{F})$ we have $\|A_\ell f\| \leq 2\sqrt{\ell} \cdot \|f\|$.*

Moreover, the A_ℓ for $\ell \in \Sigma$ pairwise commute.

In other words, the normalised operator $A'_\ell = \frac{1}{\ell+1}A_\ell$ makes functions rapidly converge to the subspace $L^2_{\deg}(\mathcal{G}_\mathcal{F})$. This operator A'_ℓ preserves the subset of probability distributions, and closely relates to the effect of a random walk of ℓ-isogenies (see the full version [PW23, Appendix A.1]). In simple cases (such as $N = 1$), the space $L^2_{\deg}(\mathcal{G}_\mathcal{F})$ has dimension 1, is generated by the constant function 1 and the theorem says that random walks in ℓ-isogeny graphs rapidly converge to the unique stationary distribution f with $f(E, x)$ proportional to $\frac{1}{\#\text{Aut}(E,x)}$. One thus sees that the classical rapid-mixing property for isogeny graphs (Proposition 2.7) is a particular case of Theorem 3.10. More details and other illustrations of Theorem 3.10 are available in the full version [PW23, Appendix A].

In general $L^2_{\deg}(\mathcal{G}_\mathcal{F})$ could have higher dimension. This reflects the fact that the graph may be disconnected or multipartite, two obstructions for random walks to converge to a unique limit. To ease the application of Theorem 3.10 in such cases, we provide the following companion proposition that gives extra information on the graph $\mathcal{G}_\mathcal{F}$ and an explicit description of the space $L^2_{\deg}(\mathcal{G}_\mathcal{F})$.

Proposition 3.11. *With the same hypotheses and notations as in Theorem 3.10:*

(1) for every isogeny φ in $\text{SS}_\Sigma(p)$, the map $\mathcal{F}(\varphi)$ is a bijection;
(2) for every $E, E' \in \text{SS}(p)$, there exists $\varphi \in \text{Hom}_\Sigma(E, E')$ of degree 1 mod N;
(3) for every $E \in \text{SS}(p)$, the morphism $\text{End}_\Sigma(E) \to (\text{End}(E)/N\text{End}(E))^\times$ is surjective, inducing an action of $G = (\text{End}(E)/N\text{End}(E))^\times$ on $\mathcal{F}(E)$.

Let $x_1, \ldots, x_n$ denote representatives of the orbits of the action of G on $\mathcal{F}(E_0)$ and for each i, let H_i denote the stabiliser of x_i in G. Let $\mathcal{G}_{\deg}$ denote the graph with edges labelled by elements of $(\mathbf{Z}/N\,\mathbf{Z})^\times$ and with

- *vertex set $\bigsqcup_i (\mathbf{Z}/N\,\mathbf{Z})^\times / \deg(H_i)$;*
- *for every i, every $a \in (\mathbf{Z}/N\,\mathbf{Z})^\times / \deg(H_i)$ and every $d \in (\mathbf{Z}/N\,\mathbf{Z})^\times$, an edge $a \to b$ labelled by d, where $b = ad \in (\mathbf{Z}/N\,\mathbf{Z})^\times / \deg(H_i)$.*

Then:

(4) there exists a unique morphism of graphs $\mathrm{Deg}\colon \mathcal{G}_\mathcal{F} \longrightarrow \mathcal{G}_{\deg}$ such that for all i we have $\mathrm{Deg}(E_0, x_i) = 1 \in (\mathbf{Z}/N\,\mathbf{Z})^\times / \deg(H_i)$ and for every edge φ of $\mathcal{G}_\mathcal{F}$, the edge $\mathrm{Deg}(\varphi)$ is labelled by $\deg(\varphi) \bmod N$;
(5) the map Deg is surjective; and
(6) $L^2_{\deg}(\mathcal{G}_\mathcal{F})$ is the space of functions that factor through Deg.

Remark 3.12.

- When $p \nmid N$, Property (3) can be used to relate $\mathcal{F}$ to the setup of [CL23], using an isomorphism $G \cong \mathrm{GL}_2(\mathbf{Z}/N\,\mathbf{Z})$. When $p \mid N$, for any $E \in \mathrm{SS}(p)$, the group $(\mathrm{End}(E)/N\,\mathrm{End}(E))^\times$ is not isomorphic to $\mathrm{GL}_2(\mathbf{Z}/N\,\mathbf{Z})$.
- The graph $\mathcal{G}_{\deg}$ is the Cayley graph of the set $\bigsqcup_i (\mathbf{Z}/N\,\mathbf{Z})^\times / \deg(H_i)$ equipped with its natural action of $(\mathbf{Z}/N\,\mathbf{Z})^\times$.
- Property (4) amounts to stating the existence of a disconnectedness and a multipartition of $\mathcal{G}_\mathcal{F}$.
- Using Properties (5) and (6), one easily obtains the spectra of the adjacency operators A_ℓ on $L^2_{\deg}(\mathcal{G}_\mathcal{F})$: for every complex character χ of $(\mathbf{Z}/N\,\mathbf{Z})^\times$, one obtains the eigenvalue $\chi(\ell)(\ell + 1)$ with multiplicity equal to the number of i such that $\chi(\deg(H_i)) = 1$.
- From Proposition 3.11 and Theorem 3.10, since $2\sqrt{\ell} < \ell + 1$, one can simply deduce connectedness and multipartition properties of $\mathcal{G}_\mathcal{F}$, its degree ℓ subgraphs, etc. For instance, the graph $\mathcal{G}_\mathcal{F}$ has exactly n connected components: the preimages of the $(\mathbf{Z}/N\,\mathbf{Z})^\times / \deg(H_i)$ via the map Deg.

Example 3.13. Assume $p \nmid N$, let Σ denote the set of all primes that do not divide pN, and apply Theorem 3.10 and Proposition 3.11 to $\mathcal{F} = \mathrm{Cyc}_N$. Then we have an isomorphism $G \cong \mathrm{GL}_2(\mathbf{Z}/N\,\mathbf{Z})$ and a compatible bijection $\mathcal{F}(E) \cong \{\mathbf{Z}/N\,\mathbf{Z}\text{-lines in } (\mathbf{Z}/N\,\mathbf{Z})^2\}$. In particular, there is a single orbit $(n = 1)$ and, choosing x_1 corresponding to the line generated by $\binom{1}{0}$, the stabiliser $H = H_1$ corresponds to the subgroup of upper-triangular matrices, so that $\deg(H) = (\mathbf{Z}/N\,\mathbf{Z})^\times$. The space $L^2_{\deg}(\mathcal{G}_{\mathrm{Cyc}_N})$ is therefore one-dimensional, generated by the constant function 1. Hence Theorem 3.10 recovers [BCC+23, Theorem 8].

3.2   Proof of Theorem 3.10 and Proposition 3.11

The proof of these results is available in the full version [PW23, Section 3].

4   Enriching a ONEEND Oracle

In this section, we show how to turn an oracle for the ONEEND problem into a richer oracle with better distributed output. The quality of this enrichment is quantified in Theorem 4.2. The proof is an application of the equidistribution results of Sect. 3. The following lemma relates conjugation-invariance of distributions to the abstract setup of Sect. 3.

Lemma 4.1. *Let $p > 3$ be a prime, let $N \geq 1$ and let $E \in \mathrm{SS}(p)$. Let $g \in (\mathrm{End}(E)/N\,\mathrm{End}(E))^\times$ be an element of degree $1 \in (\mathbf{Z}/N\,\mathbf{Z})^\times$. Define the linear operator $c_g \colon L^2(\mathcal{G}_{\mathrm{End}/N}) \to L^2(\mathcal{G}_{\mathrm{End}/N})$ by*

$$c_g F(E, \alpha) = F(E, g\alpha g^{-1}) \text{ and } c_g F(E', \alpha') = F(E', \alpha') \text{ for all } E' \neq E.$$

Then:

(1) for all $F \in L^2(\mathcal{G}_{\mathrm{End}/N})$, we have $\|c_g F\|^2 \leq 3\|F\|^2$;
(2) for all $G \in L^2_{\mathrm{deg}}(\mathcal{G}_{\mathrm{End}/N})$, we have $c_g G = G$; and
(3) for every $F = F_0 + F_1 \in L^2(\mathcal{G}_{\mathrm{End}/N})$ with $F_0 \in L^2_0(\mathcal{G}_{\mathrm{End}/N})$ and $F_1 \in L^2_{\mathrm{deg}}(\mathcal{G}_{\mathrm{End}/N})$, we have $\|F - c_g F\| \leq (1 + \sqrt{3})\|F_0\|$.

Proof.

(1) Let $F \in L^2(\mathcal{G}_{\mathrm{End}/N})$. We have, where E' ranges over the set of supersingular curves up to isomorphism except E, the elements α and β range over $\mathrm{End}(E)/N\,\mathrm{End}(E)$ and α' over $\mathrm{End}(E')/N\,\mathrm{End}(E')$,

$$\|F\|^2 = \sum_{(E,\alpha)} \frac{1}{\#\mathrm{Aut}(E,\alpha)} |F(E,\alpha)|^2 + \sum_{(E',\alpha')} \frac{1}{\#\mathrm{Aut}(E',\alpha')} |F(E',\alpha')|^2,$$

and

$$\begin{aligned}
\|c_g F\|^2 &= \sum_{(E,\alpha)} \frac{|F(E, g\alpha g^{-1})|^2}{\#\mathrm{Aut}(E,\alpha)} + \sum_{(E',\alpha')} \frac{|F(E',\alpha')|^2}{\#\mathrm{Aut}(E',\alpha')} \\
&= \sum_{(E,\beta)} \frac{|F(E,\beta)|^2}{\#\mathrm{Aut}(E, g^{-1}\beta g)} + \sum_{(E',\alpha')} \frac{|F(E',\alpha')|^2}{\#\mathrm{Aut}(E',\alpha')} \\
&= \sum_{(E,\beta)} \frac{\#\mathrm{Aut}(E,\beta)}{\#\mathrm{Aut}(E, g^{-1}\beta g)} \frac{|F(E,\beta)|^2}{\#\mathrm{Aut}(E,\beta)} + \sum_{(E',\alpha')} \frac{|F(E',\alpha')|^2}{\#\mathrm{Aut}(E',\alpha')} \\
&\leq 3 \sum_{(E,\beta)} \frac{|F(E,\beta)|^2}{\#\mathrm{Aut}(E,\beta)} + \sum_{(E',\alpha')} \frac{|F(E',\alpha')|^2}{\#\mathrm{Aut}(E',\alpha')} \leq 3\|F\|^2,
\end{aligned}$$

where the inequality comes from $\#\mathrm{Aut}(E,\beta) \leq 6$ and $\#\mathrm{Aut}(E, g^{-1}\beta g) \geq 2$.

(2) Let $h \in \mathrm{End}_\Sigma(E)$ be a lift of g, which exists by Proposition 3.11 (3). Let $G \in L^2_{\mathrm{deg}}(\mathcal{G}_{\mathrm{End}/N})$. For every $E' \neq E$ we have $c_g G(E',\alpha) = G(E',\alpha)$. Moreover, h defines an edge $(E,\alpha) \to (E, h\alpha\hat{h}) = (E, h\alpha h^{-1})$ in $\mathcal{G}_{\mathrm{End}/N}$ of degree $1 \bmod N$, so $G(E,\alpha) = G(E, h\alpha h^{-1})$. Since $c_g G(E,\alpha) = G(E, g\alpha g^{-1}) = G(E, h\alpha h^{-1})$, this proves that $c_g G = G$.

(3) Let $F = F_0 + F_1 \in L^2(\mathcal{G}_{\text{End}/N})$ with $F_0 \in L_0^2(\mathcal{G}_{\text{End}/N})$ and $F_1 \in L_{\deg}^2(\mathcal{G}_{\text{End}/N})$. Then

$$\|F - c_g F\| \leq \|F_0 - c_g F_0\| + \|F_1 - c_g F_1\|$$
$$= \|F_0 - c_g F_0\| \text{ since } c_g F_1 = F_1 \text{ by (2)}$$
$$\leq (1 + \sqrt{3})\|F_0\| \text{ by (1)}.$$

$\square$

Algorithm 1. $\text{RICH}_k^{\mathcal{O}}$: turning an oracle $\mathcal{O}$ for ONEEND into a 'richer' oracle $\text{RICH}_k^{\mathcal{O}}$, with guarantees on the distribution of the output.

Require: A supersingular elliptic curve $E/\mathbf{F}_{p^2}$, and a parameter $k \in \mathbf{Z}_{>0}$. We suppose access to an oracle $\mathcal{O}$ that solves the *ProblemOneEnd* problem.
Ensure: An endomorphism $\alpha \in \text{End}(E)$.
1: $\varphi \leftarrow$ a 2-isogenies random walk of length k from E
2: $E' \leftarrow$ endpoint of φ
3: $\alpha \leftarrow \mathcal{O}(E')$, a non-scalar endomorphism of E'
4: **return** $\hat{\varphi} \circ \alpha \circ \varphi$

We can now prove the main result of this section.

Theorem 4.2. *Let $p > 3$ be a prime and N an odd integer. Let $\mathcal{O}$ be an oracle for ONEEND. Let E be a supersingular elliptic curve defined over $\mathbf{F}_{p^2}$ and let α be the random endomorphism produced by $\text{RICH}_k^{\mathcal{O}}(E)$. Then for every element $g \in (\text{End}(E)/N \text{End}(E))^\times$ of degree $1 \in (\mathbf{Z}/N\mathbf{Z})^\times$, the statistical distance between the distribution of $\alpha \bmod N$ and the distribution of $g^{-1}(\alpha \bmod N)g$ is at most $\frac{1+\sqrt{3}}{4}(\frac{2\sqrt{2}}{3})^k N^2 \sqrt{p+13} = O((\frac{2\sqrt{2}}{3})^k N^2 \sqrt{p})$.*

Proof. Define $F \in L^2(\mathcal{G}_{\text{End}/N})$ by the following formula for every vertex (E', β):

$$F(E', \beta) = \Pr[\mathcal{O}(E') \bmod N = \beta], \text{ so that}$$
$$\left(\frac{A_2}{3}\right)^k F(E, \beta) = \Pr[\text{RICH}_k^{\mathcal{O}}(E) \bmod N = 4^k \beta].$$

Indeed, $\left(\frac{A_2}{3}\right)^k F(E, \beta)$ is the average, over all random walks $\varphi \colon E \to E'$ that Algorithm 1 could follow from E, of $\Pr[\mathcal{O}(E') \bmod N = \varphi\beta\hat{\varphi}]$, and the equality $\mathcal{O}(E') \bmod N = \varphi\beta\hat{\varphi}$ is equivalent to $\hat{\varphi}\mathcal{O}(E')\varphi \bmod N = \deg(\varphi)\beta\deg(\hat{\varphi}) = 4^k\beta$ since 2 is invertible mod N.

We have, where E' ranges over isomorphism classes in $\mathrm{SS}(p)$ and β over the set $\mathrm{End}(E')/N\,\mathrm{End}(E')$,

$$\|F\|^2 = \sum_{(E',\beta)} \frac{1}{\#\,\mathrm{Aut}(E',\beta)} \Pr[\mathscr{O}(E') \bmod N = \beta]^2$$

$$\leq \frac{1}{2} \sum_{(E',\beta)} \Pr[\mathscr{O}(E') \bmod N = \beta]$$

$$= \frac{1}{2} \sum_{E'} 1 \leq \frac{p+13}{24} \quad \text{by [Sil86, Theorem 4.1 (c)].}$$

Write $F = F_0 + F_1$ with $F_0 \in L_0^2(\mathcal{G}_{\mathrm{End}/N})$ and $F_1 \in L_{\deg}^2(\mathcal{G}_{\mathrm{End}/N})$. Since A_2 preserves the orthogonal decomposition $L_0^2(\mathcal{G}_{\mathrm{End}/N}) \oplus L_{\deg}^2(\mathcal{G}_{\mathrm{End}/N})$, we may apply Lemma 4.1 (3) to $A_2^k F = A_2^k F_0 + A_2^k F_1$, giving $\|A_2^k F - c_g A_2^k F\| \leq (1+\sqrt{3})\|A_2^k F_0\|$. On the other hand, by Theorem 3.10 we have $\|(\frac{A_2}{3})^k F_0\| \leq (\frac{2\sqrt{2}}{3})^k \|F_0\| \leq (\frac{2\sqrt{2}}{3})^k \|F\|$. Finally, with β ranging over $\mathrm{End}(E)/N\,\mathrm{End}(E)$, the statistical distance in the statement of the theorem is

$$\frac{1}{2} \sum_{\beta} \left| \Pr[\mathrm{RICH}_k^{\mathscr{O}}(E) \bmod N = \beta] - \Pr[\mathrm{RICH}_k^{\mathscr{O}}(E) \bmod N = g\beta g^{-1}] \right|$$

$$= \frac{1}{2} \sum_{\beta} \left| \left(\frac{A_2}{3}\right)^k F(E, 4^{-k}\beta) - c_g \left(\frac{A_2}{3}\right)^k F(E, 4^{-k}\beta) \right|$$

$$= \frac{1}{2} \sum_{\beta} \left| \left(\frac{A_2}{3}\right)^k F(E, \beta) - c_g \left(\frac{A_2}{3}\right)^k F(E, \beta) \right| \quad \text{since } \beta \mapsto 4^k\beta \text{ is a bijection.}$$

By the Cauchy–Schwarz inequality, this is bounded by

$$\frac{1}{2} \left(N^4 \sum_{\beta} \left| \left(\frac{A_2}{3}\right)^k F(E, \beta) - c_g \left(\frac{A_2}{3}\right)^k F(E, \beta) \right|^2 \right)^{\frac{1}{2}}$$

$$\leq \frac{1}{2} N^2 \sqrt{6} \left\| \left(\frac{A_2}{3}\right)^k F - c_g \left(\frac{A_2}{3}\right)^k F \right\| \quad \text{since } \#\,\mathrm{Aut}(E, \beta) \leq 6$$

$$\leq \frac{1}{2}(1+\sqrt{3}) N^2 \sqrt{6} \left\| \left(\frac{A_2}{3}\right)^k F_0 \right\| \leq \frac{1}{2}(1+\sqrt{3}) \left(\frac{2\sqrt{2}}{3}\right)^k N^2 \sqrt{6} \|F\|$$

$$\leq \frac{1}{2}(1+\sqrt{3}) \left(\frac{2\sqrt{2}}{3}\right)^k N^2 \sqrt{6 \cdot \frac{p+13}{24}} = \frac{1}{4}(1+\sqrt{3}) \left(\frac{2\sqrt{2}}{3}\right)^k N^2 \sqrt{p+13},$$

as claimed. $\qquad\square$

5   On Conjugacy-Invariant Distributions

Theorem 4.2 proves that given a ONEEND oracle, the randomization method allows one to sample endomorphisms from a distribution which is (locally) invariant under conjugation by $(\mathrm{End}(E)/N\,\mathrm{End}(E))^\times$. In this section, we study such conjugacy-invariant distributions, and show that with good probability, such endomorphisms generate interesting suborders. In the whole section, fix B a quaternion algebra over $\mathbf{Q}$ and $\mathcal{O} \subset B$ a maximal order.

5.1   The Local Case

We start by studying the local case. Let ℓ be a prime unramified in B. In this subsection, we study distributions on $M_2(\mathbf{F}_\ell) \cong \mathcal{O}/\ell\mathcal{O}$ and $M_2(\mathbf{Z}_\ell) \cong \mathcal{O}_\ell$.

Definition 5.1. *The distribution of a random $\alpha \in M_2(\mathbf{F}_\ell)/\mathbf{F}_\ell$ is ε-close to $\mathrm{SL}_2(\mathbf{F}_\ell)$-invariant if, for every $g \in \mathrm{SL}_2(\mathbf{F}_\ell)$, the statistical distance between the distributions of α and of $g^{-1}\alpha g$ is at most ε. When the distributions are the same (i.e., $\varepsilon = 0$), we say that the distribution of α is $\mathrm{SL}_2(\mathbf{F}_\ell)$-invariant.*

A key observation is that a conjugacy class cannot be stuck in a subspace.

Lemma 5.2. *Suppose $\ell > 2$. Let $\alpha \in M_2(\mathbf{F}_\ell) \setminus \mathbf{F}_\ell$. Let $V \subsetneq M_2(\mathbf{F}_\ell)/\mathbf{F}_\ell$ be an $\mathbf{F}_\ell$-linear subspace. Let $\beta \in M_2(\mathbf{F}_\ell)$ be a random element uniformly distributed in the $\mathrm{SL}_2(\mathbf{F}_\ell)$-conjugacy class of α. Then, $\beta \in V$ with probability at most $1/2$.*

Proof. The size of the orbit X of α is $\#\,\mathrm{SL}_2(\mathbf{F}_\ell)/\#C$, where C is the centraliser of α in $\mathrm{SL}_2(\mathbf{F}_\ell)$. The size of this centraliser can be $\ell+1, \ell-1$ or 2ℓ, so $\#X \geq \frac{\ell^2-1}{2}$.

We now bound $\#(X \cap V)$ by noting that every element v of this intersection satisfies the quadratic equation $\mathrm{disc}(v) = \mathrm{disc}(\alpha)$. The discriminant quadratic form on $M_2(\mathbf{F}_\ell)/\mathbf{F}_\ell$ is isomorphic to $x^2 - yz$, so the maximal dimension of a totally isotropic subspace is 1. If $\dim V = 1$, the number of solutions is at most ℓ. If $\dim V = 2$, either the equation is degenerate and has at most 2ℓ solutions, or it represents a conic and has at most $\ell + 1$ solutions.

So the probability of $\beta \in V$ is at most $2\ell/\frac{\ell^2-1}{2} = \frac{4\ell}{\ell^2-1}$, which is less than $1/2$ for $\ell \geq 11$. We check the bound by bruteforce enumeration for $\ell \in \{3, 5, 7\}$. □

Lemma 5.3. *Suppose $\ell > 2$. Let $\alpha_1, \alpha_2, \alpha_3 \in M_2(\mathbf{F}_\ell)/\mathbf{F}_\ell$ be independent non-zero $\mathrm{SL}_2(\mathbf{F}_\ell)$-invariant elements. Then, $(\alpha_1, \alpha_2, \alpha_3)$ is a basis of $M_2(\mathbf{F}_\ell)/\mathbf{F}_\ell$ with probability at least $1/8$.*

Proof. Let $V_1 = \{0\}$ and $V_i = V_{i-1} + \mathbf{F}_\ell \cdot \alpha_i$. By dimensionality, we have $V_i \neq M_2(\mathbf{F}_\ell)/\mathbf{F}_\ell$ for every $i < 3$. Lemma 5.2 implies that with probability at least $1/8$, we have $\alpha_i \notin V_{i-1}$ for each $i \leq 3$. When this occurs, each V_i is an $\mathbf{F}_\ell$-vector space of dimension i, hence, $V_3 = M_2(\mathbf{F}_\ell)/\mathbf{F}_\ell$. □

In our application, we will only approach $\mathrm{SL}_2(\mathbf{F}_\ell)$-invariance, so we now derive the corresponding result for distributions that are close to $\mathrm{SL}_2(\mathbf{F}_\ell)$-invariant.

Proposition 5.4. *Suppose $\ell > 2$. Let $\alpha_1, \alpha_2, \alpha_3 \in M_2(\mathbf{F}_\ell)/\mathbf{F}_\ell$ be independent non-zero random elements which are ε-close to $\mathrm{SL}_2(\mathbf{F}_\ell)$-invariant. Then, $(\alpha_1, \alpha_2, \alpha_3)$ is a basis of $M_2(\mathbf{F}_\ell)/\mathbf{F}_\ell$ with probability at least $1/8 - 3\varepsilon$.*

Proof. Let $g_i \in SL_2(\mathbf{F}_\ell)$ be uniformly distributed and independent. Let $\beta_i = g_i^{-1}\alpha_i g_i$, three independent variables. For each i, the statistical distance between α_i and β_i is at most ε. By the triangle inequality, the statistical distance between $(\alpha_1, \alpha_2, \alpha_3)$ and $(\beta_1, \beta_2, \beta_3)$ is at most 3ε. From Lemma 5.3, $(\beta_1, \beta_2, \beta_3)$ is a basis of $M_2(\mathbf{F}_\ell)/\mathbf{F}_\ell$ with probability at least $1/8$. Therefore, $(\alpha_1, \alpha_2, \alpha_3)$ is a basis of $M_2(\mathbf{F}_\ell)/\mathbf{F}_\ell$ with probability at least $1/8 - 3\varepsilon$. $\qquad\square$

We now show that these results about $M_2(\mathbf{F}_\ell)$ have consequences in $M_2(\mathbf{Z}_\ell)$.

Definition 5.5. *The* level *of $\alpha \in M_2(\mathbf{Z}_\ell) \setminus \mathbf{Z}_\ell$ at ℓ is the largest integer $\mathrm{lev}_\ell(\alpha)$ such that $\alpha \in \mathbf{Z}_\ell + \ell^{\mathrm{lev}_\ell(\alpha)} M_2(\mathbf{Z}_\ell)$.*

Proposition 5.6. *Suppose $\ell > 2$. Let $\alpha_1, \alpha_2, \alpha_3 \in M_2(\mathbf{Z}_\ell) \setminus \mathbf{Z}_\ell$ be three elements of level a. Then $(1, \alpha_1, \alpha_2, \alpha_3)$ is a $\mathbf{Z}_\ell$-basis of $\mathbf{Z}_\ell + \ell^a M_2(\mathbf{Z}_\ell)$ if and only if $(\alpha_1, \alpha_2, \alpha_3)$ is an $\mathbf{F}_\ell$-basis of $(\mathbf{Z}_\ell + \ell^a M_2(\mathbf{Z}_\ell))/(\mathbf{Z}_\ell + \ell^{a+1} M_2(\mathbf{Z}_\ell)) \cong M_2(\mathbf{F}_\ell)/\mathbf{F}_\ell$.*

Proof. The forward implication is clear. The converse is Nakayama's lemma. $\quad\square$

5.2 Dealing with Hard-to-factor Numbers

In the previous section, we have studied the properties of conjugacy-invariant distributions locally at a prime ℓ. However, in our application, we may be confronted to local obstructions at an integer N which is hard to factor; it is then not possible to isolate the primes ℓ to apply the results of the previous section.

In this section, fix a positive integer N. We imagine that N is hard to factor, and rework the previous results *"locally at N"*. We suppose that B does not ramify at any prime factor of N. Recall that $\mathcal{O} \subset B$ is a maximal order.

Definition 5.7. *An element $\alpha \in \mathcal{O}$ is N-reduced if $\alpha \notin \mathbf{Z} + N\mathcal{O}$.*

Lemma 5.8. *Let $\alpha \in \mathcal{O}$ be a random variable supported on N-reduced elements. Then, there exist a prime factor ℓ of N and an integer a such that ℓ^{a+1} divides N and $\Pr[\mathrm{lev}_\ell(\alpha) = a] \geq (\log N)^{-1}$.*

Proof. Write the prime factorisation $N = \prod_{i=1}^{t} \ell_i^{e_i}$. Let i and $a < e_i$ which maximise the probability $q = \Pr[\mathrm{lev}_{\ell_i}(\alpha) = a]$. We have

$$\sum_{j=1}^{t} \Pr[\mathrm{lev}_{\ell_j}(\alpha) < e_j] = \sum_{\beta} \Pr[\alpha = \beta] \cdot \#\{j \mid \mathrm{lev}_{\ell_j}(\beta) < e_j\} \geq 1,$$

where the last inequality follows from the fact that the distribution is supported on N-reduced elements, so for every β, there exists j such that $\mathrm{lev}_{\ell_j}(\beta) < e_j$. We get

$$1 \leq \sum_{j=1}^{t} \Pr[\mathrm{lev}_{\ell_j}(\alpha) < e_j] = \sum_{j=1}^{t} \sum_{x < e_j} \Pr[\mathrm{lev}_{\ell_j}(\alpha) = x] \leq q \sum_{j=1}^{t} e_j \leq q \log(N).$$

We deduce $q \geq (\log N)^{-1}$. $\qquad\square$

Definition 5.9. *Let M be a ring with an isomorphism $\iota\colon M_2(\mathbf{Z}/N\,\mathbf{Z}) \to M$. The distribution of a random $\alpha \in M/\iota(\mathbf{Z}/N\,\mathbf{Z})$ is ε-close to $\mathrm{SL}_2(\mathbf{Z}/N\,\mathbf{Z})$-invariant if, for every $g \in \iota(\mathrm{SL}_2(\mathbf{Z}/N\,\mathbf{Z}))$, the statistical distance between the distributions of α and of $g^{-1}\alpha g$ is at most ε.*

Lemma 5.10. *Let $R = \mathbf{Z}/N\,\mathbf{Z}$, $M = \mathcal{O}/N\mathcal{O} \cong M_2(R)$ and $\overline{M} = M/R$. Let ℓ be a prime factor of N, and a an integer such that $\ell^{a+1} \mid N$. Consider a distribution ν on $\overline{M}$ that is ε-close to $\mathrm{SL}_2(R)$-invariant. For α sampled from ν, let q be the probability that $\alpha \neq 0$ and that a is the largest integer such that $\alpha \in \ell^a\overline{M}$.*

1. *Let $\alpha_1, \alpha_2, \alpha_3 \in \overline{M}$ independent random elements with distribution ν. Let Λ be the subgroup generated by $(\alpha_1, \alpha_2, \alpha_3)$. We have $\Lambda/\ell^{a+1}\overline{M} = \ell^a\overline{M}/\ell^{a+1}\overline{M}$ with probability at least $q^3/8 - 3\varepsilon$.*
2. *Let $\alpha_1, \alpha_2, \alpha_3 \in \mathcal{O}$ be independent random elements such that $\alpha_i \bmod \mathbf{Z}+N\mathcal{O}$ follows the distribution ν. Let Λ be the lattice generated by $(1, \alpha_1, \alpha_2, \alpha_3)$. Then $\Lambda \otimes \mathbf{Z}_\ell = (\mathbf{Z}+\ell^a\mathcal{O}) \otimes \mathbf{Z}_\ell$ with probability at least $q^3/8 - 3\varepsilon$.*

Proof. **Item 1, with $\varepsilon = 0$.** For any $\alpha \in M$, let $\mathrm{lev}_\ell(\alpha)$ be the largest integer such that $\alpha \in R + \ell^a M$ when it exists, and $\mathrm{lev}_\ell(\alpha) = \infty$ otherwise. Let L be the event that $\mathrm{lev}_\ell(\alpha_i) = a$ for all $i \in \{1, 2, 3\}$. Note that the level is constant over any $\mathrm{SL}_2(R)$-conjugacy class, so conditional on L, the variables α_i are still $\mathrm{SL}_2(R)$-invariant. If L occurs, the random variables $\alpha_i \bmod \ell^{a+1}\overline{M}$ are non-zero and $\mathrm{SL}_2(R)$-invariant in $\ell^a\overline{M}/\ell^{a+1}\overline{M} \cong M_2(\mathbf{F}_\ell)/\mathbf{F}_\ell$. The result follows from Lemma 5.3 and the fact that $\Pr[L] = q^3$.

Item 1, with $\varepsilon > 0$. By the triangular inequality, the triple $(\alpha_1, \alpha_2, \alpha_3)$ is 3ε-close to a triple of $\mathrm{SL}_2(\mathbf{Z}/N\,\mathbf{Z})$-invariant elements. The result thus follows from the case $\varepsilon = 0$ and the defining property of the statistical distance.

Item 2. This is the combination of Item 1 with Proposition 5.6. $\square$

Proposition 5.11. *Assume that N is not a cube. Let $\alpha_1, \alpha_2, \alpha_3 \in \mathcal{O}$ be three independent random elements from a distribution α that satisfies the following properties:*

(1) α is supported on N-reduced elements;
(2) $\alpha \bmod \mathbf{Z}+N\mathcal{O}$ is ε-close to $\mathrm{SL}_2(\mathbf{Z}/N\,\mathbf{Z})$-invariant for $\varepsilon < \frac{1}{6000000\cdot(\log N)^{12}}$.

Let Λ be the lattice generated by $(1, \alpha_1, \alpha_2, \alpha_3)$. With probability $\Omega\left((\log N)^{-12}\right)$, either $\gcd(N, [\mathcal{O} : \Lambda]) = 1$, or $[\mathcal{O} : \Lambda] = N^n K$ with $\gcd(N, K) \notin \{1, N\}$.

Remark 5.12. The exhibited event either produces a lattice Λ that is saturated at every prime factor of N (when $\gcd(N, [\mathcal{O} : \Lambda]) = 1$), or reveals a non-trivial factor of N.

Proof. Let Success be the event that either $\gcd(N, [\mathcal{O} : \Lambda]) = 1$, or $[\mathcal{O} : \Lambda] = N^n K$ where $\gcd(N, K) \notin \{1, N\}$. Write the prime factorisation $N = \prod_{i=1}^{t} \ell_i^{e_i}$. Since N is not a cube, we may assume without loss of generality that $\gcd(e_1, 3) = 1$. Write $\mathcal{O}_i = \mathcal{O} \otimes \mathbf{Z}_{\ell_i}$ and $\Lambda_i = \Lambda \otimes \mathbf{Z}_{\ell_i}$.

We now split the proof in two cases, depending on the value of

$$q_+ = \Pr[\mathrm{lev}_{\ell_1}(\alpha) \geq e_1].$$

Case 1: suppose $q_+^3 > 1 - \frac{1}{2}\left(\frac{1}{8\cdot(\log N)^3} - 3\varepsilon\right)$. Let ℓ_i and a_i be the ℓ and a from Lemma 5.8. Let $q = \Pr[\mathrm{lev}_{\ell_i}(\alpha) = a_i] > (\log N)^{-1}$. Let E be the event that $\Lambda_i = \mathbf{Z}_{\ell_i} + \ell_i^{a_i}\mathcal{O}_i$, and let F be the event that $\Lambda_1 \subseteq \mathbf{Z}_{\ell_1} + \ell_1^{e_1}\mathcal{O}_1$. Suppose E and F both happen. In that situation, $[\mathcal{O}_i : \Lambda_i] = \ell_i^{3a_i} < \ell_i^{3e_i}$, and $[\mathcal{O}_1 : \Lambda_1] \geq [\mathcal{O}_1 : \mathbf{Z}_{\ell_1} + \ell_1^{e_1}\mathcal{O}_1] \geq \ell_1^{3e_1}$, hence if $[\mathcal{O} : \Lambda] = N^n K$, then $\gcd(K, N) \notin \{1, N\}$. So if E and F both happen, then Success happens. We have

$$\Pr[F] = \Pr\left[\bigwedge_{j=1}^{3}(\mathrm{lev}_{\ell_1}(\alpha_j) \geq e_1)\right] = \prod_{j=1}^{3}\Pr\left[\mathrm{lev}_{\ell_1}(\alpha_i) \geq e_1\right] = q_+^3.$$

From Lemma 5.10, $\Pr[E] = q^3/8 - 3\varepsilon$. We deduce

$$\Pr[\mathsf{Success}] \geq \Pr[E \wedge F] \geq \Pr[E] + \Pr[F] - 1$$

$$= \frac{q^3}{8} - 3\varepsilon + q_+^3 - 1 \geq \frac{3}{2}\left(\frac{1}{24\cdot(\log N)^3} - \varepsilon\right) \geq \frac{1}{32\cdot(\log N)^3}.$$

Case 2: suppose $q_+^3 \leq 1 - \frac{1}{2}\left(\frac{1}{8\cdot(\log N)^3} - 3\varepsilon\right)$. Let $a_1 < e_1$ which maximises the probability $q = \Pr[\mathrm{lev}_{\ell_1}(\alpha) = a_1]$. We have $1 - q_+ = \sum_{x<e_1}\Pr[\mathrm{lev}_{\ell_1}(\alpha) = x] \leq e_1 q$. Then

$$q \geq \frac{1 - q_+}{\log(N)} \geq \frac{1 - q_+^3}{3\log(N)} \geq \frac{1}{48\cdot(\log N)^4} - \frac{\varepsilon}{2\log(N)}.$$

Let G be the event that $\Lambda_1 = \mathbf{Z}_{\ell_1} + \ell_1^{a_1}M_1$. If G happens and $[\mathcal{O} : \Lambda]$ is of the form $N^n K$ with $\gcd(N, K) = 1$, then $3a_1 = ne_1$. In that situation, $\gcd(e_1, 3) = 1$ implies that 3 divides n, and $a_1 < e_1$ implies that $n < 3$; together, these imply $n = 0$, so $\gcd(N, [\mathcal{O} : \Lambda]) = 1$. This proves that when G happens, then Success happens. We deduce

$$\Pr[\mathsf{Success}] \geq \Pr[G] \geq \frac{q^3}{8} - 3\varepsilon = \left(\frac{1}{96\cdot(\log N)^4} - \frac{\varepsilon}{4\log(N)}\right)^3 - 3\varepsilon$$

$$\geq 3\left(\frac{1}{3\cdot 100^3\cdot(\log N)^{12}} - \varepsilon\right) \geq \frac{1}{2000000\cdot(\log N)^{12}},$$

which concludes the proof. $\qquad\square$

6 Saturation and Reduction

In this section, we introduce three algorithms to saturate a known order of endomorphisms of a supersingular curve, and to reduce an endomorphism (in the sense of Definition 5.7). The overall strategy is folklore, but only a crucial new ingredient allows it to work in polynomial time: the division algorithm due to Robert [Rob22] (see Proposition 2.3).

Let us start with saturation, which is used to deal with problematic primes in the main reduction.

Proposition 6.1. *There exists an algorithm* SATURATE$_\ell$ *that takes as input a suborder R_0 of* End(E) *and a prime ℓ and returns an order $R \subset$ End(E) containing R_0 such that $[$End$(E) : R]$ is coprime to ℓ, and that runs in time polynomial in ℓ and the size of the input.*

Proof. The proof is available in the full version [PW23, Proposition 6.1].

Proposition 6.2. *There exists an algorithm* SATURATERAM *that takes as input a suborder R_0 of* End(E) *and returns an order $R \subset$ End(E) containing R_0 such that $[$End$(E) : R]$ is coprime to p, and that runs in polynomial time.*

Proof. The proof is available in the full version [PW23, Proposition 6.2].

We now present an algorithm to reduce endomorphisms at odd integers.

Algorithm 2. REDUCE$_N(\alpha)$: reduces an endomorphism α at N.

Require: An endomorphism $\alpha \in$ End$(E) \setminus \mathbf{Z}$ in efficient representation, and an odd integer N.
Ensure: An N-reduced endomorphism (Definition 5.7) $\beta = \frac{\alpha - t}{N^e}$ with $t, e \in \mathbf{Z}$.
1: $\gamma \leftarrow 2\alpha - \mathrm{Tr}(\alpha)$
2: **repeat**
3:     $\beta \leftarrow \gamma$
4:     $\gamma \leftarrow$ DIVIDE(β, N) an efficient representation of β/N {Proposition 2.3}
5: **until** $\gamma = \perp$
6: **if** $\mathrm{Tr}(\alpha) \equiv 0 \mod 2$ **then**
7:     **return** DIVIDE$(\beta, 2)$
8: **else**
9:     **return** DIVIDE$(\beta + 1, 2)$
10: **end if**

Proposition 6.3. *Algorithm 2 (*REDUCE$_N$*) is correct and runs in polynomial time.*

Proof. Let e be the largest integer such that $\alpha \in \mathbf{Z} + N^e$ End(E). At Step 1, we have that $\gamma \in N^e$ End(E) and $\gamma \notin \mathbf{Z} + N^{e+1}$ End(E). Therefore, at the end of the loop, $\beta \in$ End(E) and $\beta \notin \mathbf{Z} + N$ End(E), i.e., β is N-reduced. The last division removes the extra factor 2 introduced in Step 1, to ensure the result is of the form $\beta = \frac{\alpha - t}{N^e}$ with $t \in \mathbf{Z}$.

Let us prove that it runs in polynomial time. We have $N^{2e} \mid \mathrm{disc}(\alpha)$, and at each iteration of the loop, $\mathrm{disc}(\beta)$ gets divided by N^2. So the number of iterations is bounded by $e \leq \log(\mathrm{disc}(\alpha)) = O(\log \deg(\alpha))$, which concludes the proof. $\square$

7   The Reduction

In this section, we prove the main result of the paper (Theorem 1.1). We start with a lemma putting together results from the previous sections.

Algorithm 3. Turning an oracle $\mathcal{O}$ for ONEEND into an ENDRING algorithm

---

Require: A supersingular elliptic curve $E/\mathbf{F}_{p^2}$, and a parameter $k > 0$. We suppose access to an oracle $\mathcal{O}$ that solves the *ProblemOneEnd* problem.

Ensure: The endomorphism ring $\mathrm{End}(E)$.

1: $k_1 \leftarrow \left\lceil \frac{\log\left(12 \cdot 9 \cdot (1+\sqrt{3}) \cdot \sqrt{p+13}\right)}{\log\left(\frac{3}{2\sqrt{2}}\right)} \right\rceil$

2: $R \leftarrow \mathbf{Z}$

3: **while** $\mathrm{rank}_\mathbf{Z}(R) \neq 4$ **do**

4:     $\alpha \leftarrow \mathrm{RICH}_{k_1}^{\mathcal{O}}(E)$, a random endomorphism of E {Algorithm 1}

5:     $R \leftarrow$ the ring generated by R and α

6: **end while**

7: $R \leftarrow \mathrm{SATURATE}_2(R)$ {Proposition 6.1}

8: $R \leftarrow \mathrm{SATURATERAM}(R)$ {Proposition 6.2}

9: $[\mathrm{End}(E) : R] \leftarrow \sqrt{\mathrm{disc}(R)}/p$

10: Factor $[\mathrm{End}(E) : R] = \prod_{i=1}^{t} N_i^{e_i}$ where no N_i is a cube {a complete prime factorisation is not required; the somewhat trivial factorisation $[\mathrm{End}(E) : R] = N_1^{3^n}$ where $N_1^{1/3} \notin \mathbf{Z}$ and $n \geq 0$ is sufficient as a starting point, and the subsequent steps of the algorithm may refine it}

11: **while** $[\mathrm{End}(E) : R] \neq 1$ **do**

12:     $N \leftarrow N_t$

13:     $k_2 \leftarrow \left\lceil 12 \cdot \log\left(4100000 \cdot (\log N)^{12} N^2 \sqrt{p+13}\right)\right\rceil$

14:     Let $\mathcal{O}_N$ the oracle which given E, runs $\alpha \leftarrow \mathcal{O}(E)$ and returns $\mathrm{REDUCE}_N(\alpha)$

15:     $\alpha_i \leftarrow \mathrm{RICH}_{k_2}^{\mathcal{O}_N}(E)$ for $i \in \{1, 2, 3\}$, random endomorphisms of E {Algorithm 1}

16:     $\Lambda \leftarrow$ the lattice generated by $(1, \alpha_1, \alpha_2, \alpha_3)$

17:     **if** $\mathrm{rank}_\mathbf{Z}(\Lambda) = 4$ **then**

18:         $n \leftarrow$ the largest integer such that N^n divides $[\mathrm{End}(E) : \Lambda]$

19:         $d \leftarrow \gcd([\mathrm{End}(E) : \Lambda]/N^n, N)$

20:         **if** $d \neq 1$ **then**

21:             Update the factorisation of $[\mathrm{End}(E) : R]$ with $N = d \cdot (N/d)$

22:         **end if**

23:         **if** $\Lambda \not\subset R$ **then**

24:             $R \leftarrow$ the order generated by R and Λ

25:             Recompute $[\mathrm{End}(E) : R] = \sqrt{\mathrm{disc}(R)}/p$, and update its factorisation

26:         **end if**

27:     **end if**

28: **end while**

29: **return** R

Lemma 7.1. *Let $\mathcal{O}$ be an oracle for* ONEEND*, and N an odd integer. Let $\mathcal{O}_N$ be the oracle which on input E, samples $\alpha \leftarrow \mathcal{O}(E)$, and returns* $\mathrm{REDUCE}_N(\alpha)$.

For any

$$k \geq 12 \cdot \log \left(4100000 \cdot (\log N)^{12} N^2 \sqrt{p + 13} \right),$$

the output of $\mathrm{RICH}_k^{\mathscr{O}_N}$ *satisfies the conditions of Proposition 5.11.*

Proof. Let $\varphi \colon E \to E'$ of degree a power of 2. For any endomorphism $\beta \in \mathrm{End}(E')$, since N is odd, we have that β is N-reduced if and only if $\hat{\varphi} \circ \beta \circ \varphi$ is N-reduced. The output of $\mathrm{RICH}_k^{\mathscr{O}_N}$ is of the form $\hat{\varphi} \circ \mathrm{REDUCE}_N(\alpha) \circ \varphi$, so is N-reduced. So the distribution of $\mathrm{RICH}_k^{\mathscr{O}_N}$ satisfies Item 1 of Proposition 5.11.

From Theorem 4.2, $\mathrm{RICH}_k^{\mathscr{O}_N}$ mod N is ε-close to $\mathrm{SL}_2(\mathbf{Z}/N\,\mathbf{Z})$-invariant for

$$\varepsilon = \frac{1 + \sqrt{3}}{4} \left(\frac{2\sqrt{2}}{3} \right)^k N^2 \sqrt{p + 13}.$$

With $k \geq \log \left(6000000 \cdot (\log N)^{12} \cdot \frac{1+\sqrt{3}}{4} N^2 \sqrt{p+13} \right) / \log \left(\frac{3}{2\sqrt{2}} \right)$, we have $\varepsilon \leq (6000000 \cdot (\log N)^{12})^{-1}$, satisfying Item 2 of Proposition 5.11.   □

We now have all the ingredients to prove our main result.

Theorem 7.2 (ENDRING **reduces to** ONEEND). *Algorithm 3 is a reduction from* ENDRING *to* ONEEND$_\lambda$ *of expected polynomial time in* $\log(p)$ *and* $\lambda(\log p)$.

Proof. The correctness is clear as at any time, R is a subring of $\mathrm{End}(E)$, and the success condition $[\mathrm{End}(E) : R] = 1$ implies $R = \mathrm{End}(E)$.

We now analyse the expected running time.

First loop (Step 3 to Step 6). First, let us analyse the expected number of iterations of the first loop. From Theorem 4.2, each α generated during this loop is ε-close to $\mathrm{SL}_2(\mathbf{F}_3)$-invariant with $\varepsilon = \frac{1+\sqrt{3}}{4} \left(\frac{2\sqrt{2}}{3} \right)^{k_1} 3^2 \sqrt{p + 13}$. Choosing $k_1 = O(\log p)$ as in Step 1, we have $\varepsilon \leq 1/48$.

Consider any three consecutively generated elements $\alpha_1, \alpha_2, \alpha_3$. Let $t = \max_i \mathrm{lev}_3(\alpha_i)$, and $\beta_i = 3^{t - \mathrm{lev}_3(\alpha_i)} \alpha_i$, so all β_i are at the same level t. Like the variables α_i, the variables β_i are ε-close to $\mathrm{SL}_2(\mathbf{F}_3)$-invariant. Combining Proposition 5.4 and Proposition 5.6, the tuple $(1, \beta_1, \beta_2, \beta_3)$ generates a full-rank lattice with probability at least $1/8 - 3\varepsilon$, and so does $(1, \alpha_1, \alpha_2, \alpha_3)$. Choosing k_1 as above, this probability is at least $1/16$. We deduce that the loop terminates after an expected $O(1)$ number of iterations.

Let us now analyse the output of this loop. Let R_1 be the order R obtained at the end of the first loop. Let α_i be any three elements generated during the loop such that $(1, \alpha_1, \alpha_2, \alpha_3)$ are independent. Combining the bound $\deg(\alpha_i) \leq 2^{2k_1 \lambda(\log p)}$ and Hadamard's inequality, we get

$$\mathrm{disc}(R_1) = 16 \cdot \mathrm{Vol}(R_1)^2 \leq 16 \cdot \prod_{i=1}^{3} \sqrt{\deg(\alpha_i)} \leq 16 \cdot 2^{6k_1 \lambda(\log p)}.$$

We deduce that

$$[\text{End}(E) : R_1] \leq 2^{3k_1\lambda(\log p)+2}/p = 2^{O(\log(p)\cdot\lambda(\log p))}. \tag{1}$$

Second loop (Step 11 to Step 28). It remains to analyse the second loop. An iteration of this loop is a *success* if either Step 21 or Step 24 is reached. In case of success, either a new factor of $[\text{End}(E) : R]$ is found (Step 21), or $[\text{End}(E) : R]$ gets divided by an integer at least 2 (Step 24). The number of successes is thus polynomially bounded in $\log([\text{End}(E) : R_1])$, hence in $\text{poly}(\log p, \lambda(\log p))$ (thanks to Eq. (1)). Therefore, we only have to prove that as long as $R \neq \text{End}(E)$, each iteration has a good probability of success.

The event analysed in Proposition 5.11 corresponds precisely to a success. By Lemma 7.1, the distribution of α_i satisfies the conditions of Proposition 5.11. Therefore, Proposition 5.11 implies that each iteration has a probability of success $\Omega((\log N)^{-12})$, which concludes the proof. □

8 Applications

In this section we describe four applications of our main result.

8.1 Collision Resistance of the Charles–Goren–Lauter Hash Function

The first cryptographic construction based on the supersingular isogeny problem is a hash function proposed by Charles, Goren and Lauter [CLG09], the *CGL hash function*. Fix a (small) prime number ℓ, typically $\ell = 2$. For any elliptic curve E, there are $\ell + 1$ outgoing ℓ-isogenies $E \to E'$ (up to isomorphism of the target), so given a curve and an incoming $E'' \to E$, there remain ℓ non-backtracking ℓ-isogenies from E, which can be arbitrarily labelled by the set $\{0,\ldots,\ell-1\}$. Then, fixing an initial curve E_0 and an arbitrary isogeny $E_{-1} \to E_0$, the set $\{0,\ldots,\ell-1\}^*$ encodes non-backtracking paths from E_0 in the ℓ-isogeny graph. The CGL hash function

$$\text{CGL}_{E_0} : \{0,\ldots,\ell-1\}^* \longrightarrow \mathbf{F}_{p^2}$$

associates to any sequence $(x_i)_i$ the j-invariant of the endpoint of the walk from E_0 it encodes. Clearly, this function is pre-image resistant if and only if ℓ-IsogenyPath is hard. However, if $\text{End}(E_0)$ is known, one can find collisions in polynomial time [KLPT14,EHL+18]. Therefore, it was proposed to sample the starting curve randomly. Let $\text{SampleSS}(p)$ be an algorithm sampling a uniformly random supersingular elliptic curve over $\mathbf{F}_{p^2}$. We define the advantage of a collision-finding algorithm $\mathscr{A}$ for the CGL family of hash functions as

$$\text{Adv}^{\mathscr{A}}_{\text{CGL}}(p) = \Pr\left[\begin{array}{c|c} m \neq m' \text{ and} & E \leftarrow \text{SampleSS}(p) \\ \text{CGL}_E(m) = \text{CGL}_E(m') & (m, m') \leftarrow \mathscr{A}(E) \end{array}\right].$$

It was heuristically argued in [EHL+18] that the collision resistance of this construction is equivalent to EndRing. The flaws of the heuristics are discussed in Sect. 1.2. With our main theorem, we can now prove this resistance.

Theorem 8.1 (Collision resistance of the CGL hash function). *For any algorithm $\mathscr{A}$, there is an algorithm to solve* ENDRING *in expected polynomial time in* $\log(p)$, *in* $\mathrm{Adv}_{\mathrm{CGL}}^{\mathscr{A}}(p)^{-1}$ *and in the expected running time of* $\mathscr{A}$.

Proof. Since ENDRING is equivalent to ONEEND (Theorem 1.1), it is sufficient to prove that $\mathscr{A}$ can be used to solve ONEEND. First, let us prove that a successful collision for CGL_E gives a non-scalar endomorphism of E. Let $\varphi, \psi \colon E \to E'$ be two distinct non-backtracking walks, i.e., isogenies of cyclic kernel of order ℓ^a and ℓ^b respectively. If $\hat{\varphi} \circ \psi$ is scalar, the degrees imply that $a + b$ is even and $\hat{\varphi} \circ \psi = [\ell^{\frac{a+b}{2}}]$. Without loss of generality, suppose $b \geq a$. From the defining property of the dual isogeny, we deduce that $\hat{\psi} = [\ell^{\frac{b-a}{2}}]\hat{\varphi}$. Taking the dual again, we get $\psi = [\ell^{\frac{b-a}{2}}]\varphi$. If $b > a$, then $\{0_E\} \neq E[\ell^{\frac{b-a}{2}}] \subseteq \ker \psi$, contradicting the cyclicity of $\ker \psi$. Therefore $b = a$, and we conclude that $\psi = \varphi$, a contradiction. So $\hat{\varphi} \circ \psi$ is non-scalar.

Now, given a curve E, we can solve ONEEND as follows:

1. First take a random walk $\eta \colon E \to E'$, so that E' has statistical distance $\varepsilon = O(1/p)$ from uniform (Proposition 2.7);
2. Then call $\mathscr{A}(E')$, which gives a non-scalar endomorphism α of E' with probability at least $\mathrm{Adv}_{\mathrm{CGL}}^{\mathscr{A}}(p) - \varepsilon$,
3. Return $\hat{\eta} \circ \alpha \circ \eta$.

The algorithm is successful after an expected $(\mathrm{Adv}_{\mathrm{CGL}}^{\mathscr{A}}(p) - \varepsilon)^{-1}$ number of attempts. This works within the claimed running time if $\mathrm{Adv}_{\mathrm{CGL}}^{\mathscr{A}}(p) > 2\varepsilon$. Otherwise, we have $(\mathrm{Adv}_{\mathrm{CGL}}^{\mathscr{A}}(p))^{-1} = \Omega(p)$, and one can indeed solve ENDRING in time polynomial in p (see [Koh96, Theorem 75] for the first such algorithm, in time $\tilde{O}(p)$, or Theorem 8.8 below for time $\tilde{O}(p^{1/2})$). □

8.2 Soundness of the SQIsign Identification Scheme

SQIsign is a digital signature scheme proposed in [DKL+20]. SQIsign and its variants offer the most compact public keys and signatures of all known post-quantum constructions.

Each digital signature scheme in this family is constructed as an identification protocol, turned into a signature by the Fiat–Shamir transform. The protocol proves knowledge of a witness for a problem that closely resembles ONEEND. While [DKL+20] or [DLRW23] heuristically argue that the protocol is sound if ENDRING is hard, our main theorem provides a way to prove it.

Among the several variants of SQIsign, we illustrate our result on RigorousSQIsignHD [DLRW23], which currently benefits from the cleanest security arguments. Note that the method could be applied to each variant, but the resulting statements may vary. In particular, a version of Theorem 8.2 below holds for the original SQIsign design if we assume that public keys are computationally indistinguishable from the uniform distribution on supersingular elliptic curves.

Let SQISIGNHD.PARAM be the RigorousSQIsignHD public parameter generation procedure, which on input a security level k, outputs data pp which encodes, among other things, a prime number $p = \Theta(2^{2k})$. Let SQISIGNHD.KEYGEN be the RigorousSQIsignHD key generation procedure, which on input pp, outputs a pair (pk, sk). The public key pk is a supersingular elliptic curve over $\mathbf{F}_{p^2}$, and sk is its endomorphism ring. The random elliptic curve pk is at statistical distance $\tilde{O}(p^{-1/2})$ from uniform [DLRW23, Appendix B.2].

Let $\mathscr{V}$ be a honest verifier for the RigorousSQIsignHD identification protocol. For any (malicious) prover $\mathscr{P}^*$ and parameters pp, run the following experiment: first, sample a key pair (pk, sk) $\leftarrow$ SQISIGNHD.KEYGEN(pp), and give pk to $\mathscr{P}^*$. Then, run the RigorousSQIsignHD identification protocol between $\mathscr{P}^*$ and $\mathscr{V}$ with input pk. Let $\pi^{\mathscr{P}^*}(\mathsf{pp})$ be the probability that $\mathscr{V}$ outputs $\top$ at the end of the protocol. We define the *soundness advantage* $\mathrm{Adv}^{\mathscr{P}^*}_{\mathrm{SQIsound}}(\mathsf{pp}) = \pi^{\mathscr{P}^*}(\mathsf{pp}) - 1/c$, where $c = \Theta(2^k)$ is the size of the challenge space.

In other words, $\pi^{\mathscr{P}^*}(\mathsf{pp})$ is the probability that $\mathscr{P}^*$ successfully fools a honest verifier, for a random key. Since there is a simple malicious prover achieving $\pi^{\mathscr{P}^*}(\mathsf{pp}) = 1/c$ (by guessing the challenge at the start of the protocol), the advantage $\mathrm{Adv}^{\mathscr{P}^*}_{\mathrm{SQIsound}}(\mathsf{pp})$ measures how much better $\mathscr{P}^*$ performs.

Theorem 8.2 (Soundness of RigorousSQIsignHD). *Let $\mathscr{P}^*$ be a malicious prover. Consider public parameters pp, encoding the prime p. There is an algorithm to solve* ENDRING *for curves over $\mathbf{F}_{p^2}$ in expected polynomial time in* $\log(p)$, *in* $\mathrm{Adv}^{\mathscr{P}^*}_{\mathrm{SQIsound}}(\mathsf{pp})^{-1}$ *and in the expected running time of $\mathscr{P}^*$.*

Proof. Let r denote the expected running time of $\mathscr{P}^*$. Let $\pi^{\mathscr{P}^*}(\mathsf{pp}, E)$ be the probability that $\mathscr{V}$ outputs $\top$ at the end of the protocol given that pk $= E$. For simplicity, we write $\pi = \pi^{\mathscr{P}^*}(\mathsf{pp})$ and $\pi_E = \pi^{\mathscr{P}^*}(\mathsf{pp}, E)$. Let $\varepsilon_{\mathsf{pk}} = \tilde{O}(p^{-1/2})$ be the statistical distance of pk from uniform.

As mentionned in the proof of Theorem 8.1, one can solve ENDRING in time polynomial in p (see [Koh96, Theorem 75], or Theorem 8.8 below), so we may assume that $\mathrm{Adv}^{\mathscr{P}^*}_{\mathrm{SQIsound}}(\mathsf{pp}) > 2/c + 4\varepsilon_{\mathsf{pk}} = \tilde{O}(p^{-1/2})$. In particular, we have $\pi > 3/c$, and $\pi > 4\varepsilon_{\mathsf{pk}}$.

From [DLRW23, Proposition D.1.7], RigorousSQIsignHD is a proof of knowledge with soundness error $1/c$ for the relation $\{(E, \alpha) \mid \alpha \in \mathrm{End}(E) \setminus \mathbf{Z}\}$ (and witnesses of size $O(\log p)$), hence, whenever $\pi_E > 1/c$, there is an algorithm which solves ONEEND on E with expected running time $R(E) = O\left(\frac{r}{\pi_E - 1/c}\right)$. We get an algorithm for ONEEND on arbitrary input E as follows:

1. First take a random walk $\eta \colon E \to E'$, so that E' has statistical distance $\varepsilon = O(1/p^2)$ from uniform (Proposition 2.7);
2. Run the above algorithm for ONEEND on input E', which has expected time $R(E')$ (if $\pi_{E'} > 1/c$). Upon termination, go to the step 3. While this runs, repeat from step (1) in a new concurrent session.
3. When one of the concurrent sessions terminates, say with $\eta \colon E \to E'$ and $\alpha \in \mathrm{End}(E')$, stop all other sessions, and return $\hat{\eta} \circ \alpha \circ \eta$.

The purpose of running concurrent sessions is that any single E' is not guaranteed to terminate. Let $X = \{E \mid \pi_E \geq \pi/2\} \subseteq \{E \mid \pi_E > 1/c\}$. We have

$$\pi \leq \Pr[\mathsf{pk} \in X] + \Pr[\mathsf{pk} \notin X]\frac{\pi}{2} = \left(1 - \frac{\pi}{2}\right)\Pr[\mathsf{pk} \in X] + \frac{\pi}{2},$$

hence $\Pr[\mathsf{pk} \in X] \geq \frac{\pi - \pi/2}{1 - \pi/2} \geq \pi/2$. Therefore, the curve E' generated in step 1 falls in X with probability at least $\pi/2 - \varepsilon - \varepsilon_{\mathsf{pk}} > \pi/4 - \varepsilon$. Whenever E' is in X, the expected running time $R(E')$ for that session is about

$$\frac{r}{\pi_{E'} - 1/c} \leq \frac{r}{\pi/2 - 1/c} = \frac{4r}{\pi + (\pi - 4/c)} = \frac{4r}{\pi + 1/c} = \frac{4r}{\mathrm{Adv}^{\mathscr{P}^*}_{\mathrm{SQIsound}}(\mathsf{pp})}.$$

We conclude that this algorithm for ONEEND runs in expected polynomial time in $\log(p)$, in $\mathrm{Adv}^{\mathscr{P}^*}_{\mathrm{SQIsound}}(\mathsf{pp})^{-1}$ and in r. The result follows from the equivalence between ONEEND and ENDRING (Theorem 1.1). □

Remark 8.3. Note that the proof can be adapted to prove the theorem with the quantity $\pi^{\mathscr{P}^*}(\mathsf{pp})^{-1}$ in place of $\mathrm{Adv}^{\mathscr{P}^*}_{\mathrm{SQIsound}}(\mathsf{pp})^{-1}$, which may be more natural.

8.3 The Endomorphism Ring Problem is Equivalent to the Isogeny Problem

It is known that the problem ENDRING is equivalent to the ℓ-isogeny path problem (assuming the generalised Riemann hypothesis [Wes22b]). The same technique shows that ENDRING is equivalent to the problem of finding isogenies of *smooth* degree. Lifting this restriction yields the more general ISOGENY problem.

Problem 8.4 (ISOGENY). *Given a prime p and two supersingular elliptic curves E and E' over $\mathbf{F}_{p^2}$, find an isogeny from E to E' in efficient representation.*

Given a function $\lambda\colon \mathbf{Z}_{>0} \to \mathbf{Z}_{>0}$, the ISOGENY$_\lambda$ problem denotes the ISOGENY problem where the solution φ is required to satisfy $\log(\deg\varphi) \leq \lambda(\log p)$ (the length of the output is bounded by a function of the length of the input).

From previous literature, it is easy to see that ISOGENY reduces to ENDRING.

Proposition 8.5 (ISOGENY **reduces to** ENDRING). *Assuming the generalised Riemann hypothesis, the problem ISOGENY$_\lambda$ reduces to ENDRING in probabilistic polynomial time (with respect to the length of the instance), for some function $\lambda(\log p) = O(\log p)$.*

Proof. ISOGENY immediately reduces to ℓ-ISOGENYPATH. It is already known that the ℓ-isogeny path problem (with paths of length $O(\log p)$) is equivalent to ENDRING [Wes22b], so ISOGENY$_\lambda$ reduces to ENDRING. □

The converse reduction is trickier. As a solution to ISOGENY is not guaranteed to have smooth degree, previous techniques have failed to prove that it is equivalent to ENDRING. Theorem 1.1 unlocks this equivalence. Better yet, contrary to previous results of this form, Theorem 8.6 below is unconditional. In particular, it implies that ENDRING reduces to the ℓ-isogeny path problem independently of the generalised Riemann hypothesis.

Theorem 8.6 (ENDRING **reduces to** ISOGENY). *Given an oracle for* ISOGENY$_\lambda$, *there is an algorithm for* ENDRING *that runs in expected polynomial time in* $\log(p)$ *and* $\lambda(\log p)$.

Algorithm 4. Solving ONEEND given an ISOGENY oracle.

Require: A supersingular elliptic curve $E/\mathbf{F}_{p^2}$, a parameter $\varepsilon > 0$, an oracle $\mathcal{O}_{ProblemIsogeny}$ solving the $ProblemIsogeny_\lambda$ problem.
Ensure: An endomorphism $\alpha \in \mathrm{End}(E) \setminus \mathbf{Z}$ in efficient representation.
1: $S \leftarrow$ an arbitrary nonzero point in $E[2]$
2: $n \leftarrow \lceil 2\log_3(p) - 4\log_3(\varepsilon) \rceil$
3: **while** true **do**
4:     $\varphi \leftarrow$ a non-backtracking random walk $\varphi \colon E \to E'$ of length n in the 3-isogeny graph
5:     $\nu \leftarrow$ the isogeny $\nu \colon E' \to E''$ of kernel $\langle \varphi(S) \rangle$
6:     $\psi \leftarrow \mathcal{O}_{ProblemIsogeny}(E'', E)$, an isogeny $\psi \colon E'' \to E$
7:     $\alpha \leftarrow (\psi \circ \nu \circ \varphi)/2^e \in \mathrm{End}(E)$ for the largest possible e
8:     **if** $2 \mid \deg(\alpha)$ **then**
9:         **return** α
10:     **end if**
11: **end while**

Proof. Since ENDRING is equivalent to ONEEND (Theorem 1.1), let us prove that ONEEND reduces to ISOGENY. Suppose we have an oracle $\mathcal{O}_{\text{ISOGENY}}$ for ISOGENY$_\lambda$. Let E be a supersingular curve for which we want to solve ONEEND. Consider a parameter ε. The reduction is described in Algorithm 4. Step 7 and Step 8 ensure that α is not a scalar (indeed, they ensure that upon return, at Step 9, we have $2 \nmid \alpha$ yet $2 \mid \deg(\alpha)$), so is a valid solution to ONEEND.

Let us show that the expected number of iterations of the while-loop is $O(1)$. Let $f \in \mathbf{Z}$ maximal such that $E''[2^f] \subseteq \ker(\psi)$, and let $\psi' = \psi/2^f$. If $\deg(\psi')$ is odd, then α is non-scalar (its degree is divisible by 2 but not by 4) and the loop terminates at this iteration. Now, suppose $\deg(\psi')$ is even and write $\ker(\psi') \cap E''[2] = G_\psi$, a group of order 2. The loop in the reduction terminates in the event that $\ker \hat{\nu} \neq G_\psi$. In the rest of the proof, we bound the probability of this event at each iteration.

Let P be the probability distribution of the pair $(E'', \hat{\nu})$, and Q the probability distribution of the pair (E'', η) where η is uniformly random (among the three 2-isogenies from E''). Note that by construction, the value $Q(E'', \eta)$ does not depend on η, and we also write it $\tilde{Q}(E'')$. Consider the function τ defined in [BCC+23, Lemma 14]. We have

$$\tau(p,2,3,k) = \frac{1}{4}(p-1)^{1/2}\left(1+\sqrt{3}\right)\left(k+\frac{1}{2}\right)3^{-k/2} \le p^{1/2}3^{-k/4}.$$

From [BCC+23, Lemma 14], if $\tau(p,2,3,k) \le \varepsilon$, then the statistical distance $\|P-Q\|_1/2$ is at most ε. This condition is satisfied if the 3-walk φ has length at least

$$n(p,2,3,\varepsilon) = \min\{k \mid \tau(p,2,3,k) \le \varepsilon\}$$
$$\le \min\{k \mid p^{1/2}3^{-k/4} \le \varepsilon\} = 2\log_3(p) - 4\log_3(\varepsilon).$$

We deduce that indeed $\|P-Q\|_1 < 2\varepsilon$, since φ has length $\lceil 2\log_3(p) - 4\log_3(\varepsilon)\rceil$. We now obtain the following bound:

$$\Pr[\ker\hat{\nu} = G_\psi] = \sum_{(E'',\hat{\nu})} P(E'',\hat{\nu})\Pr[\ker\hat{\nu} = G_\psi \mid (E'',\hat{\nu})]$$

$$\le \sum_{(E'',\hat{\nu})} \left(Q(E'',\hat{\nu}) + \max_\eta |P(E'',\eta) - Q(E'',\eta)|\right)\Pr[\ker\hat{\nu} = G_\psi \mid E'']$$

$$\le \sum_{E''} \tilde{Q}(E'') + \sum_{E''} \max_\eta |P(E'',\eta) - Q(E'',\eta)| \le \frac{1}{3} + 2\varepsilon.$$

The second line uses that for any fixed E'', the distribution of ψ is independent of ν. In conclusion, at each iteration, the event $\ker\hat{\nu} \ne G_\psi$ (leading to termination) happens with probability at least $2/3 - 2\varepsilon$. With $2\varepsilon < 1/3$, the expected number of iterations is at most $(2/3 - 2\varepsilon)^{-1} \le 3 = O(1)$. $\square$

8.4   An Unconditional Algorithm for ENDRING in Time $\tilde{O}(p^{1/2})$

As the foundational problem of isogeny-based cryptography, understanding the hardness of ENDRING is critical. The fastest known algorithms have complexity in $\tilde{O}(p^{1/2})$, but rely on unproven assumptions such as the generalised Riemann hypothesis. With our new results, we can now prove that ENDRING can be solved in time $\tilde{O}(p^{1/2})$ *unconditionally*. In contrast, the previous fastest unconditional algorithm had complexity $\tilde{O}(p)$ and only returned a full-rank subring of the endomorphism ring [Koh96, Theorem 75].

The first method to reach complexity $\tilde{O}(p^{1/2})$ under the generalised Riemann hypothesis consists in reducing ENDRING to ℓ-ISOGENYPATH (via [Wes22b]), and solving ℓ-ISOGENYPATH by a generic graph path-finding algorithm. Unconditionally, we can follow the same strategy, but using our new reduction from ENDRING to ℓ-ISOGENYPATH (Theorem 8.6). Let us start by recalling the following folklore solution to ℓ-ISOGENYPATH.

Proposition 8.7. *There exists an algorithm that solves the ℓ-IsogenyPath problem in expected time* $\mathrm{poly}(\ell, \log p)p^{1/2}$ *and returns paths of length* $O(\log p)$.

Proof. The proof is available in the full version [PW23, Proposition 8.7].

Theorem 8.8. *There is an algorithm solving* EndRing *in expected time* $\tilde{O}\left(p^{1/2}\right)$.

Proof. This follows from the fact that there is an algorithm of complexity $\tilde{O}\left(p^{1/2}\right)$ for the 2-isogeny path problem (Proposition 8.7), and EndRing reduces to polynomially many instances of the ℓ-isogeny path problem (Theorem 8.6). $\square$

Acknowledgements. The authors would like to thank Damien Robert for fruitful discussions. The authors were supported by the Agence Nationale de la Recherche under grant ANR-20-CE40-0013 (MELODIA) and ANR-19-CE48-0008 (CIAO), the France 2030 program under grant ANR-22-PETQ-0008 (PQ-TLS), and the European Research Council under grant No. 101116169 (AGATHA CRYPTY).

References

Arp23. Arpin, S.: Adding level structure to supersingular elliptic curve isogeny graphs. Preprint arXiv:2203.03531 (2023). https://arxiv.org/abs/2203.03531

BCC+23. Basso, A., et al.: Supersingular curves you can trust. In: Hazay, C., Stam, M. (eds.) EUROCRYPT 2023. LNCS, vol. 14005, pp. 405–437. Springer, Cham (2023). https://doi.org/10.1007/978-3-031-30617-4_14

CD23. Castryck, W., Decru, T.: An efficient key recovery attack on SIDH. In: Hazay, C., Stam, M. (eds.) EUROCRYPT 2023, Part V. LNCS, vol. 14008, pp. 423–447. Springer, Cham (2023). https://doi.org/10.1007/978-3-031-30589-4_15

CL23. Codogni, G., Lido, G.: Spectral theory of isogeny graphs. Preprint arXiv:2308.13913 (2023). https://arxiv.org/abs/2308.13913

CLG09. Charles, D.X., Lauter, K.E., Goren, E.Z.: Cryptographic hash functions from expander graphs. J. Cryptol. **22**(1), 93–113 (2009)

DKL+20. De Feo, L., Kohel, D., Leroux, A., Petit, C., Wesolowski, B.: SQISign: compact post-quantum signatures from quaternions and isogenies. In: Moriai, S., Wang, H. (eds.) ASIACRYPT 2020. LNCS, vol. 12491, pp. 64–93. Springer, Cham (2020). https://doi.org/10.1007/978-3-030-64837-4_3

DLRW23. Dartois, P., Leroux, A., Robert, D., Wesolowski, B.: SQISignHD: new dimensions in cryptography. IACR Cryptology ePrint Archive, Report 2023/436 (2023). https://eprint.iacr.org/2023/436

EHL+18. Eisenträger, K., Hallgren, S., Lauter, K., Morrison, T., Petit, C.: Supersingular isogeny graphs and endomorphism rings: reductions and solutions. In: Nielsen, J.B., Rijmen, V. (eds.) EUROCRYPT 2018. LNCS, vol. 10822, pp. 329–368. Springer, Cham (2018). https://doi.org/10.1007/978-3-319-78372-7_11

FIK+23. Fuselier, J., Iezzi, A., Kozek, M., Morrison, T., Namoijam, C.: Computing supersingular endomorphism rings using inseparable endomorphisms. Preprint arXiv:2306.03051 (2023). https://arxiv.org/abs/2306.03051

HLMW23. Le Merdy, A.H., Wesolowski, B.: The supersingular endomorphism ring problem given one endomorphism. Preprint arXiv:2309.11912 (2023). https://arxiv.org/abs/2309.11912

KLPT14. Kohel, D., Lauter, K., Petit, C., Tignol, J.-P.: On the quaternion ℓ-isogeny path problem. LMS J. Comput. Math. **17**(A), 418–432 (2014)

Koh96. Kohel, D.: Endomorphism rings of elliptic curves over finite fields. Ph.D. thesis, University of California, Berkeley (1996)

Mes86. Mestre, J.-F.: La méthode des graphes. Exemples et applications. In: Proceedings of the International Conference on Class Numbers and Fundamental Units of Algebraic Number Fields (Katata), pp. 217–242 (1986)

ML98. Lane, S.M.: Categories for the Working Mathematician. Graduate Texts in Mathematics, 2nd edn, vol. 5. Springer, New York (1998). https://doi.org/10.1007/978-1-4757-4721-8

MMP+23. Maino, L., Martindale, C., Panny, L., Pope, G., Wesolowski, B.: A direct key recovery attack on SIDH. In: Hazay, C., Stam, M. (eds.) EUROCRYPT 2023. LNCS, vol. 14008, pp. 448–471. Springer, Cham (2023). https://doi.org/10.1007/978-3-031-30589-4_16

Piz90. Pizer, A.K.: Ramanujan Graphs and Hecke Operators. Bull. Am. Math. Soc. **23**(1), 127–137 (1990)

PW23. Page, A., Wesolowski, B.: The supersingular endomorphism ring and one endomorphism problems are equivalent. IACR Cryptology ePrint Archive, Report 2023/1399 (2023). https://eprint.iacr.org/2023/1399

Rob22. Robert, D.: Some applications of higher dimensional isogenies to elliptic curves (overview of results). Cryptology ePrint Archive, Paper 2022/1704 (2022). https://eprint.iacr.org/2022/1704

Rob23. Robert, D.: Breaking SIDH in polynomial time. In: Hazay, C., Stam, M. (eds.) EUROCRYPT 2023, Part V. LNCS, vol. 14008, pp. 472–503. Springer, Cham (2023). https://doi.org/10.1007/978-3-031-30589-4_17

Sil86. Silverman, J.H.: The Arithmetic of Elliptic Curves. Gradute Texts in Mathematics, vol. 106. Springer, Heidelberg (1986). https://doi.org/10.1007/978-0-387-09494-6

Voi21. Voight, J.: Quaternion Algebras. Graduate Texts in Mathematics, vol. 288. Springer, Heidelberg (2021). https://doi.org/10.1007/978-3-030-56694-4

Wes22a. Wesolowski, B.: Orientations and the supersingular endomorphism ring problem. In: Dunkelman, O., Dziembowski, S. (eds.) EUROCRYPT 2022. LNCS, vol. 13277, pp. 345–371. Springer, Cham (2022). https://doi.org/10.1007/978-3-031-07082-2_13

Wes22b. Wesolowski, B.: The supersingular isogeny path and endomorphism ring problems are equivalent. In: FOCS 2021-62nd Annual IEEE Symposium on Foundations of Computer Science (2022)

Evaluating the Security of CRYSTALS-Dilithium in the Quantum Random Oracle Model

Kelsey A. Jackson[1] , Carl A. Miller[1,2] , and Daochen Wang[1,3(✉)]

[1] University of Maryland, College Park, USA
{kaj22475,camiller}@umd.edu, wdaochen@gmail.com
[2] National Institute of Standards and Technology, Gaithersburg, USA
[3] University of British Columbia, Vancouver, Canada

Abstract. In the wake of recent progress on quantum computing hardware, the National Institute of Standards and Technology (NIST) is standardizing cryptographic protocols that are resistant to attacks by quantum adversaries. The primary digital signature scheme that NIST has chosen is CRYSTALS-Dilithium. The hardness of this scheme is based on the hardness of three computational problems: Module Learning with Errors (MLWE), Module Short Integer Solution (MSIS), and SelfTargetMSIS. MLWE and MSIS have been well-studied and are widely believed to be secure. However, SelfTargetMSIS is novel and, though classically as hard as MSIS, its quantum hardness is unclear. In this paper, we provide the first proof of the hardness of SelfTargetMSIS via a reduction from MLWE in the Quantum Random Oracle Model (QROM). Our proof uses recently developed techniques in quantum reprogramming and rewinding. A central part of our approach is a proof that a certain hash function, derived from the MSIS problem, is collapsing. From this approach, we deduce a new security proof for Dilithium under appropriate parameter settings. Compared to the previous work by Kiltz, Lyubashevsky, and Schaffner (EUROCRYPT 2018) that gave the only other rigorous security proof for a variant of Dilithium, our proof has the advantage of being applicable under the condition $q = 1 \bmod 2n$, where q denotes the modulus and n the dimension of the underlying algebraic ring. This condition is part of the original Dilithium proposal and is crucial for the efficient implementation of the scheme. We provide new secure parameter sets for Dilithium under the condition $q = 1 \bmod 2n$, finding that our public key size and signature size are about 2.9× and 1.3× larger, respectively, than those proposed by Kiltz et al. at the same security level.

[Full version: arXiv:2312.16619]

1 Introduction

Quantum computers are theoretically capable of breaking the underlying computational hardness assumptions for many existing cryptographic schemes.

© International Association for Cryptologic Research 2024
M. Joye and G. Leander (Eds.): EUROCRYPT 2024, LNCS 14656, pp. 418–446, 2024.
https://doi.org/10.1007/978-3-031-58751-1_15

Therefore, it is vitally important to develop new cryptographic primitives and protocols that are resistant to quantum attacks.

The goal of NIST's Post-Quantum Cryptography Standardization Project is to design a new generation of cryptographic schemes that are secure against quantum adversaries. In 2022, NIST selected three new digital signature schemes for standardization [Ala+22]: Falcon, SPHINCS+, and CRYSTALS-Dilithium. Of the three, CRYSTALS-Dilithium [Bai+21], or Dilithium in shorthand, was identified as the primary choice for post-quantum digital signing.

To practically implement post-quantum cryptography, users must be provided with not only assurance that a scheme is secure in a post-quantum setting, but also the means by which to judge parameter choices and thereby balance their own needs for security and efficiency. The goal of the current work is to provide rigorous assurance of the security of Dilithium as well as implementable parameter sets. A common model for the security of digital signatures is existential unforgeability against chosen message attacks, or EUF-CMA. In this setting, an adversary is allowed to make sequential queries to a signing oracle for the signature scheme, and then afterwards the adversary attempts to forge a signature for a new message. We work in the setting of *strong* existential unforgeability (sEUF-CMA) wherein we must also guard against the possibility that an adversary could try to forge a new signature for one of the messages already signed by the oracle. (See the preliminaries section of the full version for details.)

Additionally, we utilize the quantum random oracle model (QROM) for hash functions. We recall that when a hash function $H : X \to Y$ is used as a subroutine in a digital signature scheme, the random oracle model (ROM) assumes that one can replace each instance of the function H with a black box that accepts inputs from X and returns outputs in Y according to a uniformly randomly chosen function from X to Y. (This model is useful because random functions are easier to work with in theory than actual hash functions.) The random oracle model needs to be refined in the quantum setting because queries to the hash function can be made in superposition: for any quantum state of the form $\sum_{x \in X} \alpha_x |x\rangle$, where $\forall x \in X, \alpha_x \in \mathbb{C}$, a quantum computer can efficiently prepare the superposed state $\sum_{x \in X} \alpha_x |x\rangle |H(x)\rangle$. The quantum random oracle model (QROM) therefore assumes that each use of the hash function can be simulated by a black box that accepts a quantum state supported on X and returns a quantum state supported on $X \times Y$ (computed by a truly random function from X to Y) [Bon+11]. While no efficient and truly random functions actually exist, the QROM is generally trusted and it enables the application of a number of useful proof techniques.

1.1 The Dilithium Signature Scheme

We give a brief description of CRYSTALS-Dilithium. (The reader is invited to consult [Bai+21] for a full version of the protocol and a more detailed explanation of the design.) Dilithium is based on arithmetic over the ring $R_q := \mathbb{Z}_q[X]/(X^n + 1)$, where q is an odd prime and n is a power of 2. Similar to other Dilithium literature, we generally leave the parameters q, n implicit. For any non-negative integer η, let $S_\eta \subseteq R_q$ denote the set of all polynomials with coefficients from $\{-\eta, -\eta + 1, \ldots, \eta\}$. For any positive integer $\tau \leq n$, let $B_\tau \subseteq R_q$ denote the set of all polynomials f such that exactly τ of the coefficients of f are in $\{-1, 1\}$ and the remaining coefficients are all zero.

Dilithium is an instance of a general family of lattice-based signature schemes (see [Pei16, Subsection 5.6.2]) that are obtained by applying the Fiat-Shamir transform to lattice-based interactive proofs-of-knowledge. Neglecting some optimizations that are present in the full version of the scheme, we can concisely express Dilithium as in Fig. 1. The parameters $k, \ell, \gamma_1, \gamma_2, \tau, \beta$ are positive integers, and H denotes a hash function which maps to the set B_τ. A signature for a message $M \in \{0, 1\}^*$ takes the form of an ordered pair $\sigma = (z, c)$, where $z \in R_q^\ell$ and $c \in B_\tau$.

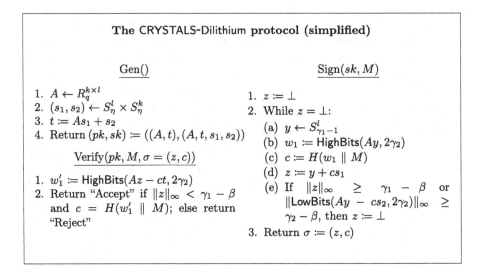

The CRYSTALS-Dilithium protocol (simplified)

Gen()

1. $A \leftarrow R_q^{k \times l}$
2. $(s_1, s_2) \leftarrow S_\eta^l \times S_\eta^k$
3. $t := As_1 + s_2$
4. Return $(pk, sk) := ((A, t), (A, t, s_1, s_2))$

Verify($pk, M, \sigma = (z, c)$)

1. $w_1' := \mathsf{HighBits}(Az - ct, 2\gamma_2)$
2. Return "Accept" if $\|z\|_\infty < \gamma_1 - \beta$ and $c = H(w_1' \| M)$; else return "Reject"

Sign(sk, M)

1. $z := \perp$
2. While $z = \perp$:
   (a) $y \leftarrow S_{\gamma_1 - 1}^l$
   (b) $w_1 := \mathsf{HighBits}(Ay, 2\gamma_2)$
   (c) $c := H(w_1 \| M)$
   (d) $z := y + cs_1$
   (e) If $\|z\|_\infty \geq \gamma_1 - \beta$ or $\|\mathsf{LowBits}(Ay - cs_2, 2\gamma_2)\|_\infty \geq \gamma_2 - \beta$, then $z := \perp$
3. Return $\sigma := (z, c)$

Fig. 1. A simplified description of the key generation algorithm (Gen), signature verification algorithm (Verify) and signing algorithm (Sign) for Dilithium.

The algorithms in Fig. 1 make use of the subroutines HighBits and LowBits which separate an R_q-vector into two parts. For any vector $x \in R_q^\ell$, the vectors $x_{\mathrm{high}} := \mathsf{HighBits}(x, 2\gamma_2)$ and $x_{\mathrm{low}} := \mathsf{LowBits}(x, 2\gamma_2)$ satisfy $x = (2\gamma_2)x_{\mathrm{high}} + x_{\mathrm{low}}$, and the polynomial coefficients in x_{low} are all from the set $\{-\gamma_2, -\gamma_2 + 1, \ldots, \gamma_2\}$.

1.2 Known Security Results for Dilithium

The security analysis for Dilithium in [Bai+21] is based on three computational problems. The first two are standard problems (Definitions 1 and 2) but the third problem is non-standard (Definition 3). The first problem is the Module

Learning With Errors (MLWE) problem. Assuming that a matrix $A \in R_q^{m \times k}$ and short vectors $s_1 \in S_\eta^k$ and $s_2 \in S_\eta^m$ are chosen uniformly at random, the MLWE problem is to distinguish the matrix-vector pair $(A, t := As_1 + s_2)$ from a uniformly random matrix-vector pair.

Definition 1 (Module Learning with Errors (MLWE)). *Let $m, k, \eta \in \mathbb{N}$. The advantage of an algorithm $\mathcal{A}$ for solving* MLWE$_{m,k,\eta}$ *is defined as:*

$$\begin{aligned}
\text{Adv}_{m,k,\eta}^{\text{MLWE}}(\mathcal{A}) := \big| &\Pr[b = 0 \mid A \leftarrow R_q^{m \times k}, \ t \leftarrow R_q^m, \ b \leftarrow \mathcal{A}(A, t)] \\
&- \Pr[b = 0 \mid A \leftarrow R_q^{m \times k}, \ (s_1, s_2) \leftarrow S_\eta^k \times S_\eta^m, \ b \leftarrow \mathcal{A}(A, As_1 + s_2)] \big|.
\end{aligned} \quad (1)$$

Here, the notation $\mathcal{A}(x)$ denotes $\mathcal{A}$ taking input x. We note that the MLWE problem is often phrased in other contexts with the short vectors s_1 and s_2 coming from a Gaussian, rather than a uniform, distribution. The use of a uniform distribution is one of the particular features of CRYSTALS-Dilithium.

The second problem, MSIS, is concerned with finding short solutions to randomly chosen linear systems over R_q.

Definition 2 (Module Short Integer Solution (MSIS)). *Let $m, k, \gamma \in \mathbb{N}$. The advantage of an algorithm $\mathcal{A}$ for solving* MSIS$_{m,k,\gamma}$ *is defined as:*

$$\text{Adv}_{m,k,\gamma}^{\text{MSIS}}(\mathcal{A}) := \Pr\big[[I_m | A] \cdot y = 0 \wedge 0 < \|y\|_\infty \le \gamma \mid A \leftarrow R_q^{m \times k}, \ y \leftarrow \mathcal{A}(A)\big]. \quad (2)$$

The third problem is a more complex variant of MSIS that incorporates a hash function H.

Definition 3 (SelfTargetMSIS). *Let $\tau, m, k, \gamma \in \mathbb{N}$ and $H: \{0,1\}^* \to B_\tau$, where $B_\tau \subseteq R_q$ is the set of polynomials with exactly τ coefficients in $\{-1, 1\}$ and all remaining coefficients zero. The advantage of an algorithm $\mathcal{A}$ for solving* SelfTargetMSIS$_{H,\tau,m,k,\gamma}$ *is defined as[1]:*

$$\begin{aligned}
\text{Adv}_{H,\tau,m,k,\gamma}^{\text{SelfTargetMSIS}}(\mathcal{A}) := \Pr\Big[&H([I_m | A] \cdot y \| M) = y_{m+k} \wedge \|y\|_\infty \le \gamma \mid \\
& A \leftarrow R_q^{m \times k}, \ (y, M) \leftarrow \mathcal{A}^{|H\rangle}(A) \Big].
\end{aligned} \quad (3)$$

The security guarantee for CRYSTALS-Dilithium is given in [KLS18, Section 4.5] by the inequality[2]

$$\text{Adv}_{\text{Dilithium}}^{\text{sEUF-CMA}}(\mathcal{A}) \le \text{Adv}_{k,l,\eta}^{\text{MLWE}}(\mathcal{B}) + \text{Adv}_{H,\tau,k,l+1,\zeta}^{\text{SelfTargetMSIS}}(\mathcal{C}) + \text{Adv}_{k,l,\zeta'}^{\text{MSIS}}(\mathcal{D}), \quad (4)$$

---

[1] $\|$ denotes string concatenation. $\mathcal{A}^{|H\rangle}$ denotes $\mathcal{A}$ with quantum query access to H — a formal definition can be found in the preliminaries section of the full version.

[2] Strictly speaking, there should be two other terms ($\text{Adv}_{\text{Sam}}^{\text{PR}}(\mathcal{E})$ and $2^{-\alpha+1}$) on the right-hand side of Eq. (4). However, we ignore them in the introduction as it is easy to set parameters such that these terms are very small. We also mention that the original proof of this inequality uses a flawed analysis of Fiat-Shamir with aborts. The flaw was found and fixed in [Bar+23, Dev+23].

where all terms on the right-hand side of the inequality depend on parameters that specify Dilithium, and sEUF-CMA stands for strong unforgeability under chosen message attacks. The interpretation of Eq. (4) is: if there exists a quantum algorithm $\mathcal{A}$ that attacks the sEUF-CMA-security of Dilithium, then there exist quantum algorithms $\mathcal{B}, \mathcal{C}, \mathcal{D}$ for MLWE, SelfTargetMSIS, and MSIS that have advantages satisfying Eq. (4) and run in time comparable to $\mathcal{A}$. Equation (4) implies that breaking the sEUF-CMA security of Dilithium is at least as hard as solving one of the MLWE, MSIS, or SelfTargetMSIS problems. MLWE and MSIS are known to be no harder than LWE and SIS, respectively. However, there are no known attacks taking advantage of their module structure so it is generally believed that they are as hard as their unstructured counterparts [LS15]. In turn, LWE and SIS are at least as hard as the (Gap) Shortest Vector Problem, which is the underlying hard problem of lattice cryptography [Ajt96, Reg09, Pei16].

However, the final problem, SelfTargetMSIS, is novel and so its difficulty is an open question. The problem is known to be as classically hard as MSIS since there exists a reduction from MSIS to SelfTargetMSIS in the ROM [KLS18, BN06]. The reduction uses the following "rewinding" argument. Any randomized algorithm can be specified by a deterministic circuit with auxiliary random bits. Therefore, given a randomized algorithm for SelfTargetMSIS, we can run its deterministic circuit with some randomly chosen bits to obtain one solution and then rewind and run it again using the same bits chosen from before, while at the same time reprogramming the random oracle at the query corresponding to the output of the first run, to obtain a second solution. Subtracting these two solutions to SelfTargetMSIS yields a solution to MSIS. However, the argument fails for the following reasons in the QROM (where a quantum algorithm can make queries in superposition to a quantum random oracle):

1. The randomness in a quantum algorithm includes the randomness of measurement outcomes. We cannot run a quantum algorithm twice and guarantee that the "random bits" will be the same in both runs because we cannot control measurement outcomes. More generally, we cannot rewind a quantum algorithm to a post-measurement state.
2. Since a quantum algorithm can make queries in superposition, it is no longer clear where to reprogram the random oracle.

Currently, the only explicit rigorous proof of Dilithium's security based on conventional hardness assumptions [KLS18] requires modifying the parameters to be such that $q = 5 \bmod 8$ and $2\gamma < \sqrt{q/2}$ (but n must remain a power of 2), where γ is a length upper bound on vectors corresponding to valid signatures. This ensures that all non-zero vectors in $S_{2\gamma}$ are invertible which equips Dilithium with a so-called "lossy mode". This variant is called Dilithium-QROM. [KLS18] then proves that a signature scheme with such a lossy mode is EUF-CMA. However, the Dilithium specification [Bai+21] uses a value of q satisfying $q = 1 \bmod 2n$ which is incompatible with the assumption that $q = 5 \bmod 8$ and $n > 2$ is a power of 2.[3] The fact that $q = 1 \bmod 2n$ is central to claims about the speed of

---

[3] The parameter n should not be 1 or 2, as that would significantly degrade Dilithium's efficiency and defeat the purpose of its use of R_q.

the algorithms in [Bai+21]: this condition implies that R_q is isomorphic to the direct product ring $\mathbb{Z}_q^{\times n}$ (or $\mathbb{Z}_q^n$ in shorthand) via the Number Theoretic Transform (NTT), which allows for fast matrix multiplication over R_q. Therefore, it is highly desirable to find a security proof that works under the assumption that $q = 1 \bmod 2n$. Moreover, when $q = 5 \bmod 8$ (and n is a power of 2), the ring R_q is *structurally* different from when $q = 1 \bmod 2n$, since in the former case R_q is isomorphic to $\mathbb{F}_{q^{n/2}} \times \mathbb{F}_{q^{n/2}}$ [LN17, Lemma 2.1]. Therefore, it may be imprudent to translate any claims of security in the case $q = 5 \bmod 8$ to the case $q = 1 \bmod 2n$.

1.3   Overview of Main Result

The main result of our paper is the first proof of the computational hardness of the SelfTargetMSIS problem, presented in Sect. 3. This hardness result implies a new security proof for Dilithium which, unlike the previous proof in [KLS18], applies to the case $q = 1 \bmod 2n$. Specifically, we reduce MLWE to SelfTargetMSIS. By Eq. (4), our result implies that the security of Dilithium (with parameters that are not too far from the original parameters) can be based on the hardness of MLWE and MSIS.

Theorem 1 (Informal version of Theorem 2). *Let $m, k, \tau, \gamma, \eta \in \mathbb{N}$. Suppose $q \geq 16$, $q = 1 \bmod 2n$, and $2\gamma\eta n(m + k) < \lfloor q/32 \rfloor$. If there exists an efficient quantum algorithm $\mathcal{A}$ that solves $\mathsf{SelfTargetMSIS}_{H,\tau,m,k,\gamma}$ with advantage ϵ, under the assumption that H is a random oracle, then there exists an efficient quantum algorithm for solving $\mathsf{MLWE}_{m+k,m,\eta}$ with advantage at least $\Omega(\epsilon^2/Q^4)$. Here, Q denotes the number of quantum queries $\mathcal{A}$ makes to H.*

We now give a high-level overview of the proof. The first step is to define two experiments: the *chosen-coordinate binding* experiment CCB and the *collapsing* experiment Collapse. These experiments are interactive protocols between a verifier and a prover. The protocols end with the verifier outputting a bit b. If $b = 1$, the prover is said to *win* the experiment. The reduction then proceeds in three steps: (i) reduce winning CCB to solving SelfTargetMSIS, (ii) reduce winning Collapse to winning CCB, and (iii) reduce solving MLWE to winning Collapse. Combining these steps together gives a reduction from MLWE to SelfTargetMSIS. The reduction can be illustrated as

$$\mathsf{SelfTargetMSIS} \xleftarrow{(i)} \mathsf{CCB} \xleftarrow{(ii)} \mathsf{Collapse} \xleftarrow{(iii)} \mathsf{MLWE}, \tag{5}$$

where the left arrow means "reduces to".

Step (i): SelfTargetMSIS $\leftarrow$ CCB. In the CCB experiment, the prover is first given a uniformly random $A \in R_q^{m \times l}$ which it uses to send the verifier some $z \in R_q^m$, the verifier then sends the prover a challenge c chosen uniformly at random from B_τ, and finally the prover sends the verifier a response $y \in R_q^l$. The prover wins if $Ay = z$, $\|y\|_\infty \leq \gamma$, and the last coordinate of y is c.

We directly apply the main result of [DFM20] to reduce winning CCB when $l = m + k$ to solving $\mathsf{SelfTargetMSIS}_{H,\tau,m,k,\gamma}$ when H is a random oracle. In more detail, the result implies that an efficient algorithm that wins SelfTargetMSIS using Q queries with probability ϵ can be used to construct another efficient algorithm that wins CCB with probability at least $\Omega(\epsilon/Q^2)$.

Step (ii): CCB $\leftarrow$ Collapse. In the Collapse experiment, the prover is first given a uniformly random $A \in R_q^{m \times l}$ which it uses to send the verifier some $z \in R_q^m$ together with a quantum state that must be supported only on $y \in R_q^l$ such that $Ay = z$, $\|y\|_\infty \leq \gamma$. Then, the verifier samples a uniformly random bit b'. If $b' = 1$, the verifier measures the quantum state in the computational basis, otherwise, it does nothing. The verifier then returns the quantum state to the prover. The prover responds by sending a bit b' to the verifier and wins if $b' = b$. The advantage of the prover is $2p - 1$ where p is its winning probability.

By using techniques in [DS23, Unr16], we reduce winning Collapse to winning CCB. More specifically, we show that an efficient algorithm that wins CCB with advantage ϵ can be used to construct another efficient algorithm that wins Collapse with advantage at least $\epsilon(\epsilon - 1/|B_\tau|)$, which is roughly ϵ^2 since $1/|B_\tau|$ is very small for the values of τ we will consider. We generalize techniques in [DS23, Unr16] to work for challenge sets of size > 2, which is necessary since the challenge set in the CCB experiment, B_τ, generally has size > 2. The key idea of first applying the quantum algorithm for winning CCB to the uniform superposition of all challenges remains the same.

Step (iii): Collapse $\leftarrow$ MLWE. We build on techniques in [LMZ23, LZ19] to reduce winning Collapse to winning MLWE. More specifically, we show that an efficient algorithm that wins Collapse with advantage ϵ can be used to construct another efficient algorithm that solves $\mathsf{MLWE}_{l,m,\eta}$ with advantage at least $\epsilon/4$. Given a quantum state supported on $y \in R_q^l$ with $Ay = z$ and $\|y\|_\infty \leq \gamma$, as promised in the Collapse experiment, [LMZ23, LZ19] considers the following two measurements. Sample $b \in R_q^l$ from one of the two distributions defined in MLWE (see Eq. (1)), compute a rounded version of $b \cdot y$ in a separate register, and measure that register. When $n = 1$, [LMZ23] shows that the effect of the measurement in one case is close to the computational basis measurement and in the other case is close to doing nothing. Therefore, an algorithm for winning Collapse can be used to solve MLWE. Our work extends [LMZ23] to arbitrary n provided $q = 1 \bmod 2n$. The extension relies on the fact that each coefficient of $b \cdot \Delta$, where $0 \neq \Delta \in R_q$ and b is chosen uniformly at random from R_q, is uniformly random in $\mathbb{Z}_q$. (This is despite the fact that $b \cdot \Delta$ is generally not uniformly random in R_q.) We establish this fact using the explicit form of the isomorphism between R_q and $\mathbb{Z}_q^n$ when $q = 1 \bmod 2n$.

Finally, in Sect. 4, we propose explicit sets of parameters using $n = 512$ and $q \approx 2^{43.5}$ such that $q = 1 \bmod 2n$. These sets of parameters achieve different security levels based on Theorem 1. We compare our sets of parameters with sets proposed by the Dilithium specifications [Bai+21] and the Dilithium-QROM construction of [KLS18]. We also compute the differences in the number of $\mathbb{Z}_q$-operations caused by using the NTT on $q = 1 \bmod 2n$ for ring element multiplication compared to a Hybrid-NTT on $q = 5 \bmod 8$. We find that our public key and signatures sizes are $\approx 11.4\times$ and $\approx 3.2\times$ larger, respectively, than the heuristically chosen parameters in the original Dilithium [Bai+21]. Compared to [KLS18], our parameters yield an increase in public key size and signature size of $\approx 2.9\times$ and $\approx 1.3\times$, respectively, while yielding a significant decrease (because of the different structure of R_q) in the number of $\mathbb{Z}_q$-operations used in key generation, signing, and verification.

Theorem 1 proves security for Dilithium in a range of parameters that preserves the algebraic structure of the original protocol [Bai+21]. Future work could explore how to optimize our approach to obtain provably secure parameters that are closer to those proposed in [Bai+21] for practical use. We also seek to generalize these results to other signature schemes that utilize the Fiat-Shamir transform.

2   Preliminaries

$\mathbb{N}$ denotes the set of positive integers. For $k \in \mathbb{N}$, $[k]$ denotes the set $\{1,\ldots,k\}$. An alphabet refers to a finite non-empty set. Given an alphabet S, the notation $s \leftarrow S$ denotes selecting an element s uniformly at random from S. Given two alphabets A and B, the notation B^A denotes the set of functions from A to B. We write the concatenation of arbitrary strings a, b as $a \parallel b$. Given matrices $A_1,\ldots,A_n$ of the same height, $[A_1|A_2|...|A_n]$ denotes the matrix that consists of the A_i matrices placed side by side. log refers to the base-2 logarithm.

We always reserve the symbol q for an odd prime and n for a positive integer that is a power of 2. R_q denotes the ring $\mathbb{Z}_q[X]/(X^n+1)$ (following the convention in other Dilithium literature [Bai+21,KLS18], we leave the n-dependence implicit). For $k \in \mathbb{N}$, a primitive kth root of unity in $\mathbb{Z}_q$ is an element $x \in \mathbb{Z}_q$ such that $x^k = 1$ and $x^j \neq 1$ for all $j \in [k-1]$; such elements exist if and only if $q = 1 \mod k$. Given $r \in \mathbb{Z}_q$, we define $r \mod^{\pm} q$ to be the unique element $r' \in \mathbb{Z}$ such that $-(q-1)/2 \leq r' \leq (q-1)/2$ and $r' = r \mod q$. For any $r = a_0 + a_1 X + \cdots + a_{n-1}X^{n-1} \in R_q$, we define $|r|_i := |a_i \mod^{\pm} q|$ for all $i \in \{0,1,\ldots,n-1\}$ and $\|r\|_\infty := \max_i |r|_i$. For $r \in R_q^m$, we define $\|r\|_\infty := \max_{i \in [m]} \|r_i\|_\infty$. For $\eta \in \mathbb{N}$, S_η denotes the set $\{r \in R_q \mid \|r\|_\infty \leq \eta\}$. For $\tau \in \mathbb{N}$, B_τ denotes the set of all elements $r \in R_q$ such that $\|r\|_\infty = 1$ and r has exactly τ nonzero coefficients. We note that $|B_\tau| = 2^\tau \binom{n}{\tau}$.

We refer the reader to the full version of this paper for further preliminaries on quantum computation and digital signature schemes.

2.1   Cryptographic Problems and Experiments

We now give the formal definitions of the chosen-coordinate binding and collapsing experiments mentioned in the introduction. More general versions of these definitions can be found in, e.g., [Unr12,DS23].

In Sect. 1.2 we defined the SelfTargetMSIS problem (Definition 3). Now we define a "plain" version of SelfTargetMSIS, where the input matrix is not given in Hermite Normal Form. First reducing SelfTargetMSIS from Plain-SelfTargetMSIS will be convenient later on.

Definition 4 (Plain-SelfTargetMSIS). *Let $\tau, m, l, \gamma \in \mathbb{N}$ and $H : \{0,1\}^* \to B_\tau$. The advantage of a quantum query algorithm $\mathcal{A}$ for solving* Plain-SelfTargetMSIS$_{H,\tau,m,l,\gamma}$ *is defined as*

$$\mathrm{Adv}_{H,\tau,m,l,\gamma}^{\text{Plain-SelfTargetMSIS}}(\mathcal{A}) := \Pr\Big[H(Ay \parallel M) = y_l \wedge \|y\|_\infty \le \gamma \mid$$
$$A \leftarrow R_q^{m \times l}, \ (y, M) \leftarrow \mathcal{A}^{|H\rangle}(A)\Big]. \tag{6}$$

Definition 5 (Chosen-Coordinate Binding (CCB)). *Let $\tau, m, l, \gamma \in \mathbb{N}$. The advantage of a quantum algorithm $\mathcal{A} = (\mathcal{A}_1, \mathcal{A}_2)$ for winning* CCB$_{\tau,m,l,\gamma}$, *denoted* $\mathrm{Adv}_{\tau,m,k,\gamma}^{\text{CCB}}(\mathcal{A})$, *is defined as the probability that the experiment below outputs 1.*

Experiment CCB$_{\tau,m,l,\gamma}$.

1. *Sample $A \leftarrow R_q^{m \times l}$.*
2. *$(z, T) \leftarrow \mathcal{A}_1(A)$, where $z \in R_q^m$ and T is an arbitrary register.*
3. *Sample $c \leftarrow B_\tau$.*
4. *$y \leftarrow \mathcal{A}_2(T, c)$, where $y \in R_q^l$.*
5. *Output 1 if $Ay = z$, $\|y\|_\infty \le \gamma$, and $y_l = c$.*

When τ, m, l, γ are functions of $\lambda \in \mathbb{N}$, we say that the MSIS *hash function is chosen-coordinate binding (CCB) if for every* $\mathrm{poly}(\lambda)$-*time quantum algorithm $\mathcal{A}$,* $\mathrm{Adv}_{\tau,m,l,\gamma}^{\text{CCB}}(\mathcal{A}) \le 1/|B_\tau| + \mathrm{negl}(\lambda)$.

Definition 6 (Collapsing (Collapse)). *Let $m, l, \gamma \in \mathbb{N}$. The advantage of a quantum algorithm $\mathcal{A} = (\mathcal{A}_1, \mathcal{A}_2)$ for winning* Collapse$_{m,l,\gamma}$, *denoted* $\mathrm{Adv}_{m,l,\gamma}^{\text{Collapse}}$, *is defined as $2p - 1$ where p is the probability the experiment below outputs 1.*

Experiment Collapse$_{m,l,\gamma}$.

1. *Sample $A \leftarrow R_q^{m \times l}$.*
2. *$(Y, Z, T) \leftarrow \mathcal{A}_1(A)$, where Y is a register on R_q^l, Z is a register on R_q^m, and T is an arbitrary register.*
3. *Sample $b \leftarrow \{0,1\}$. If $b = 1$, measure Y in the computational basis.*
4. *$b' \leftarrow \mathcal{A}_2(Y, Z, T)$.*
5. *Output 1 if $b' = b$.*

We say $\mathcal{A}$ is valid if the state on the register (Y, Z) output by $\mathcal{A}_1$ in step 2 is supported on elements $(y, z) \in R_q^l \times R_q^m$ such that $Ay = z$ and $\|y\|_\infty \le \gamma$. When m, l, γ are functions of $\lambda \in \mathbb{N}$, we say that the MSIS *hash function is collapsing if for every* $\mathrm{poly}(\lambda)$-*time quantum algorithm $\mathcal{A}$,* $\mathrm{Adv}_{m,l,\gamma}^{\text{Collapse}}(\mathcal{A}) \le 1/2 + \mathrm{negl}(\lambda)$.

3   Security Proof for SelfTargetMSIS

The main result of this subsection is the following theorem which follows from Propositions 1 to 4.

Theorem 2 (SelfTargetMSIS security). *Let $m, k, \tau, \gamma, \eta \in \mathbb{N}$. Suppose $q \geq 16$, $q = 1 \bmod 2n$, and $2\gamma\eta n(m + k) < \lfloor q/32 \rfloor$. Suppose that there exists a quantum query algorithm $\mathcal{A}$ for solving* SelfTargetMSIS$_{H,\tau,m,k,\gamma}$ *using Q queries with expected advantage ϵ over uniformly random[4] $H \colon \{0,1\}^* \to B_\tau$. Then, for all $w \in \mathbb{N}$, there exists a quantum algorithm $\mathcal{B}$ that solves* MLWE$_{m+k,m,\eta}$ *with advantage at least*

$$\frac{\epsilon - nq^{-k}}{4(2Q+1)^2}\left(\frac{\epsilon - nq^{-k}}{(2Q+1)^2} - \frac{1}{|B_\tau|}\right) - \frac{1}{4}\frac{1}{3^w}. \tag{7}$$

Moreover, Time$(\mathcal{B}) \leq$ Time$(\mathcal{A}) +$ poly$(\log|B_\tau|, w, n, \log q, m, k)$.

Assuming that the choice of parameters as functions of the security parameter λ is such that $nq^{-k} = \mathrm{negl}(\lambda)$, $1/|B_\tau| = \mathrm{negl}(\lambda)$, and $w = \mathrm{poly}(\lambda)$, Theorem 2 shows that the advantage of $\mathcal{B}$ is roughly $\Omega(\epsilon^2/Q^4)$.

The proof of Theorem 2 proceeds by the following sequence of reductions, which we have labeled by the number of the section in which they are proven:

$$\text{SelfTargetMSIS} \overset{3.2}{\Longleftarrow} \text{Plain-SelfTargetMSIS} \overset{3.3}{\Longleftarrow} \text{CCB} \overset{3.4}{\Longleftarrow} \text{Collapse} \overset{3.5}{\Longleftarrow} \text{MLWE.}$$

First, we establish some properties of R_q that will be used in Sects. 3.2 and 3.5.

3.1 Property of R_q

Lemma 1. *Suppose $q = 1 \bmod 2n$. Then, $R_q \cong \mathbb{Z}_q^n$ as algebras over $\mathbb{Z}_q$.[5]*

Proof (sketch). For q prime, the multiplicative group $\mathbb{Z}_q^*$ of non-zero elements in $\mathbb{Z}_q$ is cyclic. Let g be a generator of $\mathbb{Z}_q^*$. Let $w := g^{(q-1)/(2n)}$, which is well-defined since $q = 1 \bmod 2n$. Define $A \in (\mathbb{Z}_q^*)^{n \times n}$ by $A_{i,j} = w^{(2i-1)(j-1)}$ for all $i, j \in [n]$. Define $A' \in (\mathbb{Z}_q^*)^{n \times n}$ by $A'_{i,j} = n^{-1} \cdot w^{-(2j-1)(i-1)}$ for all $i, j \in [n]$. (n^{-1} denotes the multiplicative inverse of n in $\mathbb{Z}_q$, which exists since $q = 1 \bmod 2n \implies n < q$.) Let $\kappa \colon R_q \to \mathbb{Z}_q^n$ denote the bijection defined by $\kappa(a_0 + a_1 X + \cdots + a_{n-1} X^{n-1}) = (a_0, \ldots, a_{n-1})^\top$.

Define $\phi \colon R_q \to \mathbb{Z}_q^n$ by $\phi(p) = A \cdot \kappa(p)$. Define $\phi' \colon \mathbb{Z}_q^n \to R_q$ by $\phi'(v) = \kappa^{-1}(A' \cdot v)$. It can be verified that ϕ is an algebra homomorphism and ϕ' is its inverse, from which the lemma follows. See the full version for details.

---

[4] Let $U \subset \{0,1\}^*$ be the query set of $\mathcal{A}$, i.e., the finite subset of elements in $\{0,1\}^*$ that $\mathcal{A}$ could possibly query (in particular $|U| \leq 2^{O(\mathrm{Time}(\mathcal{A}))}$). By uniformly random $H \colon \{0,1\}^* \to B_\tau$, we mean that H restricted to domain U is uniformly random.

[5] To be clear, the algebra $\mathbb{Z}_q^n$ over $\mathbb{Z}_q$ refers to the set $\mathbb{Z}_q^n$ equipped with component-wise addition and multiplication, and scalar multiplication defined by $\alpha \cdot (c_0, \ldots, c_{n-1}) := (\alpha c_0, \ldots, \alpha c_{n-1})$, where $\alpha \in \mathbb{Z}_q$ and $(c_0, \ldots, c_{n-1}) \in \mathbb{Z}_q^n$.

3.2 Reduction from **Plain-SelfTargetMSIS** to **SelfTargetMSIS**

Proposition 1. *Suppose $q = 1 \bmod 2n$. Let $m, k, \gamma, \tau \in \mathbb{N}$ and $H: \{0,1\}^* \to B_\tau$. Suppose that there exists a quantum query algorithm $\mathcal{A}$ using Q queries that solves* $\mathsf{SelfTargetMSIS}_{H,\tau,m,k,\gamma}$ *with advantage ϵ, then there exists a quantum query algorithm $\mathcal{B}$ using Q queries for solving* Plain-$\mathsf{SelfTargetMSIS}_{H,\tau,m,m+k,\gamma}$ *with advantage at least $\epsilon - n/q^k$. Moreover,* $\mathrm{Time}(\mathcal{B}) \leq \mathrm{Time}(\mathcal{A}) + O(n \log(q) \cdot mk \min(m, k))$.

Proof. The probability that a uniformly random $B \leftarrow \mathbb{Z}_q^{m \times (m+k)}$ has row-echelon form $[I_m | B']$ (i.e., rank m) is at least $(1 - 1/q^k)$. Therefore, by Lemma 1, the probability that a uniformly random $A \leftarrow R_q^{m \times (m+k)}$ does not have row-echelon form $[I_m | A']$ is at most $1 - (1 - 1/q^k)^n \leq n/q^k$. When A has row-echelon form $[I_m | A]$, $\mathcal{B}$ first performs row reduction and then runs $\mathcal{A}$. Since the time to perform row reduction on A is $O(n \log(q) \cdot mk \min(m, k))$, the proposition follows.

3.3 Reduction from **CCB** to **Plain-SelfTargetMSIS**

Let S, U, C, R be alphabets, $V: S \times U \times C \times R \to \{0, 1\}$, and $\mathcal{B} = (\mathcal{B}_1, \mathcal{B}_2)$ be a quantum algorithm. We define the Σ-experiment by:

Σ-experiment.

1. $s \leftarrow S$.
2. $(u, T) \leftarrow \mathcal{B}_1(s)$, where $u \in U$ and T is an arbitrary register.
3. $c \leftarrow C$.
4. $r \leftarrow \mathcal{B}_2(T, c)$.
5. Output 1 if $V(s, u, c, r) = 1$.

The advantage of $\mathcal{B}$ for winning the Σ-experiment is the probability of the experiment outputting 1.

In this subsection, we use the following theorem from [DFM20].

Theorem 3 (Measure-and-reprogram [DFM20, Theorem 2]). *Let $\mathcal{A}$ be a quantum query algorithm using Q queries that takes input $s \in S$ and outputs $u \in U$ and $r \in R$. Then, there exists a two-stage quantum algorithm $\mathcal{B} = (\mathcal{B}_1, \mathcal{B}_2)$ (not using any queries) such that the advantage of $\mathcal{B}$ in the Σ-experiment is at least*

$$\frac{1}{(2Q+1)^2} \Pr\left[V(s, u, H(u), r) \;\middle|\; H \leftarrow C^U, \; s \leftarrow S, \; (u, r) \leftarrow \mathcal{A}^{|H\rangle}(s)\right]. \quad (8)$$

Moreover, $\mathrm{Time}(\mathcal{B}_1) + \mathrm{Time}(\mathcal{B}_2) \leq \mathrm{Time}(\mathcal{A})$.

In the original statement of the theorem, $\mathrm{Time}(\mathcal{B}_1) + \mathrm{Time}(\mathcal{B}_2)$ is upper bounded by $\mathrm{Time}(\mathcal{A}) - Q + \mathrm{poly}(Q, \log(|U|, \log(|C|))$. (The $-Q$ is because our definition of $\mathrm{Time}(\mathcal{A})$ includes a $+Q$ term.) The term $\mathrm{poly}(Q, \log(|U|, \log(|C|))$ accounts for the cost of instantiating Q queries to a $2(Q + 1)$-wise independent hash function family from U to C. By the well-known Vandermonde matrix method (see, e.g., [Zha12, Section 6]), this cost can be upper bounded by $O(Q^2 \cdot \log(|U|) \cdot \log(|C|))$. However, we follow the convention in [KLS18, Section 2.1] and equate this cost to Q under the fair assumption that $\mathcal{B}$, like $\mathcal{A}$, can also query a random oracle at unit cost.

Proposition 2. *Let* $m, l, \gamma, \tau \in \mathbb{N}$. *Suppose there exists a quantum query algorithm* $\mathcal{A}$ *for solving* Plain-SelfTargetMSIS$_{H,\tau,m,l,\gamma}$ *using* Q *queries with expected advantage* ϵ *over uniformly random* $H: \{0,1\}^* \to B_\tau$. *Then there exists a quantum algorithm* $\mathcal{B} = (\mathcal{B}_1, \mathcal{B}_2)$ *for winning* CCB$_{\tau,m,l,\gamma}$ *with advantage at least* $\epsilon/(2Q+1)^2$. *Moreover* $\text{Time}(\mathcal{B}_1) + \text{Time}(\mathcal{B}_2) \leq \text{Time}(\mathcal{A})$.

Proof. The quantum query algorithm $\mathcal{A}$ for Plain-SelfTargetMSIS$_{H,\tau,m,l,\gamma}$ takes input A and outputs (y, M). So there exists another quantum query algorithm $\mathcal{A}'$ using Q queries that outputs $((Ay \parallel M), y)$.

The first part of the proposition follows from applying Theorem 3 to $\mathcal{A}'$ with the following parameter settings which make the Σ-experiment identical to the CCB$_{\tau,m,l,\gamma}$ experiment

1. Set $S = R_q^{m \times l}$, U to be the query set of $\mathcal{A}'$, $C = B_\tau$, and $R = R_q^l$.
2. Set $V: R_q^{m \times l} \times U \times B_\tau \times R_q^l \to \{0,1\}$ by

$$V(A, u, c, y) = \mathbb{1}[z = Ay, \|y\|_\infty \leq \gamma, y_l = c], \qquad (9)$$

where $u \in \{0,1\}^*$ is parsed as $u = (z \parallel M)$ with $z \in R_q^m$ and $M \in \{0,1\}^*$.

3.4   Reduction from Collapse to CCB

In this subsection, we will use the following lemma, which can be found as [DS23, Proposition 29].

Lemma 2. *Let* P, Q *be projectors in* $\mathbb{C}^{d \times d}$ *and* ρ *be a density matrix in* $\mathbb{C}^d$ *such that* $\rho Q = \rho$. *Then* $\text{tr}(QP\rho P) \geq \text{tr}(P\rho)^2$.

The following proposition is similar to [Unr16, Theorem 32] and [DS23, Theorem 28] except the size of the challenge set in the CCB experiment (in step 3 of Definition 5) is not restricted to being 2.

Proposition 3. *Let* $m, l, \gamma, \tau \in \mathbb{N}$. *Suppose that there exists a quantum algorithm* $\mathcal{A} = (\mathcal{A}_1, \mathcal{A}_2)$ *that succeeds in* CCB$_{\tau,m,l,\gamma}$ *with advantage* ϵ, *then there exists a valid quantum algorithm* $\mathcal{B} = (\mathcal{B}_1, \mathcal{B}_2)$ *that succeeds in* Collapse$_{m,l,\gamma}$ *with advantage at least* $\epsilon(\epsilon - 1/|B_\tau|)$. *Moreover,* $\text{Time}(\mathcal{B}_1) \leq \text{Time}(\mathcal{A}_1) + \text{Time}(\mathcal{A}_2) + O(ml \log(q) \log(|B_\tau|))$ *and* $\text{Time}(\mathcal{B}_2) \leq \text{Time}(\mathcal{A}_2) + O(\log(|B_\tau|))$.

Proof. We assume without loss of generality (wlog) that the arbitrary register in step 2 of the CCB$_{\tau,m,l,\gamma}$ experiment (Definition 5) is of the form (Y, T'), where Y is a register on R_q^l and T' is an arbitrary register. We assume wlog that $\mathcal{A}_1$ prepares a state $|\phi\rangle$ on register (Y, Z, T'), where Z is a register on R_q^m, and measures Z in the computational basis to produce the z in step 2 of the $\mathsf{CCB}_{\tau,m,l,\gamma}$ experiment. We also assume wlog that $\mathcal{A}_2$ acts on its input register (Y, T', C), where C is a register on B_τ that contains the c from step 3 of the $\mathsf{CCB}_{\tau,m,l,\gamma}$ experiment, as follows:

1. Apply a unitary U of the form $\sum_{r \in B_\tau} U_r \otimes |r\rangle\langle r|$ on (Y, T', C).
2. Measure Y in the computational basis.

We proceed to construct $\mathcal{B} = (\mathcal{B}_1, \mathcal{B}_2)$ for the $\mathsf{Collapse}_{m,l,\gamma}$ experiment (Definition 6). We first construct $\mathcal{B}_1$, given input $A \in R_q^{m \times l}$, as follows:

1. Run $\mathcal{A}_1(A)$ to prepare state $|\phi\rangle$ on register (Y, Z, T').
2. Prepare state $|\psi\rangle := |B_\tau|^{-1/2} \sum_{r \in B_\tau} |r\rangle$ on register C in time $O(\log(|B_\tau|))$. The current state on register (Y, Z, T', C) is $\sigma := |\phi\rangle\langle\phi| \otimes |\psi\rangle\langle\psi|$. Apply U on register (Y, T', C) and then measure register (Y, Z, T', C) with the projective measurement $\{\Pi, 1 - \Pi\}$, where Π is defined by

$$\Pi := \sum_{r \in B_\tau} \sum_{\substack{(y,z) \in R_q^l \times R_q^m: \\ \|y\|_\infty \leq \gamma, \; Ay = z, \; y_l = r}} |y, z\rangle\langle y, z| \otimes 1_{T'} \otimes |r\rangle\langle r|. \tag{10}$$

   This measurement can be implemented by computing a bit indicating whether the constraints defining Π are satisfied into a separate register and then measuring that register, which takes time $O(ml \log(q) + \log(|B_\tau|))$.
3. Let B be a bit register. If Π is measured, set the bit stored in B to 1. If $(1 - \Pi)$ is measured, replace the state on register (Y, Z) with $|0^l\rangle \otimes |0^m\rangle$, set the bit stored in B to 0. Then output the register (Y, Z, T', C, B).

Let $T := (T', C, B)$. We construct $\mathcal{B}_2$, given input register (Y, Z, T):

1. If B contains 0, output a uniformly random bit $b' \in \{0, 1\}$.
2. Else apply $U^\dagger$ on register (Y, T', C). Then measure C with the projective measurement $\{|\psi\rangle\langle\psi|, 1 - |\psi\rangle\langle\psi|\}$ using (the inverse of) the preparation circuit for $|\psi\rangle$ in time $O(\log(|B_\tau|))$. If the outcome is $|\psi\rangle\langle\psi|$, output 0; else output 1.

It is clear that $\mathcal{B}$ is valid by definition. Moreover,

$$\mathrm{Time}(\mathcal{B}_1) \leq \mathrm{Time}(\mathcal{A}_1) + \mathrm{Time}(\mathcal{A}_2) + O(ml \log(q) \log(|B_\tau|)), \tag{11}$$

$$\mathrm{Time}(\mathcal{B}_2) \leq \mathrm{Time}(\mathcal{A}_2) + O(\log(|B_\tau|)). \tag{12}$$

We proceed to lower bound the success probability of $\mathcal{B}$. We analyze the probabilities of the following disjoint cases corresponding to $\mathcal{B}$ being successful.

1. Case 1: In this case, $1 - \Pi$ is measured and $b' = b$. The probability that $1 - \Pi$ is measured is $(1 - \epsilon)$. Conditioned on $1 - \Pi$ being measured, b' is a uniformly random bit so the probability $b' = b$ is $1/2$. Therefore, the overall probability of this case is $(1 - \epsilon)/2$.

2. Case 2: In this case, Π is measured, $b = 1$, and then $1 - |\psi\rangle\langle\psi|$ is measured. The probability that Π is measured is ϵ and the probability that $b = 1$ is $1/2$. We now condition on these two events happening. Since $b = 1$, the state of register C in the input to $\mathcal{B}_2$ is a mixture of states of the form $|r\rangle\langle r|$ where $r \in B_\tau$. This is because $b = 1$ means that register Y is measured in the computational basis and conditioned on Π being measured, the C register is also measured in the computational basis (see the form of Π in Eq. (10)). Therefore, the probability of $\mathcal{B}_2$ measuring $|\psi\rangle\langle\psi|$ is $1/|B_\tau|$. Thus, the overall probability of this case is $\epsilon \cdot (1/2) \cdot (1 - 1/|B_\tau|)$.
3. Case 3: In this case, Π is measured, $b = 0$, and then $|\psi\rangle\langle\psi|$ is measured. The probability that $b = 0$ is $1/2$. Conditioned on $b = 0$, Lemma 2, applied with projectors $|\psi\rangle\langle\psi|$ and $U^\dagger \Pi U$ and state σ, shows that the probability of measuring Π and then $|\psi\rangle\langle\psi|$ is least ϵ^2. Therefore, the overall probability of this case is at least $\epsilon^2/2$.

Summing up the probabilities of the above cases, we see that the success probability of $\mathcal{B}$ is at least

$$\frac{1-\epsilon}{2} + \frac{\epsilon}{2}\left(1 - \frac{1}{|B_\tau|}\right) + \frac{\epsilon^2}{2} = \frac{1}{2} + \frac{\epsilon}{2}\left(\epsilon - \frac{1}{|B_\tau|}\right). \tag{13}$$

Therefore, the advantage of $\mathcal{B}$ is at least $\epsilon(\epsilon - 1/|B_\tau|)$, as required.

3.5   Reduction from MLWE to Collapse

The proof structure of the main result of this subsection, Proposition 4, follows [LMZ23, Theorem 1]. We need to modify a number of aspects of their proof since it applies to the SIS hash function whereas here we consider its module variant, i.e., the MSIS hash function.

We will use a rounding function $\lfloor \cdot \rceil_t : \mathbb{Z}_q \to \{0, 1, \ldots, t - 1\}$, where $t \in \mathbb{N}$, that is defined as follows. For $j \in \{0, 1, \ldots, t - 1\}$, define

$$I_j := \begin{cases} \{j\lfloor q/t\rfloor, j\lfloor q/t\rfloor + 1, \ldots, j\lfloor q/t\rfloor + \lfloor q/t\rfloor - 1\} & \text{if } j \in \{0, 1, \ldots, t - 2\}, \\ \{(t-1)\lfloor q/t\rfloor, (t-1)\lfloor q/t\rfloor + 1, \ldots, q - 1\} & \text{if } j = t - 1. \end{cases} \tag{14}$$

(Note that I_j contains exactly $\lfloor q/t\rfloor$ elements for $j \in \{0, 1, \ldots, t-2\}$ and at least $\lfloor q/t\rfloor$ elements for $j = t - 1$ with the constraint that $q/t \leq |I_{t-1}| \leq q/t + t - 1$.) Then, for $a \in \mathbb{Z}_q$, define $\lfloor a\rceil_t$ to be the unique $j \in \{0, 1, \ldots, t - 1\}$ such that $a \in I_j$.

We will also use the following convenient notation. Let Y and Z be registers and $f : Y \to Z$. The measurement $y \mapsto f(y)$ on register Y refers to the measurement implemented by computing $f(y)$ into a separate register Z, measuring Z in the computational basis, and discarding the result.

Finally, we will use the following lemma.

Lemma 3. Let $0 \neq \Delta \in R_q^l$ and $\alpha \in \{0, \ldots, n - 1\}$. If $b \leftarrow R_q^l$, then $(b \cdot \Delta)_\alpha$ is uniformly distributed in $\mathbb{Z}_q$.

Proof. Writing $b = (b_1, \ldots, b_l)$ and $\Delta = (\Delta_1, \ldots, \Delta_l)$, we have

$$(b \cdot \Delta)_\alpha = (b_1 \Delta_1)_\alpha + \cdots + (b_l \Delta_l)_\alpha. \tag{15}$$

Since $\Delta \neq 0$, there exists an $i \in [l]$ such that $\Delta_i \neq 0$. To prove the lemma, it suffices to prove that $(b_i \Delta_i)_a$ is uniformly distributed in $\mathbb{Z}_q$.

Let ϕ, ϕ' be as defined in the proof of Lemma 1. Write $\phi(\Delta_i) = (c_0, \ldots, c_{n-1}) \in \mathbb{Z}_q^n$. Since $\Delta_i \neq 0$ there exists $j \in \{0, \ldots, n-1\}$ such that $c_j \neq 0$. Since b_i is a uniformly random element of R_q, $\phi(b_i)$ is a uniformly random element of $\mathbb{Z}_q^n$. Therefore, the distribution of $(b_i \Delta_i)_\alpha = \phi'(\phi(b_i)\phi(\Delta_i))_\alpha$ (where we used Lemma 1 for the equality) is the same as the distribution of

$$\phi'(d_0 c_0, \ldots, d_{n-1} c_{n-1})_\alpha, \quad \text{where} \quad d_0, \ldots, d_{n-1} \leftarrow \mathbb{Z}_q. \tag{16}$$

By the linearity of ϕ',

$$\phi'(d_0 c_0, \ldots, d_{n-1} c_{n-1})_\alpha = d_j c_j \phi'(e_j)_\alpha + \sum_{j' \neq j} d_{j'} c_{j'} \phi'(e_{j'})_\alpha, \tag{17}$$

where e_j denotes the jth standard basis vector of $\mathbb{Z}_q$.

But $\phi'(e_j)_\alpha = n^{-1} \cdot w^{-(2j+1)\alpha} \neq 0$ (see Lemma 1). Therefore $d_j c_j \phi'(e_j)_\alpha$ is uniformly distributed in $\mathbb{Z}_q$ if $d_j \leftarrow \mathbb{Z}_q$. Hence $(b_i \Delta_i)_\alpha$ is uniformly distributed in $\mathbb{Z}_q$ as required.

The main result of this subsection is the following proposition.

Proposition 4. *Let $m, l, \gamma, \eta \in \mathbb{N}$. Suppose $q \geq 16$ and $2\gamma\eta nl < \lfloor q/32 \rfloor$. Suppose there exists a quantum algorithm $\mathcal{A}$ that succeeds in* Collapse$_{m,l,\gamma}$ *with advantage ϵ. Then, for all $w \in \mathbb{N}$, there exists a quantum algorithm $\mathcal{B}$ that solves* MLWE$_{l,m,\eta}$ *with advantage at least $(\epsilon - 3^{-w})/4$. Moreover,* Time$(\mathcal{B}) \leq$ Time$(\mathcal{A}) + \mathrm{poly}(w)$.

Before proving this proposition, we first prove two lemmas. Let Y be a register on R_q^l and $A \in R_q^{m \times l}$. For $t \in \mathbb{N}$, we define the following measurements on Y:

- M_0: computational basis measurement.
- M_1^t: sample $e_1 \leftarrow S_\eta^m$, $e_2 \leftarrow S_\eta^l$, set $b := e_1^\top A + e_2^\top \in R_q^l$, sample $s \leftarrow R_q$, then perform measurement $y \mapsto \lfloor (b \cdot y + s)_0 \rfloor_t$.
- M_2^t: sample $b \leftarrow R_q^l$, $s \leftarrow R_q$, then perform measurement $y \mapsto \lfloor (b \cdot y + s)_0 \rfloor_t$.

Lemma 4. *Let $t \in \mathbb{N}$ be such that $2\gamma\eta nl < \lfloor q/t \rfloor$. For all $y, y' \in R_q^l$ with $Ay = Ay'$ and $\|y'\|_\infty, \|y\|_\infty \leq \gamma$,*

$$M_1^t(|y\rangle\langle y'|) = \left(1 - \frac{t}{q} \cdot \mathrm{E}\left[|e \cdot (y - y')|_0 \,\Big|\, e \leftarrow S_\eta^l\right]\right) |y\rangle\langle y'|. \tag{18}$$

Proof. We have

$$M_1^t(|y\rangle\langle y'|) = \Pr\left[\lfloor (b \cdot y + s)_0 \rfloor_t = \lfloor (b \cdot y' + s)_0 \rfloor_t \,\Big|\right.$$
$$\left. e_1 \leftarrow S_\eta^m, e_2 \leftarrow S_\eta^l, b := e_1^\top A + e_2^\top, s \leftarrow R_q\right] \cdot |y\rangle\langle y'| \tag{19}$$

Writing $z := Ay = Ay'$, we have

$$b \cdot y + s = (e_1 \cdot z + s) + e_2 \cdot y \quad \text{and} \quad b \cdot y' + s = (e_1 \cdot z + s) + e_2 \cdot y'. \quad (20)$$

The result follows by observing that $|e_2 \cdot (y - y')|_0 \leq \|e_2\|_\infty \cdot \|y - y'\|_\infty \cdot nl \leq 2\gamma\eta nl < \lfloor q/t \rfloor$ and $(e_1 \cdot z + s)$ is a uniformly random element of R_q.

Lemma 5. *Let $t \in \mathbb{N}$ be such that $t^2 \leq q$. Then there exists $0 \leq p_t \leq 2/t$ such that for all $y, y' \in R_q^l$ with $y' \neq y$, we have*

$$M_2^t(|y\rangle\langle y|) = |y\rangle\langle y| \quad \text{and} \quad M_2^t(|y\rangle\langle y'|) = p_t \, |y\rangle\langle y'|. \quad (21)$$

Proof. The first equality is clearly true. For the second, observe that

$$M_2^t(|y\rangle\langle y'|) = \Pr[\lfloor (b \cdot y + s)_0 \rfloor_t = \lfloor (b \cdot y' + s)_0 \rfloor_t \mid b \leftarrow R_q^l, s \leftarrow R_q]. \quad (22)$$

Write $y' = y + \Delta$ for some $0 \neq \Delta \in R_q^l$. Then, $(b \cdot \Delta)_0$ is uniformly distributed in $\mathbb{Z}_q$ by Lemma 3. Therefore, writing $p_t := \Pr[\lfloor u \rfloor_t = \lfloor u + v \rfloor_t \mid u, v \leftarrow \mathbb{Z}_q]$, we have

$$\Pr[\lfloor (b \cdot y + s)_0 \rfloor_t = \lfloor (b \cdot y' + s)_0 \rfloor_t \mid b \leftarrow R_q^l, s \leftarrow R_q]$$

$$= p_t = 1 - \left(\frac{(t-1)\lfloor q/t \rfloor}{q} \cdot \frac{q - \lfloor q/t \rfloor}{q} + \frac{|I_{t-1}|}{q} \cdot \frac{q - |I_{t-1}|}{q} \right) \quad (23)$$

$$\leq \frac{1}{t} + \frac{t}{q} \leq \frac{2}{t},$$

where the last inequality uses $t^2 \leq q$.

Combining Lemmas 4 and 5 gives the following corollary.

Corollary 1. *Let $t, d \in \mathbb{N}$ be such that $2\gamma\eta nl < \lfloor q/(td) \rfloor$ and $t^2 \leq q$. Let ρ be a density matrix on register Y. Suppose there exists $z \in R_q^m$ such that ρ is supported on $\{y \in R_q^l \mid Ay = z, \|y\|_\infty \leq \gamma\}$. Then*

$$M_1^t(\rho) = \frac{1}{d}M_1^{td}(\rho) + \left(1 - \frac{1}{d}\right)\rho, \quad (24)$$

$$M_2^t(\rho) = \frac{1}{d}M_0(M_1^{td}(\rho)) + \left(1 - \frac{1}{d} - p_t\right)M_0(\rho) + p_t\rho, \quad (25)$$

where p_t is as defined in Lemma 5.

Proof. The first equality is immediate. The second equality follows from the observation that $M_0(M_1^{td}(\rho)) = M_1^{td}(M_0(\rho))$ since M_0 and M_1 both act on ρ by entry-wise multiplication.

Given the above lemmas, Proposition 4 follows from the proof of [LMZ23, Theorem 1]. The high-level idea of the proof is that M_1^t is close to the identity operation while M_2^t is close to M_0. Therefore, if the identity operation can be efficiently distinguished from M_0, then M_1^t and M_2^t can be efficiently distinguished, which solves the MLWE problem. For completeness, we give the details below.

Proof (Proof of Proposition 4). Let $t := 4$ and $d := 8$ so that $g := 1 - 1/d - p_t \geq 3/8$ and $dg \geq 3$, where p_t is as defined in Lemma 5. Let $\mathcal{A} = (\mathcal{A}_1, \mathcal{A}_2)$ be a valid algorithm for the $\mathsf{Collapse}_{m,l,\gamma}$ experiment (Definition 6) with advantage ϵ.

Fix $w \in \mathbb{N}$ and $A \in R_q^{m \times l}$. Let $T := \sum_{j=0}^{w-1} (dg)^{-j}$ and let $\mathcal{B}$ be the quantum algorithm defined on input $b \in R_q^l$ as follows:

1. Create state ρ on register (Y, Z, T) by running $\mathcal{A}_1(A)$.
2. Sample $j \in \{0, 1, \ldots, w-1\}$ with probability $(dg)^{-j}/T$.
3. Apply M_1^{td} to ρ on the Y register for j times. Call the resulting state ρ_j.
4. Sample $s \leftarrow R_q$ and apply the measurement $x \mapsto \lfloor (b \cdot x + s)_0 \rceil_t$ to ρ_j on the Y register to give state ρ_j'.
5. Compute bit $b' \in \{0, 1\}$ by running $\mathcal{A}_2(\rho_j')$.
6. Output b' if j is even and $1 - b'$ if j is odd.

For $j \in \{0, 1, \ldots, w-1\}$, let ϵ_j denote the signed distinguishing advantage of $\mathcal{A}_2$ on inputs ρ_j versus $M_0(\rho_j)$, i.e., $\epsilon_j := \Pr[\mathcal{A}_2(\rho_j) = 0] - \Pr[\mathcal{A}_2(M_0(\rho_j)) = 0]$, and let δ_j denote the signed distinguishing advantage of $\mathcal{A}_2$ on inputs $M_1^t(\rho_j)$ versus $M_2^t(\rho_j)$. Then the signed distinguishing advantage of $\mathcal{B}$ on input distributions $[e_1 \leftarrow S_\eta^m,\ e_2 \leftarrow S_\eta^l,\ b := e_1^\top A + e_2^\top]$ versus $[b^\top \leftarrow R_q^l]$ is

$$\delta := \frac{1}{T} \sum_{j=0}^{w-1} (-dg)^{-j} \delta_j, \tag{26}$$

because $\rho_j' = M_1^t(\rho_j)$ if b is sampled according to $[e_1 \leftarrow S_\eta^m,\ e_2 \leftarrow S_\eta^l,\ b := e_1^\top A + e_2^\top]$ and $\rho_j' = M_2^t(\rho_j)$ if b is sampled according to $[b^\top \leftarrow R_q^l]$.

By Corollary 1 (which applies by the assumptions in the proposition and the validity of $\mathcal{A}$), we have $\delta_j = \frac{1}{d}\epsilon_{j+1} + g\epsilon_j$ for all $j \in \{0, 1, \ldots, w-2\}$. Therefore,

$$\epsilon_i(-dg)^{-i} = \epsilon_0 - \frac{1}{g} \sum_{j=0}^{i-1} (-dg)^{-j} \delta_j \quad \text{for all } i \in \{0, 1, \ldots, w-1\}. \tag{27}$$

Then,

$$\delta = \frac{g}{T}(\epsilon_0 - \epsilon_w(-dg)^{-w}). \tag{28}$$

We now unfix $A \in R_q^{m \times l}$ and take the expectation of Eq. (28) over $A \leftarrow R_q^{m \times l}$ to see that

$$|\mathrm{E}_A[\delta]| = \frac{g}{T}\left|\mathrm{E}_A[\epsilon_0 - \epsilon_w(-dg)^{-w}]\right| \geq \left(g - \frac{1}{d}\right)(\epsilon - (dg)^{-w}) \geq \frac{1}{4}\left(\epsilon - \frac{1}{3^w}\right), \tag{29}$$

where the first inequality uses $T \leq dg/(dg - 1)$, $|\epsilon_w| \leq 1$, and $\epsilon = |\mathrm{E}_A[\epsilon_0]|$.

Since $\mathrm{Time}(\mathcal{B}) = \mathrm{Time}(\mathcal{A}) + \mathrm{poly}(w)$ and $|\mathrm{E}_A[\delta]|$ is the advantage of $\mathcal{B}$ for solving $\mathsf{MLWE}_{l,m,\eta}$, the proposition follows.

4   Concrete Parameters

In this section, we describe how to adjust the parameter settings of Dilithium using Theorem 2 to achieve security levels comparable to those considered in the Dilithium specifications [Bai+21], Dilithium-QROM [KLS18], and the relevant NIST Federal Information Processing Standards (FIPS) [NIST23, Appendix A].

We will use the same notation as in the Dilithium specification, [Bai+21]. [Bai+21] specifies Dilithium in terms of the variables

$$q, n, k, l, H, \tau, d, \tau, \gamma_1, \gamma_2, \eta, \beta. \tag{30}$$

Except for the variable d, these variables roughly specify Dilithium according to the simplified version given in Fig. 1. The variable d specifies a further compression of the public key. To see how these variables precisely specify the full version of Dilithium, we refer the reader to [Bai+21].

The security analysis of CRYSTALS-Dilithium in [KLS18] leads to [KLS18, Eqs. (10) and (11)] which shows the following. Given a quantum query algorithm $\mathcal{A}$ for breaking the sEUF-CMA-security of Dilithium, there exist quantum algorithms $\mathcal{B}, \mathcal{D}, \mathcal{E}$ and quantum query algorithm $\mathcal{C}$ such that $\text{Time}(\mathcal{B}) = \text{Time}(\mathcal{C}) = \text{Time}(\mathcal{A})$ and $\text{Time}(\mathcal{D}) \approx \text{Time}(\mathcal{A})$ with

$$\text{Adv}_{\text{Dilithium}}^{\text{sEUF-CMA}}(\mathcal{A}) \leq 2^{-\alpha+1} + \text{Adv}_{k,l,\eta}^{\text{MLWE}}(\mathcal{B}) + \text{Adv}_{H,\tau,k,l+1,\zeta}^{\text{SelfTargetMSIS}}(\mathcal{C})$$
$$+ \text{Adv}_{k,l,\zeta'}^{\text{MSIS}}(\mathcal{D}) + \text{Adv}_{\text{Sam}}^{\text{PR}}(\mathcal{E}), \tag{31}$$

where ζ, ζ' are functions of parameters $\gamma_1, \gamma_2, \beta, d, \tau$ defined as follows:

$$\zeta := \max(\gamma_1 - \beta, 2\gamma_2 + 1 + 2^{d-1}\tau) \quad \text{and} \quad \zeta' := \max(2(\gamma_1 - \beta), 4\gamma_2 + 2). \tag{32}$$

$\text{Adv}_{\text{Sam}}^{\text{PR}}(\mathcal{E})$ is the advantage of any algorithm distinguishing between the pseudorandom function used by Dilithium and a randomly selected function; and α is a min-entropy term that can be bounded using [KLS18, Lemma C.1 of ePrint version] by

$$\alpha \geq \min\left(-n \log\left(\frac{2\gamma_1 + 1}{2\gamma_2 - 1}\right), -kl \log(n/q)\right). \tag{33}$$

In the QROM, we can construct an optimal pseudorandom function using a random oracle such that $\text{Adv}_{\text{Sam}}^{\text{PR}}(\mathcal{E})$ is asymptotically negligible and can be neglected.

Theorem 2 shows that the hardness of SelfTargetMSIS in the QROM is at least that of MLWE. Therefore, Theorem 2 and Eq. (31) rigorously imply the asymptotic result that, under suitable choices of parameters as functions of the security parameter λ, if there are no poly(λ)-time quantum algorithms that solve MLWE or MSIS then there is no poly(λ)-time quantum algorithm that breaks the sEUF-CMA security of Dilithium. This is a very positive sign for the security of Dilithium as MSIS and MLWE are far better-studied problems and there is substantial support for the assumption that they are hard problems.

We proceed to give concrete estimates of the Core-SVP security of Dilithium under several choices of parameters using Theorem 2 and Eq. (31). These estimates rely on some heuristic assumptions that we will clearly state. We remark that the concrete security estimates appearing in [KLS18, Bai+21] use similar heuristic assumptions.

We begin by dividing both sides of Eq. (31) by $\text{Time}(\mathcal{A})$. Using $\text{Time}(\mathcal{B}) = \text{Time}(\mathcal{C}) = \text{Time}(\mathcal{A})$, assuming the approximation in $\text{Time}(\mathcal{D}) \approx \text{Time}(\mathcal{A})$ can be replaced by equality, and using our work's parameters in Tables 2 to 4 for which $\alpha \geq 257$, we obtain

$$S(\mathcal{A}) \leq 2^{-256} + \frac{\text{Adv}_{k,l,\eta}^{\text{MLWE}}(\mathcal{B})}{\text{Time}(\mathcal{B})} + \frac{\text{Adv}_{H,\tau,k,l+1,\zeta}^{\text{SelfTargetMSIS}}(\mathcal{C})}{\text{Time}(\mathcal{C})} + \frac{\text{Adv}_{k,l,\zeta'}^{\text{MSIS}}(\mathcal{D})}{\text{Time}(\mathcal{D})}, \qquad (34)$$

where $S(\mathcal{A}) := \text{Adv}_{\text{Dilithium}}^{\text{sEUF-CMA}}(\mathcal{A})/\text{Time}(\mathcal{A})$.

By Theorem 2, for any $\eta' \in \mathbb{N}$ with $\eta' < \lfloor q/32 \rfloor/(2\zeta n(k+l+1))$, there exists a quantum algorithm $\mathcal{C}'$ for $\text{MLWE}_{k+l+1,k,\eta'}$, such that

$$S(\mathcal{A}) \leq 2^{-256} + \frac{\text{Adv}_{k,l,\eta}^{\text{MLWE}}(\mathcal{B})}{\text{Time}(\mathcal{B})} + \frac{8Q^2\sqrt{\text{Adv}_{k+l+1,k,\eta'}^{\text{MLWE}}(\mathcal{C}')}}{\text{Time}(\mathcal{C})} + \frac{\text{Adv}_{k,l,\zeta'}^{\text{MSIS}}(\mathcal{D})}{\text{Time}(\mathcal{D})}, \qquad (35)$$

where Q is the number of queries $\mathcal{C}$ uses and we assume that Eq. (7) is well-approximated by $\epsilon^2/(64Q^4)$, in particular, that τ is sufficiently large.

Also by Theorem 2, we have $\text{Time}(\mathcal{C}')$ is at most $\text{Time}(\mathcal{C})$ plus polynomial terms. Heuristically assuming that we can neglect the polynomial terms and using $Q \leq \text{Time}(\mathcal{C})$, we obtain

$$S(\mathcal{A}) \leq 2^{-256} + \frac{\text{Adv}_{k,l,\eta}^{\text{MLWE}}(\mathcal{B})}{\text{Time}(\mathcal{B})} + 8Q^{3/2}\sqrt{\frac{\text{Adv}_{k+l+1,k,\eta'}^{\text{MLWE}}(\mathcal{C}')}{\text{Time}(\mathcal{C}')}} + \frac{\text{Adv}_{k,l,\zeta'}^{\text{MSIS}}(\mathcal{D})}{\text{Time}(\mathcal{D})}. \qquad (36)$$

Now, for NIST security level $l \in [5]$, we upper bound Q by B_l, where B_l is given in Table 1.

From the third term on the right-hand side of Eq. (36), we see that the Quantum Core-SVP security of SelfTargetMSIS can be estimated by

$$\frac{z}{2} - \frac{3}{2}\log(B_l) - 3, \qquad (37)$$

where z is the Quantum Core-SVP security of the associated MLWE problem.

Having reduced the sEUF-NMA security of Dilithium to the security of standard lattice problems MLWE and MSIS, we proceed to estimate their security. Following the analysis in the Dilithium specifications [Bai+21], we perform our security estimates via the Core-SVP methodology introduced in [Alk+16]. In the Core-SVP methodology, we consider attacks using the Block Khorkine-Zolotarev (BKZ) algorithm [SE94, CN11]. The BKZ algorithm with block size $\mu \in \mathbb{N}$ works by making a small number of calls to an SVP solver on μ-dimensional lattices. The Core-SVP methodology conservatively assumes that the run-time of the

Table 1. Upper bounds on Q for NIST security levels 1 to 5. These numbers are based on [NIST23, Appendix A] together with well-known quantum query complexity results if we model the block ciphers and hash functions used in [NIST23, Appendix A] as random functions.[1]

NIST Security Level (SLl)	SL1	SL2	SL3	SL4	SL5
Upper bound on Q (B_l)	2^{64}	2^{86}	2^{96}	2^{128}	2^{128}

[1]Given a random function $f\colon [N] \to [N]$, the number of quantum queries to f needed to find a preimage of 1 is $\Theta(N^{1/2})$ [Gro96] and the number of quantum queries to f needed to find a collision, i.e., $i \neq j$ such that $f(i) = f(j)$, is $\Theta(N^{1/3})$ [Zha15]. (We ignore the constants hidden in the Θ-notation; more detailed analysis is possible, see, e.g., [Jaq+20].)

BKZ algorithm is equal to the cost of a single run of the SVP solver at its core. The latter cost is then estimated as $2^{0.265\mu}$ since this is the cost of the best quantum SVP solver [Bai+21, Section C.1] due to Laarhoven [Laa16, Section 14.2.10]. Therefore, to estimate the security of an MLWE or MSIS problem, it suffices to estimate the smallest $\mu \in \mathbb{N}$ such that BKZ with block-size μ can solve the problem. Then we say 0.265μ is the *Quantum Core-SVP* security of the problem.

To describe how the block-size can be estimated, it is convenient to define the function $\delta\colon \mathbb{N} \to \mathbb{R}$,

$$\delta(\mu) := \left(\frac{(\mu\pi)^{1/\mu}\mu}{2\pi e} \right)^{\frac{1}{2(\mu-1)}}. \tag{38}$$

4.1 Concrete Security of MLWE

Our security analysis of MLWE generally follows the Dilithium specifications, [Bai+21, Appendix C.2]. For $a, b, \epsilon \in \mathbb{N}$, we first follow [Bai+21, Appendix C.2] and assume that $\mathsf{MLWE}_{a,b,\epsilon}$ is as hard as the Learning With Errors problem $\mathsf{LWE}_{na,nb,\epsilon}$. Then, for $a', b' \in \mathbb{N}$, $\mathsf{LWE}_{a',b',\epsilon}$ is defined to be the same as $\mathsf{MLWE}_{a',b',\epsilon}$ with n set to 1 so that $R_q = \mathbb{Z}_q$.

Then, as done in [Bai+21, Appendix C.2], we follow the security analysis in [Alk+16]. [Alk+16] considers two attacks based on the BKZ algorithm, known as the primal attack and dual attack. The block-size is then taken as the minimum of the block-sizes for the primal and dual attacks. These attacks are analyzed as follows.

1. Primal attack [Alk+16, Section 6.3]. Let $c := na + nb + 1$. Then, to solve $\mathsf{LWE}_{na,nb,\epsilon}$, we set the BKZ block-size μ to be equal to the smallest integer ≥ 50 such that:[6] $\xi\sqrt{\mu} \leq \delta(\mu)^{2\mu-c} \cdot q^{na/c}$.

---

[6] In [Alk+16, Section 6.3], the exponent on $\delta(\mu)$ is given as $2\mu - c - 1$, but it was later corrected to $2\mu - c$ by [Alb+17, Section 3.2]. There can be spurious solutions with $0 < \mu < 50$ for which the approximations leading to the inequality break down.

2. Dual attack [Alk+16, Section 6.4]. Let $c' := na+nb$. Then to solve $\mathsf{LWE}_{na,nb,\epsilon}$, we set the BKZ block-size μ to be equal to the smallest integer ≥ 50 such that $-2\pi^2\tau(\mu)^2 \geq \ln(2^{-0.2075\mu/2})$, where $\tau(\mu) := \delta(\mu)^{c'-1}q^{nb/c'}\epsilon/q$.

4.2 Concrete Security of MSIS

Our security analysis of MSIS uses heuristics in the Dilithium specifications [Bai+21, Appendix C.3] and [Lyu12] (which is in turn based on [MR09]).[7] For $a, b, \xi \in \mathbb{N}$, we first follow [Bai+21, Appendix C.3] and assume that $\mathsf{MSIS}_{a,b,\xi}$ is as hard as the Short Integer Solutions problem $\mathsf{SIS}_{na,nb,\xi}$. Then, for $a', b' \in \mathbb{N}$, $\mathsf{SIS}_{a',b',\xi}$ is defined to be the same as $\mathsf{MSIS}_{a',b',\xi}$ with n set to 1 so that $R_q = \mathbb{Z}_q$. Following [Lyu12], we estimate the security of $\mathsf{SIS}_{na,nb,\xi}$, by considering the attack that uses the BKZ algorithm with block-size μ to find a short non-zero vector in the lattice

$$L(A) := \{y \in \mathbb{Z}^{na+nb} \mid [I_{na} \mid A] \cdot y = 0 \bmod q\}, \tag{39}$$

where $A \leftarrow \mathbb{Z}_q^{na \times nb}$. Following [Lyu12, Eq. (3) of ePrint version], the BKZ algorithm is expected to find a vector $v \in L(A)$ of Euclidean length[8]

$$2^{2\sqrt{na\log(q)\log(\delta(\mu))}}. \tag{40}$$

We assume that the entries of v have the same magnitudes since a similar assumption is made in [Bai+21, Appendix C.3]. Then, to solve $\mathsf{SIS}_{na,nb,\xi}$, we set the BKZ block-size μ to be the smallest positive integer such that

$$\frac{1}{\sqrt{na+nb}} \cdot 2^{2\sqrt{na\log(q)\log(\delta(\mu))}} \leq \xi. \tag{41}$$

4.3 Parameter Sets for Different Security Levels

To set Dilithium parameters, we also require $q = 1 \bmod 2\gamma_2$, $q > 4\gamma_2$ (see [Bai+21, Lemma 1] or [KLS18, Lemma 4.1]), and $\beta = \tau\eta$ (see [Bai+21, Table 2]). Moreover, we set parameters to minimize the following metrics [KLS18]:

1. the public key size in bytes: $(nk(\lceil\log(q)\rceil - d) + 256)/8$;
2. the signature size in bytes: $(nl\lceil\log(2\gamma_1)\rceil + nk + \tau(\log(n) + 1))/8$;
3. the expected number of repeats to sign a message: $\exp\left(n\beta\left(\frac{l}{\gamma_1} + \frac{k}{\gamma_2}\right)\right)$.

---

[7] We were unable to completely reuse the analysis in [Bai+21, Section C.3] as it is not completely described. Comparing the estimates for μ obtained by the method here with that in [Bai+21, Table 1], we find our estimates are consistently around 4/5 times that given in [Bai+21, Table 1]. Therefore, our estimates underestimate the security of MSIS compared to [Bai+21].

[8] Compared to [Lyu12, Eq. (3) of ePrint version], we do not take the min of Eq. (40) with q since "trivial" vectors of the form q times a standard basis vector have too large of an infinity-norm to be a solution to $\mathsf{SIS}_{na,nb,\xi}$ when $\xi < q$, as will be the case for our parameter choices.

In Tables 2 to 4, we give parameter sets achieving different levels of security that we calculated using the methodology described above. In all tables, we use:

$$q_0 := 12439554041857 = 2^{11} \cdot 3 \cdot 19 \cdot 1447 \cdot 73643 + 1 \approx 2^{43.5}. \qquad (42)$$

In particular, $q_0 = 1 \bmod 2n$.

Having established our attack model, we quantify the security provided by the proposed parameter sets for both Dilithium [Bai+21] and Dilithium-QROM [KLS18] using our model in Tables 2 and 3. In those tables, we also provide new parameter sets that guarantee the same security if we analyzed the security of SelfTargetMSIS using Theorem 2, in particular, Eq. (37). The new parameter sets are chosen in a way that minimizes their corresponding public key and signature sizes, as well as the expected number of repeats in Sign. In Table 4, we provide our recommended parameter sets at the five security levels specified by NIST.[9]

Compared to the original Dilithium at "SL3", we find an increase in public key size of $\approx 11.4\times$ and an increase in signature size of $\approx 3.2\times$ [Bai+21]. However, our results are provably secure based on conventional hardness assumptions for the MSIS and MLWE problems, whereas Dilithium must also assume that SelfTargetMSIS is hard for the parameters that they set. (See the discussion in Sect. 1.2.) Thus, the main advantage of our parameters compared to Dilithium is that ours are based on rigorous reductions from hard lattice problems, whereas Dilithium's are based on highly heuristic reductions. We note that the heuristic reduction from SelfTargetMSIS to (a variant of) MSIS given in [Bai+21, End of Sect. 6.2.1] has been recently challenged [Wan+22].

Compared to Dilithium-QROM at its recommended security level, we find an increase in public key size of $\approx 2.9\times$ and an increase in signature size of $\approx 1.3\times$ [KLS18]. However, while both parameter sets produce schemes that can be proven secure under the assumptions that MSIS and MLWE are hard, our parameter sets allow the use of the NTT and are therefore more efficient to implement than those of Dilithium-QROM. We analyze this difference in greater detail below.

The main reason why we must increase the public key and signature sizes is due to the loss in the reduction from MLWE to SelfTargetMSIS, as stated in Theorem 2. Concretely, the loss manifests as Eq. (37), which we used to calculate the Quantum Core-SVP numbers for the SelfTargetMSIS-based MLWE problem. An interesting open question is to understand whether this loss is intrinsic.

Next, we quantitatively compare the efficiency of ring multiplication for the parameter sets in Table 3.

Our work uses $q = q_0$ and $n = 512$. Since $q = 1 \bmod 2n$, we can multiply two elements in R_q using the NTT, which uses $\frac{3}{2}n\log(n) + 2n = 7936$ multiplications in $\mathbb{Z}_q$ and $3n\log(n) = 13824$ additions in $\mathbb{Z}_q$ [Lia+21, Section 2.2].

---

[9] The headings "SLl" appearing in Table 2 follow the headings used in [Bai+21, Table 2]. Under our attack model, they do not exactly correspond to the desired security of NIST's SLl. This explains the need for Table 4 and why Table 4 differs from Table 2.

Table 2. We give parameter sets that match the quantized security of those proposed in the Dilithium specifications [Bai+21]. q_0 is defined in Eq. (42). The "SelfTargetMSIS" block-size should be understood as the block-size of the LWE problem reduced to via Theorem 2 and Sect. 4.1.

	Dilithium [Bai+21]			Our work		
	SL2	SL3	SL5	SL2	SL3	SL5
q	$2^{23} - 8191$	$2^{23} - 8191$	$2^{23} - 8191$	q_0	q_0	q_0
n	256	256	256	512	512	512
(k, l)	(4, 4)	(6, 5)	(8, 7)	(10, 4)	(12, 8)	(16, 13)
d	13	13	13	15	15	15
τ	39	49	60	40	40	40
γ_1	2^{17}	2^{19}	2^{19}	220929	370432	555648
γ_2	95232	261888	261888	441858	740864	1111296
ζ	350209	724481	769537	1539077	2137089	2877953
ζ'	380930	1048184	1048336	1767434	2963458	4445186
η	2	4	2	2	2	2
η'	N/A	N/A	N/A	8	4	2
pk size (bytes)	1312	1952	2592	18592	22304	29728
σ size (bytes)	2476	3448	4804	5554	11058	18546
Expected Repeats	4.25	5.10	3.85	5.30	4.70	4.70
LWE BKZ Block-Size	448	669	911	605	1205	2111
Quantum Core-SVP	118	177	241	160	319	559
"SelfTargetMSIS" BKZ Block-Size	N/A	N/A	N/A	1753	2177	3025
Quantum Core-SVP	N/A	N/A	N/A	100	141	205
SIS BKZ Block-Size	363	533	773	4942	5644	7423
Quantum Core-SVP	96	141	204	1309	1495	1967

Dilithium-QROM uses a q such that $q = 5 \bmod 8$ and we can no longer use the NTT to multiply elements in R_q. Instead, we consider the Hybrid-NTT (H-NTT) [Lia+21, Section 5]. When $q = 1 \bmod (n/2^{\alpha+\beta-1})$, where α, β are non-negative integer parameters, and n is a power of 2, H-NTT can multiply two elements in R_q using

$$\frac{3}{2}n\log(n) + \left(3 \cdot 2^{\alpha+\beta-3} + 2^{\alpha-2} + 3 \cdot 2^{\beta-3} + 2^{\alpha-\beta-2} - \frac{3}{2}(\alpha+\beta) + \frac{5}{4}\right)n \quad (43)$$

multiplications in $\mathbb{Z}_q$, and

$$3n\log(n) + \left(5 \cdot 2^{\alpha+\beta-2} + 5 \cdot 2^{\beta-2} + 5 \cdot 2^{\alpha-2} - 3(\alpha+\beta) - \frac{15}{4}\right)n \quad (44)$$

additions in $\mathbb{Z}_q$. Dilithium-QROM uses $q = 2^{45} - 21283$ and $n = 512$ so the condition $q = 1 \bmod (n/2^{\alpha+\beta-1})$ requires $\alpha + \beta \in \{8, 9, 10\}$.[10] The number of

---

[10] Note that $2^{\alpha+\beta-1}$ needs to be n, $n/2$, or $n/4$ for $q = 1 \bmod (n/2^{\alpha+\beta-1})$ to be compatible with $q = 5 \bmod 8$. This means H-NTT would use $\Omega(n^2)$ multiplications and additions in $\mathbb{Z}_q$ when multiplying elements of R_q in Dilithium-QROM.

Table 3. We give parameter sets that match the quantized security of those proposed in Dilithium-QROM [KLS18]. q_0 is defined in Eq. (42). In the "Our work" columns, we assume Q is bounded by 2^{96}, which corresponds to NIST Security Level 3. The "SelfTargetMSIS" block-size should be understood as the block-size of the LWE problem reduced to via Theorem 2 and Sect. 4.1.

	Dilithium-QROM [KLS18]		Our work	
	recommended	very high	recommended	very high
q	$2^{45} - 21283$	$2^{45} - 21283$	q_0	q_0
n	512	512	512	512
(k, l)	(4, 4)	(5, 5)	(12, 5)	(13, 8)
d	15	15	15	15
τ	46	46	40	40
γ_1	905679	905679	279949	370432
γ_2	905679	905679	555648	740864
ζ	2565023	2565023	1766657	2137089
ζ'	3622718	3622718	2222594	2963458
η	7	3	2	2
η'	N/A	N/A	5	4
pk size (bytes)	7712	9632	22304	24160
σ size (bytes)	5690	7098	7218	11122
Expected Repeats	4.29	2.18	5.03	4.97
LWE BKZ Block-Size	499	620	794	1232
Quantum Core-SVP	132	164	210	326
"SelfTargetMSIS" BKZ Block-Size	N/A	N/A	2118	2374
Quantum Core-SVP	N/A	N/A	133	167
SIS BKZ Block-Size	N/A	N/A	5910	6197
Quantum Core-SVP	N/A	N/A	1566	1642

multiplications and additions in $\mathbb{Z}_q$ is minimized by setting $\alpha = \beta = 4$. Therefore, H-NTT uses $\frac{3}{2}n\log(n) + 95.5n = 55808$ multiplications and $3n\log(n) + 332.25n = 183936$ additions in $\mathbb{Z}_q$ per ring element multiplication.

We can count the number of ring element multiplications and additions used by Dilithium's (Gen, Sign, Verify) given some number r of repeats in Sign. For the count, we use the simplified descriptions of these algorithms given in Fig. 1.

Multiplications   Gen: kl,   Sign: $(kl + k + l)r$,   and   Verify: $kl + k$

Additions   Gen: kl,   Sign: $(kl + l)r$,   and   Verify: kl

Note that adding two ring elements requires n additions in $\mathbb{Z}_q$.

Now, in Table 5, we compare the number of multiplications and additions in $\mathbb{Z}_q$ used by Dilithium when instantiated with the parameter sets in Table 3.

Table 4. We give parameter sets that most closely match the security levels requested by NIST [NIST23, Appendix A]. q_0 is defined in Eq. (42). The "SelfTargetMSIS" block-size should be understood as the block-size of the LWE problem reduced to via Theorem 2 and Sect. 4.1.

	SL1	SL2	SL3	SL4/5
q	q_0	q_0	q_0	q_0
n	512	512	512	512
(k, l)	(7, 7)	(9, 9)	(10, 10)	(13, 13)
d	15	15	15	15
τ	40	40	40	40
γ_1	277824	329916	370432	555648
γ_2	555648	659832	740864	1111296
ζ	1766657	1975025	2137089	2877953
ζ'	2222594	2639330	2963458	4445186
η	2	2	2	2
η'	7	5	4	2
pk size (bytes)	13024	16736	18592	24160
σ size (bytes)	9458	12146	13490	18354
Expected Repeats	4.70	5.34	5.25	4.21
LWE BKZ Block-Size	967	1325	1509	2079
Quantum Core-SVP	256	351	399	550
"SelfTargetMSIS" BKZ Block-Size	1252	1665	1866	2454
Quantum Core-SVP	66	88	100	130
SIS BKZ Block-Size	3100	4064	4525	5822
Quantum Core-SVP	821	1076	1199	1542

Table 5 shows that Dilithium-QROM at its recommended security level would require approximately the following increases in $\mathbb{Z}_q$-operation counts when compared to our work:

Multiplications	Gen: 1.9×,	Sign: 1.9×,	and	Verify: 2.0×
Additions	Gen: 3.4×,	Sign: 3.4×,	and	Verify: 3.6×

We therefore identify a cost-benefit trade-off between the two provably secure formulations of Dilithium, our work and Dilithium-QROM, at the recommended security level. Our work's public key and signature sizes are 2.9× and 1.3× larger than Dilithium-QROM's, respectively. However, our scheme requires 1.9× to 3.6× fewer $\mathbb{Z}_q$-operations to implement. Moreover, unlike Dilithium-QROM, our work proves security on Dilithium's native ring where $q = 1 \bmod 2n$.

Table 5. The number of $\mathbb{Z}_q$ additions and $\mathbb{Z}_q$ multiplications required to implement the ring operations performed by the Gen, Sign, and Verify algorithms of Dilithium. These numbers are calculated using the parameters in Table 3 and the analysis from [Lia+21].

	Dilithium-QROM [KLS18]		Our work	
	recommended	very high	recommended	very high
Multiplications in $\mathbb{Z}_q$				
Gen	892928	1395200	476160	825344
Sign	5745992	4258150	3073692	4930240
Verify	1116160	1674240	571392	928512
Additions in $\mathbb{Z}_q$				
Gen	2951168	4611200	860160	1490944
Sign	18981980	14067802	5521572	8873160
Verify	3686912	5530880	1026048	1670656

We make a final remark on the concrete security analysis of our work as well as those originally done for Dilithium and Dilithium-QROM: no analysis accounts rigorously for potential differences in the hardness between LWE with a uniform error distribution and SIS under the ℓ_∞ norm as compared to the better-studied versions of these problems which employ a Gaussian error distribution and the ℓ_2 norm, respectively. However, the hardness of the former problems are comparable to the hardness of the latter problems over parameter regimes that are polynomially related in the security parameter [Pei07, MP13]. Therefore, like the original analyses of Dilithium and Dilithium-QROM, we assume that the differences in hardness are not significant enough to seriously threaten security.

Acknowledgments. This work was supported by the National Institute of Standards and Technology (NIST) and the Joint Center for Quantum Information and Computer Science (QuICS) at the University of Maryland. This research paper is not subject to copyright in the United States. The opinions, findings, and conclusions in the paper are those of the authors and do not necessarily reflect the views or policies of NIST or the United States Government.

We thank Marcel Dall'Agnol, Jiahui Liu, Yi-Kai Liu, and Ray Perlner for helpful feedback and correspondence. We thank Amin Shiraz Gilani for his involvement during the early stages of this project.

References

[Ajt96] Ajtai, M.: Generating hard instances of lattice problems. In: Proceedings of the 28th ACM Symposium on the Theory of Computing (STOC). Philadelphia, Pennsylvania, USA: Association for Computing Machinery, pp. 99–108 (1996). ISBN: 0897917855. https://doi.org/10.1145/237814.237838

[Ala+22] Alagic, G., et al.: Status report on the third round of the NIST postquantum cryptography standardization process. In: US Department of Commerce, NIST (2022). https://doi.org/10.6028/NIST.IR.8413-upd1

[Alb+17] Albrecht, M.R., Göpfert, F., Virdia, F., Wunderer, T.: Revisiting the expected cost of solving uSVP and applications to LWE. In: Takagi, T., Peyrin, T. (eds.) ASIACRYPT 2017. LNCS, vol. 10624, pp. 297–322. Springer, Cham (2017). https://doi.org/10.1007/978-3-319-70694-8_11

[Alk+16] Alkim, Ducas, L., Pöppelmann, T., Schwabe, P.: Post-quantum key exchange—a new hope. In: 25th USENIX Security Symposium (USENIX Security 16). Austin, TX: USENIX Association, pp. 327–343 (2016). ISBN: 978-1-931971-32-4

[Bai+21] Bai, S., et al.: CRYSTALSDilithium: algorithm specifications and supporting documentation (Version 3.1). Current: https://pq-crystals.org/dilithium/resources.shtml; Stable: https://doi.org/10.13154/tches.v2018.i1.238-268 (2021)

[Bar+23] Barbosa, M., et al.: Fixing and mechanizing the security proof of Fiat-Shamir with aborts and Dilithium. In: Handschuh, H., Lysyanskaya, A., ed. Advances in Cryptology – CRYPTO 2023, pp. 358–389. Springer Nature Switzerland, Cham (2023). ISBN: 978-3-031-38554-4. https://doi.org/10.1007/978-3-031-38554-4_12

[BN06] Bellare, M., Neven, G.: Multi-signatures in the plain public-key model and a general forking lemma. In: Proceedings of the 13th ACM Conference on Computer and Communications Security. CCS '06. Alexandria, Virginia, USA: Association for Computing Machinery, pp. 390–399 (2006). ISBN: 1595935185. https://doi.org/10.1145/1180405.1180453

[Bon+11] Boneh, D., Dagdelen, Ö., Fischlin, M., Lehmann, A., Schaffner, C., Zhandry, M.: Random oracles in a quantum world. In: Lee, D.H., Wang, X. (eds.) ASIACRYPT 2011. LNCS, vol. 7073, pp. 41–69. Springer, Heidelberg (2011). https://doi.org/10.1007/978-3-642-25385-0_3

[CN11] Chen, Y., Nguyen, P.Q.: BKZ 2.0: better lattice security estimates. In: Lee, H.D., Wang, X. ed. Advances in Cryptology – ASIACRYPT 2011, pp. 1–20. Springer Berlin Heidelberg, Berlin, Heidelberg (2011). ISBN: 978-3-642-25385-0. https://doi.org/10.1007/978-3-642-25385-0_1

[Dev+23] Devevey, J., Fallahpour, P., Passelègue, A., Stehlé, D.: A detailed analysis of Fiat-Shamir with aborts. In: Handschuh, H., Lysyanskaya, A. ed. Advances in Cryptology – CRYPTO 2023, pp. 327–357. Springer Nature Switzerland, Cham (2023). ISBN: 978-3-031-38554-4. https://doi.org/10.1007/978-3-031-38554-4_11

[DFM20] Don, J., Fehr, S., Majenz, C.: The measure-and-reprogram technique 2.0: multi-round Fiat-Shamir and more. In: Micciancio, D., Ristenpart, T. (eds.) CRYPTO 2020. LNCS, vol. 12172, pp. 602–631. Springer, Cham (2020). https://doi.org/10.1007/978-3-030-56877-1_21

[DS23] Dall'Agnol, M., Spooner, N.: On the necessity of collapsing for post-quantum and quantum commitments. In: Fawzi, O., Walter, M., 18th Conference on the Theory of Quantum Computation, Communication and Cryptography (TQC 2023), vol. 266. Leibniz International Proceedings in Informatics (LIPIcs). Dagstuhl, Germany: Schloss Dagstuhl – Leibniz-Zentrum für Informatik, pp. 2:1–2:23 (2023). ISBN: 978-3-95977-283-9. https://doi.org/10.4230/LIPIcs.TQC.2023.2

[Gro96] Grover, L.K.: A fast quantum mechanical algorithm for database search. In: Proceedings of the 28th ACM Symposium on the Theory of Computing (STOC), pp. 212–219 (1996). https://doi.org/10.1145/237814.237866

[Jaq+20] Jaques, S., Naehrig, M., Roetteler, M., Virdia, F.: Implementing Grover oracles for quantum key search on AES and LowMC. In: Canteaut, A., Ishai, Y. (eds.) EUROCRYPT 2020. LNCS, vol. 12106, pp. 280–310. Springer, Cham (2020). https://doi.org/10.1007/978-3-030-45724-2_10

[KLS18] Kiltz, E., Lyubashevsky, V., Schaffner, C.: A concrete treatment of Fiat-Shamir signatures in the quantum random-oracle model. In: Nielsen, J.B., Rijmen, V. (eds.) EUROCRYPT 2018. LNCS, vol. 10822, pp. 552–586. Springer, Cham (2018). https://doi.org/10.1007/978-3-319-78372-7_18

[Laa16] Laarhoven, T.: Search problems in cryptography: from fingerprinting to lattice sieving. English. PhD Thesis. Mathematics and Computer Science (2016). ISBN: 978-90-386-4021-1

[Lia+21] Liang, Z., et al.: Number theoretic transform: generalization, optimization, concrete analysis and applications. In: Wu, Y., Yung, M. (eds.) Inscrypt 2020. LNCS, vol. 12612, pp. 415–432. Springer, Cham (2021). https://doi.org/10.1007/978-3-030-71852-7_28

[LMZ23] Liu, J., Montgomery, H., Zhandry, M.: Another round of breaking and making quantum money: how to not build it from lattices, and more. In: Hazay, C., Stam, M., ed. Advances in Cryptology – EUROCRYPT 2023, pp. 611–638. Springer Nature Switzerland, Cham (2023). ISBN: 978-3-031-30545-0. https://doi.org/10.1007/978-3-031-30545-0_21

[LN17] Lyubashevsky, V., Neven, G.: One-shot verifiable encryption from lattices. In: Coron, J.-S., Nielsen, J.B., Advances in Cryptology – EUROCRYPT 2017. Springer International Publishing, Cham (2017). ISBN: 978-3-319-56620-7. https://doi.org/10.1007/978-3-319-56620-7_11

[LS15] Langlois, A., Stehlé, D.: Worst-case to average-case reductions for module lattices. In: Designs, Codes and Cryptography 75 (2015), pp. 565–599. https://doi.org/10.1007/s10623-014-9938-4

[Lyu12] Lyubashevsky, V.: Lattice signatures without trapdoors. In: Pointcheval, D., Johansson, T. (eds.) EUROCRYPT 2012. LNCS, vol. 7237, pp. 738–755. Springer, Heidelberg (2012). https://doi.org/10.1007/978-3-642-29011-4_43

[LZ19] Liu, Q., Zhandry, M.: Revisiting post-quantum Fiat-Shamir. In: Boldyreva, A., Micciancio, D. (eds.) CRYPTO 2019. LNCS, vol. 11693, pp. 326–355. Springer, Cham (2019). https://doi.org/10.1007/978-3-030-26951-7_12

[MP13] Micciancio, D., Peikert, C.: Hardness of SIS and LWE with small parameters. In: Canetti, R., Garay, J.A. (eds.) CRYPTO 2013. LNCS, vol. 8042, pp. 21–39. Springer, Heidelberg (2013). https://doi.org/10.1007/978-3-642-40041-4_2

[MR09] Micciancio, D., Regev, O.: Lattice-based cryptography. In: Bernstein, D.J., Buchmann, J., Dahmen, E., ed. Post-Quantum Cryptography, pp. 147–191. Springer, Berlin, Heidelberg (2009). ISBN: 978-3-540-88702-7. https://doi.org/10.1007/978-3-540-88702-7_5

[NIST23] National Institute of Standards and Technology. Module-Lattice-Based Digital Signature Standard. Tech. rep. Federal Information Processing Standards Publications (FIPS PUBS) 204. Washington, D.C.: U.S. Department of Commerce (2023). https://doi.org/10.6028/NIST.FIPS.204.ipd

[Pei07] Peikert, C.: Limits on the hardness of lattice problems in LP norms. In: Twenty-Second Annual IEEE Conference on Computational Complexity (CCC'07), pp. 333–346 (2007). https://doi.org/10.1109/CCC.2007.12

[Pei16] Peikert, C.: A decade of lattice cryptography. Found. Trends Theor. Comput. Sci. 10(4), 283–424 (2016). ISSN: 1551-305X. https://doi.org/10.1561/0400000074

[Reg09] Regev, O.: On lattices, learning with errors, random linear codes, and cryptography. J. ACM **56**(6) (2009). ISSN: 0004-5411. https://doi.org/10.1145/1568318.1568324

[SE94] Schnorr, C.P., Euchner, M.: Lattice basis reduction: improved practical algorithms and solving subset sum problems. Math. Program. **66**(1), 181–199 (1994). https://doi.org/10.1007/BF01581144

[Unr12] Unruh, D.: Quantum Proofs of Knowledge. In: Pointcheval, D., Johansson, T. (eds.) EUROCRYPT 2012. LNCS, vol. 7237, pp. 135–152. Springer, Heidelberg (2012). https://doi.org/10.1007/978-3-642-29011-4_10

[Unr16] Unruh, D.: Collapse-binding quantum commitments without random oracles. In: Cheon, J.H., Takagi, T. (eds.) ASIACRYPT 2016. LNCS, vol. 10032, pp. 166–195. Springer, Heidelberg (2016). https://doi.org/10.1007/978-3-662-53890-6_6

[Wan+22] Wang, G., Xia, W., Shi, G., Wan, M., Zhang, Y., Gu, D.: Revisiting the concrete hardness of SelfTargetMSIS in CRYSTALS-Dilithium. Cryptology ePrint Archive, Paper 2022/1601 (2022)

[Zha12] Zhandry, M.: Secure identity-based encryption in the quantum random oracle model. In: Safavi-Naini, R., Canetti, R. (eds.) CRYPTO 2012. LNCS, vol. 7417, pp. 758–775. Springer, Heidelberg (2012). https://doi.org/10.1007/978-3-642-32009-5_44

[Zha15] Zhandry, M.: A note on the quantum collision and set equality problems. Quantum Inf. Comput. **15**(7-8), 557–567 (2015). ISSN: 1533-7146. https://doi.org/10.26421/QIC15.7-8-2

Crypto Dark Matter on the Torus

Oblivious PRFs from Shallow PRFs and TFHE

Martin R. Albrecht[1,2]($\boxtimes$), Alex Davidson[3], Amit Deo[4], and Daniel Gardham[5]

[1] King's College London, London, UK
martinralbrecht@googlemail.com
[2] SandboxAQ, New York, USA
[3] NOVA LINCS & DI, FCT, Universidade NOVA de Lisboa, Lisbon, Portugal
[4] Zama, Paris, France
[5] University of Surrey, Guildford, UK

Abstract. Partially Oblivious Pseudorandom Functions (POPRFs) are 2-party protocols that allow a client to learn pseudorandom function (PRF) evaluations on inputs of its choice from a server. The client submits two inputs, one public and one private. The security properties ensure that the server cannot learn the private input, and the client cannot learn more than one evaluation per POPRF query. POPRFs have many applications including password-based key exchange and privacy-preserving authentication mechanisms. However, most constructions are based on classical assumptions, and those with post-quantum security suffer from large efficiency drawbacks.

In this work, we construct a novel POPRF from lattice assumptions and the "Crypto Dark Matter" PRF candidate (TCC'18) in the random oracle model. At a conceptual level, our scheme exploits the alignment of this family of PRF candidates, relying on mixed modulus computations, and programmable bootstrapping in the torus fully homomorphic encryption scheme (TFHE). We show that our construction achieves malicious client security based on circuit-private FHE, and client privacy from the semantic security of the FHE scheme. We further explore a heuristic approach to extend our scheme to support verifiability, based on the difficulty of computing cheating circuits in low depth. This would yield a verifiable (P)OPRF. We provide a proof-of-concept implementation and preliminary benchmarks of our construction. For the core online OPRF functionality, we require amortised 10.0 KB communication per evaluation and a one-time per-client setup communication of 2.5 MB.

Keywords: oblivious PRF · lattices · FHE

1 Introduction

Oblivious pseudorandom functions allow two parties to compute a pseudorandom function (PRF) $z := F_k(x)$ together: a server supplying a key k and a user

---

Supplementary Information The online version contains supplementary material available at https://doi.org/10.1007/978-3-031-58751-1_16.

M. Joye and G. Leander (Eds.): EUROCRYPT 2024, LNCS 14656, pp. 447–476, 2024.
https://doi.org/10.1007/978-3-031-58751-1_16

supplying a private input x. The server does not learn x or z and the user does not learn k. If the user can be convinced that z is correct (i.e. that evaluation is performed under the correct key) then the function is "verifiable oblivious" (VOPRF), otherwise it is only "oblivious" (OPRF). Both may be used in many cryptographic applications. Example applications include anonymous credentials (e.g. Cloudflare's PrivacyPass [22]) and Private Set Intersection (PSI) enabling e.g. privacy-preserving contact look-up on chat platforms [18].

The obliviousness property can be too strong in many applications where it is sufficient or even necessary to only hide part of the client's input. In this case, the public and private inputs are separated by requiring an additional public input t, called the *tag*. Then we say that we have a *Partially* Oblivious PRF (POPRF). POPRFs are typically used in protocols where a server may wish to rate-limit OPRF evaluations made by a client. Such example protocols include Password-Authenticated Key Exchanges (e.g. OPAQUE [37], which is in the process of Internet Engineering Task Force (IETF) standardisation) and the Pythia PRF service [27]. This latter work also proposed a bilinear pairing-based construction of a *Verifiable* POPRF (VPOPRF), which is the natural inclusion of both properties: some of the input is revealed to the server and the client is able to check the correct evaluation of its full input.

Despite the wide use of (VP)OPRFs, most constructions are based on classical assumptions, such as Diffie-Hellman (DH), RSA or even pairing-based assumptions. The latest in this line of research is a recent VPOPRF construction based on a novel DH-like assumption [51] and DH-based OPRFs are currently being standardised by the IETF. Their vulnerability to quantum adversaries makes it desirable to find post-quantum solutions, however, known candidates are much less efficient.

Given fully homomorphic encryption (FHE), there is a natural (P)OPRF candidate. The client FHE encrypts input x and sends it with tag t. The server then evaluates the PRF homomorphically or "blindly" using a key derived from t and its own secret key. Finally, the client decrypts the resulting ciphertext to obtain the PRF output. The first challenge with this approach is performance – PRFs tend to have sufficiently deep circuits that FHE schemes struggle to evaluate them efficiently. Even special purpose PRFs such as the LowMC construction [5] require depth ten or more, making them somewhat impractical. More generally, in a binary circuit model we expect to require depth $\Theta(\log \lambda)$ to obtain a PRF resisting attacks with complexity $2^{\Theta(\lambda)}$.

Yet, if we expand our circuit model to arithmetic circuits with both mod p and mod q gates for $p \neq q$ both primes, shallow proposals exist [11,23]. In particular, the (weak) PRF candidate in [11] is

$$z := \sum (\boldsymbol{A} \cdot \boldsymbol{x} \bmod 2) \bmod 3$$

where arithmetic operations are over the integers and $\boldsymbol{A}$ is the secret key. The same work also contains a proposal to "upgrade" this weak PRF, defined for uniformly random inputs $\boldsymbol{x}$, to a full PRF, taking any $\boldsymbol{x}$. Furthermore, the works [11,23] already provide oblivious PRF candidates based on this PRF and

MPC, but with non-optimal round complexity. Thus, a natural question to ask is if we can construct a round-optimal (or, 2 message) POPRF based on this PRF candidate using the FHE-based paradigm mentioned above.

1.1 Contributions

Our starting point is the observation that the computational model in [11] aligns well with that of the TFHE encryption scheme [21] and its "programmable bootstrapping" technique [38,46]. Programmable bootstrapping allows us to realise arbitrary, not necessarily low-degree, small look-up tables and thus function evaluations on (natively) single inputs. Thus, it is well positioned to realise the required gates.[1] Indeed, FHE schemes natively compute plaintexts modulo some $P \in \mathbb{Z}$ and we observe that programmable bootstrapping allows us to switch between these plaintext moduli, e.g. from mod P_1 to mod P_2. This implies a weak PRF with a single level of bootstrapping only. We believe this simple observation and conceptual contribution will have applications beyond this work. We further hope that by giving another application domain for the PRF candidate from [11] – it is not just MPC-friendly but also (T)FHE-friendly – we encourage further cryptanalysis of it.

After some preliminaries in Sect. 2 we specify our POPRF candidate in Sect. 3 based on programmable bootstrapping for plaintext modulus switching. In particular, we define an operation called $\mathsf{CPPBS}_{(2,3)}$ which uses a programmable bootstrap with a special negacyclic "test polynomial" and a simple linear function to "correct" and realise the desired modulus switch. To our knowledge this functionality has not been explicitly defined and used in prior work. Without the bespoke design of $\mathsf{CPPBS}_{(2,3)}$, we are forced to either use only half of the plaintext space, or use a sequence of two programmable bootstraps [42]. The former drawback prevents bootstrapping-less homomorphic addition modulo P_1, whereas the latter does not permit a depth one bootstrapping construction.

As is typical with FHE-based schemes, we require the involved parties – here the client – to prove that its inputs are well-formed. We also make use of the protected encoded-input PRF (PEI-PRF) paradigm from [11]. In particular, the client performs some computations not dependent on secret key material and then submits the output together with a NIZK proof of well-formedness to the server for processing.

We prove our construction secure in the random oracle model in Sect. 4. We show that our construction meets the security definitions from [51]: pseudorandomness even in the presence of malicious clients (POPRF security) and privacy for clients. This property has two flavours based on the capabilities of the adversary, POPRIV1 (which we achieve) captures security against an honest-but-curious server, whereas POPRIV2 ensures security even when the server is malicious. Here, the client maintains privacy by detecting malicious behaviour

---

[1] The security of the PRF candidate in [11] rests on the absence of any low-degree polynomial interpolating it, ruling out efficient implementations using FHE schemes that only provide additions and multiplications.

of the server. POPRF security for the server essentially rests on circuit-privacy obtained from TFHE bootstrapping [40] and a client NIZK. The NIZK is made online extractable in the POPRF proof using a trapdoor and thus avoids any rewinding issues outlined in e.g. [49], and similarly mitigates the problem of rewinding for post-quantum security, cf. [52]. POPRIV1 security for the client against a semi-honest server relies on the IND-CPA security of TFHE.

Targeting roughly 100 bits of security, we obtain the following performance. While the public key material sent by the client to the server is large (14.7 MB) this cost can be amortised by reusing the same material for several evaluations. Individual PRF evaluations can then cost about 48.9 KB or as little as 5.3 KB when amortising client NIZK proofs across several OPRF queries. Applying the public-key compression technique of [39], we obtain 2.5 MB of public-key material at the cost of increasing the amortised cost to 10.0 KB (see Table 1).

Initially, we focus on oblivious rather than verifiable oblivious PRFs. This is motivated by the presumed high cost associated with zero-knowledge proofs for performing FHE computations. In Sect. 5, we explore a different approach to adding verifiability to our OPRF, inspired by and based on a discussion in [2]. The idea here is that the server commits to a set of evaluation "check" points and that the client can use the oblivious nature of the PRF to request PRF evaluations of these points to catch a cheating server. However, achieving security of this "cut-and-choose" approach in our setting is non-trivial as the server may still obliviously run a cheating circuit that agrees on those check points but diverges elsewhere.

We explore the feasibility of such a cheating circuit using direct cryptanalysis. Inspired by the heuristic approach in [18] for achieving malicious security – forcing the server to compute a deep circuit in FHE parameters supporting only shallow circuits – we explore cheating circuits in bootstrapping depth one. While we were unable to find such a cheating circuit, and conjecture that none exists, we stress that this part of our work is highly speculative. Note that the assumption here depends on the bootstrapping depth of the OPRF, i.e. if depth $d > 1$ was required for OPRF evaluation, the assumption would need to be that there is no cheating circuit in depth d. Therefore, our depth one construction leads to an "optimal" assumption for the cut-and-choose method. Under the heuristic assumption that our construction is verifiable, in Sect. 5.3 we then establish that it also satisfies POPRIV2. We hope that our work encourages further exploration of such strategies, as these will have applications elsewhere to upgrade FHE-based schemes to malicious security and OPRFs to VOPRFs.

We present a proof-of-concept SageMath implementation and some indicative Rust benchmarks in Sect. 6. Our SageMath implementation covers all building blocks except for the zero-knowledge proofs, which we consider out of scope. In particular, we re-implemented TFHE [21], including circuit privacy [40] and ciphertext and public-key compression [17,39]. Our Rust benchmarks make use of Zama's `tfhe-rs` library for implementing TFHE, which – however – does not implement many of the building blocks we make use of[2] and thus mostly serves

---

[2] These are: plaintext moduli that are not powers of two, circuit privacy, ciphertext and bootstrapping-key compression.

as an initial, best-case performance evaluation. In particular, we expect circuit privacy and public-key compression to increase the runtime by a factor of, say, ten (we discuss this Sect. 6). We also did not implement the NIZKs in Rust. With these caveats in mind, the client online functions we could implement run in 28.9 ms on one core and server online functions run in 151 ms on 64 cores.

In the full version [1], we also estimate costs of the required non-interactive zero-knowledge proofs. We use a combination of [44] and [10] to show that the cost of the proofs does not add significant overhead to the communication of our protocol.

1.2 Related Work

Oblivious PRFs and variants thereof are an active area of research. A survey of constructions, variants and applications was given in [16]. In this work we are interested in plausibly post-quantum and round-optimal constructions. The first construction was given in [2], which built a verifiable oblivious PRF from lattice assumptions following the blueprint of Diffie-Hellman constructions with additive blinding (a construction for multiplicative blinding is given in an appendix of the full version of [2]). The work provides both semi-honest and malicious secure candidates with the latter being significantly more expensive. We stress that in the former, both parties are semi-honest.

In [12] two candidate constructions from isogenies were proposed. One, a VOPRF related to SIDH, was unfortunately shown to not be secure [7]. The other, an OPRF related to CSIDH, achieves sub megabyte communication in a malicious setting assuming the security of group-action decisional Diffie-Hellman. In [6] a fixed-and-improved SIDH-based candidate was proposed and in [34] an improved CSIDH-based candidate is presented, both of which rely on trusted setups. In [48] an OPRF based on the Legendre PRF is proposed based on solving sparse multi-variate quadratic systems of equations. In [23], which also builds on [11], an MPC-based OPRF is proposed that is secure against semi-honest adversaries. It achieves much smaller communication complexity compared to all other post-quantum candidates, but in a preprocessing model where correlated randomness is available to the parties. A protocol computing this correlated randomness, e.g. [14], would add two rounds (or more) and thus make the overall protocol not round-optimal. The question of upgrading security to full malicious security is left as an open problem in [23]. In [28] a generic MPC solution not relying on novel assumptions is proposed, that, while not round-optimal, reportedly provides good performance in various settings.

We give a summary comparison of our construction with prior work in Table 1. The only 2-round constructions without preprocessing or trusted-setup in Table 1 are those from [2], where our construction compares favourably by offering stronger claimed qualitative security at smaller size, albeit under novel assumptions. In particular, even in a semi-honest setting, our construction outperforms that from [2] in terms of bandwidth for $L \geq 2$ queries.[3]

---

[3] We note that while the large sizes for achieving malicious security in [2] can be avoided using improved NIZKs, the semi-honest base size of 2 MB per query stems from requiring $q \approx 2^{256}$ for statistical correctness and security arguments.

Table 1. Post-quantum (P)(V)OPRF candidates in the literature

work	assumption	r	communication cost	flavour	model
[2]	R(LWE) & SIS	2	$\approx 2\,\mathrm{MB}$	plain	semi-honest, QROM
[48]	Legendre PRF	3	$\approx \lambda \cdot 13\mathrm{K}$	plain	semi-honest, pp, ROM
[12]	CSIDH	3	424 KB	plain	malicious client
[6]	SIDH	2	3.0 MB	plain	malicious, ts, ROM
[34]	CSIDH	2	21 KB	plain	semi-honest, ts
[34]	CSIDH	4	35 KB	plain	malicious client, ts
[34]	CSIDH	258	25 KB	plain	semi-honest
[23]	[11]	2	80B	plain	semi-honest, pp
[28]	AES	?	4746 KB	plain	malicious client, pp
Sect. 3	lattices, [11]	2	14.7 MB + 90.7 KB + 0.9 KB + 44.8 KB + 3.2 KB	plain	malicious client, ROM
Sect. 3	lattices, [11]	2	14.7 MB + 90.7 KB + 0.9 KB + 1.2 KB + 3.2 KB	plain	malicious client, ROM $L = 64$, per query
Sect. 3, CBR	lattices, [11]	2	2.4 MB + 137.4 KB + 2.0 KB + 63.0 KB + 6.2 KB	plain	malicious client, ROM
Sect. 3, CBR	lattices, [11]	2	2.4 MB + 137.4 KB + 2.0 KB + 1.8 KB + 6.2 KB	plain	malicious client, ROM $L = 64$, per query
[2]	R(LWE) & SIS	2	$> 128\,\mathrm{GB}$	verifiable	malicious, QROM
[6]	SIDH	2	8.7 MB	verifiable	malicious, ts, ROM
Sect. 5	heuristic	2	256 KB + 14.7 MB + 90.7 KB + 11.1· 0.9 KB + 11.1· 44.8 KB + 11.1· 3.2 KB	verifiable	malicious, ROM
Sect. 5	heuristic	2	256 KB + 14.7 MB + 90.7 KB + 11.1· 0.9 KB + 11.1· 1.2 KB + 11.1· 3.2 KB	verifiable	malicious, ROM $L = 64$, per query
Sect. 5, CBR	heuristic	2	256 KB + 2.4 MB + 137.4 KB + 11.1· 2.0 KB + 11.1· 63.0 KB + 11.1· 6.2 KB	verifiable	malicious, ROM
Sect. 5, CBR	heuristic	2	256 KB + 2.4 MB + 137.4 KB + 11.1· 2.0 KB + 11.1· 1.8 KB + 11.1· 6.2 KB	verifiable	malicious, ROM $L = 64$, per query

The column "r" gives the number of rounds. ROM is the random oracle model, QROM the quantum random oracle model, "pp" stands for "preprocessing", and "ts" for "trusted setup". When reporting on our work, the summands are: pk size, pk proof size, client message size, client message proof size, server message size. Our client message proofs can be amortised to e.g. 79.3 KB/64 = 1.2 KB per query, when amortising over $L = 64$ queries. The factor of 11.1 accounts for the "check point" evaluations, cf. Sect. 5. The rows marked as "CBR" apply public-key compression [39]. We picked parameters targeting roughly 100 bits of security for our constructions (see [1] for full parameter sets.

1.3 Open Problems

A pressing open problem is to refine our understanding of the security of the PRF candidate from [11]. In particular, our parameter choices may prove to be too aggressive, and we hope that our work inspires cryptanalysis.

A key bottleneck for implementations will be bootstrapping, an effect that will exacerbated by the need for circuit-private bootstrapping. It is an open problem to establish if this somewhat heavy machinery is required given that we are only aiming to hide the secret key A and that we can randomise our circuit by randomly flipping signs in the additions induced by A.

Considering Table 1, we note that many candidates forgo round-optimality to achieve acceptable performance. It is an interesting open question how critical this requirement is for various applications, since dropping it seems to enable significantly more efficient post-quantum instantiations of (V)OPRFs.

Our verifiability approach throws up a range of interesting avenues to explore for VOPRFs but also for verifiable homomorphic computation, more generally. First, our OPRF construction relies on programmable bootstrapping. This restricts the choice of FHE scheme we might instantiate our protocol with, but also gives the server the choice which function to evaluate, something our application does not require. That is, we may not need to rely on *evaluator programmable bootstrapping* if it is possible for the client to define the non-linear functions available to a server (*encrypter programmable bootstrapping*). This would enable to reason about malicious server security more easily.

Related works, e.g. [18], have also used similar assumptions as our work over the hardness of computing deep circuits in low FHE depth. There is growing evidence that such assumptions allow for new, interesting or more efficient constructions of cryptographic primitives. However, the hardness of these computational problems needs to be better understood.

Finally, our VOPRF is even more speculative than our OPRF candidate. A more direct approach would be to construct a NIZK for correct bootstrapping evaluation, which would have applications beyond this work.

2   Preliminaries

We use $\lfloor \cdot \rfloor$, $\lceil \cdot \rceil$ and $\lfloor \cdot \rceil$ to denote the standard floor, ceiling and rounding to the nearest integer functions (rounding down in the case of a tie). We denote the integers by $\mathbb{Z}$ and for any positive $p \in \mathbb{Z}$, the integers modulo p are denoted by $\mathbb{Z}_p$. We typically use representatives of $\mathbb{Z}_p$ in $\{-p/2, \ldots, (p/2) - 1\}$ if p is even and $\{-\lfloor p/2 \rfloor, \ldots, \lfloor p/2 \rfloor\}$ if p is odd, but we will also consider $\mathbb{Z}_p$ as $\{0, 1, \ldots, p - 1\}$. Since it will always be clear from context or stated explicitly which representation we use, this does not create ambiguity. The p-adic decomposition of an integer $x \geq 0$ is a tuple $(x_i)_{0 \leq i < \lceil \log_p(x) \rceil}$ with $0 \leq x_i < p$ such that $x = \sum p^i \cdot x_i$. We denote the set S_m to be the permutation group of m elements.

Let $\mathbb{Z}[X]$ denote the polynomial ring in the variable X whose coefficients belong to $\mathbb{Z}$. We also denote power-of-two cyclotomic rings $\mathcal{R} := \mathbb{Z}[X]/(X^d + 1)$ where d is a power-of-two, and $\mathcal{R}_q := \mathcal{R}/(q\mathcal{R})$ for any integer "modulus" q. Bold letters denote vectors and upper case letters denote matrices. Abusing notation we write $(\boldsymbol{x}, \boldsymbol{y})$ for the concatenation of the vectors $\boldsymbol{x}$ and $\boldsymbol{y}$. We extend this notation to scalars, too. Additionally, $\| \cdot \|$ and $\| \cdot \|_\infty$ denote standard Euclidean and infinity norms respectively.

For a distribution D, we write $x \xleftarrow{\$} D$ to denote that x is sampled according to the distribution D. An example of a distribution is the discrete Gaussian distribution over $\mathbb{Z}$ with parameter $\sigma > 0$ denoted as $D_{\mathbb{Z}, \sigma}$. This distribution has its probability mass function proportional to the Gaussian function $\rho_\sigma(x) := \exp(-\pi x^2/\sigma^2)$. We use λ to denote the security parameter. We use the standard asymptotic notation ($\Omega, \mathcal{O}, \omega$ etc.) and use $\mathsf{negl}(\lambda)$ to denote a negligible function, i.e. a function that is $\lambda^{\omega(1)}$. Further, we write $\mathsf{poly}(\lambda)$ to denote a polynomial function i.e. a function that is $\mathcal{O}(n^c)$ for some constant c. An algorithm is said to be polynomially bounded if it terminates after $\mathsf{poly}(\lambda)$ steps and uses $\mathsf{poly}(\lambda)$-sized memory. Two distribution ensembles $D_1(1^\lambda)$ and $D_2(1^\lambda)$ are said to be *computationally* indistinguishable if for any probabilistic polynomially bounded algorithm $\mathcal{A}$, $\mathrm{Adv}(\mathcal{A}) := \| \Pr[1 \leftarrow_\$ \mathcal{A}_X(1^\lambda)] - \Pr[1 \leftarrow_\$ \mathcal{A}_Y(1^\lambda)]\| \leq \mathsf{negl}(\lambda)$. In such a case we write $D_1(1^\lambda) \approx_c D_2(1^\lambda)$. The distribution ensembles are said to be *statistically* indistinguishable if the same holds for all unbounded algorithms, in which case we write $D_1(1^\lambda) \approx_s D_2(1^\lambda)$.

For a key space $\mathcal{K}$, input space $\mathcal{X}$ and output space $\mathcal{Z}$, a PRF is a function $F : \mathcal{K} \times \mathcal{X} \longrightarrow \mathcal{Z}$ with a pseudorandomness property. Rather than writing $F(k, x)$ for $k \in \mathcal{K}$ and $x \in \mathcal{X}$, we write $F_k(x)$. The pseudorandomness property of a PRF requires that over a secret and random choice of $k \leftarrow_\$ \mathcal{K}$, the single input function $F_k(\cdot)$ is computationally indistinguishable from a uniformly random function. Note here that the dependence of the parameters on λ is present, but is not explicitly written for simplicity. We also use the standard cryptographic notion of a (non-interactive) zero-knowledge proof/argument. For more details on these standard cryptographic notions, see e.g. [33].

2.1   Random Oracle Model

We will prove security by modelling hash functions as random oracles. Since our schemes will make use of more than one hash function, it will be useful to have a general abstraction for the use of ideal primitives, following the treatment in [51]. A random oracle RO specifies algorithms RO.Init and RO.Eval. The initialisation algorithm has syntax $st_{\mathsf{RO}} \leftarrow_\$ \mathsf{RO.Init}(1^\lambda)$. The stateful evaluation algorithm has syntax $y \leftarrow_\$ \mathsf{RO.Eval}(x, st_{\mathsf{RO}})$. We sometimes use A^{RO} as shorthand for giving algorithm A oracle access to $\mathsf{RO.Eval}(\cdot, st_{\mathsf{RO}})$. We combine access to multiple random oracles $\mathsf{RO} = \mathsf{RO}_0 \times \ldots \times \mathsf{RO}_{m-1}$ in the obvious way. We may arbitrarily label our random oracles to aid readability e.g. $\mathsf{RO}_{\mathsf{key}}$ to denote a random oracle applied to some "key".

2.2   (Verifiable) (Partial) Oblivious Pseudorandom Functions

We adopt the notation and definitions for oblivious pseudorandom functions from [51]. An OPRF is a protocol between two parties: a server S who holds a private key and a client who wants to obtain evaluations of F_k on inputs of its choice. We write $z := F_k(x)$. We say that an OPRF is a partial OPRF (POPRF) if part of the client's input is given to the server. In this case, we write $z := F_k(t, x)$ where t is in the clear and x is hidden from S. When C can verify that the PRF was evaluated correctly we speak of a verifiable OPRF (VOPRF) or VPOPRF when the protocol also supports partially known inputs t.

Definition 1 (Partial Oblivious PRF [51]). *A partial oblivious PRF (POPRF) $\mathcal{F}$ is a tuple of PPT algorithms*

$$(\mathcal{F}.\mathsf{Setup}, \mathcal{F}.\mathsf{KeyGen}, \mathcal{F}.\mathsf{Request}, \mathcal{F}.\mathsf{BlindEal}, \mathcal{F}.\mathsf{Finalise}, \mathcal{F}.\mathsf{Eval})$$

The setup and key generation algorithm generate public parameter pp *and a public/secret key pair* (pk, sk). *Oblivious evaluation is carried out as an interactive protocol between* C *and* S, *here presented as algorithms $\mathcal{F}.\mathsf{Request}$, $\mathcal{F}.\mathsf{BlindEal}$, $\mathcal{F}.\mathsf{Finalise}$ working as follows:*

1. *First,* C *runs the algorithm* $\mathcal{F}$.Request$_{\mathsf{pp}}^{\mathsf{RO}}(\mathsf{pk}, t, x)$ *taking a public key* pk, *a tag or public input* t *and a private input* x. *It outputs a local state* st *and a request message* req, *which is sent to the server.*
2. S *runs* $\mathcal{F}$.BlindEal$_{\mathsf{pp}}^{\mathsf{RO}}(\mathsf{sk}, t, req)$ *taking as input a secret key* sk, *a tag* t *and the request message* req. *It produces a response message* rep *sent back to* C.
3. *Finally,* C *runs* $\mathcal{F}$.Finalise(rep, st) *which takes the response message and its previously constructed state* st *and either outputs a PRF evaluation or* $\perp$ *if* rep *is rejected.*

The unblinded evaluation algorithm $\mathcal{F}$.Eval *is deterministic and takes as input a secret key* sk, *an input pair* (t, x) *and outputs a PRF evaluation* z.

We also define sets $\mathcal{F}$.SK, $\mathcal{F}$.PK, $\mathcal{F}$.T, $\mathcal{F}$.X *and* $\mathcal{F}$.Out *representing the secret key, public key, tag, private input, and output space, respectively. We define the input space* $\mathcal{F}$.In $= \mathcal{F}$.T $\times \mathcal{F}$.X. *We assume efficient algorithms for sampling and membership queries on these sets.*

Remark 1. Fixing t, e.g. $t = \perp$, recovers the definition of an OPRF.

We adapt correctness from [51], permitting a small failure probability.

Definition 2 (POPRF Correctness (adapted from [51])). *A partial oblivious PRF (POPRF)*

$$(\mathcal{F}.\mathsf{Setup}, \mathcal{F}.\mathsf{KeyGen}, \mathcal{F}.\mathsf{Request}, \mathcal{F}.\mathsf{BlindEal}, \mathcal{F}.\mathsf{Finalise}, \mathcal{F}.\mathsf{Eval})$$

is correct if

$$\Pr\left[z = \mathcal{F}.\mathsf{Eval}_{\mathsf{pp}}^{\mathsf{RO}}(\mathsf{sk}, t, x) \;\middle|\; \begin{array}{l} \mathsf{pp} \leftarrow_{\$} \mathcal{F}.\mathsf{Setup}(1^{\lambda}) \\ (\mathsf{pk}, \mathsf{sk}) \leftarrow_{\$} \mathcal{F}.\mathsf{KeyGen}_{\mathsf{pp}}^{\mathsf{RO}}(1^{\lambda}) \\ (st, req) \leftarrow_{\$} \mathcal{F}.\mathsf{Request}_{\mathsf{pp}}^{\mathsf{RO}}(\mathsf{pk}, t, x) \\ rep \leftarrow_{\$} \mathcal{F}.\mathsf{BlindEal}_{\mathsf{pp}}^{\mathsf{RO}}(\mathsf{sk}, t, req) \\ z \leftarrow_{\$} \mathcal{F}.\mathsf{Finalise}_{\mathsf{pp}}^{\mathsf{RO}}(rep, st) \end{array} \right] = 1 - \mathsf{negl}(\lambda).$$

We target the same pseudorandomness guarantees against malicious clients as [51].

Definition 3 (Pseudorandomness (POPRF)) [51]. *We say a partial oblivious PRF* $\mathcal{F}$ *is pseudorandom if for all* PPT *adversaries* $\mathcal{A}$, *there exists a* PPT *simulator* S *such that the following advantage is* negl(λ):

$$\mathsf{Adv}_{\mathcal{F},\mathsf{S},\mathsf{RO},\mathcal{A}}^{\mathsf{po-prf}}(\lambda) = \left| \Pr\left[\mathsf{POPRF}_{\mathcal{F},\mathsf{S},\mathsf{RO}}^{\mathcal{A},1}(\lambda) \Rightarrow 1 \right] - \Pr\left[\mathsf{POPRF}_{\mathcal{F},\mathsf{S},\mathsf{RO}}^{\mathcal{A},0}(\lambda) \Rightarrow 1 \right] \right|.$$

Remark 2. In Fig. 1, the oracle Prim(x) captures access to the random oracle used in the POPRF construction. For $b = 0$ (the case where the adversary interacts with a simulator and a truly random function) the simulator may only use a limited number of random function queries to simulate the random oracle accessed via Prim(x).

Game $\text{POPRF}_{\mathcal{F},\text{S},\text{RO}}^{\mathcal{A},b}(\lambda)$	Oracle $\text{Eval}(t,x)$	Oracle $\text{BlindEval}(t,req)$
$q_{s,t}, q_t \leftarrow 0, 0$	$z_0 \leftarrow \text{RO}_{\text{Fn}}.\text{Eval}((t,x), st_{\text{Fn}})$	$q_t \leftarrow q_t + 1$
$st_{\text{Fn}} \leftarrow\!\!\text{\$ } \text{RO}_{\text{Fn}}.\text{Init}(1^\lambda)$ // $\mathcal{F}.\text{In} \to \mathcal{F}.\text{Out}$	$z_1 \leftarrow \mathcal{F}.\text{Eval}_{\text{pp}_1}^{\text{RO}}(sk, t, x)$	$(rep_0, st_S) \leftarrow\!\!\text{\$ } \text{S}.\text{BlindEval}^{\text{LimitEval}}(t, req, st_S)$
$st_{\text{RO}} \leftarrow\!\!\text{\$ } \text{RO}.\text{Init}(1^\lambda)$	$\textbf{return } z_b$	$rep_1 \leftarrow\!\!\text{\$ } \mathcal{F}.\text{BlindEval}_{\text{pp}_1}^{\text{RO}}(sk, t, req)$
$\text{pp}_1 \leftarrow\!\!\text{\$ } \mathcal{F}.\text{Setup}(1^\lambda)$		$\textbf{return } rep_b$
$(st_S, \text{pk}_0, \text{pp}_0) \leftarrow\!\!\text{\$ } \text{S}.\text{Init}(\text{pp}_1)$	Oracle $\text{LimitEval}(t,x)$	
$(sk, \text{pk}_1) \leftarrow\!\!\text{\$ } \mathcal{F}.\text{KeyGen}_{\text{pp}_1}^{\text{RO}}(1^\lambda)$	$q_{t,s} \leftarrow q_{t,s} + 1$	Oracle $\text{Prim}(x)$
$b' \leftarrow\!\!\text{\$ } \mathcal{A}^{\text{Eval},\text{BlindEval},\text{Prim}}(\text{pp}_b, \text{pk}_b)$	$\textbf{if } q_{t,s} \leq q_t \textbf{ then}$	$(h_0, st_S) \leftarrow\!\!\text{\$ } \text{S}.\text{Eval}^{\text{LimitEval}}(x, st_S)$
$\textbf{return } b'$	$\quad\textbf{return } \text{Eval}(t, x)$	$h_1 \leftarrow\!\!\text{\$ } \text{RO}.\text{Eval}(x, st_{\text{RO}})$
	$\textbf{return } \bot$	$\textbf{return } h_b$

Fig. 1. Pseudorandomness against malicious clients.

The intuition of this definition is that it requires the simulator to explain a random output (defined via RO_{Fn}) as an evaluation point of the PRF. The simulator provides its own public key and public parameters, but it gets at most one query to $\text{RO}_{\text{Fn}}()$ per BlindEal query that it has to simulate. The simulator queries RO_{Fn} through calls to LimitEval, where the check $q_{t,s} \leq q_t$ enforces the number of queries per BlindEal query and tag t. This implies that BlindEal and Eval queries essentially leak nothing beyond a single evaluation to the client. Moreover, the simulator is restricted in that the LimitEval oracle will error if more queries are made to it than the number of BlindEval queries (on t) at any point in the game. Meaningful relaxations of this definition are discussed in [51], but for completeness we opt for the full definition (Fig. 2).

Definition 4 (Request Privacy (POPRIV) [51]). *We say a partial oblivious PRF $\mathcal{F}$ has request privacy against honest-but-curious and malicious servers respectively if for all PPT adversary $\mathcal{A}$ the following advantage is $\text{negl}(\lambda)$ for $k = 1$ and $k = 2$ respectively:*

$$\text{Adv}_{\mathcal{F},\text{S},\text{RO},\mathcal{A}}^{\text{po-priv}k}(\lambda) = \left| \Pr\left[\text{POPRIV } k_{\mathcal{F},\text{RO}}^{\mathcal{A},1}(\lambda) \Rightarrow 1 \right] - \Pr\left[\text{POPRIV } k_{\mathcal{F},\text{RO}}^{\mathcal{A},0}(\lambda) \Rightarrow 1 \right] \right|.$$

2.3 Hard Lattice Problems

We will rely on both the M-SIS and the M-LWE problems. Instantiating these over $\mathcal{R} = \mathbb{Z}$ recovers the SIS and LWE problems respectively. Further, instantiating these over some ring of integers of some number field and with $n = 1$, recovers the Ring-SIS and Ring-LWE problems respectively.

Definition 5 (M-SIS, adapted from [41]). *Let $\mathcal{R}, q, n, \ell, \beta$ depend on λ. The Module-SIS (or M-SIS) problem, denoted M-$\text{SIS}_{\mathcal{R}_q, n, \ell, \beta^*}$, is: Given a uniform $\mathbf{A} \leftarrow\!\!\text{\$ } \mathcal{R}_q^{n \times \ell}$ find some $\mathbf{u} \neq \mathbf{0} \in \mathcal{R}^\ell$ such that $\|\mathbf{u}\| \leq \beta^*$ and $\mathbf{A} \cdot \mathbf{u} \equiv \mathbf{0} \bmod q$.*

Definition 6 (M-LWE, adapted from [41]). *Let $\mathcal{R}, q, n, m$ depend on λ and let χ_s, χ_e be distributions over $\mathcal{R}_q$. Denote by M-$\text{LWE}_{\mathcal{R}_q, n, \chi_s, \chi_e}$ the probability*

Game $\text{POPRIV1}^{\mathcal{A},b}_{\mathcal{F},\text{RO}}(\lambda)$	Game $\text{POPRIV2}^{\mathcal{A},b}_{\mathcal{F},\text{RO}}(\lambda)$
$pp \leftarrow\!\!\text{\$}\ \mathcal{F}.\text{Setup}(1^\lambda)$	$pp \leftarrow\!\!\text{\$}\ \mathcal{F}.\text{Setup}(1^\lambda)$
$(pk, sk) \leftarrow\!\!\text{\$}\ \mathcal{F}.\text{KeyGen}^{\text{RO}}_{pp}(1^\lambda)$	$i \leftarrow 0$
$b' \leftarrow\!\!\text{\$}\ \mathcal{A}^{\text{Run,RO}}(pp, pk, sk)$	$b' \leftarrow\!\!\text{\$}\ \mathcal{A}^{\text{Request,Finalise,RO}}(pp)$
return b'	**return** b'
Oracle $\text{Run}(t, x_0, x_1)$	Oracle $\text{Request}(pk, t, x_0, x_1)$
for $j \in \{0,1\}$ **do**	$i \leftarrow i + 1$
$\quad (st_j, req_j) \leftarrow\!\!\text{\$}\ \mathcal{F}.\text{Request}^{\text{RO}}_{pp}(pk, t, x_j)$	$(st_{i,0}, req_0) \leftarrow\!\!\text{\$}\ \mathcal{F}.\text{Request}^{\text{RO}}_{pp}(pk, t, x_0)$
$\quad rep_j \leftarrow\!\!\text{\$}\ \mathcal{F}.\text{BlindEval}^{\text{RO}}_{pp}(sk, t, req_j)$	$(st_{i,1}, req_1) \leftarrow\!\!\text{\$}\ \mathcal{F}.\text{Request}^{\text{RO}}_{pp}(pk, t, x_1)$
$\quad z_j \leftarrow\!\!\text{\$}\ \mathcal{F}.\text{Finalise}^{\text{RO}}_{pp}(rep_j, st_j)$	**return** (req_b, req_{1-b})
$\tau_0 \leftarrow (req_b, rep_b, z_0)$	
$\tau_1 \leftarrow (req_{1-b}, rep_{1-b}, z_1)$	Oracle $\text{Finalise}(j, rep_0, rep_1)$
return (τ_0, τ_1)	**if** $j > i$ **then return** $\bot$
	$z_b \leftarrow\!\!\text{\$}\ \mathcal{F}.\text{Finalise}^{\text{RO}}_{pp}(rep_0, st_{j,b})$
	$z_{1-b} \leftarrow\!\!\text{\$}\ \mathcal{F}.\text{Finalise}^{\text{RO}}_{pp}(rep_1, st_{j,1-b})$
	if $z_0 = \bot$ **or** $z_1 = \bot$ **then return** $\bot$
	return (z_0, z_1)

Fig. 2. Request privacy against honest-but-curious servers (left) and against malicious servers (right).

distribution on $\mathcal{R}^{m \times n}_q \times \mathcal{R}^m_q$ obtained by sampling the coordinates of the matrix $A \in \mathcal{R}^{m \times n}_q$ independently and uniformly over $\mathcal{R}_q$, sampling the coordinates of $s \in \mathcal{R}^n_q$, $e \in \mathcal{R}^m$ independently from χ_s and χ_e respectively, setting $b := A \cdot s + e \bmod q$ and outputting (A, b). The M-LWE problem is to distinguish the uniform distribution over $\mathcal{R}^{m \times n}_q \times \mathcal{R}^m_q$ from $M\text{-LWE}_{\mathcal{R}_q, n, \chi_s, \chi_e}$.

2.4 Matrix NTRU Trapdoors

The original formulation [35] of the NTRU problem considers rings of integers of number fields or polynomial rings, but a matrix version is implicit and considered for cryptanalysis in the literature.

Definition 7. *Given integers n, p, q, β where p and q are coprime, the matrix-NTRU assumption (denoted $\text{mat-NTRU}_{n,p,q,\beta}$) states that no PPT algorithm can distinguish between A and B where*

- *$A \leftarrow\!\!\text{\$}\ \mathbb{Z}^{n \times n}_q$*
- *$B = p^{-1} \cdot G^{-1} \cdot F \bmod q$ with*

$$F \leftarrow\!\!\text{\$}\ \{0, \pm 1, \ldots, \pm \beta\}^{n \times n}, G \leftarrow\!\!\text{\$}\ \{0, \pm 1, \ldots, \pm \beta\}^{n \times n} \cap \left(\mathbb{Z}^{n \times n}_q\right)^*$$

where $\left(\mathbb{Z}^{n \times n}_q\right)^*$ denotes the set of invertible $(n \times n)$ matrices over $\mathbb{Z}_q$.

We will use the matrix-NTRU assumption to define a trapdoor. In what follows, we assume an odd q and an even p that is coprime to q. In particular, we define the following algorithms:

NTRUTrapGen(n, q, p, β): Sample

$$\boldsymbol{F} \leftarrow_\$ \{0, \pm 1, \ldots, \pm \beta\}^{n \times n}, \boldsymbol{G} \leftarrow_\$ \{0, \pm 1, \ldots, \pm \beta\}^{n \times n} \cap \left(\mathbb{Z}_q^{n \times n}\right)^*$$

and output public information $\mathsf{pp} := (p^{-1} \cdot \boldsymbol{G}^{-1} \cdot \boldsymbol{F} \bmod q, q)$ and a trapdoor $\tau := (\boldsymbol{F}, \boldsymbol{G}, p)$.

NTRUDec$(\boldsymbol{c}, \tau)$: For $\boldsymbol{c} \in \mathbb{Z}_q^n$, $\tau := (\boldsymbol{F}, \boldsymbol{G}, p)$, compute $\boldsymbol{c}_1 = p \cdot \boldsymbol{G} \cdot \boldsymbol{c} \bmod q$, $\boldsymbol{c}_2 = \boldsymbol{c}_1 \bmod (p/2)$, $\boldsymbol{c}_3 = \boldsymbol{c} - p^{-1} \cdot \boldsymbol{G}^{-1} \cdot \boldsymbol{c}_2 \bmod q$. Finally, compute and output $\boldsymbol{m}' := \left\lfloor \frac{2}{q-1} \cdot \boldsymbol{c}_3 \right\rceil$ where the multiplication and rounding is done over the rationals.

The trapdoor functionality is summarised in the lemma below.

Lemma 1. *Suppose that p, q are coprime where p is even and q is odd. Suppose also that $\beta \cdot \beta_s' \cdot n < p/4$, and that $\beta_s', \beta_e' \in \mathbb{R}$ satisfies $\beta \cdot n \cdot (\beta_s' + p \cdot (2\beta_e' + 1)/2) < q/2$. Sample $(\mathsf{pp} := (\boldsymbol{B}, q), \tau) \leftarrow_\$ \mathsf{NTRUTrapGen}(n, q, p, \beta)$. Then:*

1. *$\boldsymbol{B}$ is indistinguishable from uniform over $\mathbb{Z}_q^{n \times n}$ if the mat-NTRU$_{n,p,q,\beta}$ assumption holds.*
2. *If $\boldsymbol{c} = \boldsymbol{B} \cdot \boldsymbol{s} + \boldsymbol{e} + \lfloor q/2 \rfloor \cdot \boldsymbol{m} \bmod q$ where $\boldsymbol{m} \in \mathbb{Z}_2^n$, $(\|\boldsymbol{s}\|_\infty \le \beta_s' \vee \|\boldsymbol{s}\|_2 \le \beta_s' \cdot \sqrt{n})$ and $(\|\boldsymbol{e}\|_\infty \le \beta_e' \vee \|\boldsymbol{e}\|_2 \le \beta_e' \cdot \sqrt{n})$, then $\mathsf{NTRUDec}(\boldsymbol{c}, \tau) = \boldsymbol{m}$.*

Proof. For the first part, simply note that distinguishing $\boldsymbol{B}$ from uniform is exactly the matrix-NTRU problem for (n, p, q, β). For the second part, reusing the same notation from the description of NTRUDec$(\boldsymbol{c}, \tau := (\boldsymbol{F}, \boldsymbol{G}, p))$ gives

$$\boldsymbol{c}_1 = \boldsymbol{F} \cdot \boldsymbol{s} + p \cdot \boldsymbol{G} \cdot (\boldsymbol{e} + ((q-1)/2) \cdot \boldsymbol{m}) \bmod q$$
$$= \boldsymbol{F} \cdot \boldsymbol{s} + (p/2) \cdot \boldsymbol{G} \cdot (2\boldsymbol{e} - \boldsymbol{m}) \bmod q$$
$$= \boldsymbol{F} \cdot \boldsymbol{s} + (p/2) \cdot \boldsymbol{G} \cdot (2\boldsymbol{e} - \boldsymbol{m})$$

over $\mathbb{Z}$ because $\|\boldsymbol{F} \cdot \boldsymbol{s} + (p/2) \cdot \boldsymbol{G} \cdot (2\boldsymbol{e} - \boldsymbol{m})\|_\infty < q/2$. We then have $\boldsymbol{c}_2 = \boldsymbol{F} \cdot \boldsymbol{s} \bmod p/2 = \boldsymbol{F} \cdot \boldsymbol{s}$ over $\mathbb{Z}$ because $\|\boldsymbol{F} \cdot \boldsymbol{s}\|_\infty < p/4$. Next, $\boldsymbol{c}_3 = \boldsymbol{e} + ((q-1)/2) \cdot \boldsymbol{m}$. Note that the conditions in the lemma statement imply that $2\beta_e' \cdot \sqrt{n} < (q-1)/2$. This gives the final output $\lfloor \boldsymbol{m} + \frac{2}{q-1} \cdot \boldsymbol{e} \rceil = \boldsymbol{m}$ because $\|\frac{2\boldsymbol{e}}{q-1}\|_\infty < 1/2$. $\square$

Choosing Parameters. Looking ahead, we will instantiate this trapdoor for $q \approx 2^{32}$ and $n = 2^{11}$. So, we require $\beta \cdot \beta_s' < p/(4n)$ and, say, $\beta \cdot \beta_e' < q/(4n \cdot p)$. Picking $p = 2^{16}$, we get $\log(\beta) + \log(\beta_s') < 16 - 2 - 11 = 3$ and $\log(\beta) + \log(\beta_e') < 32 - 2 - 11 - 16 = 3$. Picking $\beta \approx 2^2$ and $\beta_s' = \beta_e' \approx 2$ we obtain an NTRU instance requiring BKZ block size 333 to solve (using the (overstretched) NTRU estimator [26]) and an LWE instance requiring BKZ block size 594 to solve (using the lattice estimator [4]). According to the cost model from [45] this costs about 2^{132} classical operations.[4]

---

[4] We note that quantum algorithms offer only marginal, i.e. less than square-root, speedups here [3].

2.5   Homomorphic Encryption and TFHE

Fully homomorphic encryption (FHE) allows to perform computations on plaintexts by performing operations on ciphertexts. In slightly more detail, an FHE scheme consists of four algorithms: FHE.KeyGen, FHE.Enc, FHE.Eval, FHE.Dec. The key generation, encryption and decryption algorithms all work similarly to normal public key encryption. Together, they provide privacy (i.e. IND-CPA security) and decryption correctness. The interesting part of FHE is its homomorphic property. Assume that $\mathcal{M}$ is the message space, e.g. $\mathcal{M} := \mathbb{Z}_P$. The homomorphic property is enabled by the FHE.Eval function which takes as input a public key pk, an arbitrary function $f : \mathcal{M}^k \longrightarrow \mathcal{M}$, a sequence of ciphertexts $(c_i)_{i \in [\mathbb{Z}_k]}$ encrypting plaintexts $(m_i)_{i \in \mathbb{Z}_k}$, and outputs a ciphertext $c' \leftarrow$ FHE.Eval(pk, f, $(c_0, \ldots, c_{k-1})$). The homomorphic property ensures that c' is an encryption of $f(m_0, \ldots, m_{k-1})$. Intuitively, FHE allows arbitrary computation on encrypted data without having to decrypt. Importantly, the privacy of the plaintext is maintained. In addition, an FHE scheme may also maintain the privacy of the evaluated computation (see below).

FHE was first realised by Gentry [31]. A considerable amount of influential follow-up research provides the basis of most practically feasible schemes [15, 20, 29, 32]. We will be focusing on an extension of the third of these works known as TFHE [21] because its programmable bootstrapping technique lends enables our construction. For a summary of TFHE, see the guide [38].

Programmable Bootstrapping. A crucial ingredient of any FHE scheme is a bootstrapping procedure. Essentially, homomorphic evaluation increases ciphertext noise, meaning that after a prescribed number of evaluations, a ciphertext becomes so noisy that it cannot be decrypted correctly. Bootstrapping provides a method of resetting the size of the noise in a ciphertext to allow for correct decryption using some bootstrapping key material. Note that the bootstrapping operation can either produce a ciphertext encrypted under the original key or a new one depending on the bootstrapping key material used.[5] We also note that the FHE schemes considered in this work are additively homomorphic with very modest noise growth, meaning that many additions of plaintexts can be performed *without* bootstrapping.

In TFHE we have access to *negacyclic* look-up tables from $\mathbb{Z}_{2d}$ to $\mathbb{Z}_P$ which we will denote by $f(\cdot) : \mathbb{Z}_{2d} \to \mathcal{M}$. Here, d is the degree of a cyclotomic ring $\mathcal{R} = \mathbb{Z}[X]/(X^d + 1)$ and $\mathbb{Z}_P$ is the plaintext space. There is a slight problem here in that the look-up table does not take plaintext-space inputs, but this is overcome by approximating $\mathbb{Z}_{2d}$ as $\mathbb{Z}_P$ [21, 38]. TFHE generalises bootstrapping by applying the look-up table to the plaintext at the same time as resetting the size of the noise. The negacyclic property dictates that $f(x + d) = -f(x)$ for $x = 0, 1, \ldots, d-1$, so if the desired look-up table is not negacyclic, one must either restrict to using half the plaintext space or use more complex bootstrapping techniques [42].

---

[5] This allows to restrict the number of sequential bootstrappings that can be performed.

2.6   Circuit Private (Programmable) Bootstrapping

Circuit private FHE hides the computation performed on a ciphertext. There are generic methods of achieving circuit privacy [25] and more specific ones for GSW [13] and TFHE [40]. As our OPRF is designed within the specific framework of TFHE, we restrict discussion to the latter work. At a high level, TFHE bootstrapping consists of two steps: blind rotation and key-switching. Blind Rotation is a Generalised GSW [32] based operation that outputs an LWE ciphertext under a different key. The key-switching phase then maps back to the original key to allow for further homomorphic operations. A key contribution of Kluczniak [40] is a generalised Gaussian leftover hash lemma that shows how to randomise the blind rotation phase in order to "clean up" the noise distribution. Ultimately, this entails adding Gaussian preimage sampling to the blind rotation algorithm which affects computation time and correctness parameters. We note that we will not require key-switching (line 1 of Fig. 3 in [40]), but this does not affect the statistical distance result below in any way. We avoid giving too many details on the meaning of parameters with respect to the circuit privacy bootstrapping algorithm and refer to [40] for details. In the statement below, $\|\boldsymbol{B}_{L,Q}\|$ denotes the maximum length of a column of

$$
\boldsymbol{B}_{L,Q} := \begin{bmatrix} L & & & Q_1 \\ -1 & L & & Q_2 \\ & -1 & \ddots & \vdots \\ & & -1 & Q_\ell \end{bmatrix} \in \mathbb{Z}^{\ell \times \ell} \tag{1}
$$

where $\ell := \lceil \log_L(Q) \rceil$ and $(Q_1, \ldots, Q_\ell)$ is a base-L decomposition of Q. We recall the main circuit privacy result from [40] we will use below.

Theorem 1 ([40]). *Let $\beta_{\mathsf{br}}, \beta_R$ be noise bounds on a blind rotation key and LWE public key respectively and let $\boldsymbol{c}$ be an input LWE ciphertext with secret $\boldsymbol{s} \in \mathbb{Z}_2^n$. Furthermore, assume the use of a test polynomial $v(X)$ such that the constant of $v(X) \cdot X^{\mathsf{Phase}(c)}$ is $f(m)$. Then if*

$$
\sigma_{\mathsf{rand}} \geq \max\left(4 \left((1-\gamma) \cdot (2\epsilon)^2 \right)^{-\frac{1}{\ell_R}}, \ \sqrt{1+\beta_R} \cdot \|\boldsymbol{B}_{L_R,Q}\| \cdot \sqrt{\frac{\ln(2\ell_R(1+1/\gamma))}{\pi}} \right)
$$

and

$$
\sigma_x \geq \sqrt{1+\beta_{\mathsf{br}}} \cdot \|\boldsymbol{B}_{L_{\mathsf{br}}}\| \cdot \sqrt{\frac{\ln(4\,n \cdot d \cdot \ell_{\mathsf{br}}(1+1/\delta))}{\pi}}
$$

then

$$
\Delta(\boldsymbol{c}_{\mathsf{out}}, \boldsymbol{c}_{\mathsf{fresh}}) \leq \max(\epsilon + 2\gamma, 2\delta)
$$

where $\boldsymbol{c}_{\mathsf{out}}$ is the output of the algorithm in Fig. 3 of [40] and $\boldsymbol{c}_{\mathsf{fresh}} = (\boldsymbol{a}_{\mathsf{fresh}}, \boldsymbol{a}_{\mathsf{fresh}} \cdot \boldsymbol{s} + f(m) + e_{\mathsf{rand}} + e_{\mathsf{out}})$ is a well distributed fresh ciphertext with noise distributions $e_{\mathsf{rand}} \leftarrow_{\$} \chi_{\mathbb{Z}, \sigma_{\mathsf{rand}}\sqrt{1+\ell_R \cdot \sigma_R^2}}, \ e_{\mathsf{out}} \leftarrow_{\$} \chi_{\mathbb{Z}, \sigma_x \sqrt{1+2\,n \cdot d \cdot \sigma_{\mathsf{br}}^2}}.$

Malicious Security. Note that the definition above is required to hold for "any" FHE.pk, FHE.sk, ct$_{\text{out}}$ generated honestly. More precisely, this means for *any* possible (i.e. valid) outputs of the appropriate FHE algorithms. For example, the word "any" for an error term distributed as a discrete Gaussian would mean any value satisfying some appropriate bound. Intuitively, malicious circuit privacy requires that an adversary cannot learn anything about the circuit (or $(\boldsymbol{A}, \boldsymbol{x})$) even in the presence of maliciously generated keys and ciphertexts. Thus if we can ensure the well-formedness of keys and ciphertexts, then a semi-honest circuit-private FHE scheme is also secure against malicious adversaries. In the random oracle model, we can achieve this with NIZKs that show well-formedness of the keys and that the ciphertext is a valid ciphertext under that public key. Then, FHE.Eval can explicitly check that the proof verifies and abort otherwise.

2.7 Crypto Dark Matter PRF

Let p, q be two primes where $p < q$. We now describe the "Crypto Dark Matter" PRF candidate [11,23]. It is built from the following *weak* PRF proposal F_{weak} : $\mathbb{Z}_p^{m_p \times n_p} \times \mathbb{Z}_p^{n_p} \to \mathbb{Z}_q$ where

$$F_{\text{weak}}(\boldsymbol{A}, \boldsymbol{x}) = \sum_{j=0}^{m_p - 1} (\boldsymbol{A} \cdot \boldsymbol{x} \bmod p)_j \bmod q.$$

Here $\boldsymbol{A}$ is the secret key, $\boldsymbol{x}$ is the input and $(\boldsymbol{A} \cdot \boldsymbol{x} \bmod p)_j$ denotes the j-th component of $\boldsymbol{A} \cdot \boldsymbol{x} \bmod p$. In order to describe the strong PRF construction, we introduce a fixed public matrix $\boldsymbol{G}_{\text{inp}} \in \mathbb{Z}_q^{n_q \times n}$ and a p-adic decomposition operation $\mathsf{decomp} : \mathbb{Z}_q^{n_q} \to \mathbb{Z}_p^{\lceil \log_p(q) \rceil \cdot n_q}$ where $\lceil \log_p(q) \rceil \cdot n_q = n_p$. The *strong* PRF candidate[6] is $F_{\text{one}} : \mathbb{Z}_p^{m_p \times n_p} \times \mathbb{Z}_p^n \to \mathbb{Z}_q$ where

$$F_{\text{one}}(\boldsymbol{A}, \boldsymbol{x}) := F_{\text{weak}}(\boldsymbol{A}, \mathsf{decomp}(\boldsymbol{G}_{\text{inp}} \cdot \boldsymbol{x} \bmod q)).$$

In order to extend the small output of the above PRF constructions, the authors of [11] introduce another matrix $\boldsymbol{G}_{\text{out}} \in \mathbb{Z}_q^{m \times m_p}$ (with $m < m_p$) which is the generating matrix of some linear code. Then the full PRF is $F_{\text{strong}} : \mathbb{Z}_p^{m_p \times n_p} \times \mathbb{Z}_p^n \to \mathbb{Z}_q^m$ where

$$F_{\text{strong}}(\boldsymbol{A}, \boldsymbol{x}) := \boldsymbol{G}_{\text{out}} \cdot (\boldsymbol{A} \cdot \mathsf{decomp}(\boldsymbol{G}_{\text{inp}} \cdot \boldsymbol{x} \bmod q) \bmod p) \bmod q.$$

Given access to gates implementing mod p and mod q this PRF candidate can be implemented in a depth 3 arithmetic circuit. See the full version [1] for an example implementation, or the attachment.[7]

Note that $\mathsf{decomp}(\boldsymbol{G}_{\text{inp}} \cdot \boldsymbol{x} \bmod q) \in \mathbb{Z}_p^{n_p}$ does not depend on the PRF key. Thus, in an OPRF construction it could be precomputed and submitted by the

---

[6] As it stands, this strong PRF candidate maps zero to zero and is thus trivially distinguished from a random function, we will address this below.

[7] If the reader's PDF viewer does not support PDF attachments (e.g. Preview on MacOS does not), then e.g. pdfdetach can be used to extract these files.

Table 2. PRF Parameters

	$\lambda = 128$	Explanation		$\lambda = 128$	Explanation
p	2	modulus of x, A	n_p, m_p	256	dimensions of A
q	3	modulus of $z, G_{\text{inp}}, G_{\text{out}}$	n	128	dim. of $x \pmod{p}$
n_q	192	rows of G_{inp}	m	82	dim. of $z \pmod{q}$

client knowing x. However, in this case, we must enforce that the client is doing this honestly via a zero-knowledge proof π that $y := \text{decomp}(G_{\text{inp}} \cdot x \bmod q)$ is well-formed. Specifically, following [11], if $H_{\text{inp}} \in \mathbb{Z}_q^{(n_q-n) \times n_q}$ is the parity check matrix of G_{inp} and $G_{\text{gadget}} := (p^{\lceil \log_p(q) \rceil - 1}, \ldots, 1) \otimes I_{n_p}$ we may check

$$H_{\text{inp}} \cdot G_{\text{gadget}} \cdot y \equiv 0 \bmod q.$$

Note that as stated this does not enforce $x \in \mathbb{Z}_p^n$ but $x \in \mathbb{Z}_q^n$. Since it is unclear if this has a security implication, we may avoid this issue relying on a comment made in [11] that we may, wlog, replace G_{inp} with a matrix in systematic (or row echelon) form. That is, writing $G_{\text{inp}} = [I \mid A]^T \in \mathbb{Z}_q^{n_p \times n}$, $y = (y_0, y_1) \in \mathbb{Z}_q^{n_p}$, the *protected encoded-input* PRF is defined as

$$F_{\text{pei}}(A, y) := \begin{cases} G_{\text{out}} \cdot (A \cdot y \bmod p) \bmod q & \text{if } H_{\text{inp}} \cdot G_{\text{gadget}} \cdot y \equiv 0 \bmod q \\ & \text{and } y_0 \in \{0,1\}^n \\ \perp & \text{otherwise.} \end{cases}$$

Note that with this definition of G_{inp} the "most significant bits" of y_0 will always be zero, so there is no point in extracting those when running decomp. Thus, we adapt decomp to simply return the first n output values in $\{0,1\}$ and to perform the full decomposition on the remaining $(n_q - n)$ entries. We thus obtain $n_p := n + \lceil \log_p(q) \rceil \cdot (n_q - n)$. A similar strategy is discussed in Remark 7.13 of the full version of [11] (Table 2).

Security Analysis. The initial work [11] provided some initial cryptanalysis and relations to known hard problems to substantiate the security claims made therein. When A is chosen to be a circulant rather than a random matrix, the scheme has been shown to have degraded security [19] contrary to the expectation stated in [11]. The same work [19] also proposes a fix. Further cryptanalysis was preformed in [23], supporting the initial claims of concrete security. Our choices for $\lambda = 128$ (classically) are aggressive, especially for a post-quantum construction. This is, on the one hand, to encourage cryptanalysis. On the other hand, known cryptanalytic algorithms against the proposals in [11,23] require exponential memory in addition to exponential time, a setting where Grover-like square-root speed-ups are less plausible, cf. [3] (which, however, treats the Euclidean distance rather than Hamming distance).

3   Boostrapping Depth One OPRF Candidate

We wish to design an (P)OPRF where the server homomorphically evaluates the PRF using its secret key and uses some form of circuit-private homomorphic encryption to protect its key. The depth of bootstrapping required is one, which enhances efficiency and is useful in the security of our V(P)OPRF in Sect. 5.

3.1   Extending the PEI PRF

Here, we first note that the PRFs defined in Sect. 2.7 trivially fail to achieve pseudorandomness as they map $\mathbf{0} \in \mathbb{Z}_p^n \to \mathbf{0} \in \mathbb{Z}_q^m$, which holds with $\mathsf{negl}(\lambda)$ probability for a random function. We thus define

$$F_{\mathsf{strong}}(\boldsymbol{A}', \boldsymbol{x}) := \boldsymbol{G}_{\mathsf{out}} \cdot (\boldsymbol{A} \cdot (\mathsf{decomp}(\boldsymbol{G}_{\mathsf{inp}} \cdot \boldsymbol{x} \bmod q), 1) \bmod p) \bmod q.$$

and

$$F_{\mathsf{pei}}(\boldsymbol{A}', \boldsymbol{y}) := \begin{cases} \boldsymbol{G}_{\mathsf{out}} \cdot (\boldsymbol{A}' \cdot (\boldsymbol{y}, 1) \bmod p) \bmod q & \text{if } \boldsymbol{H}_{\mathsf{inp}} \cdot \boldsymbol{G}_{\mathsf{gadget}} \cdot \boldsymbol{y} \equiv \mathbf{0} \bmod q \\ \bot & \text{otherwise.} \end{cases}$$

for $\boldsymbol{A}' \in \mathbb{Z}_p^{m_p \times (n_p+1)}$, i.e. extended by one column. Furthermore, we wish to support an additional input $\boldsymbol{t} \in \mathbb{Z}_p^n$ to be submitted in the clear. For this, we deploy the standard technique of using a key derivation function to derive a fresh key per tag $\boldsymbol{t}$ [16,36]. In particular, let $\mathsf{RO}_{\mathsf{key}} : \mathbb{Z}_p^{m_p \times n_p} \times \mathbb{Z}_p^n \to \mathbb{Z}_p^{m_p \times (n_p+1)}$ be a random oracle, we then define our PRF candidate $F_{\boldsymbol{A}}^{\mathsf{RO}_{\mathsf{key}}}(\boldsymbol{t}, \boldsymbol{x})$ in Algorithm 1. Clearly, if $F_{\mathsf{pei}}(\boldsymbol{A}', \boldsymbol{y})$ is a PRF then $F_{\boldsymbol{A}}^{\mathsf{RO}_{\mathsf{key}}}(\cdot, \cdot)$ is a PRF with input $(\boldsymbol{t}, \boldsymbol{x})$, as $\boldsymbol{A}_t$ in Algorithm 1 is simply a fresh $F_{\mathsf{pei}}()$ key for each distinct value of $\boldsymbol{t}$.

Algorithm 1. $F_{\boldsymbol{A}}^{\mathsf{RO}_{\mathsf{key}}}(\boldsymbol{t}, \boldsymbol{x})$

Input: $\boldsymbol{A} \in \mathbb{Z}_p^{m_p \times n_p}, \quad \boldsymbol{x} \in \mathbb{Z}_p^n, \quad \boldsymbol{t} \in \mathbb{Z}_p^n$
Output: $F_{\boldsymbol{A}}(\boldsymbol{t}, \boldsymbol{x})$
$\quad \boldsymbol{A}_t \leftarrow \mathsf{RO}_{\mathsf{key}}(\boldsymbol{A}, \boldsymbol{t})$
$\quad \boldsymbol{y} \leftarrow \mathsf{decomp}(\boldsymbol{G}_{\mathsf{inp}} \cdot \boldsymbol{x} \bmod q)$
$\quad \boldsymbol{z} \leftarrow \boldsymbol{G}_{\mathsf{out}} \cdot (\boldsymbol{A}_t \cdot (\boldsymbol{y}, 1) \bmod p) \bmod q$
$\quad \textbf{return } \boldsymbol{z}$

3.2   TFHE-Based Instantiation

We ultimately show that the above PRF is highly compatible with TFHE/FHEW, so we describe the OPRF (F_{poprf}) using subroutines from the associated literature. The high-level outline of the construction is given as Fig. 3 and a full implementation of TFHE and our OPRF candidate in SageMath is given in [1].

$F_{\text{poprf}}.\text{Setup}(1^\lambda)$	$F_{\text{poprf}}.\text{KeyGen}(1^\lambda)$	$F_{\text{poprf}}.\text{Eval}(sk = A, t = t, x = x)$	$F_{\text{poprf}}.\text{Finalise}(rep = ct)$
$A_{\text{pp}} \leftarrow\!\!\$\ \mathbb{Z}_Q^{N \times N}$	$\text{pk} \leftarrow \perp$	$z' := F_A^{\text{RO}_{\text{key}}}(t, x)$	if ct' not a ctxt then return $\perp$
$\text{pp} \leftarrow A_{\text{pp}}$	$sk \leftarrow\!\!\$\ \mathbb{Z}_p^{m_p \times n_p}$	$z := \text{RO}_{\text{fin}}(t, x, z')$	$z' \leftarrow \text{FHE.Dec}(\text{FHE.sk}, ct)$
return pp	return (pk, sk)	return z	$z \leftarrow \text{RO}_{\text{fin}}(t, x, z')$
			return z

$F_{\text{poprf}}.\text{Request}(\text{pk}, t = t, x = x; \text{pp})$	$F_{\text{poprf}}.\text{BlindEval}(sk = A, t = t, req; \text{pp})$
$\text{FHE.pk}^{(\text{pp})}, \text{FHE.sk} \leftarrow\!\!\$\ \text{FHE.KeyGen}^{(\text{pp})}()$	$(\text{FHE.pk}^{(\text{pp})}, ct, \pi) \leftarrow req$
$y \leftarrow \text{decomp}(G_{\text{inp}} \cdot x \bmod p)$	$A_t \leftarrow \text{RO}_{\text{key}}(A, t)$
$ct \leftarrow\!\!\$\ \text{FHE.Enc}(\text{FHE.sk}, y)$	$ct' \leftarrow F_{\text{poprf}}.\text{HEEval}(\text{FHE.pk}^{(\text{pp})}, A_t, ct)$
$\pi \leftarrow\!\!\$\ \text{NIZKAoK}_c(\text{FHE.pk}^{(\text{pp})}, ct; \text{FHE.sk}, x)$	if π does not verify then $ct' = \perp$
$req \leftarrow (\text{FHE.pk}^{(\text{pp})}, ct, \pi, t)$	$rep \leftarrow ct'$
return req	return rep

Client   **Server**

$F_{\text{poprf}}.\text{Request}(\text{pk}, t = t, x = x; \text{pp})$

$$\xrightarrow{\quad req = (\text{FHE.pk}^{(\text{pp})}, ct, \pi, t) \quad} \quad F_{\text{poprf}}.\text{BlindEval}(sk = A, t = t, req; \text{pp})$$

$F_{\text{poprf}}.\text{Finalise}(rep)$ $\qquad \xleftarrow{\quad rep = ct' \quad}$

Output: $\text{RO}_{\text{fin}}(t, x, F_A^{\text{RO}_{\text{key}}}(t, x))$

Fig. 3. Main construction.

Plaintext Modulus Switching. The main point of interest is in the design of $F_{\text{poprf}}.\text{HEEval}$, which is given in Algorithm 2. The input LWE ciphertexts have plaintext space $\mathbb{Z}_2$ and the output LWE ciphertexts have plaintext space $\mathbb{Z}_3$. In order to perform the plaintext modulus switch, we use a variant of TFHE/FHEW bootstrapping that we denote $\text{FHE.CPPBS}_{(p,q)}$. This algorithm is a variation of the standard TFHE programmable bootstrapping algorithm (see [38] for details) augmented with the circuit-private technique of Kluczniak [40]. The difference is that we apply a simple linear transformation and a special "test polynomial", whilst forgoing the key-switching in [40, Fig. 3].

In more detail, note that general TFHE bootstrapping applies a function $f : \mathbb{Z}_{2d} \to \mathbb{Z}_q$ to a plaintext using test polynomial $v(x) = \sum_{i=0}^{d-1} f(i) \cdot x^i$, assuming the function has negacyclic form i.e. $f(x) = -f(x+d)$. Recall that TFHE encodes a plaintext $m \in \mathbb{Z}_p$ as $m \cdot \lfloor Q/p \rfloor$ during encryption and decodes intervals

$$\left[m \cdot \lfloor Q/p \rceil - \frac{\lfloor Q/p \rceil}{2}, \ m \cdot \lfloor Q/p \rceil + \frac{\lfloor Q/p \rceil}{2} \right)$$

to $m \in \mathbb{Z}_p$ during decryption. Consider the simple plaintext switch $f : \lfloor m \cdot (2d/p) \rceil + e \mapsto m \cdot (Q/q)$ for $m \in \mathbb{Z}_p$, where e denotes some LWE error. The corresponding function is not negacyclic, so we would have to restrict plaintext space so that the most significant bit is zero to overcome this. Alternatively, we could apply the techniques of [42] at the cost of two sequential programmable bootstraps. However, in the case $(p, q) = (2, 3)$ (which is the one that we use)[8], one can use the negacyclic function

$$f(x) = \begin{cases} \lfloor Q/3 \rceil & \text{if } x \in [d/2, 3d/2) \\ -\lfloor Q/3 \rceil & \text{otherwise} \end{cases}.$$

Although this is a negacyclic function, it maps regions that decrypt to $m \in \mathbb{Z}_2$ to $-(m+1) \cdot \lfloor Q/3 \rceil \bmod Q$. To correct this, $\mathsf{CPPBS}_{(2,3)}$ completes by negating the ciphertext and subtracting $\lfloor Q/3 \rceil$. To summarise, the complete $\mathsf{CPPBS}_{(2,3)}$ procedure takes as input an LWE encryption of $m \in \mathbb{Z}_2$ and outputs an LWE ciphertext that encrypts m as an element of $\mathbb{Z}_3$. We may then optionally apply the ciphertext compression technique from [17] to pack multiple answers into a single RLWE ciphertext (we suppress this step in pseudocode for brevity).

Algorithm 2. $F_{\mathsf{poprf}}.\mathsf{HEEval}$

Input: pk   ▷ HE public key with ciphertext modulus Q, plaintext modulus p
Input: $A_t \in \mathbb{Z}_p^{m_p \times n_p}$, $\mathsf{ct} \in \mathcal{C}^{n_p}$ encrypting $\boldsymbol{y} \in \mathbb{Z}_p^{n_p}$
Output: $\mathsf{ct}' \in \mathcal{C}^m$ encrypting $F_A^{\mathsf{RO}_{\mathsf{key}}}(\boldsymbol{t}, \boldsymbol{x})$ or $\bot$
 1: $\mathsf{ct}' \leftarrow_\$ \mathsf{FHE.Enc}(\mathsf{pk}, 1)$ ▷ can be e.g. $1 \cdot \lfloor Q/p \rceil$
 2: $\mathsf{ct}^{(1)} \leftarrow A_t \cdot (\mathsf{ct}, \mathsf{ct}') \bmod Q$ ▷ additive hom. plaintext space $\mathbb{Z}_p$
 3: $\mathsf{ct}_i^{(2)} \leftarrow \mathsf{FHE.CPPBS}_{(p,q)}(\mathsf{pk}, \mathsf{ct}_i^{(1)})$ $\forall i \in \mathbb{Z}_{m_p}$ ▷ plaintext space $\mathbb{Z}_q$
 4: $\mathsf{ct}^{(3)} \leftarrow G_{\mathsf{out}} \cdot \mathsf{ct}^{(2)} \bmod Q$ ▷ m LWE ciphertexts
 5: **return** $\mathsf{ct}^{(3)}$ ▷ Optionally pack into single RLWE ctxt [17]

Commitment. A further important alteration is that $\mathsf{FHE.KeyGen}^{(\mathsf{pp})}$ will output a commitment to the secret key $\mathsf{FHE.sk} = \boldsymbol{s} \in \mathbb{Z}_2^e$, in addition to the standard public key $\mathsf{FHE.pk}$. In particular, $\mathsf{FHE.KeyGen}^{(\mathsf{pp})}()$ begins by running $(\mathsf{FHE.pk}, \mathsf{FHE.sk}) \leftarrow_\$ \mathsf{FHE.KeyGen}()$ and then adds the commitment $\boldsymbol{b}_{\mathsf{pk}}$ to $\mathsf{FHE.pk}$. This commitment takes the form $\boldsymbol{b}_{\mathsf{pk}} = A_{\mathsf{pp}} \cdot \boldsymbol{r} + \boldsymbol{e} + \lfloor Q/2 \rfloor \cdot (\boldsymbol{s}, \boldsymbol{0}) \in \mathbb{Z}_Q^N$, where Q is the ciphertext modulus, and $\boldsymbol{r}, \boldsymbol{e} \leftarrow_\$ (\chi')^N$, where χ' is a discrete Gaussian of standard deviation $\beta' \approx 4$ and $N = 2048$ (as in Sect. 2.4). One can view $\boldsymbol{b}_{\mathsf{pk}}$ as a partial symmetric LWE encryption of the secret key from the (T)LWE encryption scheme within TFHE, so χ' is simply an error distribution. Therefore, using the same LWE assumption from Sect. 2.4, $\boldsymbol{b}_{\mathsf{pk}}$ is indistinguishable from random and it is easy to check that its presence does not affect the IND-CPA property of TFHE. Furthermore, since $\boldsymbol{b}_{\mathsf{pk}}$ is simply a randomised function of $(\mathsf{FHE.pk}, \mathsf{FHE.sk})$, it can be constructed by an adversarial client. Thus, its advantage against semi-honest circuit privacy of FHE in which the key also contains $\boldsymbol{b}_{\mathsf{pk}}$ remains unchanged. To summarise, the public key material output by $\mathsf{FHE.KeyGen}^{(\mathsf{pp})}$ is $\mathsf{FHE.pk}^{(\mathsf{pp})} := (\boldsymbol{b}_{\mathsf{pk}}, \mathsf{FHE.pk})$.

Public Key. Note that although the server does not need to create encryptions itself, we still use the public-key version of TFHE rather than a symmetric-key

---

[8] Note that we may pick $q \neq 3$ but require $p = 2$.

version as this is useful for circuit privacy [40]. This extra key material in the public key does not impact efficiency noticeably, as the bootstrapping key sizes are the main bottleneck. See the full version for details of NIZKAoK$_C$, and where we fully describe the generation of the bootstrapping keys.

Noise Analysis Overview. Although key-switching may help reduce the number of loops in the blind rotation phase, we will ignore it as we only have bootstrapping depth one, so it is useless in our setting. Additionally, we do not consider key compression here for simplicity (this can be added by amending β_{br} below). We assume a blind rotation base B_{br} and set $\ell_{br} = \lceil \log_{B_{br}}(Q) \rceil$. We also assume the blind rotation key has a noise bound of β_{br}. For the final re-randomisation step of circuit-private bootstrapping, we use B_R and $\lceil \ell_{B_R}(Q) \rceil$, assuming a noise bound of β_R for the LWE instances. CPPBS$_{(2,3)}$ leads to exactly the same noise term as a circuit-private bootstrapping, so we just analyse the output of a circuit-private bootstrap (without key-switching).

To describe the correctness requirement, we will use noise$_\star$ to denote an infinity-norm noise bound of ciphertext $\star$ when viewed as an encryption of the "correct" value. Moving through the computation, we can track error terms as:

- noise$_{ct^{(1)}} \leq n_p \cdot$ noise$_{ct}$
- noise$_{ct^{(2)}} \leq \sqrt{\sigma_{rand}^2(1 + \ell_R \sigma_R^2) + \sigma_x^2(1 + 2nd\sigma_{br}^2)} \cdot c$ for some appropriately chosen $c, \sigma_{rand}, \sigma_x$ (see Theorem 1)
- noise$_{ct^{(3)}} \leq m_p \cdot$ noise$_{ct^{(2)}}$.

Let e denote the TLWE secret key dimension. Then, for correctness, we require that noise$_{ct^{(1)}} \cdot \frac{2d}{Q} + \frac{e}{2} \leq d/2$ for the Q-to-$2d$ mod-switching ct $\mapsto \lfloor ct \cdot 2d/Q \rceil$ in CPPBS$_{(2,3)}$, and also that noise$_{ct^{(3)}} \leq Q/3$ for decryption correctness of the unpacked output ciphertext. For circuit privacy, the parameters σ_{rand} and σ_x must be chosen according to Theorem 1. As we see later, for POPRIV1 security, we also need the M-LWE$_{\mathbb{Z}_Q, N, \mathbb{Z}_2, \sigma}$, M-LWE$_{\mathcal{R}_q, 1, \mathbb{Z}_2, \sigma_R}$ and M-LWE$_{\mathcal{R}_q, 1, \mathbb{Z}_2, \sigma_{br}}$ assumptions with $\mathcal{R}_q := \mathbb{Z}_q[X]/(X^d + 1)$, for the security of the FHE scheme.

Ciphertext Compression. The LWE to RLWE ciphertext packing operation from [17] introduces an additional error whose variance is bounded by $\frac{d^2-1}{3} \cdot V_{ks}$, where V_{ks} is the variance of a key-switching operation. In particular, $V_{ks} = \ell_{ks} \cdot B_{ks}^2 \cdot \sigma_{ks}^2$, where $(\ell_{ksk}, B_{ksk}, \sigma_{ksk})$ are analogues to $(\ell_{br}, B_{br}, \sigma_{br})$ in a key-switching key context. Therefore, if ciphertext packing is used, the correctness property noise$_{ct^{(3)}} \leq Q/3$ becomes noise$_{ct^{(3)}} + \sqrt{\frac{d^2-1}{3} \cdot V_{ks}} \cdot c' \leq Q/3$, for some appropriately chosen c'. We further assume the hardness of M-LWE$_{\mathcal{R}_q, 1, \mathbb{Z}_2, \sigma_{ks}}$.

Choosing Parameters and Size Estimates. To pick parameters, we run the script (given in [1]), which checks the noise/correctness constraints and hardness constraints mentioned above. The script additionally includes correctness constraints for the public key compression techniques in [39]. Based on this, we estimate the size of the bootstrapping key (which may be considered an amortisable offline communication cost) as 14.7 MB. The size of the zero-knowledge proofs accompanying this key is 90.7 KB. Applying public-key compression, we instead obtain 2.4 MB and 137.4 KB respectively.

Each request then sends LWE encryptions of $n_p = 256$ bits $\boldsymbol{m}$ using protected encoded inputs, i.e. $(\boldsymbol{A}^{(0)}, \boldsymbol{b} := \boldsymbol{A}^{(0)} \cdot \boldsymbol{s} + \boldsymbol{e} + \lfloor Q/P \rfloor \cdot \boldsymbol{m})$ where $\boldsymbol{A}^{(0)} \in \mathbb{Z}_Q^{n_p \times e}$ and $\boldsymbol{b} \in \mathbb{Z}_Q^{n_p}$. Here, $\boldsymbol{A}^{(0)}$ can be computed from a small seed of 256 bits. For $\boldsymbol{b}$ we need to transmit $n_p \cdot \log Q$ bits. However, as noted in e.g. [43], we may drop the least significant bits. In total we have a ciphertext size of 2.0 KB. The accompanying zero-knowledge proofs take up 63.0 KB but can be amortised to cost about 1.8 KB per query when sending 64 queries in one shot.[9]

The message back from the server is $m = 82$ encryptions of the output elements belonging to $\mathbb{Z}_q$. Here, we cannot expand the dominant uniform matrix $\boldsymbol{A}^{(1)}$ from a small seed, but we can drop the least significant bits of $\boldsymbol{A}^{(1)}$, since $\boldsymbol{s}$ is binary. In particular, we may drop, say, the 8 least significant bits and we arrive at $e \cdot m \cdot 24$ bits for $\boldsymbol{A}^{(1)}$. We need $m \log Q$ bits for $\boldsymbol{b}$. We can use the same trick of dropping lower order bits for $\boldsymbol{b}$ again, so we obtain $82 \cdot 16$ bits. In total we get 480.6 KB. As mentioned above, it is more efficient to pack all return values into a single RLWE sample using techniques from [17], since the cost of transmitting $\boldsymbol{A}^{(1)}$ dominates here. This does not require additional key material when using public-key compression and reduces the size of response to about 6.2 KB. For more details on these values, see the full version of this paper [1]. The communication performance of our scheme without public key compression has smaller online communication cost, as reported in Table 1.

Remark 3. While our parameter selection is largely conservative in applying worst-case bounds and in adopting the noise sizes required for circuit privacy according to [40, Theorem 1], we deviate from the theorem in setting $\ell = 1$ and $L < Q$ in (1) when we do not apply public-key compression. This is because the lower-order bits of the decomposed vectors contain only noise. These random bits are then linearly composed with encryptions of $\boldsymbol{s}$. Thus, the server may simply sample its own random "$\boldsymbol{s}$" to perform this computation outputting noise. Not performing this optimisation would increase the size of the public-key by a factor of three. We use $\ell := \lceil \log(Q, L) \rceil$ when applying public-key compression.

4   Security

We first prove the pseudorandomness property against malicious clients in Theorem 2 and then privacy (POPRIV1 only) against servers in Theorem 3.

Theorem 2. *Let* FHE *denote the* TFHE *scheme with* $q \mid Q$. *The construction* F_{poprf} *from Fig. 3 satisfies the POPRF property from Definition 3, with random oracles* $\mathsf{RO}_{\mathsf{fin}}$ *and* $\mathsf{RO}_{\mathsf{key}}$, *if:*

- *The client zero-knowledge proof is sound.*

---

[9] All of these figures assume that we apply public-key compression.

- *For any valid* pk, ct = *FHE.Enc(m) for* $m \in \mathbb{Z}_p$, CPPBS$^{(p,q)}$(pk, ct) *is indistinguishable from a fresh LWE ciphertext encrypting m as a vector in* $\mathbb{Z}_q$, *with some error distribution* χ_{Sim} *as in Theorem 1.*
- *The* mat-NTRU$_{N,P',Q,B}$ *assumption holds where Q is the* FHE *modulus.*
- *P'* *is even and coprime to Q, such that* $Q > B \cdot N \cdot (\beta' + P' \cdot (2\beta' + 1)/2)$ *where* β' *is the standard deviation used in* FHE.KeyGen$^{(pp)}$.
- $F.(\cdot, \cdot)$, *defined in Sect. 3, is a PRF with output range super-polynomial in the security parameter (e.g.* 2^λ).

See full version of this paper [1] for the proof.

Remark 4. Note that the security proof asks that $q \mid Q$. However, parts of the OPRF (e.g. efficient zero-knowledge proofs) might require or benefit from Q having a specific form that is not a multiple of $q = 3$. This situation can be remedied by applying an LWE modulus switch to a nearby multiple of Q just after FHE.CPPBS is applied in Algorithm 2.

Theorem 3. *Let* FHE *denote the TFHE scheme. The construction* $\mathcal{F}$ *from Fig. 3 satisfies the POPRIV1 property if the following hold:*

- FHE *is IND-CPA.*
- *The client proof is zero-knowledge.*
- *The* M-LWE$_{\mathbb{Z}_Q,N,\chi',\chi'}$ *assumption holds where* $\chi' = D_{\mathbb{Z},\beta'}$ *is the error distribution used in* FHE.KeyGen$^{(pp)}$.

The proof is given in the full version of this paper [1].

5 Verifiability

We aim to leverage the oblivious nature of the OPRF to extend our POPRF construction to achieve verifiability. We base our technique on the heuristic trick informally discussed in [2, Sect. 3.2], but with some modifications. In particular, we identify a blind-evaluation attack on this verifiability strategy in our context, the mitigation for which requires sending more "check" material. We then use cryptanalysis to study the security of our protocol, i.e. our construction does not reduce to a known (or even new but clean) hard problem. We view our analysis as an exploration into achieving secure protocols from bounded depth circuits, which we hope has applications beyond this work.

Our verifiability procedure is based on our OPRF presented in Fig. 3 using the cut-and-choose method from [2, Sect. 3.2]. Intuitively, the client, C, sends the server, S, a set of known answer "check" points amongst genuine OPRF queries. The client checks if these check points match the known answer values. It also checks if evaluations on the same points produce the same outputs and if evaluations on different points produce different outputs, here we implicitly rely on the PRP-PRF switching lemma [9]. If these checks pass, we conjecture that the C may then assume that S computed the (P)OPRF correctly, assuming appropriate parameters. Let $\gamma = \nu \cdot \alpha + \beta$ be the number of points C submits.

1. For some fixed t, S commits to κ points $z_k^\star := F_A(t, x_k^\star)$ for $k \in \mathbb{Z}_\kappa$ and publishes them (or sends them to C); S attaches a NIZK proof that these are well-formed, i.e. they satisfy the relation

$$\mathfrak{R}_t := \{t, \{(x_k^\star, z_k^\star)\}_{k \in \mathbb{Z}_\kappa}; \; A \mid z_k^\star = F_A(t, x_k^\star)\} \tag{2}$$

2. C wishes to evaluate α distinct points $x_i^{(\alpha)}$ for $i \in \mathbb{Z}_\alpha$. It samples $x_j^{(\beta)} \leftarrow_\$ \{x_k^\star\}_{k \in \mathbb{Z}_\kappa}$ for $j \in \mathbb{Z}_\beta$. It constructs the vector

$$\left(\overbrace{x_0^{(\alpha)}, \ldots, x_0^{(\alpha)}}^{\nu \text{ copies}}, \ldots, \overbrace{x_{\alpha-1}^{(\alpha)}, \ldots, x_{\alpha-1}^{(\alpha)}}^{\nu \text{ copies}}, x_0^{(\beta)}, \ldots, x_{\beta-1}^{(\beta)} \right).$$

It then applies a secret permutation ρ, i.e. shuffles the indices, and submits these queries.

3. C applies ρ^{-1} to the responses, i.e. unshuffles the indices, and receives z_i. The client C rejects if any of the following conditions is satisfied:
   (a) For $0 \le k < \alpha$ and for $i, j \in \mathbb{Z}_k$: $z_{\nu \cdot k + i} \ne z_{\nu \cdot k + j}$, i.e. evaluations on the same point disagree.
   (b) For $0 \le k < \ell < \alpha$ and for $i, j \in \mathbb{Z}_k$: $z_{\nu \cdot k + i} = z_{\nu \cdot \ell + j}$, i.e. evaluations on different points agree.
   (c) For $0 \le k \le \beta$: $z_{\nu \cdot \alpha + k} \ne z_k^\star$, i.e. check points do not match.
   Otherwise C accepts.

We formalise the security definition with a game in Fig. 4. Since the tag t remains constant throughout we suppress it here. We say a (P)OPRF, $\mathcal{F}$, is verifiable if the following advantage is negligible in the security parameter λ:

$$\mathsf{Adv}_{\mathcal{F},\mathsf{S},\mathcal{A}}^{\mathrm{verif}}(\lambda) = \Pr\left[\mathrm{VERIF}_{\mathcal{F},\mathsf{RO}}^{\mathcal{A}}(\lambda) = 1\right].$$

Remark 5. We phrase our candidate construction above directly in a batch variant that amortises the overhead of verifiability by submitting α points together. To recover the usual definition (also used in our security game) of a single evaluation, we may either simply sample $\alpha - 1$ random points and then call our batch variant or submit more check points. This is necessary since γ is a function of α and β but affects security bounds.

5.1 Verifiability from Levelled HE

Inspired by [18], the heuristic we use to claim security is argues that evaluating a deep circuit in an FHE scheme supporting only shallow circuits is a hard problem. We pursue the same line of reasoning, albeit with significantly tighter security margins. That is, our assumption is significantly stronger than that in [18].

We will assume that the bootstrapping keys for the FHE scheme provided by C to S do not provide FHE, but restrict to a limited number of levels. More

$$\underline{\text{VERIF}_{\mathcal{F},\text{RO}}^{\mathcal{A}}}$$

pp $\leftarrow \mathcal{F}.\text{Setup}(\lambda)$

$(\text{sk}, \text{pk}, \boldsymbol{x}) \leftarrow \mathcal{A};$

$req \leftarrow \mathcal{F}.\text{Request}(\text{pk}, \boldsymbol{t}, \boldsymbol{x}; \text{pp})$

$rep \leftarrow \mathcal{A}^{\text{Request},\text{Finalise},\text{RO}}(req)$

$\boldsymbol{z}' \leftarrow \mathcal{F}.\text{Finalise}(rep)$

$\boldsymbol{z} \leftarrow \mathcal{F}.\text{Eval}(\text{sk}, \boldsymbol{t}, \boldsymbol{x})$

if $\boldsymbol{z}' \neq \boldsymbol{z}$ then return 1

return 0

Fig. 4. Verifiability Experiment for (P)OPRF

precisely, we pick parameters such that only Line 3 of Algorithm 2 costs a bootstrapping operation, i.e. all linear operations are realised without bootstrapping. This is already how Algorithm 2 is written, but we foreground this as a *security requirement* here. We stress that our POPRF in Algorithm 2 can be evaluated in depth one, and that the bootstrapping key submitted to S presumably prevents it from computing higher depth circuits. This is enabled by the removal of a key-switching key in our (VP)OPRF. See [1] for the construction.

5.2 Cryptanalysis

We explore cheating strategies of a malicious server.

Maximal-Change Guessing. Assume the adversary guesses the positions of the check points in order to make C accept incorrect outputs, i.e. the adversary behaves honestly on the check points but dishonestly yet consistent on all other points. Recall that $\gamma = \nu \cdot \alpha + \beta$ is the number of points C submits to S, where there are β such check point positions. Thus, if we assume semantic security of the underlying HE scheme then the probability of the server guessing correctly is bounded by the probability it selects the positions of a particular check point, for each of the β check points. We obtain a probability $1/\binom{\gamma}{\beta}$ of guessing correctly.

Minimal-Change Guessing. Assume the adversary's strategy is to evaluate all points honestly except for one. The consistency check that all ν evaluations of the same point must agree and that all other evaluations must disagree, means this adversary has to guess the ν positions of the target point. Since there are α evaluation points, we obtain a probability $\alpha/\binom{\gamma}{\nu}$ of making a correct guess.

Interpolation. We consider an adversarial S that uses a circuit F'_{pei}, of depth at most one, to win the verifiability experiment. At a high level, it solves a quadratic system of equations, assuming one level of bootstrapping allows to implement one multiplication with arity two. More precisely, it chooses F'_{pei} such that it agrees on the κ points with of the POPRF circuit $F_{\text{pei}}(A, t, \cdot)$, but that can differ elsewhere. Since the server knows the check points, this can be trivially done. To prevent such an attack, one would need to publish $\kappa = n + \frac{n}{2}(n+1) + \mathcal{O}(1)$ check points where n is the input/output dimension. This, implies no quadratic polynomial interpolation exists. If we let $\kappa = 128^2$, then the communication cost of check points is approximately an additional 0.5 MB, which can be reduced to 256 KB by generating the input values from a seed.

Check and Cheat. Finally, we consider that the adversary is able to construct a shallow cheating circuit, which is described in Algorithm 3, with $[\cdot]$ denoting a homomorphic encryption of a value. Intuitively, it homomorphically checks the clients inputs against known answers, and then homomorphically selects which output to return. This circuit has depth two.

Parameters. We may aim for 80-bit security against the statistical guessing attacks above while assuming $\kappa = 128$ and a depth-one check and cheat algorithm does not exist. To do so, we set $\gamma = 1165$, $\beta = 10, \nu = 11$ and thus $\alpha = 105$. This implies a multiplicative size overhead of ≈ 11.1 to heuristically upgrade the OPRF to a VOPRF.

Algorithm 3. Cheating Circuit

Input: $[y] \in \mathbb{Z}_p^{n_p}$; check points $\{y_j^*\}$; $H : \mathbb{Z}_p^{n_p} \to \mathbb{Z}_q^m$ any function
  $[r], [\text{found}] \leftarrow 0, 0$
  for all y_j^* **do**
    $[d] \leftarrow [y] - y_j^*$
    $[h] \leftarrow \sum_{i \in \mathbb{Z}_{n_p}} d_i$
    if $[h] = 0$ **then**   ▷ CMUX, depth one
      $[r] \leftarrow [r] + y_j^*$; $[\text{found}] \leftarrow [\text{found}] + 1$
    else
      $[r] \leftarrow [r] + 0$; $[\text{found}] \leftarrow [\text{found}] + 0$
    end if
  end for
  return $\mathsf{CMUX}_{[\text{found}]}([r], H([y]))$ ▷ depth one

---

5.3 Security Reduction

Finally, we establish that our verifiability property implies POPRIV2 under some additional assumptions.

Theorem 4. *Our VPOPRF construction satisfies POPRIV2 if*

- F_{vpoprf} *satisfies POPRIV1.*
- F_{vpoprf} *is verifiable.*
- *NIZKAoK$_{\mathfrak{R}_t}$ is sound for $\mathfrak{R}_t$ defined in* (2).

The proof is given in the full version of this paper [1].

6   Proof-of-Concept Implementations

SageMath. In the full version of this paper [1], we give a SageMath [50] implementation of TFHE and our OPRF candidate. This implementation is meant to establish and clarify ideas and thus we do not provide benchmarks for it. Our implementation is complete with respect to the core functionality. In particular, we provide a new from-scratch implementation of TFHE [21] in tfhe.py, of circuit-private TFHE bootstrapping [40] in cpbs.py, and ciphertext and bootstrapping-key compression [17,39] in compression.py. Our OPRF in oprf.py is then relatively simple and calls the appropriate library functions. We re-implemented the underlying machinery since we are not aware of public implementations that provide all these features yet. We did not implement the zero-knowledge proof systems from [44] and [10] since those are somewhat orthogonal to the focus of this work. We did, however, as indicated earlier, adapt or re-implement scripts for estimating their (combined) proof sizes.

Rust Benchmarks. To give a sense of performance, we also implemented the key operations relied upon by our OPRF in Rust. In particular, we use Zama's tfhe-rs FHE library [21]. Unfortunately, several functionalities we rely on are not (yet) implemented in tfhe-rs: circuit privacy, ciphertext and public-key compression. Moreover, tfhe-rs assumes throughout that plaintext moduli are powers of two, which is incompatible with our OPRF. The most costly operations are the client's F_{poprf}.KeyGen and the server's F_{poprf}.BlindEal, which we discuss next.[10]

In our benchmarks F_{poprf}.KeyGen took 1 s. While this contains neither proving well-formedness nor compressing the public-key, we expect neither to be significantly more expensive. Even so, this operation can be regarded as a one-time cost in many applications. For example, considering OPAQUE [37], clients and servers already register persistent identifiers for each other (such as the client-specific OPRF key). Therefore, the client keypair can be registered as part of this process. Similarly for Privacy Pass [22], the issuance phase of the protocol does not discount clients from registering persistent information that they use whenever they make VOPRF evaluations (which could include this key information). As a result, in many applications, clients will generate a single FHE keypair and use that over multiple interactions with the server.

For the online server-side algorithm (F_{poprf}.BlindEal), the runtime in our benchmarks was 151 ms, which may be quick enough for certain applications that have a hard requirement to ensure post-quantum security. However, as mentioned above, this costs "plain" and not circuit-private boostrapping which would be significantly more expensive.[11] On the other hand, as mentioned under open problems, it is plausible that cheaper alternatives to full circuit privacy

---

[10] F_{poprf}.Request runs in 28.9 ms and F_{poprf}.Finalise in 0.2 ms in our benchmarks. The former does not include the time to prove well-formedness, but – as below – we do not expect this to radically change this picture.

[11] Table 3 of [40] reports an overhead of 5x to 10x for circuit privacy.

might suffice for our setting. More broadly, we note that hardware acceleration of this step is a viable option, cf. [8]. In any case, previous classical constructions of (P)OPRFs, such as [51] take only a few ms to run the server evaluation, so the efficiency gap between our FHE-based approach and previous work is evident.

These results were acquired by using a server with 96 Intel Xeon Gold 6252 CPU @ 2.10 GHz cores and 768 GB of RAM. Server evaluation was run with parallelisation enabled, meaning that each multiplication of the client input encrypted vector with a matrix column is run in its own separate thread, but we only use 64 threads/cores.[12] Client evaluations use only a single core. Each of the benchmarks was established after running it ten times and taking the average runtime. Our benchmarking code is available at https://github.com/alxdavids/oprf-fhe-ec24-artifact.

Acknowledgements. We thank Christian Weinert for discussing MPC approaches with us; Ilaria Chillotti, Ben Curtis and Jean-Baptiste Orfila for answering questions about TFHE and tfhe-rs; Nicolas Gama for answering questions about TFHE. We thank Ward Beullens and Gregor Seiler for answering questions about LaBRADOR and sharing their size estimation Pari/GP script.

The research of Martin Albrecht was supported by UKRI grants EP/S02-0330/1, EP/-S02087X/1, EP/Y02432X/1 and by the European Union Horizon 2020 Research and Innovation Program Grant 780701. The research of Alex Davidson was supported by NOVA LINCS (UIDB/04516/2020), with the financial support of FCT.IP. Part of this work was done while Martin Albrecht was at Royal Holloway, University of London, while Alex Davidson was at Brave Software, and while Amit Deo was at Crypto Quantique.

References

1. Albrecht, M.R., Davidson, A., Deo, A., Gardham, D.: Crypto dark matter on the Torus: oblivious PRFs from shallow PRFs and FHE. Cryptology ePrint Archive, Report 2023/232 (2023). https://eprint.iacr.org/2023/232
2. Albrecht, M.R., Davidson, A., Deo, A., Smart, N.P.: Round-optimal verifiable oblivious pseudorandom functions from ideal lattices. In: Garay [30], pp. 261–289 (2019). https://eprint.iacr.org/2019/1271
3. Albrecht, M.R., Gheorghiu, V., Postlethwaite, E.W., Schanck, J.M.: Estimating quantum speedups for lattice sieves. In: Moriai and Wang [47], pp. 583–613 (2020)
4. Albrecht, M.R., Player, R., Scott, S.: On the concrete hardness of learning with errors. J. Math. Cryptol. **9**(3), 169–203 (2015)
5. Albrecht, M.R., Rechberger, C., Schneider, T., Tiessen, T., Zohner, M.: Ciphers for MPC and FHE. In: Oswald, E., Fischlin, M. (eds.) EUROCRYPT 2015, Part I. LNCS, vol. 9056, pp. 430–454. Springer, Heidelberg (2015). https://doi.org/10.1007/978-3-662-46800-5_17
6. Basso, A.: A post-quantum round-optimal oblivious PRF from isogenies. Cryptology ePrint Archive, Report 2023/225 (2023). https://eprint.iacr.org/2023/225

---

[12] On a single core, server blind evaluation took 7.1 s.

7. Basso, A., Kutas, P., Merz, S.-P., Petit, C., Sanso, A.: Cryptanalysis of an oblivious PRF from supersingular isogenies. In: Tibouchi, M., Wang, H. (eds.) ASIACRYPT 2021, Part I. LNCS, vol. 13090, pp. 160–184. Springer, Cham (2021). https://doi.org/10.1007/978-3-030-92062-3_6

8. Van Beirendonck, M., D'Anvers, J.-P., Verbauwhede, I.: FPT: a fixed-point accelerator for torus fully homomorphic encryption. Cryptology ePrint Archive, Report 2022/1635 (2022). https://eprint.iacr.org/2022/1635

9. Bellare, M., Rogaway, P.: The security of triple encryption and a framework for code-based game-playing proofs. In: Vaudenay, S. (ed.) EUROCRYPT 2006. LNCS, vol. 4004, pp. 409–426. Springer, Heidelberg (2006). https://doi.org/10.1007/11761679_25

10. Beullens, W., Seiler, G.: LaBRADOR: compact proofs for R1CS from module-SIS. Cryptology ePrint Archive, Report 2022/1341 (2022). https://eprint.iacr.org/2022/1341

11. Boneh, D., Ishai, Y., Passelègue, A., Sahai, A., Wu, D.J.: Exploring crypto dark matter: new simple PRF candidates and their applications. In: Beimel, A., Dziembowski, S. (eds.) TCC 2018, Part II, vol. 11240. LNCS, pp. 699–729. Springer, Heidelberg (2018). Full version available at https://eprint.iacr.org/2018/1218

12. Boneh, D., Kogan, D., Woo, K.: Oblivious pseudorandom functions from isogenies. In: Moriai and Wang [47], pp. 520–550 (2020)

13. Bourse, F., del Pino, R., Minelli, M., Wee, H.: FHE circuit privacy almost for free. In: Robshaw, M., Katz, J. (eds.) CRYPTO 2016. Part II, volume 9815 of LNCS, pp. 62–89. Springer, Heidelberg (2016)

14. Boyle, E., et al.: Correlated pseudorandomness from expand-accumulate codes. In: Dodis and Shrimpton [24], pp. 603–633 (2022)

15. Brakerski, Z., Gentry, C., Vaikuntanathan, V.: Fully homomorphic encryption without bootstrapping. Cryptology ePrint Archive, Report 2011/277 (2011). https://eprint.iacr.org/2011/277

16. Casacuberta, S., Hesse, J., Lehmann, A.: SoK: oblivious pseudorandom functions. In: 7th IEEE European Symposium on Security and Privacy, EuroS&P 2022, pp. 625–646. IEEE (2022)

17. Chen, H., Dai, W., Kim, M., Song, Y.: Efficient homomorphic conversion between (Ring) LWE ciphertexts. In: Sako, K., Tippenhauer, N.O. (eds.) ACNS 2021, Part I. LNCS, vol. 12726, pp. 460–479. Springer, Cham (2021). https://doi.org/10.1007/978-3-030-78372-3_18

18. Chen, H., Huang, Z., Laine, K., Rindal, P.: Labeled PSI from fully homomorphic encryption with malicious security. In: Lie, D., Mannan, M., Backes, M., Wang, X. (eds.) ACM CCS 2018, pp. 1223–1237. ACM Press, October 2018

19. Cheon, J.H., Cho, W., Kim, J.H., Kim, J.: Adventures in crypto dark matter: attacks and fixes for weak pseudorandom functions. In: Garay [30], pp. 739–760 (2020)

20. Cheon, J.H., Kim, A., Kim, M., Song, Y.: Homomorphic encryption for arithmetic of approximate numbers. In: Takagi, T., Peyrin, T. (eds.) ASIACRYPT 2017, Part I. LNCS, vol. 10624, pp. 409–437. Springer, Cham (2017). https://doi.org/10.1007/978-3-319-70694-8_15

21. Chillotti, I., Gama, N., Georgieva, M., Izabachène, M.: TFHE: fast fully homomorphic encryption over the torus. J. Cryptol. **33**(1), 34–91 (2020)

22. Davidson, A., Goldberg, I., Sullivan, N., Tankersley, G., Valsorda, F.: Privacy pass: bypassing internet challenges anonymously. PoPETs **2018**(3), 164–180 (2018)

23. Dinur, I., et al.: MPC-friendly symmetric cryptography from alternating moduli: candidates, protocols, and applications. In: Malkin, T., Peikert, C. (eds.) CRYPTO 2021, Part IV. LNCS, vol. 12828, pp. 517–547. Springer, Cham (2021). https://doi.org/10.1007/978-3-030-84259-8_18

24. Dodis, Y., Shrimpton, T. (eds.): CRYPTO 2022, Part II. LNCS, vol. 13508. Springer, Heidelberg (2022)

25. Ducas, L., Stehlé, D.: Sanitization of FHE ciphertexts. In: Fischlin, M., Coron, J.-S. (eds.) EUROCRYPT 2016, Part I. LNCS, vol. 9665, pp. 294–310. Springer, Heidelberg (2016). https://doi.org/10.1007/978-3-662-49890-3_12

26. Ducas, L., van Woerden, W.: NTRU fatigue: how stretched is overstretched? In: Tibouchi, M., Wang, H. (eds.) ASIACRYPT 2021, Part IV. LNCS, vol. 13093, pp. 3–32. Springer, Cham (2021). https://doi.org/10.1007/978-3-030-92068-5_1

27. Everspaugh, A., Chatterjee, R., Scott, S., Juels, A., Ristenpart, T.: The Pythia PRF service. In: Jung, J., Holz, T. (eds.) USENIX Security 2015, pp. 547–562. USENIX Association, August 2015

28. Faller, S., Ottenhues, A., Ernst, J.: Composable oblivious pseudo-random functions via garbled circuits. Cryptology ePrint Archive, Paper 2023/1176 (2023). https://eprint.iacr.org/2023/1176

29. Fan, J., Vercauteren, F.: Somewhat practical fully homomorphic encryption. Cryptology ePrint Archive, Report 2012/144 (2012). https://eprint.iacr.org/2012/144

30. Garay, J. (ed.): PKC 2021, Part II. LNCS, vol. 12711. Springer, Heidelberg (2021)

31. Gentry, C.: A fully homomorphic encryption scheme. Ph.D. thesis, Stanford University (2009). crypto.stanford.edu/craig

32. Gentry, C., Sahai, A., Waters, B.: Homomorphic encryption from learning with errors: conceptually-simpler, asymptotically-faster, attribute-based. In: Canetti, R., Garay, J.A. (eds.) CRYPTO 2013, Part I. LNCS, vol. 8042, pp. 75–92. Springer, Heidelberg (2013). https://doi.org/10.1007/978-3-642-40041-4_5

33. Goldreich, O.: Foundations of Cryptography, vol. 2. Cambridge University Press, Cambridge (2004)

34. Heimberger, L., Meisingseth, F., Rechberger, C.: OPRFs from isogenies: designs and analysis. Cryptology ePrint Archive, Paper 2023/639 (2023). https://eprint.iacr.org/2023/639

35. Hoffstein, J., Pipher, J., Silverman, J.H.: NTRU: a new high speed public key cryptosystem. Draft Distributed at Crypto (1996). http://web.securityinnovation.com/hubfs/files/ntru-orig.pdf

36. Jarecki, S., Krawczyk, H., Resch, J.: Threshold partially-oblivious PRFs with applications to key management. Cryptology ePrint Archive, Report 2018/733 (2018). https://eprint.iacr.org/2018/733

37. Jarecki, S., Krawczyk, H., Xu, J.: OPAQUE: an asymmetric PAKE protocol secure against pre-computation attacks. In: Nielsen, J.B., Rijmen, V. (eds.) EUROCRYPT 2018, Part III. LNCS, vol. 10822, pp. 456–486. Springer, Cham (2018). https://doi.org/10.1007/978-3-319-78372-7_15

38. Joye, M.: Guide to fully homomorphic encryption over the [discretized] torus. Cryptology ePrint Archive, Report 2021/1402 (2021). https://eprint.iacr.org/2021/1402

39. Kim, A., Lee, Y., Deryabin, M., Eom, J., Choi, R.: LFHE: fully homomorphic encryption with bootstrapping key size less than a megabyte. Cryptology ePrint Archive, Paper 2023/767 (2023). https://eprint.iacr.org/2023/767

40. Kluczniak, K.: Circuit privacy for FHEW/TFHE-style fully homomorphic encryption in practice. Cryptology ePrint Archive, Report 2022/1459 (2022). https://eprint.iacr.org/2022/1459

41. Langlois, A., Stehlé, D.: Worst-case to average-case reductions for module lattices. DCC **75**(3), 565–599 (2015)
42. Liu, Z., Micciancio, D., Polyakov, Y.: Large-precision homomorphic sign evaluation using FHEW/TFHE bootstrapping. In: Agrawal, S., Lin, D. (eds.) ASIACRYPT 2022. Part II, vol. 13792. LNCS, pp. 130–160. Springer, Heidelberg (2022). https://doi.org/10.1007/978-3-031-22966-4_5
43. Lyubashevsky, V., et al.: CRYSTALS-Dilithium. Technical report, National Institute of Standards and Technology (2022). https://csrc.nist.gov/Projects/post-quantum-cryptography/selected-algorithms-2022
44. Lyubashevsky, V., Nguyen, N.K., Plançon, M.: Lattice-based zero-knowledge proofs and applications: shorter, simpler, and more general. In: Dodis and Shrimpton [24], pp. 71–101 (2022)
45. MATZOV. Report on the Security of LWE: Improved Dual Lattice Attack, April 2022. https://doi.org/10.5281/zenodo.6412487
46. Micciancio, D., Polyakov, Y.: Bootstrapping in FHEW-like cryptosystems. Cryptology ePrint Archive, Report 2020/086 (2020). https://eprint.iacr.org/2020/086
47. Moriai, S., Wang, H. (eds.): ASIACRYPT 2020, Part II. LNCS, vol. 12492. Springer, Heidelberg (2020)
48. Seres, I.A., Horváth, M., Burcsi, P.: The Legendre pseudorandom function as a multivariate quadratic cryptosystem: security and applications. Cryptology ePrint Archive, Report 2021/182 (2021). https://eprint.iacr.org/2021/182
49. Shoup, V., Gennaro, R.: Securing threshold cryptosystems against chosen ciphertext attack. In: Nyberg, K. (ed.) EUROCRYPT 1998. LNCS, vol. 1403, pp. 1–16. Springer, Heidelberg (1998). https://doi.org/10.1007/BFb0054113
50. Stein, W., et al.: Sage Mathematics Software Version 9.8. The Sage Development Team (2023). http://www.sagemath.org
51. Tyagi, N., Celi, S., Ristenpart, T., Sullivan, N., Tessaro, S., Wood, C.A.: A fast and simple partially oblivious PRF, with applications. In: Dunkelman, O., Dziembowski, S. (eds.) EUROCRYPT 2022, Part II, vol. 13276. LNCS, pp. 674–705. Springer, Heidelberg (2022). https://doi.org/10.1007/978-3-031-07085-3_23
52. Unruh, D.: Quantum proofs of knowledge. In: Pointcheval, D., Johansson, T. (eds.) EUROCRYPT 2012. LNCS, vol. 7237, pp. 135–152. Springer, Heidelberg (2012). https://doi.org/10.1007/978-3-642-29011-4_10